THE STRATEGY PROCESS

THE STRATEGY PROCESS

Concepts, Contexts, Cases

FIFTH EDITION

Joseph Lampel
Henry Mintzberg
James Brian Quinn
Sumantra Ghoshal

PEARSON

Harlow, England • London • New York • Boston • San Francisco • Toronto • Sydney
Auckland • Singapore • Hong Kong • Tokyo • Seoul • Taipei • New Delhi
Cape Town • São Paulo • Mexico City • Madrid • Amsterdam • Munich • Paris • Milan

PEARSON EDUCATION LIMITED

Edinburgh Gate
Harlow CM20 2JE
Tel: +44 (0)1279 623623
Fax: +44 (0)1279 431059
Website: www.pearson.com/uk

Former European editions published 1996 and 2003 (print)
Fifth edition published 2014 (print)

ISBN: 978-0-273-71628-0 (print)

British Library Cataloguing-in-Publication Data
A catalogue record for the print edition is available from the British Library

Library of Congress Cataloging-in-Publication Data
Joseph Lampel.
The strategy process: concepts, contexts, cases / Joseph Lampel, Henry Mintzberg, James Brian Quinn, Sumantra Ghoshal. — Fifth Edition.
pages cm
Includes bibliographical references and index.
ISBN 978-0-273-71628-0 (alk. paper)
1. Strategic planning. 2. Strategic planning—Case studies. I. Title.
HD30.28.Q53 2013
658.4'012—dc23
2013008560

10 9 8 7 6 5 4 3 2 1
17 16 15 14 13

Print edition typeset in 9.75pt/11.5pt Minionpro-Regular by 75
Print edition printed and bound in the UK by Ashford Colour

BRIEF CONTENTS

CONTENTS

Section III CONTEXTS 311

Lecturer Resources

For password-protected online resources tailored to support the use of this textbook in teaching, please visit **www.pearsoned.co.uk/TheStrategyProcess**

PREFACE

In our first edition, we set out to produce a different kind of textbook in the field of strategy, or general management.

We tried to provide the reader with a richness of theory, a richness of practice, and a strong basis for linkage between the two. We rejected the strictly case study approach, which leaves theory out altogether, or soft-pedals it, and thereby denies the accumulated benefits of many years of careful research and thought about management processes. We also rejected an alternate approach that forces on readers a highly rationalistic model of how the strategy process *should* function. We collaborated on this book because we believe that in this complex world of organizations a range of concepts is needed to cut through and illuminate particular aspects of that complexity.

There is no "one best way" to create strategy, nor is there "one best form" of organization. Quite different forms work well in particular contexts. We believe that exploring a fuller variety systematically will create a deeper and more useful appreciation of the strategy process. In this revised edition, we remain loyal to these beliefs and objectives, while making major changes in the readings and cases. We kept some of the classic readings, but there are many new ones.

A host of new cases provide rich vehicles for discussing the value and limits of new management approaches and the dimensions of new management issues. There is a conscious balance among small, medium, and large-scale companies. They are entrepreneurial, innovative, rapidly growing, or slowly maturing; and they run the gamut from consumer goods to high technology. We have made an effort to select cases from new areas of the economy, such as videogames, broadband technology, software, personal computers, as well as areas that have been around for a while but are increasingly important, including media, entertainment, pharmaceuticals, and wealth management. Companies such as Pixar, Apple, Netflix, Warner Brothers, QVC, HBO, and Cirque Du Soleil represent some of the most exciting experiments in products and services, and management itself, today. We have also set out to offer the most international set of cases available. Glance down the list of cases included in this book and you realize how widely we have covered the globe.

This text, unlike most others, is therefore eclectic. Presenting published articles and portions of other books in their original form, rather than filtered through our minds and pens, is one way to reinforce this variety. Each author has his or her ideas and his or her own best way of expressing them (ourselves included!). Summarized by us, these readings would lose a good deal of their richness.

We do not apologize for contradictions among the ideas of leading thinkers. The world is full of contradictions. The real danger lies in using pat solutions to a nuanced reality, not in opening perspectives up to different interpretations. The effective strategist is one who can live with contradictions, learn to appreciate their causes and effects, and reconcile them sufficiently for effective action. The readings have, nonetheless, been ordered by chapter to suggest some ways in which reconciliation can be considered. Our own chapter introductions are also intended to assist in this task and to help place the readings in perspective.

ON THEORY

A word on theory is in order. We do not consider theory a dirty word, nor do we apologize for making it a major component of this book. To some people, to be theoretical is to be detached and impractical. But a bright social scientist once said, "There is nothing so practical as a good theory." And every successful doctor, engineer, and physicist would have to agree: They would be unable to practice their modern work without theories. Theories are useful because they shortcut the need to store masses of data. It is easier to remember a simple framework about some phenomenon than it is to consider every small detail you ever observed. In a sense theories are a bit like cataloging systems in libraries: The world would be impossibly confusing without them. They enable you to store and conveniently access your own experiences as well as those of others.

One can, however, suffer not just from an absence of theories but also from being dominated by them without realizing it. To paraphrase the words of John Maynard Keynes, most "practical men" are the slaves of some defunct theory. Whether we realize it or not, our behavior is guided by the systems of ideas that we have internalized over the years. Much can be learned by bringing these out in the open, examining them more carefully, and comparing them with alternative ways to view the world—including ones based on systematic study (that is, research). One of our prime intentions in this book is to expose the limitations of conventional theories and to offer alternate explanations that can be superior guides for understanding and taking action in specific contexts.

PRESCRIPTIVE THEORY VERSUS DESCRIPTIVE THEORY

Unlike many textbooks in this field, this one tries to explain the world as it is rather than as someone thinks it is *supposed* to be. Although there has sometimes been a tendency to disdain such *descriptive* theories, *prescriptive* (or normative) ones have often been the problem, rather than the solution, in the field of management. There is no one best way in management; no prescription works for all organizations. Even when a prescription seems effective in some context, it requires a sophisticated understanding of exactly what that context is and how it functions. In other words, one cannot decide reliably what should be done in a system as complicated as a contemporary organization without a genuine understanding of how that organization really works. In engineering, no student ever questions having to learn physics, in medicine, having to learn anatomy. Imagine an engineering student's hand shooting up in physics class: "Listen, prof, it's fine to tell us how the atom does work. But what we really want to know is how the atom *should* work." Why should a management student's similar demand in the realm of strategy or structure be considered any more appropriate? How can people manage complex systems they do not understand?

Nevertheless, we have not ignored prescriptive theory when it appears useful. A number of prescriptive techniques (industry analysis, experience curves, and so on) are discussed. But these are associated both with other readings and with cases that will help you understand the context and limitations of their usefulness. Both readings and cases offer opportunities to pursue the full complexity of strategic situations. You will find a wide range of issues and perspectives addressed. One of our main goals is to integrate a variety of views, rather than allow strategy to be fragmented into just "human issues" and "economics issues." The text and cases provide a basis for treating the full complexity of strategic management.

ON SOURCES

How were the readings selected and edited? Some textbooks boast about how new all their readings are. We make no such claim; indeed we would like to make a different boast; many of our readings have been around quite a while, long enough to mature, like fine wine. Our criterion for inclusion was not the newness of the article so much as the quality of its insight—that is, its ability to explain some aspect of the strategy process better than any other article. Time does not age the really good articles. Quite the opposite—it distinguishes their quality. So look here for classics from the 1950s still fully relevant alongside the latest thinking in this new millennium.

We are, of course, not biased toward old articles—just toward good ones. Hence, the materials in this book range from the classics to some published just before our final selection was made (as well as a few hitherto unpublished pieces). You will find articles from the most serious academic journals, the best practitioner magazines, books, and some very obscure sources. The best can sometimes be found in strange places.

We have tried to include many shorter readings rather than fewer longer ones, and we have tried to present as wide a variety of good ideas as possible while maintaining clarity. To do so we often had to cut within readings. We have, in fact, put a great deal of effort into the cutting in order to extract the key messages of each reading in as brief, concise, and clear a manner as possible. Unfortunately, our cutting sometimes forced us to eliminate interesting examples and side issues. (In the readings, as well as some of the case materials from published sources, dots . . . signify portions that have been deleted from the original, while square brackets [] signify our own insertions of minor clarifications into the original text). We apologize to you, the reader, as well as to the authors, for having done this, but hope that the overall result has rendered these changes worthwhile.

We have also included a number of our own works. Perhaps we are biased, having less objective standards by which to judge what we have written. But we have messages to convey, too, and our own writings do examine the basic themes that we feel are important in policy and strategy courses today.

ON CASES

A major danger of studying the strategy process—probably the most enticing subject in the management curriculum, and at the pinnacle of organizational processes—is that students and professors can become detached from the basics of the enterprise. The "Don't bore me with the operating details; I'm here to tackle the really big issues?" syndrome has been the death of many strategy courses (not to mention managerial practices!). Effective strategy processes always come down to specifics. For this reason, cases are the most convenient way to introduce practice into the classroom, to cap a wide variety of experiences, and to involve students actively in analysis and decision making.

Cases are the pedagogical approach of choice when it comes to studying strategy, but it is an approach with potential pitfalls and blind alleys. It is easy to lose sight of the fact that cases are selective narratives. In this respect, short and tightly focused cases can be better than long and highly detailed cases: They are less likely to mislead one into seeing the narrative as recreation of reality, as opposed to representation of reality, and a partial one at that.

Though cases are partial representation of reality, they can be revealing if used wisely. Most cases pose a dilemma or a problem. They irresistibly draw us toward prescription. An invitation to pronounce is appealing: how many can resist being the CEO of IBM or Microsoft for a day? However, this is false empowerment. It is not only based on incomplete information (made worse by the illusion of comprehensive description), it also lacks the pressure and nuance that are indispensable to decision making.

Cases are positive when they are used to illustrate and stimulate. They illustrate situations and dilemmas. They stimulate thinking by focusing minds on crucial issues, forcing the student to struggle with questions without the comfort of pretending that questions posed in the classroom can be settled in the classroom.

Our cases consciously contain both descriptive and prescriptive aspects of strategy, and as authors of this text, we have different views on which to use—description only, or description with prescription. On the one hand, the cases provide the data and background for making a major decision. Students can appraise the situation in its full context, suggest what future directions would be best for the organization in question, and discuss how their solutions can realistically be implemented. On the other hand, each case is also an opportunity to understand the dynamics of an organization—the historical context of the problems it faces, the influence of its technology, values, relationship to other organizations, its probable reactions to varying solutions, and so on. Unlike many cases which focus on only the analytical aspects of a decision, ours constantly force you to consider the messy realities of arriving at decisions in organizations and obtaining a desired response to any decision. In these respects, case study can involve a good deal of descriptive *and* prescriptive analysis.

LINKING CASES AND READINGS

The cases in this book are not intended to emphasize any particular theories, any more than the theoretical materials are included because they explain particular cases. Each case presents a slice of some specific reality, each reading a conceptual interpretation of some phenomenon. The readings are placed in particular groupings because they approach some common aspects or issues in theory.

We have provided some general guidelines for relating particular cases to sets of readings. But do not push this too far: study each case for its own sake. Cases are intrinsically richer than readings. Each contains a wide variety of issues—many awfully messy—in no particular order. The readings, in contrast, are usually neat and tidy, professing one or a few basic conceptual ideas, and providing some specific vocabulary. When the two connect—sometimes through direct effort, more often indirectly as conceptual ideas are recalled in the situation of a particular case—some powerful learning can take place in the form of clarification and, we hope, revelation.

Try to see how particular theories can help you to understand some of the issues in the cases and provide useful frameworks for drawing conclusions. Perhaps the great military theorist, Carl von Clausewitz, said it best almost two centuries ago:

> All that theory can do is give the artist or soldier points of reference, and standards of evaluation, with the ultimate purpose not of telling him how to act but of developing his judgment. (1976:15)

In relating theory to cases bear in mind that sound judgment depends on knowing the limitations of the former and the incompleteness of the latter. Theories compartmentalize reality. You should not take this compartmentalization as a given. Go beyond it when preparing each case. Use whatever concepts you find helpful both from chapters of the book and from your personal knowledge. Likewise, bear in mind that cases never tell the whole story (how could they!). This is rather evident in ones that deal with real people and real companies. Because they leave out so much, it is worthwhile to reach out to newspapers, Websites, Who's Who, or any other reference that comes to mind. Some of our cases, however, present imaginary situations, but should not for this reason be considered unreal. Their intent is to enhance awareness of key issues by avoiding the bias that comes with our accidental knowledge of actual companies and events.

CASE DISCUSSION

Management cases provide a concrete information base for students to analyze and share as they discuss management issues. Without this focus, discussions of theory can become quite confusing. You may have in mind an image of an organization or a situation that is very different from that of other discussants. As a result, what appears to be a difference in theory will—after much argument—often turn out to be simply a difference in perception of the realities surrounding these examples.

In this text we try to provide three levels of learning: first, a chance to share the generalized insights of leading theoreticians (in the readings); second, an opportunity to test the applicability and limits of these theories in specific (case) situations; third, the capacity to develop one's own special amalgam of insights based upon empirical observations and inductive reasoning (from case analyses). All are useful approaches; some students and professors will find one mix more productive for their special level of experience or mindset. Another will prefer a quite different mix. Hence, we include a wide selection of cases and readings.

The cases are not intended as examples of either weak or exceptionally good management practices. Nor, as we noted, do they provide examples of the concepts of a particular reading. They are discussion vehicles for probing the benefits and limits of various approaches. And they are analytical vehicles for applying and testing concepts and tools developed in your education and experience. Cases can have marketing, operations, accounting, financial, human relations, planning and control, external environmental, ethical, political, and quantitative dimensions. Each dimension should be addressed in preparations and classroom discussions, although some aspects will inevitably emerge as more important in one situation than another.

In each case you should look for several sets of issues. First, you should understand what went on in that situation. Why did it happen this way? What are the strong or weak features of what happened? What could have been changed to advantage? How? Why? Second, there are always issues of what should be done next. What are the key issues to be resolved? What are the major alternatives available? What outcomes could the organization expect from each? Which alternative should it select? Why? Third, there will almost always be "hard" quantitative data and "soft" qualitative impressions about each situation. Both deserve attention.

But remember, no realistic strategy situation is just an organization behavior problem or just a financial or economic analytical one. Both sets of information should be considered, and an integrated solution developed. Our cases are consciously constructed for this. Given their complexity we have tried to keep the cases as short as possible. And we have tried to capture some of the flavour of the real organization. Moreover, we have sought to mix product and services cases, technological and "non-tech" cases, entrepreneurial, small company, and large enterprise situations. In this cross section, we have tried to capture some of the most important and exciting issues, concepts, and products of our times. We believe management is fun and important. The cases try to convey this.

There is no "correct" answer to any case. There may be several "good" answers and many poor ones. The purpose of a strategy course should be to help you understand the nature of these "better" answers, what to look for, how to analyze alternatives, and how to see through the complexities of reaching solutions and implanting them in real organizations. A strategy course can only improve your probability of success, not ensure it. The total number of variables in a real strategy situation is typically beyond the control of any one person or group. Hence another caveat; do not rely excessively on performance as a criteria for evaluating the effectiveness of a strategy. A company may have succeeded or failed not because of its specific decisions, but because of luck, an outstanding personality, the bizarre action of an opponent, international actions over which it had no control, and so on. One of the products of a successful strategy course should be a little humility.

CASE STUDY GUIDES

A crucial part of reflection and analysis in the classroom, as in the real world, is coming up with the question that really matters. Asking the right question in strategy is analogous to an explorer's finding his or her bearing before starting the journey. There is no standard methodology for coming up with questions: intuition and experience play far too important a role in the process.

The cases provide a rich soil for investigating strategic realities. Their complexities always extend well below the surface. Each layer peeled back can reveal new insights and rewards. Like any good mystery story, a case provides many clues, never all, but, surprisingly, sometimes more than managers might have had time to absorb in the real situation.

Believing that no "canned approach" is viable for *all* strategic situations, we have selected cases that cut across a variety of issues and theoretical constructs. Almost any of these cases contains sufficient richness and complexity that it can be positioned at a number of different spots in a good strategy course. We leave the final case selection to the style and wisdom of the professor and his or her students.

THIS BOOK'S STRUCTURE

NOT FORMULATION, THEN IMPLEMENTATION

The first edition of this text offered a chapter format that was new to the strategy field. Unlike most others, it had no specific chapter or section devoted to "implementation" per se. The assumption in other texts is that strategy is formulated and then implemented, with organizational structures, control systems, and the like following obediently behind strategy. In this text, as in reality, formulation and implementation are intertwined as complex interactive processes in which politics, values, organizational culture, and management styles determine or constrain particular strategic decisions. And strategy, structure, and systems mix together in complicated ways to influence outcomes. While strategy formulation and implementation may be separated in some situations—perhaps in crises, in some totally new ventures, as well as in organizations facing predictable futures—these events are far from typical. We certainly do not believe in building a whole book (let alone a whole field) around this conceptual distinction.

BUT CONCEPTS, THEN CONTEXTS

The readings are divided roughly into two different parts. The first deals with *concepts*, the second with *contexts*. We introduce concepts early in the text as equal partners in the complex web of ideas that make up what we call "the strategy process." In the second half of the text we weave these concepts together in a number of distinct situations, which we call *contexts*.

Our theme diagram illustrates this. Concepts, shown on top, are divided into two groups—strategy and forces—to represent the first two sections of the book. Contexts draw all these concepts together, in a variety of situations—covered in the third section—which we consider the key ones in the field of strategy today (though hardly the only ones). The outline of the text, chapter by chapter, proceeds as follows:

Section I: Strategy

The first section is called *Strategy;* it comprises six chapters, two introductory in nature and four on the processes by which strategy making takes place. Chapter 1 introduces strategies themselves and probes the meaning of this important word to broaden your view of it. Here the pattern is set of challenging you to question conventional views, especially when these act to narrow perspectives. The themes introduced in this chapter carry throughout the book and are worth care in understanding.

Chapter 2 introduces a very important set of actors in this book, the *strategists*—all those people who play key roles in the strategy process. In examining the work of the general manager and other strategists, we shall perhaps upset a number of widely accepted notions. We do this to help you understand the very real complexities and difficulties of making strategy and managing in contemporary organizations.

Chapters 3 to 5 take up a theme that is treated extensively in the text—to the point of being reflected in its title: the development of an understanding of the *processes* by which strategies are made. Chapter 3 looks at *formulating strategy*, specifically at some widely accepted prescriptive models for how organizations should go about developing their strategies. Chapter 4 extends these ideas to more formal ways of *analyzing strategy* and considering what, if any, "generic" forms a strategy can take. While readings in later chapters will challenge some of these precepts, what will not be questioned is the importance of having to understand them. They are fundamental to appreciating the strategy process today.

Chapter 5 switches from a prescriptive to a descriptive approach. Concerned with understanding *strategy formation*, it considers how strategies actually *do* form in organizations (not necessarily by being formulated) and *why* different processes may be effective in specific circumstances. This text takes an unconventional stand by viewing planning and other formal approaches as not the only—and often indeed not even the most desirable—ways to make strategy. You will find our emphasis on the descriptive process—as an equal partner with the more traditional concerns for technical and analytical issues—to be one of the unifying themes of this book. Chapter 6 then turns attention to the nature of *strategic change*, and how this can come about.

Section II: Forces

In Section I, the readings introduced strategy, the strategist, and various ways in which strategy might be formulated and does in fact form. In Section II, entitled *Forces*, we introduce six additional concepts that constitute part of the strategy process.

In Chapter 7, the influence of *cognition* is discussed. Strategy is fundamentally a concept in people's minds, and so how we think about it—our cognitive process—must be understood. Chapter 8 looks at *organization*, how we put

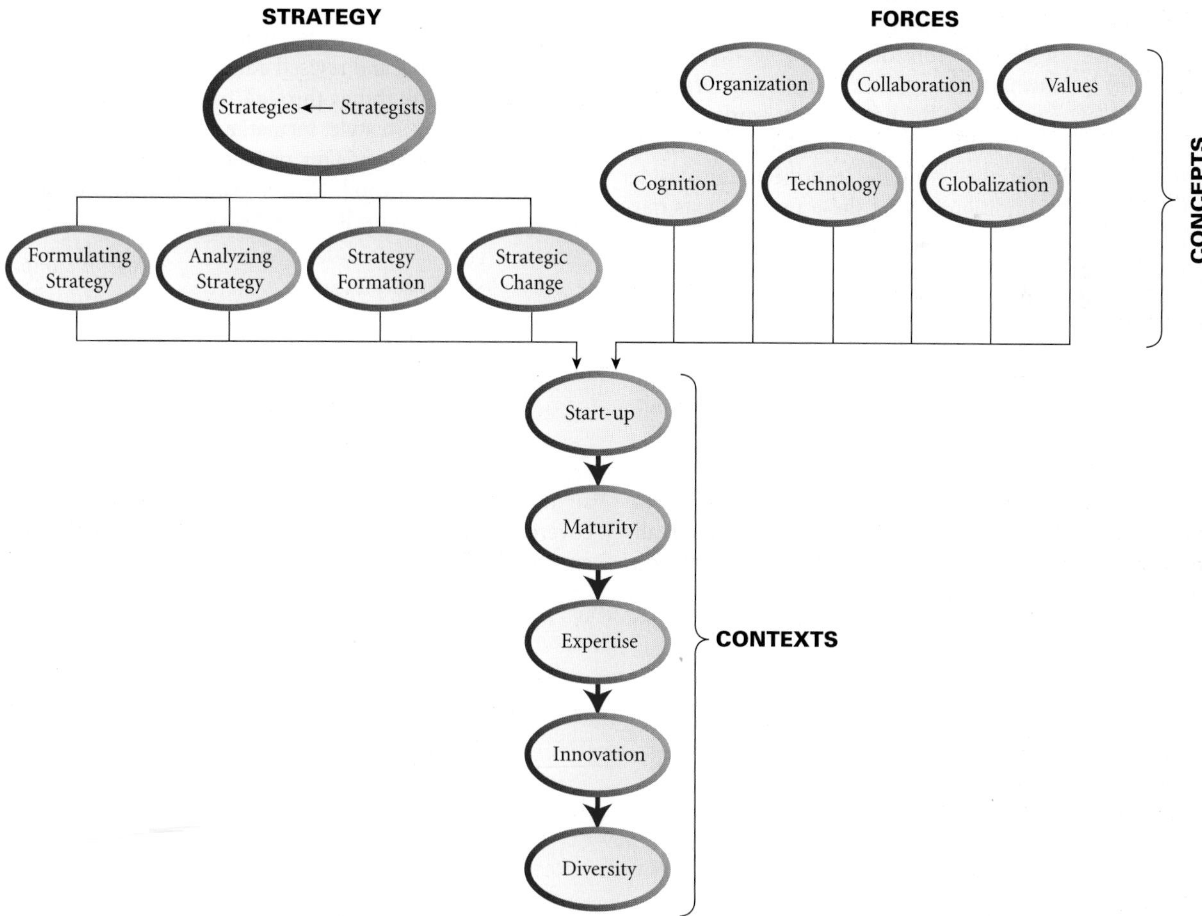

STRATEGY PROCESS THEME DIAGRAM

together and design those institutions for which strategies are created. Chapter 9 takes up another key force in the process, namely *technology*. We turn in Chapter 10 to the nature of *collaboration* as it influences the strategy process, from collaboration among individuals to alliances among corporations. Chapter 11 looks at *globalization*, that very popular yet over-hyped notion about which most of us need much more careful understanding. Last in this section, but certainly not least, is consideration of the *values* that drive us all. Together, these six forces must be understood if modern day processes of strategy making are to be appreciated.

Section III: Contexts

Section III is called *Contexts*. We consider how all of the elements introduced so far—strategies, the processes by which they are formulated and get formed, the strategists, cognition, organization, technology, collaboration, globalization and values—combine to suit particular contexts, five in all.

Chapter 13 deals with *managing start-up*, where often rather simple organizations come under the close control of strong leaders, or "entrepreneurs," frequently people with vision. Chapter 14 examines *managing maturity*, a context common to many large business and government organizations involved in the mass production and/or distribution of goods and services.

Chapters 14 and 15 consider *managing experts* and *managing innovation*, two contexts involving organizations of high expertise. In the first, experts work relatively independently in rather stable conditions, while in the innovation context, they combine in project teams under more dynamic conditions. What these two contexts have in common, however, is that they act in ways that upset many of the widely accepted notions about how organizations should be structured and make strategy.

Chapter 17 considers *managing diversity*, and deals with organizations that have diversified their product or service line and usually divisionalized their structures to deal with the greater varieties of environments they face. Finally, Chapter 18, called *Managing Otherwise*, closes the book by considering some rather unconventional views of the strategy process and of organizations that work despite being so different—and upsetting cherished beliefs. You don't have to be unusual to succeed, but you do have to be tolerant of the unusual to be a successful manager.

In considering each of these widely different contexts we seek to discuss the situation in which each is most likely to be found, the structures most suited to it, the kinds of strategies that tend to be pursued, the processes by which these strategies tend to be formed and might be formulated, and the social issues associated with the context.

Instructors' Supplements

The fifth edition of *The Strategy Process* is accompanied by a comprehensive Instructor's Manual available to download from Pearson's website. The Instructor's Manual includes detailed summaries of all readings and discussion questions for each chapter, as well as Teaching Notes for the cases in each section.

Well, there you have it. We worked hard on this book, in both the original and revised editions, to get it right. We have tried to think things through from the basics, with a resulting text that in style, format, and content is unusual for the field of strategy. Our product may not be perfect, but we believe it is good. Now it's your turn to find out if you agree. Enjoy yourself along the way.

Joseph Lampel
Henry Mintzberg

ABOUT THE AUTHORS

JOSEPH LAMPEL

Joseph Lampel is Professor of Strategy at Cass Business School, City University London. He received his doctorate in Strategic Management from McGill University in 1990, and was awarded Best Dissertation Award from the Administrative Science Association of Canada. Following his graduate studies Professor Lampel taught for seven years at the Stern School of Business, New York University. He subsequently moved to the United Kingdom where he held positions at University of St. Andrews and the University of Nottingham.

Professor Lampel has authored more than 50 journal articles and book chapters. He is also co-author with Henry Mintzberg and Bruce Ahlstrand of 'The Strategy Safari', 'Strategy Bites Back', 'and Management? It's Not What You Think'. In addition, he is co-editor with Jamal Shamsie and Theresa Lant of 'The Business of Culture: Strategic Perspectives on Entertainment and Media', and co-editor with Benson Honig and Israel Drori, of 'Handbook of Organizational and Entrepreneurial Ingenuity'.

HENRY MINTZBERG

Henry Mintzberg is Cleghorn Professor of Management Studies at McGill University in Montreal, Canada. His research has dealt with issues of general management and organizations, focusing on the nature of managerial work, forms of organizing, and the strategy formation process. Currently, he is completing a pamphlet entitled Rebalancing Society. He is also promoting the development of a family of masters programs for practicing managers (see IMPM.org and IMHL.info). His own teaching activities focus on ad hoc seminars for managers and work with doctoral students.

He received his doctorate and master of science degrees from the M.I.T. Sloan School of Management and his mechanical engineering degree from McGill, working in between in operational research for the Canadian National Railways. He has been named an Officer of the Order of Canada and of l'Ordre Nationale du Quebec and holds honorary degrees from sixteen universities. He also served as President of the Strategic Management Society from 1988 to 1991, and is an elected Fellow of the Royal Society of Canada (the first from a management faculty), the Academy of Management, and the International Academy of Management. He was named Distinguished Scholar for the year 2000 by the Academy of Management.

JAMES BRIAN QUINN

Professor Quinn was a recognized authority in the fields of strategic planning, management of technological change, entrepreneurial innovation, and management of intellect and technology in the services sector. He received both the Academy of Management's prestigious Outstanding Educator Award and its Book of the Year award (for *Intelligent Enterprise*).

SUMANTRA GHOSHAL

Sumantra Ghoshal was Professor of Strategic and International Management at the London Business School. He also served as the Founding Dean of the Indian School of Business in Hyderabad, of which LBS is a partner, and as a member of The Committee of Overseers of the Harvard Business School. *Managing Across Borders: The Transnational Solution*, a book he coauthored with Christopher Bartlett, has been listed in the *Financial Times* as one of the 50 most influential management books and has been translated into nine languages. *The Differentiated Network: Organizing the Multinational Corporation for Value Creation*, a book he coauthored with Nitin Nohria, won the George Terry Book Award in 1997. *The Individualized Corporation*, coauthored with Christopher Bartlett, won the Igor Ansoff Award in 1997, and has been translated into seven languages. His book, *Managing Radical Change*, won the Management Book of the Year award in India. With doctoral degrees from both the MIT School of Management and the Harvard Business School, Sumantra served on the editorial boards of several academic journals and was nominated to the Fellowships at the Academy of Management, the Academy of International Business, and the World Economic Forum.

ACKNOWLEDGMENTS

This book was originally brought together by James Brian Quinn and Henry Mintzberg, in the belief that the field of strategy badly needed a new kind of textbook. We wanted one that looked at process as well as analysis; that was built around dynamic strategy concepts and contexts instead of the overworked dichotomy of formulation and implementation; and that accomplished these aims in an intelligent, eclectic, and lively style. We sought to combine theory with practice, as well as description with prescription, in new ways that offered insights none could achieve alone. These goals stayed with us during the successive editions, including the current fifth edition.

What changed were the people that joined our effort. Joseph Lampel and Sumantra Ghoshal jointed Henry Mintzberg and James Brian Quinn for the fourth edition. Sadly, James Brian Quinn and Sumantra Ghoshal passed away in the decade that elapsed between the fourth and the current fifth edition. They were both seminal figures in the development of strategic management research, teaching, and practice. The two of us miss them greatly.

It was left to Joseph Lampel and Henry Mintzberg to review and edit the fifth edition of the book. We kept most of the readings from the earlier editions that worked in the belief that good readings do not go out of date; rather they age like good wine. But we have also replaced some of the readings in the fourth edition with new readings that deal with the same topics, as well as including new readings that explore issues that have become more important over the past decade.

We wish to express our warmest appreciation to a number of people who have been helpful, especially Aneesh Banerjee, Ajay Bhalla, Pushkar Jha, and Daniel Ronen. We also wish to extend our appreciation to those in Pearson Education who helped to make this book a reality. Special thanks go to Rufus Curnow and Catharine Steers, Christopher Kingston, Helen Bartlett and Philippa Fiszzon, and Kirubhagaran P. and Mahalatchoumy S.

One last word: This book is not finished. Like the subject of so much of its content, our text is an ongoing process, not a static statement. There are all kinds of opportunities for improvement. Please write to any of us with your suggestions on how to improve the readings, the cases, and the organization of the book at large and its presentation. Strategy making, we believe, is a learning process; we are also engaged in a learning process. Thank you and enjoy what follows.

Joseph Lampel
Henry Mintzberg

PUBLISHER'S ACKNOWLEDGMENTS

We are grateful to the following for permission to reproduce copyright material:

Figures

Figure 1 in Reading 1.2 adapted from *Alexander the Great*, Praeger (Green, P. 1970) p.50; Figure 1 in Reading 4.1 from *Competitive advantage*, Free Press (Porter, ME 1985) Fig. 1.2, p.6, With the permission of The Free Press, a Division of Simon & Schuster, Inc. Copyright © 1985 by Michael Porter. All rights reserved; Figure 1 in Reading 4.3 adapted from *Resources and Strategy: an IO Perspective (Working Paper)*, Harvard Business School (Ghemawat, P 1991) Fig 3, p.20; Figure 3 in Reading 4.5 from *Competitive Advantage*, Simon and Schuster (Porter, M.E. 1985) p.37, With the permission of The Free Press, a Division of Simon & Schuster, Inc. Copyright © 1985 by Michael Porter. All rights reserved; Figure 4 in Reading 4.5 from *Competitive Advantage*, Simon and Schuster (Porter, M.E. 1985) p.12, With the permission of The Free Press, a Division of Simon & Schuster, Inc. Copyright © 1985 by Michael Porter. All rights reserved; Figure 5 in Reading 4.5 adapted from *Corporate strategy: an analytic approach to business policy for growth and expansion*, McGraw-Hill (Ansoff, I. 1965) p.109; Figure 1 in Reading 5.3 from *Strategy Alternatives for the British Motorcycle Industry*, BCG/HMSO (Boston Consulting Group 1975); Figure 2 in Reading 6.1 from *Control Your Destiny or Someone Else Will*, Doubleday (Tichy, NM and Sherman, S. 1993) p.305, Copyright © 1993 by Noel M. Tichy and Stratford Sherman. Used by permission of Doubleday, a division of Random House, Inc. Any third party use of this material, outside of this publication, is prohibited. Interested parties must apply directly to Random House, Inc. for permission; Figure 3 in Reading 6.1 from Re-Energizing the Mature Organization, *Organizational Dynamics*, vol. 20(1), p.25 (Beatty, R.W., & Ulrich, D.O. 1991); Figure 7 in Reading 8.1 from *Program and project management in a matrix organization: a case study*, Bureau of Business Research and Service, Graduate School of Business, University of Wisconsin-Madison (Delbecq, A. and Filley, A 1974) p.16; Figure 3 in Reading 14.2 from Boston Consulting Group, pre 1979; Figure 5 in Reading 14.2 adapted from *Perspectives on Experience*, Boston Consulting Group (1972) p.21; Figure 3 in Reading 17.1 from *Strategy, Structure, and Economic Performance*, Harvard University Press (Rumlet, R. 1974) p.21.

Table

Table on page 189 adapted from *Forecasting, planning and strategy for the 21st century*, Free Press (Makridakis, S 1990) pp.36–37, With the permission of The Free Press, a Division of Simon & Schuster, Inc. Copyright © 1990 by S Makridakis. All rights reserved.

Text

Reading 1.1 adapted from The five P's for strategy, *California Management Review*, Vol. 30(1), pp.11–24 (Mintzberg, H. 1987), © 1987, by The Regents of the University of California. Reproduced with permission of GRADUATE SCHOOLS OF BUSINESS ADMINISTRATION, UNIVERSITY OF CALIFORNIA in the format Republish in a book via Copyright Clearance Center; Reading 1.2 adapted from *Strategies for change: logical incrementalism*, Richard D Irwin (Quinn, JB 1980) Chapters 1 & 5, © The McGraw-Hill Companies, Inc. Reproduced by permission; Reading 1.3 adapted from What is Strategy, *Harvard Business Review*, Nov–Dec (Porter, ME 1996), © 1996, by the Harvard Business School Publishing Corporation, all rights reserved. Republished by permission of the Harvard Business Review; Reading 2.1 adapted from The manager's job: folklore and fact, *Harvard Business Review*, Jul–Aug (Mintzberg, H. 1975); Reading 2.2 adapted from Balancing personality types at the top, *Business Quarterly*, vol. 58(2), pp.47–57 (Pitcher, P. 1993). One time permission to reproduce granted by Richard Ivey School of Business Foundation on 21 January 2013, Richard Ivey School of Business Foundation prohibits any form of reproduction, storage or transmission of this material without its written permission. This material is not covered under authorization from any reproduction rights organization. To order copies or request permission to reproduce materials, contact Ivey Publishing, Richard Ivey School of Business Foundation, The University of Western Ontario, London, Ontario, Canada, N6A 3K7; phone (519) 661–3208, fax (519) 661–3882, e-mail cases@ivey.uwo.ca. Copyright © (1993) Richard Ivey School of Business Foundation; Reading 2.3 adapted from Good Managers Don't Make Policy Decisions, *Harvard Business Review*, Sept–Oct (Wrapp, HE 1967); Reading 2.4 from The leader's new work: building learning organizations, *Sloan Management Review*, Fall, pp.7–23 (Senge, PM 1990), © 1990 from MIT Sloan Management Review/Massachusetts Institute of Technology. All rights reserved. Distributed by Tribune Media Services; Reading 2.5 adapted from In praise of middle managers, *Harvard Business Review*, Sep–Oct (Huy, QN 2001); Case Study on pages 489–497 from *Napoleon Bonaparte: Victim of an inferior Strategy?*, INSEAD (Sinha, A. 1999); Reading 3.1 adapted from *The concept of corporate strategy*, Richard D Irwin (Andrews, K R 1980) Chapters 2–3, © The McGraw-Hill Companies, Inc. Reproduced by permission; Reading 3.2 adapted from *The Evaluation of Business Strategy*, McGraw-Hill (Gluek, WF 1980); Reading 3.3 adapted from Strategic Intent, *Harvard Business Review*, May–June (Hamel, G & Prahlad, CK 1989); Reading 3.4 from The Real Value of Strategic Planning, *Sloan Management Review*, Jan (Sarah Kaplan and Eric D. Beinhocker 2003), © 2003 from MIT Sloan Management Review/Massachusetts Institute of Technology. All rights reserved. Distributed by Tribune Media Services; Reading 4.1 adapted from How competitive forces shape strategy, *Harvard Business Review*, March–April (Porter, ME 1979), Copyright © 1979 by the President and Fellows of Harvard College; all rights reserved. Reprinted with deletions by permission of the Harvard Business Review; Reading 4.2 adapted from Looking inside for competitive advantage, *Academy of Management Executive*, Vol.9(4), pp.49–61 (Barney, JB 1995); Reading 4.3 adapted from Sustaining superior performance: commitments and capabilities, *Harvard Business School, Case 798008* (Ghemawat, P. and Pisano, G. 1997); Reading 4.4 adapted from *Henderson on Corporate Strategy*, Abt books (Henderson, B. 1979) pp. 27–33, © 1979, The Boston Consulting Group; Reading 5.1 from The perils of bad strategy, *McKinsey Quarterly*, June (Rumelt, R 2011), This article was originally published in McKinsey Quarterly, www.mckinseyquarterly.com. Copyright © 2011 McKinsey & Company. All rights reserved. Reprinted by permission; Reading 5.2 adapted from Sustaining superior performance: commitments and capabilities, *Harvard Business School Note*, 9-798-008 July (Ghemawat, P and Pisano, G 1997), Copyright © 1987 by the President and Fellows of Harvard College; all rights reserved. Reprinted with deletions by permission of the Harvard Business Review; Reading 5.3 adapted from Strategy as Strategic Decision Making, *Sloan Management Review*, Spring, pp.65–72 (Eisenhardt, KM 1999), © 1999 from MIT Sloan Management Review/Massachusetts Institute of Technology. All rights reserved. Distributed by Tribune Media Services; Reading 5.4 adapted from The Honda Effect, *California Management Review*, Vol.38(4), pp. 78–117 (Pascale, RT 1996), Reproduced with permission of GRADUATE SCHOOLS OF BUSINESS ADMINISTRATION, UNIVERSITY OF CALIFORNIA in the format Republish in a book via Copyright Clearance Center; Reading 6.1 adapted from *Strategy Safari: a guided tour through the wilds of strategic management*, Free Press (Mintzberg, H., Ahlstrand, B. and Lampel, J. 1998), With the permission of The Free Press, a Division of Simon & Schuster, Inc. Copyright © 1998 by H. Mintzberg, B. Ahlstrand and J. Lampel, all rights reserved, and Pearson Education Ltd; Reading 6.2 adapted from Convergence and upheaval: managing the unsteady pace of organizational evolution, *California Management Review*, Vol.29(1), pp. 29–44 (Tushman, ML., Newman, WH. and Romanelli, E. 1986), Copyright © 1986, by the Regents of the University of California. Reproduced with permission of GRADUATE SCHOOLS OF BUSINESS ADMINISTRATION, UNIVERSITY OF CALIFORNIA in the format Republish in a book via Copyright Clearance Center; Reading 6.3 adapted from *The Strategy Process*, Prentice Hall (Mintzberg, H., Lampel, J., Quinn, B. & Ghoshal 1994), 3rd,

©1996. Printed and Electronically reproduced by permission of Pearson Education, Inc., Upper Saddle River, New Jersey; Case Study on pages 517–524 from *Barbie vs Bratz*, IBS Research Center (Vedpuriswar, A. and Mankad, R. 2006) Case Code: COM0006; Reading 7.1 adapted from *Strategy Safari*, The Free Press (Mintzberg, H., Ahlstrand, B. and Lampel, J. 1998) p.155–184, Pearson Education Ltd; Reading 7.2 adapted from The strategy and structure of firms in the attention economy, *Ivey Business Journal*, Mar-Apr (Davenport, TH. and Beck, JC. 2002). One time permission to reproduce granted by Richard Ivey School of Business Foundation on 21 January 2013, Richard Ivey School of Business Foundation prohibits any form of reproduction, storage or transmission of this material without its written permission. This material is not covered under authorization from any reproduction rights organization. To order copies or request permission to reproduce materials, contact Ivey Publishing, Richard Ivey School of Business Foundation, The University of Western Ontario, London, Ontario, Canada, N6A 3K7; phone (519) 661–3208, fax (519) 661-3882, e-mail cases@ivey.uwo.ca. Copyright © (2002) Richard Ivey School of Business Foundation; Reading 7.3 adapted from When it comes to real change, too much objectivity may be fatal to the process, *Strategy and Leadership*, Mar–Apr, pp.6–12 (Hurst, DK 1997), © Emerald Group Publishing Limited, all rights reserved; Case Study on pages 525–539 from *The European Airline industry: Lufthansa*, INSEAD (Gimeno J., Cool K., Fung, H. and Buccella, A. 2004) 12/2008-5125; Reading 8.2 adapted from Strategy and organization planning, *Human Resource Management*, Spring–Summer 1983 (Galbraith, JR 1983); Reading 8.3 adapted from *Wharton on Managing Emerging Technologies*, John Wiley & Sons, Inc. (The Design of New Organizational Forms 2000) pp. 376–392, Day, GS., Schoemaker, PJH., and Gunther, RE. (Eds); Reading 9.2 adapted from Avoiding the Pitfalls of Emerging Technologies, *California Management Review*, Vol. 42(2), pp.8–33 (Day, GS. and Schoemaker, PJ. 2000), Reproduced with permission of GRADUATE SCHOOLS OF BUSINESS ADMINISTRATION, UNIVERSITY OF CALIFORNIA in the format Republish in a book via Copyright Clearance Center; Reading 9.3 adapted from Reinventing your business model, *Harvard Business Review*, Vol. 86(12) (Johnson, MW., Christensen, CM., and Kagermann, H. 2008); Reading 10.1 adapted from *Collaborating to Compete: Using Strategic Alliances and Acquisitions in the Global Marketplace*, John Wiley & Sons Inc. (Bleeke, J. and Ernst, D. 1993); Reading 10.2 adapted from Why Create Alliances from 'Incorporating International Strategic Alliances into Overall Firm Strategy', *The International Executive*, Vol. 37(3), pp. 261–277 (Preece. S. 1995), Copyright © 1995 by John Wiley & Sons, Inc. Used by permission of John Wiley & Sons; Reading 10.3 adapted from Creating Knowledge Through Collaboration, *California Management Review*, Vol. 39(1), pp. 123–140 (Inkpen, A.C. 1996); Reading 11.2 adapted from Global strategy . . . in a world of nations, *Sloan Management Review*, Fall (Yip, G.S. 1989), Copyright © 1989 from MIT Sloan Management Review/Massachusetts Institute of Technology. All rights reserved. Distributed by Tribune Media Services; Reading 11.4 from *Financial Times Mastering Strategy: The Complete MBA Companion in Strategy*, Financial Times Prentice Hall (Rangan, S. 2000) pp.119–124; Case Study on pages 555–563 from *Managing European Wealth*, IMD International (Buchel, B. 2010) IMD-3-1304; Reading 12.1 adapted from *New Values, Morality, and Strategic Ethics* (Gustafsson, C.); Reading 12.2 adapted from *Leadership in Administration*, Harper and Row (Selznick, P. 1957) Chapter 1, Reproduced with permission of UNIVERSITY OF CALIFORNIA PRESS in the format Republish in a book via Copyright Clearance Center; Case Study on pages 564–571 from *A note on the U.S. wine industry 2007*, Babson College (Cummings, M & Otley, G 2010) 660-N10, One time permission to reproduce granted by Babson College on 3rd January 2013; Reading 13.2 adapted from *Competitive Strategy: Techniques for Analyzing Industries and Competitors*, The Free Press (Porter, M.E. 1980), With the permission of The Free Press, a Division of Simon & Schuster, Inc. Copyright © 1980 by Michael Porter. All rights reserved; Reading 13.3 adapted from How Entrepreneurs Craft Strategies that Work, *Harvard Business Review*, Mar–Apr, pp. 150–161 (Bhide, A. 1994), Copyright © 1994 by the President and Fellows of Harvard College; all rights reserved. Reprinted with deletions by permission of the Harvard Business Review; Reading 14.2 adapted from *Strategic Market Planning: Problems and Analytical Approaches*, Prentice Hall (Abell, D.F. and Hammond, J.S. 1979) pp.103–198, 1st edition © 1979. Printed by permission of Pearson Education, Inc., Upper Saddle River, New Jersey; Reading 14.3 adapted from *Bureaucracy: What Government Agencies Do and Why They Do It*, Basic Books (Wilson, J.Q. 1989) pp.220–232, Reproduced with permission of BASIC BOOKS in the format Republish in a book via Copyright Clearance Center; Reading 14.4 adapted from Corporate Entrepreneurship: How?, *VIKALPA: The Journal for Decision Makers*, Vol. 31(1), pp.85–93 (Ramachandran, K., Devarajan, T.P. and Ray, S. 2006), Published by the Indian Institute of Management, Ahmedabad, India. Reproduced with permission; Case Study on pages 576–581 from *The Making of the iPod*, IMD International (Fischer, WA 2009); Reading 15.3 adapted from Managing the Professional Service Firm, *Sloan Management Review*, Fall, pp.15–29 (Maister, D.H. 1982), Copyright © 1982 from MIT Sloan Management Review/Massachusetts Institute of Technology. All rights reserved. Distributed by Tribune Media Services; Reading 15.4 after Covert Leadership: Notes on Managing Professionals, *Harvard Business Review*, Nov–Dec 1998, pp.140–147 (Mintzberg, H. 1998); Case Study on pages 582–586 from *Arnold Schwarzenegger (A): Strategy or Sheer Willpower?* (Lampel, J. and Ronen, D. 2011); Reading 16.2 adapted from Managing in the Whitespace, *Harvard Business Review*, Feb, pp.103–111 (Maletz, M.C. and Nohria, N. 2001); Reading 16.3 adapted from the era of open innovation, *Sloan Management Review*, Vol. 50(1), pp.35–41 (Chesbrough, H.W. 2003), Copyright © 2003 from MIT Sloan Management Review/Massachusetts Institute of Technology. All rights reserved. Distributed by Tribune Media Services; Reading 17.2 adapted from The Management of Large Groups: Asia and Europe Compared, *European Management Journal*, Vol. 10(2), pp.157–612 (Lasserre, P. 1992), Reprinted with deletions with permission of the Journal, Elsevier Science Ltd., Pergamon Imprint, Oxford, England; Reading 17.3 adapted from From competitive advantage to corporate strategy, *Harvard Business Review*, May–June (Porter, M.E. 1987), Copyright © 1987 by the President and Fellows of Harvard College; all rights reserved. Reprinted with deletions by permission of the Harvard Business Review; Case Study on pages 589–592 from *Whisky Exchange* (Lampel, J. & Ronen, D. 2010); Reading 18.2 adapted from The Future Disposable Organizations and the Rigidities of Management, *Organization*, Nov. (March, J.G. 1995), copyright © 1995 by Sage Publications Ltd. Reprinted by Permission of SAGE; Reading 18.3 after Strategy Innovation and the Quest for Value, *Sloan Management Review*, Winter, pp.7–14 (Hamel, G. 1998), Copyright © 1998 from MIT Sloan Management Review/Massachusetts Institute of Technology. All rights reserved. Distributed by Tribune Media Services; Reading 18.4 adapted from How We Went Digital Without a Strategy, *Harvard Business Review*, Sep–Oct (Semler, R. 2000); Reading 18.5 adapted from Managing Quietly, *Leader to Leader*, Spring, pp.24–30 (Mintzberg, H 1999); Exhibit 1 on page 597 and Exhibit 2 on page 600 from Outset Contemporary Art Fund (www.outset.org.uk); Case Study on pages 608–617 from *Netflix*, Ivey Publishing (Chatterjee, S., Carroll, E. and Spencer, D. 2009) 9B09M093. One time permission to reproduce granted by Richard Ivey School of Business Foundation in Spring 2013, Richard Ivey School of Business Foundation prohibits any form of reproduction, storage or transmission of this material without its written permission. This material is not covered under authorization from any reproduction rights organization. To order copies or request permission to reproduce materials, contact Ivey Publishing, Richard Ivey School of Business Foundation, The University of Western Ontario, London, Ontario, Canada, N6A 3K7; phone (519) 661-3208, fax (519) 661-3882, e-mail cases@ivey.uwo.ca. Copyright © (2009) Richard Ivey School of Business Foundation; Case Study on pages 618–234 from *Nintendo: Fighting the Computer Game Colsole Wars*, Cass Business School (Rietveld, J. 2012); Case Study on pages 650–666 from *Natura: The magic behind Brazil's most admired company*, London Business School (Ghoshal, S., Sull, D., Tanure, B., and Escobari, M. 1999) ECCH Case 302-090-1; Case Study on pages 675–680 from *Building emotional energy: Nissan*, INSEAD (Huy, QN 2010) 04/2010-5195; Case Study on pages 681–684 from *Even a clown can do it: Cirque du Soleil*, Insead (Williamson, M. 2002) ECCH 302-058-1; Case Study on pages 687–691 from *Managing performance Haier (A)*, IMD International (Pucik, V., Xin, K. & Everatt, D. 2004) Case 3-1332.

Photographs

Pearson Education Ltd: Martin Sookias page 525, Steven Greaves © Dorling Kindersley page 682; **Shutterstock.com**: Randy Miramontez page 681.

In some instances we have been unable to trace the owners of copyright material, and we would appreciate any information that would enable us to do so.

Section I

STRATEGY

CHAPTER 1

Strategies

We open this text on its focal point: strategy. The first section is called "Strategy," the first chapter, "Strategies." Later chapters in this section describe the role of strategists and consider the processes by which strategies develop from three perspectives: deliberate formulation, systematic analysis, and emergent formation. A last chapter looks at strategic change. But in this opening chapter, we consider the central concept—strategies themselves.

What is strategy? There is no single, universally accepted definition. Various authors and managers use the term differently; for example, some include goals and objectives as part of strategy whereas others make firm distinctions between them. Our intention in including the following readings is not to promote any one view of strategy but rather to suggest a number of views that seem useful. As will be evident throughout this text, our wish is not to narrow perspectives but to broaden them by trying to clarify issues. In pursuing these readings, it will be helpful to think about the meaning of strategy, to try to understand how different people have used the term, and later to see if certain definitions hold up better in particular contexts.

The first reading, by Henry Mintzberg of McGill University in Montreal, serves to open up the concept of strategy to a variety of views, some very different from traditional writings. Mintzberg focuses on various distinct definitions of strategy as plan (as well as ploy), pattern, position, and perspective. He uses the first two of these definitions to take us beyond deliberate strategy—beyond the traditional view of the term—to the notion of *emergent* strategy. This introduces the idea that strategies can form in an organization without being consciously intended, that is, without being *formulated*. This may seem to run counter to the whole thrust of the strategy literature, but Mintzberg argues that many people implicitly use the term this way even though they would not so define it.

The two readings that follow explore at some length two of Mintzberg's definitions of strategy: planning and position. James Brian Quinn's "Strategies for Change" looks at strategy as a plan that integrates an organization's major goals and action sequences into a cohesive whole. To illustrate this definition Quinn looks to military strategy as arguably the first area in human history where strategy was consciously developed and used, often with momentous consequences. He explores at some length the battle of Chaeronea in 338 BC where Macedonia, led by King Philip and his son Alexander, defeated the Greeks and their allied troops. Quinn sees the strategy that Philip and Alexander developed and put into action in Chaeronea as a classic example of how each element of strategy, individually and in combination, should be pursued. This, he argues, is well understood by military strategists up to the present, which is why strategy can be codified into a set of enduring principles—applicable more than two thousand years ago, as it does today.

The reading that follows Quinn's, is an award-winning article by Michael Porter of the Harvard Business School, and explores strategy as a position rather than as a plan. In this reading, Porter, probably the best-known writer in the field of strategy, focuses on strategy as a tightly integrated, clearly cohesive, and highly deliberate concept that positions a firm for competitive advantage. Porter suggests that excessive concern with operational effectiveness has displaced attention to strategy. Competitive strategy is about being different from one's rivals. This consists of tailoring a set of activities to support a strategic position. Defending this position, however, depends on crafting trade-offs that competitors will find very hard to imitate.

Our fourth reading in this chapter, by coauthors Henry Mintzberg and Joseph Lampel of City University London, "reflects" on the strategy process, specifically by introducing ten perspectives, or schools of thought, that describe the field today. Strategy is an elephant, they argue, and we are all the proverbial blind men grabbing at its different parts and pretending to understand the whole. These schools—and, more importantly, their interrelationships—reappear continually throughout this book so that, in a sense, this reading helps to introduce the book, too.

Upon completion of these readings, we hope that you will be less sure of the use of the word *strategy* but more ready to tackle the study of the strategy process with a broadened perspective and an open mind. There are no universally right answers in this field (any more than there are in most other fields), but there are interesting and constructive perspectives.

USING THE CASE STUDIES

Explicit and intuitive understanding is essential for understanding strategy. Sometimes, however, the issue of what strategy is to begin with is very much at the forefront of such understanding. The Robin Hood case strongly illustrates the multiple facets of strategy. One can argue with Porter in the reading "What Is Strategy?" that Robin Hood begins to have a strategy only when he starts to ask serious questions about what he is doing and where he is going. Or one can take Mintzberg's view in "Five Ps for Strategy" and argue that Robin Hood's actions, at different times, conform to different definitions of strategy.

Porter's insistence on a single definition of strategy works best in cases such as McDonald's, Netflix, QVC, and Nintendo, where managers are asking hard questions about the future direction of the company. However, when one looks at cases such as Procter & Gamble, HBO, and Johnson & Johnson, which take the long view, it is possible to argue with Mintzberg and Lampel in "Reflecting on the Strategy Process" that there is no single school of strategy but rather different schools depending on assumptions and perspectives.

READING 1.1

Five Ps for Strategy BY HENRY MINTZBERG

Human nature insists on a definition for every concept. But the word *strategy* has long been used implicitly in different ways even if it has traditionally been defined in only one. Explicit recognition of multiple definitions can help people to maneuver through this difficult field. Accordingly, five definitions of strategy are presented here—as plan, ploy, pattern, position, and perspective—and some of their interrelationships are then considered.

STRATEGY AS PLAN

To almost anyone you care to ask, strategy is a plan—some sort of *consciously intended* course of action, a guideline (or set of guidelines) to deal with a situation. A kid has a "strategy" to get over a fence, a corporation has one to capture a market. By this definition, strategies have two essential characteristics: they are made in advance of the actions to which they apply, and they are developed consciously and purposefully. A host of definitions in a variety of fields reinforce this view. For example:

- *in the military:* Strategy is concerned with "draft[ing] the plan of war . . . shap[ing] the individual campaigns and within these, decide[ing] on the individual engagements" (von Clausewitz, 1989: 177).
- *in game theory:* Strategy is "a complete plan: a plan which specifies what choices [the player] will make in every possible situation" (von Newman and Morgenstern, 1944: 79).
- *in management:* "Strategy is a unified, comprehensive, and integrated plan . . . designed to ensure that the basic objectives of the enterprise are achieved" (Glueck, 1980: 9).

As plans, strategies may be general or they can be specific. There is one use of the word in the specific sense that should be identified here. As plan, a strategy can be a ploy, too, really just a specific "maneuver" intended to outwit an opponent or competitor. The kid may use the fence as a ploy to draw a bully into his yard, where his Doberman pinscher awaits intruders. Likewise, a corporation may threaten to expand plant capacity to discourage a competitor from building a new plant. Here the real strategy (as plan, that is, the real intention) is the threat, not the expansion itself, and as such is a ploy.

In fact, there is a growing literature in the field of strategic management, as well as on the general process of bargaining, that views strategy in this way and so focuses attention on its most dynamic and competitive aspects. For example, in his popular book, *Competitive Strategy*, Porter (1980) devotes one chapter to "Market Signals" (including discussion of the effects of announcing moves, the use of "the fighting brand," and the use of threats of private antitrust suits) and another to "Competitive Moves" (including actions to preempt competitive response). And Schelling (1980) devotes much of his famous book, *The Strategy of Conflict*, to the topic of ploys to outwit rivals in a competitive or bargaining situation.

STRATEGY AS PATTERN

But if strategies can be intended (whether as general plans or specific ploys), surely they can also be realized. In other words, defining strategy as a plan is not sufficient; we also need a definition that encompasses the resulting behavior. Thus, a third definition is proposed: strategy is a pattern—specifically, a pattern in a stream of actions (Mintzberg and Waters, 1982). By this definition, when Picasso painted blue for a time, that was a strategy, just as was the behavior of the Ford Motor Company when Henry Ford offered his Model T only in black. In other words, by this definition, strategy is *consistency* in behavior, *whether or not* intended.

This may sound like a strange definition for a word that has been so bound up with free will ("strategos" in Greek, the art of the army general [Evered, 1983]). But the fact of the matter is that while hardly anyone defines strategy in this way, many people seem at one time or another to so use it. Consider this quotation from a business executive: "Gradually the successful approaches merge into a pattern of action that becomes our strategy. We certainly don't have an overall strategy on this" (quoted in Quinn, 1980: 35). This comment is inconsistent only if we restrict ourselves to one definition of strategy: what this man seems to be saying is that his firm has strategy as pattern, but not as plan. Or consider this comment in *Business Week* on a joint venture between General Motors and Toyota:

> The tentative Toyota deal may be most significant because it is another example of how GM's strategy boils down to doing a little bit of everything until the market decides where it is going. (*Business Week*, October 31, 1983)

A journalist has inferred a pattern in the behavior of a corporation and labeled it strategy.

The point is that every time a journalist imputes a strategy to a corporation or to a government, and every time a manager does the same thing to a competitor or even to the senior management of his own firm, they are implicitly defining strategy as pattern in action—that is, inferring consistency in behavior and labeling it strategy. They may, of course, go further and impute intention to that consistency—that is, assume there is a plan behind the pattern. But that is an assumption, which may prove false.

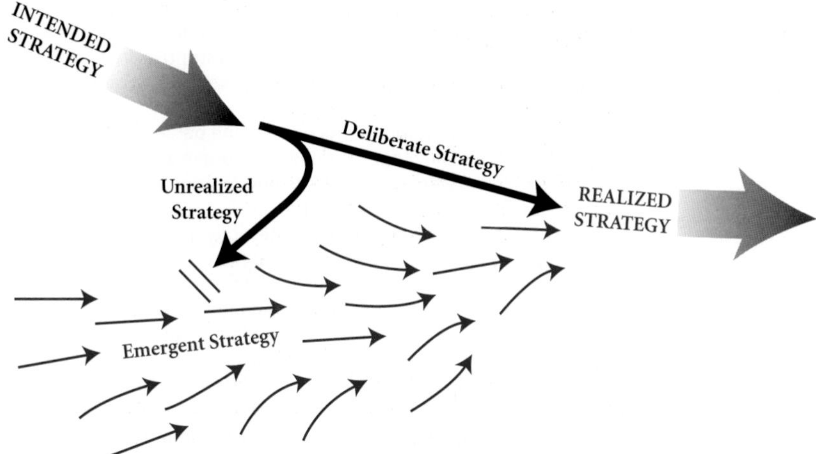

FIGURE 1
DELIBERATE AND EMERGENT STRATEGIES

Thus, the definitions of strategy as plan and pattern can be quite independent of each other: plans may go unrealized, while patterns may appear without preconception. To paraphrase Hume, strategies may result from human actions but not human designs (see Majone, 1976–77). If we label the first definition *intended* strategy and the second *realized* strategy, as shown in Figure 1, then we can distinguish *deliberate* strategies, where intentions that existed previously were realized, from *emergent* strategies, where patterns developed in the absence of intentions, or despite them (which went *unrealized*).

For a strategy to be truly deliberate—that is, for a pattern to have been intended *exactly* as realized—would seem to be a tall order. Precise intentions would have had to be stated in advance by the leadership of the organization; these would have had to be accepted as is by everyone else, and then realized with no interference by market, technological, or political forces, and so on. Likewise, a truly emergent strategy is again a tall order, requiring consistency in action without any hint of intention. (No consistency means *no* strategy, or at least unrealized strategy.) Yet some strategies do come close enough to either form, while others—probably most—sit on the continuum that exists between the two, reflecting deliberate as well as emergent aspects. Table 1 lists various kinds of strategies along this continuum.

STRATEGIES ABOUT WHAT?

Labeling strategies as plans or patterns still begs one basic question: *strategies about what?* Many writers respond by discussing the deployment of resources, but the question remains: which resources and for what purposes? An army may plan to reduce the number of nails in its shoes, or a corporation may realize a pattern of marketing only products painted black, but these hardly meet the lofty label "strategy." Or do they?

As the word has been handed down from the military, "strategy" refers to the important things, "tactics" to the details (more formally, "tactics teaches the use of armed forces in the engagement, strategy the use of engagements for the object of the war" [von Clausewitz, 1989: 128]). Nails in shoes, colors of cars; these are certainly details. The problem is that in retrospect details can sometimes prove "strategic." Even in the military: "For want of a Nail, the Shoe was lost; for want of a Shoe the Horse was lost . . . ," and so on through the rider and general to the battle, "all for want of Care about a Horseshoe Nail" (Franklin, 1977: 280). Indeed, one of the reasons Henry Ford lost his war with General Motors was that he refused to paint his cars anything but black.

Rumelt (1980) notes that "one person's strategies are another's tactics—that what is strategic depends on where you sit." It also depends on *when* you sit; what seems tactical today may prove strategic tomorrow. The point is that labels should not be used to imply that some issues are *inevitably* more important than others. There are times when it pays to manage the details and let the strategies emerge for themselves. Thus, there is good reason to refer to issues as more or less "strategic," in other words, more or less "important" in some context, whether as intended

TABLE 1
VARIOUS KINDS OF STRATEGIES, FROM RATHER DELIBERATE TO MOSTLY EMERGENT*

Planned Strategy: Precise intentions are formulated and articulated by a central leadership, and backed up by formal controls to ensure their surprise-free implementation in an environment that is benign, controllable, or predictable (to ensure no distortion of intentions); these strategies are highly deliberate.

Entrepreneurial Strategy: Intentions exist as the personal, unarticulated vision of a single leader, and so are adaptable to new opportunities; the organization is under the personal control of the leader and located in a protected niche in its environment; these strategies are relatively deliberate but can emerge too.

Ideological Strategy: Intentions exist as the collective vision of all the members of the organization, controlled through strong shared norms; the organization is often proactive vis-à -vis its environment; these strategies are rather deliberate.

Umbrella Strategy: A leadership in partial control of organizational actions defines strategic targets or boundaries within which others must act (e.g., that all new products be high priced and at the technological cutting edge, although what these actual products are to be is left to emerge); as a result, strategies are partly deliberate (the boundaries) and partly emergent (the patterns within them); this strategy can also be called deliberately emergent, in that the leadership purposefully allows others the flexibility to maneuver and form patterns within the boundaries.

Process Strategy: The leadership controls the process aspects of strategy (who gets hired and so gets a chance to influence strategy, what structures they work within, etc.), leaving the actual content of strategy to others; strategies are again partly deliberate (concerning process) and partly emergent (concerning content), and deliberately emergent.

Disconnected Strategy: Members or subunits loosely coupled to the rest of the organization produce patterns in the streams of their own actions in the absence of, or in direct contradiction to, central or common intentions of the organization at large; the strategies can be deliberate for those who make them.

Consensus Strategy: Through mutual adjustment, various members converge on patterns that pervade the organization in the absence of central or common intentions; these strategies are rather emergent in nature.

Imposed Strategy: The external environment dictates patterns in actions, either through direct imposition (say, by an outside owner or by a strong customer) or through implicitly preempting or bounding organizational choice (as in a large airline that must fly jumbo jets to remain viable); these strategies are organizationally emergent, although they may be internalized and made deliberate.

*Adapted from Mintzberg and Waters (1982: 270).

before acting or as realized after it. Accordingly, the answer to the question, strategy about what, is: potentially about anything. About products and processes, customers and citizens, social responsibilities and self-interests, control and color.

Two aspects of the content of strategies must, however, be singled out because they are of particular importance.

STRATEGY AS POSITION

The fourth definition is that strategy is a position—specifically, a means of locating an organization in what organization theorists like to call an "environment." By this definition, strategy becomes the mediating force—or "match," according to Hofer and Schendel (1978: 4)— between organization and environment, that is, between the internal and the external context. In ecological terms, strategy becomes a "niche"; in economic terms, a place that generates "rent" (i.e., "returns to [being] in a 'unique' place" [Bowman, 1974: 47]); in management terms, formally, a product-market "domain" (Thompson, 1967), the place in the environment where resources are concentrated.

Note that this definition of strategy can be compatible with either (or all) of the preceding ones; a position can be preselected and aspired to through a plan (or ploy) and/or it can be reached, perhaps even found, through a pattern of behavior.

In military and game theory views of strategy, it is generally used in the context of what is called a "two-person game," better known in business as head-on competition (where ploys are especially common). The definition of strategy as position, however, implicitly allows us to open up the concept, to so-called *n*-person games (i.e., many players), and beyond. In other words, while position can always be defined with respect to a single competitor (literally so in the military, where position becomes the site of battle), it can also be considered in the context of a number of competitors or simply with respect to markets or an environment at large. But strategy as position can extend beyond competition too, economic and otherwise. Indeed, what is the meaning of the word "niche" but a position that is occupied to *avoid* competition. Thus, we can move from the definition employed by General Ulysses Grant in the 1860s, "Strategy [is] the deployment of one's resources in a manner which is most likely to defeat the enemy," to that of Professor Richard Rumelt in the 1980s, "Strategy is creating situations for economic rents and finding ways to sustain them" (Rumelt, 1982), that is, any viable position, whether or not directly competitive.

Astley and Fombrun (1983), in fact, take the next logical step by introducing the notion of "collective" strategy, that is, strategy pursued to promote cooperation between organizations, even would-be competitors (equivalent in biology to animals herding together for protection). Such strategies can range "from informal arrangements and discussions to formal devices such as interlocking directorates, joint ventures, and mergers." In fact, considered from a slightly different angle, these can sometimes be described as *political* strategies, that is, strategies to subvert the legitimate forces of competition.

STRATEGY AS PERSPECTIVE

While the fourth definition of strategy looks out, seeking to locate the organization in the external environment, and down to concrete positions, the fifth looks inside the organization, indeed inside the heads of the collective strategist, but up to a broader view. Here, strategy is a perspective, its content consisting not just of a chosen position, but of an ingrained way of perceiving the world. There are organizations that favor marketing and build a whole ideology around that (an IBM); Hewlett-Packard has developed the "H-P way," based on its engineering culture, while McDonald's has become famous for its emphasis on quality, service, and cleanliness.

Strategy in this respect is to the organization what personality is to the individual. Indeed, one of the earliest and most influential writers on strategy (at least as his ideas have been reflected in more popular writings) was Philip Selznick (1957: 47), who wrote about the "character" of an organization—distinct and integrated "commitments to ways of acting and responding" that are built right into it. A variety of concepts from other fields also capture this notion; anthropologists refer to the "culture" of a society and sociologists to its "ideology"; military theorists write of the "grand strategy" of armies; while management theorists have used terms such as the "theory of the business" and its "driving force" (Drucker, 1974; Tregoe and Zimmerman, 1980); and Germans perhaps capture it best with their word "Weltanschauung," literally "worldview," meaning collective intuition about how the world works.

This fifth definition suggests above all that strategy is a *concept*. This has one important implication, namely, that all strategies are abstractions that exist only in the minds of interested parties. It is important to remember that no one has ever seen a strategy or touched one; every strategy is an invention, a figment of someone's imagination, whether conceived of as intentions to regulate behavior before it takes place or inferred as patterns to describe behavior that has already occurred.

What is of key importance about this fifth definition, however, is that the perspective is *shared*. As implied in the words *Weltanschauung, culture,* and *ideology* (with respect to a society), but not the word *personality*, strategy is a perspective shared by the members of an organization, through their intentions and/or by their actions. In effect, when we are talking of strategy in this context, we are entering the realm of the *collective* mind—individuals united by common thinking and/or behavior. A major issue in the study of strategy formation becomes, therefore, how to read that collective mind—to understand how intentions diffuse through the system called organization to become shared and how actions come to be exercised on a collective yet consistent basis.

INTERRELATING THE Ps

As suggested above, strategy as both position and perspective can be compatible with strategy as plan and/or pattern. But, in fact, the relationships between these different definitions can be more involved than that. For example, while some consider perspective to *be* a plan (Lapierre,

1980, writes of strategies as "dreams in search of reality"), others describe it as *giving rise* to plans (e.g., as positions and/or patterns in some kind of implicit hierarchy). But the concept of emergent strategy is that a pattern can emerge and be recognized so that it gives rise to a formal plan, perhaps within an overall perspective.

We may ask how perspective arises in the first place. Probably through earlier experiences: the organization tried various things in its formative years and gradually consolidated a perspective around what worked. In other words, organizations would appear to develop "character" much as people develop personality—by interacting with the world as they find it through the use of their innate skills and natural propensities. Thus pattern can give rise to perspective too. And so can position. Witness Perrow's (1970:161) discussion of the "wool men" and "silk men" of the textile trade, people who developed an almost religious dedication to the fibers they produced.

No matter how they appear, however, there is reason to believe that while plans and positions may be dispensable, perspectives are immutable (Brunsson, 1982). In other words, once they are established, perspectives become difficult to change. Indeed, a perspective may become so deeply ingrained in the behavior of an organization that the associated beliefs can become subconscious in the minds of its members. When that happens, perspective can come to look more like pattern than like plan—in other words, it can be found more in the consistency of behaviors than in the articulation of intentions.

Of course, if perspective is immutable, then change in plan and position within perspective is easy compared to change of perspective. In this regard, it is interesting to take up the case of Egg McMuffin. Was this product when new—the American breakfast in a bun—a strategic change for the McDonald's fast-food chain? Posed in MBA classes, this earth-shattering (or at least stomach-shattering) question inevitably evokes heated debate. Proponents (usually people sympathetic to fast food) argue that of course it was: it brought McDonald's into a new market, the breakfast one, extending the use of existing facilities. Opponents retort that this is nonsense; nothing changed but a few ingredients: this was the same old pap in a new package. Both sides are, of course, right—and wrong. It simply depends on how you define strategy. Position changed; perspective remained the same. Indeed—and this is the point—the position could be changed easily because it was compatible with the existing perspective. Egg McMuffin is pure McDonald's, not only in product and package, but also in production and propagation. But imagine a change of position at McDonald's that would require a change of perspective—say, to introduce candlelight dining with personal service (your McDuckling à l'Orange cooked to order) to capture the late evening market. We needn't say more, except perhaps to label this the "Egg McMuffin syndrome."

THE NEED FOR ECLECTICISM IN DEFINITION

While various relationships exist among the different definitions, no one relationship, nor any single definition for that matter, takes precedence over the others. In some ways, these definitions compete (in that they can substitute for each other), but in perhaps more important ways, they complement. Not all plans become patterns nor are all patterns that develop planned; some ploys are less than positions, while other strategies are more than positions yet less than perspectives. Each definition adds important elements to our understanding of strategy, indeed encourages us to address fundamental questions about organizations in general.

As plan, strategy deals with how leaders try to establish direction for organizations, to set them on predetermined courses of action. Strategy as plan also raises the fundamental issue of cognition—how intentions are conceived in the human brain in the first place, indeed, what intentions really mean. The road to hell in this field can be paved with those who take all stated intentions at face value. In studying strategy as plan, we must somehow get into the mind of the strategist, to find out what is really intended.

As ploy, strategy takes us into the realm of direct competition, where threats and feints and various other maneuvers are employed to gain advantage. This places the process of strategy formation in its most dynamic setting, with moves provoking countermoves and so on. Yet ironically, strategy itself is a concept rooted not in change but in stability—in set plans and established patterns. How then to reconcile the dynamic notions of strategy as ploy with the static ones of strategy as pattern and other forms of plan?

As pattern, strategy focuses on action, reminding us that the concept is an empty one if it does not take behavior into account. Strategy as pattern also introduces the notion of convergence, the achievement of consistency in an organization's behavior. How does this consistency form, where does it come from? Realized strategy, when considered alongside intended strategy, encourages us to consider the notion that strategies can emerge as well as be deliberately imposed.

As position, strategy encourages us to look at organizations in their competitive environments—how they find their positions and protect them in order to meet competition, avoid it, or subvert it. This enables us to think of organizations in ecological terms, as organisms in niches that struggle for survival in a world of hostility and uncertainty as well as symbiosis.

And finally as perspective, strategy raises intriguing questions about intention and behavior in a collective context. If we define organization as collective action in the pursuit of a common mission (a fancy way of saying that a group of people under a common label—whether a General Motors or a Luigi's Body Shop—somehow finds the means to cooperate in the production of specific goods and services), then strategy as perspective raises the issue of how intentions diffuse through a group of people to become shared as norms and values, and how patterns of behavior become deeply ingrained in the group.

Thus, strategy is not just a notion of how to deal with an enemy or a set of competitors or a market, as it is treated in so much of the literature and its popular usage. It also draws us into some of the most fundamental issues about organizations as instruments for collective perception and action.

To conclude, a good deal of the confusion in this field stems from contradictory and ill-defined uses of the term "strategy". By explicating and using various definitions, we may be able to avoid some of this confusion, and thereby enrich our ability to understand and manage the processes by which strategies form.

READING 1.2

Strategies for Change BY JAMES BRIAN QUINN

SOME USEFUL DEFINITIONS

Because the words *strategy, objectives, goals, policy,* and *programs* have different meanings to individual readers or to various organizational cultures, I [try] to use certain definitions consistently. . . . For clarity—not pedantry—these are set forth as follows:

A strategy is the *pattern* or *plan* that *integrates* an organization's *major* goals, policies, and action sequences into a *cohesive* whole. A well-formulated strategy helps to *marshal* and *allocate* an organization's resources into a *unique and viable posture* based on its relative *internal competencies* and *shortcomings*, anticipated *changes in the environment*, and contingent moves by *intelligent opponents*.

Goals (or objectives) state *what* is to be achieved and *when* results are to be accomplished, but they do not state *how* the results are to be achieved. All organizations have multiple goals existing in a complex hierarchy (Simon, 1964): from value objectives, which express the broad value premises toward which the company is to strive; through overall organizational objectives, which establish the intended *nature* of the enterprise and the *directions* in which it should move; to a series of less permanent goals that define targets for each organizational unit, its subunits, and finally all major program activities within each subunit. Major goals—those that affect the entity's overall direction and viability—are called *strategic goals*.

Policies are rules or guidelines that express the *limits* within which action should occur. These rules often take the form of contingent decisions for resolving conflicts among specific objectives. For example: "Don't exceed three months' inventory in any item without corporate approval." Like the objectives they support, policies exist in a hierarchy throughout the organization. Major policies—those that guide the entity's overall direction and posture or determine its viability—are called *strategic policies*.

Programs specify the *step-by-step sequence of actions* necessary to achieve major objectives. They express *how* objectives will be achieved within the limits set by policy. They ensure that resources are committed to achieve goals, and they provide the dynamic track against which progress can be measured. Those major programs that determine the entity's overall thrust and viability are called *strategic programs*.

Strategic decisions are those that determine the overall direction of an enterprise and its ultimate viability in light of the predictable, the unpredictable, and the unknowable changes that may occur in its most important surrounding environments. They intimately shape the true goals of the enterprise. They help delineate the broad limits within which the enterprise operates. They dictate both the resources the enterprise will have accessible for its tasks and the principal patterns in which these resources will be allocated. And they determine the effectiveness of the enterprise—whether its major thrusts are in the right directions given its resource potentials—rather than whether individual tasks are performed efficiently. Management for efficiency, along with the myriad decisions necessary to maintain the daily life and services of the enterprise, is the domain of operations.

STRATEGIES VERSUS TACTICS

Strategies normally exist at many different levels in any large organization. For example, in government there are world trade, national economic, treasury department, military spending, investment, fiscal, monetary supply, banking, regional development, and local reemployment strategies—all related to each other somewhat hierarchically yet each having imperatives of its own. Similarly, businesses have numerous strategies from corporate levels to department levels within divisions. Yet if strategies exist at all these levels, how do strategies and tactics differ? Often the primary difference lies in the scale of action or the perspective of the leader. What appears to be a "tactic" to the chief executive officer (or general) may be a "strategy" to the marketing head (or lieutenant) if it determines the ultimate success and viability of his or her organization. In a more precise sense, tactics can occur at either level. They are the short-duration, adaptive, action–interaction realignments that opposing forces use to accomplish limited goals after their initial contact. Strategy defines a continuing basis for ordering these adaptations toward more broadly conceived purposes.

A genuine strategy is always needed when the potential actions or responses of intelligent opponents can seriously affect the endeavor's desired outcome—regardless of that endeavor's organizational level in the total enterprise. This condition almost always pertains to the important actions taken at the top level of competitive organizations. However, game theorists quickly point out that some important top-level actions—for example, sending a peacetime fleet across the Atlantic—merely require elaborate coordinative plans and programs (Von Neumann and Morgenstern, 1944; Shubik, 1975; McDonald, 1950). A whole new set of concepts, a true strategy, is needed if some people or nations decide to oppose the fleet's purposes. And it is these concepts that in large part distinguish strategic formulation from simpler programmatic planning.

Strategies may be looked at as either a priori statements to guide action or a posteriori results of actual decision behavior. In most complex organizations . . . one would be hard pressed to find a complete a priori statement of a total strategy that actually is followed. Yet often the existence of a strategy (or strategy change) may be clear to an objective observer, although it is not yet apparent to the executives making critical decisions. One, therefore, must look at the actual emerging *pattern* of the enterprise's operant goals, policies, and major programs to see what its true strategy is (Mintzberg, 1972). Whether it is consciously set forth in advance or is simply a widely held understanding resulting from a stream of decisions, this pattern becomes the real strategy of the enterprise. And it is changes in this pattern—regardless of what any formal strategic documents may say—that either analysts or strategic decision makers must address if they wish to comprehend or alter the concern's strategic posture. . . .

THE CLASSICAL APPROACH TO STRATEGY

Military–diplomatic strategies have existed since prehistoric times. In fact, one function of the earliest historians and poets was to collect the accumulated lore of these successful and unsuccessful life-and-death strategies and convert them into wisdom and guidance for the future.

As societies grew larger and conflicts more complex, generals, statesmen, and captains studied, codified, and tested essential strategic concepts until a coherent body of principles seemed to emerge. In various forms these were ultimately distilled into the maxims of Sun Tzu (1963), Machiavelli (1950), Napoleon (1940), von Clausewitz (1989), Foch (1970), Lenin (1927), Liddell Hart (1954), Montgomery (1958), or Mao Tse-Tung (1967). Yet with a few exceptions—largely introduced by modern technology—the most basic principles of strategy were in place and recorded long before the Christian era. More modern institutions primarily adapted and modified these to their own special environments.

Although one could choose any number of classical military–diplomatic strategies as examples, Philip and Alexander's actions at Chaeronea (in 338 B.C.) contain many currently relevant concepts (Varner and Alger, 1978; Green, 1970). . . .

A Classical Strategy

A Grand Strategy

Philip and his young son, Alexander, had very *clear goals*. They sought to rid Macedonia of influence by the Greek city-states and to *establish dominance* over what was then essentially northern Greece. They also wanted Athens to join a coalition with them against Persia on their eastern flank. *Assessing their resources*, they *decided* to avoid the overwhelming superiority of the Athenian fleet and *chose to forego* attack on the powerful walled cities of Athens and Thebes where their superbly trained phalanxes and cavalry would not *have distinct advantages*.

Philip and Alexander *used an indirect approach* when an invitation by the Amphictyonic Council brought their army south to punish Amphissa. In a *planned sequence of actions and deceptive maneuvers*, they cut away from a direct line of march to Amphissa, *bypassed the enemy*, and *fortified a key base*, Elatea. They then took steps to *weaken their opponents politically and morally* by pressing restoration of the Phoenician communities earlier dispersed by the Thebans and by having Philip declared a champion of the Delphic gods. Then *using misleading messages* to make the enemy believe they had moved north to Thrace and also *using developed intelligence sources*, the Macedonians in a *surprise attack* annihilated the Greeks' positions near Amphissa. This *lured their opponents away from their defensive positions* in the nearby mountain passes to *consolidate their forces* near the town of Chaeronea.

There, *assessing the relative strengths* of their opponents, the Macedonians first *attempted to negotiate* to achieve their goals. When this was unsuccessful they had a *well-developed contingency plan* on how to *attack and overwhelm* the Greeks. Prior to this time, of course, the Macedonians had *organized* their troops into the famed phalanxes, and had *developed the full logistics* needed for their field support including a longer spear, which helped the Macedonian phalanxes penetrate the solid shield wall of the heavily massed Greek formations. *Using the natural advantages* of their terrain, the Macedonians had developed cavalry support for their phalanxes' movements far beyond the Greek capability. Finally, using a *relative advantage*—the *command structure* their hierarchical *social system* allowed—against the more democratic Greeks, the Macedonian nobles had *trained their personnel* into one of the most *disciplined and highly motivated forces* in the world.

The Battle Strategy

Supporting this was the battle strategy at Chaeronea, which emerged as follows. Philip and Alexander first *analyzed their specific strengths and weaknesses and their opponents' current alignments and probable moves*. The Macedonian strength lay in their new spear technology, the *mobility* of their superbly disciplined phalanxes, and the powerful cavalry units led by Alexander. Their weaknesses were that they were badly outnumbered and faced—in the Athenians and the Theban Band—some of the finest foot troops in the world. However, their opponents had two weak points. One was the Greek left flank with lightly armed local troops placed near the Chaeronean Acropolis and next to some more heavily armed—but hastily assembled—hoplites bridging to the strong center held by the Athenians. The famed Theban Band anchored the Greek right wing near a swamp on the Cephissus River. [See Figure 1.]

Philip and Alexander *organized their leadership to command key positions*, Philip took over the right wing and Alexander the cavalry. They *aligned their forces* into *a unique posture* that *used their strengths* and *offset their weaknesses*. They decided on those spots at which they would *concentrate their forces*, what *positions to concede*, and what *key points* they *must take and hold*. Starting with their units angled back from the Greek lines (see the map shown in Figure 1), they developed a

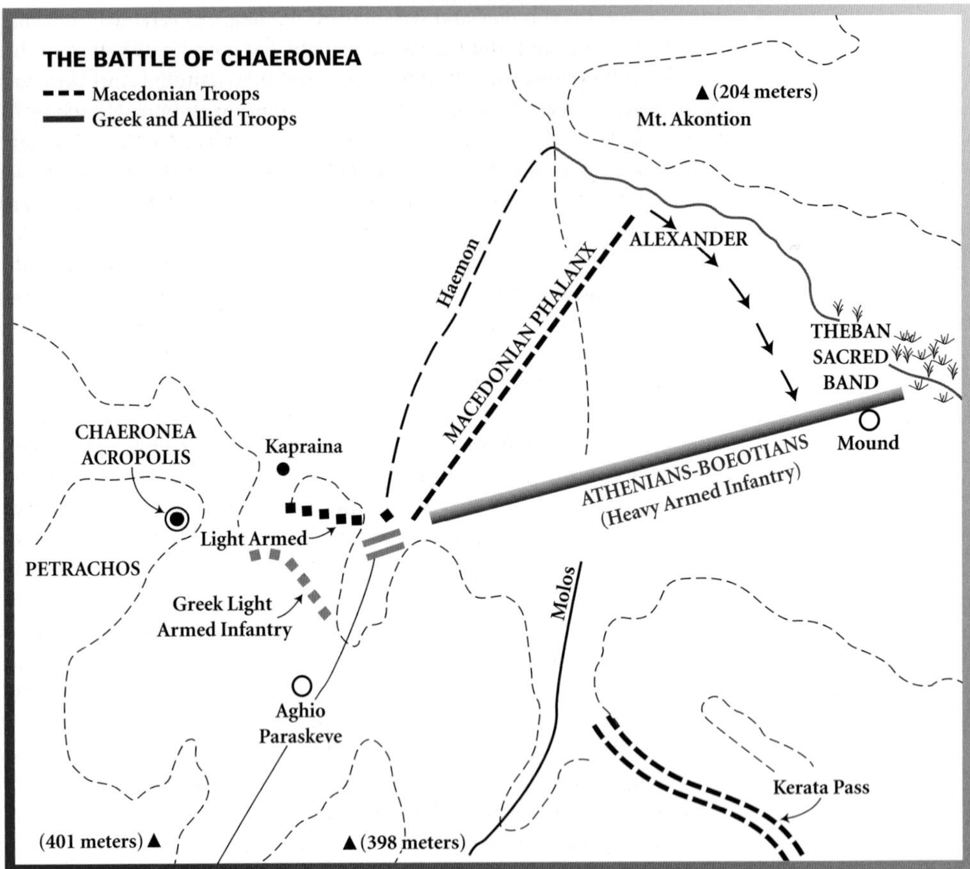

FIGURE 1
THE BATTLE OF CHAERONEA
Source: Modified with permission from P. Green, *Alexander the Great*, Praeger Publishers, New York (1970).

focused major thrust against the Greek left wing and *attacked their opponents'* weaknesses—the troops near Chaeronea—with the most disciplined of the Macedonian units, the guards' brigade. After building up pressure and stretching the Greek line to its left, the guards' brigade abruptly began a *planned withdrawal.* This *feint* caused the Greek left to break ranks and rush forward, believing the Macedonians to be in full retreat. This *stretched their opponents' resources* as the Greek center moved left to *maintain contact* with its flank and to attack the "fleeing" Macedonians.

Then *with predetermined timing,* Alexander's cavalry *attacked the exposure* of the stretched line at the same moment Philip's phalanxes *re-formed as planned* on the high ground at the edge of the Heamon River. Alexander *broke through* and *formed a bridgehead* behind the Greeks. He *refocused his forces against a segment* of the opponents' line; his cavalry *surrounded and destroyed* the Theban Band as the *overwhelming power* of the phalanxes poured through the gap he had created. From its *secured position,* the Macedonian left flank then turned and *attacked the flank* of the Athenians. With the help of Philip's *planned counterattack,* the Macedonians *expanded their dominance and overwhelmed the critical target,* that is, the Greek center. . . .

MODERN ANALOGIES

Similar concepts have continued to dominate the modern era of formal strategic thought. As this period begins, Scharnhorst still points to the need to *analyze social forces and structures* as a basis for *understanding effective command styles* and *motivational stimuli* (von Clausewitz, 1989: 8). Frederick the Great proved this point in the field. Presumably based on such analyses, he adopted *training, discipline,* and *fast maneuvers* as the central concepts for a tightly disciplined German culture that had to be constantly ready to fight on two fronts (Phillips, 1940). Von Bülow (1806) continued to emphasize the dominant strategic roles of *geographical positioning* and *logistical support systems* in strategy. Both Jomini (1971) and Von Bülow (1806) stressed the concepts of *concentration, points of domination,* and *rapidity of movement* as central strategic themes and even tried to develop them into mathematically precise principles for their time.

Still later von Clausewitz expounded on the paramountcy of *clear major objectives* in war and on developing war strategies as a component of the nation's *broader goals* with *time horizons* extending beyond the war itself. Within this context he postulated that an effective strategy should be focused around a relatively *few central principles* that can *create, guide,* and *maintain dominance* despite the enormous frictions that occur as one tries to position or maneuver large forces in war. Among these he included many of the concepts operant in Macedonian times: *spirit or morale, surprise, cunning, concentration in space, dominance of selected positions, use of strategic reserves, unification over time, tension and release,* and so on. He showed how these broad principles applied to a number of specific attack, defense, flanking, and retreat situations; but he always stressed the intangible of *leadership*. His basic positioning and organizational principles were to be mixed with boldness, perseverance, and genius. He constantly emphasized—as did Napoleon—the need for *planned flexibility* once the battle was joined.

Later strategic analysts adapted these classic themes for larger-scale conflicts. Von Schlieffen linked together the huge numerical and production *strengths* of Germany and the vast *maneuvering capabilities* of Flanders fields to pull the nation's might together conceptually behind a *unique alignment of forces* ("a giant hayrake"), which would "outflank" his French opponents, *attack weaknesses* (their supply lines and rear), capture and *hold key political centers* of France, and *dominate or destroy* its weakened army in the field (Tuchman, 1962). On the other side, Foch and Grandmaison saw *morale* ("élan"), *nerve* ("cran"), and continuous *concentrated attack* ("attaque à outrance") as *matching the values* of a volatile, recently defeated, and vengeful French nation, which had decided (for both moral and *coalition* reasons) to *set important limits* on its own actions in World War I—that is, not to attack first or through Belgium.

As these two strategies lost shape and became the head-on slaughter of trench warfare, Liddell Hart (1954) revitalized the *indirect approach*, and this became a central theme of British strategic thinking between the wars. Later in the United States, Matloff and Snell (1953) began to stress planning for *large-scale coalitions* as the giant forces of World War II developed. The Enigma group *moved secretly to develop the intelligence network* that was so crucial in the war's outcome (Stevenson, 1976). But once engaged in war, George Marshall still saw the only hope for Allied victory in *concentrating overwhelming forces* against one enemy (Germany) first, then after *conceding early losses* in the Pacific, *refocusing Allied forces* in a gigantic *sequential coordinated movement* against Japan. In the eastern theater, MacArthur first *fell back, consolidated a base* for operations, *built up his logistics, avoided his opponent's strengths, bypassed* Japan's established defensive positions, and in a *gigantic flanking maneuver* was ready to invade Japan after *softening its political and psychological will* through saturation bombing (James, 1970).

All these modern thinkers and practitioners utilized classical principles of strategy dating back to the Greek era, but perhaps the most startling analogies of World War II lay in Patton's and Rommel's battle strategies, which were almost carbon copies of the Macedonians' concepts of planned concentration, rapid breakthrough, encirclement, and attack on the enemy's rear (Essame, 1974; Farago, 1964; Irving, 1977; Young, 1974).

Similar concepts still pervade well-conceived strategies—whether they are government, diplomatic, military, sports, or business strategies. What could be more direct than the parallel between Chaeronea and a well-developed business strategy that first probes and withdraws to determine opponents' strengths, forces opponents to stretch their commitments, then concentrates resources, attacks a clear exposure, overwhelms a selected market segment, builds a bridgehead in that market, and then regroups and expands from that base to dominate a wider field? Many companies have followed just such strategies with great success. . . .

DIMENSIONS OF STRATEGY

Analysis of military–diplomatic strategies and similar analogies in other fields provides some essential insights into the basic dimensions, nature, and design of formal strategies.

First, effective formal strategies contain three essential elements: (1) the most important *goals* (or objectives) to be achieved, (2) the most significant *policies* guiding or limiting action, and

(3) the major *action sequences* (or programs) that are to accomplish the defined goals within the limits set. Since strategy determines the overall direction and action focus of the organization, its formulation cannot be regarded as the mere generation and alignment of programs to meet predetermined goals. Goal development is an integral part of strategy formulation. . . .

Second, effective strategies develop around a *few key concepts and thrusts*, which give them cohesion, balance, and focus. Some thrusts are temporary; others are carried through to the end of the strategy. Some cost more per unit gain than others. Yet resources must be *allocated in patterns* that provide sufficient resources for each thrust to succeed regardless of its relative cost/gain ratio. And organizational units must be coordinated and actions controlled to support the intended thrust pattern or else the total strategy will. . . .

Third, strategy deals not just with the unpredictable but also with the *unknowable*. For major enterprise strategies, no analyst could predict the precise ways in which all impinging forces could interact with each other, be distorted by nature or human emotions, or be modified by the imaginations and purposeful counteractions of intelligent opponents (Braybrooke and Lindblom, 1963). Many have noted how large-scale systems can respond quite counterintuitively (Forrester, 1971) to apparently rational actions or how a seemingly bizarre series of events can conspire to prevent or assist success (White, 1978; Lindblom, 1959). . . .

Consequently, the essence of strategy—whether military, diplomatic, business, sports, (or) political . . . —is to *build a posture* that is so strong (and potentially flexible) in selective ways that the organization can achieve its goals despite the unforeseeable ways external forces may actually interact when the time comes.

Fourth, just as military organizations have multiple echelons of grand, theater, area, battle, infantry, and artillery strategies, so should other complex organizations have a number of hierarchically related and mutually supporting strategies (Vancil and Lorange, 1975; Vancil, 1976). Each such strategy must be more or less complete in itself, congruent with the level of decentralization intended. Yet each must be shaped as a cohesive element of higher-level strategies. Although, for reasons cited, achieving total cohesion among all of a major organization's strategies would be a superhuman task for any chief executive officer, it is important that there be a systematic means for testing each component strategy and seeing that it fulfills the major tenets of a well-formed strategy.

The criteria derived from military–diplomatic strategies provide an excellent framework for this, yet too often one sees purported formal strategies at all organizational levels that are not strategies at all. Because they ignore or violate even the most basic strategic principles, they are little more than aggregates of philosophies or agglomerations of programs. They lack the cohesiveness, flexibility, thrust, sense of positioning against intelligent opposition, and other criteria that historical analysis suggests effective strategies must contain. Whether formally or incrementally derived, strategies should be at least intellectually tested against the proper criteria.

CRITERIA FOR EFFECTIVE STRATEGY

In devising a strategy to deal with the unknowable, what factors should one consider? Although each strategic situation is unique, are there some common criteria that tend to define a good strategy? The fact that a strategy worked in retrospect is not a sufficient criterion for judging any strategy. Was Grant really a greater strategist than Lee? Was Foch's strategy better than von Schlieffen's? Was Xerxes's strategy superior to that of Leonidas? Was it the Russians' strategy that allowed them to roll over the Czechoslovaks in 1968? Clearly, other factors than strategy—including luck, overwhelming resources, superb or stupid implementation, and enemy errors—help determine ultimate results. Besides, at the time one formulates a strategy, one cannot use the criterion of ultimate success because the outcome is still in doubt. Yet one clearly needs some guidelines to define an effective strategic structure.

A few studies have suggested some initial criteria for evaluating a strategy (Tilles, 1963; Christensen et al., 1978). These include its clarity, motivational impact, internal consistency, compatibility with the environment, appropriateness in light of resources, degree of risk, match to the personal values of key figures, time horizon, and workability. . . . In addition, historical examples—from both business and military–diplomatic settings—suggest that effective strategies should at a minimum encompass certain other critical factors and structural elements. . . .

- *Clear, decisive objectives:* Are all efforts directed toward clearly understood, decisive, and attainable overall goals? Specific goals of subordinate units may change in the heat of campaigns or competition, but the overriding goals of the strategy for all units must remain clear enough to provide continuity and cohesion for tactical choices during the time horizon of the strategy. All goals need not be written down or numerically precise, but they must be understood and be decisive—that is, if they are achieved they should ensure the continued viability and vitality of the entity vis-à-vis its opponents.

- *Maintaining the initiative:* Does the strategy preserve freedom of action and enhance commitment? Does it set the pace and determine the course of events rather than reacting to them? A prolonged reactive posture breeds unrest, lowers morale, and surrenders the advantage of timing and intangibles to opponents. Ultimately, such a posture increases costs, decreases the number of options available, and lowers the probability of achieving sufficient success to ensure independence and continuity.
- *Concentration:* Does the strategy concentrate superior power at the place and time likely to be decisive? Has the strategy defined precisely what will make the enterprise superior in power—that is, "best" in critical dimensions—in relation to its opponents. A distinctive competency yields greater success with fewer resources and is the essential basis for higher gains (or profits) than competitors. . . .
- *Flexibility:* Has the strategy purposely built in resource buffers and dimensions for flexibility and maneuver? Reserved capabilities, planned maneuverability, and repositioning allow one to use minimum resources while keeping opponents at a relative disadvantage. As corollaries of concentration and concession, they permit the strategist to reuse the same forces to overwhelm selected positions at different times. They also force less flexible opponents to use more resources to hold predetermined positions, while simultaneously requiring minimum fixed commitment of one's own resources for defensive purposes.
- *Coordinated and committed leadership:* Does the strategy provide responsible, committed leadership for each of its major goals? . . . [Leaders] must be so chosen and motivated that their own interests and values match the needs of their roles. Successful strategies require commitment, not just acceptance.
- *Surprise:* Has the strategy made use of speed, secrecy, and intelligence to attack exposed or unprepared opponents at unexpected times? With surprise and correct timing, success can be achieved out of all proportion to the energy exerted and can decisively change strategic positions. . . .
- *Security:* Does the strategy secure resource bases and all vital operating points for the enterprise? Does it develop an effective intelligence system sufficient to prevent surprises by opponents? Does it develop the full logistics to support each of its major thrusts? Does it use coalitions effectively to extend the resource base and zones of friendly acceptance for the enterprise? . . .

These are critical elements of strategy, whether in business, government, or warfare.

READING 1.3

What Is Strategy? BY MICHAEL E. PORTER

I. OPERATIONAL EFFECTIVENESS IS NOT STRATEGY

For almost two decades, managers have been learning to play by a new set of rules. Companies must be flexible to respond rapidly to competitive and market changes. They must benchmark continuously to achieve best practice. They must outsource aggressively to gain efficiencies. And they must nurture a few core competencies in the race to stay ahead of rivals.

Positioning—once the heart of strategy—is rejected as too static for today's dynamic markets and changing technologies. According to the new dogma, rivals can quickly copy any market position, and competitive advantage is, at best, temporary.

But those beliefs are dangerous half-truths, and they are leading more and more companies down the path of mutually destructive competition. True, some barriers to competition are falling as regulation eases and markets become global. True, companies have properly invested energy in becoming leaner and more nimble. In many industries, however, what some call *hypercompetition* is a self-inflicted wound, not the inevitable outcome of a changing paradigm of competition.

The root of the problem is the failure to distinguish between operational effectiveness and strategy. The quest for productivity, quality, and speed has spawned a remarkable number of management tools and techniques: total quality management, benchmarking, time-based competition, outsourcing, partnering, reengineering, change management. Although the resulting operational improvements have often been dramatic, many companies have been frustrated by their inability to translate those gains into sustainable profitability. And bit by bit, almost imperceptibly, management tools have taken the place of strategy. As managers push to improve on all fronts, they move farther away from viable competitive positions.

OPERATIONAL EFFECTIVENESS: NECESSARY BUT NOT SUFFICIENT

Operational effectiveness and strategy are both essential to superior performance, which, after all, is the primary goal of any enterprise. But they work in very different ways.

A company can outperform rivals only if it can establish a difference that it can preserve. It must deliver greater value to customers or create comparable value at a lower cost, or do both. The arithmetic of superior profitability then follows: delivering greater value allows a company to charge higher average unit prices; greater efficiency results in lower average unit costs.

Ultimately, all differences between companies in cost or price derive from the hundreds of activities required to create, produce, sell, and deliver their products or services, such as calling on customers, assembling final products, and training employees. Cost is generated by performing activities, and cost advantage arises from performing particular activities more efficiently than competitors. Similarly, differentiation arises from both the choice of activities and how they are performed. Activities, then, are the basic units of competitive advantage. Overall advantage or disadvantage results from all a company's activities, not only a few.

Operational effectiveness (OE) means performing similar activities *better* than rivals perform them. Operational effectiveness includes but is not limited to efficiency. It refers to any number of practices that allow a company to better utilize its inputs by, for example, reducing defects in products or developing better products faster. In contrast, strategic positioning means performing *different* activities from rivals or performing similar activities in *different ways*.

Differences in operational effectiveness among companies are pervasive. Some companies are able to get more out of their inputs than others because they eliminate wasted effort, employ more advanced technology, motivate employees better, or have greater insight into managing particular activities or sets of activities. Such differences in operational effectiveness are an important source of differences in profitability among competitors because they directly affect relative cost positions and levels of differentiation. . . .

Imagine for a moment a *productivity frontier* that constitutes the sum of all existing best practices at any given time. Think of it as the maximum value that a company delivering a particular product or service can create at a given cost, using the best available technologies, skills, management techniques, and purchased inputs. The productivity frontier can apply to individual activities, to groups of linked activities such as order processing and manufacturing, and to an entire company's activities. When a company improves its operational effectiveness, it moves toward the frontier. Doing so may require capital investment, different personnel, or simply new ways of managing.

The productivity frontier is constantly shifting outward as new technologies and management approaches are developed and as new inputs become available. . . .

OE competition shifts the productivity frontier outward, effectively raising the bar for everyone. But although such competition produces absolute improvement in operational effectiveness, it leads to relative improvement for no one. Consider the $5 billion-plus U.S. commercial-printing industry. The major players—R.R. Donnelley & Sons Company, Quebecor, World Color Press, and Big Flower Press—are competing head to head, serving all types of customers, offering the same array of printing technologies (gravure and web offset), investing heavily in the same new equipment, running their presses faster, and reducing crew sizes. But the resulting major productivity gains are being captured by customers and equipment suppliers, not retained in superior profitability. . . .

The second reason that improved operational effectiveness is insufficient—competitive convergence—is more subtle and insidious. The more benchmarking companies do, the more they look alike. The more that rivals outsource activities to efficient third parties, often the same ones, the more generic those activities become. As rivals imitate one another's improvements in quality, cycle times, or supplier partnerships, strategies converge and competition becomes a series of races down identical paths that no one can win. Competition based on operational effectiveness alone is mutually destructive, leading to wars of attrition that can be arrested only by limiting competition.

The recent wave of industry consolidation through mergers makes sense in the context of OE competition. Driven by performance pressures but lacking strategic vision, company after company has had no better idea than to buy up its rivals. The competitors left standing are often those that outlasted others, not companies with real advantage.

II. STRATEGY RESTS ON UNIQUE ACTIVITIES

Competitive strategy is about being different. It means deliberately choosing a different set of activities to deliver a unique mix of value.

Southwest Airlines Company, for example, offers short-haul, low-cost, point-to-point service between midsize cities and secondary airports in large cities. Southwest avoids large airports and does not fly great distances. . . .

IKEA, the global furniture retailer based in Sweden, also has a clear strategic positioning. IKEA targets young furniture buyers who want style at low cost. What turns this marketing concept into a strategic positioning is the tailored set of activities that make it work. Like Southwest, IKEA has chosen to perform activities differently from its rivals. . . .

THE ORIGINS OF STRATEGIC POSITIONS

Strategic positions emerge from three distinct sources, which are not mutually exclusive and often overlap. First, positioning can be based on producing a subset of an industry's products or services. I call this *variety-based positioning* because it is based on the choice of product or service varieties rather than customer segments. Variety-based positioning makes economic sense when a company can best produce particular products or services using distinctive sets of activities.

Jiffy Lube International, for instance, specializes in automotive lubricants and does not offer other car repair or maintenance services. Its value chain produces faster service at a lower cost than broader line repair shops, a combination so attractive that many customers subdivide their purchases, buying oil changes from the focused competitor, Jiffy Lube, and going to rivals for other services. . . .

A second basis for positioning is that of serving most or all the needs of a particular group of customers. I call this *needs-based positioning*, which comes closer to traditional thinking about targeting a segment of customers. It arises when there are groups of customers with differing needs, and when a tailored set of activities can serve those needs best. Some groups of customers are more price sensitive than others, demand different product features, and need varying amounts of information, support, and services. IKEA's customers are a good example of such a group. IKEA seeks to meet all the home furnishing needs of its target customers, not just a subset of them. . . .

It is intuitive for most managers to conceive of their business in terms of the customers' needs they are meeting. But a critical element of needs-based positioning is not at all intuitive and is often overlooked. Differences in needs will not translate into meaningful positions unless the best set of activities to satisfy them *also* differs. If that were not the case, every competitor could meet those same needs, and there would be nothing unique or valuable about the positioning. . . .

The third basis for positioning is that of segmenting customers who are accessible in different ways. Although their needs are similar to those of other customers, the best configuration of activities that reach them is different. I call this *access-based positioning.* Access can be a function of customer geography or customer scale—or of anything that requires a different set of activities to reach customers in the best way. . . .

Rural versus urban-based customers are one example of access driving differences in activities. Serving small rather than large customers or densely rather than sparsely situated customers are other examples in which the best way to configure marketing, order processing, logistics, and after-sale service activities to meet the similar needs of distinct groups will often differ. . . .

Having defined positioning, we can now begin to answer the question, "What is strategy?" Strategy is the creation of a unique and valuable position, involving a different set of activities. If there were only one ideal position, there would be no need for strategy. Companies would face a simple imperative—win the race to discover and preempt it. The essence of strategic positioning is to choose activities that are different from those of rivals. If the same set of activities were best to produce all varieties, meet all needs, and access all customers, companies could easily shift among them and operational effectiveness would determine performance.

III. A SUSTAINABLE STRATEGIC POSITION REQUIRES TRADE-OFFS

Choosing a unique position, however, is not enough to guarantee a sustainable advantage. A valuable position will attract imitation by incumbents, who are likely to copy it in one of two ways.

First, a competitor can reposition itself to match the superior performer. . . . A second and far more common type of imitation is straddling. The straddler seeks to match the benefits of a successful position while maintaining its existing position. It grafts new features, services, or technologies onto the activities it already performs.

For those who argue that competitors can copy any market position, the airline industry is a perfect test case. It would seem that nearly any competitor could imitate any other airline's activities. Any airline can buy the same planes, lease the gates, and match the menus and ticketing and baggage handling services offered by other airlines.

Continental Airlines saw how well Southwest was doing and decided to straddle. While maintaining its position as a full-service airline, Continental also set out to match Southwest on a number of point-to-point routes. The airline dubbed the new service Continental Lite. It eliminated meals and first-class service, increased departure frequency, lowered fares, and shortened turnaround time at the gate. Because Continental remained a full-service airline on other routes, it continued to use travel agents and its mixed fleet of planes and to provide baggage checking and seat assignments.

But a strategic position is not sustainable unless there are trade-offs with other positions. Trade-offs occur when activities are incompatible. Simply put, a trade-off means that more of one thing necessitates less of another. An airline can choose to serve meals—adding cost and slowing turnaround time at the gate—or it can choose not to, but it cannot do both without bearing major inefficiencies. . . .

Trade-offs arise for three reasons. The first is inconsistencies in image or reputation. A company known for delivering one kind of value may lack credibility and confuse customers—or even undermine its reputation—if it delivers another kind of value or attempts to deliver two inconsistent things at the same time. . . .

Second, and more important, trade-offs arise from activities themselves. Different positions (with their tailored activities) require different product configurations, different equipment, different employee behavior, different skills, and different management systems. Many trade-offs reflect inflexibilities in machinery, people, or systems. The more IKEA has configured its activities to lower costs by having its customers do their own assembly and delivery, the less able it is to satisfy customers who require higher levels of service. . . .

Finally, trade-offs arise from limits on internal coordination and control. By clearly choosing to compete in one way and not another, senior management makes organizational priorities clear. Companies that try to be all things to all customers, in contrast, risk confusion in the trenches as employees attempt to make day-to-day operating decisions without a clear framework.

Positioning trade-offs are pervasive in competition and essential to strategy. They create the need for choice and purposefully limit what a company offers. They deter straddling or repositioning, because competitors that engage in those approaches undermine their strategies and degrade the value of their existing activities.

Trade-offs ultimately grounded Continental Lite. The airline lost hundreds of millions of dollars, and the CEO lost his job. Its planes were delayed leaving congested hub cities or slowed at the gate by baggage transfers. . . .

Continental tried to compete in two ways at once. In trying to be low cost on some routes and full service on others, Continental paid an enormous straddling penalty. . . .

For the past decade, as managers have improved operational effectiveness greatly, they have internalized the idea that eliminating trade-offs is a good thing. But if there are no trade-offs, companies will never achieve a sustainable advantage. They will have to run faster and faster just to stay in place.

As we return to the question, What is strategy?, we see that trade-offs add a new dimension to the answer. Strategy is making trade-offs in competing. The essence of strategy is choosing what *not* to do. Without trade-offs, there would be no need for choice and thus no need for strategy. Any good idea could and would be quickly imitated. Again, performance would once again depend wholly on operational effectiveness.

IV. FIT DRIVES BOTH COMPETITIVE ADVANTAGE AND SUSTAINABILITY

Positioning choices determine not only which activities a company will perform and how it will configure individual activities but also how activities relate to one another. While operational effectiveness is about achieving excellence in individual activities, or functions, strategy is about *combining* activities. . . .

What is Southwest's core competence? Its key success factors? The correct answer is that everything matters. Southwest's strategy involves a whole system of activities, not a collection of parts. Its competitive advantage comes from the way its activities fit and reinforce one another.

Fit locks out imitators by creating a chain that is as strong as its *strongest* link. As in most companies with good strategies, Southwest's activities complement one another in ways that create real economic value. One activity's cost, for example, is lowered because of the way other activities are performed. Similarly, one activity's value to customers can be enhanced by a company's other activities. That is the way strategic fit creates competitive advantage and superior profitability.

TYPES OF FIT

The importance of fit among functional policies is one of the oldest ideas in strategy. Gradually, however, it has been supplanted on the management agenda. Rather than seeing the company as a whole, managers have turned to "core" competencies, "critical" resources, and "key" success factors. In fact, fit is a far more central component of competitive advantage than most realize. . . .

There are three types of fit, although they are not mutually exclusive. First-order fit is *simple consistency* between each activity (function) and the overall strategy. . . .

Consistency ensures that the competitive advantages of activities cumulate and do not erode or cancel themselves out. It makes the strategy easier to communicate to customers, employees, and shareholders, and improves implementation through single-mindedness in the corporation.

Second-order fit occurs when *activities are reinforcing*. . . . Bic Corporation sells a narrow line of standard, low-priced pens to virtually all major customer markets (retail, commercial, promotional, and giveaway) through virtually all available channels. As with any variety-based positioning serving a broad group of customers, Bic emphasizes a common need (low price for an acceptable pen) and uses marketing approaches with a broad reach (a large sales force and heavy television advertising). . . .

Third-order fit goes beyond activity reinforcement to what I call *optimization of effort*. The Gap, a retailer of casual clothes, considers product availability in its stores a critical element of its strategy. The Gap could keep products either by holding store inventory or by restocking from warehouses. The Gap has optimized its effort across these activities by restocking its selection of basic clothing almost daily out of three warehouses, thereby minimizing the need to carry large in-store inventories. The emphasis is on restocking because the Gap's merchandising strategy sticks to basic items in relatively few colors. . . .

In all three types of fit, the whole matters more than any individual part. Competitive advantage grows out of the *entire system* of activities. The fit among activities substantially reduces cost or increases differentiation. Beyond that, the competitive value of individual activities—or the associated skills, competencies, or resources—cannot be decoupled from the system or the strategy. Thus, in competitive companies it can be misleading to explain success by specifying individual strengths, core competencies, or critical resources. The list of strengths cuts across many functions, and one strength blends into others. It is more useful to think in terms of themes that pervade many activities, such as low cost, a particular notion of customer service, or a particular conception of the value delivered. These themes are embodied in nests of tightly linked activities.

FIT AND SUSTAINABILITY

Strategic fit among many activities is fundamental not only to competitive advantage but also to the sustainability of that advantage. It is harder for a rival to match an array of interlocked activities than it is merely to imitate a particular sales-force approach, match a process technology, or replicate a set of product features. Positions built on systems of activities are far more sustainable than those built on individual activities. . . .

The more a company's positioning rests on activity systems with second- and third-order fit, the more sustainable its advantage will be. Such systems, by their very nature, are usually difficult to untangle from outside the company and therefore hard to imitate. And even if rivals can identify the relevant interconnections, they will have difficulty replicating them. Achieving fit is difficult because it requires the integration of decisions and actions across many independent subunits. . . .

The most viable positions are those whose activity systems are incompatible because of trade-offs. Strategic positioning sets the trade-off rules that define how individual activities will be configured and integrated. Seeing strategy in terms of activity systems only makes it clearer why organizational structure, systems, and processes need to be strategy-specific. Tailoring organization to strategy, in turn, makes complementarities more achievable and contributes to sustainability.

One implication is that strategic positions should have a horizon of a decade or more, not of a single planning cycle. Frequent shifts in positioning are costly. Not only must a company reconfigure individual activities, but it must also realign entire systems. Some activities may never catch up to the vacillating strategy. The inevitable result of frequent shifts in strategy, or of failure to choose a distinct position in the first place, is "me-too" or hedged activity configurations, inconsistencies across functions, and organizational dissonance.

What is strategy? We can now complete the answer to this question. Strategy is creating fit among a company's activities. The success of a strategy depends on doing many things well—not just a few—and integrating among them. If there is no fit among activities, there is no distinctive strategy and little sustainability. Management reverts to the simpler task of overseeing independent functions, and operational effectiveness determines an organization's relative performance.

READING 1.4

Reflecting on the Strategy Process BY HENRY MINTZBERG AND JOSEPH LAMPEL

We are the blind people and strategy formation is our elephant. Each of us, in trying to cope with the mysteries of the beast, grabs hold of some part or other, and, in the words of John Godfrey Saxe's poem of the last century:

> Rail on in utter ignorance
> of what each other mean,
> And prate about an Elephant,
> Not one of [us] has seen!

Consultants have been like big game hunters embarking on their safaris for tusks and trophies, while academics have preferred photo safaris—keeping a safe distance from the animals they pretend to observe.

Managers are encouraged to take one narrow perspective or another—the glories of planning or the wonders of learning, the demands of external competitive analyses or the imperatives of an internal "resource-based" view. Much of this writing and advising has been decidedly dysfunctional, simply because managers have no choice but to cope with the entire beast.

In the first part of this chapter, we review briefly the evolution of the field in terms of ten "schools" (based on Mintzberg, Ahlstrand, and Lampel, *Strategy Safari*, 1998). We ask whether these perspectives represent fundamentally different processes of strategy making or different *parts* of the same process. In both cases, our answer is yes. We seek to show how some recent work tends to cut across these historical perspectives—in a sense, how cross-fertilization has occurred. Our historical survey of strategy literature suggests that it had been characterized by ten major schools since its inception in the 1960s—three *prescriptive* (or "ought") and seven *descriptive* (or "is").

DESIGN SCHOOL: A PROCESS OF CONCEPTION

The original perspective—dating back to Selznick (1957) followed by Chandler (1962) and given sharper definition by Andrews (in Learned et al., 1951)— sees strategy formation as achieving the essential fit between internal strengths and weaknesses and external threats and opportunities. Senior management formulates clear, simple, and unique strategies in a deliberate process of conscious thought—which is neither formally analytical nor informally intuitive—so that everyone can implement the strategies. This was the dominant view of the strategy process, at least into the 1970s, and, some might argue, to the present day, given its implicit influence on most teaching and practice. The design school did not develop, however, in the sense of giving rise to variants within its own context. Rather, it combined with other views in rather different contexts.

PLANNING SCHOOL: A FORMAL PROCESS

The planning school grew in parallel with the design school—indeed, H. Igor Ansoff's book appeared in 1965, as did the initial Andrews text. But, in sheer volume of publication, the planning school predominated by the mid-1970s, faltered in the 1980s, and yet continues to be an important branch of the literature today. Ansoff's book reflects most of the design school's assumptions except a rather significant one: that the process is not just cerebral but formal, decomposable into distinct steps, delineated by checklists, and supported by techniques (especially with regard to objectives, budgets, programs, and operating plans). This means that staff planners replaced senior managers, de facto, as the key players in the process.

POSITIONING SCHOOL: AN ANALYTICAL PROCESS

The third of the prescriptive schools, commonly labeled positioning, was the dominant view of strategy formation in the 1980s. It was given impetus especially by Michael Porter in 1980, following earlier work on strategic positioning in academe (notably by Hatten and Schendel) and in consulting by the Boston Consulting Group and the PIMS project—all preceded by a long literature on military strategy, dating back to Sun Tzu in 400 B.C. (See Sun Tzu, 1971.) In this view, strategy reduces to generic positions selected through formalized analyses of industry situations. Hence, the planners become analysts. This proved especially lucrative to consultants and academics alike, who could sink their teeth into hard data and promote their "scientific truths" to journals and companies. This literature grew in all directions to include strategic groups, value chains, game theories, and other ideas—but always with this analytical bent.

ENTREPRENEURIAL SCHOOL: A VISIONARY PROCESS

Meanwhile, on other fronts, mostly in trickles and streams rather than waves, wholly different approaches to strategy formation arose. Much like the design school, the entrepreneurial school centered the process on the chief executive; but, unlike the design school and opposite from the planning school, it rooted that process in the mysteries of intuition. That shifted strategies from precise designs, plans, or positions to vague *visions* or broad perspectives, to be seen, in a sense, often through metaphor. This focused the process on particular contexts—start-up, niche, or private ownership, as well as "turnaround" by the forceful leader—although the case was certainly put forth that every organization needs the vision of a creative leader. In this view, however, the

TABLE 1 DIMENSIONS OF THE TEN SCHOOLS, PART A

	DESIGN	PLANNING	POSITIONING	ENTREPRENEURIAL	COGNITIVE
Sources	P. Selznick (and perhaps earlier work, for example, by W.H. Newman), then K.R. Andrews.[a]	H.I. Ansoft.[b]	Purdue University work (D.E. Schendel, K.J. Hatten), then notably M.E. Porter.[c]	J.A. Schumpeter, A.H. Cole, and others in economics.[d]	H.A. Simon and J.G. March.[e]
Base Discipline	None (architecture as metaphor).	Some links to urban planning, systems theory, and cybernetics.	Economics (industrial organization) and military history.	None (although early writings come from economists).	Psychology (cognitive).
Champions	Case study teachers (especially at or from Harvard University), leadership aficionados—especially in the United States.	"Professional" managers, MBAs, staff experts (especially in finance), consultants, and government controllers—especially in France and the United States.	As in planning school, particularly analytical staff types, consulting "boutiques," and military writers—especially in the United States.	Popular business press, individualists, small business people everywhere, but most decidedly in Latin America and among overseas Chinese.	Those with a psychological bent—pessimists in one wing, optimists in the other.
Intended Message	Fit.	Formalize.	Analyze.	Envision.	Cope or create.
Realized Message	Think (strategy making as case study).	Program (rather than formulate).	Calculate (rather than create or commit).	Centralize (then hope).	Worry (being unable to cope in either case).
School Category	Prescriptive.	Prescriptive.	Prescriptive.	Descriptive (some prescriptive).	Descriptive.
Associated Homily	"Look before you leap."	"A stitch in time saves nine."	"Nothin' but the facts, ma'am."	"Take us to your leader."	"I'll see it when I believe it."

[a]P. Selznick, *Leadership in Administration: A Sociological Interpretation* (Evanston, Illinois: Row, Peterson, 1957).

[b]W.H. Newman, *Administrative Action. The Techniques of Organization and Management* (Englewood Cliffs, New Jersey: Prentice-Hall, 1951); and E.P. Learned, C.R. Christensen, K.R. Andrews, and W.D. Guth, *Business Policy: Text and Cases* (Homewood, Illinois: Irwin, 1965).

[c]K.J. Hatten and D.F. Schendel, "Heterogeneity Within an Industry: Firm Conduct in the U.S. Brewing Industry 1952–1971," *Journal of Industrial Economics* 26 (1977): 97–113. M.E. Porter, *Competitive Strategy* (New York: Free Press, 1980); and M.E. Porter, *Competitive Advantage: Creating and Sustaining Superior Performance* (New York: Free Press, 1985).

[d]J.A. Schumpeter, *The Theory of Economic Development* (Cambridge, Massachusetts: Harvard University Press, 1934); and A.H. Cole, *Business Enterprise in Its Social Setting* (Cambridge, Massachusetts: Harvard University Press, 1959).

[e]H.A. Simon, *Administrative Behavior* (New York: Macmillan, 1947); and J.G. March and H.A. Simon, *Organizations* (New York: Wiley, 1958).

leader maintains such close control over *implementing* his or her *formulated* vision that the distinction central to the three prescriptive schools begins to break down.

COGNITIVE SCHOOL: A MENTAL PROCESS

On the academic front, the origin of strategies generated considerable interest. If strategies developed in people's minds as frames, models, maps, concepts, or schemas, what could be understood about those mental processes? Particularly in the 1980s and continuing today, research has grown steadily on cognitive biases in strategy making and on cognition as information processing, knowledge structure mapping, and concept attainment—the latter important for strategy formation, yet on which progress has been minimal. Meanwhile, another newer branch of this school adopted a more subjective *interpretative* or *constructivist* view of the strategy process: that cognition is used to construct strategies as creative interpretations, rather than simply to map reality in some more or less objective way, however distorted.

TABLE 1 DIMENSIONS OF THE TEN SCHOOLS, PART B

	LEARNING	POWER	CULTURAL	ENVIRONMENTAL	CONFIGURATION
Sources	C.E. Lindblom, R.M. Cyert and J.G. March, K.E. Weick, J.B. Quinn, and C.K. Prahalad and G. Hamel.[f]	G.T. Allison (micro), J. Pfeffer and G.R. Salancik, and W.G. Astley (macro).[g]	E. Rhenman and R. Normann in Sweden. No obvious source elsewhere.[h]	M.T. Hannan and J. Freeman. Contingency theorists (e.g., D.S. Pugh et al.).[i]	A.D. Chandler, McGill University group (H. Mintzberg, D. Miller, and others), R.E. Miles and C.C. Snow.[j]
Base Discipline	None (perhaps some peripheral links to learning theory in psychology and education). Chaos theory in mathematics.	Political science.	Anthropology.	Biology.	History.
Champions	People inclined to experimentation, ambiguity, adaptability—especially in Japan and Scandinavia.	People who like power, politics, and conspiracy—especially in France.	People who like the social, the spiritual, the collective—especially in Scandinavia and Japan.	Population ecologists, some organization theorists, splitters, and positivists in general—especially in the Anglo-Saxon countries.	Lumpers and integrators in general, as well as change agents. Configuration perhaps most popular in the Netherlands. Transformation most popular in the United States.
Intended Message	Learn.	Promote.	Coalesce.	React.	Integrate, transform.
Realized Message	Play (rather than pursue).	Hoard (rather than share).	Perpetuate (rather than change).	Capitulate (rather than confront).	Lump (rather than split, adapt).
School Category	Descriptive.	Descriptive.	Descriptive.	Descriptive.	Descriptive and prescriptive.
Associated Homily	"If at first you don't succeed, try, try again."	"Look out for number one."	"An apple never falls far from the tree."	"It all depends."	"To everything there is a season. . . ."

[f]F.D. Braybrooke and C.E. Lindblom, *A Strategy of Decision* (New York: Free Press, 1963); R.M. Cyert and J.G. March, *A Behavioral Theory of the Firm* (Englewood Cliffs, New Jersey: Prentice-Hall, 1963); K.E. Weick, *The Social Psychology of Organizing* (Reading, Massachusetts: Addison-Wesley, first edition 1969, second edition 1979); J.B. Quinn, *Strategies for Change: Logical Incrementalism* (Homewood, Illinois: Irwin, 1980); and G. Hamel and C.K. Prahalad, *Competing for the Future* (Boston: Harvard Business School Press, 1994).

[g]G.T. Allison, *Essence of Decision: Explaining the Cuban Missile Crisis* (Boston: Little Brown, 1971); J. Pfeffer and G.R. Salancik, *The External Control of Organizations: A Resource Dependence Perspective* (New York: Harper & Row, 1978).

[h]E. Rhenman, *Organization Theory for Long-Range Planning* (London: Wiley, 1973); and R. Normann, *Management for Growth* (New York: Wiley, 1977).

[i]M.T. Hannan and J. Freeman, "The Population Ecology of Organizations," *American Journal of Sociology* 82 (1977): 929–64; and D.S. Pugh, D.J. Hickson, C.R. Hinings, and C. Turner, "Dimensions of Organizational Structure, Administrative Science Quarterly 13 (1968): 65–105.

[j]A.D. Chandler, *Strategy and Structure: Chapters in the History of the Industrial Enterprise* (Cambridge, Massachusetts: MIT Press, 1962); H. Mintzberg, *The Structuring of Organizations* (Englewood Cliffs, New Jersey: Prentice-Hall, 1984); D. Miller and P.H. Friesen, *Organization: A Quantum View* (Englewood Cliffs, New Jersey: Prentice-Hall, 1984); and R.E. Miles and C.C. Snow, *Organization Strategy, Structure, and Process* (New York: McGraw-Hill, 1978).

LEARNING SCHOOL: AN EMERGENT PROCESS

Of all the *descriptive* schools, the learning school grew into a veritable wave and challenged the always dominant prescriptive schools. Dating back to Lindblom's early work on disjointed incrementalism (Braybrooke and Lindblom, 1963) and running through Quinn's (1980) logical incrementalism, Bower's (1970) and Burgelman's notions of venturing, Mintzberg et al.'s ideas about emergent strategy, and Weick's (1979) notion of retrospective sense making, a model of strategy making as learning developed that differed from the earlier schools. In this view, strategies are emergent, strategists can be found throughout the organization, and so-called formulation and implementation intertwine.

POWER SCHOOL: A PROCESS OF NEGOTIATION

A thin, but quite different stream in the literature has focused on strategy making rooted in power. Two separate orientations seem to exist. *Micro* power sees the development of strategies *within* the organization as essentially political—a process involving bargaining, persuasion, and confrontation among actors who divide the power. *Macro* power views the organization as an entity that uses its power over others and among its partners in alliances, joint ventures, and other network relationships to negotiate "collective" strategies in its interest.

CULTURAL SCHOOL: A SOCIAL PROCESS

Hold power up to a mirror and its reverse image is culture. Whereas the former focuses on self-interest and fragmentation, the latter focuses on common interest and integration—strategy formation as a social process rooted in culture. Again, we find a thin stream of literature, focused particularly on the influence of culture in discouraging significant strategic change. Culture became a big issue in the U.S. literature after the impact of Japanese management was fully realized in the 1980s; later, some attention to the implications for strategy formation followed. However, interesting research developed in Sweden in the 1970s with culture as a central, although hardly exclusive, theme, stimulated by the early work of Rhenman and Normann, and carried out by people such as Hedberg and Jonsson, and others.

ENVIRONMENTAL SCHOOL: A REACTIVE PROCESS

Perhaps not strictly strategic management, if one defines the term as being concerned with how organizations use degrees of freedom to maneuver through their environments, the environmental school nevertheless deserves some attention for illuminating the demands of environment. In this category, we include so-called "contingency theory" that considers which responses are expected of organizations facing particular environmental conditions and "population ecology" writings that claim severe limits to strategic choice. "Institutional theory," which is concerned with the institutional pressures faced by organizations, is perhaps a hybrid of the power and cognitive schools.

CONFIGURATION SCHOOL: A PROCESS OF TRANSFORMATION

Finally, we come to a more extensive and integrative literature and practice. One side of this school, more academic and descriptive, sees organization as configuration—coherent clusters of characteristics and behaviors—and integrates the claims of the other schools, that is, each configuration, in effect, in its own place. Planning, for example, prevails in machine-type organizations under conditions of relative stability, while entrepreneurship can be found under more dynamic configurations of start-up and turnaround. But if organizations can be described by such *states*, change must be described as rather dramatic transformation—the leap from one state to another. And so, a literature and practice of transformation—more prescriptive and practitioner oriented (and consultant promoted)— developed. These two different literatures and practices nevertheless complement one another and so, in our opinion, belong to the same school.

PRATING ABOUT STRATEGIC MANAGEMENT

During the nineteenth century, numerous explorers went in search of the source of the Nile. In time, it became increasingly evident that the source was not definitive. This was not something the expedition backers or the public wanted to hear. After some debate, the explorers announced their discovery: the source of the Nile was Lake Victoria! This is a verdict generally rejected by contemporary geographers, who believe the headstreams of the Kagera River in the highlands Burundi is a better answer. Different views may prevail in the future. The source of a river, after all, is a matter of interpretation, not a fact waiting to be discovered.

TABLE 2
BLENDING OF THE STRATEGY FORMATION SCHOOLS

APPROACH	SCHOOLS
Dynamic capabilities	Design, Learning
Resource-based theory	Cultural, Learning
Soft techniques (e.g., scenario analysis and stakeholder analysis)	Planning, Learning or Power
Constructionism	Cognitive, Cultural
Chaos and evolutionary theory	Learning, Environmental
Institutional theory	Environmental, Power or Cognitive
Intrapreneurship (venturing)	Environmental, Entrepreneurial
Revolutionary change	Configuration, Entrepreneurial
Negotiated strategy	Power, Positioning
Strategic maneuvering	Positioning, Power

Strategic management has suffered from the problem that bedeviled the Victorian explorers. We, too, are a community of explorers, competing for discoveries, with backers eager for results and a public that demands answers.

Some explorers searching for the source of strategy have found "first principles" that explain the nature of the process. These have usually been rooted in basic disciplines, such as economics, sociology, or biology. Others have invoked a central concept, such as organization culture, to explain why some strategies succeed and others do not. The consequence has been to grasp one part of the strategic management elephant and prate about it as though none other exists. Of course, in the affairs of writing and consulting, to succeed and to sell, champions must defend their positions, erecting borders around their views while dismissing or denying others. Or, to return to our metaphor, like butchers (we include ourselves in this group), they chop up reality for their own convenience, just as poachers grab the tusks of the elephant and leave the carcass to rot.

To repeat a key issue, such behavior ultimately does not serve the practicing manager. These people, as noted, have to deal with the entire beast of strategy formation, not only to keep it alive but to help sustain some real life energy. True, they can use it in various ways—just as an elephant can be a beast of burden or a symbol of ceremony—but only if it remains intact as a living being. The greatest failings of strategic management have occurred when managers took one point of view too seriously. This field had its obsession with planning, then generic positions based on careful calculations, and now learning.

Hence, we take pleasure in noting that some of the more recent approaches to strategy formation cut across these ten schools in eclectic and interesting ways. This suggests a broadening of the literature. (See Table 2 for a list of these across-school approaches.) For example, research on stakeholder analysis links the planning and positioning schools, whereas the work of Porter and others on what can be called strategic maneuvering (first-mover advantage, use of feints, etc.) connects the positioning to the power school. And chaos theory, as applied to strategic management, might be seen as a hybrid of the learning and environmental schools. Perhaps best known is the "dynamic capabilities" approach of Prahalad and Hamel. We see their notions of core competence, strategic intent, and stretch—reminiscent of Itami's earlier work—as a hybrid of the learning and design schools: strong leadership to encourage continuous strategic learning.

ONE PROCESS OR DIFFERENT APPROACHES

Do these schools represent different processes of strategy formation, or different parts of the same process? We find either answer too constraining.

Some of the schools clearly are stages or aspects of the strategy formation process (see Figure 1):

- The cognitive school resides in the mind of the strategist located at the *center*.
- The positioning school looks *behind* at established data that is analyzed and fed into the black box of strategy making.

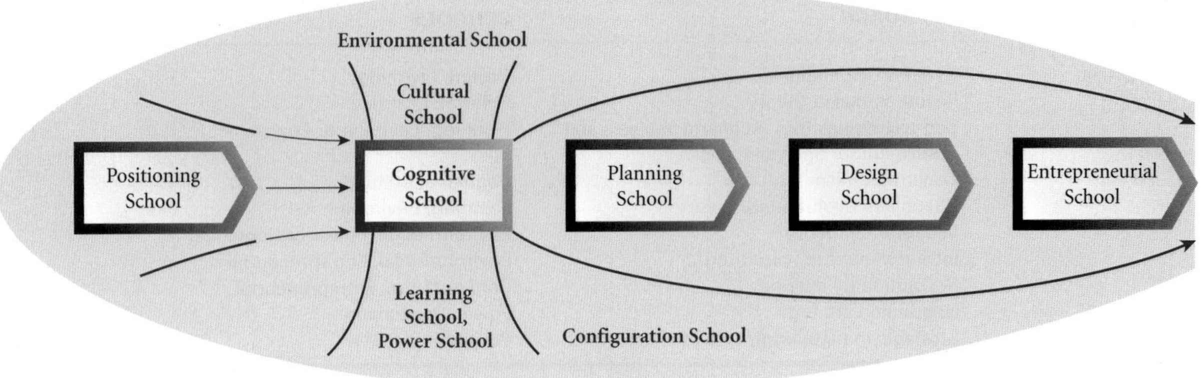

FIGURE 1 STRATEGY FORMATION AS A SINGLE PROCESS

- The planning school looks slightly *ahead*, to program the strategies created in other ways.
- The design school looks farther *ahead* to a strategic perspective.
- The entrepreneurial school looks *beyond* to a unique vision of the future.
- The learning and power schools look *below*, enmeshed in details. Learning looks into the grass roots, whereas power looks under the rocks—to places that organizations may not want to expose.
- The cultural school looks *down*, enshrouded in clouds of beliefs.
- Above the cultural school, the environmental school looks *on*, so to speak.
- The configuration school looks *at* the process, or, we might say, *all around* it, in contrast to the cognitive school that tries to look *inside* the process.

Dealing with all this complexity in one process may seem overwhelming. But that is the nature of the beast. Strategy formation *is* judgmental designing, intuitive visioning, and emergent learning; it is about transformation as well as perpetuation; it must involve individual cognition and social interaction, cooperative as well as conflictive; it has to include analyzing before and programming after as well as negotiating during; and all this must be in response to what may be a demanding environment. Try to omit any of this, and watch what happens!

Yet, just as clearly, the process can tilt toward the attributes of one school or another: toward the entrepreneurial school during start-up or when there is the need for a dramatic turnaround, toward the learning school under dynamic conditions when prediction is well nigh impossible, and so on. Sometimes the process has to be more individually cognitive than socially interactive (in small business, for example). Some strategies seem to be more rationally deliberate (especially in mature mass-production industries and government), whereas others tend to be more adaptively emergent (as in dynamic, high-technology industries). The environment can sometimes be highly demanding (during social upheaval), yet at other times (or even at the same times) entrepreneurial leaders are able to maneuver through it with ease. There are, after all, identifiable stages and periods in strategy making, not in any absolute sense but as recognizable tendencies.

Figure 2 plots the schools as different processes along two dimensions: states of the internal process and states of the external world. In this view, practitioners can pick and choose among the various processes (or combine them when appropriate)— as long as any one is not pushed to its illogical extreme (see Table 3).

IN SEARCH OF STRATEGIC MANAGEMENT

Scholars and consultants should certainly continue to probe the important elements of each school. But, more importantly, we have to get beyond the narrowness of each school: we need to know how strategy formation, which combines all these schools and more, really works.

We need to ask better questions and generate fewer hypotheses—to allow ourselves to be pulled by real-life concerns rather than being pushed by reified concepts. We need better practice,

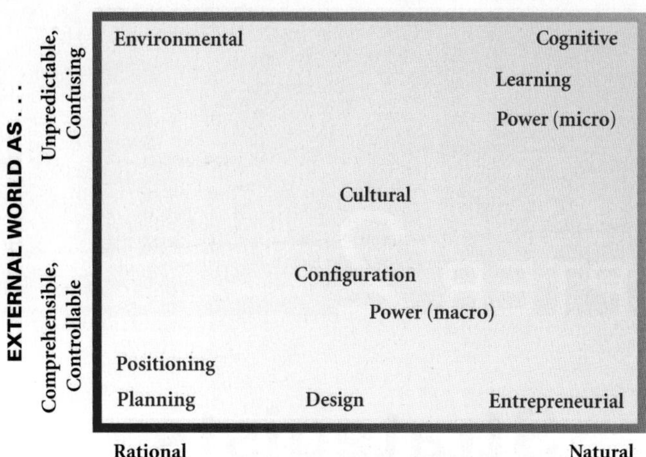

FIGURE 2 STRATEGY FORMATION AS MANY PROCESSES

TABLE 3 GOING OVER THE EDGE IN STRATEGY FORMATION

SCHOOL	ILLOGICAL EXTREME
Design	Fixation
Planning	Ritual
Positioning	Fortification
Entrepreneurial	Idolatry
Cognitive	Fantasy
Learning	Drift
Power	Intrigue
Cultural	Eccentricity
Environmental	Conformity
Configuration	Degeneration

not neater theory. So we must concern ourselves with process and content, statics and dynamics, constraint and inspiration, the cognitive and the collective, the planned and the learned, the economic and the political. In other words, we must give more attention to the entire elephant—to strategy formation as a whole. We may never see it fully, but we can certainly see it better.

CHAPTER 2

Strategists

Every conventional strategy or policy textbook focuses on the job of the general manager as a main ingredient in understanding the process of strategy formation. The discussion of emergent strategy in the last chapter suggests that we do not take such a narrow view of the strategist. Anyone in the organization who happens to control key or precedent-setting actions can be a strategist; the strategist can be a collection of people as well. Managers are obviously prime candidates for such a role because their perspective is generally broader than that of any of the people who report to them and because so much power naturally resides with them. But they are not alone.

We present five readings that describe the work of the manager. The one by Mintzberg challenges the conventional view of the manager. The image presented in this article is a job characterized by pressure, interruption, orientation to action, oral rather than written communication, and working with outsiders and colleagues as much as with so-called subordinates. The reading then goes on to describe the content of managerial work, arguing that it takes place on three levels—a rather abstract information level, an in-between people level, and a concrete action level. The roles the manager performs can be seen to fit into these levels, but, as emphasized, all managers must ultimately deal with all levels in an integrated fashion, although most will favor one level or another.

The second reading brings some of these aspects of managing to life in different styles of managing. By Patricia Pitcher of Montreal's Ecole des Hautes Etudes Commerciales, it contrasts the three styles of artists, craftsmen, and technocrats—if you like, creative visionaries, sympathetic leaders, and systematic analysts. Pitcher is no friend of the technocrats, as you shall see, believing that artists and craftsmen have to take the lead in today's organizations.

One evident and important conclusion of this reading is that managers do not always function as the strategists they are supposed to be—as leaders directing their organizations the way conductors direct their orchestras (at least the way it looks on the podium, a point we shall develop further in Chapter 15). The article by Edward Wrapp of the University of Chicago illustrates how this happens in large organizations. He depicts managers as somewhat political animals, providing broad guidance but facilitating or pushing through their strategies, bit by bit, in rather unexpected ways. They rarely state specific goals. They practice "the art of imprecision," trying to "avoid policy straitjackets," while concentrating on only a few really significant issues. They move whenever possible through "corridors of comparative indifference" to avoid undue opposition, at the same time that they are trying to ensure cohesive direction for their organizations.

The next article, by Peter Senge of the MIT Sloan School of Management and based on his highly successful book, *The Fifth Discipline,* characterizes the "leader's new work" as building the "learning organization." Senge views the ability to learn as the primary source of a company's competitive advantage and argues that facilitating organizational learning is the principal task of the strategist. Senge sees a long-term vision as the key source of tension in the organization and, therefore, of energy in the learning process. The manager must be the designer, the teacher, and the steward of the learning organization and, to play these roles, he or she must develop a new set of skills, which Senge describes in the article. Above all, the manager must promote systems thinking. On balance, Senge's new leader may well be Pitcher's craftsman (see especially the quote he uses to end his discussion—hardly the technocrat or even the artist), in which case this reading fleshes out that style in an interesting way.

Finally, there is a recent article by Quy Huy of INSEAD, the lead article in the September–October 2001 issue of the *Harvard Business Review*. Middle managers have received a bum rap, Quy believes, and so he set out to write "In Praise of Middle Managers." His point is an important one, long overdue, which helps to promote the fact that middle managers are critical components of every organization, *especially* those that wish to engage in effective processes of strategic change.

How do we reconcile these different views of the strategist? At one level, perhaps, we do not need a grand theory that integrates across all of them. There are different kinds of managers and different beliefs and styles, as well as different kinds of authors: Different lenses capture different aspects of managerial work. You may also observe similarities in the roles and tasks of the strategists described in these readings, despite the very different languages the authors use. Think, for example, about how the styles of Pitcher relate to the managerial roles Mintzberg describes.

USING THE CASE STUDIES

It is no accident that strategy was originally defined as the "art of the strategist." And, indeed, there is no shortage of fascinating strategists in our cases. Guy Laliberté of Cirque du Soleil shows how a deeply felt experience can dramatically affect strategic goals. The case on Napoleon Bonaparte shows how personal ambition creatively shaped strategy at the beginning of this general's career but distorted it as he gained more power and control. The Sportsmake case, on the other hand, deals with the impact of personality and the vision of a strategist on the organization after his untimely death. The board is faced with a decision of whom they should appoint as successor, and this raises the issue of whether such replacement should herald change or emphasize continuity.

The career and approach to work of Sukhinder Singh in Whisky Exchange show how strategic decisions are woven into daily reality, a point that is forcefully argued by Mintzberg in "The Manager's Job." Matt Walsh's quandary in Axion Consulting illustrates the crucial role that middle managers play in strategy. "In Praise of Middle Managers" by Quy argues that companies ignore this role at their peril.

The Nissan case illustrates the formidable challenge faced by Carlos Ghosn and his French team when they tackled deeply embedded management inertia in a Japanese corporation with strong traditions. The case shows that CEOs that take control of large organizations would be wise not to equate power and effectiveness, a distinction that is perceptively analyzed by Wrapp in his "Good Managers Do Not Make Policy Decisions." Steve Jobs, on the other hand, rarely had problems with organizational inertia because he single-handedly crafted the strategy of Apple. His approach is well described by Senge in "The Leader's New Work." It is a mixture of strong vision and fast learning. However, as Pitcher notes in her "Artists, Craftsmen, and Technocrats," both Ghosn and Jobs, not to mention many of the other managers who play a prominent role in this book, practice strategy with a particular style. Ghosn is clearly the craftsman, and Jobs the artist. As to which of our cases describes the strategist as technocrat, we leave you with the task of finding this out.

READING 2.1

The Manager's Job BY HENRY MINTZBERG

Tom Peters tells us that good managers are doers. (Wall Street says they "do deals.") Michael Porter suggests that they are thinkers. Not so, argue Abraham Zaleznik and Warren Bennis: good managers are really leaders. Yet, for the best part of the 20th century, the classical writers—Henri Fayol and Lyndell Urwick, among others—keep telling us that good managers are essentially controllers.

It is a curiosity of the management literature that its best-known writers all seem to emphasize one particular part of the manager's job to the exclusion of the others. Together, perhaps, they cover all the parts, but even that does not describe the whole job of managing.

Moreover, the image left by all of this of the manager's job is that it is a highly systematic, carefully controlled job. That is the folklore. The facts are quite different.

We shall begin by reviewing some of the early research findings on the *characteristics* of the manager's job, comparing that folklore with the facts, as I observed them in my first study of managerial work (published in the 1970s), reinforced by other research. Then we shall present a new framework to think about the *content* of the job—what managers really do—based on some recent observations I have made of managers in very different situations.

SOME FOLKLORE AND FACTS ABOUT MANAGERIAL WORK

There are four myths about the manager's job that do not bear up under careful scrutiny of the facts.

Folklore:
The manager is a reflective, systematic planner. The evidence on this issue is overwhelming, but not a shred of it supports this statement.

Fact:
Study after study has shown that managers work at an unrelenting pace, that their activities are characterized by brevity, variety, and discontinuity, and that they are strongly oriented to action and dislike reflective activities. Consider this evidence:

- Half the activities engaged in by the five [American] chief executives [that I studied in my own research (Mintzberg, 1973a)] lasted less than nine minutes, and only 10% exceeded one hour. A study of 56 U.S. foremen found that they averaged 583 activities per eight-hour shift, an average of 1 every 48 seconds (Guest, 1956: 478). The work pace for both chief executives and foremen was unrelenting. The chief executives met a steady stream of callers and mail from the moment they arrived in the morning until they left in the evening. Coffee breaks and lunches were inevitably work related, and ever-present subordinates seemed to usurp any free moment.
- A diary study of 160 British middle and top managers found that they worked for a half hour or more without interruption only about once every two days (Stewart, 1967).
- Of the verbal contacts of the chief executives in my study, 93% were arranged on an ad hoc basis. Only 1% of the executives' time was spent in open-ended observational tours. Only 1 out of 368 verbal contacts was unrelated to a specific issue and could be called general planning. Another researcher finds that "in *not one single case* did a manager report the obtaining of important external information from a general conversation or other undirected personal communication" (Aguilar, 1967: 102).
- No study has found important patterns in the way managers schedule their time. They seem to jump from issue to issue, continually responding to the needs of the moment.

Is this the planner that the classical view describes? Hardly. How, then, can we explain this behavior? The manager is simply responding to the pressures of the job. I found that my chief executives terminated many of their own activities, often leaving meetings before the end, and interrupted their desk work to call in subordinates. One president not only placed his desk so that he could look down a long hallway but also left his door open when he was alone—an invitation for subordinates to come in and interrupt him.

Clearly, these managers wanted to encourage the flow of current information. But more significantly, they seemed to be conditioned by their own work loads. They appreciated the opportunity cost of their own time, and they were continually aware of their ever-present obligations—mail to be answered, callers to attend to, and so on. It seems that no matter what he or she is doing, the manager is plagued by the possibilities of what he or she might do and must do.

When the manager must plan, he or she seems to do so implicitly in the context of daily actions, not in some abstract process reserved for two weeks in the organization's mountain retreat. The plans of the chief executives I studied seemed to exist only in their heads—as flexible, but often specific, intentions. The traditional literature notwithstanding, the job of managing does not breed reflective planners; the manager is a real-time responder to stimuli, an individual who is conditioned by his or her job to prefer live to delayed action.

Folklore:
The effective manager has no regular duties to perform. Managers are constantly being told to spend more time planning and delegating, and less time on operating details. These are not, after all, the true tasks of the manager. To use the popular analogy, the good manager, like the good conductor, carefully orchestrates everything in advance, then sits back to enjoy the fruits of his or her labor, responding occasionally to an unforeseeable exception. . . .

Fact:
In addition to handling exceptions, managerial work involves performing a number of regular duties, including ritual and ceremony, negotiations, and processing of soft information that links the organization with its environment. Consider some evidence from the early research studies:

- A study of the work of the presidents of small companies found that they engaged in routine activities because their companies could not afford staff specialists and were so thin on operating personnel that a single absence often required the president to substitute (Choran in Mintzberg, 1973a).
- One study of field sales managers and another of chief executives suggest that it is a natural part of both jobs to see important customers, assuming the managers wish to keep those customers (Davis, 1978; Copeman, 1963).
- Someone, only half in jest, once described the manager as that person who sees visitors so that everyone else can get his or her work done. In my study, I found that certain ceremonial duties—meeting visiting dignitaries, giving out gold watches, presiding at Christmas dinners—were an intrinsic part of the chief executive's job.
- Studies of managers' information flow suggest that managers play a key role in securing "soft" external information (much of it available only to them because of their status) and in passing it along to their subordinates.

Folklore:
The senior manager needs aggregated information, which a formal management information system best provides. In keeping with the classical view of the manager as that individual perched on the apex of a regulated, hierarchical system, the literature's manager was to receive all important information from a giant, comprehensive MIS.

But this never proved true at all. A look at how managers actually process information makes the reason quite clear. Managers have five media at their command—documents, telephone calls, scheduled and unscheduled meetings, and observational tours.

Fact:
Managers strongly favor the verbal media—namely, telephone calls and meetings. The evidence comes from every one of the early studies of managerial work: Consider the following:

- In two British studies, managers spent an average 66% and 80% of their time in verbal (oral) communication (Stewart, 1967; Burns, 1954). In my study of five American chief executives, the figure was 78%.

- These five chief executives treated mail processing as a burden to be dispensed with. One came in Saturday morning to process 142 pieces of mail in just over three hours, to "get rid of all the stuff." This same manager looked at the first piece of "hard" mail he had received all week, a standard cost report, and put it aside with the comment, "I never look at this."
- These same five chief executives responded immediately to 2 of the 40 routine reports they received during the five weeks of my study and to four items in the 104 periodicals. They skimmed most of the periodicals in seconds, almost ritualistically. In all, these chief executives of good-sized organizations initiated on their own—that is, not in response to something else—a grand total of 25 pieces of mail during the 25 days I observed them.

An analysis of the mail the executives received reveals an interesting picture—only 13% was of specific and immediate use. So now we have another piece of the puzzle: not much of the mail provides live, current information—the action of a competitor, the mood of a government legislator, or the rating of last night's television show. Yet this is the information that drove the managers, interrupting their meetings and rescheduling their workdays.

Consider another interesting finding. Managers seem to cherish "soft" information, especially gossip, hearsay, and speculation. Why? The reason is its timeliness; today's gossip may be tomorrow's fact. The manager who is not accessible for the telephone call informing him or her that the firm's biggest customer was seen golfing with its main competitor may read about a dramatic drop in sales in the next quarterly report. But then it is too late.

Consider the words of Richard Neustadt, who studied the information-collecting habits of Presidents Roosevelt, Truman, and Eisenhower.

> It is not information of a general sort that helps a President see personal stakes; not summaries, not surveys, not the *bland amalgams.* Rather . . . it is the odds and ends of *tangible detail* that pieced together in his mind illuminate the underside of issues put before him. To help himself he must reach out as widely as he can for every scrap of fact, opinion, gossip, bearing on his interests and relationships as President. He must become his own director of his own central intelligence. (1960:153–154: italics added)

The manager's emphasis on the verbal media raises two important points:

First, verbal information is stored in the brains of people. Only when people write this information down can it be stored in the files of the organization—whether in metal cabinets or computer memory—and managers apparently do not write down much of what they hear. Thus, the strategic data bank of the organization is not in the memory of its computers but in the minds of its managers.

Second, the managers' extensive use of verbal media helps to explain why they are reluctant to delegate tasks. When we note that most of the managers' important information comes in verbal form and is stored in their heads, we can well appreciate their reluctance. It is not as if they can hand a dossier over to someone; they must take the time to "dump memory"—to tell that someone all they know about the subject. But this could take so long that the managers find it easier to do the task themselves. Thus the managers are damned by their own information systems to a "dilemma of delegation"—to do too much themselves or to delegate to their subordinates with inadequate briefing.

Folklore:

Management is, or at least is quickly becoming, a science and a profession. By almost any definitions of *science* and *profession,* this statement is false. Brief observation of any manager will quickly lay to rest the notion that managers practice a science. A science involves the enaction of systematic, analytically determined procedures or programs. If we do not even know what procedures managers use, how can we prescribe them by scientific analysis? And how can we call management a profession if we cannot specify what managers are to learn?

Fact:

The managers' programs—to schedule time, process information, make decisions, and so on—remain locked deep inside their brains. Thus, to describe these programs, we rely on words like judgment and intuition, seldom stopping to realize that they are merely labels for our ignorance.

I was struck during my study by the fact that the executives I was observing—all very competent by any standard—are fundamentally indistinguishable from their counterparts of a hundred years ago (or a thousand years ago, for that matter). The information they need differs, but they seek it in the same way—by word of mouth. Their decisions concern modern technology, but the procedures they use to make them are the same as the procedures of the nineteenth-century manager. In fact, the manager is in a kind of loop, with increasingly heavy work pressures but no aid forthcoming from management science.

Considering the facts about managerial work, we can see that the manager's job is enormously complicated and difficult. The manager is overburdened with obligations; yet he or she cannot easily delegate tasks. As a result, he or she is driven to overwork and is forced to do many tasks superficially. Brevity, fragmentation, and verbal communication characterize the work. Yet these are the very characteristics of managerial work that have impeded scientific attempts to improve it. As a result, the management scientists have concentrated their efforts on the specialized functions of the organization, where they could more easily analyze the procedure and quantify the relevant information. Thus, the first step in providing managers with some help is to find out what their job really is.

TOWARD A BASIC DESCRIPTION OF MANAGERIAL WORK

Now let us try to put some of the pieces of this puzzle together. The manager can be defined as that person in charge of an organization or one of its units. Besides chief executive officers, this definition would include vice presidents, head nurses, hockey coaches, and prime ministers. Can all of these people have anything in common? Indeed, they can. Our description takes the form of a model, building the image of the manager's job from the inside out, beginning at the center with the person and his or her frame and working out from there, layer by layer.

THE PERSON IN THE JOB

We begin at the center, with the person who comes to the job. People are not neutral when they take on a new managerial job, mere putty to be molded into the required shape. Figure 1 shows that an individual comes to a managerial job with a set of *values*, by this stage in life probably rather firmly set, also a body of *experience* that, on the one hand, has forged a set of skills or *competencies*, perhaps honed by training, and, on the other, has provided a base of *knowledge*. That knowledge is, of course, used directly, but it is also converted into a set of *mental models*, key means by which managers interpret the world around them—for example, how the head nurse on a hospital ward perceives the behavior of the surgeons with whom she must work. Together, all these characteristics greatly determine how any manager approaches a given job—his or her *style* of managing. Style will come to life as we begin to see *how* a manager carries out *what* his or her job requires.

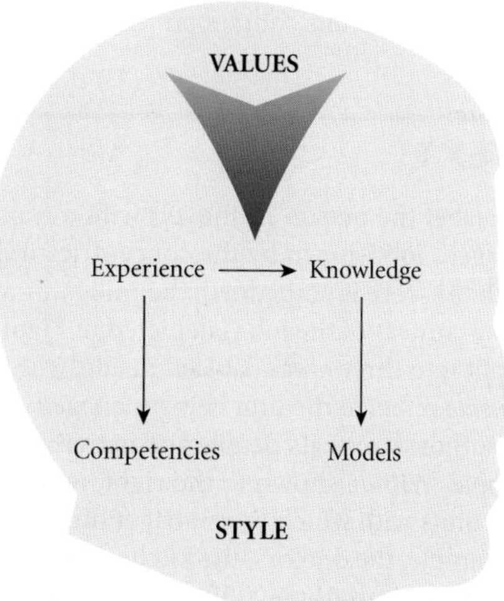

FIGURE 1
THE PERSON IN THE JOB

THE FRAME OF THE JOB

Embed the person depicted in a given managerial job and you get managerial work. At the core of it is some kind of *frame* for the job, the mental set the incumbent assumes to carry it out. Frame is strategy, to be sure, possibly even vision, but it is more than that. It is purpose, whether to create something in the first place, maintain something that has already been created or adapt it to changes, or else re-create something. Frame is also *perspective*—the broad view of the organization and its mission, and *positions*—concerning specific products, services, and markets.

Alain Noël, who studied the relationship between the frames and the work of the chief executives of three small companies, has said that managers have "occupations" and they have "preoccupations" (Noël, 1989). Frame describes the preoccupations, while roles (discussed below) describe the occupations. But frame does give rise to a first role in this model as well, which I call conceiving, namely thinking through the purpose, perspective, and positions of a particular unit to be managed over a particular period of time.

THE AGENDA OF THE WORK

Given a person in a particular managerial job with a particular frame, the question arises of how this is manifested in the form of specific activities. That happens through the *agenda* to carry out the work, and the associated role of scheduling, which has received considerable attention in the literature of management. Agenda is considered in two respects here. First, the frame gets manifested as a set of current *issues*, in effect, whatever is of concern to the manager, broken down into manageable units—what Tom Peters likes to call "chunks." Ask any manager about his or her work, and the almost inevitable first reply will be about the "issues" of central concern, those things "on the plate," as the saying goes. Or take a look at the agendas of meetings and you will likewise see a list of issues (rather than decisions). These, in effect, operationalize the frame (as well as change it, of course, by feeding in new concerns).

The sharper the frame, the more integrated the issues. The more realizable they may be as well, since it is a vague frame that gives rise to that all-too-common phenomenon of the unattainable "wishlist" in an organization. Sometimes a frame can be so sharp, and the issues therefore so tightly integrated, that they all reduce to what Noël has called one "magnificent obsession" (Noël, 1989). In effect, all the concerns of the manager revolve around one central issue, for example, making a new merger work.

Second, the frame and the issues get manifested in the more tangible *schedule*, the specific allocations of managerial time on a day-to-day basis. Also included here, however implicitly, is the setting of priorities among the issues. The scheduling of time and the prioritization of issues are obviously of great concern to all managers, and, in fact, are themselves significant consumers of managerial time. Accordingly, a great deal of attention has been devoted to these concerns, including numerous courses on "time management."

THE CORE IN CONTEXT

If we label the person in the job with a frame manifested by an agenda, the central *core* of the manager's job (shown by the concentric circles in Figure 2), then we turn next to the context in which this core is embedded, the milieu in which the work is practiced.

The context of the job is depicted in Figure 2 by the lines that surround the core. Context can be split into three areas, labeled inside, within, and outside on Figure 2.

Inside refers to the unit being managed, shown below the manager to represent his or her formal authority over its people and activities—the hospital ward in the case of the head nurse, for example. *Within*, shown to the right, refers to the rest of the organization—other members and other units with which the manager must work but over which he or she has no formal authority, for example, the doctors, the kitchen, the physiotherapists in the rest of the hospital, to continue with the same example. (Of course, in the case of the chief executive, there is no inside separate from within: that person has authority over the entire organization.) And *outside* refers to the

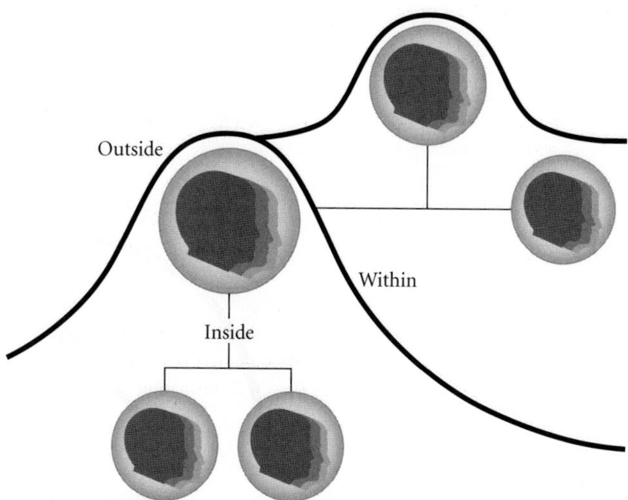

FIGURE 2
THE CORE IN CONTEXT

rest of the context not formally part of the organization with which the manager must work—in this example, patients' relatives, long-term care institutions to which some of the unit's patients are discharged, nursing associations, and so on. The importance of this distinction (for convenience, we shall mostly refer to inside versus outside) is that much of managerial work is clearly directed either to the unit itself, for which the manager has official responsibility, or at its various boundary contexts, through which the manager must act without that responsibility.

MANAGING ON THREE LEVELS

We are now ready to address the actual behaviors that managers engage in to do their jobs. The essence of the model, designed to enable us to "see" managerial work comprehensively, in one figure, is that these roles are carried out on three successive levels, each inside and outside the unit. This is depicted by concentric circles of increasing specificity, shown in Figure 3.

From the outside (or most tangible level) in, managers can manage *action* directly, they can manage *people* to encourage them to take the necessary actions, and they can manage *information* to influence the people in turn to take their necessary actions. In other words, the ultimate objective of managerial work, and of the functioning of any organizational unit, the taking of action, can be managed directly, indirectly through people, or even more indirectly by information through people. The manager can thus choose to intervene at any of the three levels, but once done, he or she must work through the remaining ones. Later we shall see that the level a given manager favors becomes an important determinant of his or her managerial style, especially distinguishing so-called "doers" who prefer direct action, "leaders" who prefer working through people, and "administrators" who prefer to work by information.

MANAGING BY INFORMATION

To manage by information is to sit two steps removed from the purpose of managerial work. The manager processes information to drive other people who, in turn, are supposed to ensure that necessary actions are taken. In other words, here the managers' own activities focus neither on people nor on actions per se, but rather on information as an indirect way to make things happen. Ironically, while this was the classic perception of managerial work for the last half of the 20th century, in recent years it has also become a newly popular, in some quarters almost obsessional, view, epitomized by the so-called "bottom line" approach to management.

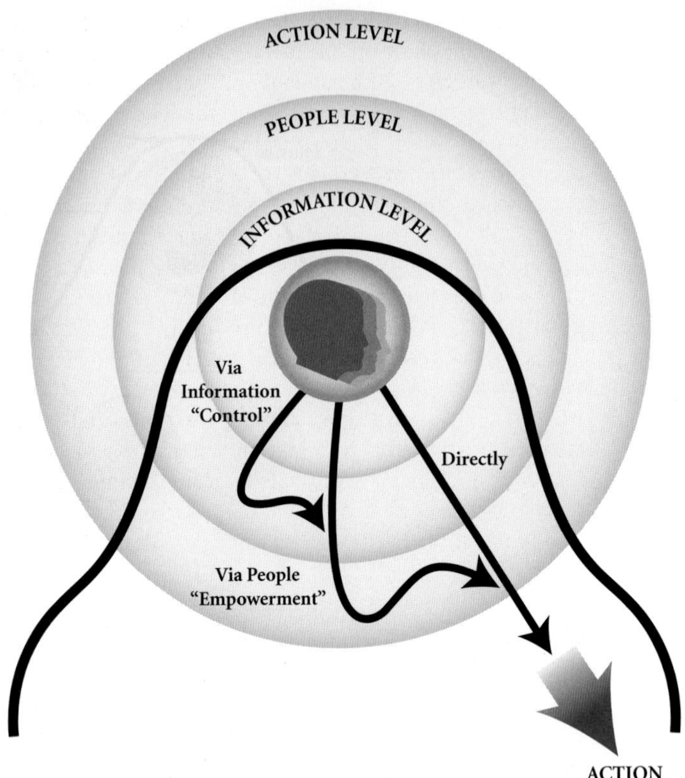

FIGURE 3
THREE LEVELS OF EVOKING ACTIONS

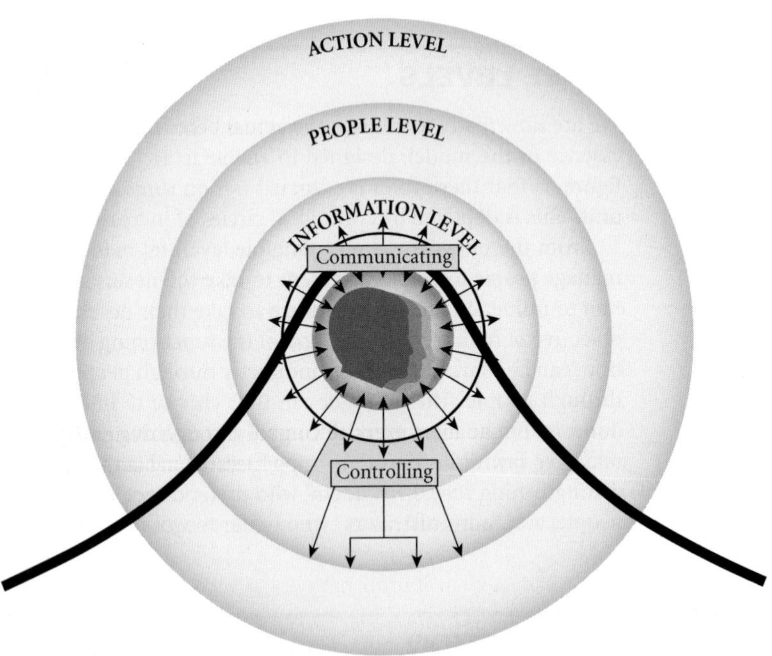

FIGURE 4
THE INFORMATION ROLES

The manager's various informational behaviors may be grouped into two broad roles, here labeled communicating and controlling, shown in Figure 4.

Communicating refers to the collection and dissemination of information. In Figure 4, communicating is shown by double arrows to indicate that managers devote a great deal of effort to the two-way flow of information with the people all around them—employees inside their own units, others in the rest of the organization, and especially, as the empirical evidence makes abundantly clear, a great number of outsiders with whom they maintain regular contact. Thus the head of one regional division of the national police force spent a good part of the day I observed him passing information back and forth between the central headquarters and the people on his staff.

Managers "scan" their environments, they monitor their own units, and they share with and disseminate to others considerable amounts of the information they pick up. Managers can be described as "nerve centers" of their units, who use their status of office to gain access to a wide variety of informational sources. Inside the unit, everyone else is a specialist who generally knows more about his or her specialty than the manager. But, because the manager is connected to all those specialists, he or she should have the broadest base of knowledge about the unit in general. This should apply to the head of a huge health care system, with regard to broad policy issues, no less than to the clinical director of one of its hospital units, with regard to the service rendered there. And externally, by virtue of their status, managers have access to other managers who are themselves nerve centers of their own units. And so they tend to be exposed to powerful sources of external information and thus emerge as external nerve centers as well. The health care chief executive can thus talk to people running health care systems in other countries and so gain access to an array of information perhaps inaccessible even to his most influential reports.

The result of all this is that a considerable amount of the manager's information turns out to be privileged, especially when we consider how much of it is oral and nonverbal. Accordingly, to function effectively with the people around them, managers have to spend considerable time sharing their information, both with outsiders (in a kind of spokesperson role) and with insiders (in a kind of disseminator role).

I found in my initial study of chief executives that perhaps 40 percent of their time was devoted almost exclusively to the communicating role—just to gaining and sharing information—leaving aside the information processing aspects of all the other roles. In other words, the job of managing is fundamentally one of processing information, notably by talking and especially listening. Thus Figure 4 shows the inner core (the person in the job, conceiving and scheduling) connected to the outer rings (the more tangible roles of managing people and action) through what can be called the membrane of information processing all around the job.

What can be called the controlling role describes the managers' efforts, not just to gain and share information, but to use it in a directive way inside their units: to evoke or provoke general action by the people who report to them. They do this in three broad ways: they develop systems, they design structures, and they impose directives. Each of these seeks to control how other people work, especially with regard to the allocation of resources, and so what actions they are inclined to take.

First, developing systems is the most general of these three, and the closest to conceiving. It uses information to control people's behaviors. Managers often take charge of establishing and even running such systems in their units, including those of planning and performance control (such as budgeting). Robert Simons has noted how chief executives tend to select one such system and make it key to their exercise of control, in a manner he calls "interactive" (Simons, 1990, 1991).

Second, managers exercise control through designing the structures of their units. By establishing responsibilities and defining hierarchical authority, they again exercise control rather passively, through the processing of information. People are informed of their duties, which in turn is expected to drive them to carry out the appropriate actions.

Third is imposing directives, which is the most direct of the three, closest to the people and action, although still informational in nature. Managers pronounce: they make specific choices and give specific orders, usually in the process of "delegating" particular responsibilities and "authorizing" particular requests. In effect, managers manage by transmitting information to people so that they can act.

If a full decision-making process can be considered in the three stages of diagnosing, designing, and deciding—in other words, identifying issues, working out possible solutions, and selecting one—then here we are dealing with a restricted view of decision making. Delegating means mostly diagnosing ("Would you please handle this problem in this context"), while authorizing means mostly deciding ("OK, you can proceed"). Either way, the richest part of the process, the stage of designing possible solutions, resides with the person being controlled rather than with the manager himself or herself, whose own behavior remains rather passive. Thus, the manager as controller seems less an *actor* with sleeves rolled up, digging in, than a *reviewer* who sits back in the office and passes judgment. That is why this role is characterized as informational: I will describe a richer approach to decision making in the section on action roles.

The controlling role is shown in Figure 4 propelling down into the manager's own unit, since that is where formal authority is exercised. The single-headed arrows represent the imposed directives, while the pitchfork shape symbolizes both the design of structure and the development of systems. The proximity of the controlling role in Figure 4 to the manager's agenda reflects the fact that informational control is the most direct way to operationalize the agenda, for example, by using budgets to impose priorities or delegation to assign responsibilities. The controlling role is, of course, what people have in mind when they refer to the "administrative" aspect of managerial work.

MANAGING THROUGH PEOPLE

To manage through people, instead of by information, is to move one step closer to action, but still to remain removed from it. That is because here the focus of managerial attention becomes affect instead of effect. Other people become the means to get things done, not the manager himself or herself, or even the substance of the manager's thoughts.

If the information roles (and controlling in particular) dominated our early thinking about managerial work, then after that, people entered the scene, or at least they entered the textbooks, as entities to be "motivated" and later "empowered." Influencing began to replace informing, and commitment began to vie with calculation for the attention of the manager. Indeed, in the 1960s and 1970s especially, the management of people, quite independent of content—of the strategies to be realized, the information to be processed, even the actions to be taken—became a virtual obsession of the literature, whether by the label of "human relations," "Theory Y," or "participative management" (and later "quality of work life," to be replaced by "total quality management").

For a long time, however, these people remained "subordinates" in more ways than one. "Participation" kept them subordinate, for this was always considered to be granted at the behest of the managers still fully in control. So does the currently popular term "empowerment," which implies that power is being granted, thanks to the managers. (Hospital directors do not "empower" physicians!) People also remained subordinates because the whole focus was on those inside the unit, not outside it. Not until serious research on managerial work began did it become evident how important to managers were contacts with individuals outside their units. Virtually every single study of how all kinds of managers spent their time has indicated that outsiders, of an enormously wide variety, generally take as much of the managers' attention as so-called "subordinates." We shall thus describe two people roles here, shown in Figure 5, one internal, called leading, and one external, called linking.

The leading role has probably received more attention in the literature of management than all other roles combined. And so we need not dwell on it here. But neither can we ignore it: managers certainly do much more than lead the people in their own units, and leading certainly infuses much else of what managers do (as, in fact, do all the roles, as we have already noted about communicating). But their work just as certainly cannot be understood without this dimension. We can describe the role of leading on three levels, as indicated in Figure 5.

First, managers lead on the *individual* level, "one on one," as the expression goes. They encourage and drive the people of their units—motivate them, inspire them, coach them, nurture them, push them, mentor them, and so on. All the managers I observed, from the chief executive of a major police force to the front-country manager in a mountain park, stopped to chat with their people informally during the day to encourage them in their work. Second, managers lead on the *group* level, especially by building and managing teams, an effort that has received considerable attention in recent years. Again, team meetings, including team building, figured in many of my observations; for example, the head of a London film company who brought film-making teams together for both effective and affective purposes. And, third, they lead on the *unit* level, especially with regard to the creation and maintenance of culture, another subject of increasing attention in recent years (thanks especially to the Japanese). Managers, for example, engage in

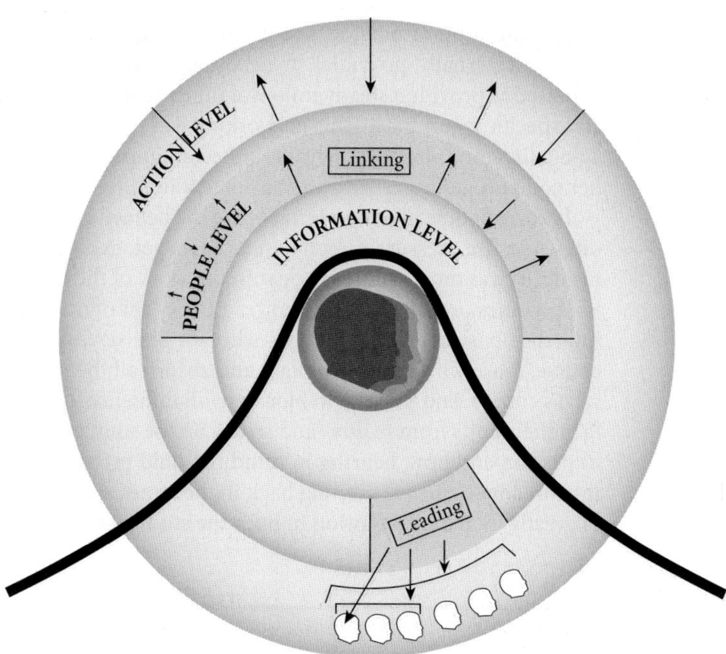

FIGURE 5
THE PEOPLE ROLES

many acts of symbolic nature ("figurehead" duties) to sustain culture, as when the head of the national police force visited its officer training institute (as he did frequently) to imbue the force's norms and attitudes in its graduating class.

All managers seem to spend time on all three levels of leadership, although, again, styles do vary according to context and personality. If the communicating role describes the manager as the nerve center of the unit, then the leading role must characterize him or her as its "energy center," a concept perhaps best captured in Maeterlinck's wonderful description of the "spirit of the hive" (Maeterlinck, 1918). Given the right managerial "chemistry" (in the case of Maeterlinck's queen bee, quite literally!), it may be the manager's mere presence that somehow draws things together. By exuding that mystical substance, the leader unites his or her people, galvanizing them into action to accomplish the unit's mission and adapt it to a changing world.

The excess attention to the role of leading has probably been matched by the inadequate attention to the role of linking. For, in their sheer allocation of time, managers have been shown to be external linkers as much as they are internal leaders, in study after study. Yet, still the point seems hardly appreciated. Indeed, now more than ever, it must be understood, given the great growth of joint ventures and other collaborating and networking relationships between organizations, as well as the gradual reconception of the "captive" employee as an autonomous "agent" who supplies labor.

Figure 5 suggests a small model of the linking role. The arrows go in and out to indicate that the manager is both an advocate of its influence outside the unit and, in turn, a recipient of much of the influence exerted on it from the outside. In the middle are two parallel lines to represent the buffering aspect of this role—that managers must regulate the receipt of external influence to protect their units. To use a popular term, they are the "gatekeepers" of influence. Or, to add a metaphor, the manager acts as a kind of valve between the unit and its environment. Nowhere was this clearer than in my observation of three levels of management in a national park system—a regional director, the head of one mountain park, and the front-country manager of that park. They sit in an immensely complex array of forces—developers who want to enhance their business opportunities, environmentalists who want to preserve the natural habitat, tourists who want to enjoy the beauty, truckers who want to drive through the park unimpeded, politicians who want to avoid negative publicity, etc. It is a delicate balancing, or buffering, act indeed!

All managers appear to spend a great deal of time "networking"—building vast arrays of contacts and intricate coalitions of supporters beyond their own units, whether within the rest of the organization or outside, in the world at large. To all these contacts, the manager represents the unit externally, promotes its needs, and lobbies for its causes. In response, these people are expected to provide a steady inflow of information to the unit as well as various means of support and specific favors for it. This networking was most evident in the case of the film company managing director I observed, who exhibited an impressive network of contacts in order to negotiate her complex contracts with various media in different countries.

In turn, people intent on influencing the behavior of an organization or one of its subunits will often exercise pressure directly on its manager, expecting that person to transmit the influence inside, as was most pointedly clear in the work of the parks manager. Here, then, the managerial job becomes one of delicate balance, a tricky act of mediation. Those managers who let external influence pass inside too freely—who act like sieves—are apt to drive their people crazy. (Of course, those who act like sponges and absorb all the influence personally are apt to drive themselves crazy!) And those who block out all influence—who act like lead to X-rays—are apt to detach their units from reality (and so dry up the sources of external support). Thus, what influence to pass on and how, bearing in mind the quid pro quo that influence exerted out is likely to be mirrored by influence coming back in, becomes another key aspect of managerial style, worthy of greatly increased attention in both the study of the job and the training of its occupants.

MANAGING ACTION

If managers manage passively by information and affectively through people, then they also manage actively and instrumentally by their own direct involvement in action. Indeed, this has been a long-established view of managerial work, although the excess attention in the last century, first to controlling and then to leading, and more recently to conceiving (of planned strategy), has obscured its importance. Leonard Sayles, however, has long and steadily insisted on this, beginning with his 1964 book and culminating in *The Working Leader* (published in 1993), in which he makes his strongest statement yet, insisting that managers must be the focal points for action in and by their units (Sayles, 1964, 1993). Their direct involvement must, in his view, take precedence over the pulling force of leadership and the pushing force of controllership.

I shall refer to this involvement as the doing role. But, in using this label—a popular one in the managerial vernacular ("Mary Ann's a doer")—it is necessary to point out that managers, in fact, hardly ever "do" anything. Many barely even dial their own telephones! Watch a manager and you will see someone whose work consists almost exclusively of talking and listening, alongside, of course, watching and "feeling." (That, incidentally, is why I show the manager at the core of the model as a head and not a full body!)

What "doing" presumably means, therefore, is getting closer to the action, ultimately being just one step removed from it. Managers as doers manage the carrying out of action directly, instead of indirectly through managing people or by processing information. In effect, a "doer" is really someone who gets it done (or, as the French put it with their expression *faire faire*, to "make" something "get made"). And the managerial vernacular is, in fact, full of expressions that reflect just this: "doing deals," "championing change," "fighting fires," "juggling projects." In the terms of decision making introduced earlier, here the manager diagnoses and designs as well as decides: he or she gets deeply and fully involved in the management of particular activities. Thus, in the day I spent with the head of the small retail chain, I saw a steady stream of all sorts of people coming and going, most involved with some aspect of store development or store operations, and there to get specific instructions on how to proceed next. He was not delegating or authorizing, but very clearly managing specific development projects step by step.

Just as they communicate all around the circle, so too do managers "do" all around it, as shown in Figure 6. *Doing inside* involves projects and problems. In other words, much "doing" has to do with changing the unit itself, both proactively and reactively. Managers champion change to exploit opportunities for their units, and they handle its problems and resolve its crises, often with "hands on" involvement. Indeed, the president I observed of a large French systems company spent part of his day in a meeting on a very specific customer contract. Asked why he attended, he said it was a leading-edge project that could well change his company. He was being informed, to be sure, but also "doing" (more than controlling): he was an active member of the team. Here, then, the

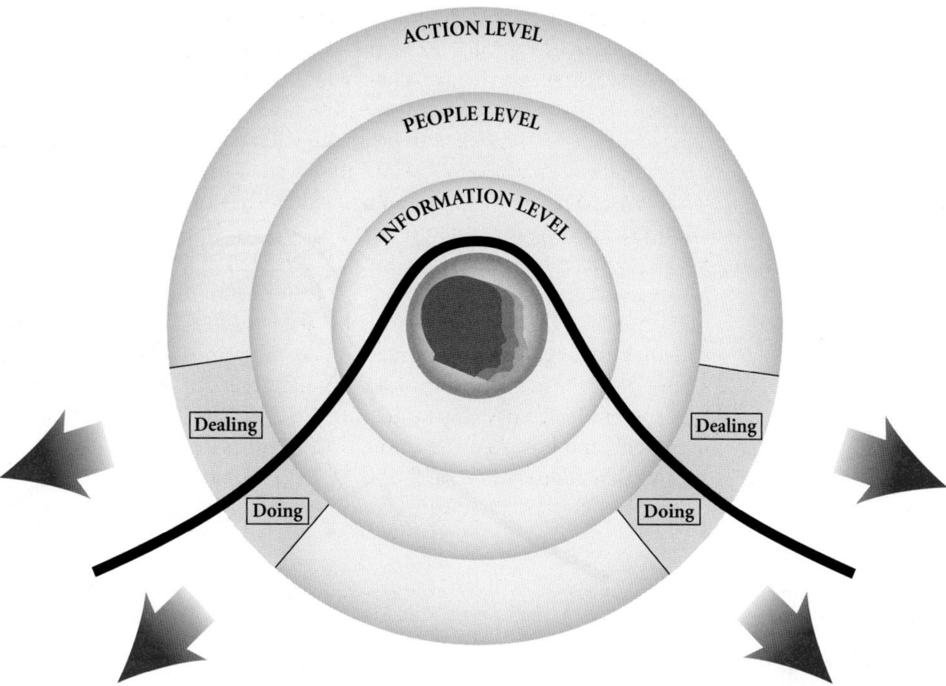

FIGURE 6
THE ACTION ROLES

manager becomes a true designer (or, in the example above, a partner in the design), not of abstract strategies or of generalized structures, but of tangible projects of change. And the evidence, in fact, is that managers at all levels typically juggle many such projects concurrently, perhaps several dozen in the case of chief executives. Hence the popularity of the term "project management."

Some managers continue to do regular work after they have become managers as well. For example, a head nurse might see a patient, just as the Pope leads prayers, or a dean might teach a class. Done for its own sake, this might be considered separate from managerial work. But such things are often done for very managerial reasons as well. This may be an effective way of "keeping in touch" with the unit's work and finding out about its problems, in which case it falls under the role of communicating. Or it may be done to demonstrate involvement and commitment with others in the unit, in which case it falls under the role of culture building in the role of leading.

Doing outside, or *dealing*, takes place in terms of deals and negotiations. Again, there is no shortage of evidence on the importance of negotiating as well as dealing in managerial work. Most evident in my observations was the managing director of the film company, who was working on one intricate deal after another. This was a small company, and making deals was a key part of her job. But even in larger organizations, senior managers have to spend considerable time on negotiations themselves, especially when critical moments arise. After all, they are the ones who have the authority to commit the resources of their unit, and it is they who are the nerve centers of its information as well as the energy centers of its activity, not to mention the conceptual centers of its strategy. All around the circles, therefore, action connects to people who connect to information, which connects to the frame.

THE WELL-ROUNDED JOB OF MANAGING

I opened this article by noting that the best-known writers of management all seem to emphasize one aspect of the job—in the terms we now have, "doing" for Tom Peters, "conceiving" for Michael Porter, "leading" for Abraham Zaleznik and Warren Bennis, "controlling" for the classical writers. Now it can be appreciated why all may well be wrong: heeding the advice of any one of them must lead to the lopsided practice of managerial work. Like an unbalanced wheel at resonant frequency, the job risks flying out of control. That is why it is important to show all

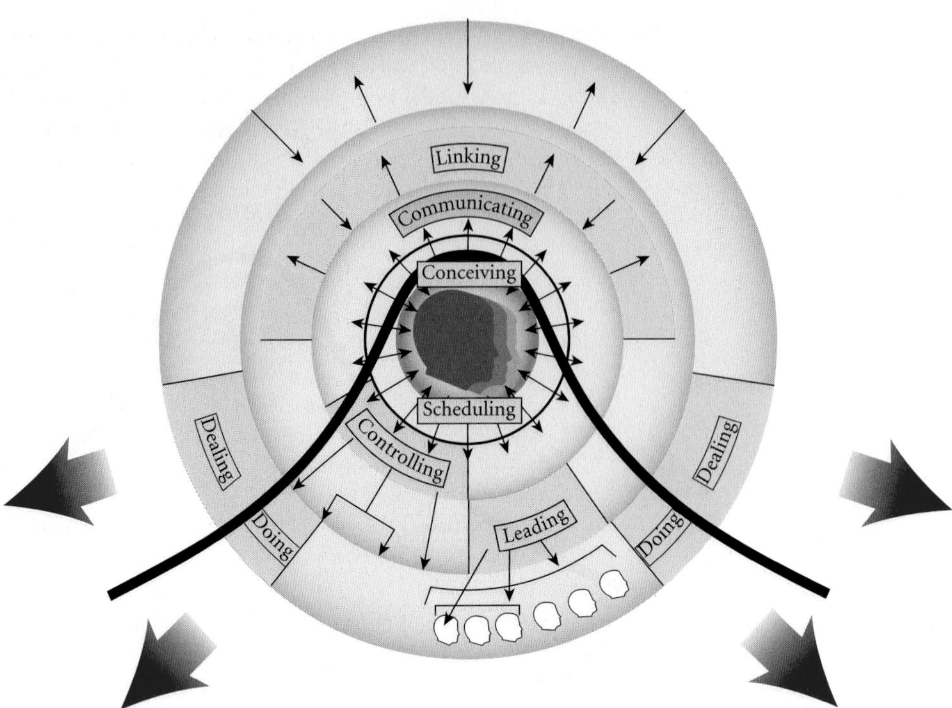

FIGURE 7
MANAGERIAL WORK ROUNDED OUT

of the components of managerial work on a single integrated diagram, as in Figure 7, to remind people, at a glance, that these components form one job and cannot be separated.

Acceptance of Tom Peters's urgings—" 'Don't think, do' is the phrase I favor"—could lead to the centrifugal explosion of the job, as it flies off in all directions, free of a strong frame anchoring it at the core. But acceptance of the spirit of Michael Porter's opposite writings—that what matters most is conception of the frame, especially of strategic positions—could produce a result no better: centripetal implosion, as the job closes in on itself cerebrally, free of the tangible connection to its outer actions. Thinking is heavy and can wear down the incumbent, while acting is light and cannot keep him or her in place. Only together do they provide the balance that seems so characteristic of effective management.

Too much leading produces a job free of content—aimless, frameless, and actionless—while too much linking produces a job detached from its internal roots—public relations instead of public service. The manager who only communicates or only conceives never gets anything done, while the manager who only "does" ends up doing it all alone. And, of course, we all know that happens to managers who believe their job is merely to control. A bad pun may thus make for good practice: the manager must practice a well-rounded job.

In fact, while we may be able to separate the components of this job conceptually, I maintain that they cannot be separated behaviorally. In other words, it may be useful, even necessary, to delineate the parts for purposes of design, selection, training, and support. But this job cannot be practiced as a set of independent parts. The core is a kind of magnet that holds the rest together, while the communication ring acts as a membrane that allows the flow of information between inner thinking and outer behaviors, which themselves tie people to action.

Indeed, the most interesting aspects of this job may well fall on the edges, between the component parts. For example, Andrew Grove, president of Intel, likes to describe what he does as "nudging," a perfect blend of controlling, leading, and doing (Grove, 1996). This can mean pushing people, tangibly but not aggressively, as might happen with pure doing, and not coldly, as with pure controlling, but with a sense of leading. There are similar edges between the inside and the outside, thinking and behaving, and communicating and controlling, as we shall see.

Managers who try to "deal" outside without "doing" inside inevitably get themselves into trouble. Just consider all those chief executives who "did the deal," acquired the company or whatever, and then dropped it into the laps of others for execution. Likewise, it makes no more sense to conceive and then fail to lead and do (as has been the tendency in so-called "strategic planning," where controlling has often been considered sufficient for "implementation") than it makes sense to do or to lead without thinking through the frame in which to embed these activities. A single managerial job may be carried out by a small team, but only if its members are so tightly knitted together—especially by that ring of communication—that they act as a single entity. This is not to argue, of course, that different managers do not emphasize different roles or different aspects of the job. For example, we can distinguish a *conceptual* style of management, which focuses on the development of the frame, an *administrative* style, which concerns itself primarily with controlling, an *interpersonal* style, which favors leading on the inside or linking on the outside, and an *action* style, which is concerned mainly with tangible doing and dealing. And as we move out in this order, the overall style of managing can be described as less *opaque*, and more *visible*.

A final aspect of managerial style has to do with the interrelationships among the various components of managerial work. For example, an important distinction can be made between *deductive* and *inductive* approaches to managerial work. The former proceeds from the core out, as the conceived frame is implemented through scheduling that uses information to drive people to get action done. We can call this a *cerebral* style of managing—highly deliberate. But there is an alternate, emergent view of the management process as well, which proceeds inductively, from the outer surface to the inner core. We might label it an *insightful* style. As Karl Weick puts it, managers act in order to think. They try things to gain experience, retain what works, and then, by interpreting the results, gradually evolve their frames (Weick, 1979).

Clearly, there is an infinity of possible contexts within which management can be practiced. But just as clearly, perhaps, a model such as the one presented here can help to order them and so come to grips with the difficult requirements of designing managerial jobs, selecting the right people to fill them, and training people accordingly.

READING 2.2

Artists, Craftsmen, and Technocrats BY PATRICIA PITCHER

. . . If you want to change corporate North America, you have to change its managers—not the culture, not the structure, but the people. All else is abstraction.

In my 20 years as an executive, a board member of multibillion dollar corporations and, recently, an academic, one lesson stands out. Give a technocrat ultimate authority and he or she will drive out everything else: vision and its carriers—artists—will be replaced; experience and its carriers—craftsmen—will follow. Dissent will be driven from the board. The organization will ossify, turn inward and short-term. . . .

HOW TO IDENTIFY A TECHNOCRAT

Technocrats are never at a loss for words, charts, or graphs. They always have a plan of action in three parts. They rarely laugh out loud, except maybe at baseball games; never at work. When they explain to you why Jim or George had to be let go, they use expressions like, "He just wasn't tough, professional, modern, rigorous, serious, hard-working enough." If they go on to mention "too emotional," watch out! You have a technocrat on your hands. This person will be described by peers and colleagues as controlled, conservative, serious, analytical, no-nonsense, intense,

Reading 2.2 is adapted from Balancing personality types at the top, *Business Quarterly*, vol. 58(2), pp.47–57 (Pitcher, P. 1993).

determined, cerebral, methodical, and meticulous. Individually, any of these words might be a compliment; together, they represent a syndrome. Here is an example of how a technocrat thinks:

> Mirroring a world-wide trend . . . , we initiated in 1989 and continued in 1990 an extensive program under which operations were regrouped, assets sold, and activities rationalized. New chief executives have been appointed and our strategy is profitability.

In this one paragraph from an annual report, we notice three things. First, the technocrat loves conventional wisdom and thus the first phase, "Mirroring a world-wide trend"; if everyone else is doing it, it must be right. Second, we see the word "rationalized"; this is the watchword. Third, we are told that all the bad guys have been fired and replaced by serious folk. When things go wrong it is always the fault of someone else.

RECOGNIZING AN ARTIST

How do you recognize artists? Well, pretty much by the opposite. What is your strategic plan for the future? Answer: "to get big," "to hit $5 billion in sales," "to beat the pants off the competition," "to be a world leader by 2020." Artists may be a little short on the details, on the how. Board presentations are sometimes a little loose—unless they are done by the chief financial officer. The artist CEO might get overtly angry or euphoric at board meetings. How does the artist CEO talk? Listen to one.

> What is strategy anyway? Grand plan? No. You try to instill a vision you have and get people to buy in. The strategy comes from astrology; quirks, dreams, love affairs, science fiction, perception of society, some madness probably, ability to guess. It is clear but fluid. Action brings precision. Very vague, but becomes clear in the act of transformation. Creation is the storm.

When CEOs like this talk to their boards about "astrology; quirks, dreams," boards have a tendency to get a little uneasy. This person's peers and colleagues describe him or her as bold, daring, exciting, volatile, intuitive, entrepreneurial, inspiring, imaginative, unpredictable, and funny. Technocrats will apply labels like "star-trekky," or more simply, nuts. The artist makes both fast friends and abiding enemies. Very few have a neutral reaction. The organization as a whole is an exciting place to be, confusing maybe, dizzying maybe, but exciting nonetheless.

AND NOW, THE CRAFTSMAN

Rosabeth Moss Kanter insists, and I think she is dead right, that people take the long view when they perceive their leaders as trustworthy, and that the sacrifices they are called upon to make are genuinely for the collective future and not to line someone else's pockets today. The organizational craftsmen embody these values. People trust them. They see the organization as an enduring institution, one that has a life of its own, a past and a future, one of which he or she is but a custodian. They tend to stay in one organization and are therefore intimately familiar with its past and infinitely careful about preserving its identity in the midst of change. The craftsman provides continuity and organizational glue, and stimulates loyalty and commitment.

Craft is fundamentally conservative, rooted in tradition. Samuel Johnson, the great British satirist, wrote, "You cannot with all the talk in the world, enable a man to make a shoe." Experience and practice are essential to judgment. What happens if you do not have experience in the firm, in the industry, in the organization? As one CEO once said, referring to a famous bright, young, professional, "He'll get hit by every blue-suede shoes man in the country." What he meant was that this brilliant young man would fall prey to idea salesmen peddling old ideas in new packages, and he would buy because he has no experience. He could not possibly know that the idea had been tried—and rejected—20 years ago. Craft demands submission to authority. Apprenticeship is long, frustrating and sometimes arduous. There are not short cuts. Polanyi argues:

> To learn by example is to submit to authority. You follow your master because you trust his manner of doing things even when you cannot analyze or account in detail for its effectiveness. A society which wants to preserve a kind of personal knowledge must submit to tradition.

Imagine the frustration of a brilliant young executive when his or her craftsman boss cannot answer the question, "Why?" Craft is inarticulate. The answer to the young manager's question is locked away in the tricks of the trade, in tacit knowledge. So, he or she thinks the boss a fool. If he or she is the boss, the employee is condemned as an old-fashioned fool and fired.

What does this tell us about craftsmen? First of all, craftsmen are patient, both with themselves and with others; they know that it took them a long time to acquire their skills and that it will be true for others. They regularly exhibit that much-sought-after commodity, judgment; judgment flows out of long experience. Young people rarely exhibit it. Their colleagues will describe them as wise, amiable, humane, honest, straightforward, responsible, trustworthy, reasonable, open-minded, and realistic. Here is a craftsman speaking about technocrats:

> Even if they had a vision, how would they get it done? There's no managerial continuity. At this year's planning meeting, there were four out of 14 people left over from two years ago. Every two years there's a new chief executive. There's no opportunity to fail, so there's no continuity. They focus directly on profit but they'll never get it because profit comes from the vision and the people and they won't invest in people. If you look after the people, the profit follows. You can't drive at it directly. Twelve and a half percent ROI is a joke; we'll be dead [in five years]. They refuse to see this. You can't correct a problem unless you see it exists. It's like me. I look in the mirror and I see a young fullback, not a balding, middle-aged man with his chest on his belly. You have to see reality to change it.

Craftsmen believe that technocrats do not have vision, and even if they did it would not do any good because they "won't invest in people." The craftsman speaking above objects to trend-line projections; "Twelve and a half percent ROI is a joke; we'll be dead [in five years]." His credo is, "If you look after the people, the profit follows." . . . (See Figure 1 for a summary of these types of managerial stereotypes.)

TEAMWORK AND THE TYPES

When serious looks at funny what does it see? Red. It sees cavalier; it sees irresponsible; it sees childish. When analytical looks at intuitive, it sees dreamer, head-in-the-clouds. When wise stares at cerebral, it sees a head without a heart, it sees brilliance devoid of judgment. And so on down the list. In short, the three types of people cannot communicate. They live in different worlds, with different values and different goals. They frame different questions and different answers to all issues confronting the corporation. They believe that their conflicts center on ideas, whereas, in fact, they center on character.

THE ARTIST	THE CRAFTSMAN	THE TECHNOCRAT
Bold	Responsible	Conservative
Daring	Wise	Methodical
Exciting	Humane	No-nonsense
Volatile	Straightforward	Controlled
Intuitive	Open-minded	Cerebral
Entrepreneurial	Realistic	Analytical
Inspiring	Trustworthy	Determined
Imaginative	Reasonable	Meticulous
Unpredictable	Honest	Intense
Funny	Amiable	Serious

FIGURE 1 MANAGERIAL STEREOTYPES

For example, recently, a major international corporation experienced pronounced difficulty with its stock price. No matter what it did, its stock traded at a 50% discount from book value. Why? Listen in on the dialogue of the deaf that goes on between senior officers and the CEO inside that corporation. They are all talking about the same subject, but you would not know it.

An *artist:* "Of course the stock price is low! (He always talks with exclamation points.) We're not doing anything to create interest, magic! We haven't bought anything, launched anything, dreamt up anything in months! Nobody believes we have an exciting future ahead of us! The stock will go up when people believe in our dream!"

A *technocrat* (firmly): "It's all the so-called dreams which have turned into cost-nightmares. We haven't showed consistent quarterly earnings over the last three years. For two quarters, our earnings have reflected some marginal improvement. As soon as the street begins to have some faith in our capacity to control costs they'll turn into believers and start to recommend our stock."

A *craftsman:* "The people on the street are not stupid. They know that we've had so much managerial turnover that we have no continuity. They know we've fallen out of touch with our traditional markets. The guy brought in to run our main widgets division wouldn't know a widget if he fell over one. The whole sales force is disillusioned. What we need is to get back in touch with what we do best."

Sticking to your knitting is not some new theoretical concept to craftsmen; it is their life. They have always done it. It comes as naturally as breathing. The cost-cutting program inevitably proposed by the technocrat strikes at the core of what the craftsman considers to be the answer to the problem. The technocrat wants to cut out the fat: inflated marketing budgets, sales training conferences, and staff development expenses. The craftsman sees the profitability problem as a symptom, a reflection of the demotivation of staff, as a diminished sense of loyalty and therefore of effort—a legacy of the last round of staff cuts and the replacement of leaders that they trusted. The technocrat is dangerous because, to the craftsman, he or she is too theoretical, "too distant from the coalface" to understand the real issues. . . .

In a major multinational I have studied for the last 10 years, the technocrats have truly triumphed. Figure 2 shows the 10-year evolution of the management team. Beginning with a healthy mix of artists, craftsmen and technocrats, by 1990 the structure had tilted irrevocably to the technocrat. Two remaining craftsmen were in the power structure only nominally; both were looking for jobs.

The result of this shift has been parallel changes in strategy and in structure. Under the aegis of the artist, the corporation had been outward-looking, increasingly internationally oriented. Fueled both by internal growth and acquisitions, assets climbed. Subsidiaries were left pretty much on their own—the power structure was decentralized—and the atmosphere, prevailing ethic, or culture if you will, was of teamwork, growth, and excitement. Out of insecurity or a simple error in judgment, the artist chose as his successor his opposite. Promoted into the number one spot, the technocrat began to install others and to rationalize, organize, and control. The by-product of rationalization, systematization, and control was centralization. The by-product of centralization was demoralization. The strategy became, in the words of the annual reports, profitability. Profitability was not and is not a strategy and it can certainly not inspire anyone as an ultimate

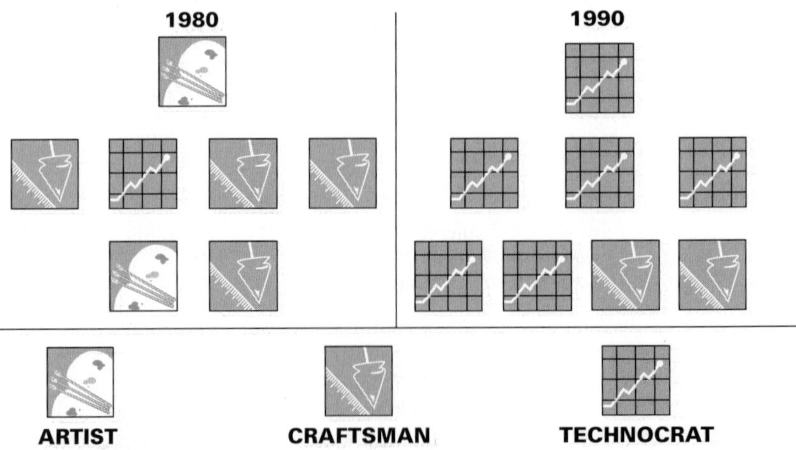

FIGURE 2
THE TECHNOCRATIC TRANSFORMATION

goal: "What do you do for a living?" "I make profit." Losing the artists, the company lost vision. Losing the craftsmen, it lost its humanity. Although profitability became the watchword, profits did not go up. Nor did share prices. The group was eventually absorbed by a more ambitious rival.

THE TRIUMPH OF THE TECHNOCRAT

. . . Technocrats have a way of making us feel secure. With their ready answers, their charts, and their graphs, they give us the feeling that everything will be all right if we just follow the rules: the rules of logic, the rules of good business practice, matrix management, participatory management, total quality management, and the new rules of globalization and strategic alliances. They make everything sound so straightforward, so rational, so comforting, so reassuring—sort of like Betty Crocker.

. . . What does a manager look like, I ask my students. "He's calm, rational, well-balanced, measured, analytical, methodological, skilled, trained, serious," they say. It occurs to me that I am listening to a liturgy—a liturgy from the gospel of the technocratic school. The person they describe is one kind of manager, and he or she is now firmly anchored as the only kind. It has become definitional.

THE LEARNING ORGANIZATION

If we concede for a moment the narcissistic presumption that ours is an age of discontinuity, then the old ways of doing things no longer work. Organizations need to learn—rapidly and continuously. How does learning take place? At the turn of the century, American philosopher George Santayana wrote, "Man's progress has a poetic phase in which he imagines the world, then a scientific phase in which he sifts and tests what he has imagined." Culturally, we have always relied on our visionaries to point us toward the new way. In science, we call a visionary a genius; in letters, a poet; in politics, a statesman; in business, a leader; generically, an artist. What all these labels have in common is the idea of someone who breaks radically with conventional wisdom, someone who sees what others do not, someone who imagines a new order. This is discontinuous learning. We call it imaginative.

Then, there is continuous learning, daily learning. What is found in art comes into use and is transformed, concretized, shaped, and sculpted by experience. A great idea, usually quite vague, is refined by practice over time. The bugs are worked out. Flesh is added to the skeleton. The slow accumulation of talent in its application is the domain of craft. We call its carrier, skilled.

Finally, there is a third form of learning. It comes from the codification of old knowledge; it comes from books and scientific papers. It comes from studying and diligence, and requires neither insight nor practice to make it our own. We call the person who possesses it knowledgeable, and if he or she possesses it to a very fine degree, brilliant.

With our religion we have eliminated both the poetic and the craft phase of learning, and tried to reduce everything to the scientific. (We are sons and daughters of the Enlightenment, after all.) We have come to believe that managers who have an MBA, can read a balance sheet, and can talk knowledgeably about strategic alliances must make good CEOs. This is nonsense. If they have no imagination, they will only mimic the competition—strategy as paint-by-numbers art. If they have no skill, they will not understand their markets. If they have no wisdom, they will tear at the fabric of the organization.

VISION, CONTINUITY, AND CONTROL

There are three ways of learning, each equally necessary. Leadership consists of knowing how to put the package together and make it work. It consists of integrating vision, continuity, and control in the managerial team.

The first step is obviously diagnostic. What does my organization look like currently? How many artists, craftsmen, and technocrats do I have, and how are they functionally distributed? What is the balance of power among them? What is the dominant ethic? Is there the freedom to fail, which is indispensable to the possibility to succeed? Is there sufficient pride of place given to emotion, to skill, to brilliance? This diagnosis is of course easier proposed than accomplished, and this for three main reasons:

1. Artists, craftsmen, and technocrats rarely exist as such; they are archetypes. Real people come in more complex packages. We may see artists, for example, with an admixture of craft. We may see conservative, cerebral craftsmen and we may see emotionally hot technocrats, or highly analytical and determined artists. Rarely do we see someone who combines all three—although we all think we do.
2. The task is made more difficult by masquerades. Faced with an artistic type, we are rarely fooled. And, with their straightforwardness and frankness, craftsmen usually give themselves away. But the technocrat, particularly of the brilliant variety, is hard to see. Technocrats revere conventional wisdom—not wisdom of a traditional sort, but new wisdom. For example, I recently had the pleasure of listening to a discourse on total quality management and empowerment from an archetypal technocratic CEO. He had systematically eliminated all artists and craftsmen from his organization. Experimentation and loyalty were dead because one false step meant being fired. Now he wanted to graft onto this moribund organization new energies of empowerment. And, what is worse, he was sincere. He really could not know that these managerial recipes, conceived procedurally, will not work. The graft will not take. But, to his board and to other observers, this man was saying all the right things. He was masquerading as a craftsman. Others, again of the brilliant variety, will masquerade as artists; knowledgeable and well-read in a superficial sort of way, they will seem to know the future. Here, we can be radically misled.
3. Finally, there is a third reason why the diagnosis is so fraught with uncertainty. It is us. What we see depends on where we sit. If I am a technocrat, I will have a tendency to see other, more brilliant technocrats as artists. I will think of them as visionary and entrepreneurial, far-sighted, and bold. If I am a pure craftsman, I will have no use for any technocrats. As one craftsman CEO put it to me recently, "They make good consultants." To him, a brilliant technocrat is dangerous as a manager because he or she is intellectually disconnected from reality. And artists, too, have their blind spots, not so much about people as about suitable objects of attention. Built into the diagnostic process, therefore, must be an element of collective judgment—judgment that does not rely too exclusively on the point of view of one or another of the archetypes. . . .

Growing frustration with formal managerial models coupled with increasing recognition of the difficulty of planning in a turbulent world, has led to the call for charismatic leadership, as though the presence of a charismatic leader could somehow take all the hard work out of managing a business. Certainly, the artists described here are charismatic and their presence is vital for success. But, they are not alone. You need artists, craftsmen, and technocrats in the right dose and in the right places. You need someone with vision, but you also need someone who can develop the people, the structures, and the systems to make the dream a reality. If you have the right people, they will do the job that comes naturally to them; you do not have to teach a fish how to swim. [The] key managerial task [of the CEO] is not to know everything but to build an executive team that can get the whole job done.

READING 2.3

Good Managers Do Not Make Policy Decisions BY H. EDWARD WRAPP

The upper reaches of management are a land of mystery and intrigue. Very few people have ever been there, and the present inhabitants frequently send back messages that are incoherent both to other levels of management and to the world in general. This may account for the myths, illusions, and caricatures that permeate the literature of management—for example, such widely held notions as these:

- Life gets less complicated as a manager reaches the top of the pyramid.
- The manager at the top level knows everything that is going on in the organization, can command whatever resources he may need, and therefore can be more decisive.

- The general manager's day is taken up with making broad policy decisions and formulating precise objectives.
- The top executive's primary activity is conceptualizing long-range plans.
- In a large company, the top executive may be seen meditating about the role of his organization in society.

I suggest that none of these versions alone, or in combination, is an accurate portrayal of what a general manager does. Perhaps students of the management process have been overly eager to develop a theory and a discipline. As one executive I know puts it, "I guess I do some of the things described in the books and articles, but the descriptions are lifeless, and my job isn't."

What common characteristics, then, do successful executives exhibit *in reality?* I shall identify five skills or talents that, in my experience, seem especially significant. . . .

KEEPING WELL INFORMED

First, each of my heroes has a special talent for keeping himself informed about a wide range of operating decisions being made at different levels in the company. As he moves up the ladder, he develops a network of information sources in many different departments. He cultivates these sources and keeps them open no matter how high he climbs in the organization. When the need arises, he bypasses the lines on the organization chart to seek more than one version of a situation.

In some instances, especially when they suspect he would not be in total agreement with their decision, his subordinates will elect to inform him in advance, before they announce a decision. In these circumstances, he is in a position to defer the decision, or redirect it, or even block further action. However, he does not insist on this procedure. Ordinarily he leaves it up to the members of his organization to decide at what stage they inform him.

Top-level managers are frequently criticized by writers, consultants, and lower levels of management for continuing to enmesh themselves in operating problems, after promotion to the top, rather than withdrawing to the "big picture." Without any doubt, some managers do get lost in a welter of detail and insist on making too many decisions. Superficially, the good manager may seem to make the same mistake—but his purposes are different. He knows that only by keeping well informed about the decisions being made can he avoid the sterility so often found in those who isolate themselves from operations. If he follows the advice to free himself from operations, he may soon find himself subsisting on a diet of abstractions, leaving the choice of what he eats in the hands of his subordinates. As Kenneth Boulding puts it, "The very purpose of a hierarchy is to prevent information from reaching higher layers. It operates as an information filter, and there are little wastebaskets all along the way" (in *Business Week*, February 18, 1967: 202). . . .

FOCUSING TIME AND ENERGY

The second skill of the good manager is that he knows how to save his energy and hours for those few particular issues, decisions, or problems to which he should give his personal attention. He knows the fine and subtle distinction between keeping fully informed about operating decisions and allowing the organization to force him into participating in these decisions, or, even worse, making them. Recognizing that he can bring his special talents to bear on only a limited number of matters, he chooses those issues which he believes will have the greatest long-term impact on the company, and on which his special abilities can be most productive. Under ordinary circumstances he will limit himself to three or four major objectives during any single period of sustained activity.

What about the situations he elects *not* to become involved in as a decision maker? He makes sure (using the skill first mentioned) that the organization keeps him informed about them at various stages; he does not want to be accused of indifference to such issues. He trains his subordinates not to bring the matters to him for a decision. The communication to him from below is essentially one of, "Here is our sizeup, and here's what we propose to do." Reserving his hearty encouragement for those projects that hold superior promise of a contribution to total corporate strategy, he simply acknowledges receipt of information on other matters. When he sees a problem where the organization needs his help, he finds a way to transmit his know-how short of giving orders—usually by asking perceptive questions.

PLAYING THE POWER GAME

To what extent do successful top executives push their ideas and proposals through the organization? The rather common notion that the "prime mover" continually creates and forces through new programs, like a powerful majority leader in a liberal Congress, is in my opinion very misleading.

The successful manager is sensitive to the power structure in the organization. In considering any major current proposal, he can plot the position of the various individuals and units in the organization on a scale ranging from complete, outspoken support down to determined, sometimes bitter, and oftentimes well-cloaked opposition. In the middle of the scale is an area of comparative indifference. Usually, several aspects of a proposal will fall into this area, and *here is where he knows he can operate*. He assesses the depth and nature of the blocs in the organization. His perception permits him to move through what I call *corridors* of comparative indifference. He seldom challenges when a corridor is blocked, preferring to pause until it has opened up.

Related to this particular skill is his ability to recognize the need for a few trial-balloon launchers in the organization. He knows that the organization will tolerate only a certain number of proposals that emanate from the apex of the pyramid. No matter how sorely he may be tempted to stimulate the organization with a flow of his own ideas, he knows he must work through idea men in different parts of the organization. As he studies the reactions of key individuals and groups to the trial balloons these men send up, he is able to make a better assessment of how to limit the emasculation of the various proposals. For seldom does he find a proposal that is supported by all quarters of the organization. The emergence of strong support in certain quarters is almost sure to evoke strong opposition in others.

VALUE OF SENSE OF TIMING

Circumstances like these mean that a good sense of timing is a priceless asset for a top executive. . . . As a good manager stands at a point in time, he can identify a set of goals he is interested in, albeit the outline of them may be pretty hazy. His timetable, which is also pretty hazy, suggests that some must be accomplished sooner than others, and that some may be safely postponed for several months or years. He has a still hazier notion of how he can reach these goals. He assesses key individuals and groups. He knows that each has its own set of goals, some of which he understands rather thoroughly and others about which he can only speculate. He knows also that these individuals and groups represent blocks to certain programs or projects, and that these points of opposition must be taken into account. As the day-to-day operating decisions are made, and as proposals are responded to both by individuals and by groups, he perceives more clearly where the corridors of comparative indifference are. He takes action accordingly.

THE ART OF IMPRECISION

The fourth skill of the successful manager is knowing how to satisfy the organization that it has a sense of direction *without ever actually getting himself committed to a specific set of objectives*. This is not to say that he does not have objectives—personal and corporate, long-term and short-term. They are significant guides to his thinking, and he modifies them continually as he better understands the resources he is working with, the competition, and the changing market demands. But as the organization clamors for statements of objectives, these are samples of what they get back from him:

> "Our company aims to be number one in its industry."
> "Our objective is growth with profit."
> "We seek the maximum return on investment."
> "Management's goal is to meet its responsibilities to stockholders, employees, and the public."

In my opinion, statements such as these provide almost no guidance to the various levels of management. Yet they are quite readily accepted as objectives by large numbers of intelligent people.

MAINTAINING VIABILITY

Why does the good manager shy away from precise statements of his objectives for the organization? The main reason is that he finds it impossible to set down specific objectives that will be relevant for any reasonable period into the future. Conditions in business change continually and rapidly, and corporate strategy must be revised to take the changes into account. The more explicit the statement of strategy, the more difficult it becomes to persuade the organization to turn to different goals when needs and conditions shift.

The public and the stockholders, to be sure, must perceive the organization as having a well-defined set of objectives and clear sense of direction. But in reality the good top manager is seldom so certain of the direction that should be taken. Better than anyone else, he senses the many, many threats to his company—threats that lie in the economy, in the actions of competitors, and, not least, within his own organization.

He also knows that it is impossible to state objectives clearly enough so that everyone in the organization understands what they mean. Objectives get communicated only over time by a consistency or pattern in operating decisions. Such decisions are more meaningful than words. In instances where precise objectives are spelled out, the organization tends to interpret them so they fit its own needs.

Subordinates who keep pressing for more precise objectives are in truth working against their own best interests. Each time the objectives are stated more specifically, a subordinate's range of possibilities for operating are reduced. The narrower field means less room to roam and to accommodate the flow of ideas coming up from his part of the organization.

AVOIDING POLICY STRAITJACKETS

The successful manager's reluctance to be precise extends into the area of policy decisions. He seldom makes a forthright statement of policy. He may be aware that in some companies there are executives who spend more time in arbitrating disputes caused by stated policies than in moving the company forward. The management textbooks contend that well-defined policies are the sine qua non of a well-managed company. My research does not bear out this contention. For example,

> The president of one company with which I am familiar deliberately leaves the assignments of his top officers vague and refuses to define policies for them. He passes out new assignments with seemingly no pattern in mind and consciously sets up competitive ventures among his subordinates. His methods, though they would never be sanctioned by a classical organization planner, are deliberate—and, incidentally, quite effective.

Since able managers do not make policy decisions, does this mean that well-managed companies operate without policies? Certainly not. But the policies are those that evolve over time from an indescribable mix of operating decisions. From any single operating decision might have come a very minor dimension of the policy as the organization understands it; from a series of decisions comes a pattern of guidelines for various levels of the organization.

The skillful manager resists the urge to write a company creed or to compile a policy manual. Preoccupation with detailed statements of corporate objectives and departmental goals and with comprehensive organization charts and job descriptions is often the first symptom of an organization that is in the early stages of atrophy.

The "management by objectives" school, so widely heralded in recent years, suggests that detailed objectives be spelled out at all levels in the corporation. This method is feasible at lower levels of management, but it becomes unworkable at the upper levels. The top manager must think out objectives in detail, but ordinarily some of the objectives must be withheld, or at least communicated to the organization in modest doses. A conditioning process that may stretch over months or years is necessary in order to prepare the organization for radical departures from what it is currently striving to attain.

Suppose, for example, that a president is convinced his company must phase out of the principal business it has been in for 35 years. Although making this change of course is one of his objectives, he may well feel that he cannot disclose the idea even to his vice presidents, whose total know-how is in the present business. A blunt announcement that the company is changing horses would be too great a shock for most of them to bear. And so he begins moving toward this goal but without a full disclosure to his management group.

A detailed spelling out of objectives may only complicate the task of reaching them. Specific, detailed statements give the opposition an opportunity to organize its defenses.

MUDDLING WITH A PURPOSE

The fifth, and most important, skill I shall describe bears little relation to the doctrine that management is (or should be) a comprehensive, systematic, logical, well-programmed science. Of all the heresies set forth here, this should strike doctrinaires as the rankest of all!

The successful manager, in my observation, recognizes the futility of trying to push total packages or programs through the organization. He is willing to take less than total acceptance in order to achieve modest progress toward his goals. Avoiding debates on principles, he tries to piece together particles that may appear to be incidentals into a program that moves at least part of the way toward his objectives. His attitude is based on optimism and persistence. Over and over he says to himself, "There must be some parts of this proposal on which we can capitalize."

Whenever he identifies relationships among the different proposals before him, he knows that they present opportunities for combination and restructuring. It follows that he is a man of wide-ranging interests and curiosity. The more things he knows about, the more opportunities he will have to discover parts that are related. This process does not require great intellectual brilliance or unusual creativity. The wider ranging his interests, the more likely that he will be able to tie together several unrelated proposals. He is skilled as an analyst, but even more talented as a conceptualizer.

If the manager has built or inherited a solid organization, it will be difficult for him to come up with an idea that no one in the company has ever thought of before. His most significant contribution may be that he can see relationships which no one else has seen. . . .

CONTRASTING PICTURES

It is interesting to note, in the writings of several students of management, the emergence of the concept that, rather than making decisions, the leader's principal task is maintaining operating conditions that permit the various decision-making systems to function effectively. The supporters of this theory, it seems to me, overlook the subtle turns of direction that the leader can provide. He cannot add purpose and structure to the balanced judgments of subordinates if he simply rubberstamps their decisions. He must weigh the issues and reach his own decision. . . .

Many of the articles about successful executives picture them as great thinkers who sit at their desks drafting master blueprints for their companies. The successful top executives I have seen at work do not operate this way. Rather than produce a full-grown decision tree, they start with a twig, help it grow, and ease themselves out on the limbs only after they have tested to see how much weight the limbs can stand.

In my picture, the general manager sits in the midst of a continuous stream of operating problems. His organization presents him with a flow of proposals to deal with the problems. Some of these proposals are contained in voluminous, well-documented, formal reports; some are as fleeting as the walk-in visit from a subordinate whose latest inspiration came during the morning's coffee break. Knowing how meaningless it is to say, "This is a finance problem," or, "That is a communications problem," the manager feels no compulsion to classify his problems. He is, in fact, undismayed by a problem that defies classification. As the late Gary Steiner, in one of his speeches, put it, "He has a high tolerance for ambiguity."

In considering each proposal, the general manager tests it against at least three criteria:

1. Will the total proposal—or, more often, will some parts of the proposal—move the organization toward the objectives that he has in mind?
2. How will the whole or parts of the proposal be received by the various groups and subgroups in the organization? Where will the strongest opposition come from, which group will furnish the strongest support, and which group will be neutral or indifferent?
3. How does the proposal relate to programs already in process or currently proposed? Can some parts of the proposal under consideration be added on to a program already under way, or can they be combined with all or parts of other proposals in a package that can be steered through the organization? . . .

To recapitulate, the general manager possesses five important skills. He knows how to:

1. *Keep open many pipelines of information*—No one will quarrel with the desirability of an early warning system that provides varied viewpoints on an issue. However, very few managers know how to practice this skill, and the books on management add precious little to our understanding of the techniques that make it practicable.
2. *Concentrate on a limited number of significant issues*—No matter how skillful the manager is in focusing his energies and talents, he is inevitably caught up in a number of inconsequential duties. Active leadership of an organization demands a high level of personal involvement, and personal involvement brings with it many time-consuming activities that have an infinitesimal impact on corporate strategy. Hence this second skill, while perhaps the most logical of the five, is by no means the easiest to apply.
3. *Identify the corridors of comparative indifference*—Are there inferences here that the good manager has no ideas of his own, that he stands by until his organization proposes solutions, that he never uses his authority to force a proposal through the organization? Such inferences are not intended. The message is that a good organization will tolerate only so much direction from the top; the good manager therefore is adept at sensing how hard he can push.
4. *Give the organization a sense of direction with open-ended objectives*—In assessing this skill, keep in mind that I am talking about top levels of management. At lower levels, the manager should be encouraged to write down his objectives, if for no other reason than to ascertain if they are consistent with corporate strategy.
5. *Spot opportunities and relationships in the stream of operating problems and decisions*—Lest it be concluded from the description of this skill that the good manager is more an improviser than a planner, let me emphasize that he is a planner and encourages planning by his subordinates. Interestingly, though, professional planners may be irritated by a good general manager. Most of them complain about his lack of vision. They devise a master plan, but the president (or other operating executive) seems to ignore it, or to give it minimum acknowledgment by borrowing bits and pieces for implementation. They seem to feel that the power of a good master plan will be obvious to everyone, and its implementation automatic. But the general manager knows that even if the plan is sound and imaginative, the job has only begun. The long, painful task of implementation will depend on his skill, not that of the planner. . . .

READING 2.4

The Leader's New Work: Building Learning Organizations BY PETER M. SENGE

Human beings are designed for learning. No one has to teach an infant to walk, or talk, or master the spatial relationships needed to stack eight building blocks that do not topple. Children come fully equipped with an insatiable drive to explore and experiment. Unfortunately, the primary institutions of our society are oriented predominantly toward controlling rather than learning, rewarding individuals for performing for others rather than for cultivating their natural curiosity and impulse to learn. The young child entering school discovers quickly that the name of the game is getting the right answer and avoiding mistakes—a mandate no less compelling to the aspiring manager.

"Our prevailing system of management has destroyed our people," writes W. Edwards Deming, leader in the quality movement (Senge, 1990). "People are born with intrinsic motivation, self-esteem, dignity, curiosity to learn, joy in learning. The forces of destruction begin with toddlers—a prize for the best Halloween costume, grades in school, gold stars, and on up through the university. On the job, people, teams, divisions are ranked—reward for the one at the top, punishment at the bottom. MBO, quotas, incentive pay, business plans, put together separately, division by division, cause further loss, unknown and unknowable."

Ironically, by focusing on performing for someone else's approval, corporations create the very conditions that predestine them to mediocre performance. Over the long run, superior performance depends on superior learning. A Shell study showed . . . that "the key to the long term survival of the large industrial enterprise was the ability to run 'experiments in the margin,' to continually explore new business and organizational opportunities that create potential new sources of growth" (de Gues, 1988: 70–74).

If anything, the need for understanding how organizations learn and accelerating that learning is greater today than ever before. The old days when a Henry Ford, Alfred Sloan, or Tom Watson *learned for the organization* are gone. In an increasingly dynamic, interdependent, and unpredictable world, it is simply no longer possible for anyone to "figure it all out at the top." The old model, "the top thinks and the local acts," must now give way to integrative thinking and acting at all levels. . . .

ADAPTIVE LEARNING AND GENERATIVE LEARNING

The prevailing view of learning organizations emphasizes increased adaptability. . . . But increasing adaptiveness is only the first stage in moving toward learning organizations. The impulse to learn in children goes deeper than desires to respond and adapt more effectively to environmental change. The impulse to learn, at its heart, is an impulse to be generative, to expand our capability. This is why leading corporations are focusing on *generative* learning, which is about creating, as well as *adaptive* learning, which is about coping. . . .

Generative learning, unlike adaptive learning, requires new ways of looking at the world, whether in understanding customers or in understanding how to better manage a business. For years, U.S. manufacturers sought competitive advantage in aggressive controls on inventories, incentives against overproduction, and rigid adherence to production forecasts. Despite these incentives, their performance was eventually eclipsed by Japanese firms who saw the challenges of manufacturing differently. They realized that eliminating delays in the production process was the key to reducing instability and improving cost, productivity, and service. They worked to build networks of relationships with trusted suppliers and to redesign physical production processes so as to reduce delays in materials procurement, production setup, and in-process inventory—a much higher-leverage approach to improving both cost and customer loyalty.

As Boston Consulting Group's George Stalk has observed, the Japanese saw the significance of delays because they saw the process of order entry, production scheduling, materials procurement, production, and distribution *as an integrated system*. "What distorts the system so badly is time," observed Stalk—the multiple delays between events and responses. "These distortions reverberate throughout the system, producing disruptions, waste, and inefficiency" (Stalk, 1988: 41–51). Generative learning requires seeing the systems that control events. When we fail to grasp the systemic source of problems, we are left to "push on" symptoms rather than eliminate underlying causes. The best we can ever do is adaptive learning.

THE LEADER'S NEW WORK

. . . Our traditional view of leaders—as special people who set the direction, make the key decisions, and energize the troops—is deeply rooted in an individualistic and nonsystemic worldview. Especially in the West, leaders are *heroes*—great men (and occasionally women) who rise to the fore in times of crisis. So long as such myths prevail, they reinforce a focus on short-term events and charismatic heroes rather than on systemic forces and collective learning.

Leadership in learning organizations centers on subtler and ultimately more important work. In a learning organization, leaders' roles differ dramatically from that of the charismatic decision maker. Leaders are designers, teachers, and stewards. These roles require new skills: the ability to build shared vision, to bring to the surface and challenge prevailing mental models, and to foster more systemic patterns of thinking. In short, leaders in learning organizations are responsible for *building organizations* where people are continually expanding their capabilities to shape their future—that is, leaders are responsible for learning.

CREATIVE TENSION: THE INTEGRATING PRINCIPLE

Leadership in a learning organization starts with the principle of creative tension (Fritz, 1989, 1990). Creative tension comes from seeing clearly where we want to be, our "vision," and telling the truth about where we are, our "current reality." The gap between the two generates a natural tension. . . .

Creative tension can be resolved in two basic ways: by raising current reality toward the vision or by lowering the vision toward current reality. Individuals, groups, and organizations who learn how to work with creative tension learn how to use the energy it generates to move reality more reliably toward their visions. . . .

Without vision there is no creative tension. Creative tension cannot be generated from current reality alone. All the analysis in the world will never generate a vision. Many who are otherwise qualified to lead fail to do so because they try to substitute analysis for vision. They believe that, if only people understood current reality, they would surely feel the motivation to change. They are then disappointed to discover that people "resist" the personal and organizational changes that must be made to alter reality. What they never grasp is that the natural energy for changing reality comes from holding a picture of what might be that is more important to people than what is.

But creative tension cannot be generated from vision alone; it demands an accurate picture of current reality as well. Just as Martin Luther King had a dream, so too did he continually strive to "dramatize the shameful conditions" of racism and prejudice so that they could no longer be ignored. Vision without an understanding of current reality will more likely foster cynicism than creativity. The principle of creative tension teaches that *an accurate picture of current reality is just as important as a compelling picture of a desired future.*

Leading through creative tension is different than solving problems. In problem solving, the energy for change comes from attempting to get away from an aspect of current reality that is undesirable. With creative tension, the energy for change comes from the vision, from what we want to create, juxtaposed with current reality. While the distinction may seem small, the consequences are not. Many people and organizations find themselves motivated to change only when their problems are bad enough to cause them to change. This works for a while, but the change process runs out of steam as soon as the problems driving the change become less pressing. With problem solving, the motivation for change is extrinsic. With creative tension, the motivation is intrinsic. This distinction mirrors the distinction between adaptive and generative learning.

NEW ROLES

The traditional authoritarian image of the leader as "the boss calling the shots" has been recognized as oversimplified and inadequate for some time. According to Edgar Schein (1985), "Leadership is intertwined with culture formation." Building an organization's culture and shaping its evolution is the "unique and essential function" of leadership. In a learning organization, the critical roles of leadership—designer, teacher, and steward—have antecedents in the ways leaders have contributed to building organizations in the past. But each role takes on new meaning in the learning organization and, as will be seen in the following sections, demands new skills and tools.

LEADER AS DESIGNER

Imagine that your organization is an ocean liner and that you are "the leader." What is your role?

I have asked this question of groups of managers many times. The most common answer, not surprisingly, is "the captain." Others say, "The navigator, setting the direction." Still others say, "The helmsman, actually controlling the direction," or "The engineer down there stoking the fire, providing energy," or "The social direction, making sure everybody's enrolled, involved, and communicating." While these are legitimate leadership roles, there is another that, in many ways, eclipses them all in importance. Yet rarely does anyone mention it.

The neglected leadership role is the *designer* of the ship. No one has a more sweeping influence than the designer. What good does it do for the captain to say, "Turn starboard 30 degrees," when the designer has built a rudder that will only turn to port, or which takes six hours to turn to starboard? It is fruitless to be the leader in an organization that is poorly designed.

The functions of design, or what some have called "social architecture," are rarely visible; they take place behind the scenes. The consequences that appear today are the result of work done long in the past, and work today will show its benefits far in the future. Those who aspire to lead out of a desire to control, or gain fame, or simply to be at the center of the action, will find little to attract them to the quiet design work of leadership.

But what, specifically, is involved in organizational design? "Organizational design is widely misconstrued as moving around boxes and lines," says Hanover Insurance Company's CEO William O'Brien. "The first task of organization design concerns designing the governing ideas of purpose, vision, and core values by which people will live." Few acts of leadership have a more enduring impact on an organization than building a foundation of purpose and core values. . . .

If governing ideas constitute the first design task of leadership, the second design task involves the policies, strategies, and structures that translate guiding ideas into business decisions. Leadership theorist Philip Selznick (1957) calls policy and structure the "institutional embodiment of purpose." "Policy making (the rules that guide decisions) ought to be separated from decision making," says Jay Forrester (1965: 5–17). "Otherwise, short-term pressures will usurp time from policy creation."

Traditionally, writers like Selznick and Forrester have tended to see policy making and implementation as the work of a small number of senior managers. But that view is changing. Both the dynamic business environment and the mandate of the learning organization to engage people at all levels now make it clear that this second design task is more subtle. Henry Mintzberg has argued that strategy is less a rational plan arrived at in the abstract and implemented throughout the organization than an "emergent phenomenon." Successful organizations "craft strategy" according to Mintzberg (1987: 66–75) as they continually learn about shifting business conditions and balance what is desired and what is possible. The key is not getting the right strategy but fostering strategic thinking. "The choice of individual action is only part of . . . the policymaker's need," according to Mason and Mitroff (1981: 16). "More important is the need to achieve insight into the nature of the complexity and to formulate concepts and world views for coping with it."

Behind appropriate policies, strategies, and structures are effective learning processes: their creation is the third key design responsibility in learning organizations. This does not absolve senior managers of their strategic responsibilities. Actually, it deepens and extends those responsibilities. Now, they are responsible not only for ensuring that an organization has well-developed strategies and policies, but also for ensuring that processes exist whereby these are continually improved.

In the early 1970s, Shell was the weakest of the big seven oil companies. Today, Shell and Exxon are arguably the strongest, both in size and in financial health. Shell's ascendance began with frustration. Around 1971 members of Shell's "Group Planning" in London began to foresee dramatic change and unpredictability in world oil markets. However, it proved impossible to persuade managers that the stable world of steady growth in oil demand and supply they had known for twenty years was about to change. Despite brilliant analysis and artful presentation, Shell's planners realized, in the words of Pierre Wack (1985: 73–89), that they "had failed to change behavior in much of the Shell organization." Progress would probably have ended there, had the frustration not given way to a radically new view of corporate thinking.

As they pondered this failure, the planners' view of their basic task shifted: "We no longer saw our task as producing a documented view of the future business environment five or ten years ahead. Our real target was the microcosm (the 'mental model') of our decision makers." Only when the planners reconceptualized their basic task as fostering learning rather than devising plans did their insights begin to have impact. The initial tool used was "scenario analysis," through which planners encouraged operating managers to think through how they would manage in the future under different possible scenarios. It mattered not that the managers believed the planners' scenarios absolutely, only that they became engaged in ferreting out the implications. In this way, Shell's planners conditioned managers to be mentally prepared for a shift from low prices to high prices and from stability to instability. The results were significant. When OPEC became a reality, Shell quickly responded by increasing local operating company control (to enhance maneuverability in the new political environment), building buffer stocks, and accelerating development of non-OPEC sources—actions that its competitors took much more slowly or not at all.

Somewhat inadvertently, Shell's planners had discovered the leverage of designing institutional learning processes, whereby, in the words of former planning director de Geus (1988), "Management teams change their shared mental models of their company, their markets, and their competitors." Since then, "planning as learning" has become a byword at Shell, and Group Planning has continually sought out new learning tools that can be integrated into the planning process. Some of these are described below.

LEADER AS TEACHER

"The first responsibility of a leader," writes retired Herman Miller CEO Max de Pree (1989: 9), "is to define reality." Much of the leverage leaders can actually exert lies in helping people achieve more accurate, more insightful, and more *empowering* views of reality.

Leader as teacher does *not* mean leader as authoritarian expert whose job it is to teach people the "correct" view of reality. Rather, it is about helping everyone in the organization, oneself included, to gain more insightful views of current reality. This is in line with a popular emerging view of leaders as coaches, guides, or facilitators. . . . In learning organizations, this teaching role is developed further by virtue of explicit attention to people's mental models and by the influence of the systems perspective.

The role of leader as teacher starts with bringing to the surface people's mental models of important issues. No one carries an organization, a market, or a state of technology in his or her head. What we carry in our heads are assumptions. These mental pictures of how the world works have a significant influence on how we perceive problems and opportunities, identify courses of action, and make choices.

One reason that mental models are so deeply entrenched is that they are largely tacit. Ian Mitroff, in his study of General Motors, argues that an assumption that prevailed for years was that, in the United States, "Cars are status symbols. Styling is therefore more important than quality" (Mitroff, 1988: 66–67). The Detroit automakers did not say, "We have a *mental model* that all people care about is styling." Few actual managers would even say publicly that all people care about is styling. So long as the view remained unexpressed, there was little possibility of challenging its validity or forming more accurate assumptions.

But working with mental models goes beyond revealing hidden assumptions. "Reality," as perceived by most people in most organizations, means pressures that must be borne, crises that must be reacted to, and limitations that must be accepted. Leaders as teachers help people *restructure their views of reality* to see beyond the superficial conditions and events into the underlying causes of problems—and therefore to see new possibilities for shaping the future.

Specifically, leaders can influence people to view reality at three distinct levels: events, patterns of behavior, and systemic structure.

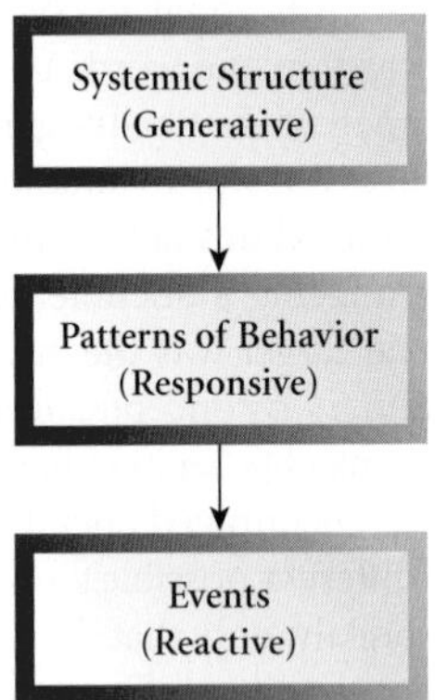

The key question becomes where do leaders predominantly focus their own and their organization's attention?

Contemporary society focuses predominantly on events. The media reinforces this perspective, with almost exclusive attention to short-term, dramatic events. This focus leads naturally to explaining what happens in terms of those events: "The Dow Jones average went up sixteen points because high fourth-quarter profits were announced yesterday."

Pattern-of-behavior explanations are rarer, in contemporary culture, than event explanations, but they do occur. "Trend analysis" is an example of seeing patterns of behavior. A good editorial that interprets a set of current events in the context of long-term historical changes is another example. Systemic, structural explanations go even further by addressing the question, "What causes the patterns of behavior?"

In some sense, all three levels of explanation are equally true. But their usefulness is quite different. Event explanations—who did what to whom—doom their holders to a reactive stance toward change. Pattern-of-behavior explanations focus on identifying long-term trends and assessing their implications. They at least suggest how, over time, we can respond to shifting conditions. Structural explanations are the most powerful. Only they address the underlying causes of behavior at a level such that patterns of behavior can be changed.

By and large, leaders of our current institutions focus their attention on events and patterns of behavior, and, under their influence, their organizations do likewise. That is why contemporary organizations are predominantly reactive, or at best responsive—rarely generative. On the other hand, leaders in learning organizations pay attention to all three levels, but focus especially on systemic structure; largely by example, they teach people throughout the organization to do likewise.

LEADER AS STEWARD

This is the subtlest role of leadership. Unlike the roles of designer and teacher, it is almost solely a matter of attitude. It is an attitude critical to learning organizations.

While stewardship has long been recognized as an aspect of leadership, its source is still not widely understood. I believe Robert Greenleaf (1977) came closest to explaining real stewardship, in his seminal book *Servant Leadership*. There, Greenleaf argues that "The servant leader *is* servant first. . . . It begins with the natural feeling that one wants to serve, to serve *first*.

This conscious choice brings one to aspire to lead. That person is sharply different from one who is leader first, perhaps because of the need to assuage an unusual power drive or to acquire material possessions."

Leaders' sense of stewardship operates on two levels: stewardship for the people they lead and stewardship for the larger purpose or mission that underlies the enterprise. The first type arises from a keen appreciation of the impact one's leadership can have on others. People can suffer economically, emotionally, and spiritually under inept leadership. If anything, people in a learning organization are more vulnerable because of their commitment and sense of shared ownership. Appreciating this naturally instills a sense of responsibility in leaders. The second type of stewardship arises from a leader's sense of personal purpose and commitment to the organization's larger mission. People's natural impulse to learn is unleashed when they are engaged in an endeavor they consider worthy of their fullest commitment. Or, as Lawrence Miller (1984) puts it, "Achieving return on equity does not, as a goal, mobilize the most noble forces of our soul."

Leaders engaged in building learning organizations naturally feel part of a larger purpose that goes beyond their organization. They are part of changing the way businesses operate, not from a vague philanthropic urge, but from a conviction that their efforts will produce more productive organizations, capable of achieving higher levels of organizational success and personal satisfaction than more traditional organizations. . . .

NEW SKILLS

New leadership roles require new leadership skills. These skills can only be developed, in my judgment, through a lifelong commitment. It is not enough for one or two individuals to develop these skills. They must be distributed widely throughout the organization. This is one reason that understanding the *disciplines* of a learning organization is so important. These disciplines embody the principles and practice that can widely foster leadership development.

Three critical areas of skills (disciplines) are building shared vision, surfacing and challenging mental models, and engaging in systems thinking.

BUILDING SHARED VISION

How do individual visions come together to create shared visions? A useful metaphor is the hologram, the three-dimensional image created by interacting light sources.

If you cut a photograph in half, each half shows only part of the whole image. But if you divide a hologram, each part, no matter how small, shows the whole image intact. Likewise, when a group of people come to share a vision for an organization, each person sees an individual picture of the organization at its best. Each shares responsibility for the whole, not just for one piece. But the component pieces of the holograms are not identical. Each represents the whole image from a different point of view. It is something like poking holes in a window shade; each hole offers a unique angle for viewing the whole image. So, too, is each individual's vision unique.

When you add up the pieces of a hologram, something interesting happens. The image becomes more intense, more lifelike. When more people come to share a vision, the vision becomes more real in the sense of a mental reality that people can truly imagine achieving. They now have partners, cocreators; the vision no longer rests on their shoulders alone. Early on, when they are nurturing an individual vision, people may say it is "my vision." But, as the shared vision develops, it becomes both "my vision" and "our vision."

The skills involved in building shared vision include the following:

- *Encouraging Personal Vision.* Shared visions emerge from personal visions. It is not that people only care about their own self-interest—in fact, people's values usually include dimensions that concern family, organization, community, and even the world. Rather, it is that people's capacity for caring is *personal.*
- *Communicating and Asking for Support.* Leaders must be willing to continually share their own vision, rather than being the official representative of the corporate vision. They also

must be prepared to ask, "Is this vision worthy of your commitment?" This can be difficult for a person used to setting goals and presuming compliance.

- *Visioning as an Ongoing Process.* Building shared vision is a never-ending process. At any one point there will be a particular image of the future that is predominant, but that image will evolve. Today, too many managers want to dispense with the "vision business" by going off and writing the Official Vision Statement. Such statements almost always lack the vitality, freshness, and excitement of a genuine vision that comes from people asking, "What do we really want to achieve?"
- *Blending Extrinsic and Intrinsic Visions.* Many energizing visions are extrinsic—that is, they focus on achieving something relative to an outsider, such as a competitor. But a goal that is limited to defeating an opponent can, once the vision is achieved, easily become a defensive posture. In contrast, intrinsic goals like creating a new type of product, taking an established product to a new level, or setting a new standard for customer satisfaction can call forth a new level of creativity and innovation. Intrinsic and extrinsic visions need to coexist; a vision solely predicated on defeating an adversary will eventually weaken an organization.
- *Distinguishing Positive from Negative Visions.* Many organizations only truly pull together when their survival is threatened. Similarly, most social movements aim at eliminating what people do not want: for example, anti-drugs, anti-smoking, or anti-nuclear arms movements. Negative visions carry a subtle message of powerlessness: people will only pull together when there is sufficient threat. Negative visions also tend to be short term. Two fundamental sources of energy can motivate organizations: fear and aspiration. Fear, the energy source behind negative visions, can produce extraordinary changes in shorter periods, but aspiration endures as a continuing source of learning and growth.

SURFACING AND TESTING MENTAL MODELS

Many of the best ideas in organizations never get put into practice. One reason is that new insights and initiatives often conflict with established mental models. The leadership task of challenging assumptions without invoking defensiveness requires reflection and inquiry skills possessed by few leaders in traditional controlling organizations.

- *Seeing Leaps of Abstraction.* Our minds literally move at lightning speed. Ironically, this often slows our learning, because we leap to generalizations so quickly that we never think to test them. We then confuse our generalizations with the observable data upon which they are based, treating the generalizations *as if they were data*. . . .
- *Balancing Inquiry and Advocacy.* Most managers are skilled at articulating their views and presenting them persuasively. While important, advocacy skills can become counterproductive as managers rise in responsibility and confront increasingly complex issues that require collaborative learning among different, equally knowledgeable people. Leaders in learning organizations need to have both inquiry *and* advocacy skills. . . .
- *Distinguished Espoused Theory from Theory in Use.* We all like to think that we hold certain views, but often our actions reveal deeper views. For example, I may proclaim that people are trustworthy, but never lend friends money and jealously guard my possessions. Obviously, my deeper mental model (my theory in use) differs from my espoused theory. Recognizing gaps between espoused views and theories in use (which often requires the help of others) can be pivotal to deeper learning.
- *Recognizing and Defusing Defensive Routines.* As one CEO in our research program puts it, "Nobody ever talks about an issue at the 8:00 business meeting exactly the same way they talk about it at home that evening or over drinks at the end of the day." The reason is what Chris Argyris calls "defensive routines," entrenched habits used to protect ourselves from the embarrassment and threat that come with exposing our thinking. For most of us, such defenses began to build early in life in response to pressures to have the right answers in school or at home. Organizations add new levels of performance anxiety and thereby amplify and exacerbate this defensiveness. Ironically, this makes it even more difficult to expose hidden mental models, and thereby lessens learning.

The first challenge is to recognize defensive routines, then to inquire into their operation. Those who are best at revealing and defusing defensive routines operate with a high degree of self-disclosure regarding their own defensiveness (e.g., I notice that I am feeling uneasy about how this conversation is going. Perhaps I do not understand it or it is threatening to me in ways I do not yet see. Can you help me see this better?).

SYSTEMS THINKING

We all know that leaders should help people see the big picture. But the actual skills whereby leaders are supposed to achieve this are not well understood. In my experience, successful leaders often are "systems thinkers" to a considerable extent. They focus less on day-to-day events and more on underlying trends and forces of change. But they do this almost completely intuitively. The consequence is that they are often unable to explain their intuitions to others and feel frustrated that others cannot see the world the way they do.

One of the most significant developments in management science today is the gradual coalescence of managerial systems thinking as a field study and practice. This field suggests some key skills for future leaders:

- *Seeing Interrelationships, Not Things, and Processes, Not Snapshots.* Most of us have been conditioned throughout our lives to focus on things and to see the world in static images. This leads us to linear explanations of systemic phenomena. For instance, in an arms race each party is convinced that the other is *the cause* of problems. They react to each new move as an isolated event, not as part of a process. So long as they fail to see the interrelationships of these actions, they are trapped.
- *Moving beyond Blame.* We tend to blame each other or outside circumstances for our problems. But it is poorly designed systems, not incompetent or unmotivated individuals, that cause most organizational problems. Systems thinking shows us that there is no outside—that you and the cause of your problems are part of a single system.
- *Distinguishing Detail Complexity from Dynamic Complexity.* Some types of complexity are more important strategically than others. Detail complexity arises when there are many variables. Dynamic complexity arises when cause and effect are distant in time and space, and when the consequences over time of interventions are subtle and not obvious to many participants in the system. The leverage in most management situations lies in understanding dynamic complexity, not detail complexity.
- *Focusing on Areas of High Leverage.* Some have called systems thinking the "new dismal science" because it teaches that most obvious solutions do not work—at best, they improve matters in the short run, only to make things worse in the long run. But there is another side to the story. Systems thinking also shows that small, well-focused actions can produce significant, enduring improvements, if they are in the right place. Systems thinkers refer to this idea as the principle of "leverage." Tackling a difficult problem is often a matter of seeing where the high leverage lies, where a change—with a minimum of effort—would lead to lasting, significant improvement.
- *Avoiding Symptomatic Solutions.* The pressures to intervene in management systems that are going awry can be overwhelming. Unfortunately, given the linear thinking that predominates in most organizations, interventions usually focus on symptomatic fixes, not underlying causes. This results in only temporary relief, and it tends to create still more pressures later on for further, low-leverage intervention. If leaders acquiesce to these pressures, they can be sucked into an endless spiral of increasing intervention. Sometimes the most difficult leadership acts are to refrain from intervening through popular quick fixes and to keep the pressure on everyone to identify more enduring solutions.

While leaders who can articulate systemic explanations are not rare, those who *can* will leave their stamp on an organization. . . . The consequence of leaders who lack systems thinking skills can be devastating. Many charismatic leaders manage almost exclusively at the level of events. They deal in visions and in crises, and little in between. Under their leadership, an organization hurtles from crisis to crisis. Eventually, the worldview of people in the organization becomes dominated by events and reactiveness. Many, especially those who are deeply committed, become burned out. Eventually, cynicism comes to pervade the organization. People have no control over their time, let alone their destiny.

Similar problems arise with the "visionary strategist," the leader with vision who sees both patterns of change and events. This leader is better prepared to manage change. He or she can explain strategies in terms of emerging trends, and thereby fosters a climate that is less reactive. But such leaders impart a responsive orientation rather than a generative one.

Many talented leaders have rich, highly systemic intuitions but cannot explain those intuitions to others. Ironically, they often end up being authoritarian leaders, even if they do not want to, because only they see the decisions that need to be made. They are unable to conceptualize their strategic insights so that these can become public knowledge, open to challenge and further improvement. . . .

I believe that [a] new sort of management development will focus on the roles, skills, and tools for leadership in learning organizations. Undoubtedly, the ideas offered above are only a rough approximation of this new territory. The sooner we begin seriously exploring the territory, the sooner the initial map can be improved—and the sooner we will realize an age-old vision of leadership:

The wicked leader is he who the people despise.
The good leader is he who the people revere.
The great leader is he who the people say, "We did it ourselves."

Lao Tsu

READING 2.5

In Praise of Middle Managers BY QUY NGUYEN HUY

The very phrase "middle manager" evokes mediocrity: a person who stubbornly defends the status quo because he is too unimaginative to dream up anything better—or, worse, someone who sabotages others' attempts to change the organization for the better.

The popular press and a couple of generations' worth of change-management consultants have reinforced this stereotype. Introducing a major change initiative? Watch out for the middle managers—that is where you will find the most resistance. Reengineering your business processes? Start by sweeping out the middle managers—they are just intermediaries; they do not add value. Until very recently, anyone who spent time reading about management practices, as opposed to watching real managers at work, might have concluded that middle managers are doomed to extinction or should be.

But do not pull out the pink slips just yet. Middle managers, it turns out, make valuable contributions to the realization of radical change at a company—contributions that go largely unrecognized by most senior executives. These contributions occur in four major areas. First, middle managers often have value-adding entrepreneurial ideas that they are able and willing to realize—if only they can get a hearing. Second, they are far better than most senior executives are at leveraging the informal networks at a company that make substantive, lasting change possible. Third, they stay attuned to employees' moods and emotional needs, thereby ensuring that the change initiative's momentum is maintained. And, finally, they manage the tension between continuity and change—they keep the organization from falling into extreme inertia, on the one hand, or extreme chaos, on the other.

Of course, not every middle manager in every organization is a paragon of entrepreneurial vigor and energy. But I would argue that if senior managers dismiss the role that middle managers play—and carelessly reduce their ranks—they will drastically diminish their chances of realizing radical change. Indeed, middle managers may be corner-office executives' most effective allies when it is time to make a major change in a business. Let us take a closer look at their underestimated strengths.

THE ENTREPRENEUR

When it comes to envisioning and implementing change, middle managers stand in a unique organizational position. They are close to day-to-day operations, customers, and frontline employees—closer than senior managers are—so they know better than anyone where the problems are. But they are also far enough away from frontline work that they can see the big picture, which allows them to see new possibilities, both for solving problems and for encouraging growth. Taken as a group, middle managers are more diverse than their senior counterparts are in, for instance, functional area, work experience, geography, gender, and ethnic background. As a result, their insights are more diverse. Middle management is thus fertile ground for creative ideas about how to grow and change a business. In fact, middle managers' ideas are often better than their bosses' ideas.

Consider a large telecommunications company that I studied. When it initiated a radical change program a few years ago, 117 separate projects were funded. Of the projects that senior executives had proposed, 80% fell short of expectations or failed outright. Meanwhile, 80% of the projects that middle managers had initiated succeeded, bringing in at least $300 million in annual profits.

Middle managers were equally successful at spurring innovation at other companies I studied. It was, for example, a middle-management team that developed Super Dry Beer, an innovative product that allowed Japanese brewer Asahi to capture new market share. That success set the stage for the struggling company's turnaround.

The more closely I looked at companies, the more examples I saw of senior executives failing to listen to their middle managers. Good ideas routinely died before they ever saw the light of day.

Not getting credit is [another] pervasive problem. When the telecom company I studied embraced its radical change program, it had a new leadership team. The top managers very sensibly pushed the task of generating new ideas down to a group of long-standing middle managers, whose ideas turned out to be more grounded and profitable than the senior managers' ideas. But that is not how the outside world saw it. Shareholders and the media perceived that the new team had come in, cleaned up, and turned the company around. In a sense they had, but they had not done it alone, and they had not done it by cleaning house.

THE COMMUNICATOR

Aside from being an important source of entrepreneurial ideas, middle managers are also uniquely suited to communicating proposed changes across an organization. Change initiatives have two stages, conception and implementation, and it is widely understood that failure most often occurs at the second stage. What is less understood is the central role that middle managers play during this stage. Successful implementation requires clear and compelling communication throughout the organization. Middle managers can spread the word and get people on board because they usually have the best social networks in the company. Many of them start their careers as operations workers or technical specialists. Over time and through various job rotations at the same company, they build webs of relationships that are both broad and deep. They know who really knows what and how to get things done. Typically their networks include unwritten obligations and favors traded, giving effective middle managers a significant amount of informal leverage.

Senior managers have their own networks, of course, but these tend to be less powerful because many of these executives have been at their companies for shorter periods of time. . . .

If the middle managers with the best networks—and the most credibility—genuinely buy into the change program, they will sell it to the rest of the organization in subtle and nonthreatening ways. And they will know which groups or individuals most need to be on board and how to customize the message for different audiences.

Sometimes senior executives themselves can be barriers to change, and it requires tactful communication by middle managers to keep the company on track. For instance, a middle manager at a large airline I studied realized that most of the senior executives barely knew how to use a PC. Few of them understood the capabilities or limitations of the Web well enough to make complex strategic decisions about the company's use of the Internet and e-commerce. To educate them, the middle manager developed a reverse-mentoring program: Younger employees would teach experienced executives about the Internet. In turn, the executives would expose their young mentors to more senior-level business issues, decisions, and practices. Each member of the pair was separated by several hierarchical levels, and each came from different business units. The middle manager correctly assumed that this degree of separation would make the executives more comfortable about admitting their weaknesses with computers. The program was a success; eventually, hundreds of executives at the airline became more technology literate and less fearful of change. . . .

THE THERAPIST

Radical changes in the workplace can stir up high levels of fear among employees. Uncertainty about change can deflate morale and trigger anxiety that, unchecked, can degenerate into depression and paralysis. Once people are depressed, they stop learning, adapting, or helping to move the group forward. Senior managers cannot do much to alleviate this pain; they are too removed from most workers to help, and they are also focused externally more than internally.

Middle managers, though, have no choice but to address their employees' emotional well-being during times of radical change. If they ignore it, most useful work will come to a grinding halt as people either leave the company or become afraid to act. Even as they privately deplore the lack of attention from their own bosses, many middle managers make sure that their own sense of alienation does not seep down to their subordinates. They do a host of things to create a psychologically safe work environment. They are able to do this, once again, because of their position within the organization. They know the people who report to them—as well as those reports' direct reports—and they can communicate directly and personally, rather than in vague corporate-speak. They can also tailor individual conversations to individual needs. Some employees will have big concerns about whether a new strategic direction is right for the organization; others will be far more interested in whether they are going to be forced to move or to give up a flexible schedule. . . .

THE TIGHTROPE ARTIST

Successful organizational change requires attention not only to employee morale but also to the balance between change and continuity. If too much change happens too fast, chaos ensues. If too little change happens too slowly, it results in organizational inertia. Both extremes can lead to severe underperformance. Even during normal times, middle managers allot considerable energy to finding the right mix of the two. When radical change is being imposed from the top, this balancing act becomes even more important—and far more difficult.

Middle managers, like the people who report to them, are overburdened and stressed out during periods of profound change—but I noticed that they found personal and professional fulfillment by taking on this particular balancing act. They are problem solvers, typically, and they find relief in rolling up their sleeves and figuring out how to make the whole messy thing work. They do not all do it the same way, of course—and, from a senior-management point of view, that is a good thing. Some middle managers pay more attention to the continuity side of the equation, and some tend more to the change side.

We have already looked at what middle managers do to ensure continuity. They "keep the company working," as one of them said to me with some pride. At the telecom company I studied, middle managers' focus on continuity contributed to a relatively smooth downsizing of 13,000 positions. By showing flexibility and fairness, and by working closely with union representatives, managers defused resentment and avoided a strike. Their concern for employees kept anxiety at manageable levels. Their loyalty to the organization probably slowed turnover rates. And as a result of the middle managers' actions, the telecom company was able to generate revenues at decent levels during an extraordinarily difficult time, thus providing needed cash for the multitude of change projects. Other middle managers are more interested in promoting change. They champion projects, putting intense pressure on the people who control resources and equally intense pressure on their own people.

The challenge [today] is figuring out how to hold on to core values and capabilities while simultaneously changing how work gets done and shifting the organization in new strategic directions. This simply will not happen unless people throughout the organization help make it happen. Middle managers understand—in a deep way—those core values and competencies. They are the ones who can translate and synthesize; who can implement strategy because they know how to get things done; who can keep work groups from spinning into alienated, paralyzed chaos; and who can be persuaded to put their credibility on the line to turn vision into reality.

The senior executive who learns to recognize, respect, and deal fairly with the most influential middle managers in an organization will gain trusted allies—and improve the odds of realizing a complex but necessary organizational change.

CHAPTER 3

Formulating Strategy

Most of what has been published on the strategy process deals with how strategy *should* be designed or consciously *formulated*. On how this works, there has been a good deal of consensus, although, as we shall see later, this is now eroding. Perhaps we should properly conclude that there have been two waves of consensus. The first, which developed in the 1960s, is presented in this chapter; the second, which began in the 1980s, did not challenge the first so much as build on it. This is presented in Chapter 4. Both are very much alive—we should say, still dominant.

Ken Andrews of the Harvard Business School is the person most commonly associated with the first wave, although Bill Newman of Columbia wrote on some of these issues much earlier, and Igor Ansoff simultaneously outlined very similar views while he was at Carnegie-Mellon. But the Andrews text became the best known, in part because it was so simply and clearly written, in part because it was embodied in a popular textbook (with cases) emanating from the Harvard Business School.

We reproduce parts of the Andrews text (as revised in its own publication in 1980 but based on the original 1965 edition). These serve to introduce the basic point that strategy ultimately requires the achievement of fit between the external situation (opportunities and threats) and internal capability (strengths and weaknesses). As you read the Andrews text, a number of basic premises will quickly become evident. Among these are the clear distinction made between strategy formulation and strategy implementation (in effect, between thinking and action); the belief that strategy (or at least intended strategy) should be made explicit; the notion that structure should follow strategy (in other words, be designed in accordance with it); and the assumption that strategy emanates from the formal leadership of the organization. Similar premises underlie most of the prescriptive literature of strategic management.

This "model" (if we can call it that) has proven very useful in many circumstances as a broad way to analyze a strategic situation and to think about making strategy. A careful strategist should certainly touch all the bases suggested in this approach. But in many circumstances the model cannot or should not be followed to the letter, as shall be discussed in Chapter 5 and later.

The Rumelt reading elaborates on one element in this traditional model—the evaluation of strategies. Although the Andrews text contains a similar discussion, Rumelt, a graduate of the Harvard Business School and strategy professor at UCLA, develops it in a particularly elegant way.

The third reading is by Gary Hamel, who has built up quite a reputation in the strategy field as a consultant, author, and academic, and C. K. Prahalad, equally well known and associated with the University of Michigan. They make the case for "strategic intent," their take on vision, in a sense. The challenge of leadership is to create "an obsession with winning" that will energize the collective action of all employees. Managers have to build such an ambition, they believe, in order to help people develop faith in their own ability to deliver on tough goals, to motivate them to do so, and to channel their energies into a step-by-step progression that they compare with "running a marathon in 400-meter sprints." The traditional view of strategy formulation is that it requires an accurate idea of the future and a plan for achieving this future. Andrews outlines a systematic process for carrying this out. Rumelt provides a methodology for judging whether this can be done. In practice, however, unfolding events tend to frustrate the most carefully formulated strategies. For some, this suggests that strategies should be allowed to evolve. Others, however, insist that strategy requires direction. Hamel and Prahalad argue that strategy formulation should consist of general goals that capture the essence of what the organization is trying to do. Correctly formulated and properly invested with energy and commitment, the resulting "strategic intent" challenges the organization to push boundaries and constraints beyond current limits.

Whereas traditional strategy formulation entails instructions from the top, strategic intent entails empowerment. The goals set direction, but not a road map. They are sufficiently general to allow members of the organization to infuse their own perspective into implementation. This works nicely when perspectives are not too disparate. When they are, implementation can lead to fragmentation and incoherence. The temptation at that point is to revert to a top-down strategy formulation that leaves little scope for initiative on the part of the rest of the organization. Sarah Kaplan from the Rotman School of Management in Toronto and Eric D. Beinhocker from McKinsey and Company argue that this temptation should be resisted. There is real value in the strategic planning process provided that the organization knows how to weave together formal and informal planning processes. Kaplan and Beinhocker point to the pitfalls of formal strategic planning, but at the same time argue that astute management that takes into account individual and group failings can get the best out of strategic planning.

USING THE CASE STUDIES

In one sense, companies are always formulating (or reformulating) their strategy. Formulating strategy, however, comes to the surface and becomes explicit when companies are at a crossroads, facing new threats or attractive opportunities. The Nintendo case describes a company that has undergone an explicit formulation and reformulation of its strategy. The Lufthansa case deals with a company that overcame the threat of bankruptcy, in part by pursuing an alliance strategy. How will it go about formulating strategy jointly with other airlines? In the reading "The Concept of Corporate Strategy" Andrews lays out an orderly process that Lufthansa could follow for best results.

The Sportsmake case, however, suggests that many corporations do not see strategy as an orderly process. They move from opportunity to opportunity, usually driven by the vision and personality of their CEO. And when this CEO unexpectedly departs from the scene, as he does in this case, the choice of a successor raises issues of strategic direction that are not easily addressed using the standard planning process. The same can be said of Edwin Catmull, president of Pixar. Under his leadership Pixar has gone from strength to strength, pioneering computer animated feature films. Following the acquisition of Pixar by Disney he must come up with a plan to combine the iconoclastic Silicon Valley management style with Disney's staid management style. This is strategy formulation under pressure.

Rumelt's "Evaluating Business Strategy" puts forward criteria by which this strategy (or any other) can be judged. McDonald's CEO, Jim Skinner, must evaluate whether to stick to the strategy that his predecessor put in place or respond to new trends by offering lattes, cappuccinos, ice-blended frappe in direct competition to Starbucks. McDonald's certainly has the resources to do it, but is such a move consistent with its strategy? Rumelt's framework is a useful starting point for analyzing the dilemma faced by Skinner, but it does not resolve the tensions between the different criteria that emerge in practice. This has to be done by the managers.

Systematically evaluating a strategy during the formulation phase makes sense. Analyze before you jump and you will have less to regret afterward. But as Hamel and Prahalad point out, this view of the strategy process leads to imitation. When you generate options, and then filter these options through fixed criteria, you usually end up with a strategy that is closer to what has been attempted by others. To avoid this, companies should have ambitions that exceed their resources and capabilities. By pursuing "strategic intent," companies develop strategies that could not have come about by the traditional formulation/implementation approach.

The making of the iPod case certainly demonstrates how strategic intent creates strategies that few in the computer industry would have foreseen, let alone dared pursue. Not surprisingly, Pixar, a company that Apple's Steve Jobs guided to success, also demonstrates the power of strategic intent to transform not only the fortunes of a company but in addition to change the industry as well.

READING 3.1

The Concept of Corporate Strategy BY KENNETH R. ANDREWS

THE STRATEGY CONCEPT

WHAT STRATEGY IS

Corporate strategy is the pattern of decisions in a company that determines and reveals its objectives, purposes, or goals, produces the principal policies and plans for achieving those goals, and defines the range of business the company is to pursue, the kind of economic and human organization it is or intends to be, and the nature of the economic and noneconomic contribution it intends to make to its shareholders, employees, customers, and communities. . . .

The strategic decision contributing to this pattern is one that is effective over long periods of time, affects the company in many different ways, and focuses and commits a significant portion of its resources to the expected outcomes. The pattern resulting from a series of such decisions will probably define the central character and image of a company, the individuality it has for its members and various publics, and the position it will occupy in its industry and markets. It will permit the specification of particular objectives to be attained through a timed sequence of investment and implementation decisions and will govern directly the deployment or redeployment of resources to make these decisions effective.

Some aspects of such a pattern of decisions may be in an established corporation unchanging over long periods of time, like a commitment to quality, or high technology, or certain raw materials or good labor relations. Other aspects of strategy must change as or before the world changes, such as product line, manufacturing process, or merchandising and styling practices. The basic determinants of company character, if purposefully institutionalized, are likely to persist through and shape the nature of substantial changes in product-market choices and allocation of resources. . . .

It is important, however, not to take the idea apart in another way, that is, to separate goals from the policies designed to achieve those goals. The essence of the definition of strategy I have just recorded is *pattern*. The interdependence of purposes, policies, and organized action is crucial to the particularity of an individual strategy and its opportunity to identify competitive advantage. It is the unity, coherence, and internal consistency of a company's strategic decisions that position the company in its environment and give the firm its identity, its power to mobilize its strengths, and its likelihood of success in the marketplace. It is the interrelationship of a set of goals and policies that crystallizes from the formless reality of a company's environment a set of problems an organization can seize upon and solve.

What you are doing, in short, is never meaningful unless you can say or imply what you are doing it for: the quality of administrative action and the motivation lending it power cannot be appraised without knowing its relationship to purpose. Breaking up the system of corporate goals and the character-determining major policies for attainment leads to narrow and mechanical conceptions of strategic management and endless logic chopping. . . .

SUMMARY STATEMENTS OF STRATEGY

Before we proceed to clarification of this concept by application, we should specify the terms in which strategy is usually expressed. A summary statement of strategy will characterize the product line and services offered or planned by the company, the markets and market segments for which products and services are now or will be designed, and the channels through which these markets will be reached. The means by which the operation is to be financed will be specified, as will the profit objectives and the emphasis to be placed on the safety of capital versus level of return. Major policy in central functions such as marketing, manufacturing, procurement, research and development, labor relations, and personnel will be stated where they distinguish the company from others, and usually the intended size, form, and climate of the organization will be included.

Each company, if it were to construct a summary strategy from what it understands itself to be aiming at, would have a different statement with different categories of decision emphasized to indicate what it wanted to be or do. . . .

FORMULATION OF STRATEGY

Corporate strategy is an organization process, in many ways inseparable from the structure, behavior, and culture of the company in which it takes place. Nevertheless, we may abstract from the process two important aspects, interrelated in real life but separable for the purposes of analysis. The first of these we may call *formulation*, the second *implementation*. Deciding what strategy should be may be approached as a rational undertaking, even if in life emotional attachments . . . may complicate choice among future alternatives. . . .

The principal subactivities of strategy formulation as a logical activity include identifying opportunities and threats in the company's environment and attaching some estimate of risk to the discernible alternatives. Before a choice can be made, the company's strengths and weaknesses should be appraised together with the resources on hand and available. Its actual or potential capacity to take advantage of perceived market needs or to cope with attendant risks should be estimated as objectively as possible. The strategic alternative which results from matching opportunity and corporate capability at an acceptable level of risk is what we may call an *economic strategy*.

The process described thus far assumes that strategists are analytically objective in estimating the relative capacity of their company and the opportunity they see or anticipate in developing markets. The extent to which they wish to undertake low or high risk presumably depends on their profit objectives. The higher they set the latter, the more willing they must be to assume a correspondingly high risk that the market opportunity they see will not develop or that the corporate competence required to excel competition will not be forthcoming.

So far we have described the intellectual processes of ascertaining what a company *might do* in terms of environmental opportunity, of deciding what it can *do* in terms of ability and power, and of bringing these two considerations together in optimal equilibrium. The determination of strategy also requires consideration of what alternatives are preferred by the chief executive and perhaps by his or her immediate associates as well, quite apart from economic considerations. Personal values, aspirations, and ideals do, and in our judgment quite properly should, influence the final choice of purposes. Thus, what the executives of a company *want to do* must be brought into the strategic decision.

Finally, strategic choice has an ethical aspect—a fact much more dramatically illustrated in some industries than in others. Just as alternatives may be ordered in terms of the degree of risk that they entail, so may they be examined against the standards of responsiveness to the expectations of society that the strategist elects. Some alternatives may seem to the executive considering them more attractive than others when the public good or service to society is considered. What a company *should do* thus appears as a fourth element of the strategic decision. . . .

THE IMPLEMENTATION OF STRATEGY

Since effective implementation can make a sound strategic decision ineffective or a debatable choice successful, it is as important to examine the processes of implementation as to weigh the advantages of available strategic alternatives. The implementation of strategy is comprised of a series of subactivities which are primarily administrative. If purpose is determined, then the resources of a company can be mobilized to accomplish it. An organizational structure appropriate for the efficient performance of the required tasks must be made effective by information systems and relationships permitting coordination of subdivided activities. The organizational processes of performance measurement, compensation, management development—all of them enmeshed in systems of incentives and controls—must be directed toward the kind of behavior required by organizational purpose. The role of personal leadership is important and sometimes decisive in the accomplishment of strategy. Although we know that organization structure and processes of compensation, incentives, control, and management development influence and constrain the formulation of strategy, we should look first at the logical proposition that structure should follow strategy in order to cope later with the organizational reality that strategy also follows structure. When we have examined both tendencies, we will understand and to some extent be prepared to deal with the interdependence of the formulation and implementation of corporate purpose. Figure 1 may be useful in understanding the analysis of strategy as a pattern of interrelated decisions. . . .

RELATING OPPORTUNITIES TO RESOURCES

Determination of a suitable strategy for a company begins in identifying the opportunities and risks in its environment. This [discussion] is concerned with the identification of a range of strategic alternatives, the narrowing of this range by recognizing the constraints imposed by corporate capability, and the determination of one or more economic strategies at acceptable levels of risk. . . .

THE NATURE OF THE COMPANY'S ENVIRONMENT

The environment of an organization in business, like that of any other organic entity, is the pattern of all the external conditions and influences that affect its life and development. The environmental influences relevant to strategic decision operate in a company's industry, the total

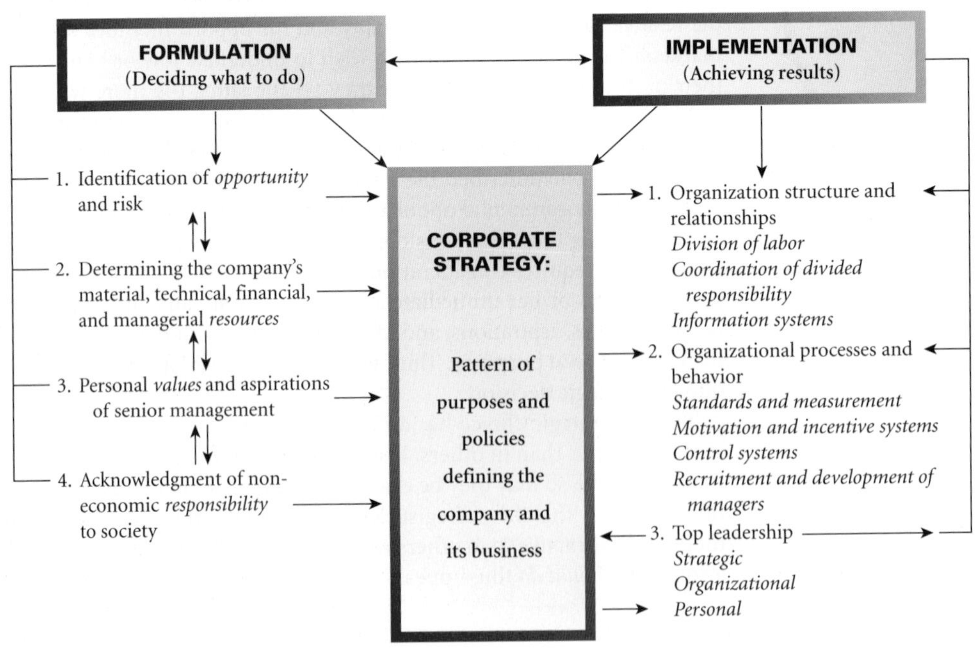

FIGURE 1
RELATING OPPORTUNITIES TO RESOURCES

business community, its city, its country, and the world. They are technological, economic, physical, social, and political in kind. The corporate strategist is usually at least intuitively aware of these features of the current environment. But in all these categories change is taking place at varying rates—fastest in technology, less rapidly in politics. Change in the environment of business necessitates continuous monitoring of a company's definition of its business, lest it falter, blur, or become obsolete. Since by definition the formulation of strategy is performed with the future in mind, executives who take part in the strategic planning process must be aware of those aspects of their company's environment especially susceptible to the kind of change that will affect their company's future.

Technology

From the point of view of the corporate strategist, technological developments are not only the fastest unfolding but the most far-reaching in extending or contracting opportunity for an established company. They include the discoveries of science, the impact of related product development, the less dramatic machinery and process improvements, and the progress of automation and data processing. . . .

Ecology

It used to be possible to take for granted the physical characteristics of the environment and find them favorable to industrial development. Plant sites were chosen using criteria like availability of process and cooling water, accessibility to various forms of transportation, and stability of soil conditions. With the increase in sensitivity to the impact on the physical environment of all industrial activity, it becomes essential, often to comply with law, to consider how planned expansion and even continued operation under changing standards will affect and be perceived to affect the air, water, traffic density, and quality of life generally of any area which a company would like to enter. . . .

Economics

Because business is more accustomed to monitoring economic trends than those in other spheres, it is less likely to be taken by surprise by such massive developments as the internationalization of competition, the return of China and Russia to trade with the West, the slower than projected development of the Third World countries, the Americanization of demand and culture in the developing countries and the resulting backlash of nationalism, the increased importance of the large multinational corporations and the consequences of host-country hostility, the recurrence of recession, and the persistence of inflation in all phases of the business cycle. The consequences of world economic trends need to be monitored in much greater detail for any one industry or company.

Industry

Although the industry environment is the one most company strategists believe they know most about, the opportunities and risks that reside there are often blurred by familiarity and the uncritical acceptance of the established relative position of competitors. . . .

Society

Social developments of which strategists keep aware include such influential forces as the quest for equality for minority groups, the demand of women for opportunity and recognition, the changing patterns of work and leisure, the effects of urbanization upon the individual, family, and neighborhood, the rise of crime, the decline of conventional morality, and the changing composition of world population.

Politics

The political forces important to the business firm are similarly extensive and complex—the changing relations between communist and noncommunist countries (East and West) and between prosperous and poor countries (North and South), the relation between private enterprise and government, between workers and management, the impact of national planning on corporate planning, and the rise of what George Lodge (1975) calls the communitarian ideology. . . .

Although it is not possible to know or spell out here the significance of such technical, economic, social, and political trends, and possibilities for the strategist of a given business or company, some simple things are clear. Changing values will lead to different expectations of the role business should perform. Business will be expected to perform its mission not only with economy in the use of energy but with sensitivity to the ecological environment. Organizations in all walks of life will be called upon to be more explicit about their goals and to meet the needs and aspirations (for example, for education) of their membership.

In any case, change threatens all established strategies. We know that a thriving company—itself a living system—is bound up in a variety of interrelationships with larger systems comprising its technological, economic, ecological, social, and political environment. If environmental developments are destroying and creating business opportunities, advance notice of specific instances relevant to a single company is essential to intelligent planning. Risk and opportunity in the last quarter of the twentieth century require of executives a keen interest in what is going on outside their companies. More than that, a practical means of tracking developments promising good or ill, and profit or loss, needs to be devised. . . .

For the firm that has not determined what its strategy dictates it needs to know or has not embarked upon the systematic surveillance of environmental change, a few simple questions kept constantly in mind will highlight changing opportunity and risk. In examining your own company or one you are interested in, these questions should lead to an estimate of opportunity and danger in the present and predicted company setting.

1. What are the essential economic, technical, and physical characteristics of the industry in which the company participates? . . .
2. What trends suggesting future change in economic and technical characteristics are apparent? . . .
3. What is the nature of competition both within the industry and across industries? . . .
4. What are the requirements for success in competition in the company's industry? . . .
5. Given the technical, economic, social, and political developments that most directly apply, what is the range of strategy available to any company in this industry? . . .

IDENTIFYING CORPORATE COMPETENCE AND RESOURCES

The first step in validating a tentative choice among several opportunities is to determine whether the organization has the capacity to prosecute it successfully. The capability of an organization is its demonstrated and potential ability to accomplish, against the opposition of circumstance or competition, whatever it sets out to do. Every organization has actual and potential strengths and weaknesses. Since it is prudent in formulating strategy to extend or maximize the one and contain or minimize the other, it is important to try to determine what they are and to distinguish one from the other.

It is just as possible, though much more difficult, for a company to know its own strengths and limitations as it is to maintain a workable surveillance of its changing environment. Subjectivity, lack of confidence, and unwillingness to face reality may make it hard for organizations as well as for individuals to know themselves. But just as it is essential, though difficult, that a maturing person achieve reasonable self-awareness, so an organization can identify approximately its central strength and critical vulnerability. . . .

To make an effective contribution to strategic planning, the key attributes to be appraised should be identified and consistent criteria established for judging them. If attention is directed to strategies, policy commitments, and past practices in the context of discrepancy between organization goals and attainment, an outcome useful to an individual manager's strategic planning is possible. The assessment of strengths and weaknesses associated with the attainment of specific objectives becomes in Stevenson's (1976) words a "key link in a feedback loop" which allows managers to learn from the success or failures of the policies they institute.

Although [a] study by Stevenson did not find or establish a systematic way of developing or using such knowledge, members of organizations develop judgments about what the company can do particularly well—its core of competence. If consensus can be reached about this capability, no matter how subjectively arrived at, its application to identified opportunity can be estimated.

Sources of Capabilities

The powers of a company constituting a resource for growth and diversification accrue primarily from experience in making and marketing a product line or providing a service. They inhere as well in (1) the developing strengths and weaknesses of the individuals comprising the organization, (2) the degree to which individual capability is effectively applied to the common task, and (3) the quality of coordination of individual and group effort.

The experience gained through successful execution of a strategy centered upon one goal may unexpectedly develop capabilities which could be applied to different ends. Whether they should be so applied is another question. For example, a manufacturer of salt can strengthen his competitive position by offering his customers salt-dispensing equipment. If, in the course of making engineering improvements in this equipment, a new solenoid principle is perfected that has application to many industrial switching problems, should this patentable and marketable innovation be exploited? The answer would turn not only on whether economic analysis of the opportunity shows this to be a durable and profitable possibility, but also on whether the organization can muster the financial, manufacturing, and marketing strength to exploit the discovery and live with its success. The former question is likely to have a more positive answer than the latter. In this connection, it seems important to remember that individual and unsupported flashes of strength are not as dependable as the gradually accumulated product and market-related fruits of experience.

Even where competence to exploit an opportunity is nurtured by experience in related fields, the level of that competence may be too low for any great reliance to be placed upon it. Thus a chain of children's clothing stores might well acquire the administrative, merchandising, buying, and selling skills that would permit it to add departments in women's wear. Similarly, a sales force effective in distributing typewriters might gain proficiency in selling office machinery and supplies. But even here it would be well to ask what *distinctive* ability these companies could bring to the retailing of soft goods or office equipment to attract customers away from a plethora of competitors.

Identifying Strengths

The distinctive competence of an organization is more than what it can do; it is what it can do particularly well. To identify the less obvious or by-product strengths of an organization that may well be transferable to some more profitable new opportunity, one might well begin by examining the organization's current product line and by defining the functions it serves in its markets. Almost any important consumer product has functions which are related to others into which a qualified company might move. The typewriter, for example, is more than the simple machine for mechanizing handwriting that it once appeared to be when looked at only from the point of view of its designer and manufacturer. Closely analyzed from the point of view of the potential user, the typewriter is found to contribute to a broad range of information processing functions. Any one of these might have suggested an area to be exploited by a typewriter manufacturer. Tacitly defining a typewriter as a replacement for a fountain pen as a writing instrument rather than as an input–output device for word processing is the explanation provided by hindsight for the failure of the old-line typewriter companies to develop before IBM did the electric typewriter and the computer-related input–output devices it made possible. The definition of product which would lead to identification of transferable skills must be expressed in terms of the market needs it may fill rather than the engineering specifications to which it conforms.

Besides looking at the uses or functions to which present products contribute, the would-be diversifier might profitably identify the skills that underlie whatever success has been achieved. The qualifications of an organization efficient at performing its long-accustomed tasks come to be taken for granted and considered humdrum, like the steady provision of first-class service. The insight required to identify the essential strength justifying new ventures does not come naturally. Its cultivation can probably be helped by recognition of the need for analysis. In any case, we should look beyond the company's capacity to invent new products. Product leadership is not possible for a majority of companies, so it is fortunate that patentable new products are not the only major highway to new opportunities. Other avenues include new marketing services, new methods of distribution, new values in quality–price combinations, and creative merchandising. The effort to find or to create a competence that is truly distinctive may hold the real key to a company's success or even to its future development. For example, the ability of a cement manufacturer to run a truck fleet more effectively than its competitors may constitute one of its principal competitive strengths in selling an undifferentiated product.

Matching Opportunity and Competence

The way to narrow the range of alternatives, made extensive by imaginative identification of new possibilities, is to match opportunity to competence, once each has been accurately identified and its future significance estimated. It is this combination which establishes a company's economic mission and its position in its environment. The combination is designed to minimize organizational weakness and to maximize strength. In every case, risk attends it. And when opportunity seems to outrun present distinctive competence, the willingness to gamble that the latter can be built up to the required level is almost indispensable to a strategy that challenges the organization and the people in it. Figure 2 diagrams the matching of opportunity and resources that results in an economic strategy.

Before we leave the creative act of putting together a company's unique internal capability and opportunity evolving in the external world, we should note that—aside from distinctive competence—the principal resources found in any company are money and people—technical and managerial people. At an advanced stage of economic development, money seems less a problem than technical competence, and the latter less critical than managerial ability. Do not assume that managerial capacity can rise to any occasion. The diversification of American industry is marked by hundreds of instances in which a company strong in one endeavor lacked the ability to manage an enterprise requiring different skills. The right to make handsome profits over a long period must be earned. Opportunism without competence is a path to fairyland.

Besides equating an appraisal of market opportunity and organizational capability, the decision to make and market a particular product or service should be accompanied by an

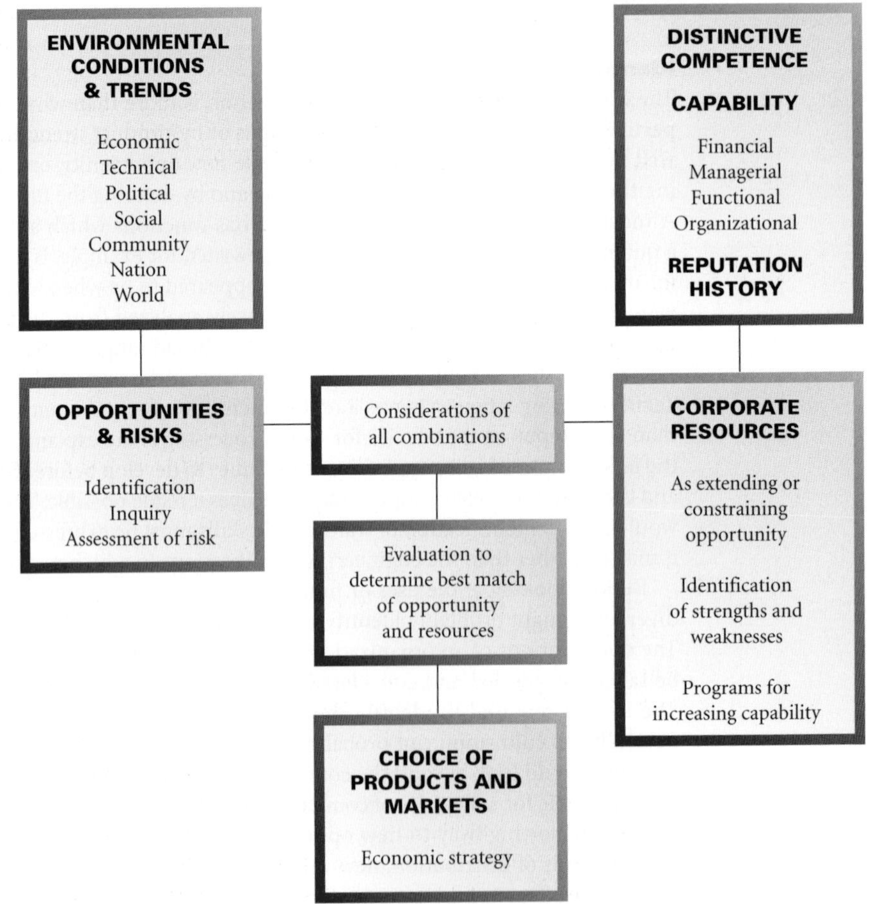

FIGURE 2
THE CHALLENGE OF EVALUATION

identification of the nature of the business and the kind of company its management desires. Such a guiding concept is a product of many considerations, including the managers' personal values. . . .

Uniqueness of Strategy

In each company, the way in which distinctive competence, organizational resources, and organizational values are combined is or should be unique. Differences among companies are as numerous as differences among individuals. The combinations of opportunity to which distinctive competencies, resources, and values may be applied are equally extensive. Generalizing about how to make an effective match is less rewarding than working at it. The effort is a highly stimulating and challenging exercise. The outcome will be unique for each company and each situation.

READING 3.2

Evaluating Business Strategy BY RICHARD R. RUMELT

Strategy can neither be formulated nor adjusted to changing circumstances without a process of strategy evaluation. Whether performed by an individual or as part of an organizational review procedure, strategy evaluation forms an essential step in the process of guiding an enterprise.

For many executives strategy evaluation is simply an appraisal of how well a business performs. Has it grown? Is the profit rate normal or better? If the answers to these questions are affirmative, it is argued that the firm's strategy must be sound. Despite its unassailable simplicity, this line of reasoning misses the whole point of strategy—that the critical factors determining the quality of current results are often not directly observable or simply measured, and that by the time strategic opportunities or threats do directly affect operating results, it may well be too late for an effective response. Thus, strategy evaluation is an attempt to look beyond the obvious facts regarding the short-term health of a business and appraise instead those more fundamental factors and trends that govern success in the chosen field of endeavor.

THE CHALLENGE OF EVALUATION

However it is accomplished, the products of a business strategy evaluation are answers to these three questions:

- Are the objectives of the business appropriate?
- Are the major policies and plans appropriate?
- Do the results obtained to date confirm or refute critical assumptions on which the strategy rests?

Devising adequate answers to these questions is neither simple nor straightforward. It requires a reasonable store of situation-based knowledge and more than the usual degree of insight. In particular, the major issues which make evaluation difficult and with which the analyst must come to grips are these:

- Each business strategy is unique. For example, one paper manufacturer might rely on its vast timber holdings to weather almost any storm while another might place primary reliance in modern machinery and an extensive distribution system. Neither strategy is "wrong" nor "right" in any absolute sense; both may be right or wrong for the firms in question. Strategy evaluation must, then, rest on a type of situational logic that does not focus on "one best way" but which can be tailored to each problem as it is faced.
- Strategy is centrally concerned with this selection of goals and objectives. Many people, including seasoned executives, find it much easier to set or try to achieve goals than to evaluate them.

In part this is a consequence of training in problem solving rather than in problem structuring. It also arises out of a tendency to confuse values, which are fundamental expressions of human personality, with objectives, which are devices for lending coherence to action.

- Formal systems of strategic review, while appealing in principle, can create explosive conflict situations. Not only are there serious questions as to who is qualified to give an objective evaluation, the whole idea of strategy evaluation implies management by "much more than results" and runs counter to much of currently popular management philosophy.

THE GENERAL PRINCIPLES OF STRATEGY EVALUATION

The term "strategy" has been so widely used for different purposes that it has lost any clearly defined meaning. For our purposes a strategy is a set of objectives, policies, and plans that, taken together, define the scope of the enterprise and its approach to survival and success. Alternatively, we could say that the particular policies, plans, and objectives of a business express its strategy for coping with a complex competitive environment.

One of the fundamental tenets of science is that a theory can never be proven to be absolutely true. A theory can, however, be declared absolutely false if it fails to stand up to testing. Similarly, it is impossible to demonstrate conclusively that a particular business strategy is optimal or even to guarantee that it will work. One can, nevertheless, test it for critical flaws. Of the many tests which could be justifiably applied to a business strategy, most will fit within one of these broad criteria:

- *Consistency:* The strategy must not present mutually inconsistent goals and policies.
- *Consonance:* The strategy must represent an adaptive response to the external environment and to the critical changes occurring within it.
- *Advantage:* The strategy must provide for the creation and/or maintenance of a competitive advantage in the selected area of activity.
- *Feasibility:* The strategy must neither overtax available resources nor create unsolvable subproblems.

A strategy that fails to meet one or more of these criteria is strongly suspect. It fails to perform at least one of the key functions that are necessary for the survival of the business. Experience within a particular industry or other setting will permit the analyst to sharpen these criteria and add others that are appropriate to the situation at hand.

CONSISTENCY

Gross inconsistency within a strategy seems unlikely until it is realized that many strategies have not been explicitly formulated but have evolved over time in an ad hoc fashion. Even strategies that are the result of formal procedures may easily contain compromise arrangements between opposing power groups.

Inconsistency in strategy is not simply a flaw in logic. A key function of strategy is to provide coherence to organizational action. A clear and explicit concept of strategy can foster a climate of tacit coordination that is more efficient than most administrative mechanisms. Many high-technology firms, for example, face a basic strategic choice between offering high-cost products with high custom-engineering content and lower-cost products that are more standardized and sold at higher volume. If senior management does not enunciate a clear consistent sense of where the corporation stands on these issues, there will be continuing conflict between sales, design, engineering, and manufacturing people. A clear consistent strategy, by contrast, allows a sales engineer to negotiate a contract with a minimum of coordination—the trade-offs are an explicit part of the firm's posture.

Organizational conflict and interdepartmental bickering are often symptoms of a managerial disorder but may also indicate problems of strategic inconsistency. Here are some indicators that can help sort out these two different problems:

- If problems in coordination and planning continue despite changes in personnel and tend to be issue- rather than people-based, they are probably due to inconsistencies in strategy.

- If success for one organizational department means, or is interpreted to mean, failure for another department, either the basic objective structure is inconsistent or the organizational structure is wastefully duplicative.
- If, despite attempts to delegate authority, operating problems continue to be brought to the top for the resolution of policy issues, the basic strategy is probably inconsistent.

A final type of consistency that must be sought in strategy is between organizational objectives and the values of the management group. Inconsistency in this area is more of a problem in strategy formulation than in the evaluation of a strategy that has already been implemented. It can still arise, however, if the future direction of the business requires changes that conflict with managerial values. The most frequent source of such conflict is growth. As a business expands beyond the scale that allows an easy informal method of operation, many executives experience a sharp sense of loss. While growth can of course be curtailed, it often will require special attention to a firm's competitive position if survival without growth is desired. The same basic issues arise when other types of personal or social values come into conflict with existing or apparently necessary policies: the resolution of the conflict will normally require an adjustment in the competitive strategy.

CONSONANCE

The way in which a business relates to its environment has two aspects: the business must both match and be adapted to its environment and it must at the same time compete with other firms that are also trying to adapt. This dual character of the relationship between the firm and its environment has its analog in two different aspects of strategic choice and two different methods of strategy evaluation.

The first aspect of fit deals with the basic mission or scope of the business and the second with its special competitive position or "edge." Analysis of the first is normally done by looking at changing economic and social conditions over time. Analysis of the second, by contrast, typically focuses on the differences across firms at a given time. We call the first the *generic* aspect of strategy and the second *competitive* strategy. Generic strategy deals with the creation of social value—with the question of whether the products and services being created are worth more than their cost. Competitive strategy, by contrast, deals with the firm's need to capture some of the social value as profit. Exhibit 1 summarizes the differences between these concepts.

The notion of consonance, or matching, therefore, invites a focus on generic strategy. The role of the evaluator in this case is to examine the basic pattern of economic relationships that characterize the business and determine whether or not sufficient value is being created to sustain the strategy. Most macroanalysis of changing economic conditions is oriented toward the formulation or evaluation of generic strategies. For example, a planning department forecasts that within six years flat-panel liquid crystal displays will replace CRT-based video displays in computers. The basic message here to makers of CRT-based video displays is that their generic strategies are becoming obsolete. Note that the threat in this case is not to a particular firm, competitive position, or individual approach to the marketplace but to the basic generic mission.

One major difficulty in evaluating consonance is that most of the critical threats to a business are those which come from without, threatening an entire group of firms. Management, however, is often so engrossed in competitive thinking that such threats are only recognized after the damage has reached considerable proportions.

EXHIBIT 1
GENERIC VERSUS COMPETITIVE STRATEGY

	GENERIC STRATEGY	COMPETITIVE STRATEGY
Value Issue	Social value	Corporate value
Value Constraint	Customer value > cost	Price > Cost
Success Indicator	Sales growth	Increased corporate worth
Basic Strategic Task	Adapting to change	Innovating, impeding imitation, deterring rivals
How Strategy Is Expressed	Product-market definition	Advantage, position, and policies supporting them
Basic Approach to Analysis	Study of an industry over time	Comparison across rivals

Another difficulty in appraising the fit between a firm's mission and the environment is that trend analysis does not normally reveal the most critical changes—they are the result of interactions among trends. The supermarket, for example, comes into being only when home refrigeration and the widespread use of automobiles allow shoppers to buy in significantly larger volumes. The supermarket, the automobile, and the move to suburbia together form the nexus which gives rise to shopping centers. These, in turn, change the nature of retailing and, together with the decline of urban centers, create new forms of enterprise, such as the suburban film theater with four screens. Thus, while gross economic or demographic trends might appear steady for many years, there are waves of change going on at the institutional level.

The key to evaluating consonance is an understanding of why the business, as it currently stands, exists at all and how it assumed its current pattern. Once the analyst obtains a good grasp of the basic economic foundation that supports and defines the business, it is possible to study the consequences of key trends and changes. Without such an understanding, there is no good way of deciding what kinds of changes are most crucial and the analyst can be quickly overwhelmed with data.

ADVANTAGE

It is no exaggeration to say that competitive strategy is the art of creating or exploiting those advantages that are most telling, enduring, and most difficult to duplicate.

Competitive strategy, in contrast with generic strategy, focuses on the differences among firms rather than their common missions. The problem it addresses is not so much "how can this function be performed" but "how can we perform it either better than, or at least instead of, our rivals?" The chain supermarket, for example, represents a successful generic strategy. As a way of doing business, of organizing economic transactions, it has replaced almost all the smaller owner-managed food shops of an earlier era. Yet a potential or actual participant in the retail food business must go beyond this generic strategy and find a way of competing in this business. As another illustration, IBM's early success in the PC industry was generic—other firms soon copied the basic product concept. Once this happened, IBM had to try to either forge a strong competitive strategy in this area or seek a different type of competitive arena.

Competitive advantages can normally be traced to one of the three roots:

- Superior skills
- Superior resources
- Superior position

In examining a potential advantage, the critical question is "What sustains this advantage, keeping competitors from imitating or replicating it?" A firm's skills can be a source of advantage if they are based on its own history of learning-by-doing and if they are rooted in the coordinated behavior of many people. By contrast, skills that are based on generally understood scientific principles, on training that can be purchased by competitors, or which can be analyzed and replicated by others are not sources of sustained advantage.

The *skills* which compose advantages are usually organizational, rather than individual, skills. They involve the adept coordination or collaboration of individual specialists and are built through the interplay of investment, work, and learning. Unlike physical assets, skills are enhanced by their use. Skills that are not continually used and improved will atrophy.

Resources include patents, trademark rights, specialized physical assets, and the firm's working relationships with suppliers and distribution channels. In addition, a firm's reputation with its employees, suppliers, and customers is a resource. Resources that constitute advantages are specialized to the firm, are built up slowly over time through the accumulated exercise of superior skills, or are obtained through being an insightful first mover, or by just plain luck. For example, Nucor's special skills in mini-mill construction are embodied in superior physical plants. Goldman Sachs's reputation as the premier U.S. investment banking house has been built up over many years and is now a major resource in its own right.

A firm's *position* consists of the products or services it provides, the market segments it sells to, and the degree to which it is isolated from direct competition. In general, the best positions involve supplying very uniquely valuable products to price-insensitive buyers, whereas poor positions involve being one of many firms supplying marginally valuable products to very well-informed, price-sensitive buyers.

Positional advantage can be gained by foresight, superior skill and/or resources, or just plain luck. Once gained, a good position is defensible. This means that it (1) returns enough value to warrant its continued maintenance and (2) would be so costly to capture that rivals are deterred from full-scale attacks on the core of the business. Position, it must be noted, tends to be self-sustaining as long as the basic environmental factors that underlie it remain stable. Thus, entrenched firms can be almost impossible to unseat, even if their raw skill levels are only average. And when a shifting environment allows position to be gained by a new entrant or innovator, the results can be spectacular.

Positional advantages are of two types: (1) first mover advantages and (2) reinforcers. The most basic *first mover advantage* occurs when the minimum scale to be efficient requires a large (sunk) investment relative to the market. Thus, the first firm to open a large discount retail store in a rural area precludes, through its relative scale, close followers. More subtle first mover advantages occur when standardization effects "lock in" customers to the first mover's product (e.g., Lotus 1-2-3). Buyer learning and related phenomena can increase the buyer's switching costs, protecting an incumbent's customer base from attack. Frequent flyer programs are aimed in this direction. First movers may also gain advantages in building distribution channels, in tying up specialized suppliers, or in gaining the attention of customers. The first product of a class to engage in mass advertising, for example, tends to impress itself more deeply in people's minds than the second, third, or fourth. In a careful study of frequently purchased consumer products, Urban et al. (1986) found that (other things being equal) the first entrant will have a market share that is $\sqrt{n}$ times as large as that of the *n*th entrant.

Reinforcers are policies or practices acting to strengthen or preserve a strong market position and which are easier to carry out because of the position. The idea that certain arrangements of one's resources can enhance their combined effectiveness, and perhaps even put rival forces in a state of disarray, is at the heart of the traditional notion of strategy. It is reinforcers which provide positional advantage, the strategic quality familiar to military theorists, chess players, and diplomats.

A firm with a larger market share, due to being an early mover or to having a technological lead, can typically build a more efficient production and distribution system. Competitors with less demand simply cannot cover the fixed costs of the larger more efficient facilities, so for them larger facilities are not an economic choice. In this case, scale economies are a reinforcer of market position, not the cause of market position. The firm that has a strong brand can use it as a reinforcer in the introduction of related brands. A company that sells a specialty coating to a broader variety of users may have better data on how to adapt the coating to special conditions than a competitor with more limited sales—properly used, this information is a reinforcer. A famous brand will appear on TV and in films because it is famous, another reinforcer. An example given by Porter (1985: 145) is that of Steinway and Sons, the premier U.S. maker of fine pianos. Steinway maintains a dispersed inventory of grand pianos that approved pianists are permitted to use for concerts at very low rental rates. The policy is less expensive for a leader than for a follower and helps maintain leadership.

The positive feedback provided by reinforcers is the source of the power of position-based advantages—the policies that act to enhance position may not require unusual skills; they simply work most effectively for those who are already in the position in the first place.

While it is not true that larger businesses always have the advantages, it is true that larger businesses will tend to operate in markets and use procedures that turn their size to advantage. Large national consumer-products firms, for example, will normally have an advantage over smaller regional firms in the efficient use of mass advertising, especially network TV. The larger firm will, then, tend to deal in those products where the marginal effect of advertising is most potent, while the smaller firms will seek product/market positions that exploit other types of advantage.

Other position-based advantages follow from such factors as:

- The ownership of special raw material sources or advantageous long-term supply contracts.
- Being geographically located near key customers in a business involving significant fixed investment and high transport costs.
- Being a leader in a service field that permits or requires the building of a unique experience base while serving clients.

- Being a full-line producer in a market with heavy trade-up phenomena.
- Having a wide reputation for providing a needed product or service trait reliably and dependably.

In each case, the position permits competitive policies to be adopted that can serve to reinforce the position. Whenever this type of positive-feedback phenomena is encountered, the particular policy mix that creates it will be found to be a defensible business position. The key factors that sparked industrial success stories such as IBM and Eastman Kodak were the early and rapid domination of strong positions opened up by new technologies.

FEASIBILITY

The final broad test of strategy is its feasibility. Can the strategy be attempted within the physical, human, and financial resources available? The financial resources of a business are the easiest to quantify and are normally the first limitations against which strategy is tested. It is sometimes forgotten, however, that innovative approaches to financing expansion can both stretch the ultimate limitations and provide a competitive advantage, even if it is only temporary. Devices such as captive finance subsidiaries, sale–leaseback arrangements, and tying plant mortgages to long-term contracts have all been used effectively to help win key positions in suddenly expanding industries.

The less quantifiable but actually more rigid limitation on strategic choice is that imposed by the individual and organization capabilities that are available.

In assessing the organization's ability to carry out a strategy, it is helpful to ask three separate questions:

1. Has the organization demonstrated that it possesses the problem-solving abilities and/or special competencies required by the strategy? A strategy, as such, does not and cannot specify in detail each action that must be carried out. Its purpose is to provide structure to the general issue of the business's goals and approaches to coping with its environment. It is up to the members and departments of the organization to carry out the tasks defined by strategy. A strategy that requires tasks to be accomplished which fall outside the realm of available or easily obtainable skill and knowledge cannot be accepted. It is either unfeasible or incomplete.
2. Has the organization demonstrated the degree of coordinative and integrative skill necessary to carry out the strategy? The key tasks required of a strategy not only require specialized skill, but often make considerable demands on the organization's ability to integrate disparate activities. A manufacturer of standard office furniture may find, for example, that its primary difficulty in entering the new market for modular office systems is a lack of sophisticated interaction between its field sales offices and its manufacturing plant. Firms that hope to span national boundaries with integrated worldwide systems of production and marketing may also find that organizational process, rather than functional skill per se or isolated competitive strength, becomes the weak link in the strategic posture.
3. Does the strategy challenge and motivate key personnel and is it acceptable to those who must lend their support? The purpose of strategy is to effectively deploy the unique and distinctive resources of an enterprise. If key managers are unmoved by a strategy, not excited by its goals or methods, or strongly support an alternative, it fails in a major way.

THE PROCESS OF STRATEGY EVALUATION

Strategy evaluation can take place as an abstract analytic task, perhaps performed by consultants. But most often it is an integral part of an organization's process of planning, review, and control. In some organizations, evaluation is informal, only occasional, brief, and cursory. Others have created elaborate systems containing formal periodic strategy review sessions. In either case, the quality of strategy evaluation, and, ultimately, the quality of corporate performance, will be determined more by the organization's capacity for self-appraisal and learning than by the particular analytic technique employed.

In their study of organizational learning, Argyris and Schon distinguish between single-loop and double-loop learning. They argue that normal organizational learning is of the feedback-control type—deviations between expected and actual performance lead to problem solving which brings the system back under control. They note that

> [Single-loop learning] is concerned primarily with effectiveness—that is, with how best to achieve existing goals and objectives and how best to keep organizational performance within the range specified by existing norms. In some cases, however, error correction requires a learning cycle in which organizational norms themselves are modified. . . . We call this sort of learning "double-loop." There is . . . a double feedback loop which connects the detection of error not only to strategies and assumptions for effective performance but to the very norms which define effective performance. (1978: 20)

These ideas parallel those of Ashby, a cyberneticist. Ashby (1954) has argued that all feedback systems require more than single-loop error control for stability; they also need a way of monitoring certain critical variables and changing the system "goals" when old control methods are no longer working.

These viewpoints help to remind us that the real strategic processes in any organization are not found by looking at those things that happen to be labeled "strategic" or "long range." Rather, the real components of the strategic process are, by definition, those activities which most strongly affect the selection and modification of objectives and which influence the irreversible commitment of important resources. They also suggest that appropriate methods of strategy evaluation cannot be specified in abstract terms. Instead, an organization's approach to evaluation must fit its strategic posture and work in conjunction with its methods of planning and control.

In most firms comprehensive strategy evaluation is infrequent and, if it occurs, is normally triggered by a change in leadership or financial performance. The fact that comprehensive strategy evaluation is neither a regular event nor part of a formal system tends to be deplored by some theorists, but there are several good reasons for this state of affairs. Most obviously, any activity that becomes an annual procedure is bound to become more automatic. While evaluating strategy on an annual basis might lead to some sorts of efficiencies in data collection and analysis, it would also tend to strongly channel the types of questions asked and inhibit broad-ranging reflection.

Second, a good strategy does not need constant reformulation. It is a framework for continuing problem solving, not the problem solving itself. One senior executive expressed it this way: "If you play from strength you don't always need to be rethinking the whole plan; you can concentrate on details. So when you see us talking about slight changes in tooling, it isn't because we forgot the big picture, it's because we took care of it."

Strategy also represents a political alignment within the firm and embodies the past convictions and commitments of key executives. Comprehensive strategy evaluation is not just an analytical exercise, it calls into question this basic pattern of commitments and policies. Most organizations would be hurt rather than helped to have their mission's validity called into question on a regular basis. Zero-based budgeting, for example, was an attempt to get agencies to rejustify their existence each time a new budget is drawn up. If this were literally true, there would be little time or energy remaining for any but political activity.

Finally, there are competitive reasons for not reviewing the validity of a strategy too freely! There are a wide range of rivalrous confrontations in which it is crucial to be able to convince others that one's position, or strategy, is fixed and unshakable. Schelling's (1963) analysis of bargaining and conflict shows that a great deal of what is involved in negotiating is finding ways to bind or commit oneself convincingly. This is the principle underlying the concept of deterrence and what lies behind the union leader's tactic of claiming that while he would go along with management's desire for moderation, he cannot control the members if the less moderate demands are not met. In business strategy, such situations occur in classic oligopoly, plant-capacity duels, new-product conflicts, and other situations in which the winner may be the party whose policies are most credibly unswayable. Japanese electronics firms, for example, have gained such strong reputations as low-cost committed players that their very entry into a market has come to induce rivals to give up. If such firms had instead the reputation of continually reviewing the advisability of continuing each product, they would be much less threatening, and thus less effective, competitors. . . .

CONCLUSIONS

Strategy evaluation is the appraisal of plans and the results of plans that centrally concern or affect the basic mission of an enterprise. Its special focus is the separation between obvious current operating results and those factors which underlie success or failure in the chosen domain of activity. Its result is the rejection, modification, or ratification of existing strategies and plans. . . .

In most medium- to large-size firms, strategy evaluation is not a purely intellectual task. The issues involved are too important and too closely associated with the distribution of power and authority for either strategy formulation or evaluation to take place in an ivory tower environment. In fact, most firms rarely engage in explicit formal strategy evaluation. Rather, the evaluation of current strategy is a continuing process and one that is difficult to separate from the normal planning, reporting, control, and reward systems of the firm. From this point of view, strategy evaluation is not so much an intellectual task as it is an organizational process.

Ultimately, a firm's ability to maintain its competitive position in a world of rivalry and change may be best served by managers who can maintain a dual view of strategy and strategy evaluation—they must be willing and able to perceive the strategy within the welter of daily activity and to build and maintain structures and systems that make strategic factors the object of current activity.

READING 3.3

Strategic Intent BY GARY HAMEL AND C. K. PRAHALAD

Today managers in many industries are working hard to match the competitive advantages of their new global rivals. They are moving manufacturing offshore in search of low labor costs, rationalizing product lines to capture global scale economics, instituting quality circles and just-in-time production, and adopting Japanese human resource practices. When competitiveness still seems out of reach, they form strategic alliances, often with the very companies that upset the competitive balance in the first place.

Important as these initiatives are, few of them go beyond mere imitation. . . . For these executives and their companies, regaining competitiveness will mean rethinking many of the basic concepts of strategy. . . . The new global competitors approach strategy from a perspective that is fundamentally different from that which underpins Western management thought. . . .

Companies that have risen to global leadership over the past 20 years invariably began with ambitions that were out of all proportion to their resources and capabilities. But they created an obsession with winning at all levels of the organization and then sustained that obsession over the 10- to 20-year quest for global leadership. We term this obsession "strategic intent."

On the one hand, strategic intent envisions a desired leadership position and establishes the criteria the organization will use to chart its progress. Komatsu set out to "Encircle Caterpillar." Canon sought to "Beat Xerox." Honda strove to become a second Ford—an automotive pioneer. All are expressions of strategic intent.

At the same time, strategic intent is more than simply unfettered ambition. (Many companies possess an ambitious strategic intent yet fall short of their goals.) The concept also encompasses an active management process that includes: focusing the organization's attention on the essence of winning; motivating people by communicating the value of the target; leaving room for individual and team contributions; sustaining enthusiasm by providing new operations definitions as circumstances change; and using intent consistently to guide resource allocations.

Strategic intent captures the essence of winning. The Apollo program—landing a man on the moon ahead of the Soviets—was as competitively focused as Komatsu's drive against Caterpillar. The space program became the scorecard for America's technology race with the USSR. . . . For Coca-Cola, strategic intent has been to put Coke within "arm's reach" of every consumer in the world.

Strategic intent is stable over time. In battles for global leadership, one of the most critical tasks is to lengthen the organization's attention span. Strategic intent provides consistency to short-term action, while leaving room for reinterpretation as new opportunities emerge. . . .

Strategic intent sets a target that deserves personal effort and commitment. Ask the chairmen of many American corporations how they measure their contributions to their companies' success and you're likely to get an answer expressed in terms of shareholder wealth. In a company that possesses a strategic intent, top management is more likely to talk in terms of global market leadership. Market share leadership typically yields shareholder wealth, to be sure. But the two goals do not have the same motivational impact. It is hard to imagine middle managers, let alone blue-collar employees, waking up each day with the sole thought of creating more shareholder wealth. But mightn't they feel different given the challenge to "Beat Benz"— the rallying cry at one Japanese auto producer? Strategic intent gives employees the only goal that is worthy of commitment: to unseat the best or remain the best, worldwide. . . .

Just as you cannot plan a 10- to 20-year quest for global leadership, the chance of falling into a leadership position by accident is also remote. We don't believe that global leadership comes from an undirected process of intrapreneurship. Nor is it the product of skunkworks or other techniques for internal venturing. Behind such programs lies a nihilistic assumption: the organization is so hide-bound, so orthodox ridden that the only way to innovate is to put a few bright people in a dark room, pour in some money, and hope that something wonderful will happen. In the "Silicon Valley" approach to innovation, the only role for top managers is to retrofit their corporate strategy to the entrepreneurial successes that emerge from below. Here the value added of top management is low indeed. . . .

In companies that overcame resource constraints to build leadership positions, we see a different relationship between means and ends. While strategic intent is clear about ends, it is flexible as to means—it leaves room for improvisation. Achieving strategic intent requires enormous creativity with respect to means. . . . But this creativity comes in the service of a clearly prescribed end. Creativity is unbridled, but not uncorraled, because top management establishes the criterion against which employees can pretest the logic of their initiatives. Middle managers must do more than deliver on promised financial targets; they must also deliver on the broad direction implicit in their organization's strategic intent.

Strategic intent implies a sizable stretch for an organization. Current capabilities and resources will not suffice. This forces the organization to be more inventive, to make the most of limited resources. Whereas the traditional view of strategy focuses on the degree of fit between existing resources and current opportunities, strategic intent creates an extreme misfit between resources and ambitions. Top management then challenges the organization to close the gap by systematically building new advantages. For Canon this meant first understanding Xerox's patents, then licensing technology to create a product that would yield early market experience, then gearing up internal R&D efforts, then licensing its own technology to other manufacturers to fund further R&D, then entering marketing segments in Japan and Europe where Xerox was weak, and so on.

In this respect, strategic intent is like a marathon run in 400-meter sprints. No one knows what the terrain will look like at mile 26, so the role of top management is to focus the organization's attention on the ground to be covered in the next 400 meters. In several companies, management did this by presenting the organization with a series of corporate challenges, each specifying the next hill in the race to achieve strategic intent. One year the challenge might be quality, the next total customer care, the next entry into new markets, the next a rejuvenated product line. As this example indicates, corporate challenges are a way to stage the acquisition of new competitive advantages, a way to identify the focal point for employees' efforts in the near to medium term. As with strategic intent, top management is specific about the ends (reducing product development times by 75%, for example) but less prescriptive about the means.

Like strategic intent, challenges stretch the organization. To preempt Xerox in the personal copier business, Canon set its engineers a target price of $1,000 for a home copier. At the time, Canon's least expensive copier sold for several thousand dollars. . . . Canon engineers were challenged to reinvent the copier—a challenge they met by substituting a disposable cartridge for the complex image-transfer mechanism used in other copiers. . . .

For a challenge to be effective, individuals and teams throughout the organization must understand it and see its implications for their own jobs. Companies that set corporate challenges to create new competitive advantages (as Ford and IBM did with quality improvement) quickly discover that engaging the entire organization requires top management to:

Create a sense of urgency, or quasi-crisis, by amplifying weak signals in the environment that point up the need to improve, instead of allowing inaction to precipitate a real crisis. . . .

Develop a competitor focus at every level through widespread use of competitive intelligence. Every employee should be able to benchmark his or her efforts against best-in-class competitors so that the challenge becomes personal. . . .

Provide employees with the skills they need to work effectively—training in statistical tools, problem solving, value engineering, and team building, for example.

Give the organization time to digest one challenge before launching another. When competing initiatives overload the organization, middle managers often try to protect their people from the whipsaw of shifting priorities. But this "wait and see if they're serious this time" attitude ultimately destroys the credibility of corporate challenges.

Establish clear milestones and review mechanisms to track progress and ensure that internal recognition and rewards reinforce desired behavior. The goal is to make the challenge inescapable for everyone in the company. . . .

Reciprocal responsibility means shared gain and shared pain . . . at Nissan when the yen strengthened top management took a big pay cut and then asked middle managers and line employees to sacrifice relatively less. In too many companies, the pain of revitalization falls almost exclusively on the employees least responsible for the enterprise's decline. . . .This one-sided approach to regaining competitiveness keeps many companies from harnessing the intellectual horsepower of their employees.

Creating a sense of reciprocal responsibility is crucial because competitiveness ultimately depends on the pace at which a company embeds new advantages deep within its organization, not on its stock of advantages at any given time. Thus we need to expand the concept of competitive advantage beyond the scorecard many managers now use: Are my costs lower? Will my product command a price premium?

Few competitive advantages are long-lasting. Uncovering a new competitive advantage is a bit like getting a hot tip on a stock: the first person to act on the insight makes more money than the last. . . .

Keeping score of existing advantages is not the same as building new advantages. The essence of strategy lies in creating tomorrow's competitive advantages faster than competitors mimic the ones you possess today. In the 1960s, Japanese producers relied on labor and capital cost advantages. As Western manufacturers began to move production offshore, Japanese companies accelerated their investment in process technology and created scale and quality advantages. Then as their U.S. and European competitors rationalized manufacturing, they added another string to their bow by accelerating the rate of product development. Then they built global brands. Then they deskilled competitors through alliances and outsourcing deals. The moral? An organization's capacity to improve existing skills and learn new ones is the most defensible competitive advantage of all.

To achieve strategic intent, a company must usually take on larger, better financed competitors. That means carefully managing competitive engagements so that scarce resources are conserved. Managers cannot do that simply by playing the same game better—making marginal improvement to competitors' technology and business practices. Instead, they must fundamentally change the game in ways that disadvantage incumbents—designing novel approaches to market entry, advantage building, and competitive warfare. For smart competitors, the goal is not competitive imitation but competitive innovation, the art of containing competitive risks within manageable proportions.

Four approaches to competitive innovation are evident in the global expansion of Japanese companies. These are: building layers of advantage, searching for loose bricks, changing the terms of engagement, and competing through collaboration.

The wider a company's portfolio of advantages, the less risk it faces in competitive battles. New global competitors have built such portfolios by steadily expanding their arsenals of competitive weapons. They have moved inexorably from less defensible advantages such as low wage costs to more defensible advantages like global brands. . . .

Business schools have perpetuated the notion that a manager with new present value calculations in one hand and portfolio planning in the other can manage any business anywhere.

In many diversified companies, top management evaluates line managers on numbers alone because no other basis for dialogue exists. Managers move so many times as part of their "career development" that they often do not understand the nuances of the businesses they are managing. At GE, for example, one fast-track manager heading an important new venture had moved across five businesses in five years. His series of quick successes finally came to an end when he confronted a Japanese competitor whose managers had been plodding along in the same business for more than a decade.

Regardless of ability and effort, fast-track managers are unlikely to develop the deep business knowledge they need to discuss technology options, competitors' strategies, and global opportunities substantively. Invariably, therefore, discussions gravitate to "the numbers," while the value added of managers is limited to the financial and planning savvy they carry from job to job. Knowledge of the company's internal planning and accounting systems substitutes for substantive knowledge of the business, making competitive innovation unlikely.

When managers know that their assignments have a two- to three-year time frame, they feel great pressure to create a good track record fast. This pressure often takes on one of two forms. Either the manager does not commit to goals whose time line extends beyond his or her expected tenure, or ambitious goals are adopted and squeezed into an unrealistically short time frame. Aiming to be number one in a business is the essence of strategic intent; but imposing a three- to four-year horizon on that effort simply invites disaster. Acquisitions are made with little attention to the problems of integration. The organization becomes overloaded with initiatives. Collaborative ventures are formed without adequate attention to competitive consequences.

Almost every strategic management theory and nearly every corporate planning system is premised on a strategy hierarchy in which corporate goals guide business-unit strategies and business-unit strategies guide functional tactics. In this hierarchy, senior management makes strategy and low levels execute it. The dichotomy between formulation and implementation is familiar and widely accepted. But the strategy hierarchy undermines competitiveness by fostering an elitist view of management that tends to disenfranchise most of the organization. Employees fail to identify with corporate goals or involve themselves deeply in the work of becoming more competitive.

The strategy hierarchy isn't the only explanation for an elitist view of management, of course. The myths that grow up around successful top managers . . . perpetuate it. So does the turbulent business environment. Middle managers buffeted by circumstances that seem to be beyond their control desperately want to believe that top management has all the answers. And top management, in turn, hesitates to admit it does not for fear of demoralizing lower-level employees. . . .

Unfortunately, a threat that everyone perceives but no one talks about creates more anxiety than a threat that has been clearly identified and made the focal point for the problem-solving efforts of the entire company. That is one reason honesty and humility on the part of top management may be the first prerequisite of revitalization. Another reason is the need to make participation more than a buzzword.

Programs such as quality circles and total customer service often fall short of expectations because management does not recognize that successful implementation requires more than administrative structures. Difficulties in embedding new capabilities are typically put down to "communication" problems, with the unstated assumption that if only downward communication were more effective— "if only middle management would get the message straight"— the new program would quickly take root. The need for upward communication is often ignored, or assumed to mean nothing more than feedback. In contrast, Japanese companies win, not because they have smarter managers, but because they have developed ways to harness the "wisdom of the anthill." They realize the top managers are a bit like the astronauts who circle the earth in the space shuttle. It may be the astronauts who get all the glory, but everyone knows that the real intelligence behind the mission is located firmly on the ground. . . .

Developing faith in the organization's ability to deliver on tough goals, motivating it to do so, focusing its attention long enough to internalize new capabilities—this is the real challenge for top management. Only by rising to this challenge will senior managers gain the courage they need to commit themselves and their companies to global leadership.

READING 3.4

The Real Value of Strategic Planning BY SARAH KAPLAN AND ERIC D. BEINHOCKER

Most companies invest a significant amount of time and effort in a formal, annual strategic planning process—but many executives see little benefit from the investment. One manager told us, "Our planning process is like a primitive tribal ritual—there is a lot of dancing, waving of feathers and beating of drums. No one is exactly sure why we do it, but there is an almost mystical hope that something good will come out of it." Another said, "It's like the old Communist system: We pretend to make strategy and they pretend to follow it."

Management thinker Henry Mintzberg has gone so far as to label the phrase "strategic planning" an oxymoron (n1). He notes that real strategy is made informally—in hallway conversations, in working groups, and in quiet moments of reflection on long plane flights—and rarely in the paneled conference rooms where formal planning meetings are held. Our own research on strategic planning supports Mintzberg's observation: We found that few truly strategic decisions are made in the context of a formal process. But we also found that, when approached with the right goal in mind, formal planning need not be a waste of time and can, in fact, be a real source of competitive advantage. Companies that achieved such success used strategic planning not to generate strategic plans but as a learning tool to create "prepared minds" within their management teams (to paraphrase Louis Pasteur) (n2).

A former senior executive at GE Capital explained the logic of such thinking to us: Business is often unpredictable—two competitors merge, another develops a new technology, the government issues new regulations, market demand swings in a different direction. It is often during these real-time developments that a company's most important strategic decisions are made. Too often, however, companies react poorly under the pressure. Because they are not well prepared, discussions among top managers are often based more on opinion than fact, and the subsequent decisions end up being based on gut instinct rather than thoughtful analysis. GE Capital, however, believes it gains a competitive advantage by following a disciplined strategy process that focuses on preparing it for the uncertainties ahead.

As this analysis makes clear, real strategy is made in real time. It follows, then, that the goal of a formal strategic planning process is to make sure that key decision makers have a solid understanding of the business, share a common fact base, and agree on important assumptions. These elements of the prepared mind serve as the foundation upon which good strategic decisions can be made throughout the year. And one of the most important ways of building that foundation is by getting the central elements of the process right.

HOW TO CREATE PREPARED MINDS

Most strategic planning processes are built around a set of annual (or other time period) meetings in which the chief executive officer and senior corporate team review the strategies of the company's business units or divisions. The CEO and top team typically meet separately to discuss corporate strategy as well.

We found that the key to transforming these review meetings from dog and pony shows into effective vehicles for learning was to view them not as "reviews by the CEO" but as conversations. The difference is that a conversation is a two-way street in which participants learn from and challenge one another—the goal is for everyone to leave the room much better informed than when they went in. Achieving that outcome requires a lot of preparation by all the participants. The devil, it turns out, is in a host of seemingly mundane, but actually critical, details:

Who should attend the reviews? Real conversations take place in groups of 3 to 10 people; they simply do not happen in large groups for both logistical and political reasons. Once the group grows in size, it is difficult to ensure that everyone can participate meaningfully, so hierarchical forces are more likely to come into play. Rather than frank discussion, in larger groups one is more likely to see posturing and politicking. Some companies in our study, tempted by the values of inclusion, brought in groups as large as 30 or 40 people to their strategy reviews. These discussions were inhibited, and people came away feeling that the exercise had been more of a slide show than a real dialogue about critical business issues.

In reality, there are only two essential participants in a business-unit strategy review: the CEO and the business-unit head. Everyone else is discretionary and should be included only if he or she is truly a decision maker. The number of decision makers varies from company to company but typically includes the corporate CFO, the group executive (if there is one) that the business unit reports to, the head of corporate HR, one or two senior corporate executives, and two to three senior members of the business-unit team. The corporate head of strategy also usually attends as the person responsible for making sure the conversation is effective. Thus the total number of participants can be kept to between 5 and 10, with 12 as the maximum. People will fight to be included in these meetings, but other forums can be set up to keep them informed and get their buy-in.

How long should the reviews be? It's not possible to have an in-depth strategy discussion about a significant business in less than a day. There are simply too many topics to cover: customers, competitors, technology, regulation, risks, investments and more. Spending less time prevents the careful poking and prodding of issues required to get the full benefit from the effort. It may sound like a lot to commit a full day to each major business unit, but most CEOs we interviewed said they wanted to spend about a third of their time on strategy. Given 240 working days, that leaves 80 days to devote to strategy. In that context, it seems reasonable to expect the CEO to spend 10 to 30 days in intensive, well-prepared strategy discussions. Former CEO Charles E. Knight said that "more than half my time each year is blocked out strictly for planning," a commitment to strategy that has been carried on by his successor David Farr.

Where should they be held? It is best to hold planning meetings at the business-unit site; they will then feel less like a "summons from corporate." Holding the meeting at the business unit also minimizes the distractions of day-to-day business at corporate headquarters, and the CEO's presence at the site signals the importance of strategy to the entire organization. The CEO can often use additional time at the site to take the temperature of the business by attending formal and informal events with employees, taking a plant tour, and visiting important local customers.

What should be discussed? Many companies combine their strategy reviews with a discussion of budgets and financial targets. That is a big mistake. When the two are combined, the discussion is dominated by a focus on the numbers and short-term issues; long-term strategy questions receive only cursory attention. Likewise, if there is no other forum in which to discuss the financials, they will inevitably come up in the strategy meetings. Ideally, companies should have two clearly demarcated meetings: one full day on business-unit strategy and another meeting at a different time of the year to set financial targets. The two should then be linked with a common, rolling five- to seven-year financial plan that ties together strategic initiatives with budgets. Such linking is crucial: We have seen some companies use the strategy review to advocate a major change in direction but, in a separate process, build a budget that looks like an update of last year's financials. The lack of connection is sure to stymie the change effort.

Rather than near-term financial targets, the conversation should focus on long-term trends, opportunities, challenges and decisions. In businesses where decisions have a long lifetime and are difficult to reverse, such as aerospace or telecommunications, "long term" might mean 5 to 10 years. In those where commitments have a shorter life, such as software or consumer goods, it might mean two to five years. The discussion should focus on questions over the appropriate time horizon such as: What are our aspirations? What are the critical trends regarding customers, competitors, technology and regulation? How is our business model performing, and how will it likely evolve? What are the key challenges and opportunities we face? What capabilities do we need to build for the future? What are the key risks and uncertainties we face, and what can we do to ensure our adaptability?

How should the conversation be conducted? The main purpose of the discussions is to challenge the strategy by testing assumptions about the market, checking that a full range of strategic choices is considered, exploring potential opportunities and risks, and forcing an honest assessment of the business's strengths and weaknesses.

An organization's culture will dictate the tone of the discussions, and we discovered that there is no one right culture for planning; good strategic planning can emerge from the in-your-face culture of Emerson Electric or the more genteel culture of Hewlett-Packard. There are, however, certainly some wrong ways to conduct strategic planning conversations. Sometimes business-unit heads, resentful of what they see as "interference from corporate," try to reveal as little information as possible; on the other side, senior corporate leaders at times turn the meetings into a game of "gotcha," seeking all the skeletons in the business unit's closets.

The conversations can be hard-nosed, but it's important to create an environment that doesn't become "us versus them." In companies where people are able to challenge one another, that is done by exploring the boundaries of the strategy: pushing the business team to explore worst-case scenarios and understand what might make them come true, testing to see if aspirations could be ratcheted upward, or investigating the competitive implications of a radical cost reduction or product performance improvement. It's also fine to have a collegial atmosphere, as long as it doesn't devolve to the point where uncomfortable issues are glossed over or buried. One company we studied never made an effective strategic plan because it was so consensus-oriented. Tough issues simply were postponed until another meeting because the members of the management team were not able to confront one another.

How much preparation is necessary? Preparation by the principals is the key to making a full-day strategy discussion pay off. The tasks should not be outsourced to staff people. A document detailing the strategy should be sent out at least a week before the meeting, allowing participants the time they'll need to study it. That will prevent people from having to take the time to read and understand the slides for the first time; instead, the participants will come ready to ask questions and debate the issues.

The corporate center should provide the business units with certain "must haves"—a template that serves as a guideline for analysis. The template should define the company's current position in terms of customers, products or services, and market segments; assess the future direction of the industry, including customer trends, competitor actions, technology changes, and globalization; and determine the major opportunities and threats facing the business. It is also helpful to share with units the best plan of the previous year to create a "gold standard" of what is expected and instigate some competition among the business units.

Each unit, however, should be given a lot of latitude. For one thing, every business unit is different, and one-size-fits-all templates are likely to obscure more than they reveal. For another, strategy reviews are a great way for a CEO to check out the quality of the company's managers. If there is too much corporate guidance, it becomes harder to tell the real strategists from those who are merely good at filling out templates.

What kind of follow-up is needed? Disciplined follow-up is essential. Long-term strategic goals should be tied to shorter-term budgets, financial targets, operating plans, and human resource strategies. In companies that had a good process, the CEO personally took detailed notes; wrote a three- to four-page memo to the business unit or division management summarizing the main themes, implications, and commitments; and used the notes as the starting point for next year's review. The goals should also be incorporated into the compensation plans of the unit management team. This level of follow-up assures that the strategic plans do not lie ignored on the executive bookshelf but are living documents that drive actions and performance.

PREPARED MINDS IN ACTION

How does one judge the success or failure of the strategic planning process? Not by whether the written plans were good, or whether everyone felt good afterward, or even whether any big decisions were made during the meetings. Again, the ultimate criterion is whether all the participants came out of the process better prepared for the real-time job of strategic decision making. In our research, we saw many examples in which the right process led to that result.

Consider how rigorous planning processes helped a multibusiness industrial goods company expand internationally. Quite unexpectedly, its automotive parts division was faced with the opportunity to acquire two large businesses in Germany, where it had not been a significant player. Because the company would be new to the market and would need to commit significant resources in order to succeed in it, the decision was risky. Fortunately, the CEO, the top corporate team, and the top business-unit team had engaged in extensive strategy discussions and therefore already had a point of view on the German market and the strategic fit presented by the opportunity, as well as a thorough understanding of the economics of the product area in question. The company was able to make a decision quite quickly and outnegotiate a slower-moving rival that was not as well prepared. The acquisitions were critical to the success of the company's growth strategy.

Prepared minds can also help companies reject moves that don't make sense. A company with a large aerospace and defense division, for example, invested a lot of time in its strategy reviews to ensure that top managers understood the economic implications of consolidation in its industry. Instead of accepting the standard line from the industry press and pundits, the participants looked in detail at what it meant for their specific subsectors of the industry and their own future economics. They weren't gullible, then, when their investment bankers came to town, arguing that the company needed greater economies of scale to survive and proposing a specific acquisition target that would soon be for sale. Armed with an appreciation of the business and aware of the strengths and weaknesses of competitors, top management chose not to do the deal—which in hindsight proved to be the right decision. Their preparation enabled them to sort out sensible deals from foolish ones and avoid a potentially costly and distracting mistake.

Contrast that outcome with events at an agrochemical company whose processes did not do an adequate job of preparing its leaders to respond to challenges posed by the market. Growth in the company's industry had come primarily from the development and sale of genetically modified (GM) seeds. At one point, the company's seed division held a brainstorming session to talk about new growth opportunities. European colleagues raised the possibility of a backlash in their home countries against food grown from GM seeds, but a corporate senior executive who had joined the discussion, unhappy with this negative view of the business, struck the topic off the table. Later, European consumers did indeed object to GM foods, and the company was blindsided by the rapid decline of its European seed business. That outcome might have been avoided if the company had had a formal process (and forum) for fact-based, open-minded discussions of business-unit risks among senior corporate and business-unit executives. In the absence of such a process, the whim of one senior executive overrode the concerns of the local business unit.

As these examples suggest, there's no reason strategic planning should be the butt of cynical jokes—it's one of the most important tasks for senior corporate and business-unit executives. Companies whose processes look more like tribal rituals waste valuable executive time at a minimum; more seriously, they may leave corporate leaders unprepared to respond properly when the inevitable moments of truth arise. When repositioned as a learning process, formal strategic planning can help managers make solidly grounded strategic decisions in a world of turbulence and uncertainty.

REFERENCES

(n1.) Henry Mintzberg, *The Rise and Fall of Strategic Planning*, New York: Free Press, 1994 (p. 321).
(n2.) Pasteur famously said that "chance favors the prepared mind" in describing his own breakthrough research.

CHAPTER 4

Analyzing Strategy

As noted in the introduction to Chapter 3, a second prescriptive view of how strategy should be formulated developed in the 1980s. Its contribution is less as a new conceptual model—in fact, it embraces most of the assumptions of the traditional model—and more as a careful structuring of the kinds of formal analyses that should be undertaken to develop a successful strategy. One outcome of this more formal approach is that many of its adherents came to see strategies as fitting certain "generic" classifications—not being created individually so much as being selected from a limited set of options. This approach has proved to be powerful and useful in specific situations.

Michael Porter became the leader of this school after studying at the doctoral level in Harvard's economics department. By building intellectual bridges between the fields of management policy and industrial organization—the latter a branch of economics concerned with the performance of industries as a function of their competitive characteristics—Porter elaborated on the earlier views of Andrews, Ansoff, Newman, and others.

We open this chapter with Porter's basic model of competitive and industry analysis, probably his best-known work in the area of strategy analysis. As presented in this award-winning *Harvard Business Review* article, it proposes a framework of five forces that in his view defines the basic posture of competition in an industry—the bargaining power of existing suppliers and buyers, the threat of substitutes and new entrants, and the intensity of existing rivalry. The model is a powerful one, as you shall see in references to it in subsequent readings as well as in applications of it in the case studies.

The next two articles, by Jay Barney of Ohio State University and Pankaj Ghemawat and Gary Pisano of Harvard Business School, take this analytical perspective further into new aspects that developed since Porter wrote his path-breaking books of the 1980s. Sustainable competitive advantage is the holy grail of what we like to call the "content" approach to strategy. It is, however, a surprisingly elusive goal. Porter's five-forces model suggests that sustainable competitive advantage can be discovered by proper industry analysis. The only problem with his model is that the same analysis often applies equally well to more than one company (hence, the notion of "strategic groups"). Barney's article takes up the challenge, putting forward what has come to be known as the resource-based view of the firm. This argues that sustainable competitive advantage is not the product of correct position in the external environment but is derived from the firm's internal resources. More specifically, resources must meet four criteria to confer sustainable competitive advantage. They must be valuable, inimitable, rare, and nonsubstitutable.

In "Sustaining Superior Performance: Commitments and Capabilities" Ghemawat and Pisano maintain that Barney's criteria are not sufficient for ensuring sustainable advantage. Sustainability must address other conditions—in particular the need to prevent other firms from imitating and appropriating resources, and the need to ensure that employees (or other agents of the organization) refrain from abusing their position through underperformance or by covertly appropriating resources. Large-scale investments in the right resources can help companies meet these conditions, but in addition to these discrete actions, companies should make regular small-scale investments that build their capabilities.

Porter is also known for a number of other concepts: "generic strategies," of which he argues there are three in particular—cost leadership, differentiation, and focus (or scope); the "value chain," as a way of decomposing the activities of a business to apply strategy analyses of various kinds; strategic groups, where firms with like sets of strategies compete in subsegments of an industry; and "generic industry environments," such as "fragmented" and "mature," which reflect similar characteristics.

We shall hear from Porter again on the last of these in our third section. But his three generic strategies as well as his value chain concept are summarized in the next reading in this chapter. Here Mintzberg seeks to present a more comprehensive picture of the various generic strategies that firms commonly pursue. These generic strategies are described at four levels as strategies concerned with locating the core business, with distinguishing the core business by means of "differentiation" and scope," with elaborating the core business, and with extending the core business.

The fourth reading of the chapter looks at strategic analysis quite differently, in a kind of political way. You may recall one of the definitions of strategy introduced in Chapter 1 that has not been heard from since—that of ploy. In this reading, ploy comes to life in the form of "competitive maneuvering" and the various means strategists use to outwit competitors. This reading is based on two short articles entitled "Brinkmanship in Business" and "The Nonlogical Strategy" by Bruce Henderson, drawn from his book, *Henderson on Corporate Strategy,* which is a collection of short, pithy, and rather opinionated views. Henderson founded the Boston Consulting Group and built it into a major international force in management consulting.

The literature of strategic analysis, or "positioning" as it is sometimes called, tends like analysis itself to be rather decomposed in that it is more concerned with probing into parts than combining into wholes. Accordingly, the concepts tend to come and go at a frantic pace, confusing reader and writer alike. Thus, Mintzberg has prepared for this book an integrative piece called "A Guide to Strategic Positioning," which sets out to place these many concepts into a single framework. To do so, he uses the metaphor of a launching vehicle that projects its products and services into the terrain of markets. You should have some fun with this new contribution to the strategic management literature.

USING THE CASE STUDIES

Porter's five-forces model is arguably the most influential analytical model in strategy. In principle, it can be applied to most of the cases in this book. In practice, it is best applied to cases in which strategic decision making is tightly coupled to industry conditions. This is very much in evidence in the cases that deal with entire industries such as the casino industry, the European wealth management industry, and the U.S. wine industry. But it also works well with cases that deal with companies such as Heineken, McDonald's, and QVC, whose strategy flows directly from industry position.

Porter's emphasis on the importance of external context is balanced by Barney's insistence that sustainable advantage depends as much or more on the internal resources of the firm. These resources are fairly easy to identify in the case of HBO, Pixar, or Apple, but much harder to pinpoint when we turn to companies such as Lufthansa, Nissan, and Natura, and Cirque du Soleil. (Try it; it can be an interesting exercise.) Ghemawat and Pisano, of course, would argue that capabilities, not resources, are the key to sustainability. Johnson & Johnson demonstrates this most persuasively. However, capabilities, like resources, are a difficult analytical construct. It is often best approached when trying to explain the success of a company such as HBO, which seemingly violates every rule in its industry.

Effective strategic analysis may rely less on "grand" theories, such as those of Porter or Barney, and more on finding the right framework for identifying moves and positions. Henderson's "Competitive Maneuvering" brings Porter's model down to earth. Cases such as Barbie versus Bartz, Nintendo, Netflix and QVC show how companies focus on their competitors. In "Generic Business Strategies" and "A Guide to Strategic Positioning," Mintzberg opens up Porter's typology to new kinds of business strategies. This may be valuable for the top managers in the U.S. wine industry as they confront the challenge of direct-to-consumer shipping. How they position their companies as a value chain that has persisted for more than thirty years begins to disintegrate?

READING 4.1

How Competitive Forces Shape Strategy* BY MICHAEL E. PORTER

The essence of strategy formulation is coping with competition. Yet it is easy to view competition too narrowly and too pessimistically. While one sometimes hears executives complaining to the contrary, intense competition in an industry is neither coincidence nor bad luck.

Moreover, in the fight for market share, competition is not manifested only in the other players. Rather, competition in an industry is rooted in its underlying economics, and competitive forces exist that go well beyond the established combatants in a particular industry. Customers, suppliers, potential entrants, and substitute products are all competitors that may be more or less prominent or active depending on the industry.

The state of competition in an industry depends on five basic forces, which are diagrammed in Figure 1. The collective strength of these forces determines the ultimate profit potential of an industry. It ranges from *intense* in industries like tires, metal cans, and steel, where no company earns spectacular returns on investment, to *mild* in industries like oil field services and equipment, soft drinks, and toiletries, where there is room for quite high returns.

In the economists' "perfectly competitive" industry, jockeying for position is unbridled and entry to the industry very easy. This kind of industry structure, of course, offers the worst prospect for long-run profitability. The weaker the forces collectively, however, the greater the opportunity for superior performance.

Whatever their collective strength, the corporate strategist's goal is to find a position in the industry where his or her company can best defend itself against these forces or can influence them in its favor. The collective strength of the forces may be painfully apparent to all the antagonists; but to cope with them, the strategist must delve below the surface and analyze the sources of each. For example, what makes the industry vulnerable to entry? What determines the bargaining powers of suppliers?

Knowledge of these underlying sources of competitive pressure provides the groundwork for a strategic agenda of action. They highlight the critical strengths and weaknesses of the company, animate the positioning of the company in its industry, clarify the areas where strategic changes may yield the greatest payoff, and highlight the places where industry trends promise to hold the greatest significance as either opportunities or threats. Understanding these sources also proves to be of help in considering areas for diversification.

CONTENDING FORCES

The strongest competitive force or forces determine the profitability of an industry and so are of greatest importance in strategy formulation. For example, even a company with a strong position in an industry unthreatened by potential entrants will earn low returns if it faces a superior or lower-cost substitute product—as the leading manufacturers of vacuum tubes and coffee percolators have learned to their sorrow. In such a situation, coping with the substitute product becomes the number one strategy priority.

*Originally published in the *Harvard Business Review* (March–April 1979) and winner of the McKinsey prize for the best article in the *Review* in 1979.

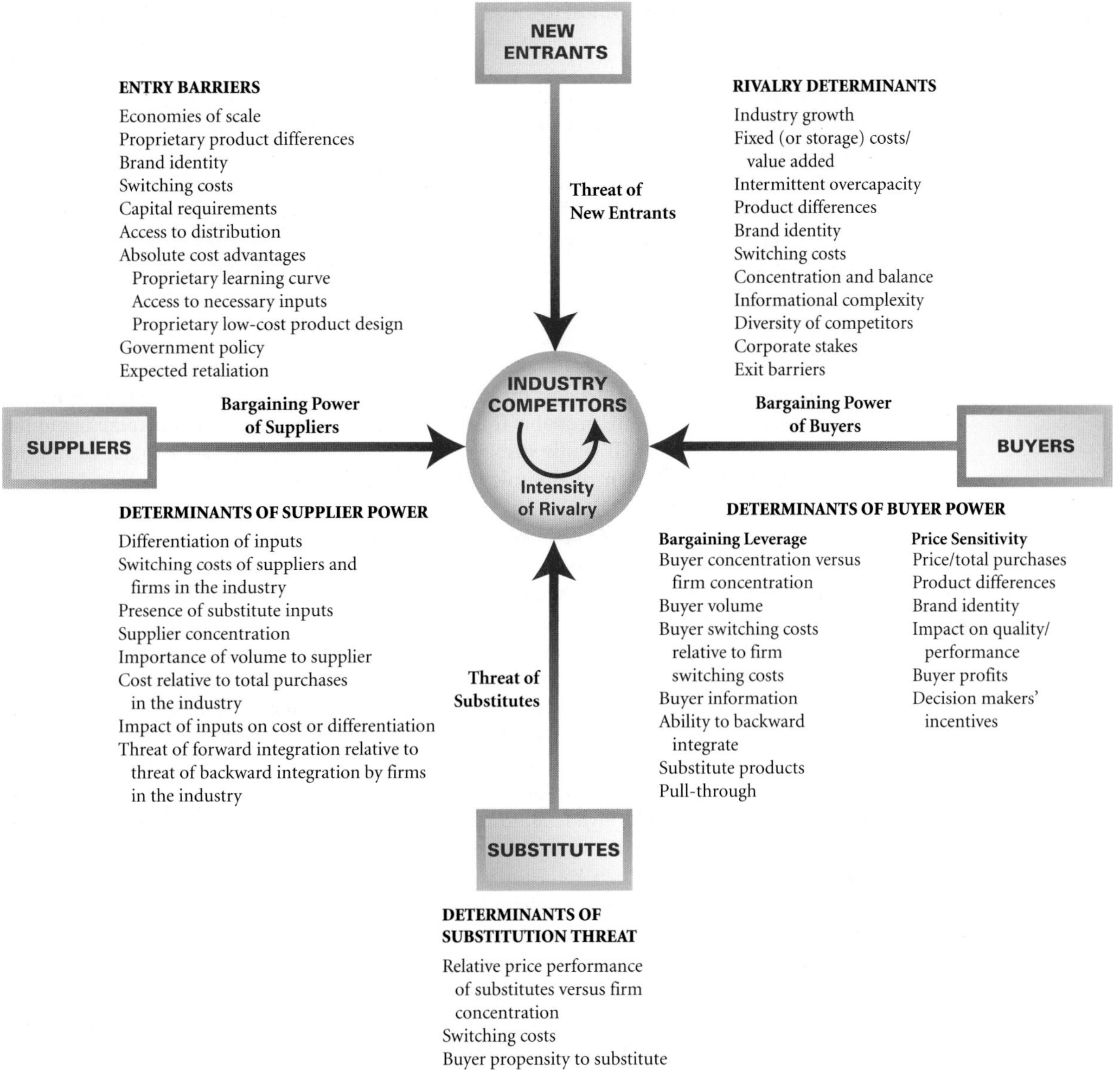

FIGURE 1 ELEMENTS OF INDUSTRY STRUCTURE

Source: Competitive Advantage, Free Press (Porter, M.E. 1985) Fig. 1.2, p.6. Used with the permission ofThe Free Press, a Division of Simon & Schuster, Inc. Copyright © 1985 by Michael Porter. All rights reserved.

Different forces take on prominence, of course, in shaping competition in each industry. In the oceangoing tanker industry the key force is probably the buyers (the major oil companies), while in tires it is powerful OEM buyers coupled with tough competitors. In the steel industry the key forces are foreign competitors and substitute materials.

Every industry has an underlying structure, or a set of fundamental economic and technical characteristics, that gives rise to these competitive forces. The strategist, wanting to position his company to cope best with its industry environment or to influence the environment in the company's favor, must learn what makes the environment tick.

This view of competition pertains equally to industries dealing in services and to those selling products. To avoid monotony in this article, I refer to both products and services as "products." The same general principles apply to all types of business.

A few characteristics are critical to the strength of each competitive force. I shall discuss them in this section.

THREAT OF ENTRY

New entrants to an industry bring new capacity, the desire to gain market share, and often substantial resources. Companies diversifying through acquisition into the industry from other markets often leverage their resources to cause a shakeup, as Philip Morris did with Miller beer.

The seriousness of the threat of entry depends on the barriers present and on the reaction from existing competitors that the entrant can expect. If barriers to entry are high and a newcomer can expect sharp retaliation from the entrenched competitors, obviously he will not pose a serious threat of entering.

There are six major sources of barriers to entry:

1. *Economies of scale*—These economies deter entry by forcing the aspirant either to come in on a large scale or to accept a cost disadvantage. Scale economies in production, research, marketing, and service are probably the key barriers to entry in the mainframe computer industry, as Xerox and GE sadly discovered. Economies of scale can also act as hurdles in distribution, utilization of the sales force, financing, and nearly any other part of a business.
2. *Product differentiation*—Brand identification creates a barrier by forcing entrants to spend heavily to overcome customer loyalty. Advertising, customer service, being first in the industry, and product differences are among the factors fostering brand identification. It is perhaps the most important entry barrier in soft drinks, over-the-counter drugs, cosmetics, investment banking, and public accounting. To create high fences around their businesses, brewers couple brand identification with economies of scale in production, distribution, and marketing.
3. *Capital requirements*—The need to invest large financial resources in order to compete creates a barrier to entry, particularly if the capital is required for unrecoverable expenditures in upfront advertising or R&D. Capital is necessary not only for fixed facilities but also for customer credit, inventories, and absorbing start-up losses. While major corporations have the financial resources to invade almost any industry, the huge capital requirements in certain fields, such as computer manufacturing and mineral extraction, limit the pool of likely entrants.
4. *Cost disadvantages independent of size*—Entrenched companies may have cost advantages not available to potential rivals, no matter what their size and attainable economies of scale. These advantages can stem from the effects of the learning curve (and of its first cousin, the experience curve), proprietary technology, access to the best raw materials sources, assets purchased at preinflation prices, government subsidies, or favorable locations. Sometimes cost advantages are legally enforceable, as they are through patents. . . .
5. *Access to distribution channels*—The new boy on the block must, of course, secure distribution of his product or service. A new food product, for example, must displace others from the supermarket shelf via price breaks, promotions, intense selling efforts, or some other means. The more limited the wholesale or retail channels are and the more that existing competitors have these tied up, obviously the tougher that entry into the industry will be. Sometimes this barrier is so high that, to surmount it, a new contestant must create its own distribution channels, as Timex did in the watch industry in the 1950s.
6. *Government policy*—The government can limit or even foreclose industries with such controls as license requirements and limits on access to raw materials. Regulated industries like trucking, liquor retailing, and freight forwarding are noticeable examples; more subtle government restrictions operate in fields like ski-area development and coal mining. The government also can play a major indirect role by affecting entry barriers through controls such as air and water pollution standards and safety regulations.

The potential rival's expectations about the reaction of existing competitors also will influence its decision on whether to enter. The company is likely to have second thoughts if incumbents have previously lashed out at new entrants or if:

- The incumbents possess substantial resources to fight back, including excess cash and unused borrowing power, productive capacity, or clout with distribution channels and customers.

- The incumbents seem likely to cut prices because of a desire to keep market shares or because of industrywide excess capacity.
- Industry growth is slow, affecting its ability to absorb the new arrival and probably causing the financial performance of all the parties involved to decline.

Changing Conditions

From a strategic standpoint there are two important additional points to note about the threat of entry.

First, it changes, of course, as these conditions change. The expiration of Polaroid's basic patents on instant photography, for instance, greatly reduced its absolute cost entry barrier built by proprietary technology. It is not surprising that Kodak plunged into the market. Product differentiation in printing has all but disappeared. Conversely, in the auto industry economies of scale increased enormously with post-World War II automation and vertical integration—virtually stopping successful new entry.

Second, strategic decisions involving a large segment of an industry can have a major impact on the conditions determining the threat of entry. For example, the actions of many U.S. wine producers in the 1960s to step up product introductions, raise advertising levels, and expand distribution nationally surely strengthened the entry roadblocks by raising economies of scale and making access to distribution channels more difficult. Similarly, decisions by members of the recreational vehicle industry to vertically integrate in order to lower costs have greatly increased the economies of scale and raised the capital cost barriers.

POWERFUL SUPPLIERS AND BUYERS

Suppliers can exert bargaining power on participants in an industry by raising prices or reducing the quality of purchased goods and services. Powerful suppliers can thereby squeeze profitability out of an industry unable to recover cost increases in its own prices. By raising their prices, soft drink concentrate producers have contributed to the erosion of profitability of bottling companies because the bottlers, facing intense competition from powdered mixes, fruit drinks, and other beverages, have limited freedom to raise *their* prices accordingly. Customers likewise can force down prices, demand higher quality or more service, and play competitors off against each other—all at the expense of industry profits.

The power of each important supplier or buyer group depends on a number of characteristics of its market situation and on the relative importance of its sales or purchases to the industry compared with its overall business.

A *supplier* group is powerful if:

- It is dominated by a few companies and is more concentrated than the industry it sells to.
- Its product is unique or at least differentiated, or if it has built up switching costs. Switching costs are fixed costs buyers face in changing suppliers. These arise because, among other things, a buyer's product specifications tie it to particular suppliers, it has invested heavily in specialized ancillary equipment or in learning how to operate a supplier's equipment (as in computer software), or its production lines are connected to the supplier's manufacturing facilities (as in some manufacture of beverage containers).
- It is not obliged to contend with other products for sale to the industry. For instance, the competition between the steel companies and the aluminum companies to sell to the can industry checks the power of each supplier.
- It poses a credible threat of integrating forward into the industry's business. This provides a check against the industry's ability to improve the terms on which it purchases.
- The industry is not an important customer of the supplier group. If the industry *is* an important customer, suppliers' fortunes will be closely tied to the industry, and they will want to protect the industry through reasonable pricing and assistance in activities like R&D and lobbying.

A *buyer* group is powerful if:

- It is concentrated or purchases in large volumes. Large-volume buyers are particularly potent forces if heavy fixed costs characterize the industry—as they do in mental containers, corn refining, and bulk chemicals, for example—which raise the stakes to keep capacity filled.

- The products it purchases from the industry are standard or undifferentiated. The buyers, sure that they can always find alternative suppliers, may play one company against another, as they do in aluminum extrusion.
- The products it purchases from the industry form a component of its product and represent a significant fraction of its cost. The buyers are likely to shop for a favorable price and purchase selectively. Where the product sold by the industry in question is a small fraction of buyers' costs, buyers are usually much less price sensitive.
- It earns low profits, which create great incentive to lower its purchasing costs. Highly profitable buyers, however, are generally less price sensitive (that is, of course, if the item does not represent a large fraction of their costs).
- The industry's product is unimportant to the quality of the buyers' products or services. Where the quality of the buyers' products is very much affected by the industry's product, buyers are generally less price sensitive. Industries in which this situation exists include oil field equipment, where a malfunction can lead to large losses, and enclosures for electronic medical and test instruments, where the quality of the enclosure can influence the user's impression about the quality of the equipment inside.
- The industry's product does not save the buyer money. Where the industry's product or service can pay for itself many times over, the buyer is rarely price sensitive; rather, he is interested in quality. This is true in services like investment banking and public accounting, where errors in judgment can be costly and embarrassing, and in businesses like the logging of oil wells, where an accurate survey can save thousands of dollars in drilling costs.
- The buyers pose a credible threat of integrating backward to make the industry's product. The Big Three auto producers and major buyers of cars have often used the threat of self-manufacture as a bargaining lever. But sometimes an industry engenders a threat to buyers that its members may integrate forward.

Most of these sources of buyer power can be attributed to consumers as a group as well as to industrial and commercial buyers; only a modification of the frame of reference is necessary. Consumers tend to be more price sensitive if they are purchasing products that are undifferentiated, expensive relative to their incomes, and of a sort where quality is not particularly important.

The buying power of retailers is determined by the same rules, with one important addition. Retailers can gain significant bargaining power over manufacturers when they can influence consumers' purchasing decisions, as they do in audio components, jewelry, appliances, sporting goods, and other goods.

Strategic Action

A company's choice of suppliers to buy from or buyer groups to sell to should be viewed as crucial strategic decisions. A company can improve its strategic posture by finding suppliers or buyers who possess the least power to influence it adversely.

Most common is the situation of a company being able to choose whom it will sell to—in other words, buyer selection. Rarely do all the buyer groups a company sells to enjoy equal power. Even if a company sells to a single industry, segments usually exist within that industry that exercise less power (and that are therefore less price sensitive) than others. For example, the replacement market for most products is less price sensitive than the overall market.

As a rule, a company can sell to powerful buyers and still come away with above-average profitability only if it is a low-cost producer in its industry or if its product enjoys some unusual, if not unique, features. In supplying large customers with electric motors, Emerson Electric earns high returns because its low-cost position permits the company to meet or undercut competitors' prices.

If the company lacks a low-cost position or a unique product, selling to everyone is self-defeating because the more sales it achieves, the more vulnerable it becomes. The company may have to muster the courage to turn away business and sell only to less potent customers.

Buyer selection has been a key to the success of National Can and Crown Cork & Seal. They focus on the segments of the can industry where they can create product differentiation, minimize the threat of backward integration, and otherwise mitigate the awesome power of their customers. Of course, some industries do not enjoy the luxury of selecting "good" buyers.

As the factors creating supplier and buyer power change with time or as a result of a company's strategic decisions, naturally the power of these groups rises or declines. In the ready-to-wear clothing industry, as the buyers (department stores and clothing stores) have become more concentrated and control has passed to large chains, the industry has come under increasing pressure and suffered falling margins. The industry has been unable to differentiate its product or engender switching costs that lock in its buyers enough to neutralize these trends.

SUBSTITUTE PRODUCTS

By placing a ceiling on prices that can be charged, substitute products or services limit the potential of an industry. Unless it can upgrade the quality of the product or differentiate it somehow (as via marketing), the industry will suffer in earnings and possibly in growth.

Manifestly, the more attractive the price–performance trade-off offered by substitute products, the firmer the lid placed on the industry's profit potential. Sugar producers confronted with the large-scale commercialization of high-fructose corn syrup, a sugar substitute, are learning this lesson today.

Substitutes not only limit profits in normal times; they also reduce the bonanza an industry can reap in boom times. In 1978 the producers of fiberglass insulation enjoyed unprecedented demand as a result of high energy costs and severe winter weather. But the industry's ability to raise prices were tempered by the plethora of insulation substitutes, including cellulose, rock wool, and styrofoam. These substitutes are bound to become an even stronger force once the current round of plant additions by fiberglass insulation producers has boosted capacity enough to meet demand (and then some).

Substitute products that deserve the most attention strategically are those that (1) are subject to trends improving their price–performance trade-off with the industry's product, or (2) are produced by industries earning high profits. Substitutes often come rapidly into play if some development increases competition in their industries and causes price reduction or performance improvement.

JOCKEYING FOR POSITION

Rivalry among existing competitors takes the familiar form of jockeying for position—using tactics like price competition, product introduction, and advertising slugfests. Intense rivalry is related to the presence of a number of factors:

- Competitors are numerous or are roughly equal in size and power. In many U.S. industries in recent years foreign contenders, of course, have become part of the competitive picture.
- Industry growth is slow, precipitating fights for market share that involve expansion-minded members.
- The product or service lacks differentiation or switching costs, which lock in buyers and protect one combatant from raids on its customers by another.
- Fixed costs are high or the product is perishable, creating a strong temptation to cut prices. Many basic materials businesses, like paper and aluminum, suffer from this problem when demand slackens.
- Capacity is normally augmented in large increments. Such additions, as in the chlorine and vinyl chloride businesses, disrupt the industry's supply–demand balance and often lead to periods of overcapacity and price cutting.
- Exit barriers are high. Exit barriers, like very specialized assets or management's loyalty to a particular business, keep companies competing even though they may be earning low or even negative returns on investment. Excess capacity remains functioning, and the profitability of the healthy competitors suffers as the sick ones hang on. If the entire industry suffers from overcapacity, it may seek government help—particularly if foreign competition is present.
- The rivals are diverse in strategies, origins, and "personalities." They have different ideas about how to compete and continually run head on into each other in the process. . . .

While a company must live with many of these factors—because they are built into industry economics—it may have some latitude for improving matters through strategic shifts. For example, it may try to raise buyers' switching costs or increase product differentiation. A focus on selling efforts in the fastest-growing segments of the industry or on market areas with the lowest fixed costs can reduce the impact of industry rivalry. If it is feasible, a company can try to avoid confrontation with competitors having high exit barriers and can thus sidestep involvement in bitter price cutting.

FORMULATION OF STRATEGY

Once the corporate strategist has assessed the forces affecting competition in his industry and their underlying causes, he can identify his company's strengths and weaknesses. The crucial strengths and weaknesses from a strategic standpoint are the company's posture vis-à-vis the underlying causes of each force. Where does it stand against substitutes? Against the sources of entry barriers?

Then the strategist can devise a plan of action that may include (1) positioning the company so that its capabilities provide the best defense against the competitive force; and/or (2) influencing the balance of the forces through strategic moves, thereby improving the company's position; and/or (3) anticipating shifts in the factors underlying the forces and responding to them, with the hope of exploiting change by choosing a strategy appropriate for the new competitive balance before opponents recognize it. I shall consider each strategic approach in turn.

POSITIONING THE COMPANY

The first approach takes the structure of the industry as given and matches the company's strengths and weaknesses to it. Strategy can be viewed as building defenses against the competitive forces or as finding positions in the industry where the forces are weakest.

Knowledge of the company's capabilities and of the causes of the competitive forces will highlight the areas where the company should confront competition and where avoid it. If the company is a low-cost producer, it may choose to confront powerful buyers while it takes care to sell them only products not vulnerable to competition from substitutes. . . .

INFLUENCING THE BALANCE

When dealing with the forces that drive industry competition, a company can devise a strategy that takes the offensive. This posture is designed to do more than merely cope with the forces themselves; it is meant to alter their causes.

Innovations in marketing can raise brand identification or otherwise differentiate the product. Capital investments in large-scale facilities or vertical integration affect entry barriers. The balance of forces is partly a result of external factors and partly in the company's control.

EXPLOITING INDUSTRY CHANGE

Industry evolution is important strategically because evolution, of course, brings with it changes in the sources of competition I have identified. In the familiar product life-cycle pattern, for example, growth rates change, product differentiation is said to decline as the business becomes more mature, and the companies tend to integrate vertically.

These trends are not so important in themselves; what is critical is whether they affect the sources of competition. . . .

Obviously, the trends carrying the highest priority from a strategic standpoint are those that affect the most important sources of competition in the industry and those that elevate new causes to the forefront. . . .

The framework for analyzing competition that I have described can also be used to predict the eventual profitability of an industry. In long-range planning the task is to examine each competitive force, forecast the magnitude of each underlying cause, and then construct a composite picture of the likely profit potential of the industry. . . .

The key to growth—even survival—is to stake out a position that is less vulnerable to attack from head-to-head opponents, whether established or new, and less vulnerable to erosion from the direction of buyers, suppliers, and substitute goods. Establishing such a position can take many forms—solidifying relationships with favorable customers, differentiating the product either substantively or psychologically through marketing, integrating forward or backward, establishing technological leadership.

READING 4.2

Looking Inside for Competitive Advantage* BY JAY B. BARNEY

The history of strategic management research can be understood as an attempt to "fill in the blanks" created by the SWOT framework; i.e., to move beyond suggesting that strengths, weaknesses, opportunities, and threats are important for understanding competitive advantage to suggest models and frameworks that can be used to analyze and evaluate these phenomena. Michael Porter (1980, 1985) and his associates have developed a number of these models and frameworks for analyzing environmental opportunities and threats. Porter's work on the "five-forces model," the relationship between industry structure and strategic opportunities, and strategic groups can all be understood as an effort to unpack the concepts of environmental opportunities and threats in a theoretically rigorous, yet highly applicable way.

However, the SWOT framework tells us that environmental analysis—no matter how rigorous—is only half the story. A complete understanding of sources of competitive advantage requires the analysis of a firm's internal strengths and weaknesses as well. The importance of integrating internal with environmental analyses can be seen when evaluating the sources of competitive advantage of many firms. Consider, for example,

- WalMart, a firm that has, for the last twenty years, consistently earned a return on sales twice the average of its industry;
- Southwest Airlines, a firm whose profits continued to increase, despite losses at other U.S. airlines that totaled almost $10 billion from 1990 to 1993; and
- Nucor Steel, a firm whose stock price continued to soar through the 1980s and 1990s, despite the fact that the market value of most steel companies has remained flat or fallen during the same time period.

These firms, and many others, have all gained competitive advantages—despite the unattractive, high-threat, low-opportunity environments within which they operate. Even the most careful and complete analysis of these firms' competitive environments cannot, by itself, explain their success. Such explanations must also include these firms' internal attributes—their strengths and weaknesses—as sources of competitive advantage. Following more recent practice, internal attributes will be referred to as *resources* and *capabilities* throughout the following discussion.

A firm's resources and capabilities include all of the financial, physical, human, and organizational assets used by a firm to develop, manufacture, and deliver products or services to its customers. Financial resources include debt, equity, retained earnings, and so forth. Physical resources include the machines, manufacturing facilities, and buildings firms use in their operations. Human resources include all the experience, knowledge, judgment, risk-taking propensity, and wisdom of individuals associated with a firm. Organizational resources include the history, relationships, trust, and organizational culture that are attributes of groups of individuals associated with a firm, along with a firm's formal reporting structure, explicit management control systems, and compensation policies.

In the process of filling in the "internal blanks" created by SWOT analysis, managers must address four important questions about their resources and capabilities: (1) the question of value, (2) the question of rareness, (3) the question of imitability, and (4) the question of organization.

THE QUESTION OF VALUE

To begin evaluating the competitive implications of a firm's resources and capabilities, managers must first answer the question of value: Do a firm's resources and capabilities add value by enabling it to exploit opportunities and/or neutralize threats?

*Reprinted with deletions from "Looking Inside for Competitive Advantage," Jay B. Barney, *Academy of Management Executive*, 1995, Vol. 9(4), 49–61.

The answer to this question, for some firms, has been yes. Sony, for example, has a great deal of experience in designing, manufacturing, and selling miniaturized electronic technology. Sony has used these resources to exploit numerous market opportunities, including portable tape players, portable disc players, portable televisions, and easy-to-hold 8 mm video cameras. . . .

Unfortunately, for other firms, the answer to the question of value has been no. . . . Sears was unable to recognize or respond to changes in the retail market that had been created by WalMart and specialty retail stores. In a sense, Sears's historical success, along with a commitment to stick with a traditional way of doing things, led it to miss some significant market opportunities.

Although a firm's resources and capabilities may have added value in the past, changes in customer tastes, industry structure, or technology can render them less valuable in the future. General Electric's capabilities in transistor manufacturing became much less valuable when semiconductors were invented. . . .

Some environmental changes are so significant that few, if any, of a firm's resources remain valuable in any environmental context. However, this kind of radical environmental change is unusual. More commonly, changes in a firm's environment may reduce the value of a firm's resources in their current use, while leaving the value of those resources in other uses unchanged. . . .

Numerous firms have weathered these environmental shifts by finding new ways to apply their traditional strengths. AT&T had developed a reputation for providing high-quality long distance telephone service. It moved rapidly to exploit this reputation in the newly competitive long distance market by aggressively marketing its services against MCI, Sprint, and other carriers. . . .

By answering the question of value, managers link the analysis of internal resources and capabilities with the analysis of environmental opportunities and threats. A firm's resources are not valuable in a vacuum, but rather are valuable only when they exploit opportunities and/or neutralize threats. The models developed by Porter and his associates can be used to isolate potential opportunities and threats that the resources a firm controls can exploit or neutralize. . . .

THE QUESTION OF RARENESS

That a firm's resources and capabilities are valuable is an important first consideration in understanding internal sources of competitive advantage. However, if a particular resource and capability is controlled by numerous competing firms, then that resource is unlikely to be a source of competitive advantage for any one of them. Instead, valuable but common (i.e., not rare) resources and capabilities are sources of competitive parity. For managers evaluating the competitive implications of their resources and capabilities, these observations lead to the second critical issue: How many competing firms already possess these valuable resources and capabilities? . . .

While resources and capabilities must be rare among competing firms in order to be a source of competitive advantage, this does not mean that common, but valuable, resources are not important. Indeed, such resources and capabilities may be essential for a firm's survival. On the other hand, if a firm's resources are valuable and rare, those resources may enable a firm to gain at least a temporary competitive advantage. WalMart's skills in developing and using point-of-purchase data collection to control inventory have given it a competitive advantage over K-Mart, a firm that until recently has not had access to this timely information. . . .

THE QUESTION OF IMITABILITY

A firm that possesses valuable and rare resources and capabilities can gain, at least, a temporary competitive advantage. If, in addition, competing firms face a cost disadvantage in imitating these resources and capabilities, firms with these special abilities can obtain a sustained competitive advantage. These observations lead to the questions of imitability: Do firms without a resource or capability face a cost disadvantage in obtaining it compared to firms that already possess it?

Obviously, imitation is critical to understanding the ability of resources and capabilities to generate sustained competitive advantages. Imitation can occur in at least two ways: duplication and substitution. Duplication occurs when an imitating firm builds the same kinds of resources as the firm it is imitating. If one firm has a competitive advantage because of its research and development skills, then a duplicating firm will try to imitate that resource by developing its own research and development skills. In addition, firms may be able to substitute some resources for other resources. If these substitute resources have the same strategic implications and are no more costly to develop, then imitation through substitution will lead to competitive parity in the long run. . . .

As firms evolve, they pick up skills, abilities, and resources that are unique to them, reflecting their particular path through history. These resources and capabilities reflect the unique personalities, experiences, and relationships that exist in only a single firm. . . .

[Consider] The Mailbox, Inc., a very successful firm in the bulk mailing business in the Dallas–Ft. Worth market. If there was ever a business where it seems unlikely that a firm would have a sustained competitive advantage, it is bulk mailing. Firms in this industry gather mail from customers, sort it by postal code, and then take it to the post office to be mailed. Where is the competitive advantage here? And yet, The Mailbox has enjoyed an enormous market share advantage in the Dallas–Ft. Worth area for several years. Why?

When asked, managers at The Mailbox have a difficult time describing the sources of their sustained advantages. Indeed, they can point to *no* "Big Decisions" they have made to generate this advantage. However, as these managers begin to discuss their firm, what becomes clear is that their success does not depend on doing a few big things right, but on doing lots of little things right. The way they manage accounting, finance, human resources, production, or other business functions, separately, is not exceptional. However, to manage all these functions so well, and so consistently over time is truly exceptional. Firms seeking to compete against The Mailbox will not have to imitate just a few internal attributes; they will have to imitate thousands, or even hundreds of thousands of such attributes—a daunting task indeed.

[Another] reason that firms may be at a cost disadvantage in imitating resources and capabilities is that these resources may be socially complex. Some physical resources (e.g., computers, robots, and other machines) controlled by firms are very complex. However, firms seeking to imitate these physical resources need only purchase them, take them apart, and duplicate the technology in question. With just a couple of exceptions (including the pharmaceutical and specialty chemicals industries), patents provide little protection from the imitation of a firm's physical resources. On the other hand, socially complex resources and capabilities—organizational phenomena like reputation, trust, friendship, teamwork and culture—while not patentable, are much more difficult to imitate. Imagine the difficulty of imitating Hewlett-Packard's (HP) powerful and enabling culture. . . .

THE QUESTION OF ORGANIZATION

A firm's competitive advantage potential depends on the value, rareness, and imitability of its resources and capabilities. However, to fully realize this potential, a firm must also be organized to exploit its resources and capabilities. These observations lead to the question of organization: Is a firm organized to exploit the full competitive potential of its resources and capabilities?

Numerous components of a firm's organization are relevant when answering the question of organization, including its formal reporting structure, its explicit management control systems, and its compensation policies. These components are referred to as *complementary resources* because they have limited ability to generate competitive advantage in isolation. However, in combination with other resources and capabilities, they can enable a firm to realize its full competitive advantage.

. . . WalMart's continuing competitive advantage in the discount retailing industry can be attributed to its early entry into rural markets in the southern United States. However, to fully exploit this geographic advantage, WalMart needed to implement appropriate reporting structures, control systems, and compensation policies. We have already seen that one of these components of WalMart's organization—its point-of-purchase inventory control system—is being imitated by K-Mart, and thus, by itself, is not likely to be a source of sustained competitive advantage. However, this inventory control system has enabled WalMart to take full advantage of its rural locations by decreasing the probability of stockouts and by reducing inventory costs. . . .

THE MANAGEMENT CHALLENGE

In the end, this discussion reminds us that sustained competitive advantage cannot be created simply by evaluating environmental opportunities and threats, and then conducting business only in high-opportunity, low-threat environments. Rather, creating sustained competitive advantage depends on the unique resources and capabilities that a firm brings to competition in its environment. To discover these resources and capabilities, managers must look inside their firm for valuable, rare, and costly-to-imitate resources, and then exploit these resources through their organization.

READING 4.3

Sustaining Superior Performance: Commitments and Capabilities* BY PANKAJ GHEMAWAT AND GARY PISANO

. . .A competitive advantage is generally necessary for sustained superior performance. But experience suggests that it is far from sufficient. . . .

THREATS TO SUSTAINABILITY

A superior product market position is likely to yield sustained superior performance to the extent that it satisfies two conditions: *scarcity* and *appropriability*. The importance of scarcity in this context can be highlighted with the air *versus* diamond example beloved by economists. Why is the air in your lungs worth less, at market prices, than the gemstone that may be on your finger? Part of the reason is that less cost is incurred in transforming the air in the atmosphere into something that you are willing to breathe than in transforming a diamond in the rough into something that you are willing to wear. But this cost differential is not the only element of the difference in prices. Differential scarcity also takes a hand. Breathable air is available in such abundant quantities that it has virtually no scarcity value in most locations. Gem-quality diamonds are clearly much scarcer. The implied difference in scarcity values accounts for most of the sustained difference in the prices that air and diamonds can command.

To test whether a strategic position or option offers sustainable scarcity value, it is useful to ask two kinds of questions. The first question is why scarcity won't induce competitors, actual or potential, to copy the superior position: this is the threat of *imitation*. The second question is whether competitors, even if they are unable to attack scarcity value directly, won't be able to find a way around it: this is the threat of *substitution*.

The second condition for sustainability, appropriability, is of distinct interest because even when an organization can count on sustained scarcity value, the ability of its owners to pocket that value cannot be taken for granted. Nonowners out to further their own interests may be able to siphon off some of that value: this is the threat of *holdup*. They, particularly employees, may also squander some of it: this is the threat of *slack*. In other words, holdup threatens to divert scarcity value and slack to dissipate it.

All four threats to sustainability—imitation, substitution, holdup, and slack—have two things in common: the intensity of each tends to increase with the amount of (positioning) value generated, and each tends to take time to make its effects felt. They will be elaborated and illustrated in detail one at a time, beginning with threats external to the organization and working in.

*Reprinted with deletions from P. Ghemawat and G. Pisano, "Sustaining Superior Performance: Commitments and Capabilities," Harvard Business School Note: 9-798-008, July 31, 1997.

IMITATION

Imitation is the most direct and obvious threat to sustainability. According to the cross-sectional evidence, imitation is endemic. In capacity-driven industries, an addition by one player usually triggers additions by others aimed at preserving their capacity shares. . . .

The most obvious way of analyzing the threat of imitation (as well as the other threats to sustainability discussed in this note) is to figure out which players will be most affected by the organization's strategic choice, assess their likely responses, and, to the extent that those responses appear threatening, think about how they can be thwarted or blunted. . . .

When the number of competitors to be considered is [large], or when the analysis focuses on the long run, it makes . . . sense to look for impediments to imitation. . . . Such impediments are usually categorized as different types of *early-mover advantages*. There seem to be five principal forms of early-mover advantages [based on earlier work by Ghemawat and Teece (ed.), 1987].

Private Information. One possible reason for moving early is better information. To the extent that this information can be kept private—to the extent that it is costly for would-be imitators to tap into it—imitation will be inhibited. Privacy is most likely obtained when information is tacit rather than specifiable (i.e., doesn't lend itself to blueprinting), and when no one party can carry it out of the organization.

Size Economies. Size economies refer to the (possible) advantages of being large. They come in three different varieties: scale economies, which are the advantages of being large in a particular business at a particular point in time; learning economies, which are the advantages of being large in a particular business over time; and scope economies, which are the advantages of being large across interrelated businesses. If there are size economies, the early mover may be able to deter imitation by committing itself to exploiting them. That possibility depends on the would-be imitator's fear that if it tried to match the early mover's size, supply might exceed demand by enough to make it rue the effort.

Enforceable Contracts/Relationships. Early movers may be able to enter contracts or establish relationships on better terms than those available to late movers. . . .

Threats of Retaliation. There are a number of reasons . . . why early movers may be able to deter imitation by threatening massive retaliation. Talk of retaliation is, however, cheap. To be credible, it must be backed up by both the ability and the willingness to retaliate. Retaliatory moves that satisfy both conditions may either be directly profitable or reflect the early mover's demonstrated willingness to be tough with interlopers in spite of the immediate losses to itself.

Response Lags. Even if information isn't impacted, size isn't a source of economies, contracts/relationships aren't enforceable, and retaliation isn't credible, imitation usually requires a minimum time lag. From the early mover's perspective, this can be described as a response lag. . . .The only sensible conclusion about early versus late timing is the one drawn long ago by Alfred P. Sloan: If you are late, you have to be better.

SUBSTITUTION

Scarcity value may be threatened by substitution as well as by imitation: capacity in place may be displaced by newer and better capacity, customer preferences changed in ways that erode established customer bases, and existing know-how improved upon. While they blur into each other at the boundaries, there are two respects in which substitution is less direct a threat to scarcity value than is imitation. First, substitution threats are less likely to be confined to direct competitors. Second, successful substitution involves finding a way around scarcity, not carrying out a direct attack on it. . . .

Substitution threats depend on environmental changes that create enough of a mismatch between established positions and market opportunities to override early-mover advantages. While such changes can take a variety of forms, changes in technology, in demand, and in the availability or prices of inputs seem, in that order, to be the most significant gateways to successful substitution. Note the implication that substitution threats are likely to be most frequent in technology-intensive, fashion-intensive, and other *creative* industries in which the salient sticky factors have short half-lives (i.e. are obsolesced relatively rapidly). . . .

HOLDUP

Even if scarcity value can be preserved from imitation and substitution the ability of the organization to appropriate the proceeds cannot be taken for granted. The possibility of expropriation is a consequence of the gap between ownership and control: there typically is such a gap, and it typically leaves room for self-serving behavior by non-owners. Such behavior can reduce either the owners' share of total scarcity value (holdup) or the total amount of scarcity value available to be divided among them and non-owners (slack), or both. The diversionary threat of holdup will be discussed in this subsection, and the dissipative threat of slack in the next one.

Holdup is a problem in negotiation rather than competition, conventionally defined. Holdup is a threat whenever the perpetuation of a superior competitive position depends on the continued cooperation of complementors. . . .

An example will help make this description more concrete. It concerns the holdup of the owners of National Football League (NFL) franchises in the 1970s and 1980s.* The NFL consists of independently owned franchises that have managed, for the most part, to function as a cartel on the basis of selective antitrust exemptions. Since 1970, the NFL has weathered threats of imitation by the World Football League (WFL) and the United States Football League (USFL), each of which operated less than three seasons. It has withstood substitution threats to sustain much higher broadcast ratings than any other sport. As a result, it managed to sign lucrative multiyear contracts with the three TV networks in 1978 and in 1982, contracts that increased the total revenue available to the average NFL team by 77% in *real* terms between 1970 and 1984. In spite of this winning record, however, the average team's operating income fell by a third between those years. Why?

Holdup by NFL players seems to have been the principal reason for decrease. People of the size, skill, and recklessness necessary to play professional football are obviously specialized resources. The essential complementarity of their services to the scarcity value of football franchises has been evident from the inception of professional football: crowds of 70,000 people. . . .

Recognizing the resultant potential for holdup, the NFL evolved a number of practices to contain it. Players were signed to enforceable multiyear contracts . . . [there were] exclusive rights to draft rookies and restrictions on free agency by veterans [etc.].

SLACK

Slack is the final threat to sustainability that must be taken into account. Slack measures the extent to which the scarcity value realized by the organization falls short of the amount potentially available to it. The conceptual distinction between slack and holdup is that the former shrinks the total size of the pie available to owners and non-owners while the latter shrinks the owners' slice of that pie. . . .

Slack cannot, be definition, be less than zero. An upper bound on it is implicit in the condition that organizations cannot sustain losses indefinitely. As a result, particularly valuable product market positions can be expected to afford the most scope for slack. Or in plainer language, rich diets tend to lead to a hardening of organizational arteries. Estimates of the fraction of revenues dissipated, on average, in this fashion tend to range from 10% to 40% [see, for instance, Caves and Barton, 1990]. These estimates hint at both the significance of slack and the difficulty of measuring it precisely.

[Consider] Xerox's copier business in the 1970s and 1980s. The information assembled . . . indicates that the 1980s marked a period of substantial turnaround for the company. Its managers seem to have achieved these improvements in a number of ways. They . . . establish[ed] targets for improvement and incentives to achieve them. And they reinforced these incentives by trying to create an organizational culture that emphasized quality, responsiveness, and other good things. Xerox's management deserves considerable credit for successful implementation of all these initiatives in the 1980s.

It is also clear, however, that Xerox could not have wrung such significant improvements out of its copier business in the 1980s unless it had accumulated stupendous amounts of slack there in the 1970s. Xerox's own statements about the savings achieved in the 1980s as well as other estimates suggest that by the late 1970s, slack was dissipating at least 20% of the company's sales revenues. . . .

---

*The description that follows is based, in part, on Michael E. Porter, "The NFL vs. the USFL," HBS Case No. 9-386-168.

The suggestion that Xerox squandered much of its birthright in the 1970s is strongly borne out by what happened to its shareholders during the 1970s and early 1980s: the ratio of shareholder enrichment to retained earnings over the 1970s and early 1980s was 2220% for Xerox. . . .

BUILDING SUSTAINABLE COMPETITIVE ADVANTAGES

Multiple, potent threats to sustainability imply that managers cannot afford to take the sustainability of an actual or targeted competitive advantage for granted. Much has been written recently about the roots of sustained superior performance. Most of these contributions can be classified in terms of the debate about whether sustainability is *really* rooted in resources or activities.

The resource-based view seems to have won more adherents in academia. Partly as a result, there is no single authoritative statement of the resource-based view of sustainability. But writers in this tradition tend to flag resources that are *intrinsically inimitable*—resources for which imitation is, in effect, infinitely costly—as companies' crown jewels. Examples include physically unique resources (e.g., the best retail location in town), resources whose imitation is legally infeasible (e.g., patents) and composite resources which may be impossible to imitate because of *causal ambiguity* (the inability to figure out what makes a successful firm tick) or *social complexity* which may place them "beyond the ability of firms to systematically manage and influence" (e.g., corporate culture) [Barney, 1991].

The activity-based approach, in contrast, focuses on the activities that firms perform rather than the resources that they possess. While the activity-based approach has long been employed to analyze competitive positioning, fit among many discrete but interactive activities has recently been proposed as an explanation of sustainability as well, as in Porter's "What Is Strategy?" article [1991]. The basic idea here is that imitation may take longer, cost more, and offer less certain prospects for success when a competitor must be matched along many dimensions rather than just one or two.

We think that both these approaches are useful, especially if they are seen as complementary. Based on the conventional definition of resources as factors that are fixed in the short run, a firm's resource endowment determines the activities that it can perform at any given point in time. Those activities, in turn, are important because it is only with reference to them that competitive advantage or disadvantage can be evaluated.

We also think, however, that both of these approaches—even if taken together—are incomplete, . . . resource-based theorists typically take the firm's resource endowment as given and focus on the short-run deployment of those fixed factors in the product market. And the activity-based approach, while insisting that it may take longer and cost more to match a competitor along many dimensions rather than just one or two, fails to explain, by itself, why strategic innovation, in the sense of constructing an activity system that fits together, is any easier or more profitable than strategic imitation.

Remedying this deficiency seems to require integration and generalization of the resource- and activity-based approaches. . . . Figure 1 provides a simple dynamic framework of this sort in which both history and management matter. The two feedback loops (the dashed lines in the figure) that run from right to left capture the ways in which the activities that a firm performs, and the resource commitments that it makes, affect its future resource endowment or opportunity set. The bold arrows running from left to right indicate that choices about what activities to perform and how to perform them are constrained by resources that can be varied only in the long run. And the first bold arrow that runs from resource endowments to resource commitments also serves as a reminder that the terms on which an organization can make

FIGURE 1
A DYNAMIC VIEW OF THE FIRM

Source: Adapted from Figure 3, Pankaj Ghemawat, "Resources and Strategy: An IO Perspective," Harvard Business School Working Paper (1991), p. 20.

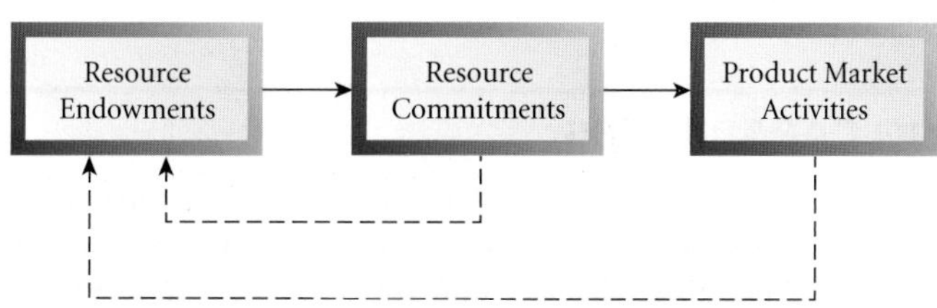

resource commitments depend, in part, on the undepreciated residue of the choices that it has made in the past. . . .

MAKING COMMITMENTS

By commitments, we mean to refer to a few large, lumpy decisions—such as acquiring another company, launching a new product, engaging in a major capacity expansion, and so on—that will have significant and lasting effects on possible future courses of action. The irreversibility of such major decisions or, equivalently, the costs of changing one's mind about them, mandates a deep look into the future. . . .

Irreversibility, not the amount of money involved, is the correct measure of whether a particular decision is commitment-intensive or not. There are three economic indicators of such irreversibility: significant sunk costs, opportunity costs, and time lags. Consider these indicators in turn.

Sunk costs create irreversibility through *lock-in*. When a company sinks a lot of money into resources specialized to a particular course of action that cannot easily be sold off, there is a presumption in favor of continuing to use them. Otherwise, they would be valueless. Boeing's decision to develop the wide-bodied airframe for the 747 provides an example. At some point, the company's net investment in the project considerably exceeded its net worth. As a result, it was sunk unless it could make the plane fly. That meant Boeing was committed to the 747 once it was well into its development. . . .

Opportunity costs create irreversibility through *lock-out*, which is the mirror image of lock-in. Lock-out effects persist because of the difficulty of reactivating dormant resources, reacquiring discarded resources, or recreating lapsed opportunities to deploy particular resources in particular ways. Take, for example, the decision of Reynolds Metals to shut down its alumina refinery at Hurricane Creek, Arkansas, after years of unprofitable operations. This shutdown decision locked Reynolds out of ever using that refinery again—even if aluminum prices were to recover. . . .

The third economic indicator of irreversibility is the *time lag* in altering a firm's endowment of resources. For example, when Coors began to take its beer national in the late 1970s and early 1980s, everyone knew from the outset that the switch from a regional to a national position would require at least the better part of a decade. . . .

The Coors example also illustrates the point that choices of competitive position are themselves commitment-intensive (and therefore strategic) because they typically involve a host of hard-to-reverse commitments to performing particular activities in particular ways. If choices of positioning weren't hard to reverse, a firm could simply try out a particular position and, if it didn't work out, costlessly change it!

Having identified the factors that determine whether a particular decision represents a major commitment, it is time to turn to the ways in which commitments can lead to sustained superior performance. It is convenient to start with the two threats to scarcity, imitation and substitution. The way in which commitments can blunt the threat of imitation is fairly obvious: by staking out particular opportunities through commitments, a company may be able to create sustainable early-mover advantages for itself of the sort that were discussed in the previous section. . . .

The final threat to sustainability, slack, is the one that is the least tightly coupled to the kinds of commitments discussed in this section. While financial commitments (e.g., taking on debt) and other contractual mechanisms can sometimes help reduce slack, many other methods of improving organizational efficiency are hard to interpret in irreversibility-related terms. This is one reason why commitments need not always lead to superior performance: internal organization matters as well.

A second, even more important reason why commitments need not always lead to superior performance stems from uncertainty. In an uncertain world, many commitments fail, which is why commitments can lead to the persistence of inferior as well as superior performance. . . .

DEVELOPING CAPABILITIES

The previous section of this note highlighted how large-scale commitments to appropriate input factors can enable a company to build scarcity and maintain appropriability. Not all commitments, however, are "lumpy." In many cases, firms can build scarcity and maintain appropriability through a series of cumulative smaller-scale investments made over long periods of time. For instance, over many years and hundreds of individual product and process development projects, Intel has accumulated relatively unique knowledge about microprocessor design and manufacturing—knowledge that has proven to be a powerful and durable source of competitive advantage. How should one think about such "capabilities" that are developed incrementally over time?

One way to get a handle on the concept of organization capabilities is to reflect on what organizations do. At any given time, an organization—be it a bank, a biotech firm, or an academic institution—is engaged in a whole set of activities or processes (processing loans, researching drugs, teaching students, etc.) geared toward the development, production, and/or delivery of chosen sets of services and products. An organization's capabilities characterize what activities the organization can undertake within some predictable range of proficiency. . . .

Part of the reason [capabilities can be hard to imitate] seems to be related to private information . . . knowledge that capabilities are based on often seems to be tacit rather than specifiable . . . because it is rooted in detailed and complex organizational processes which, as a bonus, are often hard for competitors to observe. Cumulative learning, particularly localized learning-by-doing, and time lags also seem to play a prominent role in making capabilities hard to imitate. And finally, "metacapabilities" associated with integration, transformation, and reconfiguration may also be subject to similar barriers to imitation, although our understanding of them is, at this point, woefully underdeveloped.*

Of course, imitation is just one of the threats to scarcity: scarcity value can also be eroded through substitution. As with imitation threats, substitution threats cannot be entirely blocked. They can be mitigated, however, through investments in "upstream" or "basic" capabilities that provide a foundation for shifting a firm's product market positions. . . .

Having said as much, we must add that the ability of firms to hedge substitution threats is limited: there is no such thing as an all-purpose capability that will give a firm competitive advantage under all circumstances. . . .

Finally, the competitive advantages afforded by superior capabilities must be resistant to threats of appropriability as well as scarcity if they are to afford a basis for sustained superior performance. Because capabilities are rooted in organizational processes that span many individuals and may link multiple firms, they are less subject to holdup and, arguably, slack than some other types of assets. Where a competitive advantage rests on access to one person or a small group of people, or requires the services of one particular supplier, sustainability will be highly vulnerable to holdup problems. . . .

Summing up across the various threats to sustainability, superior capabilities can indeed support sustained superior performance. But there are several challenges that have to be confronted in making this capability a reality. First of all, the competitive superiority of a capability must be demonstrable: the lack of an objective test along this dimension is likely to lead managers to designate anything the organization does that they care about as one of its core capabilities (or competencies). Unfortunately, many of the characteristics of capabilities that make them potential sources of sustainable competitive advantage also make them hard to benchmark competitively.

Second, given the incremental nature of capability development, firms that seek to develop superior capabilities as the basis of sustainable competitive advantages must prevent the overall coherence of their capability development efforts from being nibbled away, choice by choice, by drop-in-the-bucket biases and the like. Somewhat paradoxically, this makes the choice of which capabilities to develop, and how, a relatively lumpy choice. . . .The similarity becomes less paradoxical when one notes that a capability development thrust has the same lock-in, lock-out, and lag effects associated with conventionally lumpy commitment decisions.

Third, the similarity with lumpy commitment decisions has some of the same awkward effects: specific capabilities also imply specific rigidities that can, in an uncertain world, result in inferior rather than superior performance [see Leonard-Barton, 1992]. In other words, neither capability development nor commitment affords foolproof recipes for success. Instead, careful thinking about strategy reveals what mathematicians call an impossibility theorem: no firm can

---

*For the original discussion that frames these and other issues concerning capabilities, see David J. Teece and Gary P. Pisano, "The Dynamic Capabilities of Firms: an Introduction," *Industrial and Corporate Change* (1994 No. 3), pp. 537–556.

hope to sustain a competitive advantage unless it has superior specialized resources or knowledge. Making commitments or developing firm-specific capabilities is therefore necessary for sustained success but may not be sufficient. This is a sobering note on which to end. Given the evidence on the extent of (un)sustainability, we think that that is appropriate.

READING 4.4

Competitive Maneuvering* BY BRUCE HENDERSON

BRINKMANSHIP IN BUSINESS

A businessman often convinces himself that he is completely logical in his behavior when in fact the critical factor is his emotional bias compared to the emotional bias of his opposition. Unfortunately, some businessmen and students perceive competition as some kind of impersonal, objective, colorless affair, with a company competing against the field as a golfer competes in medal play. A better case can be made that business competition is a major battle in which there are many contenders, each of whom must be dealt with individually. Victory, if achieved, is more often won in the mind of a competitor than in the economic arena.

I shall emphasize two points. The first is that the management of a company must persuade each competitor voluntarily to stop short of a maximum effort to acquire customers and profits. The second point is that persuasion depends on emotional and intuitive factors rather than on analysis or deduction.

The negotiator's skill lies in being as arbitrary as necessary to obtain the best possible compromise without actually destroying the basis for voluntary mutual cooperation of self-restraint. There are some commonsense rules for success in such an endeavor:

1. Be sure that your rival is fully aware of what he can gain if he cooperates and what it will cost him if he does not.
2. Avoid any action which will arouse your competitor's emotions, since it is essential that he behave in a logical, reasonable fashion.
3. Convince your opponent that you are emotionally dedicated to your position and are completely convinced that it is reasonable.

It is worth emphasizing that your competitor is under the maximum handicap if he acts in a completely rational, objective, and logical fashion. For then he will cooperate as long as he thinks he can benefit. In fact, if he is completely logical, he will not forgo the profit of cooperation as long as there is *any* net benefit.

FRIENDLY COMPETITORS

It may strike most businessmen as strange to talk about cooperation with competitors. But it is hard to visualize a situation in which it would be worthwhile to pursue competition to the utter destruction of a competitor. In every case there is a greater advantage to reducing the competition on the condition that the competitor does likewise. Such mutual restraint is cooperation, whether recognized as such or not.

Without cooperation on the part of competitors, there can be no stability. We see this most clearly in international relationships during times of peace. There are constant encroachments and aggressive acts. And the eventual consequence is always either voluntarily imposed self-restraint or mutual destruction. Thus, international diplomacy has only one purpose: to stabilize

*"Brinkmanship in Business" and "The Nonlogical Strategy," in *Henderson on Corporate Strategy* (Cambridge, MA: Abt Books, 1979), pp. 27–33, title selected for this book; section on "Rules for the Strategist" originally at the end of "Brinkmanship in Business" moved to the end of "The Nonlogical Strategy," reprinted by permission of publisher.

cooperation between independent nations on the most favorable basis possible. Diplomacy can be described as the art of being stubborn, arbitrary, and unreasonable without arousing emotional responses.

Businessmen should notice the similarity between economic competition and the peacetime behavior of nations. The object in both cases is to achieve a voluntary, cooperative restraint on the part of otherwise aggressive competitors. Complete elimination of competition is almost inconceivable. The goal of the hottest economic war is an agreement for coexistence, not annihilation. The competition and mutual encroachment do not stop; they go on forever. But they do so under some measure of mutual restraint.

"COLD WAR" TACTICS

A breakdown in negotiations is inevitable if both parties persist in arbitrary positions which are incompatible. Yet there are major areas in business where some degree of arbitrary behavior is essential for protecting a company's self-interest. In effect, a type of brinkmanship is necessary. The term was coined to describe cold war international diplomacy, but it describes a normal pattern in business, too.

In a confrontation between parties who are in part competitors and in part cooperators, deciding what to accept is essentially emotional or arbitrary. Deciding what is attainable requires an evaluation of the other party's degree of intransigence. The purpose is to convince him that you are arbitrary and emotionally committed while trying to discover what he would really accept in settlement. The competitor known to be coldly logical is at a great disadvantage. Logically, he can afford to compromise until there is no advantage left in cooperation. If, instead, he is emotional, irrational, and arbitrary, he has a great advantage.

CONSEQUENCE

The heart of business strategy for a company is to promote attitudes on the part of its competitors that will cause them either to restrain themselves or to act in a fashion which management deems advantageous. In diplomacy and military strategy the key to success is very much the same.

The most easily recognized way of enforcing cooperation is to exhibit obvious willingness to use irresistible or overwhelming force. This requires little strategic skill, but there is the problem of convincing the competing organization that the force will be used without actually resorting to it (which would be expensive and inconvenient).

In industry, however, the available force is usually not overwhelming, although one company may be able to inflict major punishment on another. In the classic case, each party can inflict such punishment on the other. If there were open conflict, then both parties would lose. If they cooperate, both parties are better off, but not necessarily equally so—particularly if one is trying to change the status quo.

When each party can punish the other, the prospects of agreement depend on three things:

1. Each party's willingness to accept the risk of punishment
2. Each party's belief that the other party is willing to accept the risk of punishment
3. The degree of rationality in the behavior of each party

If these conclusions are correct, what can we deduce about how advantages are gained and lost in business competition?

First, management's unwillingness to accept the risk of punishment is almost certain to produce either the punishment or progressively more onerous conditions for cooperation—provided the competition recognized the attitude.

Second, beliefs about a competitor's future behavior or response are all that determine competitive cooperation. In other words, it is the judgment not of actual capability but of probable use of capability that counts.

Third, the less rational or less predictable the behavior of a competitor appears to be, the greater the advantage he possesses in establishing a favorable competitive balance. This advantage is limited only by his need to avoid forcing his competitors into an untenable position or creating an emotional antagonism that will lead them to be unreasonable and irrational (as he is).

THE NONLOGICAL STRATEGY

The goal of strategy in business, diplomacy, and war is to produce a stable relationship favorable to you with the consent of your competitors. By definition, restraint by a competitor is cooperation. Such cooperation from a competitor must seem to be profitable to him. *Any competition which does not eventually eliminate a competitor requires his cooperation to stabilize the situation.* The agreement is usually that of tacit nonaggression; the alternative is death for all but one competitor. A stable competitive situation requires an agreement between competing parties to maintain self-restraint. Such agreement cannot be arrived at by logic. It must be achieved by an emotional balance of forces. This is why it is necessary to appear irrational to competitors. For the same reason, you must seem unreasonable and arbitrary in negotiations with customers and suppliers.

Competition and cooperation go hand in hand in all real-life situations. Otherwise, conflict could only end in extermination of the competitor. There is a point in all situations of conflict where both parties gain more or lose less from peace than they can hope to gain from any foreseeable victory. Beyond that point cooperation is more profitable than conflict. But how will the benefits be shared?

In negotiated conflict situations, the participant who is coldly logical is at a great disadvantage. Logically, he can afford to compromise until there is no advantage left in cooperation. The negotiator/competitor whose behavior is irrational or arbitrary has a great advantage if he can depend upon his opponent being logical and unemotional. The arbitrary or irrational competitor can demand far more than a reasonable share and yet his logical opponent can still gain by compromise rather than breaking off the cooperation.

Absence of monopoly in business requires voluntary restraint of competition. At some point there must be a tactic agreement not to compete. Unless the restraint of trade were acceptable to all competitors, the resulting aggression would inevitably eliminate the less efficient competitors leaving only one. Antitrust laws represent a formal attempt to limit competition. All antimonopoly and fair trade laws constitute restraint of competition.

Utter destruction of a competitor is almost never profitable unless the competitor is unwilling to accept peace. In our daily social contracts, in our international affairs, and in our business affairs, we have far more ability to damage those around us than we ever dare use. Others have the same power to damage us. The implied agreement to restrain our potential aggression is all that stands between us and eventual elimination of one by the other. Both war and diplomacy are mechanisms for establishing or maintaining this self-imposed restraint on all competitors. The conflict continues, but within the implied area of cooperative agreement.

There is a definite limit to the range within which competitors can expect to achieve an equilibrium or negotiate a shift in equilibrium even by implication. Arbitrary, uncooperative, or aggressive attitudes will produce equally emotional reactions. These emotional reactions are in turn the basis for nonlogical and arbitrary responses. Thus, nonlogical behavior is self-limiting.

This is why the art of diplomacy can be described as the ability to be unreasonable without arousing resentment. It is worth remembering that the objective of diplomacy is to include cooperation on terms that are relatively more favorable to you than to your protagonist without actual force being used.

More business victories are won in the minds of competitors than in the laboratory, the factory, or the marketplace. The competitor's conviction that you are emotional, dogmatic, or otherwise nonlogical in your business strategy can be a great asset. This conviction on his part can result in an acceptance of your actions without retaliation, which would otherwise be unthinkable. More important, the anticipation of nonlogical or unrestrained reactions on your part can inhibit his competitive aggression.

RULES FOR THE STRATEGIST

If I were asked to distill the conditions and forces described into advice for the business strategist, I would suggest five rules:

1. You must know as accurately as possible just what your competition has at stake in his contact with you. It is not what you gain or lose, but what he gains or loses that sets the limit on his ability to compromise with you.
2. The less the competition knows about your stakes, the less advantage he has. Without a reference point, he does not even know whether you are being unreasonable.

3. It is absolutely essential to know the character, attitudes, motives, and habitual behavior of a competitor if you wish to have a negotiating advantage.
4. The more arbitrary your demands are, the better your relative competitive position—provided you do not arouse an emotional reaction.
5. The less arbitrary you seem, the more arbitrary you can in fact be.

These rules make up the art of business brinkmanship. They are guidelines for winning a strategic victory in the minds of competitors. Once this victory has been won, it can be converted into a competitive victory in terms of sales volume, costs, and profits.

READING 4.5

Generic Strategies* BY HENRY MINTZBERG

Almost every serious author concerned with "content" issues in strategic management, not to mention strategy consulting "boutiques," has his, her, or its own list of strategies commonly pursued by different organizations. The problem is that these lists almost always either focus narrowly on special types of strategies or aggregate arbitrarily across all varieties of them with no real order.

In 1965, Igor Ansoff proposed a matrix of four strategies which became quite well known—market penetration, product development, market development, and diversification (1965: 109). But this was hardly comprehensive. Fifteen years later, Michael Porter (1980) introduced what became the best-known list of "generic strategies": cost leadership, differentiation, and focus. But the Porter list was also incomplete: while Ansoff focused on *extensions* of business strategy, Porter focused on *identifying* business strategy in the first place.

We believe that families of strategies may be divided into five broad groupings. These are:

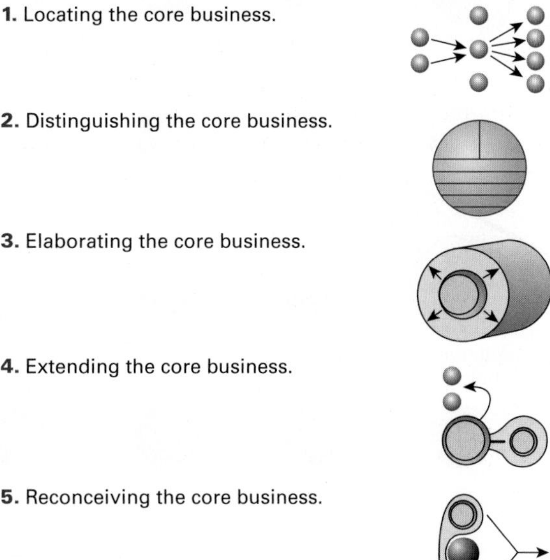

1. Locating the core business.
2. Distinguishing the core business.
3. Elaborating the core business.
4. Extending the core business.
5. Reconceiving the core business.

These five groupings of strategies are presented as a logical hierarchy, although it should be emphasized that strategies do not necessarily develop that way in organizations.

*Abbreviated version prepared for this book of an article by Henry Mintzberg, "Generic Strategies Toward a Comprehensive Framework," originally published in *Advances in Strategic Management*, Vol. 5 (Greenwich, CT: JAI Press, 1988) pp. 1–67.

LOCATING THE CORE BUSINESS

A business can be thought to exist at a junction in a network of industries that take raw materials and through selling to and buying from each other produce various finished products (or services). Figure 1, for example, shows a hypothetical canoe business in such a network. Core location strategies can be described with respect to the stage of the business in the network and the particular industry in question.

STRATEGIES OF STAGE OF OPERATIONS

Traditionally, industries have been categorized as being in the primary (raw materials extraction and conversion), secondary (manufacturing), or tertiary (delivery or other service) stage of operations. More recently, however, state in the "stream" has been the favored form of description:

Upstream Business Strategy

Upstream businesses function close to the raw material. The flow of product tends to be divergent, from a basic material (wood, aluminum) to a variety of uses for it. Upstream business tends to be technology- and capital-intensive rather than people-intensive, and more inclined to search for advantage through low costs than through high margins and to favor sales push over market pull (Galbraith, 1983: 65–66).

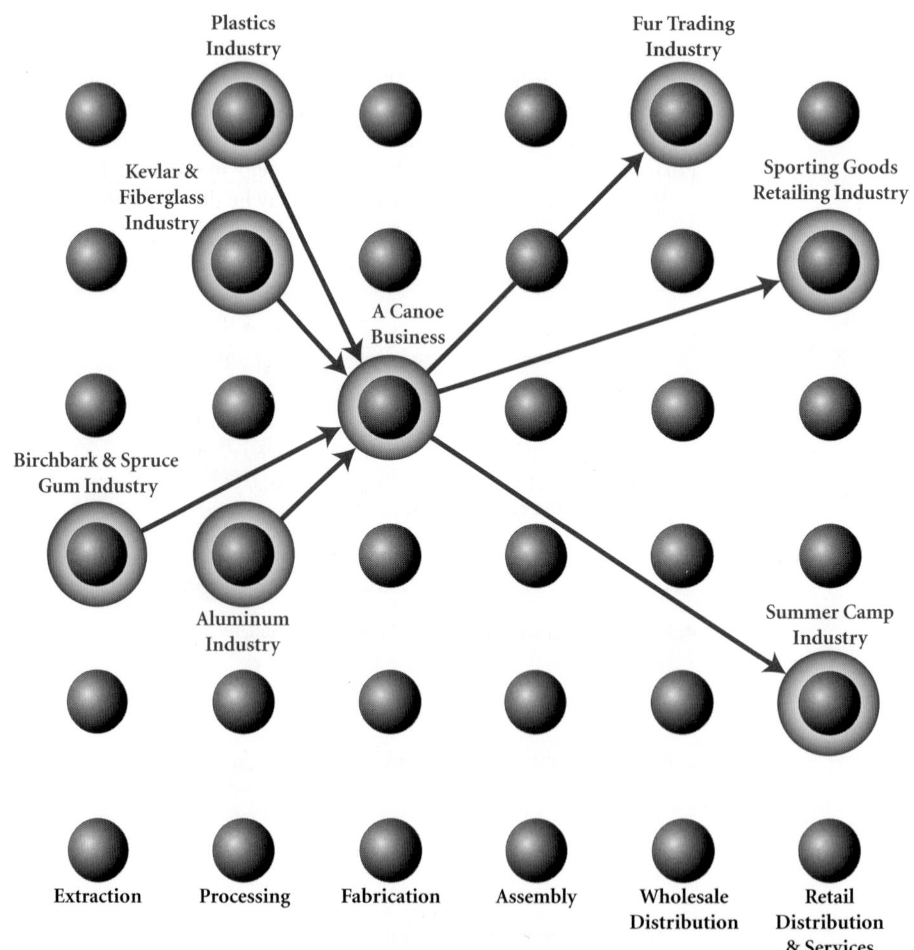

FIGURE 1
LOCATING A CORE BUSINESS AS A JUNCTION IN A NETWORK OF INDUSTRIES

Midstream Business Strategy

Here the organization sits at the neck of an hour-glass, drawing a variety of inputs into a single production process out of which flows the product to a variety of users, much as the canoe business is shown in Figure 1.

Downstream Business Strategy

Here a wide variety of inputs converge into a narrow funnel, as in the many products sold by a department store.

STRATEGIES OF INDUSTRY

Many factors are involved in the identification of an industry, so many that it would be difficult to develop a concise set of generic labels. Moreover, change continually renders the boundaries between "industries" arbitrary. Diverse products get bundled together so that two industries become one, while traditionally bundled products get separated so that one industry becomes two. Economists in government and elsewhere spend a great deal of time trying to pin these things down, via Standard Industrial Classification codes and the like. In effect, they try to fix what strategists try to change: competitive advantage often comes from reconceiving the definition of an industry.

DISTINGUISHING THE CORE BUSINESS

Having located the circle that identifies the core business, the next step is to open it up—to distinguish the characteristics that enable an organization to achieve competitive advantage and so to survive in its own context.

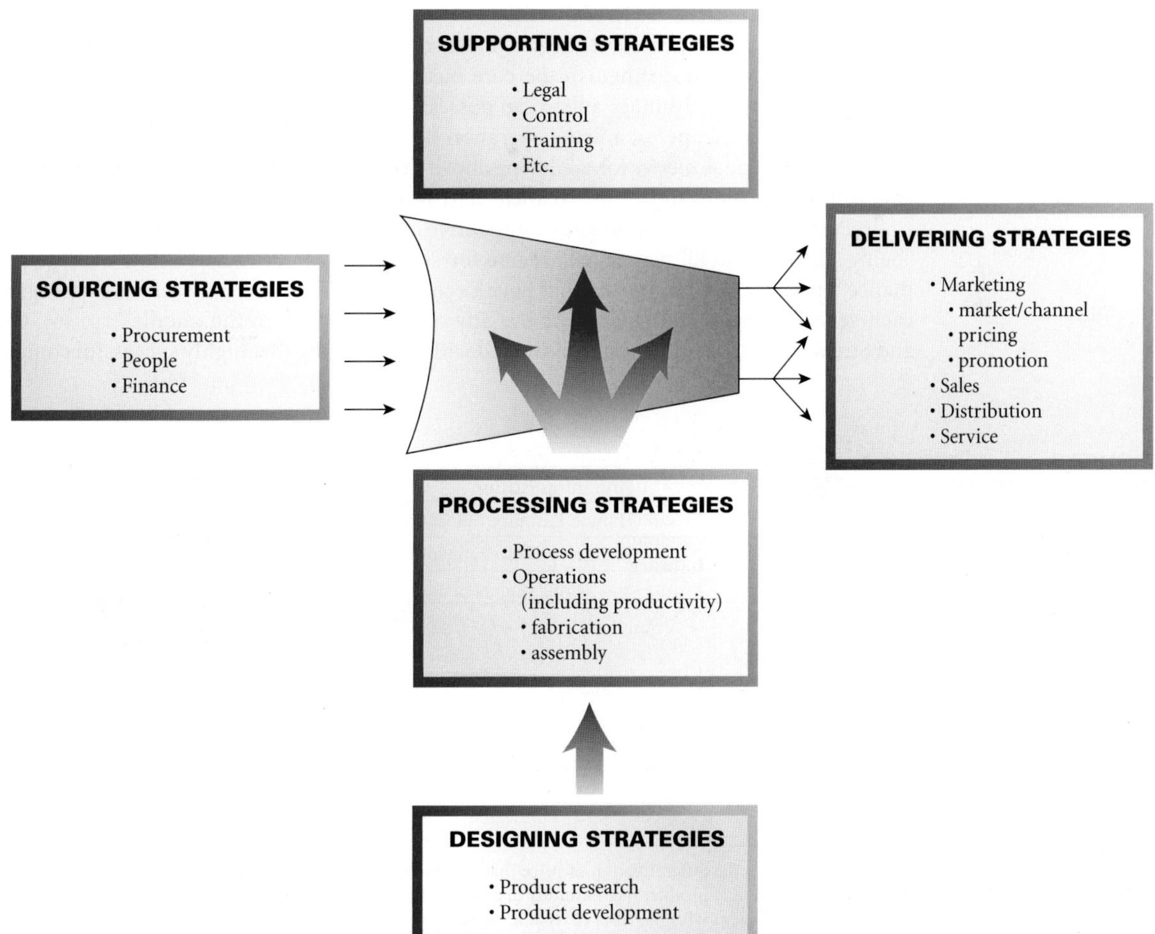

FIGURE 2 FUNCTIONAL AREAS IN SYSTEMS TERMS

THE FUNCTIONAL AREAS

The second level of strategy can encompass a whole host of strategies in the various functional areas. As shown in Figure 2, they may include input "sourcing" strategies, throughput "processing" strategies, and output "delivery" strategies, all reinforced by a set of "supporting" strategies.

It has been popular to describe organizations in this way, especially since Michael Porter built his 1985 book around the "generic value chain," shown in Figure 3. Porter presents it as "a systematic way of examining all the activities a firm performs and how they interact . . . for analyzing the sources of competitive advantage" (1985: 33). Such a chain, and how it performs individual activities, reflects a firm's "history, its strategy, its approach to implementing its strategy, and the underlying economies of the activities themselves" (p. 36). According to Porter,

> "the goal of any generic strategy" is to "create value for buyers" at a profit. Accordingly, the value chain displays total value, and consists of *value activities* and *margin*. Value activities are the physically and technologically distinct activities a firm performs. These are the building blocks by which a firm creates a product valuable to its buyers. Margin is the difference between total value and the collective cost of performing the value activities. . . .

Value activities can be divided into two broad types, *primary* activities and *support* activities. Primary activities, listed along the bottom of Figure 3, are the activities involved in the physical creation of the product and its sale and transfer to the buyer as well as after-sale assistance. In any firm, primary activities can be divided into the five generic categories shown in Figure 3. Support activities support the primary activities and each other by providing purchased inputs, technology, human resources, and various firmwide functions (p. 38).*

PORTER'S GENERIC STRATEGIES

Porter's framework of "generic strategies" has also become quite widely used. In our terms, these constitute strategies to distinguish the core business. Porter believes there are but two "basic types of competitive advantage a firm can possess: low costs or differentiation" (1985: 11). These combine with the "scope" of a firm's operation (the range of market segments targeted) to produce "three *generic strategies* for achieving above-average performance in an industry: cost leadership, differentiation, and focus" (namely, narrow scope), shown in Figure 4.

To Porter, firms that wish to gain competitive advantage must "make a choice" among these: "being 'all things to all people' is a recipe for strategic mediocrity and below-average performance" (p. 12). Or in the words that have become more controversial, "a firm that engages in each generic strategy but fails to achieve any of them is 'stuck in the middle'" (p. 16). Gilbert and Strebel (1992), however, have disagreed with this, arguing that highly successful companies,

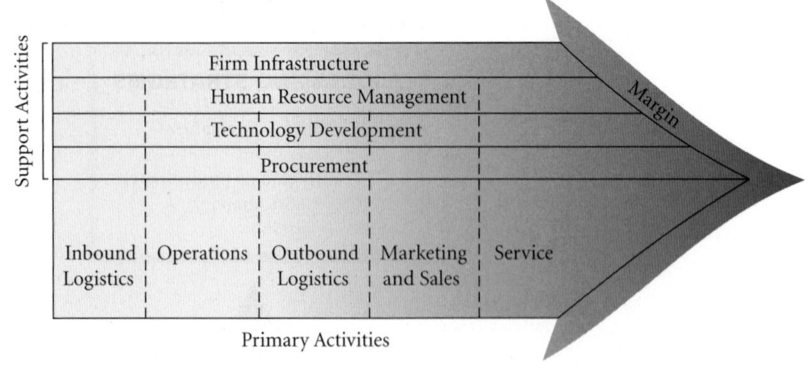

FIGURE 3
THE GENERIC VALUE CHAIN

Source: Competitive Advantage, Simon and Schuster (Porter, M.E. 1985) p.37. Used with the permission of The Free Press, a Division of Simon & Schuster, Inc.

*In other words, it is the differentiation of price that naturally drives the functional strategy of reducing costs just as it is the differentiation of product that naturally drives the functional strategies of enhancing quality or creating innovation. (To be consistent with the label of "cost leadership," Porter would have had to call his differentiation strategy "product leadership.") A company could, of course, cut costs while holding prices equivalent to competitors'. But often that means less service, lower quality, fewer features, etc., and so the customers would have to be attracted by lower prices. [See Mintzberg (1988: 14–17) for a fuller discussion of this point.]

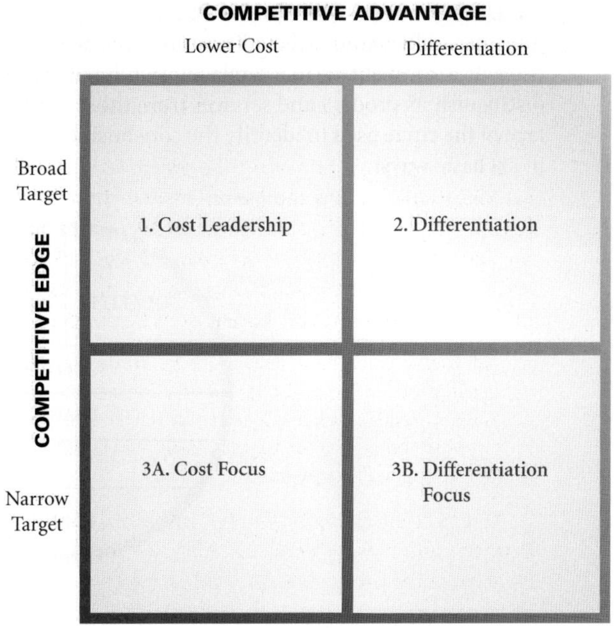

FIGURE 4
PORTER'S GENERIC STRATEGIES

Source: Competitive Advantage, Simon and Schuster (Porter, M.E. 1985) p.12. Used with the permission of The Free Press, a Division of Simon & Schuster, Inc. Copyright © 1985 by Michael Porter. All rights reserved.

COMPETITIVE ADVANTAGE

COMPETITIVE EDGE	Lower Cost	Differentiation
Broad Target	1. Cost Leadership	2. Differentiation
Narrow Target	3A. Cost Focus	3B. Differentiation Focus

such as some of the Japanese automobile manufacturers, have adopted "outpacing strategies." First they use a low-cost strategy to secure markets, and then, by "proactive" differentiation moves (say an increase in quality), they capture certain important market segments. Or else firms begin with value differentiation and follow that up with "preemptive" price cutting. In effect, the authors argue that companies can achieve both forms of Porter's competitive advantage simultaneously.

The strategies we describe in this section take their lead from Porter, but depart in some respects. We shall distinguish scope and differentiation, as Porter did in his 1980 book (focus being introduced as narrow scope in his later book), but we shall include cost leadership as a form of differentiation (namely, with regard to low price). If, as Porter argues, the intention of generic strategies is to seize and sustain competitive advantage, then it is not just taking leadership on cutting costs that matters so much as using that cost leadership to underprice competitors and so to attract buyers.*

Thus two types of strategy for distinguishing a core business are presented in the figure on p. 116. First is a set of increasingly extensive strategies of *differentiation,* shown on the face of the circle. These identify what is fundamentally distinct about a business in the marketplace, in effect as perceived by its customers. Second is a set of decreasingly extensive strategies of *scope*. These identify what markets the business is after, as perceived by itself.

---

*Our figure differs from Porter's in certain ways. Because he places his major emphasis on the flow of physical materials (for example, referring to "inbound logistics" as encompassing materials handling, warehousing, inventory control, vehicle scheduling, and returns to suppliers), he shows procurement and human resource management as support activities, whereas by taking more of a general system orientation, our Figure 2 shows them as inputs, among the sourcing strategies. Likewise, he considers technology development as support whereas Figure 2 considers it as part of processing. (Among the reasons Porter gives for doing this is that such development can pertain to "outbound logistics" or delivery as well as processing. While true, it also seems true that far more technology development pertains to operations than to delivery, especially in the manufacturing firms that are the focus of Porter's attention. Likewise, Porter describes procurement as pertaining to any of the primary activities, or other support activities for that matter. But in our terms that does not make it any less an aspect of sourcing on the inbound side.) In fact, Porter's description would relegate engineering and product design (not to mention human resources and purchasing) to staff rather than line activities, a place that would certainly be disputed in many manufacturing firms (with product design, for example, being mentioned only peripherally in his text (p. 42) alongside other "technology development" activities such as media research and servicing procedures).

STRATEGIES OF DIFFERENTIATION

As is generally agreed in the literature of strategic management, an organization distinguishes itself in a competitive marketplace by differentiating its offerings in some way—by acting to distinguish its product and services from those of its competitors. Hence, differentiation fills the face of the circle used to identify the core business. An organization can differentiate its offerings in six basic ways:

Price Differentiation Strategy

The most basic way to differentiate a product (or service) is simply to charge a lower price for it. All things being equal, or not too unequal, some people at least will always beat a path to the door of the cheaper product. Price differentiation may be used with a product undifferentiated in any other way—in effect, a standard design, perhaps a commodity. The producer simply absorbs the lost margin, or makes it up through a higher volume of sales. But other times, backing up price differentiation is a strategy of design intended to create a product that is intrinsically cheaper.

Image Differentiation Strategy

Marketing is sometimes used to feign differentiation where it does not otherwise exist—an image is created for the product. This can also include cosmetic differences to a product that do not enhance its performance in any serious way, for example, putting a fancier package around yogurt. (Of course, if it is the image that is for sale, in other words if the product is intrinsically cosmetic, as, say, in "designer" jeans, then cosmetic differences would have to be described in design differentiation.)

Support Differentiation Strategy

More substantial, yet still having no effect on the product itself, is to differentiate on the basis of something that goes alongside the product, some basis of support. This may have to do with selling the product (such as special credit or 24-hour delivery), servicing the product (such as exceptional after-sales service), or providing a related product or service alongside the basic one (paddling lessons with the canoe you buy). In an article entitled "Marketing Success Through Differentiation—of Anything," Theodore Levitt has argued the interesting point that "there is no such thing as a commodity" (1980: 8). His basic point is that no matter how difficult it may be to achieve differentiation by design, there is always a basis to achieve another substantial form of differentiation, especially by support.

Quality Differentiation Strategy

Quality differentiation has to do with features of the product that make it better—not fundamentally different, just better. The product performs with (1) greater initial reliability, (2) greater long-term durability, and/or (3) superior performance.

Design Differentiation Strategy

Last but certainly not the least is differentiation on the basis of design—offering something that is truly different, that breaks away from the "dominant design" if there is one, to provide unique features. When everyone else was making cameras whose pictures could be seen next week, Edward Land made one whose pictures could be seen in the next minute.

Undifferentiation Strategy

To have no basis for differentiation is a strategy: indeed by all observation a common one, and in fact one that may be pursued deliberately. Hence there is a blank space in the circle. Given enough room in a market, and a management without the skill or the will to differentiate what it does, there can be a place for copycats.

SCOPE STRATEGIES

The second dimension to distinguish the core business is by the *scope* of the products and services offered, in effect the extent of the markets in which they are sold. Scope is essentially a demand-driven concept, taking its lead from the market for what exists out there. Differentiation, in contrast, is a supply-driven concern, rooted in the nature of the product itself—what is offered to the market (Smith, 1956). Differentiation, by concentrating on the product offered, adopts the perspective of the customer, existing only when that person perceives some characteristic of the product that adds value. And scope, by focusing on the market served, adopts the perspective of the producer, existing only in the collective mind of the organization—in terms of how it diffuses and disaggregates its markets (in other words, what marketing people call segmentation).

Unsegmentation Strategy

"One size fits all": the Ford Model T, table salt. In fact, it is difficult to think of any product today that is not segmented in some way. What the unsegmented strategy really means then is that the organization tries to capture a wide chunk of the market with a basic configuration of the product.

Segmentation Strategies

The possibilities for segmentation are limitless, as are the possible degrees. We can, however, distinguish a range of this, from a simple segmentation strategy (three basic sizes of paper clips) to a hyperfine segmentation strategy (as in designer lighting). Also, some organizations seek to be *comprehensive,* to serve all segments (department stores, large cereal manufacturers), others to be *selective,* targeting carefully only certain segments (e.g., "clean" mutual funds).

Niche Strategy

Niche strategies focus on a single segment. Just as the panda bear has found its biological niche in the consumption of bamboo shoots, so too is there the canoe company that has found its market niche in the fabrication of racing canoes, or the many firms which are distinguished only by the fact that they provide their highly standardized offerings in a unique place, a geographical niche—the corner grocery store, the regional cement producer, the national Red Cross office. All tend to follow "industry" recipes to the letter, providing them to their particular community. In a sense, all strategies are in some sense niche, characterized as much by what they exclude as by what they include. No organization can be all things to all people. The all-encompassing strategy is no strategy at all.

Customizing Strategies

Customization is the limiting case of segmentation: disaggregation of the market to the point where each customer constitutes a unique segment. *Pure* customization, in which the product is developed from scratch for each customer, is found in the architecturally designed house and the special purpose machine. It infiltrates the entire value chain: the product is not only delivered in a personalized way, not only assembled and even fabricated to order, but is also designed for the individual customer in the first place. Less ambitious but probably more common is *tailored* customization: a basic design is modified, usually in the fabrication stage, to the customer's needs or specifications (certain housing, prostheses modified to fit the bone joints of each consumer, and so on). *Standardized customization* means that final products are assembled to individual request for standard components—as in automobiles in which the customer is allowed to choose color, engine, and various accessories. Advances in computer-aided design and manufacturing (CAD, CAM) have caused a proliferation of standardized customization, as well as tailored customization.

ELABORATING THE CORE BUSINESS

An organization can elaborate a business in a number of ways. It can develop its product offerings within that business, it can develop its market via new segments, new channels or new geographical areas, or it can simply push the same products more vigorously through the same markets. Back in 1965, Igor Ansoff showed these strategies as presented in Figure 5.

Penetration Strategies

Penetration strategies work from a base of existing products and existing markets, seeking to penetrate the market by increasing the organization's share of it. This may be done by straight *expansion* or by the *takeover* of existing competitors. Trying to expand sales with no fundamental change in product or market (buying market share through more promotion, etc.) is at one and the same time the most obvious thing to do and perhaps the most difficult to succeed at, because, at least in a relatively stable market, it means extracting market share from other firms, which logically leads to increased competition. Takeover, where possible, obviously avoids this, but perhaps at a high cost. The harvesting strategy, popularized in the 1970s by the Boston Consulting Group, in some ways represents the opposite of the penetration strategies. The way to deal with "cash cows"—businesses with high market shares but low growth potential—was to harvest them, cease investment, and exploit whatever potential remained. The mixing of the metaphors may have been an indication of the dubiousness of the strategy since to harvest a cow is, of course, to kill it.

Market Development Strategies

A predominant strategy here is *market elaboration,* which means promoting existing products in new markets—in effect broadening the scope of the business by finding new market segments, perhaps served by new channels. Product substitution is a particular case of market elaboration, where uses for a product are promoted which enable it to substitute for other products. *Market consolidation* is the inverse of market elaboration, namely reducing the number of segments. But this is not just a strategy of failure. Given the common tendency to proliferate market segments, it makes sense for the healthy organization to rationalize them periodically, to purge the excesses.

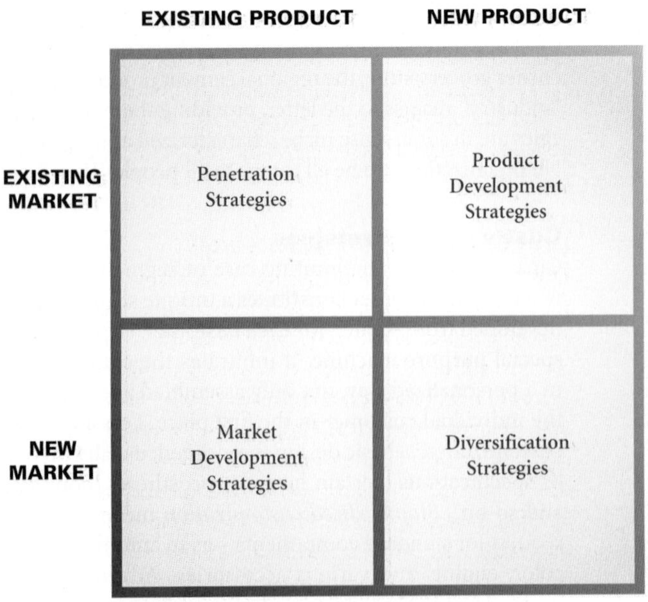

	EXISTING PRODUCT	NEW PRODUCT
EXISTING MARKET	Penetration Strategies	Product Development Strategies
NEW MARKET	Market Development Strategies	Diversification Strategies

FIGURE 5
WAYS TO ELABORATE A GIVEN BUSINESS

Source: Ansoff (1965: 109) with minor modifications; see also Johnson and Jones (1957: 52).

Geographic Expansion Strategies

An important form of market development can be geographic expansion—carrying the existing product offering to new geographical areas, anywhere from the next block to across the world. When this also involves a strategy of geographic rationalization—locating different business functions in different places—it is sometimes referred to as a "global strategy." The IKEA furniture company, for example, designs in Scandinavia, sources in Eastern Europe among other places, and markets in Western Europe and North America.

Product Development Strategies

Here we can distinguish a simple *product extension* strategy from a more extensive *product line proliferation* strategy, and their counterparts, *product line rationalization*. Offering new or modified products in the same basic business is another obvious way to elaborate a core business—from cornflakes to bran flakes and rice crispies, eventually offering every permutation and combination of the edible grains. This may amount to differentiation by design, if the products are new and distinctive, or else to no more than increased scope through segmentation, if standardized products are added to the line. Product line proliferation means aiming at comprehensive product segmentation—the complete coverage of a given business. Rationalization means culling products and thinning the line to get rid of overlaps or unprofitable excesses. Again we might expect cycles of product extension and rationalization, at least in businesses (such as cosmetics and textiles) predisposed to proliferation in their product lines.

Extending the Core Business

Next comes the question of what strategies of a generic nature are available to extend and reconceive that core business. These are approaches designed to answer the corporate-level question, "What business should we be in?"

Strategies designed to take organizations beyond their core business can be pursued in so-called vertical or horizontal ways, as well as combinations of the two. "Vertical" means backward or forward in the operating chain, the strategy being known formally as "vertical integration," although why this has been designated vertical is difficult to understand, especially since the flow of product and the chain itself are almost always drawn horizontally! Hence this will here be labeled chain integration. "Horizontal" diversification (its own geometry no more evident), which will be called here just plain diversification, refers to encompassing within the organization other parallel businesses, not in the same chain of operations.

CHAIN INTEGRATION STRATEGIES

Organizations can extend their operating chains downstream or upstream, encompassing within their own operations the activities of their customers on the delivery end or their suppliers on the sourcing end. In effect, they choose to "make" rather than to "buy" or sell. *Impartation* (Barreyre, 1984) is a label that has been proposed to describe the opposite strategy, where the organization chooses to buy what it previously made (also called "outsourcing"), or sell what it previously transferred.

DIVERSIFICATION STRATEGIES

Diversification refers to the entry into some business not in the same chain of operation. It may be *related* to some distinctive competence or asset of the core business itself (also called *concentric* diversification); otherwise, it is referred to as *unrelated* or *conglomerate* diversification. In related diversification, there is evident potential synergy between the new business and the core one, based on a common facility, asset, channel, skill, even opportunity. Porter (1985: 323–4) makes the distinction here between "intangible" and "tangible" relatedness. The former is based on some functional or managerial skill considered common across the businesses, as in a Philip Morris using its marketing capabilities in Kraft. The latter refers to businesses that actually "share activities in the value chain" (p. 323), for example, different products sold by the same sales force. It should be emphasized here that no matter what its basis, every related diversification is also fundamentally an unrelated one, as many diversifying organizations have discovered to their regret. That is, no matter what is common between two different businesses, many other things are not.

STRATEGIES OF ENTRY AND CONTROL

Chain integration or diversification may be achieved by *internal development* or *acquisition.* In other words, an organization can enter a new business by developing it itself or by buying an organization already in business. Both internal development and acquisition involve complete ownership and formal control of the diversified business. But there are a host of other possible strategies, as follows:

STRATEGIES OF ENTRY AND CONTROL	
Full ownership and control	• Internal development • Acquisition

Partial ownership and control	• Majority, minority
	• Partnership, including
	  • Joint venture
	  • Turnkey (temporary control)

Partial control without ownership	• Licensing • Franchising • Long-term contracting

COMBINED INTEGRATION–DIVERSIFICATION STRATEGIES

Among the most interesting are those strategies that combine chain integration with business diversification, sometimes leading organizations into whole networks of new businesses. *By-product diversification* involves selling off the by-products of the operating chain in separate markets, as when an airline offers its maintenance services to other carriers. The new activity amounts to a form of market development at some intermediate point in the operating chain. *Linked diversification* extends by-product diversification: one business simply leads to another, whether integrated "vertically" or diversified "horizontally." The organization pursues its operating chain upstream, downstream, sidestream; it exploits pre-products, end-products, and by-products of its core products as well as of each other, ending up with a network of businesses. *Crystalline diversification* pushes the previous strategy to the limit, so that it becomes difficult and perhaps irrelevant to distinguish integration from diversification, core activities from peripheral activities, closely related businesses from distantly related ones. What were once clear links in a few chains now metamorphose into what looks like a form of crystalline growth, as business after business gets added literally right and left as well as up and down. Here businesses tend to be related, at least initially, through internal development of core competencies, as in the "coating and bonding technologies" that are common to many of 3M's products.

WITHDRAWAL STRATEGIES

Finally there are strategies that reverse all those of diversification: organizations cut back on the businesses they are in. "Exit" has been one popular label for this, withdrawal is another. Sometimes organizations *shrink* their activities, canceling long-term licenses, ceasing to sell by-products, reducing their crystalline networks. Other times they abandon or *liquidate* businesses (the opposite of internal development), or else they *divest* them (the opposite of acquisition).

RECONCEIVING THE CORE BUSINESS(ES)

It may seem strange to end a discussion of strategies of ever more elaborate development of a business with ones involving reconception of the business. But in one important sense, there is a logic to this: after a core business has been identified, distinguished, elaborated, and extended, there often follows the need not just to consolidate it but also to redefine it and reconfigure it—in essence, to reconceive it. As they develop, through all the waves of expansion, integration, diversification, and so on, some organizations lose a sense of themselves. Then reconception becomes the ultimate form of consolidation: rationalizing not just excesses in product offerings or market segments or even new businesses, but all of these things together and more—the essence of the entire strategy itself. We can identify three basic reconception strategies.

BUSINESS REDEFINITION STRATEGY

A business, as Abell (1980) has pointed out, may be defined in a variety of ways—by the function it performs, the market it serves, the product it produces. All businesses have popular conceptions. Some are narrow and tangible, such as the canoe business, others broader and vague, such as the financial services business. All such definitions, no matter how tangible, are ultimately concepts that exist in the minds of actors and observers. It therefore becomes possible, with a little effort and imagination, to *redefine* a particular business—reconceive the "recipe" for how that business is conducted (Grinyer and Spender, 1979; Spender, 1989)—as Edwin Land did when he developed the Polaroid camera.*

BUSINESS RECOMBINATION STRATEGIES

As Porter notes, through the waves of diversification that swept American business in the 1960s and 1970s, "the concept of synergy has become widely regarded as passe"—a "nice idea" but "one that rarely occurred in practice" (1985: 317–18). Businesses were elements in a portfolio to be bought and sold, or, at best, grown and harvested. Deploring that conclusion, Porter devoted three chapters of his 1985 book to "horizontal strategy," which we shall refer to here (given our problems with the geometry of this field) as *business recombination strategies*—efforts to recombine different businesses in some way, at the limit to reconceive various businesses as one. Businesses can be recombined tangibly or only conceptually. The latter was encouraged by Levitt's "Marketing Myopia" (1960) article. By a stroke of the pen, railroads could be in the transportation business, ball-bearing manufacturers in the friction reduction business. Realizing some practical change in behavior often proved much more difficult, however. But when some substantial basis exists for combining different activities, a strategy of business recombination can be very effective. There may never have been a transportation business, but 3M was able to draw on common technological capabilities to create a coating and bonding business.** Business recombination can also be more tangible, based on shared activities in the value chain, as in a strategy of *bundling,* where complementary products are sold together for a single price (e.g., automobile service with the new car). Of course, *unbundling* can be an equally viable strategy, such as selling "term" insurance free of any investment obligation. Carried to their logical extreme, the more tangible recombination strategies lead to a "systems view" of the business, where all products and services are conceived to be tightly interrelated.

CORE RELOCATION STRATEGIES

Finally we come full circle by closing the discussion where we began, on the location of the core business. An organization in addition to having one or more strategic positions in a marketplace tends to have what Jay Galbraith (1983) calls a single "center of gravity," some conceptual place where are concentrated not only its core skills but also its cultural heart, as in a Procter & Gamble focusing its efforts on "branded consumer products," each "sold primarily by advertising to the homemaker and managed by a brand manager" (p. 13). But as changes in strategic position take place, shifts can also take place in this center of gravity, in various ways. First, the organization

---

*MacMillian refers to the business redefinition strategy as "reshaping the industry infrastructure" (1983:18), while Porter calls it "reconfiguration" (1985: 519–523), although his notion of product *substitution* (273–314) could sometimes also constitute a form of business redefinition.

**Our suspicion, we should note, is that such labels often emerge after the fact, as the organization seeks a way to rationalize the diversification that has already taken place. In effect, the strategy is emergent. (See Chapter 1 on "Five Ps for Strategy.")

can move *along the operating chain,* upstream or downstream, as did General Mills "from a flour miller to a related diversified provider of products for the homemaker"; eventually the company sold off its flour milling operation altogether (p. 76). Second, there can be a shift *between dominant functions,* say from production to marketing. Third is the shift *to a new business,* whether or not at the same stage of the operating chain. Such shifts can be awfully demanding, simply because each industry is a culture with its own ways of thinking and acting. Finally is the shift *to a new core theme,* as in the reorientation from a single function or product to a broader concept, for example, when Procter & Gamble changed from being a soap company to being in the personal care business.

This brings us to the end of our discussion of generic strategies—our loop from locating a business to distinguishing it, elaborating it, extending it, and finally reconceiving it.

We should close with a warning that while a framework of generic strategies may help to think about positioning an organization, use of it as a pat list may put that organization at a disadvantage against competitors that develop their strategies in more creative ways.

READING 4.6

A Guide to Strategic Positioning* By Henry Mintzberg

In the large literature of strategic management that deals with positioning, the concepts come and go at a frantic pace. There is thus a need to pin them down—to develop a framework to see them all, as well as to provide a "glossary" of what they are, even for experts who tend to beaver away in one area or another. There is woefully little synthesis in the world of analysis!

Thus, a little model is offered here. It is visual because, in a sense, all of this needs to be seen to be believed. The model is a metaphor of sorts, consisting of a launching device, representing an organization, that sends projectiles, namely products and services, at a landscape of targets, meaning markets, faced with rivals, or competition, in the hope of attaining fit.

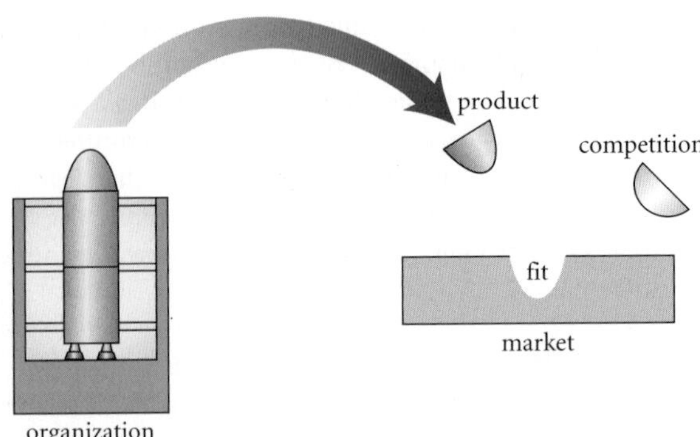

We should add that we have not chosen this metaphor casually: the hunting or military (or any other) implication very much reflects how writers of this school tend to see the world. We use the model to locate, explain, illustrate, and especially link the various concepts that make up this school.

* He would like to express his appreciation to Richard Rumelt, who provided invaluable help in the development of this model.

THE VEHICLE (ORGANIZATION)

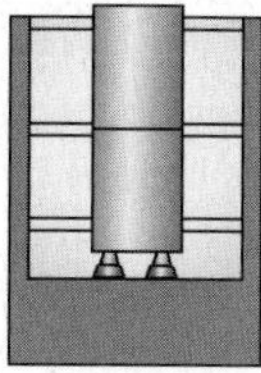

The organization is depicted as a launching device which develops, produces and distributes its products and services into markets. To do that, it performs a series of business functions that sequence themselves into what Michael Porter (1985) has labeled a value chain. As depicted in our figure, design (of product and process) and production are the basic platform, while supply and sourcing (including financing) form one tower, and administration and support (such as public relations and industrial relations) form the other. The launch vehicle has two booster rockets (which fall away during the product's voyage)—the first for sales and marketing, the second for physical distribution.

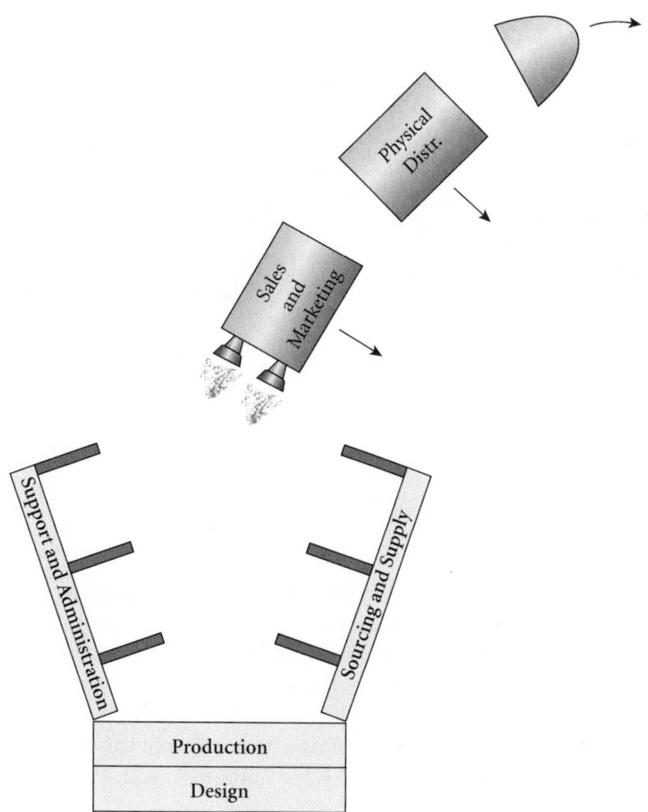

The business functions are executed by using a bundle of competences or capabilities of various kinds (such as the ability to do research or to produce products inexpensively) and supported by all sorts of resources or assets (including patents, machinery, and so on). Itami (1987) has referred to key competences as invisible assets, while Prahalad and Hamel (1990) have drawn attention to core competences, the ones that have developed deep within the organization over its history and explain its comparative and competitive advantages (as in the example of product venturing in 3M or quality design in Maytag). These can perhaps be distinguished from shallow or common competences, more tangible, codified and so imitable in nature (such as selling groceries in the corner shop). These are easily acquired and so easily lost too—more generic than genetic.

These core competences must be sustained and enhanced as the key to the organization's future. In part, this is done by accumulating experience, according to a theory popularized by the Boston Consulting Group in the 1970s (see Henderson, 1979): the more the organization produces, the more it engages in learning, and so the faster it reduces its costs.

Indeed, currently popular theory has it that the organization should shed as many of its non-core competences as it can, in order to become lean and flexible, and so be able to focus attention on doing what it does best. The rest should be bought from suppliers. Thus, the old strategy of vertical integration—encompassing your suppliers upstream as well as your intermediate customers downstream so that you can control their activities tightly—gets replaced by the new one of outsourcing, resulting in the virtual organization.

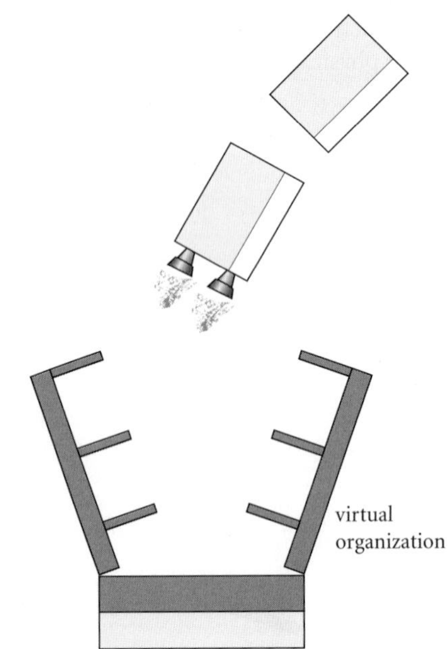

Competences can be combined in various ways, for example, through joint ventures or other forms of alliances with partners, licensing agreements, franchising relationships and long-term contracts, the extensive combinations of which result in networks. This can happen in parallel, as when an electronics firm combines its research capabilities with that of a mechanical products firm to develop new electromagnetic products together. Or it can happen sequentially, as when the design capability of one firm is combined with the production capability of another. These result in synergy, the 2 + 2 = 5 effect (Ansoff, 1965).

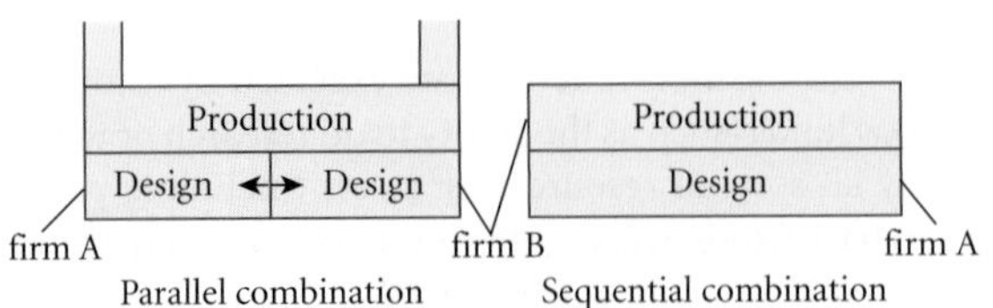

THE PROJECTILE (PRODUCTS AND SERVICES)

Proceeding along the value chain eventually creates a product (or service) which is launched at a target market. The ways in which this can be done are described, according to the positioning school, by a set of generic strategies (Porter, 1980). We can use our metaphor to describe a broad array of these (based on Mintzberg, 1988), according to the nature of the projectile (size, shape, surrounding, etc.) and the sequence of projectiles launched (frequency, direction, etc.). First are the generic strategies that characterize the product itself:

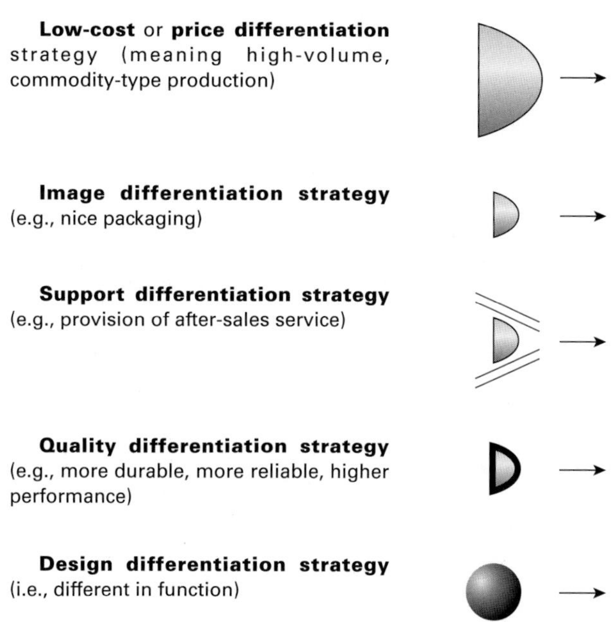

Then there are the strategies that elaborate or extend the range of products offered:

Penetration strategy (targeting the same product more intensely at the same market, for example, through increased advertising)

Bundling strategy (selling two products together, such as computer software with hardware)

Market development strategy (targeting the same product at new markets)

Product development strategy (targeting new products at the same market)

Diversification strategy (targeting different products at different markets)

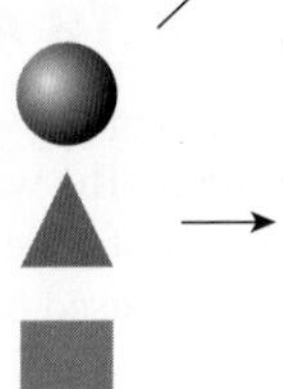

whether the different .products are **unrelated** or **related**

and whether this is done by the **acquisition** of other companies

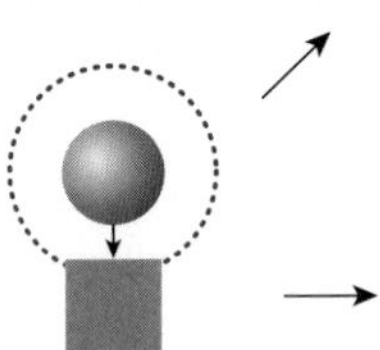

or **internal development** of the new product/market

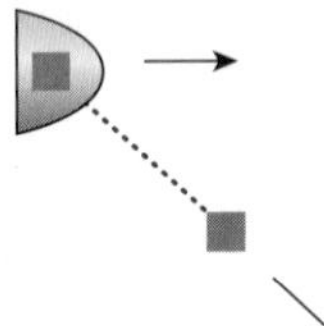

THE TARGET (MARKETS)

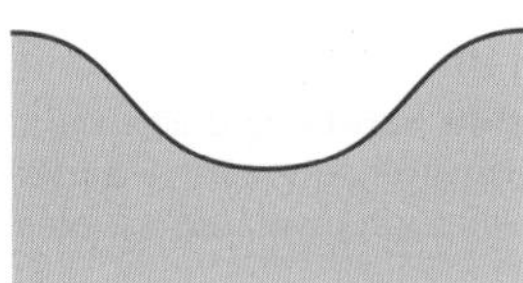

Again, the metaphor can be used for purposes of illustration, but here we show the generic characteristics of markets (the targeted place), first by size and divisibility, then by location, and finally by stage of evolution or change.

Mass market (large, homogeneous)

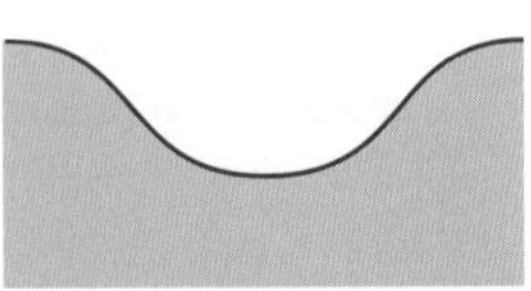

Fragmented market (many small niches)

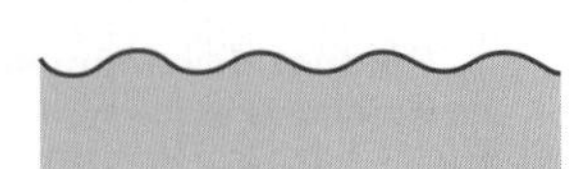

Segmented market (differing demand segments)

Thin market (few, occasional buyers, as in nuclear reactors)

Geographic markets (looked at from the perspective of place)

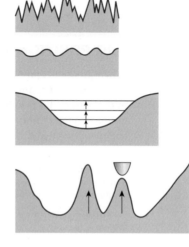

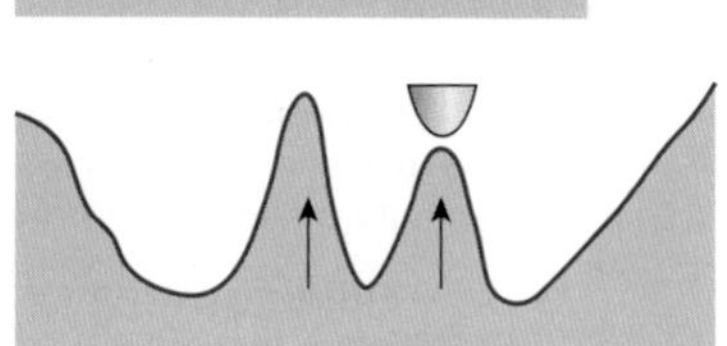

Emerging market (young, not yet clearly defined)

Established (mature) market (clearly defined)

Eroding market

Erupting market (undergoing destabilizing changes)

INDUSTRY AND GROUP

Where does one market end and another begin? In our discussion, we have spanned the concerns of various disciplines associated with strategy, from those of organization theory (the launching device) to strategic management (the projectile) and then to marketing (the target). Here, in further elaborating the target, or more exactly the nature of the targeted terrain, we move into the realm of economics, with its focus on "industry."

Economists spend a lot of time worrying about identifying industries (through the definition of SIC codes and the like). However, much of this is arbitrary, since they often no sooner find one than a strategist destroys it (because one job of the strategist is to break up the very industries that economists identify, as in the case of a CNN that took the news program and turned it into a subindustry, namely a television network, in its own right).

In our terms here, an industry can be defined as a landscape of associated markets, isolated from others by blockages in the terrain. In the literature of economics and strategic positioning, these are known as barriers to entry—for example, some kind of special know-how or close ties to the customers that keep potential new competitors out. Michael Porter (1980) elaborated on this with his notion of strategic group, really a kind of subindustry, housing companies that pursue similar strategies (for example, national news magazines, as opposed to magazines targeted at specific audiences, such as amateur photographers). These are distinguished by barriers to mobility, in other words, difficulties of shifting into the group even though it is within the overall industry. These concepts map easily into our metaphor, with higher barriers shown for industries and lower ones for strategic groups, as follows:

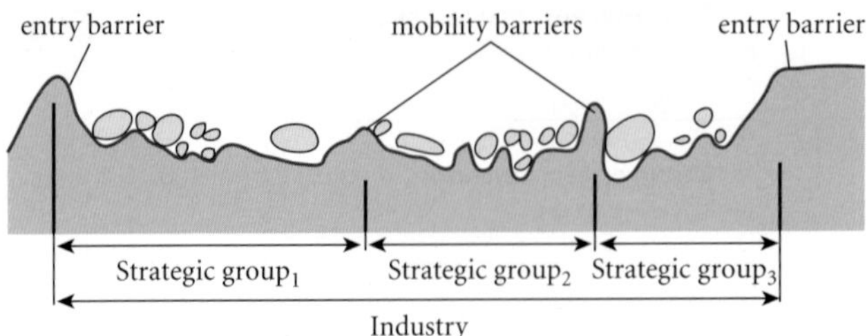

THE FIT (STRATEGIC POSITIONS)

When products and markets (projectiles and targets) come together, we reach the central concept of strategic management, namely fit, or the strategic position itself—how the product sits in the market. Fit is logically discussed, first in terms of the match between the breadth of the products offered and markets served (which Porter calls scope). After this, we shall turn to the quality of the fit and ways to improve it.

Commodity strategy targets a (perceived) mass market with a single, standardized product

Segmentation strategy targets a (perceived) segmented market with a range of products, geared to each of the different segments

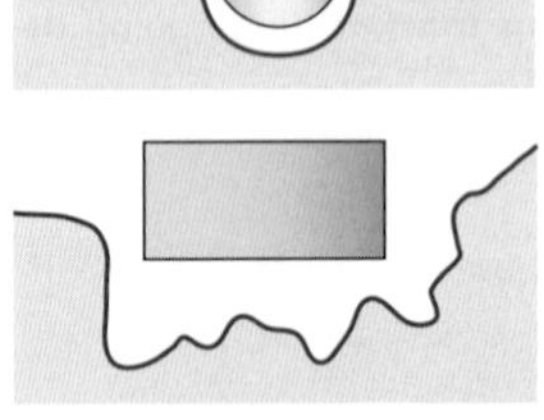

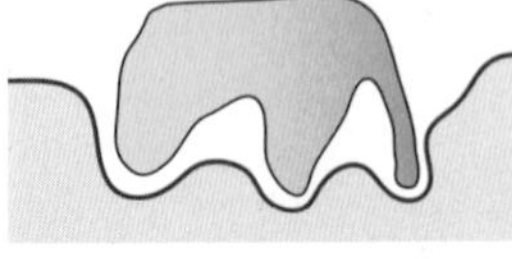

Niche strategy targets a small isolated market segment with a sharply delineated product

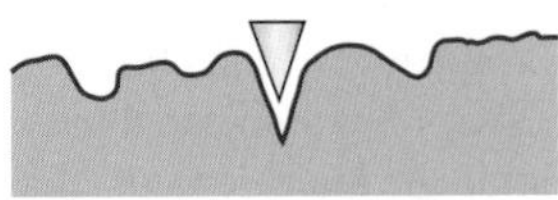

Customization strategy (the ultimate in both niching and segmentation) designs or tailors each specific product to one particular customer need (such as the architecturally designed home)

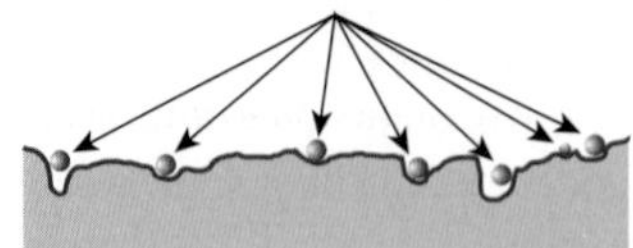

Once fit, or scope, is established, then attention turns to its strength, namely how secure it is—its durability, or sustainability. Here the concepts of the positioning school are less developed, so we use our metaphor to introduce some new ones that might prove useful.

First of all, we identify natural fit—where the product and market fit each other quite naturally, whether it was the product that created the market or the market that encouraged the development of the product. Natural fit is inherently sustainable (for example, because there is usually intrinsic customer loyalty, perhaps secured by high switching costs).

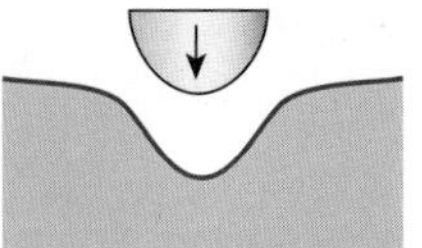

Natural fit: product push

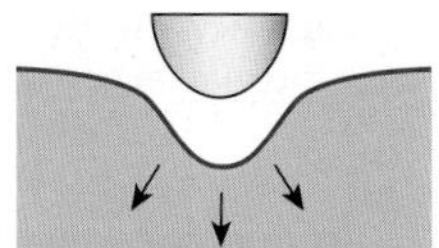

Natural fit: market pull

This can be distinguished from forced fit, as well as vulnerable fit, which is weak and so easily dislodged, whether by attack from competitors or loss of interest from customers.

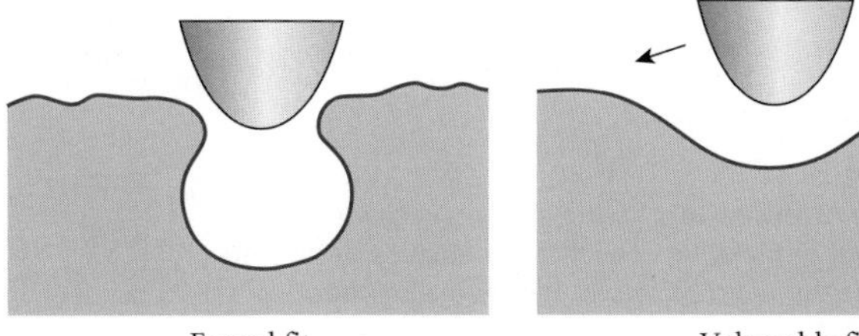

Forced fit

Vulnerable fit

When fit is not perfect (as is always true in an imperfect world), and so not easily sustainable, attention has to be given to what can be called reinforcing mechanisms, to improve it, or isolating mechanisms, to protect it. Inspired by the metaphor itself, we suggest three types of these:

Burrowing strategy (driving into the market deeper, for example, by using advertising to strengthen brand loyalty—but this could prove costly)

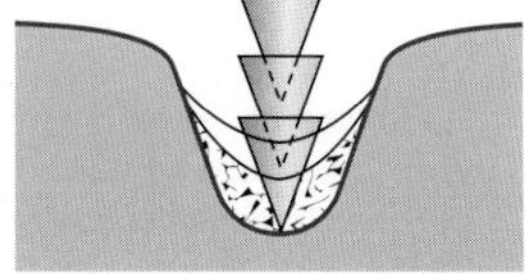

Packing strategy (tightening the fit by adding supporting elements, such as strong after-sales services, or the use of supporting brands—but the seller can get stuck too)

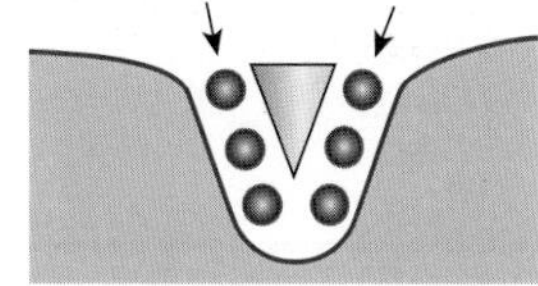

Fortifying strategy (building up barriers or shelters around the fit, such as seeking tariff or patent protection, or creating long-term contracts with customers—but these can topple, or else, in fact, blind the seller to changes occurring elsewhere)

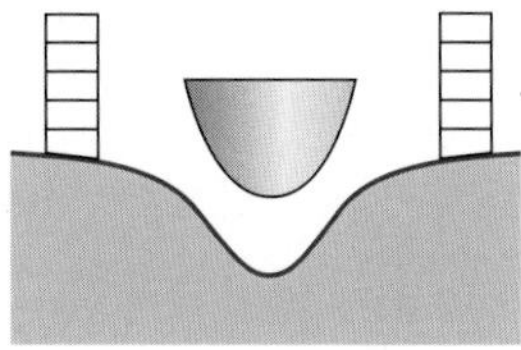

There can also be a **learning strategy** to improve fit through adaptability, for example, by riding the **experience curve** to take advantage of the steady stream of learning that comes from producing more and more of the product, or simply by coming to know better the needs of the customers, or by taking advantage of the complementarities that come from different parts of a strategy that reinforce each other, such as franchising and mass preparation in fast food retailing

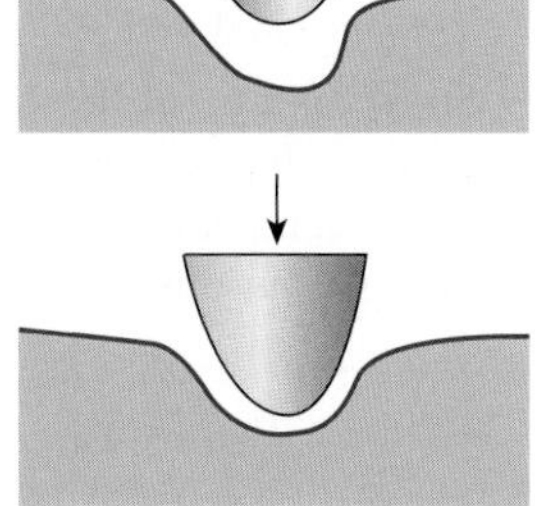

Of course, if there can be natural fit and forced fit and vulnerable fit, then there can also be misfit. This concept has not been much developed in the literature, but we can at least offer a few ideas here:

Capacity misfit (what is offered exceeds what the market can take)

Competence misfit (the competences of the producer do not match the needs of the market)

Design misfit (the design is wrong for the market)

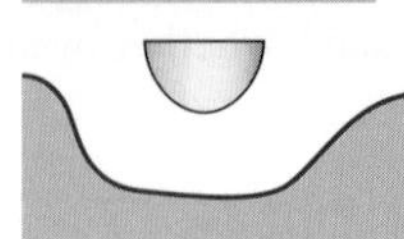

Sunk misfit (being stuck in a market due to exit barriers, as in sunk costs such as dedicated machinery that cannot be used elsewhere)

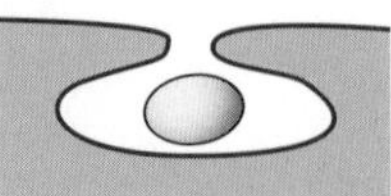

Myopic misfit (the producer cannot see the market—perhaps because of too long concentration on other markets)

Location misfit (the producer is in the wrong place, and cannot reach the market—perhaps because some barrier is too high)

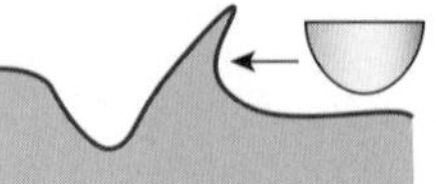

RIVALRY (COMPENSATION)

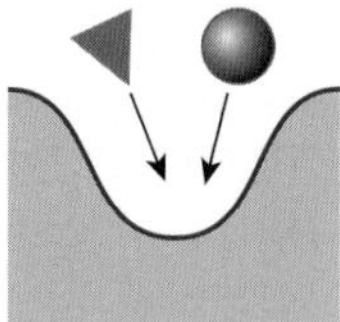

So far, almost all these relationships have been between a single seller and one or more target markets. But sellers are no more found alone than are buyers. There is rivalry in markets, consisting of competitors—capable of doing better or doing differently. So we return to economics to describe various competitive situations.

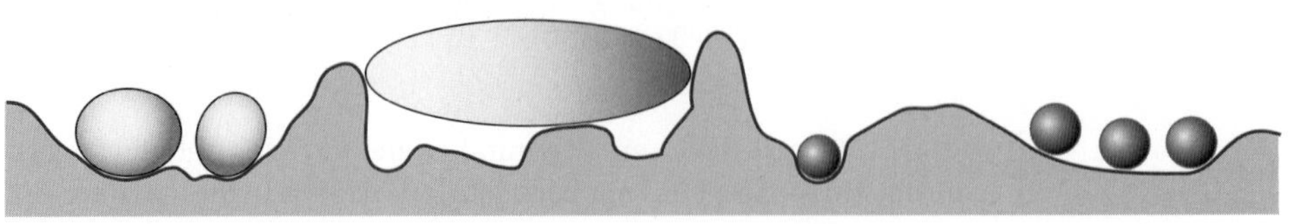

Market Leader (or **dominant firm**)

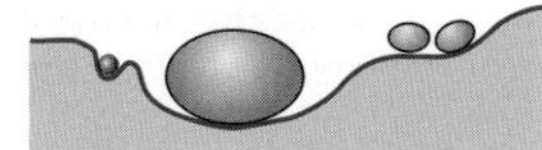

Stable Competition

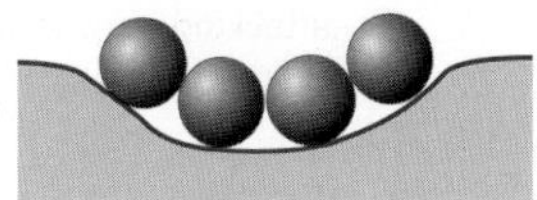

Multipoint Competition (ability to take action in one market to influence competitor's actions in another)

Unstable Competition (in a mature market)

Unstable Competition (in an emerging market)

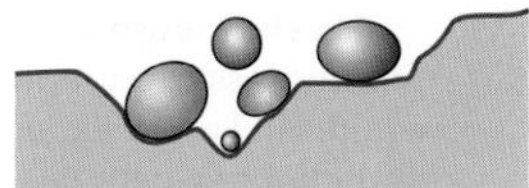

CONTESTABILITY

Obviously, markets are contestable. New competitors can seek to drive themselves in. Here we draw especially on the literature of military strategy, adapted to business by such writers as Quinn (1980) and Porter (1980).

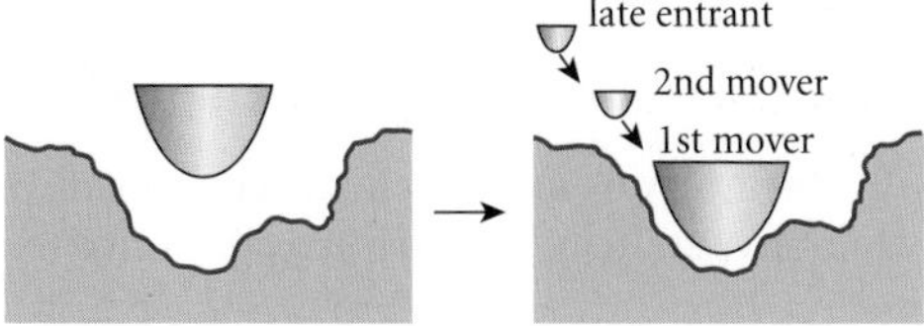

First movers seek to position themselves in new markets to keep rivals out. But later entrants (including second movers) come along and seek a share, if not to displace their rivals altogether. (Strategic window refers to the period of opportunity when an initial or later move becomes possible, for example, because the rival is having trouble, such as a strike in the factory, or because customers are suddenly vulnerable to a brand change.) Later entrants use various military-type strategies:

Frontal attack (by the **concentration of forces**, e.g., cost cutting)

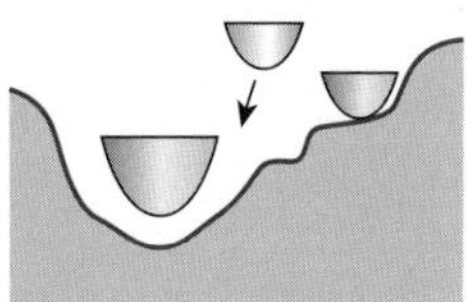

Lateral (or **indirect** or **flanking**) attack, perhaps by

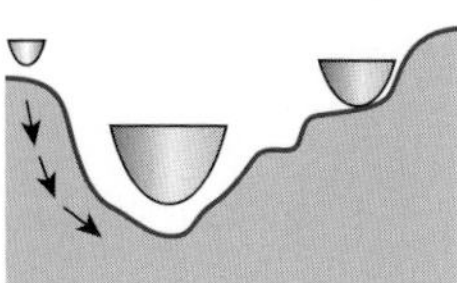

—undermining (e.g., taking away the least loyal customers through lower prices)

—attacking a supporting brand (to dislodge the main one)

—attacking fortifications, through a battering strategy (e.g., lobbying for the elimination of tariff barriers)

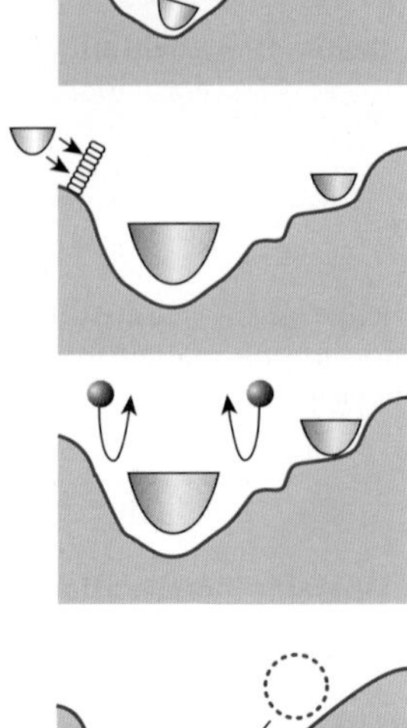

Guerrilla attack (series of small "hit and run" attacks, such as sudden moves of deep discounting)

Market signaling by feint (giving the impression of doing something, such as pretending to expand plant to scare off potential competitor)

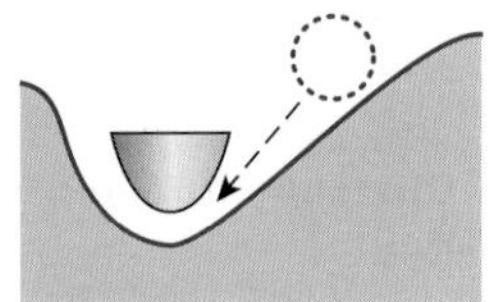

Later entrants may also seek to carve out small territories through niche strategies (sometimes called "picking up the crumbs").

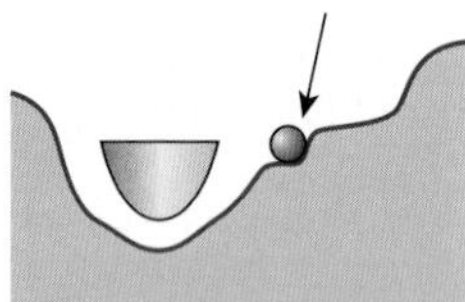

Finally, rivals may reach an accord with the existing players so that all settle down to a collaborative strategy, perhaps in a cozy price fixing or market allocating cartel.

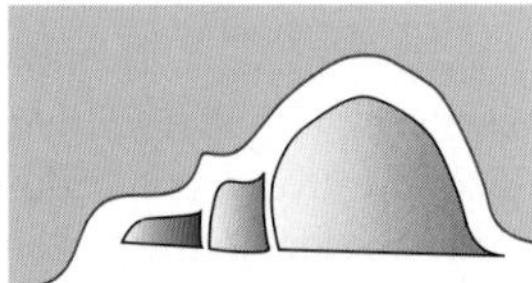

The truly creative strategist, however, shuns all of these categories, or at least recombines them in innovative ways, to develop a novel strategy, for which there is no diagram, since no one can tell what it might look like!

CHAPTER 5

Strategy Formation

The readings of the last two chapters describe how strategies are supposed to be made and thereby illustrate the prescriptive side of the field. This chapter presents readings that describe how strategies really do seem to be made, the *descriptive side.* We title this chapter "Strategy Formation" to emphasize the point introduced in Chapter 1 that strategies can form implicitly as well as be formulated explicitly.

The preceding chapters may seem to deal with an unattainable utopia and this one with an imperfect reality. But a better conclusion may be that prescription offers useful guidelines for thinking about ends and how to order physical resources efficiently to achieve them, whereas description provides a useful frame of reference for considering how these ends must be related to real-world patterns of behavior in organizations. Another way to say this is that although the analytical tools and models prescribed earlier are vital to thinking about strategy, they must also be rooted in a genuine understanding of the realities of organizations. Unfortunately, management writers have often been quick to prescribe without offering enough appreciation of why managers and organizations act in the ways they do.

We open with a reading by Richard Rumelt called "Good Strategy/Bad Strategy," an excerpt from his book by the same name. One of the things that motivated Rumelt to write the book was his observation that far too many organizational leaders said that they have a strategy, when in fact what they have are statements of broad goals, ambition, vision, and values that satisfy the need to have a strategy, but rarely translate into effective action. Good strategy, argues Rumelt, is made up of diagnosing situations correctly, adopting an overall policy for dealing with the problems and opportunities identified by the diagnosis, and finally coordinating a set of steps that support this policy. Bad strategy does not follow this process, or does it badly. This may come about because organizations are unable to face their real problems, treat goals as the be all and end all of strategy, compound this problem by choosing bad objectives, or simply reduce strategy to abstractions and clichés.

If Rumelt draws a sharp line between good and bad strategy process, Henry Mintzberg in the second reading called "Crafting Strategy" portrays strategy as more nuanced interplay between actions and ideas, and between experience and inspiration. The governing metaphor in this reading is the potter and her lump of clay. Managers mold strategies the way craftspersons mold clay, interacting, reflecting, experimenting, converging on a shape that makes sense, and sometimes taking this shape apart and starting anew. This reading also builds on Mintzberg's reading of Chapter 1 on the different forms of strategy, developing further the concept of emergent strategy.

Following this reading, Kathy Eisenhardt of Stanford University describes strategy as a process of decision making. Suited especially to more contemporary, dynamic conditions of many industries (which she calls "high velocity"), Eisenhardt sees the strategy process as a set of fast moves that uses collective intuition in an enterprise, stimulates conflict to improve thinking, and maintains a disciplined pace of decision making, while defusing wasteful political behavior.

In a chapter that challenges many of the accepted notions about how strategy should be made, the next reading may be the most upsetting of all. In it Richard Pascale, a well-known consultant, writer, and lecturer at Stanford Business School, challenges head on not only the whole approach to strategy analysis (as represented in the last chapter), especially as practiced by the Boston Consulting Group (BCG), one of the better-known "strategy boutiques," but also the very concept of strategy formulation itself.

As his point of departure, Pascale describes a Boston Consulting Group (BCG) study carried out for the British government to explain how manufacturers in that country lost the American motorcycle market to the Japanese and to Honda in particular. The analysis seems impeccable and eminently logical: The Japanese were simply more clever, by thinking through a brilliant strategy before they acted. But then Pascale flew to Japan and interviewed those clever executives who pulled off this coup. We shall save the story for Pascale, who tells it with a great deal of color, except to note here its basic message: An openness to learning and a fierce commitment to an organization and its markets may count for more in strategy making than all the brilliant analysis one can imagine. (Ask yourself while reading these accounts how the strategic behavior of the British motorcycle manufacturers who received the BCG report might have differed if they had instead received Pascale's story.) Pascale in effect takes the arguments for incrementalism and strategy making as a crafting and learning process to their natural conclusions.

No one who reads Pascale's account can ever feel quite so smug about rational strategy analysis again. We include this reading, however, not to encourage rejection of analysis or the very solid thinking that has gone into the works of Porter, Ansoff, and others. Rather, we wish to balance the message conveyed in so much of the strategy literature with the practical lessons from the field. The point is that successful strategies can no more rely exclusively on such analysis than they can do without it.

As we suggested in the introduction to this book, there is no truth, only closer approximations to the truth—by seeking to reconcile opposing perspectives, each with its own grain of truth. As Alfred North Whitehead remarked, "Seek simplicity, and distrust it."

USING THE CASE STUDIES

Rumelt's "Good Strategy/Bad Strategy" works well with cases where organizations follow or violate his clear guidelines. Most people would consider Napoleon's campaigns as examples of brilliant strategy. Reading the case one finds both good strategy and bad strategy. Cadbury Schweppes thought it had a good strategy, but performance increasingly indicates otherwise. Can it find its way to good strategy?

Mintzberg's "Crafting Strategy" suggests that strategy formation is often strongly emergent. This is best seen when we take the long view as, for example, in the case of Airbus and Boeing strategy evolves over a long period; but what about short periods? Surely, here there is not much scope for emergence.

As unlikely as it seems, the case on Napoleon Bonaparte suggests otherwise. In the popular mind Napoleon's approach to strategy is the antithesis of emergence. He is often portrayed as a masterful strategist who planned his way to victory. The case, however, suggests that Napoleon developed a strategy process that was oriented toward taking advantage of the unexpected rather than anticipating it.

The myth of Napoleon grew out of a tendency to attribute superior rationality to superior results. The Pascale reading suggests that rationality is a seductive concept that often obscures truly effective strategic process. The British motorcycle industry was very rational in the way it approached its business, whereas as Pascale shows the Japanese behavior was counterintuitive. Yet, the Japanese succeeded because they were not bound by rational analysis that would tell them what is possible and what is not. Apple, Pixar, Cirque du Soleil, Whisky Exchange, and Outset are all cases that demonstrate the importance of engaging with the environment, without necessarily starting with a plan.

At the same time, these cases also show that in most instances strategy formation is both emergent and deliberate. Eisenhardt's more detailed picture of strategy formation suggests how this happens. Her reading argues that strategy can be stimulated by constructive conflict, humor, and a disciplined pace that drives the strategy process forward. Carlos Ghosn turnaround of Nissan illustrates the approach and the limits of the approach she advocates.

Finally, we have the case of Arnold Schwarzenegger, bodybuilder, movie star, governor of California. On the face of it, Ghosn and Schwarzenegger are a world apart. But closer scrutiny reveals that they both had indomitable willpower which they brought to a succession of careers, usually with brilliant results. In the Ghosn case we looked at how his strategy evolved as he dealt with culture with which he was wholly unfamiliar. Ghosn had worked in difficult and unfamiliar environments before. Schwarzenegger likewise had multiple careers as champion bodybuilder, one of the most successful movie stars in his time, a real estate developer, and two-time governor of California. He did not have the same professional advantages as Ghosn, but the same question applies to both: Did they owe their success to willpower, or they did have a strategy? The Ghosn case focuses mostly on his time in Nissan, but we know that his problem solving skills and ability to drive strategic change are effective in other instances. Schwarzenegger recounts his life from his humble beginnings to the present. It shows willpower, but it also shows an exceptional ability to learn and adapt. At a deeper level the case also shows that the secret to successful strategy is not pure adaptation to circumstances, but a willingness to adapt while maintaining a direction and set of principles. Everybody told Schwarzenegger that his name and accent made a successful movie career impossible. He retained his name, and selected roles that highlighted his strengths and minimized his limitations. He married into the Kennedys, the most famous political family in the United States, but remained a Republican even though it would have been more convenient to become a Democrat. When he became governor against all odds, he tried to impose his will on the legislature. When this backfired, he learned, and changed, but he did not discard his basic principles. Schwarzenegger is a man of extraordinary willpower, but he is also a strategist.

READING 5.1

Good Strategy/Bad Strategy BY RICHARD RUMELT

Horatio Nelson had a problem. The British admiral's fleet was outnumbered at Trafalgar by an armada of French and Spanish ships that Napoleon had ordered to disrupt Britain's commerce and prepare for a cross-channel invasion. The prevailing tactics in 1805 were for the two opposing fleets to stay in line, firing broadsides at each other. But Nelson had a strategic insight into how to deal with being outnumbered. He broke the British fleet into two columns and drove them at the Franco-Spanish fleet, hitting its line perpendicularly. The lead British ships took a great risk, but Nelson judged that the less trained Franco-Spanish gunners would not be able to compensate for the heavy swell that day and that the enemy fleet, with its coherence lost, would be no match for the more experienced British captains and gunners in the ensuing melee. He was proved right: the French and Spanish lost 22 ships, two-thirds of their fleet. The British lost none.

Nelson's victory is a classic example of good strategy, which almost always looks this simple and obvious in retrospect. It does not pop out of some strategic-management tool, matrix, triangle, or fill-in-the blanks scheme. Instead, a talented leader has identified the one or two critical issues in a situation—the pivot points that can multiply the effectiveness of effort—and then focused and concentrated action and resources on them. A good strategy does more than urge us forward toward a goal or vision; it honestly acknowledges the challenges we face and provides an approach to overcoming them.

Too many organizational leaders say they have a strategy when they do not. Instead, they espouse what I call "bad strategy." Bad strategy ignores the power of choice and focus, trying instead to accommodate a multitude of conflicting demands and interests. Like a quarterback whose only advice to his teammates is "let's win," bad strategy covers up its failure to guide by embracing the language of broad goals, ambition, vision, and values. Each of these elements is, of course, an important part of human life. But, by themselves, they are not substitutes for the hard work of strategy.

In this article, I try to lay out the attributes of bad strategy and explain why it is so prevalent. Make no mistake: the creeping spread of bad strategy affects us all. Heavy with goals and slogans, governments have become less and less able to solve problems. Corporate boards sign off on strategic plans that are little more than wishful thinking. The U.S. education system is rich with targets and standards but poor at comprehending and countering the sources of underperformance. The only remedy is for us to demand more from those who lead. More than charisma and vision, we must demand good strategy.

THE HALLMARKS OF BAD STRATEGY

I coined the term bad strategy in 2007 at a Washington, DC, seminar on national-security strategy. My role was to provide a business and corporate-strategy perspective. The participants expected, I think, that my remarks would detail the seriousness and growing competence with which business strategy was created. Using words and slides, I told the group that many businesses did have powerful, effective strategies. But in my personal experiences with corporate practice, I saw a growing profusion of bad strategy.

In the years since that seminar, I have had the opportunity to discuss the bad-strategy concept with a number of senior executives. In the process, I have condensed my list of its key hallmarks to four points: the failure to face the challenge, mistaking goals for strategy, bad strategic objectives, and fluff.

FAILURE TO FACE THE PROBLEM

A strategy is a way through a difficulty, an approach to overcoming an obstacle, a response to a challenge. If the challenge is not defined, it is difficult or impossible to assess the quality of the strategy. And, if you cannot assess that, you cannot reject a bad strategy or improve a good one.

International Harvester learned about this element of bad strategy the hard way. In July 1979, the company's strategic and financial planners produced a thick sheaf of paper titled "Corporate Strategic Plan: International Harvester." It was an amalgam of five separate strategic plans, each created by one of the operating divisions. The strategic plan did not lack for texture and detail. Looking, for example, within the agricultural-equipment group—International Harvester's core, dating back to the McCormick reaper, which was a foundation of the company—there is information and discussion about each segment. The overall intent was to strengthen the dealer/distributor network and to reduce manufacturing costs. Market share in agricultural equipment was also projected to increase, from 16 percent to 20 percent.

That was typical of the overall strategy, which was to increase the company's share in each market, cut costs in each business, and thereby ramp up revenue and profit. A summary graph, showing past and forecast profit, forms an almost perfect hockey stick, with an immediate recovery from decline followed by a steady rise.

The problem with all this was that the plan didn't even mention Harvester's grossly inefficient production facilities, especially in its agricultural-equipment business, or the fact that Harvester had the worst labor relations in U.S. industry. As a result, the company's profit margin had been about one-half of its competitors' for a long time. As a corporation, International Harvester's main problem was its inefficient work organization—a problem that would not be solved by investing in new equipment or pressing managers to increase market share.

By cutting administrative overhead, Harvester boosted reported profits for a year or two. But following a disastrous six-month strike, the company quickly began to collapse. It sold off various businesses, including its agricultural-equipment business, to Tenneco. The truck division, renamed Navistar, is today a leading maker of heavy trucks and engines.

To summarize, if you fail to identify and analyze the obstacles, you don't have a strategy. Instead, you have a stretch goal or a budget or a list of things you wish would happen.

MISTAKING GOALS FOR STRATEGY

A few years ago, a CEO I'll call Chad Logan asked me to work with the management team of his graphic-arts company on "strategic thinking." Logan explained that his overall goal was simple—he called it the "20/20 plan." Revenues were to grow at 20 percent a year, and the profit margin was to be 20 percent or higher.

"This 20/20 plan is a very aggressive financial goal," I said. "What has to happen for it to be realized?" Logan tapped the plan with a blunt forefinger. "The thing I learned as a football player is that winning requires strength and skill, but more than anything it requires the will to win—the drive to succeed. . . . Sure, 20/20 is a stretch, but the secret of success is setting your sights high. We are going to keep pushing until we get there."

I tried again: "Chad, when a company makes the kind of jump in performance your plan envisions, there is usually a key strength you are building on or a change in the industry that opens up new opportunities. Can you clarify what the point of leverage might be here, in your company?"

Logan frowned and pressed his lips together, expressing frustration that I didn't understand him. He pulled a sheet of paper out of his briefcase and ran a finger under the highlighted text. "This is what Jack Welch says," he told me. The text read: "We have found that by reaching for what appears to be the impossible, we often actually do the impossible." (Logan's reading of Welch was, of course, highly selective. Yes, Welch believed in stretch goals. But he also said, "If you don't have a competitive advantage, don't compete.")

The reference to "pushing until we get there" triggered in my mind an association with the great pushes of 1915–17 during World War I, which led to the deaths of a generation of European youths. Maybe that's why motivational speakers are not the staple on the European management-lecture circuit that they are in the United States. For the slaughtered troops did not suffer from a lack of motivation. They suffered from a lack of competent strategic leadership. A leader may justly ask for "one last push," but the leader's job is more than that. The job of the leader—the strategist—is also to create the conditions that will make the push effective, to have a strategy worthy of the effort called upon.

BAD STRATEGIC OBJECTIVES

Another sign of bad strategy is fuzzy strategic objectives. One form this problem can take is a scrambled mess of things to accomplish—a dog's dinner of goals. A long list of things to do, often mislabeled as strategies or objectives, is not a strategy. It is just a list of things to do. Such lists usually grow out of planning meetings in which a wide variety of stakeholders suggest things they would like to see accomplished. Rather than focus on a few important items, the group sweeps the whole day's collection into the strategic plan. Then, in recognition that it is a dog's dinner, the label "long term" is added, implying that none of these things need be done today. As a vivid example, I recently had the chance to discuss strategy with the mayor of a small city in the Pacific Northwest. His planning committee's strategic plan contained 47 strategies and 178 action items. Action item number 122 was "create a strategic plan."

A second type of weak strategic objective is one that is "blue sky"—typically a simple restatement of the desired state of affairs or of the challenge. It skips over the annoying fact that no one has a clue as to how to get there. A leader may successfully identify the key challenge and propose an overall approach to dealing with the challenge. But if the consequent strategic objectives are just as difficult to meet as the original challenge, the strategy has added little value.

Good strategy, in contrast, works by focusing energy and resources on one, or a very few, pivotal objectives whose accomplishment will lead to a cascade of favorable outcomes.

It also builds a bridge between the critical challenge at the heart of the strategy and action—between desire and immediate objectives that lie within grasp. Thus, the objectives that a good strategy sets stand a good chance of being accomplished, given existing resources and competencies.

FLUFF

A final hallmark of mediocrity and bad strategy is superficial abstraction—a flurry of fluff—designed to mask the absence of thought. Fluff is a restatement of the obvious, combined with a generous sprinkling of buzzwords that masquerade as expertise. Here is a quote from a major retail bank's internal strategy memoranda: "Our fundamental strategy is one of customer-centric intermediation." Intermediation means that the company accepts deposits and then lends out the money. In other words, it is a bank. The buzz phrase "customer-centric" could mean that the bank competes by offering better terms and service, but an examination of its policies does not reveal any distinction in this regard. The phrase "customer-centric intermediation" is pure fluff. Remove the fluff and you learn that the bank's fundamental strategy is being a bank.

WHY SO MUCH BAD STRATEGY?

Bad strategy has many roots, but I'll focus on two here: the inability to choose and template-style planning—filling in the blanks with "vision, mission, values, strategies."

THE INABILITY TO CHOOSE

Strategy involves focus and, therefore, choice. And choice means setting aside some goals in favor of others. When this hard work is not done, weak strategy is the result. In 1992, I sat in on a strategy discussion among senior executives at Digital Equipment Corporation (DEC). A leader of the minicomputer revolution of the 1960s and 1970s, DEC had been losing ground for several years to the newer 32-bit personal computers. There were serious doubts that the company could survive for long without dramatic changes. To simplify matters, I will pretend that only three executives were present. "Alec" argued that DEC had always been a computer company and should continue integrating hardware and software into usable systems. "Beverly" felt that the only distinctive resource DEC had to build on was its customer relationships. Hence, she derided Alec's "Boxes" strategy and argued in favor of a "Solutions" strategy that solved customer problems. "Craig" held that the heart of the computer industry was semiconductor technology and that the company should focus its resources on designing and building better "Chips."

Choice was necessary: both the Chips and Solutions strategies represented dramatic transformations of the firm, and each would require wholly new skills and work practices. One wouldn't choose either risky alternative unless the status quo Boxes strategy was likely to fail. And one wouldn't choose to do both Chips and Solutions at the same time, because there was little common ground between them. It is not feasible to do two separate, deep transformations of a company's core at once.

With equally powerful executives arguing for each of the three conflicting strategies, the meeting was intense. DEC's chief executive, Ken Olsen, had made the mistake of asking the group to reach a consensus. It was unable to do that, because a majority preferred Solutions to Boxes, a majority preferred Boxes to Chips, and a majority also preferred Chips to Solutions. No matter which of the three paths was chosen, a majority preferred something else.

Not surprisingly, the group compromised on a statement: "DEC is committed to providing high-quality products and services and being a leader in data processing." This fluffy, amorphous statement was, of course, not a strategy. It was a political outcome reached by individuals who, forced to reach a consensus, could not agree on which interests and concepts to forego.

Ken Olsen was replaced, in June 1992, by Robert Palmer, who had headed the company's semiconductor engineering. Palmer made it clear that the strategy would be Chips. One point of view had finally won. But by then it was five years too late. Palmer stopped the losses for a while but could not stem the tide of ever more powerful personal computers that were overtaking the firm. In 1998, DEC was acquired by Compaq, which, in turn, was acquired by Hewlett-Packard three years later.

TEMPLATE-STYLE STRATEGY

The Jack Welch quote about "reaching for what appears to be the impossible" is fairly standard motivational fare, available from literally hundreds of motivational speakers, books, calendars, memo pads, and websites. This fascination with positive thinking has helped inspire ideas about charismatic leadership and the power of a shared vision, reducing them to something of a formula. The general outline goes like this: the transformational leader (1) develops or has a vision, (2) inspires people to sacrifice (change) for the good of the organization, and (3) empowers people to accomplish the vision.

By the early 2000s, the juxtaposition of vision-led leadership and strategy work had produced a template-style system of strategic planning. (Type "vision mission strategy" into a search engine and you'll find thousands of examples of this kind of template for sale and in use.)

The template looks like this:

> The Vision. Fill in your vision of what the school/business/nation will be like in the future. Currently popular visions are to be the best or the leading or the best known.
>
> The Mission. Fill in a high-sounding, politically correct statement of the purpose of the school/business/nation. Innovation, human progress, and sustainable solutions are popular elements of a mission statement.
>
> The Values. Fill in a statement that describes the company's values. Make sure they are noncontroversial. Key words include "integrity," "respect," and "excellence."
>
> The Strategies. Fill in some aspirations/goals but call them strategies. For example, "to invest in a portfolio of performance businesses that create value for our shareholders and growth for our customers."

This template-style planning has been enthusiastically adopted by corporations, school boards, university presidents, and government agencies. Scan through such documents and you will find pious statements of the obvious presented as if they were decisive insights. The enormous problem all this creates is that someone who actually wishes to conceive and implement an effective strategy is surrounded by empty rhetoric and bad examples.

THE KERNEL OF GOOD STRATEGY

By now, I hope you are fully awake to the dramatic differences between good and bad strategy. Let me close by trying to give you a leg up in crafting good strategies, which have a basic underlying structure:

1. A diagnosis: an explanation of the nature of the challenge. A good diagnosis simplifies the often overwhelming complexity of reality by identifying certain aspects of the situation as being the critical ones.
2. A guiding policy: an overall approach chosen to cope with or overcome the obstacles identified in the diagnosis.
3. Coherent actions: steps that are coordinated with one another to support the accomplishment of the guiding policy.

I'll illustrate by describing Nvidia's journey from troubled start-up to market leader for 3-D graphics chips. Nvidia's first product, a PC add-in board for video, audio, and 3-D graphics, was a commercial failure. In 1995, rival start-up 3Dfx Interactive took the lead in serving the burgeoning demand of gamers for fast 3-D graphics chips. Furthermore, there were rumors that industry giant Intel was thinking about introducing its own 3-D graphics chip. The diagnosis: "We are losing the performance race."

Nvidia CEO Jen-Hsun Huang's key insight was that given the rapid state of advance in 3-D graphics, releasing a new chip every 6 months, instead of at the industry standard rate of every 18 months, would make a critical difference. The guiding policy, in short, was to "release a faster, better chip three times faster than the industry norm."

To accomplish this fast release cycle, the company emphasized several coherent actions: it formed three development teams, which worked on overlapping schedules; it invested in massive simulation and emulation facilities to avoid delays in the fabrication of chips and in the development of software drivers; and, over time, it regained control of driver development from the branded add-in board makers.

Over the next decade, the strategy worked brilliantly. Intel introduced its 3-D graphics chip in 1998 but did not keep up the pace, exiting the business of discrete 3-D graphics chips a year later. In 2000, creditors of 3Dfx initiated bankruptcy proceedings against the company, which was struggling to keep up with Nvidia. In 2007, Forbes named Nvidia the "Company of the Year."

* * *

Despite the roar of voices equating strategy with ambition, leadership, vision, or planning, strategy is none of these. Rather, it is coherent action backed by an argument. And the core of the strategist's work is always the same: discover the crucial factors in a situation and design a way to coordinate and focus actions to deal with them.

READING 5.2

Crafting Strategy* BY HENRY MINTZBERG

Imagine someone planning strategy. What likely springs to mind is an image of orderly thinking: a senior manager, or a group of them, sitting in an office formulating courses of action that everyone else will implement on schedule. The keynote is reason—rational control, the systematic analysis of competitors and markets, of company strengths and weaknesses, the combination of these analyses producing clear, explicit, full-blown strategies.

Now imagine someone *crafting* strategy. A wholly different image likely results, as different from planning as craft is from mechanization. Craft evokes traditional skill, dedication, perfection through the mastery of detail. What springs to mind is not so much thinking and reason as involvement, a feeling of intimacy and harmony with the materials at hand, developed through long experience and commitment. Formulation and implementation merge into a fluid process of learning through which creative strategies evolve.

My thesis is simple: the crafting image better captures the process by which effective strategies come to be. The planning image, long popular in the literature, distorts these processes and thereby misguides organizations that embrace it unreservedly.

In developing this thesis, I shall draw on the experiences of a single craftsperson, a potter, and compare them with the results of a research project that tracked the strategies of a number of corporations across several decades. Because the two contexts are so obviously different, my metaphor, like my assertion, may seem farfetched at first. Yet if we think of a craftsperson as an organization of one, we can see that he or she must also resolve one of the great challenges the corporate strategist faces: knowing the organization's capabilities well enough to think deeply enough about its strategic direction. By considering strategy making from the perspective of one person, free of all the paraphernalia of what has been called the strategy industry, we can learn something about the formation of strategy in the corporation. For much as our potter has to manage her craft, so too managers have to craft their strategy.

---

*Originally published in the *Harvard Business Review* (July–August 1987) and winner of McKinsey prize for second best article in the *Review* 1987. Reprinted with deletions by permission of the *Harvard Business Review*.

At work, the potter sits before a lump of clay on the wheel. Her mind is on the clay, but she is also aware of sitting between her past experiences and her future prospects. She knows exactly what has and has not worked for her in the past. She has an intimate knowledge of her work, her capabilities, and her markets. As a craftsperson, she senses rather than analyzes these things; her knowledge is "tacit." All these things are working in her mind as her hands are working the clay. The product that emerges on the wheel is likely to be in the tradition of her past work, but she may break away and embark on a new direction. Even so, the past is no less present, projecting itself into the future.

In my metaphor, managers are craftspersons and strategy is their clay. Like the potter, they sit between the past of corporate capabilities and a future of market opportunities. And if they are truly craftspersons, they bring to their work an equally intimate knowledge of the materials at hand. That is the essence of crafting strategy.

1. STRATEGIES ARE BOTH PLANS FOR THE FUTURE AND PATTERNS FROM THE PAST

Ask almost anyone what strategy is, and they will define it as a plan of some sort, an explicit guide to future behavior. Then ask them what strategy a competitor or a government or even they themselves have actually pursued. Chances are they will describe consistency in *past* behavior—a pattern in action over time. Strategy, it turns out, is one of those words that people define in one way and often use in another, without realizing the difference.

The reason for this is simple. Strategy's formal definition and its Greek military origins notwithstanding, we need the word as much to explain past actions as to describe intended behavior. After all, if strategies can be planned and intended, they can also be pursued and realized (or not realized, as the case may be). And pattern in action, or what we call realized strategy, explains that pursuit. Moreover, just as a plan need not produce a pattern (some strategies that are intended are simply not realized), so too a pattern need not result from a plan. An organization can have a pattern (or realized strategy) without knowing it, let alone making it explicit.

Patterns, like beauty, are in the mind of the beholder, of course. But finding them in organizations is not very difficult. But what about intended strategies, those formal plans and pronouncements we think of when we use the term *strategy*? Ironically, here we run into all kinds of problems. Even with a single craftsperson, how can we know what her intended strategies really were? If we could go back, would we find expressions of intention? And if we could, would we be able to trust them? We often fool ourselves, as well as others, by denying our subconscious motives. And remember that intentions are cheap, at least when compared with realizations.

READING THE ORGANIZATION'S MIND

If you believe all this has more to do with the Freudian recesses of a craftsperson's mind than with the practical realities of producing automobiles, then think again. For who knows what the intended strategies of an organization really mean, let alone what they are? Can we simply assume in this collective context that the company's intended strategies are represented by its formal plans or by other statements emanating from the executive suite? Might these be just vain hopes or rationalizations or ploys to fool the competition? And even if expressed intentions do exist, to what extent do various people in the organization share them? How do we read the collective mind? Who is the strategist anyway?

The traditional view of strategic management resolves these problems quite simply, by what organizational theorists call attribution. You see it all the time in the business press. When General Motors acts, it's because its CEO has made a strategy. Given realization, there must have been intention, and that is automatically attributed to the chief.

In a short magazine article, this assumption is understandable. Journalists don't have a lot of time to uncover the origins of strategy, and GM is a large, complicated organization. But just consider all the complexity and confusion that gets tucked under this assumption—all the meetings and debates, the many people, the dead ends, the folding and unfolding of ideas. Now imagine trying to build a formal strategy-making system around that assumption. Is it any wonder that formal strategic planning is often such a resounding failure?

To unravel some of the confusion—and move away from the artificial complexity we have piled around the strategy-making process—we need to get back to some basic concepts. The most basic of all is the intimate connection between thought and action. That is the key to craft, and so also to the crafting of strategy.

2. STRATEGIES NEED NOT BE DELIBERATE—THEY CAN ALSO EMERGE, MORE OR LESS

Virtually everything that has been written about strategy making depicts it as a deliberate process. First we think, then we act. We formulate, then we implement. The progression seems so perfectly sensible. Why would anybody want to proceed differently?

Our potter is in the studio, rolling the clay to make a waferlike sculpture. The clay sticks to the rolling pin, and a round form appears. Why not make a cylindrical vase? One idea leads to another, until a new pattern forms. Action has driven thinking: a strategy has emerged.

Out in the field, a salesman visits a customer. The product isn't quite right, and together they work out some modifications. The salesman returns to his company and puts the changes through; after two or three more rounds, they finally get it right. A new product emerges, which eventually opens up a new market. The company has changed strategic course.

In fact, most salespeople are less fortunate than this one or than our craftsperson. In an organization of one, the implementor is the formulator, so innovations can be incorporated into strategy quickly and easily. In a large organization, the innovator may be ten levels removed from the leader who is supposed to dictate strategy and may also have to sell the idea to dozens of peers doing the same job.

Some salespeople, of course, can proceed on their own, modifying products to suit their customers and convincing skunkworks in the factory to produce them. In effect, they pursue their own strategies. Maybe no one else notices or cares. Sometimes, however, their innovations do get noticed, perhaps years later, when the company's prevalent strategies have broken down and its leaders are groping for something new. Then the salesperson's strategy may be allowed to pervade the system, to become organizational.

Is this story farfetched? Certainly not. We've all heard stories like it. But since we tend to see only what we believe, if we believe that strategies have to be planned, we're unlikely to see the real meaning such stories hold.

Consider how the National Film Board of Canada (NFB) came to adopt a feature-film strategy. The NFB is a federal government agency, famous for its creativity and expert in the production of short documentaries. Some years back, it funded a filmmaker on a project that unexpectedly ran long. To distribute his film, the NFB turned to theaters and so inadvertently gained experience in marketing feature-length films. Other filmmakers caught on to the idea, and eventually the NFB found itself pursuing a feature-film strategy—a pattern of producing such films.

My point is simple, deceptively simple: strategies can *form* as well as be *formulated*. A realized strategy can emerge in response to an evolving situation, or it can be brought about deliberately, through a process of formulation followed by implementation. But when these planned intentions do not produce the desired actions, organizations are left with unrealized strategies.

Today we hear a great deal about unrealized strategies, almost always in concert with the claim that implementation has failed. Management has been lax, controls have been loose, people haven't been committed. Excuses abound. At times, indeed, they may be valid. But often these explanations prove too easy. So some people look beyond implementation to formulation. The strategists haven't been smart enough.

While it is certainly true that many intended strategies are ill conceived, I believe that the problem often lies one step beyond, in the distinction we make between formulation and implementation, the common assumption that thought must be independent of and precede action. Sure, people could be smarter—but not only by conceiving more clever strategies. Sometimes they can be smarter by allowing their strategies to develop gradually, through the organization's actions and experiences. Smart strategists appreciate that they cannot always be smart enough to think through everything in advance.

HANDS AND MINDS

No craftsperson thinks some days and works others. The craftsperson's mind is going constantly, in tandem with her hands. Yet large organizations try to separate the work of minds and hands. In so doing, they often sever the vital feedback linking between the two. The salesperson who finds a customer with an unmet need may possess the most strategic bit of information in the entire organization. But that information is useless if he or she cannot create a strategy in response to it or else convey the information to someone who can—because the channels are blocked or because the formulators have simply finished formulating. The notion that strategy is something that should happen way up there, far removed from the details of running an organization on a daily basis, is one of the great fallacies of conventional strategic management. And it explains a good many of the most dramatic failures in business and public policy today.

Strategies like the NFB's that appear without clear intentions—or in spite of them—can be called emergent. Actions simply converge into patterns. They may become deliberate, of course, if the pattern is recognized and then legitimated by senior management. But that's after the fact.

All this may sound rather strange, I know. Strategies that emerge? Managers who acknowledge strategies already formed? Over the years we have met with a good deal of resistance from people upset by what they perceive to be our passive definition of a word so bound up with proactive behavior and free will. After all, strategy means control—the ancient Greeks used it to describe the art of the army general.

STRATEGIC LEARNING

But we have persisted in this usage for one reason: learning. Purely deliberate strategy precludes learning once the strategy is formulated; emergent strategy fosters it. People take actions one by one and respond to them, so that patterns eventually form.

Our craftsperson tries to make a freestanding sculptural form. It doesn't work, so she rounds it a bit here, flattens it a bit there. The result looks better, but still isn't quite right. She makes another and another and another. Eventually, after days or months or years, she finally has what she wants. She is off on a new strategy.

In practice, of course, all strategy making walks on two feet: one deliberate, the other emergent. For just as purely deliberate strategy making precludes learning, so purely emergent strategy making precludes control. Pushed to the limit, neither approach makes much sense. Learning must be coupled with control. That is why we use the word *strategy* for both emergent and deliberate behavior.

Likewise, there is no such thing as a purely deliberate strategy or a purely emergent one. No organization—not even the ones commanded by those ancient Greek generals—knows enough to work everything out in advance, to ignore learning en route. And no one—not even a solitary potter—can be flexible enough to leave everything to happenstance, to give up all control. Craft requires control just as it requires responsiveness to the material at hand. Thus deliberate and emergent strategy form the end points of a continuum along which the strategies that are crafted in the real world may be found. Some strategies may approach either end, but many more fall at intermediate points.

3. EFFECTIVE STRATEGIES DEVELOP IN ALL KINDS OF STRANGE WAYS

Effective strategies can show up in the strangest places and develop through the most unexpected means. There is no one best way to make strategy.

The form for a ceramic cat collapses on the wheel, and our potter sees a bull taking shape. Clay sticks to a rolling pin, and a line of cylinders results. Wafers come into being because of a shortage of clay and limited kiln space while visiting a studio in France. Thus errors become opportunities, and limitations stimulate creativity. The natural propensity to experiment, even boredom, likewise stimulates strategic change.

Organizations that craft their strategies have similar experiences. Recall the National Film Board with its inadvertently long film. Or consider its experiences with experimental films, which made special use of animation and sound. For 20 years, the NFB produced a bare but steady trickle of such films. In fact, every film but one in that trickle was produced by a single person, Norman McLaren, the NFB's most celebrated filmmaker. McLaren pursued a *personal strategy* of experimentation, deliberate for him perhaps (though who can know whether he had the whole stream in mind or simply planned one film at a time?) but not for the organization. Then 20 years later, others followed his lead and the trickle widened, his personal strategy becoming more broadly organizational.

While the NFB may seem like an extreme case, it highlights behavior that can be found, albeit in muted form, in all organizations. Those who doubt this might read Richard Pascale's account of how Honda stumbled into its enormous success in the American motorcycle market (the following article in this book).

GRASS-ROOTS STRATEGY MAKING

These strategies all reflect, in whole or part, what we like to call a grass-roots approach to strategic management. Strategies grow like weeds in a garden. They take root in all kinds of places, wherever people have the capacity to learn (because they are in touch with the situation) and the resources to support that capacity. These strategies become organizational when they become collective, that is, when they proliferate to guide the behavior of the organization at large.

Of course, this view is overstated. But it is no less extreme than the conventional view of strategic management, which might be labeled the hothouse approach. Neither is right. Reality falls between the two. Some of the most effective strategies we uncovered in our research combined deliberation and control with flexibility and organizational learning.

Consider first what we call the *umbrella strategy*. Here senior management sets out broad guidelines (say, to produce only high-margin products at the cutting edge of technology or to favor products using bonding technology) and leaves the specifics (such as what these products will be) to others lower down in the organization. This strategy is not only deliberate (in its guidelines) and emergent (in its specifics), but it is also deliberately emergent, in that the process is consciously managed to allow strategies to emerge en route. IBM used the umbrella strategy in the early 1960s with the impending 360 series, when its senior management approved a set of broad criteria for the design of a family of computers later developed in detail throughout the organization. (See the IBM case in this section.)

Deliberately emergent, too, is what we call the *process strategy*. Here management controls the process of strategy formation—concerning itself with the design of the structure, its staffing, procedures, and so on—while leaving the actual content to others.

Both process and umbrella strategies seem to be especially prevalent in businesses that require great expertise and creativity—a 3M, a Hewlett-Packard, a National Film Board. Such organizations can be effective only if their implementors are allowed to be formulators, because it is people way down in the hierarchy who are in touch with the situation at hand and have the requisite technical expertise. In a sense, these are organizations peopled with craftspersons, all of whom must be strategists.

4. STRATEGIC REORIENTATIONS HAPPEN IN BRIEF, QUANTUM LEAPS

The conventional view of strategic management, especially in the planning literature, claims that change must be continuous: the organization should be adapting all the time. Yet this view proves to be ironic because the very concept of strategy is rooted in stability, not change. As this same literature makes clear, organizations pursue strategies to set direction, to lay out courses of action, and to elicit cooperation from their members around common, established guidelines. By any definition, strategy imposes stability on an organization. No stability means no strategy (no course to the future, no pattern from the past). Indeed, the very fact of having a strategy, and especially of making it explicit (as the conventional literature implores managers to do), creates resistance to strategic change!

What the conventional view fails to come to grips with, then, is how and when to promote change. A fundamental dilemma of strategy making is the need to reconcile the forces for stability and for change—to focus efforts and gain operating efficiencies on the one hand, yet adapt and maintain currency with a changing external environment on the other.

QUANTUM LEAPS

Our own research and that of colleagues suggest that organizations resolve these opposing forces by attending first to one and then to the other. Clear periods of stability and change can usually be distinguished in any organization: while it is true that particular strategies may always be changing marginally, it seems equally true that major shifts in strategic orientation occur only rarely.

In our study of Steinberg, Inc., a large Quebec supermarket chain headquartered in Montreal, we found only two important reorientations in the 60 years from its founding to the mid-1970s: a shift to self-service in 1933 and the introduction of shopping centers and public financing in 1953. At Volkswagenwerk, we saw only one between the late 1940s and the 1970s, the tumultuous shift from the traditional Beetle to the Audi-type design. And at Air Canada, we found none over the airline's first four decades, following its initial positioning.

Our colleagues at McGill, Danny Miller and Peter Friesen (1984), found this pattern of change so common in their studies of large numbers of companies (especially the high-performance ones) that they built a theory around it, which they labeled the quantum theory of strategic change. Their basic point is that organizations adopt two distinctly different modes of behavior at different times.

Most of the time they pursue a given strategic orientation. Change may seem continuous, but it occurs in the context of that orientation (perfecting a given retailing formula, for example) and usually amounts to doing more of the same, perhaps better as well. Most organizations favor these periods of stability because they achieve success not by changing strategies but by exploiting the ones they have. They, like craftspersons, seek continuous improvement by using their distinctive competencies on established courses.

While this goes on, however, the world continues to change, sometimes slowly, occasionally in dramatic shifts. Thus gradually or suddenly, the organization's strategic orientation moves out of sync with its environment. Then what Miller and Friesen call a strategic revolution must take place. That long period of evolutionary change is suddenly punctuated by a brief bout of revolutionary turmoil in which the organization quickly alters many of its established patterns. In effect, it tries to leap to a new stability quickly to reestablish an integrated posture among a new set of strategies, structures, and culture.

But what about all those emergent strategies, growing like weeds around the organization? What the quantum theory suggests is that the really novel ones are generally held in check in some corner of the organization until a strategic revolution becomes necessary. Then, as an alternative to having to develop new strategies from scratch or having to import generic strategies from competitors, the organization can turn to its own emerging patterns to find its new orientation. As the old, established strategy disintegrates, the seeds of the new one begin to spread.

This quantum theory of change seems to apply particularly well to large established, mass-production companies, like a Volkswagenwerk. Because they are especially reliant on standardized procedures, their resistance to strategic reorientation tends to be especially fierce. So we find long periods of stability broken by short disruptive periods of revolutionary change. Strategic reorientations really are cultural revolutions.

In more creative organizations we see a somewhat different pattern of change and stability, one that is more balanced. Companies in the business of producing novel outputs apparently need to run off in all directions from time to time to sustain their creativity. Yet they also need to settle down after such periods to find some order in the resulting chaos—convergence following divergence.

Whether through quantum revolutions or cycles of convergence and divergence, however, organizations seem to need to separate in time the basic forces for change and stability, reconciling them by attending to each in turn. Many strategic failures can be attributed either to mixing the two or to an obsession with one of these forces at the expense of the other.

The problems are evident in the work of many craftspersons. On the one hand, there are those who seize on the perfection of a single theme and never change. Eventually the creativity disappears from their work and the world passes them by—much as it did Volkswagenwerk until the company was shocked into its strategic revolution. And then there are those who are always changing, who flit from one idea to another and never settle down. Because no theme or strategy ever emerges in their work, they cannot exploit or even develop any distinctive competence.

And because their work lacks definition, identity crises are likely to develop, with neither the craftspersons nor their clientele knowing what to make of it. Miller and Friesen (1978: 921) found this behavior in conventional business too; they label it "the impulsive firm running blind." How often have we seen it in companies that go on acquisition sprees?

5. TO MANAGE STRATEGY, THEN, IS TO CRAFT THOUGHT AND ACTION, CONTROL AND LEARNING, STABILITY AND CHANGE

The popular view sees the strategist as a planner or as a visionary, someone sitting on a pedestal dictating brilliant strategies for everyone else to implement. While recognizing the importance of thinking ahead and especially of the need for creative vision in this pedantic world, I wish to propose an additional view of the strategist—as a pattern recognizer, a learner if you will—who manages a process in which strategies (and visions) can emerge as well as be deliberately conceived. I also wish to redefine that strategist, to extend that someone into the collective entity made up of the many actors whose interplay speaks an organization's mind. This strategist *finds* strategies no less than creates them, often in patterns that form inadvertently in his or her own behavior.

What, then, does it mean to craft strategy? Let us return to the words associated with craft: dedication, experience, involvement with the material, the personal touch, mastery of detail, a sense of harmony and integration. Managers who craft strategy do not spend much time in executive suites reading MIS reports or industry analyses. They are involved, responsive to their materials, learning about their organizations and industries through personal touch. They are also sensitive to experience, recognizing that while individual vision may be important, other factors must help determine strategy as well.

Manage Stability

Managing strategy is mostly managing stability, not change. Indeed, most of the time senior managers should not be formulating strategy at all; they should be getting on with making their organizations as effective as possible in pursuing the strategies they already have. Like distinguished craftspersons, organizations become distinguished because they master the details.

To manage strategy, then, at least in the first instance, is not so much to promote change as to know *when* to do so. Advocates of strategic planning often urge managers to plan for perpetual instability in the environment (for example, by rolling over five-year plans annually). But this obsession with change is dysfunctional. Organizations that reassess their strategies continuously are like individuals who reassess their jobs or their marriages continuously—in both cases, they will drive themselves crazy or else reduce themselves to inaction. The formal planning process repeats itself so often and so mechanically that it desensitizes the organization to real change, programs it more and more deeply into set patterns, and thereby encourages it to make only minor adaptations.

So-called strategic planning must be recognized for what it is: a means not to create strategy but to program a strategy already created—to work out its implications formally. It is essentially analytic in nature, based on decomposition, while strategy creation is essentially a process of synthesis. That is why trying to create strategies through formal planning most often leads to extrapolating existing ones or copying those of competitors.

This is not to say that planners have no role to play in strategy formation. In addition to programming strategies created by other means, they can feed ad hoc analyses into the strategy-making process at the front end to be sure that the hard data are taken into consideration. They can also stimulate others to think strategically. And of course people called planners can be strategists too, so long as they are creative thinkers who are in touch with what is relevant. But that has nothing to do with the technology of formal planning.

Detect Discontinuity

Environments don't change on any regular or orderly basis. And they seldom undergo continuous dramatic change, claims about our "age of discontinuity" and environmental "turbulence" notwithstanding. (Go tell people who lived through the Great Depression or survivors of the siege of Leningrad during World War II that ours are turbulent times.) Much of the time, change is minor and even temporary and requires no strategic response. Once in a while there is a truly significant discontinuity or, even less often, a gestalt shift in the environment, where everything important seems to change at once. But these events, while critical, are also easy to recognize.

The real challenge in crafting strategy lies in detecting the subtle discontinuities that may undermine a business in the future. And for that, there is no technique, no program, just a sharp mind in touch with the situation. Such discontinuities are unexpected and irregular, essentially unprecedented. They can be dealt with only by minds that are attuned to existing patterns yet able to perceive important breaks in them. Unfortunately, this form of strategic thinking tends to atrophy during the long periods of stability that most organizations experience. So the trick is to manage within a given strategic orientation most of the time yet be able to pick out the occasional discontinuity that really matters. The ability to make that kind of switch in thinking is the essence of strategic management. And it has more to do with vision and involvement than it does with analytic technique.

Know the Business

Note the kind of knowledge involved in strategic thinking: not intellectual knowledge, not analytical reports or abstracted facts and figures (though these can certainly help), but personal knowledge, intimate understanding, equivalent to the craftsperson's feel for the clay. Facts are available to anyone; this kind of knowledge is not. Wisdom is the word that captures it best. But wisdom is a word that has been lost in the bureaucracies we have built for ourselves, systems designed to distance leaders from operating details. Show me managers who think they can rely on formal planning to create their strategies, and I'll show you managers who lack intimate knowledge of their businesses or the creativity to do something with it.

Craftspersons have to train themselves to see, to pick up things other people miss. The same holds true for managers of strategy. It is those with a kind of peripheral vision who are best able to detect and take advantage of events as they unfold.

Manage Patterns

Whether in an executive suite in Manhattan or a pottery studio in Montreal, a key to managing strategy is the ability to detect emerging patterns and help them take shape. The job of the manager is not just to preconceive specific strategies but also to recognize their emergence elsewhere in the organization and intervene when appropriate.

Like weeds that appear unexpectedly in a garden, some emergent strategies may need to be uprooted immediately. But management cannot be too quick to cut off the unexpected, for tomorrow's vision may grow out of today's aberration. (Europeans, after all, enjoy salads made from the leaves of the dandelion, America's most notorious weed.) Thus some patterns are worth watching until their effects have more clearly manifested themselves. Then those that prove useful can be made deliberate and be incorporated into the formal strategy, even if that means shifting the strategic umbrella to cover them.

To manage in this context, then, is to create the climate within which a wide variety of strategies can grow. In more complex organizations, this may mean building flexible structures, hiring creative people, defining broad umbrella strategies, and watching for the patterns that emerge.

Reconcile Change and Continuity

Finally, managers considering radical departures need to keep the quantum theory of change in mind. As Ecclesiastes reminds us, there is a time to sow and a time to reap. Some new patterns must be held in check until the organization is ready for a strategic revolution, or at least a period of divergence. Managers who are obsessed with either change or stability are bound eventually to harm their organizations. As pattern recognizer, the manager has to be able to sense when to exploit an established crop of strategies and when to encourage new strains to displace the old.

While strategy is a word that is usually associated with the future, its link to the past is no less central. As Kierkegaard once observed, life is lived forward but understood backward. Managers may have to live strategy in the future, but they must understand it through the past.

Like potters at the wheel, organizations must make sense of the past if they hope to manage the future. Only by coming to understand the patterns that form in their own behavior do they get to know their capabilities and their potential. Thus crafting strategy, like managing craft, requires a natural synthesis of the future, present, and past.

READING 5.3

Strategy as Strategic Decision Making* BY KATHLEEN M. EISENHARDT

Many executives realize that to prosper in the coming decade, they need to turn to the fundamental issue of strategy. What is strategy? To use a simple yet powerful definition from *The Economist,* strategy answers two basic questions: "Where do you want to go?" and "How do you want to get there?"

Traditional approaches to strategy focus on the first question. They involve selecting an attractive market, choosing a defensible strategic position, or building core competencies. Only later, if at all, do executives address the second question. Yet in today's high-velocity, hotly competitive markets, these approaches are incomplete. They overemphasize executives' ability to analyze and predict which industries, competencies, or strategic positions will be viable and for how long, and they underemphasize the challenge of actually creating effective strategies.

Many managers of successful corporations have adopted a different perspective on strategy that Shona Brown and I call "competing on the edge." At the heart of this approach lies the recognition that strategy combines the questions of "where" and "how" to create a continuing flow of temporary and shifting competitive advantages. . . .

This article describes strategy as strategic decision making, especially in rapidly changing markets. Its underlying assumption is that "bet the company" decisions—those that change the firm's direction and generate new competitive advantages—arise much more often in these markets. Therefore, the ability to make fast, widely supported, and high-quality strategic decisions on a frequent basis is the cornerstone of effective strategy. To use the language of contemporary strategy thinking, strategic decision making is the fundamental dynamic capability in excellent firms. . . .

In both studies (done with colleagues), clear differences stood out between the strategic decision-making processes in the more and less effective firms. Strikingly, these differences counter commonly held beliefs that conflict slows down choice, politicking is typical, and fast decisions are autocratic. In other words, these findings challenge the assumption of trade-offs among speed, quality, and support. Instead, the most effective strategic decision makers made choices that were fast, high-quality, and widely supported. How did they do it? Four approaches emerged from this research and my other work with executives. Effective decision makers create strategy by:

- Building collective intuition that enhances the ability of a top-management team to see threats and opportunities sooner and more accurately.
- Stimulating quick conflict to improve the quality of strategic thinking without sacrificing significant time.
- Maintaining a disciplined pace that drives the decision process to a timely conclusion.
- Defusing political behavior that creates unproductive conflict and wastes time.

BUILD COLLECTIVE INTUITION

One myth of strategic decision making in high-velocity markets is that there is no time for formal meetings and no place for the careful consideration of extensive information. Executives, the thinking goes, should consider limited, decision-specific data, concentrate on one or two alternatives, and make decisions on the fly.

Effective strategic decision makers do not follow that approach. They use as much as or more information than ineffective executives, and they are far more likely to hold regularly scheduled, "don't miss" meetings. They rely on extensive, real-time information about internal and external

*Excerpted from "Strategy as Strategic Decision Making" by Kathleen M. Eisenhardt, *MIT Sloan Management Review,* Spring 1999, pp. 65–72, by permission of the publisher.

operations, which they discuss in intensive meetings. They avoid both accounting-based information because it tends to lag behind the realities of the business and predictions of the future because these are likely to be wrong. From extensive, real-time information, these executives build a collective intuition that allows them to move quickly and accurately as opportunities arise. . . .

Why do real-time information and "must attend" meetings lead to more effective strategic decision making? Intense interaction creates teams of managers who know each other well. Familiarity and friendship make frank conversation easier because people are less constrained by politeness and more willing to express diverse views. The strategic decision process then moves more quickly and benefits from high-quality information . . . when intense interaction focuses on the operating metrics of today's businesses, a deep intuition, or "gut feeling," is created, giving managers a superior grasp of changing competitive dynamics. Artificial intelligence research on championship chess players indicates how this intuition is formed. These players, for example, develop their so-called intuition through experience. Through frequent play, they gain the ability to recognize and process information in patterns or blocks that form the basis of intuition. This patterned processing (what we term "intuition") is faster and more accurate than processing single pieces of information. Consistent with this research, many effective decision makers were described by their colleagues as having "an immense instinctive feel," "a high quality of understanding," and "an intuitive sense of the business." This intuition gives managers a head start in recognizing and understanding strategic issues.

STIMULATE QUICK CONFLICT

In high-velocity markets, many executives are tempted to avoid conflict. They assume that conflict will bog down the decision-making process in endless debate and degenerate into personal attacks. They seek to move quickly toward a few alternatives, analyze the best ones, and make a quick choice that beats the competition to the punch.

Reality is different. In dynamic markets, conflict is a natural feature of high-stakes decision making because reasonable managers will often diverge in their views on how the marketplace will unfold. Furthermore, as research demonstrates, conflict stimulates innovative thinking, creates a fuller understanding of options, and improves decision effectiveness. Without conflict, decision makers commonly miss opportunities to question assumptions and overlook key elements of the decision. Given the value of conflict, effective strategic decision makers in rapidly changing markets not only tolerate conflict, they accelerate it.

One way that executives accelerate conflict is by assembling executive teams that are diverse in age, gender, functional background, and corporate experience. . . .

Another way that effective strategic decision makers accelerate conflict is by using "frame-breaking" tactics that create alternatives to obvious points of view. One technique is scenario planning: teams systematically consider strategic decisions in the light of several possible future states. Other techniques have executives advocate alternatives that they may or may not favor and perform role plays of competitors. The details of the techniques are not crucial. Rather, the point is to use and switch among them to prevent stale thinking. . . .

Perhaps the most powerful way to accelerate conflict is by creating multiple alternatives. The idea is to develop alternatives as quickly as possible so that the team can work with an array of possibilities simultaneously. As one executive commented, "We play a larger set of options than most people." It is considered entirely appropriate for executives to advocate options that they may not prefer simply to encourage debate. . . .

Why do diverse teams, frame-breaking techniques, and multiple alternatives lead to faster conflict and ultimately more effective decisions? The rationale for diverse teams is clear: these teams come up with more varied viewpoints than homogeneous teams. The value of frame-breaking techniques is more subtle. In addition to the obvious benefit of generating many different perspectives, these techniques establish the norm that constructive conflict is an expected part of the strategic decision-making process. It is acceptable and even desirable to engage in conflict. Furthermore, frame-breaking techniques are intellectually engaging and even fun. They can motivate even apathetic executives to participate more actively in expansive strategic thinking.

The power of multiple alternatives comes from several sources. Clearly, pushing for multiple alternatives speeds up conflict by stimulating executives to develop divergent options. It also enables them to rapidly compare alternatives, helping them to better understand their own preferences. Furthermore, multiple alternatives provide executives with the confidence that they have not overlooked a superior option. That confidence is crucial in rapidly changing markets, where the blocks to effective decision making are emotional as much as cognitive. Finally, multiple alternatives defuse the interpersonal tension that can accompany conflict by giving team members room to maneuver and save face when they disagree. . . .

MAINTAIN THE PACE

Less effective strategic decision makers face a dilemma. On the one hand, they believe that every strategic decision is unique. Each requires its own analytical approach, and each unfolds in its own way. On the other hand, these same decision makers believe that they must decide as quickly as possible. Yet making quick choices conflicts with making one-of-a-kind choices.

Effective strategic decision makers avoid this dilemma by focusing on maintaining decision pace, not pushing decision speed. They launch the decision-making process promptly, keep up the energy surrounding the process, and cut off debate at the appropriate moment. They drive strategic decision-making momentum. . . .

Effective strategic decision makers skillfully cut off debate, typically using a two-step method called "consensus with qualification" to bring decision making to a close. First, managers conduct the decision process itself with the goal of consensus in mind. If they reach consensus, the choice is made. If consensus does not emerge, they break the deadlock using a decision rule such as voting or, more commonly, allowing the manager with the largest stake in the outcome to make the decision. . . .

Decision-making rhythm helps managers plan their progress and forces them to recognize the familiar aspects of decision making that make the process more predictable. As significant, it emphasizes that hitting decision timing is more critical than forging consensus or developing massive data analyses. As one manager told us, "The worst decision is no decision at all." . . .

DEFUSE POLITICS

Some executives believe that politics are a natural part of strategic choice. They see strategic decision making as involving high stakes that compel managers to lobby one another, manipulate information, and form coalitions. The game quickly becomes a competition among ambitious managers.

More effective strategic decision makers take a negative view of politicking. Since politicking often involves managers using information to their own advantage, it distorts the information base, leading to a poor strategic decision-making process. Furthermore, these executives see political activity as wasting valuable time. Their perspective is collaborative, not competitive, setting limits on politics and, more generally, interpersonal conflict.

One way in which effective executives defuse politics is by creating common goals. These goals do not imply homogeneous thinking. Rather, they suggest that managers have a shared vision of where they want to be or who their external competitors are. Managers at Neptune, a successful multibusiness computing firm, are highly aware of their external competition. At their monthly meetings, they pay close attention to the moves of the competition and personalize that competition by referring to individual managers in competitor companies, particularly their direct counterparts. They have a clear collective goal for their own ranking and market share position in the industry. It is to be number one. At Intel, managers typically contend that "only the paranoid survive." . . .

A more direct way to defuse politics is through a balanced power structure in which each key decision maker has a clear area of responsibility, but in which the leader is the most powerful decision maker. . . .

Humor defuses politics. Effective strategic decision makers often relieve tension by making business fun. They emphasize the excitement of fast-paced markets and the "rush" of competing in these settings. . . . Humor strengthens the collaborative outlook. It puts people into a positive mood. Research has shown that people whose frame of mind is positive have more accurate perceptions of each other's arguments and are more optimistic, creative in their problem solving, forgiving, and collaborative. Humor also allows managers to convey negative information in a less threatening way. Managers can say something as a joke that might otherwise be offensive.

READING 5.4

The Honda Effect* BY RICHARD T. PASCALE

At face value, "strategy" is an innocent noun. Webster defines it as the large-scale planning and direction of operations. In the business context, it pertains to a process by which a firm searches and analyzes its environment and resources in order to (1) select opportunities defined in terms of markets to be served and products to serve them and (2) make discrete decisions to invest resources in order to achieve identified objectives (Bower, 1970: 7–8).

But for a vast and influential population of executives, planners, academics, and consultants, strategy is more than a conventional English noun. It embodies an implicit model of how organizations should be guided and, consequently, preconfigures our way of thinking. Strategy formulation (1) is generally assumed to be driven by senior management whom we expect to set strategic direction, (2) has been extensively influenced by empirical models and concepts, and (3) is often associated with a laborious strategic planning process that, in some companies, has produced more paper than insight.

A $500-million-a-year "strategy" industry has emerged in the United States and Europe comprised of management consultants, strategic planning staffs, and business school academics. It caters to the unique emphasis that American and European companies place upon this particular aspect of managing and directing corporations.

Words often derive meaning from their cultural context. *Strategy* is one such word and nowhere is the contrast of meanings more pronounced than between Japan and the United States. The Japanese view the emphasis we place on "strategy" as we might regard their enthusiasm for Kabuki or sumo wrestling. They note our interests not with an intent of acquiring similar ones but for insight into our peculiarities. The Japanese are somewhat distrustful of a single "strategy" for in their view any idea that focuses attention does so at the expense of peripheral vision. They strongly believe that *peripheral vision* is essential to discerning changes in the customer, the technology, or competition, and is the key to corporate survival over the long haul. They regard any propensity to be driven by a single-minded strategy as a weakness.

The Japanese have particular discomfort with strategic concepts. While they do not reject ideas such as the experience curve or portfolio theory outright they regard them as a stimulus to perception. They have often ferreted out the "formula" of their concept-driven American competitors and exploited their inflexibility. In musical instruments, for example (a mature industry facing stagnation as birthrates in the United States and Japan declined), Yamaha might have classified its products as "cash cows" and gone on to better things (as its chief U.S. competitor, Baldwin United, had done). Instead, beginning with a negligible share of the U.S. market, Yamaha plowed ahead and destroyed Baldwin's seemingly unchallengeable dominance. YKK's success in zippers against Talon (a Textron division) and Honda's outflanking of Harley-Davidson (a former AMF subsidiary) in the motorcycle field provide parallel illustrations. All three cases involved American conglomerates, wedded to the portfolio concept, that had classified pianos, zippers, and motorcycles as mature businesses to be harvested rather than nourished and defended.

Of course, those who developed portfolio theory and other strategic concepts protest that they were never intended to be mindlessly applied in setting strategic direction. But most would also agree that there is a widespread tendency in American corporations to misapply concepts and to otherwise become strategically myopic—ignoring the marketplace, the customer, and the problems of execution. This tendency toward misapplication, being both pervasive and persistent over several decades, is a phenomenon that the literature has largely ignored (for exceptions, see Hayes and Abernathy, 1980: 67; Hayes and Garvin, 1982: 71). There is a need to identify explicitly the factors that influence how we conceptualize strategy—and which foster its misuse.

HONDA: THE STRATEGY MODEL

In 1975, the Boston Consulting Group (BCG) presented the British government its final report: *Strategy Alternatives for the British Motorcycle Industry*. This 120-page document identified two key factors leading to the British demise in the world's motorcycle industry:

- Market share loss and profitability declines
- Scale economy disadvantages in technology, distribution, and manufacturing

During the period 1959 to 1973, the British share of the U.S. motorcycle industry had dropped from 49% to 9%. Introducing BCG's recommended strategy (of targeting market segments where sufficient production volumes could be attained to be price competitive) the report states:

> The success of the Japanese manufacturers originated with the growth of their domestic market during the 1950s. As recently as 1960, only 4 percent of Japanese motorcycle production was exported. By this time, however, the Japanese had developed huge production volumes in small motorcycles in their domestic market, and volume-related cost reductions had followed. This resulted in a highly competitive cost position which the Japanese used as a springboard for penetration of world markets with small motorcycles in the early 1960s. (BCG, 1975: xiv)

The BCG study was made public by the British government and rapidly disseminated in the United States. It exemplifies the necessary (and, I argue, insufficient) strategist's perspective of:

- examining competition primarily from an intercompany perspective
- at a high level of abstraction
- with heavy reliance on macroeconomic concepts (such as the experience curve)

Case writers at Harvard Business School, UCLA, and the University of Virginia quickly condensed the BCG report for classroom use in case discussions. It currently enjoys extensive use in first-term courses in business policy.

Of particular note in the BCG study, and in the subsequent Harvard Business School rendition, is the historical treatment of Honda.

> The mix of competitors in the U.S. motorcycle market underwent a major shift in the 1960s. Motorcycle registrations increased from 575,000 in 1960 to 1,382,000 in 1965. Prior to 1960 the U.S. market was served mainly by Harley-Davidson of U.S.A., BSA, Triumph and Norton of U.K., and Moto-Guzzi of Italy. Harley was the market leader with total 1959 sales of $16.6 million. After the Second World War, motorcycles in the United States attracted a very limited group of people other than police and army personnel who used motorcycles on the job. While most motorcyclists were no doubt decent people, groups of rowdies who went around on motorcycles and called themselves by such names as "Hell's Angels," "Satan's Slaves" gave motorcycling a bad image. Even leather jackets which were worn by motorcyclists as a protective device acquired an unsavory image. A 1953 movie called *The Wild Ones* starring a 650cc Triumph, a black leather jacket, and Marlon Brando gave the rowdy motorcyclists wide media coverage. The stereotype of the motorcyclist was a leather-jacketed, teenage troublemaker.
>
> Honda established an American subsidiary in 1959—American Honda Motor Company. This was in sharp contrast to other foreign producers who relied on distributors. Honda's marketing strategy was described in the 1963 annual report as "With its policy of selling, not primarily to confirmed motorcyclists but rather to members of the general public who had never before given a second thought to a motorcycle. . . ." Honda started its push in the U.S. market with the smallest, lightweight motorcycles. It had a three-speed transmission, an automatic clutch, five horsepower (the American cycle only had two and a half), an electric starter, and step through frame for female riders. And it was easier to

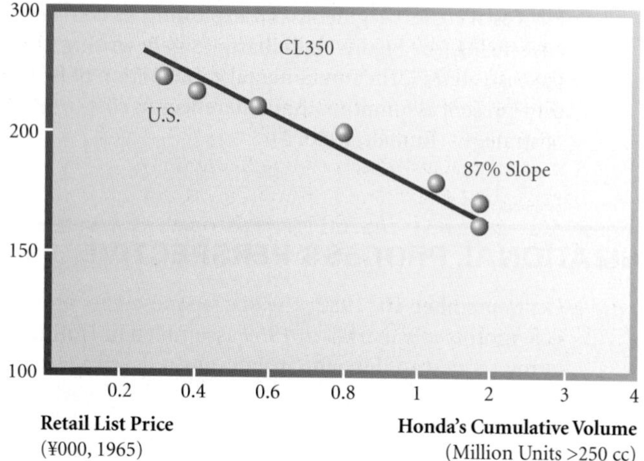

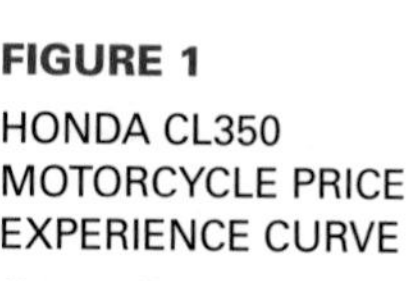

FIGURE 1

HONDA CL350 MOTORCYCLE PRICE EXPERIENCE CURVE

Source: Boston Consulting Group, Strategic Alternatives for the British Motorcycle Industry, House of Commons, London: Her Majesty's Stationary Office, July 1975, p. 41.

handle. The Honda machines sold for under $250 in retail compared with $1,000–$1,500 for the bigger American or British machines. Even at that early date Honda was probably superior to other competitors in productivity.

By June 1960 Honda's Research and Development effort was staffed with 700 designers/engineers. This might be contrasted with 100 engineers/draftsmen employed by . . . (European and American competitors). In 1962 production per man-year was running at 159 units (a figure not matched by Harley-Davidson until 1974). Honda's net fixed asset investment was $8170 per employee . . . (more than twice its European and American competitors). With 1959 sales of $55 million Honda was already the largest motorcycle producer in the world.

Honda followed a policy of developing the market region by region. They started on the West Coast and moved eastward over a period of four to five years. Honda sold 2,500 machines in the United States in 1960. In 1961 they lined up 125 distributors and spent $150,000 on regional advertising. Their advertising was directed to the young families, their advertising theme was "You Meet the Nicest People on a Honda." This was a deliberate attempt to dissociate motorcycles from rowdy, Hell's Angels type people.

Honda's success in creating demand for lightweight motorcycles was phenomenal. American Honda's sales went from $500,000 in 1960 to $77 million in 1965. By 1966 the market share data showed the ascendancy of Japanese producers and their success in selling lightweight motorcycles. (Honda had 63% of the market) . . .Starting from virtually nothing in 1960, the lightweight motorcycles had clearly established their lead. (Purkayastha, 1981: 5, 10, 11, 12)

QUOTING FROM THE BCG REPORT

The Japanese motorcycle industry, and in particular Honda, the market leader, present a [consistent] picture. The basic philosophy of the Japanese manufacturers is that high volumes per model provide the potential for high productivity as a result of using capital intensive and highly automated techniques. Their marketing strategies are therefore directed towards developing these high model volumes, hence the careful attention that we have observed them giving to growth and market share.

The overall result of this philosophy over time has been that the Japanese have now developed an entrenched and leading position in terms of technology and production methods. . . . The major factors which appear to account for the Japanese superiority in both these areas are . . . (specialized production systems, balancing engineering and market requirements, and the cost efficiency and reliability of suppliers). (Boston Consulting Group, 1975: 59, 40)

As evidence of Honda's strategy of taking position as low-cost producer and exploiting economies of scale, other sources cite Honda's construction in 1959 of a plant to manufacture 30,000 motorcycles per month well ahead of existing demand at the time. Up until then Honda's most popular models sold 2,000–3,000 units per month (Sakiya, 1982: 119).

The overall picture as depicted by the quotes exemplifies the "strategy model." Honda is portrayed as a firm dedicated to being the low-price producer, utilizing its dominant market position in Japan to force entry into the U.S. market, expanding that market by redefining a leisure class

("Nicest People") segment, and exploiting its comparative advantage via aggressive pricing and advertising (see Figure 1). Richard Rumelt, writing the teaching note for the UCLA adaptation of the case, states: "The fundamental contribution of BCG is not the experience curve per se but the ever-present assumption that differences in cost (or efficiency) are the fundamental components of strategy" (Rumelt, 1980: 2).

THE ORGANIZATIONAL PROCESS PERSPECTIVE

On September 10, 1982, the six Japanese executives responsible for Honda's entry into the U.S. motorcycle market in 1959 assembled in Honda's Tokyo headquarters. They had gathered at my request to describe in fine-grain detail the sequence of events that had led to Honda's ultimate position of dominance in the U.S. market. All were in their sixties; three were retired. The story that unfolded, greatly abbreviated below, highlights miscalculation, serendipity, and organizational learning—counterpoints to the streamlined "strategy" version related earlier. . . .

Any account of Honda's successes must grasp at the outset the unusual character of its founder, Sochiro Honda, and his partner, Takeo Fujisawa. Honda was an inventive genius with a large ego and mercurial temperament, given to bouts of "philandering" (to use his expression) (Sakiya, 1979). . . .

Postwar Japan was in desperate need of transportation. Motorcycle manufacturers proliferated, producing clip-on engines that converted bicycles into makeshift "mopeds." Honda was among these but it was not until he teamed up with Fujisawa in 1949 that the elements of a successful enterprise began to take shape. Fujisawa provided money as well as financial and marketing strengths. In 1950 their first D-type motorcycle was introduced. They were, at that juncture, participating in a fragmented industry along with 247 other manufacturers. Other than its sturdy frame, this introductory product was unnoteworthy and did not enjoy great commercial success (Sakiya, 1979, 1982).

Honda embodied a rare combination of inventive ability and ultimate self-confidence. His motivation was not primarily commercial. Rather, the company served as a vehicle to give expression to his inventive abilities. A successful company would provide a resource base to pursue, in Fujisawa's words, his "grandiose dream." Fujisawa continues, "There was no end to his pursuit of technology" (Sakiya, 1982).

Fujisawa, in an effort to save the faltering company, pressed Honda to abandon their noisy two-stroke engine and pursue a four-stroke design. The quieter four-stroke engines were appearing on competitive motorcycles, therefore threatening Honda with extinction. Mr. Honda balked. But a year later, Honda stunned Fujisawa with a breakthrough design that doubled the horsepower of competitive four-stroke engines. With this innovation, the firm was off, and by 1951 demand was brisk. There was no organization, however, and the plant was chaotic (Sakiya, 1982). Strong demand, however, required early investment in a simplified mass-production process. As a result, *primarily* due to design advantages, and secondarily to production methods, Honda became one of the four or five industry leaders by 1954 with 15 percent market share (data provided by company). . . .

For Fujisawa, the engine innovation meant increased sales and easier access to financing. For Mr. Honda, the higher horsepower engine opened the possibility of pursuing one of his central ambitions in life—to race his motorcycle and win. . . .

Fujisawa, throughout the fifties, sought to turn Honda's attention from his enthusiasm with racing to the more mundane requirements of running an enterprise. By 1956, as the innovations gained from racing had begun to pay off in vastly more efficient engines, Fujisawa pressed Honda to adapt this technology for a commercial motorcycle (Sakiya, 1979, 1982). Fujisawa had a particular segment in mind. Most motorcyclists in Japan were male and the machines were used primarily as an alternative form of transportation to trains and buses. There were, however, a vast number of small commercial establishments in Japan that still delivered goods and ran errands on bicycles. Trains and buses were inconvenient for these activities. The pursestrings of these small enterprises were controlled by the Japanese wife—who resisted buying conventional motorcycles because they were expensive, dangerous, and hard to handle. Fujisawa challenged Honda: Can you use what you've learned from racing to come up with an inexpensive, safe-looking motorcycle that can be driven with one hand (to facilitate carrying packages).

In 1958, the Honda 50cc Supercub was introduced—with an automatic clutch, three-speed transmission, automatic starter, and the safe, friendly look of a bicycle (without the stigma of the outmoded mopeds). Owing almost entirely to its high horsepower but *lightweight 50cc engine* (not to production efficiencies), it was affordable. Overnight, the firm was overwhelmed with orders. Engulfed by demand, they sought financing to build a new plant with a 30,000 unit per month capacity. "It wasn't a speculative investment," recalls one executive. "We had the proprietary technology, we had the market and the demand was enormous." (The plant was completed in mid-1960.) Prior to its opening, demand was met through makeshift, high-cost, company-owned assembly and farmed-out assembly through subcontractors. By the end of 1959, Honda had skyrocketed into first place among Japanese motorcycle manufacturers. Of its total sales that year of 285,000 units, 168,000 were Supercubs.

Fujisawa utilized the Supercub to restructure Honda's channels of distribution. For many years, Honda had rankled under the two-tier distribution system that prevailed in the industry. These problems had been exacerbated by the fact that Honda was a late entry and had been carried as a secondary line by distributors whose loyalties lay with their older manufacturers. Further weakening Honda's leverage, all manufacturer sales were on a consignment basis.

Deftly, Fujisawa had characterized the Supercub to Honda's distributors as "something much more like a bicycle than a motorcycle." The traditional channels, to their later regret, agreed. Under amicable terms Fujisawa began selling the Supercub directly to retailers—and primarily through bicycle shops. Since these shops were small and numerous (approximately 12,000 in Japan), sales on consignment were unthinkable. A cash-on-delivery system was installed, giving Honda significantly more leverage over its dealerships than the other motorcycle manufacturers enjoyed.

The stage was now set for exploration of the U.S. market. Mr. Honda's racing conquests in the late 1950s had given substance to his convictions about his abilities. . . .

Two Honda executives—the soon-to-be-named president of American Honda, Kihachiro Kawashima, and his assistant—arrived in the United States in late 1958. Their itinerary: San Francisco, Los Angeles, Dallas, New York, and Columbus. Mr. Kawashima recounts his impressions:

> My first reaction after travelling across the United States was: how could we have been so stupid as to start a war with such a vast and wealthy country! My second reaction was discomfort. I spoke poor English. We dropped in on motorcycle dealers who treated us discourteously and in addition, gave the general impression of being motorcycle enthusiasts who, secondarily, were in business. There were only 3,000 motorcycle dealers in the United States at the time and only 1,000 of them were open five days a week. The remainder were open on nights and weekends. Inventory was poor, manufacturers sold motorcycles to dealers on consignment, the retailers provided consumer financing; after-sales service was poor. It was discouraging.
>
> My other impression was that everyone in the United States drove an automobile—making it doubtful that motorcycles could ever do very well in the market. However, with 450,000 motorcycle registrations in the U.S. and 60,000 motorcycles imported from Europe each year it didn't seem unreasonable to shoot for 10 percent of the import market. I returned to Japan with that report.
>
> In truth, we had no strategy other than the idea of seeing if we could sell something in the United States. It was a new frontier, a new challenge and it fit the "success against all odds" culture that Mr. Honda had cultivated. I reported my impressions to Fujisawa—including the seat-of-the-pants target of trying, over several years, to attain a 10 percent share of U.S. imports. He didn't probe that target quantitatively. We did not discuss profits or deadlines for breakeven. Fujisawa told me if anyone could succeed, I could and authorized $1 million for the venture.
>
> The next hurdle was to obtain a currency allocation from the Ministry of Finance. They were extraordinarily skeptical. Toyota had launched the Toyopet in the U.S. in 1958 and had failed miserably. "How could Honda succeed?" they asked. Months went by. We put the project on hold. Suddenly, five months after our application, we were given the go-ahead—but at only a fraction of our expected level of commitment. "You can invest $250,000 in the U.S. market," they said, "but only $110,000 in cash." The remainder of our assets had to be in parts and motorcycle inventory.

We moved into frantic activity as the government, hoping we would give up on the idea, continued to hold us to the July 1959 start-up timetable. Our focus, as mentioned earlier, was to compete with the European exports. We knew our products at the time were good but not far superior. Mr. Honda was especially confident of the 250cc and 305cc machines. The shape of the handlebar on these larger machines looked like the eyebrow of Buddha, which he felt was a strong selling point. Thus, after some discussion and with no compelling criteria for selection, we configured our start-up inventory with 25 percent of each of our four products—the 50cc Supercub and the 125cc, 250cc, and 305cc machines. In dollar value terms, of course, the inventory was heavily weighted toward the larger bikes.

The stringent monetary controls of the Japanese government together with the unfriendly reception we had received during our 1958 visit caused us to start small. We chose Los Angeles where there was a large second and third generation Japanese community, a climate suitable for motorcycle use, and a growing population. We were so strapped for cash that the three of us shared a furnished apartment that rented for $80 per month. Two of us slept on the floor. We obtained a warehouse in a run-down section of the city and waited for the ship to arrive. Not daring to spare our funds for equipment, the three of us stacked the motorcycle crates three high—by hand, swept the floors, and built and maintained the parts bin.

We were entirely in the dark the first year. We were not aware the motorcycle business in the United States occurs during a seasonable April-to-August window—and our timing coincided with the closing of the 1959 season. Our hard-learned experiences with distributorships in Japan convinced us to try to go to the retailers direct. We ran ads in the motorcycle trade magazine for dealers. A few responded. By spring of 1960, we had forty dealers and some of our inventory in their stores—mostly larger bikes. A few of the 250cc and 305cc bikes began to sell. Then disaster struck.

By the first week of April 1960, reports were coming in that our machines were leaking oil and encountering clutch failure. This was our lowest moment. Honda's fragile reputation was being destroyed before it could be established. As it turned out, motorcycles in the United States are driven much farther and much faster than in Japan. We dug deeply into our precious cash reserves to air freight our motorcycles to the Honda testing lab in Japan. Through the dark month of April, Pan Am was the only enterprise in the U.S. that was nice to us. Our testing lab worked twenty-four-hour days bench testing the bikes to try to replicate the failure. Within a month, a redesigned head gasket and clutch spring solved the problem. But in the meantime, events had taken a surprising turn.

Throughout our first eight months, following Mr. Honda's and our own instincts, we had not attempted to move the 50cc Supercubs. While they were a smash success in Japan (and manufacturing couldn't keep up with demand there), they seemed wholly unsuitable for the U.S. market where everything was bigger and more luxurious. As a clincher, we had our sights on the import market—and the Europeans, like the American manufacturers, emphasized the larger machines.

We used the Honda 50s ourselves to ride around Los Angeles on errands. They attracted a lot of attention. One day we had a call from a Sears buyer. While persisting in our refusal to sell through an intermediary, we took note of Sears' interest. But we still hesitated to push the 50cc bikes out of fear they might harm our image in a heavily macho market. But when the larger bikes started breaking, we had no choice. We let the 50cc bikes move. And surprisingly, the retailers who wanted to sell them weren't motorcycle dealers, they were sporting goods stores.

The excitement created by the Honda Supercub began to gain momentum. Under restrictions from the Japanese government, we were still on a cash basis. Working with our initial cash and inventory, we sold machines, reinvested in inventory, and sunk the profits into additional inventory and advertising. Our advertising tried to straddle the market. While retailers continued to inform us that our Supercub customers were normal everyday Americans, we hesitated to target toward this segment out of fear of alienating the high margin end of our business—sold through the traditional motorcycle dealers to a more traditional "black leather jacket" customer.

Honda's phenomenal sales and share gains over the ensuing years have been previously reported. History has it that Honda "redefined" the U.S. motorcycle industry. In the view of American Honda's start-up team, this was an innovation they backed into—and reluctantly. It was certainly not the strategy they embarked on in 1959. As late as 1963, Honda was still working with its original Los Angeles advertising agency, its ad campaigns straddling all customers so as not to antagonize one market in pursuit of another.

In the spring of 1963, an undergraduate advertising major at UCLA submitted, in fulfillment of a routine course assignment, an ad campaign for Honda. Its theme: You Meet the Nicest People on a Honda. Encouraged by his instructor, the student passed his work on to a friend at Grey Advertising. Grey had been soliciting the Honda account—which with a $5 million a year budget was becoming an attractive potential client. Grey purchased the student's idea—on a tightly kept nondisclosure basis. Grey attempted to sell the idea to Honda.

Interestingly, the Honda management team, which by 1963 had grown to five Japanese executives, was badly split on this advertising decision. The president and treasurer favored another proposal from another agency. The director of sales, however, felt strongly that the Nicest People campaign was the right one—and his commitment eventually held sway. Thus, in 1963, through an inadvertent sequence of events, Honda came to adopt a strategy that directly identified and targeted that large untapped segment of the marketplace that has since become inseparable from the Honda legend.

The Nicest People campaign drove Honda's sales at an even greater rate. By 1964, nearly one out of every two motorcycles sold was a Honda. As a result of the influx of medium-income leisure-class consumers, banks and other consumer credit companies began to finance motorcycles—shifting away from dealer credit, which had been the traditional purchasing mechanism available. Honda, seizing the opportunity of soaring demand for its products, took a courageous and seemingly risky position. Late in 1964, they announced that thereafter, they would cease to ship on a consignment basis but would require cash on delivery. Honda braced itself for revolt. While nearly every dealer questioned, appealed, or complained, none relinquished his franchise. In one fell swoop, Honda shifted the power relationship from the dealer to the manufacturer. Within three years, this would become the pattern for the industry.

THE "HONDA EFFECT"

The preceding account of Honda's inroads in the U.S. motorcycle industry provides more than a second perspective on reality. It focuses our attention on different issues and raises different questions. What factors permitted two men as unlike one another as Honda and Fujisawa to function effectively as a team? What incentives and understandings permitted the Japanese executives at American Honda to respond to the market as it emerged rather than doggedly pursue the 250cc and 305cc strategy that Mr. Honda favored? What decision process permitted the relatively junior sales director to overturn the bosses' preferences and choose the Nicest People campaign? What values or commitment drove Honda to take the enormous risk of alienating its dealers in 1964 in shifting from a consignment to cash? In hindsight, these pivotal events all seem ho-hum common sense. But each day, as organizations live out their lives without the benefit of hindsight, few choose so well and so consistently.

The juxtaposed perspectives reveal what I shall call the "Honda Effect." Western consultants, academics, and executives express a preference for oversimplifications of reality and cognitively linear explanations of events. To be sure, they have always acknowledged that the "human factor" must be taken into account. But extensive reading of strategy cases at business schools, consultants' reports, strategic planning documents as well as the coverage of the popular press, reveals a widespread tendency to overlook the process through which organizations experiment, adapt, and learn. We tend to impute coherence and purposive rationality to events when the opposite may be closer to the truth. How an organization deals with miscalculation, mistakes, and serendipitous events *outside its field of vision is often crucial to success over time.* It is this realm that requires better understanding and further research if we are to enhance our ability to guide an organization's destiny. . . .

An earlier section has addressed the shortcomings of the narrowly defined macroeconomic strategy model. The Japanese avoid this pitfall by adopting a broader notion of "strategy." In our recent awe of things Japanese, most Americans forget that the original products of the Japanese automotive manufacturers badly missed the mark. Toyota's Toyopet was square, sexless, and mechanically defective. It failed miserably, as did Datsun's first several entries into the U.S. market. More recently, Mazda miscalculated badly with its first rotary engine and nearly went bankrupt. Contrary to myth, the Japanese did not from the onset embark on a strategy to seize the high-quality small-car market. They manufactured what they were accustomed to building in Japan and tried to sell it abroad. Their success, as any Japanese automotive executive will readily agree, did not result from a bold insight by a few big brains at the top. On the contrary, success was achieved by senior managers humble enough not to take their initial strategic positions too seriously. What saved Japan's near-failures was the cumulative impact of "little brains" in the form of salesmen and dealers and production workers, all contributing incrementally to the quality and market position these companies enjoy today. Middle and upper management saw their primary task as guiding and orchestrating this input from below rather than steering the organization from above along a predetermined strategic course.

The Japanese don't use the term "strategy" to describe a crisp business definition or competitive master plan. They think more in terms of "strategic accommodation," or "adaptive persistence," underscoring their belief that corporate direction evolves from an incremental adjustment to unfolding events. Rarely, in their view, does one leader (or a strategic planning group) produce a bold strategy that guides a firm unerringly. Far more frequently, the input is from below. It is this ability of an organization to move information and ideas from the bottom to the top and back again in continuous dialogue that the Japanese value above all things. As this dialogue is pursued, what in hindsight may be "strategy" evolves. In sum, "strategy" is defined as "all the things necessary for the successful functioning of organization as an adaptive mechanism." . . .

Section II

FORCES

CHAPTER 6

Strategic Change

Strategy is technically about continuity rather than change: After all, it is concerned with imposing structured patterns of behavior on an organization, whether these take the form of intentions in advance that become deliberate strategies or actions after the fact that fall into the consistent patterns of emergent strategies. But to manage strategy today is frequently to manage change—to recognize when a shift of a strategic nature is possible, desirable, and necessary, and then to act—possibly putting into place mechanisms for continuous change.

Managing strategic change is generally far more difficult than it may at first appear. The need for reorientation occurs rather infrequently, and when it does, it means moving from a familiar domain into a less well-defined future where many of the old rules no longer apply. People must often abandon the roots of their past successes and develop entirely new skills and attitudes. This is clearly a demanding situation—and often, therefore, the most difficult challenge facing a manager.

The causes of such change also vary, from an ignored steady decline in performance, which ultimately demands a turnaround, to a sudden radical shift in a base technology that requires a reconceptualization of everything the organization does; from the gradual shift into the next stage of an organization's life cycle to the appearance of a new chief executive who wishes to put his or her particular stamp on the organization. The resulting strategic alignments may also take a variety of forms, from a shift of strategic position within the same industry to a whole new perspective in a new industry. Some changes require rapid transitions; others are accompanied by slower shifts. Each transition has its own management prerequisites and problems.

This chapter covers a number of these aspects of organizational change, presenting ideas on what evokes them in the first place, what forms they can take, and how they can and should be managed in differing situations.

We begin with an overview of the change process, excerpted from the Mintzberg, Ahlstrand, and Lampel book *Strategy Safari*, which was the basis for the "Reflections on the Strategy Process" readings about the ten schools in Chapter 1. Here, on strategy formation as a process of transformation, the authors provide a framework to think about the content of change (called the "change cube"), a map of the various popular techniques used to promote change in organizations, and a consideration of different programs that have been used to promote change in organizations, from rather "top down" to significantly "bottom up."

Our second reading on change considers the "Unsteady Pace of Organizational Evolution" in terms of distinct periods of convergence and upheaval. Related to the literature on organizational life cycles, its three authors, Michael Tushman, William Newman, and Elaine Romanelli, argue for what has also been referred to as a "quantum theory" of organizational change (Miller and Freisen, 1984). The essence of the argument is that organizations prefer to stay on course most of the time, accepting incremental changes to improve their strategies, processes, and structures. But periodically they must submit to dramatic shifts in these—"strategic revolutions" of a sort—to realign their overall orientation.

A very different perspective follows, from coauthor James Brian Quinn at the Dartmouth Tuck School and John Voyer of the University of Maine. Drawn from Quinn's book *Strategies for Change: Logical Incrementalism,* it develops a particular view of the strategy-making process based on intensive interviews in some of America's and Europe's best-known corporations. Planning does not capture the essence of strategy formation, according to Quinn and Voyer, although it does play an important role in developing new data and in confirming strategies derived in other ways. The traditional view of incrementalism does not fit observed behavior patterns either. The processes may seem randomly incremental on the surface, but a powerful logic underlies them. And, unlike the other incremental processes, these are not so much reactive as subtly proactive. Executives use incremental approaches to deal simultaneously with the informational, motivational, and political aspects of creating a strategy.

Above all, Quinn and Voyer depict strategy formation as a managed, interactive *learning* process in which the chief strategist gradually works out strategy in his or her own mind and orchestrates the organization's acceptance of it. In emphasizing the role of a central strategist—or small groups managing "subsystems" of strategy—Quinn and Voyer often seem close to Andrews's views. But the two differ markedly in other important respects. In their emphasis on the political and motivational dimensions of strategy, they may be closer to Wrapp, whose managers "don't make policy decisions." In fact, Quinn and Voyer attempt to integrate their views with the traditional one, noting that although the strategies themselves "emerge" from an incremental process, they have many of the characteristics of the highly deliberate ones of Andrews's strategists. This reading ends with practical advice on how to foster strategy making as an incremental process.

How do we reconcile this view of incrementalism with the previous view of quantum change, since both seem plausible? Perhaps they are not as contradictory as they may seem. Consider three dimensions: (1) the specific aspects of the strategy change process that each considers, (2) the time frames of the two viewpoints, and (3) the types of organizations involved. Quinn and Voyer's incrementalist view focuses on the processes going on in senior managers' minds as they think about new strategies. Because of the complexities involved, effective strategic thinking requires an incremental, interactive, learning process for all key players.

The quantum approach, in contrast, focuses not on the strategists' thinking as much as on the organization's actions—the strategies it actually pursues (referred to in Chapter 5 as the realized strategies of the organization). It is these that often seem to change in quantum fashion. It may be, therefore, that managers conceive and promote their intended strategies incrementally, but once that is accomplished they change their organizations in rapid, quantum fashion. But then again, each of these two approaches may also occur in its own situation. For example, quantum changes may more often take place in crisis situations, when external environments compress time frames often because of technological or regulatory shifts.

The last reading of the chapter, by Quy Nguyen Huy and Henry Mintzberg, casts a skeptical eye at the widespread and deeply held belief that we live in an age of ceaseless and radical change. Our tendency to invoke change as mantra, they point out, stands in the way of effectively managing change. To manage change, argue Quy and Mintzberg, it is important to understand that it always takes place against the background of stability. Managing change effectively therefore requires deciding what not to change as much as it requires knowing what to change. For the strategic manager this goes hand in hand with appreciating the "rhythm of change" making a distinction between revolution and reform, and between change that is induced from the top as opposed to change that spreads from the heart of the organization. Making these distinctions becomes particularly important the longer organizations stay in business. As organizations grow older they must play catch-up with younger and more nimble competitors if they wish to stay in business. In a word, they must rejuvenate, that is, recapture the energy and vitality that made them successful in the first place. Rejuvenation, argue Quy and Mintzberg, depends on encouraging small steps and the little initiatives that normally escape attention, as well as using unexpected and dramatic events to pursue a change agenda.

USING THE CASE STUDIES

The strategy process is more often than not about change rather than continuity. Thus, it would be difficult to single out a case in this book that is not about change. Nevertheless, some cases deal with change that is dramatic even by normal standards of strategy. Napoleon comes to power during one of the most tumultuous periods in European history. The politics of change so often evident in this case may be less visible arguably play an important role in strategic change processes, as seen in the Cadbury Schweppes case. The Lufthansa and Nissan cases deal with strategic change faced repeatedly by two companies with global ambitions. Both the Tushman, Newman, and Romanelli reading and that by Huy and Mintzberg are relevant to how these companies attempted to retain their vitality. And these readings are also relevant to the case of Nintendo, a successful video game company that is reluctant to face up to the challenge of online gaming. The Warner Brothers case describes a company that has fallen on hard times, in part because top managers developed a successful formula that outlived its usefulness. A comparison of these two companies should make for an interesting discussion, and the excerpt by Mintzberg, Ahlstrand, and Lampel from *Strategy Safari* describes frameworks that can be useful for doing this.

READING 6.1

Transforming Organization* BY HENRY MINTZBERG, BRUCE AHLSTRAND, AND JOSEPH LAMPEL

There is an enormous literature and consulting practice aimed at helping managers deal with major change in their organizations—turnaround, revitalization, downsizing, and the like. . . . Here, we seek to provide some overall structure for this work as well as some illustrations of it.

One word of caution before we begin. All of this is about "managed change." But a case can well be made . . . that this term is an oxymoron, that change should not be "managed," at least when this word is used to mean forced, made to happen. Managers often claim that people in their organizations resist changing. True enough. But maybe that is because these people have for so long been *over*managed. The cure might actually prove to be just more of the cause. If so, then perhaps the best way to "manage" change is to allow for it to happen—to set up the conditions whereby people will follow their natural instincts to experiment and transform their behaviors. . . . "You deal with change by improving you. And then your time must come" (Clemmer, 1995).

CHANGING WHAT?

The first question is: *what* can be changed in an organization? One way to think of this is as a change cube, discussed in the accompanying box. It indicates what comprehensive change in an organization really means: it is about strategy and structure, ranging from the conceptual to the concrete and from highly formal behaviors to rather informal ones.

*Adapted from *Strategy Safari: A guided tour through the wilds of strategic management*, Free Press (Mintzberg, H., Ahlstrand, B. and Lampel, J. 1998), with the permission of The Free Press, a Division of Simon & Schuster, Inc., copyright © 1998 by H. Mintzberg, B. Ahlstrand and J. Lampel, all rights reserved, and Pearson Education Ltd.

THE CHANGE CUBE

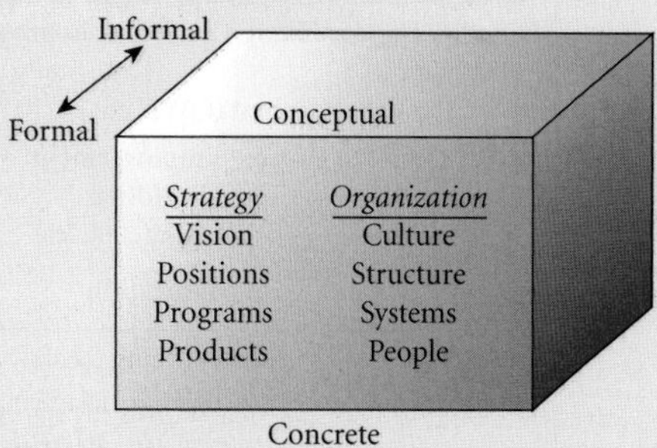

Change in organizations is greatly spoken about, yet all too often done in bits and pieces. We hear about turnaround, revitalization, cultural change, total quality management, venturing, new product development, and so on. Somehow all of this has to be put into perspective. The change cube is designed to do that.

The face of the cube shows two major dimensions of change. On the left side, change can be about *strategy*, the direction an organization is headed, and on the right, about *organization*, the state it is in. Both have to be considered when changing an organization.

Looking up and down the cube, both strategy and organization can range from the highly conceptual, or abstract, to the rather concrete, or tangible. On the strategy dimension, vision (or strategic perspective) is the most conceptual (rethinking, reconceiving), as is culture on the organization dimension (reenergizing, revitalizing). And going down the cube toward the more concrete, you can change, on the two sides, strategic positions (repositioning, reconfiguring) and organization structure (reorganizing, reducing), then programs and systems (reprogramming, reworking, reengineering), finally products and people (redesigning, retraining, replacing), which can also be thought of as changing actions on one side and actors on the other. Put differently, the broadest but most abstract things you can change in an organization are vision and culture, the most specific, actual products and real people (either by replacing the people who are there or by changing their behavior).

An organization can easily change a single product or an individual. But changing, say, a vision or a structure without changing anything else is silly, just an empty gesture. In other words, wherever you intervene on this cube, you have to change everything below. For example, it makes no sense to change structure without changing systems and people, or to change vision without rethinking strategic positions as well as redesigning programs and products.

Finally, all of this can range from the overt and formal, shown on the front face of the cube, to the rather more implicit and informal, shown on the back face. For example, a strategic position can be more deliberate (formal) or more emergent (informal), while people can be changed formally through education or informally through coaching and mentoring.

The point of this description is that serious change in organizations includes the entire cube: strategy and organization, from the most conceptual to the most concrete, informally as well as formally.

Now we can consider the methods of change. Needed here is some kind of *map*, to sort out and place into perspective the confusing array of approaches that have been developed over the years to change organizations. Figure 1 presents such a map, in which the methods of change are plotted on two dimensions. Along the top is a scale of the breadth of change, which runs from micro to macro. Micro change is focused within the organization: it might involve, for example, job redesign in a factory or the development of a new product. Macro change is aimed at the entire organization, for example, repositioning its place in the market or shifting all of its physical facilities.* David Hurst has expressed this in another way: "The *helmsman* manages change all the time. But the *navigator*

*Micro change tends to focus on the concrete level of the change cube, but it need not. One can change the vision of work design in a factory. Likewise, macro change, while it often starts at the conceptual level, need not. The organization can shift all its physical facilities without any overarching vision, although that would hardly seem to be logical (which does not mean it never happens!).

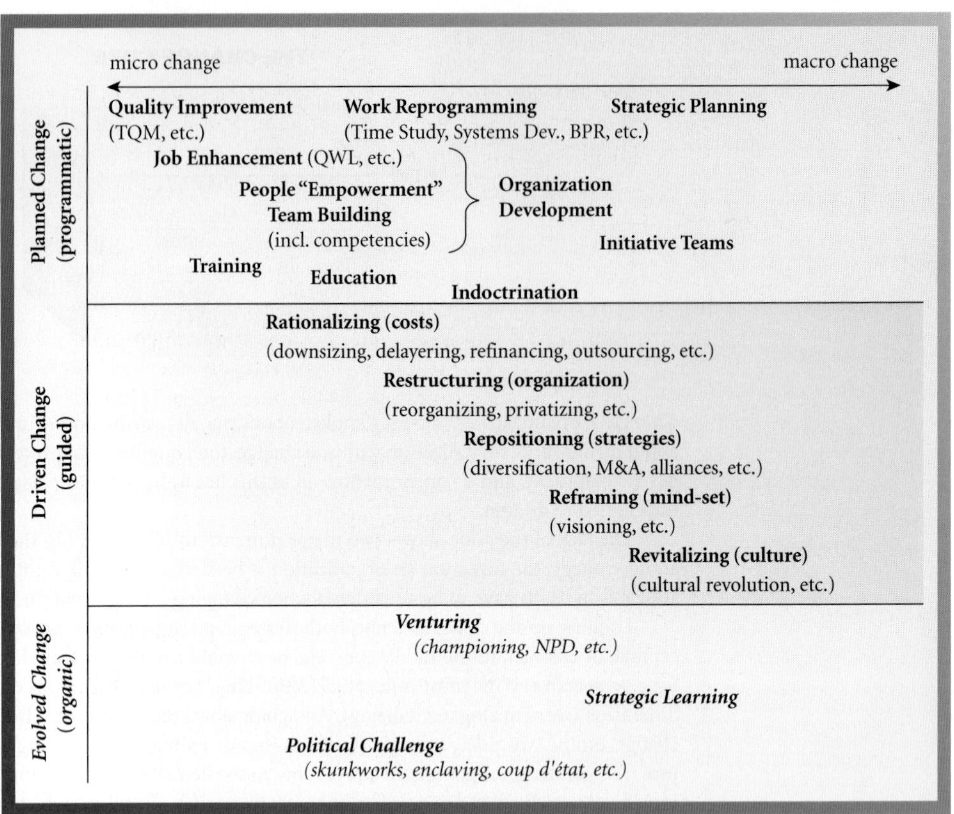

FIGURE 1
MAP OF CHANGE METHODS

changes course quite infrequently and then only as circumstances dictate. Changes in destination can be made by the *captain* even less frequently, for they require a total value change in the organization. And *discoverers* may find a new world only once in a lifetime" (unpublished material). . . .

On the horizontal scale of Figure 1, we suggest that there are three basic approaches to the process of change: planned change, driven change, and evolved change. *Planned* change is programmatic: there exists a system or set of procedures to be followed. These range from programs of quality improvement and training (micro) to ones of organizational development and strategic planning (more macro). Consider, for example, this classic statement of organization development:

> Organizational development is an effort (1) *planned,* (2) *organization-wide,* and (3) *managed* from the *top,* to (4) increase organization *effectiveness* and *health* through (5) *planned interventions* in the organization's "processes" using *behavioral science* knowledge. (Beckhard, 1969: 9; italics in original)

Driven change is guided: a single individual or small group, usually in an influential position of authority, oversees the change and ensures that it happens. Here we find all the currently popular (mostly) "re" words, ranging from rationalization through restructuring to revitalizing. Doz and Thanheiser (1996) have referred to various among these as changing the strategic context, the organizational context, and the emotional context (culture). The sequence of these driven changes shown in the diagram, reading diagonally from more micro and closer to planned to more macro and closer to evolved, include changing operating costs, organizational structure, strategic positions, managerial mind-set, and overall culture. . . .

Finally, *evolved* change is organic: it kind of happens, or at least is guided by people outside positions of significant authority, often in obscure places in the organization. Unlike the first two approaches, which are driven, or "managed" in some sense, whether more formally by procedures or less formally by managers, this third approach to change is neither managed nor even under the firm control of managers. More to the micro side, we show political challenge (which can, of course, be rather macro too, as in the coup d'état discussed in the power school), in the middle, we see venturing, and on the more macro side, we find strategic learning (the last two discussed in the learning school). . . .

PROGRAMS OF COMPREHENSIVE CHANGE

A manager can simply pick something and try to change it: enhance the training of the sales force, for example, or reorganize the research laboratory. Most change is of this *piecemeal* type; it goes on all the time, here and there. Indeed, Tom Peters has long been a fan of such change, which he has called "chunking." Don't get bogged down, he suggests, just grab something and change it.

The change cube suggests, however, that this probably works better at the more concrete (and micro) level than the conceptual (and macro) end. You can retrain a group of workers or reorganize one department, perhaps, but you cannot reposition strategy or change culture without making a lot of other associated changes. Indeed, "changing culture" alone is just a lot of empty words: as noted earlier, culture is not changed at all when nothing else changes.

So there has arisen a great deal of literature and consulting practice on massive programs of comprehensive change, namely *transformation*. These propose how to combine the various methods of change into logical sequences to "turn around" or "renew" an organization. (Turnaround implies quick, dramatic revolution; renewal, a slower building up of comprehensive change.) But this is a confusing body of work: just about every writer and consulting firm has his, her, or its own formula for success. There is no consensus at all as to what works best, although there are certainly periodic fads—galore. But all this seems to reveal mainly what *doesn't* work—namely last year's fad.

Here, then, as everywhere else, there are no magic formulas. Just as chunking can be suboptimal, so too can renewing be excessive. Despite all the current hype about change, not all organizations need to change everything all the time. The word for that is "anarchy." The trick is to balance change with continuity: to achieve change when and where necessary while maintaining order. Embracing the new while sweeping out the old may be the very modern thing to do, but it is generally a lot more effective—as well as difficult—to find ways to integrate the best of the new with most useful of the old. Too many organizations these days are subjected to too much ill-conceived change. Just because there is a new chief executive or some new fad does not mean that everything has to be thrown into turmoil.

Nevertheless, there are times when an organization has to be changed in a serious, comprehensive, way. Then the trick for management is to figure out where it can intervene, what it can change and leave others to change, when, how fast, and in what sequence. Start small and build up, or do something dramatic? Begin by replacing people, reconceiving vision, or redoing the chart? After that, concentrate on strategy, structure, culture, or shareholder value? Change everything at once or "chunk" along?

But might these questions set the wrong context: maybe management should just create the conditions for change and then let it happen? Perhaps it should lay off altogether. Maybe the best change begins on the ground, in the corner of some factory or a visit to some customers and then flows from there. Must change always end at the "bottom" after having been driven by the "top"? What about ending at the top after the people in touch with the customers have finally convinced the management of the problems? Or maybe the whole thing has to be driven organically from the outside?

It always seems so terribly confusing, especially when one considers all the evidence about resistance to change in organizations. Yet some do change. The French philosopher Alain provides hope with his comment that "All change seems impossible. But once accomplished, it is the state you are no longer in that seems impossible." When you do get there, "How did we ever tolerate that?" may be the reaction. With this in mind, let us sample some of the frameworks for comprehensive change.

In 1995, three McKinsey consultants, Dickhout, Denham, and Blackwell, published an interesting article on change, outlining six basic "strategies" used by the 25 companies studied:

- Evolutionary/institution building: a gradual reshaping of the "company's values, top-level structures and performance measures so that line managers could drive the change."
- Jolt and refocus: to "shake up a gridlocked power structure," leaders "in one fell swoop . . . delayered top management, defined new business units, and redesigned management processes."

- Follow the leader: for immediate results, leaders "initiated major changes from the top," for example, by selling off weak businesses, "while removing only the most critical organizational bottlenecks."
- Multifront focus: in this case, "change is driven by task teams whose targets are more wide ranging"—cost reduction, sales stimulation, etc.
- Systematic redesign: again task teams drive the process to boost performance, but "core process redesign and other organizational changes tend to be planned in parallel."
- Unit-level mobilizing: "change leaders empower task teams to tap into the pent-up ideas of middle managers and front-line employees." (102–104)

These describe mainly initial or focal activities. But a key question for many people working in this area is how the different activities should be sequenced over time to effect a major transformation. Let us consider first top-down change and then bottom-up.

TOP-DOWN CHANGE?

Perhaps most popular is the approach stimulated by the changes at General Electric under the leadership of Jack Welch over the past decade and a half. Tichy and Sherman (1993) have described these as a "three-act drama": *awakening, envisioning,* and *rearchitecturing,* as shown in Figure 2.

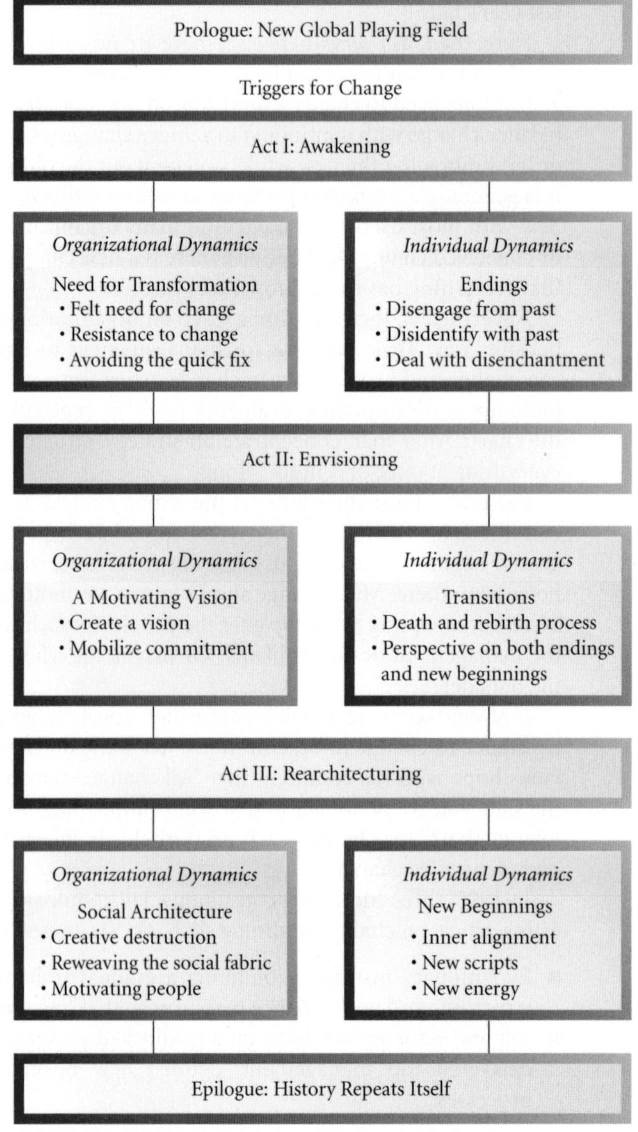

FIGURE 2
TRANSFORMATIONAL LEADERSHIP: A THREE-ACT DRAMA

Source: From Tichy and Sherman (1993: 305).

David Ulrich, who has also worked closely with Welch, in an article with Richard Beatty (1991) characterized this a bit differently. They describe a five-step process (which may occur simultaneously as well as in sequence), including both the "hardware" of the organization (strategy, structure, systems) and its "software" (employee behavior and mind-set). Their description begins with *restructuring,* by which they mean downsizing and delayering, followed by *bureaucracy bashing,* to "get rid of unnecessary reports, approvals, meetings, measures," and the like. Then there is a stage of *employee empowerment,* which gives rise to one of *continuous improvement,* before, as "an outgrowth of the other four," the culture is fundamentally changed (1991: 22, 24, 29). This is illustrated in Figure 3.

Baden-Fuller and Stopford's "crescendo model of rejuvenation" is similar:

1. Galvanize: create a top team dedicated to renewal.
2. Simplify: cut unnecessary and confusing complexity.
3. Build: develop new capabilities.
4. Leverage: maintain momentum and stretch the advantages (1992).

Doz and Thanheiser (1996) noted in a survey of forty companies that almost all included in their transformational efforts portfolio restructuring, downsizing and outsourcing, benchmarking, and some sort of process improvement and quality management efforts. They found "periods of intense activity where high energy . . . [was] typically triggered by various 'turning points' [or 'crucible'] events such as retreats, workshops, or other employee–manager gatherings" (7), as in General Electric's "work out/team meetings." In the "more effective, longer term" transformations, they describe the following pattern:

- "from internal to external focus": first improve efficiency, then create new opportunities.
- "from top-down to delegated action": "the inertia breaking process was usually strongly driven from the top" even though "the transformation was sometimes piloted in a subunit . . . before being implemented in the whole company"; subsequent activities were often "at the initiative of subunits."
- "from emotion and intellect to organization": "in nearly all the cases . . . the initial transformation cycle was driven by a new strategic understanding that was brought into focus through an emotional process (part and parcel of 'crucible' events), then later reflected in more extensive, subtle, and multifaced changes in organizational context." (10–11)

In effect, the chief executive took some quick initial strategic actions, such as divesting some business or replacing key executives, but "winning the hearts" of others was key to the next step. These "changes in the emotional context permitted further, more subtle changes in strategic

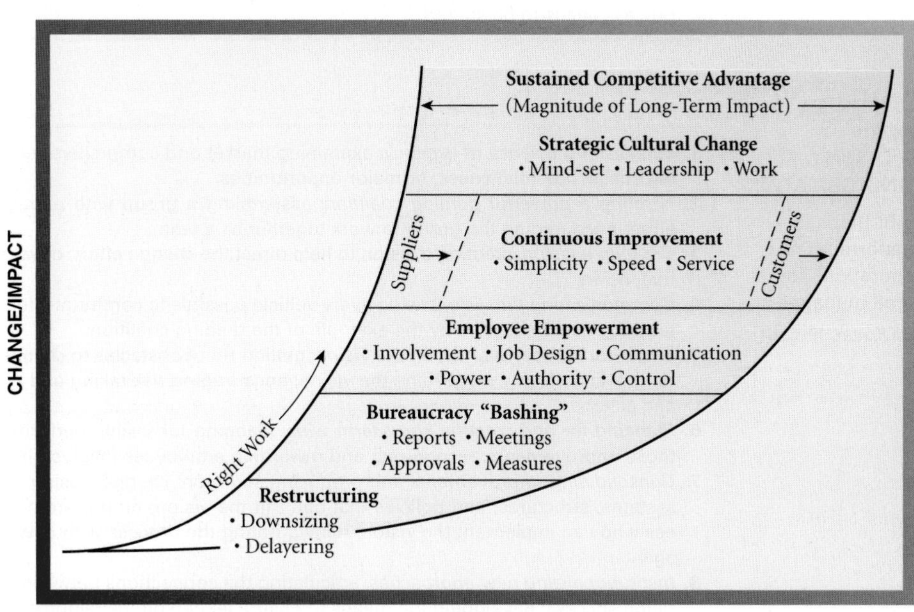

FIGURE 3
A PROCESS FOR REENGINEERING MATURE ORGANIZATIONS
Source: From Beatty and Ulrich (1991: 25).

context," as well as in the organizational context, so that the chief executive could "let go" to allow for more "decentralized emergent initiatives."

> In summary, over time the nature of the transformation process kept alternating from cycle to cycle between *bursts* of energy concentration and *periods* of energy diffusion, to smaller, less visible pulsations. Successful transformation processes shifted from corporate upheavals to ongoing learning and renewal. (11)

BOTTOM-UP CHANGE?

The above has been the view very much from strategic management: top-down, at least initially, leader-driven, and strategic. But, stemming from earlier work in "organizational development," others have described transformation as far more of a bottom-up process, in which small changes taken within pockets of the organization drive the overall change process. Change to these people is an exploratory journey rather than a predetermined trajectory, more of a learning process than a planned or driven one. Yet if it works, it can end up being significantly strategic.

This is the spirit of a 1990 article by Beer et al. in the *Harvard Business Review*, entitled "Why Change Programs Don't Produce Change." After discussing "the fallacy of programmatic change," they discuss the "more successful transformations" they studied that "usually started at

BOX 1
BOTTOM-UP CHANGE

"Six Steps to Effective Change" for managers at the business unit or plant level

(from Beer, Eisentat, and Spector, 1990: 161–164)

1. Mobilize commitment to change through joint diagnosis of business problems. . . . By helping people develop a shared diagnosis of what is wrong in an organization and what can and must be improved, a general manager [of a unit] mobilizes the initial commitment that is necessary to begin the change process. . . .
2. Develop a shared vision of how to organize and manage for competitiveness. Once a core group of people is committed to a particular analysis of the problem, the general manager can lead employees toward a task-aligned vision of the organization that defines new roles and responsibilities. . . .
3. Foster consensus for the new vision, competence to enact it, and cohesion to move it along. . . .
4. Spread revitalization to all departments without pushing it from the top. . . . The temptation to force newfound insights on the rest of the organization can be great, particularly when rapid change is needed, but it would be the same mistake that senior managers make when they try to push programmatic change throughout a company. It short-circuits the change process. It's better to let each department "reinvent the wheel"—that is, to find its own way to the new organization. . . .
5. Institutionalize revitalization through formal policies, systems, and structures. . . . The new approach has to become entrenched. . . .
6. Monitor and adjust strategies in response to problems in the revitalization process. The purpose of change is to create . . . a learning organization capable of adapting to a changing competitive environment. . . . Some might say that this is the general manager's responsibility. But monitoring the change process needs to be shared. . . .

BOX 2
TOP-DOWN TRANSFORMATION

"Eight Steps to Transforming Your Corporation" for its overall managers

(from Kotter, 1995: 61)

1. *Establishing a sense of urgency:* examining market and competitive realities; identifying and discussing crises, potential crises, or major opportunities.
2. *Forming a powerful guiding coalition:* assembling a group with enough power to lead the change effort; encouraging the group to work together as a team.
3. *Creating a vision:* creating a vision to help direct the change effort; developing strategies for achieving that vision.
4. *Communicating the vision:* using every vehicle possible to communicate the new vision and strategies; teaching new behaviors by the example of the guiding coalition.
5. *Empowering others to act on the vision:* getting rid of obstacles to change; changing systems or structures that seriously undermine the vision; encouraging risk taking and nontraditional ideas, activities, and actions.
6. *Planning for and creating short-term wins:* planning for visible performance improvements; creating those improvements; recognizing and rewarding employees involved in the improvements.
7. *Consolidating improvements and producing still more changes:* using increased credibility to change systems, structures, and policies that don't fit the vision; hiring, promoting, and developing employees who can implement the vision; reinvigorating the process with new projects, themes, and change agents.
8. *Institutionalizing new approaches:* articulating the connections between the new behaviors and corporation success; developing the means to ensure leadership development and succession.

the periphery of the corporation in a few plants and divisions far from corporate headquarters" and were "led by the general managers of those units, not by the CEO or corporate staff people" (159). The best chief executives created "a market for change," but let others decide how to initiate changes and then used the most successfully revitalized units as models for the rest of the company. The accompanying box presents their "Six Steps to Effective Change" for the managers of such units.

Opposite this box we juxtapose another, from an article that appeared a few years later in the *Harvard Business Review,* with a remarkably similar title, "Leading Change: Why Transformation Efforts Fail." This was written by John Kotter, a colleague of Beer, in the same department at the Harvard Business School. But Kotter's "Eight Steps to Transforming Your Corporation" are very much top-down. "Change, by definition," Kotter wrote, "requires creating a new system, which in turn always demands leadership. [The start of] a renewal process typically goes nowhere until enough real leaders are promoted or hired into senior-level jobs" (1995: 60).

So should the change process be top-down or bottom-up? If you are to believe the experts, then you will have to flip a coin. Or else try to understand what is broken in your own organization before you decide how to fix it. There is no formula for transforming any organization, and that includes the very notion that the organization needs transforming in the first place.

In fact, the McKinsey consultants, Dickhout and colleagues, whose set of change strategies were presented (earlier in) this discussion, are among the few in this literature who have made the welcome claim that which approach you use *depends* on your organization's goals, needs, and capabilities. In their study, "each transformation was a unique response to a specific set of problems and opportunities. . . . The leader appeared to have 'cracked a code' embedded within the organization . . . [so that] energy was released and channeled to improve performance . . . " (20). Wise words to end discussion of a literature and a practice that have not always been terribly wise.

READING 6.2

Convergence and Upheaval: Managing the Unsteady Pace of Organizational Evolution* BY MICHAEL L. TUSHMAN, WILLIAM H. NEWMAN, AND ELAINE ROMANELLI

A snug fit of external opportunity, company strategy, and internal structure is a hallmark of successful companies. The real test of executive leadership, however, is in maintaining this alignment in the race of changing competitive conditions.

Consider the Polaroid or Caterpillar corporations. Both firms virtually dominated their respective industries for decades, only to be caught offguard by major environmental changes. The same strategic and organizational factors which were so effective for decades became the seeds of complacency and organization decline.

Recent studies of companies over long periods show that the most successful firms maintain a workable equilibrium for several years (or decades), but are also able to initiate and carry out sharp, widespread changes (referred to here as reorientations) when their environments shift. Such upheaval may bring renewed vigor to the enterprise. Less successful firms, on the other hand, get stuck in a particular pattern. The leaders of these firms either do not see the need for reorientation or are unable to carry through the necessary frame-breaking changes. While not all reorientations succeed, those organizations which do not initiate reorientations as environments shift underperform.

This reading focuses on reasons why for long periods most companies make only incremental changes, and why they then need to make painful, discontinuous, system-wide shifts. We are particularly concerned with the role of executive leadership in managing this pattern of convergence punctuated by upheaval. . . .

The task of managing incremental change, or convergence, differs sharply from managing frame-breaking change. Incremental change is compatible with the existing structure of a company and is reinforced over a period of years. In contrast, frame-breaking change is abrupt, painful to participants, and often resisted by the old guard. Forging these new strategy–structure–people–process consistencies and laying the basis for the next period of incremental change calls for distinctive skills.

Because the future health, and even survival, of a company or business unit is at stake, we need to take a closer look at the nature and consequences of convergent change and of differences imposed by frame-breaking change. We need to explore when and why these painful and risky revolutions interrupt previously successful patterns, and whether these discontinuities can be avoided and/or initiated prior to crisis. Finally, we need to examine what managers can and should do to guide their organizations through periods of convergence and upheaval over time. . . .

The following discussion is based on the history of companies in many different industries, different countries, both large and small organizations, and organizations in various stages of their product class's life cycle. We are dealing with a widespread phenomenon—not just a few dramatic sequences. Our research strongly suggests that the convergence/upheaval pattern occurs within departments at the business-unit level . . . and at the corporate level of analysis. . . . The problem of managing both convergent periods and upheaval is not just for the CEO, but necessarily involves general managers as well as functional managers.

PATTERNS IN ORGANIZATIONAL EVOLUTION: CONVERGENCE AND UPHEAVAL

BUILDING ON STRENGTH: PERIODS OF CONVERGENCE

Successful companies wisely stick to what works well. . . .

. . . [C]onvergence starts out with an effective dovetailing of strategy, structure, people, and processes. . . . The formal system includes decisions about grouping and linking resources as well as planning and control systems, rewards and evaluation procedures, and human resource management systems. The informal system includes core values, beliefs, norms, communication patterns, and actual decision making and conflict resolution patterns. It is the whole fabric of structure, systems, people, and processes which must be suited to company strategy (Nadler and Tushman, 1986).

As the fit between strategy, structure, people, and processes is never perfect, convergence is an ongoing process characterized by incremental change. Over time, in all companies studied, two types of converging changes were common: fine-tuning and incremental adaptations.

- Converging change: Fine-tuning—Even with good strategy–structure–process fits, well-run companies seek even better ways of exploiting (and defending) their missions. Such effort typically deals with one or more of the following:
  - Refining policies, methods, and procedures.
  - Creating specialized units and linking mechanisms to permit increased volume and increased attention to unit quality and cost.
  - Developing personnel especially suited to the present strategy—through improved selection and training, and tailoring reward systems to match strategic thrusts.
  - Fostering individual and group commitments to the company mission and to the excellence of one's own department.
  - Promoting confidence in the accepted norms, beliefs, and myths.
  - Clarifying established roles, power, status, dependencies, and allocation mechanism.

The fine-tuning fills out and elaborates the consistencies between strategy, structure, people, and processes. These incremental changes lead to an ever more interconnected (and therefore more stable) social system. Convergent periods fit the happy, stick-with-a-winner situations romanticized by Peters and Waterman (1982).

- Converging change: Incremental adjustments to environmental shifts—In addition to fine-tuning changes, minor shifts in the environment will call for some organizational response. Even the most conservative of organizations expect, even welcome, small changes which do not make too many waves.

A popular expression is that almost any organization can tolerate a "10 percent change." At any one time, only a few changes are being made; but these changes are still compatible with the prevailing structures, systems, and processes. Examples of such adjustments are an expansion in sales territory, a shift in emphasis among products in the product line, or improved processing technology in production.

The usual process of making changes of this sort is well known: wide acceptance of the need for change, openness to possible alternatives, objective examination of the pros and cons of each plausible alternative, participation of those directly affected in the preceding analysis, a market test or pilot operation where feasible, time to learn the new activities, established role models, known rewards for positive success, evaluation, and refinement.

The role of executive leadership during convergent periods is to reemphasize mission and core values and to delegate incremental decisions to middle-level managers. Note that the uncertainty created for people affected by such changes is well within tolerable limits. Opportunity is provided to anticipate and learn what is new, while most features of the structure remain unchanged.

The overall system adapts, but it is not transformed.

Converging Change: Some Consequences

For those companies whose strategies fit environmental conditions, convergence brings about better and better effectiveness. Incremental change is relatively easy to implement and ever more optimizes the consistencies between strategy, structure, people, and processes. At AT&T, for example, the period between 1913 and 1980 was one of ever more incremental change to further bolster the "Ma Bell" culture, systems, and structure all in service of developing the telephone network.

Convergent periods are, however, a double-edged sword. As organizations grow and become more successful, they develop internal forces for stability. Organizational structures and systems become so interlinked that they only allow compatible changes. Further, over time, employees develop habits, patterned behaviors begin to take on values (e.g., "service is good"), and employees develop a sense of competence in knowing how to get work done within the system. These self-reinforcing patterns of behavior, norms, and values contribute to increased organizational momentum and complacency and, over time, to a sense of organizational history. This organizational history—epitomized by common stories, heroes, and standards—specifies "how we work here" and "what we hold important here."

This organizational momentum is profoundly functional as long as the organization's strategy is appropriate. The Ma Bell . . . culture, structure, and systems—and associated internal momentum—were critical to [the] organization's success. However, if (and when) strategy must change, this momentum cuts the other way. Organizational history is a source of tradition, precedent, and pride which are, in turn, anchors to the past. A proud history often restricts vigilant problem solving and may be a source of resistance to change.

When faced with environmental threat, organizations with strong momentum

- may not register the threat due to organization complacency and/or stunted external vigilance (e.g., the automobile or steel industries), or
- if the threat is recognized, the response is frequently heightened conformity to the status quo and/or increased commitment to "what we do best."

For example, the response of dominant firms to technological threat is frequently increased commitment to the obsolete technology (e.g., telegraph/telephone; vacuum tube/transistor; core/semiconductor memory). A paradoxical result of long periods of success may be heightened organizational complacency, decreased organizational flexibility, and a stunted ability to learn.

Converging change is a double-edged sword. Those very social and technical consistencies which are key sources of success may also be the seeds of failure if environments change. The longer the convergent periods, the greater these internal forces for stability. This momentum seems to be particularly accentuated in those most successful firms in a product class . . . in historically regulated organizations . . . or in organizations that have been traditionally shielded from competition. . . .

ON FRAME-BREAKING CHANGE

Forces Leading to Frame-Breaking Change

What, then, leads to frame-breaking change? Why defy tradition? Simply stated, frame-breaking change occurs in response to or, better yet, in anticipation of major environmental changes—changes which require more than incremental adjustments. The need for discontinuous change springs from one or a combination of the following:

- Industry discontinuities—Sharp changes in legal, political, or technological conditions shift the basis of competition within industries. Deregulation has dramatically transformed the financial services and airlines industries. Substitute product technologies . . . or substitute process technologies . . . may transform the bases of competition within industries. Similarly, the emergence of industry standards, or dominant designs (such as the DC-3, IBM 360, or PDP-8), signal a shift in competition away from product innovation and toward increased process innovation. Finally, major economic changes (e.g., oil crises) and legal shifts (e.g., patent protection in biotechnology or trade/regulator barriers in pharmaceuticals or cigarettes) also directly affect bases of competition.
- Product life-cycle shifts—Over the course of a product class life cycle, different strategies are appropriate. In the emergence phase of a product class, competition is based on product innovation and performance, where in the maturity stage, competition centers on cost, volume, and efficiency. Shifts in patterns of demand alter key factors for success. For example, the demand and nature of competition for mini-computers, cellular telephones, wide-body aircraft, and bowling alley equipment was transformed as these products gained acceptance and their product classes evolved. Powerful international competition may compound these forces.
- Internal company dynamics—Entwined with these external forces are breaking points within the firm. Sheer size may require a basically new management design. For example, few inventor-entrepreneurs can tolerate the formality that is linked with large volume. . . . Key people die. Family investors may become more concerned with their inheritance taxes than with company development. Revised corporate portfolio strategy may sharply alter the role and resources assigned to business units or functional areas. Such pressures, especially when coupled with external changes, may trigger frame-breaking change.

Scope of Frame-Breaking Change

Frame-breaking change is driven by shifts in business strategy. As strategy shifts so too must structure, people, and organizational processes. Quite unlike convergent change, frame-breaking reforms involve discontinuous changes throughout the organization. These bursts of change do not reinforce the existing system and are implemented rapidly. . . . Frame-breaking changes are revolutionary changes *of* the system as opposed to incremental changes *in* the system.

The following features are usually involved in frame-breaking change:

- Reformed mission and core values—A strategy shift involves a new definition of company mission. Entering or withdrawing from an industry may be involved; at least the way the company expects to be outstanding is altered. . . .
- Altered power and status—Frame-breaking change always alters the distribution of power. Some groups lose in the shift while others gain. . . . These dramatically altered power distributions reflect shifts in bases of competition and resource allocation. A new strategy must be backed up with a shift in the balance of power and status.
- Reorganization—A new strategy requires a modification in structure, systems, and procedures. As strategic requirements shift, so too must the choice of organization form. A new direction calls for added activity in some areas and less in others. Changes in structure and systems are means to ensure that this reallocation of effort takes place. New structures and revised roles deliberately break business-as-usual behavior.
- Revised interaction patterns—The way people in the organization work together has to adapt during frame-breaking change. As strategy is different, new procedures, work flows, communication networks, and decision-making patterns must be established. With these changes in work flows and procedures must also come revised norms, informal decision-making/conflict-resolution procedures, and informal roles.

- New executives—Frame-breaking change also involves new executives, usually brought in from outside the organization (or business unit) and placed in key managerial positions. Commitment to the new mission, energy to overcome prevailing inertia, and freedom from prior obligations are all needed to refocus the organization. A few exceptional members of the old guard may attempt to make this shift, but habits and expectations of their associations are difficult to break. New executives are most likely to provide both the necessary drive and an enhanced set of skills more appropriate for the new strategy. While the overall number of executive changes is usually relatively small, these new executives have substantial symbolic and substantive effects on the organization. . . .

Why All at Once?

Frame-breaking change is revolutionary in that the shifts reshape the entire nature of the organization. Those more effective examples of frame-breaking change were implemented rapidly. . . . It appears that a piecemeal approach to frame-breaking changes gets bogged down in politics, individual resistance to change, and organizational inertia. . . . Frame-breaking change requires discontinuous shifts in strategy, structure, people, and processes concurrently—or at least in a short period of time. Reasons for rapid, simultaneous implementation include:

- Synergy within the new structure can be a powerful aid. New executives with a fresh mission, working in a redesigned organization with revised norms and values, backed up with power and status, provide strong reinforcement. The pieces of the revitalized organization pull together, as opposed to piecemeal change where one part of the new organization is out of synch with the old organization.
- Pockets of resistance have a chance to grow and develop when frame-breaking change is implemented slowly. The new mission, shifts in organization, and other frame-breaking changes upset the comfortable routines and precedent. Resistance to such fundamental change is natural. If frame-breaking change is implemented slowly, then individuals have a greater opportunity to undermine the changes and organizational inertia works to further stifle fundamental change.
- Typically, there is a pent-up need for change. During convergent periods, basic adjustments are postponed. Boat rocking is discouraged. Once constraints are relaxed, a variety of desirable improvements press for attention. The exhilaration and momentum of a fresh effort (and new team) make difficult moves more acceptable. Change is in fashion.
- Frame-breaking change is an inherently risky and uncertain venture. The longer the implementation period, the greater the period of uncertainty and instability. The most effective frame-breaking changes initiate the new strategy, structure, processes, and systems rapidly and begin the next period of stability and convergent change. The sooner fundamental uncertainty is removed, the better the chances of organizational survival and growth. While the pacing of change is important, the overall time to implement frame-breaking change will be contingent on the size and age of the organization.

Patterns in Organization Evolution

This historical approach to organization evolution focuses on convergent periods punctuated by reorientation—discontinuous, organization-wide upheavals. The most effective firms take advantage of relatively long convergent periods. These periods of incremental change build on and take advantage of organization inertia. Frame-breaking change is quite dysfunctional if the organization is successful and the environment is stable. If, however, the organization is performing poorly and/or if the environment changes substantially, frame-breaking change is the only way to realign the organization with its competitive environment. Not all reorientations will be successful. . . . However, inaction in the face of performance crisis and/or environmental shifts is a certain recipe for failure.

Because reorientations are so disruptive and fraught with uncertainty, the more rapidly they are implemented, the more quickly the organization can reap the benefits of the following convergent period. High-performing firms initiate reorientations when environmental conditions shift and implement these reorientations rapidly. . . . Low-performing organizations either do not reorient or reorient all the time as they root around to find an effective alignment with environmental conditions. . . .

EXECUTIVE LEADERSHIP AND ORGANIZATION EVOLUTION

Executive leadership plays a key role in reinforcing system-wide momentum during convergent periods and in initiating and implementing bursts of change that characterize strategic reorientations. The nature of the leadership task differs sharply during these contrasting periods of organization evolution.

During convergent periods, the executive team focuses on *maintaining* congruence and fit within the organization. Because strategy, structure, processes, and systems are fundamentally sound, the myriad of incremental substantive decisions can be delegated to middle-level management, where direct expertise and information reside. The key role for executive leadership during convergent periods is to reemphasize strategy, mission, and core values and to keep a vigilant eye on external opportunities and/or threats.

Frame-breaking change, however, requires direct executive involvement in all aspects of the change. Given the enormity of the change and inherent internal forces for stability, executive leadership must be involved in the specification of strategy, structure, people, and organizational processes *and* in the development of implementation plans. . . .

The most effective executives in our studies foresaw the need for major change. They recognized the external threats and opportunities, and took bold steps to deal with them. . . . Indeed, by acting before being forced to do so, they had more time to plan their transitions.

Such visionary executive teams are the exceptions. Most frame-breaking change is postponed until a financial crisis forces drastic action. The momentum, and frequently the success, of convergent periods breeds reluctance to change. . . .

. . . [M]ost frame-breaking upheavals are managed by executives brought in from outside the company. The Columbia research program finds that externally recruited executives are more than three times more likely to initiate frame-breaking change than existing executive teams. Frame-breaking change was coupled with CEO succession in more than 80% of the cases. . . .

There are several reasons why a fresh set of executives is typically used in company transformations. The new executive team brings different skills and a fresh perspective. Often they arrive with a strong belief in the new mission. Moreover, they are unfettered by prior commitments linked to the status quo; instead, this new top team symbolizes the need for change. Excitement of a new challenge adds to the energy devoted to it.

We should note that many of the executives who could not, or would not, implement frame-breaking change went on to be quite successful in other organizations. . . . The stimulation of a fresh start and of jobs matched to personal competence applies to individuals as well as to organizations.

Although typical patterns for the when and who of frame-breaking change are clear—wait for a financial crisis and then bring in an outsider, along with a revised executive team, to revamp the company—this is clearly less than satisfactory for a particular organization. Clearly, some companies benefit from transforming themselves before a crisis forces them to do so, and a few exceptional executives have the vision and drive to reorient a business which they nurtured during its preceding period of convergence. The vital tasks are to manage incremental change during convergent periods; to have the vision to initiate and implement frame-breaking change prior to the competition; and to mobilize an executive team which can initiate and implement both kinds of change.

CONCLUSION

. . . Managers should anticipate that when environments change sharply:

- Frame-breaking change cannot be avoided. These discontinuous organizational changes will be either made proactively or initiated under crisis/turnaround conditions.
- Discontinuous changes need to be made in strategy, structure, people, and processes concurrently. Tentative change runs the risk of being smothered by individual, group, and organizational inertia.

- Frame-breaking change requires direct executive involvement in all aspects of the change, usually bolstered with new executives from outside the organization.
- There are no patterns in the sequence of frame-breaking changes, and not all strategies will be effective. Strategy and, in turn, structure, systems, and processes must meet industry-specific competitive issues.

Finally, our historical analysis of organizations highlights the following issues for executive leadership:

- Need to manage for balance, consistency, or fit during convergent period.
- Need to be vigilant for environmental shifts in order to anticipate the need for frame-breaking change.
- Need to manage effectively incremental as well as frame-breaking change.
- Need to build (or rebuild) a top team to help initiate and implement frame-breaking change.
- Need to develop core values which can be used as an anchor as organizations evolve through frame-breaking changes (e.g., IBM, Hewlett-Packard).
- Need to develop and use organizational history as a way to infuse pride in an organization's past and for its future.
- Need to bolster technical, social, and conceptual skills with visionary skills. Visionary skills add energy, direction, and excitement so critical during frame-breaking change. . . .

READING 6.3

Logical Incrementalism: Managing Strategy Formation* BY JAMES BRIAN QUINN AND JOHN VOYER

THE LOGIC OF LOGICAL INCREMENTALISM

Strategy change processes in well-managed major organizations rarely resemble the rational–analytical systems touted in the literature. Instead, strategic change processes are typically fragmented, evolutionary, and intuitive. Real strategy *evolves* as internal decisions and external events flow together to create a new, widely shared consensus for action.

THE FORMAL SYSTEMS PLANNING APPROACH

There is a strong literature stating which actors *should* be included in a systematically planned strategy. This systems planning approach focuses on quantitative factors, and underemphasizes qualitative, organizational, and power factors. Systems planning *can* make a contribution, but it should be just one building block in the continuous stream of events that creates organizational strategy.

THE POWER-BEHAVIORAL APPROACH

Another body of literature has enhanced our understanding of *multiple goal structures,* the *politics* of strategic decisions, *bargaining* and *negotiation* processes, *satisficing* in decision making, the role of *coalitions,* and the practice of "muddling" in public sector management. The shortcomings of this body of literature are that it has typically been far removed from strategy making, it has ignored the contributions of useful analytical approaches, and it has offered few practical recommendations for the strategist.

---

*Originally published in the collegiate edition of *The Strategy Process,* Prentice Hall, 1994. Based on James Brian Quinn, "Strategic Change: Logical Incrementalism," *Sloan Management Review,* Fall 1978, pp. 1–21, and James Brian Quinn, "Managing Strategies Incrementally," *Omega: The International Journal of Management Science,* 1982, drawn from his book *Strategies for Change: Logical Incrementalism* (Irwin, 1980).

SUMMARY FINDINGS FROM STUDY OF ACTUAL CHANGE PROCESSES

Recognizing the strengths and weaknesses of each of these approaches, the change processes in ten major organizations were documented. Several important findings emerged from these investigations.

- Neither approach above adequately describes strategy processes.
- Effective strategies tend to emerge incrementally and opportunistically, as subsystems of organizational activity (e.g., acquisitions, divestitures, major reorganizations, even formal plans) are blended into a coherent pattern.
- The logic behind this process is so powerful that it may be the best approach to recommend for strategy formation in large companies.
- Because of cognitive and process limits, this approach must be managed and linked together in a way best described as "logical incrementalism."
- Such incrementalism is not "muddling." It is a purposeful, effective, active management technique for improving and integrating both the analytical and behavioral aspects of strategy formation.

CRITICAL STRATEGIC ISSUES

Though "hard data" decisions dominate the literature, there are various "soft" kinds of changes that affect strategy:

- The design of an organization's structure
- The characteristic management style in the firm
- A firm's external (especially government) relations
- Acquisitions, divestitures, or divisional control issues
- A firm's international posture and relationships
- An organization's innovative capabilities
- The effects of an organization's growth on the motivation of its personnel
- Value and expectation changes, and their effects on worker and professional relationships in the organization
- Technological changes that affect the organization

Top executives made several important points about these kinds of changes. Few of these issues lend themselves to quantitative modeling or financial analysis. Most firms use different subsystems to handle different types of strategic changes, yet the subsystems were similar across firms. Lastly, no single formal analytical process could handle all strategic variables simultaneously using a planning approach.

Precipitating Events and Incremental Logic

Executives reported that various events often resulted in interim decisions that shaped the company's future strategy. This was evident in the decisions forced on General Motors by the 1973–74 oil crisis, in the shift in posture pressed upon Exxon by the Prince William Sound oil spill, or in the dramatic opportunities allowed for Haloid Corporation and Pilkington Brothers by the unexpected inventions of xerography and float glass. No organization—no matter how brilliant, rational, or imaginative—could possibly have foreseen the timing, severity, or even the nature of all such precipitating events.

Recognizing this, top executives tried to respond incrementally. They kept early commitments broadly formative, tentative, and subject to later review. Future implications were too hard to understand, so parties wanted to test assumptions and have an opportunity to learn. Also, top executives were sensitive to social and political structures in the organization; they tried to handle things in a way that would make the change process a good one.

The Diversification Subsystem

Strategies for diversification provide excellent examples of the value of proceeding incrementally. Incremental processes aid both the formal aspects of diversification (price and strategic fit, for example) and the psychological and political aspects. Most important among the latter are generating a genuine, top-level psychological commitment to diversification, consciously preparing the firm to move opportunistically, building a "comfort factor" for risk taking, and developing a new ethos based on the success of new divisions.

The Major Reorganization Subsystem

Large-scale organizational moves may have negative effects on organizational politics and social structure. Logical incrementalism makes it easier to avoid those negative effects. As the organization proceeds incrementally, it can assess the new roles, capabilities, and individual reactions of those involved in the restructuring. It allows new people to be trained and tested, perhaps for extended periods. Logical incrementalism allows organizational actors to modify the idea behind the reorganization as more is learned. It also gives executives the luxury of making final commitments as late as possible. Executives may move opportunistically, step by step, selectively moving people as developments warrant (events seldom come together at one convenient time). They may also articulate the broad organizational concept in detail only when the last pieces fit together. Lastly, logical incrementalism works well in large-scale reorganization because it allows for testing, flexibility, and feedback.

FORMAL PLANNING IN CORPORATE STRATEGY

Formal planning techniques do serve some essential functions. They discipline managers to look ahead, and to express goals and resource allocations. Long-term planning encourages longer time horizons, and eases the evaluation of short-term plans. Long-term plans create a psychological backdrop and an information framework about the future against which managers can calibrate short-term or interim decisions. Lastly, "special studies," like the white papers used at Pillsbury to inform the chicken-business divestiture decision, have a large effect at key junctures for specific decisions.

Planning may make incrementalism standard organizational practice, for two reasons. First, most planning is "bottom up," and the people at the bottom have an interest in their existing products and processes. Second, executives want most plans to be "living" or "ever green," intended to be only frameworks, providing guidance and consistency for incremental decisions. To do otherwise would be to deny that further information could have value. Thus, properly used formal planning can be part of incremental logic.

Total Posture Planning

Occasionally, managements did attempt very broad assessments of their companies' total posture. But these major product thrusts were usually unsuccessful. Actual strategies *evolved,* as each company overextended, consolidated, made errors, and rebalanced various thrusts over time. The executives thought that this was both logical and expected.

LOGICAL INCREMENTALISM

Strategic decisions cannot be aggregated into a single decision matrix, with factors treated simultaneously to achieve an optimum solution. There are cognitive limits, but also "process limits"—timing and sequencing requirements, the needs to create awareness, to build comfort levels, to develop consensus, to select and train people, and so forth.

A Strategy Emerges

Successful executives connect and sequentially arrange a series of strategic processes and decisions over a period of years. They attempt to build a resource base and posture that are strong enough to withstand all but the most devastating events. They constantly reconfigure corporate structure and strategy as new information suggests better—but never perfect—alignments. The process is dynamic, with no definite beginning or end.

CONCLUSIONS

Strategy deals with the unknowable, not the uncertain. It involves so many forces, most of which have great strength and the power to combine, that one cannot, in a probabilistic sense, predict events. Therefore, logic dictates that one proceeds flexibly and experimentally from broad ideas toward specific commitments. Making the latter concrete as late as possible narrows the bands of uncertainty, and allows the firm to benefit from the best available information. This is the process of "logical incrementalism." It is not "muddling." Logical incrementalism is conscious, purposeful, active, good management. It allows executives to blend analysis, organizational politics, and individual needs into a cohesive new direction.

MANAGING INCREMENTALLY

How can one actively manage the logical incremental process? The study discussed here shows that executives tend to use similar incremental processes as they manage complex strategy shifts.

Being Ahead of the Formal Information System

The earliest signals for strategy change rarely come from formal company systems. Using multiple internal and external sources, managers "sense" the need for change before the formal systems do. T. Vincent Learson at IBM drove the company to develop the 360 series of computers based on his feeling that, despite its current success, IBM was heading toward market confusion. IBM's formal intelligence system did not pick up any market signals until three years after Learson launched the development process.

Building Organizational Awareness

This is essential when key players lack information or psychological stimulation to change. At early stages, management processes are broad, tentative, formative, information seeking, and purposely avoid irreversible commitments. They also try to avoid provoking potential opponents of an idea.

Building Credibility/Changing Symbols

Symbols may help managers signal to the organization that certain types of changes are coming, even when specific solutions are not yet in hand. Highly visible symbolic actions can communicate effectively to large numbers of people. Grapevines can amplify signals of pending change. Symbolic moves often verify the intention of a new strategy, or give it credibility in its early stages. Without such actions, people may interpret even forceful verbiage as mere rhetoric and delay their commitment to new strategic ideas.

Legitimizing New Viewpoints

Planned delays allow the organization to debate and discuss threatening issues, work out implications of new solutions, or gain an improved information base. Sometimes, strategic ideas that are initially resisted can gain acceptance and commitment simply by the passage of time and open discussion of new information. Many top executives, planners, and change agents consciously arrange such "gestation periods." For example, William Spoor at Pillsbury allowed more than a year of discussion and information gathering before the company decided to divest its chicken business.

Tactical Shifts and Partial Solutions

These are typical steps in developing a new strategic posture, especially when early problem resolutions need to be partial, tentative, or experimental. Tactical adjustments, or a series of small programs, typically encounter little opposition, while a broad strategic change could encounter much opposition. These approaches allow the continuation of ongoing strengths while shifting momentum at the margin. Experimentation can occur with minimized risk, leading to many different ways to succeed.

As events unfurl, the solutions to several problems, which may initially have seemed unrelated, tend to flow together into a new combination. When possible, strategic logic (risk minimization) dictates starting broad initiatives that can be flexibly guided in any of several possible desirable directions.

Broadening Political Support

This is an essential and consciously active step in major strategy changes. Committees, task forces, or retreats tend to be favored mechanisms. By selecting such groups' chairpersons, membership, timing, and agenda the guiding executives can largely influence and predict a desired outcome, yet nudge other executives toward a consensus. Interactive consensus building also improves the quality of decisions, and encourages positive and innovative help when things go wrong.

Overcoming Opposition

Unnecessary alienation of managers from an earlier era in the organization's history should be avoided; their talents may be needed. But overcoming opposition is usually necessary. Preferred methods are persuasion, co-optation, neutralization, or moving through zones of indifference (i.e., pushing those portions of a project that are non controversial to most of the interested parties). To be sure, successful executives honor and even stimulate legitimate differences. Opponents sometimes thoughtfully shape new strategies into more effective directions; sometimes they even change their views. Occasionally, though, strong-minded executives may need to be moved to less influential positions, or be stimulated to leave.

Consciously Structured Flexibility

Flexibility is essential in dealing with the many "unknowables" in the environment. Successful organizations actively create flexibility. This requires active horizon scanning, creating resource buffers, developing and positioning champions, and shortening decision lines. These are the keys to *real* contingency planning, not the usual pre-capsuled (and shelved) programs designed to respond to stimuli that never occur quite as expected.

Trial Balloons and Systematic Waiting

Strategists may have to wait patiently for the proper option to appear or precipitating event to occur. For example, although he wanted to divest Pillsbury's chicken business, William Spoor waited until his investment bankers found a buyer at a good price. Executives may also consciously launch trial ideas, like Spoor's "Super Box" at Pillsbury, to attract options and concrete proposals. Without making a commitment to any specific solution, the executive mobilizes the organization's creative abilities.

Creating Pockets of Commitment

Executives often need this tactic when they are trying to get organizations to adopt entirely new strategic directions. Small projects, deep within the organization, are used to test options, create skills, or build commitments for several possible options. The executive provides broad goals, proper climate, and flexible resource support, without public commitment. This avoids attention on, and identification with, any project. Yet executives can stimulate the good options, make life harder for the poorer options, or even kill the weakest ones.

Crystallizing the Focus

At some point, this becomes vital. Early commitments are necessarily vague, but once executives develop information or consensus on desirable ways to proceed, they may use their prestige or power to push or crystallize a particular formulation. This should not be done too early, as it might inadvertently centralize the organization or preempt interesting options. Focusing too early might also provide a common target for otherwise fragmented opposition, or cause the organization to undertake undesirable actions just to carry out a stated commitment. When to crystallize viewpoints and when to maintain open options is a true art of strategic management.

Formalizing Commitment

This is the final step in the logical incremental strategy formation process. It usually occurs after general acceptance exists, and when the timing is right. Typically, the decision is announced publicly, programs and budgets are formed, and control and reward systems are aligned to reflect intended strategic emphases.

Continuing the Dynamics and Mutating the Consensus

Advocates of the "new" strategy can become as strong a source of inflexible resistance to new ideas as were the advocates of the "old" strategy. Effective strategic managers immediately introduce new ideas and stimuli at the top, to maintain the adaptability of the strategic thrusts they have just solidified. This is a most difficult, but essential, psychological task.

Not a Linear Process

While generation of a strategy generally flows along the sequence presented above, the stages are usually not ordered or discrete. The process is more like fermentation in biochemistry, instead of being like an industrial assembly line. Segments of major strategies are likely to be at different stages of development. They are usually integrated in the minds of top executives, each of whom may nevertheless see things differently. Lastly, the process is so continuous that it may be hard to discern the particular point in time when specific clear-cut decisions are made.

An important point to remember is that the validity of a strategy lies not in its pristine clarity or rigorously maintained structure. Its value lies in its capacity to capture the initiative, to deal with unknowable events, and to redeploy and concentrate resources as new opportunities and thrusts emerge. This allows the organization to use resources most effectively toward selected goals.

INTEGRATING THE STRATEGY

The process described above may be incremental, but it is not piecemeal. Effective executives constantly reassess the total organization, its capacities, and its needs as related to the surrounding environment.

Concentrating on a Few Key Thrusts

Effective strategic managers constantly seek to distill a few (six to ten) "central themes" that draw the firm's actions together. These maintain focus and consistency in the strategy. They make it easier to discuss and monitor intended directions. By contrast, formal models, designed to keep track of divisional progress toward realizing strategy, tend to become bound up in red tape, procedure, and rigid bureaucracy.

Coalition Management

The heart of all controlled strategy development is coalition management. Top managers act at the confluence of pressures from all stakeholders. These stakeholders will form coalitions, so managers must be active in forming their own. People selection and coalition management are the ultimate controls top executives have in guiding and coordinating their companies' strategies.

CONCLUSIONS

Many recent attempts to devise strategy-using approaches that emphasize formal planning have failed because of poor implementation. This results from the classic trap of thinking about strategy formulation and implementation as separate and sequential processes. Successful managers, who operate logically and actively, in an *incremental* mode, build the seeds of understanding, identity, and commitment into the very processes that create their strategies. Strategy "formulation" and strategy "implementation" interact in the organization's continuing stream of events.

READING 6.4

The Rhythm of Change BY QUY NGUYEN HUY AND HENRY MINTZBERG

We are all familiar with the modern-day manager's mantra that we live in times of great and constant change. Because the world is turbulent, it is said, and the competition is hyperturbulent, managers must take seriously the job of continually initiating and adjusting to change. Change, by definition, is good. Resistance to change is bad.

Might we suggest that you turn off the hype and look out the window? Do you notice anything out there resembling all that supposed change and turbulence? We perceive our environment to be in constant flux because *we only notice the things that do change*. We are not as keenly aware, however, of the vast majority of things that remain unchanged—the engine of the automobile you drive (basically the same as that used in Ford Motor Co.'s Model T), even the buttons on the shirt you wear (the same technology used by your grandparents). This, indeed, is a good thing, because prolonged and pervasive change means anarchy—and hardly anybody wants to live with that. Sure, important changes have been taking place recently, but the truth is that stability and continuity also form the basis of our experience. In fact, *change has no meaning unless it is juxtaposed against continuity*. Because many things remain stable, change has to be managed with a profound appreciation of stability. Accordingly, there are times when *change is sensibly resisted*; for example, when an organization should simply continue to pursue a perfectly good strategy. What's needed is a framework whereby pragmatic, coherent approaches to thinking about change can be explored.

Dramatic, Systematic and Organic Change

Today's obsession with change focuses on that which is imposed dramatically from the "top." This view should be tempered, however, by the realization that effective organizational change often emerges inadvertently (organic change) or develops in a more orderly fashion (systematic change). (See "The Change Triangle.")

Dramatic change is frequently initiated in times of crisis or of great opportunity when power is concentrated and there is great slack to be leveraged (for example, in the sale of assets). It can range from rationalizing costs, restructuring the organization and repositioning strategy to

BOX 6.1
THE CHANGE TRIANGLE

The dynamic rhythm of organizational change has always been a constant: Dramatic change descends from the top (from senior management), systematic change is generated laterally and organic change emerges from the grass roots. These three forces interact dynamically, each providing the primary, but not sole, thrust for a key transformation process: Dramatic change incites revolution, which provides impetus; systematic change orchestrates reform, which instills order; and organic change nurtures rejuvenation, which spurs initiative.

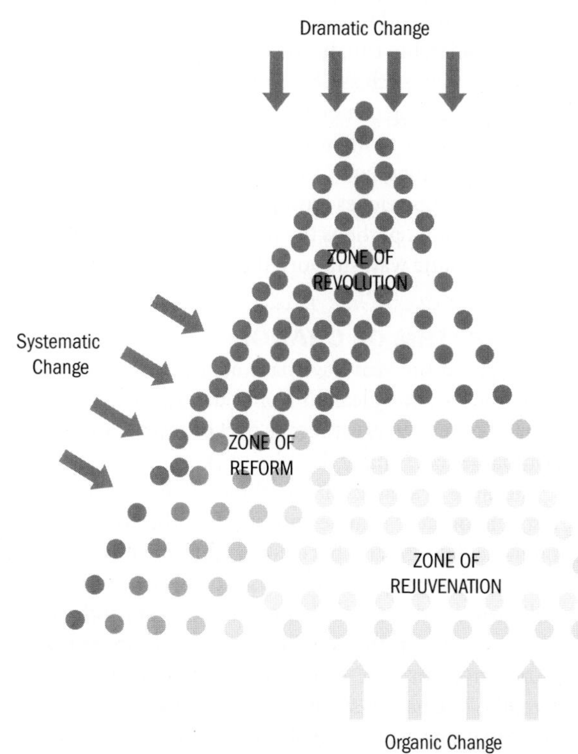

reframing the organization's mindset and revitalizing its culture. Usually, a company's leadership commands this dramatic change in the expectation of compliance by everyone else. Although this kind of initiative can be effective, it can also be misguided and engender covert resistance. For example, consider the case of Vivendi Universal. In a five-year buying spree in the late 1990s, former CEO Jean-Marie Messier borrowed heavily against Vivendi's water-utility business, acquiring numerous telecommunications, media and entertainment firms, including Seagram Co.'s Universal Studios and the Universal Music Group, in an ill-fated attempt to build a vertically integrated media conglomerate. When the stock bubble burst, Vivendi's market value plummeted, and Messier was fired. Seeing no synergistic benefit in these disparate holdings, his successor, Jean-René Foutou, is now selling off most of them.

Systematic change is slower, less ambitious, more focused, and more carefully constructed and sequenced than dramatic change. In a word, it is more orderly. Often it is promoted by staff groups and consultants who handle planning and organizational development. Over the years, many approaches to systematic change have appeared, including quality improvement, work reprogramming, benchmarking, strategic planning, and so on. As the nature of these approaches suggests, systematic change draws heavily on technique and, in that sense, is change imported to the organization. But it can also be overly formalized and so stifle initiative in the organization.

Whereas dramatic change is usually driven by the formal leadership and systematic change is usually promoted by specialists, organic change tends to arise from the ranks without being formally managed. It often involves messy processes with vague labels like venturing, learning, and politicking and is nurtured behind the scenes in the skunkworks of big companies such as 3M Co. or Intel Corp. and in those near-legendary garage startups that spawned industry giants like Apple Computer Inc. and Dell Computer Corp.

The trouble is that the organic approach can be splintered and is itself anarchical. Groups may begin to work at cross-purposes and fight each other over resources. When informal groups indulge in experiential learning, narrowed competences can result if each focuses on promoting only what it knows best to serve its own interests.

The important thing to understand about organic change is that it is not systematically organized when it begins or dramatically consequential in its intentions, and it does not depend on managerial authority or specialized change agents. Indeed, it often proceeds as a challenge to that authority and those agents, sometimes in rather quirky ways. Yet its results can be dramatic. Clever leadership can, however, stimulate organic change by socializing the organization to prize it. Companies, such as 3M, Honda, Sony, and Intel, have recognized that managerial support and network building can be the key to generating change initiatives at the grass-roots level.

In our view, neither dramatic nor systematic nor organic change works well in isolation. Dramatic change has to be balanced by order and engagement throughout the organization. Systematic approaches require leadership and, again, depend on broad engagement. And organic change, though perhaps the most natural of the three approaches, eventually must be manifested in a systematic way, supported by the leadership.

THE RHYTHM OF CHANGE

Throughout the years, we have acquired in-depth familiarity with many organizational change situations—some gleaned from our experiences as consultants or when working in managerial capacities ourselves, others as part of research projects to track the strategies actually realized by companies over many decades (n1).

Because dramatic change alone can be just drama, systematic change by itself can be deadening, and organic change without the other two can be chaotic, they must be combined or, more often, sequenced and paced over time, creating a rhythm of change. When functioning in a kind of dynamic symbiosis, dramatic change can instead provide impetus, systematic change can instill order, and organic change can generate enthusiasm.

We have seen this symbiosis arising in three main modes. Revolution is dramatic, but often comes from organic origins and later requires systematic consolidation. Reform is largely systematic, but has to stimulate the organic and can sometimes be driven by the dramatic. And rejuvenation is fundamentally organic, but usually must make use of the systematic, and its consequences can be inadvertently dramatic (n2). In illustrating this framework, we cite older examples alongside newer ones, which helps us to make another crucial point: The problem with change is the present. That is, an obsession with the new tends to blind managers to the fact that the basic processes of change and continuity do not change. So older examples, because their consequences have settled, can be more insightful than newer ones.

CORPORATE REVOLUTION

We associate revolution with dramatic acts that change a society. Yet many revolutions actually begin with small organic actions—a "tea party" in Boston or the storming of the Bastille in Paris (that released only a handful of prisoners!). These acts spark the drama; then leadership arises, but only if the conditions, organically, are right. Consider the following:

"The [American] Revolution was effected before the war commenced" John Adams wrote. "The Revolution was in the hearts and minds of the people. . . . This radical change in the principles, opinions, sentiments and affections of the people was the real American Revolution." A revolution without a prior reformation would collapse or become a totalitarian tyranny (n3).

Think of all the totalitarian tyrannies in today's corporations—all the dramatic change devoid of organic underpinnings and lacking systematic support. The leader acts alone, heroically it seems, and everyone else is supposed to follow. Thus we get the great mergers (Daimler-Benz and Chrysler, AOL and Time Warner, Compaq and Hewlett-Packard), the grand strategies (Jean-Marie Messier at Vivendi, L. Dennis Kozlowski at Tyco) and the dramatic downsizings ("Chainsaw Al" Dunlap at Scott Paper Co. and Sunbeam Corp.). There are, however, two forms of revolution that can work.

Driven Revolution. To appreciate when leader-initiated revolution can work, consider the case of Steinberg, Inc., a major Canadian grocery chain whose strategies we tracked over 60 years. Entrepreneur Sam Steinberg propelled two major changes in 1933 and 1968, which despite their 35-year separation, were remarkably similar.

In 1933, one of the company's eight stores "struck it bad," as Steinberg phrased it, incurring "unacceptable" losses of $125 a week. He closed the store one Friday evening, converted it to self-service (a new concept for Montreal), changed its name, slashed its prices by 15–20%, printed handbills, stuffed them into neighborhood mailboxes and reopened on Monday morning. That certainly seems dramatic, but he did this in just a single store. Only when the changes proved successful did he convert the other stores—systematically. Then, in Steinberg's words, "We grew like Topsy," at least until the mid-1960s, when the company—then much larger with almost 200 stores—faced fierce competition. In 1968, the company initiated large, permanent, across-the-board price reductions, coupled with a complete shift in merchandising philosophy. It eliminated specials, games, and gimmicks, and reduced service and advertising, returning to what it knew best. But these changes too began in one store before being allowed to spread to the rest of the operation, with enormous success.

Fomented Revolution. In their organic origins, corporate revolutions can also resemble the political ones of eighteenth-century America and France. For instance, organic changes helped to undermine established behaviors and induce new learning at Volkswagen AG, a company whose strategic evolution we have studied by looking back to the inception of its first automobile in 1934. In the 1960s, many middle managers at the company believed it had to move away from its reliance on the Beetle, but their consistent lobbying was to no avail. With the arrival of a new, deeply knowledgeable chief executive, however, that pent-up organic foment was catalyzed into revolution, and Volkswagen quickly began to produce more stylish, front-wheel-drive, water-cooled cars.

Such stories are, in fact, common. Organic changes infiltrate and bypass skeptical areas of the organization and, through gradual experimentation and persistent small victories, open up the system to really dramatic change.

Consolidating the Revolution. Revolutions must be consolidated: They have to get beyond the dramatic to the systematic and the organic. Companies are judged on the products and services they deliver, not on the changes they make. As the experiences of British Airways Plc show, there are better and worse ways to pace the consolidation of dramatic change.

In the late 1970s, British Airways was ranked among the worst air carriers for customer service and was losing money rapidly. By 1993, however, it had become Europe's most profitable carrier and was benchmarked as a provider of world-class customer service. How did this occur? Upon his arrival in 1983, Colin Marshall, the new CEO, wasted no time in commanding dramatic change. His first two years were characterized by ambitious and rapid change: The workforce was downsized and assets were sold because of poor performance; in one 24-hour period, Marshall terminated 161 managers and executives.

Two years later, sensing that a slower, more tolerable rhythm would be appreciated, Marshall launched systematic consolidation through training programs that encouraged managers to enhance customer service. By 1985, the company opted for organic change to complement the systematic initiatives: Employees with proven interpersonal skills were asked to develop a "family" climate for customer-facing employees. In 1987, systematic and faster-paced reengineering of work processes was introduced, as BA invested heavily in information technology to build a new reservation system. Thus, BA was transformed into a profitable carrier with an enviable reputation for customer service.

In 1996, as British Airways was at its peak in profitability and customer service, Marshall stepped down and a new CEO, Bob Ayling, was appointed. Ayling anticipated higher competitive pressures in the long term and thus wanted to streamline the airline cost structure immediately. The business logic seemed to make sense, but the way he went about it backfired. Ayling suddenly announced dramatic change through major cost cutting and staff reductions on the same day when the company announced record profits. Most employees were shocked because they had not been informed, and the announcement's timing and the magnitude of sacrifices demanded of them did little to win them over. Flight attendants went on strike. BA leadership fanned the fires of dissension by declaring the strike illegal and using intimidation tactics. In subsequent years, systematic efforts to boost low morale and declining customer service were treated with cynicism by employees. Eventually, Ayling resigned, as BA once again became an unprofitable airline with dismal customer service.

Clearly, corporate revolutions are not uniformly effective, and many times something else is called for.

CORPORATE REFORM

Reform—by which we mean "re-forming" a social system in an orderly way—used to be favored in politics and in business. The carefully developed Marshall Plan, the subsequent growth of the European Community (now the European Union), and the successful redevelopment of postwar Japan are outstanding examples of change driven largely by systematic efforts. These are cases where the cumulative effects of the initiatives amounted to changes as massive as those of many full-fledged revolutions.

Planned Reform. In practice, systematic change must be realized organically, not only around conference tables where plans are hatched, but also in operations, where real things happen. Even strategies are not created in a formal planning process; so-called "strategic planning" is, in fact, usually strategic programming (n4), which takes place throughout an organization in the minds and actions of creative individuals. This is the essence of planned reform. However, like a revolution that never advances beyond its drama, reform that becomes mired in procedures is equally useless. In one study of an airline, we found that an obsession with planning impeded strategic thinking. When operational planning takes precedence, everything can become too systematic.

Two variants of reform, though, are especially effective in stimulating organic change.

Educated Reform. Many organizations use systematic training and development programs to breed an atmosphere conducive to organic change, most notably General Electric Co.'s Work-Out process that had been launched to encourage frontline workers to improve workplace efficiency. Another interesting example described by Richard Pascale (n5) and his coauthors is that undertaken by the United States Army. Over a grueling 14-day period, an organizational unit of 3,000 to 4,000 people goes head to head with a competitor of like size in a highly realistic simulation, including desert tank battles and aircraft support. Six hundred instructors are involved, one for each person with managerial responsibility; they shadow their trainees through the 18-hour days. The debriefing event (or "After Action Review, where hardship and insight meet") can be harassing, with officers often cowering under the intense scrutiny. But according to the commander of the exercise, it "has changed the Army dramatically. . . . It has instilled a discipline of relentlessly questioning everything we do."

Energized Reform. Here the emphasis of the reform is to drive organic change directly. General Electric's Six-Sigma efforts come to mind, as does *kaizen* (total quality management), used so successfully by Japanese companies like Toyota Motor Co.

While initially showing shades of revolution and later rejuvenation, Louis Gerstner's changes at IBM Corp. might be best described as energized reform—steady and consistent. No great new vision or revolution emerged. The company simply returned to listening to customers and managing relationships, focusing once again on key business results, devolving more authority and accountability from staff groups to line managers and carefully reengineering work processes to reduce long-term costs.

CORPORATE REJUVENATION

Often, significant corporate change comes about largely, although not exclusively, as the result of organic efforts embedded deep within an organization. This corporate rejuvenation can come about in a variety of ways.

Inadvertent Rejuvenation. Organizations often learn by trying new things, by engaging in all kinds of messy little experiments. The best learners are those closest to the operations and the customers. Indeed, this is probably how most of the really interesting changes in business and even society happen. Sometimes a single, seemingly peripheral or even inadvertent initiative remakes an organization. This is not revolution, although the consequences may be revolutionary.

One of our favorite examples of this sort of inadvertent rejuvenation cum revolution is Pilkington PLC, a glass manufacturer based in St. Helens, England. Years ago, one of its engineers was doing the dishes at home, so the story goes, when he got an idea for a new way to make glass, by floating it on a bath of liquid tin. After seven years of experimentation (supported by the board) and 100,000 tons of wasted glass, he had yet to prove he could make soluble glass. As each problem was solved, a new one took its place. The engineer remained optimistic and persistent, the board remained remarkably patient, and both were rewarded with eventual success. Patents were granted, and the company licensed the process worldwide. A grass-roots, production-process redesign had transformed into a successful strategy, revolutionizing the company and its industry.

Imperative Rejuvenation. In one of our most intensive studies of change, a large telecommunications company under fierce global competition was losing market share and money rapidly. Seeking new ways to address customer needs and reduce costs, new leadership brought a wave of dramatic changes: a new executive team, a 25% downsizing, a wide array of consultants, and all manner of big-change projects, including three restructurings in three years. (One of us closely studied 117 of these projects.) Only about one in five of the large change initiatives launched by their senior managers met with demonstrable success. At the same time, a host of smaller initiatives launched by middle management fared much better, with about four out of five producing good results. Whereas the dramatic revolutionary actions largely failed, the more organic initiatives sustained and revitalized the company well after the new leadership was gone (n6).

Steady Rejuvenation. Companies such as HP or 3M have been able to sustain their innovative capacities over long periods of time by finding a workable combination of steady organic change supported by systematic change. As Shona Brown and Kathleen Eisenhardt put it, balancing tensions between the organic and the systematic tends to keep an organization "on the edge of order and chaos" and so helps to sustain its innovative capability (n7). Such organizations systematically invest in a wide variety of low-cost experiments to continuously probe new markets and technologies; they pace the rhythm of change to balance chaos and inertia by applying steady pressure on product-development cycles and market launches; and they maintain speed and flexibility by calibrating the size of their business units to avoid the chaos that is characteristic of too many small units and the inertia associated with most large bureaucracies. This kind of continuous innovation can be found not only in high-tech firms, but also in so-called staid academic institutions.

When, for example, one of us studied the realized strategies of McGill University between 1829 and 1980, he found neither evidence of anything faintly resembling a revolution in that century and a half nor any stage when many strategies were changing simultaneously. Although there was little deliberate overall strategic change—especially with regard to the essential missions of the university, namely, teaching and research—McGill was, in fact, changing all the time. Programs, courses, and research projects were under constant revision and updated by the faculty. Of course, the university administration systematically facilitated the organic changes through budget allocations, facilities construction, new procedures for hiring and tenure, and so on.

Although universities are unusual in many respects, they are akin to manufacturing corporations in an important way. While both organizations may tolerate occasional bursts of dramatic change, mostly they hum along, experiencing less pervasive streams of small changes (n8)—here and there, organic and systematic—pursuing a process that Eric Abrahamson has labeled "dynamic stability" (n9).

Driven Rejuvenation. Rather than foment revolution, a leader can induce change by personal example or by recalibrating an organization's culture to encourage its people to undertake organic initiatives. Perhaps the classic example of this is Mahatma Gandhi, the ultimate organic leader. Gandhi lived and functioned far from the centers of conventional power; he never sought election and never led by edict, but through example he inspired the Indian people to rise up and take control of their destiny. He did not drive dramatic change so much as foment popular rejuvenation.

Certainly few, if any, stories from business come close to matching that degree of poignancy, but there are many business leaders who do energize people with the palpable force of their authentic acts. Take Tsutomu Murai, who in 1982 became the new CEO of the then lackluster and beleaguered Japanese beer producer Asahi Breweries, Ltd. Murai spurred the development of the innovative Asahi Super Dry product that revolutionized Japanese drinking taste and Asahi's fortunes by gently pushing a basic theme: He simply got the production and marketing people to talk to each other. Or consider Christian Blanc, the CEO whose first step toward revitalizing the Air France Group was to disclose that his compensation was 255th within the company—after which he took an additional 15% cut. Similarly, Roger Sant and Dennis Bakke of AES Corp., a global electricity company based in Arlington, Virginia, continually encourage frontline workers to expand their expertise and autonomy—not just by providing them with training, but also with the kind of sensitive strategic and financial information usually reserved only for senior managers. Such basic acts of conviction and faith can inspire rejuvenations tantamount to organic revolutions (n10).

Dramatic change makes for grand stories in the popular press, first about its promises and later about its often dramatic collapses. Unlike the phoenix of mythology, which could rise from its own ashes but once every 500 years, companies cannot continue to rely solely upon the mythical promise of dramatic reemergence. This is not to argue that companies should abandon dramatic initiatives, but rather that lasting, effective change arises from the natural, rhythmic combination of organic and systematic change with the well-placed syncopation of dramatic transformation. The world continues to move ahead in small steps, punctuated by the occasional big one—just as it always has. It is now time to manage change with an appreciation for continuity.

REFERENCES

(n1.) H. Mintzberg, "Crafting Strategy," *Harvard Business Review* 65 (July–August 1987): 66–75.

(n2.) S.J. Mezias and M.A. Glynn, "The 3 Faces of Corporate Renewal: Institution, Revolution and Evolution," *Strategic Management Journal* 14 (February 1993): 77–101. Evolution is similar to our rejuvenation, except that it is described as working within the rules; revolution disregards or breaks the rules and so is closer to what we call organic change; and institution is akin to our reform.

(n3.) S.D. Alinsky, *Rules for Radicals: A Practical Primer for Realistic Radicals* (New York: Vintage Books, 1989), xxii.

(n4.) H. Mintzberg, *The Rise and Fall of Strategic Planning* (New York: Free Press, 1994).

(n5.) R. Pascale, M. Millemann and L. Gioja, "Changing the Way We Change," *Harvard Business Review* 75 (November–December 1997): 126–139.

(n6.) Q.N. Huy, "Emotional Balancing of Organizational Continuity and Radical Change: The Contribution of Middle Managers," *Administrative Science Quarterly* 47 (March 2002): 31–69.

(n7.) S.L. Brown and K.M. Eisenhardt, *Competing on the Edge: Strategy as Structured Chaos* (Boston: Harvard Business School Press, 1998).

(n8.) D. Miller *Organizations: A Quantum View* (Englewood Cliffs, New Jersey: Prentice-Hall, 1984).

(n9.) E. Abrahamson, "Change without Pain," *Harvard Business Review* 78 (July–August 2000): 75–79.

(n10.) Q.N. Huy, "Time, Temporal Capability and Change," *Academy of Management Review* 26 (October 2001): 601–623.

CHAPTER 7

Cognition

The first section of this book has taken us through strategy in its various aspects. Now we turn to the *forces* that drive the strategy process, including human cognition, organization, technology, collaboration, globalization, and values.

We begin here with cognition, to get inside the head of the strategists. No one has ever seen a strategy or touched one. Strategies don't exist in any concrete form; they are nothing more than concepts in people's heads. So cognition—namely, how people think about, conceive, and perceive strategy—has to figure importantly in any book about the strategy process.

We include three readings here. The first draws on the cognitive school chapter of the Mintzberg, Ahlstrand, and Lampel *Strategy Safari* book to review various views of "Strategy as Cognition": for example, the limitations of cognition and the mistakes people make when faced with strategic complexity; cognition as the processing of information; cognition as "mapping" through the use of mental models; and the currently popular view of cognition as "construction"—that we don't *see* our world of strategy out there so much as *create* it inside our brains.

The human brain today is very much the same brain that our ancestors used so effectively in the African savannah. But is this brain sufficient to deal with today's realities? The second reading by Thomas H. Davenport, Professor in Information Technology and Management at Babson College, and John C. Beck, Professor and Director at Hult International Business School, answers this question in the negative. They argue that managers confront a mismatch between the exponential increase in the information they are exposed to, and their brains' attention capacity. What managers face, argue these authors, is nothing less than an "attention crisis." Tackling this attention crisis requires managers to think differently about their strategy and organizational structure. Both strategy and organizational structure must be oriented toward managing attention resources. This means looking not only at the way that strategy and organization capture and direct attention, but also at the adverse impact that popular strategies such as mergers and acquisitions have on the effective allocation of attention resources.

If you think that managing attention resources is sufficient to solve the problem of information overload then you may be mistaken. David Hurst, formerly a business executive and now a management writer and consultant in Toronto, argues that one of the seductive ideas of management past and present is managerial objectivity: ". . . the power to stand outside of a situation, to map it onto a logical framework and initiate the action it suggests." This aspiration is not only futile; it is downright dangerous, particularly when organizations embark on change. Change is risky, so it is not surprising that managers often believe that change processes that are rational and objective are less risky. Hurst suggests that contrary to this belief successful change processes may actually be harmed by too much rationality. As he puts it: "When it comes to real change, too much objectivity may be fatal to the process."

The final reading by Mintzberg suggests objectivity can be fatal to change because change, like strategy more generally, is about the future. To impose objectivity on the future is to accept that in some way an "object" already exists. But, of course, the future is inchoate—in other words, it is rudimentary, and imperfectly formed. Thinking strategically must take this into account. The final reading by Henry Mintzberg, "Strategic thinking as 'seeing,' provides guidelines on how managers can look into the future without becoming trapped by the illusion that in some way they are actually seeing the future as they move towards it (or alternately as it comes towards them)."

USING THE CASE STUDIES

Mintzberg, Ahlstrand, and Lampel suggest in "Strategy as Cognition" that the way that you process information can have an important bearing on the strategy that eventually develops. The Procter & Gamble case illustrates most vividly the dangers of self-inflicted information overload in a rapidly changing environment that Davenport and Beck analyze. Durk I. Jaeger introduces a raft of new products without getting rid of old ones. Doing this, while at the same time attempting culture change, was contentious and confusing. As Davenport and Beck predict, employees shift their attention to political infighting when they should be trying to make sense of the new product lines. The Airbus versus Boeing case affirms Hurst's main contention: That what seems objective to managers is often not the case. Boeing was convinced that there was insufficient demand to accommodate two suppliers of very large commercial aircraft, the so-called "superjumbo." Boeing presented a lot of "objective" data to argue its case. For Airbus, the strategic logic of the aircraft trumped the financial and market data on which Boeing based its calculation. The European aircraft manufacturer followed Mintzberg's guidelines: It looked at the market from a variety of perspectives without getting bogged down in data which extrapolated today's conditions into the future. Has Airbus made the right decision? It is too early to say. It usually takes decades before aircraft projects of this magnitude begin to pay off. What is certain is that the superjumbo project would not have taken off the ground without the vision of Airbus' top management. Mintzberg's article suggests that this vision can benefit from graphic representation. The Haier case describes the use of such graphic by top management, though in the Haier case the representation owes more to incline plane physics than to optics.

READING 7.1

Strategy as Cognition* BY HENRY MINTZBERG, BRUCE AHLSTRAND, AND JOSEPH LAMPEL

I'll see it when I believe it.

Anonymous

If we are really serious about understanding strategic vision as well as how strategies form under other circumstances, then we had better probe into the mind of the strategist . . . to get at what this process means in the sphere of human cognition, drawing especially on the field of cognitive psychology.

. . . [S]trategists are largely self-taught: they develop their knowledge structures and thinking processes mainly through direct experience. That experience shapes what they know, which in turn shapes what they do, thereby shaping their subsequent experience. This duality plays a central role in [cognition], giving rise to two rather different wings.

One wing, more positivistic, treats the processing and structuring of knowledge as an effort to produce some kind of *objective* motion picture of the world. The mind's eye is thus seen as a kind of camera: it scans the world, zooming in and out in response to its owner's will, although the pictures it takes are considered in this school to be rather distorted.

*Adapted from *Strategy Safari*, The Free Press (Mintzberg, H., Ahlstrand, B. and Lampel, J. 1998) pp.155–184, with the permission of The Free Press, a Division of Simon & Schuster, Inc., and Pearson Education Ltd., copyright © 1998 by H. Mintzberg, B. Ahlstrand and J. Lampel, all rights reserved, and Pearson Education Ltd.

The other wing sees all of this as *subjective*: strategy is some kind of *interpretation* of the world. Here the mind's eye turns inward, on how the mind does its "take" on what it sees out there—the events, the symbols, the behavior of customers, and so on. So while the other wing seeks to understand cognition as some kind of *re-creation* of the world, this wing drops the prefix and instead believes that cognition *creates* the world. . . .

COGNITION AS CONFUSION

Scholars have long been fascinated by the peculiarities of how individuals process information to make decisions, especially the biases and distortions that they exhibit. Management researchers have been especially stimulated by the brilliant work of Herbert Simon (1947, 1957; see also March and Simon, 1958) . . . [who] popularized the notion that the world is large and complex, while human brains and their information-processing capacities are highly limited in comparison. Decision making thus becomes not so much rational as a vain effort to be rational.

A large research literature on judgmental biases followed . . . some of the results of which [are] reproduced in the table below. All have obvious consequences for strategy making. These include the search for evidence that supports rather than denies beliefs, the favoring of more easily remembered recent information over earlier information, the tendency to see a causal effect between two variables that may simply be correlated, the power of wishful thinking, and so on.

BIASES IN DECISION MAKING

TYPE OF BIAS	DESCRIPTION OF BIAS
Search for supportive evidence	Willingness to gather facts which lead toward certain conclusions and to disregard other facts which threaten them
Inconsistency	Inability to apply the same decision criteria in similar situations
Conservatism	Failure to change (or changing slowly) one's own mind in light of new information/evidence
Recency	The most recent events dominate those in the less recent past, which are downgraded or ignored
Availability	Reliance upon specific events easily recalled from memory, to the exclusion of other pertinent information
Anchoring	Predictions are unduly influenced by initial information which is given more weight in the forecasting process
Illusory correlations	Belief that patterns are evident and/or two variables are causally related when they are not
Selective perception	People tend to see problems in terms of their own background and experience
Regression effects	Persistent increases [in some phenomenon] might be due to random reasons which, if true, would [raise] the chance of a [subsequent] decrease. Alternatively, persistent decreases might [raise] the chances of [subsequent] increases
Attribution of success and failure	Success is attributed to one's skills while failure to bad luck, or someone else's error. This inhibits learning as it does not allow recognition of one's mistakes
Optimism, wishful thinking	People's preferences for future outcomes affect their forecasts of such outcomes
Underestimating uncertainty	Excessive optimism, illusory correlation, and the need to reduce anxiety result in underestimating future uncertainty

Source: Adapted from *Forecasting, Planning and Strategy for the 21st Century,* Free Press (Makridakis, S. 1990) pp.36–37, with the permission of The Free Press, a Division of Simon & Schuster, Inc.

COGNITION AS INFORMATION PROCESSING

Beyond the biases in individual cognition are the effects of working in the collective system for processing information that is called an organization. Managers are information workers. They serve their own needs for information as well as that of their colleagues and of the managers who supervise them. In large organizations especially, this creates all sorts of well-known problems. Senior managers have limited time to oversee vast arrays of activities. Hence much of the information they receive has to be aggregated, which can pile distortions upon distortions. If the original inputs have been subjected to all the biases discussed above, then think about what happens when all of this gets combined and presented to the "boss." No wonder so many senior managers become the captives of their information-processing organizations.

COGNITION AS MAPPING

... [O]n one point there is widespread agreement: an essential prerequisite for strategic cognition is the existence of mental structures to organize knowledge. These are the "frames" referred to above, although a host of other labels have been used over the years, including schema, concept, script, plan, mental model, and map.

Map is a currently popular label, perhaps because of its metaphoric value. It implies the navigation through confusing terrain with some kind of representative model. . . .

All experienced managers carry around in their heads all kinds of . . . *causal maps,* or *mental models* as they are sometimes called. And their impact on behavior can be profound. For example, Barr, Stimpert, and Huff (1992) compared two railroads, Rock Island and C&NW, over a twenty-five-year period (1949–1973). They were similar to begin with, but one eventually went bankrupt while the other survived. The researchers attributed this to their managers' causal maps about the environment. Initially, both firms ascribed poor performance to bad weather, government programs, and regulations. Then one firm's maps shifted to a focus on the relationships between costs, productivity, and management style, and that provoked the necessary changes.

COGNITION AS CONCEPT ATTAINMENT

Managers are, of course, map makers as well as map users. How they create their cognitive maps is key to our understanding of strategy formation. Indeed, in the most fundamental sense, this *is* strategy formation. A strategy is a *concept,* and so, to draw on an old term from cognitive psychology, strategy making is "concept attainment."

["Insight" and "intuition" may be key here.] With reference to the Japanese executive, Shimizu (1980) has referred to insight as "intuitive sensibility," and "ability to grasp instantly an understanding of the whole structure of new information." He mentioned the "sixth sense or *kan*" which, in contrast to the "sequential steps of logical thinking," entails the "fitting together of memory fragments that had until then been mere accumulation of various connected information" (23). *In*-sight, seeing inside, seems to come to the decision maker when he or she can see beyond given facts to understand the deeper meaning of an issue. "If the soldier's lot is months of boredom interrupted by moments of terror, to cite an old adage, then the lot of organizations may likewise be described as years of routine reconfigured by flashes of insight. . . . " (Langley et al., 1995: 268). . . . We need to understand, therefore, how it is that strategists are sometimes able to synthesize vast arrays of soft information into new perspectives. Perhaps this will require less study of words and other "recognizable chunks" and more recognition of images. . . . The work of Roger Sperry (1974), who won a Nobel Prize in physiology for his work on split brain research, at least suggests the existence of two very different sets of processes operating within the human brain. One, accessible to verbalization, is usually associated with the left hemisphere, while the other, more spatial, is apparently often found in the mute right hemisphere. Have we, therefore, focused too much of our research and technique of strategic management on the wrong side of the human brain? . . .

COGNITION AS CONSTRUCTION

There is another side to the cognitive school (at least as we interpret it), very different and potentially, perhaps, more fruitful. . . . This views strategy as interpretation, based on cognition as construction.

To proponents of this view, the world "out there" does not simply drive behavior "in here," even if through the filters of distortion, bias, and simplification. There is more to cognition than some kind of effort to mirror reality—to be out there with the best map of the market. . . . These people ask: What about those strategies that change the world? Where do they come from?

For the *interpretative* or *constructionist* view, what is inside the human mind is not a reproduction of the external world. All that information flowing in through those filters, supposedly to be decoded by those cognitive maps, in fact interacts with cognition and is shaped by it. The mind, in other words, imposes some interpretation on the environment—it constructs its world. In a sense, the mind has a mind of its own—it marches to its own cognitive dynamics. Or perhaps we might better say *they* march, because there is a collective dimension to this too: people interact to create their mental worlds. . . .

One obvious conclusion is that . . . managers need a rich repertoire of frames—alternate views of their world, so as not to be imprisoned by any one. Hence the success of books such as Gareth Morgan's *Images of Organizations* (1986), which offers chapters on seeing organizations as machines, as organisms, as brains, and so on. Bolman and Deal's *Reframing Organizations* (1997) suggests that managerial insight hinges on a willingness to use multiple lenses or vantage points, which they too present. . . .

The problem, of course, is that the practice of management requires focus, sometimes . . . even obsession. "On the one hand, on the other hand" is hardly the best route to decisive action. However, opening up perspectives is also critical for effective management.

IS THE "ENVIRONMENT" CONSTRUCTED?

The social constructionist view begins with a strong premise: no one in an organization "sees" the environment. Instead, organizations construct it from rich and ambiguous information in which even such basic categories as "inside" and "outside" can be very fuzzy. While this premise is strongly supported by evidence, what the social constructionists do with it is more controversial. They argue that since environments are constructed within the organization, they are little more than the product of managerial beliefs. Harking back to the Andrews reading, we now find that the big box on the SWOT chart—the one that deals with environment and of which Michael Porter has made so much—suddenly gets relegated to a minor role. . . . And in its place appears that most obscure box on the chart—the beliefs of the managers.

Many people balk at this conclusion. Surely, they say, there is an environment out there. Markets are, after all, littered with the debris of companies that got them wrong, regardless (or some would say because) of what their managers believed. To which social constructionists reply: this objection itself represents a simplistic assumption about the meaning of "environment." Is it "objective," "perceived," or "enacted?" (Smircich and Stubbart, 1985).

Under this constructionist perspective, strategy formation takes on a whole new color. Metaphors become important, as do symbolic actions and communications . . . all based on the manager's total life experience. . . . And vision emerges as more than an instrument for guidance: it becomes the leader's interpretation of the world made into a collective reality. . . .

READING 7.2

The Strategy and Structure of Firms in the Attention Economy BY THOMAS H. DAVENPORT AND JOHN C. BECK

> *What information consumes is rather obvious: It consumes the attention of its recipients. Hence a wealth of information creates a poverty of attention.*
>
> ***Herbert Simon, economist and Nobel Prize recipient***

One of the striking realities of our time is that we have catapulted forward from an era of information overload to one of information assault. Today, the best and the brightest of CEOs

Reading 7.2 is adapted from The strategy and structure of firms in the attention economy, *Ivey Business Journal*, Mar–Apr (Davenport, TH. and Beck, JC. 2002).

are being challenged to absorb and manage the torrent of information—and the requests for information—that comes their way every day. That challenge underlines one of the most pressing problems for leaders: They simply do not have enough attention to give and to go around, to meet the unrelenting demands of and for information. Yes, we are living in the New Economy. At the same time, however, we are also living in the Attention Economy.

Today, there is no shortage of capital, labor, knowledge and, of course, information. There is, however, at least one glaring scarcity, human attention. There is a shortage not of telecommunications bandwidth, but rather of human bandwidth. Businesses today have an attention deficit, and the implications for business—especially for issues of strategy and structure—can be surprising. Our research has convinced us that, in today's economy, attention is the scarce resource. Consequently, corporate leaders need to help the people in their organizations manage attention. The starting points, we suggest, are strategy and structure.

THE ATTENTION CRISIS

There is an attention deficit, partly, but only partly, because the price of information has been growing less expensive for many, many years. By one analysis, there are more facts in a single edition of the *Sunday New York Times* than anyone in the world could have commanded in, say, the fifteenth century. In 1472, for example, the best university library in the world, at Queens' College in Cambridge, had 199 books. Today, more than 300,000 new books spew forth from worldwide presses every year. The Web includes at least two billion pages, a large chunk of which can't be found even with the best search engine. (And let's not forget that there are 11,339 distinct electronic databases, up from just 301 in 1975.)

It's not just library-type information that overwhelms us. The typical viewer today can choose from 80 percent more new feature films than were released in 1990. The average grocery store stocks about 40,000 different items or SKUs; roughly 15,000 new grocery products are introduced each year. Think of this business problem: In this environment, how can your new product become one of the only 150 SKUs the average household buys each year? The problem is not only one of reaching consumers; it is a problem that affects the B2B market and internal management as well. Today's manager can, with just a few mouse clicks, call up more information than any of us can ever fully absorb—all the while dealing with an increasing number of phone calls, faxes, and mail.

MORE THAN INFORMATION OVERLOAD

It is important to understand that the growing importance of attention management is far more than a response to information overload. An equally important challenge is the increasing speed and complexity of our business lives. Decades of global competition have produced lean organizations, very high customer expectations, short cycle times, and a need for just-in-time everything. These challenges can be described in an information context, but they really go much further afield.

We all know about the attention deficit problem at some level; we live with it every day. And reflecting on our own experience may be the best indication of how serious this problem is for any business. Think of your own behavior, and that of your colleagues. Do you know anyone who isn't becoming used to having his or her attention skip from topic to topic like a fairy sprite? Who doesn't have the nagging sense that there are far more people, tasks, topics, inputs and decisions than anyone could manage? In this environment, attention management becomes a question of survival. What if attention is focused on the wrong topics, or just wanders about randomly? Can we focus organizational attention at all? Can we stretch the organizational attention span when we need to? And if we can, then how can we?

There are answers, and they are ones your firm can live with. Having conducted substantial research on the Attention Economy, we have concluded that attention can be managed. Indeed, it must be. In this economy, every business faces two basic problems: How can it get and hold attention (consumers, stockholders, potential employees, etc.), and how should it allocate its own attention (in the face of overwhelming options)? Companies who fail in these tasks will fail—period. But those who succeed will find that winning the battle for attention pays handsome rewards.

Winning that battle begins with understanding the attributes of the Attention Economy. This will allow you to manipulate this era's zero-sum resource more effectively both outside and inside the firm. In this article, we want to focus on just two topics: strategy and structure. These topics are the right starting place not only because they are so important, but because strategy and structure are, in essence, vehicles for focusing organizational attention.

ATTENTION AND STRATEGY: IS THERE A DIFFERENCE?

For virtually any firm you can name, making the right key decisions is, more than ever, a matter of attention management. Perhaps the main reason is that attention is the bridge between awareness and action. If an issue doesn't receive attention, it won't be resolved; attention, we know, is always the precursor of action. So attention is a vital resource indeed. That alone makes it a key in developing effective strategy. Likewise with structure; an organization chart is, among other things, a map of who controls the firm's resources.

Strategy and structure are fundamentally about attention. After all, in the world of everyday decision making, what are strategy and structure? We answer from the behavioral perspective (exemplified by the management scholars Henry Mintzberg, James Brian Quinn, and Richard Pascale). Both strategy and structure are mental constructs, important not in themselves, but for their impact on the people in the organization. There is no absolute reality of a firm's strategy or its structure, or at least not one that we can all agree on. Rather, strategies and structures are tools to help us think. They matter only to the extent that they help executives, managers, and employees work effectively. In other words, they are vehicles for focusing attention.

Consider the example of Jack Welch at General Electric. When he announced that all GE business units had to be first or second in market share by 1990, or no longer be part of GE, he was first and foremost focusing attention. After all, businesses below that level are often profitable. There might even have been a GE-owned business where it made sense to remain number three. But, in general, huge revenues and fat profit margins go to market leaders. Welch's vision of GE as a stable of champions not only conveyed that message in a memorable way, it also focused the mind wonderfully. Its very lack of attention to the exceptional case told people that this was a serious commitment.

ATTENDING TO STRUCTURE

We've seen that business strategy is largely about focusing managers' and employees' attention on some things rather than others. But strategy is a soft discipline. What about something hard, like organizational structure? After all, M&A decisions are ultimately about the numbers, right? And internal organization is about what it takes to get the job done. What does attention have to do with all that?

Actually, quite a bit. Organizational structure is the plan for, and the reality of, how power and responsibility are distributed across an organization. We humans are social animals. So, inside our groups, we focus on hierarchy; outside, we focus on the identifiable groups or individuals who represent opportunity or threat. Thus, organizational structure is a powerful vehicle for focusing employees' and external stakeholders' attention on a particular aspect of the business. It sends a message that some issues are more important than others. To create a focus on customers, we can organize around types of customers. To show employees, customers, and external observers that quality is important, we can create a department for it and put a heavy hitter in charge. Structure is not the only means for focusing attention on a goal, but it often pulls other means along with it, including performance evaluation and compensation systems, organizational communications, and informal social networks. For individuals, the weight of an organizational title and a position in the organization chart are powerful forces that channel attention toward a formally structured objective.

Consider one specific structural challenge, process management. The traditional organizational chart creates an attention problem: The organization is focused on lines of business or functional distinctions, not on the activities by which work gets done. Not surprisingly, it is widely believed that focusing on these processes is always good—and critical when a company is trying to improve efficiency, reduce cycle time, and improve customer service. So some attention must be shifted from managers and employees. Some observers suggest that firms adopt process management as the primary or even only dimension of organizational structure. But many firms have found that this suggestion goes too far; that other, existing dimensions require attention. Typically, if other dimensions such as functional skills, geographical variations, and different markets for products and services no longer receive attention, performance will begin to suffer.

One example, of both a problem and a solution, is the Chrysler division of DaimlerChrysler. In the early 1990s, it shifted to cross-functional "platform teams" that managed the entire process of developing a new vehicle. Overall, these teams worked well, producing both successful new car designs and shorter development cycles. But the functional organization that had focused attention on producing and maintaining technical skills was no longer in place. Soon, technical experts found themselves working not with others of their ilk, but with manufacturers, marketers, and financial experts on cross-functional issues. The result? A recurrence of quality problems that Chrysler had previously solved. The company is now attempting to turn some of its attention to increasing functional and technical knowledge by organizing "Tech Clubs," so that engineers in specific domains of car development can meet with each other and exchange ideas. In general, matrix structures such as these create attention problems; our innate focus on hierarchy and threat/reward does not match well with situations where it is not clear which dimension is the primary one. But Chrysler's Tech Club approach, a kind of "stealth" matrix, avoids this problem by giving only informal legitimacy to a second dimension of structure. It is important to understand that the balancing act here is not about power, but rather about attention; Chrysler needs employees to stay focused on the process of developing new vehicles, but not forget about enhancing their technical skills. The Tech Club structure seems to get that balance just about right.

THE URGE TO MERGE

The lens of attention can be especially useful in deciding on, and managing, structural initiatives such as joint ventures and mergers and acquisitions. Again, the principle is simple: Scarce attention is paid to how your organization deals with both external and internal information. But the implications can seem contradictory. One of the best ways to get more attention in the market is to get bigger, so M&A activity makes sense. But the very process of deciding on, closing, and absorbing a merger or acquisition fragments internal attention. A recent energy-industry joint venture illustrates the point: The JV confronted employees with new management that had an unclear agenda, was uncertain about organizational structure (including function, business unit, and geography), and had literally 158 various business-improvement initiatives. Even with high oil prices, the company's financial performance was poor. Does that mean mergers are bad?

Not at all. It means that no matter how useful mergers are for focusing external attention, they are challenges for the internal attention market. But they can be managed. In this case, a new CEO was brought in from one of the parent companies. He reduced the number of improvement initiatives to three or four, concluded that process management was important but not something that the company was ready for, and postponed some e-commerce initiatives. "We don't have the attention to do all this stuff," he said.

Of course, another way of dealing with an internal attention shortage is the opposite of merging—spinning off or outsourcing. Spin-offs are much more rare than mergers, but they can have very positive bottom-line results; less to consider means more attention focused on the remaining elements . . . By essentially splitting a corporation into two or more autonomous entities, employee attention is enhanced, not hampered. Not only is their group mission clearer, but individuals in the spin-offs who had never been eligible for stock options before suddenly become eligible. They now are paying more voluntary attention to the stock price of the unit, which seems tied more directly to their own performance. Because a spun-off firm usually has a narrow strategic focus, its value is clearer to analysts and investors. The business model is usually easier to understand and attend to, hence the market values of both the original company and the spin-off may go up.

PROCESS MATTERS

Spin-offs and outsourcing can be great, but the urge to merge is strong for financial and psychological reasons, if nothing else. Attention analysis may sometimes suggest another path. In our experience, when acquisitions and mergers fail, attention is the issue more often than not. No matter what the external drivers are, the attention of both upper management and employees immediately shifts to internal issues once the merger is announced. In other words, in an attention-scarce environment, attention that was given to customers, suppliers, partners, and other stakeholders is suddenly allocated to answering questions such as "Will I be fired?" "Will my product line be cut?" and "Who will I report to?" And while your customers may not care deeply about these issues, everyone inside your firm does; they have to. So the longer these issues remain unresolved, the faster the merger's strategic value disappears.

PAY ATTENTION. IT PAYS

Our research reveals that attention is a valuable lens for viewing strategy and structure. But does attention alone determine success or failure? Of course not. However, attention is the right place to start, and a perspective worth monitoring consistently. Attention is the scarce resource of our time, and a resource that is innately tied to what the human beings in the organization actually do. Leaders who understand and manage it are a long stride ahead of their competitors.

READING 7.3

The Dangers of Objectivity* BY DAVID K. HURST

Enthusiasm for reengineering may be fading, but it will not be the last management formula offered to us. It is the objectivity that frameworks such as reengineering give their users that undermines the social dynamics leading to fundamental change. Indeed, the intellectual detachment of the designers and managers of change from the process itself should be identified as a leading cause of the failure of such change efforts. Perhaps the frameworks should come with a warning label: *When it comes to real change, too much objectivity may be fatal to the process.*

Managerial objectivity is the power to stand outside of a situation, to map it onto a logical framework and initiate the action it suggests. Usually these frameworks are abstracted from the experiences of other prominent organizations, and their plausibility depends upon the cause–effect relationships that they explain. These explanations usually take the form of likely stories

*Excerpted from an article originally published as "When it Comes to Real Change, too much Objectivity May Be Fatal to the Process," by David K. Hurst, *Strategy and Leadership,* March/April 1997, pp. 6–12.

about how successful companies became successful or how failing companies turned themselves around. . . . The assumption implicit in each story is that the logic is context-free. The implication is that "you, too" can use these techniques to achieve similar results. The assumption these likely stories share is that managers can behave rationally in the achievement of desirable organizational goals. That is, they can think before they take action, identify cause–effect relationships, start organizational processes, and monitor progress toward these goals.

This assumption is flawed. While nobody suggests that managers can never be instrumentally rational (as this form of rationality is known), the unasked question is whether they can or should be rational in this way *at all times, especially during periods of radical change.* There are two reasons why managers cannot and should not try to behave in this way at such times: the first is intellectual, the second is social.

The intellectual problem is that business realities do not exist independently of their observers. Economies, markets, organizations, and strategies are constructed rather than natural objects. Thus, objectivity is never absolute—it is always relative to some frame of reference developed from the past. Because real change means that the frames themselves have to be altered, a rigid objectivity freezes this process, preventing the examination of the assumptions that support the framework. Some explicit assumptions can be examined, but most assumptions are tacit—they are the answers to the questions we never asked. *They can be tested only from outside the framework of logic in use.* And that takes action—experience. We can't just rethink our way into a better way of thinking.

Take the trade-off between cost and quality for example. For years, everyone in North America who had ever taken Economics 101 knew that there was a negative relationship between the two—the more quality one put into a product, the more it would cost. The power of this model is probably the single most important reason why North American business academics were so comprehensively surprised by the quality revolution. It took the success of the lean Japanese automobile manufacturing system to show us that quality could be systemically improved without adding costs. In fact, costs might drop if the production system was changed. The assumptions of manufacturing economics made it impossible for us to conceive of an alternative to mass manufacturing—until we saw one. Thus, the systems logic that supports "lean-flow" principles was developed after the practical results had been confirmed. As a result, all the books on quality have been rewritten.

The second reason why an excess of objectivity is a hindrance to change is demonstrated by the senior executive . . . [who sees him- or herself] outside the change process, diagnosing the condition of those within it. The implication [is] that *they* [have to change. He or she does] not. For much of the time in every change initiative, the situation demands that *everyone* in the organization be seen and felt to share a common fate. Suggestions that the change process is entirely objective and rational introduce a fatal distance between managers and the managed. This distance is lethal to the change effort, for it leads to cynicism in the workers, arouses their suspicion that they are being manipulated, and increases their resistance—not to change itself, but to *being changed.* Instead of feeling empowered, workers feel exhausted and drained by the change process. A typical response: "Why should I change the system if it's going to cost me my job?" (O'Neill and Lenn, 1995).

SELF-SEALING BELIEFS

. . . Reengineering . . . developed [a] self-sealing quality to its rhetoric. Managers were warned to expect resistance, to anticipate where it would come from, and to motivate and involve people. Communication had to "anticipate what people will want to know at every stage," and so on. But this meant that senior managers had to know more about the direction of the change process than those within it. They were on the outside, manipulating those within. Anticipating this, the gurus even warned management to expect feelings of disaster midway through the change process and of the need to stay the course. The implication was that there was nothing wrong with the process or the assumptions that underpinned it; all one had to do was apply them properly. Without any feedback loops, many organizations set out upon a series of escalating commitments to a doomed course of action. Cyberneticists call this condition "systems runaway."

. . .[T]he essence of empowerment [is] that people genuinely feel that the future is up to them to invent, not someone else's plan that they have to implement. And they will get this feeling only if the senior managers behave in a way that expresses these open, egalitarian values. . . .

SENIOR MANAGERS AREN'T COOKS, THEY'RE INGREDIENTS

In the final analysis, when it comes to fundamental change in organizations, there can be no *final analysis*. For it is the very frameworks of analysis that need to be changed. In fundamental organizational change, *it takes behavior to change behavior: change cannot be managed, it can only be led*. Thus, managers of change are not just cooks preparing a meal by following a recipe, they are also key ingredients. Senior managers are powerful role models, and their key contribution to the process of change is to lead by modeling the new behaviors that they expect of their people. They can plan and orchestrate the arrangements only up to a point. Then they have to throw themselves into the mixture with everyone else and trust that their behavior will be copied by others. . . .

Our Western bias is to believe that we can think our way into a better way of *acting*. Experience with real change suggests that just the opposite is true—we have to *act* our way into a better way of *thinking*. As managers, the only behavior we can hope to change directly is our own.

READING 7.4

Strategic Thinking as "Seeing" BY HENRY MINTZBERG

If strategies are visions, then what role does seeing play in strategic thinking?

Three pairs of factors are presented below, together with a seventh that knits them together into a framework of strategic thinking.

Almost everyone would agree that strategic thinking means seeing ahead. But, you cannot see ahead unless you can see behind, because any good vision of the future has to be rooted in an understanding of the past.

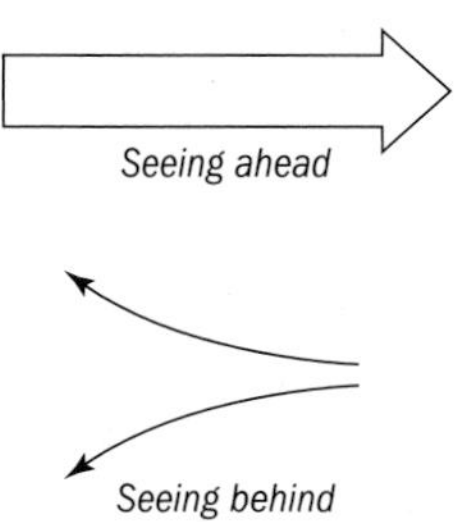

Many people also claim that strategic thinking is seeing above. It is as if strategists should take helicopters, to be able to see the "big picture," to distinguish "the forest from the trees." But can anyone really get the big picture just by seeing above? The forest looks like a rug from a helicopter. Anyone who has taken a walk in a forest knows that it doesn't look much like that on the ground. Forestry people who stay in helicopters don't understand much more than strategists who stay in offices.

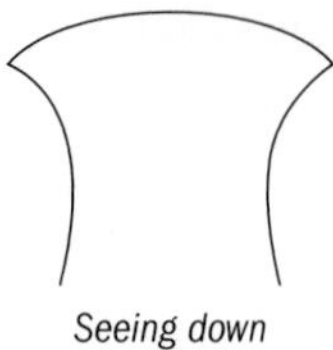

Seeing down

Finding the diamond in the rough might be a better metaphor. Strategic thinkers have to find the gem of an idea that changes their organization. And that comes from a lot of hard and messy digging. There is no big picture ready for the seeing; each strategist has to construct his or her own. Thus, strategic thinking is also inductive thinking: seeing above must be supported by *seeing below*.

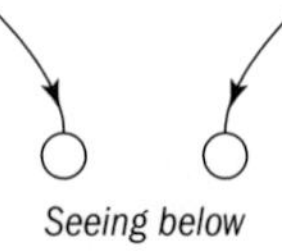

Seeing below

You can, however, see ahead by seeing behind and see above by seeing below and still not be a strategic thinker. That takes more—creativity for one thing.

Strategic thinkers see differently from other people; they pick out the precious gems that others miss. They challenge conventional wisdom—the industry recipe, the traditional strategy—and thereby distinguish their organizations. Since creative thinking has been referred to as lateral thinking, this could be called *seeing beside*.

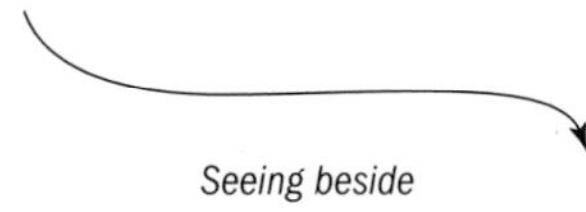

Seeing beside

But there are many creative ideas in this world, far more than it can handle—just visit any art gallery. And so, beside seeing beside, strategic thinkers have to *see beyond*. Creative ideas have to be placed into context, to be seen in a world that is to unfold. Seeing beyond is different from seeing ahead. Seeing ahead foresees an expected future by constructing a framework out of the events of the past—it intuitively forecasts discontinuities. Seeing beyond constructs the future—it invents a world that would not otherwise be.

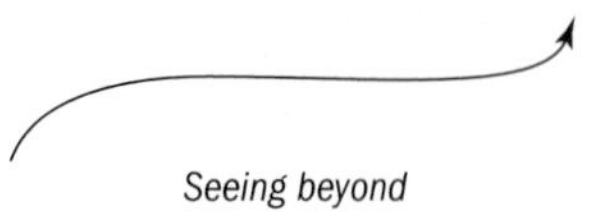

Seeing beyond

But there remains one last element. What is the use of doing all this seeing—ahead and behind, above and below, beside and beyond—if nothing gets done?

In other words, for a thinker to deserve the label *strategic,* he or she must also *see it through.*

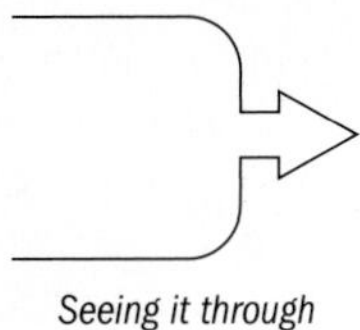

Seeing it through

Put this all together and you get *strategic thinking as seeing.*

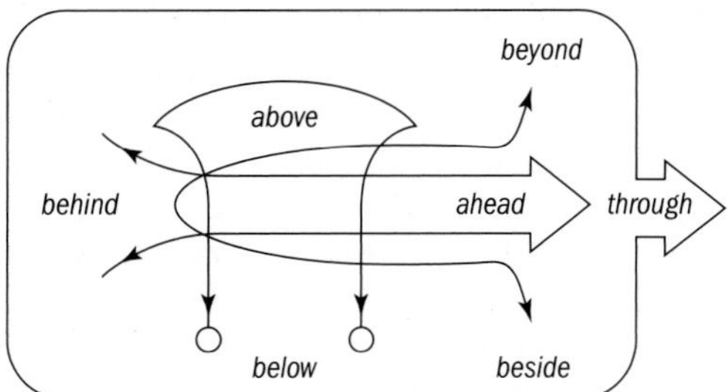

CHAPTER 8

Organization

Organization is a major force in society today: We are born in organizations called hospitals and buried by organizations called funeral homes; most everything that happens in between involves formal organizations in one way or another. So we had better understand them by appreciating the strategy process.

Organizational structure, in our view, no more follows strategy than the left foot follows the right in walking. The two exist interdependently, each influencing the other. There are certainly times when a structure is redesigned to carry out a new strategy. But the choice of any new strategy is likewise influenced by the realities and potentials of the existing structure. Indeed, the classical model of strategy formulation (discussed in Chapter 3) implicitly recognizes this by showing the strengths and weaknesses of the organization as an input to the creation of strategies. Surely, these strengths and weaknesses are deeply rooted within the existing structure, indeed often part and parcel of it. Hence, we introduce here organization and the associated structures that make it work as essential factors to consider in the strategy process. Later we present the various contexts within which strategy and structure interact.

We begin with a reading, excerpted originally from Mintzberg's book *The Structuring of Organizations,* that probes comprehensively the design of organizations. It seeks to do two things: first to delineate the basic dimensions of organizations, and then to combine these to identify various basic types of organizations, called "configurations." The dimensions introduced include mechanisms used to coordinate work in organizations, parameters to consider in designing structures, and situational factors that influence choices among these design parameters. This reading also introduces a somewhat novel diagram to depict organizations—not as the usual organizational chart or cybernetic flow process but as a visual combination of the key parts of an organization. This reading then clusters all these dimensions into a set of configurations, each introduced briefly here and discussed at length in the later chapters on context. In fact, the choice of the chapters on context was really based on these types, so this reading will introduce you to Section III.

In his article "Strategy and Organization Planning," Jay Galbraith, who worked as an independent management consultant for several years and now teaches at the University of Southern California, also views structure broadly, as encompassing support systems of various kinds. Building on concepts such as "driving force" and "center of gravity," Galbraith links various strategies (of vertical integration and diversification) to forms of structure, ranging from the functional to the increasingly diversified. Galbraith covers a wide body of important literature and uses visual imagery to make his points. The result is one of the best articles in print on the relationship between the strategy of diversification and the structure of divisionalization.

In "The Design of New Organizational Forms," authors Herber from Goldman Sachs and Singh and Useem from the Wharton School faculty describe a number of interesting new forms of organization to deal with changing environments. These include the virtual organization, network organization (external and internal), spin-out organization, ambidextrous organization, front-back organization, and sense-and-respond organization.

USING THE CASE STUDIES

The relationship between strategy and organization is explored in many of the cases. In several, however, the organization or, more specifically, organizational structure plays a central role in the strategy process. Robin Hood allocates responsibility for different areas to his key lieutenant, thereby transforming the Merrymen from a loose band into a functional organization. Nissan's difficulties can be traced back to functional structure that laid the groundwork to its success, but ultimately proved to be dysfunctional when the company had to undertake radical change. "The Structuring of Organizations" by Mintzberg provides a general framework for analyzing the relationship between strategy and organization in this case. "Strategy and Organization Planning" by Galbraith focuses on organizational structure in diversified corporations. Structure is central to strategy in both Johnson and Johnson and Procter and Gamble. It also throws light on why Cadbury Schweppes, a highly diversified company geographically that is structured into two product lines—confectionary and soft drinks—can contemplate splitting the company in two without disrupting operations.

The last 20 years have been a period of extraordinary organizational experimentation and innovation. Herber, Singh, and Useem examine many of the new organizational forms that have emerged. Their analysis relates to several cases of companies involved in organizational experimentation. Apple is one of Silicon Valley's iconic companies not only because of its products, but also because it has experimented with different ways of organizing. The same can be said of Pixar, which was also set up by Steve Jobs. Less well known outside Brazil but no less innovative is Natura's experimentation with the so-called "5-company" structure. This structure was instrumental in propelling growth at Natura, but was eventually abandoned when it became a disabling constraint. Managers must accept that organizational experiments, like other kind of experiments, do not always succeed.

READING 8.1

The Structuring of Organizations* BY HENRY MINTZBERG

The "one best way" approach has dominated our thinking about organizational structure since the turn of the century. There is a right way and a wrong way to design an organization. A variety of failures, however, has made it clear that organizations differ, that, for example, long-range planning systems or organizational development programs are good for some but not others. And so recent management theory has moved away from the "one best way" approach toward an "it all depends" approach, formally known as "contingency theory." Structure should reflect the organization's situation—for example, its age, size, type of production system, the extent to which its environment is complex and dynamic.

This reading argues that the "it all depends" approach does not go far enough, that structures are rightfully designed on the basis of a third approach, which might be called the "getting it all together" or "configuration" approach. Spans of control, types of formalization and decentralization, planning systems, and matrix structures should not be picked and chosen independently, the way a shopper picks vegetables at the market. Rather, these and other elements of organizational design should logically configure into internally consistent groupings.

---

*Excerpted originally from *The Structuring of Organizations* (Prentice Hall, 1979), with added sections from *Power in and Around Organizations* (Prentice Hall, 1983). This chapter was rewritten for this edition of the text, based on two other excerpts: "A Typology of Organizational Structure," published as Chapter 3 in Danny Miller and Peter Friesen, *Organizations: A Quantum View* (Prentice Hall, 1984) and "Deriving Configurations," Chapter 6 in *Mintzberg on Management: Inside Our Strange World of Organizations* (Free Press, 1989).

When the enormous amount of research that has been done on organizational structure is looked at in the light of this conclusion, much of its confusion falls away, and a convergence is evident around several configurations, which are distinct in their structural designs, in the situations in which they are found, and even in the periods of history in which they first developed.

To understand these configurations, we must first understand each of the elements that make them up. Accordingly, the first four sections of this reading discuss the basic parts of organizations, the mechanisms by which organizations coordinate their activities, the parameters they use to design their structures, and their contingency, or situational, factors. The final section introduces the structural configurations, each of which will be discussed at length in Section III of this text.

SIX BASIC PARTS OF THE ORGANIZATION

At the base of any organization can be found its operators, those people who perform the basic work of producing the products and rendering the services. They form the *operating core.* All but the simplest organizations also require at least one full-time manager who occupies what we shall call the *strategic apex,* where the whole system is overseen. And as the organization grows, more managers are needed—not only managers of operators but also managers of managers. A *middle line* is created, a hierarchy of authority between the operating core and the strategic apex.

As the organization becomes still more complex, it generally requires another group of people, whom we shall call the analysts. They, too, perform administrative duties—to plan and control formally the work of others—but of a different nature, often labeled "staff." These analysts form what we shall call the *technostructure,* outside the hierarchy of line authority. Most organizations also add staff units of a different kind, to provide various internal services, from a cafeteria or mailroom to a legal counsel or public relations office. We shall call these units and the part of the organization they form the *support staff.*

Finally, every active organization has a sixth part, which we call its *ideology* (by which is meant a strong "culture"). Ideology encompasses the traditions and beliefs of an organization that distinguish it from other organizations and infuse a certain life into the skeleton of its structure.

This gives us six basic parts of an organization. As shown in Figure 1, we have a small strategic apex connected by a flaring middle line to a large, flat operating core at the base. These three parts of the organization are drawn in one uninterrupted sequence to indicate that they are typically connected through a single chain of formal authority. The technostructure and the support staff are shown off to either side to indicate that they are separate from this main line of authority, influencing the operating core only indirectly. The ideology is shown as a kind of halo that surrounds the entire system.

These people, all of whom work inside the organization to make its decisions and take its actions—full-time employees or, in some cases, committed volunteers—may be thought of as *influencers* who form a kind of internal coalition. By this term, we mean a system within which people vie among themselves to determine the distribution of power.

In addition, various outside people also try to exert influence on the organization, seeking to affect the decisions and actions taken inside. These external influencers, who create a field of

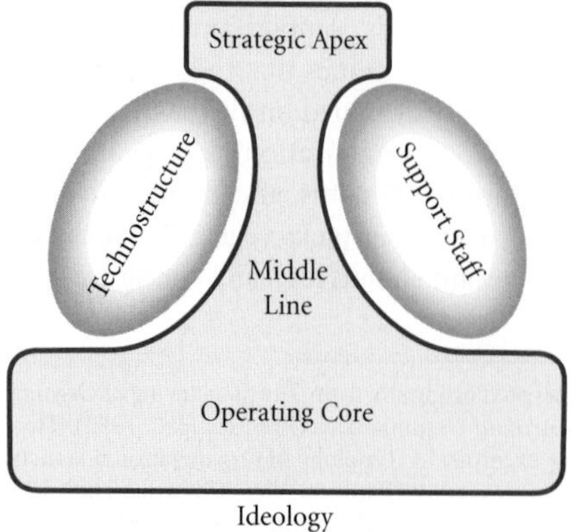

FIGURE 1
THE SIX BASIC PARTS OF THE ORGANIZATION

forces around the organization, can include owners, unions and other employee associations, suppliers, clients, partners, competitors, and all kinds of publics, in the form of governments, special interest groups, and so forth. Together they can all be thought to form an *external coalition.*

Sometimes the external coalition is relatively *passive* (as in the typical behavior of the shareholders of a widely held corporation or the members of a large union). Other times it is *dominated* by one active influencer or some group of them acting in concert (such as an outside owner of a business firm or a community intent on imposing a certain philosophy on its school system). And in still other cases, the external coalition may be *divided,* as different groups seek to impose contradictory pressures on the organization (as in a prison buffeted between two community groups, one favoring custody, the other rehabilitation).

SIX BASIC COORDINATING MECHANISMS

Every organized human activity—from the making of pottery to the placing of a man on the moon—gives rise to two fundamental and opposing requirements: the *division of labor* into various tasks to be performed and the *coordination* of those tasks to accomplish the activity. The structure of an organization can be defined simply as the total of the ways in which its labor is divided into distinct tasks and then its coordination achieved among those tasks.

1. *Mutual adjustment* achieves coordination of work by the simple process of informal communication. The people who do the work interact with one another to coordinate, much as two canoeists in the rapids adjust to one another's actions. Figure 2a shows mutual adjustment in terms of an arrow between two operators. Mutual adjustment is obviously used in the simplest of organizations—it is the most obvious way to coordinate. But, paradoxically, it is also used in the most complex, because it is the only means that can be relied upon under extremely difficult circumstances, such as trying to figure out how to put a man on the moon for the first time.

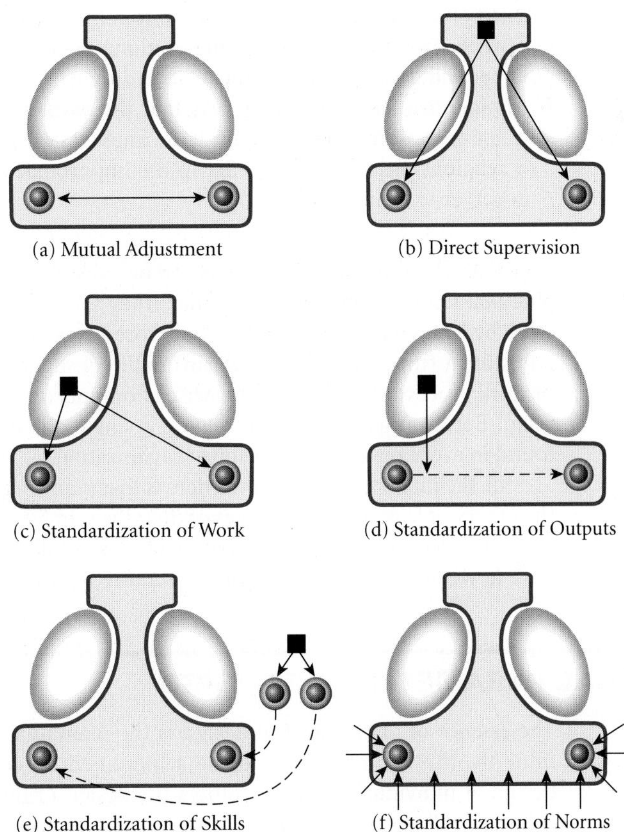

FIGURE 2
THE BASIC MECHANISMS OF COORDINATION

2. *Direct supervision* in which one person coordinates by giving orders to others tends to come into play after a certain number of people must work together. Thus, fifteen people in a war canoe cannot coordinate by mutual adjustment; they need a leader who, by virtue of instructions, coordinates their work, much as a football team requires a quarterback to call the plays. Figure 2b shows the leader as a manager with the instructions as arrows to the operators.

Coordination can also be achieved by *standardization*—in effect, automatically, by virtue of standards that predetermine what people do and so ensure that their work is coordinated. We can consider four forms—the standardization of the work processes themselves, of the outputs of the work, of the knowledge and skills that serve as inputs to the work, or of the norms that more generally guide the work.

3. *Standardization of work processes* means the specification—that is, the programming—of the content of the work directly, the procedures to be followed, as in the case of the assembly instructions that come with many children's toys. As shown in Figure 2c, it is typically the job of the analysts to so program the work of different people in order to coordinate it tightly.
4. *Standardization of outputs* means the specification not of what is to be done but of its results. In that way, the interfaces between jobs is predetermined, as when a machinist is told to drill holes in a certain place on a fender so that they will fit the bolts being welded by someone else, or a division manager is told to achieve a sales growth of 10% so that the corporation can meet some overall sales target. Again, such standards generally emanate from the analysts, as shown in Figure 2d.
5. *Standardization of skills,* as well as knowledge, is another, though looser way to achieve coordination. Here, it is the worker rather than the work or the outputs that is standardized. He or she is taught a body of knowledge and a set of skills which are subsequently applied to the work. Such standardization typically takes place outside the organization—for example, in a professional school of a university before the worker takes his or her first job—indicated in Figure 2e. In effect, the standards do not come from the analyst; they are internalized by the operator as inputs to the job he or she takes. Coordination is then achieved by virtue of various operators' having learned what to expect of each other. When an anesthetist and a surgeon meet in the operating room to remove an appendix, they need hardly communicate (that is, use mutual adjustment, let alone direct supervision); each knows exactly what the other will do and can coordinate accordingly.
6. *Standardization of norms* means that the workers share a common set of beliefs and can achieve coordination based on it, as implied in Figure 2f. For example, if every member of a religious order shares a belief in the importance of attracting converts, then all will work together to achieve this aim.

These coordinating mechanisms can be considered the most basic elements of structure, the glue that holds organizations together. They seem to fall into a rough order. As organizational work becomes more complicated, the favored means of coordination seems to shift from mutual adjustment (the simplest mechanism) to direct supervision, then to standardization, preferably of work processes or norms, otherwise of outputs or of skills, finally reverting to mutual adjustment. But no organization can rely on a single one of those mechanisms; all will typically be found in every reasonably developed organization.

Still, the important point for us here is that many organizations do favor one mechanism over the others, at least at certain stages of their lives. In fact, organizations that favor none seem most prone to becoming politicized, simply because of the conflicts that naturally arise when people have to vie for influence in a relative vacuum of power.

THE ESSENTIAL PARAMETERS OF DESIGN

The essence of organizational design is the manipulation of a series of parameters that determine the division of labor and the achievement of coordination. Some of these concern the design of individual positions, others the design of the superstructure (the overall network of subunits, reflected in the organizational chart), some the design of lateral linkages to flesh out that superstructure, and a final group concerns the design of the decision-making system of the organization. Listed as follows are the main parameters of structural design, with links to the coordinating mechanisms:

- Job specialization refers to the number of tasks in a given job and the workers' control over these tasks. A job is *horizontally* specialized to the extent that it encompasses a few narrowly defined tasks, *vertically* specialized to the extent that the worker lacks control of the tasks performed. *Unskilled* jobs are typically highly specialized in both dimensions; skilled or *professional* jobs are typically specialized horizontally but not vertically. "Job enrichment" refers to the enlargement of jobs in both the vertical and horizontal dimension.
- Behavior formalization refers to the standardization of work processes by the imposition of operating instructions, job descriptions, rules, regulations, and the like. Structures that rely on any form of standardization for coordination may be defined as *bureaucratic,* those that do not as *organic.*
- Training refers to the use of formal instructional programs to establish and standardize in people the requisite skills and knowledge to do particular jobs in organizations. Training is a key design parameter in all work we call professional. Training and formalization are basically substitutes for achieving the standardization (in effect, the bureaucratization) of behavior. In one, the standards are learned as skills, in the other they are imposed on the job as rules.
- Indoctrination refers to programs and techniques by which the norms of the members of an organization are standardized, so that they become responsive to its ideological needs and can thereby be trusted to make its decisions and take its actions. Indoctrination too is a substitute for formalization, as well as for skill training, in this case the standards being internalized as deeply rooted beliefs.
- Unit grouping refers to the choice of the bases by which positions are grouped together into units, and those units into higher-order units (typically shown on the organization chart). Grouping encourages coordination by putting different jobs under common supervision, by requiring them to share common resources and achieve common measures of performance, and by using proximity to facilitate mutual adjustment among them. The various bases for grouping—by work process, product, client, place, and so on—can be reduced to two fundamental ones—the *function* performed and the *market* served. The former (illustrated in Figure 3) refers to means, that is, to a single link in the chain of processes by which products or services are produced; the latter (in Figure 4) to ends, that is, the whole chain for specific end products, services, or markets. On what criteria should the choice of a basis for grouping be made? First, there is the consideration of workflow linkages, or "interdependencies." Obviously, the more tightly linked are positions or units in the workflow, the more desirable that they be grouped together to facilitate their coordination. Second is the consideration of process interdependencies—for example, across people doing the same kind of work but in different workflows (such as maintenance men working on different machines). It sometimes makes sense to group them together to facilitate their sharing of equipment or ideas, to encourage the improvement of their skills, and so on. Third is the question of scale interdependencies. For example, all maintenance people in a factory may have to be grouped together because no single department has enough maintenance work for one person. Finally, there are the social interdependencies, the need to group people together for social reasons, as in coal mines where mutual support under dangerous working conditions can be a factor in deciding

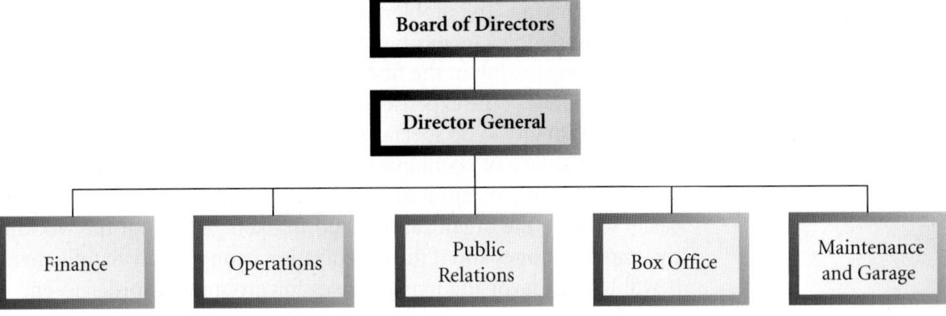

FIGURE 3
GROUPING BY FUNCTION: A CULTURAL CENTER

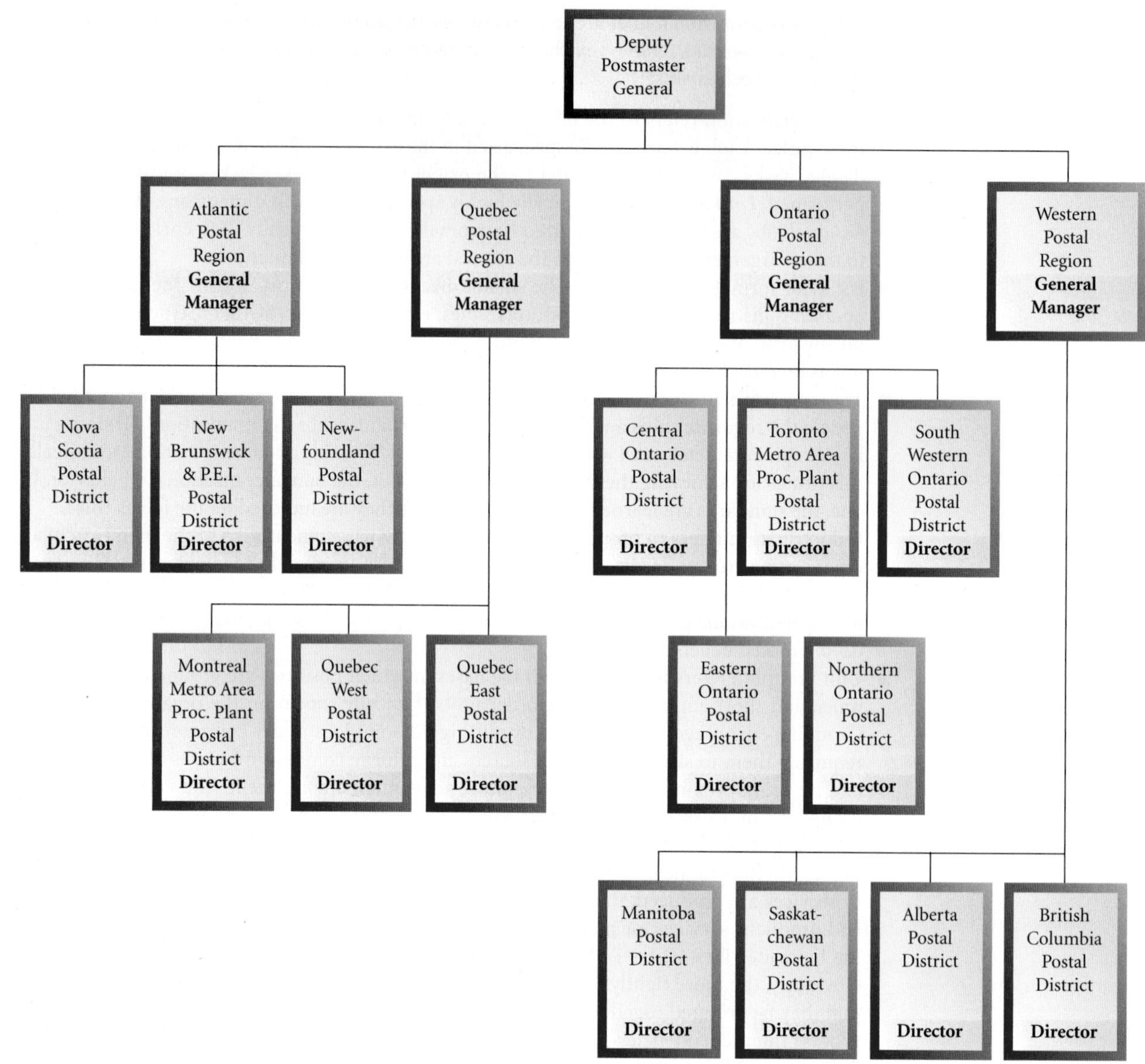

FIGURE 4
GROUPING BY MARKET: THE CANADIAN POST OFFICE*
*Headquarter staff groups deleted.

how to group people. Clearly, grouping by function is favored by process and scale interdependencies, and to a lesser extent by social interdependencies (in the sense that people who do the same kind of job often tend to get along better). Grouping by function also encourages specialization, for example, by allowing specialists to come together under the supervision of one of their own kind. The problem with functional grouping, however, is that it narrows perspectives, encouraging a focus on means instead of ends—the way to do the job instead of the reason for doing the job in the first place. Thus grouping by market is used to favor coordination in the workflow at the expense of process and scale specialization. In general, market grouping reduces the ability to do specialized or repetitive tasks well and is more wasteful, being less able to take advantage of economies of scale and often requiring the duplication of resources. But it enables the organization to accomplish a wider variety of tasks and to change its tasks more easily to serve the organization's end markets. And so if the workflow interdependencies are the important ones and if the organization cannot easily handle them by standardization, then it will tend to favor the market bases for grouping in order to encourage mutual adjustment and direct supervision. But if the workflow is irregular (as in a tion can easily contain the important workflow interdependencies, interdependencies are the important ones, then the organization will be advantages of specialization and group on the basis of function instead. Of cou smallest organizations, the question is not so much *which* basis of grouping, but in Much as fires are built by stacking logs first one way and then the other, so too are organi built by varying the different bases for grouping to take care of various interdependencies.

- Unit size refers to the number of positions (or units) contained in a single unit. The equivalent term, *span of control,* is not used here, because sometimes units are kept small despite an absence of close supervisory control. For example, when experts coordinate extensively by mutual adjustment, as in an engineering team in a space agency, they will form into small units. In this case, unit size is small and span of control is low despite a relative absence of direct supervision. In contrast, when work is highly standardized (because of either formalization or training), unit size can be very large, because there is little need for direct supervision. One foreman can supervise dozens of assemblers, because they work according to very tight instructions.
- Planning and control systems are used to standardize outputs. They may be divided into two types: *action planning* systems, which specify the results of specific actions before they are taken (for example, that holes should be drilled with diameters of 3 centimeters); and *performance control* systems, which specify the desired results of whole ranges of actions after the fact (for example, that sales of a division should grow by 10% in a given year).
- Liaison devices refer to a whole series of mechanisms used to encourage mutual adjustment within and between units. Four are of particular importance:
  - *Liaison positions* are jobs created to coordinate the work of two units directly, without having to pass through managerial channels, for example, the purchasing engineer who sits between purchasing and engineering or the sales liaison person who mediates between the sales force and the factory. These positions carry no formal authority per se; rather, those who serve in them must use their powers of persuasion, negotiation, and so on to bring the two sides together.
  - *Task forces and standing committees* are institutionalized forms of meetings which bring members of a number of different units together on a more intensive basis, in the first case to deal with a temporary issue, in the second, in a more permanent and regular way to discuss issues of common interest.
  - *Integrating managers*—essentially liaison personnel with formal authority—provide for stronger coordination. These "managers" are given authority not over the units they link, but over something important to those units, for example, their budgets. One example is the brand manager in a consumer goods firm who is responsible for a certain product but who must negotiate its production and marketing with different functional departments.
  - *Matrix structure* carries liaison to its natural conclusion. No matter what the bases of grouping at one level in an organization, some interdependencies always remain. Figure 5 suggests various ways to deal with these "residual interdependencies": a different type of grouping can be used at the next level in the hierarchy; staff units can be formed next to line units to advise on the problems; or one of the liaison devices already discussed can be overlaid on the grouping. But in each case, one basis of grouping is favored over the others. The concept of matrix structure is balance between two (or more) bases of grouping, for example, functional with market (or for that matter, one kind of market with another—say, regional with product). This is done by the creation of a dual authority structure—two (or more) managers, units, or individuals are made jointly and equally responsible for the same decisions. We can distinguish a *permanent* form of matrix structure, where the units and the people in them remain more or less in place, as shown in the example of a whimsical multinational firm in Figure 6, and a *shifting* form, suited to project work, where the units and the people in them move around frequently. Shifting matrix structures are common in high-technology industries, which group specialists in functional departments for housekeeping purposes (process interdependencies, etc.) but deploy them from various departments in project teams to do the work, as shown for NASA in Figure 7.
- Decentralization refers to the diffusion of decision-making power. When all the power rests at a single point in an organization, we call its structure centralized; to the extent that the

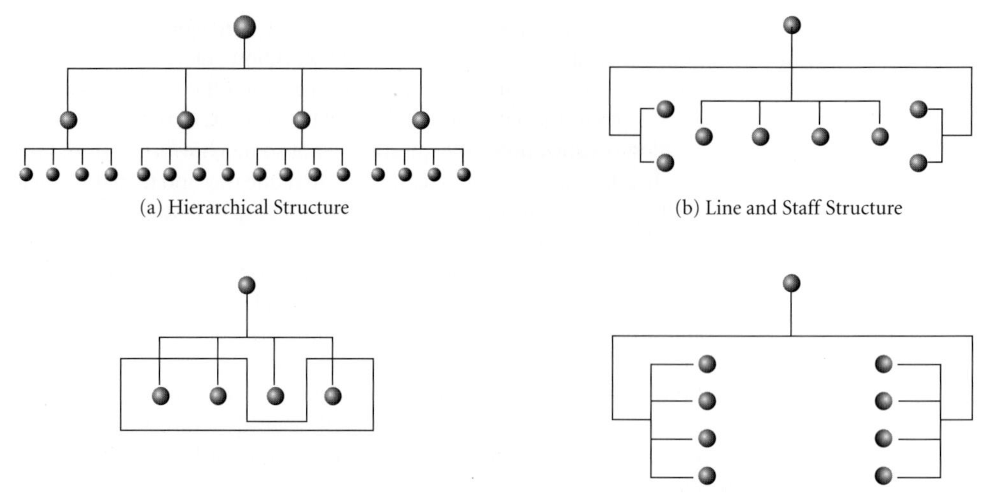

FIGURE 5
STRUCTURES TO DEAL WITH RESIDUAL INTERDEPENDENCIES

power is dispersed among many individuals, we call it relatively decentralized. We can distinguish *vertical decentralization*—the delegation of formal power down the hierarchy to line managers—from *horizontal decentralization*—the extent to which formal or informal power is dispersed out of the line hierarchy to nonmanagers (operators, analysts, and support staffers). We can also distinguish *selective* decentralization—the dispersal of power over different decisions to different places in the organization—from *parallel* decentralization—where the power over various kinds of decisions is delegated to the same place. Six forms of decentralization may thus be described: (1) vertical and horizontal centralization, where all the power rests at the strategic apex; (2) limited horizontal decentralization (selective), where the strategic apex shares some power with the technostructure that standardizes everybody else's work; (3) limited vertical decentralization (parallel), where managers of market-based units are delegated the power to control most of the decisions concerning their line units; (4) vertical and horizontal decentralization, where most of the power rests in the operating core, at the bottom of the structure; (5) selective vertical and horizontal decentralization, where the power over different decisions is dispersed to various places in the organization, among managers, staff experts, and operators who work in teams at various levels in the hierarchy; and (6) pure decentralization, where power is shared more or less equally by all members of the organization.

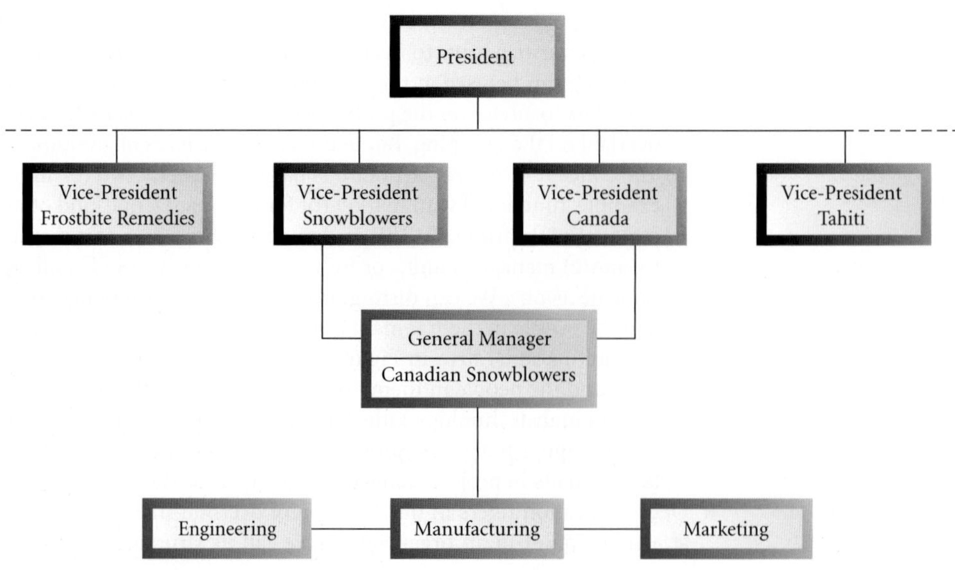

FIGURE 6
A PERMANENT MATRIX STRUCTURE IN AN INTERNATIONAL FIRM

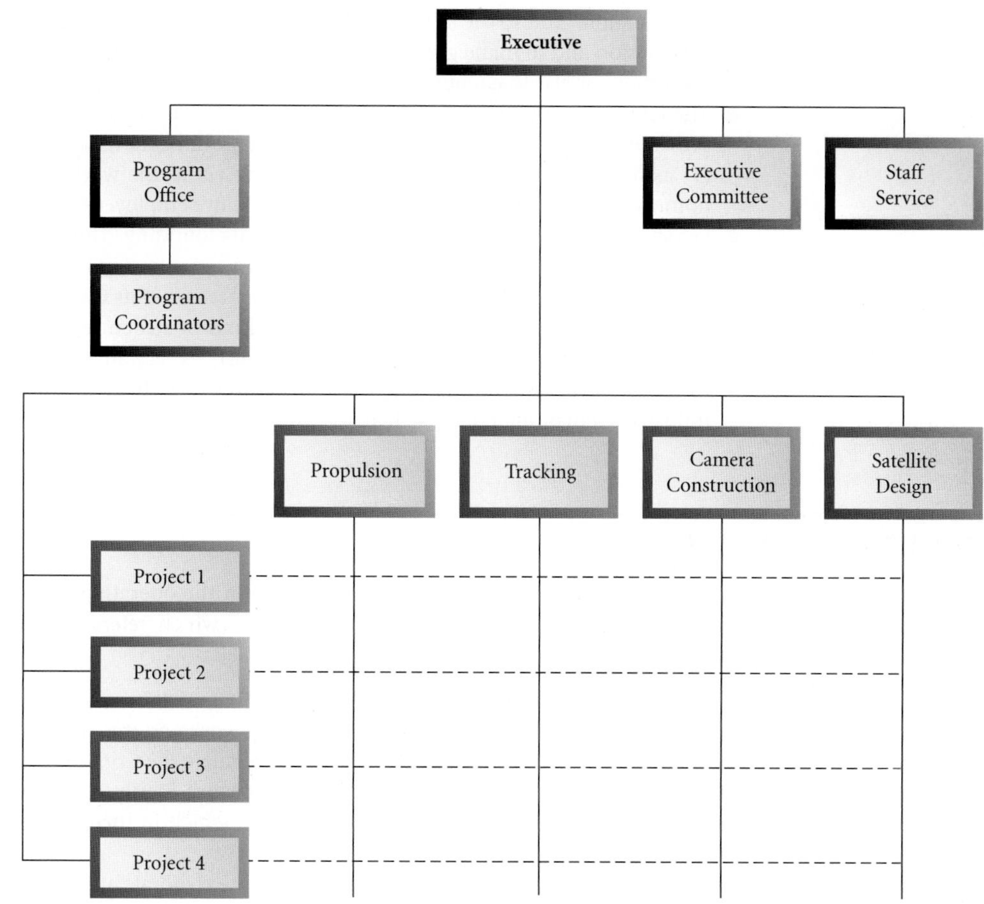

FIGURE 7
SHIFTING MATRIX STRUCTURE IN THE NASA WEATHER SATELLITE PROGRAM

Source: Modified from Delbecq and Filley (1974: 16).

THE SITUATIONAL FACTORS

A number of "contingency" or "situational" factors influence the choice of these design parameters, and vice versa. They include the age and size of the organization; its technical system of production; various characteristics of its environment, such as stability and complexity; and its power system, for example, whether or not it is tightly controlled by outside influencers. Some of the effects of these factors, as found in an extensive body of research literature, are summarized below as hypotheses.

AGE AND SIZE

- The older an organization, the more formalized its behavior. What we have here is the "we've-seen-it-all-before" syndrome. As organizations age, they tend to repeat their behaviors: as a result, these become more predictable and so more amenable to formalization.
- The larger an organization, the more formalized its behavior. Just as the older organization formalizes what it has seen before, so the larger organization formalizes what it sees often. ("Listen mister, I've heard that story at least five times today. Just fill in the form like it says.")
- The larger an organization, the more elaborate its structure; that is, the more specialized its jobs and units and the more developed its administrative components. As organizations grow in size, they are able to specialize their jobs more finely. (The big barbershop can afford a specialist to cut children's hair; the small one cannot.) As a result, they can also specialize—or "differentiate"—the work of their units more extensively. This requires more effort at

coordination. And so the larger organization tends also to enlarge its hierarchy to effect direct supervision and to make greater use of its technostructure to achieve coordination by standardization, or else to encourage more coordination by mutual adjustment.

- The larger the organization, the larger the size of its average unit. This finding relates to the previous two, the size of units growing larger as organizations themselves grow larger because (1) as behavior becomes more formalized, and (2) as the work of each unit becomes more homogeneous, managers are able to supervise more employees.
- Structure reflects the age of the industry from its founding. This is a curious finding, but one that we shall see holds up remarkably well. An organization's structure seems to reflect the age of the industry in which it operates, no matter what its own age. Industries that predate the Industrial Revolution seem to favor one kind of structure, those of the age of the early railroads another, and so on. We should obviously expect different structures in different periods; the surprising thing is that these structures seem to carry through to new periods, old industries remaining relatively true to earlier structures.

TECHNICAL SYSTEM

Technical system refers to the instruments used in the operating core to produce the outputs. (This should be distinguished from "technology," which refers to the knowledge base of an organization.)

- The more regulating the technical system—that is, the more it controls the work of the operators—the more formalized the operating work and the more bureaucratic the structure of the operating core. Technical systems that regulate the work of the operators—for example, mass production assembly lines—render that work highly routine and predictable, and so encourage its specialization and formalization, which in turn create the conditions for bureaucracy in the operating core.
- The more complex the technical system, the more elaborate and professional the support staff. Essentially, if an organization is to use complex machinery, it must hire staff experts who can understand that machinery—who have the capability to design, select, and modify it. And then it must give them considerable power to make decisions concerning that machinery, and encourage them to use the liaison devices to ensure mutual adjustment among them.
- The automation of the operating core forms a bureaucratic administrative structure into an organic one. When unskilled work is coordinated by the standardization of work processes, we tend to get bureaucratic structure throughout the organization, because a control mentality pervades the whole system. But when the work of the operating core becomes automated, social relationships tend to change. Now it is machines, not people, that are regulated. So the obsession with control tends to disappear—machines do not need to be watched over—and with it go many of the managers and analysts who were needed to control the operators. In their place come the support specialists to look after the machinery, coordinating their own work by mutual adjustment. Thus, automation reduces line authority in favor of staff expertise and reduces the tendency to rely on standardization for coordination.

ENVIRONMENT

Environment refers to various characteristics of the organization's outside context, related to markets, political climate, economic conditions, and so on.

- The more dynamic an organization's environment, the more organic its structure. It stands to reason that in a stable environment—where nothing changes—an organization can predict its future conditions and so, all other things being equal, can easily rely on standardization for coordination. But when conditions become dynamic—when the need for product change is frequent, labor turnover is high, and political conditions are unstable—the organization cannot standardize but must instead remain flexible through the use of direct supervision or mutual adjustment for coordination, and so it must use a more organic structure. Thus, for example, armies, which tend to be highly bureaucratic institutions in peacetime, can become rather organic when engaged in highly dynamic, guerilla-type warfare.

- The more complex an organization's environment, the more decentralized its structure. The prime reason to decentralize a structure is that all the information needed to make decisions cannot be comprehended in one head. Thus, when the operations of an organization are based on a complex body of knowledge, there is usually a need to decentralize decision-making power. Note that a simple environment can be stable or dynamic (the manufacturer of dresses faces a simple environment yet cannot predict style from one season to another), as can a complex one (the specialist in perfected open heart surgery faces a complex task, yet knows what to expect).
- The more diversified an organization's markets, the greater the propensity to split it into market-based units, or divisions, given favorable economies of scale. When an organization can identify distinct markets—geographical regions, clients, but especially products and services—it will be predisposed to split itself into high-level units on that basis, and to give each a good deal of control over its own operations (that is, to use what we called "limited vertical decentralization"). In simple terms, diversification breeds divisionalization. Each unit can be given all the functions associated with its own markets. But this assumes favorable economies of scale: If the operating core cannot be divided, as in the case of an aluminum smelter, also if some critical function must be centrally coordinated, as in purchasing in a retail chain, then full divisionalization may not be possible.
- Extreme hostility in its environment drives any organization to centralize its structure temporarily. When threatened by extreme hostility in its environment, the tendency for an organization is to centralize power, in other words, to fall back on its tightest coordinating mechanism, direct supervision. Here a single leader can ensure fast and tightly coordinated response to the threat (at least temporarily).

POWER

- The greater the external control of an organization, the more centralized and formalized its structure. This important hypothesis claims that to the extent that an organization is controlled externally—for example, by a parent firm or a government that dominates its external coalition—it tends to centralize power at the strategic apex and to formalize its behavior. The reason is that the two most effective ways to control an organization from the outside are to hold its chief executive officer responsible for its actions and to impose clearly defined standards on it. Moreover, external control forces the organization to be especially careful about its actions.
- A divided external coalition will tend to give rise to a politicized internal coalition, and vice versa. In effect, conflict in one of the coalitions tends to spill over to the other, as one set of influencers seeks to enlist the support of the others.
- Fashion favors the structure of the day (and the culture), sometimes even when inappropriate. Ideally, the design parameters are chosen according to the dictates of age, size, technical system, and environment. In fact, however, fashion seems to play a role too, encouraging many organizations to adopt currently popular design parameters that are inappropriate for themselves. Paris has its salons of haute couture; likewise, New York has its offices of "haute structure," the consulting firms that sometimes tend to oversell the latest in structural fashion.

THE CONFIGURATIONS

We have now introduced various attributes of organizations—parts, coordinating mechanisms, design parameters, situational factors. How do they all combine?

We proceed here on the assumption that a limited number of configurations can help explain much of what is observed in organizations. We have introduced in our discussion six basic parts

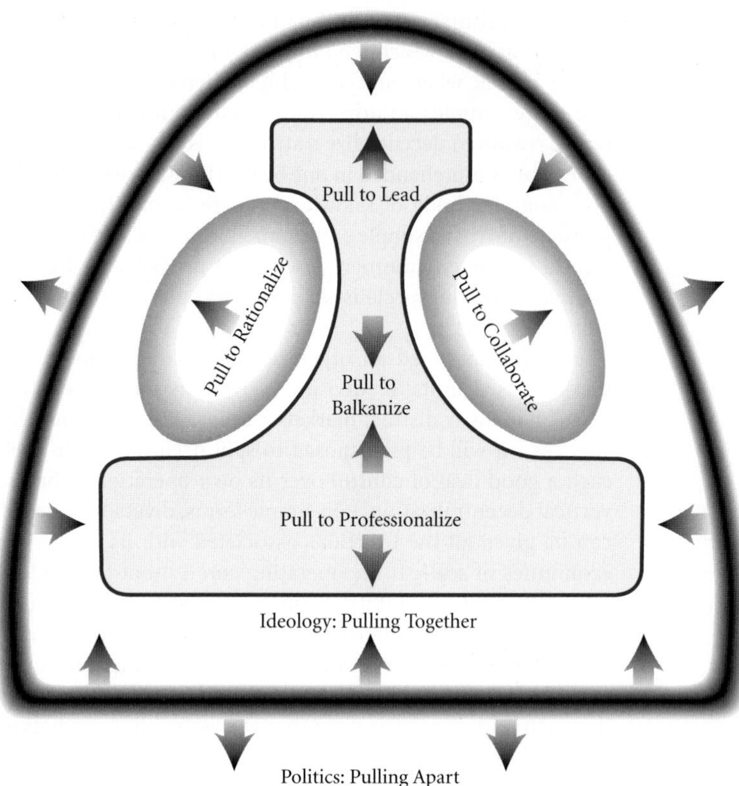

FIGURE 8
BASIC PULLS ON
THE ORGANIZATION

of the organization, six basic mechanisms of coordination, as well as six basic types of decentralization. In fact, there seems to be a fundamental correspondence between all of these sixes, which can be explained by a set of pulls exerted on the organization by each of its six parts, as shown in Figure 8. When conditions favor one of these pulls, the associated part of the organization becomes key, the coordinating mechanism appropriate to itself becomes prime, and the form of decentralization that passes power to itself emerges. The organization is thus drawn to design itself as a particular configuration. We list here (see Table 1) and then introduce briefly the six resulting configurations, together with a seventh that tends to appear when no one pull or part dominates.

THE ENTREPRENEURIAL ORGANIZATION

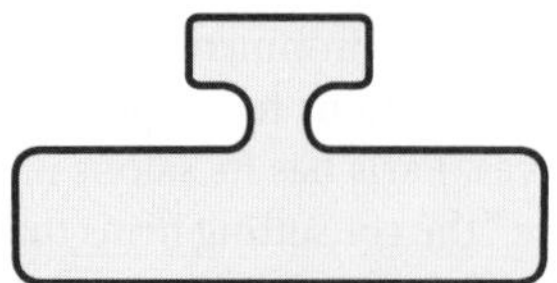

The name tells it all. And the figure above shows it all. The structure is simple, not much more than one large unit consisting of one or a few top managers, one of whom dominates by the pull to lead, and a group of operators who do the basic work. Little of the behavior in the organization is formalized and minimal use is made of planning, training, or the liaison devices. The absence of standardization means that the structure is organic and has little need for staff analysts. Likewise, there are few middle-line managers because so much of the coordination is handled at

TABLE 1

CONFIGURATION	PRIME COORDINATING MECHANISM	PART OF ORGANIZATION	TYPE OF DECENTRALIZATION
Entrepreneurial organization	Direct supervision	Strategic apex	Vertical and horizontal centralization
Machine organization	Standardization of work processes	Technostructure	Limited horizontal decentralization
Professional organization	Standardization of skills	Operating core	Horizontal decentralization
Diversified organization	Standardization of outputs	Middle line	Limited vertical decentralization
Innovative organization	Mutual adjustment	Support staff	Selected decentralization
Missionary organization	Standardization of norms	Ideology	Decentralization

the top. Even the support staff is minimized, in order to keep the structure lean, the organization flexible.

The organization must be flexible because it operates in a dynamic environment, often by choice since that is the only place where it can outsmart the bureaucracies. But that environment must be simple, as must the production system, or else the chief executive could not for long hold on to the lion's share of the power. The organization is often young, in part because time drives it toward bureaucracy, in part because the vulnerability of its simple structure often causes it to fail. And many of these organizations are often small, since size too drives the structure toward bureaucracy. Not infrequently the chief executive purposely keeps the organization small in order to retain his or her personal control.

The classic case is of course the small entrepreneurial firm, controlled tightly and personally by its owner. Sometimes, however, under the control of a strong leader the organization can grow too large. Likewise, entrepreneurial organizations can be found in other sectors too, like government, where strong leaders personally control particular agencies, often ones they have founded. Sometimes under crisis conditions, large organizations also revert temporarily to the entrepreneurial form to allow forceful leaders to try to save them.

THE MACHINE ORGANIZATION

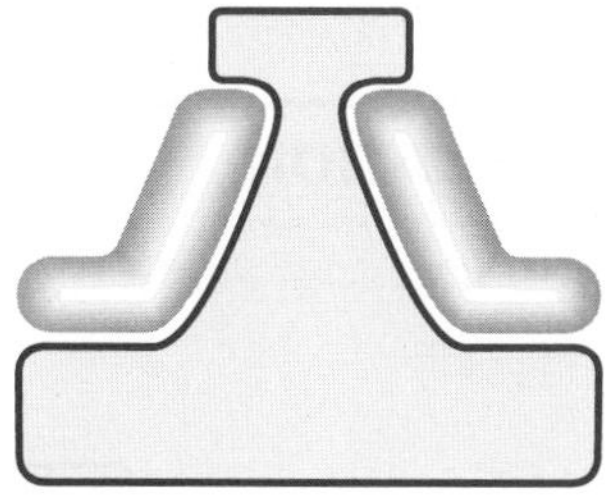

The machine organization is the offspring of the Industrial Revolution, when jobs became highly specialized and work became highly standardized. As can be seen in the figure above, in contrast to entrepreneurial organizations, the machine one elaborates its administration. First, it requires a large technostructure to design and maintain its systems of standardization, notably those that formalize its behaviors and plan its actions. And by virtue of the organization's dependence on these systems, the technostructure gains a good deal of informal power, resulting in a limited amount of horizontal decentralization reflecting the pull to rationalize. A large hierarchy of middle-line managers emerges to control the highly specialized work of the operating core. But the middle-line hierarchy is usually structured on a functional basis all the way up to the top, where the real power of coordination lies. So the structure tends to be rather centralized in the vertical sense.

To enable the top managers to maintain centralized control, both the environment and the production system of the machine organization must be fairly simple, the latter regulating the work of the operators but not itself automated. In fact, machine organizations fit most naturally with mass production. Indeed, it is interesting that this structure is most prevalent in industries that date back to the period from the Industrial Revolution to the early part of 20th century.

THE PROFESSIONAL ORGANIZATION

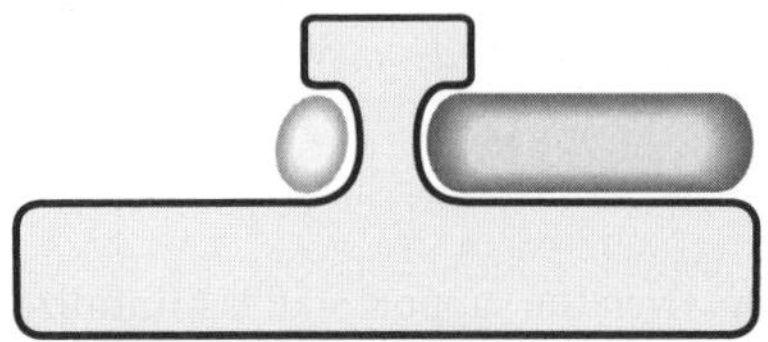

There is another bureaucratic configuration, but because this one relies on the standardization of skills rather than of work processes or outputs for its coordination, it emerges as dramatically different from the machine one. Here the pull to professionalize dominates. In having to rely on trained professionals—people highly specialized, but with considerable control over their work, as in hospitals or universities—to do its operating tasks, the organization surrenders a good deal of its power not only to the professionals themselves but also to the associations and institutions that select and train them in the first place. So the structure emerges as highly decentralized horizontally; power over many decisions, both operating and strategic, flows all the way down the hierarchy, to the professionals of the operating core.

Above the operating core we find a rather unique structure. There is little need for a technostructure, since the main standardization occurs as a result of training that takes place outside the organization. Because the professionals work so independently, the size of operating units can be very large, and few first-line managers are needed. The support staff is typically very large too, in order to back up the high-priced professionals.

The professional organization is called for whenever an organization finds itself in an environment that is stable yet complex. Complexity requires decentralization to highly trained individuals, and stability enables them to apply standardized skills and so to work with a good deal of autonomy. To ensure that autonomy, the production system must be neither highly regulating, complex, nor automated.

THE DIVERSIFIED ORGANIZATION

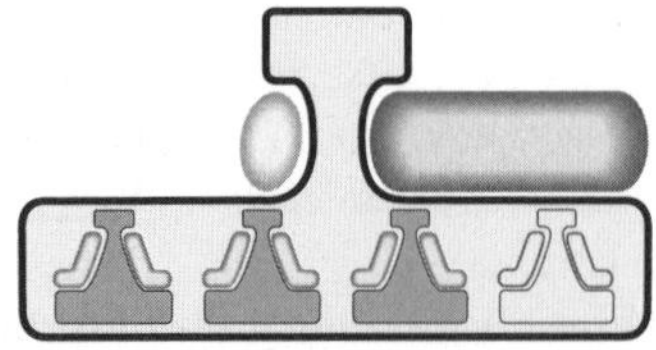

Like the professional organization, the diversified one is not so much an integrated organization as a set of rather independent entities coupled together by a loose administrative structure. But whereas those entities of the professional organization are individuals, in the diversified one they are units in the middle line, generally called "divisions," exerting a dominant pull to balkanize. This configuration differs from the others in one major respect: it is not a complete structure, but a partial one superimposed on the others. Each division has its own structure.

An organization divisionalizes for one reason above all, because its product lines are diversified. And that tends to happen most often in the largest and most mature organizations, the ones that have run out of opportunities—or have become bored—in their traditional markets. Such diversification encourages the organization to replace functional by market-based units, one for each distinct product line (as shown in the diversified organization figure), and to grant considerable autonomy to each to run its own business. The result is a limited form of decentralization down the chain of command.

How does the central headquarters maintain a semblance of control over the divisions? Some direction supervision is used. But too much of that interferes with the necessary divisional autonomy. So the headquarters relies on performance control systems, in other words, the standardization of outputs. To design these control systems, headquarters creates a small technostructure. This is shown in the figure, across from the small central support staff that headquarters sets up to provide certain services common to the divisions such as legal counsel and public relations. And because headquarters' control constitutes external control, as discussed in the first hypothesis on power, the structure of the divisions tend to be drawn toward the machine form.

THE INNOVATIVE ORGANIZATION

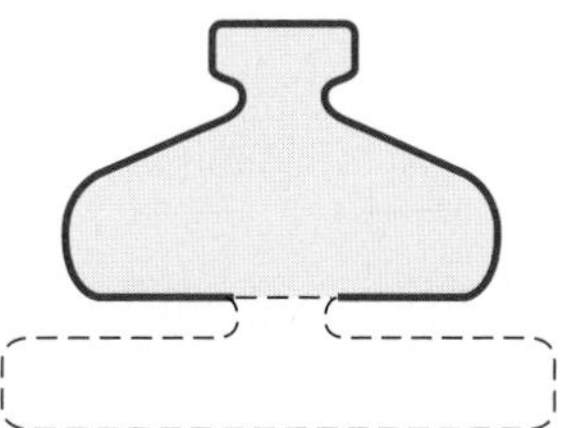

None of the structures so far discussed suits the industries of our age, industries such as aerospace, petrochemicals, think-tank consulting, and film making. These organizations need above all to innovate in very complex ways. The bureaucratic structures are too inflexible, and the entrepreneurial one too centralized. These industries require "project structures," ones that can fuse experts drawn from different specialties into smoothly functioning creative teams. That is the role of our fifth configuration, the innovative organization, which we shall also call "adhocracy," dominated by the experts' pull to collaborate.

Adhocracy is an organic structure that relies for coordination on mutual adjustment among its highly trained and highly specialized experts, which it encourages by the extensive use of the liaison devices—integrating managers, standing committees, and above all task forces and matrix structure. Typically the experts are grouped in functional units for housekeeping purposes but deployed in small market-based project teams to do their work. To these teams, located all over the structure in accordance with the decisions to be made, is delegated power over different kinds of decisions. So the structure becomes decentralized selectively in the vertical and horizontal dimensions, that is, power is distributed unevenly, all over the structure, according to expertise and need.

All the distinctions of conventional structure disappear in the innovative organization, as can be seen in the figure above. With power based on expertise, the line–staff distinction evaporates. With power distributed throughout the structure, the distinction between the strategic apex and the rest of the structure blurs.

These organizations are found in environments that are both complex and dynamic, because those are the ones that require sophisticated innovation, the type that calls for the cooperative efforts of many different kinds of experts. One type of adhocracy is often associated with a production system that is very complex, sometimes automated, and so requires a highly skilled and influential support staff to design and maintain the technical system of the operating core. (The dashed lines of the figure designate the separation of the operating core from the adhocratic administrative structure.) Here the projects take place in the administration to bring new operating facilities on line (as when a new complex is designed in a petrochemicals firm). Another type of adhocracy produces its projects directly for its clients (as in a think-tank consulting firm or manufacturer of engineering prototypes). Here, as a result, the operators also take part in the projects, bringing their expertise to bear on them; hence the operating core blends into the administrative structure (as indicated in the figure above the dashed line). This second type of adhocracy tends to be young on average, because with no standard products or services, many tend to fail while others escape their vulnerability by standardizing some products or services and so converting themselves to a form of bureaucracy.*

THE MISSIONARY ORGANIZATION

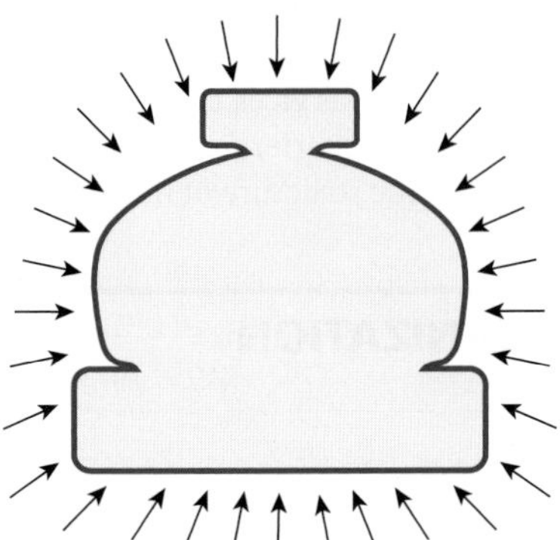

Our sixth configuration forms another rather distinct combination of the elements we have been discussing. When an organization is dominated by its ideology, its members are encouraged to pull together, and so there tends to be a loose division of labor, little job specialization, as well as a reduction of the various forms of differentiation found in the other configurations—of the strategic apex from the rest, of staff from line or administration from operations, between operators, between divisions, and so on.

What holds the missionary together—that is, provides for its coordination—is the standardization of norms, the sharing of values and beliefs among all its members. And the key to ensuring this is their socialization, effected through the design parameter of indoctrination. Once the new member has been indoctrinated into the organization—once he or she identifies strongly with the common beliefs—then he or she can be given considerable freedom to make decisions. Thus the result of effective indoctrination is the most complete form of decentralization. And because other forms of coordination need not be relied upon, the missionary organization formalizes little of its behavior as such and makes minimal use of planning and control systems. As a result, it has little technostructure. Likewise, external professional training is not relied upon, because that would force the organization to surrender a certain control to external agencies.

Hence, the missionary organization ends up as an amorphous mass of members, with little specialization as to job, differentiation as to part, division as to status.

Missionaries tend not to be very young organizations—it takes time for a set of beliefs to become institutionalized as an ideology. Many missionaries do not get a chance to grow very old either (with notable exceptions, such as certain long-standing religious orders). Missionary organizations cannot grow very large per se—they rely on personal contacts among their members—although some tend to spin off other enclaves in the form of relatively independent units sharing the same ideology. Neither the environment nor the technical system of the missionary organization can be very complex, because that would require the use of highly skilled specialists, who would hold a certain power and status over others and thereby serve to differentiate the structure. Thus we would expect to find the simplest technical systems in these organizations, usually hardly any at all, as in religious orders or in the primitive farm cooperatives.

---

*We shall clarify in a later reading these two basic types of adhocracies. Toffler employed the term *adhocracy* in his popular book *Future Shock,* but it can be found in print at least as far back as 1964.

THE POLITICAL ORGANIZATION

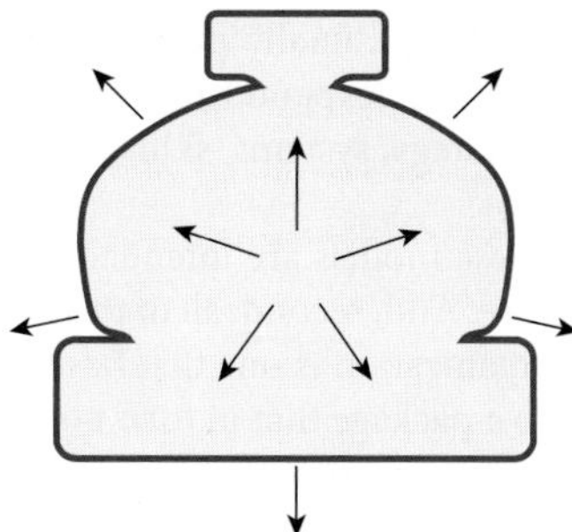

Finally, we come to a form of organization characterized, structurally at least, by what it lacks. When an organization has no dominant part, no dominant mechanism of coordination, and no stable form of centralization or decentralization, it may have difficulty tempering the conflicts within its midst, and a form of organization called the *political* may result. What characterizes its behavior is the pulling apart of its different parts, as shown in the figure above.

Political organizations can take on different forms. Some are temporary, reflecting difficult transitions in strategy or structure that evoke conflict. Others are more permanent, perhaps because the organization must face competing internal forces (say, between necessarily strong marketing and production departments), perhaps because a kind of political rot has set in but the organization is sufficiently entrenched to support it (being, for example, a monopoly or a protected government unit).

Together, all these configurations seem to encompass and integrate a good deal of what we know about organizations. It should be emphasized, however, that as presented, each configuration is idealized—a simplification, really a caricature of reality. No real organization is ever exactly like any one of them, although some do come remarkably close, while others seem to reflect combinations of them, sometimes in transition from one to another.

The first five represent what seem to be the most common forms of organizations; thus these will form the basis for the "context" section of this book—labeled entrepreneurial, mature, diversified, innovation, and professional. There, a reading in each chapter will be devoted to each of these configurations, describing its structure, functioning, conditions, strategy-making process, and the issues that surround it. Other readings in these chapters will look at specific strategies in each of these contexts, industry conditions, strategy techniques, and so on.

The other two configurations—the missionary and the political—seem to be less common, represented more by the forces of culture and conflict that exist in all organizations than by distinct forms as such. Hence they will not be discussed further as such. But because all these configurations themselves must not be taken as hard and fast, a reading in the final chapter, called "Beyond Configuration: Forces and Forms in Effective Organizations," has been included to broaden this view of organizations.

READING 8.2

Strategy and Organization Planning* BY JAY R. GALBRAITH

. . . There has been a great deal of progress in the knowledge base supporting organization planning in the last twenty-five years. Modern research on corporate structures probably started with Chandler's *Strategy and Structure*. Subsequent research has been aimed at expanding the

*Originally published in *Human Resource Management* (Spring–Summer 1983). Copyright © 1983 John Wiley & Sons, Inc. Reprinted with deletions by permission of John Wiley & Sons, Inc.

number of attributes of an organization beyond that of just structure. I have used the model shown in Figure 1 to indicate that organization consists of structure, processes that cut the structural lines like budgeting, planning, teams, and so on, reward systems like promotions and compensation, and finally people practices like selection and development (Galbraith, 1977). The trend . . . is to expand to more attributes like the 7-Ss (Waterman et al., 1980), comprising structure, strategy, systems, skills, style, staff, and superordinate goals and to "softer" attributes like culture.

All of these models are intended to convey the same ideas. First, organization is more than just structure. And, second, all of the elements must "fit" to be in "harmony" with each other. The effective organization is one that has blended its structure, management practices, rewards, and people into a package that in turn fits with its strategy. However, strategies change and therefore the organization must change.

The research of the past few years is creating some evidence by which organizations and strategies are matched. Some of the strategies are proving more successful than others. One of the explanations is organizational in nature. Also, the evidence shows that for any strategy, the high performers are those who have achieved a fit between their strategy and their organization.

These findings give organization planning a base from which to work. The organization planner should become a member of the strategic team in order to guide management to choose the appropriate strategies for which the organization is developed or to choose the appropriate organization for the new strategy.

In the sections that follow, the strategic changes that are made by organizations are described. Then the strategy and organization evidence is presented. Finally the data on economic performance and fit is discussed.

STRATEGY AND ORGANIZATION

There has been a good deal of recent attention given to the match between strategy and organization. Much of this work consists of empirical tests of Chandler's ideas presented in *Strategy and Structure* (1962). Most of this material is reviewed elsewhere (Galbraith and Nathanson, 1978).

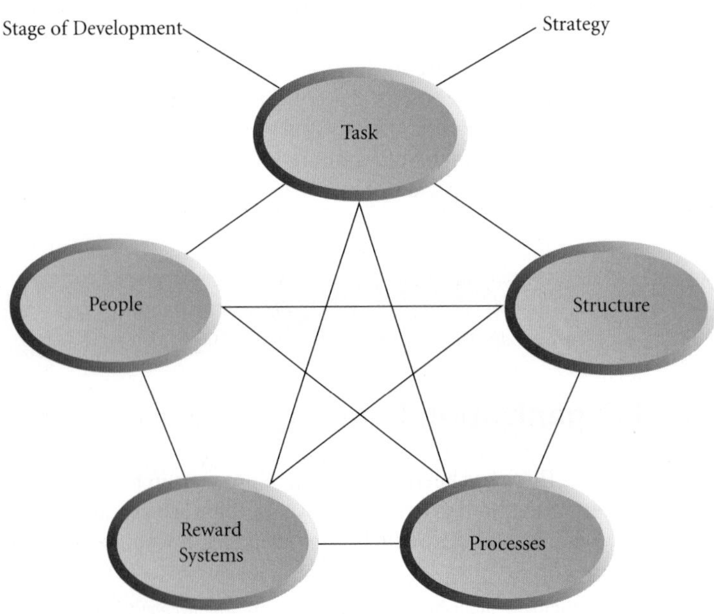

FIGURE 1
MODEL OF ORGANIZATION STRUCTURE

However, some recent work and ideas hold out considerable potential for understanding how different patterns of strategic change lead to different organization structures, management systems, and company cultures. In addition, some good relationships with economic performance are also attained.

The ideas rest on the concept of an organization having a center of gravity or driving force (Tregoe and Zimmerman, 1980). This center of gravity arises from the firm's initial success in the industry in which it grew up. Let us first explore the concept of center of gravity, then the patterns of strategic change that have been followed by American enterprises.

The center of gravity of a company depends on where in the industry supply chain the company started. In order to explain the concept, manufacturing industries will be used. Figure 2 depicts the stages of supply in an industry chain. Six stages are shown here. Each industry may have more or fewer stages. Service industries typically have fewer stages.

The chain begins with a raw material extraction stage which supplies crude oil, iron ore, logs, or bauxite to the second stage of primary manufacturing. The second stage is a variety-reducing stage to produce a standardized output (petrochemicals, steel, paper pulp, or aluminum ingots). The next stage fabricates commodity products from this primary material. Fabricators produce polyethylene, cans, sheet steel, cardboard cartons, and semiconductor components. The next stage is the product producers who add value, usually through product development, patents, and proprietary products. The next stage is the marketer and distributors. These are the consumer branded product manufacturers and various distributors. Finally, there are the retailers who have the direct contact with the ultimate consumer.

The line splitting the chain into two segments divides the industry into upstream and downstream halves. While there are differences between each of the stages, the differences between the upstream and downstream stages are striking. The upstream stages add value by reducing the variety of raw materials found on the earth's surface to a few standard commodities. The purpose is to produce flexible, predictable raw materials and intermediate products from which an increasing variety of downstream products are made. The downstream stages add value through producing a variety of products to meet varying customer needs. The downstream value is added through advertising, product positioning, marketing channels, and R&D. Thus, the upstream and downstream companies face very different business problems and tasks.

The reason for distinguishing between upstream and downstream companies is that the factors for success, the lessons learned by managers, and the organizations used are fundamentally different. The successful, experienced manager has been shaped and formed in fundamentally different ways in the different stages. The management processes are different, as are the dominant functions. In short, the company's culture is shaped by where it began in the industry chain. Listed are some fundamental differences that illustrate the contrast:

UPSTREAM	DOWNSTREAM
Standardize/homogenize	Customize/segment
Low-cost producer	High margins/proprietary positions
Process innovation	Product innovation
Capital budget	R&D/advertising budget
Technology/capital intensive	People intensive
Supply/trader/engineering	R&D/marketing dominated
Line driven	Line/staff
Maximize end users	Target end users
.	.
.	.
.	.
Sales push	Market pull

The mindset of the upstream manager is geared toward standardization and efficiency. They are the producers of standardized commodity products. In contrast, downstream managers try to customize and tailor output to diverse customer needs. They segment markets and target

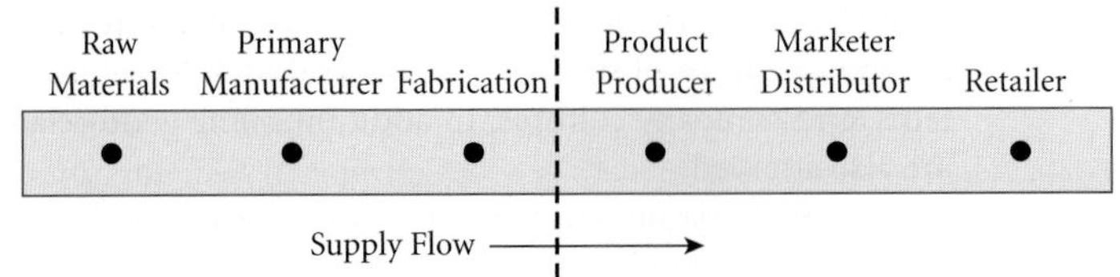

FIGURE 2
SUPPLY STAGES IN AN INDUSTRY CHAIN

individual users. The upstream company wants to standardize in order to maximize the number of end users and get volume to lower costs. The downstream company wants to target particular sets of end users. Therefore, the upstreamers have a divergent view of the world based on their commodity. For example, the cover of the 1981 annual report of Intel (a fabricator of commodity semiconductors) is a listing of the 10,000 uses to which microprocessors have been put. The downstreamers have a convergent view of the world based on customer needs and will select whatever commodity will best serve that need. In the electronics industry there is always a conflict between the upstream component types and the downstream systems types because of this contrast in mindsets.

The basis of competition is different in the two stages. Commodities compete on price since the products are the same. Therefore, it is essential that the successful upstreamer be the low-cost producer. Their organizations are the lean and mean ones with a minimum of overheads. Low cost is also important for the downstreamer, but it is proprietary features that generate high margins. That feature may be a brand image, such as Maxwell House, a patented technology, an endorsement (such as the American Dental Association's endorsement of Crest toothpaste), customer service policy, and so on. Competition revolves around product features and product positioning and less on price. This means that marketing and product management sets prices. Products move by marketing pull. In contrast, the upstream company pushes the product through a strong sales force. Often salespeople negotiate prices within limits set by top management.

The organizations are different as well. The upstream companies are functional and line driven. They seek a minimum of staff, and even those staffs that are used are in supporting roles. The downstream company with multiple products and multiple markets learns to manage diversity early. Profit centers emerge and resources need to be allocated across products and markets. Larger staffs arise to assist top management in priority setting across competing product/market advocates. Higher margins permit the overhead to exist.

Both upstream and downstream companies use research and development. However, the upstream company invests in process development in order to lower costs. The downstream company invests primarily in product development in order to achieve proprietary positions.

The key managerial processes also vary. The upstream companies are driven by the capital budget and have various capital appropriations controls. The downstream companies also have a capital budget but are driven by the R&D budget (product producers) or the advertising budget (marketers). Further downstream it is working capital that becomes paramount. Managers learn to control the business by managing the turnover of inventory and accounts receivable. Thus, the upstream company is capital intensive and technological "know-how" is critical. Downstream companies are more people intensive. Therefore, the critical skills revolve around human resources management.

The dominant functions also vary with stages. The raw material processor is dominated by geologists, petroleum engineers, and traders. The supply and distribution function which searches for the most economical end use is powerful. The manufacturers of commodities are dominated by engineers who come up through manufacturing. The downstream companies are dominated first by technologists in research and product development. Farther downstream, it is marketing and then merchandising that emerge as the power centers. The line of succession to the CEO usually runs through this dominant function.

In summary, the upstream and downstream companies are very different entities. The differences, a bit exaggerated here because of the dichotomy, lead to differences in organization structure, management processes, dominant functions, succession paths, management beliefs and values or, in short, the management way of life. Thus, companies can be in the same industry but be very different because they developed from a beginning at a particular stage of the industry. This beginning, and the initial successes, teaches management the lessons of that stage. The firm develops an integrated organization (structure, processes, rewards, and people) which is peculiar to that stage and forms the center of gravity.

STRATEGIC CHANGE

The first strategic change that an organization makes is to vertically integrate within its industry. At a certain size, the organization can move backward to prior stages to guarantee sources of supply and secure bargaining leverage on vendors. And/or it can move forward to guarantee markets and volume for capital investments and become a customer to feed back data for new products. This initial strategic move does not change the center of gravity because the prior and subsequent stages are usually operated for the benefit of the center-of-gravity stage.

The paper industry is used to illustrate the concepts of center of gravity and vertical integration. Figure 3 depicts five paper companies which operate from different centers of gravity. The first is Weyerhauser. Its center of gravity is at the land and timber stage of the industry. Weyerhauser seeks the highest return use for a log. They make pulp and paper rolls. They make containers and milk cartons. But they are a timber company. If the returns are better in lumber, the pulp mills get fed with sawdust and chips. International Paper (the name of the company tells it all), by contrast, is a primary manufacturer of paper. It also has timber lands, container plants, and works on new products around aseptic packaging. However, if the pulp mills ran out of logs, the manager of the woodlands used to be fired. The raw material stage is to supply the manufacturing stage, not seek the highest return for its timber. The Container Corporation (again, the name describes the company) is the example of the fabricator. It also has woodlands and pulp mills, but they are to supply the container making operations. The product producer is Appleton. It makes specialty paper products. For example, Appleton produces a paper with globules of ink embedded in it. The globules burst and form a letter or number when struck with an impact printer.

The last company is Procter & Gamble. P&G is a consumer products company. And, like the other companies, it operates pulp mills and owns timber lands. However, it is driven by the advertising or marketing function. If one wanted to be CEO of P&G, one would not run a pulp mill or the woodlands. The path to CEO is through the brand manager for Charmin or Pampers.

Thus, each of these companies is in the paper industry. Each operates at a number of stages in the industry. Yet each is a very different company because it has its center of gravity at a different

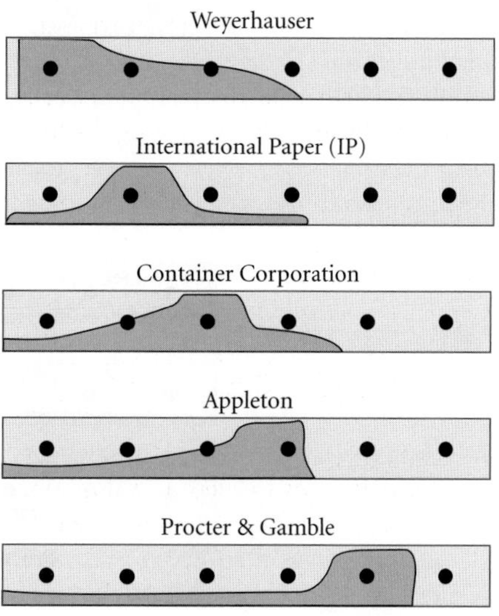

FIGURE 3
EXAMPLES OF FIVE PAPER COMPANIES OPERATING AT DIFFERENT CENTERS OF GRAVITY

stage. The center of gravity establishes a base from which subsequent strategic changes take place. That is, as a company's industry matures, the company feels a need to change its center of gravity in order to move to a place in the industry where better returns can be obtained, or move to a new industry but use its same center of gravity and skills in that industry, or make some combination of industry and center-of-gravity change. These options lead to different patterns of corporate developments.

BY-PRODUCTS DIVERSIFICATION

One of the first diversification moves that a vertically integrated company makes is to sell by-products from points along the industry chain. Figure 4 depicts this strategy. These companies appear to be diversified if one attributes revenue to the various industries in which the company operates. But the company has changed neither its industry nor its center of gravity. The company is behaving intelligently by seeking additional sources of revenue and profit. However, it is still psychologically committed to its center of gravity and to its industry. Alcoa is such a firm. Even though they operate in several industries, their output varies directly with the aluminum cycle. They have not reduced their dependence on a single industry, as one would with real diversification.

RELATED DIVERSIFICATION

Another strategic change is the diversification into new industries but at the same center of gravity. This is called "related diversification." The firm diversifies into new businesses, but they are all related. The relationship revolves around the company's center of gravity. Figure 5 depicts the diversification moves of Procter & Gamble. After beginning in the soap industry, P&G vertically integrated back into doing its own chemical processing (fatty acids) and seed crushing. Then, in order to pursue new growth opportunities, it has been diversifying into paper, food, beverages, pharmaceuticals, coffee, and so on. But each move into a new industry is made at the company's center of gravity. The new businesses are all consumer products which are driven out of advertising by brand managers. The 3M Company also follows a related diversification strategy, but theirs is based on technology. They have 40,000 different products which are produced by some

FIGURE 4
BY-PRODUCT DIVERSIFICATION

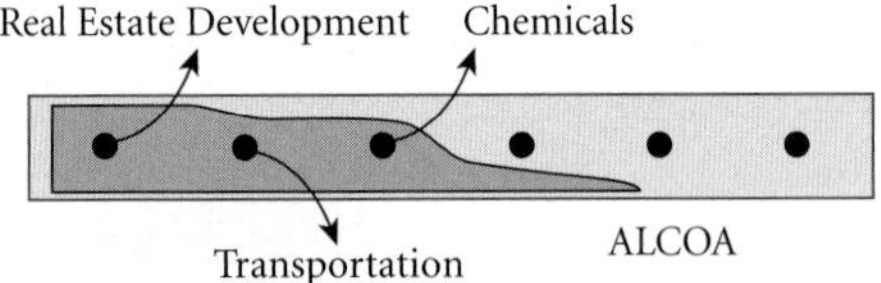

FIGURE 5
RELATED DIVERSIFICATION

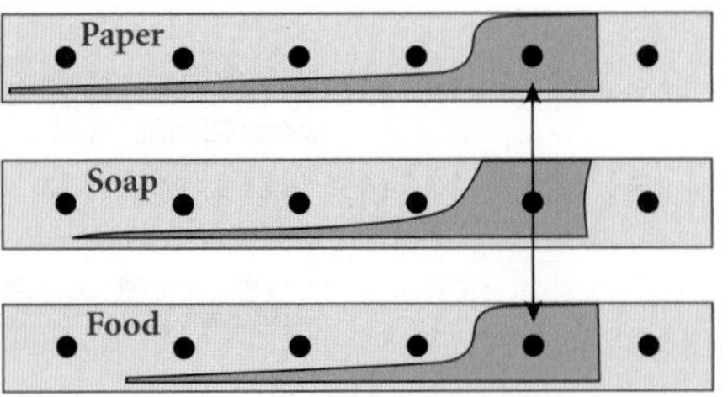

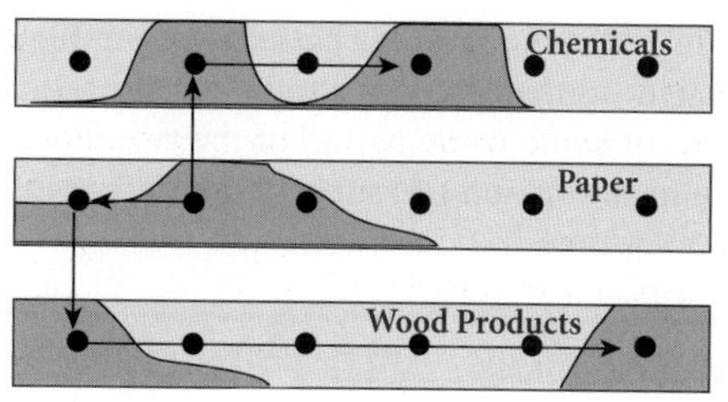

FIGURE 6
LINKED DIVERSIFICATION

seventy divisions. However, 95% of the products are based on coating and bonding technologies. Its center of gravity is a product producer, and it adds value through R&D.

LINKED DIVERSIFICATION

A third type of diversification involves moving into new industries and operating at different centers of gravity in those new industries. However, there is a linkage of some type among various businesses. Figure 6 depicts Union Camp as following this pattern of corporate development. Union Camp is a primary producer of paper products. As such, it vertically integrated backward to its own woodlands. From there, it moved downstream within the wood products industry by running sawmills and fabricating plants. However, they recently purchased a retail lumber business.

They also moved into the chemical business by selling by-products from the pulping process. This business was successful and expanded. Recently, Union Camp was bidding for a flavors and fragrances (F&F) company. The F&F company is a product producer which adds value through creating flavors and fragrances for mostly consumer products companies.

Thus, Union Camp is an upstream company that is acquiring downstream companies. However, these new companies are in industries in which the company already diversified from its upstream center of gravity. But these new acquisitions are not operated for the benefit of the center of gravity but are stand-alone profit centers.

UNRELATED DIVERSIFICATION

The final type of strategic change is to diversify into unrelated businesses. Like the linked diversifiers, unrelated diversifiers move into new industries often at a different centers of gravity. They almost always use acquisition, while related and linked companies use some acquisitions but rely heavily on internal development. There is often very little relation between the industries into which the unrelated company diversifies. Textron and Teledyne have been the paradigm examples. They operate in industrial equipment, aerospace, consumer products, insurance, and so on. Others have spread into retailing, services, and entertainment. The purpose is to insulate the company's earnings from the uncertainties of any one industry, or from the business cycle.

CENTER-OF-GRAVITY CHANGE

Another possibility is for an organization to stay in the same industry but change its center of gravity in that industry. Recent articles describe the attempts of chemical companies to move downstream into higher margin, proprietary products. They want to move away from the overcapacity/undercapacity cycles of commodity businesses with their low margins and high capital intensity. In aerospace, some of the system integration houses are moving backward into making electronic components. For example, there are going to be fewer airplanes and more effort on the avionics, radars, weapons, and so on that go into airplanes. In either case, it means a shift in the center of gravity of the company.

In summary, several patterns of strategic change can occur in a company. These involve changes to the company's industry of origination, changes to the center of gravity of the company, or some combination of the two. For some of the strategic changes there are appropriate organizations and measures of their economic performance.

STRATEGY, ORGANIZATION, AND PERFORMANCE

For a number of years now, studies have been made of strategy and structure of the *Fortune* 500. Most of these were conducted by the Harvard Business School. These studies were reviewed in previous work (Galbraith and Nathanson, 1978). The current view is illustrated in Table 1. If one samples the *Fortune* 500 and categorizes them by strategy and structure, the following relationships hold.

TABLE 1

STRATEGY	STRUCTURE
Single business	Functional
Vertical by-products	Functional with P&Ls
Related businesses	Divisional
Linked businesses	Mixed structures
Unrelated businesses	Holding company

One can still find organizations staying in their same original business. Such a single business is Wrigley Chewing Gum. These organizations are run by centralized functional organizations. The next strategic type is the vertically integrated by-product seller. Again, these companies have some diversification but remain committed to their industry and center of gravity. The companies are also functional, but the sequential stages are often operated as profit and loss divisions. The companies are usually quite centralized and run by collegial management groups. The profit centers are not true ones in being independent to run their own businesses. These are almost all upstream companies.

The related businesses are those that move into new industries at their center of gravity. Usually these are downstream companies. They adopt the decentralized profit center divisions. However, the divisions are not completely decentralized. There are usually strong corporate staffs and some centralized marketing, manufacturing, and R&D. There may be several thousand people on the corporate payroll.

The clearest contrast to the related diversifier is the unrelated business company. These companies enter a variety of businesses at several centers of gravity. The organization they adopt is the very decentralized holding company. Their outstanding feature is the small corporate staff. Depending on their size, the numbers range between fifty and two hundred. Usually these are support staffs. All of the marketing, manufacturing, and R&D is decentralized to the divisions. Group executives have no staffs and are generally corporate oriented.

The linked companies are neither of these extremes. Often linked forms are transitory. The organizations that they utilize are usually mixed forms that are not easily classified. Some divisions are autonomous, while others are managed out of the corporate HQ. Still others have strong group executives with group staffs. Some work has been done on classifying these structures (Allen, 1978).

There has been virtually no work done on center-of-gravity changes and their changes in structure. Likewise, there has been nothing done on comparisons for economic performance. But for the other categories and structures, there is emerging some good data on relative economic performance.

The studies of economic performance have compared the various strategic patterns and the concept of fit between strategy and organization. Both sets of results have organization design implications. The economic studies use return on equity as the performance measure. If one compares the strategic categories listed in Table 1, there are distinct performance differences. The high performers are consistently the related diversifiers (Rumelt, 1974; Galbraith and Nathanson, 1978; Nathanson and Cassano, 1982; Bettis, 1981; Rumelt, 1982). There are several explanations for this performance difference. One explanation is that the related diversifiers are all downstream companies in businesses with high R&D and advertising expenditures. These businesses have higher margins and returns than other businesses. Thus, it may not be the strategy but the businesses the relateds happen to be in. However, if the unrelateds are good acquirers, why do they not enter the high-return businesses?

The other explanation is that the relateds learn a set of core skills and design an organization to perform at a particular center of gravity. Then, when they diversify, they take on the task of learning a new business, but at the same center of gravity. Therefore, they get a diversified portfolio of businesses but each with a system of management and an organization that is understood by everyone. The management understands the business and is not spread thin.

The unrelateds, however, have to learn new industries and also how to operate to a different center of gravity. This latter change is the most difficult to accomplish. One upstream company diversified via acquisition into downstream companies. It consistently encountered control troubles. It instituted a capital appropriation process for each investment of $50,000 or more. It still had problems, however. The retail division opened a couple of stores with leases for $40,000. It didn't use the capital process. The company got blindsided because the stores required $40 million in working capital for inventory and receivables. Thus, the management systems did not fit the new downstream business. It appears that organizational fit makes a difference. . . .

One additional piece of evidence results from the studies of economic performance. This result is that the poorest performer of the strategic categories is the vertically integrated by-product seller. Recall these companies are all upstream, raw material, and primary manufacturers. They make up a good portion of "Smokestack America." In some respects, these companies made their money early in the century, and their value added is shifting to lesser developed countries in the natural course of industrial development. However, what is significant here is their inability to change. It is no secret to anyone that they have been underperformers, yet they have continued to put money back into the same business.

My explanation revolves around the center of gravity. These previously successful companies put together an organization that fit their industry and stage. When the industry declined, they were unable to change as well as the downstream companies. The reason is that upstream companies were functional organizations with few general managers. Their resource allocation was within a single business, not across multiple products. The management skill is partly technological know-how. This technology does not transfer across industries at the primary manufacturing center of gravity. The knowledge of paper making does not help very much in glass making. Yet both might be combined in a package company. Also, the capital intensity of these industries limits the diversification. Usually one industry must be chosen and capital invested to be the low-cost producer. So there are a number of reasons why these companies have been notoriously poor diversifiers.

In addition, it appears to be very difficult to change centers of gravity no matter where an organization is along the industry chain. The reason is that a center of gravity shift requires a dismantling of the current power structure, rejection of parts of the old culture, and establishing all new management systems. The related diversification works for exactly the opposite reasons. They can move into new businesses with minimal change to the power structure and accepted ways of doing things. Changes in the center of gravity usually occur by new start-ups at a new center of gravity rather than a shift in the center of established firms. . . .

There are some exceptions that prove the rule. Some organizations have shifted from upstream commodity producers to downstream product producers and consumer product firms. General Mills moved from a flour miller to a related diversified provider of products for the homemaker. Over a long period of time they shifted downstream into consumer food products from their cake mix product beginnings. From there, they diversified into related areas after selling off the milling operations, the old core of the company. . . . [In these cases], however, new management was brought in and acquisition and divestment used to make the transition. So, even though vestiges of the old name remain, these are substantially different companies. . . .

The vast majority of our research has examined one kind of strategic change—diversification. The far more difficult one, the change in center of gravity, has received far less [attention]. For the most part, the concept is difficult to measure and not publicly reported like the number of industries in which a company operates. Case studies will have to be used. But there is a need for more systematic knowledge around this kind of strategic change.

READING 8.3

The Design of New Organizational Forms* BY JENNIFER HERBER, JITENDRA V. SINGH, AND MICHAEL USEEM

. . . One of the more hallowed management truisms is that organizations should adapt to changing environmental conditions. But successful organizations frequently have trouble responding to discontinuous, competence-destroying change such as the advent of the Internet. Dominant players often fail to adapt because it means dismantling the very organizations that have led to their success. They had mastered current technologies and customer needs, but by virtue of having established that expertise and focus they had also become ill prepared to face innovative technologies and new customers. Past adaptations become inertial constraints, leading to a kind of "competency trap." The organizational architectures that companies have built to propel their success can become as outmoded as feudal kingdoms in an age of democracy.

Yet we have entered an era of intense experimentation with new organizational forms, as innovative technologies have created radically different opportunities for doing business. As a result, company architectures are changing, reporting relations are flattening, work designs are empowering, and markets are opening. We examine new organizational forms that are emerging in response to the discontinuous technological breaks of recent years. We seek to understand what makes these organizational forms distinctive and how they provide competitive advantage. . . .

Experimenting managers have generally designed these new forms to capture two capabilities viewed as critical for success in environments of discontinuous technological change. The first capability is an effective balancing [of] exploration and exploitation. When a company focuses entirely on the exploitation of its current competitive advantages, it certainly becomes better at what it is doing well, but at the same time it becomes vulnerable to abrupt changes that negate the value of what it does best. On the other hand, if a firm focuses solely on exploration of future capabilities, it risks near-term failure for lack of tangible results. A balance, then, of both building the future and exploiting the past is seen as essential. The second capability is a recombination of established competencies. Organizations that take what they already do well and create fresh blends can capitalize on existing competencies without being locked into them.

Distinctive organizational forms are defined by unique reconfigurations of six elements:

1. *Organizational goals* are the firm's broad objectives and performance-related outcomes ranging from market share and customer satisfaction to total shareholder return. They implicitly contain time frames for measuring the extent to which they are achieved. A company goal, for instance, might be to establish the dominant market share in an emerging area over the next three years, much as Amazon.com has achieved in online bookselling.
2. *Strategies* concern intended and emergent patterns of long-term methods for achieving goals at both the firm and business unit levels.
3. *Authority relations* include organizational architecture and reporting structures.
4. *Technologies* refer to information, communication, and production methods.
5. *Markets* include relationships with customers, suppliers, partners, and competitors.
6. *Processes* refer to dynamic links among these elements, such as recruitment, budgeting, compensation, and performance evaluation.

. . . Among the emerging forms, we see six relatively different and potentially enduring organizational models. They are not necessarily mutually exclusive, with some companies simultaneously building two or more at the same time. Nor are the boundaries between them precisely defined. Still, they are coming to represent relatively distinct responses to emerging technologies of production, communication, and distribution. The six new organizational forms are (1) virtual

*Excerpted from Jennifer Herber, Jitendra V. Singh, and Michael Useem, "The Design of New Organizational Forms" in *Wharton on Managing Emerging Technologies*, 2000, pp. 376–392.

organization, (2) network organization, (3) spin-out organization, (4) ambidextrous organization, (5) front-back organization, and (6) sense-and-respond organization.

VIRTUAL ORGANIZATION

The virtual form is an organization in which employees, suppliers, and customers are geographically dispersed but united by technology. A network of distributed organizational units and individuals act in concert to serve widely scattered customers. New information technologies have driven the rise of this form, as customers and companies come to utilize high-speed, broadband communication systems to buy and sell products and services anywhere rather than at a point of direct contact in a store or office. These technologies have also created mechanisms for inexpensively weaving together far-flung organizations and operations. The virtual organization is largely boundary-less, with tasks performed, suppliers accessed, and products delivered in hundreds if not thousands of widely strewn physical locations. Headquarters may be little more than the chief executive's home computer and an Internet connection.

The virtual form minimizes asset commitments, resulting in greater flexibility, lower costs, and consequentially, faster growth. Its application and value can be well seen in the experience of Dell Computer Corporation. Founded in 1984, Dell seized on emergent technologies and information management to integrate supplier partnership, mass customization, and just-in-time manufacturing for fast and precise responsiveness to fast-evolving customer demand. It introduced virtual organizational forms across the entire value chain, from suppliers to manufacturers to customers.

The backbone of Dell's exceptional productivity, efficiency, and mass customization has been its company-wide coordination across businesses, customers, and suppliers. In maintaining real-time links with its suppliers, for instance, Dell could provide the kind of detailed data that would allow them to reduce inventory, enhance speed, and improve logistics. The sharing of information with the suppliers enhanced their incentives to collaborate. And Dell's use of electronic logs rather than written forms reduced the cost for many functions ranging from order taking to quality inspection. The technology thus enabled Dell to benefit from a de facto vertical integration without the liabilities and inflexibilities of owning the supply chain.

Dell Computer's virtual linkage with customers via Internet and voice channels also permitted Dell to circumvent traditional dealership channels and thereby create a sustainable competitive advantage of lower selling cost and higher customer responsiveness. By the late 1990s, Dell had become the world's second largest computer maker, with 30,000 employees, annual revenues of $21 billion, and $30 million in daily Internet sales.

Electronic technologies have been used by other companies to push the limits of virtual relationships. In such relationships, products never appear in showrooms, customers never meet salespeople, and dollars never physically change hands. Amazon.com, CDNow, and thousands of kindred e-commerce start-ups have mastered the use of cyber catalogs in place of storefronts, credit cards instead of cash, and e-mail confirmations in place of paper receipts.

Virtual companies have also learned to exploit the unique potential of the two-way medium through which they both sell and learn. They have created more enduring and more customized relations with individual customers and they have constructed communities among customers. . . .

Yet this flexibility of the virtual organizational form created its own new set of challenges, especially in the area of authority relations. The ties of communication technologies were strong enough that it no longer mattered if employees sat next to each other or even nearby. They could as well work from home offices miles away or even business offices a continent removed. They need not work full-time or from 9 to 5 either. But in that lessening of physical proximity and contact frequency, the traditional role of supervisors would change from overseeing work processes to job outcomes, from exercising authority over tasks to delegating responsibility for results. Supervisors would also no longer stand at the center of communication and coordination since the increasing horizontal collaboration negated the necessity of going up the organization to obtain downward cooperation in other operations. An enduring by-product has been for bosses to become less central in giving feedback and appraising performance—and peers to become more central. Vertical organization gives way to lateral relations. . . .

The virtual organizational form brings many advantages to companies that are themselves building and marketing emerging technologies. This form serves as a magnet for attracting creative and energetic employees who eschew bureaucracy and favor sovereignty. This advantage can turn to disadvantage, however, when pushing the emerging technologies to their next stage of development depends on a critical mass of creative people working intensively together. The need for geographic proximity partially explains why even the most technologically advanced industries—which would seemingly lend themselves best to virtual forms—are often geographically concentrated, as seen in computer making in Silicon Valley and telecommunication services in Northern Virginia.

NETWORK ORGANIZATION

The network form is based on an organized set of relationships among autonomous or semi-autonomous work units for delivering a complete product or service to a customer. Network forms are found both inside companies and across sets of companies.

EXTERNAL NETWORK FORM

External networks among companies can be viewed as outsourcing in the extreme. At the core are organizations that have chosen to concentrate on a particular competence or specific slice of the value chain. The central organizations create symbiotic ties among a host of legally independent entities to aggregate the necessary skills, assembly, and services. They rely on other entities from suppliers and distributors to complete the value chain in the delivery of a complete product or service.

Some external networks can be described as *federated* in that a set of loosely affiliated firms work relatively autonomously but nonetheless engage in mutual monitoring and control of one another. Other external networks can be viewed more as evanescent *organizational webs* in which constellations of players coalesce around an emerging business opportunity and dissipate just as rapidly once it runs its course. Still another subspecies is the *strategic partnership* in which companies form cooperative deals, often across continents, with suppliers to achieve lowest-cost manufacturing, or collaborate with research companies worldwide to acquire highest-quality innovation.

External networks are stitched together with a variety of methods, ranging from joint ventures and formal partnerships to franchising systems and research consortia. Whatever the specific type of external network, they transform the competitive fray to one of rivalries between constellations of collaborating enterprises.

The textile industry in Prato, Italy, during the 1980s exemplifies the external network. Here, tiny firms came to specialize in a particular niche of the industry in response to customer demand for lower prices and greater variety. No single company dominated, and independent master brokers—*impannatores*—served as the customer interface, taking orders that far exceeded the capacity of any one producer. They divided and dispatched the orders to hundreds of producers over which they held no formal authority. The region's 15,000 independent firms, with an average of just five employees each, collectively produced what would ordinarily have only been available from a few massive companies. Though these miniature producers competed vigorously against one another, they also established strong cooperatives for tasks where economies of scale and joint practices proved . . . lucrative. . . .

The external network organizational form brings distinctive authority and market relations, relying on lateral communication instead of vertical clout to achieve coordination. . . .

INTERNAL NETWORK FORM

The internal network structure builds on much the same premise that undergirds the external network—aligned but loose relations among a set of operations can often beat a hierarchy of control among the operations—but here the premise is applied inside the firm. Strategic business units, microenterprises, and autonomous work teams are the building blocks, and their work is coordinated and disciplined but rarely directed by the top of the pyramid. Headquarters sets global strategy, allocates assets, and monitors results, but is otherwise little concerned with daily operations. Top executives establish a cultural esprit and common mindset across the operating units and teams, and then the upper echelon leaves it almost entirely to each of the operations to devise its own methods for making and selling.

An exemplary case is the Zurich-based ABB, Asea Brown Boveri, which has networked its many fully owned subsidiaries and business units to an extreme. This engineering and technology company employed 200,000 people in more than 100 countries during the late 1990s, and in 1998 it earned $2 billion on $31 billion in revenue. Yet its home office housed fewer than 100 managers, and virtually all of its decisions were centered in 1,300 operating units and 5,000 profit centers around the world. Described as "obsessively decentralized," the ABB pyramid is about as flat as they come, with a single layer of management between top executives and field managers. The field managers as a result have the autonomy to do what they want so long as their decisions are aligned with the firm's goals. . . .

Both external and internal network organization forms benefit from the adaptive flexibility that comes with their built-in modularity. Whether inside a company or across a lattice of companies, units can be opened, moved, or closed, and each is far closer to its respective customers than anybody else in the operation. . . .

This organizational form may be particularly useful in industries with fast-moving technological change and rapidly emergent new ways of producing and selling. When uncertainty is high, risk is great, and time is punishing, the modularity of the network form provides for quick response. The customer focus of the network form provides for nuanced response. And the local autonomy of the network form provides for a creative response.

SPIN-OUT ORGANIZATION

The spin-out organizational form is built when companies establish fresh entities inside from new business concepts and then send them off at least partially on their own. The parent organization, sometimes resembling a holding company, serves as venture capitalist, protective incubator, and proud mentor, but the successful units are sooner or later pushed out of the nest. The parent may relinquish all ownership and control, or it may choose to retain a 20, 50, or 70 percent stake. Whatever the lingering tether, the spin-out is left largely to its own devices to sink or swim.

During the spin-out process, authority relations between the company and business unit evolve from parental control to adult independence. The goals of the spin-out will diverge from the parent's objectives once the offspring is legally separate. Still, gentle parental advice is frequently continued, and some offspring continue to make good use of the parent's accounting, legal, and investment functions.

. . .Thermo Electron has long served as an "innovation incubator" for thermodynamic, medical, and technology-related products for well-defined market niches. . . .Founded in 1956, the company in 1982 began "spinning out" promising technologies and services by offering minority shares in newly created subsidiaries to the public. To ensure that its managers of the spin-outs continued to produce great returns even when they could no longer be required to do so, Thermo Electron created highly leveraged incentive packages. Given a chance to behave like an entrepreneur and be rewarded for doing so, and with a proven product in hand from the incubation period, spin-out managers have often outperformed the market. So, too, has Thermo Electron, which by 1999 had grown into a $4 billion enterprise with 26,000 employees worldwide. . . .

Spin-outs can . . . constitute an excellent vehicle for not only developing but also commercializing expensive and risky emerging technologies. Because they become legally separate from the corporate parent, they can pursue variant growth strategies, financing objectives, and performance goals, permitting greater responsiveness to fast-changing market conditions and emerging possibilities. They can use stock options to attract and retain talent who might otherwise exit the parent firm for the lack of real wealth incentives. And once the spin-outs are on their own in the market, the joint forces of demanding investors and aggressive competitors impose a financial discipline with an intensity rarely felt inside a large parent.

AMBIDEXTROUS ORGANIZATION

If the spin-out form is designed to take a new venture out of the sometimes inhospitable environment of a large organization, the ambidextrous organizational form creates an environment in which both established and emerging businesses flourish side by side. Some parts of the organization are working on incremental improvements in technologies, others are looking for breakthroughs. The ambidextrous form overcomes the "innovator's dilemma," the conundrum of listening so well to current customers that the company never anticipates radically new technologies that customers have not yet come to appreciate but will eventually demand. This organizational scheme is designed to ensure simultaneous dexterity in both continuous improvement and discontinuous innovation.

With 125,000 employees and sales of $47 billion in 1998, Hewlett-Packard was concerned that the success of existing products would dampen new products because champions of the latter would not have the political clout to obtain funding and attention. The firm thus created an internal consulting group to help its autonomous business units do two things at once. As characterized by Stu Winby, its director of Strategic Change Services, the objective is to improve a business unit's sale of today's technologies, with a focus on raising volumes and lowering costs. But a concurrent objective is to organize part of the same business unit around future technologies, with an emphasis on entrepreneurship and speed to market. The latter's products sometimes compete head on with existing products or even threaten to cannibalize them entirely, and managers of well-established product lines are predictably wary. Still, Hewlett-Packard's experience confirms that ways can be found to keep both agendas successfully working under the same roof.

The ambidextrous form can be especially useful for fostering emerging technologies without abandoning the old. Doing both at the same time runs the risk of sowing conflict, but when well orchestrated, this form helps reconcile otherwise opposed agendas. A critical feature is limiting their separation: Those responsible for traditional products are brought into active dialogue with those at the forefront of new ideas. Lateral linkages rather than segregated operations become important here for mutual stimulation. And when well incentivized to share rather than hoard knowledge, to communicate rather than isolate, both sides contribute more to the company's ultimate objectives and devote less energy to thwarting the other party.

FRONT-BACK ORGANIZATION

The front-back organizational form is organized around customers in the front, with all company functions placed at the back to serve the front. The purpose is to provide customers with fast, responsive, and customized solutions.

One type of front-back form is an inverted organization in which all line executives, systems, and support staff in effect work for the front-line person, allowing him or her to concentrate the company's capabilities on satisfying the customer. With the firm's systems and procedures so focused, the front-line person commands the resources to respond swiftly and precisely to evolving customer needs. The organization chart is turned upside down, with customers on top, customer-contact people next, and the rest below.

The front-back form can be seen in many health maintenance organizations. They still divide medical practices into specialties such as radiology, anesthesiology, and cardiology, but many now also designate a primary care provider to coordinate the back-end functions to deliver a complete health package to the patient.

A second variant of the front-back form is a hybrid of vertical and horizontal process teams. Here, companies are divided into units with vertical reporting lines, but they also establish formal means for transcending vertical barriers when they get in the way. Sometimes front-back companies are focused on products, in other cases on geography or distribution channels. However configured, they come to resemble a "centerless corporation" in which resources are directed at whatever part is most in frontal contact with customers.

The hybrid model with horizontal work that transects vertical reporting lines can be found in many management consulting firms. Partners and associates at McKinsey & Company, Andersen Consulting, and kindred companies are organized into specialized practices, such as strategy, information, and change, but they also create temporary client teams drawn from several of the practices. Team leaders have command over the resources of the specialized practices for the duration of the engagement to ensure that their clients receive the right combination of technical expertise to solve the problems they face. . . .

Front-back organizations differ from traditional forms most starkly in their reconfigured authority relations. Health maintenance organizations, for example, realign incentives to foster cooperation instead of adversarial relationships among physicians, health workers, and medical plans. . . .

SENSE-AND-RESPOND ORGANIZATION

The sense-and-respond organizational form is focused even more intensely on identifying emerging customer needs. While the front-back form develops a distinctive relationship with customers, the sense-and-respond form orients the entire organization around meeting ever-changing customer demands. The working premise is that unpredictable change is inevitable in the marketplace, and the challenge is to ready the organization to capitalize on whatever discontinuity confronts it.

Adaptability is among the foremost capacities of sense-and-respond firms. They tend to plan from the bottom up with few predetermined long-term plans, reacting almost daily to market movements. They occupy a middle ground between a strategy of "control your own destiny" and a strategy of "let your destiny happen to you." One variation of this form is what has been termed a "MegaStrategic Business Entity," found among giant, diversified companies that continuously change to stay with their same customers for years.

Westpac Banking Corporation, an Australian-based firm with 31,000 employees and $6 billion in revenue in 1998, illustrates the sense-and-respond form. For a decade it has worked as a collection of capabilities and assets managed to adapt to customer requests. It is not especially efficient at processing, but its modularity ensures that it gathers detailed information from customers and responds with precisely what each needs. It sets as its main objective continuously responding to customers and anticipating their coming needs. Authority relations necessarily are more fluid to ensure flexible response to customer requests. . . .

CONCLUSIONS

. . . For managers asking which of the six organizational forms holds greatest promise for their firm, the choice is a contingent one. As summarized in Table 1, the selection depends on the unique configuration of a company's goals and authority relations on the one hand, and the nature of its changing technologies and markets on the other. When a firm's technologies and markets are relatively fresh but its goals and authority relationships are not, the ambidextrous form may be most appropriate. When an enterprise's goals and authority relations are new but its technologies and markets are less so, the spin-out form may be most suited. When a company is facing change in both areas, the sense-and-respond form may well be more appropriate.

TABLE 1
ORGANIZATIONAL FORMS AND CHANGING ENVIRONMENTS

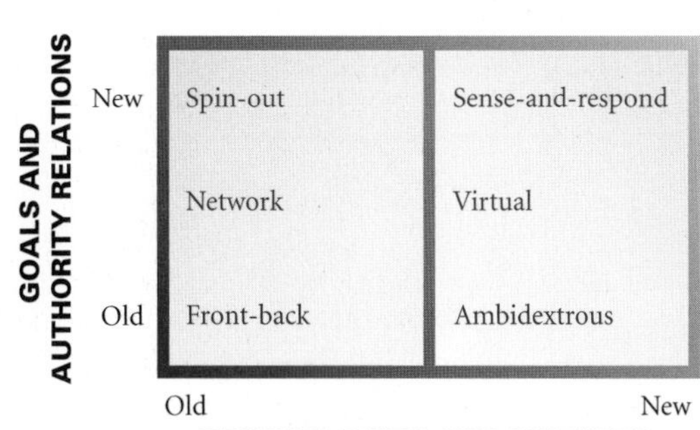

Organizations must look carefully at their competitive environments and internal capacities in selecting the right organizational form. The six forms described here represent distinctive models, but hybrids can be found among each and some companies have simultaneously adopted two or more at the same time. The six forms can best be seen as a starting point for thinking about a form that is uniquely tailored to meet the specific challenges facing a company. Because those challenges are so varied, we are likely to see a host of organizational forms that borrow no model intact and custom-build what will be needed to develop, manage, use, and sell emerging technologies during the years ahead.

CHAPTER 9

Technology

Technology is a key factor in almost any conceivable strategy process today. So, in a sense, the choice of readings to include was vast. We settled on three to give a flavor of how technology can shape strategy (and, it should be noted, various readings in other chapters return to technology themes).

New technologies often lead to completely new strategies. Not surprisingly, this can be very exciting for managers who are looking for the "killer application." Sometimes, however, the reality of new technologies is more complicated than the headlines. Lampel and Mintzberg look at "customization," an old practice made popular by revolutionary developments in data processing and communication technologies. Many expect customization to completely transform the relationship between companies and their customers. But as Lampel and Mintzberg show, the new technologies create more strategic choice, rather than across-the-board revolution. After laying out a framework to think about what customization really means, they conclude that most of what is called customization, and especially so-called "mass customization," actually sits at a midpoint between pure customization and pure standardization. New technologies allow companies to create strategies that blend pure customization and pure standardization, or go exclusively for one or the other. It does not mean that strategies will switch from one end of the spectrum, that is, standardization, to pure customization.

To some extent, the second reading, by George Day and Paul Schoemaker of the Wharton School of Business, reinforces the message that technologies allow for new strategies, but do not automatically create them. Day and Schoemaker lay out the pitfalls to be avoided in emerging technologies. They examine what may be called the "rational conservatism" of most firms in the face of new technologies. It is rational to stick to what you know best and wait for the new technology to be proven in the marketplace. It is rational to commit to a technology if it is promising, but only up to a point. And it is rational to throw in the towel if the technology fails to live up to its early promise. These are precisely the reasons why so many established and ostensibly well-managed companies lose their business to new technologies. The remedy, these authors suggest, is for companies to be mindful of the paradoxical nature of new technologies and to pay attention to information from the periphery of one's business, to challenge deep-rooted assumptions, to experiment and learn, and to remain flexible in the face of new technological options.

The third reading is by Mark W. Johnson, senior partner in Innosight, a management consulting firm, Clayton M. Christensen, professor at Harvard Business School, and Henning Kagermann, former chairman of SAP AG. These authors look at the increasingly popular concept of the "business model." The term "business model" is a child of the dot.com boom of the 1990s. For many scholars the success of companies such as Amazon and eBay can be traced to visionary entrepreneurs who distilled complex operations into simple building blocks, and then used the Internet to reconfigure these building blocks. Because these entrepreneurs often spoke of their "business models," the term gained wide currency with practitioners and later with scholars. Unfortunately, the popularity of the concept also led to much confusion about what the term meant. Johnson, Christensen, and Kagermann put forward a clear definition of "business models." They show that in principle all companies have some sort of business model. But they also show that understanding the company's business model is a crucial first step toward successfully reinventing it.

USING THE CASE STUDIES

Strategy is often focused on pioneering technologically innovative products. Apple is a company created by new technology. It also has to contend with the threat of rapidly changing technology. The fluctuating fortunes of many high-technology firms are discussed by Day and Schoemaker in their reading "Avoiding the Pitfalls of Emerging Technologies." Tiscali (UK) deals with an Internet provider that struggles to catch up with competitors that can bundle together more services. Wipro, by contrast, looks at a company that has built a global strategy providing technology consulting services to firms such as Tiscali.

For Wipro the pitfalls of emerging strategy are an opportunity rather than a threat. Wipro customizes solutions for clients, but only up to a point. Netflix, on the other hand, lets the customer do its own customization—taking advantage of the new capabilities offered by the Internet. In all these cases, we see how the flexibility of new technologies allows companies to craft a strategy that blends customization and standardization along the range of options described by Lampel and Mintzberg.

READING 9.1

Customizing Customization* BY JOSEPH LAMPEL AND HENRY MINTZBERG

The history of U.S. business during the past 100 years has been a story of mass production and mass distribution of standardized goods. Scholars and practitioners who examined the economic landscape have generally been drawn to large corporations that built their fortunes by transforming fragmented and heterogeneous markets into unified industries. At the heart of this transformation were strategies based on standardization: standardization of taste that allowed for standardized design, standardization of design that allowed for mechanized mass production, and a resulting standardization of products that allowed for mass distribution.

Recently, a growing number of economists and management scholars have declared that this era is over. Numerous books and articles have posited that we are witnessing the dawn of a new age of customization, an age in which new technologies, increased competition, and more assertive customers are leading firms toward customization of their products and services. Not surprisingly, firms that have adopted customization strategies have attracted considerable attention as models of what is expected to become commonplace in the near future.

We begin by describing these two logics. We then argue that this conceptual polarization, which took firm root in the theory and practice of management, led management thinkers to ignore strategies that combine these logics. Put simply, this view itself represents an inappropriate standardization of management theory—or, more exactly, continuation of the standardization mentality that has long pervaded such theory. Since the days of Frederick Taylor, the notion that managers should single-mindedly pursue the "one best way" has led management writers to seize on one solution or another (or, more often, one solution and *then* another) as the best practice. Indeed, the enthusiasm for customization today was paralleled by an even greater enthusiasm for standardization many years ago.

*Excerpted from "Customizing Customization," Joseph Lampel and Henry Mintzberg, *Sloan Management Review*, Fall 1996, Conclusions Vol. 38(1), 21–30.

What has been ignored in all this is that customization and standardization do not define alternative models of strategic action but, rather, poles of a continuum of real-world strategies. By promoting customization as the answer to what ails many organizations, we may be replacing one extreme with another. Managers need to locate their strategies along the continuum, and the role of management writers is to provide the conceptual tools to make this easier.

It is not an accident of history that customization is now promoted with the same enthusiasm with which standardization was promoted almost a century ago. Today's customization movement is a reaction to significant economic and technological forces, much as the standardization movement was in its time. But these developments must be viewed with a clear perspective. Therefore, we begin by reviewing how the standardization and customization distinction emerged in the first place.

THE LOGIC OF AGGREGATION

Economic theory takes a bird's-eye view of markets. It strips them of their complexity and variability, aggregating firms and individuals into two groups: buyers and sellers. In contrast, management theory, especially in strategy, starts with the relationships of specific firms to their environments. Sellers are therefore disaggregated. Customers, however, continue to be viewed collectively as a group (or a set of segmented groups) that shares common characteristics. This has led managers and researchers alike to emphasize the advantage of economies of scale in every part of the value chain, from development to production to distribution, which in turn has promoted a focus on industries in which customers' shared characteristics are easily established. Thus, in his 1980 book, Porter draws on 196 industries to illustrate his ideas. By our count, 176 of these have been dominated by the logic of aggregation, while only 20 can be considered to have tilted toward that of disaggregation.

The following maxims capture the basic imperative of the logic of aggregation: (1) reduce the impact of customers' variability on internal operations, (2) do so by identifying general product and customer categories, and then (3) simplify and streamline interactions with the customer. Over time, these coalesced into a well-defined set of strategies that promoted the advantages of scale economies and standardization with particular success.

By 1929, a survey of eighty-four product classes showed a reduction in variety at times amounting to 98 percent of its 1921 level. For example, the number of bed blanket sizes dropped from seventy-eight to twelve; hospital beds that had come in thirty-three different sizes were all standardized to a single size by 1929. . . . As one manager explained, "Over a period of years of experience with builders and architects, as well as homeowners, we have found that the five-foot tub is on the average an adequate size bathtub for the average size person."

The practical lessons learned during this period were subsequently incorporated into the mindset of the newly emerging management "profession." When the study of business became a scholarly pursuit at the turn of the century, the mass production and mass distribution firm was singled out as the most rational approach to gaining competitive advantage. Management thinkers counseled against the proliferation of products, and even such an influential writer as Lyndall Urwick warned that the temptation to respond to customers' demands could be ruinous: "To allow the individual idiosyncrasies of a wide range of customers to drive administration away from the principles on which it can manufacture most economically is suicidal—the kind of good intention with which the road to hell or bankruptcy is proverbially paved."

In the mid-1950s, there began a gradual move away from the extreme forms of aggregation, under the label of "market segmentation." Encouraged by automation in manufacturing as well as the shift from rail to road in transportation and changes in the mass media, companies began to target specific groups of consumers. Nevertheless, the logic remained the same, for this was not a movement toward serious customization so much as toward the aggregation of the submarket or the market class. Indeed, the mass market in many industries had reached such a large scale that segmentation posed few real dangers to efficiency in production if not strictly in distribution.

THE LOGIC OF INDIVIDUALIZATION

Although the logic of aggregation became dominant in many industries, there remained areas of economic activity where it failed to take over. Obvious examples are certain traditional crafts, such as personal tailoring, fine jewelry making, fine restaurant cooking, and grinding prescription eyeglass lenses. More significant, perhaps, is the capital goods sector, where products continue to be designed to customer specifications and manufactured in job-shop facilities. In industries such as pulp and paper machinery, steam turbines, commercial aircraft, flight simulators, and construction, the individual customer can be deeply involved in every aspect of the transaction and expects key product decisions to be negotiated jointly.

More recently, of course, there has been a move to greater customization in a wide variety of industries, including services. In some cases, the change has been highly visible. The standard telephone service of the past has given way to a varied menu of features from which customers may select their own preferred combination.

In industries where the logic of individualization is pervasive, different forms of marketing, production, and product development dominate. In marketing, firms seek to develop a direct relationship with the individual customer. In production, products can be "made to order" or "tailor made." And since products can be designed for particular customers, research and design can lose much of their isolation from the marketplace. In effect, the orientation is toward the management of each transaction. But, as we shall see, there are industries where product, process, and transaction vary markedly in their degree of customization.

BETWEEN AGGREGATION AND INDIVIDUALIZATION: A CONTINUUM OF STRATEGIES

Although pure aggregation and pure individualization are perceived as opposing logics, this influence has not led to the emergence of two distinct groups of strategies. Instead, we find a continuum of strategies, depending on which functions lean to standardization and which to customization. In the manufacturing firm, to take a common example, production managers often see aggregation as the best way to increase efficiency, whereas sales managers often consider individualization as the surest approach to increase sales. It is perhaps not a coincidence that the term *customer* looms large in sales managers' vocabularies, while production managers prefer to speak of outputs and schedules.

But the best solution is not necessarily a compromise. In just the operating processes, some firms tilt one way or the other because of the needs of the customers they choose to serve, while others favor intermediate positions. The latter reflect an organization's ability to customize partway back in its value chain, while retaining standardization for the rest. Since the cost of customization tends to increase in proportion to the number of product changes, it makes sense to customize the downstream functions first. Firms may offer customers special delivery services or individualized financing, while refusing to allow changes in production. Or, beyond this, they may be prepared to assemble on demand, according to customers' requests, while refusing to modify a product's core design and the standardized fabrication of its parts.

Thus value chain customization begins with the downstream activities, closest to the marketplace, and may then spread upstream. Standardization, in contrast, begins upstream, with fundamental design, and then progressively embraces fabrication, assembly, and distribution. These two approaches give rise to the continuum of strategies based on standardization and customization that we introduce here.

We develop this continuum for a manufacturing firm with four stages in its value chain: design, fabrication, assembly, and distribution. These refer, respectively, to the extent to which the firm conceives the product initially with regard to a single customer's needs, constructs and then assembles the product with regard to those needs, and distributes it individually to the single customer (as opposed to selling it generically, as in "over the counter"). Stepping customization back one notch at a time along this chain gives rise to five different strategies (see Figure 1):

- *Pure Standardization.* Ford Motor Company's strategy during the era of the Model T was the quintessential example of pure standardization—any color so long as it was black. This

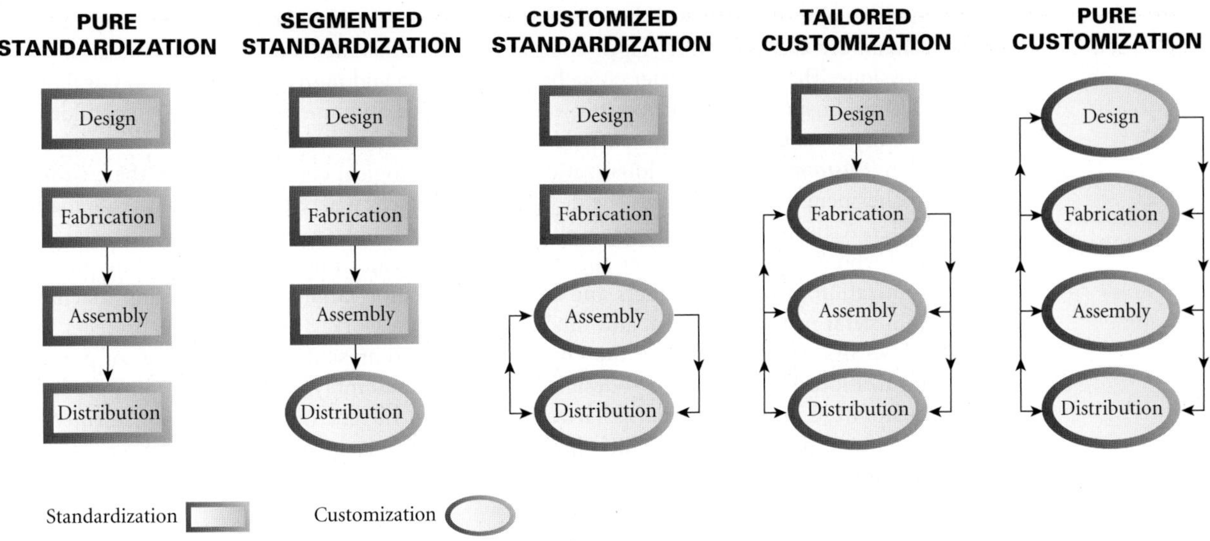

FIGURE 1 A CONTINUUM OF STRATEGIES

strategy is based on a "dominant design" targeted to the broadest possible group of buyers, produced on as large a scale as possible, and then distributed commonly to all. Under such a strategy of pure standardization, there are no distinctions between different customers. The buyer has to adapt or else switch to another product. He or she has no direct influence over design, production, or even distribution decisions. The entire organization is geared to pushing the product from one stage to the next, beginning with design and ending in the marketplace.

- *Segmented Standardization.* The proliferation of cereal brands and the variety of automobiles that followed the Model T are examples of segmented standardization. Firms respond to the needs of different clusters of buyers, but each cluster remains aggregated. Thus the products offered are standardized within a narrow range of features. A basic design is modified and multiplied to cover various product dimensions but not at the request of individual buyers. Individual choice is thus anticipated but not directly catered to. A segmented standardization strategy therefore increases the choices available to customers without increasing their direct influence over design or production decisions. At most, there may be a somewhat greater tendency to customize the distribution process, for example, in the delivery schedules of major appliances. When pushed to the limit, the segmented standardization strategy results in hyperfine distribution—as in the market for designer lamps, which offers almost limitless variety, but not at the customer's request.
- *Customized Standardization.* Automobile companies that offer the buyer the option of selecting his or her own set of components engage in customized standardization, as do hamburger chains that allow customers to specify their preferences for mustard, ketchup, mayonnaise, tomatoes, and so on. In other words, products are made to order from standardized components. The assembly is thus customized, while the fabrication is not, hence our label of customized standardization, although we might also call this standardized customization, "modularization," or "configuration." Basic design is not customized, and the components are all mass produced for the aggregate market. Each customer thus gets his or her own configuration but constrained by the range of available components. This is sometimes constructed around a central standard core, such as a hamburger or an automobile body.
- *Tailored Customization.* A tailored suit, a rug woven to order, or a birthday cake with your name on it are examples of tailored customization. The company presents a product prototype to a potential buyer and then adapts or tailors it to the individual's wishes or needs. Here customization works backward to the fabrication stage but not to the design stage. Thus the

traditional men's tailor will show the client standard fabrics and cuts that he can adapt to the client—for example, wider lapels than normal or adjustments to accommodate an unusual physique. The client will later come back for a fitting and more tailoring. A good deal of traditional business is conducted this way; for example, in home construction, the builder will modify a standard design for particular customer wishes.

- *Pure Customization.* Individualization reaches its logical conclusion when the customer's wishes penetrate deeply into the design process itself, where the product is truly made to order. Artisans who do this are well known, for example, a jeweler or a residential architect who designs to customer specifications. Of greater impact, perhaps, is the pure customization of major products and services, including large-scale production machinery, industrial instrumentation, and much construction work. So-called "megaprojects," such as NASA's Apollo project or the Olympic Games, represent major instances of pure customization. Here, all stages—design, fabrication, assembly, and distribution—are largely customized. The traditional polarization between buyers and sellers is transformed into a genuine partnership in which both sides are deeply involved in each other's decision making.

TOWARD THE CUSTOMIZATION OF PERSPECTIVES

A flood of recent publications attests to the widespread belief that we are in the midst of a fundamental technological change in manufacturing, communications, distribution, and retailing—a virtual renaissance of customization.

The initial impetus is generally considered to have come from new information, engineering, and manufacturing technologies that have blurred the traditional barriers between batch and mass production, have opened the way to the restoration of individualization in business areas hitherto dominated by the logic of aggregation, and have served to uncouple formerly tight relationships between manufacturing and design. In our opinion, however, these new technologies have not had the effects accorded them, specifically the dramatic shift to customization. Rather, all sorts of situations continue to exist. Indeed, if there is one dominant trend—which, we repeat, must coexist with all kinds of countertrends—it is from both ends of our strategy continuum toward the middle, namely toward the strategy of customized standardization, as a number of our examples show.

The shift from pure or segmented standardization to customized standardization has certainly been most obvious. The effects of computer-aided design and manufacturing have produced striking examples of previously standardized products that can now be customized.

Yet the shift from the other end of the continuum—from pure or tailored customization to that same middle position of customized standardization—while less publicized, may in fact be equally noteworthy and, in fact, driven by the same technologies. The high-rise building that was once uniquely designed may today look like a combination of rather standardized components.

An important consequence of this trend is that, as consumers, we lose flexibility in one area while gaining it in another. And, ironically, we lose individuality as we settle in the middle, on customized standardization. The right to specify mayonnaise on a hamburger or a bigger engine in an automobile may give some individuals more choice, to be sure, but can hardly be described as constituting great freedom, in the marketplace or the body politic. In a sense, we lose choice as we all become categories of generic consumers in an assembly operation.

Our new theory may be about customization, but our thinking remains standardized. Our temptation to standardize concepts is ultimately rooted in the wish to simplify the world and make our frameworks as general as possible. Yet one secret of successful management today, as at the turn of the century, is to customize standard concepts to fit specific applications. After a century in which management writing has been dominated by the search for the standardized solution, isn't it time to customize our concepts too?

READING 9.2

Avoiding the Pitfalls of Emerging Technologies* BY GEORGE S. DAY AND PAUL J. H. SCHOEMAKER

Emerging technologies**—such as gene therapy, interactivity and electronic commerce, intelligent sensors, digital imaging, micro-machines, or super conductivity—have the potential to remake entire industries and obsolete established strategies. This is exhilarating for the attackers who can write—and exploit—the new rules of competition, especially if they are not encumbered by an existing business.

For incumbents, however, emerging technologies are often traumatic. Most of these firms feel they must participate in the markets that emerge. Their first reason is defensive, driven by the belief that the newcomers are plotting to use the new functionalities to attack their core markets. Home banking via the Internet is already happening, although no one knows how widely it will be adopted. Yet many bankers are filled with trepidation that the banking industry will be profoundly reshaped (see Bowers and Singer, 1996). Their second reason is the converse of the first: if the emerging technology realizes its potential, it will be too attractive to ignore. However, the odds of large, established incumbents prevailing in these emerging markets are generally poor. . . . In this article, we address the questions of *why* these incumbents have so much difficulty with disruptive technologies, and *how* they can anticipate and overcome their handicaps. . . .

PITFALLS FOR ESTABLISHED FIRMS

The emergence of a challenging technology such as interactive computing or electronic commerce is seldom a surprise. Most managers attend industry conferences, read the trade press, buy consulting studies, talk with customers, and generally monitor developments in their field. The problem is that each of these sources tends to offer conflicting opinions that are reflected in divergent views within the firm. The inherent ambiguity of an emerging technology, and the new markets it creates, coupled with the dominance of traditional thinking frameworks, make established firms vulnerable to four related sequential pitfalls: delayed participation; sticking with the known technology; reluctance to commit fully; and lack of persistence.

PITFALL ONE: DELAYED PARTICIPATION

When faced with high uncertainty, it is tempting and perhaps rational to just "watch and wait." A watching brief may be assigned to a development group or to a consulting team commissioned to study the implications. Whether there is any organizational energy behind these probes depends critically on whether there is a credible champion for the emerging technology within the firm, who offers an alternative paradigm for encoding the weak external signals.

Managers use mental models to simplify and impose order on ambiguous and volatile situations in order to reduce uncertainty to manageable levels. These are sensible adaptations to what the managers have learned from their past experience. (Supporting evidence can be found in Day and Nedungadi (1994).) Managers see what they are prepared to see and either filter out or distort what does not fit their mental maps.

---

*Reprinted with deletions from "Avoiding the Pitfalls of Emerging Technologies," George S. Day and Paul J. H. Schoemaker, *California Management Review*, Vol. 42(2), Winter 2000, 8–33.

**We define emerging technologies as science-based innovations that have the potential to create a new industry or transform an existing one. They include discontinuous innovations derived from radical innovations (e.g., microrobots) as well as more evolutionary technologies formed by the convergence of previously separate research streams (e.g., the fax machine or the Internet).

The mental models of established firms are helpful for incremental innovations within familiar settings, but they become myopic and dysfunctional when applied to unfamiliar situations such as emerging technologies. Using the lens of the familiar may lead to an inappropriate framing of the opportunity. When IBM considered adding the Haloid-Xerox 914 copier in 1958, the main concern was whether the existing electric typewriter sales force could handle the product. The focus was on spreading the selling cost of this division over two product lines, rather than viewing it as an entirely new business for IBM. Since copiers did not look attractive within this narrow frame, the opportunity was rejected.*

Emerging technologies are often framed as suitable only for narrow applications that are not demanded by existing customers, who often favor the current features. It is easy to dismiss such unproven technologies on the grounds that their small markets will not solve the growth needs of large firms. Of course, all large markets were once in an embryonic state with their origins in limited applications. IBM at first did not see the great opportunity in PCs. They were deemed to be entry systems from which buyers would eventually move to mainframes.

Managers tend to compare the first imperfect and costly versions of the emerging technology against the refined versions of the established technology. Of course, pictures from electronic cameras initially lacked the resolution of chemical emulsion film . . . the first electronic watches were bulky and unattractive. . . . This makes it easy to dismiss or underestimate the long-run possibilities.

PITFALL TWO: STICKING WITH THE FAMILIAR

The choice of technology path is inherently difficult because of doubts about whether the technical hurdles can be overcome and which standard or architecture will prevail as the dominant design. The problem is most acute with emerging technologies derived from radical innovations. . . .

The most demanding technology choices are those where there are competing and multiple versions vying to be the dominant design, as occurred historically with the light bulb and more recently with VCRs, modems, and digital wireless telephones. A design dominates when it commands allegiance of the market, so that competitors and suppliers are forced to adopt it if they want to participate in the market. This represents a milestone in the emergence of a technology for it enforces standardization that enables product or network economics to be realized, and it removes a major inhibitor to the wide adoption of the technology.

Often there is fierce competition among firms to set the industry standard around their approach in hopes of gaining an enduring advantage. . . . The stakes may be very large, for if another design or standard prevails, the losers are trapped. Witness the struggle to set standards for HDTV, which encompasses the display technology to be used for television receivers as well as standards for delivery, transmission, and emission of images. (See Hariharan and Prahalad, 1994.)

The odds of picking the familiar but wrong technology path go up when:

- Past success reinforces certain ways of problem solving. Previous choices about appropriate technology solutions may lead the firm to search in areas that are closely related to their current skills and technologies. Thus, their capabilities limit what they can perceive and develop effectively.
- The firm lacks in-house capability to appraise the emerging technology fully. Thus, it may be underestimated or feared. Running a branch banking network is very different from electronic commerce, for example. Consequently, banks may at first shy away from offering electronic services.
- A proprietary mindset gets in the way. The instinct of a large company with a proprietary position in its core market is to find a comparable proprietary position with the new technology that will lock in customers. Such a move makes customers suspicious, however, especially in today's open system environment.

*See Vincent Barabba (1995), *Meeting of the Minds: Creating the Market-Based Enterprise*. IBM's study of the potential for copiers also overlooked the huge demand for the copying of copies, beyond simply copying originals.

Pitfalls one and two are both rooted in two familiar decision-making biases. First, most people have an aversion to ambiguity and risk (Hogarth and Kunreuther, 1989; also Schoemaker, 1991) such that a relatively known prospect usually is preferred over an unknown prospect of equal expected value (Kahneman and Tversky, 1979). Second, a deep-seated preference for the status quo puts the burden of proof on those wanting change. This status quo bias is partly due to our greater sensitivity to losses than to comparable gains (Kahneman et al., 1990).

PITFALL THREE: RELUCTANCE TO FULLY COMMIT

When firms from an established industry attempt to adopt a threatening technology, such as mechanical typewriter firms making electric typewriters or steam locomotive firms making diesel locomotives, they often enter reluctantly with token or staged commitments. One study of 27 established firms found that only four entered aggressively while three didn't participate at all in the threatening technology (Smith and Cooper, 1994). The remaining 20 made a modest initial commitment which gave the entrants from outside the established industry enough time to secure a strong market position. Why are leading firms repeatedly unable or unwilling to make aggressive commitments to an emerging technology once they decide to participate? Five plausible explanations or causes have been proposed.

The first is that managers are rightfully concerned about the possibility of cannibalizing existing profitable products or about resistance from channel partners, and thus they hold back their full support. . . .

Second, there is a paradox in managerial risk taking in that managers tend toward *bold* forecasts on the one hand and toward *timid* choices on the other (Kahneman and Lovallo, 1993). Bold forecasts can stem from overconfidence in general or, more specifically, a limited ability to see arguments contrary to the prediction. Timid choices reflect an inclination toward risk aversion and a tendency to look at choices in isolation (rather than from a portfolio perspective) (Kahneman and Tversky, 1979). So, even if strong beliefs exist about the potential of a new technology, the corresponding actions may be inadequate—as evidenced today by most newspapers' weak responses to the threats and opportunities of the Internet.

Third, when the profit prospects are unclear and appear less attractive than the current business, investments are difficult to justify under strict ROI criteria. The customary decision processes and choice criteria are biased against risky, long-term investments . . . For emerging technologies, the payouts are often staged, with further investments being contingent on reaching key milestones or resolving key uncertainties. . . .

Furthermore, the projected returns from an emerging technology are often worse than those from established or new technologies that address the predictable performance needs of current customers. . . .

Fourth, the attention of managers is primarily focused on their current customers. Thus, they dismiss or overlook new technologies that seem mostly applicable to smaller market segments they do not serve or don't understand (Christensen and Rosenbloom, 1995). This makes them vulnerable to unexpected attacks by outsiders who use the emerging technology as their entry platform. For example, the large copying centers that were the core of Xerox's and Kodak's traditional market failed to appreciate the value of small, slow tabletop copiers. This oversight opened the way for Canon. . . .

Finally, successful organizations are not naturally ambidextrous. They encounter numerous, debilitating problems in balancing the familiar demands of competing in markets presently served with the unfamiliar requirements of an emerging and potentially threatening technology. Within the core business there is usually close alignment among the strategy, capabilities, structure, and culture, which in turn is supported by well-established processes and routines for keeping these elements in balance. This gives the organization a great deal of stability, which must be overcome before the new routines and capabilities needed to compete with the emerging technology can be developed (Tushman and O'Reilly, 1997). Indeed, the more successful the firm, the more closely the elements of strategy, capabilities, structure, and culture will be aligned and the more difficult and time-consuming discontinuous changes become.

These five explanations are not independent; instead they commingle and reinforce each other to impair decision making, erode the necessary enthusiasm of the advocates, and cause firms to hesitate or hedge before making major commitments. These afflictions do not inhibit the new entrants who often sense the opportunity earlier, better comprehend or believe in the benefits of the new technology, and do not have any misleading history or culture to contend with.

PITFALL FOUR: LACK OF PERSISTENCE

Suppose, however, that an established firm has managed to avoid the first three pitfalls and has made significant investments in a newly emerging technology. Will it have the fortitude to stay the course? Large companies typically have little patience for continuing adverse results. Yet, missed forecasts and dashed hopes are commonly experienced during the gestation of new technologies that eventually do succeed. Market demand may not materialize as soon as expected, too many competitors might crowd into the market, or the technology may veer off in a new and unexpected direction. In time, the initial enthusiasm may be replaced with skepticism about when—if ever—the new technology will become a profitable business reality. This trap of weak commitment is the flip side of another well-known trap—the sunk cost fallacy. The irony is that the very firms that are overly committed to their core business (the sunk cost trap) are often too quick to pull the plug on investments in emerging technologies.

Those who truly appreciate the possibilities of the emerging technology and feel enthusiasm for any given new project are often deep in the organization and may have little influence on high-level strategic thinking. Thus, if a company's core business begins to struggle and senior managers are looking for ways to cut costs or reduce assets, the new venture is an easy target. . . . The established firms that do prevail follow a more aggressive path that balances flexibility of posture with sustained commitment and follow through. This path entails four approaches: widening peripheral vision, creating a learning culture, staying flexible in strategic ways, and providing organizational autonomy. . . .

ATTENDING TO SIGNALS FROM THE PERIPHERY

Emerging technologies signal their arrival long before they bloom into full-fledged commercial successes. However, the signal-to-noise ratio is initially low so one has to work hard to appreciate the early indicators. This means looking past the disappointing results, limited functionality, and modest initial applications to anticipate the possibilities. Many signals are available to those who look: other signals can only be seen by the prepared mind. As the philosopher Kant noted, we can only see what we are prepared to see. The winners are those who hear the weak signals and can anticipate and imagine future possibilities faster than the competition. . . .

The weak signals to be captured usually come from the periphery, where new competitors are making inroads, unfamiliar customers are participating in early applications, and unfamiliar technology or business paradigms are used. However, the periphery is very noisy, with many possible emerging technologies that might be relevant. . . .

BUILDING A LEARNING CAPACITY

The diverse sources of information flowing from the periphery create a lot of noise. There will be confusion and immobility rather than insight and action unless this information is absorbed, communicated widely, and discussed intensively so that the full implications are understood. This requires a learning capacity that is characterized by:

- an openness to a diversity of viewpoints within and across organizational units,
- a willingness to challenge deep-seated assumptions of entrenched mental models while facilitating the forgetting of outmoded approaches, and
- continuous experimentation in an organizational climate that encourages and rewards "well-intentioned" failure.

ENCOURAGING OPENNESS TO DIVERSE VIEWPOINTS

The uncertainties surrounding disruptive emerging technologies require thorough debate. The early emphasis should be on encouraging *divergent* opinions about technological solutions, market opportunities, and strategies for participating. As learning evolves, one or multiple views may emerge as a basis for *convergence* toward a few commercializable solutions that can be tested. The tone of this extended debate should be set by senior management through their willingness to bring in outsiders with nontraditional backgrounds, to immerse themselves in the stream of data, and to ask challenging questions. They must be outside their office, having conversations with informed insiders, outside experts, and customers. They must study competitive moves and analogous situations, float ideas, and seek collaborations. This can be done in diverse forums, including team meetings, outside conferences, and electronic bulletin boards. Top-down involvement will only be productive if there is active bottom-up participation. Employees from different levels bring different points of view and expertise, and they are typically closer to market and technology realities. . . . Organizations need a mechanism for coalescing and focusing the ongoing dialogue while reducing the various uncertainties to manageable chunks. Scenario analysis achieves this through a process of collectively envisioning a limited set of plausible futures that are internally consistent and detailed. Each scenario can be used to generate strategic options, evaluate prospective investments, and assess their robustness (Schoemaker, 1991).

CHALLENGE THE PREVAILING MINDSET

Diverse viewpoints will not have an impact on the prevailing mindset if the organization prevents it from absorbing these insights. Expansive thinking about the future is readily subverted by the rigidities and restrictions of the prevailing mental models, industry success formulas, conventional wisdom, and false analogies from the past. The limiting and simplifying operation of deeply embedded mental models raises serious questions about whether even scenario approaches can deal with profoundly disruptive and discontinuous change. The concern is that the scenario-building process anchors on the present—as shaped by the prevailing mindset—and then projects forward to what *might* happen. By contrast, firms that successfully exploit discontinuities may have to separate their thinking from current beliefs and realities to envision what *could be* and then work back to what must be done to ensure this aspired future will be realized. . . .

EXPERIMENT CONTINUALLY

Successful adaptation to the vagaries of emerging technologies requires a willingness to experiment and an openness to learn from the inevitable failures and setbacks. There are several facets to the call for continual experimentation. Sometimes it means a willingness to create a diverse portfolio of technological solutions by endorsing parallel development activities. . . .

Continually experimenting and improvising with a new technology produces insights about the possibilities and limits of the technology, the responses of diverse market segments, and the competitive options that customers consider. Once important uncertainties are resolved, such learning organizations are ready to act. . . .

Experimentation requires a tolerance for failure. The trial-and-error learning that relies on experimentation is quickly subverted if there is a fear-of-failure syndrome. Organizations that reward those who play it safe and blame risk takers for "well-intentioned" failures will quickly discourage learning. The path of learning is marked by serendipity and the knowledge gleaned from careful diagnoses of the possible reasons for failure. . . . It takes concerted leadership to create a more open climate that rewards improvisation and makes learning from failures possible. . . .

MAINTAINING FLEXIBILITY: BALANCING COMMITMENT AND OPTIONS

Investments in emerging technologies present a dilemma. On the one hand there is compelling evidence that long-run winners are often early movers who committed quickly and unequivocally to a technology path. Andy Grove (1996) of Intel argues that it takes all the energy of an organization to pursue one clear and simple strategic aim—especially in the face of aggressive and focused competitors—and that hedging by exploring a number of alternative directions is expensive and dilutes commitment. . . .

On the other hand, there are persuasive arguments that investments in emerging technologies should be viewed as creating a portfolio of options where the commitment of additional resources is subject to attaining defined milestones and resolving key uncertainties. These options are investments that give the investor the right but not the obligation to make further investments. Additional funds are provided only if the project continues to appear promising. . . .

At first glance, commitment seems to be the opposite of flexibility and you may not be able to have it both ways (Ghemawat, 1991). However, only if the commitment is *irreversible* does it directly contravene flexibility. For instance, if you make a commitment to make a cruise voyage and pay the full amount upfront, it may seem that your flexibility has been diminished. However, if you also purchase cancellation insurance (in case of illness or a death in the family) you preserve considerable flexibility to change course when needed. This is the art of options management: it involves creativity, hedging, and an ability to imagine diverse scenarios. The only downside of creating flexibility is that it may reduce the strategic signaling value of making a commitment, which truly requires irreversibility to be credible. . . .

MANAGING REAL OPTIONS

The basic issue is when to make an aggressive commitment that does not have a high risk of failure. Best practice suggests it is desirable in the early stages of exploration of an emerging technology to keep a number of options open by only committing investments in stages, following multiple technology paths, and delaying some projects. Once uncertainty has been reduced to a tolerable level and there is a widespread consensus within the organization on an appropriate technology path that can utilize the firm's internal development capabilities—as in the case with Intel's choice of personal computer over television as the preferred information appliance—then full-scale internal development can begin.

However, what if there are many plausible technology paths, the risks of pursuing one to the exclusion of others are unacceptable, and the firm lacks the necessary internal capabilities?... Ultimately, the optimal approach (ranging from betting the farm to "watch and wait") depends on the choice set a company and its competitors face. Only careful analysis can sort out the best path for any one company guided by its long-term vision.

ORGANIZATIONAL SEPARATION

The culture, mindset, risk-avoidance tendencies, and controls of an existing organization are usually stifling to an embryonic initiative based on an emerging technology. This is why large companies are counseled to set up separate organizations dedicated to pursuing a new endeavor (such as GM's Saturn division, IBM's PC unit, or Roche's Genentech investment). The objective of "cocooning" the new business is to create a boundary that enables the new group to do things differently while still permitting the sharing of resources and ideas with the parent. This also permits separate objectives, tolerance for long development cycles, and continuing cash drains, as well as differentiated measurement criteria so that the performance of managers in the rest of the organization is not jeopardized. Above all, it creates flexibility. . . . (See Bahrami, 1992).

HOW MUCH INDEPENDENCE IS OPTIMAL?

This depends on the magnitude of the technological discontinuity and whether it threatens to erode or obsolete the competencies of the core business, the extent to which the activities and customers of the two businesses are different, and the difference in profitability. The greater the differences, the more important it is that the new business not be evaluated using the lens of the old. For completely new and disruptive technologies both *physical* and *structural* separation may be necessary and involve setting up a separate division that reports to senior management. Even when such a full degree of separation is not warranted, it is still desirable to have separate *funding* and *accounting,* so losses from the new projects are not carried by an established business unit.

The new venture also needs distinct *policies* that match the realities of building a new business. The new venture must be able to attract the best personnel and it must have the latitude to do fast prototyping and probe ill-defined markets while keeping restrictive controls and burdensome overhead to a minimum. They must be exempted from much of the routine planning and budgeting required of their more mature siblings. Above all, the new unit should be allowed and indeed encouraged to cannibalize the established business. . . .

WHAT ABOUT "SYNERGY"?

When should the two structures cooperate? One view is that internal competition and some redundancy should always be encouraged, with different business units championing different models (based on Chandy and Tellis, 1999). A more nuanced view is that the separated venture should be able to leverage the parent's strengths while avoiding absorption or subservience. It is ironic and instructive that IBM, in its quest to develop a truly new personal computer, set up a separate and geographically removed unit in 1980 that failed to tap into any of IBM's formidable technological capabilities. The IBM PC was an assembled product without any proprietary systems or semiconductors, and it quickly attracted clones. . . .

CONCLUSIONS

How can established firms compete, survive, and succeed in industries that are being created or transformed by emerging technologies? Success requires continuing support from senior management, separation of the new venture from continuing activities, and a willingness to take risks and learn from experiments. Investments should be treated as options to position the company to make informed investments at some later time—if and when the uncertainties are reduced. There should be a diversity of viewpoints that can challenge prevailing mindsets, misleading precedents, and potentially myopic views of new ventures. The best innovators seem to be able to think broadly and to entertain a wide range of possibilities before they converge on any one solution.

These prescriptions appear directionally correct, but need tailoring to the distinctive character of each emerging technology and the particular organization involved. The design challenge is to create a high-commitment organization that can cope with the tensions of high uncertainty of results while achieving alignment of all levels and functions in support of the strategic choices made. The main point is that managing emerging technologies constitutes a different game for established firms, with its own pitfalls and solutions.

READING 9.3

Reinventing Your Business Model BY MARK W. JOHNSON, CLAYTON M. CHRISTENSEN, AND HENNING KAGERMANN

In 2003, Apple introduced the iPod with the iTunes store, revolutionizing portable entertainment, creating a new market, and transforming the company. In just three years, the iPod/iTunes combination became a nearly $10 billion product, accounting for almost 50% of Apple's revenue. Apple's market capitalization catapulted from around $1 billion in early 2003 to over $150 billion by late 2007.

This success story is well known; what's less well known is that Apple was not the first to bring digital music players to market. A company called Diamond Multimedia introduced the Rio in 1998. Another firm, Best Data, introduced the Cabo 64 in 2000. Both products worked well and were portable and stylish. So why did the iPod, rather than the Rio or Cabo, succeed?

Apple did something far smarter than take a good technology and wrap it in a snazzy design. It took a good technology and wrapped it in a great business model. Apple's true innovation was to make downloading digital music easy and convenient. To do that, the company built a groundbreaking business model that combined hardware, software, and service. This approach worked like Gillette's famous blades-and-razor model in reverse: Apple essentially gave away the "blades" (low-margin iTunes music) to lock in purchase of the "razor" (the high-margin iPod). That model defined value in a new way and provided game-changing convenience to the consumer.

Business model innovations have reshaped entire industries and redistributed billions of dollars of value. Retail discounters such as Wal-Mart and Target, which entered the market with pioneering business models, now account for 75% of the total valuation of the retail sector. Low-cost U.S. airlines grew from a blip on the radar screen to 55% of the market value of all carriers. Fully 11 of the 27 companies born in the last quarter century that grew their way into the Fortune 500 in the past 10 years did so through business model innovation.

Stories of business model innovation from well-established companies like Apple, however, are rare. An analysis of major innovations within existing corporations in the past decade shows that precious few have been business model related.

Senior managers at incumbent companies thus confront a frustrating question: Why is it so difficult to pull off the new growth that business model innovation can bring? Our research suggests two problems. The first is a lack of definition: Very little formal study has been done into the dynamics and processes of business model development. Second, few companies understand their existing business model well enough—the premise behind its development, its natural interdependencies, and its strengths and limitations. So they don't know when they can leverage their core business and when success requires a new business model.

After tackling these problems with dozens of companies, we have found that new business models often look unattractive to internal and external stakeholders—at the outset. To see past the borders of what is and into the land of the new, companies need a road map.

Ours consists of three simple steps. The first is to realize that success starts by not thinking about business models at all. It starts with thinking about the opportunity to satisfy a real customer who needs a job done. The second is to construct a blueprint laying out how your company will fulfill that need at a profit. In our model, that plan has four elements. The third is to compare that model to your existing model to see how much you'd have to change it to capture the opportunity. Once you do, you will know if you can use your existing model and organization or need to separate out a new unit to execute a new model. Every successful company is already fulfilling a real customer need with an effective business model, whether that model is explicitly understood or not. Let's take a look at what that entails.

BUSINESS MODEL: A DEFINITION

A business model, from our point of view, consists of four interlocking elements that, taken together, create and deliver value. The most important to get right, by far, is the first.

Customer value proposition (CVP). A successful company is one that has found a way to create value for customers—that is, a way to help customers get an important job done. By "job" we mean a fundamental problem in a given situation that needs a solution. Once we understand the job and all its dimensions, including the full process for how to get it done, we can design the offering. The more important the job is to the customer, the lower the level of customer satisfaction with current options for getting the job done, and the better your solution is than existing alternatives at getting the job done (and, of course, the lower the price), the greater the CVP. Opportunities for creating a CVP are at their most potent, we have found, when alternative products and services have not been designed with the real job in mind and you can design an offering that gets that job—and only that job—done perfectly. We'll come back to that point later.

Profit formula. The profit formula is the blueprint that defines how the company creates value for itself while providing value to the customer. It consists of the following:

Revenue model: price × volume
Cost structure: direct costs, indirect costs, economies of scale. Cost structure will be predominantly driven by the cost of the key resources required by the business model.
Margin model: given the expected volume and cost structure, the contribution needed from each transaction to achieve desired profits.
Resource velocity: how fast we need to turn over inventory, fixed assets, and other assets—and, overall, how well we need to utilize resources—to support our expected volume and achieve our anticipated profits.

People often think the terms "profit formulas" and "business models" are interchangeable. But how you make a profit is only one piece of the model. We've found it most useful to start by setting the price required to deliver the CVP and then work backward from there to determine what the variable costs and gross margins must be. This then determines what the scale and resource velocity needs to be to achieve the desired profits.

Key resources. The key resources are assets such as the people, technology, products, facilities, equipment, channels, and brand required to deliver the value proposition to the targeted customer. The focus here is on the key elements that create value for the customer and the company, and the way those elements interact. (Every company also has generic resources that do not create competitive differentiation.)

Key processes. Successful companies have operational and managerial processes that allow them to deliver value in a way they can successfully repeat and increase in scale. These may include such recurrent tasks as training, development, manufacturing, budgeting, planning, sales, and service. Key processes also include a company's rules, metrics, and norms.

These four elements form the building blocks of any business. The customer value proposition and the profit formula define value for the customer and the company, respectively; key resources and key processes describe how that value will be delivered to both the customer and the company.

As simple as this framework may seem, its power lies in the complex interdependencies of its parts (see Figure 1). Major changes to any of these four elements affect the others and the whole. Successful businesses devise a more or less stable system in which these elements bond to one another in consistent and complementary ways.

HOW GREAT MODELS ARE BUILT

To illustrate the elements of our business model framework, we will look at what's behind two companies' game-changing business model innovations.

Creating a customer value proposition. It's not possible to invent or reinvent a business model without first identifying a clear customer value proposition. Often, it starts as a quite simple realization.

TABLE 1 BUSINESS MODELS IN PRACTICE

Established companies don't succeed with radically new product offerings unless they understand exactly how the opportunity relates to their current business model and proceed accordingly. In the authors' formulation, that work happens in several steps. Start by developing a strong customer value proposition. Many companies begin with a product idea and a business model and then go in search of a market. Success comes from figuring out how to satisfy a real customer who needs to get a real job done.

- EXAMPLE: When Ratan Tata of Tata Group looked out over the streets of Mumbai, he saw motorcycles in traffic carrying entire families—father, mother, and children. What if he could provide these scooter families with a safe, enclosed car at a price they could afford? That would be a powerful customer value proposition.

Construct a profit formula that allows you to deliver value to your company. Then decide what resources and processes you'll need. A customer value proposition without a profit formula is just pie in the sky, as many a dot-com start-up found out. Stuck? Start with a goal for total profits and work back from there.

- EXAMPLE: In seeking to build a car for 100,000 rupees, or $2,500, Tata knew that sufficient profit would be generated through high volume if the company could persuade the huge number of nonconsumers—the scooter families—to buy. That goal required radical changes in the cost structure of making a car. To build the Nano, a team of young engineers developed new processes—outsourcing 85% of the car's components, using 60% fewer vendors, and eventually employing a network of assemblers to build to order.

Compare the model to your current one to determine whether you can implement it within your organization or should set up a separate unit.

- EXAMPLE: Procter & Gamble introduced the game-changing Swiffer using its existing business model because the profit formula and key resources weren't radically different from those of its other household consumables. But when Dow Corning, a master at providing high-margin silicone products with sophisticated technical support, sought to serve the low end with a low-touch, standardized offering, executive Don Sheets found that he needed to set up a new business unit with a new brand identity. Simulations had quickly told him that existing processes and entrenched habits would thwart any attempt to implement the new model.

Hilti, a Liechtenstein-based manufacturer of high-end power tools for the construction industry, reconsidered the real job to be done for many of its current customers. A contractor makes money by finishing projects; if the required tools aren't available and functioning properly, the job doesn't get done. Contractors don't make money by owning tools; they make it by using them as efficiently as possible. Hilti could help contractors get the job done by selling tool use instead of the tools themselves—managing its customers' tool inventory by providing the best tool at the right time and quickly furnishing tool repairs, replacements, and upgrades, all for a monthly fee. To deliver on that value proposition, the company needed to create a fleet-management program for tools and in the process shift its focus from manufacturing and distribution to service. That meant Hilti had to construct a new profit formula and develop new resources and new processes.

The most important attribute of a customer value proposition is its precision: how perfectly it nails the customer job to be done—and nothing else. But such precision is often the most difficult thing to achieve. Companies trying to create the new often neglect to focus on one job; they dilute their efforts by attempting to do lots of things. In doing lots of things, they do nothing really well.

One way to generate a precise customer value proposition is to think about the four most common barriers keeping people from getting particular jobs done: insufficient wealth, access, skill, or time. Software maker Intuit devised QuickBooks to fulfill small-business owners' need to avoid running out of cash. By fulfilling that job with greatly simplified accounting software, Intuit broke the skills barrier that kept untrained small-business owners from using more complicated accounting packages. MinuteClinic, the drugstore-based basic health care provider, broke the time barrier that kept people from visiting a doctor's office with minor health issues by making nurse practitioners available without appointments.

Designing a profit formula. For Hilti, moving to a contract management program required shifting assets from customers' balance sheets to its own and generating revenue through a lease/subscription model. For a monthly fee, customers could have a full complement of tools at their fingertips, with repair and maintenance included. This would require a fundamental shift in all major components of the profit formula: the revenue stream (pricing, the staging of payments, and how to think about volume), the cost structure (including added sales development and contract management costs), and the supporting margins and transaction velocity.

Identifying key resources and processes. Having articulated the value proposition for both the customer and the business, companies must then consider the key resources and processes needed to deliver that value. For a professional services firm, for example, the key resources are generally its people, and the key processes are naturally people related (training and development, for instance). For a packaged goods company, strong brands and well-selected channel retailers might be the key resources, and associated brand-building and channel-management processes among the critical processes.

Oftentimes, it's not the individual resources and processes that make the difference but their relationship to one another. Companies will almost always need to integrate their key resources and processes in a unique way to get a job done perfectly for a set of customers. When they do, they almost always create enduring competitive advantage. Focusing first on the value proposition and the profit formula makes clear how those resources and processes need to interrelate. For example, most general hospitals offer a value proposition that might be described as, "We'll do anything for anybody." Being all things to all people requires these hospitals to have a vast collection of resources (specialists, equipment, and so on) that can't be knit together in any proprietary way. The result is not just a lack of differentiation but dissatisfaction.

By contrast, a hospital that focuses on a specific value proposition can integrate its resources and processes in a unique way that delights customers. National Jewish Health in Denver, for example, is organized around a focused value proposition we'd characterize as, "If you have a disease of the pulmonary system, bring it here. We'll define its root cause and prescribe an effective therapy." Narrowing its focus has allowed National Jewish to develop processes that integrate the ways in which its specialists and specialized equipment work together.

For Tata Motors to fulfill the requirements of its customer value proposition and profit formula for the Nano, it had to reconceive how a car is designed, manufactured, and distributed. Tata built a small team of fairly young engineers who would not, like the company's more experienced designers, be influenced and constrained in their thinking by the automaker's existing profit formulas. This team dramatically minimized the number of parts in the vehicle, resulting in a significant cost saving. Tata also reconceived its supplier strategy, choosing to outsource a remarkable 85% of the Nano's components and use nearly 60% fewer vendors than normal to reduce transaction costs and achieve better economies of scale.

At the other end of the manufacturing line, Tata is envisioning an entirely new way of assembling and distributing its cars. The ultimate plan is to ship the modular components of the vehicles to a combined network of company-owned and independent entrepreneur-owned assembly plants, which will build them to order. The Nano will be designed, built, distributed, and serviced in a radically new way—one that could not be accomplished without a new business model. And while the jury is still out, Ratan Tata may solve a traffic safety problem in the process.

For Hilti, the greatest challenge lay in training its sales representatives to do a thoroughly new task. Fleet management is not a half-hour sale; it takes days, weeks, even months of meetings to persuade customers to buy a program instead of a product. Suddenly, field reps accustomed to dealing with crew leaders and on-site purchasing managers in mobile trailers found themselves staring down CEOs and CFOs across conference tables.

Additionally, leasing required new resources—new people, more robust IT systems, and other new technologies—to design and develop the appropriate packages and then come to an agreement on monthly payments. Hilti needed a process for maintaining large arsenals of tools more inexpensively and effectively than its customers had. This required warehousing, an inventory management system, and a supply of replacement tools. On the customer management side, Hilti developed a website that enabled construction managers to view all the tools in their fleet and their usage rates. With that information readily available, the managers could easily handle the cost accounting associated with those assets.

Rules, norms, and metrics are often the last element to emerge in a developing business model. They may not be fully envisioned until the new product or service has been road tested. Nor should they be. Business models need to have the flexibility to change in their early years.

WHEN A NEW BUSINESS MODEL IS NEEDED

Established companies should not undertake business model innovation lightly. They can often create new products that disrupt competitors without fundamentally changing their own business model. Procter & Gamble, for example, developed a number of what it calls "disruptive market innovations" with such products as the Swiffer disposable mop and duster and Febreze, a new kind of air freshener. Both innovations built on P&G's existing business model and its established dominance in household consumables.

There are clearly times, however, when creating new growth requires venturing not only into unknown market territory but also into unknown business model territory. When? The short answer is "When significant changes are needed to all four elements of your existing model." But it's not always that simple. Management judgment is clearly required. That said, we have observed five strategic circumstances that often require business model change:

- The opportunity to address through disruptive innovation the needs of large groups of potential customers who are shut out of a market entirely because existing solutions are too expensive or complicated for them.
- The opportunity to capitalize on a brand new technology by wrapping a new business model around it (Apple and MP3 players) or the opportunity to leverage a tested technology by bringing it to a whole new market (say, by offering military technologies in the commercial space or vice versa).
- The opportunity to bring a job-to-be-done focus where one does not yet exist. That's common in industries where companies focus on products or customer segments, which leads them to refine existing products more and more, increasing commoditization over time. A jobs focus allows companies to redefine industry profitability. For example, when FedEx entered the package delivery market, it did not try to compete through lower prices or better marketing. Instead, it concentrated on fulfilling an entirely unmet customer need to receive packages far, far faster, and more reliably, than any service then could. To do so, it had to integrate its key processes and resources in a vastly more efficient way. The business model that resulted from

Customer Value Proposition (CVP)

- **Target customer**
- **Job to be done** to solve an Important problem or fulfill an Important need for the target customer
- **Offering,** which satisfies the problem or fulfills the need. This is defined not only by what is sold but also by how It's sold.

PROFIT FORMULA

- **Revenue model** How much money can be made: price x volume. Volume can be thought of in terms of market size, purchase frequency, ancillary sales, etc.
- **Cost structure** How costs are allocated: Includes cost of key assets, direct costs, Indirect costs, economies of scale.
- **Margin model** How much each transaction should net to achieve desired profit levels.
- **Resource velocity** How quickly resources need to be used to support target volume. Includes lead time, throughout inventory turns, asset utilization, and so on.

KEY RESOURCES

needed to deliver the customer value proposition profitably. Might include:

- **People**
- **Technology, products**
- **Equipment**
- **Information**
- **Channels**
- **Partnerships, alliances**
- **Brand**

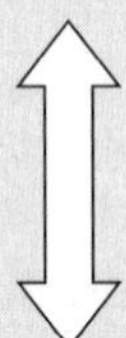

KEY PROCESSES, as well as rules metrics, and norms, that make the profitable delivery of the customer value proposition repeatable and scalable. Might include:

- **Processes:** design, product development, sourcing, manufacturing, marketing, hiring and training, IT
- **Rules and metrics:** margin requirements for investment, credit terms, lead times, supplier terms
- **Norms:** opportunity size needed for investment, approach to customers and channels

FIGURE 1 THE ELEMENTS OF A SUCCESSFUL BUSINESS MODEL

this job-to-be-done emphasis gave FedEx a significant competitive advantage that took UPS many years to copy.

- The need to fend off low-end disrupters. . . . .much as minimills threatened the integrated steel mills a generation ago by making steel at significantly lower cost.
- The need to respond to a shifting basis of competition. Inevitably, what defines an acceptable solution in a market will change over time, leading core market segments to commoditize. Hilti needed to change its business model in part because of lower global manufacturing costs; "good enough" low-end entrants had begun chipping away at the market for high-quality power tools.

Of course, companies should not pursue business model reinvention unless they are confident that the opportunity is large enough to warrant the effort. And, there's really no point in instituting a new business model unless it's not only new to the company but in some way new or game changing to the industry or market. To do otherwise would be a waste of time and money.

These questions will help you evaluate whether the challenge of business model innovation will yield acceptable results. Answering "yes" to all four greatly increases the odds of successful execution:

- Can you nail the job with a focused, compelling customer value proposition?
- Can you devise a model in which all the elements—the customer value proposition, the profit formula, the key resources, and the key processes—work together to get the job done in the most efficient way possible?
- Can you create a new business development process unfettered by the often negative influences of your core business?
- Will the new business model disrupt competitors?

Creating a new model for a new business does not mean the current model is threatened or should be changed. A new model often reinforces and complements the core business, (see Table 1).

The secret sauce: patience. Successful new businesses typically revise their business models four times or so on the road to profitability. While a well-considered business model-innovation process can often shorten this cycle, successful incumbents must tolerate initial failure and grasp the need for course correction. In effect, companies have to focus on learning and adjusting as much as on executing. We recommend companies with new business models be patient for growth (to allow the market opportunity to unfold) but impatient for profit (as an early validation that the model works). A profitable business is the best early indication of a viable model.

Established companies' attempts at transformative growth typically spring from product or technology innovations. Their efforts are often characterized by prolonged development cycles and fitful attempts to find a market. As the Apple iPod story that opened this article suggests, truly transformative businesses are never exclusively about the discovery and commercialization of a great technology. Their success comes from enveloping the new technology in an appropriate, powerful business model.

CHAPTER 10

Collaboration

It all used to be so easy. You developed a strategy, negotiated arrangements with suppliers (better still, bought them up to become "vertically integrated"), and off you went. Today's world of partnerships, alliances and outsourcing makes the strategy process much more complicated. In place of a good deal of competition, collaboration has become king.

Our first reading, called "Collaborating to Compete", reviews alliances. This article is adapted from the recent book of that title by two McKinsey and Company consultants, Joel Bleeke and David Ernst, who sought to capture the company's experiences with such activities. The old style of competition is out, they argue, replaced by a more collaborative style. And to succeed at it, companies must arbitrage their skills and gain access to market and capital, and they must see this as a flexible sequence of actions.

The second reading by Stephen Preece of Wilfred Laurier University in Canada, explains why firms create alliances in the first place—for learning, for leaving, for leveraging, for linking, for leaping, and for locking out. Very colorful! Very relevant!

The third reading by Andrew Inkpen of Thunderbird, The American Graduate School of International Management, looks inside collaborative arrangements to describe how knowledge, both tacit and explicit, is created by technology sharing, by interactions with parent firms or joint ventures, by the movement of personnel across cooperating units, and by the linkage between parent strategies and alliance strategies. All of this requires flexible learning objectives, a committed leadership, a climate of trust alongside a tolerance for redundancy, and some good old-fashioned creative chaos.

USING THE CASE STUDIES

To understand joint ventures and alliances, we need to appreciate the forces leading to their formation and examine their management. In practice, as many of the cases show, the two are closely related. The Lufthansa case examines the formation and management of the Star Alliance. By banding together, airlines changed the structure of their industry, thereby increasing pressure on other airlines to join forces. The case can be used in conjunction with Bleeke and Ernst's "Collaborating to Compete," which deals with the motives and pressures that lead firms to seek joint ventures and alliances. The Pixar case deals with the consequences of a close alliance between Pixar and Disney. Both are animation pioneers with extraordinary records. But whereas Pixar has broken new ground with computer animation, Disney's breakthroughs are in the past. Disney, however, has spent more than seventy years building a highly sophisticated distribution and marketing system. Pixar can make popular animated feature films, but lacks these capabilities. They therefore agree to collaborate: Pixar will make the feature films, and Disney will distribute. Both benefit, but as time wears on, Steve Jobs, the owner of Pixar, believes that making successful animated features is more difficult than distributing them. If this was not the case, he reasons, Disney would not have made the deal in the first place. The relationship is on the verge of breaking down, but surprisingly the two decide to marry, that is, merge, rather than divorce. Preece's "Why Create Alliances" is especially relevant to this case. Outset contemporary art fund describes how the founders created a network of allied organizations. When Outset works to build an alliance in Turkey it discovers that each partner has unique requirements and each presents special challenges.

In "Creating Knowledge through Collaboration," Andrew Inkpen argues that ultimately the most enduring payoff from collaboration is acquisition of knowledge. The Tiscali case describes the risks of relying on partners to provide key technological knowledge. Tiscali relies on Wipro to provide key broadband applications. When the project suffered delays and cost overruns the two sides parted company somewhat acrimoniously. Tiscali turned to Mahindra British Telecommunications (MBT) to complete the project. The case is written mostly from Tiscali's point of view. Wipro of course had its own version of the events. You can use this case in combination with the Wipro case to consider whether Tiscali was it inexperienced when it comes to managing collaboration, or was simply too small to get Wipro's full attention.

READING 10.1

Collaborating to Compete* BY JOEL BLEEKE AND DAVID ERNST

For most global businesses, the days of flat-out, predatory competition are over. The traditional drive to pit one company against the rest of an industry, to pit supplier against supplier, distributor against distributor, on and on through every aspect of a business no longer guarantees the lowest cost, best products or services, or highest profits for winners of this Darwinian game. In businesses as diverse as pharmaceuticals, jet engines, banking, and computers, managers have learned that fighting long, head-to-head battles leaves their companies financially exhausted, intellectually depleted, and vulnerable to the next wave of competition and innovation.

In place of predation, many multinational companies are learning that they must collaborate to compete. Multinationals can create the highest value for customers and stakeholders by selectively sharing and trading control, costs, capital, access to markets, information, and technology with competitors and suppliers alike. Competition does not vanish. The computer and commercial aircraft markets are still brutally competitive.

Instead of competing blindly, companies should increasingly compete only in those precise areas where they have a durable advantage or where participation is necessary to preserve industry power or capture value. In packaged goods, that power comes from controlling distribution; in pharmaceuticals, having blockbuster drugs and access to doctors. Managers are beginning to see that many necessary elements of a global business are so costly (like R&D in semiconductors), so generic (like assembly), or so impenetrable (like some of the Asian markets) that it makes no sense to have a traditional competitive stance. The best approach is to find partners that already have the cash, scale, skills, or access you seek.

When a company reaches across borders, its ability and willingness to collaborate is the best predictor of success. The more equal the partnership, the brighter its future. This means that both partners must be strong financially and in the product or function that they bring to the venture. Of 49 alliances that we examined in detail, two thirds of those between equally matched strong partners succeeded, while about 60% of those involving unequal partners failed. So, too, with ownership. Fifty–fifty partnerships had the highest rate of success of any deal structure that we have examined.

---

*Excerpted from "Collaborating to Compete," *Directors and Boards* (Winter 1994); used with the permission of McKinsey & Company.

THREE THEMES

The need for better understanding of cross-border alliances and acquisitions is increasingly clear. Cross-border linkages are booming, driven by globalization, Europe 1992, the opening of Eastern European and Asian markets, and an increased need for foreign sales to cover the large fixed costs of playing in high-technology businesses. Go-it-alone strategies often take too long, cost too much, or fail to provide insider access to markets. Yet, large numbers of strategic alliances and cross-border acquisitions are failing. When we examined the cross-border alliances and acquisitions of the largest 150 companies in the United States, Europe, and Japan, we found that only half of these linkages succeed. The average life expectancy for most alliances is approximately seven years. Common lessons from the wide experience of many companies in cross-border strategies are beginning to emerge.

In general, three themes emerge from our studies of alliances:

- First, as we have mentioned, companies are learning that they must collaborate to compete. This requires different measurements of "success" from those used for traditional competition.
- Second, alliances between companies that are potential competitors represent an arbitrage of skills, market access, and capital between the companies. Maintaining a fair balance in this arbitrage is essential for success.
- Third, it is important for managers to develop a vision of international strategy and to see cross-border acquisitions and alliances as a flexible sequence of actions—not one-off deals driven by temporary competitive or financial benefit. The remainder of this article discusses each of these three themes in more detail. . . .

Old measures such as financial hurdles and strategic goals only have meaning in the new context of collaboration. As markets become increasingly competitive, managers are beginning to measure success based on the scarcest resources, including skills and access, not only capital. In the global marketplace, maximizing the value of skills and access can often be achieved only if managers are willing to share ownership with and learn from companies much *different* from their own. Success increasingly comes in proportion to a company's willingness to accept differences.

Successful collaboration also requires flexibility. Most alliances that endure are redefined in terms of geographic or product scope. The success rate for alliances that have changed their scope over time is more than twice that of alliances where the scope has not evolved. Alliances with legal or financial structures that do not permit change are nearly certain to fail. (See Table 1, which gives Kenichi Ohmae's Tips for Collaboration.)

ALLIANCES AS ARBITRAGE

If all markets were equally accessible, all management equally skilled, all information readily available, and all balance sheets equally solid, there would be little need for collaboration among competitors. But they are not, so companies increasingly benefit by trading these "chips" across borders.

The global arbitrage reflected in cross-border alliances and acquisitions takes place at a slower pace than in capital markets, but the mechanism is similar. Each player uses the quirks, irrational differences, and inefficiencies in the marketplace as well as each company's advantages to mutual benefit. This concept applies mostly to alliances, but cross-border acquisitions can also be viewed as an extreme example of arbitrage: all cash or shares from the buyer, for all the skills, products, and access of the other company. . . .

Successful alliance partners follow several patterns in handling the inherent tensions of arbitrating with potential competitors. To begin with, they approach the negotiation phase with a win–win situation. As one executive said, "Do not sit down to negotiate a deal—build links between the companies."

Successful partners also build in conflict-resolution mechanisms such as powerful boards of directors (for joint ventures) and frequent communication between top management of

TABLE 1
KENICHI OHMAE'S TIPS FOR COLLABORATION

1. Treat the collaboration as a personal commitment. It's people that make partnerships work.
2. Anticipate that it will take up management time. If you can't spare the time, don't start it.
3. Mutual respect and trust are essential. If you don't trust the people you are negotiating with, forget it.
4. Remember that both partners must get something out of it (money, eventually). Mutual benefit is vital. This will probably mean you've got to give something up. Recognize this from the outset.
5. Make sure you tie up a tight legal contract. Don't put off resolving unpleasant or contentious issues until "later." Once signed, however, the contract should be put away. If you refer to it, something is wrong with the relationship.
6. Recognize that during the course of a collaboration, circumstances and markets change. Recognize your partner's problems and be flexible.
7. Make sure that you and your partner have mutual expectations of the collaboration and its time scale. One happy and one unhappy partner is a formula for failure.
8. Get to know your opposite numbers at all levels socially. Friends take longer to fall out.
9. Appreciate that cultures—both geographic and corporate—are different. Don't expect a partner to act or respond identically to you. Find out the true reason for a particular response.
10. Recognize your partner's interests and independence.
11. Even if the arrangement is tactical in your eyes, make sure you have corporate approval. Your tactical activity may be a key piece in an overall strategic jigsaw puzzle. With corporate commitment to the partnership, you can act with the positive authority needed in these relationships.
12. Celebrate achievement together. It's a shared elation, and you'll have earned it!

Postscript

Two further things to bear in mind:

1. If you're negotiating a product original equipment manufacturer (OEM) deal, look for a quid pro quo. Remember that another product may offer more in return.
2. Joint development agreements must include joint marketing arrangements. You need the largest market possible to recover development costs and to get volume/margin benefits.

—Kenichi Ohmae
Kenichi Ohmae is Chairman of McKinsey & Co.'s offices in Japan.

the parent companies and the alliance. The CEOs of the parent companies need to be absolutely clear on where cooperation is expected and where the "old rules" of competition will apply.

In approaching alliances as arbitrage, managers should recognize that the value of "chips" is likely to change over time. The key is to maximize your bargaining power—that is, the value of your company's contribution to the alliance—while also being ready to renegotiate the alliance as necessary. Some of the best alliances have had built-in timetables for assessing partner contributions and clear rules for valuing the contributions going forward.

A SEQUENCE OF ACTIONS

Beyond the themes of collaboration and arbitrage involved in individual deals, cross-border alliances and acquisitions need to be viewed as a *sequence* of actions in the context of overall international strategy—not as one-off transactions. Companies that take a purely financial, deal-driven approach to cross-border alliances and acquisitions usually wind up in trouble.

Looking at cross-border M&A [mergers and acquisitions], the most successful companies make a series of acquisitions that build presence in core businesses over time in the target country. One consumer goods company, for example, made an "anchor" acquisition of a leading brand to establish a solid presence in an important European market, then used its enhanced distribution clout to ensure the acceptance of several brands that were subsequently acquired.

In our study of the cross-border acquisition programs of the largest Triad companies [Asia, Europe, North America], successful acquirers had nearly twice the average and median number of purchases as unsuccessful companies. Through initial acquisitions, the acquirer refines M&A skills and becomes more comfortable with, and proficient at, using M&A for international expansion. And by completing a sequence of transactions, particularly in the same geography, it is possible to gain economies through integrating operations and eliminating overlapping functions.

WILLINGNESS TO RETHINK

It is important to think about cross-border alliances, as well as acquisitions, as a part of a sequence of actions. Most alliances evolve over time, so the initial charter and contract often are not meaningful within a few years. Since trouble is the rule, not the exception, and since two thirds of all cross-border alliances run into management trouble during the first few years, alliances require a willingness by partners to rethink their situation on a constant basis—and renegotiate as necessary.

Alliances should usually be considered as an intermediate strategic device that needs other transactions surrounding it. Approximately half of all cross-border alliances terminate within seven years, so it is critical that managers have a point of view early on of "what's next?"

Most terminating alliances are purchased by one of the partners, and termination need not mean failure. But the high rate of termination suggests that both parties should think hard early on about likely roles as a buyer or seller—the probabilities are high that alliance partners eventually will be one or the other.

The companies that can bring the largest short-term synergies to an alliance are often those companies that will most likely be direct competitors in the long term. So, if the desired sequence of management action does not include selling the business, a different, more complementary partner may need to be found at the outset. Understanding the probable sequence of transactions is therefore important in selecting even early alliance of acquisition partners. As our colleagues in Japan remind us, nothing is worse in cross-border alliances or acquisitions than to have "partners in the same bed with different dreams."

POSTSCRIPT: A LOOK AHEAD

Global corporations of the future will be rather like amoebas. The single-celled aquatic animal is among the most ancient life-forms on earth. It gets all its nourishment directly from its environment through its permeable outer walls. These walls define the creature as distinct from its environment, but allow much of what is inside to flow out and much of what is outside to come in. The amoeba is always changing shape, taking and giving with the surroundings, yet it always retains its integrity and identity as a unique creature.

To be truly global and not merely "big," organizations of the future must hold this permeability as one of their highest values. When managers enter a new market, they should first ask these questions: "How is business here different? What do I need to learn?" They have to seek partners that can share costs and swap skills and access to markets. In the fluid global marketplace, it is no longer possible or desirable for single organizations to be entirely self-sufficient. Collaboration is the value of the future. Alliances are the structure of the future.

This has enormous impact on corporate strategy. It makes the world very complex, because there is no single valid rule book for all markets. As our studies have demonstrated, alliances are based on arbitrating the unique differences between markets and partners. And so it is impossible to standardize an approach to the topic. Managers at the corporate center must be able to tolerate and in fact encourage variation: 10 different markets, 10 different partners, 10 different organization charts, 10 reporting systems, and so on. Policies and procedures must be fluid. The word *schizophrenia* has negative connotations, but it captures this idea that a truly global organization must entertain two seemingly contradictory aspects—a strong identity, along with an openness to different ways of doing business, to the values of different cultures and localities.

This duality is going to be very difficult for many of the "global" companies of today. Companies with a sales-based culture, where senior executives all come from a sales background, will have a particularly hard time adapting to this new collaborative world. Such companies see the world as "us and them." They reject ideas from the outside world, even if the concept is helpful. They find it hard to live without standardization. They find it hard to collaborate with partners. Deep down, they are trying to convert everyone to their own way of doing things.

This makes them inflexible and confrontational. They don't know how to communicate and work with the outside world on its own terms. They cannot be like the amoeba, with its permeable walls and changing shape, its openness to take from every environment. These companies may survive because they are large and powerful, but they will cease to be leaders.

READING 10.2

Why Create Alliances* BY STEPHEN B. PREECE

In response to global competitive forces, business leaders are increasingly turning to cooperative arrangements to advance their competitive edge internationally.

The rise of ISA (International Strategic Alliances) formation has brought about euphoria over the potential of such arrangements to meet the intensifying demands of global competition, as well as disappointment over the challenges inherent in their implementation. Important to the success of these arrangements is that managers be clear about their overall strategic purpose. Alliances are often spoken of in terms of specific functions performed (i.e., market extension, technology sharing). However, the decision to engage a company in a major alliance often represents a substantive strategic alternative having wide-ranging implications for overall firm competitiveness, both positive and negative. The way in which an ISA is incorporated into the overall firm strategy, the long-run strategic objective assumed by management, is critical to the effectiveness of this competitive tool. This article suggests that there are multiple objectives managers can take regarding the integration of ISAs into the strategic management of the organization, with varying consequences.

The three ways to conceptualize ISAs are: structures, functions, and objectives (see Table 1). Perhaps the most common way of thinking about ISAs focuses on alliance organizational structures. The most prevalent organizational structure is the joint venture, where two firms contribute equity in order to create a new and separate entity; some have described this new organization as the "child" with contributing firms assuming the role of "parents" (Harrigan and Newman, 1990). A variation on the joint venture is the minority-equity investment, where one firm takes a minority-equity position in another ongoing firm. Nonequity cooperative arrangements are also possible where firms agree to share efforts, assets, and profits without engaging in equity ties. The extent of collaborative intensity is not necessarily obvious when comparing equity with nonequity arrangements, despite the obvious tangible effect equity provides.

Other efforts to analyze the structure of alliances have focused on issues such as the impact of varying levels of partnership equity on performance, small versus large firm alliances, specific industry sectors, and nationality issues. The prevailing message of this literature is that certain structural arrangements are to be avoided or pursued in the formation and implementation of ISAs.

A second conceptualization of ISAs relates to the various functions of alliances. The primary areas targeted for alliance formation are often collapsed into four primary categories: technology, finance, markets, and production. Technology-driven alliances include such activities as technology development, commercialization, sharing, or licensing. Finance-driven alliances focus on gaining access to financial markets at least cost and the sharing of risk where the product gestation period is long. Market-driven alliances emphasize the penetration of new foreign markets, sharing distribution channels, or extending a brand name. Production-driven alliances include

TABLE 1 ISA STRUCTURES, FUNCTIONS, AND OBJECTIVES

Structures	The organizational form chosen for the collaboration. May include joint venture, minority-equity, licensing, nonequity contractual, etc.
Functions	The specific activities to be performed by the alliance. May include market access, technology development, production sharing, financial access, risk sharing, etc.
Objectives	The overall contribution the alliance is intended to have on the strategic direction and capabilities of the firm, i.e., its long-run significance.

*Excerpted from "Why Create Alliances" from "Incorporating International Strategic Alliances into Overall Firm Strategy" by S. Preece found in *The International Executive,* Vol. 37 (3), May/June 1995, pp. 261–277. Copyright © 1995 by John Wiley & Sons, Inc. Used by permission of John Wiley & Sons, Inc.

TABLE 2
SIX ISA OBJECTIVES

OBJECTIVE	DESCRIPTION	POSITIVE ASPECTS	NEGATIVE ASPECTS
Learning	Acquire needed know-how (markets, technology, management)	Inexpensive and efficient acquisition	Partner opportunism, organizational challenges
Leaning	Replace value-chain activities, fill in missing firm infrastructure	Specialization advantages	Partner dependency
Leveraging	Fully integrate firm operations with partner	Entirely new portfolio of resources	Decision paralysis, evolving environment
Linking	Closer links with suppliers and customers	Closer coordination of vertical activities	Greater inflexibility in vertical relations
Leaping	Pursue radically new area of endeavor	Expanding universe of market opportunity	Cultural incompatibility
Locking out	Reduce competitive pressure from non partners	Temporary competitive hiatus	Static strategic position, ephemeral advantage

the sharing of production facilities, rationalizing manufacturing, or integrating supplier relationships. A large amount of literature focuses on the functions relevant to technology, finance, markets, and production, and although the term "international strategic alliances" assumes a strategic activity, the actual link to overall firm strategy is not always clear.

Although the structure and functional conceptualizations address important elements of collaborative activity, it is the third category, ISA strategic objectives, that will potentially have the greatest impact on the overall strategic direction and future organizational capabilities of the firm. The variety of options available to managers in approaching strategic alliance objectives and their consequences has not been well developed in the literature. This article presents a typology defining six cooperative objectives [see Table 2], in hopes that it will assist managers in assessing their own vision of strategic alliances and contribute to the understanding of how such relationships can work to their advantage both cooperatively and competitively. . . . It is important to emphasize that both structural and functional issues are important, and inextricably linked, to the various strategic objectives that will be discussed. It is also evident that while one alliance objective will likely dominate, others may play secondary roles.

LEARNING

The first strategic objective is *learning*. In this case the firm enters into the alliance with the intention of acquiring needed know-how from the partner through the learning process. Learning becomes attractive when a firm is incapable of performing certain value-chain activities that have the potential to make it either more powerful or more profitable. Two important assumptions linked to this objective are: there is an advantage to maintaining the function/technology within the firm hierarchy; and the function/technology is embedded within the firm, making an arm's-length (market) transaction difficult.

It is unlikely that the learning alliance will actually be described by the participants in these terms. The stated rationale will be defined as an agreement to combine R&D efforts, jointly manufacture a product, and/or share distribution outlets (all functional arrangements). However, one or both sides may aggressively use the alliance to acquire valuable know-how, gradually becoming independent of the "teaching" partner once the learning process is complete.

The positive elements of pursuing alliances as a learning vehicle are speed, efficiency, and cost. Rather than developing a new capability (process, market, or technology) by trial and error through internal development, the alliance provides immediate access to the desired skill. An alternative to alliance learning would be to acquire a firm that carries the needed know-how.

However, this strategy can prove to be confrontational and ultimately result in losing the desired skills by way of workplace disruptions, distrust, and defections. Licensing can also serve as an alternative for developing needed know-how; however, some of the most valuable technologies (management, process, and product) are often so embedded in the organizational framework that they are difficult to separate and transfer effectively to a new organization. In short, the strategic alliance relationship with learning as a primary intent has many advantages over the alternatives—acquisition, in-house development, or licensing.

The negative elements of learning alliances primarily accrue to the nonlearner. If an alliance partner does not have a learning motive, it may view partner learning efforts to be predatory or in bad faith, resulting in conflict or even dissolution. Further, the learning alliance assumes an organizational ability to learn and a willingness of the partner to allow learning to take place. . . . The potential for learning in alliances to dramatically impact the competitive dynamics among competing firms makes it an alliance objective that must be seriously considered and appropriately grappled with.

LEANING

The second objective in ISA relationships is *leaning*. In this case the alliance is entered with the intention of having the partner replace an element of the firm's value-chain activities that was previously performed internally. An important assumption is that by ceding out certain operational segments, firms will be able to focus on what they do best, placing an emphasis on their core competence. The firm picking up the value-chain activity is assumed to have its own core competence in that particular area. Leaning objectives, to the extent that the firm is moving away from unattractive value-chain activities, may be considered to be the opposite of the learning objective that seeks to take on particular activities and competencies.

A natural opportunity for leaning in ISAs occurs through cooperative relationships with firms located in countries that provide a comparative advantage in specific value-added activities.

The advantage of such a strategy can result in substantial short-term gains in a production cost structure. Both parties benefit through specialization in the functions that are most amenable to their environments or organizations. The risk in a leaning strategy is in determining which activities are not critical to the core competence of the firm. If a firm mistakenly cedes out crucial activities it can severely cripple its long-term strategy.

A central problem to this alliance objective is functional impotence resulting from a loss of skills. When a set of operations is removed from the "vocabulary" of the firm, the organization may forget how to use it and end up losing it forever. This can lead to a dependency relationship where the original firm can no longer perform production or other functions internally without incurring substantial costs.

Another problem with the leaning strategy is associated with the geographic and organizational separation of value-chain functions. Performing design and research functions in one country while production takes place on the other side of the world can lead to inefficiencies and slower response times. In addition, important feedback and interactive development and production processes are noticeably absent.

Finally, the risk of creating a competitor is great. The number of industries that have relied on cooperative relationships to substitute internal processes only to be later overtaken by the partners are numerous.

LEVERAGING

The third strategic objective to be addressed in ISA relationships is *leveraging*. In this case the alliance represents a major integration of firm functions between partners in order to benefit from size and/or scope advantages. The competitive structure of numerous global industries often requires a critical mass in areas such as market reach, R&D dollars, and product offerings to compete with other dominant global players. While the costs of amassing the necessary size or scope may be prohibitive for an individual firm, two or more smaller firms can enter into an ISA to achieve similar results. The outcome is the leveraging of individual firm strengths with those of a partner for size and/or scope advantages.

In early 1991 Sterling Drug (U.S.) and Sanoñ S.A. (France) joined their pharmaceutical operations in what could be considered a leveraging alliance. The arrangement, which involved no equity exchange, enabled Sanoñ to market its products through the extensive Sterling distribution system in both North and Latin America, while Sterling gained access to the extensive Sanoñ distribution system throughout Europe (Ansberry, 1991). In addition to market sharing arrangements, the alliance included a significant R&D component.

. . . Two medium-sized pharmaceutical companies with complementary markets, product capabilities, and research budgets combined efforts to become a powerhouse in a global industry. The extensiveness of this relationship was such that the two companies had to coordinate activities on virtually every level of business practice. The obvious advantage of this kind of alliance objective is the opportunity to expand assets, resources, capabilities, and opportunities significantly in a very short time frame. . . .

Two negative elements stand out in the leveraging strategy. Organizational inertia and bureaucratic stagnation are possible when any organization reaches the point of having multiple management layers and departments . . . combining two large bureaucracies increases complexity and the potential for decision hang-ups. Procedural issues as well as trust, reciprocity, and monitoring issues affect the commitment and durability of the relationship. . . .

The other negative aspect of this strategy is the problem of a changing world. The top management of two major companies may see eye to eye regarding industry and competitive factors that make such an alliance favorable today. However, the question becomes, will this consensus in "world view" exist 1, 2, or 5 years from now? Extensive research suggests that industry evolution and the shifting of the competitive landscape are major contributors to alliance instability. . . .

LINKING

The fourth ISA objective considered in this analysis is *linking*. This particular relationship approach is most frequently associated with vertical relationships (as opposed to horizontal) and are often singular in their functional scope. Strategic supplier and customer relationships are becoming much more prevalent as a specific example of this relationship type. . . .

The traditional model in the United States has been to maintain multiple suppliers for any given component and then to foster an environment that makes them compete against one another. Annual or biannual bidding arrangements would lead to constant competitive pressure through low-price seeking and the willingness to shift suppliers with virtually interchangeable component parts. A changing trend, however, is for manufacturers to seek tighter links with supplier companies, based on the belief that closer cooperation and coordination will lead to a more effective relationship, because the sharing of information, specifications, and expertise over time will result in shorter lead times, higher quality, and greater control in the manufacturing process.

The advantage to the linking strategic objective is that it brings about opportunities for greater coordination and a tighter relationship between partners than would be available in an arm's-length supplier relationship.

The major negative element of this strategy is inflexibility. When a traditional supplier relationship is reevaluated annually or biannually, there is little problem in severing a relationship when it becomes necessary; with an alliance relationship it becomes much more difficult. As the relationship deepens and intensifies over time, specific assets and personnel are exclusively devoted to the relationship. If the firm encounters a downturn in business or a reduction in customer orders, it is much more difficult to sever the relationship with the one supplier with which the firm has developed an involved relationship than it would be otherwise, and the damage to both may be severe.

LEAPING

The fifth alliance objective is *leaping*. In this case a company benefits from the expertise of another firm whose core competency is substantially different, thereby allowing the former to expand into largely disparate but potentially viable areas in which it would otherwise not venture.

This objective is called leaping because the areas of expertise sought for in the partner enable the firm to explore product or market opportunities, leaping over otherwise formidable entry barriers, that would be difficult to exploit internally due to a lack of specific firm capabilities.

An example of leaping is the strategic alliance between Sony and ESPN to develop and jointly market a new line of sports video games. In this case Sony had an established expertise in consumer electronics applications in many areas. ESPN, through its sports cable broadcasting, had established a solid reputation with, and understanding of, sports fans.

. . . [L]eaping may represent cultural or geographic expansions necessary to access foreign markets. In many cases companies may have products that are appropriate for a particular country or market, but may have little expertise in the cultural practices of the residents. This is particularly true of less-developed countries, and may explain why culturally sensitive sectors such as retailing involve alliances.

Leaping differs from learning in that the leaping firm is not likely to have the desire to internalize the expertise of its partner. The technological infrastructure is so different that this would be a far too onerous task. In the Sony example, Sony is unlikely to have the interest or capacity to develop the sports knowledge and understanding of ESPN; likewise, ESPN is unlikely to digress into consumer electronics. Leaping differs from leveraging in that the leaping segment of the firm typically does not represent the core technological thrust and integration that the leveraging relationship would encompass.

The negatives associated with leaping alliances are primarily those of cultural incompatibility. Any ISA arrangement presents challenges to the successful integration of management styles as well as bridging the cultural gap between nations. However, efforts to cooperate between companies that occupy *radically* different industry and technological capabilities can prove to be particularly difficult to manage due to organizational cultural differences. Organizational traditions in such areas as decision-making processes, risk preferences, and managerial styles can represent enormous invisible barriers to the successful implementation of desired alliance objectives.

LOCKING OUT

The sixth ISA strategic objective to be considered is *locking out*. In this scenario two or more partners come together in order to thwart competition and benefit from the combined market power or structural relationship of the cooperating firms. The intention is not particularly to advance a new technology, innovation, or market, but rather to protect existing advantages from potential competition.

Examples of such alliances may include large manufacturers consolidating supplier networks to make it more difficult for competing firms to gain access.

The primary negative element of locking-out alliances is their ephemeral nature. The antitrust issues related to strategic alliances are often complex and untested in many countries. As potential competitors fall to unfair market obstructions and as customers complain about the lack of competition, governments may quickly disallow an alliance and threaten a competitive advantage stronghold. Additionally, alliances used to neutralize competition may make the involved firms enjoy a false sense of competitive advantage, ultimately making them vulnerable to more innovative and nimble competitors.

CONCLUSION

In conclusion, there are three important steps in developing appropriate ISA arrangements. The first is to conceive of and adequately define a primary objective for the alliance arrangement. This article has argued that several alliance objectives are possible and can have significantly differing implications for the firm. The next step is to ensure that such an objective is appropriate given the firm's broader strategies and objectives. If there is a good alliance/strategy fit, then the final step is to ensure that the partner's alliance objects are compatible. Such strategic planning activities are likely to reduce conflictual foundations for ISAs and increase the possibility that they will ultimately contribute to firm competitive advantages as planned.

READING 10.3

Creating Knowledge through Collaboration* BY ANDREW C. INKPEN

Increasingly, the creation of new organizational knowledge is becoming a managerial priority. New knowledge provides the basis for organizational renewal and sustainable competitive advantage (Quinn, 1992). By examining knowledge creation through alliance strategies, this article provides insights into how firms manage knowledge.

In the past five years, the number of domestic and international alliances has grown by more than 25 percent annually (Bleeke and Ernst, 1995). Peter Drucker (1995) has suggested that the greatest change in the way business is being conducted is in the accelerating growth of relationships based not on ownership but on partnership. Many firms have now realized that self-sufficiency is becoming increasingly difficult in a business environment that demands strategic focus, flexibility, and innovation. Alliances provide firms with a unique opportunity to leverage their strengths with the help of partners.

Many firms enter into alliances with specific learning objectives. Although learning through alliances can and does occur successfully, it is a difficult, frustrating, and often misunderstood process. The primary obstacle to success is a failure to execute the specific organizational processes necessary to access, assimilate, and disseminate alliance knowledge. Successful firms exploit learning opportunities by acquiring knowledge through "grafting," a process of internalizing knowledge not previously available within the organization. . . . **

This research study examined two main questions: Do alliance parents recognize and seek to exploit alliance learning opportunities? What organizational conditions facilitate effective or ineffective learning? The sample of alliance organizations for the research consisted of 40 American–Japanese joint ventures (JVs) located in North America and involved interviews with their managers. All of the JVs were suppliers to the automotive industry and, with two exceptions, all were startup or greenfield organizations. In terms of ownership, 17 ventures were 50–50, in 15 ventures the Japanese partners had majority equity, and in 8 ventures the American partners had majority equity. Five cases from the initial study were selected for further study.

EXPLOITING COLLABORATIVE KNOWLEDGE

There are four critical knowledge management processes used by firms to access and transform knowledge from an alliance context to a partner context: technology sharing; JV–parent interactions; personnel movement; and linkages between parent and alliance strategies. These processes create connections for individual managers through which they can communicate their alliance experiences to others and form the foundation for the integration of knowledge into the parent's collective knowledge base.

TACIT AND EXPLICIT KNOWLEDGE

Organizational knowledge creation involves a continuous interplay between tacit and explicit knowledge (Nonaka and Takeuchi, 1995). Tacit knowledge is hard to formalize, making it difficult to communicate or share with others. Tacit knowledge involves intangible factors embedded in personal beliefs, experiences, and values. Explicit knowledge is systematic and easily

*Excerpted from "Creating Knowledge through Collaboration," Andrew C. Inkpen, *California Management Review*, Vol. 39 (1), Fall 1996, pp. 123–140.

**Huber (1991) has explored the various ways by which organizations are exposed to new knowledge: congenital learning, experiential learning, vicarious learning, searching, and grafting. Of specific interest in this study is grafting knowledge from outside the organization's boundaries; for example, through mergers and acquisitions.

TABLE 1 KNOWLEDGE MANAGEMENT PROCESSES AND TYPES OF KNOWLEDGE

KNOWLEDGE MANAGEMENT PROCESSES	TYPES OF KNOWLEDGE	EXAMPLES OF KNOWLEDGE POTENTIALLY USEFUL TO AMERICAN JV PARENTS
Technology Sharing	Explicit	• Quality control processes • Product designs • Scheduling systems
JV–Parent Interactions	Explicit	• Specific human resource practices
	Tacit	• Expectations of Japanese customers
Personnel Movement	Tacit	• Continuous improvement objectives • Commitment to customer satisfaction
Linkages between Parent and Alliance Strategies	Explicit	• Market intelligence
	Tacit	• Visions for the future • Partner's *keiretsu* relationships

communicated in the form of hard data or codified procedures. Often there will be a strong tacit dimension associated with how to use and implement explicit knowledge. Table 1 shows the four knowledge management processes and the primary types of knowledge associated with each process.

TECHNOLOGY SHARING

In the cases studied, parent firms had put into place various mechanisms to gain access to JV manufacturing process and product technology. The most common approach was also the most straightforward—meetings between JV and parent managers. In one case, monthly meetings were held, with the location alternating between the JV and one of the American parent plants. In attendance at the meetings were plant managers, heads of quality control, R&D managers, the VP of manufacturing at the American parent head office, and several senior JV managers. In addition, quarterly R&D meetings were held involving the JV and American parent.

Access to partner technology skills also occurred through direct linkages between Japanese and American partners. In two cases, there were regular visits by American parent personnel to Japanese parent facilities.

In another case, the partners signed a very broad global technology agreement. Both partners agreed to be completely open in sharing both product and manufacturing technology.

Not all American parents were interested in access to Japanese partner technology. In one case, a Japanese partner offered to share its manufacturing technology with its American partner. The Japanese partner had developed some proprietary process technology and was willing to share it at no cost. The technology was used in the JV and was very visible to American partner managers. The offer was communicated in a written memo from a JV manager to the American partner president. The American firm never followed up on the offer. Why was the offer refused? One JV manager's opinion was that "the people from the American parent do not want to learn because they see the JV as an upstart."

JV–PARENT INTERACTIONS

The JV–parent relationship plays a key role in knowledge management. In addition to the technology-sharing initiatives discussed above, other JV–parent interactions can create the social context necessary to bring JV knowledge into a wider arena. JV–parent interactions can provide the basis for what have been referred to as "communities of practice" (Brown and Duguid, 1991). A community of practice is a group of individuals that is not necessarily recognizable within strict organizational boundaries. The members share community knowledge and may be willing to challenge the organization's conventional wisdom. Communities emerge not when the members absorb abstract knowledge, but when the members become "insiders" and acquire the particular community's subjective viewpoint and learn to speak its language.

Visits and tours of JV facilities were an effective means for parent managers to learn about their JVs. JV managers were generally convinced that differences embodied in the JV were visible and parent managers would appreciate the differences if they spent more time in the JV.

Customer–supplier relationships between the JV and the American parent also created a basis for extensive JV–parent interaction. In one case, the American parent substantially increased its quality because of pressure from the JV customer, which in turn was under pressure from its Japanese transplant supplier. Until the JV was formed, the American parent had not had any extensive interactions with Japanese customers. In supplying the JV, and indirectly becoming a transplant supplier, the American parent was forced to evaluate some of its manufacturing operations.

PERSONNEL MOVEMENT

The rotation of personnel between the alliance and the parent can be a very effective means of "mobilizing" personal knowledge. Rotation helps members of an organization understand the business from a multiplicity of perspectives, which in turn makes knowledge more fluid and easier to put into practice. In this study, the rotation of interest was a two-way movement of personnel between the JV and parent. If there is only one-way movement, such as from the parent to the JV, this was not considered rotation.

The attitude of the Japanese parent sometimes constrained rotation. In one case, the Japanese parent preferred that JV personnel not move to the American parent. The Japanese parent saw the JV as distinct and separate from the American parent. Despite this concern, the American parent has moved personnel from the JV to the parent. In another case, personnel were willing to move from the parent to the JV but less willing to return to the American parent. This prompted the American parent to ask its JV not to "poach" any more personnel from the parent.

LINKAGES BETWEEN PARENT AND ALLIANCE STRATEGIES

The degree to which the parent and alliance strategies are linked plays an important role in the management of alliance knowledge. A JV perceived as peripheral to the parent organization's strategy will likely yield few opportunities for the transfer of alliance knowledge to the parent. A JV viewed as important may receive more attention from the parent organization, leading to substantial parent–JV interaction and a greater commitment of resources to the management of the collaboration.

Through strategic linkages between the JV and the parent, the partners can gain important insights into each other's businesses. For example, an American parent won a contract to supply a part but was unable to meet the target cost. The parent decided to use its JV to produce the parts because of the JV's superior process technology. This type of linkage indicates that the American parent has internalized the differences between the parent and JV. It also opens the door for more knowledge sharing and cooperation in the future.

FACILITATING FACTORS

Why do some firms actively seek to leverage alliance knowledge while others make only a minimal effort? Why are some firms more effective at leveraging alliance knowledge? There are six factors that facilitate effective knowledge management: flexible learning objectives; leadership commitment; a climate of trust; a tolerance for redundancy; creative chaos; and an absence of performance myopia.

FLEXIBLE LEARNING OBJECTIVES

The collaborative objectives of the JV partners are a key element in alliance knowledge creation. However, it is not enough to enter a JV with a learning objective. Initial learning objectives may have little impact on the effectiveness of knowledge creation efforts. This is not to suggest that learning objectives are unimportant. If learning objectives are associated with the formation of a JV, a parent firm may enter more actively into the search for knowledge. However, if the initial learning objective is not correctly focused and management is unwilling or unable to adjust the objective, knowledge management efforts may be ineffective. For example, in one case the American partner had a very explicit technology learning objective. However, this firm's knowledge management efforts were weak and inconsistent because the firm did not have a clear understanding of its partner's skills. . . .

In another JV, the situation was almost the reverse. The American parent was interested in forming a JV primarily to gain access to the Japanese transplant market. When negotiations to form the JV were started, American parent management made it clear that they were only willing to be involved if they managed the JV. According to the JV president, "We have a quality reputation which we should be able to carry over to the JV." But, after working together for several years, American parent management realized that alliance knowledge could be important to their firm and greater effort was made to gain access to the JV operations and JV partner knowledge. . . .

LEADERSHIP COMMITMENT

Top management's role in managing knowledge should be one of architect and catalyst. While multiple advocates are important, there must be at least one strong champion of knowledge creation in a leadership position. The leader's role is especially important in initiating linkages between parent and alliance strategies. In one JV, the primary impetus for this close relationship came from the president of the American parent. The president had a long-standing personal relationship with the chairman of the Japanese partner. The president was committed to building the JV relationship and leveraging the JV experience to strengthen the American parent business. Through the president's efforts, explicit knowledge management efforts designed to transfer specific technologies as well as more exploratory exchanges of personnel and ideas were initiated. . . .

CLIMATE OF TRUST

A climate of trust between both the JV partners and between the JV and parent organizations is critical to the free exchange of information. Trust between the partners appeared to be both a function of top management involvement in the relationship and a history of cooperation prior to the formation of the JV. . . .

TOLERANCE FOR REDUNDANCY

Redundancy means the conscious overlapping of company information, activities, and management responsibilities. Redundancy encourages frequent dialogue and, as Peter Senge (1990) argues, dialogue is a key element of collective learning. In a dialogue, complex issues are explored with the objective of collectively achieving common meaning. Dialogue involves conversations and connections between people at different organization levels. Inevitably, as issues are debated and assumptions questioned, dialogue will lead to some redundancy in information. Without a tolerance for redundancy, sharing of ideas and effective dialogue will be difficult. . . .

CREATIVE CHAOS

Chaos is created naturally when an organization faces a crisis, such as a rapid decline in performance. Chaos can also occur when differences or discrepancies disrupt normal routines. Chaos increases tension within the organization and focuses attention on forming and solving new problems. The job of managers in the knowledge-creating company is to orient the chaos toward knowledge creation by providing managers with a conceptual framework that can be used to interpret experience (Nonaka, 1991).

PERFORMANCE MYOPIA

Managers seeking to create knowledge must cope with confusing experiences. One such "experience" for JV parents was the assessment of JV performance. Several managers in the American parent companies pointed to the poor financial performance of the JVs as evidence that learning was not occurring, or could not occur. More generally, a myopic preoccupation with short-term issues was a common characteristic of the American partners. Although it is too simplistic to describe Japanese management as long-term oriented and American management as short-term oriented, the Japanese partner firms in this study appeared to focus on customer satisfaction and product quality rather than on profit-based performance. Consistent with other studies (for example, Abbeglen and Stalk, 1985), the Japanese firms seemed less constrained by issues of share price and by impatient boards of directors than their American counterparts. While North Americans focused on the bottom line, the Japanese focused on improving productivity, quality, and delivery.

When a firm is heavily focused on financial performance issues, learning will often be a secondary and less tangible concern. In the poorly performing JVs, American managers found it difficult to conceive that learning could be occurring in the face of poor performance. . . .

CONCLUSION

Knowledge creation is a dynamic process involving interactions at various organizational levels and it encompasses a community of individuals that enlarge, amplify, and disseminate their knowledge. It can be haphazard and idiosyncratic and should be viewed as a continuous process, rather than one with identifiable input–output phases. It may occur unintentionally and it may occur even if success cannot be assessed in terms of objective outcomes. Given its haphazard and idiosyncratic nature, firms may view resources committed to knowledge creation as extravagant and wasteful. The view here is that the ability to create knowledge and move it from one part of the organization to another is the basis for competitive advantage. While not all knowledge creation efforts will be successful, some will yield surprisingly important results. Also, not all knowledge creation efforts will have immediate performance payoffs. However, over the long term, successful knowledge creation should strengthen and reinforce a firm's competitive strategy.

CHAPTER 11

Globalization

The attention to the international dimension in this book is hardly casual or cosmetic. A glance at the list of cases reveals just how international this book is. Here we turn to the conceptual side under the label of globalization, which is certainly a major force in business today.

Operating in an international rather than a domestic arena presents managers with many new opportunities. Having worldwide operations not only gives a company access to new markets and specialized resources, but it also opens up new sources of information to stimulate future product development. And it broadens the options of strategic moves and countermoves the company might make in competing with its domestic or international rivals. However, with all these new opportunities comes the challenge of managing strategy, organization, and operations that are innately more complex, diverse, and uncertain. We include four readings here to help consider this.

The first, by Christopher Bartlett of the Harvard Business School and coauthor Sumantra Ghoshal of the London Business School, deals with the organizational aspects of managing in the international context. To operate effectively on a worldwide basis, Bartlett and Ghoshal suggest, companies must learn to differentiate how they manage different businesses, countries, and functions; create interdependence among units instead of either dependence or independence; and focus on coordination and co-option rather than control. The key to such organizational capability lies in shared vision and values.

The second reading by George Yip, who is at the London Business School, focuses on the strategic aspects of managing in an international context. Yip's views on global strategy reflect the same orientation of industrial organization economies that influenced Porter's work: In deciding on markets in which to participate, products and services to offer, and location of specific activities and tasks, managers must analyze the "globalization drivers" in their industries and find the right strategic fit.

The third reading by Joseph Lampel and Ajay Bhalla, who are both at Cass Business School, looks at "offshoring," a strategy that has had profound impact not only on the operations of many companies, but on entire countries. For many corporations, offshoring seemed an ideal answer to cost pressures and rapidly moving technological change. But, as is often the case in strategy, what they discovered is that offshoring has its risks as well as advantages, and that it is not a one-size-fits-all strategy. Lampel and Bhalla show there are in fact four different models of offshoring, each with its own advantages and risks. Companies should therefore pursue the offshoring model that is consistent with their global strategy.

Finally, Subramanian Rangan of INSEAD offers "seven myths" about global strategy, another set of warnings that *globalism* is not as simple as the word implies. This kind of sobering advice is central in a world perhaps a little too casual about terms like *globalization*.

USING THE CASE STUDIES

There is a distinction to be made between going global and operating as a global company. Many of the cases describe companies that have long been global. Cases such as McDonald's, Procter and Gamble, Cadbury Schweppes, and Lufthansa deal with the problems of running organizations that span the globe. Ghoshal's reading, "Managing across Borders," considers how global companies can deal with this challenge. By contrast, cases such as the Whisky Exchange and Outset consider the pitfalls of going global. It is a good illustration of Rangan's warning in "Seven Myths Regarding Global Strategies" that going global may be fashionable, but doing it right is more important. Lampel and Bhalla suggest that going global often takes the form of offshoring, another fashionable strategy made possible by IT technology. The Tiscali case illustrates how companies can get offshoring both right and wrong. The Wipro case examines a company that is a major player in providing global companies with offshoring services and facilities. The case reminds us that for some companies making globalization possible is a business in itself.

Of course, it should be remembered that one does not have to be global or go global to face the challenge of globalization. Ben and Jerry, and the U.S. wine industry are the cases that deals with the consequences of globalization for firms that have deep roots in their local environment. Yip examines the dilemma of going global. It is useful for analyzing companies such as Nissan and Haier, that began as local and then went global, but it is also useful for analyzing companies that have to deal with the consequences of globalization without going global themselves.

READING 11.1

Managing across Borders: New Organizational Responses* BY CHRISTOPHER A. BARTLETT AND SUMANTRA GHOSHAL

. . . Recent changes in the international operating environment have forced companies to optimize *efficiency, responsiveness,* and *learning* simultaneously in their worldwide operations. To companies that previously concentrated on developing and managing one of these capabilities, this new challenge implie[s] not only a total strategic reorientation but a major change in organizational capability as well.

Implementing such a complex, three-pronged strategic objective would be difficult under any circumstances, but in a worldwide company the task is complicated even further. The very act of "going international" multiplies a company's organizational complexity. Typically, doing so requires adding a third dimension to the existing business- and function-oriented management structure. It is difficult enough balancing product divisions that bring efficiency and focus to domestic product market strategies with corporate staffs whose functional expertise allows them to play an important counterbalance and control role. The thought of adding capable, geographically oriented management—and maintaining a three-way balance of organizational perspectives and capabilities among product, function, and area—is intimidating to most managers. The difficulty is increased because the resolution of tensions among product, function, and area managers must be accomplished in an organization whose operating units are often divided by distance and time, and whose key members are separated by culture and language.

*Originally published in *Sloan Management Review* 43 (Autumn 1987). Reprinted with deletions by permission of the *Review*.

FROM UNIDIMENSIONAL TO MULTIDIMENSIONAL CAPABILITIES

Faced with the task of building multiple strategic capabilities in highly complex organizations, managers in almost every company we studied* made the simplifying assumption that they were faced with a series of dichotomous choices. They discussed the relative merits of pursuing a strategy of national responsiveness as opposed to one based on global integration; they considered whether key assets and resources should be centralized or decentralized; and they debated the need for strong central control versus greater subsidiary autonomy. How a company resolved these dilemmas typically reflected influences exerted and choices made during its historical development. In telecommunications, ITT's need to develop an organization responsive to national political demands and local specification differences was as important to its survival in the pre- and post–World War II era as was NEC's need to build its highly centralized technological manufacturing and marketing skills and resources in order to expand abroad in the same industry in the 1960s and 1970s.

When new competitive challenges emerged, however, such unidimensional biases became strategically limiting. As ITT demonstrated by its outstanding historic success and NEC showed by its more delayed international expansion, strong *geographic management* is essential for development of dispersed responsiveness. Geographic management allows worldwide companies to sense, analyze, and respond to the needs of different national markets.

Effective competitors also need to build strong *business management* with global product responsibilities if they are to achieve global efficiency and integration. These managers act as champions of manufacturing rationalization, product standardization, and low-cost global sourcing. (As the telecommunications switching industry globalized, NEC's organizational capability in this area gave it a major competitive advantage.) Unencumbered by either territorial or functional loyalties, central product groups remain sensitive to overall competitive issues and become agents to facilitate changes that, though painful, are necessary for competitive viability.

Finally, a strong, worldwide *functional management* allows an organization to build and transfer its core competencies—a capability vital to worldwide learning. Links between functional managers allow the company to accumulate specialized knowledge and skills and to apply them wherever they are required in the worldwide operations. Functional management acts as the repository of organizational learning and as the prime mover for its consolidation and circulation within the company. It was for want of a strongly linked research and technical function across subsidiaries that ITT failed in its attempt to coordinate the development and diffusion of its System 12 digital switch.

Thus, to respond to the needs for efficiency, responsiveness, and learning *simultaneously,* the company must develop a multidimensional organization in which the effectiveness of each management group is maintained *and* in which each group is prevented from dominating the others. As we saw in company after company, the most difficult challenge for managers trying to respond to broad, emerging strategic demands was to develop the new elements of multidimensional organization without eroding the effectiveness of their current unidimensional capability.

OVERCOMING SIMPLIFYING ASSUMPTIONS

For all nine companies at the core of our study, the challenge of breaking down biases and building a truly multidimensional organization proved difficult. Behind the pervasive either/or mentality that led to the development of unidimensional capabilities, we identified three simplifying assumptions that blocked the necessary organizational development. The need to reduce

*The findings presented in this article are based on a three-year research project on the organization and management of multinational corporations. Extensive discussions were held with 250 managers in nine of the world's largest multinational companies, in the United States, Europe, and Japan. Complete findings are presented in *Managing across Borders: The Transnational Solution* (Boston: Harvard Business School Press, 1988).

organizational and strategic complexity has made these assumptions almost universal in worldwide companies, regardless of industry, national origin, or management culture.

- There is a widespread, often implicit assumption that roles of different organizational units are uniform and symmetrical; different businesses should be managed in the same way, as should different functions and national operations.
- Most companies, some consciously, most unconsciously, create internal interunit relationships on clear patterns of dependence or independence, on the assumption that such relationships *should* be clear and unambiguous.
- Finally, there is the assumption that one of corporate management's principal tasks is to institutionalize clearly understood mechanisms for decision making and to implement simple means of exercising control.

Those companies most successful in developing truly multidimensional organizations were the ones that challenged these assumptions and replaced them with some very different attitudes and norms. Instead of treating different businesses, functions and subsidiaries similarly, they systematically *differentiated* tasks and responsibilities. Instead of seeking organizational clarity by basing relationships on dependence or independence, they built and managed *interdependence* among the different units of the companies. And instead of considering control their key task, corporate managers searched for complex mechanisms to *coordinate and co-opt* the differentiated and interdependent organizational units into sharing a vision of the company's strategic tasks. These are the central organizational characteristics of what we described in the earlier article as transnational corporations—those most effective in managing across borders in today's environment of intense competition and rapid, often discontinuous change.

FROM SYMMETRY TO DIFFERENTIATION

... Just as they saw the need to change symmetrical structures and homogeneous processes imposed on different businesses and functions, most companies we observed eventually recognized the importance of differentiating the management of diverse geographic operations. Despite the fact that various national subsidiaries operated with very different external environments and internal constraints, they all traditionally reported through the same channels, operated under similar planning and control systems, and worked under a set of common and generalized mandates.

Increasingly, however, managers recognized that such symmetrical treatment can constrain strategic capabilities. At Unilever, for example, it became clear that Europe's highly competitive markets and closely linked economies meant that its operating companies in that region required more coordination and control than those in, say, Latin America. Little by little, management increased the product coordination groups' role in Europe until they had direct line responsibility for all operating companies in their businesses. Elsewhere, however, national management maintained its historic line management role, and product coordinators acted only as advisors. Unilever has thus moved in sequence from a symmetrical organization to a much more differentiated one: differentiating by product, then by function, and finally by geography. ...

But Unilever is far from unique. In all of the companies we studied, senior management was working to differentiate its organizational structure and processes in increasingly sophisticated ways. For example, ... Procter & Gamble is differentiating the roles of its subsidiaries by giving some of them responsibilities as "lead countries" in product strategy development, then rotating that leadership role from product to product. ... Thus, instead of deciding the overall roles of product, functional, and geographic management on the basis of simplistic dichotomies such as global versus domestic businesses or centralized versus decentralized organizations, many companies are creating different levels of influence for different groups as they perform different activities. Doing this allows the relatively underdeveloped management perspectives to be built in a gradual, complementary manner rather than in the sudden, adversarial environment often associated with either/or choices. Internal heterogeneity has made the change from unidimensional to multidimensional organization easier by breaking the problem up into many small, differentiated parts and by allowing for a step-by-step process of organizational change.

FROM DEPENDENCE OR INDEPENDENCE TO INTERDEPENDENCE

. . . New strategic demands make organizational models of simple interunit dependence *or* independence inappropriate. The reality of today's worldwide competitive environment demands collaborative information sharing and problem solving, cooperative support and resource sharing, and collective action and implementation. Independent units risk being picked off one by one by competitors whose coordinated global approach gives them two important strategic advantages—the ability to integrate research, manufacturing, and other scale-efficient operations and the opportunity to cross-subsidize the losses from battles in one market with funds generated by profitable operations in home markets or protected environments. . . .

On the other hand, foreign operations totally dependent on a central unit must deal with problems reaching beyond the loss of local market responsiveness. . . . They also risk being unable to respond effectively to strong national competitors or to sense potentially important local market or technical intelligence. This was the problem Procter & Gamble's Japan subsidiary faced in an environment where local competitors began challenging P&G's previously secure position with successive, innovative product changes and novel market strategies, particularly in the disposable nappies business. After suffering major losses in market share, management recognized that a local operation focused primarily on implementing the company's classic marketing strategy was no longer sufficient; the Japanese subsidiary needed the freedom and incentive to be more innovative. Not only to ensure the viability of the Japanese subsidiary, but also to protect its global strategic position, P&G realized it had to expand the role of the local unit and change its relationship with the parent company to enhance two-way learning and mutual support.

But it is not easy to change relationships of dependence or independence that have been built up over a long history. Many companies have tried to address the increasing need for interunit collaboration by adding layer upon layer of administrative mechanisms to foster greater cooperation. Top managers have extolled the virtues of teamwork and have even created special departments to audit management response to this need. In most cases these efforts to obtain cooperation by fiat or by administrative mechanisms have been disappointing. The independent units have feigned compliance while fiercely protecting their independence. The dependent units have found that the new cooperative spirit implies little more than the right to agree with those on whom they depend.

Yet some companies have gradually developed the capability to achieve such cooperation and to build what Rosabeth Kanter (1983) calls an "integrative organization." Of the companies we studied, the most successful did so not by creating new units, but by changing the basis of the relationships among product, functional, and geographic management groups. From relations based on dependence or independence, they moved to relations based on formidable levels of explicit, genuine interdependence. In essence, they made integration and collaboration self-enforcing by making it necessary for each group to cooperate in order to achieve its own interests. . . .

Procter & Gamble . . . in Europe, for example, [has] formed a number of Eurobrand teams for developing product-market strategies for different product lines.* Each team is headed by the general manager of a subsidiary that has a particularly well-developed competence in that business. It also includes the appropriate product and advertising managers from the other subsidiaries and relevant functional managers from the company's European headquarters. . . .

In observing many such examples of companies building and extending interdependence among units, we were able to identify three important flows, which seem to be at the centre of the emerging organizational relationships. Most fundamental was the product interdependence which most companies were building as they specialized and integrated their worldwide manufacturing operations to achieve greater efficiency, while retaining sourcing flexibility and sensitivity to host country interests. The resulting *flow of parts, components, and finished goods* increased the interdependence of the worldwide operations in an obvious and fundamental manner.

We also observed companies developing a resource interdependence that often contrasted sharply with earlier policies that had either encouraged local self-sufficiency or required the centralization of all surplus resources. . . .

---

*For a full description of the development of Eurobrand in P&G, see C. A. Bartlett, "Proctor & Gamble Europe: Vizir Launch" (Boston: Harvard Business School, Case Services 9-384-139).

Finally, the worldwide diffusion of technology, the development of international markets, and the globalization of competitive strategies have meant that vital strategic information now exists in many different locations worldwide. Furthermore, the growing dispersion of assets and delegation of responsibilities to foreign operations have resulted in the development of local knowledge and expertise that has implications for the broader organization. With these changes, the need to manage the *flow of intelligence, ideas, and knowledge* has become central to the learning process and has reinforced the growing interdependence of worldwide operations, as P&G's Eurobrand teams illustrate.

It is important to emphasize that the relationships we are highlighting are different from the interdependencies commonly observed in multi-unit organizations. Traditionally, MNC managers have attempted to highlight what has been called "pooled interdependence" to make subunit managers responsive to global rather than local interests. (Before the Euroteam approach, for instance, P&G's European vice-president often tried to convince independent-minded subsidiary managers to transfer surplus generated funds to other, more needy subsidiaries, in the overall corporate interest, arguing that, "Someday when you're in need they might be able to fund a major product launch for you.")

As the example illustrates, pooled interdependence is often too broad and amorphous to affect day-to-day management behavior. The interdependencies we described earlier are more clearly reciprocal, and each unit's ability to achieve its goals is made conditional upon its willingness to help other units achieve their own goals. Such interdependencies more effectively promote the organization's ability to share the perspectives and link the resources of different components, and thereby to expand its organizational capabilities.*

FROM CONTROL TO COORDINATION AND CO-OPTION

The simplifying assumptions of organizational symmetry and dependence (or independence) had allowed the management processes in many companies to be dominated by simple controls—tight operational controls in subsidiaries dependent on the center, and a looser system of administrative or financial controls in decentralized units. When companies began to challenge the assumptions underlying organizational relationships, however, they found they also had to adapt their management processes. The growing interdependence of organizational units strained the simple control-dominated systems and underlined the need to supplement existing processes with more sophisticated ones. Furthermore, the differentiation of organizational tasks and roles amplified the diversity of management perspectives and capabilities and forced management to differentiate management processes.

As organizations became, at the same time, more diverse and more interdependent, there was an explosion in the number of issues that had to be linked, reconciled, or integrated. The rapidly increasing flows of goods, resources, and information among organizational units increased the need for *coordination* as a central management function. But the costs of coordination are high, both in financial and human terms, and coordinating capabilities are always limited. Most companies, though, tended to concentrate on a primary means of coordination and control—the company's way of doing things. . . .

In a number of companies, we saw a . . . broadening of administrative processes as managers learned to operate with previously underutilized means of coordination. Unilever's heavy reliance on the socialization of managers to provide the coordination "glue" was supplemented by the growing role of the central product coordination departments. In contrast, NEC reduced central management's coordination role by developing formal systems and social processes in a way that created a more robust and flexible coordinative capability.

Having developed diverse new means of coordination, management's main task is carefully to ration their usage and application. . . . it is important to distinguish where tasks can be formalized and managed through systems, where social linkages can be fostered to encourage informal

---

*The distinction among sequential, reciprocal, and pooled interdependencies has been made in J. D. Thompson, *Organizations in Action* (New York: McGraw-Hill, 1967).

agreements and cooperation, and where the coordination task is so vital or sensitive that it must use the scarce resource of central management arbitration. . . .

We have described briefly how companies began to . . . differentiat[e] roles and responsibilities within the organization. Depending on their internal capabilities and on the strategic importance of their external environments, organizational units might be asked to take on roles ranging from that of strategic leader with primary corporate-wide responsibility for a particular business or function, to simple implementer responsible only for executing strategies and decisions developed elsewhere.

Clearly, these roles must be managed in quite different ways. The unit with strategic leadership responsibility must be given freedom to develop responsibility in an entrepreneurial fashion, yet must also be strongly supported by headquarters. For this unit, operating controls may be light and quite routine, but coordination of information and resource flows to and from the unit will probably require intensive involvement from senior management. In contrast, units with implementation responsibility might be managed through tight operating controls, with standardized systems used to handle much of the coordination—primarily of goods flows. Because the tasks are more routine, the use of scarce coordinating resources could be minimized.

Differentiating organizational roles and management processes can have a fragmenting and sometimes demotivating effect, however. Nowhere was this more clearly illustrated than in the many companies that unquestioningly assigned units the "dog" and "cash cow" roles defined by the Boston Consulting Group's growth-share matrix in the 1970s. (See Haspeslagh, 1982.) Their experience showed that there is another equally important corporate management task, which complements and facilitates coordination effectiveness. We call this task *co-option:* the process of uniting the organization with a common understanding of, identification with, and commitment to the corporation's objectives, priorities, and values.

A clear example of the importance of co-option was provided by the contrast between ITT and NEC managers. At ITT, corporate objectives were communicated more in financial than in strategic terms, and the company's national entities identified almost exclusively with their local environment. When corporate management tried to superimpose a more unified and integrated global strategy, its local subsidiaries neither understood nor accepted the need to do so. For years they resisted giving up their autonomy, and management was unable to replace the interunit rivalry with a more cooperative and collaborative process.

In contrast, NEC developed an explicitly defined and clearly communicated global strategy enshrined in the company's "C&C" motto—a corporate-wide dedication to building business and basing competitive strategy on the strong link between computers and communications. For over a decade, the C&C philosophy was constantly interpreted, refined, elaborated, and eventually institutionalized in organizational units dedicated to various C&C missions (e.g., the C&C Systems Research Laboratories, the C&C Corporate Planning Committee, and eventually the C&C Systems Division). Top management recognized that one of its major tasks was to inculcate the worldwide organization with an understanding of the C&C strategy and philosophy and to raise managers' consciousness about the global implications of competing in these converging businesses. By the mid-1980s, the company was confident that every NEC employee in every operating unit had a clear understanding of NEC's global strategy as well as of his or her role in it. Indeed, it was this homogeneity that allowed the company to begin the successful decentralization of its management processes.

Thus the management process that distinguished transnational organizations from simpler unidimensional forms was one in which control was made less dominant by the increased importance of interunit integration and collaboration. These new processes required corporate management to supplement its control role with the more subtle tasks of coordination and co-option, giving rise to a much more complex and sophisticated management process.

SUSTAINING A DYNAMIC BALANCE: ROLE OF THE "MIND MATRIX"

Developing multidimensional perspectives and capabilities does not mean that product, functional, and geographic management must have the same level of influence on all key decisions. Quite the contrary. It means that the organization must possess a differentiated influence structure—one in which different groups have different roles for different activities. These roles cannot be fixed but must change continually to respond to new environmental demands and evolving industry characteristics. Not only is it necessary to prevent any one perspective from dominating the others, it is equally important not to be locked into a mode of operation that prevents reassignment of responsibilities, realignment of relationships, and rebalancing of power distribution. This ability to manage the multidimensional organization capability in a flexible manner is the hallmark of a transnational company.

In the change processes we have described, managers were clearly employing some powerful organizational tools to create and control the desired flexible management process. They used the classic tool of formal structure to strengthen, weaken, or shift roles and responsibilities over time, and they employed management systems effectively to redirect corporate resources and to channel information in a way that shifted the balance of power. By controlling the ebb and flow of responsibilities, and by rebalancing power relationships, they were able to prevent any of the multidimensional perspectives from atrophying. Simultaneously, they prevented the establishment of entrenched power bases.

But the most successful companies had an additional element at the core of their management processes. We were always conscious that a substantial amount of senior management attention focused on the *individual* members of the organization. NEC's continual efforts to inculcate all corporate members with a common vision of goals and priorities; P&G's careful assignment of managers to teams and task forces to broaden their perspectives; Philips's frequent use of conferences and meetings as forums to reconcile differences; and Unilever's extensive use of training as a powerful socialization process and its well-planned career path management that provided diverse experience across businesses, functions, and geographic locations—all are examples of companies trying to develop multidimensional perspectives and flexible approaches at the level of the individual manager.

What is critical, then, is not just the structure, but also the mentality of those who constitute the structure. The common thread that holds together the diverse tasks we have described is a managerial mindset that understands the need for multiple strategic capabilities, that is able to view problems from both local and global perspectives, and that accepts the importance of a flexible approach. This pattern suggests that managers should resist the temptation to view their task in the traditional terms of building a formal global matrix structure—an organizational form that in practice has proved extraordinarily difficult to manage in the international environment. They might be better guided by the perspective of one top manager who described the challenge as "creating a matrix in the minds of managers."

Our study has led us to conclude that a company's ability to develop transnational organizational capability and management mentality will be the key factor that separates the winners from the mere survivors in the emerging international environment.

READING 11.2

Global Strategy . . . in a World of Nations* BY GEORGE S. YIP

Whether to globalize, and how to globalize, have become two of the most burning strategy issues for managers around the world. Many forces are driving companies around the world to globalize by expanding their participation in foreign markets. Almost every product market in the major world economies—computers, fast food, nuts and bolts—has foreign competitors. Trade barriers are also falling; the recent United States/Canada trade agreement and the impending 1992 harmonization in the European Community are the two most dramatic examples. Japan is

*My framework, developed in this article, is based in part on M. E. Porter's (1986) pioneering work on global strategy. Bartlett and Ghoshal (1987) define a "transnational industry" that is somewhat similar to Porter's "global industry." Originally published in the *Sloan Management Review* (Fall 1989). [FN]

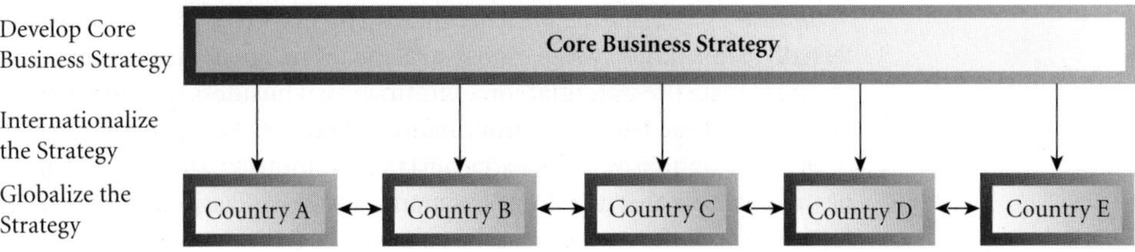

FIGURE 1
TOTAL GLOBAL STRATEGY

gradually opening up its long barricaded markets. Maturity in domestic markets is also driving companies to seek international expansion. This is particularly true of U.S. companies that, nourished by the huge domestic market, have typically lagged behind their European and Japanese rivals in internationalization.

Companies are also seeking to globalize by integrating their worldwide strategy. Such global integration contrasts with the multinational approach whereby companies set up country subsidiaries that design, produce, and market products or services tailored to local needs. This multinational model (also described as a "multidomestic strategy") is now in question (Hout et al., 1982). Several changes seem to increase the likelihood that, in some industries, a global strategy will be more successful than a multidomestic one. One of these changes, as argued forcefully and controversially by Levitt (1983), is the growing similarity of what citizens of different countries want to buy. Other changes include the reduction of tariff and nontariff barriers, technology investments that are becoming too expensive to amortize in one market only, and competitors that are globalizing the rules of the game.

Companies want to know how to globalize—in other words, expand market participation—and how to develop an integrated worldwide strategy. As depicted in Figure 1, three steps are essential in developing a total worldwide strategy:

- Developing the core strategy—the basis of sustainable competitive advantage. It is usually developed for the home country first.
- Internationalizing the core strategy through international expansion of activities and through adaptation.
- Globalizing the international strategy by integrating the strategy across countries.

Multinational companies know the first two steps well. They know the third step less well since globalization runs counter to the accepted wisdom of tailoring for national markets (Douglas and Wind, 1987).

This article makes a case for how a global strategy might work and directs managers toward opportunities to exploit globalization. It also presents the drawbacks and costs of globalization. Figure 2 lays out a framework for thinking through globalization issues.

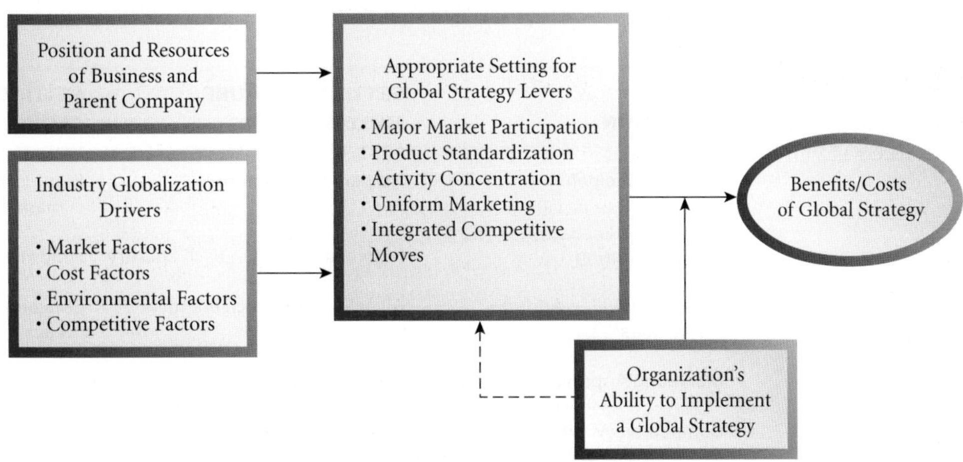

FIGURE 2
FRAMEWORK OF GLOBAL STRATEGY FORCES

Industry globalization drivers (underlying market, cost, and other industry conditions) are externally determined, while global strategy levers are choices available to the worldwide business. Drivers create the potential for a multinational business to achieve the benefits of global strategy. To achieve these benefits, a multinational business needs to set its *global strategy levers* (e.g., use of product standardization) appropriately to industry drivers, and to the position and resources of the business and its parent company. The organization's ability to implement the strategy affects how well the benefits can be achieved.

WHAT IS GLOBAL STRATEGY?

Setting strategy for a worldwide business requires making choices along a number of strategic dimensions. Table 1 lists five such dimensions or "global strategy levels" and their respective positions under a pure multidomestic strategy and a pure global strategy. Intermediate positions are, of course, feasible. For each dimension, a multidomestic strategy seeks to maximize worldwide performance by maximizing local competitive advantage, revenues, or profits; a global strategy seeks to maximize worldwide performance through sharing and integration.

MARKET PARTICIPATION

In a multidomestic strategy, countries are selected on the basis of their stand-alone potential for revenues and profits. In a global strategy, countries need to be selected for their potential contribution to globalization benefits. This may mean entering a market that is unattractive in its own right, but has global strategic significance, such as the home market of a global competitor. Or it may mean building share in a limited number of key markets rather than undertaking more widespread coverage. . . . The Electrolux Group, the Swedish appliance giant, is pursing a strategy of building significant share in major world markets. The company aims to be the first global appliance maker.

PRODUCT OFFERING

In a multidomestic strategy, the products offered in each country are tailored to local needs. In a global strategy, the ideal is a standardized core product that requires minimal local adaptation. Cost reduction is usually the most important benefit of product standardization. . . . Differing worldwide needs can be met by adapting a standardized core product. In the early 1970s, sales of the Boeing 737 began to level off. Boeing turned to developing countries as an attractive new market, but found initially that its product did not fit the new environments. Because of the

TABLE 1
GLOBALIZATION DIMENSIONS/GLOBAL STRATEGY LEVERS

DIMENSION	SETTING FOR PURE MULTIDOMESTIC	SETTING FOR PURE GLOBAL STRATEGY
Market Participation	No particular pattern	Significant share in major markets
Product Offering	Fully customized in each country	Fully standardized worldwide
Location of Value-Added Activities	All activities in each country	Concentrated—one activity in each (different) country
Marketing Approach	Local	Uniform worldwide
Competitive Moves	Stand-alone by country	Integrated across countries

shortness of runways, their greater softness, and the lower technical expertise of their pilots, the planes tended to bounce a great deal. When the planes bounced on landing, the brakes failed. To fix this problem, Boeing modified the design by adding thrust to the engines, redesigning the wings and landing gear, and installing tires with lower pressure. These adaptations to a standardized core product enabled the 737 to become the best selling plane in history.

LOCATION OF VALUE-ADDED ACTIVITIES

In a multidomestic strategy, all or most of the value chain is reproduced in every country. In another type of international strategy—exporting—most of the value chain is kept in one country. In a global strategy, costs are reduced by breaking up the value chain so each activity may be conducted in a different country. . . .

MARKETING APPROACH

In a multidomestic strategy, marketing is fully tailored for each country, being developed locally. In a global strategy, a uniform marketing approach is applied around the world, although not all elements of the marketing mix need be uniform. Unilever achieved great success with a fabric softener that used a globally common positioning, advertising theme, and symbol (a teddy bear), but a brand name that varied by country. Similarly, a product that serves a common need can be geographically expanded with a uniform marketing program, despite differences in marketing environments.

COMPETITIVE MOVES

In a multidomestic strategy, the managers in each country make competitive moves without regard for what happens in other countries. In a global strategy, competitive moves are integrated across countries at the same time or in a systematic sequence: a competitor is attacked in one country in order to drain its resources for another country, or a competitive attack in one country is countered in a different country. Perhaps the best example is the counterattack in a competitor's home market as a parry to an attack on one's own home market. Integration of competitive strategy is rarely practiced, except perhaps by some Japanese companies.

Bridgestone Corporation, the Japanese tire manufacturer, tried to integrate its competitive moves in response to global consolidation by its major competitors. . . . These competitive actions forced Bridgestone to establish a presence in the major U.S. market in order to maintain its position in the world tire market. To this end, Bridgestone formed a joint venture to own and manage Firestone Corporation's worldwide tire business. This joint venture also allowed Bridgestone to gain access to Firestone's European plants.

BENEFITS OF A GLOBAL STRATEGY

Companies that use global strategy levels can achieve one or more of these benefits. . . .

- cost reductions
- improved quality of products and programs
- enhanced customer preference
- increased competitive leverage

COST REDUCTIONS

An integrated global strategy can reduce worldwide costs in several ways. A company can increase the benefits from economies of scale by *pooling production or other activities* for two or more countries. Understanding the potential benefit of these economies of scale, Sony

Corporation has concentrated its compact disc production in Terre Haute, Indiana, and Salzburg, Austria.

A second way to cut costs is by *exploiting lower factor costs* by moving manufacturing or other activities to low-cost countries. This approach has, of course, motivated the recent surge of offshore manufacturing, particularly by U.S. firms. For example, the Mexican side of the U.S.–Mexico border is now crowded with "maquiladoras"—manufacturing plants set up and run by U.S. companies using Mexican labor.

Global strategy can also cut costs by *exploiting flexibility*. A company with manufacturing locations in several countries can move production from location to location on short notice to take advantage of the lowest costs at a given time. Dow Chemicals takes this approach to minimize the cost of producing chemicals. Dow uses a linear programming model that takes account of international differences in exchange rates, tax rates, and transportation and labor costs. The model comes up with the best mix of production volume by location for each planning period.

An integrated global strategy can also reduce costs by *enhancing bargaining power*. A company whose strategy allows for switching production among different countries greatly increases its bargaining power with suppliers, workers, and host governments. . . .

IMPROVED QUALITY OF PRODUCTS AND PROGRAMS

Under a global strategy, companies focus on a smaller number of products and programs than under a multidomestic strategy. This concentration can improve both product and program quality. Global focus is one reason for Japanese success in automobiles. Toyota markets a far smaller number of models around the world than does General Motors, even allowing for its unit sales being half that of General Motors. . . .

ENHANCED CUSTOMER PREFERENCE

Global availability, serviceability, and recognition can enhance customer preference through reinforcement. Soft drink and fast food companies are, of course, leading exponents of this strategy. Many suppliers of financial services, such as credit cards, must have a global presence because their service is travel related. . . .

INCREASED COMPETITIVE LEVERAGE

A global strategy provides more points from which to attack and counterattack competitors. In an effort to prevent the Japanese from becoming a competitive nuisance in disposable syringes, Becton Dickinson, a major U.S. medical products company, decided to enter three markets in Japan's backyard. Becton entered the Hong Kong, Singapore, and Philippine markets to prevent further Japanese expansion (Cvar, 1986).

DRAWBACKS OF A GLOBAL STRATEGY

Globalization can incur significant management costs through increased coordination, reporting requirements, and even added staff. It can also reduce the firm's effectiveness in individual countries if overcentralization hurts local motivation and morale. In addition, each global strategy lever has particular drawbacks.

A global strategy approach to *market participation* can incur an earlier or greater commitment to a market than is warranted on its own merits. Many American companies, such as Motorola, are struggling to penetrate Japanese markets, more in order to enhance their global competitive position than to make money in Japan for its own sake.

Product standardization can result in a product that does not entirely satisfy *any* customers. When companies first internationalize, they often offer their standard domestic product without adapting it for other countries, and suffer the consequences. . . .

A globally standardized product is designed for the global market but can seldom satisfy all needs in all countries. For instance, Canon, a Japanese company, sacrificed the ability to copy certain Japanese paper sizes when it first designed a photocopier for the global market.

Activity concentration distances customers and can result in lower responsiveness and flexibility. It also increases currency risk by incurring costs and revenues in different countries. Recently volatile exchange rates have required companies that concentrate their production to hedge their currency exposure.

Uniform marketing can reduce adaptation to local customer behavior. For example, the head office of British Airways mandated that every country use the "Manhattan Landing" television commercial developed by advertising agency Saatchi and Saatchi. While the commercial did win many awards, it has been criticized for using a visual image (New York City) that was not widely recognized in many countries.

Integrated competitive moves can mean sacrificing revenues, profits, or competitive position in individual countries, particularly when the subsidiary in one country is asked to attack a global competitor in order to send a signal or to divert that competitor's resources from another country.

FINDING THE BALANCE

The most successful worldwide strategies find a balance between overglobalizing and underglobalizing. The ideal strategy matches the level of strategy globalization to the globalization potential of the industry. . . .

INDUSTRY GLOBALIZATION DRIVERS

To achieve the benefits of globalization, the managers of a worldwide business need to recognize when industry globalization drivers (industry conditions) provide the opportunity to use global strategy levers. These drivers can be grouped in four categories: market, cost, governmental, and competitive. Each industry globalization driver affects the potential use of global strategy levers. . . .

MARKET DRIVERS

Market globalization drivers depend on customer behavior and the structure of distribution channels. These drivers affect the use of all five global strategy levers.

HOMOGENEOUS CUSTOMER NEEDS

When customers in different countries want essentially the same type of product or service (or can be so persuaded), opportunities arise to market a standardized product. Understanding which aspects of the product can be standardized and which should be customized is key. In addition, homogeneous needs make participation in a large number of markets easier because fewer different product offerings need to be developed and supported.

GLOBAL CUSTOMERS

Global customers buy on a centralized or coordinated basis for decentralized use. The existence of global customers both allows and requires a uniform marketing program. There are two types of global customers: national and multinational. A national global customer searches the world for suppliers but uses the purchased product or service in one country. National defense agencies are a good example. A multinational global customer also searches the world for suppliers, but uses the purchased product or service in many countries. The World Health Organization's purchase of medical products is an example. Multinational global customers are particularly challenging to serve and often require a global account management program. . . .

GLOBAL CHANNELS

Analogous to global customers, channels of distribution may buy on a global or at least a regional basis. Global channels or middlemen are also important in exploiting differences in prices by buying at a lower price in one country and selling at a higher price in another country. Their presence makes it more necessary for a business to rationalize its worldwide pricing. Global channels are rare, but regionwide channels are increasing in number, particularly in European grocery distribution and retailing.

TRANSFERABLE MARKETING

The buying decision may be such that marketing elements, such as brand names and advertising, require little local adaptation. Such transferability enables firms to use uniform marketing strategies and facilitates expanded participation in markets. A worldwide business can also adapt its brand names and advertising campaigns to make them more transferable, or, even better, design global ones to start with. Offsetting risks include the blandness of uniformly acceptable brand names or advertising, and the vulnerability of relying on a single brand franchise.

COST DRIVERS

Cost drivers depend on the economics of the business; they particularly affect activity concentration.

ECONOMIES OF SCALE AND SCOPE

A single-country market may not be large enough for the local business to achieve all possible economies of scale or scope. Scale at a given location can be increased through participation in multiple markets combined with product standardization or concentration of selected value activities. Corresponding risks include rigidity and vulnerability to disruption. . . .

LEARNING AND EXPERIENCE

Even if economies of scope and scale are exhausted, expanded market participation and activity concentration can accelerate the accumulation of learning and experience. The steeper the learning and experience curves, the greater the potential benefit will be. Managers should beware, though, of the usual danger in pursuing experience curve strategies—overaggressive pricing that destroyed not just the competition but the market as well. Prices get so low that profit is insufficient to sustain any competitor.

SOURCING EFFICIENCIES

Centralized purchasing of new materials can significantly lower costs. . . .

FAVORABLE LOGISTICS

A favorable ratio of sales value to transportation cost enhances the company's ability to concentrate production. Other logistical factors include nonperishability, the absence of time urgency, and little need for location close to customer facilities. . . .

DIFFERENCES IN COUNTRY COSTS AND SKILLS

Factor costs generally vary across countries; this is particularly true in certain industries. The availability of particular skills also varies. Concentration of activities in low-cost or high-skill countries can increase productivity and reduce costs, but managers need to anticipate the danger of training future offshore competitors. . . .

PRODUCT DEVELOPMENT COSTS

Product development costs can be reduced by developing a few global or regional products rather than many national products. The automobile industry is characterized by long product development periods and high product development costs. One reason for the high costs is duplication of effort across countries. The Ford Motor Company's "Centers of Excellence" program aims to reduce these duplicating efforts and to exploit the differing expertise of Ford specialists worldwide. As part of the concentrated effort, Ford of Europe is designing a common platform for all compacts, while Ford of North America is developing platforms for the replacement of the mid-sized Taurus and Sable. This concentration of design is estimated to save "hundreds of millions of dollars per model by eliminating duplicative efforts and saving on retooling factories" (*Business Week,* 1967).

GOVERNMENTAL DRIVERS

Government globalization drivers depend on the rules set by national governments and affect the use of all global strategy levers.

FAVORABLE TRADE POLICIES

Host governments affect globalization potential through import tariffs and quotas, nontariff barriers, export subsidies, local content requirements, currency and capital flow restrictions, and requirements on technology transfer. Host government policies can make it difficult to use the global levers of major market participation, product standardization, activity concentration, and uniform marketing; they also affect the integrated-competitive moves lever. . . .

COMPATIBLE TECHNICAL STANDARDS

Differences in technical standards, especially government-imposed standards, limit the extent to which products can be standardized. Often, standards are set with protectionism in mind. Motorola found that many of their electronics products were excluded from the Japanese market because these products operated at a higher frequency than was permitted in Japan.

COMMON MARKETING REGULATIONS

The marketing environment of individual countries affects the extent to which uniform global marketing approaches can be used. Certain types of media may be prohibited or restricted. For example, the United States is far more liberal than Europe about the kinds of advertising claims that can be made on television. The British authorities even veto the depiction of socially undesirable behavior. For example, British television authorities do not allow scenes of children pestering their parents to buy a product. . . .

COMPETITIVE DRIVERS

Market, cost, and governmental globalization drivers are essentially fixed for an industry at any given time. Competitors can play only a limited role in affecting these factors (although a sustained effort can bring about change, particularly in the case of consumer preferences). In contrast, competitive drivers are entirely in the realm of competitor choice. Competitors can raise the globalization potential of their industry and spur the need for a response on the global strategy levers.

INTERDEPENDENCE OF COUNTRIES

A competitor may create competitive interdependence among countries by pursuing a global strategy. The basic mechanism is through sharing of activities. When activities such as production are shared among countries, a competitor's market share in one country affects its scale and overall cost position in the shared activities. Changes in that scale and cost will affect its competitive position in all countries dependent on the shared activities. Less directly, customers may view market position in a lead country as an indicator of overall quality. Companies frequently promote a product as, for example, "the leading brand in the United States." Other competitors then need to respond via increased market participation, uniform marketing, or integrated competitive strategy to avoid a downward spiral of sequentially weakened positions in individual countries.

In the automobile industry, where economies of scale are significant and where sharing activities can lower costs, markets have significant competitive interdependence. As companies like Ford and Volkswagen concentrate production and become more cost competitive with the Japanese manufacturers, the Japanese are pressured to enter more markets so that increased production volume will lower costs. Whether conscious of this or not, Toyota has begun a concentrated effort to penetrate the German market: between 1984 and 1987, Toyota doubled the number of cars produced for the German market.

GLOBALIZED COMPETITORS

More specifically, matching or preempting individual competitor moves may be necessary. These moves include expanding into or within major markets, being the first to introduce a standardized product, or being the first to use a uniform marketing program.

The need to preempt a global competitor can spur increased market participation. In 1986, Unilever, the European consumer products company, sought to increase its participation in the U.S. market by launching a hostile takeover bid for Richardson-Vicks Inc. Unilever's global archrival, Procter & Gamble, saw the threat to its home turf and outbid Unilever to capture Richardson-Vicks. With the Richardson-Vicks' European system, P&G was able to greatly strengthen its European positioning. So Unilever's attempt to expand participation in a rival's home market backfired to allow the rival to expand participation in Unilever's home markets.

In summary, industry globalization drivers provide opportunities to use global strategy levers in many ways. Some industries, such as civil aircraft, can score high on most dimensions of globalization (Yoshino, 1986). Others, such as the cement industry, seem to be inherently local. But more and more industries are developing a globalization potential. Even the food industry in Europe, renowned for its diversity of taste, is now a globalization target for major food multinationals.

CHANGES OVER TIME

Finally, industry evolution plays a role. As each of the industry globalization drivers changes over time, so too will the appropriate global strategy change. For example, in the European major appliance industry, globalization forces seem to have reversed. In the late 1960s and early 1970s, a regional standardization strategy was successful for some key competitors (Levitt, 1983). But in the 1980s the situation appears to have turned around, and the most successful strategies seem to be national (Baden-Fuller et al., 1987).

In some cases, the actions of individual competitors can affect the direction and pace of change; competitors positioned to take advantage of globalization forces will want to hasten them. . . .

MORE THAN ONE STRATEGY IS VIABLE

Although they are powerful, industry globalization drivers do not dictate one formula for success. More than one type of international strategy can be viable in a given industry.

INDUSTRIES VARY ACROSS DRIVERS

No industry is high on every one of the many globalization drivers. A particular competitor may be in a strong position to exploit a driver that scores low on globalization. . . . The hotel industry provides examples of both successful global and successful local competitors.

GLOBAL EFFECTS ARE INCREMENTAL

Globalization drivers are not deterministic for a second reason: the appropriate use of strategy levers adds competitive advantage to existing sources. These other sources may allow individual competitors to thrive with international strategies that are mismatched with industry globalization drivers. For example, superior technology is a major source of competitive advantage in most industries, but can be quite independent of globalization drivers. A competitor with sufficiently superior technology can use it to offset globalization disadvantages.

BUSINESS AND PARENT COMPANY POSITION AND RESOURCES ARE CRUCIAL

The third reason that drivers are not deterministic is related to resources. A worldwide business may face industry drivers that strongly favor a global strategy. But global strategies are typically expensive to implement initially even though great cost savings and revenue gains should follow.

High initial investments may be needed to expand within or into major markets, to develop standardized products, to relocate value activities, to create global brands, to create new organization units or coordination processes, and to implement other aspects of a global strategy. The strategic position of the business is also relevant. Even though a global strategy may improve the business's long-term strategic position, its immediate position may be so weak that resources should be devoted to short-term, country-by-country improvements. Despite the automobile industry's very strong globalization drivers, Chrysler Corporation had to deglobalize by selling off most of its international automotive businesses to avoid bankruptcy. Lastly, investing in non-global sources of competitive advantage, such as superior technology, may yield greater returns than global ones, such as centralized manufacturing.

ORGANIZATIONS HAVE LIMITATIONS

Finally, factors such as organization structure, management processes, people, and culture affect how well a desired global strategy can be implemented. Organizational differences among companies in the same industry can, or should, constrain the companies' pursuit of the same global strategy. . .

READING 11.3

Globalization and the Offshoring of Services BY JOSEPH LAMPEL AND AJAY BHALLA

1. THE OFFSHORING DILEMMA

Few trends in business have had greater impact on global operations in recent years than offshoring. Offshoring is a strategic move that involves the transfer of certain firm activities to a related business unit that is located offshore and functions as a host, or a separate firm that acts as an outsourcing provider while being located in an offshore location. As such the term offshoring encompasses offshore outsourcing and offshoring to fully owned business units located offshore that may create an internal market for their services. Offshoring is now widely touted as a strategy for cutting costs, promoting flexibility, and accessing a global talent pool. Broadly speaking, companies turn to offshoring because they must deal with persistent and increasing pressures on operating margins, or alternately because they are interested in accelerating their value chain activities. But as with any other strategy, offshoring is a move with associated risks as well as potential advantages. What is more, the advantages and risks vary, depending on the model of offshoring that the firm decides to pursue. In order to successfully undertake offshoring, it is therefore important to select the right model. Selecting the right model in turn calls for a proper appreciation of the advantages and risks that are inherent in offshoring in general.

Although offshoring covers a range of related activities and investments, closer examination suggests that beneath the diversity there are commonalities that cut across sectors and industries. This is particularly apparent in offshoring of IT enabled services (ITES), which encompass IT services such as software development and maintenance, business processes such as transaction processing, human resource management, and customer interaction and support. Advances in information and communication technologies have enabled the disaggregation of value chain and business processes that can be located elsewhere entirely or in parts to secure benefits such as cost savings, economies of scale, and quality improvements. Overwhelmingly, most of the large corporations today rely heavily on these IT enabled services, and many of these firms have pursued, or are pursuing, offshoring in this area.

Our analysis has led us to conclude that offshoring initiatives that involve IT enabled services have seen the emergence of four distinct models. This paper explores the background of these offshoring models, their nature and dynamics, and the factors that influence their adoption. To understand this background, we begin with a general discussion of the drivers that lead many firms to offshore. These drivers are front-and-center when firms decide to pursue offshoring rather than retaining activities onshore. However, alongside the advantages of these drivers, offshoring also has associated risks. Understanding these risks is useful in deciding not only whether and when offshoring is the right strategy for the firm, but it is also important in deciding which model of offshoring the firm should pursue.

Our discussion of key offshoring drivers and their associated risks therefore forms the background for describing and analyzing the four offshoring models which our research suggests are currently in use. These offshoring models represent strategic design configurations—their choice is mainly influenced by two factors: pressures on operating margins and the need to accelerate key value chain activities.

2. OFFSHORING IN IT ENABLED SERVICES: DRIVERS AND RISKS

Offshoring as such is hardly a new phenomenon. What has changed the character of current offshoring is the advent of new technologies, in particular new information technologies. New information technologies have allowed firms to create new value chain capabilities, specifically in the provision of so-called IT enabled services, which, as pointed out earlier, encompass transaction processing, customer interaction and support, software development and maintenance, and human resource management. IT enabled services have allowed firms not only to devise novel methods that address current challenges of their business environments, but also to develop value chain configurations that open new strategic opportunities.

IT enablement of services allows firms to overcome some of the difficulties that have previously constrained their ability to transfer and manage activities in countries that are not only geographically distant, but also different socially and economically. But as the use of IT enabled services increases, firms confront the limitations of retaining these services onshore. To begin with, scarcities of specialized skills emerge as large numbers of firms simultaneously seek to develop IT enabled services in their home markets. These scarcities hamper the ability of firms to fully develop and take advantage of IT enabled services, and they also raise the costs. Thus, as IT enabled services grow in importance they consume an increasing share of corporate resources. Many firms therefore turn to offshoring of IT enabled services as a way of expanding their use while at the same time reducing their burden on corporate overheads.

To understand the dynamics of offshoring IT enabled services it is important to recognize that the process that leads firms to transfer these services offshore often begins with an analysis of current or comparable operations at home. Since managers face problems of creating and delivering these services at home, they look to offshoring as a way of resolving these difficulties, and, whenever appropriate, use offshoring to gain additional advantage. The drivers of IT enabled service offshoring are therefore relatively explicit because they are based on benchmarking similar operations in different locations. What is not readily apparent are the risks that go with this move, precisely because these risks are not evident in the onshore operations, and beyond that because they are often specific to the offshoring location. In what follows, we therefore look at drivers that firms cite as their reasons for offshoring IT enabled services, but then explore the risks associated with these drivers.

DRIVER 1: COST CONTAINMENT AND REDUCTION

Cost reduction and containment are often cited as key reasons for offshoring IT enabled services. Senior managers are attracted to offshoring by claims of cost savings that may be as high as 40% to 50%. These cost savings are often associated with "hot spots," such as Bangalore, India, where highly skilled and easily recruited labor is available at lower labor costs than in home markets. What this fails to take into account are associated costs that do not show in simple comparison of employee costs. Full-time equivalent employees in India may cost 40% less than in North America, but the growing demand for offshoring services in hubs such as Bangalore and Hyderabad has resulted in the shortage of a skilled labor pool. This has driven up pay rates, and though starting salaries for software engineers in Bangalore are about one sixth of those in the United States, annual wage inflation in India points to erosion of offshoring labor cost advantage.

Many firms also fail to factor in the hidden costs involved in offshoring because they are not easily quantifiable. Ancillary costs, such as legal and advisory fees, and travel expenses, are difficult to forecast but they can easily escalate. Likewise, when making the decision to offshore, many companies do not take into consideration the substantial costs of selecting a vendor. The costs of documenting requirements, sending out requests for proposals, evaluating the responses, and negotiating the contract can vary from 1% to 10% in addition to the annual cost of the deal, the average being 3%. In other words, if a firm is sending $10 million worth of work to India, selecting a vendor could cost up to $300,000 each year.

DRIVER 2: FOCUSING ON CRUCIAL CORE COMPETENCIES

Externalizing non-crucial activities, especially support functions, has always been an attractive route to combining the advantages of focus with greater organizational flexibility. Constraints in the home market, for example, the difficulty of developing local cost-effective alternatives to in-house activities, have tended to hamper the move away from non-core activities. New technologies and the growth of offshoring hubs have allowed firms to use offshoring as a way of refocusing their strategy on core competencies. The key difficulty in using offshoring to refocus on core competencies is judging correctly which activities to retain and which to offshore. IT functions are seen as a non-core activity mainly because of claims that as technologies become more standardized the role of IT as a source of strategic differentiation diminishes—often because firms can easily replicate some of their competitors' "best practices" by sourcing from specialist vendors. Closer scrutiny suggests the contrary: Human IT resources and IT intangibles underpin core IT capabilities—they take a long time to build, and benefit from their embeddedness in the operations. Thus what appears as a non-core activity at one level becomes an important part of strategic advantage at another.

DRIVER 3: SPURRING INNOVATION

Proponents of offshoring argue that it enhances innovation capabilities. For example, many firms find it increasingly difficult to acquire, develop, and retain the people and technical know-how needed to sustain the current pace of technological innovation. Others discover a mismatch between rapid growth and the difficulty of growing key value chain activities that require strong technical human resources. Offshoring offers a quick expansion of internal capabilities without having to undergo the difficult process of building them up internally.

The assumption that one can "buy" technological capabilities runs counter to studies that suggest that when technology is changing rapidly, firms that choose to outsource may actually fall behind. Expanding capabilities may work if the firm has plenty of time to coordinate innovation with its offshoring partners, but it becomes a crucial barrier if speed is important.

3. FOUR MODELS OF OFFSHORING IT ENABLED SERVICES

As offshoring initiatives gain popularity, there is a transition from early enthusiasm about the potential of this strategic move to a more nuanced view that includes pitfalls and risks. Managers must now engage in a broader and more complex calculation before committing to an offshoring strategy. This commitment, however, depends on whether managers can find an offshoring strategy that delivers superior results relative to the same activity onshore, but in addition, it also depends on whether the advantages associated with this strategy justify the risks. Research suggests that when faced with the complex task of developing an offshoring strategy, managers tend to examine this approach by looking at strategic models that are already in use. In the case of offshoring, our research suggests the following four models (see Table 1).

3.1 CAPTIVE CENTERS

Offshoring via a captive center involves setting up a company-owned and operated facility in offshore locations. A captive center allows managers to retain the advantages of internal communications and coordination, while deriving cost benefits from recruiting locally. This means direct oversight of new product introduction, with the capability of ensuring that schedules are met. It also means effective retention of knowledge generated during offshoring activities.

TABLE 1 MODELS OF OFFSHORING

	MODEL	DESCRIPTION	POTENTIAL BENEFITS	POTENTIAL RISKS
1	Captive centers	The vendor builds, owns, staffs, and operates offshore facility.	Internalization of knowledge, ability to control costs and service level, potential for continuous focus on ongoing learning and innovation.	High set-up and high fixed costs, internal bureaucratization, exposure to locational risks such as geopolitical and exchange risks.
2	Build–operate–transfer agreements	The vendor owns, builds, staffs, and operates the facility on behalf of the customer. The customer has the option where ownership and employees are transferred at a pre-agreed future date.	Cost efficiencies, scalability, benefits from specialist know-how, transferable skills.	Problems of transferring knowledge, dependence on external vendor for training, lack of visible incentives to innovate for vendor.
3	Dedicated offshore centers	The vendor owning the operation dedicates part of its facility to the customer.	Low set-up costs, scalable, by-pass political resistance, capitalize on external skills.	Reduced ability to control output and introduce innovation, potential for vendor opportunism, no transferable skills.
4	Fee-for-service relationships	A fixed or tiered fee is payable to the vendor for his services.	No set-up costs, low financial risk.	Potential for cost escalations, forced cost–service trade-off, low potential for building on innovations.

By operating an internal offshore center the firm can more easily transfer practices and processes from the home office to the offshoring center, and back, often by rotating managers.

3.2 BUILD–OPERATE–TRANSFER AGREEMENTS

The build–operate–transfer (BOT) model is essentially a strategic alliance with an outsourcing vendor. The vendor sets up and manages the offshore facility, and the offshoring firm has an option to own the facility at the end of a specified period. Managerial motivations may be efficiency-related, for example, cost and risk sharing, and mutual specialization of tasks; or strategic, in the sense of entering a new geographic market, and developing new capabilities.

Currently, BOT is a relatively rare form of offshoring, at least in the sample we examined. This could be because vendors may not see benefits in setting up and running a facility, which they have to transfer to the offshoring firm in a set period of time. Offshoring firms too may be reluctant in opting for this model, as not only do they have to pay a management fee to the vendor for running the captive facility, they also gain little managerial experience in starting and running an offshore facility. Consider two Fortune 500 firms which set up BOT as an offshoring model—Aviva, an insurance firm, and Lloyds TSB, a financial services firm. Both were running BOT centers which provided back-office and customer service support. Aviva started to offshore by outsourcing software development and claims administration to specialist vendors in India. In 2003, it reinforced its commitment to offshoring when it negotiated BOT agreements with three Indian vendors, WNS, EXL, and 24X7. The vendor 24X7 was selected to build and operate Aviva's customer service call center in Bangalore, India, while EXL and WNS built and managed the business processing centers in Pune and Colombo, Sri Lanka. Signing up the four-year BOT contracts with best of the breed vendors enabled Aviva to ramp up rapidly and gain the speed to market. In January 2007, following its original plan, it began transferring third party vendor staff in sequence starting with Bangalore, and more recently Colombo to Aviva Global Services, a newly set up offshore entity. Today, both firms run their offshore centers as captive facilities.

3.3 DEDICATED OFFSHORE CENTERS

The dedicated offshore center is an offshoring model in which the vendor enters into a contract to set up the dedicated center for the offshoring firm within its existing facility. Setting up such a facility requires little upfront financial commitment, and hence is likely to face little inside resistance. Managers can still specify processes, such as employee recruitment and culture, which enable the facility to replicate certain aspects of the organization. For instance, Sony's European division engaged one of the leading offshore vendors in India, to set up a dedicated offshore development center in Bangalore. In justifying its choice to partially relocate its in-house onshore IT service, Sony claimed that offshoring to a specialist vendor would enable its infrastructure services team to focus on core activities such as platform enhancement, optimization and innovation, while the vendor handles IT development for Sony sales and distribution, warehouse management, finance and business intelligence systems.

3.4 FEE-FOR-SERVICE RELATIONSHIPS

Finally, managers may engage in purely transactional offshoring by opting for a fee-for-service model. A fixed or tiered fee is payable to the vendor for its services. Often managers choose this model because of cost, speed, or the specialist nature of the service they require. When Airbus, one of the world's leading aircraft manufacturers, wanted a reduction in the development time of the A340 flight warning system, it contracted with HCL Technologies, an Indian-based offshore vendor, to develop the sophisticated embedded software. The project followed a phased approach, which involved Airbus remunerating HCL in the first phase for migrating the embedded software development environment from an older technology platform to a newer platform and for the development of new software in the second phase.

4. FACTORS INFLUENCING SELECTION OF OFFSHORING MODELS

Studies of effective strategic decision making suggest that the process tends to be iterative: Firms look at the reasons for the proposed move; they then look at feasible strategic options, and having done this, they more often than not go back and look at the reasons once again. This iterative back-and-forth process clarifies the thinking behind the decision, and allows more time to fully understand the options. In the process, firms not only come to see how the proposed move fits into their overall strategy, but also which strategic options would be a good starting point for thinking concretely about how they should proceed.

In the case of offshoring, a good first step for thinking about reasons for taking activities offshore is to ask why the same activities cannot be performed in the home market: Why offshore abroad if you can outsource at home? Our research suggests that pressure on two key areas tends to drive firms to offshore: First, offshoring is often motivated by pressure on operating margins—either because firms are facing stiff price competition or because their costs are rising, or sometimes both. Second, firms confront the need to accelerate key value chain activities, in particular product development activities. These twin pressures operate differentially for different firms, depending on the sector or industry in which they do business. In the case of some firms pressures on operating margins predominate as they confront declining margins. Other firms do not confront declining operating margins, but they operate in industries where there is pressure to accelerate the rate at which they introduce innovative products. And of course, there are firms that confront pressures on both fronts.

Selecting which offshoring models the firm should explore must begin with clear understanding of which of these pressures it is confronting. Is the firm confronting pressures on its operating margins, pressures to accelerate key value chain activities, or both? Having assessed the extent of these pressures, it is possible to match the analysis against offshoring models as explained below.

4.1 OFFSHORING AS A RESPONSE TO PRESSURES ON OPERATING MARGINS

Firms that face strong pressures on operating margins, but are not technologically racing to develop new markets, tend to look toward offshoring as means of reducing cost and creating a leaner organization set-up. Large companies with substantial resources that are able to pursue a long-term strategy of reducing operating margins usually opt for dedicated offshore centers. For these firms, dedicated offshore centers that allow the offshoring firm to control key activities offer a balance between cost savings and quality risks.

By contrast, companies that face urgent demand to alleviate pressure on their operating margins, and lack resource depth, usually pursue fee-for-service offshoring. The firm contracts with an offshoring provider to deliver an existing activity at lower costs than it is possible to do at home. The contract specifies the term of delivery, and can usually be terminated under relatively short notice if these terms are not met. The option to terminate, however, is cold comfort when providers purchase cost savings by cutting corners. Short of a truly desperate financial situation, fee-for-service offshoring will for this reason be rarely adopted by firms that are in a business where reputational damage can adversely impact market position. The airline industry is a good example. Most of the firms in this industry have experienced operating margin squeeze as a result of rising operating costs, and have moved many back- and front-office functions, such as accounting, ticket processing, and customer reservation to providers in India or the Philippines. At the same time, however, these firms have opted for dedicated offshore centers rather than fee-for-service because they wanted to retain control and exercise oversight over these activities.

4.2 OFFSHORING AS A RESPONSE TO PRESSURES ON KEY VALUE-CHAIN ACTIVITIES

Firms that operate in environments where strategy calls for accelerating key value-chain activities, such as research and development, engineering, or product development, often see offshoring as an attractive route to breaking constraints they face at home. Offshoring firms operate in close proximity to extensive pools of specialized human resources, and also have greater flexibility when it comes to mobilizing and deploying these resources.

Notwithstanding these advantages, when firms turn their attention to selecting offshoring models they must be aware of the risks of relying on outside firms for knowledge-intensive activities such as engineering or product development where contracts are normally difficult to write. This precludes offshoring models such as fee-for-service where the offshoring firm must be able to specify in some detail what it expects from the provider. Alongside the difficulties of writing contracts for these activities, there is also the risk of losing crucial knowledge to providers who may pass it on to other competitors, or turn into competitors themselves.

For these reasons, captive centers are probably the best offshoring model when it comes to combining simplicity of coordination with security against misappropriation. This is indeed the choice made by many firms that operate in environments where technology and competition demand ramping up of research, development, and engineering activities. For instance, firms such as Google, Oracle, Sun Microsystems, and Microsoft all have offshore captive research centers in India.

Offshoring to accelerate value-chain activities is not just limited to industries where new scientific or technological breakthroughs could quickly transform the competitive landscape; it could also occur in other parts of the value chain characterized by continuous improvement. For instance, increasingly firms are experiencing the disintegration of the product development process, and thus look to offshoring to capture benefits at various stages ranging from concept to definition to high-level design or testing in production to support stages. Activities in these stages may involve industrial design, systems engineering, conceptual computer aided design (CAD) work, development of embedded software, and prototype designing.

4.3 OFFSHORING AS A RESPONSE TO PRESSURES ON OPERATING MARGINS AND VALUE-CHAIN ACTIVITIES

We next turn to firms who are in the unenviable position of confronting both strong pressures on their operating margins and increasing demands to accelerate key value-chain activities. For these firms the consideration of cost, the difficulties of negotiating contracts, and the peril of losing key knowledge assets must all simultaneously be taken into account. This normally rules out fee-for-service agreements because they lack adequate provisions for securing knowledge assets, but also captive centers because they do not offer sufficient cost savings. In effect, for firms facing these twin pressures, the build–operate–transfer offshoring model is usually the most attractive. It not only offers substantial cost savings, but also allows firms to assert control if they believe that the provider's behavior may in the future pose a problem.

If the firm is operating in an environment where pressures to accelerate key value-chain activities do not stem primarily from radical technological change, it can attain further cost savings and an adequate degree of protection against loss of proprietary knowledge by selecting dedicated offshore centers.

5. CONCLUSION

As with many other strategic innovations, offshoring is widely imitated even when external environment conditions do not demand it. In many industries, one finds offshoring first movers: firms that offshore not only to stay ahead of competitors, but also because the advantages offered by the move are intrinsically attractive. The offshoring model that these firms decide to pursue will often depend on their specific strategic requirements, but will also be a function of their own perspective of how the future of their industry will unfold.

It is important to remember that because firms often operate in different environments, different offshoring models are often selected. Since environments also change, choice of offshoring model may also vary over time. Organizations may therefore settle on a particular offshoring model, but when it comes to making the choice once again, another offshoring model may appear better suited—sometimes because top management thinking has changed, but often because the previous choice has not been entirely satisfactory.

The last point directs attention to one of the more important reasons why we see diversity of offshoring choices within the same organization. Many organizations learn from their offshoring experiences. They learn how to negotiate, how to set up operations, how to understand their providers, and how to evaluate their partners. This learning is often idiosyncratic because it is so strongly influenced by initial offshoring experience. For this reason, strategically smart organizations see early offshoring experience as opportunities to engage with a strategic option that has considerable upside potential but also significant risks. The particular offshoring model selected early on can therefore be seen from a dual perspective: First as an answer to specific strategic issues confronting the organization and second as a learning opportunity. The first may or may not succeed, depending on a variety of industry and business factors. The second is more likely to succeed if the company focuses on capturing and analyzing the offshoring experience, and then taking the trouble to introduce lessons learned into the planning and implementation of future offshoring moves.

READING 11.4

Seven Myths Regarding Global Strategy* BY SUBRAMANIAN RANGAN

Companies of all shapes and sizes are pondering global strategies. While there are many useful ideas and opinions on this topic, there are also unfortunately a number of myths. In this article I will highlight seven common ones and discuss them briefly below.

1. ANY COMPANY WITH MONEY CAN GO GLOBAL

The flaw with this is that going global and going global successfully are not the same thing. The Paris department store Galeries Lafayette went global with much fanfare, setting up shop in New York some years ago. However, success proved elusive and the store folded its operations after sustained losses, returning to its home base a wiser company. Expansion into Europe by Whirlpool, the U.S. home appliances manufacturer, has not exactly been smooth either.

The reasons are rooted in an idea known as "the liability of foreignness." A company attempting to sell into a foreign market tends to face an inherent handicap relative to local rivals. Customer needs and tastes in the foreign market are likely to be different; obstacles may abound, from identifying good local suppliers to dealing with skeptical host authorities; and the very model of business may be different. Crucially, on all these fronts, local rivals are likely to have

*Reprinted from S. Rangan, "Seven Myths Regarding Global Strategy," in *Financial Times Mastering Strategy: The Complete MBA Companion in Strategy.* Harlow: Pearson Education Limited: Financial Times Prentice Hall, 2000.

the home advantage. If a company is to succeed abroad, it must possess some valuable intangible asset that will enable it to meet and beat local rivals in their own home market. This could be advanced technology (as with Canon, the copier and camera maker); an appreciably superior value proposition (such as that developed by IKEA, the Swedish furniture group); a well-known brand name (e.g., Coca-Cola); low unit costs deriving from scale or process know-how (e.g., Dell in PCs, or South African Breweries in beer); or some combination of the above (e.g., Toyota, L'Oréal, and Citibank).

When Galeries Lafayette went to New York, it faced established rivals as diverse as Macy's and Bloomingdale's, as well as Saks Fifth Avenue, and it did not have any valuable intangible asset that would set it apart. Whirlpool faces similar challenges in Europe.

Implications: If the urge to expand internationally should strike your company, first study local rivals abroad and look for concrete evidence that you can beat them. A track record of solid and growing exports into the target market can be a credible sign that you can deliver value that local rivals either do not or cannot deliver themselves. This is why companies tend to export before they set up shop abroad. Also, ensure that you dominate your home market. As the foreign market poses inherent handicaps, you may not be ready for global expansion if you are not a domestic leader (if you are not, in other words, a Samsung, a Telefónica, or a Cemex). The broader point is that a global strategy is no substitute for a good business strategy. Also, remember that low growth at home is neither a necessary nor sufficient condition for global expansion. So, if your company does not possess valuable intangible assets, then, no matter how deep its pockets, expansion abroad is unlikely to be profitable (and hence should be postponed).

2. INTERNATIONALIZATION IN SERVICES IS DIFFERENT

Companies in the services sector are indeed, in many important ways, different from companies in the manufacturing and primary sectors. Services tend to be less transportable (and, hence, less tradable), less storable, more regulated. But, when it comes to internationalization, services are no different. From hotels to healthcare, retail to real estate, financial services to fast food, service-sector companies are subject to the viability test stated above. That is, if a service company does not possess a valuable intangible asset, internationalization is not going to be profitable.

Before embarking on international expansion, service companies, as much as manufacturers, must also respond affirmatively to two other questions. First, is there sufficient and steady demand abroad (backed by purchasing power) for the service offered? French cuisine, Spanish bullfighting, and U.S. football might not meet this test. Second, is the service experience replicable abroad? Disney may (with some difficulty) be able to re-create its theme parks in Japan and France, and Club Med can offer its convivial holiday village atmosphere not only in southern Europe but also in North Africa—but Virgin Airways, Toys "R" Us, and Indian diamond cutters may be less able to replicate their value proposition abroad. Reasons include regulatory hurdles, costly access to key inputs, and the difficulty of transferring competences abroad.

Implications: Internationalization in services is no different from that in manufacturing. A service company can internationalize successfully as long as it meets the intangible asset test, the effective demand test, and the replicability test. Companies as diverse as Blockbuster Video, the U.S. video rental operator, Sodexho Alliance, the French in-house catering company, and Goldman Sachs, the U.S. investment bank have met these tests and expanded abroad profitably. But fail one or more of the three, and expansion abroad is unlikely to be profitable.

3. DISTANCE AND NATIONAL BORDERS MATTER NO MORE

Spurred by developments like the Internet, some observers have proclaimed the demise of distance. Others, perhaps persuaded by the omnipresence (from Mexico to Malaysia, from Iceland to New Zealand) of the U.S.-based broadcaster CNN and of McDonald's fast-food outlets, believe that national cultures have converged and can be safely disregarded when it comes to global business. In the latter view, the only culture that matters now is corporate culture; national borders are passé.

There may sometimes be some truth in these assertions, but they should, at least for now, be treated with skepticism. Indeed, besides being exaggerated they are plainly incorrect as generalizations. Take distance. In books and CDs, software and remote diagnostics, new technologies continue to shrink physical distance; but in most spheres of economic activity transport and telecommunication costs, small though they may have become, are still positive and still increase with distance.

Moreover, as every executive knows, reliable information is the lifeblood of economic decisions. And, even in this day and age, reliable information is acquired more readily and more reliably locally than from afar. This is partly why companies tend to cluster close to others in their industry—part of the explanation perhaps for the "home bias" that economists have documented in trade and investment. It is also why, even after controlling for transport costs, distance has a significant (and negative) influence on economic exchange.

National culture and borders are also still significant. National cultures shape national institutions and influence economic values and ethos. Although patterns are changing, economic organization in Japan still seems to favor business above labor and consumers; in parts of Europe labor comes first, followed by producers and consumers; in the United States consumers tend to rank ahead of producers and labor.

Cultural values aid interpretation and are an input in business decisions. The relationship of a company to its customers, national and local governments, rivals, shareholders, financial institutions, and the local community, all tend to be influenced by national culture. From language to labor policy, punctuality to property rights, taxation to transfer pricing, accounting rules to supplier relationships, business still operates differently across nations and regions. As a result, companies that cross national borders tend to face sharp discontinuities and those that disregard or fail to anticipate the latter are likely to see successful home-grown strategies meet a poor reception abroad (just ask Lincoln Electric Holdings, the welding systems equipment maker, or Otis, the lifts and elevators manufacturer).

National borders represent the combined forces of national history, institutions, and conditioning, and give potent meaning to the terms insiders and outsiders. Even the seemingly innocuous U.S.–Canada border appears to operate in this way. Empirically, language and national borders show up as significant and large determinants of international trade and investment. Even in our increasingly digital and anglicized global economy, national language and cultural affinity are still a crucial determinant of trade and investment decisions. U.S. companies still head for Canada first, Portuguese companies for Brazil, Spanish companies for Latin America, Japanese companies for other parts of Asia.

Implications: In view of the above, it continues to make sense to expand regionally before entering more distant markets: to head for familiar markets before unfamiliar ones. Companies that respect national borders and cultures are more likely to win back respect from employees, suppliers, customers, and national authorities. This hardly means forsaking "globality"; it just means placing added emphasis on being both local and global. Indeed, companies that embrace this ambiguity will more likely be rewarded with profitable growth.

4. DEVELOPING COUNTRIES ARE WHERE THE ACTION IS

In much public discourse on globalization, there is a view that the big markets are in the large developing countries (such as Mexico, Brazil, China, and India). In fact, globalization is still very much a concentrated, rich country game. Of the 100 largest multinationals, only two are from developing countries. In terms of international trade and inward and outward foreign direct investment, ten nations—Canada, the United States, the United Kingdom, Germany, France, the Netherlands, Sweden, Switzerland, Japan, and Australia—account for 50, 70, and 90 percent of respective world totals. Their purchasing power is still unrivaled despite recent economic convergence.

Implications: No company that wants to be counted as world class can afford to ignore developed country markets. Indeed, as Japan restructures its economy and recovers from a prolonged slump, it should not be surprising to see the U.S.–European cross-border merger mania being followed by a similar Europe–Japan and U.S.–Japan company-driven integration. The 1999 Renault–Nissan deal may only be a harbinger of things to come.

5. MANUFACTURE WHERE LABOR COSTS ARE CHEAPEST

During the debate on the North American Free Trade Agreement or NAFTA, the "sucking sound" hypothesis—that multinationals will shift their operations to nations where labor costs are lowest—was elevated to new heights. In reality, of course, the only sounds that low wages should stir are loud yawns. As every business executive knows, what matters first off is delivered unit costs and not just wage costs. Materials are typically a big chunk of total costs and by levying import duties and such, developing countries (that boast low wages) often make local manufacturing expensive. Second, where wages are low, productivity tends to be low too. Consequently, hourly wage costs may appear ridiculously low, but unit costs tend to be high. Lastly, it is generally optimal to manufacturers in (or the least near) the big markets. Not only does such a strategy minimize tariffs, transport costs, and logistical problems, it also creates a structural hedge against unfavorable changes in real exchange rates. If, for instance, Mercedes had opened its plants in Mexico rather than in the United States, it would have traded off its deutschmark–dollar currency exposure for peso–dollar exposure.

Implications: As a generalization (but not as a rule), make where you sell. For large companies that sell in the triad (Europe, Japan, the United States), this means operating in that triad. Young European managers might care to concentrate on learning Japanese; as European consumers warm to Japanese products, Japanese companies will continue to raise their presence in Europe significantly. For similar reasons, young Japanese managers should brush up on their English; foreign investment into Japan is likely to rise significantly as well. Envy the British and the Americans; when it comes to foreign tongues, the default status of English as the language of international business offers them a free ride.

6. GLOBALIZATION IS HERE TO STAY

A sentiment that is often part of the hype surrounding the "new economy" is that globalization, like a genie, is out of the bottle and cannot be pushed back in. Here again, there is some truth to the claim, but serious skepticism is also warranted. To see why, consider the key developments that have enabled globalization.

First and most familiar are technology changes. It would appear that these are unlikely to be reversed. Second is the phenomenon referred to as economic convergence. As per capita incomes converge across nations, demand patterns tend to converge (people in more and more nations want fast food, cars, and JVCs), and capabilities converge as well (people in more and more nations can now write software, make new medicines, and build fancy products). This convergence process might suffer interruptions (witness the recent Asian crisis), but it appears unlikely to be arrested for long, let alone reversed.

The most important driver of globalization, though, is the spread of economic liberalism. The recent and widespread change in ideology—from state socialism to market capitalism—has unleashed much internal deregulation and external liberalization, from France to the former Soviet Union. The embrace of openness that took hold during the late 1980s and early 1990s trailed a half-century of economic growth and global peace. Take away either of the latter two conditions and liberalization might become a potential casualty. Globalization has been willed into existence due to the changed beliefs and acts of national governments. Bring serious war or sustained high unemployment into the picture and governments may start to act in ways that could reverse globalizing trends. Even at the end of 1999, with just 5 percent unemployment and a seemingly unstoppable economy, the United States sometimes appeared to be ambiguous on globalization. What would the attitude be if it faced Europe's double-digit unemployment?

Implications: Economic growth is key if globalization is to continue apace. In a "winner takes all" economy, we are building a shaky enterprise and a fragile society if all cannot (sooner or later) be winners. Companies need to explore issues such as unemployment, employee retraining, and equality of opportunity, if not incomes. If business does not become more sensitive to this possibility, expect to see much more resistance to the structural adjustment that globalization tends to bring, and expect to see governments reasserting themselves.

7. GOVERNMENTS DON'T MATTER ANYMORE

Beneath a headline saying that 1998 sales by the world's 100 largest multinational enterprises were one-and-a-half times the gross domestic product (GDP) of France, a cartoon in *Le Monde* newspaper showed executives (atop skyscrapers) clasping their stomachs and roaring with laughter at a remark by Prime Minister Lionel Jospin, "L'état ne peut pas tout" (roughly, "the state cannot do everything"). The cartoon's implicit message: multinationals are the masters of today's world, governments are powerless. Move over Lionel Jospin, make way for Bill Gates.

Those who fail to treat this as an exaggerated claim are likely to be in for some unpleasant surprises. As long as people attach value to a collective national identity and as long as they value local representation in decision making, governments will continue to matter greatly. The reality is that people are not very mobile across national borders; we tend to become part of the local and national communities where we are born. In this kind of society, concepts such as local and national interests have real meaning, and local and national governments have evolved to be the key institutions that promise to advance those interests with any constancy. After all, companies come and companies go (take Digital Equipment in Massachusetts); their identities may change through acquisitions (as in DaimlerChrysler or Renault–Nissan). To the extent that corporate interests align with those of the local community this may be welcome, but it is no longer to be counted on (just ask the community living in Clermont-Ferrand, home town of the French tire maker Michelin).

In a world where people no longer expect companies to give primacy to local interests, local and national governments will be viewed as a necessary counterweight. Governments know this and will willingly serve that function. Of course, to do so credibly, from time to time governments will push their weight around. They may break up large firms, prevent foreign investment in so-called culture industries, and tie up the hands of companies in other ways. All this is easier to do when the companies are foreign and the voters local. As Raymond Vernon warned in his book *In the Hurricane's Eye,* multinationals and governments—both legitimate entities—will confront one another again; when this happens, it will be seen that power has not slipped away from sovereign nations.

Equally importantly, a working global economy needs global rules. There are too many countries (with perhaps as many interests) and they can't all be invited to make those rules. Global rules are therefore still the prerogative of governments, and so long as rules matter (and, in the future, they are likely to matter more not less), governments will continue to matter.

Implications: Companies should resist the temptation to write off governments as ineffective anachronisms. Rather, they should recognize governments as important and legitimate institutions in the world economy. Indeed, if companies are to benefit from globalization and wish to encourage its spread, they should work with governments to establish how local and global can evolve in an acceptably balanced manner. Jobs and profits might be traded off in the short but not the long run. Managers must recognize this. In the twentieth century, prime responsibility for jobs fell on governments, while that for profits fell on companies. If we are to rest on the tremendous economic gains made in that century, this division of labor might work well. Without engagement and imaginative coordination among private enterprises and governments, neither the concept of the market nor that of democracy is likely to deliver its full promise. To avoid that outcome should be the goal of all economic entities.

CHAPTER 12

Values

Right from the early days, when Kenneth Andrews wrote about strategy in the mid-1960s, values were included as an integral part of the process. In a way, that has been forgotten with all the attention to strategic analysis. It should not have been, and we include three rather interesting readings here to put the spotlight on values in this chapter.

First is a paper by Claes Gustafsson of Abo Akademi University in Finland. "Why strategy?" he asks, and what does an "ethical strategy" mean? He then goes on to consider the moral responsibility of managers—necessary words, perhaps, in a world obsessed with shareholder value. This launches Gustafsson into a general discussion of ethics in today's world—and tomorrow's. A most unusual and welcome paper!

Our second reading on values actually predates Andrews's early writings on strategy and, in fact, can be seen as a predecessor to it. From a book published in 1957 by sociologist Philip Selznick of the Berkeley campus of the University of California entitled *Leadership in Administration,* this excerpt introduces the wonderful ideas of organizations as sustained "institutions" and of managers as people who "infuse" them with value. That is leadership! This reading, almost 50 years old, is perfectly contemporary; indeed, it contains messages that we need to heed perhaps now more than ever.

Finally, in "A New Manifesto for Management," Sumantra Ghoshal and Chris Bartlett team up with Ghoshal's colleague at the London Business School, Peter Moran, to present this unusual "manifesto." We need to rethink our very basis of managing, they argue, to move away from tight controls and narrow theories to a new philosophy that recognizes companies as value creators that reclaim their legitimacy by engaging their people.

USING THE CASE STUDIES

Values can be a driving force and a stabilizing influence in strategy. Zhang Ruimin takes over an ailing refrigerator manufacturer in China with a reputation for low quality. To signal his determination to improve quality he orders his workers to smash with sledgehammers 76 refrigerators that have just come off the production line with defects that are often minor (e.g. chips in the paintwork). The message to his employees is clear: from now on quality will be at the heart of the company. Likewise, Candida Gertler and Yana Peel's evangelical belief in contemporary art guides strategic decisions at Outset. Likewise, Sukhinder Singh's passionate quest for the next batch of fine whiskies stays as the constant thread that runs through the evolution of strategy of Whisky Exchange. In the Reorganization at Axion Consulting case, Matt Walsh, a member of the executive committee, must decide whether advancing his career should take precedence over loyalty to the values and mission of his organization. In all these instances, what we see in action is consistent with Selznick's argument in "Leadership in Administration," namely that values provide the "backbone" for strategy formation during times of considerable change. Ghoshal, Bartlett, and Moran expand on this argument in "A

New Manifesto for Management." The Natura case, which deals with a Brazilian consumer goods company that puts ethics and honesty at the center of its strategy, is a good illustration of the basic thesis. And if Gustafsson's argument in "New Values, Morality, and Strategic Ethics" is to be believed, companies such as Natura are harbingers of a future trend.

READING 12.1

New Values, Morality, and Strategic Ethics* BY CLAES GUSTAFSSON

1. WHY STRATEGY?

The idea of an ethical strategy is, you might say, a contradiction of moral logic. You should behave ethically, we could say, out of personal conviction and of moral feeling, not out of sheer strategic calculation of self-interest. Ethics should not be an instrument for furthering possibly unethical aims. Or, put in another way, ethics is a question of values and goals, not of methods. . . .

. . . [W]e can choose to study the morality of the actors in the "business game"—"are managers ethical and what are their values?"—or of the organizations as such, provided, of course, that we believe "organizations" can have a morality apart from that of their members. On the other hand, we can direct our interest to the specific ethical position of, e.g., business firms. What are the norms or norm structures important for economic action, where are the moral traps and fallacies, what should the firm—or rather the managers—do in order to avoid these traps? What is good and right in connection with the business world, and what kinds of difficulties can we expect to meet?

Into this perspective I want to put the question of an "ethical strategy." For many reasons the modern corporation is doomed to stumble into all kinds of moral conflicts, even insoluble paradoxical ones. There are several reasons for this. On the one hand, you could say that the modern corporation lives at the crossroads of many legitimate groups of stakeholders, with rightful and legitimate interests. On the other hand, corporate activities are large-scale, highly efficient, and often have long-range effects. A single individual can usually only commit small sins; a large firm can commit grandiose ones. The latter capacity was earlier a prerogative of the state—for good or bad. As it is now, we do not know for sure which one has the greater potential for doing good or evil, the large firm or the state.

If you are doing something wrong, and somebody points this out to you, then, being a good person, you change your ways of acting. That is the simple logic of being a morally "good" person. It is always possible to make mistakes, but you try to avoid them and to correct yourself whenever you find that you have been wrong. Of course, it is better to know in advance what to do—a really good person knows that. But you should, in any case, try your best.

For the modern corporation the question of doing right is, however, not so easy. Doing the wrong thing may, as such, be expensive, and doing it on a large scale multiplies the damage. Doing something on a large scale usually implies doing it far into the future. Large-scale organized action is usually planned years in advance and is slow to change. It is, in other words, not always so easy to change your ways when told that you are wrong. Or you can do it only at great cost. The problem is further aggravated by the obvious fact that conceptions regarding good and bad change over time. Thus it is possible, at least in theory, that a certain act or state is considered "good" or at least acceptable when it is planned and put into action, but that it has changed to be "bad" or unacceptable, when it is about to be implemented.

All this makes talk about an ethical strategy legitimate. As a good man tries to act in the right way and to search for knowledge about good and bad in order to be able to act accordingly, so

*Claes Gustafsson, "New Values, Morality, and Strategic Ethics," working paper; reprinted with deletions by permission of the author.

does a good corporation. The good man needs to know what is good and bad just now. The good corporation, however, needs to know what is good and bad not only just now, but also within the action-relevant future.

2. IS THERE A MORAL RESPONSIBILITY?

You might, of course, argue that the corporation—or its managers—have no moral responsibility outside that given by the law. You might add, like Milton Friedman (1962), that the managers of the firm have no moral responsibility except for taking care of the interests of the owners. In that perspective the question of an ethical strategy will not even arise.

This view is, however, simplistic and misleading. Regarding the moral responsibility of the firm as such, we can note that it is not and never has acted in a vacuum. Every business activity means taking part in a grand social play, where the acceptance of the surrounding social network is a conditio sine qua non. Ordered economic activity—leaving robbery and some other marginally extreme, economically directed activities aside—is always a question of legitimation and institutionalization. If the surrounding social network—society—does not accept your behavior, it will react quickly and harshly. There has never been a society where business activities have been exempt from social regulations and moral demands. Moral responsibility is not only something you decide yourselves; it is determined by the moral demands of the environment. Immoral action or gross neglect of moral responsibilities may, thus, become costly. This means that even for a subjectively amoral person, morality exists as a question of cost/benefit.

There is, however, another aspect of corporate ethics, too. No firm exists as a technical and economic unit only—it lives and works in the form of human decisions and choices. On a trivial level of conceptual definition we can see that everybody has some kind of moral conceptions—even the mafia or the robber on the street. Any social grouping rests on some set of generalized normative expectations regarding the actions of others. Human reasoning, moreover, seems to be based, at least partly, on moral-like normative conceptions.

On the other hand, business as such is strongly moralistic. Textbooks in business administration are probably among the most moralistic found, constantly stressing the importance of loyalty, credibility, diligence, and effective management of whatever activity you are supposed to be in charge of. It is in this case interesting to note that, whereas the mythology of business mostly stresses speculative greed and the possibility of enriching yourselves, corporate logic, both in theory and in practice, as stubbornly tells us about how professional managers take care of somebody else's interests. The modern corporation does not depend on the unrestricted personal greed of a set of free agents, but instead, and very much so, on highly restricted personal interests, on loyal cooperation, reliable mutual expectations, and skillful management. Even those few who, perhaps for romantic reasons, maintain that they are in business "just for the money," at the same time demand extreme loyalty of their subordinates.

The truth is, of course, that even if street robbery might be possible for a totally immoral loner, highly organized cooperation is impossible without strong moral ties. This is found to be the fact empirically, too. The most constant characteristic you will find when interviewing managers is that they all have strong moralistic conceptions regarding business activities.

There are, in other words, two arguments for the concern regarding ethical strategy: firstly, the fact that most managers, at least within certain limits, personally would not like to be caught with their hand in the till. There are things, for all of us, that we would not like to be part of, and there are things that we do not want our children to accuse us of. Secondly, stumbling into moral pitfalls may be extremely expensive—even in the way that rather small sins can lead to excessive losses.

3. STRUCTURES OF ETHICAL REASONING

When discussing business ethics, it might be a good idea first to point out certain traits that are specifically manifest in business firms. The private corporation is a child of the "invisible hand." Its basic existential assumption is that of free and unregulated action. The corporation is expected to pursue its own internal interests in ways it sees fit, as long as it does not break the laws of the land. The manager, forming the will of the firm, is supposed to choose the best ways of action available, considering the specific resources and interests of the corporation. In this way, as a matter of principle, the horizon of action is open to the private firm—only the sky is the limit.

Business firms are highly instrumental social constructs. They are social structures and meeting places where people converge under the common tacit assumption of rationally planned and effective action. The basic idea of the firm is premeditated action, not spontaneous socializing, it is goal-directed and goal-attaining action. . . .

If you study the moral—more or less moral—argumentation of business managers, you are bound to find, rather quickly, that "rationality," "efficiency," and "the will to work" (diligence) form dominant structures of moralizing norms in economic action. The same is true, to a very high degree, of textbooks in management and business administration. Behind the normatively instrumental discussion, we find a strong moralistic tone, stressing the unavoidable importance of rationality, efficiency, and hard work. . . .*

There are other moral values to be found in business firms, of course. Loyalty and trustworthiness—to tell the truth and not to tell lies, to keep your word and your promises—form a large and important ethical structure of argument. . . .

Instrumentality and cooperation, thus, form the bases for the moral backbone of managerial logic. Add to this all other "normal" moral considerations from the culture of the surrounding society—humanity, integrity, equality, justice, altruism, environmental concerns, and so on. Even if these do not necessarily derive from the logic of large-scale organized instrumental action, everybody working in the corporation accepts them.

4. PREDICTING CHANGES IN VALUE PATTERNS

Moral values change over time. Some change slowly, over centuries, at a pace which is not detectable in ordinary life. Some change more quickly, needing only decades. Sometimes they change abruptly, usually in connection with some socially catastrophic event like natural disasters—not, perhaps, earthquakes, but rather epidemic diseases—war, genocide, and the like. Studying the history of ideas you lose the belief that any moral value will hold for ever. . . . The astonishing 180 degree turn in "Western" culture, from the social altruism of the late sixties, to the neo-liberal egoism of the late eighties, is an example of [rapid] change. . . .

5. WHAT CAN WE EXPECT IN THE NEAR FUTURE?

What, then, can we expect in the near future? Where are the ethical minefields to be found? That we do not know; as noted above, we cannot know for sure. We can, however, try to develop some reasonable expectations. These expectations concern, for obvious reasons, the action-relevant future of ten to fifteen years.

Even if moral values seem to change unpredictably, there is usually a pattern to be found. Morality is an aspect of culture, in the sense that different cultures have different moral systems—or, turning the question around, that cultural differences to a great degree consist of moral differences. If we want to know how moral values change, we have to look at the dynamics of cultural change.

Culture is as such a complex and elusive phenomenon, a kind of generalized space of values, ideas, habits, expectations, traditions, artifacts, and techniques. Culture forms behavioral regularities and patterns which are not genetically determined. . . .

Predicting changes in moral values is always a question of guessing. I shall make two guesses regarding social and cultural changes which could lead to ethical problems in the future, and which, in my opinion, are questions of strategic concern. They concern the effects of our rapid

*The work ethic, which in fact has become a household word in day-to-day moralizing discussions, is eminently handled in Weber's (1978) famous treatise on the relation between the Protestant ethic and the spirit of Western capitalism.

technological development, and, possibly more destructive, the cultural effects of environmental changes.

The fact of technological development is nothing new. Especially in the field of computerization and robotization, technological innovations come at an increasing pace. The cultural effects, however, are yet to be seen. During the coming decade or two we can expect not only new technology, but also the first generations of a working force that has been born and grown up in the computerized world. We have, thus, a two-sided change: on the one side, a technological breakthrough which must be expected to have immense cultural side effects, and on the other side, a population which, being tuned to that technology, is more able than ever to use and develop that technology further. Several areas of concern may arise out of this. There is a strong risk of techniques and practices leading to infringement of the personal integrity of almost anybody coming into contact with the modern corporation. This concerns not only employees, but customers, the general public, competitors, etc. On the other hand, the fast pace of action made possible may lead to ethical concerns just because there is no time left for reflection, and because of new possibilities for a quick unethical rip-off. The virulent ethical problems connected with the stock exchange might partly derive from these kinds of processes. Legitimate business practices, which as a whole determine much of what is morally right in business, depend on accumulated experience from a relatively stable world. The faster the pace of change in that world, the weaker the moral agreement.

In the relatively short time of about thirty years, i.e., since Rachel Carson published her book *The Silent Spring* in the beginning of the sixties, the question of disturbing refuse and dirty swimming water has turned into a problem for the twenty-first century. It has at the same time formed a new class of knowledge—"environmental pollution" and, connected with it, a new category of moral concern.

A closer look at what might be called "environmental ethics" shows that there is a common base forming something like a "future-directed morality." There is, deeply embedded in human reasoning, a tendency to transcendental empathy, i.e., a tendency to feel empathy and responsibility for coming generations, for humanity as such. . . .

6. ETHICAL STRATEGY FOR THE FUTURE?

I shall finish by asking what can be done in a strategic perspective to meet possible dramatic ethical conflicts. As always, when discussing strategy, the answers seem somewhat elusive. On the other hand, it would seem that some kind of preparedness is better than just waiting for it all to happen.

There is always a reason for some kind of ethical strategic concern, as long as there is reason to assume that moral values change. The forms of change, however, are unclear. What we need, then, is some kind of ethic sensitivity in the corporation. This can be organized, to some degree. Some firms do it by establishing ethical committees. The important thing to remember, in the case of ethical committees, is that they should aim not just at handling hot potatoes and exploding ethical conflicts. Rather, they ought to establish some kind of routine for probing into the general ethical climate of the firm.

The ethical problems are to be found partly inside the organization, when the ethical climate begins to deviate too sharply from that of the surrounding culture. An internal organization culture heavily dominated by greed, for example, can be expected to produce behavior leading to ethical conflicts over a broad spectrum from insider crimes to embezzlement, both on the individual level and on the level of organizational action. This might be important especially in banking and finance, and among stockbrokers. It is important to remember that moral values constitute a truth-forming logic of action. In a culture of greed, its members really "believe" that economic egoism is good and virtuous—not exclusively, but to a high degree. Their activities are then formed according to that logic. This does not mean that everybody instantly starts breaking laws or acting unethically, but rather that the probability of ethical transgressions increases.

It is not enough, of course, to acknowledge the problem. Something ought to be done, too. One central question regarding business ethics concerns the possibilities of influencing the ethical climate in the corporation. I shall here limit myself to some superficial comments.

Codes of conduct, in use in many places, may have some positive effect—not in the form, however, of some kind of local organizational law, linked to control systems and sanctions. The logical structure of norms quickly neutralizes this approach, because strict rules lead to all kinds of dysfunctional behavior in the form of cheating, hypocrisy, and evasion. On the other hand, codes of conduct, especially if management visibly supports and emphasizes them, often have a good educating effect. In a way they form a statement of corporate vision. A clear and consistent show of personal corporate vision and moral conviction may have strong unifying cultural effects in the organization. On the other hand, it should never take too heavy a "preaching" form.

By consistently trying to strengthen the moral base in a firm, you may give it the intellectual power to handle coming ethical conflicts and to evade the most critical pitfalls.

The other side of an ethical strategy concerns predicting and preparing for the future. This is not easy, as is known. The two fields of value change depicted above, however, seem to have such a high probability, even if the patterns are not clear, as to warrant closer scrutiny. Detecting the pattern of change in advance, perhaps by some kind of scenario technique, by forming discussion groups in the tradition of early operations analysis, may be one way. The question is not so much about meteorological, climatological, and technical knowledge, but more about the knowledge given by historians, sociologists, cultural anthropologists, philosophers, and their like.

READING 12.2

Leadership in Administration* BY PHILIP SELZNICK

The nature and quality of leadership, in the sense of statesmanship, is an elusive but persistent theme in the history of ideas. Most writers have centered their attention on *political* statesmen, leaders of whole communities who sit in the high places where great issues are joined and settled. In our time, there is no abatement of the need to continue the great discussion, to learn how to reconcile idealism with expediency, freedom with organization.

But an additional emphasis is necessary. Ours is a pluralist society made up of many large, influential, relatively autonomous groups. The U.S. government itself consists of independently powerful agencies which do a great deal on their own initiative and are largely self-governing. These, and the institutions of industry, politics, education, and other fields, often command large resources; their leaders are inevitably responsible for the material and psychological well-being of numerous constituents; and they have become increasingly *public* in nature, attached to such interests and dealing with such problems as affect the welfare of the entire community. In our society the need for statesmanship is widely diffused and beset by special problems. An understanding of leadership in both public and private organizations must have a high place on the agenda of social inquiry. . . .

The argument of this essay is quite simply stated: *The executive becomes a statesman as he makes the transition from administrative management to institutional leadership.* This shift entails a reassessment of his own tasks and of the needs of the enterprise. It is marked by a concern for the evolution of the organization as a whole, including its changing aims and capabilities. In a word, it means viewing the organization as an institution. To understand the nature of institutional leadership, we must have some notion of the meaning and significance of the term "institution" itself.

ORGANIZATIONS AND INSTITUTIONS

The most striking and obvious thing about an administrative organization is its formal system of rules and objectives. Here tasks, powers, and procedures are set out according to some officially approved pattern. This pattern purports to say how the work of the organization is to be carried on, whether it be producing steel, winning votes, teaching children, or saving souls. The organization thus designed is a technical instrument for mobilizing human energies and directing them toward set aims. We allocate tasks, delegate authority, channel communication, and find some

*Excerpted from *Leadership in Administration,* by Philip Selznick, New York: Harper and Row, 1957.

way of coordinating all that has been divided up and parceled out. All this is conceived as an exercise in engineering; it is governed by the related ideals of rationality and discipline.

The term "organization" thus suggests a certain bareness, a lean, no-nonsense system of consciously coordinated activities (Barnard, 1938: 73). It refers to an *expendable tool,* a rational instrument engineered to do a job. An "institution," on the other hand, is more nearly a natural product of social needs and pressures—a responsive, adaptive organism. This distinction is a matter of analysis, not of direct description. It does not mean that any given enterprise must be either one or the other. While an extreme case may closely approach either an "ideal" organization or an "ideal" institution, most living associations resist so easy a classification. They are complex mixtures of both designed and responsive behavior. . . .

In what is perhaps its most significant meaning, "to institutionalize" is to *infuse with value* beyond the technical requirements of the task at hand. The prizing of social machinery beyond its technical role is largely a reflection of the unique way in which it fulfills personal or group needs. Whenever individuals become attached to an organization or a way of doing things as persons rather than as technicians, the result is a prizing of the device for its own sake. From the standpoint of the committed person, the organization is changed from an expendable tool into a valued source of personal satisfaction. Some manifestations of this process are quite obvious; others are less easily recognized. It is commonplace that administrative changes are difficult when individuals have become habituated to and identified with long-established procedures. For example, the shifting of personnel is inhibited when business relations become personal ones and there is resistance to any change that threatens rewarding ties. A great deal of energy in organizations is expended in a continuous effort to preserve the rational, technical, impersonal system against such counterpressures. . . .

The test of infusion with value is *expendability*. If an organization is merely an instrument, it will be readily altered or cast aside when a more efficient tool becomes available. Most organizations are thus expendable. When value infusion takes place, however, there is a resistance to change. People feel a sense of personal loss; the "identity" of the group or community seems somehow to be violated; they bow to economic or technological considerations only reluctantly, with regret. A case in point is the perennial effort to save San Francisco's cable cars from replacement by more economical forms of transportation. The Marine Corps has this institutional halo, and it resists administrative measures that would submerge its identity. . . .

To summarize: organizations are technical instruments, designed as means to definite goals. They are judged on engineering premises; they are expendable. Institutions, whether conceived as groups or practices, may be partly engineered, but they have also a "natural" dimension. They are products of interaction and adaptation; they become the receptacles of group idealism; they are less readily expendable. . . .

THE DEFAULT OF LEADERSHIP

When institutional leadership fails, it is perhaps more often by default than by positive error or sin. Leadership is lacking when it is needed; and the institution drifts, exposed to vagrant pressures, readily influenced by short-run opportunistic trends. This default is partly a failure of nerve, partly a failure of understanding. It takes nerve to hold a course; it takes understanding to recognize and deal with the basic sources of institutional vulnerability.

One type of default is the failure to set goals. Once an organization becomes a "going concern," with many forces working to keep it alive, the people who run it can readily escape the task of defining its purposes. This evasion stems partly from the hard intellectual labor involved, a labor that often seems but to increase the burden of already onerous daily operations. In part, also, there is the wish to avoid conflicts with those in and out of the organization who would be threatened by a sharp definition of purpose, with its attendant claims and responsibilities. Even business firms find it easy to fall back on conventional phrases, such as that "our goal is to make profit," phrases which offer little guidance in the formulation of policy.

A critique of leadership, we shall argue, must include this emphasis on the leader's responsibility to define the mission of the enterprise. This view is not new. It is important because so much of administrative analysis takes the goal of the organization as given, whereas in many crucial instances this is precisely what is problematic. We shall also suggest that the analysis of goals is itself dependent on an understanding of the organization's social structure. In other words, the purposes we have or can have depend on what we are or what we can be. In statesmanship no less than in the search for personal wisdom, the Socratic dictum—know thyself—provides the ultimate guide.

Another type of default occurs when goals, however neatly formulated, enjoy only a superficial acceptance and do not genuinely influence the total structure of the enterprise. Truly accepted values must infuse the organization at many levels, affecting the perspectives and attitudes of personnel, the relative importance of staff activities, the distribution of authority, relations with outside groups, and many other matters. Thus if a large corporation asserts a wish to change its role in the community from a narrow emphasis on profit making to a larger social responsibility (even though the ultimate goal remains some combination of survival and profit-making ability), it must explore the implications of such a change for decision making in a wide variety of organizational activities. We shall stress that the task of building special values and a distinctive competence into the organization is a prime function of leadership. . . .

Finally, the role of the institutional leader should be clearly distinguished from that of the "interpersonal" leader. The latter's task is to smooth the path of human interaction, ease communication, evoke personal devotion, and allay anxiety. His expertness has relatively little to do with content; he is more concerned with persons than with policies. His main contribution is to the efficiency of the enterprise. The institutional leader, on the other hand, *is primarily an expert in the promotion and protection of values*. The interpretation that follows takes this idea as a starting point, exploring its meaning and implications. . . .

It is in the realm of policy—including the areas where policy formation and organization building meet—that the distinctive quality of institutional leadership is found. Ultimately, this is the quality of statesmanship which deals with current issues, not for themselves alone but according to their long-run implications for the role and meaning of the group. Group leadership is far more than the capacity to mobilize personal support; it is more than the maintenance of equilibrium through the routine solution of everyday problems; it is the function of the leader-statesman—whether of a nation or a private association—to define the ends of group existence, to design an enterprise distinctively adapted to these ends, and to see that that design becomes a living reality. These tasks are not routine; they call for continuous self-appraisal on the part of the leaders; and they may require only a few critical decisions over a long period of time. "Mere speed, frequency, and vigor in coming to decisions may have little relevance at the top executive level, where a man's basic contribution to the enterprise may turn on his making two or three significant decisions a year" (Learned, Ulrich, and Booz, 1951: 57). This basic contribution is not always aided by the traits often associated with psychological leadership, such as aggressive self-confidence, intuitive sureness, ability to inspire. . . .

CHARACTER AS DISTINCTIVE COMPETENCE

In studying character we are interested in the *distinctive competence or inadequacy* that an organization has acquired. In doing so, we look beyond the formal aspects to examine the commitments that have been accepted in the course of adaptation to internal and external pressures. . . . Commitments to ways of acting and responding are built into the organization. When integrated, these commitments define the "character" of the organization. . . .

THE FUNCTIONS OF INSTITUTIONAL LEADERSHIP

We have argued that policy and administration are interdependent in the special sense that certain areas of organizational activity are peculiarly sensitive to policy matters. Because these areas exist, creative men are needed—more in some circumstances than in others—who know how to transform a neutral body of men into a committed polity. These men are called leaders; their profession is politics. . . .

Leadership sets goals, but in doing so takes account of the conditions that have already determined what the organization can do and to some extent what it must do. Leadership creates and molds an organization embodying—in thought and feeling and habit—the value premises of policy. Leadership reconciles internal strivings and environmental pressures, paying close attention to the way adaptive behavior brings about changes in organizational character. When an organization lacks leadership, these tasks are inadequately fulfilled, however expert the flow of paper and however smooth the channels of communication and command. And this fulfillment requires a continuous scrutiny of how the changing social structure affects the evolution of policy.

The relation of leadership to organizational character may be more closely explored if we examine some of the key tasks leaders are called on to perform:

1. *The definition of institutional mission and role.* The setting of goals is a creative task. It entails a self-assessment to discover the true commitments of the organization, as set by effective internal and external demands. The failure to set aims in the light of these commitments is a major source of irresponsibility in leadership.
2. *The institutional embodiment of purpose.* The task of leadership is not only to make policy but to build it into the organization's social structure. This, too, is a creative task. It means shaping the "character" of the organization, sensitizing it to ways of thinking and responding, so that increased reliability in the execution and elaboration of policy will be achieved according to its spirit as well as its letter.
3. *The defense of institutional integrity.* The leadership of any polity fails when it concentrates on sheer survival: institutional survival, properly understood, is a matter of maintaining values and distinctive identity. This is at once one of the most important and least understood functions of leadership. This area (like that of defining institutional mission) is a place where the intuitively knowledgeable leader and the administrative analyst often part company, because the latter has no tools to deal with it. The fallacy of combining agencies on the basis of "logical" association of functions is a characteristic result of the failure to take account of institutional integrity.
4. *The ordering of internal conflict.* Internal interest groups form naturally in large-scale organizations, since the total enterprise is in one sense a polity composed of a number of suborganizations. The struggle among competing interests always has a high claim on the attention of leadership. This is so because the direction of the enterprise as a whole may be seriously influenced by changes in the internal balance of power. In exercising control, leadership has a dual task. It must win the consent of constituent units, in order to maximize voluntary cooperation, and therefore must permit emergent interest blocs a wide degree of representation. At the same time, in order to hold the helm, it must see that a balance of power appropriate to the fulfillment of key commitments will be maintained.

READING 12.3

A New Manifesto for Management* BY SUMANTRA GHOSHAL, CHRISTOPHER A. BARTLETT, AND PETER MORAN

Why do corporations elicit such powerful love–hate responses? On the one hand, amid the decay of influence and legitimacy of other institutions—such as states, political parties, churches, monarchies, or even families—the corporation has emerged as perhaps the most powerful social and economic institution of modern society. Versatile and creative, the corporation is a prodigious amplifier of human effort across national and cultural boundaries. Corporations, not abstract economic forces or governments, create and distribute most of an economy's wealth, innovate, trade, and raise living standards. Historically, they have served as a pervasive force for civilization, promoting honesty, trust, and respect for contracts. As the market sphere has grown to

*Reprinted with deletions from "A New Manifesto for Management," S. Ghoshal, C. A. Bartlett, and P. Moran, *Sloan Management Review*, Spring 1999, 9–20.

annex areas such as health and sports, companies loom even larger in the lives of individuals. People look to them for community and identity as well as economic well-being.

Yet, in the closing year of the century, corporations and managers suffer from a profound social ambivalence. Hero-worshipped by the few, they are deeply distrusted by the many. In popular mythology, the corporate manager is Gordon Gekko, the financier who preaches the gospel of greed in Hollywood's *Wall Street*. Corporations are "job killers."

There is so much uncertainty about what companies represent that Bill Clinton in the United States and Tony Blair in the United Kingdom set up reviews of companies' roles. Big business arouses big suspicion in France, Korea, and Germany. Even in the United States, executive salaries have caused a public furor, while the equally astronomical remuneration of entertainers, entrepreneurs, and bond traders raises scarcely an eyebrow. When asked by pollsters to rank professionals by ethical standing, people consistently rate managers the lowest of the low—below even politicians and journalists.

People are *right* in their intuition that something is wrong. But this is not because large corporations or management are inherently harmful or evil. It is because of the deeply unrealistic, pessimistic assumptions about the nature of individuals and corporations that underlie current management doctrine and that, in practice, cause managers to undermine their own worth. . . . It is time to expose the old, disabling assumptions and replace them with a different, more realistic set that calls on managers to act out a positive role that can release the vast potential still trapped in the old model. The new role for management breaks from the narrow economic assumptions of the past to recognize that:

- Modern societies are not market economies, they are organizational economies in which companies are the chief actors in creating value and advancing economic progress.
- The growth of firms and, therefore, economies is primarily dependent on the quality of their management.
- The foundation of a firm's activity is a new "moral contract" with employees and society, replacing paternalistic exploitation and value appropriation with employability and value creation in a relationship of shared destiny.

BETWEEN A ROCK AND A HARD PLACE

To understand why rethinking is necessary, start by looking at what happened to the corporate world in the 1980s. Driven by vociferous shareholders and global competition, managers have concentrated on enhancing competitiveness by improving their operating efficiencies. Managers have enlisted an array of techniques such as total quality, continuous improvement, and process reengineering to this end. Firms have cut costs, eliminated waste, focused, outsourced, downsized, let go, and generally pared themselves to the bone. The result has been victory—of a sort. Shareholder returns (and senior executives' pay) have, in many cases, soared. Value has been extracted, but at what price?

Explicit or implicit past contracts with both employees and suppliers were broken. Employee loyalty and commitment have been shattered. So has management confidence in its ability to create instead of cut; witness the vogue of high-growth companies like Reuters handing back cash to shareholders via share buybacks and special dividends instead of investing it to pursue emerging opportunities. Michael Porter (1996) expressed alarm that the obsession with operating efficiencies was "leading more and more companies down the path of mutually destructive competition." Stephen Roach (1998), chief economist of Morgan Stanley, reversed his previous enthusiasm for downsizing and warned that if cutting labor costs and hollowing companies were all there was to the productivity-led recovery, "the nation could well be on a path toward industrial extinction." . . .

GENEEN'S MONKEY

The top jaw of the pincer is the doctrine by which managers run their companies.

Two generations of top managers have learned to frame their task through the viewfinder of the three Ss: crafting *strategy*, designing the *structure* to fit, and locking both in place with supporting *systems*. In its time, the strategy–structure–systems trilogy was a revolutionary discovery. Invented in the 1920s by Alfred Sloan and others as a technology to support their pioneering strategy of diversification, it served companies well for decades. It supported vertical and horizontal integration, the wave of conglomerate diversification in the 1960s, and the start of globalization in the 1970s and 1980s. But then it began to break down. However sophisticated their structure and systems, the great companies that had been bidding fair to inherit the earth—a French intellectual warned in the early 1980s that IBM had everything it needed to become a world power—were suddenly transformed into stumbling giants. The decline of excellence is well known. So what went wrong?

What happened was the "real world" changed. The strength—and fundamental weakness—of the classic strategy–structure–systems model was the primacy it gave to control. As Frederick Taylor had made complex assembly repeatable by breaking it down to its simplest component tasks, so the new doctrine, the managerial equivalent of Taylorism, aimed to make the management of complex corporations systematic and predictable. Once strategy had been set at the top, structures and systems would banish troublesome human idiosyncrasy, enabling large, diversified companies to be run in the same machine-like ways. Like the workers on Henry Ford's assembly lines, all employees were replaceable parts. Harold Geneen, the accountant who ran the quintessential 1970s conglomerate ITT, used to boast that he was building a system that "a monkey will be able to run when I'm gone."

Famous last words. In the world that today's companies operate in—a world of converging technologies and markets, swirling competition, and innovation that can outdate established industry structures overnight—machine-like systems of control aren't helpful. In a situation where the most important corporate resources are not the financial funds in the hands of top management but the knowledge and expertise of the people on the front lines, they are downright unhelpful. To say that they stifle initiative, creativity, and diversity is true—but that was their point. They were designed for an organization man who has turned out to be an evolutionary dead end.

THE TYRANNY OF THEORY

The second jaw of the pincer in which companies are gripped is theory. Instead of providing remedies, academic prescriptions mostly have tightened the squeeze on managers and companies. They are part of the problem. Consider two strands of theory that have dominated managerial discourse, both academic and practical, for the past decade.

The first is Michael Porter's theory of strategy, grounded in industrial organization economics. Crudely, under Porter's theory, the essence of strategy is competition to appropriate value. Companies strive to seize and keep for themselves as much as they can of the value embodied in the products and services they deal with, while allowing as little of this value as possible to fall into the hands of others. Employees, customers, suppliers, and direct or potential competitors are all trying to do the same thing. In short, strategy is positioning to grab all you can, while preventing anyone else from eating your lunch.

The difficulty is that, in this view, the interests of the company are incompatible with those of society. For society, the freer the competition among companies the better. But for individual firms, the purpose of strategy is precisely to restrict the play of competition to get as much as possible for themselves. To do their jobs, managers must prevent free competition, at the cost of social welfare. The destruction of social welfare is not just a coincidental by-product of strategy; it is the fundamental objective of profit-seeking firms and, therefore, of their managers.

The second influential strand of theory addresses a very basic question. Why do companies exist? The answer provided by most economists is so straightforward that it appears compelling; companies exist simply because markets fail. Accept this and it's only a short step toward the dangerously misleading belief that markets represent some sort of ideal way to organize all economic activities. According to "transaction-cost economics," the dominant branch of theorizing on this subject, a company is an inferior substitute for markets. Oliver Williamson (1985), a key contributor to one strand of this theory, refers to companies as the organizing means of "last resort, to be employed when all else fails." Markets fail, Williamson presumes, because people are weak. It is only because we, as humans, are limited in our ability to act rationally and because at least some of us are prone to acting "opportunistically" that we need organizations to save us from ourselves. In some of our dealings with others, particularly those requiring complex coordination of tasks, our opportunity to behave strategically is too great for markets to restrain. In these cases, companies are necessary because managers, with their hierarchical authority and their power to monitor and control, can keep the opportunism of employees in check.

Unfortunately, the practical consequence of these two theories is to make managers not architects but wreckers of their own corporations. What they have in common, apart from their narrow, instrumental, and largely pessimistic view of human enterprise, is an emphasis on static rather than dynamic efficiencies. Static efficiency is about exploiting available economic options as efficiently as possible—making the economy more efficient by shifting existing resources to their highest valued use. Dynamic efficiency comes from the innovations that create new options and new resources—moving the economy to a different level. Porter's theory is static in that it focuses strategic think-firms into the market logic of static efficiency. Fit the pieces together and we can see why this unholy alliance of theory and practice should have destructive consequences. In its constant struggle for appropriating value, the company is pitted against its own employees as well as business rivals and the rest of society. The economic challenge for society is to keep human discretion in check. This is accomplished in markets through a focus on individualism and the power of sharp incentives and, within the firm, through hierarchical control. In other words, as Williamson wrote, and Geneen practiced, companies must act as if they were "a continuation of market relations, by other means." Caught as it is, between the sound logic of efficiency and the harsh reality of human frailties and pathologies, it is no wonder that dominant doctrine focuses managers' attention almost exclusively on concerns of appropriation and control. The resulting pathological economic role for companies and individuals should also be no surprise. It follows naturally from the premise that "markets rule" that any and all failures to heed the market's corrective discipline are likely to be futile for firms and individuals and inefficient for society.

When in a hole, the first thing to do is to stop digging. The outlines are beginning to take shape of a different management model, based on a better understanding of both individual and corporate motivation. If downsizing, cost cutting, and "getting lean and mean" were the mantras of the past decade, the desire for growth and renewal will be the major concern of the next.

A NEW MANAGEMENT PHILOSOPHY

Start by turning the conventional justification for the existence of the company around: markets begin where firms leave off. As Nobel laureate Herbert Simon (1957) has put it, "modern societies are not primarily market but *organizational economies*." That is, most of their value is created not by individuals transacting individually in the market, as in the economists' ideal, but by organizations involving people acting collectively, with their motives empowered and their actions coordinated by their companies' purpose. Far from destroying social welfare, the rise of the corporation over the past century has coincided with a sustained and unprecedented improvement in living standards, fueled by the ability of companies to enhance productivity and create new products and services. Indeed, the clearest evidence for Simon's contention lies in a strong positive correlation between the relative prosperity of an economy and its quotient of large, healthy companies. Growing, efficient companies help create growing, efficient economies. Not only is the premise of a fundamental conflict between corporate well-being and social welfare wrong; the reality is exactly the reverse.

In terms of static efficiency, much of what happens inside a company *is* inefficient. That's its point. It exists precisely to provide a haven and (temporary) respite from the laws of the market in which humans can combine to do something that markets aren't very good at: innovating. From a static viewpoint, the 15 percent of their time that 3M encourages its employees to spend on their own projects is wasted. And, indeed, a lot of it is. But the company willingly makes this sacrifice, banking that out of their efforts will come products that alter the bounds of the existing market. Sony and Intel duplicate development teams for the same purpose. Companies create fresh value for society by developing new products and services and finding better ways for providing existing ones. Markets relentlessly force the same companies eventually to "hand off" most of the newly created value to others, increasing, not diminishing, social welfare. In this symbiotic coexistence, they jointly drive the process of "creative destruction" that the Austrian economist Joseph Schumpeter identified sixty years ago as the engine of economic progress.

Reversing the logic pries companies from the crushing hold of the pincer, with liberating effect for their managers and employees. The difference between old and new is not just economic but also philosophical. In an organizational economy in which the essence of the company is value creation, the corporation and society are no longer in conflict. They are interdependent, and the starting point is a new moral contract between them. In this framework, management too wins back its legitimacy: not only is the "destroy it to save it" nightmare banished, but the success of the company and the economy as a whole can be seen to depend on how well management does its job. Far from being villainous or exploitative, management as a profession can be seen for what it is—the primary engine of social and economic progress. Individual inventors and entrepreneurs develop new products and, sometimes, new businesses. A vast majority of new products and new businesses, however, are created by established organizations. Managers build organizations, the embodiments of an economy's social capital—a factor that is beginning to be recognized as perhaps the key driver of economic growth.

COMPANIES AS VALUE CREATORS

The contrast between these two views of a company comes sharply into focus if we compare the management approaches of Norton and 3M, or of Westinghouse and ABB. As we have described elsewhere, managers at Norton and Westinghouse lived in the zero-sum, dog-eat-dog world of traditional management theory. When they found a company that had created an attractive new product or business, they bought it. When they found the market for a product to be too competitive for them to dictate terms to their buyers and suppliers, they sold those businesses. Their primary management focus was on value appropriation—not only vis-à-vis their customers and suppliers, but also vis-à-vis their own employees.

At 3M and ABB, in contrast, a very different management philosophy was at work. While Norton tried to develop increasingly sophisticated strategic resource allocation models, 3M's entire strategy was based on the value-creating logic of continuous innovation. The same power equipment business that Westinghouse abandoned as unattractive (that is, not enough opportunity for value appropriation), ABB rejuvenated, in part by its own investments in productivity and in new technologies to enhance products' functionality or their appropriateness for new markets.

Norton and Westinghouse managers thought of their companies in market terms: they bought and sold businesses, created internal markets whenever they could, and dealt with their people with market rules. Through the power of sharp, marketlike incentives, they got what they wanted. People began to behave as they would in a market—acting alone as independent agents with an atomistic concern only for their self-interest.

By thinking of their companies in market terms, Norton and Westinghouse became the victims of the very logic that both companies sought to live by—a market logic that left little choice but to squeeze out more efficiency in everything that was attempted. Their strategy focused entirely on productivity improvement and cost cutting. Their structures for controlling behavior rewarded autonomy, while their elaborate systems for monitoring performance were finely tuned to eliminate even the smallest pools of waste. Yet, they could not create any value that was new. . . . people [were] unable to cooperate among themselves or to pool their resources and capabilities in order to create new combinations—particularly, new combinations of knowledge and expertise—that most innovations require.

Visions like ABB's purpose "to make economic growth and improved living standards a reality for all nations throughout the world," values such as Kao Corporation's espoused belief that "we are, first of all, an educational institution," and norms like 3M's acceptance that "products belong to divisions but technologies belong to the company" all emphasize the non-marketlike nature of a company, encouraging people to work collectively toward shared goals and values rather than more restrictively, within their narrow self-interests. They can share resources, including knowledge, without having to be certain of how precisely each of them will benefit personally—as long as they believe that the company overall will benefit, to their collective gain. . . .

The manager's primary task is redefined from institutionalizing control to embedding trust, from maintaining the status quo to leading change. As opposed to being the designers of strategy, managers take on the role of establishing a sense of *purpose* within the company. Defined in terms of how the company will create value for society, purpose allows strategy to emerge from within the organization, from the energy and alignment created by that sense of purpose. As opposed to playing with the boxes and lines that represent the company's formal structure, managers focus on building the core organizational processes that would release the entrepreneurs held hostage in the front-line units of that structure; integrate the resources and capabilities across those units to create new combinations of resources and knowledge; and create the stretch that would drive the whole organization into continuously striving for new value creation. And, from being the builders of systems, managers transform into the developers of people, helping each individual in the company become the best he or she can be. The three Ss of strategy, structure, and systems that were at the core of the managerial role give way to the three Ps: purpose, process, and people.

CREATING VALUE FOR PEOPLE

This kind of management also demands a qualitatively different employment relationship from that of the past. The contrast is perhaps the clearest statement of the new management philosophy in action. In a value-appropriating, cost-cutting mode, part of the firm's advantage comes from its monopoly power over people's capabilities. In return, it takes on, or was understood to take on, responsibility for the employees' careers. Counterintuitively, the offer of job security has allowed companies to extract the maximum value from their people in the past.

Unlike machines, people cannot be owned. Yet, like machines, the way people become most valuable to a company is by becoming specialized to the company's businesses and activities. The more specific the employee's knowledge and skills are to a company's unique set of customers, technologies, equipment, and so on, the more productive they become and the more efficient the company becomes in all that it does. Without employment security, employees hesitate to invest their time and energy to acquire such specialized knowledge and skills that may be very useful to the company, but may have limited value outside of it. Without any assurance of a long-term association, companies too lack the incentive to commit resources to help employees develop such company-specific expertise. Employment security provides a viable basis for both to make such investments. . . .*

But even if they wanted to, companies can no longer meaningfully give the kind of job security that was their side of the bargain. One reason is the hyper-competition they have brought on themselves. In any case, security could hardly survive in an unstable world in which competitive advantage in one period becomes competitive disadvantage in another. . . .

At the same time, a free-market hire-and-fire regime is no alternative, as many companies have come to recognize. Paradoxically, the same forces of ferocious competition and turbulent change that make job security impossible also increase the need for trust and teamwork. These can't be fostered in an affection-free environment of reciprocal opportunism and continuous spot contracting. On the contrary, firms such as Intel and 3M have intuited that value creation demands something much more inspiring than individual self-interest: a community of purpose in which individuals can share resources, including knowledge, without knowing precisely how they will benefit, but confident of collective gain. In other words, innovation depends on a company acting as a social and an economic institution, in which individuals can behave accordingly.

This requirement is embodied in a new moral contract with employees to anchor the similar contract with society. In the new contract, employees take responsibility for the competitiveness of both themselves and the part of the company to which they belong. In return, the company offers not the dependence of employment security but the independence of employability—a guarantee that they fulfill through continuous education and development. Says GE's Welch:

*This is a core argument of the theory of internal labor markets. See P. B. Doeringer and M. J. Piore, *Internal Labor Markets and Manpower Analysis* (Lexington, MA: D. C. Heath, 1971).

"The new psychological contract . . . is that jobs at GE are the best in the world for people who are willing to compete. We have the best in training and development resources, and an environment committed to providing opportunities for personal and professional growth." . . .

Few companies take their commitment to employability of people more seriously than Motorola. In a context of radical decentralization of resources and decisions to the divisional level, employee education is one activity that Motorola manages at the corporate level, through the large and well-funded Motorola University that has branches all over the world. Each employee, including the chief executive, has to undertake a minimum of forty hours of formal coursework each year. Courses span a wide range of topics—from state-of-the-art coverage of new technologies to broad general management topics and issues, so as to allow Motorola employees around the world to update knowledge and skills in their chosen areas. It is this commitment to adding value to people that allowed Motorola to launch and implement its much-imitated "Six Sigma" total quality initiative. At the same time, the reputation of Motorola University increasingly has become a key source of the company's competitive advantage in recruiting and retaining the best graduates from leading schools in every country in which it operates.

More recently, Motorola has further upped the ante on its commitment to employability by launching the "Individual Dignity Entitlement" (or IDE) program. The program requires all supervisors to discuss, on a quarterly basis, six questions with everyone whose work they supervise. A negative response from any employee to any one of these questions is treated as a quality failure, to be redressed in accordance with the principles of total quality management. Yet even Motorola, a company that has invested more in its people than most and that has long been an adherent of employability, was surprised to learn that some of its units reported failures in excess of 70 percent the first time that IDE was implemented. Beginning in 1995, the company began addressing the negatives systematically by identifying and then eliminating their root causes. This is the hard edge of the new moral contract on management's side—the commitment to help people become the best they can be—that counterbalances the new demands on people which the "employability for competitiveness" contract creates.

WHAT THE NEW CONTRACT IS NOT

It is important to emphasize that this new moral contract is not a catchy new slogan to free managers from a sense of responsibility to protect the jobs of their staff. At Intel, Andy Grove could make the kind of demands he did because his own past actions had established, beyond any doubt, the extent to which he was willing to go to protect the interests of his employees. During the memory-products blood bath in the early 1980s, when every other semiconductor company in the United States immediately laid off many people, Grove adopted the 90 percent rule, with everyone, from the chairman down, accepting a 10 percent pay cut, to avoid layoffs. Then, to tide the company over the bad period without losing people he had nurtured for years, Grove sold 20 percent of the company to IBM for $350 million in cash. When cost pressures continued to mount, he implemented the 125 percent rule by asking everyone to work an extra ten hours a week with no pay increase, again to avoid cutbacks. Only after all these efforts proved insufficient did he finally close some operations, with the attending job losses. This kind of proven commitment to people makes a contract based on employability credible, and its hard-edged demands on people acceptable. . . .

. . . [T]he contract based on employability is not some program that can be installed by a company's HR department. Rather, it must be inculcated as a very different philosophy—one that requires management at every level to work hard, on an ongoing basis, to create an exciting and invigorating work environment, a place of enormous pride and satisfaction that bonds people to the company even more tightly than any bond of dependency that employment security could create. The combination of a moral contract based on employability and a management commitment to empowerment leads, as a consequence, to the durable long-term and mutually satisfying relationship between the individual and the organization that the traditional employment contract abandoned. But, by building the new company–employee relationship on a platform of mutual value-adding and continuous choice, rather than on a self-degrading acceptance of one-way dependence, the new contract is not just functional. It is also moral. . . .

A MANIFESTO FOR RECLAIMING MANAGERIAL LEGITIMACY

Institutions decline when they lose their source of legitimacy. This happened to the monarchy, to organized religion, and to the state. This will happen to companies unless managers accord the same priority to the collective task of rebuilding the credibility and legitimacy of their institutions as they do to the individual task of enhancing their company's economic performance.

Ideas matter. In a practical discipline like management, the normative influence of ideas can be powerful, as they can manifest themselves as uniquely beneficial or uniquely dangerous. Bad theory and a philosophical vacuum have caused managers to subvert their own practice, trapping them in a vicious circle. But there is a choice. Management can continue down the well-worn path to illegitimacy or begin to chart a new course by laying claim to a higher purpose. When the solution to a recurring problem is always "try harder," there is usually something wrong with the terms, not the execution. Get out of the pincer's grip. Throw out the old paradigm while you still can, before the growing gap between companies' economic power and their social legitimacy proves it right. Take responsibility before management is held to blame for stunting the growth potential of individuals, companies, and society.

Section III

CONTEXTS

CHAPTER 13

Managing Start-Ups

The text of this book really divides into two basic parts, although there are three sections. The first, encompassing Chapters 1 through 12 and Sections I and II, introduces a variety of important concepts: strategy, strategist, process, organization, values, and so on. The second, beginning here with Section III and Chapter 13, considers how these concepts combine to form major contexts of organizations. In effect, a context is a type of situation wherein can be found particular strategies, structures, and processes.

Traditionally, policy and strategy textbooks are divided into two very different parts—a first part on the formulation of strategy and a second part on its implementation (including discussion of structure, systems, culture, etc.). As some of the readings of Chapter 5 have already made clear, we believe this is often a false dichotomy: In many situations (i.e., contexts), formulation and implementation can be so intertwined that it makes no sense to separate them. Likewise, to build a textbook around a questionable dichotomy makes no sense to us, and so we have instead proceeded by introducing all the concepts related to the strategy process first and then considered the various ways in which they might interact in specific situations.

There is no "one best way" to manage the strategy process. The notion that there are several possible "good ways,"—various contexts appropriate to strategic management—was first developed in the Mintzberg reading in Chapter 8. In fact, his *configurations* of organization serve as the basis for determining the set of contexts we include here. These are as follows.

We start in Chapter 13 with what seems to be the simplest context, certainly one that has had much good press in America since Horatio Alger first went into business—that of the *start-up.* Here a single leader usually takes personal charge in a highly dynamic situation, as in a new firm or a small one operating in a growing market, or even sometimes in a large organization facing turnaround.

We next consider in Chapter 14 a contrasting context that often dominates large business as well as big government. We label it the *mature* context, although it might equally be referred to as the stable context or the mass-production or mass-service context. Here rather formal structures combine with strategy processes that are heavily analytical.

Our third and fourth contexts are those of organizations largely dependent on specialists and experts. These contexts are called *expert* when the environment is stable, *innovative* when it is dynamic. Here responsibility for strategy making tends to diffuse throughout the organization, sometimes even lodging itself at the bottom of the hierarchy. The strategy process tends to become rather emergent in nature.

Fifth, we consider the context of the *diversified* organization, which became increasingly important as waves of mergers swept across various Western economies. Because product-market strategies are diversified, the structures tend to get divisionalized, and the focus of strategy shifts to two levels: the corporate or portfolio level and the divisional or business level.

In the chapter on each context, our intention is to include material that describes all the basic concepts as they take shape in that context. We wish to describe the form of organization and strategic leadership found there, the nature of the strategy-making process, including its favored forms of strategic analysis and its most appropriate types of strategies (generic and otherwise) and social issues that surround it. Unfortunately, appropriate readings on all these aspects are not available—in part we do not yet know all that we must about each context.

Before beginning, we should warn you of one danger in focusing this discussion on contexts such as these: It may make the world of organizations appear to be more pat and ordered than it really is. Many organizations certainly seem to fit one context or another, as numerous examples will make clear. But none ever does so quite perfectly—the world is too nuanced for that. And then there are the organizations that do not fit a single context. We believe and have included arguments in a concluding chapter to this section that, in fact, the whole set of contexts forms a framework by which to understand better all kinds of organizations. But until we get to this, you should bear in mind that much of this material caricatures reality as much as it mirrors it.

Of course, such caricaturing is a necessary part of formal learning and of acting. Managers, for example, would never get anything done if they could not use simplified frameworks to comprehend their experiences in order to act on them. As Miller and Mintzberg have argued in a paper called "The Case for Configuration," managers are attracted to a particular, well-defined context because that allows them to achieve a certain consistency and coherence in the design of their organization and so to facilitate its effective performance. Each context, as you will see, has its own logic—its own integrated way of dealing with its part of the world—that makes things more manageable.

This chapter of Section III discusses managing the start-up. At least in its traditional form, this encompasses situations in which a single individual, typically with a clear and distinct vision of purpose, directs an organization that is structured to be as responsive as possible to his or her personal wishes. Strategy making, thus, revolves around a single brain, unconstrained by forces of bureaucratic momentum.

Such entrepreneurship is commonly found in young organizations, especially ones in new or emerging industries, where vision may be essential because of long delays between the conception of an idea and its commercial success. But in crisis situations, a similar type of strong and visionary leadership may offer the best hope for successful turnaround. And it can thrive as well in highly fragmented industries, where small, flexible organizations can move quickly into and out of specialized market niches and so outmaneuver the big bureaucracies.

The word *entrepreneurship* has also been associated with change and innovation inside larger, more bureaucratic organizations—sometimes under the label *intrapreneurship*. In these situations, it is often not the boss but someone in an odd corner of the organization—a champion for some technology or strategic issue—who takes on the entrepreneurial role. We believe, however, for reasons that will become evident that intrapreneurship better fits into our chapter on the innovation context.

To describe the structure that seems to be most logically associated with start-ups and entrepreneurship in general, we open with material on the entrepreneurial form of organization from Mintzberg's book, *The Structuring of Organizations*. Combined with this is a discussion of strategy making in the entrepreneurial context, especially with regard to strategic vision, based on research carried out at McGill University. In one, strategies of visionary leadership were studied through biographies and autobiographies; in the other, the strategies of entrepreneurial firms were tracked across several decades of their histories.

Then to investigate the external situation that seems to be most commonly (although not exclusively) associated with this context, we present excerpts from a chapter on emerging industries from Michael Porter's book *Competitive Strategy*.

The final reading of this chapter is based on research by Amar Bhide of the Harvard Business School, and his associates. It tells how entrepreneurs go about crafting their strategies. Entrepreneurs select carefully but are also careful not to be too analytical (recall Pitcher's artists versus the technocrats of Chapter 2), and they maintain their ability to maneuver and to "hustle." Action must be integrated with analysis.

USING THE CASE STUDIES

Many of the cases deal with companies that began life as an entrepreneurial start-up. Some of the cases, for example, Apple and Whisky Exchange shows how early decisions by entrepreneurs shape the company long after it has outgrown its formative stage. Other cases, such as Pixar, Netflix, and Outset, illustrate the approach to start-ups presented by Mintzberg's reading "The Entrepreneurial Organization." Pixar and Netflix are particularly relevant to Porter's discussion of "Competitive Strategy in Emerging Industries." Arguably, however, the Robin Hood case deals with a start-up, albeit not in the usual sense of the term. Bhide's advice to entrepreneurial start-ups would have been surprisingly useful to Robin, as it is for more conventional entrepreneurs.

READING 13.1

The Entrepreneurial Organization* BY HENRY MINTZBERG

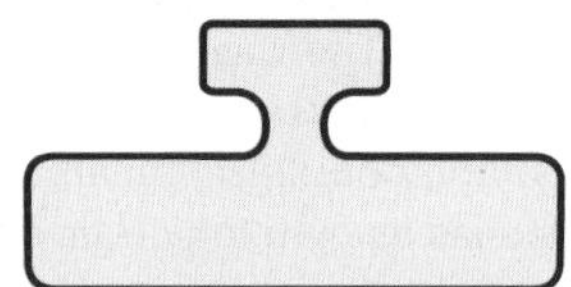

Consider an automobile dealership with a flamboyant owner, a brand-new government department, a corporation or even a nation run by an autocratic leader, or a school system in a state of crisis. In many respects, those are vastly different organizations. But the evidence suggests that they share a number of basic characteristics. They form a configuration we shall call the *entrepreneurial organization*.

THE BASIC STRUCTURE

The structure of the entrepreneurial organization is often very simple, characterized above all by what it is not: elaborated. As shown in the opening figure, typically it has little or no staff, a loose division of labor, and a small managerial hierarchy. Little of its activity is formalized, and it makes minimal use of planning procedures or training routines. In a sense, it is nonstructure; in my "structuring" book, I called it *simple structure*.

Power tends to focus on the chief executive, who exercises a high personal profile. Formal controls are discouraged as a threat to the chief's flexibility. He or she drives the organization by sheer force of personality or by more direct interventions. Under the leader's watchful eye, politics cannot easily arise. Should outsiders, such as particular customers or suppliers, seek to exert influence, such leaders are as likely as not to take the organizations to a less exposed niche in the marketplace.

Thus, it is not uncommon in small entrepreneurial organizations for everyone to report to the chief. Even in ones not so small, communication flows informally, much of it between the chief executive and others. As one group of McGill MBA students commented in their study of a small manufacturer of pumps: "It is not unusual to see the president of the company engaged in casual

*Adapted from *The Structuring of Organizations* (Prentice Hall, 1979, Chap. 17 on "The Simple Structure"), *Power In and Around Organizations* (Prentice Hall, 1983, Chap. 20 on "The Autocracy"), and the material on strategy formation from "Visionary Leadership and Strategic Management," *Strategic Management Journal* (1989), coauthored with Frances Westley; see also, "Tracking Strategy in an Entrepreneurial Firm," *Academy of Management Journal* (1982), and "Researching the Formation of Strategies: The History of a Canadian Lady, 1939–1976," in R. B. Lamb, ed., *Competitive Strategic Management* (Prentice Hall, 1984), the last two coauthored with James A. Waters. A chapter similar to this appeared in *Mintzberg on Management: Inside Our Strange World of Organizations* (Free Press, 1989).

conversation with a machine shop mechanic. [That way he is] informed of a machine breakdown even before the shop superintendent is advised."

Decision making is likewise flexible, with a highly centralized power system allowing for rapid response. The creation of strategy is, of course, the responsibility of the chief executive, the process tending to be highly intuitive, often oriented to the aggressive search for opportunities. It is not surprising, therefore, that the resulting strategy tends to reflect the chief executive's implicit vision of the world, often an extrapolation of his or her own personality.

Handling disturbances and innovating in an entrepreneurial way are perhaps the most important aspects of the chief executive's work. In contrast, the more formal aspects of managerial work—figurehead duties, for example—receive less attention, as does the need to disseminate information and allocate resources internally, since knowledge and power remain at the top.

CONDITIONS OF THE ENTREPRENEURIAL ORGANIZATION

A centrist entrepreneurial configuration is fostered by an external context that is both simple and dynamic. Simpler environments (say, retailing food as opposed to designing computer systems) enable one person at the top to retain so much influence, while it is a dynamic environment that requires a flexible structure, which in turn enables the organization to outmaneuver the bureaucracies. Entrepreneurial leaders are naturally attracted to such conditions.

The classic case of this is, of course, the entrepreneurial firm, where the leader is the owner. Entrepreneurs often found their own firms to escape the procedures and control of the bureaucracies where they previously worked. At the helm of their own enterprises, they continue to loathe the ways of bureaucracy, and the staff analysts that accompany them, and so they keep their organizations lean and flexible. Figure 1 shows the organigram for Steinberg's, a supermarket chain we shall be discussing shortly, during its most classically entrepreneurial years. Notice the identification of people above positions, the simplicity of the structure (the firm's sales by this time were on the order of $27 million), and the focus on the chief executive (not to mention the obvious family connections).

Entrepreneurial firms are often young and aggressive, continually searching for the risky markets that scare off the bigger bureaucracies. But they are also careful to avoid the complex markets, preferring to remain in niches that their leaders can comprehend. Their small size and focused strategies allow their structures to remain simple, so that the leaders can retain tight control and maneuver flexibly. Moreover, business entrepreneurs are often visionary, sometimes charismatic or autocratic as well (sometimes both, in sequence!). Of course, not all "entrepreneurs" are so aggressive or visionary; many settle down to pursue common strategies in small geographic niches. Labeled the *local producers,* these firms can include the corner restaurant, the town bakery, the regional supermarket chain.

But an organization need not be owned by an entrepreneur, indeed need not even operate in the profit sector, to adopt the configuration we call entrepreneurial. In fact, most new organizations seem to adopt this configuration, whatever their sector, because they generally have to rely on personalized leadership to get themselves going—to establish their basic direction, or *strategic vision,* to hire their first people and set up their initial procedures. Of course, strong leaders are likewise attracted to new organizations, where they can put their own stamp on things. Thus, we can conclude that most organizations in business, government, and not-for-profit areas pass through the entrepreneurial configuration in their formative years, during *start-up*.

Moreover, while new organizations that quickly grow large or that require specialized forms of expertise may make a relatively quick transition to another configuration, many others seem to remain in the entrepreneurial form, more or less, as long as their founding leaders remain in office. This reflects the fact that the structure has often been built around the personal needs and orientation of the leader and has been staffed with people loyal to him or her.

This last comment suggests that the personal power needs of a leader can also, by themselves, give rise to this configuration in an existing organization. When a chief executive hoards power and avoids or destroys the formalization of activity as an infringement on his or her right to rule by fiat, then an autocratic form of the entrepreneurial organization will tend to appear. This can be seen in the cult of personality of the leader, in business (the last days of Henry Ford) no less

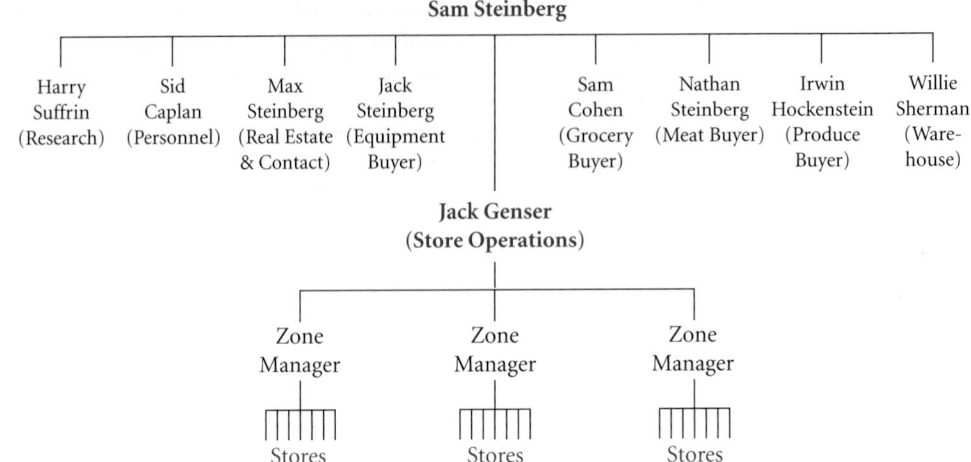

FIGURE 1 ORGANIZATION OF STEINBERG'S, AN ENTREPRENEURIAL FIRM (CIRCA 1948)

than in government (the leadership of Stalin in the Soviet Union). Charisma can have a similar effect, though different consequences, when the leader gains personal power not because he or she hoards it but because the followers lavish it on the leader.

The entrepreneurial configuration also tends to arise in any other type of organization that faces severe crisis. Backed up against a wall, with its survival at stake, an organization will typically turn to a strong leader for salvation. The structure thus becomes effectively (if not formally) simple, as the normal powers of existing groups—whether staff analysts, line managers, or professional operators, and so on, with their perhaps more standardized forms of control—are suspended to allow the chief to impose a new integrated vision through his or her personalized control. The leader may cut costs and expenses in an attempt to effect what is known in the strategic management literature as an *operating turnaround,* or else reconceive the basic product and service orientation, to achieve *strategic turnaround.* Of course, once the turnaround is realized, the organization may revert to its traditional operations, and, in the bargain, spew out its entrepreneurial leader, now viewed as an impediment to its smooth functioning.

STRATEGY FORMATION IN THE ENTREPRENEURIAL ORGANIZATION

How does strategy develop in the entrepreneurial organization? And what role does that mysterious concept known as "strategic vision" play? We know something of the entrepreneurial mode of strategy making, but less of strategic vision itself, since it is locked in the head of the individual. But some studies we have done at McGill do shed some light on both these questions. Let us consider strategic vision first.

VISIONARY LEADERSHIP

In a paper she coauthored with me, my McGill colleague Frances Westley contrasted two views of visionary leadership. One she likened to a hypodermic needle, in which the active ingredient (vision) is loaded into a syringe (words) which is injected into the employees to stimulate all kinds of energy. There is surely some truth to this, but Frances prefers another image, that of drama. Drawing from a book on theater by Peter Brook (1968), the legendary director of the Royal Shakespeare Company, she conceives strategic vision, like drama, as becoming magical in that moment when fiction and life blend together. In drama, this moment is the result of endless "rehearsal," the "performance" itself, and the "attendance" of the audience. But Brook prefers the more dynamic equivalent words in French, all of which have English meanings—"repetition," "representation," and "assistance." Frances likewise applies these words to strategic vision.

"Repetition" suggests that success comes from deep knowledge of the subject at hand. Just as Sir Laurence Olivier would repeat his lines again and again until he had trained his tongue muscles to say them effortlessly (Brook, p. 154), so too Lee Iacocca "grew up" in the automobile business, going to Chrysler after Ford because cars were "in his blood" (Iacocca, 1984: 141). The visionary's inspiration stems not from luck, although chance encounters can play a role, but from endless experience in a particular context.

"Representation" means not just to perform but to make the past live again, giving it immediacy, vitality. To the strategist, that is vision articulated, in words and actions. What distinguishes visionary leaders is their profound ability with language, often in symbolic form, as metaphor. It is not just that they "see" things from a new perspective but that they get others to so see them.

Edwin Land, who built a great company around the Polaroid camera he invented, has written of the duty of "the inventor to build a new gestalt for the old one in the framework of society" (1975: 50). He himself described photography as helping "to focus some aspect of [your] life"; as you look through the viewfinder, "it's not merely the camera you are focusing: you are focusing yourself . . . when you touch the button, what is inside of you comes out. It's the most basic form of creativity. Part of you is now permanent" (*Time,* 1972: 84). Lofty words for 50 tourists filing out of a bus to record some pat scene, but powerful imagery for someone trying to build an organization to promote a novel camera. Steve Jobs, visionary (for a time) in his promotion, if not invention, of the personal computer, placed a grand piano and a BMW in Apple's central foyer, with the claim that "I believe people get great ideas from seeing great products" (in Wise, 1984: 146).

"Assistance" means that the audience for drama, whether in the theater or in the organization, empowers the actor no less than the actor empowers the audience. Leaders become visionary because they appeal powerfully to specific constituencies at specific periods of time. That is why leaders once perceived as visionary can fall so dramatically from grace—a Steve Jobs, a Winston Churchill. Or to take a more dramatic example, here is how Albert Speer, arriving skeptical, reacted to the first lecture he heard by his future leader: "Hitler no longer seemed to be speaking to convince; rather, he seemed to feel that he was experiencing what the audience, by now transformed into a single mass, expected of him" (1970: 16).

Of course, management is not theater; the leader who becomes a stage actor, playing a part he or she does not live, is destined to fall from grace. It is integrity—a genuine feeling behind what the leader says and does—that makes leadership truly visionary, and that is what makes impossible the transition of such leadership into any formula.

This visionary leadership is style and strategy, coupled together. It is drama, but not playacting. The strategic visionary is born and made, the product of a historical moment. Brook closes his book with the following quotation:

> In everyday life, "if" is a fiction, in the theatre "if" is an experiment.
> In everyday life, "if" is an evasion, in the theatre "if" is the truth.
> When we are persuaded to believe in this truth, then the theatre and life are one.
> This is a high aim. It sounds like hard work.
> To play needs much work. But when we experience the work as play, then it is not work anymore.
> A play is play. (p. 157)

In the entrepreneurial organization, at best, "theater," namely strategic vision, becomes one with "life," namely organization. That way leadership creates drama; it turns work into play.

Let us now consider the entrepreneurial approach to strategy formation in terms of two specific studies we have done, one of a supermarket chain, the other of a manufacturer of women's undergarments.

THE ENTREPRENEURIAL APPROACH TO STRATEGY FORMATION IN A SUPERMARKET CHAIN

Steinberg's is a Canadian retail chain that began with a tiny food store in Montreal in 1917 and grew to sales in the billion-dollar range during the almost 60-year reign of its leader. Most of that growth came from supermarket operations. In many ways, Steinberg's fits the entrepreneurial model rather well. Sam Steinberg, who joined his mother in the first store at the age of 11 and personally made a quick decision to expand it 2 years later, maintained complete formal control of the firm (including every single voting share) to the day of his death in 1978. He also exercised close managerial control over all its major decisions, at least until the firm began to diversify after 1960, primarily into other forms of retailing.

It has been popular to describe the "bold stroke" of the entrepreneur (Cole, 1959). In Steinberg's we saw only two major reorientations of strategy in the sixty years, moves into self-service in the 1930s and into the shopping center business in the 1950s. But the stroke was not bold so much as tested. The story of the move into self-service is indicative. In 1933 one of the company's eight stores "struck it bad," in the chief executive's words, incurring "unacceptable" losses ($125 a week). Sam Steinberg closed the store one Friday evening, converted it to self-service, changed its name from "Steinberg's Service Stores" to "Wholesale Groceteria," slashed its prices by 15–20%, printed handbills, stuffed them into neighborhood mailboxes, and reopened on Monday morning. That's strategic change! But only once these changes proved successful did he convert the other stores. Then, in his words, "We grew like Topsy."

This anecdote tells us something about the bold stroke of the entrepreneur—"controlled boldness" is a better expression. The ideas were bold, the execution careful. Sam Steinberg could have simply closed the one unprofitable store. Instead he used it to create a new vision, but he tested that vision, however ambitiously, before leaping into it. Notice the interplay here of problems and opportunities. Steinberg took what most businessmen would probably have perceived as a *problem* (how to cut the losses in one store) and by treating it as a *crisis* (what is wrong with our *general* operation that produces these losses) turned it into an *opportunity* (we can grow more effectively with a new concept of retailing). That was how he got energy behind actions and kept ahead of his competitors. He "oversolved" his problem and thereby remade his company, a characteristic of some of the most effective forms of entrepreneurship.

But absolutely central to this form of entrepreneurship is intimate, detailed knowledge of the business or of analogous business situations, the "repetition" discussed earlier. The leader as conventional strategic "planner"—the so-called architect of strategy—sits on a pedestal and is fed aggregate data that he or she uses to "formulate" strategies that are "implemented" by others. But the history of Steinberg's belies that image. It suggests that clear, imaginative, integrated strategic vision depends on an involvement with detail, an intimate knowledge of specifics. And by closely controlling "implementation" personally, the leader is able to reformulate en route, to adapt the evolving vision through his or her own process of learning. That is why Steinberg tried his new ideas in one store first. And that is why, in discussing his firm's competitive advantage, he told us: "Nobody knew the grocery business like we did. Everything has to do with your knowledge." He added: "I knew merchandise, I knew cost. I knew selling, I knew customers. I knew everything . . . and I passed on all my knowledge; I kept teaching my people. That's the advantage we had. They couldn't touch us."

Such knowledge can be incredibly effective when concentrated in one individual who is fully in charge (having no need to convince others, not subordinates below, not superiors at some distant headquarters, nor market analysts looking for superficial pronouncements) and who retains a strong, long-term commitment to the organization. So long as the business is simple and focused enough to be comprehended in one brain, the entrepreneurial approach is powerful, indeed unexcelled. Nothing else can provide so clear and complete a vision, yet also allow the flexibility to elaborate and rework that vision when necessary. The conception of a new strategy is an exercise in synthesis, which is typically best carried out in a single, informed brain. That is why the entrepreneurial approach is at the center of the most glorious corporate success.

But in its strength lies entrepreneurship's weakness. Bear in mind that strategy for the entrepreneurial leader is not a formal, detailed plan on paper. It is a personal vision, a concept of the business, locked in a single brain. It may need to get "represented," in words and metaphors, but that must remain general if the leader is to maintain the richness and flexibility of his or her concept. But success breeds a large organization, public financing, and the need for formal planning. The vision must be articulated to drive others and gain their support, and that threatens the personal nature of the vision. At the limit, as we shall see later in the case of Steinberg's, the leader can get captured by his or her very successes.

In Steinberg's, moreover, when success in the traditional business encouraged diversification into new ones (new regions, new forms of retailing, new industries), the organization moved beyond the realm of its leader's personal comprehension, and the entrepreneurial mode of strategy formation lost its viability. Strategy making became more decentralized, more analytic, in some ways more careful, but at the same time less visionary, less integrated, less flexible, and ironically, less deliberate.

CONCEIVING A NEW VISION IN A GARMENT FIRM

The genius of an entrepreneur like Sam Steinberg was his ability to pursue one vision (self-service and everything that entailed) faithfully for decades and then, based on a weak signal in the environment (the building of the first small shopping center in Montreal), to realize the need to shift that vision. The planning literature makes a big issue of forecasting such discontinuities, but as far as I know there are no formal techniques to do so effectively (claims about "scenario analysis" notwithstanding). The ability to perceive a sudden shift in an established pattern and then to conceive a new vision to deal with it appears to remain largely in the realm of informed intuition, generally the purview of the wise, experienced, and energetic leader. Again, the literature is largely silent on this. But another of our studies, also concerning entrepreneurship, did reveal some aspects of this process.

Canadelle produces women's undergarments, primarily brassieres. It was a highly successful organization, although not on the same scale as Steinberg's. Things were going well for the company in the late 1960s, under the personal leadership of Larry Nadler, the son of its founder, when suddenly everything changed. A sexual revolution of sorts was accompanying broader social manifestations, with bra burning a symbol of its resistance. For a manufacturer of brassieres the threat was obvious. For many other women the miniskirt had come to dominate the fashion scene, obsoleting the girdle and giving rise to pantyhose. As the executives of Canadelle put it, "the bottom fell out of the girdle business." The whole environment—long so receptive to the company's strategies—seemed to turn on it all at once.

At the time, a French company had entered the Quebec market with a light, sexy, molded garment called "Huit," using the theme, "just like not wearing a bra." Their target market was 15–20-year-olds. Though the product was expensive when it landed in Quebec and did not fit well in Nadler's opinion, it sold well. Nadler flew to France in an attempt to license the product for manufacture in Canada. The French firm refused, but, in Nadler's words, what he learned in "that one hour in their offices made the trip worthwhile." He realized that what women wanted was a more natural look, not no bra but less bra. Another trip shortly afterward, to a sister American firm, convinced him of the importance of market segmentation by age and life-style. That led him to the realization that the firm had two markets, one for the more mature customer, for whom the brassiere was a cosmetic to look and feel more attractive, and another for the younger customer who wanted to look and feel more natural.

Those two events led to a major shift in strategic vision. The CEO described it as sudden, the confluence of different ideas to create a new mental set. In his words, "all of a sudden the idea forms." Canadelle reconfirmed its commitment to the brassiere business, seeking greater market share while its competitors were cutting back. It introduced a new line of more natural brassieres for the younger customers, for which the firm had to work out the molding technology as well as a new approach to promotion.

We can draw on Kurt Lewin's (1951) three-stage model of unfreezing, changing, and refreezing to explain such a gestalt shift in vision. The process of *unfreezing* is essentially one of overcoming the natural defense mechanisms, the established "mental set" of how an industry is supposed to operate, to realize that things have changed fundamentally. The old assumptions no longer hold. Effective managers, especially effective strategic managers, are supposed to scan their environments continually, looking for such changes. But doing so continuously, or worse, trying to use technique to do so, may have exactly the opposite effect. So much attention may be given to strategic monitoring when nothing important is happening that when something really does, it may not even be noticed. The trick, of course, is to pick out the discontinuities that matter, and as noted earlier that seems to have more to do with informed intuition than anything else.

A second step in unfreezing is the willingness to step into the void, so to speak, for the leader to shed his or her conventional notions of how a business is supposed to function. The leader must above all avoid premature closure—seizing on a new thrust before it has become clear what its signals really mean. That takes a special kind of management, one able to live with a good deal of uncertainty and discomfort. "There is a period of confusion," Nadler told us, "you sleep on it . . . start looking for patterns . . . become an information hound, searching for [explanations] everywhere."

Strategic *change* of this magnitude seems to require a shift in mind-set before a new strategy can be conceived. And the thinking is fundamentally conceptual and inductive, probably stimulated (as in this case) by just one or two key insights. Continuous bombardment of facts, opinions, problems, and so on may prepare the mind for the shift, but it is the sudden *insight* that is likely to drive the synthesis—to bring all the disparate elements together in one "eureka"-type flash.

Once the strategist's mind is set, assuming he or she has read the new situation correctly and has not closed prematurely, then the *refreezing* process begins. Here the object is not to read the situation, at least not in a global sense, but in effect to block it out. It is a time to work out the consequences of the new strategic vision.

It has been claimed that obsession is an ingredient in effective organizations (Peters, 1980). Only for the period of refreezing would we agree, when the organization must focus on the pursuit of the new orientation—the new mind-set—with full vigor. A management that was open and divergent in its thinking must now become closed and convergent. But that means that the uncomfortable period of uncertainty has passed, and people can now get down to the exciting task of accomplishing something new. Now the organization knows where it is going; the object of the exercise is to get there using all the skills at its command, many of them formal and analytic. Of course, not everyone accepts the new vision. For those steeped in old strategies, *this* is the period of discomfort, and they can put up considerable resistance, forcing the leader to make greater use of his or her formal powers and political skills. Thus, refreezing of the leader's mind-set often involves the unfreezing, changing, and refreezing of the organization itself! But when the structure is simple, as it is in the entrepreneurial organization, that problem is relatively minor.

LEADERSHIP TAKING PRECEDENCE IN THE ENTREPRENEURIAL CONFIGURATION

To conclude, entrepreneurship is very much tied up with the creation of strategic vision, often with the attainment of a new concept. Strategies can be characterized as largely deliberate, since they reside in the intentions of a single leader. But being largely personal as well, the details of those strategies can emerge as they develop. In fact, the vision can change too. The leader can adapt en route, can learn, which means new visions can emerge too, sometimes, as we have seen, rather quickly.

In the entrepreneurial organization, as shown in Figure 2, the focus of attention is on the leader. The organization is malleable and responsive to that person's initiatives, while the environment remains benign for the most part, the result of the leader's selecting (or "enacting") the correct niche for his or her organization. The environment can, of course, flare up occasionally to challenge the organization, and then the leader must adapt, perhaps seeking out a new and more appropriate niche in which to operate.

SOME ISSUES ASSOCIATED WITH THE ENTREPRENEURIAL ORGANIZATION

We conclude briefly with some broad issues associated with the entrepreneurial organization. In this configuration, decisions concerning both strategy and operations tend to be centralized in the office of the chief executive. This centralization has the important advantage of rooting strategic response in deep knowledge of the operations. It also allows for flexibility and adaptability: Only one person need act. But this same executive can get so enmeshed in operating problems that he or she loses sight of strategy; alternatively, he or she may become so enthusiastic about strategic

FIGURE 2
LEADERSHIP TAKING PRECEDENCE IN THE ENTREPRENEURIAL ORGANIZATION

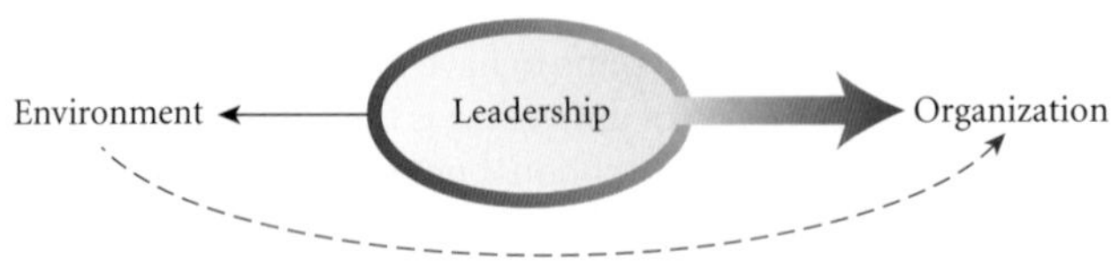

opportunities that the more routine operations can wither for lack of attention and eventually pull down the whole organization. Both are frequent occurrences in entrepreneurial organizations.

This is also the riskiest of organizations, hinging on the activities of one individual. One heart attack can literally wipe out the organization's prime means of coordination. Even a leader in place can be risky. When change becomes necessary, everything hinges on the chief's response to it. If he or she resists, as is not uncommon where that person developed the existing strategy in the first place, then the organization may have no means to adapt. Then the great strength of the entrepreneurial organization—the vision of its leader plus its capacity to respond quickly—becomes its chief liability.

Another great advantage of the entrepreneurial organization is its sense of mission. Many people enjoy working in a small, intimate organization where the leader—often charismatic—knows where he or she is taking it. As a result, the organization tends to grow rapidly, with great enthusiasm. Employees can develop a solid identification with such an organization.

But other people perceive this configuration as highly restrictive. Because one person calls all the shots, they feel not like the participants on an exciting journey, but like cattle being led to market for someone else's benefit. In fact, the broadening of democratic norms into the sphere of organizations has rendered the entrepreneurial organization unfashionable in some quarters of contemporary society. It has been described as paternalistic and sometimes autocratic, and accused of concentrating too much power at the top. Certainly, without countervailing powers in the organization the chief executive can easily abuse his or her authority.

Perhaps the entrepreneurial organization is an anachronism in societies that call themselves democratic. Yet there have always been such organizations, and there always will be. This was probably the only structure known to those who first discovered the benefits of coordinating their activities in some formal way. And it probably reached its heyday in the era of the great American trusts of the late nineteenth century, when powerful entrepreneurs personally controlled huge empires. Since then, at least in Western society, the entrepreneurial organization has been on the decline. Nonetheless, it remains a prevalent and important configuration, and will continue to be so as long as society faces the conditions that require it: the prizing of entrepreneurial initiative and the resultant encouragement of new organizations, the need for small and informal organizations in some spheres and of strong personalized leadership despite larger size in others, and the need periodically to turn around ailing organizations of all types.

READING 13.2

Competitive Strategy in Emerging Industries* BY MICHAEL E. PORTER

Emerging industries are newly formed or reformed industries that have been created by technological innovations, shifts in relative cost relationships, emergence of new consumer needs, or other economic and sociological changes that elevate a new product or service to the level of a potentially viable business opportunity. . . .

The essential characteristic of an emerging industry from the viewpoint of formulating strategy is that there are no rules of the game. The competitive problem in an emerging industry is that all the rules must be established such that the firm can cope with and prosper under them.

THE STRUCTURAL ENVIRONMENT

Although emerging industries can differ a great deal in their structures, there are some common structural factors that seem to characterize many industries in this stage of their development. Most of them relate either to the absence of established bases for competition or other rules of the game or to the initial small size and newness of the industry.

*Adapted from *Competitive Strategy: Techniques for analyzing industries and competitors*, The Free Press (Porter, M.E. 1980), with the permission of The Free Press, a Division of Simon & Schuster, Inc.

COMMON STRUCTURAL CHARACTERISTICS

TECHNOLOGICAL UNCERTAINTY

There is usually a great deal of uncertainty about the technology in an emerging industry: What product configuration will ultimately prove to be the best? Which production technology will prove to be the most efficient? . . .

STRATEGIC UNCERTAINTY

. . . No "right" strategy has been clearly identified, and different firms are groping with different approaches to product/market positioning, marketing, servicing, and so on, as well as betting on different product configurations or production technologies. . . . Closely related to this problem, firms often have poor information about competitors, characteristics of customers, and industry conditions in the emerging phase. No one knows who all the competitors are, and reliable industry sales and market share data are often simply unavailable, for example.

HIGH INITIAL COSTS BUT STEEP COST REDUCTION

Small production volume and newness usually combine to produce high costs in the emerging industry relative to those the industry can potentially achieve. . . . Ideas come rapidly in terms of improved procedures, plant layout, and so on, and employees achieve major gains in productivity as job familiarity increases. Increasing sales make major additions to the scale and total accumulated volume of output produced by firms. . . .

EMBRYONIC COMPANIES AND SPIN-OFFS

The emerging phase of the industry is usually accompanied by the presence of the greatest proportion of newly formed companies (to be contrasted with newly formed units of established firms) that the industry will ever experience. . . .

FIRST-TIME BUYERS

Buyers of the emerging industry's product or service are inherently first-time buyers. The marketing task is thus one of inducing substitution, or getting the buyer to purchase the new product or service instead of something else. . . .

SHORT TIME HORIZON

In many emerging industries the pressure to develop customers or produce products to meet demand is so great that bottlenecks and problems are dealt with expediently rather than as a result of an analysis of future conditions. At the same time, industry conventions are often born out of pure chance. . . .

SUBSIDY

In many emerging industries, especially those with radical new technology or that address areas of societal concern, there may be subsidization of early entrants. Subsidy may come from a variety of government and nongovernment sources. . . . Subsidies often add a great degree of instability to an industry, which is made dependent on political decisions that can be quickly reversed or modified. . . .

EARLY MOBILITY BARRIERS

In an emerging industry, the configuration of mobility barriers is often predictably different from that which will characterize the industry later in its development. Common early barriers are the following:

- proprietary technology
- access to distribution channels
- access to raw materials and other inputs (skilled labor) of appropriate cost and quality

- cost advantages due to experience, made more significant by the technological and competitive uncertainties
- risk, which raises the effective opportunity cost of capital and thereby effective capital barriers

. . . The nature of the early barriers is a key reason why we observe newly created companies in emerging industries. The typical early barriers stem less from the need to command massive resources than from the ability to bear risk, be creative technologically, and make forward-looking decisions to garner input supplies and distribution channels. . . . There may be some advantages to late entry, however. . . .

STRATEGIC CHOICES

Formulation of strategy in emerging industries must cope with the uncertainty and risk of this period of an industry's development. The rules of the competitive game are largely undefined, the structure of the industry unsettled and probably changing, and competitors hard to diagnose. Yet all these factors have another side—the emerging phase of an industry's development is probably the period when the strategic degrees of freedom are the greatest and when the leverage from good strategic choices is the highest in determining performance.

SHAPING INDUSTRY STRUCTURE

The overriding strategic issue in emerging industries is the ability of the firm to shape industry structure. Through its choices, the firm can try to set the rules of the game in areas like product policy, marketing approach, and pricing strategy. . . .

EXTERNALITIES IN INDUSTRY DEVELOPMENT

In an emerging industry, a key strategic issue is the balance the firm strikes between industry advocacy and pursuing its own narrow self-interest. Because of potential problems with industry image, credibility, and confusion of buyers . . . in the emerging phase the firm is in part dependent on others in the industry for its own success. The overriding problem for the industry is inducing substitution and attracting first-time buyers, and it is usually in the firm's interest during this phase to help promote standardization, police substandard quality and fly-by-night producers, and present a consistent front to suppliers, customers, government, and the financial community. . . .

It is probably a valid generalization that the balance between industry outlook and firm outlook must shift in the direction of the firm as the industry begins to achieve significant penetration. Sometimes firms who have taken very high profiles as industry spokespersons, much to their and the industry's benefit, fail to recognize that they must shift their orientation. As a result, they can be left behind as the industry matures. . . .

CHANGING ROLE OF SUPPLIERS AND CHANNELS

Strategically, the firm in an emerging industry must be prepared for a possible shift in the orientation of its suppliers and distribution channels as the industry grows in size and proves itself. Suppliers may become increasingly willing (or can be forced) to respond to the industry's special needs in terms of varieties, service, and delivery. Similarly, distribution channels may become more receptive to investing in facilities, advertising, and so forth in partnership with the firms. Early exploitation of these changes in orientation can give the firm strategic leverage.

SHIFTING MOBILITY BARRIERS

As outlined earlier . . . the early mobility barriers may erode quickly in an emerging industry, often to be replaced by very different ones as the industry grows in size and as the technology matures. This factor has a number of implications. The most obvious is that the firm must be prepared to find new ways to defend its position and must not rely solely on things like proprietary technology and a unique product variety on which it has succeeded in the past. Responding to shifting mobility barriers may involve commitments of capital that far exceed those that have been necessary in the early phases.

Another implication is that the *nature of entrants* into the industry may shift to more established firms attracted to the larger and increasingly proven (less risky) industry, often competing on the basis of the newer forms of mobility barriers, like scale and marketing clout. . . .

TIMING ENTRY

A crucial strategic choice for competing in emerging industries is the appropriate timing of entry. Early entry (or pioneering) involves high risk but may involve otherwise low entry barriers and can offer a large return. Early entry is appropriate when the following general circumstances hold:

- Image and reputation of the firm are important to the buyer, and the firm can develop an enhanced reputation by being a pioneer.
- Early entry can initiate the learning process in a business in which the learning curve is important, experience is difficult to imitate, and it will not be nullified by successive technological generations.
- Customer loyalty will be great, so that benefits will accrue to the firm that sells to the customer first.
- Absolute cost advantages can be gained by early commitment to supplies of raw materials, distribution channels, and so on. . . .

TACTICAL MOVES

The problems limiting development of an emerging industry suggest some tactical moves that may improve the firm's strategic position:

- Early commitments to suppliers of raw materials will yield favorable priorities in times of shortages.
- Financing can be timed to take advantage of a Wall Street love affair with the industry if it happens, even if financing is ahead of actual needs. This step lowers the firm's cost of capital. . . .

The choice of which emerging industry to enter is dependent on the outcome of a predictive exercise such as the one described above. An emerging industry is attractive if its ultimate structure (not its *initial* structure) is one that is consistent with above-average returns and if the firm can create a defendable position in the industry in the long run. The latter will depend on its resources relative to the mobility barriers that will evolve.

Too often firms enter emerging industries because they are growing rapidly, because incumbents are currently very profitable, or because ultimate industry size promises to be large. These may be contributing reasons, but the decision to enter must ultimately depend on a structural analysis. . . .

READING 13.3

How Entrepreneurs Craft Strategies that Work* BY AMAR BHIDE

However popular it may be in the corporate world, a comprehensive analytical approach to planning doesn't suit most start-ups. Entrepreneurs typically lack the time and money to interview a representative cross section of potential customers, let alone analyze substitutes, reconstruct competitors' cost structures, or project alternative technology scenarios. In fact, too much analysis can be harmful; by the time an opportunity is investigated fully, it may no longer exist.

---

*Originally published as "How Entrepreneurs Craft Strategies that Work," in the *Harvard Business Review*, March–April 1994, pp. 150–161. Reprinted with deletions by permission of the *Harvard Business Review*.

A city map and restaurant guide on a CD may be a winner in January but worthless if delayed until December.

Interviews with the founders of 100 companies on the 1989 Inc. "500" list of the fastest growing private companies in the United States and recent research on more than 100 other thriving ventures by my MBA students suggest that many successful entrepreneurs spend little time researching and analyzing. . . . And those who do often have to scrap their strategies and start over. Furthermore, a 1990 National Federation of Independent Business study of 2,994 start-ups showed that founders who spent a long time in study, reflection, and planning were no more likely to survive their first three years than people who seized opportunities without planning. In fact, many corporations that revere comprehensive analysis develop a refined incapacity for seizing opportunities. Analysis can delay entry until it's too late or kill ideas by identifying numerous problems.

Yet all ventures merit some analysis and planning. Appearances to the contrary, successful entrepreneurs don't take risks blindly. Rather, they use a quick, cheap approach that represents a middle ground between planning paralysis and no planning at all. They don't expect perfection—even the most astute entrepreneurs have their share of false starts. Compared to typical corporate practice, however, the entrepreneurial approach is more economical and timely.

What are the critical elements of winning entrepreneurial approaches? Our evidence suggests three general guidelines for aspiring founders:

1. Screen opportunities quickly to weed out unpromising ventures.
2. Analyze ideas parsimoniously. Focus on a few important ideas.
3. Integrate action and analysis. Don't wait for all the answers, and be ready to change course.

SCREENING OUT LOSERS

Individuals who seek entrepreneurial opportunities usually generate lots of ideas. Quickly discarding those that have low potential frees aspirants to concentrate on the few ideas that merit refinement and study.

Screening out unpromising ventures requires judgment and reflection, not new data. The entrepreneur should already be familiar with the facts needed to determine whether an idea has prima facie merit. Our evidence suggests that new ventures are usually started to solve problems the founders have grappled with personally as customers or employees. . . . Companies like Federal Express, which grew out of a paper its founder wrote in college, are rare.

Profitable survival requires an edge derived from some combination of a creative idea and a superior capacity for execution. . . . The entrepreneur's creativity may involve an innovative product or a process that changes the existing order. Or the entrepreneur may have a unique insight about the course or consequence of an external change: the California gold rush, for example, made paupers of the thousands caught in the frenzy, but Levi Strauss started a company—and a legend—by recognizing the opportunity to supply rugged canvas and later denim trousers to prospectors.

But entrepreneurs cannot rely on just inventing new products or anticipating a trend. They must also execute well, especially if their concepts can be copied easily. For example, if an innovation cannot be patented or kept secret, entrepreneurs must acquire and manage the resource needed to build a brand name or other barrier that will deter imitators. Superior execution can also compensate for a me-too concept in emerging or rapidly growing industries where doing it quickly and doing it right are more important than brilliant strategy.

Ventures that obviously lack a creative concept or any special capacity to execute—the ex-consultant's scheme to exploit grandmother's cookie recipe, for instance—can be discarded without much thought. In other cases, entrepreneurs must reflect on the adequacy of their ideas and their capacities to execute them.

Successful start-ups don't need an edge on every front. The creativity of successful entrepreneurs varies considerably. Some implement a radical idea, some modify, and some show no originality. Capacity for execution also varies among entrepreneurs. Selling an industrial niche product doesn't call for the charisma that's required to pitch trinkets through infomercials. Our evidence suggests that there is no ideal entrepreneurial profile either: successful founders can be gregarious or taciturn, analytical or intuitive, good or terrible with details, risk averse or thrill seeking. They can be delegators or control freaks, pillars of the community or outsiders. In assessing the viability of a potential venture, therefore, each aspiring entrepreneur should consider three interacting factors:

1. OBJECTIVES OF THE VENTURE

Is the entrepreneur's goal to build a large, enduring enterprise, carve out a niche, or merely turn a quick profit? Ambitious goals require great creativity. Building a large enterprise quickly, either by seizing a significant share of an existing market or by creating a large new market, usually calls for a revolutionary idea. . . .

Requirements for execution are also stiff. Big ideas often necessitate big money and strong organizations. Successful entrepreneurs, therefore, require an evangelical ability to attract, retain, and balance the interests of investors, customers, employees, and suppliers for a seemingly outlandish vision, as well as the organizational and leadership skills to build a large, complex company quickly. In addition, the entrepreneur may require considerable technical know-how in deal making, strategic planning, managing overhead, and other business skills. The revolutionary entrepreneur, in other words, would appear to require almost superhuman qualities: ordinary mortals need not apply.

Consider Federal Express founder Fred Smith. His creativity lay in recognizing that customers would pay a significant premium for reliable overnight delivery and in figuring out a way to provide the service for them. Smith ruled out using existing commercial flights, whose schedules were designed to serve passenger traffic. Instead, he had the audacious idea of acquiring a dedicated fleet of jets and shipping all packages through a central hub that was located in Memphis.

As with most big ideas, the concept was difficult to execute. Smith, 28 years old at the time, had to raise $91 million in venture funding. The jets, the hub, operations in 25 states, and several hundred trained employees had to be in place before the company could open for business. And Smith needed great fortitude and skill to prevent the fledgling enterprise from going under: Federal Express lost over $40 million in its first three years. Some investors tried to remove Smith, and creditors tried to seize assets. Yet Smith somehow preserved morale and mollified investors and lenders while the company expanded its operations and launched national advertising and direct-mail campaigns to build market share.

In contrast, ventures that seek to capture a market niche, not transform or create an industry, don't need extraordinary ideas. Some ingenuity is necessary to design a product that will draw customers away from mainstream offerings and overcome the cost penalty of serving a small market. But features that are too novel can be a hindrance; a niche market will rarely justify the investment required to educate customers and distributors about the benefits of a radically new product. Similarly, a niche venture cannot support too much production or distribution innovation; unlike Federal Express, the Cape Cod Potato Company, for example, must work within the limits of its distributors and truckers.

And since niche markets cannot support much investment or overhead, entrepreneurs do not need the revolutionary's ability to raise capital and build large organizations. Rather, the entrepreneur must be able to secure others' resources on favorable terms and make do with less, building brand awareness through guerilla marketing and word of mouth instead of national advertising, for example.

Jay Boberg and Miles Copeland, who launched International Record Syndicate (IRS) in 1979, used a niche strategy, my students Elisabeth Bentel and Victoria Hackett found, to create one of the most successful new music labels in North America. Lacking the funds or a great innovation to compete against the major labels, Boberg and Copeland promoted "alternative" music—undiscovered British groups like the buzzcocks and Skafish—which the major labels were ignoring because their potential sales were too small. And IRS used low-cost, alternative marketing methods to promote their alternative music. At the time, the major record labels had not yet realized that music videos on television could be used effectively to promote their products. Boberg, however, jumped at the opportunity to produce a rock show, "The Cutting Edge," for MTV. The show proved to be a hit with fans and an effective promotional tool for IRS. Before "The Cutting Edge," Boberg had to plead with radio stations to play his songs. Afterward, the MTV audience demanded that disc jockeys play the songs they had heard on the show.

2. LEVERAGE PROVIDED BY EXTERNAL CHANGE

Exploiting opportunities in a new or changing industry is generally easier than making waves in a mature industry. Enormous creativity, experience, and contacts are needed to take business away from competitors in a mature industry, where market forces have long shaken out weak technologies, strategies, and organizations.

But new markets are different. There start-ups often face rough-around-the-edges rivals, customers who tolerate inexperienced vendors and imperfect products, and opportunities to profit from shortages. Small insights and marginal innovations, a little skill or expertise (in the land of the blind, the one-eyed person is king), and the willingness to act quickly can go a long way. In fact, with great external uncertainty, customers and investors may be hesitant to back a radical product and technology until the environment settles down. Strategic choices in a new industry are often very limited; entrepreneurs have to adhere to the emerging standards for product features, components, or distribution channels.

The leverage provided by external change is illustrated by the success of numerous start-ups in hardware, software, training, retailing, and systems integration that emerged from the personal computer revolution of the 1980s. Installing or fixing a computer system is probably easier than repairing a car; but because people with the initiative or foresight to acquire the skill were scarce, entrepreneurs like Bohdan's Peter Zacharkiw built successful dealerships by providing what customers saw as exceptional service. . . . As one midwestern dealer told me, "We have a joke slogan around here: We aren't as incompetent as our competitors!"

Bill Gates turned Microsoft into a multibillion-dollar company without a breakthrough product by showing up in the industry early and capitalizing on the opportunities that came his way. Gates, then 19, and his partner Paul Allen, 21, launched Microsoft in 1975 to sell software they had created. By 1979, Microsoft had grown to 25 employees and $2.5 million in sales. Then in November 1980, IBM chose Microsoft to provide an operating system for its personal computer. Microsoft thereupon bought an operating system from Seattle Computer Products, which it modified into the now ubiquitous MS-DOS. The IBM name and the huge success of the 1-2-3 spreadsheet, which only ran on DOS computers, soon helped make Microsoft the dominant supplier of operating systems.

3. BASIS OF COMPETITION: PROPRIETARY ASSETS VERSUS HUSTLE

In some industries, such as pharmaceuticals, luxury hotels, and consumer goods, a company's profitability depends significantly on the assets it owns or controls—patents, location, or brands, for example. Good management practices like listening to customers, maintaining quality, and paying attention to costs, which can improve the profits of a going business, cannot propel a start-up over such structural barriers. Here a creative new technology, product, or strategy is a must.

Companies in fragmented service industries, such as investment management, investment banking, head hunting, or consulting cannot establish proprietary advantages easily but can nonetheless enjoy high profits by involving exceptional service tailored to client demands. Start-ups in those fields rely mainly on their hustle (Bhide, 1986). Successful entrepreneurs depend on personal selling skills, contacts, their reputations for expertise, and their ability to convince clients of the value of the services rendered. They also have the capacity for institution building—skills such as recruiting and motivating stellar professionals and articulating and reinforcing company values. Where there are few natural economies of scale, an entrepreneur cannot create a going concern out of a one-man-band or ad hoc ensemble without a lot of expertise in organizational development. . . .

GAUGING ATTRACTIVENESS

Entrepreneurs should also screen potential ventures for their attractiveness—their risks and rewards—compared to other opportunities. Several factors should be considered. Capital requirements, for example, matter to the entrepreneur who lacks easy access to financial markets. An unexpected need for cash because, say, one large customer is unable to make a timely payment may shut down a venture or force a fire sale of the founder's equity. Therefore, entrepreneurs should favor ventures that aren't capital intensive and have the profit margins to sustain rapid growth with internally generated funds. In a similar fashion, entrepreneurs should look for a high margin for error, ventures with simple operations and low fixed costs that are less likely to face a cash crunch because of factors such as technical delays, cost overruns, and slow buildup of sales.

Other criteria reflect the typical entrepreneur's inability to undertake multiple projects: an attractive venture should provide a substantial enough reward to compensate the entrepreneur's exclusive commitment to it. Shut-down costs should be low: the payback should be quick, or failure soon recognized so that the venture can be terminated without a significant loss of time, money, or reputation. And the entrepreneur should have the option to cash in, for example, by selling all or part of the equity. An entrepreneur locked into an illiquid business cannot easily pursue other opportunities and risks fatigue and burnout. . . .

Ventures must also fit what the individual entrepreneur values and wants to do. Surviving the inevitable disappointments and near disasters one encounters on the rough road to success requires a passion for the chosen business. . . .

Surprisingly, small endeavors often hold more financial promise than large ones. Often the founders can keep a larger share of the profits because they don't dilute their equity interest through multiple rounds of financings. But entrepreneurs must be willing to prosper in a backwater; dominating a neglected market segment is sometimes more profitable than intellectually stimulating or glamorous. Niche enterprises can also enter the "land of the living dead" because their market is too small for the business to thrive but the entrepreneur has invested too much effort to be willing to quit. . . .

PARSIMONIOUS PLANNING AND ANALYSIS

To conserve time and money, successful entrepreneurs minimize the resources they devote to researching their ideas. Unlike the corporate world, where foil mastery and completed staff work can make a career, the entrepreneur only does as much planning and analysis as seems useful and makes subjective judgment calls when necessary. . . .

In setting their analytical priorities, entrepreneurs must recognize that some critical uncertainties cannot be resolved through more research. For example, focus groups and surveys often have little value in predicting demand for products that are truly novel. At first, consumers had dismissed the need for copiers, for instance, and told researchers they were satisfied with using carbon paper. With issues like this, entrepreneurs have to resist the temptation of endless investigation and trust their judgment. . . .

Revenues are notoriously difficult to predict. At best, entrepreneurs may satisfy themselves that their novel product or service delivers considerably greater value than current offerings do; how quickly the product catches on is a blind guess. Leverage may be obtained, however, from analyzing how customers might buy and use the product or service. Understanding the purchase can help identify the right decision makers for the new offering. With Federal Express, for instance, it was important to go beyond the mailroom managers who traditionally bought delivery services. Understanding how products are used can also help by revealing obstacles that must be overcome before consumers can benefit from a new offering.

Visionary entrepreneurs must guard against making competitors rich from their work. Many concepts are difficult to prove but, once proven, easy to imitate. Unless the pioneer is protected by sustainable barriers to entry, the benefits of a hard-fought revolution can become a public good rather than a boon to the innovator. . . .

Entrepreneurs who hope to secure a niche face different problems: they often fail because the costs of serving a specialized segment exceed the benefits to customers. Entrepreneurs should therefore analyze carefully the incremental costs of serving a niche and take into account their lack of scale and the difficulty of marketing to a small, diffused segment. And especially if the cost disadvantage is significant, entrepreneurs should determine whether their offering provides a significant performance benefit. Whereas established companies can vie for share through line extensions or marginal tailoring of their products and services, the start-up must really wow its target customers. A marginally tastier cereal won't knock Kellogg's Cornflakes off supermarket shelves.

Inadequate payoffs also pose a risk for ventures that address small markets. For example, a niche venture that can't support a direct sales force may not generate enough commissions to attract an independent broker or manufacturer's rep. Entrepreneurs will eventually lose interest too if the rewards aren't commensurate with their efforts. Therefore, the entrepreneur should make sure that everyone who contributes can expect a high, quick, or sustainable return even if the venture's total profits are small.

Entrepreneurs who seek to leverage factors like changing technologies, customer preferences, or regulations should avoid extensive analysis. Research conducted under conditions of such turbulence isn't reliable, and the importance of a quick response precludes spending the time to make sure every detail is covered. . . .

Analyzing whether or not the rewards for winning are commensurate with the risks, however, can be a more feasible and worthwhile exercise. In some technology races, success is predictably short-lived. In the disk-drive industry, for example, companies that succeed with one generation of products are often leap-frogged when the next generation arrives. In engineering workstations, however, Sun enjoyed long-term gains from its early success because it established a durable architectural standard. If success is unlikely to be sustained, entrepreneurs should have a plan for making a good return while it lasts. . . .

INTEGRATING ACTION AND ANALYSIS

Standard operating procedure in large corporations usually makes a clear distinction between analysis and execution. In contemplating a new venture, managers in established companies face issues about its fit with ongoing activities. Does the proposed venture leverage corporate strengths? Will the resources and attention it requires reduce the company's ability to build customer loyalty and improve quality in core markets? These concerns dictate a deliberate, "trustee" approach: before they can launch a venture, managers must investigate an opportunity extensively, seek the counsel of people higher up, submit a formal plan, respond to criticisms by bosses and corporate staff, and secure a headcount and capital allocation.

Entrepreneurs who start with a clean slate, however, don't have to know all the answers before they act. In fact, they often can't easily separate action and analysis. The attractiveness of a new restaurant, for example, may depend on the terms of the lease; low rents can change the venture from a mediocre proposition into a money machine. But an entrepreneur's ability to negotiate a good lease cannot be easily determined from a general prior analysis; he or she must enter into a serious negotiation with a specific landlord for a specific property.

Acting before an opportunity is fully analyzed has many benefits. Doing something concrete builds confidence in oneself and in others. Key employees and investors will often follow the individual who has committed to action, for instance, by quitting a job, incorporating, or signing a lease. By taking a personal risk, the entrepreneur convinces other people that the venture *will* proceed, and they may believe that if they don't sign up, they could be left behind.

Early action can generate more robust, better informed strategies too. Extensive surveys and focus-group research about a concept can produce misleading evidence: slippage can arise between research and reality because the potential customers interviewed are not representative of the market, their enthusiasm for the concept wanes when they see the actual product, or they lack the authority to sign purchase orders. More robust strategies may be developed by first building a working prototype and asking customers to use it before conducting extensive market research.

The ability of individual entrepreneurs to execute quickly will naturally vary. Trial and error is less feasible with large-scale, capital-intensive ventures like Orbital Sciences, which had to raise over $50 million to build rockets for NASA, than with a consulting firm start-up. Nevertheless, some characteristics are common to an approach that integrates action and analysis:

HANDLING ANALYTICAL TASKS IN STAGES

Rather than resolve all issues at once, the entrepreneur does only enough research to justify the next action or investment. For example, an individual who has developed a new medical technology may first obtain crude estimates of market demand to determine whether it's worth seeing a patent lawyer. If the estimates and lawyer are encouraging, the individual may do more analysis to investigate the wisdom of spending money to obtain a patent. Several more iterations of analysis and action will follow before the entrepreneur prepares and circulates a formal business plan to venture capitalists.

PLUGGING HOLES QUICKLY

As soon as any problems or risks show up, the entrepreneur begins looking for solutions. For example, suppose that an entrepreneur sees it will be difficult to raise capital. Rather than kill the idea, he or she thinks creatively about solving the problem. Perhaps the investment can be reduced by modifying technology to use more standard equipment that can be rented instead of bought. Or under the right terms, a customer might underwrite the risk by providing a large initial order. Or expectations and goals for growth might be scaled down, and a niche market could be tackled first. Except with obviously unviable ideas that can be ruled out through elementary logic, the purpose of analysis is not to find fault with new ventures or find reasons for abandoning them. Analysis is an exercise in what to do next more than what not to do.

EVANGELICAL INVESTIGATION

Entrepreneurs often blur the line between research and selling. As one founder recalls, "My market research consisted of taking a prototype to a trade show and seeing if I could write orders." Software industry "beta sites" provide another example of simultaneous research and selling; customers actually pay to help vendors test early versions of their software and will often place larger orders if they are satisfied with the product.

From the beginning, entrepreneurs don't just seek opinions and information, they also look for commitment from other people. Entrepreneurs treat everyone whom they talk to as a potential customer, investor, employee, or supplier, or at least as a possible source of leads down the road. Even if they don't actually ask for an order, they take the time to build enough interest and rapport so they can come back later. This simultaneous listening and selling approach may not produce truly objective market research and statistically significant results. But the resource-constrained entrepreneur doesn't have much choice in the matter. Besides, in the initial stages, the deep knowledge and support of a few is often more valuable then broad, impersonal data.

SMART ARROGANCE

An entrepreneur's willingness to act on sketchy plans and inconclusive data is often sustained by an almost arrogant self-confidence. One successful high-tech entrepreneur likens his kind to "gamblers in a casino who know they are good at craps and are therefore likely to win. They believe: 'I'm smarter, more creative, and harder working than most people. With my unique and rare skills, I'm doing investors a favor by taking their money.'" Moreover, the entrepreneur's arrogance must stand the test of adversity. Entrepreneurs must have great confidence in their talent and ideas to persevere as customers stay away in droves, the product doesn't work, or the business runs out of cash.

But entrepreneurs who believe they are more capable or venturesome than others must also have the smarts to recognize their mistakes and to change their strategies as events unfold. Successful ventures don't always proceed in the direction on which they initially set out. A significant proportion develop entirely new markets, products, and sources of competitive advantage. Therefore, although perseverance and tenacity are valuable entrepreneurial traits, they must be complemented with flexibility and a willingness to learn. If prospects who were expected to place orders don't, the entrepreneur should consider reworking the concept. Similarly, the entrepreneur should also be prepared to exploit opportunities that didn't figure in the initial plan. . . .

The apparently sketchy planning and haphazard evolution of many successful ventures . . . doesn't mean that entrepreneurs should follow a ready–fire–aim approach. Despite appearances, astute entrepreneurs do analyze and strategize extensively. They realize, however, that businesses cannot be launched like space shuttles, with every detail of the mission planned in advance. Initial analyses only provide plausible hypotheses, which must be tested and modified. Entrepreneurs should play with and explore ideas, letting their strategies evolve through a seamless process of guesswork, analysis, and action.

CHAPTER 14

Managing Maturity

In this chapter, we focus on what has historically been one of the more common contexts for organizations. Whether we refer to this by its form of operations (usually mass production or the mass provision of services), by the form of structure adopted (machine-like bureaucracy), by the type of environment it prefers (a stable one in a mature industry), or by the specific generic strategy often found there (low cost), the context tends to give rise to a certain relatively well-defined configuration.

Although this context has received bad press lately, don't think that it has gone away. Amidst all the talk of change, turbulence, and hypercompetition, this context remains common, indeed quite possibly still the most likely that a manager will encounter. Bureaucracy is alive, if not always well, we assure you!

The readings on what we shall refer to as the mature context cover these different aspects and examine some of the problems and opportunities of functioning in this realm. The first reading on the machine organization from Mintzberg's work describes the organization for this context as well as the environment in which it tends to be found and also investigates some of the social issues surrounding this particular form of organization. This reading also probes the nature of the strategy-making process in this context. Here we can see what happens when large organizations accustomed to stability suddenly have to change their strategies dramatically. The careful formal planning, on which they tend to rely so heavily in stable times, seems ill-suited to dealing with changes that may require virtual revolutions in their functioning. A section of this reading, thus, considers what the role of planners can be when their formal procedures fail to come to grips with the needs of strategy making.

A particular technique designed for use with this strategy and the mature context in general is the subject of the second reading. Called "Cost Dynamics: Scale and Experience Effects" and written by Derek Abell and John Hammond for a marketing textbook, it probes the "experience curve." Developed by the Boston Consulting Group some years ago, this technique became quite popular in the 1970s. Although its limitations are now widely recognized, it still has certain applications to firms operating in the mature context.

When machine-like, mature organizations do have to change, the next two readings explain how this can be done. James Q. Wilson of the Andreson School at University of California at Los Angeles has written a widely respected book entitled *Bureaucracy*. Here we reprint excerpts from the chapter on innovation. The book is about government, but as will become evident, the reading applies no less obviously to business or to mature organizations in any other sphere of activity. Wilson points out that the main reason that people in bureaucracy resist change is because they are supposed to: These organizations are designed for stability. But entrepreneurs do bring about changes by acting on the periphery, at least initially. Wilson also points out in this sophisticated piece that changes can be bad as well as good, and he discusses most insightfully what role executives can play in effective change processes.

One of the things that executives can do to fight the negative effects of maturity is to inject entrepreneurial vitality into their organizations. In the last reading by K. Ramachandran and T. P. Devarajan, both from the Indian School of Business, at Hyderabad, and Sougata Ray from the Indian Institute of Management, Calcutta, direct their attention to "corporate entrepreneurship," systems that encourage and reward entrepreneurial initiative in mature organizations. The idea of corporate entrepreneurship in mature organizations seems paradoxical at first. After all, mature organizations frown on innovation and initiative that is not approved in detail beforehand. Ramachandran, Devarajan, and Ray show that top management can create internal contexts where employees are empowered to develop ideas and pursue opportunities. This does not mean that employees have the same decision-making freedom as entrepreneurs who start their own companies—corporate entrepreneurs must at some point justify the use of corporate resources to the organization—but it does mean that creativity and initiative that are suppressed by the proliferation of rules and directives have an outlet. Effective corporate entrepreneurship, however, is not simply giving employees an outlet for their creativity and initiative; it must be linked to corporate strategy. For this reason, as Ramachandran, Devarajan, and Ray show, different types of corporate entrepreneurship, from focused initiatives to organization-wide programs of corporate entrepreneurship, have arisen that serve different strategic purposes.

USING THE CASE STUDIES

Many of the cases struggle with the consequences of longevity, both in terms of absolute age and in terms of product and industry maturity. Procter and Gamble, Nissan, and Johnson and Johnson examine how companies of approximately the same age deal with the need to regain their vitality. All these organizations are to some extent an example of Mintzberg's "Machine Organization." Firms such as Nissan, and Johnson and Johnson must by the very nature of their business, have to manage maturity, which involves attaining efficiency through the use of scale and experience effects, as described in the reading by Abell and Hammond—while at the same time, they also have to manage technological discontinuities. Wilson's discussion of "Innovation in Bureaucracy" and Ramachandran, Devarajan, and Ray go a long way toward explaining how Nissan and Johnson and Johnson address this problem.

READING 14.1

The Machine Organization* BY HENRY MINTZBERG

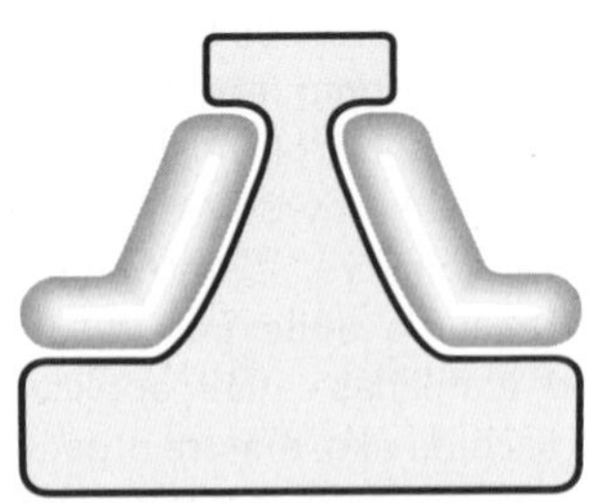

*Adapted from *The Structure of Organizations* (Prentice Hall, 1979), Chap. 18 on "The Machine Bureaucracy"; also *Power In and Around Organizations* (Prentice Hall, 1983), Chap. 18 "The Instrument", and Chap. 19 "The Closed System"; the material on strategy formation from "Patterns in Strategy Formation," *Management Science* (1978); "Does Planning Impede Strategic Thinking? Tracking the Strategies of Air Canada, from 1937–1976" (coauthored with Pierre Brunet and Jim Waters), in R. B. Lamb and P. Shrivastava, eds., *Advances in Strategic Management,* Volume IV (JAI Press, 1986); and "The Mind of the Strategist(s)" (coauthored with Jim Waters), in S. Srivastva, ed., *The Executive Mind* (Jossey-Bass, 1983); the section on the role of planning, plans, and planners is drawn from a book in progress on strategic planning. A chapter similar to this appeared in *Mintzberg on Management: Inside Our Strange World of Organizations* (Free Press, 1989).

A national post office, a custodial prison, an airline, a giant automobile company, even a small security agency—all these organizations appear to have a number of characteristics in common. Above all, their operating work is routine, the greatest part of it rather simple and repetitive; as a result, their work processes are highly standardized. These characteristics give rise to the machine organizations of our society, structures fine-tuned to run as integrated, regulated, highly bureaucratic machines.

THE BASIC STRUCTURE

A clear configuration of the attributes has appeared consistently in the research: highly specialized, routine operating tasks; very formalized communication throughout the organization; large-size operating units; reliance on the functional basis for grouping tasks; relatively centralized power for decision making; and an elaborate administrative structure with a sharp distinction between line and staff.

THE OPERATING CORE AND ADMINISTRATION

The obvious starting point is the operating core, with its highly rationalized work flow. This means that the operating tasks are made simple and repetitive, generally requiring a minimum of skill and training, the latter often taking only hours, seldom more than a few weeks, and usually in-house. This in turn results in narrowly defined jobs and an emphasis on the standardization of work processes for coordination, with activities highly formalized. The workers are left with little discretion, as are their supervisors, who can therefore handle very large spans of control.

To achieve such high regulation of the operating work, the organization has need for an elaborate administrative structure—fully developed middle-line hierarchy and technostructure—but the two are clearly distinguished.

The managers of the middle line have three prime tasks. One is to handle the disturbances that arise in the operating core. The work is so standardized that when things fall through the cracks, conflict flares, because the problems cannot be worked out informally. So it falls to managers to resolve them by direct supervision. Indeed, many problems get bumped up successive steps in the hierarchy until they reach a level of common supervision where they can be resolved by authority (as with a dispute in a company between manufacturing and marketing that may have to be resolved by the chief executive). A second task of the middle-line managers is to work with the staff analysts to incorporate their standards down into the operating units. And a third task is to support the vertical flows in the organization—the elaboration of action plans flowing down the hierarchy and the communication of feedback information back up.

The technostructure must also be highly elaborated. In fact this structure was first identified with the rise of technocratic personnel in early-nineteenth-century industries such as textiles and banking. Because the machine organization depends primarily on the standardization of its operating work for coordination, the technostructure—which houses the staff analysts who do the standardizing—emerges as the key part of the structure. To the line managers may be delegated the formal authority for the operating units, but without the standardizers—the cadre of work-study analysts, schedulers, quality control engineers, planners, budgeters, accountants, operations researchers, and many more—these structures simply could not function. Hence, despite their lack of formal authority, considerable informal power rests with these staff analysts, who standardize everyone else's work. Rules and regulations permeate the entire system: The emphasis on standardization extends well beyond the operating core of the machine organization, and with it follows the analysts' influence.

A further reflection of this formalization of behavior are the sharp divisions of labor all over the machine organization. Job specialization in the operating core and the pronounced formal distinction between line and staff have already been mentioned. In addition, the administrative structure is clearly distinguished from the operating core; unlike the entrepreneurial organization, here managers seldom work alongside operators. And they themselves tend to be organized along functional lines, meaning that each runs a unit that performs a single function in the chain that produces the final outputs. Figure 1 shows this, for example, in the organigram of a large steel company, traditionally machine-like in structure.

All this suggests that the machine organization is a structure with an obsession—namely, control. A control mentality pervades it from top to bottom. At the bottom, consider how a Ford Assembly Division general foreman described his work:

> I refer to my watch all the time. I check different items. About every hour I tour my line. About six thirty, I'll tour labor relations to find out who is absent. At seven, I hit the end of the line. I'll check paint, check my scratches and damage. Around ten I'll start talking to all the foremen. I make sure they're all awake. We can't have no holes, no nothing.

And at the top, consider the words of a chief executive:

> When I was president of this big corporation, we lived in a small Ohio town, where the main plant was located. The corporation specified who you could socialize with, and on what level. (His wife interjects: "Who were the wives you could play bridge with.") In a small town they didn't have to keep check on you. Everybody knew. There are certain sets of rules. (Terkel, 1972: 186, 406)

The obsession with control reflects two central facts about these organizations. First, attempts are made to eliminate all possible uncertainty, so that the bureaucratic machine can run smoothly, without interruption, the operating core perfectly sealed off from external influence. Second, these are structures ridden with conflict; the control systems are required to contain it. The problem in the machine organization is not to develop an open atmosphere where people can talk the conflicts out, but to enforce a closed, tightly controlled one where the work can get done despite them.

The obsession with control also helps to explain the frequent proliferation of support staff in these organizations. Many of the staff services could be purchased from outside suppliers. But that would expose the machine organization to the uncertainties of the open market. So it "makes" rather than "buys," that is, it envelops as many of the support services as it can within its own structure in order to control them, everything from the cafeteria in the factory to the law office at headquarters.

THE STRATEGIC APEX

The managers at the strategic apex of these organizations are concerned in large part with the fine-tuning of their bureaucratic machines. Theirs is a perpetual search for more efficient ways to produce the given outputs.

But not all is strictly improvement of performance. Just keeping the structure together in the face of its conflicts also consumes a good deal of the energy of top management. As noted, conflict is not resolved in the machine organization; rather, it is bottled up so that the work can get done. And as in the case of a bottle, the cork is applied at the top: Ultimately, it is the top managers who must keep the lid on the conflicts through their role of handling disturbances. Moreover, the managers of the strategic apex must intervene frequently in the activities of the middle line to ensure that coordination is achieved there. The top managers are the only generalists in the structure, the only managers with a perspective broad enough to see all the functions.

All this leads us to the conclusion that considerable power in the machine organization rests with the managers of the strategic apex. These are, in other words, rather centralized structures: The formal power clearly rests at the top; hierarchy and chain of authority are paramount concepts. But so also does much of the informal power, since that resides in knowledge, and only at the top of the hierarchy does the formally segmented knowledge of the organization come together.

Thus, our introductory figure shows the machine organization with a fully elaborated administrative and support structure—both parts of the staff component being focused on the operating core—together with large units in the operating core but narrower ones in the middle line to reflect the tall hierarchy of authority.

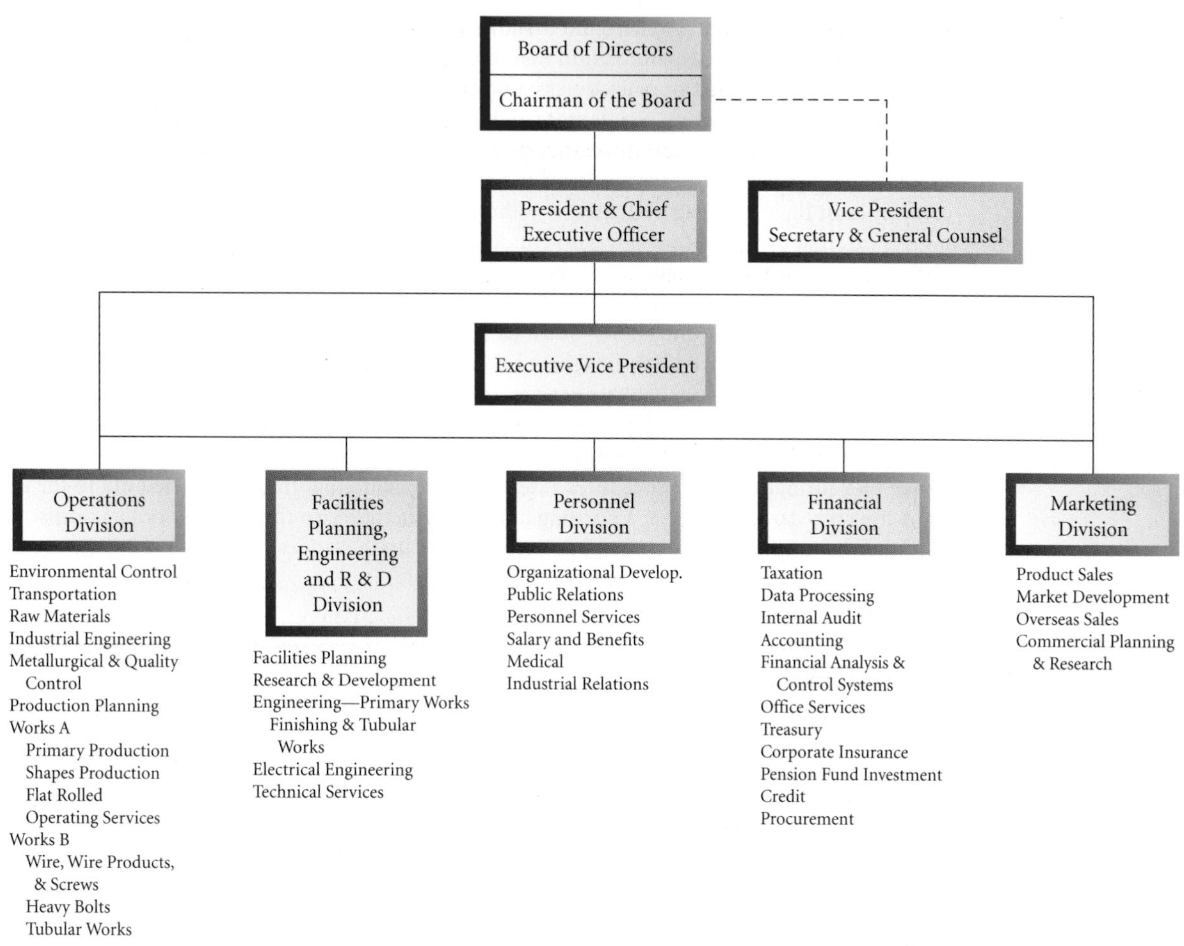

FIGURE 1 ORGANIGRAM OF A LARGE STEEL COMPANY

CONDITIONS OF THE MACHINE ORGANIZATION

Work of a machine bureaucratic nature is found, above all, in environments that are simple and stable. The work associated with complex environments cannot be rationalized into simple tasks, and that associated with dynamic environments cannot be predicted, made repetitive, and so standardized.

In addition, the machine configuration is typically found in mature organizations, large enough to have the volume of operating work needed for repetition and standardization, and old enough to have been able to settle on the standards they wish to use. These are the organizations that have seen it all before and have established standard procedures to deal with it. Likewise, machine organizations tend to be identified with technical systems that regulate the operating work, so that it can easily be programmed. Such technical systems cannot be very sophisticated or automated (for reasons that will be discussed later).

Mass production firms are perhaps the best-known machine organizations. Their operating work flows through an integrated chain, open at one end to accept raw materials, and after that functioning as a sealed system that processes them through sequences of standardized operations. Thus, the environment may be stable because the organization has acted aggressively to stabilize it. Giant firms in such industries as transportation, tobacco, and metals are well known for their attempts to influence the forces of supply and demand by the use of advertising, the development of long-term supply contacts, sometimes the establishment of cartels. They also tend to adopt strategies of "vertical integration," that is, extend their production chains at both ends, becoming both their own suppliers and their own customers. In that way they can bring some of the forces of supply and demand within their own planning processes.

Of course, the machine organization is not restricted to large, or manufacturing, or even private enterprise organizations. Small manufacturers—for example, producers of discount furniture or paper products—may sometimes prefer this structure because their operating work is simple and repetitive. Many service firms use it for the same reason, such as banks or insurance companies in their retailing activities. Another condition often found with machine organizations is external control. Many government departments, such as post offices and tax collection agencies, are machine bureaucratic not only because their operating work is routine but also because they must be accountable to the public for their actions. Everything they do—treating clients, hiring employees, and so on—must be seen to be fair, and so they proliferate regulations.

Since control is the forte of the machine bureaucracy, it stands to reason that organizations in the business of control—regulatory agencies, custodial prisons, police forces—are drawn to this configuration, sometimes in spite of contradictory conditions. The same is true for the special need for safety. Organizations that fly airplanes or put out fires must minimize the risks they take. Hence they formalize their procedures extensively to ensure that they are carried out to the letter. A fire crew cannot arrive at a burning house and then turn to the chief for orders or discuss informally who will connect the hose and who will go up the ladder.

MACHINE ORGANIZATIONS AS INSTRUMENTS AND CLOSED SYSTEMS

Control raises another issue about machine organizations. Being so pervasively regulated, they themselves can easily be controlled externally, as the *instruments* of outside influencers. In contrast, however, their obsession with control runs not only up the hierarchy but beyond, to control of their own environments, so that they can become *closed systems* immune to external influence. From the perspective of power, the instrument and the closed system constitute two main types of machine organizations.

In our terms, the instrument form of machine organization is dominated by one external influencer or by a group of them acting in concert. In the "closely held" corporation, the dominant influencer is the outside owner; in some prisons, it is a community concerned with the custody rather than the rehabilitation of prisoners.

Outside influencers render an organization their instrument by appointing the chief executive, charging that person with the pursuit of clear goals (ideally quantifiable, such as return on investment or prisoner escape measures), and then holding the chief responsible for performance. That way outsiders can control an organization without actually having to manage it. And such control, by virtue of the power put in the hands of the chief executive and the numerical nature of the goals, acts to centralize and bureaucratize the internal structure, in other words, to drive it to the machine form.

In contrast to this, Charles Perrow, the colorful and outspoken organizational sociologist, does not quite see the machine organization as anyone's instrument:

> Society is adaptive to organizations, to the large, powerful organizations controlled by a few, often overlapping, leaders. To see these organizations as adaptive to a "turbulent," dynamic, very changing environment is to indulge in fantasy. The environment of most powerful organizations is well controlled by them, quite stable, and made up of other organizations with similar interests, or ones they control. (1972: 199)

Perrow is, of course, describing the closed system form of machine organization, the one that uses its bureaucratic procedures to seal itself off from external control and control others instead. It controls not only its own people but its environment as well: perhaps its suppliers, customers, competitors, even government and owners too.

Of course, autonomy can be achieved not only by controlling others (for example, buying up customers and suppliers in so-called vertical integration) but simply by avoiding the control of others. Thus, for example, closed system organizations sometimes form cartels with ostensible competitors or, less blatantly, diversify markets to avoid dependence on particular customers, finance internally to avoid dependence on particular financial groups, and even buy back their own shares to weaken the influence of their own owners. Key to being a closed system is to ensure wide dispersal, and therefore pacification, of all groups of potential external influence.

What goals does the closed system organization pursue? Remember that to sustain centralized bureaucracy the goals should be operational, ideally quantifiable. What operational goals enable an organization to serve itself, as a system closed to external influence? The most obvious answer is growth. Survival may be an indispensable goal and efficiency a necessary one, but beyond those what really matters here is making the system larger. Growth serves the system by providing greater rewards for its insiders—bigger empires for managers to run or fancier private jets to fly, greater programs for analysts to design, even more power for unions to wield by virtue of having more members. (The unions may be external influencers, but the management can keep them passive by allowing them more of the spoils of the closed system.) Thus the classic closed system machine organization, the large, widely held industrial corporation, has long been described as oriented far more to growth than to the maximization of profit per se (Galbraith, 1967).

Of course, the closed system form of machine organization can exist outside the private sector too, for example, in the fundraising agency that, relatively free from external control, becomes increasingly charitable to itself (as indicated by the plushness of its managers' offices), the agricultural or retail cooperative that ignores those who collectively own it, even government that becomes more intent on serving itself than the citizens for which it supposedly exists.

The communist state, at least up until very recently, seemed to fit all the characteristics of the closed system bureaucracy. It had no dominant external influencer (at least in the case of the Soviet Union, if not the other East European states, which were its "instruments"). And the population to which it is ostensibly responsible had to respond to its own plethora of rules and regulations. Its election procedures, traditionally offering a choice of one, were similar to those for the directors of the "widely held" Western corporation. The government's own structure was heavily bureaucratic, with a single hierarchy of authority and a very elaborate technostructure, ranging from state planners to KGB agents. (As James Worthy [1959: 77] noted, Frederick Taylor's "Scientific Management had its fullest flowering not in America but in Soviet Russia.") All significant resources were the property of the state—the collective system—not the individual. And, as in other closed systems, the administrators tend to take the lion's share of the benefits.

SOME ISSUES ASSOCIATED WITH THE MACHINE ORGANIZATION

No structure has evoked more heated debate than the machine organization. As Michel Crozier, one of its most eminent students, has noted,

> On the one hand, most authors consider the bureaucratic organization to be the embodiment of rationality in the modern world, and, as such, to be intrinsically superior to all other possible forms of organizations. On the other hand, many authors—often the same ones—consider it a sort of Leviathan, preparing the enslavement of the human race. (1964: 176)

Max Weber, who first wrote about this form of organization, emphasized its rationality; in fact, the word *machine* comes directly from his writings (see Gerth and Wright Mills, 1958). A machine is certainly precise; it is also reliable and easy to control; and it is efficient—at least when restricted to the job it has been designed to do. Those are the reasons many organizations are structured as machine bureaucracies. When an integrated set of simple, repetitive tasks must be performed precisely and consistently by human beings, this is the most efficient structure—indeed, the only conceivable one.

But in these same advantages of machine-like efficiency lie all the disadvantages of this configuration. Machines consist of mechanical parts; organizational structures also include human beings—and that is where the analogy breaks down.

HUMAN PROBLEMS IN THE OPERATING CORE

James Worthy, when he was an executive of Sears, wrote a penetrating and scathing criticism of the machine organization in his book *Big Business and Free Men*. Worthy traced the root of the human problems in these structures to the "scientific management" movement led by Frederick

Taylor that swept America early in the 20th century. Worthy acknowledged Taylor's contribution to efficiency, narrowly defined. Worker initiative did not, however, enter into his efficiency equation. Taylor's pleas to remove "all possible brain work" from the shop floor also removed all possible initiative from the people who worked there: the "machine has no will of its own. Its parts have no urge to independent action. Thinking, direction—even purpose— must be provided from outside or above." This had the "consequence of destroying the meaning of work itself," which has been "fantastically wasteful for industry and society," resulting in excessive absenteeism, high worker turnover, sloppy workmanship, costly strikes, and even outright sabotage (1959: 67, 79, 70). Of course, there are people who like to work in highly structured situations. But increasing numbers do not, at least not *that* highly structured.

Taylor was fond of saying, "In the past the man has been first; in the future the system must be first" (in Worthy, 1959: 73). Prophetic words, indeed. Modern man seems to exist for his systems; many of the organizations he created to serve him have come to enslave him. The result is that several of what Victor Thompson (1961) has called "bureaupathologies"—dysfunctional behaviors of these structures—reinforce each other to form a vicious circle in the machine organization. The concentration on means at the expense of ends, the mistreatment of clients, the various manifestations of worker alienation—all lead to the tightening of controls on behavior. The implicit motto of the machine organization seems to be, "When in doubt, control." All problems have to be solved by the turning of the technocratic screws. But since that is what caused the bureaupathologies in the first place, increasing the controls serves only to magnify the problems, leading to the imposition of further controls, and so on.

COORDINATION PROBLEMS IN THE ADMINISTRATIVE CENTER

Since the operating core of the machine organization is not designed to handle conflict, many of the human problems that arise there spill up and over, into the administrative structure.

It is one of the ironies of the machine configuration that to achieve the control it requires, it must mirror the narrow specialization of its operating core in its administrative structure (for example, differentiating marketing managers from manufacturing managers, much as salesmen are differentiated from factory workers). This, in turn, means problems of communication and coordination. The fact is that the administrative structure of the machine organization is also ill suited to the resolution of problems through mutual adjustment. All the communication barriers in these structures—horizontal, vertical, status, line/staff—impede informal communication among managers and with staff people. "Each unit becomes jealous of its own prerogatives and finds ways to protect itself against the pressure or encroachments of others" (Worthy, 1950: 176). Thus narrow functionalism not only impedes coordination; it also encourages the building of private empires, which tends to produce top-heavy organizations that can be more concerned with the political games to be won than with the clients to be served.

ADAPTATION PROBLEMS IN THE STRATEGIC APEX

But if mutual adjustment does not work in the administrative center—generating more political heat than cooperative light—how does the machine organization resolve its coordination problems? Instinctively, it tries standardization, for example, by tightening job descriptions or proliferating rules. But standardization is not suited to handling the nonroutine problems of the administrative center. Indeed, it only aggravates them, undermining the influence of the line managers and increasing the conflict. So to reconcile these coordination problems, the machine organization is left with only one coordinating mechanism, direct supervision from above. Specifically, nonroutine coordination problems between units are "bumped" up the line hierarchy until they reach a common level of supervision, often at the top of the structure. The result can be excessive centralization of power, which in turn produces a host of other problems. In effect, just as the human problems in the operating core become coordination problems in the administrative center, so too do the coordination problems in the administrative center become adaptation problems at the strategic apex. Let us take a closer look at these by concluding with a discussion of strategic change in the machine configuration.

STRATEGY FORMATION IN THE MACHINE ORGANIZATION

Strategy in the machine organization is supposed to emanate from the top of the hierarchy, where the perspective is broadest and the power most focused. All the relevant information is to be sent up the hierarchy, in aggregated, MIS-type form, there to be formulated into integrated strategy (with the aid of the technostructure). Implementation then follows, with the intended strategies sent down the hierarchy to be turned into successively more elaborated programs and action plans. Notice the clear division of labor assumed between the formulators at the top and the implementers down below, based on the assumption of perfectly deliberate strategy produced through a process of planning.

That is the theory. The practice has been shown to be another matter. Drawing on our strategy research at McGill University, we shall consider first what planning really proved to be in one machine-like organization, how it may in fact have impeded strategic thinking in a second, and how a third really did change its strategy. From there we shall consider the problems of strategic change in machine organizations and their possible resolution.

PLANNING AS PROGRAMMING IN A SUPERMARKET CHAIN

What really is the role of formal planning? Does it produce original strategies? Let us return to the case of Steinberg's in the later years of its founder, as large size drove this retailing chain toward the machine form, and as is common in that form, toward a planning mode of management at the expense of entrepreneurship.

One event in particular encouraged the start of planning at Steinberg's: the company's entry into capital markets in 1953. Months before it floated its first bond issue (stock, always nonvoting, came later), Sam Steinberg boasted to a newspaper reporter that "not a cent of any money outside the family is invested in the company." And asked about future plans, he replied: "Who knows? We will try to go everywhere there seems to be a need for us." A few months later he announced a $5 million debt issue and with it a $15 million five-year expansion program, one new store every two months for a total of thirty, the doubling of sales, new stores to average double the size of existing ones.

What happened in those ensuing months was Sam Steinberg's realization, after the opening of Montreal's first shopping center, that he needed to enter the shopping center business himself to protect his supermarket chain and that he could not do so with the company's traditional methods of short-term and internal financing. And, of course, no company is allowed to go to capital markets without a plan. You can't just say: "I'm Sam Steinberg and I'm good," though that was really the issue. In a "rational" society, you have to plan (or at least appear to do so).

But what exactly was that planning? One thing for certain: It did not formulate a strategy. Sam Steinberg already had that. What planning did was justify, elaborate, and articulate the strategy that already existed in Sam Steinberg's mind. Planning operationalized his strategic vision, programmed it. It gave order to that vision, imposing form on it to comply with the needs of the organization and its environment. Thus, planning followed the strategy-making process, which had been essentially entrepreneurial.

But its effect on that process was not incidental. By specifying and articulating the vision, planning constrained it and rendered it less flexible. Sam Steinberg retained formal control of the company to the day of his death. But his control over strategy did not remain so absolute. The entrepreneur, by keeping his vision personal, is able to adapt it at will to a changing environment. But by being forced to program it, the leader loses that flexibility. The danger, ultimately, is that the planning mode forces out the entrepreneurial one; procedure replaces vision. As its structure became more machine-like, Steinberg's required planning in the form of strategic programming. But that planning also accelerated the firm's transition toward the machine form of organization.

Is there, then, such a thing as "strategic planning"? I suspect not. To be more explicit, I do not find that major new strategies are formulated through any formal procedure. Organizations that rely on formal planning procedures to formulate strategies seem to extrapolate existing strategies, perhaps with marginal changes in them, or else copy the strategies of other organizations. This came out most clearly in another of our McGill studies.

PLANNING AS AN IMPEDIMENT TO STRATEGIC THINKING IN AN AIRLINE

From about the mid-1950s, Air Canada engaged heavily in planning. Once the airline was established, particularly once it developed its basic route structure, a number of factors drove it strongly to the planning mode. Above all was the need for coordination, both of flight schedules with aircraft, crews, and maintenance and of the purchase of expensive aircraft with the structure of the route system. (Imagine someone calling out in the hangar: "Hey, Fred, this guy says he has two 747s for us; do you know who ordered them?") Safety was another factor. The intense need for safety in the air breeds a mentality of being very careful about what the organization does on the ground, too. This is the airlines' obsession with control. Other factors included the lead times inherent in key decisions, such as ordering new airplanes or introducing new routes, the sheer cost of the capital equipment, and the size of the organization. You don't run an intricate system like an airline, necessarily very machine-like, without a great deal of formal planning.

But what we found to be the consequence of planning at Air Canada was the absence of a major reorientation of strategy during our study period (up to the mid-1970s). Aircraft certainly changed—they became larger and faster—but the basic route system did not, nor did markets. Air Canada gave only marginal attention, for example, to cargo, charter, and shuttle operations. Formal planning, in our view, impeded strategic thinking.

The problem is that planning, too, proceeds from the machine perspective, much as an assembly line or a conventional machine produces a product. It all depends on the decomposition of analysis: You split the process into a series of steps or components parts, specify each, and then by following the specifications in sequence you get the desired product. There is a fallacy in this, however. Assembly lines and conventional machines produce standardized products, while planning is supposed to produce a novel strategy. It is as if the machine is supposed to design the machine; the planning machine is expected to create the original blueprint—the strategy. To put this another way, planning is analysis oriented to decomposition, while strategy making depends on synthesis oriented to integration. That is why the term "strategic planning" has proved to be an oxymoron.

ROLES OF PLANNING, PLANS, PLANNERS

If planning does not create strategy, then what purpose does it serve? We have suggested a role above, which has to do with the programming of strategies already created in other ways. This is shown in Figure 2, coming out of a box labeled strategy formation—meant to represent what is to planning a mysterious "black box." But if planning is restricted to programming strategy, plans and planners nonetheless have other roles in play, shown in Figure 2 and discussed alongside that of planning itself.

ROLE OF PLANNING

Why do organizations engage in formal planning? The answer seems to be: not to create strategies, but to program the strategies they already have, that is, to elaborate and operationalize the consequences of those strategies formally. We should really say that *effective* organizations so engage in planning, at least when they require the formalized implementation of their strategies. Thus strategy is not the *consequence* of planning but its starting point. Planning helps to translate the intended strategy into realized ones, taking the first step that leads ultimately to implementation.

This *strategic programming,* as it might properly be labeled, can be considered to involve a series of steps, namely the *codification* of given strategy, including its clarification and articulation, the *elaboration* of that strategy into substrategies, ad hoc action programs, and plans

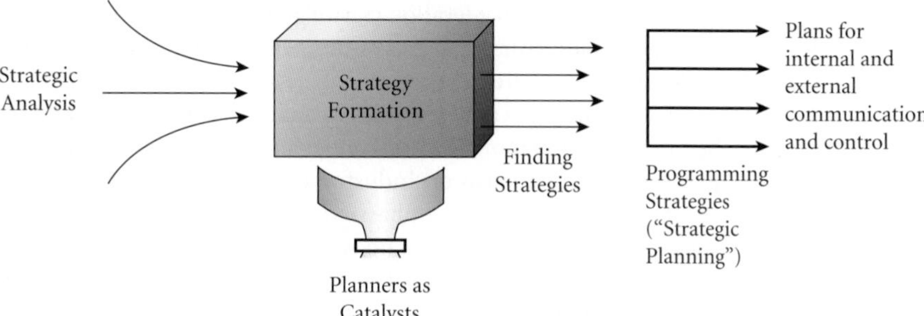

FIGURE 2
SPECIFIC ROLLS OF PLANNERS

of various kinds, and the *translation* of those substrategies, programs, and plans into routine budgets and objectives. In these steps, we see planning as an analytical process that takes over after the synthesis of strategic formation is completed.

Thus formal planning properly belongs in the *implementation* of strategy, not in its formulation. But it should be emphasized that strategic programming makes sense when viable intended strategies are available, in other words when the world is expected to hold still while these strategies unfold, so that formulation can logically precede implementation, and when the organization that does the implementing in fact requires clearly codified and elaborated strategies. In other circumstances, strategic programming can do organizations harm by preempting the flexibility that managers and others may need to respond to changes in the environment, or to their own internal processes of learning.

ROLES OF PLANS

If planning is programming, then plans clearly serve two roles. They are a medium for communication and a device for control. Both roles draw on the analytical character of plans, namely, that they represent strategies in decomposed and articulated form, if not quantified then often at least quantifiable.

Why program strategy? Most obviously for coordination, to ensure that everyone in the organization pulls in the same direction, a direction that may have to be specified as precisely as possible. In Air Canada, to use our earlier example, that means linking the acquisition of new aircraft with the particular routes that are to be flown, and scheduling crews and planes to show up when the flights are to take off, and so on. Plans, as they emerge from strategic programming as programs, schedules, budgets, and so on, can be prime media to communicate not just strategic intention but also the role each individual must play to realize it.

Plans, as communication media, inform people of intended strategy and its consequences. But as control devices they can go further, specifying what role departments and individuals must play in helping to realize strategy and then comparing that with performance in order to feed control information back into the strategy-making process.

Plans can help to effect control in a number of ways. The most obvious is control of the strategy itself. Indeed what has long paraded under the label of "strategy planning" has probably had more to do with "strategic control" than many people may realize. Strategic control has to do with keeping organizations on their strategic tracks: to ensure the realization of intended strategy, its implementation as expected, with resources appropriately allocated. But there is more to strategic control than this. Another aspect includes the assessment of the realization of strategies in the first place, namely, whether the patterns realized corresponded to the intentions specified beforehand. In other words, strategic control must assess behavior as well as performance. Then the more routine and traditional form of control can come in to consider whether the strategies that were in fact realized proved effective.

ROLES OF PLANNERS

Planners, of course, play key roles in planning (namely, strategic programming), and in using the resulting plans for purposes of communication and control. But many of the most important things planners do have little to do with planning or even plans per se. Three roles seem key here.

First, planners can play a role in finding strategies. This may seem curious, but if strategies really do emerge in organizations, the planners can help to identify the patterns that are becoming strategies, so that consideration can be given to formalizing them, that is, making them deliberate. Of course, finding the strategies of competitors—for assessment and possible modified adoption—is also important here.

Second, planners play the roles of analysts, carrying out ad hoc studies to feed into the black box of strategy making. Indeed, one could argue that this is precisely what Michael Porter proposes with his emphasis on industry and competitive analysis. The ad hoc nature of such studies should, however, be emphasized because they feed into a strategy-making process that is itself irregular, proceeding on no schedule and following no standard sequence of steps. Indeed, regularity in the planning process can interfere with strategic thinking, which must be flexible, responsive, and creative.

Third, the role of the planner is as a catalyst. This refers not to the traditional role long promoted in the literature of selling formal planning as some kind of religion, but to encourage strategic *thinking* throughout the organization. Here the planner encourages *informal* strategy making, trying to get others to think about the future in a creative way. He or she does not enter the black box of strategy making so much as ensure that the box is occupied with active line managers.

A PLANNER FOR EACH SIDE OF THE BRAIN

We have discussed various roles for planning, plans, and planners, summarized around the black box of strategy formation in Figure 2. These roles suggest two different orientations for planners.

On the one hand (so to speak), the planner must be a highly analytic, convergent type of thinker, dedicated to bringing order to the organization. Above all, this planner programs intended strategies and sees to it that they are communicated clearly and used for purposes of control. He or she also carries out studies to ensure that the managers concerned with strategy formation take into account the necessary hard data that they may be inclined to miss and that the strategies they formulate are carefully and systematically evaluated before they are implemented.

On the other hand, there is another type of planner, less conventional, a creative, divergent thinker, rather intuitive, who seeks to open up the strategy-making process. As a "soft analyst," he or she tends to conduct "quick and dirty" studies, to find strategies in strange places, and to encourage others to think strategically. This planner is inclined toward the intuitive process identified with the brain's right hemisphere. We might call him or her a *left-handed planner*. Some organizations need to emphasize one type of planner, others the other type. But most complex organizations probably need some of both.

STRATEGIC CHANGE IN AN AUTOMOBILE FIRM

Given planning itself is not strategic, how does the planning-oriented machine bureaucracy change its strategy when it has to? Volkswagenwerk was an organization that had to. We interpreted its history from 1934 to 1974 as one long cycle of a single strategic perspective. The original "people's car," the famous "Beetle," was conceived by Ferdinand Porsche: the factory to produce it was built just before the war but did not go into civilian automobile production until after. In 1948, a man named Heinrich Nordhoff was given control of the devastated plant and began the rebuilding of it, as well as of the organization and the strategy itself, rounding out Porsche's original conception. The firm's success was dramatic.

By the late 1950s, however, problems began to appear. Demand in Germany was moving away from the Beetle. The typically machine-bureaucratic response was not to rethink the basic strategy—"it's okay" was the reaction—but rather to graft another piece onto it. A new automobile model was added, larger than the Beetle but with a similar no-nonsense approach to motoring, again air-cooled with the engine in the back. Volkswagenwerk added position but did not change perspective.

But that did not solve the basic problem, and by the mid-1960s the company was in crisis. Nordhoff, who had resisted strategic change, died in office and was replaced by a lawyer from outside the business. The company then underwent a frantic search for new models, designing, developing, or acquiring a whole host of them with engines in the front, middle, and rear; air and water cooled; front- and rear-wheel drive. To paraphrase the humorist Stephen Leacock, Volkswagenwerk leaped onto its strategic horse and rode off in all directions. Only when another leader came in, a man steeped in the company and the automobile business, did the firm consolidate itself around a new strategic perspective, based on the stylish front-wheel drive, water-cooled designs of one of its acquired firms, and thereby turn its fortunes around.

What this story suggests, first of all, is the great force of bureaucratic momentum in the machine organization. Even leaving planning aside, the immense effort of producing and marketing a new line of automobiles locks a company into a certain posture. But here the momentum was psychological, too. Nordhoff, who had been the driving force behind the great success of the organization, became a major liability when the environment demanded change. Over the years, he too had been captured by bureaucratic momentum. Moreover, the uniqueness and tight integration of Volkswagenwerk's strategy—we labeled it *gestalt*—impeded strategic change. Change an element of a tightly integrated gestalt and it *dis*integrates. Thus does success eventually breed failure.

BOTTLENECK AT THE TOP

Why the great difficulty in changing strategy in the machine organization? Here we take up that question and show how changes generally have to be achieved in a different configuration, if at all.

As discussed earlier, unanticipated problems in the machine organization tend to get bumped up the hierarchy. When these are few, which mean conditions are relatively stable, things work smoothly enough. But in times of rapid change, just when new strategies are called for, the number of such problems magnifies, resulting in a bottleneck at the top, where senior managers get overloaded. And that tends either to impede strategic change or else to render it ill considered.

A major part of the problem is information. Senior managers face an organization decomposed into parts, like a machine itself. Marketing information comes up one channel, manufacturing information up another, and so on. Somehow it is the senior managers themselves who must integrate all that information. But the very machine bureaucratic premise of separating the administration of work from the doing of it means that the top managers often lack the intimate, detailed knowledge of issues necessary to effect such an integration. In essence, the necessary power is at the top of the structure, but the necessary knowledge is often at the bottom.

Of course, there is a machine-like solution to that problem too—not surprisingly in the form of a system. It is called a management information system, or MIS, and what it does is combine all the necessary information and package it neatly so that top managers can be informed about what is going on—the perfect solution for the overloaded executive. At least in theory.

Unfortunately, a number of real-world problems arise in the MIS. For one thing, in the tall administrative hierarchy of the machine organization, information must pass through many levels before it reaches the top. Losses take place at each one. Good news gets highlighted while bad news gets blocked on the way up. And "soft" information, so necessary for strategy information, cannot easily pass through, while much of the hard MIS-type information arrives only slowly. In a stable environment, the manager may be able to wait; in a rapidly changing one, he or she cannot. The president wants to be told right away that the firm's most important customer was seen playing golf yesterday with a main competitor, not to find out six months later in the form of a drop in a sales report. Gossip, hearsay, speculation—the softest kinds of information—warn the manager of impeding problems; the MIS all too often records for posterity ones that have already been felt. The manager who depends on an MIS in a changing environment generally finds himself or herself out of touch.

The obvious solution for top managers is to bypass the MIS and set up their own informal information systems, networks of contacts that bring them the rich, tangible, instant information they need. But that violates the machine organization's presuppositions of formality and respect for the chain of authority. Also, that takes the managers' time, the lack of which caused the bottleneck in the first place. So a fundamental dilemma faces the top managers of the machine organization as a result of its very own design: in times of change, when they most need the time to inform themselves, the system overburdens them with other pressures. They are thus reduced to acting superficially, with inadequate, abstract information.

THE FORMULATION/IMPLEMENTATION DICHOTOMY

The essential problem lies in one of the chief tenets of the machine organization, that strategy formation must be sharply separated from strategy implementation. One is thought out at the top, the other then acted out lower down. For this to work assume two conditions: first, that the formulator has full and sufficient information, and, second, that the world will hold still, or at least change in predictable ways, during the implementation, so that there is no need for *re*formulation.

Now consider why the organization needs a new strategy in the first place. It is because its world has changed in an unpredictable way, indeed may continue to do so. We have just seen how the machine bureaucratic structure tends to violate the first condition—it misinforms the senior manager during such times of change. And when change continues in an unpredictable way (or at least the world unfolds in a way not yet predicted by an ill-informed management), then the second condition is violated too—it hardly makes sense to lock in by implementation a strategy that does not reflect changes in the world around it.

What all this amounts to is a need to collapse the formulation/implementation dichotomy precisely when the strategy of machine bureaucracy must be changed. This can be done in one of two ways.

In one case, the formulator implements. In other words, power is concentrated at the top, not only for creating the strategy but also for implementing it, step by step, in a personalized way. The strategist is put in close personal touch with the situation at hand (more commonly a strategist is appointed who has or can develop that touch) so that he or she can, on the one hand, be properly informed and, on the other, control the implementation en route in order to reformulate when necessary. This of course describes the entrepreneurial configuration, at least at the strategic apex.

In the other case, the implementers formulate. In other words, power is concentrated lower down, where the necessary information resides. As people who are naturally in touch with the specific situations at hand take individual actions—approach new customers, develop new products, et cetera—patterns form, in other words, strategies emerge. And this describes the innovative configuration, where strategic initiatives often originate in the grass roots of the organization, and then are championed by managers at middle levels who integrate them with one another or with existing strategies in order to gain their acceptance by senior management.

We conclude, therefore, that the machine configuration is ill suited to change its fundamental strategy, that the organization must in effect change configuration temporarily in order to change strategy. Either it reverts to the entrepreneurial form, to allow a single leader to develop vision (or proceed with one developed earlier), or else it overlays an innovative form on its conventional structure (for example, creates an informed network of lateral teams and task forces) so that the necessary strategies can emerge. The former can obviously function faster than the latter; that is why it tends to be used for drastic *turnaround,* while the latter tends to proceed by the slower process of *revitalization.* (Of course, quick turnaround may be necessary because there has been no slow revitalization.) In any event, both are characterized by a capacity to *learn*—that is the essence of the entrepreneurial and innovative configurations, in one case learning centralized for the simpler context, in the other, decentralized for the more complex one. The machine configuration is not so characterized.

This, however, should come as no surprise. After all, machines are specialized instruments, designed for productivity, not for adaptation. In Hunt's (1970) words, machine bureaucracies are performance systems, not problem-solving ones. Efficiency is their forte, not innovation. An organization cannot put blinders on its personnel and then expect peripheral vision. Managers here are rewarded for cutting costs and improving standards, not for taking risks and ignoring procedures. Change makes a mess of the operating systems: change one link in a carefully coupled system, and the whole chain must be reconceived. Why, then, should we be surprised when our bureaucratic machines fail to adapt?

Of course, it is fair to ask why we spend so much time trying to make them adapt. After all, when an ordinary machine becomes redundant, we simply scrap it, happy that it served us for as long and as well as it did. Converting it to another use generally proves more expensive than simply starting over. I suspect the same is often true for bureaucratic machines. But here, of course, the context is social and political. Mechanical parts don't protest, nor do displaced raw materials. Workers, suppliers, and customers do, however, protest the scrapping of organizations, for obvious reasons. But that the cost of this is awfully high in a society of giant machine organizations will be the subject of the final chapter of this book.

STRATEGIC REVOLUTIONS IN MACHINE ORGANIZATIONS

Machine organizations do sometimes change, however, at times effectively but more often it would seem at great cost and pain. The lucky ones are able to overlay an innovative structure for periodic revitalization, while many of the other survivors somehow manage to get turned around in entrepreneurial fashion.

Overall, the machine organizations seem to follow what my colleagues Danny Miller and Peter Friesen (1984) call a "quantum theory" of organization change. They pursue their set strategies through long periods of stability (naturally occurring or created by themselves as closed systems), using planning and other procedures to do so efficiently. Periodically these are interrupted by short bursts of change, which Miller and Friesen characterize as "strategic revolutions" (although another colleague, Mihaela Firsirotu [1985], perhaps better labels it "strategic turnaround as cultural revolution").

ORGANIZATION TAKING PRECEDENCE IN THE MACHINE ORGANIZATION

To conclude, as shown in Figure 3, it is organization—with its systems and procedures, its planning and its bureaucratic momentum—that takes precedence over leadership and environment in the machine configuration. Environment fits organization, either because the organization has slotted itself into a context that matches its procedures, or else because it has forced the environment to do so. And leadership generally falls into place too, supporting the organization, indeed often becoming part of its bureaucratic momentum.

This generally works effectively, though hardly nonproblematically, at least in times of stability. But in times of change, efficiency becomes ineffective and the organization will falter unless it can find a different way to organize for adaptation.

All of this is another way of saying that the machine organization is a configuration, a species, like the others, suited to its own context but ill suited to others. But unlike the others, it is the dominant configuration in our specialized societies. As long as we demand inexpensive and so necessarily standardized goods and services, and as long as people continue to be more efficient than real machines at providing them, and remain willing to do so, then the machine organization will remain with us—and so will all its problems.

FIGURE 3
ORGANIZATION TAKES PRECEDENCE

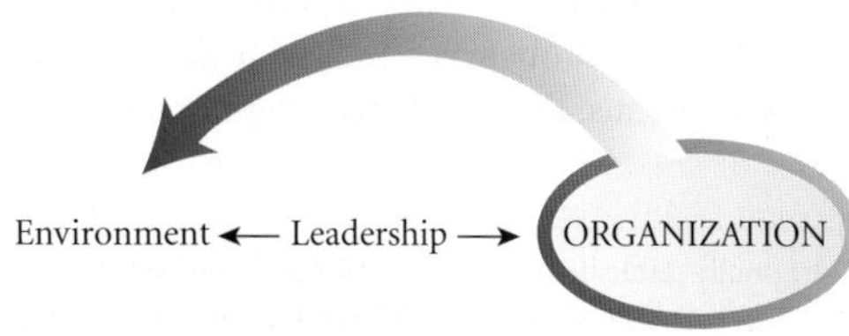

READING 14.2

Cost Dynamics: Scale and Experience Effects* BY DEREK F. ABELL AND JOHN S. HAMMOND

Market share is one of the primary determinants of business profitability; other things being equal, businesses with a larger share of a market are more profitable than their smaller-share competitors. For instance, a study by the PIMS Program (Buzzell, Gale and Sultan, 1975) . . . found that, on average, a difference of 10 percentage points in market share is accompanied by a difference of about 5 points in pretax ROI ("pretax operating profits" divided by "long-term debt plus equity"). Additional evidence is that companies having large market shares in their primary product markets—such as General Motors, IBM, Gillette, Eastman Kodak, and Xerox—tend to be highly profitable.

An important reason for the increase in profitability with market share is that large-share firms usually have *lower costs*. The lower costs are due in part to economies of scale; for instance, very large plants cost less per unit of production to build and are often more efficient than smaller plants. Lower costs are also due in part to the so-called *experience effect*, whereby the cost of many (if not most) products declines by 10–30 percent each time a company's experience at producing and selling them doubles. In this context *experience* has a precise meaning: it is the cumulative number of units produced to date. Since at any point in time, businesses with large market shares typically (but not always) have more experience than their smaller-share competitors, they would be expected to have lower cost. . . .

This [reading] considers how costs decline due to scale and to experience, practical problems in analyzing the experience effect, strategic implications of scale and experience, and limitations of strategies based on cost reduction. . . .

SCALE EFFECT

As mentioned earlier, scale effect refers to the fact that large businesses have the potential to operate at lower unit costs than their smaller counterparts. The increased efficiency due to size is often referred to as "economy of scale"; it could equally be called "economy of size."

Most people think of economy of scale as a manufacturing phenomenon because large manufacturing facilities can be constructed at a lower cost per unit of capacity and can be operated more efficiently than smaller ones. . . .

Just as they cost less to build, large-scale plants have lower *operating* costs per unit of output. . . . While substantial in manufacturing, scale effect is also significant in other cost elements, such as marketing, sales, distribution, administration, R&D, and service. For instance, a chain with 30 supermarkets in a metropolitan area needs much less than three times as much advertising as a chain of 10 stores. . . . Economies of scale are also achieved with purchased items such as raw material and shipping. . . .

Although scale economies potentially exist in all cost elements of a business in both the short and long run, large size alone doesn't assure the benefits of scale. It is evident from the above illustrations that size provides an *opportunity* for scale economies; to achieve them requires strategies and actions consciously designed to seize the opportunity, especially with operating costs. . . .

EXPERIENCE EFFECT

The experience effect, whereby costs fall with cumulative production, is measurable and predictable; it has been observed in a wide range of products including automobiles, semi conductors, petrochemicals, long-distance telephone calls, synthetic fibers, airline transportation, the cost of

---

*Originally published in *Strategic Market Planning: Problems and Analytical Approaches* (Prentice Hall, 1979), Chap. 3.

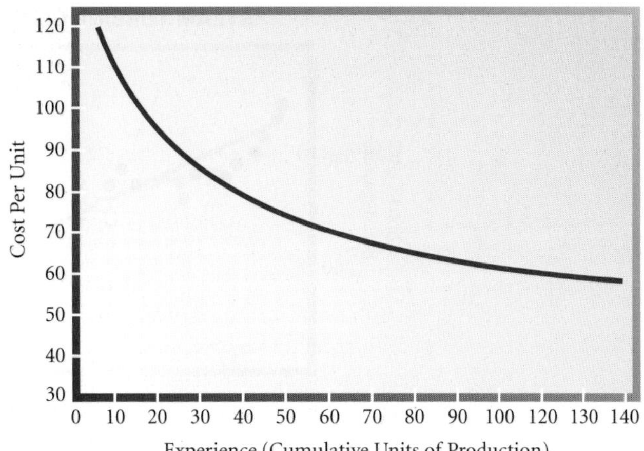

FIGURE 1
A TYPICAL EXPERIENCE CURVE [85%]

administering life insurance, and crushed limestone, to mention a few. Note that this list ranges from high-technology to low-technology products, service to manufacturing industries, consumer to industrial products, new to mature products, and process to assembly-oriented products, indicating the wide range of applicability. . . .

. . . [I]t is only comparatively recently that this phenomenon has been carefully measured and quantified; at first it was thought to apply only to the labor portion of *manufacturing* costs. . . . In the 1960s evidence mounted that the phenomenon was broader. Personnel from the Boston Consulting Group and others showed that each time cumulative volume of a product doubled, total value added costs—including administration, sales, marketing, distribution, and so on in addition to manufacturing—fell by a constant and predictable percentage. In addition, the costs of purchased items usually fell as suppliers reduced prices as their costs fell, due also to the experience effect. The relationship between costs and experience was called the *experience curve* (Boston Consulting Group, 1972).

An experience curve is plotted with the cumulative units produced on the horizontal axis, and cost per unit on the vertical axis. An "85%" experience curve is shown in Figure 1. The "85%" means that every time experience doubles, costs per unit drop to 85% of the original level. It is known as the *learning rate*. Stated differently, costs per unit decrease 15 percent for every doubling of cumulative production. For example, the cost of the 20th unit produced is about 85% of the cost of the 10th unit. . . .

An experience curve appears as a straight line when plotted on a double log paper (logarithmic scale for both the horizontal and vertical axes). Figure 2 shows the "85 percent" experience curve from Figure 1 on the double logarithmic scale. . . . Figure 3 provides illustrations for [some specific] products.

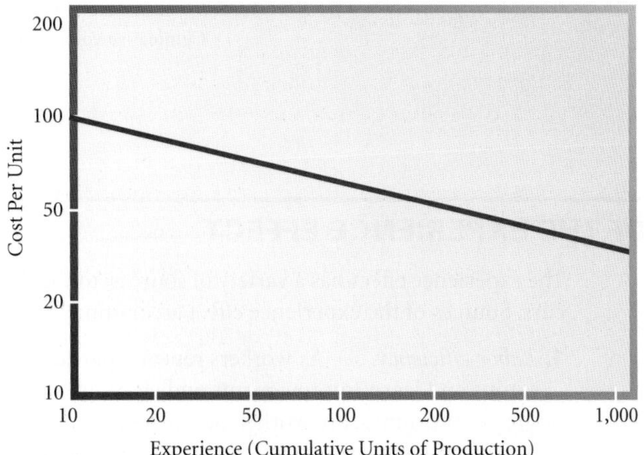

FIGURE 2
AN 85% EXPERIENCE CURVE DISPLAYED ON LOG-LOG SCALES

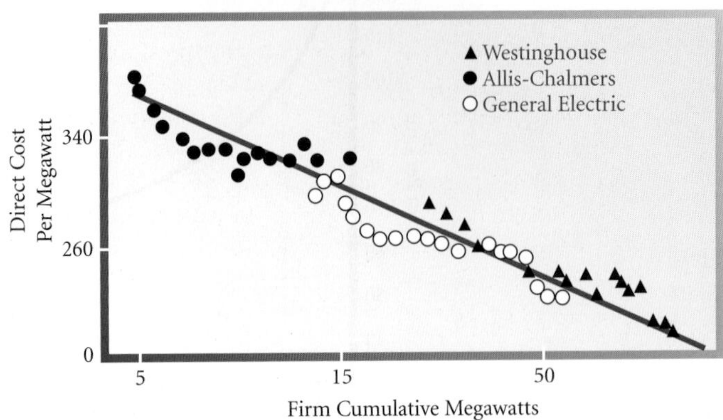

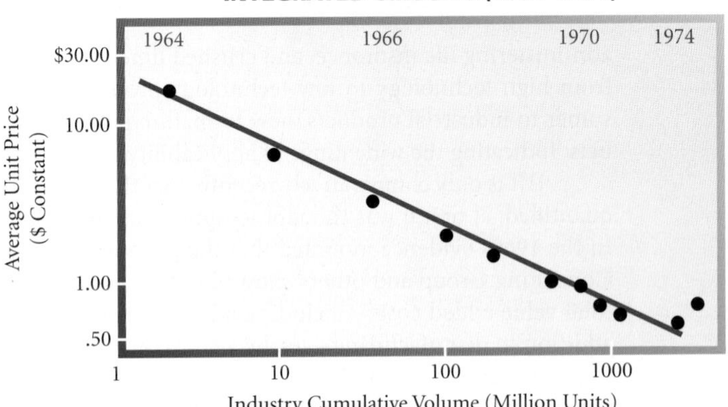
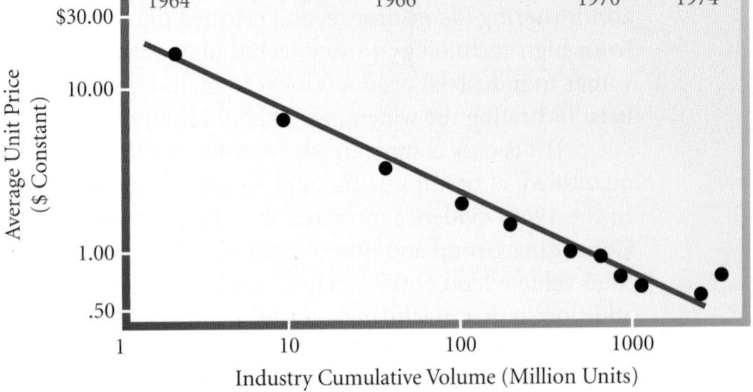

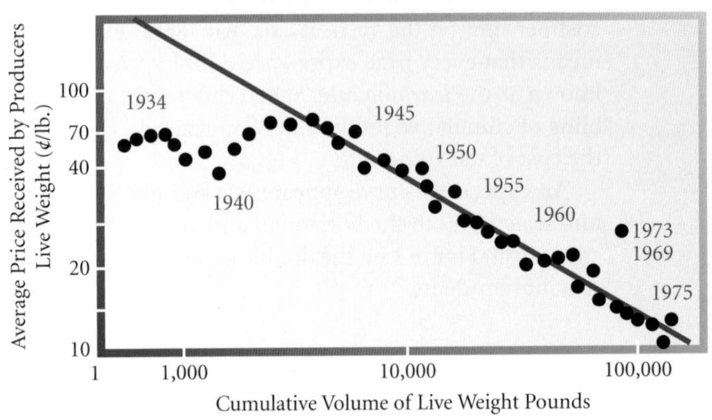

FIGURE 3
SOME SAMPLE EXPERIENCE CURVES

Note: Technically an experience curve shows the relationship between cost and experience. However, cost figures are seldom publicly available: therefore most of the above experience curves show industry price (in constant dollars) vs. experience.

Source: The Boston Consulting Group.

SOURCES OF THE EXPERIENCE EFFECT

The experience effect has a variety of sources; to capitalize on it requires knowledge of why it occurs. Sources of the experience effect are outlined as follows:

1. *Labor efficiency*. . . . As workers repeat a particular production task, they become more dexterous and learn improvements and shortcuts which increase their collective efficiency. The greater the number of worker-paced operations, the greater the amount of learning which can accrue with experience. . . .

2. *Work specialization and methods improvements.* Specialization increases worker proficiency at a given task. . . .
3. *New production processes.* Process innovations and improvements can be an important source of cost reductions, especially in capital-intensive industries. . . .
4. *Getting better performance from production equipment.* When first designed, a piece of production equipment may have a conservatively rated output. Experience may reveal innovative ways of increasing its output. . . .
5. *Changes in the resource mix.* As experience accumulates, a producer can often incorporate different or less expensive resources in the operation. . . .
6. *Product standardization.* Standardization allows the replication of tasks necessary for worker learning. Production of the Ford Model T, for example, followed a strategy of deliberate standardization; as a result, from 1909 to 1923 its price was repeatedly reduced, following an 85 percent experience curve (Abernathy and Wayne, 1974). . . .
7. *Product redesign.* As experience is gained with a product, both the manufacturer and customers gain a clearer understanding of its performance requirements. This understanding allows the product to be redesigned to conserve material, allows greater efficiency in manufacture, and substitutes less costly materials and resources, while at the same time improving performance on relevant dimensions. . . .

The foregoing list of sources dramatizes the observation that cost reductions due to experience don't occur by natural inclination; they are the result of substantial, concerted effort and pressure to lower costs. In fact, left unmanaged, costs rise. Thus, experience does not cause reductions but rather provides an opportunity that alert managements can exploit. . . .

The list of reasons for the experience effect raises perplexing questions on the difference between experience and scale effects. For instance, isn't it true that work specialization and project standardization, mentioned in the experience list, become possible because of the *size* of an operation? Therefore, aren't they each really scale effects? The answer is that they are probably both.

The confusion arises because growth in experience usually coincides with growth in size of an operation. We consider the experience effect to arise primarily due to ingenuity, cleverness, skill, and dexterity derived from experience as embodied in the adages "practice makes perfect" and "experience is the best teacher." On the other hand, scale effect comes from capitalizing on the size of an operation. . . .

Usually the overlap between the two effects is so great that it is difficult (and not too important) to separate them. This is the practice we will adopt from here on. . . .

PRICES AND EXPERIENCE

In stable competitive markets, one would expect that as costs decrease due to experience, prices will decrease similarly. (The price–experience curves in Figure 3 are examples of prices falling with experience.) If profit margins remain at a constant percentage of price, average industry costs and prices should follow identically sloped experience curves (on double logarithmic scales). The constant gap separating them will equal the profit margin percentage; Figure 4 illustrates such an idealized situation.

In many cases, however, prices and costs exhibit a relationship similar to the one shown in Figure 5, where prices start briefly below cost, then cost reductions exceed price reductions until prices suddenly tumble. Ultimately the price and cost curves parallel, as they do in Figure 4. Specifically, in the development phase, new product prices are below average industry costs due to pricing based on anticipated costs. In the price umbrella phase, when demand exceeds supply, prices remain firm under a price umbrella supported by the market leader. This is unstable. At some point a shakeout phase starts; one producer will almost certainly reduce prices to gain share. If this does not precipitate a price decline, the high profit margins will attract enough new entrants to produce temporary overcapacity, causing prices to tumble faster than costs, and marginal producers to be forced out of the market. The stability phase starts when profit margins return to normal levels and prices begin to follow industry costs down the experience curve. . . .

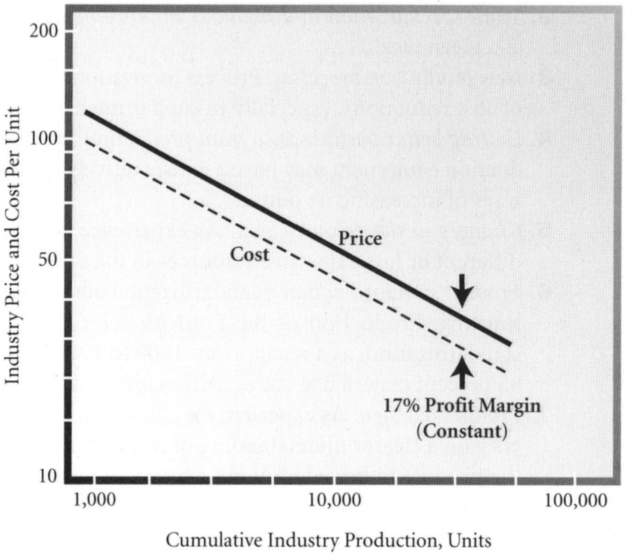

FIGURE 4
AN IDEALIZED PRICE–COST RELATIONSHIP WHEN PROFIT MARGIN IS CONSTANT

COST–PRICE PHASE

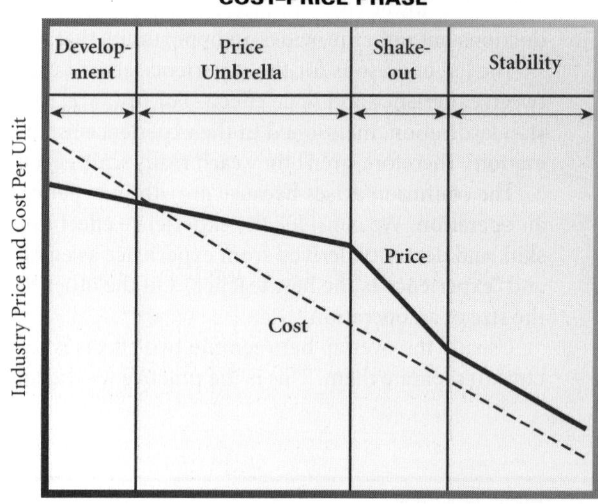

FIGURE 5
TYPICAL PRICE–COST RELATIONSHIP

Source: Adapted from *Perspectives on Experience* (Boston: The Boston Consulting Group, 1972), p. 21.

STRATEGIC IMPLICATIONS

In industries where a significant portion of total cost can be reduced due to scale or experience, important cost advantages can usually be achieved by pursuing a strategy geared to accumulating experience faster than competitors. (Such a strategy will ultimately require that the firm acquire the largest market share relative to competition.)

The dominant producer can greatly influence industry profitability. The rate of decline of competitors' costs must at least keep pace with the leader if they are to maintain profitability. If their costs decrease more slowly, because they either are pursuing cost reductions less aggressively or are growing more slowly than the leader, then their profits will eventually disappear, thus eliminating them from the market.

. . . [T]he advantage of being the leader is obvious. Leadership is usually best seized at the start when experience doubles quickly (e.g., experience increases tenfold as you move from the 20th to the 2,000th unit, but only doubles as you move from the 2,000th to the 4,000th unit). Then a firm can build an unassailable cost advantage and at the same time gain price leadership.

The best course of action for a product depends on a number of factors, one of the most important being the market growth rate. In fast-growing markets, experience can be gained by taking a disproportionate share of new sales, thereby avoiding taking sales away from competitors (which would be vigorously resisted). Therefore, with high rates of growth, aggressive action may be called for. But share-gaining tactics are usually costly in the short run, due to reduced margins from lower prices, added advertising and marketing expense, new product development costs, and the like. This means that if it lacks the resources (product, financial, and other) for leadership and in particular if it is opposed by a very aggressive competitor, a firm may find it wise to abandon the market entirely or focus on a segment it can dominate. On the other hand, in no-growth or slowly growing markets it is hard to take share from competitors and the time it takes to acquire superior experience is usually too long and the cost too great to favor aggressive strategies.

In stable competitive markets, usually the firm with the largest share of a market has the greatest experience and it is often the case that each firm's experience is roughly proportional to market share. A notable exception occurs when a late entrant to a market quickly obtains a commanding market share. It may have less experience than some early entrants. . . .

EFFICIENCY VERSUS EFFECTIVENESS: LIMITATIONS TO STRATEGIES BASED ON EXPERIENCE OR SCALE

The selection of a competitive strategy based on cost reduction due to experience or scale often involves a fundamental choice. It is the selection of cost–price *efficiency* over noncost–price marketing *effectiveness*. However, when the market is more concerned with product and service features and up-to-date technology, a firm pursuing efficiency can find itself offering a low-priced product that few customers want. Thus two basic questions arise: (1) when to use an efficiency strategy and (2) if used, how far to push it before running into dangers of losing effectiveness. . . .

Whether to pursue an efficiency strategy depends on answers to questions such as:

1. Does the industry offer significant cost advantages from experience or scale (as in semiconductors or chemicals)?
2. Are there significant market segments that will reward competitors with low prices?
3. Is the firm well equipped (financially, managerially, technologically, etc.) for or already geared up for strategies relying heavily on having the lowest cost. . . . ?

If the answer is "yes" to all these questions, then "efficiency" strategies should probably be pursued.

Once it decided to pursue an "efficiency" strategy a firm must guard against going so far that it loses effectiveness, primarily through inability to respond to changes. For instance, experience-based strategies frequently require a highly specialized work force, facilities, and organization, making it difficult to respond to changes in consumer demand, to respond to competitors' innovations, or to initiate them. In addition, large-scale plants are vulnerable to changes in process technology, and the heavy cost of operation below capacity.

For example, Ford's Model T automobile ultimately suffered the consequences of inflexibility due to overemphasizing "efficiency" (Abernathy and Wayne, 1974). Ford followed a classic experience-based strategy; over time it slashed its product line to a single model (the Model T), built modern plants, pushed division of labor, introduced the continuous assembly line, obtained economies in purchased parts through high-volume, backward integrated, increased mechanization, and cut prices as costs fell. The lower prices increased Ford's share of a growing market to a high of 55.4% by 1921.

In the meantime, consumer demand began shifting to heavier, closed-body cars and to more comfort. Ford's chief rival, General Motors, had the flexibility to respond quickly with new designs. Ford responded by adding features to its existing standard design. While the features softened the inroads of GM, the basic Model T design, upon which Ford's "efficiency" strategy was based, inadequately met the market's new performance standards. To make matters worse, the turmoil in production due to constant design changes slowed experience-based efficiency gains. Finally Ford was forced, at enormous cost, to close for a whole year beginning May 1927 while it retooled to introduce its Model A. Hence experience or scale-based *efficiency* was carried too far and thus it ultimately limited *effectiveness* to meet consumer needs, to innovate, and to respond.

Thus the challenge is to decide when to emphasize efficiency and when to emphasize effectiveness, and further to design efficiency strategies that maintain effectiveness and vice versa. . . .

READING 14.3

Innovation in Bureaucracy* BY JAMES Q. WILSON

. . . At one level, the history of the United States Army since World War II provides little support for the common view that bureaucracies never change. At the level of doctrine, and to some degree of organization, there has been little *but* change since 1945. . . .

But at a deeper level, very little changed. As Kevin Sheehan makes clear . . . the army limited its innovations to thinking about better ways to counter a Soviet invasion of Western Europe. Every alteration in doctrine and structure was based on the assumption that the war for which the army should prepare itself was a conventional war on the plains of Germany. But during this period there was no such war. Instead the army found itself fighting in Korea, Vietnam, the Dominican Republic, and Grenada, and threatened with the prospect of having to fight in the Middle East and Central America. None of these *actual* or *likely* wars produced the same degree of rethinking and experimentation that was induced by the *possibility* of a war in Europe. As a result, changes in the army were essentially limited to trying to find ways to take advantage of new technological developments in the kind of weaponry that either it or its adversary might employ in Bavaria.

INNOVATION AND TASKS

We ought not to be surprised that organizations resist innovation. They are supposed to resist it. The reason an organization is created is in large part to replace the uncertain expectations and haphazard activities of voluntary endeavors with the stability and routine of organized relationships. The standard operating procedure (SOP) is not the enemy of organization; it is the essence of organization. . . .

For the purposes of this discussion what I mean by innovation is not any new program or technology, but only those that involve the performance of new tasks or a significant alteration in the way in which existing tasks are performed. Organizations will readily accept (or at least not bitterly resist) inventions that facilitate the performance of existing tasks in a way consistent with existing managerial arrangements. Armies did not resist substituting trucks for horse-drawn carts. It is striking, however, how many technical inventions whose value seems self-evident to an outsider are resisted to varying degrees because their use changes operator tasks and managerial controls. When breech-loading rifles and machine guns became available, they dramatically increased the firepower of armies. But the improved firepower forced commanders either to disperse their infantry on the battlefield or to hide them in trenches and bunkers. The former response required decentralizing the command system; the latter permitted command to remain centralized. . . .

This bias toward maintaining existing task definitions often leads bureaucracies to adopt new technologies without understanding their significance. The tank made its appearance in World War I. Armies did not ignore this machine, they purchased it in large numbers—but as a more efficient way of performing a traditional task, that of cavalry scouting. The true innovation occurred when some armies (but not most) saw that the tank was not a mechanical horse but the means for a wholly new way of conducting battles. . . . Similarly, many navies purchased airplanes before World War II but most viewed them simply as an improved means of reconnaissance.

*Reprinted with deletions from *Bureaucracy: What Government Agencies Do and Why They Do It*, James Q. Wilson, 1989, Basic Books.

Thus, the first naval planes were launched by catapults from battleships in order to extend the vision of the battleship's captain. The organizational innovation occurred when aviation was recognized as a new form of naval warfare and the aircraft were massed on carriers deployed in fast-moving task forces.

Changes that are consistent with existing task definitions will be accepted; those that require a redefinition of those tasks will be resisted. . . .

The tendency to resist innovations that alter tasks is not limited to the military or even to government agencies. Take the computer. Its use spread quickly in some firms and was resisted in others. Without a close understanding of the core tasks of these organizations it is impossible to explain why some bought early and others late. When the core task was writing, filing, or calculating, the computer was seen as faster and more efficient, and so it was adopted. It was an improvement rather than an innovation (as the word is used here). For example, department stores were quick to acquire computers to make their accounting programs more efficient, but slow to make extensive use of computers for inventory control. The reason, as Harvey Sapolsky has shown, is that inventory control touches on the core task in a department store, that of the buyer: the person in charge of a line of goods (sportswear, budget dresses, men's furnishings) who in exchange for a share of the profits takes responsibility for buying, displaying, and selling that line. The use of a computer to manage inventory threatened to alter the role of buyer by taking decisions (over what and how much to buy) out of the hands of the buyer, who traditionally was a nearly autonomous businessperson, and placing them in the hands of central managers and staff officers. In time the computer advocates won out and the power of the buyers was diminished. . . .

Government agencies change all the time, but the most common changes are add-ons: a new program is added on to existing tasks without changing the core tasks or altering the organizational culture. The State Department accepted the job of improving security in American embassies by adding on a unit designed to do this; . . . the add-on did not significantly change the way foreign service officers behaved (and thus did not do much to improve embassy security). . . .

Real innovations are those that alter core tasks; most changes add to or alter peripheral tasks. These peripheral changes often are a response to a demand in the agency's environment. Many observers have noted that most educational changes (they always seem to be called "reforms" without regard to whether in fact they make things better) were forced on the schools by the political system. Many important changes in the military also were reactions to political demands: Some key air force generals were at first reluctant to develop the intercontinental missile; the navy for a long time was unsure about the desirability of a submarine-launched missile program; the army bowed to presidential demands for a counterinsurgency unit. Outside forces—academic scientists, industrial engineers, civilian theorists, members of Congress, and presidential aides—all helped induce the military to embrace programs that initially seemed irrelevant to (or at odds with) their core tasks.

Sometimes entrepreneurs within an agency bring about the peripheral changes. In many cases their success depends on their ability to persuade others that the changes *are* peripheral and threaten no core interests. Despite the myths about General Billy Mitchell shaming the navy into acknowledging the military potential of the airplane, the navy had taken a keen interest in aviation from the very first. At issue was the role the airplane was to play. The organizational culture of the navy—the black-shoe, battleship navy—was very much inclined to view the airplane as a scout. The first chief of the Bureau of Aeronautics, Rear Admiral William Moffett, took pains not to contradict this view. As a former battleship commander he had the credentials that line naval officers would respect. He endorsed the idea of the airplane as a scout for the battleship, suggesting only that this scouting function might be served more efficiently if the planes were on aircraft carriers that would accompany the battleship. But quietly, if not secretly, Moffett was promoting the idea of naval aviation as a separate striking force operating independently of battleships. He did this in confidential memos, by getting contracts for high-speed carriers approved, and by intervening in the promotion process to insure that a lot of aviators rose in rank. (By 1926 there were already four admirals, two captains, and sixty-three commanders who were aviators.) So successful was he that a full year before Pearl Harbor ten fast carriers were under construction.

Had it not been for Pearl Harbor, however, the carrier task force might never have become the core of the surface navy. But after December 7, 1941, there was no alternative; five American battleships were sunk or put out of action. To fight a war in the Pacific it now would be carriers or nothing. . . .

EXECUTIVES AND INNOVATION

Whether changes are core or peripheral, externally imposed or internally generated, understanding why they occur at all requires one to understand the behavior of the agency executive. As persons responsible for maintaining the organization it is executives who identify the external pressures to which the agency must react. As individuals who must balance competing interests inside the agency it is they who must decide whether to protect or to ignore managers who wish to promote changes. Almost every important study of bureaucratic innovation points to the great importance of executives in explaining change. For example, Jerald Hage and Robert Dewar studied changes that occurred in sixteen social welfare agencies in a midwestern city and found that the beliefs of the top executives were better predictors of the change than any structural features of the organizations. If John Russell had not been commandant of the Marine Corps or William Moffett had not been chief of the Bureau of Aeronautics, the Fleet Marine Force and carrier-based naval aviation would not have emerged when and as they did.

It is for this reason, I think, that little progress has been made in developing theories of innovation. Not only do innovations differ so greatly in character that trying to find one theory to explain them all is like trying to find one medical theory to explain all diseases, but innovations are so heavily dependent on executive interests and beliefs as to make the chance appearance of a change-oriented personality enormously important in explaining change. It is not easy to build a useful social science theory out of "chance appearances."

In this regard the study of innovation in government agencies is not very different from its study in business firms. In a purely competitive marketplace there would never be any entrepreneurship because anybody producing a better product would immediately attract competitors who would drive the price down (and thus the entrepreneur's profits), possibly to the point where the entrepreneur's earnings from his or her new venture would be zero. Yet new firms and new products are created. The people who create them are willing to run greater than ordinary risks. Predicting who they will be is not easy; so far as it has turned out to be impossible.

Executives are important but also can be perverse. Innovation is not inevitably good; there are at least as many bad changes as good. And government agencies are especially vulnerable to bad changes because, absent a market that would impose a fitness test on any organizational change, a changed public bureaucracy can persist in doing the wrong thing for years. The Ford Motor Company should not have made the Edsel, but if the government had owned Ford it would still be making Edsels. . . .

Uncertainty, as Jonathan Bendor has written, is to organizations what original sin is to individuals—they are born into it. Government organizations are steeped in uncertainty because it is so hard to know what might produce success or even what constitutes success. Executives and higher-level managers have an understandable urge to reduce that uncertainty. They also have a less understandable belief that more information means less uncertainty. That may be true if what they obtain by sophisticated communications and computation equipment is actually information—that is, a full, accurate, and properly nuanced body of knowledge about important matters. Often what they get is instead a torrent of incomplete facts, opinions, guesses, and self-serving statements about distant events.

The reason is not simply the limitations in information-gathering and -transmitting processes. It is also that the very creation of such processes alters the incentives operating on subordinates. These include the following:

1. If higher authority can be sent a message about a decision, then higher authority will be sent a message asking it to make the decision.
2. If higher authority can hear a lot, then higher authority will be told what it wants to hear.
3. Since processing information requires the creation of specialized bureaus, then these units will demand more and more information as a way of justifying their existence.

A good example of all of these incentives at work can be found in the consequences for some armies of the invention of the railroad and the telegraph. Now troop movement could be centrally planned (only headquarters could coordinate all the complex railroad timetables). Now army commanders could spend more time communicating with headquarters (because the telegraph and telephone lines running to the rear were likely to be intact) than with the troops at the front (where communication lines were often broken). As a result, commanders found it easier to yield to the temptation to adopt a headquarters perspective on the battle (which often was hopelessly distorted) than to take a fighting-front view of the battle. The reliance on railroads and telegraphs enhanced the power of engineering units at headquarters; soon the direction of the war itself came to be seen as an engineering matter only. Creveld quotes an Austrian officer who wrote in 1861 that as a result of better communications a commander now "has two enemies to defeat, one in front and another in the rear." . . .

It is not simply that some innovations are perverse; it is also the case that any top-down change is risky. When government executives are the source of a change, they are likely to overestimate its benefits and underestimate its costs. This is true not only because executives lack the detailed and specialized knowledge possessed by operators and lower-level managers, but also because of the incentives operating on the executives. Often they are drawn from outside the agency to serve for a brief period. Their rewards come not from the agency but from what outsiders (peers, the media, Congress) think of them. A "go-getter" who "makes a difference" and does not "go native" usually wins more praise than someone who is cautious and slow-moving. . . .

Sometimes being bold about top-down innovations is desirable, since operators not only have detailed knowledge, they have cultural and mission-oriented biases. Had they been listened to, battleship admirals might well have blocked the creation of a carrier navy until it was too late. . . .

Moreover, there are kinds of innovations that almost no subordinate will support. If an executive sees that an agency ought to be abolished, he or she is not likely to find many supporters among the rank and file, even though in this case *how* it is abolished or drastically reduced in size ought to be guided by the knowledge that only operators possess. . . .

When should executives defer to subordinates and when should they overrule them? If this were a book about how to run an agency, the answer would be: "It all depends. Use good judgment." Not very helpful comments. Moreover, the organizational arrangements that encourage members to propose an innovation often are different from those that make it easy to implement one, once proposed. An agency that wants its managers and operators to suggest new ways of doing their tasks will be open, collegial, and supportive; an agency that wishes to implement an innovation over the opposition of some of its members often needs to concentrate power in the hands of the boss sufficient to permit him or her to ignore (or even dismiss) opponents. . . .

However authority is distributed, the executive who wishes to make changes has to create incentives for subordinates to think about, propose, and help refine such changes, and this means convincing them that if they join the innovative efforts of a (usually) short-term executive, their careers will not be blighted if the innovation fails or the executive departs before it is implemented. Admiral Moffett did this in the navy. . . .

To implement a proposed change often requires either creating a specialized subunit that will take on the new tasks (such as the Bureau of Aeronautics in the navy) or if the task cannot be confined to a subunit, retraining or replacing subordinates who oppose the change. Caspar Weinberger did this at the Federal Trade Commission where, in order to instill a new sense of vigor and commitment to consumer protection, he replaced eighteen of the thirty-one top staff members and about two hundred of the nearly six hundred staff attorneys. Weinberger and his successors as FTC chairman brought in new people specially recruited because they supported a new way of defining the agency's core tasks (namely, to attack deceptive advertising and monopolistic structures rather than to prosecute small-scale price-fixing cases). . . .

None of this implies that agency members always oppose innovations and therefore must be bypassed, dismissed, or reeducated. The reaction of operators to a proposed change will be governed by the incentives to which they respond; in government agencies that are limited in their ability to use money as a reward, one important set of incentives is that derived from the way tasks are defined. Tasks that are familiar, easy, professionally rewarded, or well adapted to the circumstances in which operators find themselves will be preferred because performing them is less costly than undertaking tasks that are new, difficult, or professionally unrewarded or that place the operator in conflict with his or her environment. . . .

The longer an agency exists the more likely that its core tasks will be defined in ways that minimize the costs to the operators performing them, and thus in ways that maximize the costs of changing them. The most dramatic and revealing stories of bureaucratic innovation are therefore found in organizations . . . that have acquired settled habits and comfortable routines. Innovation in these cases requires an exercise of judgment, personal skill, and misdirection, qualities that are rare among government executives. And so innovation is rare.

READING 14.4

Corporate Entrepreneurship: How? BY K. RAMACHANDRAN, T.P. DEVARAJAN, AND SOUGATA RAY

The competitive landscape in many industries today is marked by intense competition among existing players and the emergence of many focused competitors targeting specific segments of the market. In addition, the macro environment is characterized by rapid technological progress in many fields resulting in current solutions to customer problems becoming obsolete. In this scenario, any company that is not continually developing, acquiring, and adapting to new technological advances and to the changing business environment may be making. . . . the unintentional strategic decision to be out of business within a few years.

These changes have highlighted the need for companies to become more entrepreneurial. Many companies have succeeded in their endeavor to do so and have developed new approaches to innovate and to create new businesses and achieve profitable growth. Change, innovation, and entrepreneurship describe what such successful companies do to compete. At the same time, a larger question looming is the challenge of sustaining such changes, both in growing and in mature organizations, particularly when the charismatic leadership that inspired the change disappears from the scene. It is an organizational paradox that, while the existing capabilities provide the basis for the current performance of a company, without renewal, they are likely to constrain the future ability to compete. Institutionalizing entrepreneurship, therefore, is a major challenge for the companies in the current competitive scenario.

WHAT IS CORPORATE ENTREPRENEURSHIP?

The essence of entrepreneurship is innovation leading to wealth creation and sustained growth . . . Corporate entrepreneurship (CE) is the process by which individuals inside organizations pursue opportunities without regard to the resources they currently control. An entrepreneurial manager links up discrete pieces of new technical knowledge that would provide a solution to a customer problem, matches this technical capability with the satisfaction of the market, and garners resources and skills needed to take the venture to the next stage. This process leads to the birth of new businesses and to the transformation of companies through a renewal of their key ideas.

Within the realm of existing firms, CE encompasses three types of phenomena that may or may not be interrelated. These are:

- the birth of new businesses within an existing firm
- the transformation of the existing firms through the renewal or reshaping of the key ideas on which they are built
- innovation

Corporate entrepreneurial efforts that lead to the creation of new business organizations within the corporate organization are called corporate venturing. They may follow from or lead to innovations that exploit new markets or new product offerings or both. If corporate venturing activities result in the creation of semi-autonomous or autonomous organizational entities that reside outside the existing organizational domain, it is called external corporate venturing. If corporate venturing activities result in the creation of organizational entities that reside within an existing organizational domain, it is called internal corporate venturing.

Strategic renewal refers to the corporate entrepreneurial efforts that result in significant changes in an organization's business or corporate level strategy or structure. These changes alter the pre-existing relationships within the organization or between the organization and its external environment and in most cases will involve some sort of innovation.

FOSTERING ENTREPRENEURSHIP—HOW?

Most organizations lose their entrepreneurial spirit once they cross the start-up phase. The transition from an entrepreneurial growth company to a "well-managed" business is usually accompanied by a decreasing ability to identify and pursue opportunities. Initiatives and excitement give place to structure and systems. Organizations become blind to opportunities in the process.

Some of the practices that contribute to the successful management of resources inhibit the pursuit of opportunity. In recent years, the assumptions about strategic and operational environments of the firm have been undergoing rapid changes and the mix of organizational resources necessary to keep pace with them will have to essentially be different. Most organizations, however, do not realize when and what changes are required and how to accomplish them especially when the managers do not feel compelled.

In order to enable the organization to constantly breathe an air of innovation and excitement, . . . firms must create systems that focus the attention of individual participants on innovation as an important and expected activity and direct group and firm behaviors toward entrepreneurial ends.

An entrepreneurial organization will institutionalize practices that establish an organizational environment in which innovation is considered an accepted and appropriate response to organizational problems. These practices build commitment and enthusiasm by creating a shared sense of purpose and meaning in the organization. This ensures that all the firm's technical and business skills are brought to bear to achieve its purpose. This also helps in developing a culture that encourages creativity and creates a passion for innovation in the firm.

This is a challenge [for organizations] but they have a range of options to choose from depending on the size, competition, and industry structure to achieve entrepreneurial excellence. At one end of this spectrum lies the focused initiatives covering specific parts of the organization and at the other initiatives that attempt to breathe entrepreneurship across the organization. The former is called "surface entrepreneurship" and the latter "deep entrepreneurship."

FOCUSED ENTREPRENEURSHIP

Organizations that are "mature" in a number of aspects such as product-market strategy, people's attitudes, and structure and control systems would most often not like to upset their existing applecart in any way while exploring new growth avenues. Since their ability to identify and exploit opportunities has declined, they attempt to promote entrepreneurship by mandating it as a corporate objective. In some cases, entrepreneurship is "injected" into the organization through the appointment of one or more "proven" independent entrepreneurs. In others, someone from within who may have shown some of the attributes of entrepreneurship such as initiative, innovativeness, and change leadership is chosen to lead the effort. They develop new products/services and often lead their implementation insulated from the restrictive approach of the rest of the organization. Such attempts are often accompanied by the use of steep financial incentives to match the potential rewards of independent entrepreneurship.

In this process, the entire organization does not become entrepreneurial and the existing product-market strategy is not threatened, but it is able to add new products/services to its matured portfolio. This is a low-risk approach considering that changing the "chemistry" of an organization is not easy.

CHALLENGES WITH FOCUSED INITIATIVES

Entrepreneurship needs passionate managers who are excited about championing entrepreneurial initiatives . . . Promoting entrepreneurship through a mandating process results in the appointment of managers into the role of an entrepreneur—a role for which they may be unsuited. Such managers may follow a mechanical or a superficial search process in pursuit of presumed opportunities. While they may be good at preparing an attractive business plan, the quality of the basic idea itself may be questionable if the team lacks entrepreneurial qualities. This is particularly so if the environmental characteristics are not conducive. Some organizations have gone to the extent of literally recruiting start-up entrepreneurs. However, appointment of independent entrepreneurs in the role of corporate entrepreneurs leads to difficulties as they neither have the patience nor the experience to navigate the political and cultural realities of the organizations.

While the use of steep financial incentives creates perceptions of inequity that could even result in the sabotage of the entrepreneurial initiative, use of existing financial control systems to monitor entrepreneurial ventures leads to frequent intervention and misguided direction during the progress of these ventures. The root cause of these difficulties is the use of the classical approach of setting objectives, motivating people to accomplish them, and monitoring and controlling such accomplishment. This approach works for activities for which expected results and the process to achieve them are well known. By its very nature, entrepreneurial activity seldom fits this mold.

However, there are evidences of variations of this approach existing that actually encourage small experimental initiatives by managers who always demonstrate entrepreneurial qualities such as initiatives, idea generation, and networking . . . The path to be adopted begins with individual entrepreneurship by some key managers which broadens into renewal of the entire organization. The resources and capabilities created in the process of renewal provide a platform on which far-reaching industry changes can be built.

ORGANIZATION-WIDE ENTREPRENEURSHIP

At the other end of the spectrum are the organizations that whole-heartedly support entrepreneurial initiatives of any kind such as a small improvement in products or processes to totally unrelated diversification ideas. Most often, such companies start driving entrepreneurial initiatives while the organization is still young without the rigidities of a mature organization. Of course, that does not mean that a mature organization cannot imbibe the spirit of entrepreneurship right across the organization. Depending on the circumstances, even mature organizations can become flexible.

Entrepreneurship in such companies is a shared value and drives managerial behavior in conscious and subconscious ways. Sathe (1988) characterized such entrepreneurship as "deep entrepreneurship" and identified many of its key attributes which have been described below. Over the years, variations of the same have appeared but the essential features have remained the same.

- Socialized into an entrepreneurial culture, managers who are so inclined seek out opportunities to make their mark. Those who succeed move into bigger jobs where they undertake such activities in a larger scale. Opportunities are perceived and pursued by such entrepreneurs on the basis of an in-depth knowledge of the industry and personal conviction rather than through superficial analysis and mechanical selection.
- Money is neither offered nor seen as a primary motivator. Entrepreneurial contributions are rewarded with recognition through playing up and promoting company's success stories and champions' enhanced status and the opportunity to engage in entrepreneurial activity on a bigger scale. For instance, very often, idea champions get an opportunity to drive the new project into a new business division. Moreover, failure is considered normal for such activity. Even when failure occurs, the focus is on problem solving and learning from failure rather than on apportioning blame. Therefore, managers perceive low personal/career risk.
- Although companies displaying the pattern of deep entrepreneurship use state-of-the-art analytical techniques, their risk-taking philosophy is rooted not in these techniques or their judgment but in their willingness to bet on entrepreneurs. When faced with difficult decisions regarding opportunities, it is the conviction of the person engaged in entrepreneurial activity that carries the day.
- These companies normally have excellent information and control systems and the top management keeps itself informed of the progress of each venture; great emphasis is placed on the quality and integrity of information supplied. Ventures are frequently reviewed with the purpose of challenging the entrepreneur's thinking to help uncover blind spots and not to issue edicts about the venture. Along with this, a certain amount of insubordination is tolerated provided it is within reasonable bounds; results indicate that it is justified in achieving the results. The management is also very careful in cutting budgets and believes that such cuts can help or harm a venture.

- One of the most difficult decisions in such ventures is to decide when to pull the plug and bury the project or at least send it to cold storage when faced with uncertainties. In reality, most projects do not show sudden unattractiveness; since the quality of assumptions is judgmental, a decision to discontinue which is always painful, is difficult. The challenge is in building a "detached passion"; though it sounds like an oxymoron, in reality, the manager should feel totally passionate about the project when it is pursued but should be able to agree with an objective evaluation and discard the project, if required. Royer (2003) found the need to have exit champions to kill bad projects since many managers have difficulty in giving up a project. One reason for this is lack of another project with the same individual. Hence, exit champions need to have both the temperament and the credibility to question the prevailing belief. Most often, they demand hard data on viability and are able to make a forceful case for killing bad projects.

The contrast between the patterns of focused and organization-wide deep entrepreneurship runs across every element of the organization starting with its mission and covering strategy, structure, systems, processes, and people skills and attitude. New knowledge creation is normal in such organizations.

They allow new organizational units to form and disband without fanfare or prejudice and provide for flexible boundaries among organizational subunits.

DEVELOPING ORGANIZATION-WIDE ENTREPRENEURSHIP

Companies interested in developing and preserving entrepreneurship should strive to create a corporate environment in which those who believe in the attractiveness of opportunities feel encouraged to pursue them. In such an environment, a process of self-selection takes place whereby entrepreneurs "bubble up" to the surface. Since entrepreneurial activity involves high levels of uncertainty, management under such conditions requires rapid information processing abilities and high levels of trust in entrepreneurial individuals and teams. In this process, management ensures a high level of interaction between the individual, the organization, and the external environment at all levels. The purpose is to identify areas of inefficiencies and ineffectiveness and find new solutions to customer needs. Innovations may be at any link on the value chain and not limited to new products and services in a traditional sense.

Managements interested in promoting entrepreneurship at lower levels must be willing and able to appreciate the perceptions and judgments of people at those levels. The two major challenges here are related to ensuring that the freedom granted is not misused and that the risks inherent in entrepreneurial activity are contained.

The challenges of containing risks of the entrepreneurial activity are met through constructive control mechanisms that help avoid irresponsible behavior. To promote entrepreneurship, individuals must be allowed the freedom to think and act in unconventional ways. Proscribed behavior sets the limit for the exercise of this freedom and defines what is considered irresponsible and not be tolerated. In order to contain the risks, the management must control the entrepreneurial process and not the specific initiatives. If the process is right, a certain percentage of success will follow. Also, projects, small and big, will not be judged by the outcome but the quality of the processes followed. As evidence of its commitment, several organizations have created separate venture funds for supporting innovative ideas.

Organizations follow different criteria while selecting entrepreneurial initiatives for support . . . CE activities create new knowledge that enhances the company's competencies and results in the development of new ones. This knowledge is of three types. The first type is specific to the present line of activities of the company and is the key to future product refinements and product line extensions. Such knowledge is predominantly technical and is seldom sufficient for a company to develop a sustainable competitive advantage. The second type of knowledge is integrative in nature. It brings together many elements and is firm-specific in nature. This interlinking of existing competencies in idiosyncratic ways can frustrate the rivals' efforts aimed at imitating the firm's products thus giving the firm a competitive advantage.

The third type of knowledge incorporates new ways of exploiting the technical and integrative knowledge of the firm and can lead to the commercialization of new products and services.

Creating value from the wide range of new knowledge generated in CE activities through the introduction of a new product, process, technology, system, technique, resource or capability in the firm or its markets requires management of the process of articulating, focusing, sharing, and transferring this knowledge.

INSTITUTIONALIZING ENTREPRENEURSHIP

The quality of leadership represented by the top management plays a very critical role in driving innovation in firms and in mastering its dynamics. Firm success is determined by the collective leadership of top management teams with skills complementing each other. The top management which believes that CE can make a significant difference in a company's ability to compete and achieve successful performance will pursue an entrepreneurial strategy. This represents a policy decision to seek competitive advantage through innovation on a sustained basis and will involve:

- designing an organizational context conducive to the autonomous generation of entrepreneurial initiatives by creation of structures and a culture that facilitates entrepreneurial behavior.
- providing a sense of overall direction for innovation initiatives through an entrepreneurial vision.
- ensuring that promising ventures receive necessary resources as they move through the uncertain development process.

A top management team that adopts an entrepreneurial strategy and creates a milieu in the firm such that this strategy can be executed displays entrepreneurial leadership.

Thus, the role of the top management team in firms that pursue an entrepreneurial strategy is to build an organizational setting that stimulates exchange of information between individuals and develop a culture that encourages innovation. The team also fulfills the role of recognizing the value and opportunities presented by specialized knowledge and integrating it to create rents.

The top management team, in the context of an entrepreneurial organization, must function in such a way that it solves problems, particularly in relation to innovation, in a well-honed, effortless, and effective manner so that innovation activity thrives in the firm and the value of specialized knowledge created is recognized and integrated to create rents. Deftness is a quality in a group which permits such functioning. For a top management team to perform with deftness, clear and shared goals and roles must exist, communication must be accurate, sharing of information should be rapid, constructive confrontation needs to be encouraged, and belief and trust in each other and in the team should be built.

CHAPTER 15

Managing Experts

Although most large organizations draw on a variety of experts to get their jobs done, there has been a growing interest in recent years in those organizations whose work, because it is highly complex, is organized primarily around experts. These range from hospitals, universities, and research centers to consulting firms, space agencies, and biomedical companies.

This context is a rather unusual one, at least when judged against the more traditional contexts discussed in previous chapters. Both its processes and its structures tend to take on forms quite different from those presented earlier. Organizations of experts, in fact, seem to divide into two somewhat different contexts. In one, the experts work in rapidly changing situations that demand a good deal of collaborative innovation (as in biotechnology) whereas in the other, experts work more or less alone in more stable situations involving slower-changing bodies of skill or knowledge (as in law, university teaching, and accounting). This chapter takes up the latter with regard to managing experts (since the focus is on them, not their processes). The next chapter discusses the context of innovation and managing experts when they have to work together.

We open this chapter with a description of the type of organization that seems best suited to the context of the more stable application of expertise. Drawn from Mintzberg's work, primarily his original description of "professional bureaucracy," it looks at the structure of the professional organization, including its important characteristic of "pigeonholing" work. The chapter also looks at the management of professionals and the unusual nature of strategy in such organizations (drawing from a paper Mintzberg coauthored with Cynthia Hardy, Ann Langley, and Janet Rose) and at some issues associated with these organizations.

In "Managing Intellect," the second reading, Quinn, Anderson, and Finkelstein, all from the Tuck School at Dartmouth College in New Hampshire, address the question of managing experts head-on. After describing the characteristics of intellect—for example, its pursuit of perfection rather than creativity (which puts this reading squarely in this chapter, not the next)—they suggest various interesting new forms by which companies can manage intellect: the "infinitely flat" organization, the inverted organization, the starburst, and the "spider's web."

The third reading in this chapter, written by consultant David Maister and originally published in the *Sloan Management Review,* focuses on one particular instance of the professional context that has become an increasingly important career option for management students: the professional service firm. Maister describes how companies in businesses such as consulting, investment banking, accounting, architecture, and law manage the interactions among revenue generation, compensation, and staffing to ensure long-term balanced growth.

Finally, in "Covert Leadership: Notes on Managing Professionals," Mintzberg turns around the old metaphor of the manager as orchestra conductor to see how the orchestra conductor really manages. What comes out is not the image of the leader on a pedestal in absolute control but one perhaps akin to what it really means to lead an organization of professional experts.

Overall, these readings suggest that the traditional concepts of managing and organization simply do not work as we move away from conventional mass production—which has long served as the model for "one best way" concepts in management. Whether it be highly expert work in general or service work subjected to new technologies and skills in particular, our thinking has to be opened up to some very different needs. In a widely discussed article "The Coming of the New Organization," (*Harvard Business Review,* January–February 1988), Peter Drucker has argued that work in general is becoming more skilled and so structures of organizations in general are moving toward what we would call the professional form. Although we would not go that far—we maintain our contingency view of different needs for different contexts—we do believe this is becoming a much more important form of organization.

USING THE CASE STUDIES

Managing experts and expertise is a crucial issue in many organizations where knowledge is central to strategy. The management of experts, however, acquires special significance when the experts have strong professional identity, as it does in the HBO and Pixar cases. Mintzberg's "The Professional Organization" is a good reading for analyzing how these organizations approach strategy making. The Cirque due Soleil case looks at the problems that emerge in organizations where professional and artistic identities are closely related. Quinn, Anderson, and Finkelstein's "Managing Intellect" provides a useful framework for evaluating Johnson & Johnson's strategy of decentralizing research and development, and the growing realization that the advantages of granting autonomy to business divisions future growth may depend on getting experts to collaborate and share ideas across organizational boundaries.

Johnson and Johnson also examines at some length the inevitable tension between individual professional identities that are rooted in different medical and research fields. Maister's "Balancing the Professional Service Firm" deals with this dilemma and, hence, is relevant. Mintzberg's "Covert Leadership" opens up the wider issue of how professionals can be managed without suppressing their initiative.

READING 15.1

The Professional Organization* BY HENRY MINTZBERG

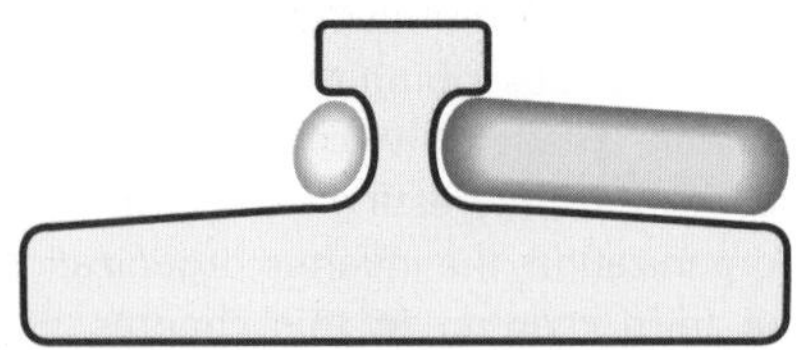

*Adapted from *The Structuring of Organizations* (Prentice Hall, 1979), specifically Chap. 19 on "The Professional Bureaucracy"; additional material included is from *Power In and Around Organizations* (Prentice Hall, 1983), specifically Chap. 22 on "The Meritocracy"; the material on strategy formation is from "Strategy Formation in the University Setting," coauthored with Cynthia Hardy, Ann Langley, and Janet Rose, in J. L. Bess (ed.),*College and University Organization* (New York University Press, 1984). A chapter similar to this one appeared in *Mintzberg on Management: Inside Our Strange World of Organizations* (Free Press, 1989).

THE BASIC STRUCTURE

An organization can be bureaucratic without being centralized. This happens when its work is complex, requiring that it be carried out and controlled by professionals, yet at the same time remains stable, so that the skills of those professionals can be perfected through standardized operating programs. The structure takes on the form of professional bureaucracy, which is common in universities, general hospitals, public accounting firms, social work agencies, and firms doing fairly routine engineering or craft work. All rely on the skills and knowledge of their operating professionals to function; all produce standardized products or services.

THE WORK OF THE PROFESSIONAL OPERATORS

Here again we have a tightly knit configuration of the attributes of structure. Most important, the professional organization relies for coordination on the standardization of skills, which is achieved primarily through formal training. It hires duly trained specialists—professionals—for the operating core, then gives them considerable control over their own work.

Control over their work means that professionals work relatively independently of their colleagues but closely with the clients they serve—doctors treating their own patients and accountants who maintain personal contact with the companies whose books they audit. Most of the necessary coordination among the operating professionals is then handled automatically by their set skills and knowledge—in effect, by what they have learned to expect from each other. During an operation as long and as complex as open-heart surgery, "very little needs to be said [between the anesthesiologist and the surgeon] preceding chest opening and during the procedure on the heart itself . . . [most of the operation is] performed in absolute silence" (Gosselin, 1978). The point is perhaps best made in reverse by the cartoon that shows six surgeons standing around a patient on an operating table with one saying, "Who opens?"

Just how standardized the complex work of professionals can be is illustrated in a paper read by Spencer before a meeting of the International Cardiovascular Society. Spencer notes that an important feature of surgical training is "repetitive practice" to evoke "an automatic reflex." So automatic, in fact, that this doctor keeps a series of surgical "cookbooks" in which he lists, even for "complex" operations, the essential steps as chains of thirty to forty symbols on a single sheet, to "be reviewed mentally in sixty to 120 seconds at some time during the day preceding the operation" (1976: 1179, 1182).

But no matter how standardized the knowledge and skills, their complexity ensures that considerable discretion remains in their application. No two professionals—no two surgeons or engineers or social workers—ever apply them in exactly the same way. Many judgments are required.

Training, reinforced by indoctrination, is a complicated affair in the professional organization. The initial training typically takes place over a period of years in a university or special institution, during which the skills and knowledge of the profession are formally programmed into the students. There typically follows a long period of on-the-job training, such as internship in medicine or articling in accounting, where the formal knowledge is applied and the practice of skills perfected. On-the-job training also completes the process of indoctrination, which began during the formal education. As new knowledge is generated and new skills develop, of course (so it is hoped) the professional upgrades his or her expertise.

All that training is geared to one goal, the internalization of the set procedures, which is what makes the structure technically bureaucratic (structure defined earlier as relying on standardization for coordination). But the professional bureaucracy differs markedly from the machine bureaucracy. Whereas the latter generates its own standards—through its technostructure, enforced by its line managers—many of the standards of the professional bureaucracy originate outside its own structure, in the self-governing associations its professionals belong to with their colleagues from other institutions. These associations set universal standards, which they ensure are taught by the universities and are used by all the organizations practicing the profession. So whereas the machine bureaucracy relies on authority of a hierarchical nature—the power of office—the professional bureaucracy emphasizes authority of a professional nature—the power of expertise.

Other forms of standardization are, in fact, difficult to rely on in the professional organization. The work processes themselves are too complex to be standardized directly by analysts. One need only try to imagine a work-study analyst following a cardiologist on rounds or timing the activities of a teacher in a classroom. Similarly, the outputs of professional work cannot easily be measured and so do not lend themselves to standardization. Imagine a planner trying to define a cure in psychiatry, the amount of learning that takes place in a classroom, or the quality of an accountant's audit. Likewise, direct supervision and mutual adjustment cannot be relied upon for coordination, for both impede professional autonomy.

THE PIGEONHOLING PROCESS

To understand how the professional organization functions at the operating level, it is helpful to think of it as a set of standard programs—in effect, the repertoire of skills the professionals stand ready to use—that are applied to known situations, called contingencies, also standardized. As Weick notes of one case in point, "schools are in the business of building and maintaining categories" (1976: 8). The process is sometimes known as *pigeonholing*. In this regard, the professional has two basic tasks: (1) to categorize, or "diagnose," the client's need in terms of one of the contingencies, which indicates which standard program to apply, and (2) to apply, or execute, that program. For example, the management consultant carries a bag of standard acronymic tricks: MBO, MIS, LRP, OD. The client with information needs gets MIS; the one with managerial conflicts, OD. Such pigeonholing, of course, simplifies matters enormously; it is also what enables each professional to work in a relatively autonomous manner.

It is in the pigeonholing process that the fundamental differences among the machine organization, the professional organization, and the innovative organization (to be discussed next) can best be seen. The machine organization is a single-purpose structure. Presented with a stimulus, it executes its one standard sequence of programs, just as we kick when tapped on the knee. No diagnosis is involved. In the professional organization, diagnosis is a fundamental task, but one highly circumscribed. The organization seeks to match a predetermined contingency to a standardized program. Fully open-ended diagnosis—that which seeks a creative solution to a unique problem—requires the innovative form of organization. No standard contingencies or programs can be relied upon there.

THE ADMINISTRATIVE STRUCTURE

Everything we have discussed so far suggests that the operating core is the key part of the professional organization. The only other part that is fully elaborated is the support staff, but that is focused very much on serving the activities of the operating core. Given the high cost of the professionals, it makes sense to back them up with as much support as possible. Thus, universities have printing facilities, faculty clubs, alma mater funds, publishing houses, archives, libraries, computer facilities, and many, many other support units.

The technostructure and middle-line management are not highly elaborated in the professional organization. They can do little to coordinate the professional work. Moreover, with so little need for direct supervision of, or mutual adjustment among, the professionals, the operating units can be very large. For example, the McGill Faculty of Management functions effectively with 50 professors under a single manager, its dean, and the rest of the university's academic hierarchy is likewise thin.

Thus, the diagram at the beginning of this reading shows the professional organization, in terms of our logo, as a flat structure with a thin middle line, a tiny technostructure, but a fully elaborated support staff. All these characteristics are reflected in the organigram of a university hospital, shown in Figure 1.

Coordination within the administrative structure is another matter, however. Because these configurations are so decentralized, the professionals not only control their own work but they also gain much collective control over the administrative decisions that affect them—decisions, for example, to hire colleagues, to promote them, and to distribute resources. This they do partly by doing some of the administrative work themselves (most university professors, for example, sit on various administrative committees) and partly by ensuring that important administrative posts are staffed by professionals or at least sympathetic people appointed with the professionals' blessing. What emerges, therefore, is a rather democratic administrative structure. But because the administrative work requires mutual adjustment for coordination among the various people involved, task forces and especially standing committees abound at this level, as is in fact suggested in Figure 1.

Because of the power of their professional operators, these organizations are sometimes described as inverse pyramids, with the professional operators on top and the administrators down below to serve them—to ensure that the surgical facilities are kept clean and the classrooms well supplied with chalk. Such a description slights the power of the administrators of professional work, however, although it may be an accurate description of those who manage the support units. For the support staff—often more numerous than the professional staff, but generally less skilled—there is no democracy in the professional organization, only the oligarchy of the professionals. Such support units as housekeeping in the hospital or printing in the university are likely to be managed tightly from the top, in effect as machinelike enclaves within the professional configuration. Thus, what frequently emerges in the professional organization are parallel and separate administrative hierarchies, one democratic and bottom-up for the professionals, a second machinelike and top-down for the support staff.

THE ROLES OF THE ADMINISTRATORS OF PROFESSIONAL WORK

Where does all this leave the administrators of the professional hierarchy, the executive directors and chiefs of the hospitals and the presidents and deans of the universities? Are they powerless? Compared with their counterparts in the entrepreneurial and machine organizations, they certainly lack a good deal of power. But that is far from the whole story. The administrator of professional work may not be able to control the professionals directly, but he or she does perform a series of roles that can provide considerable indirect power.

First, this administrator spends much time handling disturbances in the structure. The pigeonholing process is an imperfect one at best, leading to all kinds of jurisdictional disputes between the professionals. Who should perform mastectomies in the hospitals, surgeons who look after cutting or gynecologists who look after women? Seldom, however, can one administrator impose a solution on the professionals involved in a dispute. Rather, various administrators must often sit down together and negotiate a solution on behalf of their constituencies.

Second, the administrators of professional work—especially those at higher levels—serve in key roles at the boundary of the organization, between the professionals inside and the influencers outside: governments, client associations, benefactors, and so on. On the one hand, the administrators are expected to protect the professionals' autonomy, to "buffer" them from external pressures. On the other hand, they are expected to woo those outsiders to support the organization, both morally and financially. And that often leads the outsiders to expect these administrators, in turn, to control the professionals, in machine bureaucratic ways. Thus, the external roles of the manager—maintaining liaison contacts, acting as figurehead and spokesman in a public relations capacity, negotiating with outside agencies—emerge as primary ones in the administration of professional work.

Some view the roles these administrators are called upon to perform as signs of weakness. They see these people as the errand boys of the professionals, or else as pawns caught in various tugs of war—between one professional and another, between support staffer and professional, between outsider and professional. In fact, however, these roles are the very sources of administrators' power. Power is, after all, gained at the locus of uncertainty, and that is exactly where the administrators of professionals sit. The administrator who succeeds in raising extra funds for his or her organization gains a say in how they are distributed; the one who can reconcile conflicts in favor of his or her unit or who can effectively buffer the professionals from external influence becomes a valued, and therefore powerful, member of the organization.

We can conclude that power in these structures does flow to those professionals who care to devote effort to doing administrative instead of professional work, so long as they do it well. But that, it should be stressed, is not laissez-faire power; the professional administrator maintains power only as long as the professionals perceive him or her to be serving their interests effectively.

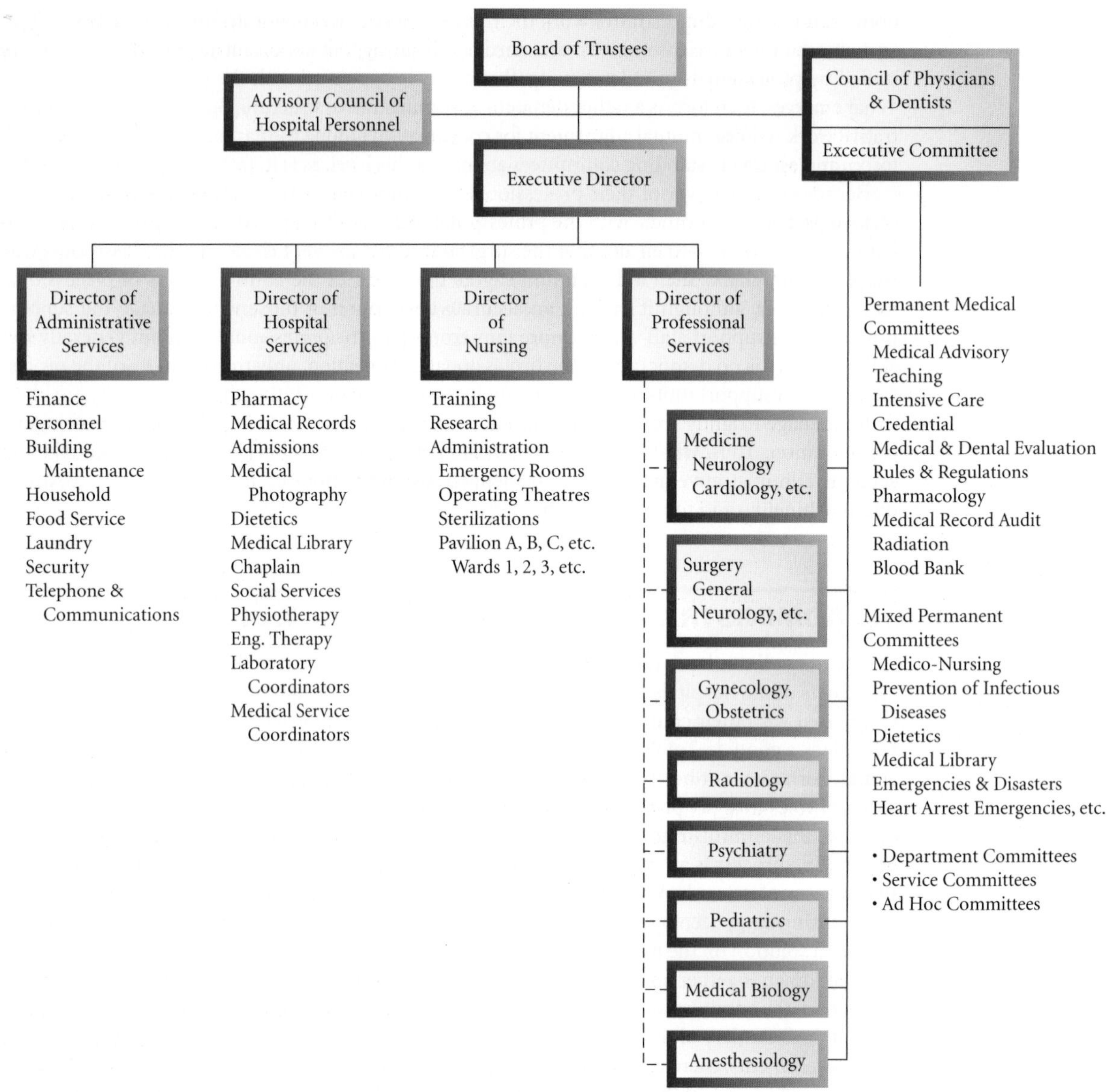

FIGURE 1 ORGANIZATION OF A UNIVERSITY HOSPITAL

CONDITIONS OF THE PROFESSIONAL ORGANIZATION

The professional form of organization appears wherever the operating work of an organization is dominated by skilled workers who use procedures that are difficult to learn yet are well defined. This means a situation that is both complex and stable—complex enough to require procedures that can be learned only through extensive training yet stable enough so that their use can become standardized.

Note that an elaborate technical system can work against this configuration. If highly regulating or automated, the professionals' skills might be amenable to rationalization, in other words, to be divided into simple, highly programmed steps that would destroy the basis for professional autonomy and thereby drive the structure to the machine form. And if highly complicated, the technical system would reduce the professionals' autonomy by forcing them to work in multidisciplinary teams, thereby driving the organization toward the innovative form. Thus the surgeon uses a scalpel, and the accountant a pencil. Both must be sharp, but both are otherwise simple and commonplace instruments. Yet both allow their users to perform independently what can be exceedingly complex functions.

The prime example of the professional configuration is the personal-service organization, at least the one with complex, stable work not reliant on a fancy technical system. Schools and universities, consulting firms, law and accounting offices, and social work agencies all rely on this form of organization, more or less, so long as they concentrate not on innovating in the solution of new problems but on applying standard programs to well-defined ones. The same seems to be true of hospitals, at least to the extent that their technical systems are simple. (In those areas that call for more sophisticated equipment—apparently a growing number, especially in teaching institutions—the hospital is driven toward a hybrid structure, with characteristics of the innovative form. But this tendency is mitigated by the hospital's overriding concern with safety. Only the tried and true can be relied upon, which produces a natural aversion to the looser innovative configuration.)

So far, our examples have come from the service sector. But the professional form can be found in manufacturing too, where the above conditions hold up. Such is the case of the craft enterprise, for example, the factory using skilled workers to produce ceramic products. The very term *craftsman* implies a kind of professional who learns traditional skills through long apprentice training and then is allowed to practice them free of direct supervision. Craft enterprises seem typically to have few administrators, who tend to work, in any event, alongside the operating personnel. The same would seem to be true for engineering work oriented not to creative design so much as to modification of existing dominant designs.

STRATEGY FORMATION IN THE PROFESSIONAL ORGANIZATION

It is commonly assumed that strategies are formulated before they are implemented, that planning is the central process of formulation, and that structures must be designed to implement these strategies. At least this is what one reads in the conventional literature of strategic management. In the professional organization, these imperatives stand almost totally at odds with what really happens, leading to the conclusion either that such organizations are confused about how to make strategy or that the strategy writers are confused about how professional organizations must function. I subscribe to the latter explanation.

Using the definition of strategy as pattern in action, strategy formation in the professional organization takes on a new meaning. Rather than simply throwing up our hands at its resistance to formal strategic planning, or, at the other extreme, dismissing professional organizations as "organized anarchies" with strategy-making processes as mere "garbage cans" (March and Olsen, 1976) we can focus on how decisions and actions in such organizations order themselves into patterns over time.

Taking strategy as pattern in action, the obvious question becomes, which actions? The key area of strategy making in most organizations concerns the elaboration of the basic mission (the products or services offered to the public); in professional organizations, we shall argue, this is significantly controlled by individual professionals. Other important areas of strategy here include the inputs to the system (notably the choice of professional staff, the determination of clients, and the raising of external funds), the means to perform the mission (the construction of buildings and facilities, the purchase of research equipment, and so on), the structure and forms of governance (design of the committee system, the hierarchies, and so on), and the various means to support the mission.

Were professional organizations to formulate strategies in the conventional ways, central administrators would develop detailed and integrated plans about these issues. This sometimes happens, but in a very limited number of cases. Many strategic issues come under the direct control of individual professionals, while others can be decided neither by individual professionals nor by central administrators, but instead require the participation of a variety of people in a complex collective process. As illustrated in Figure 2, we examine in turn the decisions controlled by individual professionals, by central administrators, and by the collectivity.

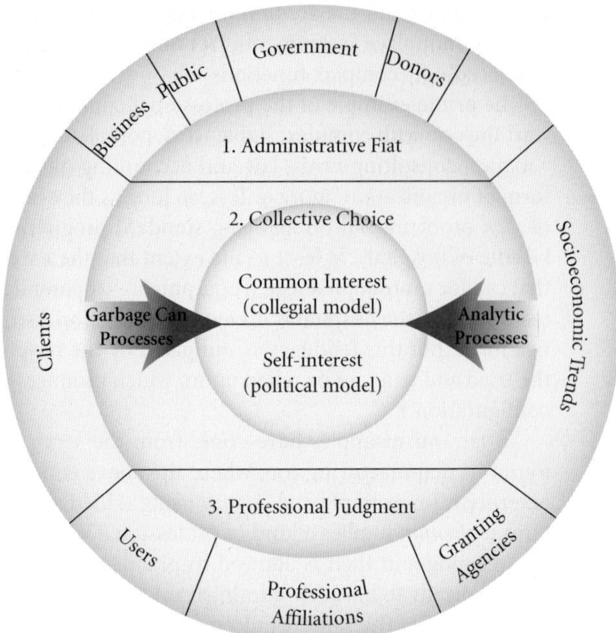

FIGURE 2
THREE LEVELS OF DECISION MAKING IN THE PROFESSIONAL ORGANIZATION

DECISIONS MADE BY PROFESSIONAL JUDGMENT

Professional organizations are distinguished by the fact that the determination of the basic mission—the specific services to be offered and to whom—is in good part left to the judgment of professionals as individuals. In the university, for example, each professor has a good deal of control over what is taught and how, as well as what is researched and how. Thus the overall product-market strategy of McGill University must be seen as the composite of the individual teaching and research postures of its 1,200 professors.

That, however, does not quite constitute full autonomy, because there is a subtle but not insignificant constraint on that power. Professionals are left to decide on their own only because years of training have ensured that they will decide in ways generally accepted in their professions. Thus professors choose course contents and adopt teaching methods highly regarded by their colleagues, sometimes even formally sanctioned by their disciplines; they research subjects that will be funded by the granting agencies (which usually come under professional controls); and they publish articles acceptable to the journals refereed by their peers. Pushed to the limit, then, individual freedom becomes professional control. It may be explicit freedom from administrators, even from peers in other disciplines, but it is not implicit freedom from colleagues in their own discipline. Thus we use the label "professional judgment" to imply that while judgment may be the mode of choice, it is informed judgment, mightily influenced by professional training and affiliation.

DECISIONS MADE BY ADMINISTRATIVE FIAT

Professional expertise and autonomy, reinforced by the pigeonholing process, sharply circumscribe the capacity of central administrators to manage the professionals in the ways of conventional bureaucracy—through direct supervision and the designation of internal standards (rules, job descriptions, policies). Even the designation of standards of output or performance is discouraged by the intractable problem of operationalizing the goals of professional work.

Certain types of decisions, less related to the professional work per se, do however fall into the realm of what can be called administrative fiat, in other words, become the exclusive prerogative of the administrators. They include some financial decisions, for example, to buy and sell property and embark on fund-raising campaigns. Because many of the support services are organized in a conventional top-down hierarchy, they too tend to fall under the control of the central administration. Support services more critical to professional matters, however, such as libraries or computers in the universities, tend to fall into the realm of collective decision making, where the central administrators join the professionals in the making of choices.

Central administrators may also play a prominent role in determining the procedures by which the collective process functions: what committees exist, who gets nominated to them, and so on. It is the administrators, after all, who have the time to devote to administration. This role can give skillful administrators considerable influence, however indirect, over the decisions made by others. In addition, in times of crisis administrators may acquire more extensive powers, as the professionals become more inclined to defer to leadership to resolve the issues.

DECISIONS MADE BY COLLECTIVE CHOICE

Many decisions are, however, determined neither by administrators nor by individual professionals. Instead, they are handled in interactive processes that combine professionals with administrators from a variety of levels and units. Among the most important of these decisions seem to be ones related to the definition, creation, design, and discontinuation of the pigeonholes, that is, the programs and departments of various kinds. Other important decisions here include the hiring and promotion of professionals and, in some cases, budgeting and the establishment and design of the interactive procedures themselves (if they do not fall under administrative fiat).

Decision making may be considered to involve the three phases of *identification* of the need for decision, *development* of solutions, and *selection* of one of them. Identification seems to depend largely on individual initiative. Given the complexities of professional work and the rigidities of pigeonholing, change in this configuration is difficult to imagine without an initiating "sponsor" or "champion." Development may involve the same individual but often requires the efforts of collective task forces as well. And selection tends to be a fully interactive process, involving several layers of standing committees composed of professionals and administrators, and sometimes outsiders as well (such as government representatives). It is in this last phase that we find the full impact and complexity of mutual adjustment in the administration of professional organizations.

MODELS OF COLLECTIVE CHOICE

How do these interactive processes in fact work? Some writers have traditionally associated professional organizations with a *collegial* model, where decisions are made by a "community of individuals and groups, all of whom may have different roles and specialties, but who share common goals and objectives for the organization" (Taylor, 1983: 18). *Common interest* is the guiding force, and decision making is therefore by consensus. Other writers instead propose a political model, in which the differences of interest groups are irreconcilable. Participants thus seek to serve their *self-interest,* and political factors become instrumental in determining outcomes.

Clearly, neither common interest nor self-interest will dominate decision processes all the time; some combination is naturally to be expected. Professionals may agree on goals yet conflict over how they should be achieved; alternatively, consensus can sometimes be achieved even where goals differ—Democrats do, after all, sometimes vote with Republicans in the U.S. Congress. In fact, we need to consider motivation, not just behavior, in order to distinguish collegiality from politics. Political success sometimes requires a collegial posture—one must cloak self-interest in the mantle of the common good. Likewise, collegial ends sometimes require political means. Thus, we should take as collegial any behavior that is *motivated* by a genuine concern for the good of the institution, and politics as any behavior driven fundamentally by self-interest (of the individual or his or her unit).

A third model that has been used to explain decision making in universities is the *garbage can.* Here decision making is characterized by "collections of choices looking for problems, issues and feelings looking for decision situations in which they may be aired, solutions looking for issues to which they might be an answer, and decision makers looking for work" (Cohen and Olsen, 1972: 1). Behavior is, in other words, nonpurposeful and often random, because goals are unclear and the means to achieve them problematic. Furthermore, participation is fluid because of the cost of time and energy. Thus, in place of the common interest of the collegial model and the self-interest of the political model, the garbage can model suggests a kind of *disinterest.*

The important question is not whether garbage can processes exist—we have all experienced them—but whether they matter. Do they apply to key issues or only to incidental ones? Of course, decisions that are not significant to anyone may well end up in the garbage can, so to speak. There is always someone with free time willing to challenge a proposal for the sake of so doing. But I have difficulty accepting that individuals to whom decisions are important do not invest the effort necessary to influence them. Thus, like common interest and self-interest, I conclude that disinterest neither dominates decision processes nor is absent from them.

Finally, *analysis* may be considered a fourth model of decision making. Here calculation is used, if not to select the best alternative, then at least to assess the acceptability of different ones. Such an approach seems consistent with the machine configuration, where a technostructure stands ready to calculate the costs and benefits of every proposal. But, in fact, analysis figures prominently in the professional configuration too, but here carried out mostly by professional operators themselves. Rational analysis structures arguments for communication and debate and enables champions and their opponents to support their respective positions. In fact, as each side seeks to pick holes in the position of the other, the real issues are more likely to emerge.

Thus, as indicated in Figure 2, the important collective decisions of the professional organization seem to be most influenced by collegial and political processes, with garbage can pressures encouraging a kind of haphazardness on one side (especially for less important decisions) and analytical interventions on the other side encouraging a certain rationality (serving as an invisible hand to keep the lid on the garbage can, so to speak!).

STRATEGIES IN THE PROFESSIONAL ORGANIZATION

Thus, we find here a very different process of strategy making, and very different resulting strategies, compared with conventional (especially machine) organizations. While it may seem difficult to create strategies in these organizations, due to the fragmentation of activity, the politics, and the garbage can phenomenon, in fact the professional organization is inundated with strategies (meaning patterning in its actions). The standardization of skills encourages patterning, as do the pigeonholing process and the professional affiliations. Collegiality promotes consistency of behavior; even politics works to resist changing existing patterns. As for the garbage can model, perhaps it just represents the unexplained variance in the system; that is, whatever is not understood looks to the outside observer like organized anarchy.

Many different people get involved in the strategy-making process here, including administrators and the various professionals, individually and collectively, so that the resulting strategies can be very fragmented (at the limit, each professional pursues his or her own product-market strategy). There are, of course, forces that encourage some overall cohesion in strategy too: the common forces of administrative fiat, the broad negotiations that take place in the collective process (for example, on new tenure regulations in a university), even the forces of habit and tradition, at the limit ideology, that can pervade a professional organization (such as hiring certain kinds of people or favoring certain styles of teaching or of surgery).

Overall, the strategies of the professional organization tend to exhibit a remarkable degree of stability. Major reorientations in strategy—"strategic revolutions"—are discouraged by the fragmentation of activity and the influence of the individual professionals and their outside associates. But at a narrower level, change is ubiquitous. Inside tiny pigeonholes, services are continually being altered, procedure redesigned, and clientele shifted, while in the collective process, pigeonholes are constantly being added and rearranged. Thus, the professional organization is, paradoxically, extremely stable at the broadest level and in a state of perpetual change at the narrowest one.

SOME ISSUES ASSOCIATED WITH THE PROFESSIONAL ORGANIZATION

The professional organization is unique among the different configurations in answering two of the paramount needs of contemporary men and women. It is democratic, disseminating its power directly to its workers (at least those lucky enough to be professional). And it provides them with extensive autonomy, freeing them even from the need to coordinate closely with their colleagues. Thus, the professional has the best of both worlds. He or she is attached to an organization yet is free to serve clients in his or her own way constrained only by the established standards of the profession.

The result is that professionals tend to emerge as highly motivated individuals, dedicated to their work and to the clients they serve. Unlike the machine organization, which places barriers between the operator and the client, this configuration removes them, allowing a personal relationship to develop. Moreover, autonomy enables the professionals to perfect their skills free of interference, as they repeat the same complex programs time after time.

But in these same characteristics, democracy and autonomy, lie the chief problems of the professional organization. For there is no evident way to control the work, outside of that exercised by the profession itself, no way to correct deficiencies that the professionals choose to overlook. What they tend to overlook are the problems of coordination, of discretion, and of innovation that arise in these configurations.

PROBLEMS OF COORDINATION

The professional organization can coordinate effectively in its operating core only by relying on the standardization of skills. But that is a loose coordinating mechanism at best; it fails to cope with many of the needs that arise in these organizations. One need is to coordinate the work of professionals with that of support staffers. The professionals want to give the orders. But that can catch the support staffers between the vertical power of line authority and the horizontal power of professional expertise. Another need is to achieve overriding coordination among the professionals themselves. Professional organizations, at the limit, may be viewed as collections of independent individuals who come together only to draw on common resources and support services. Though the pigeonholing process facilitates this, some things inevitably fall through the cracks between the pigeonholes. But because the professional organization lacks any obvious coordinating mechanism to deal with these, they inevitably provoke a great deal of conflict. Much political blood is spilled in the continual reassessment of contingencies and programs that are either imperfectly conceived or artificially distinguished.

PROBLEMS OF DISCRETION

Pigeonholing raises another serious problem. It focuses most of the discretion in the hands of single professionals, whose complex skills, no matter how standardized, require the exercise of considerable judgment. Such discretion works fine when professionals are competent and conscientious. But it plays havoc when they are not. Inevitably, some professionals are simply lazy or incompetent. Others confuse the needs of their clients with the skills of their trade. They thus concentrate on a favored program to the exclusion of all others (like the psychiatrist who thinks that all patients, indeed all people, need psychoanalysis). Clients incorrectly sent their way get mistreated (in both senses of that word).

Various factors confound efforts to deal with this inversion of means and ends. One is that professionals are notoriously reluctant to act against their own, for example, to censure irresponsible behavior through their professional associations. Another (which perhaps helps to explain the first) is the intrinsic difficulty of measuring the outputs of professional work. When psychiatrists cannot even define the word *cure* or *healthy,* how are they to prove that psychoanalysis is better for schizophrenics than is chemical therapy?

Discretion allows professionals to ignore not only the needs of their clients but also those of the organization itself. Many professionals focus their loyalty on their profession, not on the place where they happen to practice it. But professional organizations have needs for loyalty too—to support their overall strategies, to staff their administrative committees, to see them through conflicts with the professional associations. Cooperation is crucial to the functioning of the administrative structure, yet many professionals resist it furiously.

PROBLEMS OF INNOVATION

In the professional organization, major innovation also depends on cooperation. Existing programs may be perfected by the single professional, but new ones usually cut across the established specialties—in essence, they require a rearrangement of the pigeonholes—and so call for collective action. As a result, the reluctance of the professionals to cooperate with each other and the complexity of the collective processes can produce resistance to innovation. These are, after all, professional *bureaucracies,* in essence, performance structures designed to perfect given programs in stable environments, not problem-solving structures to create new programs for unanticipated needs.

The problems of innovation in the professional organization find their roots in convergent thinking, in the deductive reasoning of the professional who sees the specific situation in terms of the general concept. That means new problems are forced into old pigeonholes, as is excellently illustrated in Spencer's comments: "All patients developing significant complications or death among our three hospitals . . . are reported to a central office with a narrative description of the sequence of events, with reports varying in length from a third to an entire page." And six to eight of these cases are discussed in the one-hour weekly "mortality–morbidity" conferences, including presentation of it by the surgeon and "questions and comments" by the audience (1978: 118). An "entire" page and ten minutes of discussion for a case with "significant complications"! Maybe that is enough to list the symptoms and slot them into pigeonholes. But it is hardly enough even to begin to think about creative solutions. As Lucy once told Charlie Brown, great art cannot be done in half an hour; it takes at least 45 minutes!

The fact is that great art and innovative problem solving require *inductive* reasoning—that is, inference of the new general solution from the particular experience. And that kind of thinking is *divergent*; it breaks away from old routines or standards rather than perfecting existing ones. And that flies in the face of everything the professional organization is designed to do.

PUBLIC RESPONSES TO THESE PROBLEMS

What responses do the problems of coordination, discretion, and innovation evoke? Most commonly, those outside the profession see the problems as resulting from a lack of external control of the professional and the profession. So they do the obvious: try to control the work through other, more traditional means. One is direct supervision, which typically means imposing an intermediate level of supervision to watch over the professionals. But we already discussed why this cannot work for jobs that are complex. Another is to try to standardize the work or its outputs. But we also discussed why complex work cannot be formalized by rules, regulations, or measures of performance. All these types of controls really do, by transferring the responsibility for the service from the professional to the administrative structure, is destroy the effectiveness of the work. It is not the government that educates the student, not even the school system or the school itself; it is not the hospital that delivers the baby. These things are done by the individual professional. If that professional is incompetent, no plan or rule fashioned in the technostructure, no order from any administrator or government official, can ever make him or her competent. But such plans, rules, and orders can impede the competent professional from providing his or her service effectively.

Are there then no solutions for a society concerned about the performance of its professional organizations? Financial control of them and legislation against irresponsible professional behavior are obviously in order. But beyond that solutions must grow from a recognition of professional work for what it is. Change in the professional organization does not *sweep* in from new administrators taking office to announce wide reforms, or from government officials intent on bringing the professionals under technocratic control. Rather, change *seeps* in through the slow process of changing the professionals—changing who enters the profession in the first place, what they learn in its professional schools (norms as well as skills and knowledge), and thereafter how they upgrade their skills. Where desired changes are resisted, society may be best off to call on its professionals' sense of public responsibility or, failing that, to bring pressure on the professional associations rather than on the professional bureaucracies.

READING 15.2

Managing Intellect*

BY JAMES BRIAN QUINN, PHILIP ANDERSON, AND SYDNEY FINKELSTEIN

With rare exceptions, the economic and producing power of a modern corporation or nation lies more in its intellectual and systems capabilities than in its hard assets—raw materials, land, plant, and equipment. Intellectual and information processes create most of the value added for firms in the large service industries—like software, medical care, communications, education, entertainment, accounting, law, publishing, consulting, advertising, retailing, wholesaling, and transportation—which provide 79 percent of all jobs and 76 percent of all U.S. GNP. In manufacturing as well, intellectual activities—like R&D, process design, product design, logistics, marketing, marketing research, systems management, or technological innovation—generate the preponderance of value added. . . .

The capacity to manage intellect and to convert it into useful outputs has become the critical executive skill of the era. Yet few managements have systematic answers to even these basic questions:

- What is intellect? Where does it reside? How do we capture it? Leverage it?
- What special skills are needed to manage professional versus creative intellect? How can a firm measure the value of its intellect? How can managers leverage their firm's intellectual resources to the maximum?

WHAT IS INTELLECT?

Webster's Dictionary defines intellect as "knowing or understanding: the capacity for knowledge, for rational or highly developed use of intelligence." The intellect of an organization—in order of increasing importance—includes: (1) *cognitive knowledge* (or know what); (2) *advanced skills* (know-how); (3) *system understanding* and *trained intuition* (know why); and (4) *self-motivated creativity* (care why). Intellect clearly resides inside the firm's human brains. The first three levels can also exist in the organization's systems, databases, or operating technologies. If properly nurtured, intellect in each form is both highly leverageable and protectable. *Cognitive knowledge* is essential, but usually far from sufficient for success. Many may know the rules for performance—on a football field, piano, or accounting ledger—but lack the higher skills necessary to make money at it in competition.

Similarly, some possess advanced skills but lack system understanding: they can perform selected tasks well, but often do not fully understand how their actions affect other elements of the organization or how to improve the total entity's effectiveness. Similarly, some people may possess both the knowledge to perform a task and the *advanced skills* to compete, but lack the will, motivation, or adaptability for success. Highly *motivated* and *creative* groups often outperform others with greater physical or fiscal endowments.

The value of a firm's intellect increases markedly as one moves up the intellectual scale from cognitive knowledge toward motivated creativity. Yet, in a strange and costly anomaly, most enterprises reverse this priority in their training and systems development expenditures, focusing virtually all their attention on basic (rather than advanced) skills development and little or none on systems, motivational, or creative skills. . . .

*Reprinted with deletions from "Managing Expertise," J. B. Quinn, P. Anderson, and S. Finkelstein, *Academy of Management Executive*, Vol. 10 (3), 1996, 7–27.

CHARACTERISTICS OF INTELLECT

The best managed companies avoid this by exploiting certain critical characteristics of intellect at both the strategic and operational levels.

EXPONENTIALITY

Properly stimulated, knowledge and intellect grow exponentially. All learning and experience curves have this characteristic. As knowledge is captured or internalized, the available knowledge base itself becomes higher. . . . The effect accelerates as higher levels of knowledge allow the organization to attack more complex problems and to interrelate with other knowledge sources it earlier could not access. . . .

The strategic consequences of exploiting exponentiality are profound. Once a firm obtains a knowledge-based competitive edge, it becomes ever easier to maintain its lead and harder for competitors to catch up. The most serious threat is that through complacency intellectual leaders may lose their knowledge advantage. . . . This is why the highest level of intellect, self-motivated creativity, is so vital. Firms that nurture "care why" are able to thrive on today's rapid changes. . . .

SHARING

Another important characteristic is that knowledge is one of the few assets that grows most—also usually exponentially—when shared. . . . The core intellectual competency of many financial firms . . . lies in the human experts and the systems software that collect and analyze the data surrounding their investment specialties. Access to the internals of these centralized software systems is tightly limited to a few specialists working at headquarters. Here they share and leverage their own specialized analytical skills through close interactions with other financial specialists, "rocket scientist" modelers, and the unique access the firm has to massive transactions data. . . .

EXPANDABILITY

Unlike physical assets, intellect: (a) increases in value with use; (b) tends to have much underutilized capacity; (c) can be self-organizing; and (d) is greatly expandable under pressure. How can a company exploit these characteristics? . . . The processes they use resemble successful coaching more than anything else. The critical activities are: (1) recruiting the right people; (2) stimulating them to internalize the information knowledge, skills, and attitudes needed for success; (3) creating systematic technological and organizational structures to capture, focus, and leverage intellect to the greatest possible extent; and (4) demanding and rewarding top performance from all players. . . .

There are important differences between managing professional versus creative intellect. Although much attention has been given to managing creativity, little has been written about managing professionals. Yet professionals are the most important source of intellect for most organizations. For every truly creative organization, there are probably 20 to 100 professional groups creating high value deep within integrated firms or directly for customers. What characterizes such professionals?

PERFECTION, NOT CREATIVITY

While no precise delineation applies in all cases, most (90 to 98 percent) of a typical professional's activity is directed at perfection, not creativity (Schön, 1983). The true professional commands a complete body of knowledge—a discipline—and updates that knowledge constantly. In most cases, the customer wants the knowledge delivered reliably with the most advanced skill available. Although there is an occasional call for creativity, the preponderance of work in actuarial units, dentistry, hospitals, accounting units, opera companies, universities, law firms, aircraft operations, equipment maintenance, etc. requires the repeated use of highly developed skills on relatively similar, though complex, problems. People rarely want their surgeons, accountants, airline pilots, maintenance personnel, or nuclear plant operators to be very creative, except in emergencies. . . . Finding and developing extraordinary talent is thus the first critical managerial prerequisite. McKinsey long focused on only the top 1 percent of graduates from the top five business schools and screened heavily from these. . . .

INTENSE TRAINING, MENTORING, AND PEER PRESSURE

These factors literally force professionals to the top of their knowledge ziggurat. The best students go to the most demanding schools. The top graduate schools—whether in law, business, engineering, science, or medicine—further reselect and drive these students with greater challenges and with 100-hour work weeks. Then upon graduation the best of the survivors go back to even more intense "boot camps" in medical internships, law associate programs, or other outrageously demanding training situations as pilots, consultants, or technical specialists. The result is to drive the best professionals up a learning curve that is steeper than anyone else's. . . . The keys are forcing professional trainees' growth with constantly heightened (preferably customer-induced) complexity, thoroughly planned mentoring, high rewards for performance, and strong stimuli to understand, systematize, and advance their professional disciplines. . . .

CONSTANTLY INCREASING CHALLENGES

Intellect grows most when challenged. Hence, heavy internal competition and constant performance appraisal are common. . . . The best organizations constantly push their professionals beyond the comfort of their catalogued book knowledge, simulation models, and controlled laboratories. They relentlessly drive associates to deal with the more complex intellectual realms of live customers, real operating systems, and highly differentiated external environments and cultural differences. They insist on and actively support mentoring by those nearest the top of their fields. And they reward associates for their competencies. Mediocre organizations do not.

MANAGING AN ELITE

Each profession tends to regard itself as an elite. Members look to their profession and to their peers to determine codes for behavior and acceptable performance standards. They often disdain the values and evaluations of those "outside their discipline." This is the source of many professional organizations' problems. Professionals tend to surround themselves with people having similar backgrounds and values. Unless consciously fractured, these discipline-based cocoons quickly become inward-looking bureaucracies, resistant to change, and detached from customers. Because professionals' knowledge is their power base, many are reluctant to share it with others unless there are powerful inducements. . . .

Because they have unique knowledge and have been trained as an elite, professionals tend to regard their judgment in all realms as sacrosanct. Professionals hesitate to subordinate themselves to others to support organizational goals not completely congruent with their special viewpoint. This is why most professional firms operate as partnerships and not hierarchies, and why it is so hard for them to adopt a distinctive strategy. . . .

FEW SCALE ECONOMIES?

Yet many enterprises seem to overlook or violate all these critical characteristics in developing, leveraging, and measuring professionals' capabilities. One reason: conventional wisdom has long held that there are few scale economies—which allow leverages—in professional activities. A pilot can only handle one aircraft; a great chef can cook only so many different dishes at once; a top researcher can conduct only so many unique experiments; a doctor can only diagnose one patient's illness at a time; and so on. In such situations, adding professionals at a minimum multiplies costs at the same rates as outputs. In fact, most often, growth brought *diseconomies* of scale as the bureaucracies coordinating, monitoring, or supporting the professionals actually expanded faster than the professional base. . . .

But new technologies and management approaches now enable firms to develop, capture, and leverage intellectual resources to much higher levels. The keys are: (1) to design organizations and technology systems around *intellectual flows* rather than command and control concepts; (2) to develop performance measurements and incentive systems that reward managers for developing intellectual assets and customer value—and not just for producing current profits and using physical assets more efficiently. . . .

The crux of leveraging intellect is to focus one's own resources on those things—important to customers—where the company can create uniquely high value for its customers. Conceptually, this means disaggregating both corporate staff activities and the value chain into manageable intellectual clusters. . . . Such activities can either be performed internally or outsourced depending on one's own relative costs and competencies. For maximum effectiveness, a company should concentrate its own resources and executive time on those few activities where it performs at "best-in-world" levels. . . .

ORGANIZING AROUND INTELLECT

Exploiting these new intellectually based strategies often calls for new organization concepts. . . . we expect much greater use of four [of these] basic organizational forms that leverage professional intellect uniquely well. These are the infinitely flat, inverted, starburst, and spider's web forms. . . .

All the forms tend to push responsibility outward to the point at which the company contacts the customer. All tend to flatten the organization and remove layers of hierarchy. All seek faster, more responsive action to deal with the customization and personalization an affluent and complex marketplace demands. All require breaking away from traditional thinking about lines of command, one person–one boss structures, the center as a directing force, and management of physical assets as the key to success. But each differs substantially in its purpose and management. . . .

"INFINITELY FLAT" ORGANIZATIONS

[The] infinitely flat organizations [are] so called because there is no inherent limit to their span. . . . Single centers in such organizations presently can coordinate anywhere from 20 to 18,000 individual nodes. Common examples include highly dispersed fast-food, brokerage, shipping, mail order, or airline flight operations.

Several other characteristics are also important. The nodes themselves rarely communicate with each other, operating quite independently. The center rarely needs to give direct orders to the line organization. Instead, it is primarily an information source, a communications coordinator, and a reference desk for unusual inquiries. Lower organizational levels generally connect into the center to obtain information to improve their performances, rather than for instructions or specific guidance. Most operating rules are programmed into the system and changed automatically by software. . . . For example, Merrill Lynch's 480 domestic brokerage offices each connect directly into the parent's central information office to satisfy the bulk of their information and analytic needs. . . .

Infinitely flat organizations present certain inherent management problems. Lower-level personnel wonder how to advance in a career path when there is no "up." Those at the center require totally different skills from those at the nodes. Traditional job evaluation systems break down, and new compensation systems based on professional capability, individual performance, and customer satisfaction become imperative. . . .[T]he essence of . . . management is capturing,

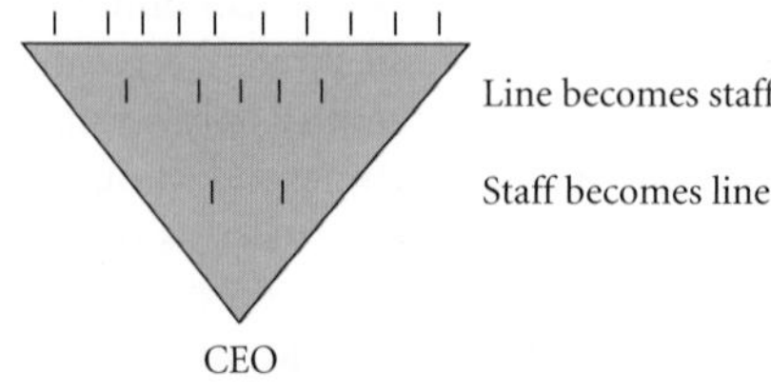

FIGURE 1
THE INVERTED ORGANIZATION

analyzing, and disseminating the most detailed possible level of customer-relevant information from the center to the contact nodes.

THE INVERTED ORGANIZATION

In the inverted form, the major locus of *both* knowledge and the conversion of knowledge into solutions is at the point of contact with customers, not at the center. Hospitals or medical clinics, therapeutic care-giving units, or consulting-engineering firms provide typical examples. These "nodes" tend to be highly professional and self-sufficient. Accordingly, there is no need for direct linkage between the nodes. When critical knowledge about operations diffuses, it usually does so informally from node to node—or formally from node to center—the opposite of the infinitely flat organization. . . .

In inverted organizations, the former line hierarchy becomes a "support" structure, only intervening in extreme emergencies—as might the CEO of a hospital or the chief pilot of an airline (see Figure 1). The function of "line" managers becomes bottleneck breaking, culture development, communication of values, developing special studies, consulting on request, expediting resource movements, and providing service economies of scale. . . . Generally . . . what was "line" (order giving) management now performs essentially "staff" (analytical or support) activities.

A well-known example is NovaCare, the largest provider of rehabilitation care in the United States and one of the fastest-growing health care companies of the last decade. With its central resource—well-trained physical, occupational, and speech therapists in short supply—NovaCare provides the business infrastructure for over 4,000 therapists, arranging and merging contracts with nursing homes and chains, handling accounting and credit activities, providing training updates, and stabilizing and enhancing therapists' earnings. However, the key to performance is the therapists' knowledge and their capability to deliver this individually to patients. . . .

The inverted organization poses certain unique challenges. The apparent loss of formal authority can be very traumatic for former "line managers." Given acknowledged formal power, contact people may tend to act ever more like specialists with strictly "professional" outlooks, and to resist any set of organization rules or business norms. Given their predilections, contact people often don't stay current with details about the firm's own complex internal systems. And their empowerment without adequate information and controls (embedded in the firm's technology systems) can be extremely dangerous. A classic example is the rapid decline of People Express, which enjoyed highly empowered and motivated point people, but lacked the systems or computer infrastructures to enable them to self-coordinate as the organization grew. . . .

THE STARBURST

Another highly leverageable form, the starburst, serves well when there is highly specialized and valuable intellect at *both* the nodes and the center. Starbursts are common in creative organizations that constantly peel off more permanent, but separate, units like shooting stars from their core competencies (see Figure 2). These spin-offs remain partially or wholly owned by the parent, usually can raise external resources independently, and are controlled primarily by market mechanisms. Some common examples . . . include movie studios, mutual fund groups, or venture capitalists. . . .

Unlike holding companies, starbursts contain some central core of intellectual competency. They are not merely banks or portfolio managers. The nodes—essentially separate permanent business units, not individuals or temporary clusters—have continuing relationships with given marketplaces and are the locus of important, specialized, market, or production knowledge. The nodes may in time spin out further enterprises from their core. . . .

Starburst organizations work well when the core embodies an expensive or complex set of competencies and houses a few knowledgeable risk takers who realize they cannot micromanage the diverse entities at the nodes. . . . Usually they occur in environments where entrepreneurship—not

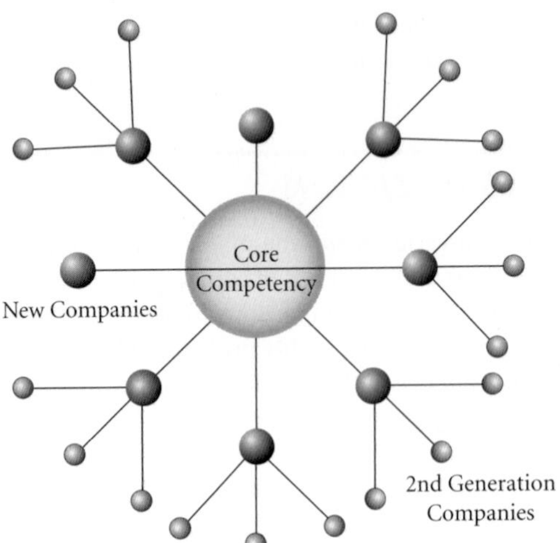

FIGURE 2
THE STARBURST ORGANIZATION

merely flexible response—is critical. . . . In addition to maintaining the core competency, the corporate center generally manages the culture, sets broad priorities, selects key people, and raises resources more efficiently than could the nodes. Unlike conglomerates, starbursts maintain some cohesive, constantly renewed, and critical intellectual competencies at their center.

The classic problem of this organizational form is that managements often lose faith in their freestanding "shooting stars." After some time they try to consolidate functions in the name of efficiency or economies of scale—as some movie studios, HP, TI, and 3M did to their regret—and only recover by reversing such policies.

THE "SPIDER'S WEB"

The spider's web form is a true network. (The term "spider's web" avoids confusion with other "network-like" forms, particularly those that are more akin to holding company or matrix organizations.) In the spider's web there is often *no* intervening hierarchy or order-giving center among the nodes. In fact it may be hard to define where the center is. The locus of intellect is highly dispersed, residing largely at the contact nodes (as in the inverted organization). However, solutions are developed around a project or problem that requires the nodes to interact intimately or to seek others who happen to have the knowledge or special capabilities that a particular problem requires.

The purest example of a spider's web is the Internet, which is managed by no one. Other common examples include most open markets, securities exchanges, library consortia, diagnostic teams, research, or political action groups.

Individual nodes may operate quite independently, when it is not essential to tap the knowledge of other sources to solve a problem efficiently. On a given project there may or may not be a single authority center. Often decisions will merely occur through informal processes if the parties agree. . . . This form of organizing releases the imaginations of many different searchers in diverse locations, multiplies the numbers of possible opportunity encounters, and encourages the formation of entirely new solutions from a variety of disciplines.

While they are usually effective for problem finding and analysis, spider's webs present important challenges when used for decision making. Dawdling is common, as nodes work on refining their specialist solutions instead of solving the complete problem together. Assigning credit for intellectual contributions is difficult, and cross-competition among nodes can inhibit the sharing on which such networks depend (see Figure 3).

Each organization form performs best for a specific set of intellectual tasks. Hence most large enterprises will require a mixture of these basic building blocks, combined with more traditional hierarchical structures (see Figure 4).

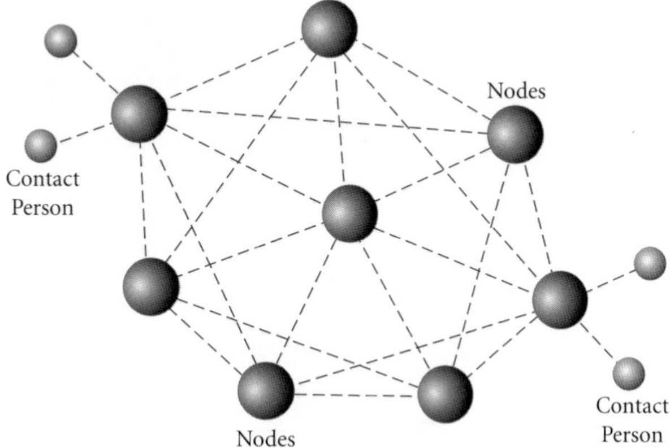

FIGURE 3
SPIDER'S WEB ORGANIZATIONS

TYPE OF INTELLECT	INFINITELY FLAT	INVERTED	STARBURST	SPIDER'S WEB
Cognitive (know what)	Deep knowledge and information at center	Primary intellect at nodes, support services from center	Depth at center (technical) and (markets) at the nodes	Dispersed, brought together for projects
Advanced Skill (know how)	Programmed into systems	Professionalized skills informally transferred node to node	Transferred from center to node, then node to node via the core	Latent until a project assembles a skill collection
Systems Knowledge (know why)	Systems experts at the center. Customer knowledge at the nodes	Systems and customer expertise at the nodes	Split: between central technical competency at the core, systematic market knowledge at nodes	Discovered in interaction or created via search enabled by the network
Motivated Creativity (care why)	Frees employees from routine for more skilled work	Great professional autonomy	Entrepreneurial incentives	Personal interest, leveraged through active interdependence stimulation

FIGURE 4
HOW DIFFERENT ORGANIZING FORMS DEVELOP INTELLECT

READING 15.3

Balancing the Professional Service Firm* BY DAVID H. MAISTER

The topic of managing professional service firms (PSFs) (including law, consulting, investment banking, accountancy, architecture, engineering, and others) has been relatively neglected by management researchers. . . . Yet in recent years large (if not giant) PSFs have emerged in most of the professional service industries. . . .

The professional service firm is the ultimate embodiment of that familiar phrase "Our assets are our people." Frequently, a PSF tends to sell to its clients the services of particular individuals (or a team of such individuals) more than the services of the firm. Professional services usually

*Reprinted with deletions from the *Sloan Management Review* (Fall, 1982), pp. 15–29, by permission of the publisher. Copyright 1982 by the Sloan Management Review Association, all rights reserved.

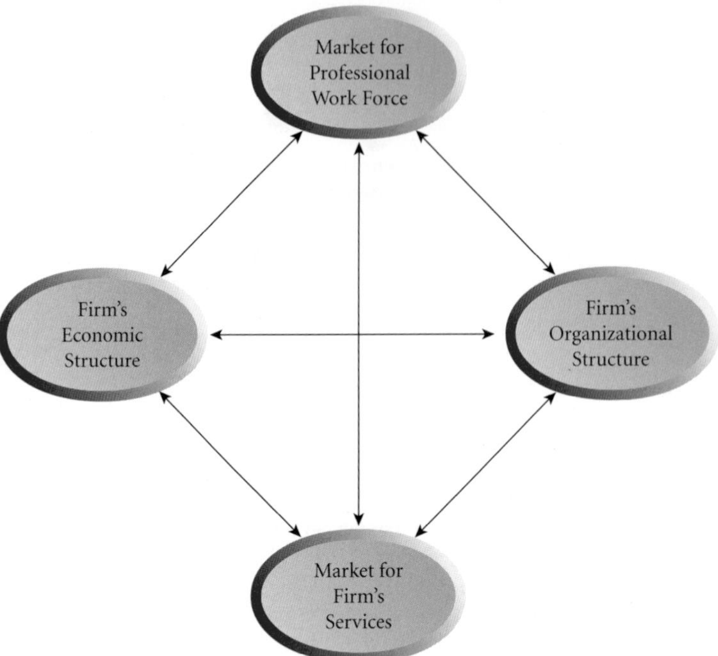

FIGURE 1
FRAMEWORK FOR ANALYZING THE PSF

involve a high degree of interaction with the client, together with a high degree of customization. Both of these characteristics demand that the firm attract (and retain) highly skilled individuals. The PSF, therefore, competes in two markets simultaneously: the "output" market for its services and the "input" market for its productive resources—the professional workforce. It is the need to balance the often conflicting demands and constraints imposed by these two markets that constitutes the special challenge for managers of the professional service firm.

This article explores the interaction of these forces inside the professional service firm, and examines some of the major variables that firm management can attempt to manipulate in order to bring these forces into balance. The framework employed for this examination is shown in Figure 1, which illustrates the proposition that balancing the demands of the two markets is accomplished through the firm's economic and organizational structures. All four of these elements—the two markets and the two structures—are tightly interrelated. By examining each in turn, we shall attempt to identify the major variables which form the links shown in Figure 1. First, the article will examine the typical organizational structure of the firm; second, it will explore the economic structure and its relation to other elements. It shall then consider the market for professional labor, and finally discuss the market for the firm's services. As we shall see, successful PSF management is a question of balance among the four elements of Figure 1.

THE ORGANIZATIONAL STRUCTURE OF THE PSF

The archetypal structure of the professional service firm is an organization containing three professional levels which serve as a normal or expected career path. In a consulting organization, these levels might be labeled junior consultant, manager, and vice-president. In a CPA firm they might be referred to as staff accountant, manager, and partner. Law firms tend to have only two levels, associate and partner, although there is an increasing tendency in large law firms to formally recognize what has long been an informal distinction between junior and senior partners. Whatever the precise structure, nearly all PSFs have the pyramid form shown in Figure 2.

There is nothing magical about the common occurrence of three levels (a greater or lesser number may be found), but it is instructive to consider other organizations that have this pattern. One example is the university which has assistant professors, associate professors, and full professors. These ranks may be signs of status as well as function (reminding us of another

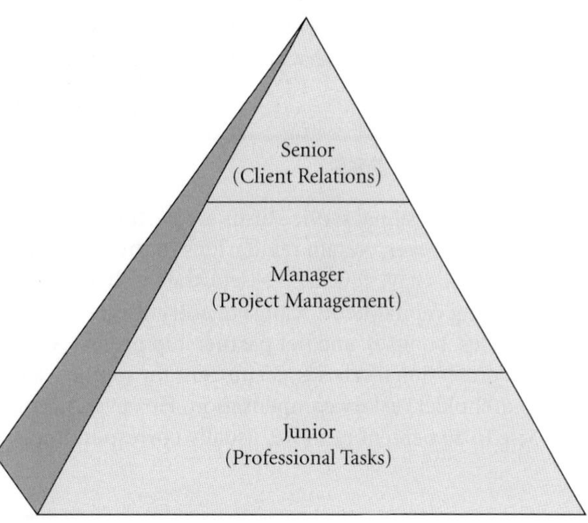

FIGURE 2
THE PROFESSIONAL PYRAMID

three-level status structure: the common people, the peerage, and royalty). Another analogy is found in the organization of the medieval craftsman's shop which had apprentices, journeymen, and master craftsmen. Indeed, the early years of an individual's association with a PSF are usually viewed as an apprenticeship: the senior craftsmen repay the hard work and assistance of the juniors by teaching them their craft.

PROJECT TEAM STRUCTURE

What determines the shape or architecture of the organization—the relative mix of juniors, managers, and seniors that the organization requires? Fundamentally, this depends on the nature of the professional services that the firm provides, and how these services are delivered. Because of their customized nature, most professional activities are organized on a project basis: the professional service firms are the job shops of the service sector. The project nature of the work means that there are basically three major activities in the delivery of professional services: client relations, project management, and the performance of the detailed professional tasks.

In most PSFs, primary responsibility for these three tasks is allocated to the three levels of the organization: seniors (partners or vice-presidents) are responsible for client relations; managers, for the day-to-day supervision and coordination of projects; and juniors, for the many technical tasks necessary to complete the study. In the vernacular, the three levels are "the finders, the minders and the grinders" of the business.* Naturally, such an allocation of tasks need not (indeed, should not) be as rigid as this suggests. In a well-run PSF, juniors are increasingly given "manager" tasks to perform (in order to test their competence and worthiness to be promoted to the manager level), and managers are gradually given tasks that enable them to develop client-relations skills to prepare for promotion to the senior level. Nevertheless, it is still meaningful to talk of "senior tasks," "manager tasks," and "junior tasks."

CAPACITY PLANNING

The required shape of the PSF is thus primarily influenced by the mix of client relations, project management, and professional tasks involved in the firm's projects. If the PSF is a job shop, then its professional staff members are its "machines" (productive resources). As with any job shop, a balance

*This characteristic is, of course, simplified. Additional "levels" or functions can be identified at both the top and the bottom of the pyramid. To the top we can add those individuals responsible for managing the firm (rather than managing projects). At the bottom of the pyramid lie both "nonprofessional" support staff and trainees.

must be established between the types of work performed and the number of different types of "machines" (people) that are required. The PSF is a "factory," and the firm must plan its capacity. . . .

THE ECONOMICS OF THE PSF

Most professional service firms are partnerships; some are corporations. Regardless of the precise form, however, certain regularities in the economic structure are observable. For example, since most PSFs have few fixed assets, they only require capital to fund accounts receivable and other working capital items. Consequently, the vast majority of revenues are disbursed in the form of salaries, bonuses, and net partnership profits. A typical division of revenues might be 33 percent for professional salaries, 33 percent for support staff and overhead, and 33 percent for senior (or shareholder) salary compensation. However, in some PSFs, partnership salary and profits might rise to 50 percent or more, usually corresponding to lower support staff and overhead costs.

GENERATING REVENUES

If revenues are typically disbursed in this way, how are they generated?. . . The relevant variable is, of course, the billing rate—the hourly charge to clients for the services of individuals at different levels of the hierarchy. The ratio between the lowest and highest rates in some firms can exceed 3 or 4 to 1. The "rewards of partnership" come only in part from the high rates that top professionals can charge their clients. Partners' rewards are also derived, in large part, from the firm's ability, through its project team structure, to *leverage* the professional skills of the seniors with the efforts of juniors. As the managing senior of a top consulting firm observed, "How is it that a young MBA, straight from graduate school, can give advice to top corporate officers?" The answer lies in the synergy of the PSF's project team. Acting independently, the juniors could not "bill out" the results of their efforts at the rates that can be charged by the PSF. The firm can obtain higher rates for the juniors' efforts because they are combined with the expertise and guidance of the seniors. . . .

THE BILLING MULTIPLE

It is also instructive to compare the net weighted billing rate to compensation levels within the firm. This (conventional) calculation is known as the billing multiple, and is calculated (for either the firm or an individual) as the billing rate per hour divided by the total compensation per hour. . . . The average multiple for most firms is between 2.5 and 4.

The appropriate billing multiple that the firm can achieve will, of course, be influenced by the added value that the firm provides and by the relative supply and demand conditions for the firm's services. The market for the firm's services will determine the fees it can command for a given project. The firm's costs will be determined by its ability to deliver the service with a "profitable" mix of junior, manager, and senior time. If the firm . . . can find a way to deliver the service with a higher proportion of juniors to seniors, it will be able to achieve lower costs and hence a higher multiple. The project team structure of the firm is, therefore, an important component of firm profitability.

The billing multiple is intimately related to the breakeven economics of the firm. If total professional salaries are taken as an amount \$*Y*, and support staff and overhead cost approximate, say, an equivalent amount \$*Y*, then breakeven will be attained when the firm bills \$2*Y*. This could be attained by charging clients a multiple of 2 for professional services, but only if all available time was billed out. If the firm wishes to break even at 50 percent target utilization (a common figure in many PSFs), then the required net billing multiple will be 4. . . .

THE PSF AND THE MARKET FOR PROFESSIONAL LABOR

One of the key characteristics of the PSF is that the three levels (junior, manager, senior) constitute a well-defined career path. Individuals joining the organization normally begin at the bottom, with strong expectations of progressing through the organization at some pace agreed to (explicitly or implicitly) in advance. While this pace may not be a rigid one ("up or out in the *X* years"), both the individual and the organization usually share strong expectations about what constitutes a reasonable period of time. Individuals that are not promoted within this period will seek greener pastures elsewhere, either by their own choice or career ambitions or at the strong suggestion of those who do not consider them promotable. Intermediate levels in the hierarchy are not considered by the individual or the organization as career positions. It is this characteristic, perhaps more than any other, that distinguishes the PSF from other types of organizations.

PROMOTION POLICY

While there are many considerations that attract young professionals to a particular firm, career opportunities within the firm usually play a large role. Two dimensions of this rate of progress are important: the normal amount of time spent at each level before being considered for promotion and the "odds of making it" (the proportion promoted). These promotion policy variables perform an important screening function. Not all young professionals are able to develop the managerial and client-relations skills required at the higher levels. While good recruiting procedures may reduce the degree of screening required through the promotion process, they can rarely eliminate the need for the promotion process to serve this important function. The "risk of not making it" also serves the firm by placing pressure on junior personnel to work hard and succeed. This pressure can be an important motivating tool in light of the discretion which many PSF professionals have over their working schedules. . . .

ACCOMMODATING RAPID GROWTH

. . . What adjustments can be made to allow faster growth? Basically, there are four strategies. First, the firm can devote more attention and resources to its hiring process so that a higher proportion of juniors can be routinely promoted to managers. (In effect, this shifts the quality-of-personnel screen from the promotion system to the hiring system, where it is often more difficult and speculative.) Second, the firm can attempt to hasten the "apprenticeship" process through more formal training and professional development programs, rather than the " learn by example" and mentoring relationships commonly found in smaller firms and those growing at a more leisurely pace. In fact, it is the rate of growth, rather than the size of the firm, which necessitates formal development programs. . . .*

The third mechanism that the firm can adopt to accelerate its target growth rate is to make use of "lateral hires": bringing in experienced professionals at other than the junior level. In most PSFs, this strategy is avoided because of its adverse effect upon the morale of junior personnel, who tend to view such actions as reducing their own chances for promotion. Even if these have been accelerated by the fast growth rate, juniors will still tend to feel that they have been less than fairly dealt with.

Modifying the project team structure is the final strategy for accommodating rapid growth without throwing out of balance the relationships between organizational structure, promotion incentives, and economic structure. In effect, the firm would alter the mix of senior, manager, and junior time devoted to a project. This strategy will be discussed in a later section.

TURNOVER

. . . In most PSF industries, one or more firms can be identified that have a high target rate of turnover (or alternatively, choose to grow at less than their optimal rate). Yet individuals routinely join these organizations knowing that the odds of "making it" are very low. Such "churning" strategies have some clear disadvantages *and* benefits for the PSF itself. One of the benefits is that the firm's partners (or shareholders) can routinely earn the surplus value of the juniors without having to repay them in the form of promotion. The high turnover rate also allows a significant degree of screening so that only the "best" stay in the organization. Not surprisingly, firms following this strategy tend to be among the most prestigious in their industry.

---

*Speeding the development of individuals so that the firm can grow faster is, of course, not the only role for formal training programs. They can also be a device to allow the firm to hire less (initially) qualified and hence lower wage individuals, thereby reducing its costs for juniors.

This last comment gives us a clue as to why such firms are able to maintain this strategy over time. For many recruits, the experience, training, and association with a prestigious firm compensate for poor promotion opportunities. Young professionals view a short period of time at such a firm as a form of " post-postgraduate" degree, and often leave for prime positions they could not have achieved (as quickly) by another route. Indeed, most of the prestigious PSFs following this strategy not only encourage this, but also provide active "outplacement" assistance. Apart from the beneficial effects that such activities provide in recruiting the next generation of juniors, such "alumni/ae" are often the source of future business for the PSF when they recommend that their corporate employers hire their old firm (which they know and understand) over other competitors. The ability to place ex-staff in prestigious positions is one of the prerequisites of a successful churning strategy. . . .

THE MARKET FOR THE FIRM'S SERVICES

The final element in our model is the market for the firm's services. We have already explored some of the ways in which this market is linked to the firm's economic structure (through the billing rates the firm charges) and to the organizational structure (through the project team structure and target growth rate).

We must add to our model one of the most basic linkages in the dynamics of the PSF: the direct link between the market for professional labor and the market for the firm's services. The key variable that links these two markets is the quality of professional labor that the firm requires and can attract. Earlier, when we considered the factors that attract professionals to a given PSF, we omitted a major variable that often enters into the decision process: the types of projects undertaken by the firm. Top professionals are likely to be attracted to the firm that engages in exciting or challenging projects, or that provides opportunities for professional fulfillment and development. In turn, firms engaged in such projects *need* to attract the best professionals. It is, therefore, necessary to consider different types of professional service activity.

PROJECT TYPES

While there are many dimensions which may distinguish one type of professional service activity from another, one in particular is crucial: the degree of customization required in the delivery of the service. To explore this, we will characterize professional service projects into three types: "Brains," "Gray Hair," and "Procedure."

In the first type (Brains), the client's problem is likely to be extremely complex, perhaps at the forefront of professional or technical knowledge. The PSF that targets this market will be attempting to sell its services on the basis of the high professional craft of its staff. In essence, this firm's appeal to its market is "hire us because we're smart." The key elements of this type of professional service are creativity, innovation, and the pioneering of new approaches, concepts, or techniques—in effect, new solutions to new problems. [See next chapter on the innovative context.]

Gray Hair projects may require highly customized "output," but they usually involve a lesser degree of innovation and creativity than a Brains' project. The general nature of the problem is familiar, and the activities necessary to complete the project may be similar to those performed on other projects. Clients with Gray Hair problems seek out PSFs with experience in their particular type of problem. The PSF sells its knowledge, its experience, and its judgment. In effect, it is saying: "Hire us because we have been through this before. We have practice in solving this type of problem."

The third type of project (Procedure) usually involves a well-recognized and familiar type of problem, at least within the professional community. While some customization is still required, the steps necessary to accomplish this are somewhat programmatic. Although clients may have the ability and resources to perform the work themselves, they may turn to the PSF because it can perform the service more efficiently; because it is an outsider; or because the clients' staff capabilities may be employed better elsewhere. In essence, the PSF is selling its procedures, its efficiency, and its availability: "Hire us because we know how to do this and can deliver it effectively."

PROJECT TEAM STRUCTURE

One of the most significant differences between the three types of projects is the project team structure required to deliver the firm's services. Brains projects are usually denoted by an extreme job-shop operation, involving highly skilled and highly paid professionals. Few procedures are routinizable: each project is a "one-off." Accordingly, the opportunities for leveraging the top professionals with juniors are relatively limited. Even though such projects may involve significant data collection and analysis (usually done by juniors), even these activities cannot be clearly specified in advance and require the involvement of at least middle-level (project management) professionals on a continuous basis. Consequently, the ratio of junior time to middle-level and senior time on Brains projects tends to be low. The project team structure of a firm with a high proportion of Brains projects will tend to have a relatively low emphasis on juniors, with a corresponding impact on the shape of the organization.

Since the problems to be addressed in Gray Hair projects are somewhat familiar, some of the tasks to be performed (particularly the early ones) are known in advance and can be specified and delegated. More juniors can be employed to accomplish these tasks, which are then assembled and jointly evaluated at some middle stage of the process. Unlike the "pure job-shop" nature of Brains projects, the appropriate process to create and deliver a Gray Hair project more closely resembles a disconnected assembly line.

Procedure projects usually involve the highest proportion of junior time relative to senior time, and hence imply a different organizational shape for firms that specialize in such projects. The problems to be addressed in such projects, and the steps necessary to complete the analysis, diagnosis, and conclusions, are usually sufficiently well established so that they can be easily delegated to junior staff (with supervision). Whereas in Gray Hair projects senior- or middle-level staff must evaluate the results of one stage of the project before deciding how to proceed, in Procedure projects the range of possible outcomes for some steps may be so well known that the appropriate responses can be "programmed." The operating procedure takes on even more of the characteristics of an assembly line.

While the three categories described are only points along a spectrum of project types, it is a simple task in any PSF industry to identify types of problems that fit these categories. The choice that the firm makes in its mix of project types is one of the most important variables available to balance the firm. As we have shown, this choice determines the firm's project team structure, thereby influencing significantly the economic and organizational structures of the firm.

CONCLUSIONS: BALANCING THE PROFESSIONAL SERVICE FIRM

Figure 3 summarizes our review of the four major elements involved in balancing the PSF and the major variables linking these elements. What may we conclude from this review? Our discussion has shown that the four elements are, indeed, tightly linked. The firm cannot change one element without making corresponding changes in one or more of the other three. . . .

In performing these balance analyses, the firm must distinguish between the "levers" (variables that it controls) and the "rocks" (variables substantially constrained by the forces of the market). . . .

Perhaps the most significant management variable is the mix of projects undertaken and the implications this has for the project team structure. This variable is a significant force in influencing the economics of the firm, its organizational structure, and both markets. The project team structure as defined in this article (i.e., the *average* or typical proportion of time required from professionals at different levels) has not been a variable that is routinely monitored by PSF management. However, as we have shown, its role in balancing the firm is critical.

It is possible, and not uncommon, for the firm's project team structure to change over time. If it is possible to deliver the firm's services with a greater proportion of juniors, this will reduce the costs of the project. Competition in the market will, over time, require the firm to seek lower costs for projects, thus creating opportunities for more juniors to be used on projects that required a high proportion of senior time in the past. Projects that, in the past, had Brains or Gray Hair characteristics may be accomplished as Procedure projects in future years.*

*This argument suggests that there is a "life cycle " to professional "products" in the same way that such cycles exist for tangible products.

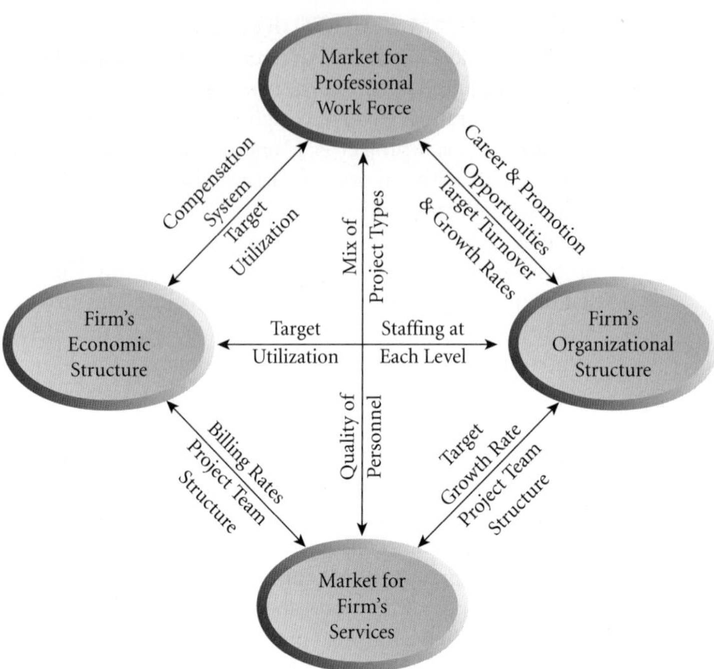

FIGURE 3
BALANCING THE PSF

When considering new projects to undertake, it is usually more profitable for the firm to engage in a project similar to one recently performed for a previous client. The knowledge, expertise, and basic approaches to the problem that were developed (often through significant personal and financial investment) can be capitalized upon by applying them to a similar or related problem. Frequently, the second project can be billed out to the client at a similar (or only slightly lower) rate, since the client perceives (and receives) something equally custom-tailored: the solution to his or her problem. However, the savings in PSF costs in delivering this customization are not all shared with the client (if, indeed, any are). The firm thus makes its most money by "leading the market": selling a service with reproducible, standardizable elements as a fully customized service at a fully customized price.

Unfortunately, even before the market catches up and refuses to bear the fully customized price, the firm may encounter an internal behavior problem. While it is in the best interest of the *firm* to undertake similar or repetitive engagements, often this does not coincide with the desires of the *individuals* involved. Apart from any reasons of status, financial rewards, or fulfillment derived from serving the clients' needs, most individuals join PSFs to experience the professional challenge and variety and to avoid routine repetition. While individuals may be content to undertake a similar project for the second or third time, they will not be for the fourth, sixth, or eighth. Yet it is in the interest of the firm (particularly if the market has not yet caught up) to take advantage of the experience and expertise that it has acquired. One solution, of course, is to convert the past experience and expertise of the individual into the expertise of the firm by accepting a similar project, but utilizing a greater proportion of juniors on it. Besides requiring a lesser commitment of time from the experienced seniors, this device serves to train the juniors.

For all these reasons, we might suspect that the proportion of juniors to seniors required by the firm *in a particular practice area* will tend to increase over time. If this is allowed to proceed without corresponding adjustments in the range of practice areas, the project team structure of the firms will be altered, causing significant impacts on the economics and organization of the firm. The dangers of failing to monitor the project team structure are thus clearly revealed. Examples of this failure abound in many PSF industries. One consulting firm that learned how to increasingly utilize junior professionals began to aggressively hire new junior staff. After a reasonable period of time for the promotion decision, the firm realized that, at its current growth rate, it could not promote its "normal" proportion of promotion candidates: it did not need as many partners and managers in relation to the number of juniors it now had. Morale and productivity in the junior ranks suffered. . . . Successful PSF management is a question of balance.

READING 15.4

Covert Leadership: Notes on Managing Professionals* BY HENRY MINTZBERG

Bramwell Tovey, artistic director and conductor of the Winnipeg Symphony Orchestra, may not seem like your typical manager. Indeed, in comparison with, say, the usual *New Yorker* cartoon of the nicely manicured executive surrounded by performance charts sitting in a corner office, orchestra conducting may seem like a rather quirky form of management. Yet as knowledge work has grown in importance—and as more and more work is done by trained and trusted professionals—the way Bramwell leads his orchestra may illustrate a good deal of what today's managing is all about.

I have been studying the work of managers on and off throughout my career, more recently spending days with a wide variety of managers. Because the metaphor of the orchestra leader is so often used to represent what business leaders do, I thought that spending time with a conductor might prove instructive. The day with Bramwell was intended to explore, and perhaps explode, the myth of the manager as the great conductor at the podium—the leader in complete control.

When you reflect on it, the symphony orchestra is like many other professional organizations—for example, consulting firms and hospitals—in that it is structured around the work of highly trained individuals who know what they have to do and just do it. Such professionals hardly need in-house procedures or time-study analysts to tell them how to do their jobs. That fundamental reality challenges many preconceptions that we have about management and leadership. Indeed, in such environments, *covert leadership* may matter more than overt leadership.

WHO CONTROLS?

When the maestro walks up to the podium and raises his baton, the musicians respond in unison. Another motion, and they all stop. It's the image of absolute control—management captured perfectly in caricature. And yet it is all a great myth.

What does Bramwell Tovey really control? What choices does he really have? Bramwell says his job consists of selecting the program, determining how the pieces are played, choosing guest artists, staffing the orchestra, and managing some external relations. (Conductors apparently vary in their propensity to engage in external work. Bramwell enjoys it.) The administrative and finance side of the orchestra is handled by an executive director—at the time, Max Tapper, who comanaged the orchestra with Bramwell.

So much of the classic literature on management has been about the need for *controlling,* which is about designing systems, creating structures, and making choices. There are systems galore in symphony orchestras, all meant to control the work. But they are systems inherent to the profession, not to management. Bramwell inherited them all. The same can be said about structures; in fact, even more so. Just look at how everyone sits, in prearranged rows, according to a very strict and externally imposed pecking order; how they tune their instruments before playing and stomp their feet after a good solo rehearsal. These rituals imply a high degree of structure, and yet they all come with the job.

The profession itself, not the manager, supplies much of the structure and coordination. While the work of some experts takes place in small teams and task forces with a great deal of informal communication, professional work here consists of applying standard operating routines: the composer started work with a blank sheet of paper, but the musicians start with the composer's score. The object is to play it well—interpreting it but hardly inventing something new. Indeed, the work, the workers, their tools—almost everything in a symphony is highly standardized. . . .

---

*Reprinted with deletions from "Covert Leadership: Notes on Managing Professionals," *Harvard Business Review,* November-December 1998, 140–147.

In organizations where standard operating routines are applied, the experts work largely on their own, free of the need to coordinate with their colleagues. This happens almost automatically. . . . They are able to coordinate their efforts because of the standardization of their skills and by what they were trained to expect from each other. . . . in the orchestra, even though the musicians play together, each and every one of them plays alone. They each follow a score and know precisely when to contribute. The instrument not only identifies each player but also distinguishes him or her from the other musicians.

Most professional workers require little direct supervision from managers. . . . Surgeons [for example] hardly expect a medical chief or a hospital director to appear, let alone set the pace for one of their operations. That observation may not seem to hold for a symphony orchestra, where the conductor certainly sets the pace. But it is a lot more relevant than it might at first appear.

Along with *controlling* and *coordinating, directing* is one of the oldest and most common words used to describe managerial work. Among other things, directing means issuing directives, delegating tasks, and authorizing decisions. Yet despite his designation as orchestra director, Bramwell's actual "directing" is highly circumscribed. The day I was with him, he hardly ran around giving orders. Indeed, he explained that even comments made during rehearsals have to be aimed at sections rather than at individuals. . . . conducting has changed considerably, Bramwell points out, since the days of the great autocrats like Toscanini.

A great deal of the conventional manager's control is exercised through formal information. Such information plays a rather limited role for the orchestra conductor. When Bramwell reads or processes information on the job, it is more about scores than about budgets. For him, musical information provides a much more relevant and direct way of judging performance. Just by listening with a trained ear, the conductor knows immediately how well the orchestra has done. Nothing needs to be measured. How could it be? One is led to wonder how much of the music of more conventional managing gets drowned out by the numbers. Of course, there is a need to count here, too—for example, the number of seats occupied in the hall. But by making that the job of the executive director, Bramwell is left free to focus his attention on the real music of managing.

What, then, do conductors control? Although they choose the program and decide how the score should be played, they are constrained by the music that has been written, by the degree to which it can be interpreted, by the sounds the audience will be receptive to, and by the ability and willingness of the orchestra to produce the music. . . . On this particular day, Hindemith and Stravinsky were pulling the strings—of the conductor no less than of the violinists.

Leonard Sayles, who has written extensively on middle management, once reversed the myth of manager as magisterial conductor. In his book *Managerial Behavior: Administration in Complex Organizations* (McGraw-Hill, 1964), Sayles wrote, "[The manager] is like a symphony orchestra conductor, endeavoring to maintain a melodious performance . . . while the orchestra members are having various personal difficulties, stage hands are moving music stands, alternating excessive heat and cold are creating audience and instrument problems, and the sponsor of the concert is insisting on irrational changes in the program." When I read this to Bramwell, he laughed. All of this had happened to him. . . .

Taken together, the various constraints within which the orchestra conductor works describe a very common condition among managers—not being in absolute control of others nor being completely powerless, but functioning somewhere in between.

LEADING IS COVERT

When someone asked Indian-born Zubin Mehta about the difficulties of conducting the Israel Philharmonic, where everyone is said to consider himself or herself a soloist, he reportedly replied, "I'm the only Indian; they're all the chiefs!" Leadership is clearly a tricky business in professional organizations. It was very much on Bramwell's mind in our discussions. He pointed out the qualifications of many of the players—some trained at Juilliard and Curtis, many of them with doctorates in music—and he expressed his discomfort in having to be a leader among ostensible equals. "I think of myself as a soccer coach who plays," he said, adding that "there are moments when I have to exert my authority in a fairly robust fashion . . . although it always puzzles me why I have to."

Watching Bramwell in a day of rehearsals, I saw a lot more *doing* than what we conventionally think of as *leading*. More like a first-line supervisor than a hands-off executive, Bramwell was taking direct and personal charge of what was getting done. Rehearsals themselves are about results—about pace, pattern, tempo, and about smoothing, harmonizing, perfecting. The preparation for a concert could itself be described as a project, with the conductor as a hands-on project manager. This, if you like, is orchestra *operating*, not orchestra *leading*, let alone *directing*.

In the course of my day with Bramwell, which involved many hours of rehearsal, I saw only one overt act of leadership. As the afternoon wore on, Bramwell was dissatisfied. "Come on guys—you're all asleep. You need to do this. It's not good enough." Later, he told me if he had to do that all the time, it would be intrusive. Fortunately, he does not. The fear of censure by the conductor is very powerful, he explained, because "instruments are the extensions of their souls!"

In conducting an orchestra, it seems that *covert leadership*—to use Bramwell's own phrase—may be far more important than overt leadership. Leadership infused everything Bramwell did, however invisibly. His "doing," in other words, was influenced by all the interpersonal concerns in the back of his mind: players' sensitivities, union contracts, and so on. Perhaps we need a greater appreciation in all managerial work of this kind of covert leadership: not leadership actions in and of themselves—motivating, coaching, and all that—but rather unobtrusive actions that infuse all the other things a manager does.

Bramwell, in fact, expressed discomfort with overt leadership. After all, the players are there because they are excellent performers—they all know the score, so to speak. Anyone who cannot play properly can be replaced. Rehearsals are not about enhancing skills but about coordinating the skills that are present.

Nevertheless, a symphony orchestra is not a jazz quartet any more than a racing scull is a canoe. With a large number of people, someone has to take the lead, set the pace, call the stroke. The Russians tried to achieve a leaderless orchestra in the heady days after the revolution, but all they succeeded in doing was relabeling the conductor. Given that all the musicians have to play in perfect harmony, the role of conductor emerges naturally. "I completely control the orchestra's timing—and timing is everything," Bramwell said, maybe because timing is one of the few things he can completely control.

Hence, a good symphony orchestra requires both highly trained professionals and clear personal leadership. And that has the potential to produce cleavage along the line where those two centers of power meet. If the players do not accept the conductor's authority or if the conductor does not accept the players' expertise, the whole system breaks down.

Bramwell's deepest concerns seem to focus precisely on this potential fault line. How can he remain true to his profession, which is music, while properly performing his job, which is management? He seems to find little comfort in that tension. Indeed, he appears most comfortable when he retreats back into the profession. Bramwell loves to play the piano by himself; he also composes music. Both of those activities, it should be noted, are pointedly free of the need to manage or be managed.

THE CULTURE IS IN THE SYSTEM

Leadership is generally exercised on three different levels. At the *individual* level, leaders mentor, coach, and motivate; at the *group* level, they build teams and resolve conflicts; at the *organizational* level, leaders build culture. In most organizations, these three levels are discrete and easily identifiable.

Not so in the symphony orchestra. Here we have a most curious phenomenon: one great big team with approximately 70 people and a single leader. (There are sections, but they have no levels of supervision). The members of this team sit together, in one space, to be heard at one time. How often do customers see the whole product being delivered by the entire operating core of the organization?

As already noted, leadership at the individual level is highly circumscribed. Empowerment is a silly notion here. Musicians hardly need to be empowered by conductors. Inspired maybe—infused with feeling and energy—but not empowered. Leaders energize people by treating them not as detachable "human resources" . . . but as respected members of a cohesive social system. When people are trusted, they do not have to be empowered.

Furthermore, in an orchestra, all these people come together for rehearsals and then disperse. How and where is the culture to be built up? The answers take us back to an earlier point: culture building, too, is covert, infused in everything the conductor does. Moreover, much of this culture is already built into the system. This is a culture of symphony orchestras—not just the Winnipeg Symphony Orchestra. A new player can to a large extent join days before a concert and still harmonize, socially as well as musically. This is not to deny the effects of the conductor's charisma or the effect that Bramwell Tovey can have on the culture of the Winnipeg Symphony Orchestra. It is only to argue that any conductor begins with several centuries of established cultural tradition.

This reality should make the job of leading at the cultural level that much easier. Culture does not have to be created so much as enhanced. People come together knowing what to expect and how they have to work. The leader has to use this culture to define the uniqueness of the group and its spirit in comparison with other orchestras. Indeed, maybe the culture, and not the personal chemistry, is the key to the ostensible "charisma" of all those famous conductors—and perhaps many other managers as well.

This point is reinforced by the fact that about half the time, symphony orchestras are not even led by their own conductors. An outsider comes in to perform the job—a so-called guest conductor. Imagine a "guest manager" almost anywhere else. Yet here it works—sometimes remarkably well—precisely because everything is so programmed by both the composer and the profession. That leaves the conductor free to inject his or her style and energy into the system.

MANAGING ALL AROUND

As noted above, Bramwell Tovey is a doer, right there on the floor. He doesn't read reports in some corner office. (Indeed, he took almost 18 months to give me feedback on my report.) He doesn't take his team off to some distant retreat to climb ropes so that they will come to trust one another. He simply ensures that a group of talented people come together to make beautiful music. In that sense, he is like a first-line supervisor, like a foreman in a factory or a head nurse of a hospital ward.

Yet at the end of our day together, Bramwell also turned around to maintain personal relationships with key stakeholders of the organization, the elite of the symphony's municipal society. In other words, the foreman acting on the factory floor by day becomes the statesman out networking in the Maestro's Circle—a group of the orchestra's most generous supporters—by night. The whole hierarchy gets compressed into the job of just one person.

Connecting to important outsiders—what is called *linking*—is an important aspect of all managerial work. There are always people to be convinced so that deals can be done. In Bramwell's case, this involves networking to represent the orchestra in the community to help it gain legitimacy and support. The other side of the linking role is serving as the conduit for social pressures on the organization. As we have seen, professionals require little direction and supervision. What they do require is protection and support. And so their managers have to pay a lot of attention to managing the boundary condition of the organization. In consulting firms, for example, it is top management that does the selling.

CODA

So what kind of organization is this in which one Indian has to put up with all those chiefs and someone like Bramwell Tovey can be so reticent about having to exercise leadership? More specifically, can we really call Bramwell a manager? Does he even want to be? Will the musicians let him be?

The answer has to be yes.

Uncomfortable as it may be to manage a group of such talented people, I believe Bramwell loves it. After all, he still gets to play often, and, when he does, no one is waving a baton at him. He is able to conduct the pieces he likes best, at least most of the time, and he experiences the extraordinary joy of seeing the work of the organization all come together at the wave of his hand—even if the composer is really pulling the strings. How many managers get this kind of satisfaction from their work?

And not only do the musicians let him do this, they actually encourage him, no matter how disagreeable some of them may find it. After all, they need him as much as he needs them. Bramwell commented, "I don't see myself as a manager. I consider myself more of a lion tamer." It is a good line, always likely to get a good laugh, and it echoes the popular description of managing professionals as "herding cats." But it hardly captures the image of 70 rather tame people sitting in neatly ordered rows ready to play together at the flick of a wand.

So even if he does not see his job as a manager, which I doubt, I certainly do. Get past the myth of the conductor in complete control and you may learn from this example what a good deal of today's managing is all about. Not obedience and harmony, but nuances and constraints. So maybe it is time for conventional managers to step down from their podiums, get rid of their budgeting batons, and see the conductor for who he or she really is. Only then can anyone appreciate the myth of the manager up there as well as the reality of the conductor down here. Perhaps that is how the manager and the organization can make beautiful music together.

CHAPTER 16

Managing Innovation

Although often seen as a high-technology event involving inventor-entrepreneurs, innovation may, of course, occur in high- or low-technology, product or service, large or small organizational situations. Innovation may be thought of as the *first reduction to practice* of an idea in a culture. The more radical the idea, the more traumatic and profound its impact will tend to be. But there are no absolutes. Whatever is newest and most difficult to understand becomes the "high technology" of its age. As Jim Utterback of MIT is fond of pointing out, the delivery of ice was high technology at the turn of the twentieth century, and later it was the production of automobiles. By the same token, 50 years from now, electronics may be considered mundane.

Our focus here, however, is not on innovation per se but on the innovation *context*, that is, the situation in which steady or frequent innovation of a complex nature is an intrinsic part of the organization and the industry segment in which it chooses to operate. Such organizations depend not on a single entrepreneurial individual but on teams of experts molded together.

The innovation context is one in which the organization often must deal with complex technologies or systems under conditions of dynamic change. Typically, major innovations require that a variety of experts work toward a common goal, often led by a single champion or a small group of committed individuals. In recent years much has been learned from research on such organizations. Although this knowledge may seem less structured than that of previous chapters, several dominant themes have emerged.

This chapter opens with a description of the fifth of Mintzberg's structures, here titled the innovative organization. This is the structure that, in a sense, achieves its effectiveness by being inefficient. This reading probes into the unusual ways in which strategies evolve in the context of work that is both highly complex and highly dynamic. Here we see the full flowering of the notion of emergent strategy, culminating in a description of a grass-roots model of the process. We also see here a strategic leadership less concerned with formulating and then implementing strategies and more with managing a process through which strategies almost seem to *form* by themselves.

When it is successful, intrapreneurship—implying the stimulation and diffusion of innovative capacity throughout a larger organization, with many champions of innovations—tends to follow most of Quinn's precepts. As such, it seems to belong more to this context than the entrepreneurial one, which focuses on organizations highly centralized around the initiatives of their single leaders, whether or not innovative.

From this description of the nature of the adhocratic organization, we move to articles on how organizations can manage in the context of innovation. Mark Maletz of Bobson College and Nitin Nohria of Harvard Business School write about "Managing in the Whitespace"— that unoccupied territory in every organization where everything is vague. The keys are to establish legitimacy, mobilize resources, build momentum—and have understanding managers!

The next reading, by Henry W. Chesbrough, of Harvard Business School, contrasts "closed innovation" with "open innovation." Closed innovation is innovation carried out in the confines of the organization, with the organization providing the resources and laying claim to the results. This model dominated thinking in the twentieth century, forming the basic framework for innovation in the large public and private organizations. The internal costs needed to maintain this model, not to mention the rigidity of administrative structures in the face of rapidly shifting business and technological environments, have led organizations to turn to "open innovation." Open innovation mobilizes knowledge and solutions from sources located outside established organization boundaries, and in many cases can deliver results that are superior to innovation that it is kept strictly within the organization. Chesbrough discusses the role of open innovation in funding, generating, or commercializing innovation, as well as the various actors that play a role in each of these activities.

The final reading of this chapter by Joseph Lampel considers the challenge of innovating in 'project-based firms': organizations that focus on the design, development, and delivery of projects. The challenge is particularly acute for project-based firms whose primary business is designing, building, and supplying large projects such as power plants, oil platforms, and mass transit systems. Lampel discusses the entrepreneurial, technical, evaluative, and relational competencies of these firms—and then compares strategies of focusing on core competencies with those of pursuing far-flung opportunities. Lampel argues that the main challenge facing firms whose main business depends on projects is balancing efficiency and flexibility under conditions of diversity. Striking this balance takes place at the operating and strategic levels. At the operating level, project-based firms build core competencies that contain the tacit and codified knowledge needed to effectively execute projects. At the strategic level, project-based firms face trade-offs between pursuing opportunities and developing their competencies.

USING THE CASE STUDIES

Managing innovation is crucial for the vitality of established as well as new companies. The Whisky Exchange case, which deals with e-business pioneering, is an example of the latter. Cases such as Pixar, Apple, and Cirque de Soleil deal with consistent efforts to manage innovation successfully. This often involves experimentation with organizational forms that facilitate innovation. The reading by Maletz and Nohria provides a framework for appreciating that innovation often take place in "whitespaces"—parts of the organization where rules are vague, authority is fuzzy, and budgets are nonexistent. Johnson and Johnson is one such organization. The problem facing William C. Weldon, J&J's CEO, is how to rein in the whitespaces without killing their innovative potential. Apple faced the same dilemma throughout its history, and so did Wipro.

Innovations are often closely tied to projects. Almost every film project of Pixar has pushed the boundaries of animation. Outset has used the funding of projects to create relationships, and then used these relationships to generate more patrons. In the reading "The Core Competencies of Project-Based Firms," Lampel outlines a typology of key competencies that are needed to manage firms in project-based industries, such as motion pictures, consulting, pharmaceuticals, aircraft, and construction. Pixar, HBO, Airbus versus Boeing cases go well with this reading.

READING 16.1

The Innovative Organization* BY HENRY MINTZBERG

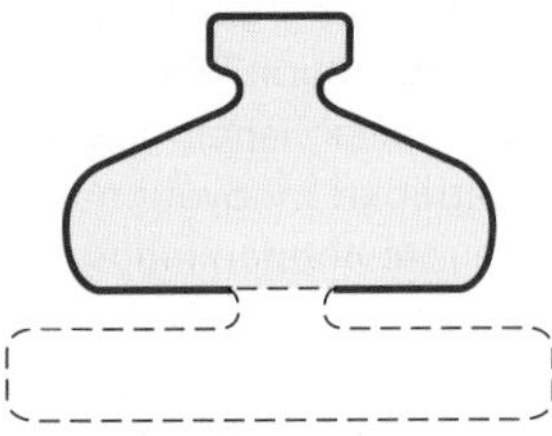

None of the organization forms so far discussed is capable of sophisticated innovation, the kind required of a high-technology research organization, an avant-garde film company, or a factory manufacturing complex prototypes. The entrepreneurial organization can certainly innovate, but only in relatively simple ways. The machine and professional organizations are performance, not problem-solving types, designed to perfect standardized programs, not to invent new ones. And although the diversified organization resolves some problem of strategic inflexibility found in the machine organization, as noted earlier it too is not a true innovator. A focus on control by standardizing outputs does not encourage innovation.

Sophisticated innovation requires a very different configuration, one that is able to fuse experts drawn from different disciplines into smoothly functioning ad hoc project teams. To borrow the word coined by Bennis and Slator in 1964 and later popularized in Alvin Toffler's *Future Shock* (1970), these are the *adhocracies* of our society.

THE BASIC STRUCTURE

Here again we have a distinct configuration of the attributes of design: highly organic structure, with little formalization of behavior; specialized jobs based on expert training; a tendency to group the specialists in functional units for housekeeping purposes but to deploy them in small project teams to do their work; a reliance on teams, on task forces, and on integrating managers of various sorts in order to encourage mutual adjustment, the key mechanism of coordination, within and between these teams; and considerable decentralization to and within these teams, which are located at various places in the organization and involve various mixtures of line managers and staff and operating experts.

To innovate means to break away from established patterns. Thus the innovative organization cannot rely on any form of standardization for coordination. In other words, it must avoid all the trappings of bureaucratic structure, notably sharp divisions of labor, extensive unit differentiation, highly formalized behaviors, and an emphasis on planning and control systems. Above all, it must remain flexible. A search for organigrams to illustrate this description elicited the following response from one corporation thought to have an adhocracy structure: "[We] would prefer not to supply an organization chart, since it would change too quickly to serve any useful purpose." Of all the configurations, this one shows the least reverence for the classical principles of management, especially unity of command. Information and decision processes flow flexibly and informally, wherever they must, to promote innovation. And that means overriding the chain of authority if need be.

---

*Adapted from *The Structuring of Organizations* (Prentice Hall, 1979), Chap. 21 on the adhocracy; on strategy formation from "Strategy Formation in an Adhocracy," coauthored with Alexandra McHugh, *Administrative Science Quarterly* (1985: 160–197), and "Strategy of Design: A Study of Architects in Co-Partnership," coauthored with Suzanne Otis, Jamal Shamsie, and James A. Waters, in J. Grant (ed.), *Strategic Management Frontiers* (JAI Press, 1988). A chapter similar to this one appeared in *Mintzberg on Management: Inside Our Strange World of Organizations* (Free Press, 1989).

The entrepreneurial configuration also retains a flexible, organic structure, and so is likewise able to innovate. But that innovation is restricted to simple situations, ones easily comprehended by a single leader. Innovation of the sophisticated variety requires another kind of flexible structure, one that can draw together different forms of expertise. Thus the adhocracy must hire and give power to experts, people whose knowledge and skills have been highly developed in training programs. But unlike the professional organization, the adhocracy cannot rely on the standardized skills of its experts to achieve coordination, because that would discourage innovation. Rather, it must treat existing knowledge and skills as bases on which to combine and build new ones. Thus the adhocracy must break through the boundaries of conventional specialization and differentiation, which it does by assigning problems not to individual experts in preestablished pigeonholes but to multidisciplinary teams that merge their efforts. Each team forms around one specific project.

Despite organizing around market-based projects, the organization must still support and encourage particular types of specialized expertise. And so the adhocracy tends to use a matrix structure: Its experts are grouped in functional units for specialized housekeeping purposes—hiring, training, professional communication, and the like—but are then deployed in the project teams to carry out the basic work of innovation.

As for coordination in and between these project teams, as noted earlier standardization is precluded as a significant coordinating mechanism. The efforts must be innovative, not routine. So, too, is direct supervision precluded because of the complexity of the work: Coordination must be accomplished by those with the knowledge, namely the experts themselves, not those with just authority. That leaves just one of our coordinating mechanisms, mutual adjustment, which we consider foremost in adhocracy. And, to encourage this, the organization makes use of a whole set of liaison devices, liaison personnel, and integrating managers of all kinds, in addition to the various teams and task forces.

The result is that managers abound in the adhocracy: functional managers, integrating managers, project managers. The last named are particularly numerous, since the project teams must be small to encourage mutual adjustment among their members, and each, of course, needs a designated manager. The consequence is that "spans of control" found in adhocracy tend to be small. But the implication of this is misleading, because the term is suited to the machine, not the innovative configuration: The managers of adhocracy seldom "manage" in the usual sense of giving orders; instead, they spend a good deal of time acting in a liaison capacity, to coordinate the work laterally among the various teams and units.

With its reliance on highly trained experts the adhocracy emerges as highly decentralized, in the "selective" sense. That means power over its decisions and actions is distributed to various places and at various levels according to the needs of the particular issue. In effect, power flows to wherever the relevant expertise happens to reside—among managers or specialists (or teams of those) in the line structure, the staff units, and the operating core.

To proceed with our discussion and to elaborate on how the innovative organization makes decisions and forms strategies, we need to distinguish two basic forms that it takes.

THE OPERATING ADHOCRACY

The *operating adhocracy* innovates and solves problems directly on behalf of its clients. Its multidisciplinary teams of experts often work under contract, as in the think-tank consulting firm, creative advertising agency, or manufacturer of engineering prototypes.

In fact, for every operating adhocracy, there is a corresponding professional bureaucracy, one that does similar work but with a narrower orientation. Faced with a client problem, the operating adhocracy engages in creative efforts to find a novel solution; the professional bureaucracy pigeonholes it into a known contingency to which it can apply a standard program. One engages in divergent thinking aimed at innovation, the other in convergent thinking aimed at perfection. Thus, one theater company might seek out new avant-garde plays to perform, while another might perfect its performance of Shakespeare year after year.

A key feature of the operating adhocracy is that its administrative and operating work tend to blend into a single effort. That is, in ad hoc project work it is difficult to separate the planning and design of the work from its execution. Both require the same specialized skills, on a project-by-project basis. Thus it can be difficult to distinguish the middle levels of the organization from its operating core, since line managers and staff specialists may take their place alongside operating specialists on the project teams.

Figure 1 shows the organigram of the National Film Board of Canada, a classic operating adhocracy (even though it does produce a chart—one that changes frequently it might be added). The Board is an agency of the Canadian federal government and produces mostly short films, many of them documentaries. At the time of this organigram, the characteristics of adhocracy were particularly in evidence: It shows a large number of support units as well as liaison positions (for example, research, technical, and production coordinators), with the operating core containing loose concurrent functional and market groupings, the latter by region as well as by type of film produced and, as can be seen, some not even connected to the line hierarchy!

THE ADMINISTRATIVE ADHOCRACY

The second type of adhocracy also functions with project teams, but toward a different end. Whereas the operating adhocracy undertakes projects to serve its clients, the *administrative adhocracy* undertakes projects to serve itself, to bring new facilities or activities on line, as in the administrative structure of a highly automated company. And in sharp contrast to the operating adhocracy, the administrative adhocracy makes a clear distinction between its administrative component and its operating core. That core is truncated—cut right off from the rest of the organization—so that the administrative component that remains can be structured as an adhocracy.

This truncation may take place in a number of ways. First, when the operations have to be machinelike and so could impede innovation in the administration (because of the associated need for control), it may be established as an independent organization. Second, the operating core may be done away with altogether—in effect, contracted out to other organizations. That leaves the organization free to concentrate on the development work, as did NASA during the Apollo project. A third form of truncation arises when the operating core becomes automated. This enables it to run itself, largely independent of the need for direct controls from the administrative component, leaving the latter free to structure itself as an adhocracy to bring new facilities on line or to modify old ones.

Oil companies, because of the high degree of automation of their production process, are in part at least drawn toward administrative adhocracy. Figure 2 shows the organigram for one oil company, reproduced exactly as presented by the company (except for modifications to mask its identity, done at the company's request). Note the domination of "Administration and Services," shown at the bottom of the chart; the operating functions, particularly "Production," are lost by comparison. Note also the description of the strategic apex in terms of standing committees instead of individual executives.

THE ADMINISTRATIVE COMPONENT OF THE ADHOCRACIES

The important conclusion to be drawn from this discussion is that in both types of adhocracy the relation between the operating core and the administrative component is unlike that in any other configuration. In the administrative adhocracy, the operating core is truncated and becomes a relatively unimportant part of the organization; in the operating adhocracy, the two merge into a single entity. Either way, the need for traditional direct supervision is diminished, so managers derive their influence more from their expertise and interpersonal skills than from formal position. And that means the distinction between line and staff blurs. It no longer makes sense to distinguish those who have the formal power to decide from those who have only the informal right to advise. Power over decision making in the adhocracy flows to anyone with the required expertise, regardless of position.

In fact, the support staff plays a key role in adhocracy, because that is where many of the experts reside (especially in administrative adhocracy). As suggested, however, that staff is not sharply differentiated from the other parts of the organization, not off to one side, to speak only

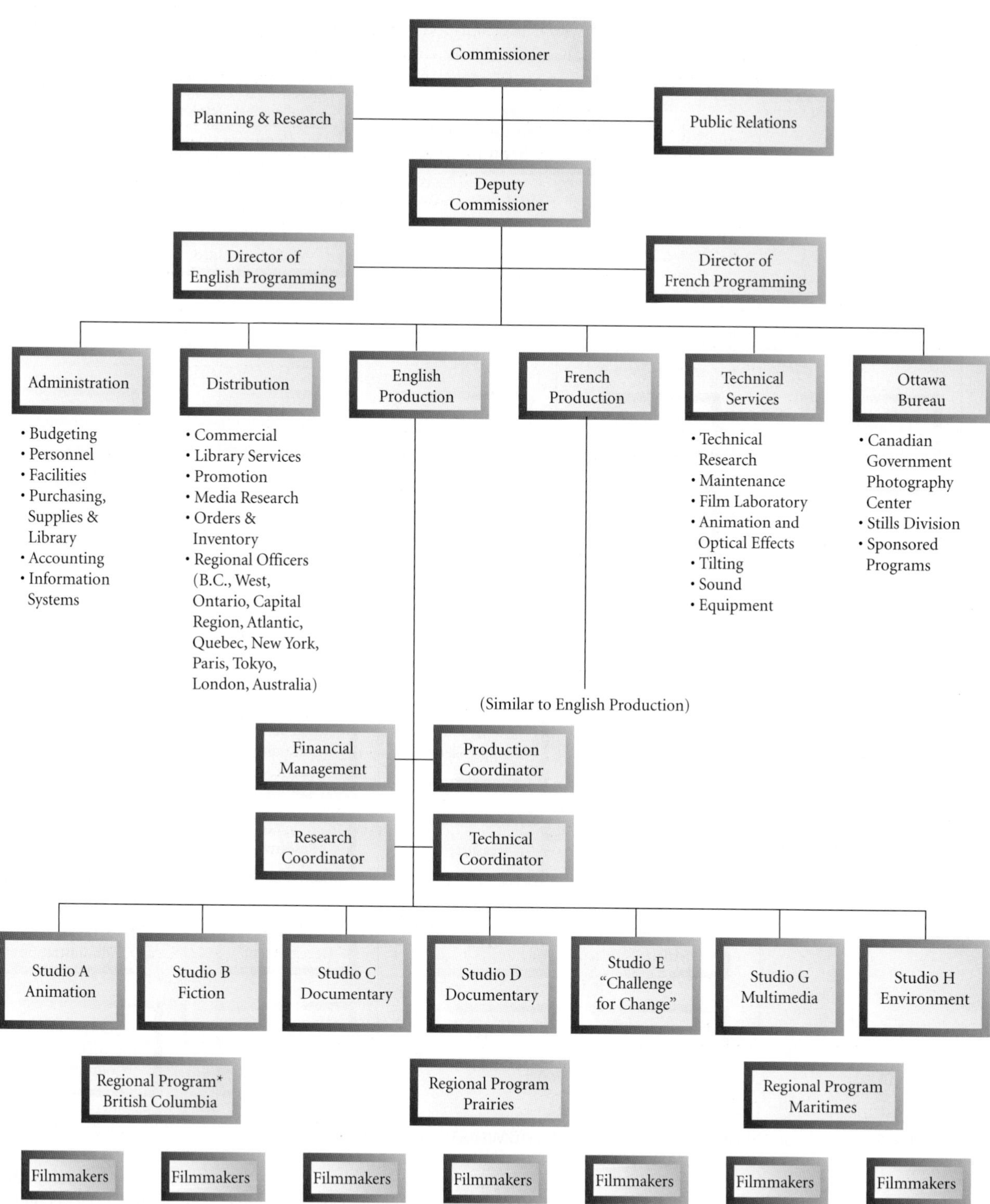

FIGURE 1 THE NATIONAL FILM BOARD OF CANADA: AN OPERATING ADHOCRACY (CIRCA 1975; USED WITH PERMISSION)

*No lines shown on original organigram connecting Regional Programs to Studios or Filmmakers.

when spoken to, as in the bureaucratic configurations. The other type of staff, however, the technostructure, is less important here, because the adhocracy does not rely for coordination on standards that it develops. Technostructure analysts may, of course, be used for some action planning and other forms of analysis—marketing research and economic forecasting, for

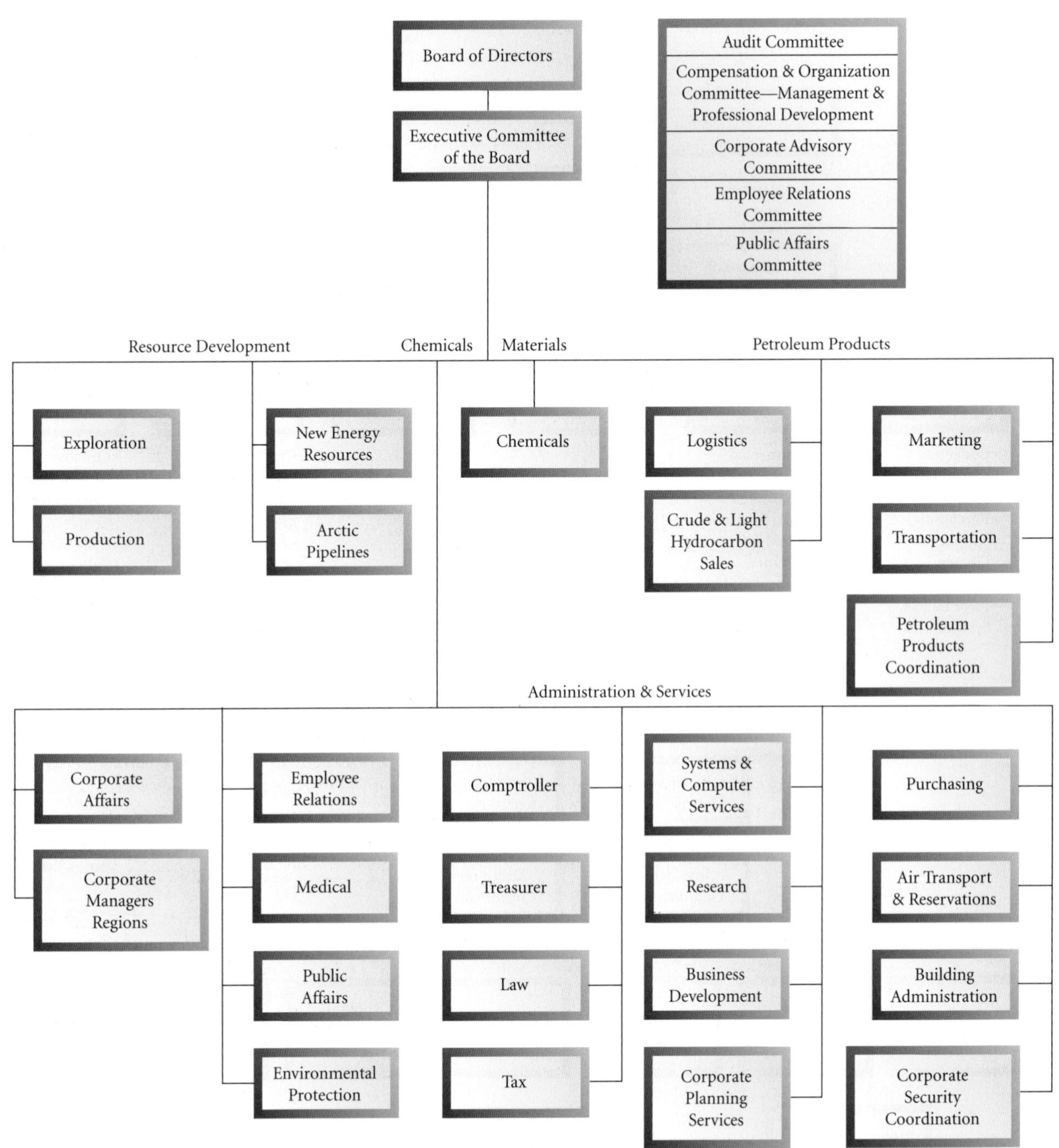

FIGURE 2 ORGANIGRAM OF AN OIL COMPANY: AN ADMINISTRATIVE ADHOCRACY

example—but these analysts are as likely to take their place alongside the other specialists on the project teams as to stand back and design systems to control them.

To summarize, the administrative component of the adhocracy emerges as an organic mass of line managers and staff experts, combined with operators in the operating adhocracy, working together in ever-shifting relationships on ad hoc projects. Our logo figure at the start of this reading shows adhocracy with its parts mingled together in one amorphous mass in the middle. In the operating adhocracy, that mass includes the middle line, support staff, technostructure, and operating core. Of these, the administrative adhocracy excludes just the operating core, which is truncated, as shown by the dotted section below the central mass. The reader will also note that the strategic apex of the figure is shown partly merged into the central mass as well, for reasons we shall present in our discussion of strategy formation.

THE ROLES OF THE STRATEGIC APEX

The top managers of the strategic apex of this configuration do not spend much time formulating explicit strategies (as we shall see). But they must spend a good deal of their time in the battles that ensue over strategic choices and in handling the many other disturbances that arise all over these fluid structures. The innovative configuration combines fluid working arrangements with power based on expertise, not authority. Together those breed aggressiveness and conflict. But the job of the managers here, at all levels, is not to bottle up that aggression and conflict so much as to channel them to productive ends. Thus, the managers of adhocracy must be masters of human relations, able to use persuasion, negotiation, coalition, reputation, and rapport to fuse the individualistic experts into smoothly functioning teams.

Top managers must also devote a good deal of time to monitoring the projects. Innovative project work is notoriously difficult to control. No MIS can be relied upon to provide complete, unambiguous results. So there must be careful personal monitoring of projects to ensure that they are completed according to specifications, on schedule, and within budget (or, more likely, not excessively late and not too far in excess of cost estimates).

Perhaps the most important single role of the top management of this configuration (especially the operating adhocracy form) is liaison with the external environment. The other configurations tend to focus their attention on clearly defined markets and so are more or less assured of a steady flow of work. Not so the operating adhocracy, which lives from project to project and disappears when it can find no more. Since each project is different, the organization can never be sure where the next one will come from. So the top managers must devote a great deal of their time to ensuring a steady and balanced stream of incoming projects. That means developing liaison contacts with potential customers and negotiating contracts with them. Nowhere is this more clearly illustrated than in the consulting business, particularly where the approach is innovative. When a consultant becomes a partner in one of these firms, he or she normally hangs up the calculator and becomes virtually a full-time salesperson. It is a distinguishing characteristic of many an operating adhocracy that the selling function literally takes place at the strategic apex.

Project work poses related problems in the administrative adhocracy. Reeser asked a group of managers in three aerospace companies, "What are some of the human problems of project management?" Among the common answers: "[M]embers of the organization who are displaced because of the phasing out of [their] work . . . may have to wait a long time before they get another assignment at as high a level of responsibility" and "the temporary nature of the organization often necessitates 'make work' assignments for [these] displaced members" (1969: 463). Thus senior managers must again concern themselves with a steady flow of projects, although in this case, internally generated.

CONDITIONS OF THE INNOVATIVE ORGANIZATION

This configuration is found in environments that are both dynamic and complex. A dynamic environment, being unpredictable, calls for organic structure; a complex one calls for decentralized structure. This configuration is the only type that provides both. Thus we tend to find the innovative organization wherever these conditions prevail, ranging from guerrilla warfare to space agencies. There appears to be no other way to fight a war in the jungle or to put the first man on the moon.

As we have noted for all the configurations, organizations that prefer particular structures also try to "choose" environments appropriate to them. This is especially clear in the case of the operating adhocracy. Advertising agencies and consulting firms that prefer to structure themselves as professional bureaucracies seek out stable environments; those that prefer the innovative form find environments that are dynamic, where the client needs are difficult and unpredictable.*

A number of organizations are drawn toward this configuration because of the dynamic conditions that result from very frequent product change. The extreme case is the unit producer, the manufacturing firm that custom-makes each of its products to order, as in the engineering company that produces prototypes or the fabricator of extremely expensive machinery. Because each customer order constitutes a new project, the organization is encouraged to structure itself as an operating adhocracy.

Some manufacturers of consumer goods operate in markets so competitive that they must be constantly changing their product offerings, even though each product may itself be mass produced. A company that records rock music would be a prime example, as would some cosmetic and pharmaceutical companies. Here again, dynamic conditions, when coupled with some complexity, drive the organization toward the innovative configuration, with the mass production operations truncated to allow for adhocracy in product development.

Youth is another condition often associated with this type of organization. That is because it is difficult to sustain any structure in a state of adhocracy for a long period—to keep behaviors from formalizing and thereby discouraging innovation. All kinds of forces drive the innovative configuration to bureaucratize itself as it ages. On the other hand, young organizations prefer naturally organic structures, since they must find their own ways and tend to be eager to innovate. Unless they are entrepreneurial, they tend to become intrapreneurial.

The operating adhocracy is particularly prone to a short life, since it faces a risky market which can quickly destroy it. The loss of one major contract can literally close it down overnight. But if some operating adhocracies have short lives because they fail, others have short lives because they succeed. Success over time encourages metamorphosis, driving the organization toward a more stable environment and a more bureaucratic structure. As it ages, the successful organization develops a reputation for what it does best. That encourages it to repeat certain activities, which may suit the employees who, themselves aging, may welcome more stability in their work. So operating adhocracy is driven over time toward professional bureaucracy to perfect the activities it does best, perhaps even toward the machine bureaucracy to exploit a single invention. The organization survives, but the configuration dies.

Administrative adhocracies typically live longer. They, too, feel the pressures to bureaucratize as they age, which can lead them to stop innovating or else to innovate in stereotyped ways and thereby to adopt bureaucratic structure. But this will not work if the organization functions in an industry that requires sophisticated innovation from all its participants. Since many of the industries where administrative adhocracies are found do, organizations that survive in them tend to retain this configuration for long periods.

In recognition of the tendency for organizations to bureaucratize as they age, a variant of the innovative configuration has emerged— "the organizational equivalent of paper dresses or throw-away tissues" (Toffler, 1970: 133)— which might be called the "temporary adhocracy." It draws together specialists from various organizations to carry out a project, and then it disbands. Temporary adhocracies are becoming increasingly common in modern society: the production group that performs a single play, the election campaign committee that promotes a single candidate, the guerrilla group that overthrows a single government, the Olympic committee that plans a single game. Related is what can be called the "mammoth project adhocracy," a giant temporary adhocracy that draws on thousands of experts for a number of years to carry out a single major task, the Manhattan Project of World War II being one famous example.

Sophisticated and automated technical systems also tend to drive organizations toward the administrative adhocracy. When an organization's technical system is sophisticated, it requires an elaborate, highly trained support staff, working in teams, to design or purchase, modify, and maintain the equipment. In other words, complex machinery requires specialists who have the

---

*I like to tell a story of the hospital patient with an appendix about to burst who presents himself to a hospital organized as an adhocracy: "Who wants to do another appendectomy? We're into livers now," as they go about exploring new procedures. But the patient returning from a trip to the jungle with a rare tropical disease had better beware of the hospital organized as a professional bureaucracy. A student came up to me after I once said this and explained how hospital doctors puzzled by her bloated stomach and not knowing what to do took out her appendix. Luckily, her problem resolved itself, some time later. Another time, a surgeon told me that his hospital no longer does appendectomies!

knowledge, power, and flexible working arrangements to cope with it, which generally requires the organization to structure itself as an adhocracy.

Automation of a technical system can evoke even stronger forces in the same direction. That is why a machine organization that succeeds in automating its operating core tends to undergo a dramatic metamorphosis. The problem of motivating bored workers disappears, and with it goes the control mentality that permeates the structure; the distinction between line and staff blurs (machines being indifferent to who turns their knobs), which leads to another important reduction in conflict; the technostructure loses its influence, since control is built into the machinery by its own designers rather than having to be imposed on workers by the standards of the analysts. Overall, then, the administrative structure becomes more decentralized and organic, emerging as an adhocracy. Of course, for automated organizations with simple technical systems (as in the production of hand creams), the entrepreneurial configuration may suffice instead of the innovative one.

Fashion is most decidedly another condition of the innovative configuration. Every one of its characteristics is very much in vogue today: emphasis on expertise, organic structure, project teams, task forces, decentralization of power, matrix structure, sophisticated technical systems, automation, and young organizations. Thus, if the entrepreneurial and machine forms were earlier configurations, and the professional and the diversified forms yesterday's, then the innovative is clearly today's. This is the configuration for a population growing ever better educated and more specialized, yet under constant encouragement to adopt the "systems" approach—to view the world as an integrated whole instead of a collection of loosely coupled parts. It is the configuration for environments that are becoming more complex and more insistent on innovation, and for technical systems that are growing more sophisticated and more highly automated. It is the only configuration among our types appropriate for those who believe organizations must become at the same time more democratic and less bureaucratic.

Yet despite our current infatuation with it, adhocracy is not the structure for all organizations. Like all the others, it too has its place. And that place, as our examples make clear, seems to be in the new industries of our age—aerospace, electronics, think-tank consulting, research, advertising, filmmaking, petrochemicals—virtually all of which experienced their greatest development since World War II. The innovative adhocracy appears to be the configuration for the industries of the last half of the twentieth century.

STRATEGY FORMATION IN THE INNOVATIVE ORGANIZATION

The structure of the innovative organization may seem unconventional, but its strategy making is even more so, upsetting virtually everything we have been taught to believe about that process.

Because the innovative organization must respond continuously to a complex, unpredictable environment, it cannot rely on deliberate strategy. In other words, it cannot predetermine precise patterns in its activities and then impose them on its work through some kind of formal planning process. Rather, many of its actions must be decided upon individually, according to the needs of the moment. It proceeds incrementally; to use Charles Lindblom's words, it prefers "continual nibbling" to a "good bite" (1968: 25).

Here, then, the process is best thought of as strategy *formation*, because strategy is not formulated consciously in one place so much as formed implicitly by the specific actions taken in many places. That is why action planning cannot be extensively relied upon in these organizations: Any process that separates thinking from action—planning from execution, formalization from implementation—would impede the flexibility of the organization to respond creatively to its dynamic environment.

STRATEGY FORMATION IN THE OPERATING ADHOCRACY

In the operating adhocracy, a project organization is never quite sure what it will do next, the strategy never really stabilizes totally but is responsive to new projects, which themselves involve the activities of a whole host of people. Take the example of the National Film Board. Among its most important strategies are those related to the content of the hundred or so mostly short, documentary-type films that it makes each year. Were the Board structured as a machine bureaucracy, the word on what films to make would come down from on high. Instead, when we studied it some years ago, proposals for new films were submitted to a standing committee, which included elected filmmakers, marketing people, and the heads of production and programming—in other words, operators, line managers, and staff specialists. The chief executive had to approve the committee's choices, and usually did, but the vast majority of the proposals were initiated by the filmmakers and the executive producers lower down. Strategies formed as themes developed among these individual proposals. The operating adhocracy's strategy thus evolves continuously as all kinds of such decisions are made, each leaving its imprint on the strategy by creating a precedent or reinforcing an existing one.

STRATEGY FORMATION IN THE ADMINISTRATIVE ADHOCRACY

Similar things can be said about the administrative adhocracy, although the strategy-making process is slightly neater there. That is because the organization tends to concentrate its attention on fewer projects, which involve more people. NASA's Apollo project, for example, involved most of its personnel for almost ten years.

Administrative adhocracies also need to give more attention to action planning, but of a loose kind—to specify perhaps the ends to be reached while leaving flexibility to work out the means en route. Again, therefore, it is only through the making of specific decisions—namely, those that determine which projects are undertaken and how these projects unfold—that strategies can evolve.

STRATEGIES NONETHELESS

With their activities so disjointed, one might wonder whether adhocracies (of either type) can form strategies (that is, patterns) at all. In fact, they do, at least at certain times.

At the Film Board, despite the little direction from the management, the content of films did converge on certain clear themes periodically and then diverge, in remarkably regular cycles. In the early 1940s, there was a focus on films related to the war effort. After the war, having lost that raison d'être as well as its founding leader, the Board's films went off in all directions. They converged again in the mid-1950s around series of films for television, but by the late 1950s were again diverging widely. And in the mid-1960s and again in the early 1970s (with a brief period of divergence in between), the Board again showed a certain degree of convergence, this time on the themes of social commentary and experimentation.

The habit of cycling in and out of focus is quite unlike what takes place in the other configurations. In the machine organization especially, and somewhat in the entrepreneurial one, convergence proves much stronger and much longer (recall Volkswagenwerk's concentration on the Beetle for twenty years), while divergence tends to be very brief. The machine organization, in particular, cannot tolerate the ambiguity of change and so tries to leap from one strategic orientation to another. The innovative organization, in contrast, seems not only able to function at times without strategic focus, but positively to thrive on it. Perhaps that is the way it keeps itself innovative—by periodically cleansing itself of some of its existing strategic baggage.

THE VARIED STRATEGIES OF ADHOCRACY

Where do the strategies of adhocracy come from? While some may be imposed deliberately by the central management (as in staff cuts at the Film Board), most seem to emerge in a variety of other ways.

In some cases, a single ad hoc decision sets a precedent which evokes a pattern. That is how the National Film Board got into making series of films for television. While a debate raged over the issue, with management hesitant, one filmmaker slipped out and made one such series, and when many of his colleagues quickly followed suite, the organization suddenly found itself deeply, if unintentionally, committed to a major new strategy. It was, in effect, a strategy of spontaneous but implicit consensus on the part of its operating employees. In another case, even the initial precedent-setting decision wasn't deliberate. One film inadvertently ran longer than expected, it had to be distributed as a feature, the first for the organization, and as some other filmmakers took advantage of the precedent, a feature film strategy emerged.

Sometimes a strategy will be pursued in a pocket of an organization (perhaps in a clandestine manner, in a so-called "skunkworks"), which then later becomes more broadly organizational when the organization, in need of change and casting about for new strategies, seizes upon it. Some salesman has been pursuing a new market, or some engineer has developed a new product, and is ignored until the organization has need for some fresh strategic thinking. Then it finds it, not in the vision of its leaders or the procedures of its planners, not elsewhere in its industry, but hidden in the bowels of its own operations, developed through the learning of its workers.

What then becomes the role of the leadership of the innovative configuration in making strategy? If it cannot impose deliberate strategies, what does it do? The answer is that it manages patterns, seeking partial control over strategies but otherwise attempting to influence what happens to those strategies that do emerge lower down.

These are the organizations in which trying to manage strategy is a little like trying to drive an automobile without having your hands on the steering wheel. You can accelerate and brake but cannot determine direction. But there do remain important forms of control. First the leaders can manage the *process* of strategy making if not the content of strategy. In other words, they can set up the structures to encourage certain kinds of activities and hire the people who themselves will carry out these activities. Second, they can provide general guidelines for strategy—what we have called *umbrella* strategies—seeking to define certain boundaries outside of which the specific patterns developed below should not stray. Then they can watch the patterns that do emerge and use the umbrella to decide which to encourage and which to discourage, remembering, however, that the umbrella can be shifted too.

A GRASS-ROOTS MODEL OF STRATEGY FORMATION

We can summarize this discussion in terms of a "grass-roots" model of strategy formation, comprising six points.

1. *Strategies grow initially like weeds in a garden, they are not cultivated like tomatoes in a hothouse.* In other words, the process of strategy formation can be overmanaged; sometimes it is more important to let patterns emerge than to force an artificial consistency upon an organization prematurely. The hothouse, if needed, can come later.
2. *These strategies can take root in all kinds of places, virtually anywhere people have the capacity to learn and the resources to support that capacity.* Sometimes an individual or unit in touch with a particular opportunity creates his, her, or its own pattern. This may happen inadvertently, when an initial action sets a precedent. Even senior managers can fall into strategies by experimenting with ideas until they converge on something that works (though the final result may appear to the observer to have been deliberately designed). At other times, a variety of actions converge on a strategic theme through the mutual adjustment of various people, whether gradually or spontaneously. And then the external environment can impose a pattern on an unsuspecting organization. The point is that organizations cannot always plan where their strategies will emerge, let alone plan the strategies themselves.
3. *Such strategies become organizational when they become collective, that is, when the patterns proliferate to pervade the behavior of the organization at large.* Weeds can proliferate and encompass a whole garden; then the conventional plants may look out of place. Likewise, emergent strategies can sometimes displace the existing deliberate ones. But, of course, what is a weed but a plant that wasn't expected? With a change of perspective, the emergent strategy, like the weed, can become what is valued (just as Europeans enjoy salads of the leaves of America's most notorious weed, the dandelion!).
4. *The processes of proliferation may be conscious but need not be; likewise, they may be managed but need not be.* The processes by which the initial patterns work their way through the organization need not be consciously intended, by formal leaders or even informal ones. Patterns may simply spread by collective action, much as plants proliferate themselves. Of course, once strategies are recognized as valuable, the processes by which they proliferate can be managed, just as plants can be selectively propagated.
5. *New strategies, which may be emerging continuously, tend to pervade the organization during periods of change, which punctuate periods of more integrated continuity.* Put more simply,

organizations, like gardens, may accept the biblical maxim of a time to sow and a time to reap (even though they can sometimes reap what they did not mean to sow). Periods of convergence, during which the organization exploits its prevalent, established strategies, tend to be interrupted periodically by periods of divergence, during which the organization experiments with and subsequently accepts new strategic themes. The blurring of the separation between these two types of periods may have the same effect on an organization that the blurring of the separation between sowing and reaping has on a garden—the destruction of the system's productive capacity.

6. *To manage this process is not to preconceive strategies but to recognize their emergence and intervene when appropriate.* A destructive weed, once noticed, is best uprooted immediately. But one that seems capable of bearing fruit is worth watching, indeed sometimes even worth building a hothouse around. To manage in this context is to create the climate within which a wide variety of strategies can grow (to establish flexible structures, develop appropriate processes, encourage supporting ideologies, and define guiding "umbrella" strategies) and then to watch what does in fact come up. The strategic initiatives that do come "up" may in fact originate anywhere, although often low down in the organization, where the detailed knowledge of products and markets resides. (In fact, to be successful in some organizations, these initiatives must be recognized by middle-level managers and "championed" by combining them with each other or with existing strategies before promoting them to the senior management.) In effect, the management encourages those initiatives that appear to have potential, otherwise it discourages them. But it must not be too quick to cut off the unexpected: Sometimes it is better to pretend not to notice an emerging pattern to allow it more time to unfold. Likewise, there are times when it makes sense to shift or enlarge an umbrella to encompass a new pattern—in other words, to let the organization adapt to the initiative rather than vice versa. Moreover, a management must know when to resist change for the sake of internal efficiency and when to promote it for the sake of external adaptation. In other words, it must sense when to exploit an established crop of strategies and when to encourage new strains to displace them. It is the excesses of either—failure to focus (running blind) or failure to change (bureaucratic momentum)— that most harms organizations.

I call this a "grass-roots" model because the strategies grow up from the base of the organization, rooted in the solid earth of its operations rather than the ethereal abstractions of its administration. (Even the strategic initiatives of the senior management itself are in this model rooted in its tangible involvement with the operations.)

Of course, the model is overstated. But no more so than the more widely accepted deliberate one, which we might call the "hothouse" model of strategy formulation. Management theory must encompass both, perhaps more broadly labeled the *learning* model and the *planning* model, as well as a third, the *visionary* model.

I have discussed the learning model under the innovative configuration, the planning model under the machine configuration, and the visionary model under the entrepreneurial configuration. But in truth, all organizations need to mix these approaches in various ways at different times in their development. For example, our discussion of strategic change in the machine organization concluded, in effect, that they had to revert to the learning model for revitalization and the visionary model for turnaround. Of course, the visionary leader must learn, as must the learning organization evolve a kind of strategic vision, and both sometimes need planning to program the strategies they develop. And overall, no organization can function with strategies that are always and purely emergent; that would amount to a complete abdication of will and leadership, not to mention conscious thought. But none can function either with strategies that are always and purely deliberate; that would amount to an unwillingness to learn, a blindness to whatever is unexpected.

ENVIRONMENT TAKING PRECEDENCE IN THE INNOVATIVE ORGANIZATION

To conclude our discussion of strategy formation, as shown in Figure 3 in the innovative configuration it is the environment that takes precedence. It drives the organization, which responds continuously and eclectically, but does nevertheless achieve convergence during certain

FIGURE 3
ENVIRONMENT TAKING THE LEAD IN ADHOCRACY

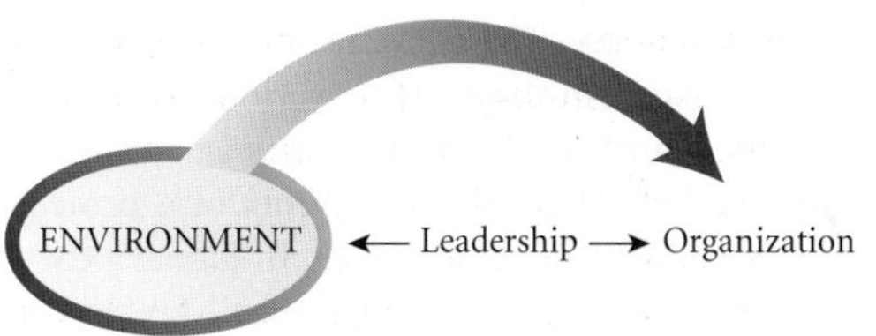

periods.* The formal leadership seeks somehow to influence both sides in this relationship, negotiating with the environment for support and attempting to impose some broad general (umbrella) guidelines on the organization.

If the strategist of the entrepreneurial organization is largely a concept attainer and that of the machine organization largely a planner, then the strategist of the innovative organization is largely a *pattern recognizer*, seeking to detect emerging patterns within and outside the strategic umbrella. Then strategies deemed unsuitable can be discouraged while those that seem appropriate can be encouraged, even if that means moving the umbrella. Here, then, we may find the curious situation of leadership changing its intentions to fit the realized behavior of its organization. But that is curious only in the perspective of traditional management theory.

SOME ISSUES ASSOCIATED WITH THE INNOVATIVE ORGANIZATION

Three issues associated with the innovative configuration merit attention here: its ambiguities and the reactions of people who must live with them, its inefficiencies, and its propensity to make inappropriate transitions to other configurations.

HUMAN REACTIONS TO AMBIGUITY

Many people, especially creative ones, dislike both structural rigidity and the concentration of power. That leaves them only one configuration, the innovative, which is both organic and decentralized. Thus they find it a great place to work. In essence, adhocracy is the only structure for people who believe in more democracy with less bureaucracy.

But not everyone shares those values (not even everyone who professes to). Many people need order, and so prefer the machine or professional type of organization. They see adhocracy as a nice place to visit but no place to spend a career. Even dedicated members of adhocracies periodically get frustrated with this structure's fluidity, confusion, and ambiguity. "In these situations, all managers some of the time and many managers all the time yearn for more definition and structure" (Burns and Stalker, 1966: 122–123). The managers of innovative organizations report anxiety related to the eventual phaseout of projects; confusion as to who their boss is, whom to impress to get promoted; a lack of clarity in job definitions, authority relationships, and lines of communication; and intense competition for resources, recognition, and rewards (Reeser, 1969). This last point suggests another serious problem of ambiguity here, the politicization of these configurations. Combining its ambiguities with its interdependencies, the innovative form can emerge as a rather politicized and ruthless organization—supportive of the fit, as long as they remain fit, but destructive of the weak.

PROBLEMS OF EFFICIENCY

No configuration is better suited to solving complex, ill-structured problems than this one. None can match it for sophisticated innovation. Or, unfortunately, for the costs of that innovation. This is simply not an efficient way to function. Although it is ideally suited for the one-of-a-kind project, the innovative configuration is not competent at doing *ordinary* things. It is designed for the *extra*ordinary. The bureaucracies are all mass producers; they gain efficiency through

*We might take this convergence as the expression of an "organization's mind"— the focusing on a strategic theme as a result of the mutual adjustments among its many actors.

standardization. The adhocracy is a custom producer, unable to standardize and so be efficient. It gains its effectiveness (innovation) at the price of efficiency.

One source of inefficiency lies in the unbalanced workload, mentioned earlier. It is almost impossible to keep the personnel of a project structure—high-priced specialists, it should be noted—busy on a steady basis. In January they may be working overtime with no hope of completing the new project on time; by May they may be playing cards for want of work.

But the real root of inefficiency is the high cost of communication. People talk a lot in these organizations; that is how they combine their knowledge to develop new ideas. But that takes time, a great deal of time. Faced with the need to make a decision in the machine organization, someone up above gives an order and that is that. Not so in the innovative one, where everyone must get into the act—managers of all kinds (functional, project, liaison), as well as all the specialists who believe their point of view should be represented. A meeting is called, probably to schedule another meeting, eventually to decide who should participate in the decision. The problem then gets defined and redefined, ideas for its solution get generated and debated, alliances build and fall around different solutions, until eventually everyone settles down to the hard bargaining over which one to adopt. Finally a decision emerges—that in itself is an accomplishment—although it is typically late and will probably be modified later.

THE DANGERS OF INAPPROPRIATE TRANSITION

Of course, one solution to the problems of ambiguity and inefficiency is to change the configuration. Employees no longer able to tolerate the ambiguity and customers fed up with the inefficiency may try to drive the organization to a more stable, bureaucratic form.

That is relatively easily done in the operating adhocracy, as noted earlier. The organization simply selects the set of standard programs it does best, reverting to the professional configuration, or else innovates one last time to find a lucrative market niche in which to mass produce, and then becomes a machine configuration. But those transitions, however easily effected, are not always appropriate. The organization came into being to solve problems imaginatively, not to apply standards indiscriminately. In many spheres, society has more mass producers than it needs; what it lacks are true problem solvers—the consulting firm that can handle a unique problem instead of applying a pat solution, the advertising agency that can come up with a novel campaign instead of the common imitation, the research laboratory that can make the really serious breakthrough instead of just modifying an existing design. The television networks seem to be classic examples of bureaucracies that provide largely standardized fare when the creativity of adhocracy is called for (except, perhaps, for the newsrooms and the specials, where an ad hoc orientation encourages more creativity).

The administrative adhocracy can run into more serious difficulties when it succumbs to the pressures to bureaucratize. It exists to innovate for itself, in its own industry. Unlike the operating adhocracy, it often cannot change orientation while remaining in the same industry. And so its conversion to the machine configuration (the natural transition for administrative adhocracy tired of perpetual change), by destroying the organization's ability to innovate, can eventually destroy the organization itself.

READING 16.2

Managing in the Whitespace* BY MARK C. MALETZ AND NITIN NOHRIA

The wisdom of the day is that your business is doomed to fail if you don't overturn the status quo. You have to think outside the box, start a revolution, break all the rules—pick your own overheated rhetoric. The assumption is that new value in a company can be created only when

*Reprinted with deletions from "Managing in the Whitespace," M. C. Maletz and N. Nohria, *Harvard Business Review*, February 2001, 103–111.

people shed their suits, don khakis and Hawaiian shirts, and think and act like the most passionate entrepreneurs. The problem is, they're rarely told when it makes sense to do those things—or how to do them.

We recently conducted a unique research project that tried to fill in those gaps. The project focused on what we call the whitespace: the large but mostly unoccupied territory in every company where rules are vague, authority is fuzzy, budgets are nonexistent, and strategy is unclear—and where, as a consequence, entrepreneurial activity that helps reinvent and renew an organization takes place. The project worked on two levels: trained ethnographers shadowed entrepreneurial managers who were actually operating in the whitespace, while a steering committee of senior organization specialists met with top managers about their efforts to oversee whitespace activities. . . .

Whitespace exists in all companies, and enterprising people are everywhere testing the waters with unofficial efforts to boost the bottom line. The managers who operate in these uncharted seas are often the ones most successful at driving innovation, incubating new businesses, and finding new markets. The task for senior managers is to avoid letting whitespace efforts "just happen." Instead, they should actively support and monitor these activities, even as they keep them separate from the organization's formal work. If companies leave this valuable territory to the scattershot whims and talents of individual managers, they are likely to miss out on many of the opportunities that come from exploring the next frontier.

MOVING INTO THE WHITESPACE

The blackspace encompasses all the business opportunities that a company has formally targeted and organized itself to capture. The whitespace, then, contains all the opportunities that fall outside the scope of formal planning, budgeting, and management.

Whether you're an entrepreneurial middle manager or a senior executive trying to keep an eye on whitespace activities, the first challenge is knowing when it's appropriate to leave the blackspace. The simple truth is that most projects should be conceived, developed, and managed within the organization's formal structures: that's what they're there for. Managers, then, should consider shifting to the whitespace only if one or more of three conditions exists.

Great uncertainty over a recognizable business opportunity is the first condition. We don't mean the garden variety uncertainty that all managers grapple with; successful managers make a career of taking on tough problems, creating plans, building consensus, and moving forward through regular company channels. We're talking about the kind of uncertainty that surrounds, for example, e-commerce, where it's unclear who has the best idea, how it should be implemented, who should be in charge, which unit should house the opportunity—and if taking the time to figure all that out would mean the opportunity would vanish altogether.

The second condition has to do with organizational politics. Sometimes turf battles make it impossible to proceed in the blackspace. . . .[O]ther times, the problem stems from the need to get resources from several groups that are generally uncooperative. In those situations, it's certainly not worth reorganizing around a new opportunity until it's proven viable. An entrepreneurial manager working in the whitespace can often bootstrap resources from competing groups without their formal involvement—and often, even without their explicit approval.

The third condition, linked to the first two, is that the company's blackspace operations are performing extremely well and would likely be profoundly disrupted by the opportunity at hand. In those circumstances, it's too risky to interfere with the existing business by formally redirecting resources. Instead, it makes sense to place some bets on the new opportunity in the whitespace and see what emerges. . . .

Knowing when to leave the blackspace is an important first step, but the actual leap to whitespace can be hazardous. It's unfamiliar ground for most managers, and it requires a different way of thinking about how work gets completed, measured, and recognized. The next step is understanding the particular challenges of operating in the whitespace and how to meet them.

MANAGING IN THE WHITESPACE

Although navigating in the whitespace requires a new compass, the rewards from successful voyages can be great. Consider this example: An executive at a major global bank developed a virtual trust business that managed assets of more than $1 billion without even appearing on top management's (or financial control's) radar screen. She designed and assembled products and services that had been manufactured for her by the bank's asset management division and sold for her by the bank's retail-banking division. The bank's organization chart indicated that the executive was a bit player without P&L responsibility or staff. And yet she was responsible for the trust business's P&L, and more than 70 people throughout the bank looked to her as their informal leader. . . .

Through examples like [this] and many others, we have identified four challenges faced by managers operating in the whitespace: establishing legitimacy, mobilizing resources, building momentum, and measuring results. The first challenge is peculiar to the whitespace; the remaining three also play out in the blackspace but much differently.

ESTABLISHING LEGITIMACY

Blackspace projects begin with a formal launch, a process that confers automatic legitimacy on them. Whitespace activities don't have that benefit; their managers must work to actively establish their legitimacy at the start if they are to get off the ground. We observed managers using a variety of techniques to show others in the organization that they deserved support.

Some traded on their superior technical skills, which made them appear uniquely qualified to lead an informal project. . . .

Depending on how whitespace efforts emerge, managers have to walk a fine line in communicating their existence to the rest of the organization and the outside world. Invisibility can protect whitespace managers while they wrestle with how best to operate, but it also makes it more difficult to mobilize needed resources.

MOBILIZING RESOURCES

Possessing a degree of legitimacy—even if it is informal—allows whitespace managers to move on to the next task: gathering the resources they'll need to move projects forward. Managers in the blackspace have a clear sense of their budgets and other resources at their disposal; the whitespace managers in our study had to beg, borrow, and steal to get what they needed.

Like fund-raisers at college telethons or on National Public Radio, effective whitespace managers recognize that you can raise a fair amount of money by asking a lot of people for a little at a time. Once people have contributed a little and been embraced as co-owners, they're likely to give again. . . .

Managers can bootstrap resources in many ways, but several characteristics are necessary regardless of one's approach: persistence, creativity, and a willingness to work with what you can get rather than what you think you need.

BUILDING MOMENTUM

Even after a whitespace project has been able to attract some resources, its managers must find ways to build momentum and prevent the initiative from fizzling out or getting mired in corporate politics. They constantly look for ways to rapidly prototype their ideas, run experiments, create pilots, and so on. These visible products make it harder for others to kill whitespace efforts, although they also heighten the risk that blackspace managers might see such efforts as a competitive threat. . . .

Presenting visible products is one way to build momentum; another is to share any wealth generated by a project. Blackspace managers are often suspicious of whitespace efforts; they believe that whitespace managers are pursuing their personal agendas rather than organizational objectives. To win over people in the blackspace—and to ensure that their resources are not cut off—effective whitespace managers share credit for their successes with others. . . .

Once a whitespace project has been launched, the key is to show some clear returns from the initial investments of time, money, and people. Effective whitespace managers recognize that their best bet is to make converts of their blackspace counterparts by spreading the wealth.

MEASURING RESULTS

Clearly, wealth—revenue—is one marker of a whitespace effort's progress. In general, however, results in the whitespace are difficult to measure. A product prototype, while potentially valuable, may not bring in much money in its initial form. A rapidly increasing number of hits to a website may be valuable but not in ways that translate directly to the bottom line. Even revenue earned in the whitespace is tricky: when the organization doesn't officially recognize the costs or the benefits involved with a product or project, crunching the numbers can get complicated. . . .

When measuring whitespace results, creativity matters. Revenues, website hits, and the existence of prototypes are all important, but they won't lead to the clear answers about an initiative's success that one would expect to find with a blackspace project. This is just one of the areas where senior managers, with their bird's-eye view of the company, can help the process work.

SENIOR MANAGERS AND THE WHITESPACE

Individual whitespace efforts can succeed without help from senior executives, but their chances are much improved when high-level people do get involved—provided they understand that traditional blackspace levers (planning, organizing, and controlling) have limited utility in the whitespace. To reap the full benefit of whitespace activities for their companies, senior managers must learn to nurture these informal efforts in the following ways.

FRAME THE STRATEGY

In whitespace, strategic imperatives typically emerge over time. Thus rather than being prematurely precise, the trick is to frame the whitespace work as broadly as possible. . . .

PROVIDE SUPPORT

Whitespace initiatives shouldn't be starved of resources, but they shouldn't be overfed, either. When whitespace managers are forced to sell their ideas to the organization to obtain resources, only the most persuasive ideas, supported by the most credible managers, will take off. Keeping funding tight also makes it easier to halt whitespace activities that are clearly failing.

Senior managers can provide something more valuable than money to whitespace managers: organizational and moral support. . . .

BUILD ENTHUSIASM

Senior executives should not only support those working in the whitespace, they should also communicate whitespace achievements to others within and outside the organization. But they have to be careful about how much light they shine on whitespace efforts, particularly in the early stages. At times, delaying the release of information to allow the whitespace activity to gain more credibility will be the wisest course. On other occasions, it may be more helpful to quickly announce results so the activity can gain momentum. . . .

MONITOR PROGRESS

Senior managers must track whitespace activities and, more important, decide what constitutes success for the projects. Only they have the broad perspective necessary to make that kind of call.

We observed senior managers staying on top of whitespace activities by using monitors throughout the organization. In a large global bank, a senior manager created a loose network of respected opinion leaders who generally heard about whitespace activities early on. By remaining in regular contact with these individuals, the senior manager had a good sense of the progress of whitespace efforts over time.

Judging the success or failure of a project can be difficult. In some cases, a project that doesn't generate a lot of revenue by company standards will be considered a failure. In other cases, where the investment is low, simply picking up the money lying on the table may be enough. Or there may be other considerations: a whitespace effort that generates only $5 million at a bank may be considered paltry by the whitespace manager, and yet if that money comes through cross-selling and leads to higher customer retention rates, it may be considered extremely valuable by senior managers.

Once senior managers have judged that a whitespace effort is valuable, they'll face the final challenge: deciding whether to keep it in the whitespace or migrate it into the blackspace.

MOVING TO BLACKSPACE

If a whitespace effort becomes successful, it will likely end up migrating to the blackspace. Ideally, there should come a point when a whitespace manager voluntarily lets go. Senior managers usually have to step in, however, and make a conscious decision to move the activity into the blackspace, leave it in the whitespace, or kill it altogether.

If an activity has reached critical mass—meaning that it has significant value to the company and a high degree of organizational support and visibility—it should probably be moved. At that point, it's likely that the effort will require such large investments and affect such important clients that it will have passed out of the whitespace comfort zone. It's also true that as the effort scales up, a problem that seemed small at first (a channel conflict, for example) may become unmanageable and will require the control found in the blackspace.

Some efforts, however, have value only in the whitespace and should be kept there indefinitely. For example, an initiative at an investment bank that is valuable to customers—say, the introduction of estate planning services at a bank that didn't have a significant trust business—would be killed immediately in the blackspace unless it brought in revenue, even though it could contribute to higher revenues by boosting customer retention. It also makes sense to keep a project going in the whitespace if bringing it into the blackspace would require the forced reconciliation of warring organizations. In that case, better to just let the whitespace informally maintain connections between the two.

Some whitespace efforts add little value, and most of the failures will die a natural death because they won't be able to attract the resources needed for continued survival. But others survive simply because they don't appear to create any obvious harm or because they generate some positive results while quietly draining away resources that could be better deployed elsewhere. Senior managers have to be aggressive about killing off such efforts. Sometimes that's not easy to do; whitespace activities have a way of reappearing in different guises. The most effective way of preventing a failed effort from resurfacing may simply be to shift the people involved to a more interesting whitespace project.

Whether the decision is to migrate a project to the blackspace, keep it alive in the whitespace, or kill it off, the important thing is to avoid letting the whitespace drift, unmonitored and unnoticed.

In an era when speed and flexibility are the watchwords, opportunities in the whitespace are likely to emerge in great profusion in most industries and companies. Some entrepreneurial managers, through their own force of will and talent, will produce huge successes. Others will pursue personal agendas, waste resources, build private empires, and suck value from other parts of the company. Whether—and how—senior managers oversee the whitespace will be a significant factor in their companies' success. Those that leave it to the luck of the draw, hoping that their entrepreneurs hold aces, risk coming up empty. Those that carefully nurture the space won't always win, but they'll have a much better sense of which bets are likely to pay off.

READING 16.3

Strategy in the Era of Open Innovation BY HENRY W. CHESBROUGH

Companies are increasingly rethinking the fundamental ways in which they generate ideas and bring them to market—harnessing external ideas while leveraging their in-house R&D outside their current operations.

In the past, internal R&D was a valuable strategic asset, even a formidable barrier to entry by competitors in many markets. Only large corporations like DuPont, IBM, and AT&T could compete by doing the most R&D in their respective industries (and subsequently reaping most of the profits as well). Rivals who sought to unseat those powerhouses had to ante up considerable resources to create their own labs, if they were to have any chance of succeeding. These days, however, the leading industrial enterprises of the past have been encountering remarkably strong competition from many upstarts. Surprisingly, these newcomers conduct little or no basic research on their own, but instead get new ideas to market through a different process.

FROM CLOSED TO OPEN

Is innovation dead? Hardly, as punctuated by the recent advances in the life sciences, including revolutionary breakthroughs in genomics and cloning. Then why is internal R&D no longer the strategic asset it once was? The answer lies in a fundamental shift in how companies generate new ideas and bring them to market. In the old model of closed innovation, firms adhered to the following philosophy: Successful innovation requires control. In other words, companies must generate their own ideas that they would then develop, manufacture, market, distribute, and service themselves (see "The Closed Innovation Model", Figure 1).This approach calls for self-reliance: If you want something done right, you've got to do it yourself.

For years, the logic of closed innovation was tacitly held to be self-evident as the "right way" to bring new ideas to market and successful companies all played by certain implicit rules. They invested more heavily in internal R&D than their competitors and they hired the best and the brightest (to reap the rewards of the industry's smartest people). Thanks to such investments, they were able to discover the best and greatest number of ideas, which allowed them to get to

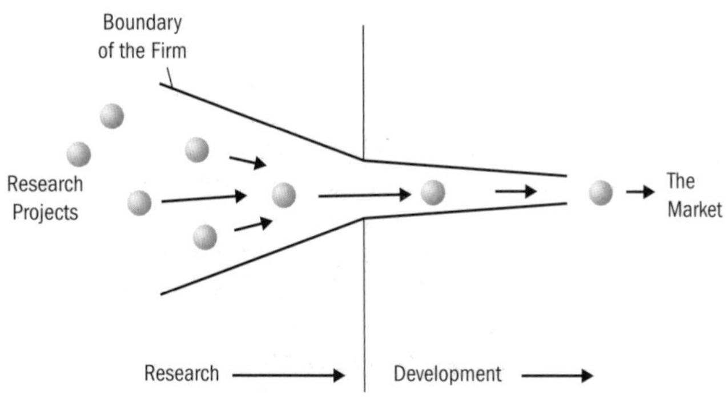

FIGURE 1
THE CLOSED INNOVATION MODEL

market first. This, in turn, enabled them to reap most of the profits, which they protected by aggressively controlling their intellectual property (IP) to prevent competitors from exploiting it. They could then reinvest the profits in conducting more R&D, which then led to additional breakthrough discoveries, creating a virtuous cycle of innovation.

For most of the twentieth century, the model worked—and it worked well. Thanks to it, Thomas Edison was able to invent a number of landmark devices, including the phonograph and the electric light bulb, which paved the way for the establishment of General Electric's famed Global Research Center in Niskayuna, New York. In the chemical industry, companies like DuPont established central research labs to identify and commercialize a stunning variety of new products, such as the synthetic fibers nylon, Kevlar, and Lycra. Bell Labs researchers discovered amazing physical phenomena and harnessed those discoveries to create a host of revolutionary products, including transistors and lasers.

Toward the end of the twentieth century, though, a number of factors combined to erode the underpinnings of closed innovation in the United States. Perhaps chief among these factors was the dramatic rise in the number and mobility of knowledge workers, making it increasingly difficult for companies to control their proprietary ideas and expertise. Another important factor was the growing availability of private venture capital, which has helped to finance new firms and their efforts to commercialize ideas that have spilled outside the silos of corporate research labs.

Such factors have wreaked havoc with the virtuous cycle that sustained closed innovation. Now, when breakthroughs occur, the scientists and engineers who made them have an outside option that they previously lacked. If a company that funded a discovery doesn't pursue it in a timely fashion, the people involved could pursue it on their own—in a startup financed by venture capital. If that fledgling firm were to become successful, it could gain additional financing through a stock offering or it could be acquired at an attractive price. In either case, the successful startup would generally not reinvest in new fundamental discoveries, but instead, like Cisco, it would look outside for another technology to commercialize. Thus, the virtuous cycle of innovation was shattered: The company that originally funded a breakthrough did not profit from the investment, and the firm that did reap the benefits did not reinvest its proceeds to finance the next generation of discoveries.

In this new model of open innovation, firms commercialize external (as well as internal) ideas by deploying outside (as well as in-house) pathways to the market. Specifically, companies can commercialize internal ideas through channels outside of their current businesses in order to generate value for the organization. Some vehicles for accomplishing this include startup companies (which might be financed and staffed with some of the company's own personnel) and licensing agreements. In addition, ideas can also originate outside the firm's own labs and be brought inside for commercialization. In other words, the boundary between a firm and its surrounding environment is more porous, enabling innovation to move easily between the two (see "The Open Innovation Model, Figure 2)."

At its root, open innovation is based on a landscape of abundant knowledge, which must be used readily if it is to provide value for the company that created it. However, an organization should not restrict the knowledge that it uncovers in its research to its internal market pathways, nor should those internal pathways necessarily be constrained to bringing only the

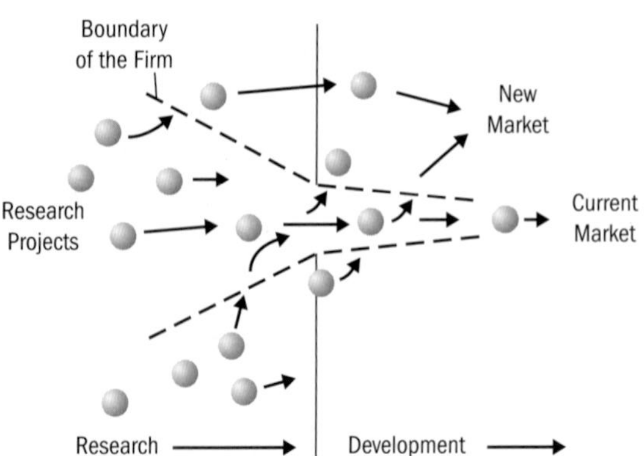

FIGURE 2
THE OPEN
INNOVATION MODEL

company's internal knowledge to market. This perspective suggests some very different rules. For example, no longer should a company lock up its IP, but instead it should find ways to profit from others' use of that technology through licensing agreements, joint ventures, and other arrangements.

One major difference between closed and open innovation lies in how companies screen their ideas. In any R&D process, researchers and their managers must separate the bad proposals from the good ones so that they can discard the former while pursuing and commercializing the latter. Both the closed and open models are adept at weeding out "false positives" (that is, bad ideas that initially look promising), but open innovation also incorporates the ability to rescue "false negatives" (projects that initially seem to lack promise but turn out to be surprisingly valuable). A company that is focused too internally—that is, a firm with a closed innovation approach—is prone to miss a number of those opportunities because many will fall outside the organization's current businesses or will need to be combined with external technologies to unlock their potential. This can be especially painful for corporations that have made substantial long-term investments in research, only to discover later that some of the projects they abandoned had tremendous commercial value.

The classic example is Xerox and its Palo Alto Research Center (PARC). Researchers there developed numerous computer hardware and software technologies—Ethernet and the graphical user interface (GUI) are two such examples. However, these inventions were not viewed as promising businesses for Xerox, which was focused on high-speed copiers and printers. In other words, the technologies were false negative and they languished inside Xerox, only to be commercialized by other companies that, in the process, reaped tremendous benefits. Apple Computer, for instance, exploited the GUI in its Macintosh operating system while Microsoft did the same in its Windows operating system.

HOW PREVALENT IS OPEN INNOVATION?

This is not to argue that all industries have been (or will be) migrating to open innovation. At this point, different businesses can be located on a continuum, from essentially closed to completely open. An example of the former is the nuclear-reactor industry, which depends mainly on internal ideas and has low labor mobility, little venture capital, few (and weak) startups, and relatively little research being conducted at universities. Whether this industry will ever migrate toward open innovation is questionable.

At the other extreme, some industries have been open innovators for some time now. Consider Hollywood, which for decades has innovated through a network of partnerships and alliances between production studios, directors, talent agencies, actors, scriptwriters, independent producers, and specialized subcontractors (such as the suppliers of special effects). The mobility of this workforce is legendary: Every waitress is a budding actress; every parking attendant has a screenplay he is working on.

Many industries—including copiers, computers, disk drives, semiconductors, telecommunications equipment, pharmaceuticals, biotechnology and even military weapons and communications systems—are currently transitioning from closed to open innovation. For such businesses, a number of critically important innovations have emerged from seemingly unlikely sources. Indeed, the locus of innovation in these industries has migrated beyond the confines of the central R&D laboratories of the largest companies and is now situated among various startups, universities, research consortia, and other outside organizations. This trend goes well beyond high technology—other industries such as automotive, health care, banking, insurance, and consumer packaged goods have also been leaning toward open innovation.

THE DIFFERENT MODES OF INNOVATION

Indeed, many companies have been defining new strategies for exploiting the principles of open innovation, exploring ways in which external technologies can fill gaps in their current businesses and looking at how their internal technologies can spawn the seeds of new businesses outside the current organization. In doing so, many firms have focused their activities into one of three primary areas: funding, generating, or commercializing innovation.

FUNDING INNOVATION

Two types of organizations—innovation investors and benefactors are focused primarily on supplying fuel for the innovation fire. The original innovation investor was the corporate R&D budget but now a wide range of other types has emerged, including venture capital (VC) firms, angel investors, corporate VC entities, private equity investors and the Small Business Investment Companies (SBICs), which provide VC to small, independent businesses and are licensed and regulated by the U.S. Small Business Administration. Their capital helps move ideas out of corporations and universities and into the market, typically through the creation of startups. In addition to financing, innovation investors can supply valuable advice for helping startups avoid the common growing pains that afflict many fledgling firms.

With the recent economic downturn and the implosion of numerous dot-com firms, innovation investors have understandably turned somewhat gun-shy. However, though it seems these players are down, they are hardly out. VCs currently have about \$250 billion in capital under management, of which \$90 billion is idle. When the economy rebounds, innovation investors will likely spot and fund new developments in areas like genomics and nanotechnology, which will likely spur the next economic wave of innovation.

Innovation benefactors provide new sources of research funding. Unlike investors, benefactors focus on the early stages of research discovery. The classic example here is the National Science Foundation (NSF), an independent agency of the U.S. government. Through its awards and grants programs, the NSF provides about 20% of federal support for academic institutions to conduct basic research. The Defense Advanced Research Projects Agency (DARPA) has also been a key benefactor, particularly for the early work in much of the computer industry.

Some companies are devoting a portion of their resources to playing the role of benefactor. By funding promising early-stage work, they get a first look at the ideas and can selectively fund those that seem favorable for their industry. An interesting development with innovation benefactors is the possible rise in philanthropy from private foundations, especially those backed by wealthy individuals. For example, the billionaire Larry Ellison, chairman and CEO of software giant Oracle, has founded an organization that provides about \$50 million annually for basic research in cancer, Parkinson's and Alzheimer's diseases, as well as other disorders. Interestingly, the foundation was set up specifically for early exploration—research so embryonic that scientists aren't able to obtain funds through traditional grants, such as those awarded by the NSF.

GENERATING INNOVATION

There are four types of organizations that primarily generate innovation: innovation explorers, merchants, architects, and missionaries. Innovation explorers specialize in performing the discovery research function that previously took place primarily within corporate R&D laboratories. Interestingly, a number of explorers evolved as spinoffs of laboratories that used to be a part of a larger organization. Just a year ago, for example, PARC became a separate, independent entity from Xerox. Similarly, Telcordia Technologies was formed from the divestiture of the Bell System and is now home to about 400 researchers with a broad range of expertise, from software engineering to optical networking.

An interesting development with explorers has been taking place with the major government labs, such as Sandia National Laboratories, Lawrence Livermore National Laboratory, and the MIT Lincoln Laboratory. In the aftermath of the end of the Cold War, these organizations have been seeking new missions for their work and much of their basic research is finding applications in commercial markets. Consider Lincoln Laboratory, which has conducted radar and other defense research since the 1950s. Technology developed there for missile detection has recently been adapted to cancer treatment, enabling microwave energy to be focused more effectively at tumors.

Innovation merchants must also explore, but their activities are focused on a narrow set of technologies that are then codified into intellectual property and aggressively sold to (and brought to market by) others. In other words, innovation merchants will innovate but only with specific commercial goals in mind, whereas explorers tend to innovate for innovation's sake. For the merchants, royalties from their IP enable them to do more research in their areas of focus. Indeed, such companies rise and fall with the strength of their IP portfolios.

One example of an innovation merchant is Qualcomm, which conducts extensive internal research on telecommunications, including code division multiple access (CDMA), a standard for wireless technology. Originally, Qualcomm manufactured cellular phones and software products such as the Eudora e-mail program, but today it focuses on licensing its CDMA technology and producing the associated chipsets for use by other cell phone manufacturers. Qualcomm currently boasts more than 100 licensees, including Motorola, Nokia, and Kyocera.

Innovation architects provide a valuable service in complicated technology worlds. In order to create value for their customers, they develop architectures that partition this complexity, enabling numerous other companies to provide pieces of the system, all the while ensuring that those parts fit together in a coherent way. Boeing, for example, will engineer the overall design of an aircraft like the 747, after which companies like GE can then develop and manufacture the jet engines and other constituent parts. Innovation architects work in areas that are complex and fast-moving, which disfavors the "do-it-yourself" approach. To be successful, innovation architects must establish their systems solution, communicate it, persuade others to support it, and develop it in the future. They must also devise a way to capture some portion of the value they create, otherwise they will find it impossible to sustain and advance their architecture.

For example, the dramatic rise of Nokia in wireless communications has been due, in part, to the strong lead it took in establishing the global system for mobile communication (GSM) technology as a standard for cellular phones. Accomplishing that required working closely with a number of other companies, as well as the governments of many European countries. Specifically, Nokia research helped define the now accepted standards for moving GSM from a narrow- to broad-bandwidth spectrum and the company pushed hard to establish that technology: It willingly licensed the research to others and partnered with companies (including competitors) to develop the chipsets necessary for implementing the standard. Those efforts have helped Nokia to become the world's dominant supplier of wireless-phone handsets, controlling nearly 40% of the global market.

Innovation missionaries consist of people and organizations that create and advance technologies to serve a cause. Unlike the innovation merchants and architects, they do not seek financial profits from their work. Instead, the mission is what motivates them. This is characteristic of many community-based nonprofits and religious groups but also occurs in the software industry. Here, user groups help define how a particular software program will evolve. These organizations, which include professional programmers as well as hobbyists, not only identify bugs (and possible ways to fix them), but additionally might even create a "wish list" of potential features that the next generation of a software product might include.

The evolution of the computer operating system Linux exemplifies this approach. Originally developed by Linus Torvalds, Linux has advanced over the years thanks to the arduous efforts of an informal network of programmers around the world. The software is freely available to anyone, and it has become a viable alternative to commercial offerings such as Microsoft Windows NT.

COMMERCIALIZING INNOVATION

Lastly, two types of organization are focused on bringing innovations to market: innovation marketers and one-stop centers. Innovation marketers often perform at least some of the functions of the other types of organization, but their defining attribute is their keen ability to profitably market ideas, both their own and those of others. To do so, marketers focus on developing a deep understanding of the current and potential needs in the market and this helps them to identify which outside ideas to bring in-house. Most of the drugs that are currently in Pfizer's pipeline, for instance, originated outside the company.

Innovation one-stop centers provide comprehensive products and services. They take the best ideas (from whatever source) and deliver those offerings to their customers at competitive prices. Like innovation marketers, they thrive by selling others' ideas, but are different in that they typically form unshakable connections to the end users, increasingly managing a customer's resources to his or her specifications. For example, the website for Yahoo! enables people to shop, send e-mail, manage their personal finances, hunt for jobs, and keep up-to-date on current events.

While Yahoo! targets consumers, other one-stop centers are focused on business-to-business interactions. IBM's Global Services division, for instance, sells IT solutions to other companies, and interestingly, will install and service hardware and software from any vendor, including IBM's competitors. In other words, it will provide the best solution to its customers, regardless of the origin of those products.

Although many companies are focusing on just funding, generating, or commercializing innovation, some are continuing to do all three. As mentioned earlier, industrial powerhouses like GE, DuPont, and AT&T (with Bell Labs) were the exemplars of this approach in the United States during the twentieth century, and the success of those corporations has cast the mold for most central R&D organizations. To this day, a number of companies, called fully integrated innovators, continue to espouse the closed innovation credo of "innovation through total control."

IBM in the mainframe computer market is one such example. ...IBM's mainframe business raises an important point: A corporation can deploy different modes of innovation in different markets. Specifically, IBM is a one-stop center for consulting services and a fully integrated innovator with respect to mainframes. Another important point is that competing modes can coexist in the same industry. In pharmaceuticals, for example, Merck has remained a fully integrated innovator while Pfizer is becoming an innovation marketer. It remains to be seen which of those modes (or perhaps another) will dominate.

All of the different modes will evolve in an open innovation environment, and future ones will probably emerge as well. One possible development is the rise of specialized intermediaries that function as brokers or middlemen to create markets for IP. More than likely, there won't be one "best way" to innovate, although some modes will face greater challenges than others.

Fully integrated innovators, for instance, have become an endangered species in many industries. As ideas spill out of the central R&D labs of large corporations, the other modes of innovation are in a position to profit from them. In fact, these other modes have risen in prominence in response to the perceived limitations of fully integrated innovators. Much of IBM's innovation, for instance, has been migrating from the fully integrated mode toward the one-stop center approach.

The explorer mode depends on external sources of funding because of the considerable resources and uncertainty of conducting long-term research. Outside of the life sciences, this support has dwindled substantially in the past decade, making a number of explorers vulnerable.

Innovation merchants also face significant challenges. Although the concept of supplying innovation to a "marketplace for ideas" is attractive in theory, it is devilishly tricky to accomplish. For one thing, merchants must determine how best to gain access to the complementary assets that might be needed to commercialize an innovation. Another issue is that the laws for IP protection are ill-defined at best, making it risky for merchants to limit their revenue stream solely to the marketing of their IP.

Innovation architects encounter a different set of challenges in their roles of organizing and coordinating complex technologies. Although ideas are plentiful, that very abundance can make it extremely difficult to create useful systems. Furthermore, innovation architects, through the harnessing of a broad network of companies, must balance the creation of value with the need to capture a portion of that value. Boeing, for instance, is able to do so by acting as the systems assembler for its aircraft. With other technologies, however, the means by which innovation architects can benefit from their roles is not so straightforward.

Several of the modes of innovation rely on a continued supply of useful ideas and technologies from the outside. Although university research is now more abundant and of higher quality than in the past, the flow of that knowledge into the commercial sector faces several obstacles. Such research is necessarily filtered through the silos of academic departments and that process tends to discourage cross-discipline breakthroughs. In addition, universities are now allowed to patent their discoveries, and although the change has benefited professors (who are able to form their own commercial ventures), it has also taxed the efforts of companies, particularly small firms, to profit from that source of innovation.

LONG LIVE OPEN INNOVATION

Today, in many industries, the logic that supports an internally oriented, centralized approach to R&D has become obsolete. Useful knowledge has become widespread and ideas must be used with alacrity. If not, they will be lost. Such factors create a new logic of open innovation that embraces external ideas and knowledge in conjunction with internal R&D. This change offers novel ways to create value—along with new opportunities to claim portions of that value.

However, companies must still perform the difficult and arduous work necessary to convert promising research results into products and services that satisfy customers' needs. Specifically, the role of R&D needs to extend far beyond the boundaries of the firm. Innovators must integrate their ideas, expertise, and skills with those of others outside the organization to deliver the result to the marketplace, using the most effective means possible. In short, firms that can harness outside ideas to advance their own businesses while leveraging their internal ideas outside their current operations will likely thrive in this new era of open innovation.

READING 16.4

The Core Competencies of Project-Based Firms* BY JOSEPH LAMPEL

"Project-based firms" focus on the design, development, and delivery of projects. Examples of such firms can be found in areas as disparate as motion pictures, software engineering, or satellite launching. Their challenge is to reconcile flexibility with efficiency: finding a workable balance between the demand of clients for customized and highly specific products, and the imperative of remaining commercially viable (Turner and Keegan, 1999).

The challenge is particularly acute for project-based firms whose primary business is designing, building, and supplying large projects such as power plants, oil platforms, mass transit systems, and toll roads. Collectively, project-based firms that specialize in this area are often known as EPC firms, or "engineering–procurement–construction" firms. Dealing with diversity stretches the resource base of EPC firms to the limit, principally because they are required to configure and reconfigure their resources on a project-by-project basis. Achieving the flexibility necessary for addressing project variation calls for a matrix structure, but this is at best a partial solution to the essential problem of diversity (Bartlett and Ghoshal, 1990). In this paper, we argue that EPC firms develop a more robust approach that is based on developing core competencies that support reconfiguration of resources in response to shifting design and market demands.

THE COMPETENCY BASE OF ENGINEERING-CONSTRUCTION FIRMS

Flexibility in this context means an ability to configure and reconfigure a bundle of resources according to the demands of a particular project. This ability is in turn an expression of what Prahalad and Hamel (1990) term the firm's "core competencies." For them, the key characteristics were the following:

a. Core competencies embody the collective learning of the organization: it is the tested and proven knowledge the firm acquires in the process of learning its business.

---

*Adapted from "The Core Competencies of Project-Based Firms," *International Journal of Project Management*, 2001.

b. Core competencies embody coordinating skills: skills to coordinate diverse operations, skills to harmonize different technologies, and skills to coordinate relationships with a heterogeneous customer base.
c. Core competencies embody a shared understanding of customer needs, even before these become explicit to the customer.
d. Core competencies embody the deep understanding of the product and market possibilities that are inherent in the firm's technological knowledge base.
e. Core competencies embody intangibles such as culture and ideology that serve to bind the firm's various businesses together.

Strategy for diversified corporations, argue Prahalad and Hamel, is not based on static synergies or on finding the optimal portfolio of businesses, but on constantly renewing the firm's market position. Core competencies are the key to this renewal. Their relationship to the market is not, however, direct. Core competencies nourish core products and technologies. These core products and technologies in turn generate the products that are sold in the marketplace. In project-based service firms, however, where final products are defined by the unique requirements of individual consumers, there are no core products or core technologies to link final products with core competencies. Instead, what we have are core processes that describe the life cycle of most, if not all, large projects, from an exploratory phase involving formulation of the basic project concept—usually involving contacts with potential clients and sponsors—which leads to detailed technical studies and costing estimates, and then uses the analysis to prepare bids. Bids may be won directly, or they may form the basis for further negotiations with clients and sponsors. EPC firms that win contracts become part of the execution phase during which the project becomes a reality. The project comes to an end when the system is commissioned and put into operation.

Applying the Prahalad and Hamel (1990) framework to the EPC sector suggests that these core processes form an intermediate link between specific projects and core competencies. They structure activities and routines of projects but they do not account for the quality of outcome because they do not contain the full range of knowledge, both explicit and tacit, needed to tackle the key problems of project planning and execution. This knowledge is contained in the core competencies of EPC firms.

My research on EPC firms in the United States, Canada, the United Kingdom, France, Malaysia, and Japan suggests that they base their operations on essentially four types of core competencies: entrepreneurial competencies, technical competencies, evaluative competencies, and relational competencies.

ENTREPRENEURIAL COMPETENCIES

Entrepreneurial competencies are by their nature experience based. Capturing contracts depends on detecting opportunities as they emerge, or even better, of stimulating the emergence of opportunities by bringing project ideas to the attention of potential clients. To do this well, EPC firms must be able to "sell" the idea to potential clients. Selling ideas is intrinsically difficult. Clients are naturally risk averse when it comes to large projects—large projects call for large investments with pay-offs that are many years in the future. They are even more risk averse when the projects do not originate from within their own organization, or from organizations and institutions with which they have a long-standing relationship.

Entrepreneurial competencies are the product of experience, but they also depend on intuition, which in turn makes them almost impossible to articulate and share. This makes it difficult for organizations to evaluate the quality of entrepreneurial decision making by individuals who are assumed to have these competencies. It is generally difficult in retrospect to isolate the reasons that led to the success or failure of particular projects. Much depends ultimately on the history of the organization. Some EPC firms begin their life highly entrepreneurial and gradually lose these competencies, becoming highly bureaucratic. Other EPC firms are highly bureaucratic to begin with but subsequently make strenuous efforts to acquire entrepreneurial competencies (e.g., utilities that undertake projects overseas).

TECHNICAL COMPETENCIES

There is a curious paradox in the large project game: Owners and sponsors have the power to define the project broadly, but only the EPC firm has the knowledge to fill in the details. Bridging this gap is costly and time-consuming for the owners and sponsors. They would like to place a limit on the number of bids they must evaluate, and they would also like to avoid costly evaluation of bids from EPC firms that lack the knowledge and experience needed to undertake the project in the first place. In order to achieve this aim owners and sponsors institute a qualifying process, which allows only a selected number of firms to participate in the competitive bidding. The key question this process seeks to answer is: Can this firm develop a technically proficient bid, and if it can, will it be able to execute the contract successfully?

The qualifying process highlights the technical competencies of the EPC firm. Engineering, procurement, construction, and operations are embedded and supported by a wide array of activities that are technical in both the narrow and broad sense of this term. Technical competencies relate first and foremost to the effective use of technological assets and engineering know-how.

Technical competencies target areas that are programmable. Programmable activities are activities that can be broken down, analyzed, and described in detail. They can be acquired via traditional education methods and are widely available in books, monographs, and manuals. The knowledge base of programmable competencies is, therefore, relatively accessible. In this respect it is relatively shallow, representing the minimum necessary for qualifying in bidding but in itself not sufficient for translating this into contracts. To do this, technical competencies must be able to identify crucial knowledge and move it to the place where it is needed in a timely fashion; it must be able to rapidly absorb knowledge from the wider environment; it must be able to learn from its own experience; and it must be able to innovate solutions for both old and new problems.

None of these activities is programmable in the strict sense of the term. They simply resist being broken down, analyzed, described, and codified. They are richly tacit precisely because they require a large amount of experience and sensitivity to context.

EVALUATIVE COMPETENCIES

It is not sufficient for EPC firms to transform opportunities into contracts, it must do so at a profit. A crucial stage in this process arrives when the EPC firm must move beyond exploration to commitment: what is it willing to do, and at what price? In the game of large projects, this overt declaration is crucial because EPC firms are stuck with their initial estimates of what they are willing to do and at what price. There is rarely much latitude for revision once the contract has been signed.

Given the complexity and uncertainty of projects these estimates are guesswork, but they are guesswork on which the welfare of the firm depends. A low-cost estimate or an overly ambitious schedule may result in losses or may even bankrupt the company. A high-cost estimate or an excessively cautious schedule may lose a promising contract to a competitor. The EPC firm must navigate between these two undesirable outcomes, and it must also do it in such a way as to make as much money as possible. Ultimately, this is a judgment of risks.

Every EPC firm that surveyed for purposes of this study had in place a system charged with this task. The system was invariably a mixture of formal analysis and informal organizational processes. With the advent of high-power information systems there have been determined efforts by many organizations to shift the process as far toward the formal as possible. However, even these organizations recognize that there are limits to how far this can be accomplished. Large projects are customized systems; they are intrinsically complex and almost always contain features that are unique to the particular project. Estimating the cost of large projects is ultimately an art, not a science; the task is simply not programmable. An assessment of the cost of a project in light of a given design and customer requirement must rely on the tacit expertise of experience of engineers and managers. But tapping this expertise requires an elaborate review system in which potential problems are identified and collectively discussed.

The review system is based on two elements: judgment and memory. Both have explicit and tacit elements, and the balance between the two varies, depending on the organizations. Almost every organization employs checklists and other formal methods to break down and weigh the elements of the project that may impact on cost, performance, or schedule. These methods, however, are supplemented and modified by managerial judgment. The process is social: managers and engineers discuss and debate their judgments. It is also often aided by specialist organizational units which deal with financial engineering and bid preparation.

The other aspect of the review system is memory. Evaluation always relies on what the organization has learned from other projects. This learning is embedded in human recollection: those who were involved in previous projects can provide information about the problems that were encountered in similar projects in the past. Memory, however, is also based on documentation. Many organizations systematically collect and analyze data about every project in which they have been involved. This data is often transformed into "work books" which are consulted when a new project is evaluated. Many organizations are also beginning to use information systems to create databases which can be consulted more efficiently and thoroughly.

RELATIONAL COMPETENCIES

Large projects are interdependent and evolving relational systems (Fonfara, 1989). They bring together a wide range of actors and institutions in different capacities, with different degree of involvement, and different amount of power to facilitate or hinder the development of the project. The interaction among these actors and institutions is unpredictable and prone to breakdowns. A manager in one of the firms I interviewed reflected on the fragility of the process in the following way: "A project is a life-organism that is subject to a lot of unexpected shocks and discontinuities. The attempt of all involved is to keep this organism moving forward. The unexpected is almost inevitable, and there is always a need for a lot of adjustment."

Getting all involved to adjust to unforeseen circumstances is essential in all projects. There are always unforeseen contingencies that call for improvisation and creative problem solving. In projects that are largely confined to a single organization, adjustment is greatly facilitated by the existence of centralized coordination. But large projects are normally a collaborative effort by a group of organizations in which none wields complete control. Adjustment in such a situation may unleash conflicts that can threaten the foundations of the collaborative process. The threat is present throughout the project but is particularly acute during the front-end part when many issues have yet to be resolved and final commitments have yet to be made.

Forestalling this threat, or dealing with it effectively when it arises, calls for a range of relational skills. The skills are an expression of relational competencies that combine both individual and organizational experiences. Their primary relevance is for managing the business interaction, but by having an impact on the interaction process, relational competencies have a substantial impact on its content as well.

Nowhere is this more important than in the interaction between EPC firms and their primary clients. The relationship is fraught with paradox. EPC firms and their clients begin with opposing interests. Each one wants to strike a deal that will maximize its own advantage, but each also knows that the relentless pursuit of advantage may undermine the very goal they are seeking, which is concluding a deal.

This transforming of an adversarial interaction into a cooperative relationship, and then making this relationship last through the vicissitudes of the project, is the basic challenge confronting EPC firms. Relational competencies are crucial to this process, but until recently these competencies were confined largely to the marketing and sales department of most EPC firms. It was their task to inform and persuade clients, and to act as liaison between the client and the rest of the organization when difficulties arise. The disadvantage of this approach is that it did not deal with adversarial attitude in the rest of the organization, in particular in the engineering and execution areas. This may result in organizational polarization to the point where, as one manager put it: "The salesman is Mr. Nice Guy, and the project manager is Mr. Nasty."

Submerging conflict during project development and contractual discussion, only to have it surface subsequently, can be costly and destructive. Otherwise, there is much recrimination. Since many projects do not end well, it is not surprising that the history of large projects is rife with bitter disputes between EPC firms and their clients. Playing Mr. Nice Guy at the beginning works when one side, or both, prefer to look the other way with the hope or intention of dealing with the downside of the agreement when it suits them. As one manager put it: "The clients like to perceive a 'cozy' relationship. In reality it is mayhem. We renegotiate all the time."

A new model is currently emerging which relies heavily on relational competencies: partnering. The essence of partnering is the joint exploration of scoping and design prior to agreement. Instead of negotiating the project from a zero-sum perspective, the firms involved explore options that maximize performance and reduce costs simultaneously. Teamwork is the operative intent. Let the professionals get together without the interfering presence of pure commercial and legal considerations, and they will come up with solutions that would not have emerged from an adversarial process.

THE STRATEGIES OF EPC FIRMS FROM A CORE COMPETENCE PERSPECTIVE

The notion of strategy revolves around creating a close relationship between actions and preferred outcomes. In most industries gaining and holding high market share is a preferred outcome. Failure to do this is seen as a sign either that the company is undertaking the wrong actions or that the actions that it is undertaking have no impact on outcomes. This model cannot be applied to EPC firms. Large projects are too heterogeneous to allow for meaningful and stable market definition; and without market definition the concept of market share also has no meaning.

My research suggests that when it comes to addressing this issue EPC firms are pulled in two opposing directions. On the one hand there is the pressure to remain close to what the EPC firm knows and does best; to leverage rather than stretch core competencies (Prahalad and Hamel, 1993). On the other hand, there is the pressure to focus on the portfolio; to generate volume, build economies of scale, and reduce overall risk. My study suggests that EPC firms respond to these forces by developing three generic strategies. The first, which I call "focusing strategy," is to target opportunities that are close to their existing competencies. The second, which I call "switching strategy," is at the opposite extreme of the spectrum. It involves targeting lucrative opportunities almost anywhere that they can be found, stretching existing competencies as far as they allow. Finally, a third strategy, which we call "combining strategy," attempts to find a balance between existing competencies and lucrative opportunities.

FOCUSING STRATEGY

A focusing strategy sees opportunities through the lens of competencies. The strategic cycle of EPC firms that pursue a focusing strategy begins with competencies and from there it leads to opportunities. Competencies should beget lucrative opportunities rather than the other way around. First, because a firm with strong competencies has a better chance when it comes to bidding. And, second, because having strong competencies not only improves quality and performance, but it also reduces costly errors.

But what are strong competencies? EPC firms that follow a focusing strategy see strong competencies as competencies that provide the greatest leverage. This inevitably leads to an emphasis on competency depth at the expense of breadth. Experience and knowledge are cultivated as much as possible along a narrow front, rather than seeking a broad coverage of many different types of projects.

SWITCHING STRATEGIES

EPC firms that follow a switching strategy fall on the other side of the competencies–opportunities spectrum. They are determinedly opportunity driven. This means seeking high-quality opportunities wherever they may be found; trying to capture these opportunities, and then turning their attention to transforming these opportunities into revenues.

The advantage of this strategy resides in the fact that it deals directly with the key uncertainty of the large project game: the difficulty of predicting the flow or composition of projects.

A switching strategy seeks to avoid the perils of specializing in a particular region or type of projects by maintaining a flexible set of competencies. The intent is not so much to create a diversified project portfolio as it is to have the ability to track changes in the stream of projects. The key to switching strategy is the ability to stretch competencies to cover a multitude of contexts and requirements. By definition, this is easier to do when competencies are broad rather than deep.

COMBINING STRATEGY

Focusing strategy and switching strategy represent two poles of a continuum. For firms that wish neither to be dominated by their competencies nor to be driven by opportunities, the third choice is to find a middle ground. This middle ground is grounded in competencies but is on the whole still oriented toward opportunities. The main difference here, however, is that there is a systematic attempt to focus on related opportunities areas and then work backward to the competencies necessary to serve these areas.

If firms that follow a focusing strategy are specialists when it comes to their approach to competencies and opportunities, firms that follow a combining strategy are specialists when it comes to pursing opportunities, and generalists when it comes to competencies. Careful attention to organizational design helps to balance the inevitable tension that exists between these two opposing imperatives. There is no one way of achieving this goal; each organization evolves its own approach.

CONCLUSION

In this paper I argue that the life cycle of large projects can be described by core processes that structure activities and routines. The transition from one process to the next is often punctuated by key events during which the impact of core competencies becomes strongly evident. Perhaps the main event confronting EPC firms is the moment when they discover whether they have succeeded or failed in winning the contract. EPC firms use their competencies to accomplish this goal, but they are aware that they cannot craft their strategies with a view to winning specific projects. All they can do is craft their strategies to maximize their chances of winning certain projects on advantageous terms.

The key to doing this successfully is developing a positively reinforcing relationship among core competencies, project choice, and project portfolio. Crucial to achieving this virtuous cycle is acquiring, developing, and managing the correct mix of key competencies: technical, which contains basic know-how and the ability to design and execute a particular project; entrepreneurial, which contains marketing and project opportunity know-how; relational, which contains skills and know-how for developing and negotiating projects; and evaluative, which contains routines designed to evaluate costs and measure risks.

EPC firms must cultivate all four competencies because each competency addresses problems that are intrinsic to the business they are in. They are also in principle insoluble: economic change, political turmoil, and technological innovations are constantly changing the nature of the problems facing EPC firms and, hence, reducing the effectiveness of proven practices and solutions. To maintain their strategic position EPC firms must, therefore, not only possess competencies that deal with current problems, they must also have the ability to reshape these competencies in the light of new circumstances.

How do EPC firms do this? To some extent competencies evolve indirectly as a result of the inevitable learning that takes place when EPC firms tackle new projects. Such evolution, however, is haphazard. It is contingent on organizational processes that are often poorly understood and mostly difficult to control. Factors such as top management thinking, team dynamics, and political rivalries can hinder as well as facilitate the development of competencies. Ultimately, however, strategy exercises an important influence on competence development, and EPC strategy, as noted earlier, is shaped by pervasive tension between the imperative of competencies and the lure of market opportunities.

CHAPTER 17

Managing Diversity

A good deal of evidence has accumulated on the relationship between diversification and divisionalization. Once organizations diversify their product or service lines, they tend to create distinct divisions to deal with each business. This relationship was perhaps first carefully documented in the classic historical study by Alfred D. Chandler, *Strategy and Structure: Chapters in the History of the Great American Enterprise*. Chandler traced the origins of diversification and divisionalization in Du Pont and General Motors in the 1920s, which were followed later by other major firms. A number of other studies elaborated on Chandler's conclusions, as discussed in the readings of this chapter.

The first reading, drawn from Mintzberg's work on structuring, probes the structure of divisionalization—how it works, what brings it about, what intermediate variations of it exist, and what problems it poses for organizations that use it and for society at large. It concludes on a rather pessimistic note about conglomerate diversification and about the purer forms of divisionalization.

Across the world, diversified corporations take many different forms. That is why we have included the next reading by Philippe Lasserre of INSEAD. Lasserre describes three forms that such organizations take in the West, which he labels industrial group, industrial holdings, and financial conglomerates. Then he describes three that are common in Asia, labeled entrepreneurial conglomerates, *keiretsus*, and national holdings. When he compares them, an interesting result emerges: Whereas organizations in the West tend to control impersonally (or analytically) and yet in some ways more loosely (or less synergistically), the Asians favor softer and more personalized forms of control but often achieve tighter connections. (Harking back to Pitcher's three styles of managing, the technocrats are more common in the West apparently, whereas the artists and craftsmen are easier to find in the East.) Lasserre warns, however, that you cannot just adopt an approach because it looks good: Beware of the limitations of your own culture!

Aspects of the diversified organization, particularly in its more conglomerate form, come under some heavy criticism in this chapter and in the next reading, too. But it quickly turns to the more constructive question of how to use strategy to combine a cluster of different businesses into an effective corporate entity. This is Michael Porter's article entitled "From Competitive Advantage to Corporate Strategy." Porter discusses in a most insightful way various types of overall corporate strategies, including portfolio management, restructuring, transferring skills, and sharing activities (the last two are referred to in his 1985 book *Competitive Advantage* as "horizontal strategies"). The former deals with "intangible" whereas the latter deals with "tangible" interrelationships among business units and are conceived in terms of his value chain.

USING THE CASE STUDIES

The strategy process in diversified firms can be strongly influenced by the size and geographic reach of the firm in question. The Johnson & Johnson case deals with an American healthcare conglomerate. Heineken, and Cadbury Schweppes, on the other hand, deals with a company that has been involved in a highly ambitious program of geographic diversification. The challenge for both these companies is finding the right structure to manage diversity effectively. The article that examines the different structural options available to diversified corporations is relevant for analysis of these cases, as well as for Procter and Gamble, which also deal with geographic and product diversity. The reading by Phillip Lasserre, "Managing Large Groups in the East and West," suggests that different approaches to diversity are more likely to emerge in the East as opposed to Europe or North America. The book contains a number of cases that deal with diversified Asian corporations, for example, Haier, and Wipro, but also Western diversified corporations such as Procter and Gamble, and Natura. A number of these are expanding into Asia. It would be interesting to see if they shift structure in response to their new environment.

Porter's reading opens up the issue of managing diversity to wider consideration. Diversity is often a by-product of growth, but it is growth with potential pitfalls. Porter's analysis of the advantages and disadvantages of corporate diversification is relevant to cases such as Johnson and Johnson. It can also be used to explain Procter and Gamble's diversification into prestige fragrances, and the difficulties confronting Cadbury Schweppes's push into soft drinks in North America, and to evaluate if Howard Fisk, the head of Axion Consulting, is right to pursue a merger with a management consulting firm.

READING 17.1

The Diversified Organization* BY HENRY MINTZBERG

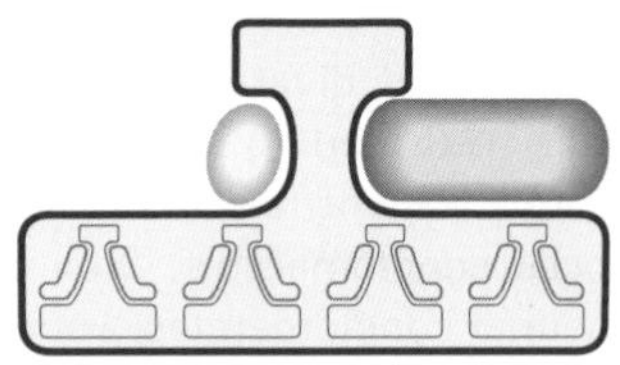

THE BASIC DIVISIONALIZED STRUCTURE

The diversified organization is not so much an integrated entity as a set of semiautonomous units coupled together by a central administrative structure. The units are generally called *divisions*, and the central administration, the *headquarters*. This is a widely used configuration in the private sector of the industrialized economy; the vast majority of the *Fortune* 500, America's largest corporations, use this structure or a variant of it. But, as we shall see, it is also found in other sectors as well.

In what is commonly called the "divisionalized" form of structure, units, called "divisions," are created to serve distinct markets and are given control over the operating functions necessary to do so, as shown in Figure 1. Each is therefore relatively free of direct control by headquarters or even of the need to coordinate activities with other divisions. Each, in other words, appears to be a self-standing business. Of course, none is. There *is* a headquarters, and it has a series of roles that distinguish this overall configuration from a collection of independent businesses providing the same set of products and services.

*Adapted from *The Structuring of Organizations* (Prentice Hall, 1979), Chap. 20 on "The Divisionalized Form." A chapter similar to this appeared in *Mintzberg on Management: Inside Our Strange World of Organizations* (Free Press, 1989).

ROLES OF THE HEADQUARTERS

Above all, the headquarters exercises performance control. It sets standards of achievement, generally in quantitative terms (such as return on investment or growth in sales), and then monitors the results. Coordination between headquarters and the divisions thus reduces largely to the standardization of outputs. Of course, there is some direct supervision—headquarters' managers have to have personal contact with and knowledge of the divisions. But that is largely circumscribed by the key assumption in this configuration that if the division managers are to be responsible for the performance of their divisions, they must have considerable autonomy to manage them as they see fit. Hence there is extensive delegation of authority from headquarters to the level of division manager.

Certain important tasks do, however, remain for the headquarters. One is to develop the overall *corporate* strategy, meaning to establish the portfolio of businesses in which the organization will operate. The headquarters establishes, acquires, divests, and closes down divisions in order to change its portfolio. Popular in the 1970s in this regard was the Boston Consulting Group's "growth share matrix," where corporate managers were supposed to allocate funds to divisions on the basis of their falling into the categories of dogs, cash cows, wildcats, and stars. But enthusiasm for that technique waned, perhaps mindful of Pope's warning that a little learning can be a dangerous thing.

Second, the headquarters manages the movement of funds between the divisions, taking the excess profits of some to support the greater growth potential of others. Third, of course, the headquarters, through its own technostructure, designs and operates the performance control system. Fourth, it appoints and therefore retains the right to replace the division managers. For a headquarters that does not directly manage any division, its most tangible power when the performance of a division lags—short of riding out an industry downturn or divesting the division—is to replace its leader. Finally, the headquarters provides certain support services that are common to all the divisions—a corporate public relations office or legal counsel, for example.

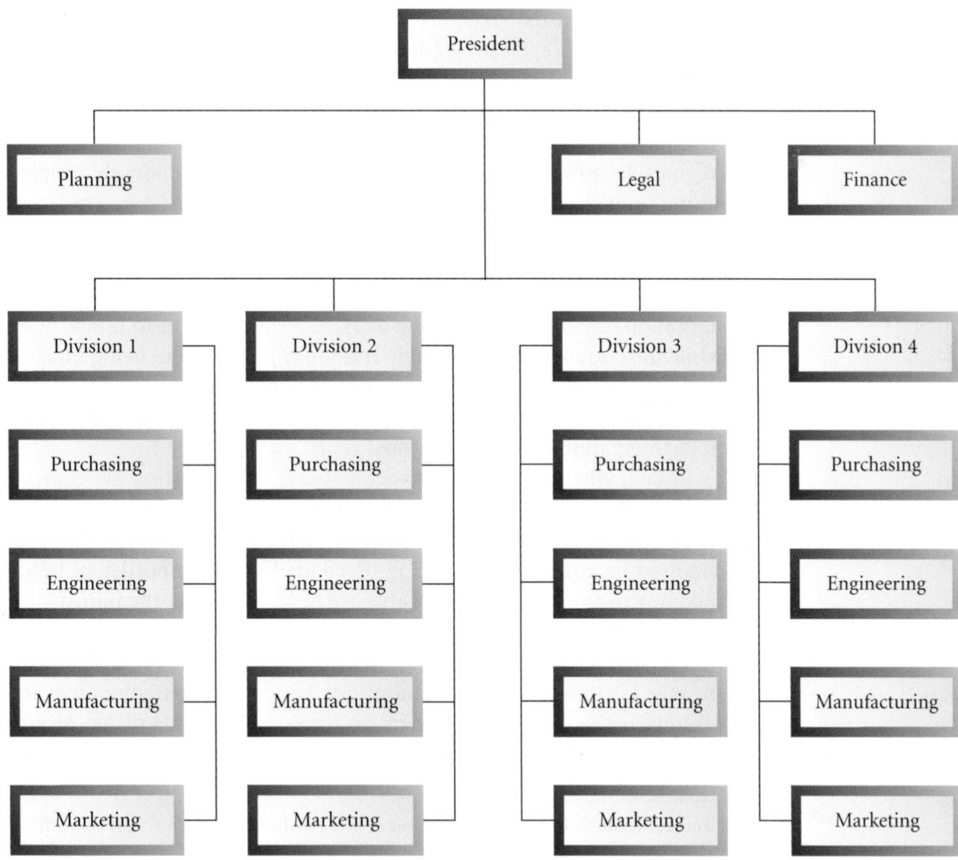

FIGURE 1
TYPICAL ORGANIGRAM FOR A DIVISIONALIZED MANUFACTURING FIRM

STRUCTURE OF THE DIVISIONS

It has been common to label divisionalized organizations "decentralized." That is a reflection of how *certain* of them came to be, most notably Du Pont early in this century. When organizations that were structured functionally (for example, in departments of marketing, manufacturing, and engineering, etc.) diversified, they found that coordination of their different product lines across the functions became increasingly complicated. The central managers had to spend great amounts of time intervening to resolve disputes. But once these corporations switched to a divisionalized form of structure, where all the functions for a given business could be contained in a single unit dedicated to that business, management became much simpler. In effect, their structures became *more* decentralized, power over distinct businesses being delegated to the division managers.

But more decentralized does not mean *decentralized.* That word refers to the dispersal of decision-making power in an organization, and in many of the diversified corporations much of the power tended to remain with the few managers who ran the businesses. Indeed, the most famous case of divisionalization was one of relative *centralization*: Alfred P. Sloan introduced the divisionalized structure to General Motors in the 1920s to *reduce* the power of its autonomous business units, to impose systems of financial controls on what had been a largely unmanaged agglomeration of different automobile businesses.

In fact, I would argue that it is the *centralization* of power within the divisions that is most compatible with the divisionalized form of structure. In other words, the effect of having a headquarters over the divisions is to drive them toward the machine configuration, namely a structure of centralized bureaucracy. That is the structure most compatible with headquarters control, in my opinion. If true, this would seem to be an important point, because it means that the proliferation of the diversified configuration in many spheres—business, government, and the rest—has the effect of driving many suborganizations toward machine bureaucracy, even where that configuration may be inappropriate (school systems, for example, or government departments charged with innovative project work).

The explanation for this lies in the standardization of outputs, the key to the functioning of the divisionalized structure. Bear in mind the headquarters' dilemma: to respect divisional autonomy while exercising control over performance. This it seeks to resolve by after-the-fact monitoring of divisional results, based on clearly defined performance standards. But two main assumptions underlie such standards.

First, each division must be treated as a single integrated system with a single, consistent set of goals. In other words, although the divisions may be loosely coupled with each other, the assumption is that each is tightly coupled internally.*

Second, these goals must be operational ones, in other words, lend themselves to quantitative measurement. But in the less formal configurations—entrepreneurial and innovative—which are less stable, such performance standards are difficult to establish, while in the professional configuration, the complexity of the work makes it difficult to establish such standards. Moreover, while the entrepreneurial configuration may lend itself to being integrated around a single set of goals, the innovative and professional configurations do not. Thus, only the machine configuration of the major types fits comfortably into the conventional divisionalized structure, by virtue of its integration and its operational goals.

In fact, when organizations with another configuration are drawn under the umbrella of a divisionalized structure, they tend to be forced toward the machine bureaucratic form, to make them conform with *its* needs. How often have we heard stories of entrepreneurial firms recently acquired by conglomerates being descended upon by hordes of headquarters technocrats bemoaning the loose controls, the absence of organigrams, the informality of the systems? In many cases, of course, the very purpose of the acquisition was to do just this, tighten up the organization so that its strategies can be pursued more pervasively and systematically. But other times, the effect is to destroy the organization's basic strengths, sometimes including its flexibility and responsiveness. Similarly, how many times have we heard tell of government administrators

*Unless, of course, there is a second layer of divisionalization, which simply takes this conclusion down another level in the hierarchy.

complaining about being unable to control public hospitals or universities through conventional (meaning machine bureaucratic) planning systems?

This conclusion is, in fact, a prime manifestation of the hypothesis that concentrated external control of an organization has the effect of formalizing and centralizing its structure, in other words, of driving it toward the machine configuration. Headquarters' control of divisions is, of course, concentrated; indeed, when the diversified organization is itself a *closed system*, as I shall argue later many tend to be, then it is a most concentrated form of control. And, the effect of that control is to render the divisions its *instruments*.

There is, in fact, an interesting irony in this, in that the less society controls the overall diversified organization, the more the organization itself controls its individual units. The result is increased autonomy for the largest organizations coupled with decreased autonomy for their many activities.

To conclude this discussion of the basic structure, the diversified configuration is represented in the opening figure, symbolically in terms of our logo, as follows. Headquarters has three parts: a small strategic apex of top managers, a small technostructure to the left concerned with the design and operation of the performance control system, and a slightly larger staff support group to the right to provide support services common to all the divisions. Each of the divisions is shown below the headquarters as a machine configuration.

CONDITIONS OF THE DIVERSIFIED ORGANIZATION

While the diversified configuration may arise from the federation of different organizations, which come together under a common headquarters umbrella, more often it appears to be the structural response to a machine organization that has diversified its range of product or service offerings. In either case, it is the diversity of markets above all that drives an organization to use this configuration. An organization faced with a single integrated market simply cannot split itself into autonomous divisions; the one with distinct markets, however, has an incentive to create a unit to deal with each.

There are three main kinds of market diversity—product and service, client, and region. In theory, all three can lead to divisionalization. But when diversification is based on variations in clients or regions as opposed to products or services, divisionalization often turns out to be incomplete. With identical products or services in each region or for each group of clients, the headquarters is encouraged to maintain central control of certain critical functions, to ensure common operating standards for all the divisions. And that seriously reduces divisional autonomy, and so leads to a less than complete form of divisionalization.

Thus, one study found that insurance companies concentrate at headquarters the critical function of investment, and retailers concentrate that of purchasing, also controlling product range, pricing, and volume (Channon, 1975). One need only look at the individual outlets of a typical retail chain to recognize the absence of divisional autonomy: usually they all look alike. The same conclusion tends to hold for other businesses organized by regions, such as bakeries, breweries, cement producers, and soft drink bottlers: Their "divisions," distinguished only by geographical location, lack the autonomy normally associated with ones that produce distinct products or services.

What about the conditions of size? Although large size itself does not bring on divisionalization, surely it is not coincidental that most of America's largest corporations use some variant of this configuration. The fact is that as organizations grow large, they become inclined to diversify and then to divisionalize. One reason is protection: large organizations tend to be risk averse—they have too much to lose—and diversification spreads the risk. Another is that as firms grow large, they come to dominate their traditional market, and so must often find growth opportunities elsewhere, through diversification. Moreover, diversification feeds on itself. It creates a cadre of aggressive general managers, each running his or her own division, who push for further diversification and further growth. Thus, most of the giant corporations—with the exception of the "heavies," those with enormously high fixed-cost operating systems, such as the oil or aluminum producers—were able to not only reach their status by diversifying but also feel great pressures to continue to do so.

Age is another factor associated with this configuration, much like size. In larger organizations, the management runs out of places to expand in its traditional markets; in older ones, the managers sometimes get bored with the traditional markets and find diversion through diversification. Also, time brings new competitors into old markets, forcing the management to look elsewhere for growth opportunities.

As governments grow large, they too tend to adopt a kind of divisionalized structure. The central administrators, unable to control all the agencies and departments directly, settle for granting their managers considerable autonomy and then trying to control their results through planning and performance controls. Indeed the "accountability" buzzword so often heard in governments these days reflects just this trend—to move closer to a divisionalized structure.

One can, in fact, view the entire government as a giant diversified configuration (admittedly an oversimplification, since all kinds of links exist among the departments), with its three main coordinating agencies corresponding to the three main forms of control used by the headquarters of the large corporation. The budgetary agency, technocratic in nature, concerns itself with performance control of the departments; the public service commission, also partly technocratic, concerns itself with the recruiting and training of government managers; and the executive office, top management in nature, reviews the principal proposals and initiatives of the departments.

In the preceding chapter, the communist state was described as a closed-system machine bureaucracy. But it may also be characterized as the ultimate closed-system diversified configuration, with the various state enterprises and agencies its instruments, machine bureaucracies tightly regulated by the planning and control systems of the central government.

STAGES IN THE TRANSITION TO THE DIVERSIFIED ORGANIZATION

There has been a good deal of research on the transition of the corporation from the functional to the diversified form. Figure 2 and the discussion that follows borrow from this research to describe four stages in that transition.

At the top of Figure 2 is the pure *functional* structure, used by the corporation whose operating activities form one integrated, unbroken chain from purchasing through production to marketing and sales. Only the final output is sold to the customers.* Autonomy cannot, therefore, be granted to the units, so the organization tends to take on the form of one overall machine configuration.

As an integrated firm seeks wider markets, it may introduce a variety of new end products and so shift all the way to the pure diversified form. A less risky alternative, however, is to start by marketing its intermediate products on the open market. This introduces small breaks in its processing chain, which in turn calls for a measure of divisionalization in its structure, giving rise to the *by-product* form. But because the processing chain remains more or less intact, central coordination must largely remain. Organizations that fall into this category tend to be vertically integrated, basing their operations on a single raw material, such as wood, oil, or aluminum, which they process to a variety of consumable end products. The example of Alcoa is shown in Figure 3.

Some corporations further diversify their by-product markets, breaking down their processing chain until what the divisions sell on the open market becomes more important than what they supply to each other. The organization then moves to the *related-product* form. For example, a firm manufacturing washing machines may set up a division to produce the motors. When the motor division sells more motors to outside customers than to its own sister division, a more serious form of divisionalization is called for. What typically hold the divisions of these firms together is some common thread among their products, perhaps a core skill or technology, perhaps a central market theme, as in a corporation such as 3M that likes to describe itself as being in the coating and bonding business. A good deal of the control over the specific product-market strategies can now revert to the divisions, such as research and development.

As a related-product firm expands into new markets or acquires other firms with less regard to a central strategic theme, the organization moves to the *conglomerate* form and so adopts a pure diversified configuration, the one described at the beginning of this reading. Each division serves its own markets, producing products unrelated to those of the other divisions—chinaware

*It should be noted that this is in fact the definition of a functional structure: Each activity contributes just one step in a chain toward the creation of the final product. Thus, for example, engineering is a functionally organized unit in the firm that produces and markets its own designs, while it would be a market organized unit in a consulting firm that sells its design services, among others, directly to clients.

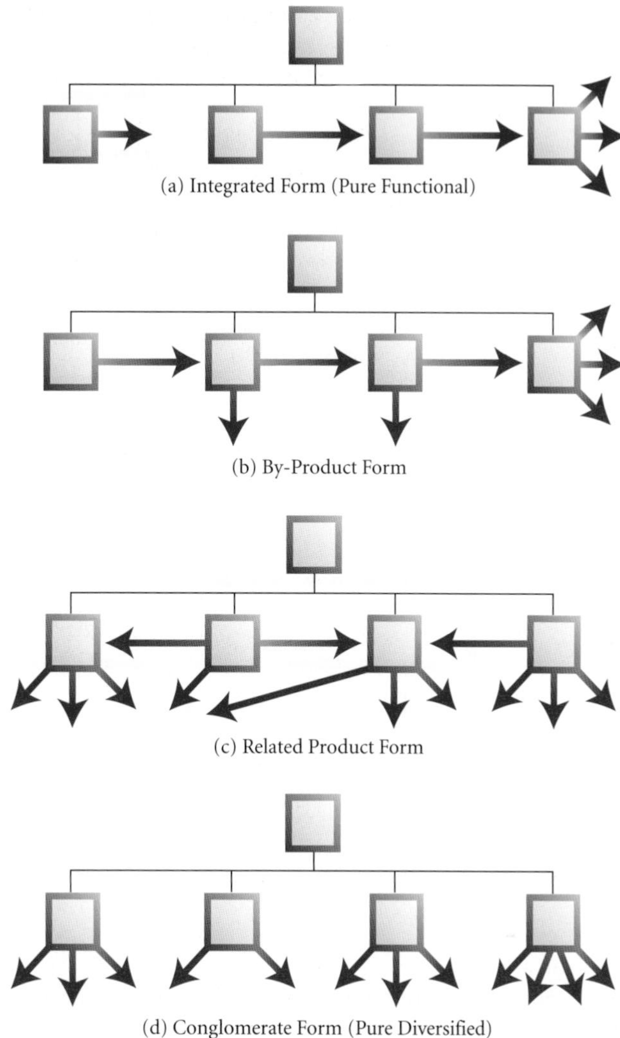

FIGURE 2
STAGES IN THE TRANSITION TO THE PURE DIVERSIFIED FORM

in one, steam shovels in a second, and so on.* The result is that the headquarters planning and control system becomes simply a vehicle for regulating performance, and the headquarters staff can diminish to almost nothing—a few general and group managers supported by a few financial analysts with a minimum of support services.

SOME ISSUES ASSOCIATED WITH THE DIVERSIFIED ORGANIZATION

THE ECONOMIC ADVANTAGES OF DIVERSIFICATION?

It has been argued that the diversified configuration offers four basic advantages over the functional structure with integrated operations, namely an overall machine configuration. First, it encourages the efficient allocation of capital. Headquarters can choose where to put its money and so can concentrate on its strongest markets, milking the surpluses of some divisions to help others grow. Second, by opening up opportunities to run individual businesses, the diversified configuration helps to train general managers. Third, this configuration spreads its risk across different markets, whereas the focused machine bureaucracy has all its strategic eggs in one market basket, so to speak.

*I wrote this example here somewhat whimsically before I encountered a firm in Finland with divisions that actually produce, among other things, the world's largest icebreaker ships and fine pottery!

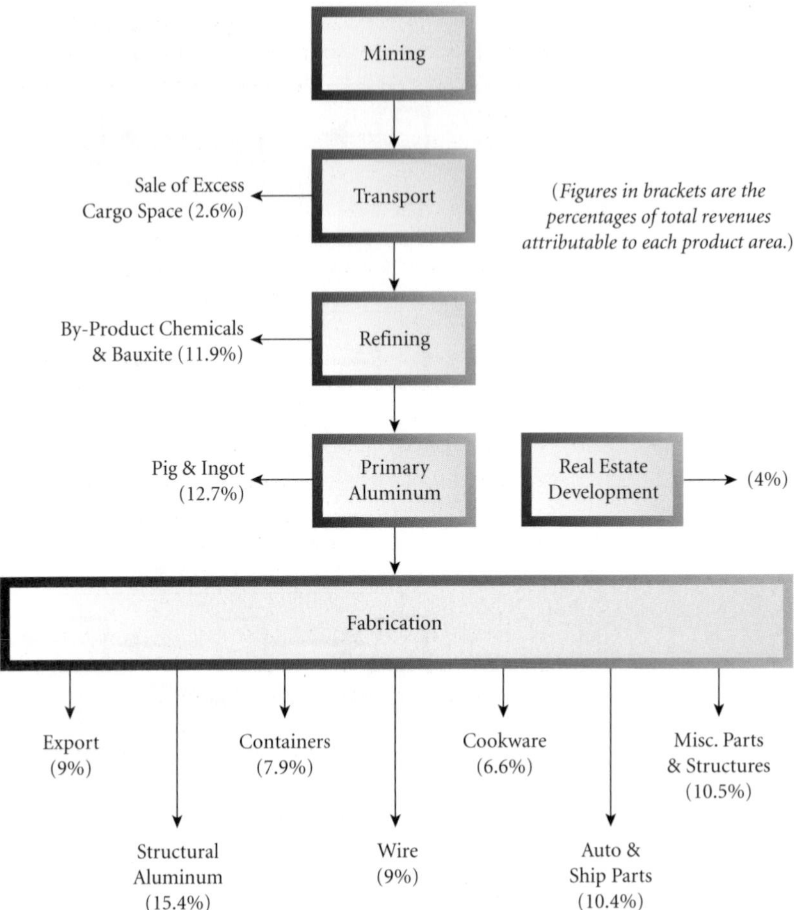

FIGURE 3
BY-PRODUCT AND END-PRODUCT SALES OF ALCOA

(from Rumelt, 1974: 21)
Note: Percentages for 1969 prepared by Richard Rumelt from data in company's annual reports.

Fourth, and perhaps most important, the diversified configuration is strategically responsive. The divisions can fine-tune their bureaucratic machines while the headquarters can concentrate on the strategic portfolio. It can acquire new businesses and divest itself of old, unproductive ones.

But is the single machine organization the correct basis of comparison? Is not the real alternative, at least from society's perspective, the taking of a further step along the same path, to the point of eliminating the headquarters altogether and allowing the divisions to function as independent organizations? Beatrice Foods, described in a 1976 *Fortune* magazine article, had 397 different divisions (Martin, 1976). The issue is whether this arrangement was more efficient than 397 separate corporations.* In this regard, let us reconsider the four advantages discussed earlier.

In the diversified corporation, headquarters allocates the capital resources among the divisions. In the case of 397 independent corporations, the capital markets do that job instead. Which does it better? Studies suggest that the answer is not simple.

Some people, such as the economist Oliver Williamson (1975, 1985), have argued that the diversified organization may do a better job of allocating money because the capital markets are inefficient. Managers at headquarters who know their divisions can move the money around faster and more effectively. But others find that arrangement more costly and, in some ways, less flexible. Moyer (1970), for example, argued early on that conglomerates pay a premium above stock market prices to acquire businesses, whereas the independent investor need pay only small

*The example of Beatrice was first written as presented here in the 1970s, when the company was the subject of a good deal of attention and praise in the business press. At the time of our first revision, in 1988, the company was being disassembled. It seemed appropriate to leave the example as first presented, among other reasons to question the tendency to favor fashion over investigation in the business press.

brokerage fees to diversify his or her own portfolio, and can do so easier and more flexibly. Moreover, that provides the investor with full information on all the businesses owned, whereas the diversified corporation provides only limited information to stockholders on the details inside its portfolio.

On the issue of management development, the question becomes whether the division managers receive better training and experience than they would as company presidents. The diversified organization is able to put on training courses and to rotate its managers to vary their experience; the independent firm is limited in those respects. But if, as the proponents of diversification claim, autonomy is the key to management development, then presumably the more autonomy the better. The division managers have a headquarters to lean on—and to be leaned on by. Company presidents, in contrast, are on their own to make their own mistakes and to learn from them.

On the third issue, risk, the argument from the diversified perspective is that the independent organization is vulnerable during periods of internal crisis or economic slump; conglomeration offers support to see individual businesses through such periods. The counterargument, however, is that diversification may conceal bankruptcies, that ailing divisions are sometimes supported longer than necessary, whereas the market bankrupts the independent firm and is done with it. Moreover, just as diversification spreads the risk, so too does it spread the consequences of that risk. A single division cannot go bankrupt; the whole organization is legally responsible for its debts. So a massive enough problem in one division can pull down the whole organization. Loose coupling may turn out to be riskier than no coupling!

Finally, there is the issue of strategic responsiveness. Loosely coupled divisions may be more responsive than tightly coupled functions. But how responsive do they really prove to be? The answer appears to be negative: this configuration appears to inhibit, not encourage, the taking of strategic initiatives. The problem seems to lie, again, in its control system. It is designed to keep the carrot just the right distance in front of the divisional managers, encouraging them to strive for better and better financial performance. At the same time, however, it seems to dampen their inclination to innovate. It is that famous "bottom line" that creates the problem, encouraging short-term thinking and shortsightedness; attention is focused on the carrot just in front instead of the fields of vegetables beyond. As Bower has noted,

> [T]he risk to the division manager of a major innovation can be considerable if he is measured on short-run, year-to-year, earnings performance. The result is a tendency to avoid big risk bets, and the concomitant phenomenon that major new developments are, with few exceptions, made outside the major firms in the industry. Those exceptions tend to be single-product companies whose top managements are committed to true product leadership. . . . Instead the diversified companies give us a steady diet of small incremental change. (1970: 194)

Innovation requires entrepreneurship, or intrapreneurship, and these, as we have already argued, do not thrive under the diversified configuration. The entrepreneur takes his or her own risks to earn his or her own rewards; the intrapreneur (as we shall see) functions best in the loose structure of the innovative adhocracy. Indeed, many diversified corporations depend on those configurations for their strategic responsiveness, since they diversify not by innovating themselves but by acquiring the innovative results of independent firms. Of course, that may be their role—to exploit rather than create those innovations—but we should not, as a result, justify diversification on the basis of its innovative capacity.

THE CONTRIBUTION OF HEADQUARTERS

To assess the effectiveness of conglomeration, it is necessary to assess what actual contribution the headquarters makes to the divisions. Since what the headquarters does in a diversified organization is otherwise performed by the various boards of directors of a set of independent firms, the question then becomes, what does a headquarters offer to the divisions that the independent board of directors of the autonomous organization does not?

One thing that neither can offer is the management of the individual business. Both are involved with it only on a part-time basis. The management is, therefore, logically left to the full-time managers, who have the required time and information. Among the functions a headquarters *does* perform, as noted earlier, are the establishment of objectives for the divisions, the monitoring of their performance in terms of these objectives, and the maintenance of limited personal contacts with division managers, for example to approve large capital expenditures. Interestingly, those are also the responsibilities of the directors of the individual firm, at least in theory.

In practice, however, many boards of directors—notably, those of widely held corporations—do those things rather ineffectively, leaving business managements carte blanche to do what they like. Here, then, we seem to have a major advantage to the diversified configuration. It exists as an administrative mechanism to overcome another prominent weakness of the free-market system, the ineffective board.

There is a catch in this argument, however, for diversification by enhancing an organization's size and expanding its number of markets renders the corporation more difficult to understand and so to control by its board of part-time directors. Moreover, as Moyer has noted, one common effect of conglomerate acquisition is to increase the number of shareholders, and so to make the corporation more widely held, and therefore less amenable to director control. Thus, the diversified configuration in some sense resolves a problem of its own making—it offers the control that its own existence has rendered difficult. Had the corporation remained in one business, it might have been more narrowly held and easier to understand, and so its directors might have been able to perform their functions more effectively. Diversification thus helped to create the problem that divisionalization is said to solve. Indeed, it is ironic that many a diversified corporation that does such a vigorous job of monitoring the performance of its own divisions is itself so poorly monitored by its own board of directors!

All of this suggests that large diversified organizations tend to be classic closed systems, powerful enough to seal themselves off from much external influence while able to exercise a good deal of control over not only their own divisions, as instruments, but also their external environments. For example, one study of all 5,995 directors of the *Fortune* 500 found that only 1.6 percent of them represented major shareholder interests (Smith, 1978), while another survey of 855 corporations found that 84 percent of them did not even formally require their directors to hold any stock at all (Bacon, 1973: 40)!

What does happen when problems arise in a division? What can a headquarters do that various boards of directors cannot? The chairman of one major conglomerate told a meeting of the New York Society of Security Analysts, in reference to the headquarters vice presidents who oversee the divisions, that "it is not too difficult to coordinate five companies that are well run" (in Wrigley, 1970: V78). True enough. But what about five that are badly run? What could the small staff of administrators at a corporation's headquarters really do to correct problems in that firm's thirty operating divisions or in Beatrice's 397? The natural tendency to tighten the control screws does not usually help once the problem has manifested itself, nor does exercising close surveillance. As noted earlier, the headquarters managers cannot manage the divisions. Essentially, that leaves them with two choices. They can replace the division manager, or they can divest the corporation of the division. Of course, a board of directors can also replace the management. Indeed, that seems to be its only real prerogative; the management does everything else.

On balance, then, the economic case for one headquarters versus a set of separate boards of directors appears to be mixed. It should, therefore, come as no surprise that one important study found that corporations with "controlled diversity" had better profits than those with conglomerate diversity (Rumelt, 1974). Overall, the pure diversified configuration (the conglomerate) may offer some advantages over a weak system of separate boards of directors and inefficient capital markets, but most of those advantages would probably disappear if certain problems in capital markets and boards of directors were rectified. And there is reason to argue, from a social no less than an economic standpoint, that society would be better off trying to correct fundamental inefficiencies in its economic system rather than encourage private administrative arrangements to circumvent them, as we shall now see.

THE SOCIAL PERFORMANCE OF THE PERFORMANCE CONTROL SYSTEM

This configuration requires that headquarters control the divisions primarily by quantitative performance criteria, and that typically means financial ones—profit, sales growth, return on investment, and the like. The problem is that these performance measures often become virtual obsessions in the diversified organization, driving out goals that cannot be measured—product quality, pride in work, customers well served. In effect, the economic goals drive out the social ones. As the chief of a famous conglomerate once remarked, "We, in Textron, worship the god of Net Worth" (in Wrigley, 1970: V86).

That would pose no problem if the social and economic consequences of decisions could easily be separated. Governments would look after the former, corporations the latter. But the fact is that the two are intertwined; every strategic decision of every large corporation involves both, largely inseparable. As a result, its control systems, by focusing on economic measures, drive the diversified organization to act in ways that are, at best, socially unresponsive, at worst, socially irresponsible. Forced to concentrate on the economic consequences of decisions, the division manager is driven to ignore their social consequences. (Indeed, that manager is also driven to ignore the intangible economic consequences as well, such as product quality or research effort, another manifestation of the problem of the short-term, bottom-line thinking mentioned earlier.) Thus, Bower found that "the best records in the race relations area are those of single-product companies whose strong top managements are deeply involved in the business" (1970: 193).

Robert Ackerman, in a study carried out at the Harvard Business School, investigated this point. He found that social benefits such as "a rosier public image . . . pride among managers . . . an attractive posture for recruiting on campus" could not easily be measured and so could not be plugged into the performance control system. The result was that

> . . . the financial reporting system may actually inhibit social responsiveness. By focusing on economic performance, even with appropriate safeguards to protect against sacrificing long-term benefits, such a system directs energy and resources to achieving results measured in financial terms. It is the only game in town, so to speak, at least the only one with an official scoreboard. (1975: 55, 56)

Headquarters managers who are concerned about legal liabilities or the public relations effects of decisions, or even ones personally interested in broader social issues, may be tempted to intervene directly in the divisions' decision-making process to ensure proper attention to social matters. But they are discouraged from doing so by this configuration's strict division of labor: divisional autonomy requires no meddling by the headquarters in specific business decisions.

As long as the screws of the performance control system are not turned too tight, the division managers may retain enough discretion to consider the social consequences of their actions, if they so choose. But when those screws are turned tight, as they often are in the diversified corporation with a bottom-line orientation, then the division managers wishing to keep their jobs may have no choice but to act socially unresponsively, if not actually irresponsibly. As Bower has noted of the General Electric price-fixing scandal of the 1960s, "a very severely managed system of reward and punishment that demanded yearly improvements in earnings, return and market share, applied indiscriminately to all divisions, yielded a situation which was—at the very least—conducive to collusion in the oligopolistic and mature electric equipment markets" (1970: 193).

THE DIVERSIFIED ORGANIZATION IN THE PUBLIC SPHERE

Ironically, for a government intent on dealing with these social problems, solutions are indicated in the very arguments used to support the diversified configuration. Or so it would appear.

For example, if the administrative arrangements are efficient while the capital markets are not, then why should a government hesitate to interfere with the capital markets? And why shouldn't it use those same administrative arrangements to deal with the problems? If Beatrice Foods really can control those 397 divisions, then what is to stop Washington from believing it can control 397 Beatrices? After all, the capital markets don't much matter. In his book on "countervailing power," John Kenneth Galbraith (1952) argued that bigness in one sector, such as business, promotes bigness in other sectors, such as unions and government. That has already happened. How long before government pursues that logical next step and exercises direct controls?

While such steps may prove irresistible to some governments, the fact is that they will not resolve the problems of power concentration and social irresponsibility but rather will aggravate them, but not just in the ways usually assumed in Western economics. All the existing problems would simply be bumped up to another level, and there increase. By making use of the diversified configuration, government would magnify the problems of size. Moreover, government, like the corporation, would be driven to favor measurable economic goals over intangible social ones, and that would add to the problems of social irresponsibility—a phenomenon of which we have already seen a good deal in the public sector.

In fact, these problems would be worse in government, because its sphere is social, and so its goals are largely ill suited to performance control systems. In other words, many of the goals most important for the public sector—and this applies to not-for-profit organizations in spheres such as health and education as well—simply do not lend themselves to measurement, no matter how long and how hard public officials continue to try. And without measurement, the conventional diversified configuration cannot work.

There are, of course, other problems with the application of this form of organization in the public sphere. For example, government cannot divest itself of subunits quite so easily as can corporations. And public service regulations on appointments and the like, as well as a host of other rules, preclude the degree of division manager autonomy available in the private sector. (It is, in fact, these central rules and regulations that make governments resemble integrated machine configurations as much as loosely coupled diversified ones, and that undermine their efforts at "accountability.")

Thus, we conclude that, appearances and even trends notwithstanding, the diversified configuration is generally not suited to the public and not-for-profit sectors of society. Governments and other public-type institutions that wish to divisionalize to avoid centralized machine bureaucracy may often find the imposition of performance standards an artificial exercise. They may thus be better off trying to exercise control of their units in a different way. For example, they can select unit managers who reflect their desired values, or indoctrinate them in those values, and then let them manage freely, the control in effect being normative rather than quantitative. But managing ideology, even creating it in the first place, is no simple matter, especially in a highly diversified organization.

IN CONCLUSION: A STRUCTURE ON THE EDGE OF A CLIFF

Our discussion has led to a "damned if you do, damned if you don't" conclusion. The pure (conglomerate) diversified configuration emerges as an organization perched symbolically on the edge of the cliff, at the end of a long path. Ahead, it is one step away from disintegration—breaking up into separate organizations on the rocks below. Behind it is the way back to a more stable integration, in the form of the machine configuration at the start of that path. And ever hovering above is the eagle, representing the broader social control of the state, attracted by the organization's position on the edge of the cliff and waiting for the chance to pull it up to a higher cliff, perhaps more dangerous still. The edge of the cliff is an uncomfortable place to be, perhaps even a temporary one that must inevitably lead to disintegration on the rocks below, a trip to that cliff above, or a return to a safer resting place somewhere on that path behind.

READING 17.2

Managing Large Groups in the East and West* BY PHILIPPE LASSERRE

. . . [T]here is no one single best method for managing groups of businesses, and the globalization of markets and competition has revealed the emergence of organizational forms of business, particularly in the Asia Pacific region, which differ significantly from the one adopted in Europe and North America. The purpose of this article is to underline some of the salient differences

*Originally published as 'The Management of Large Groups: Asia and Europe Compared," in *European Management Journal*, Vol. 10, No. 2, June 1992, 157–162. Reprinted with deletions with permission of the Journal, Elsevier Science Ltd., Pergamon Imprint, Oxford, England.

between corporations in Asia and in Europe, to analyze the basis of those differences and finally to draw some recommendations.

In the first and second parts one will identify some prominent types of corporations in Europe and in the Asia Pacific region. In a third part, their organizational forms and their corporate control styles will be compared. Finally, some recommendations . . . will be proposed.

EUROPEAN CORPORATE ARCHETYPES

European groups can be broadly classified into three major types: industrial groups, industrial holdings, and financial conglomerates.

A first type of corporation is characterized by a portfolio of business activities which share a common set of competences and in which a high degree of synergy is achieved by managing key interdependencies at corporate level. Andrew Campbell and Michael Goold at the Ashridge Strategic Management Center in the United Kingdom, in their study of British corporations, have named this type "Strategic Planning" groups (Campbell and Goold, 1987), because of the strong input from corporate headquarters in those groups into the strategy formulation of business units. Here, those groups are identified as *industrial groups*. Examples of industrial groups in Europe are British Petroleum or Glaxo in the United Kingdom, Daimler Benz or Henkel in Germany, Philips in the Netherlands, or l'Air Liquide and Michelin in France.

Industrial holdings are corporations in which the business units are clustered into subgroups or sectors. In this type of corporate grouping, synergies are strong within subgroups and weak between subgroups. In industrial holdings, the task of value creation through synergies is delegated to the subgroup level of management, while the corporate role is to impose management discipline through the implementation of planning and control systems, to manage acquisitions, and to leverage and allocate human and financial resources. Campbell and Goold call these groups "Strategic Control" groups, because of their intensive use of planning and control systems to regulate the relationships between business units and corporate headquarters. Examples of industrial holdings are: ICI or Courtaulds in the United Kingdom, BSN or Alsthom-Alcatel in France, Siemens or BASF in Germany.

Financial conglomerates are characterized by a constellation of business units which do not necessarily share any common source of synergies and whose corporate value is essentially created by the imposition of management discipline, financial leverage, and the management of acquisitions and restructuring. Heavy reliance on financial control systems as the major mechanisms of corporate governance have led Campbell and Goold to call these "Financial Control" groups. Hanson Trust or BTR in the United Kingdom are examples of financial conglomerates. A more recent and extreme version of financial conglomerates has appeared in the United States under the form of what Professor Michael Jensen at the Harvard Business School has identified as "LBO Partnerships," in which value is extracted through corporate restructuring and financial discipline imposed on business units under the form of heavy debts, as in the case of Kohlberg Kravis Roberts (Jensen, 1989).

In Europe one can find examples of the three types of groups in a variety of corporate ownership arrangements, whether private or government-owned. In France one can find in the public sector industrial groups such as Renault, SNECMA, or Aerospatiale or, in the private sector, Peugeot, Dassault, or Michelin. Similarly, Rhône Poulenc, a government-owned group, is managed as an industrial holding like BSN, which is a privately owned group. . . .

ASIAN CORPORATE ARCHETYPES

In the Asia Pacific region, where in the past three decades local corporations have emerged as strong competitors, one can possibly identify three major types: the entrepreneurial conglomerates, the Japanese Keiretsus, and the national holdings.

The *entrepreneurial conglomerate* is a prevailing form of corporate organization in South East Asia, Korea, Taiwan and Hong Kong. Entrepreneurial conglomerates are widely diversified into a large number of unrelated activities ranging from banking, trading, real estate, manufacturing, and services. These groups are usually under the leadership of a father figure who exercises control over the strategic decisions of business units and is the driving force behind any strategic move. Very little attempt is made in Asian entrepreneurial conglomerates to manage synergies. The major source of value in those groups emanates from the ability of the entrepreneur to leverage financial and human resources, to establish political connections, to conclude deals with governments and business partners, and to impose loyalty and discipline upon business units. One can distinguish three major types of entrepreneurial conglomerates in Asia: the large Korean groups or Chaebols such as Samsung, Daewoo, or Hyundai; the Overseas Chinese groups such as Liem Sioe Liong or Astra International in Indonesia, Formosa Plastics in Taiwan, Charoen Pokphand in Thailand or Li Ka Shing in Hong Kong; and the colonial "Hongs" such as Swire or Jardine Matheson in Hong Kong.

The *Keiretsus* are a unique feature of Japanese corporate organization. They constitute super groups, or clusters of groups in which businesses are either vertically integrated as in the case of Honda, NEC, Toyota, or Matsushita or horizontally connected as in the case of Mitsubishi, Mitsui, or Sumitomo. Although some companies in the groups exercise greater "power" than others, Keiretsus are not hierarchically organized. They are like a club of organizations which share common interests. Linkages across companies are made through cross shareholdings, the regular meeting of a "Presidential council" in which chairmen of leading companies exchange views. Transfer of staff and, in some cases, long-term supplier–client relationships are also mechanisms used among the vertical Keiretsus. Value is added in Keiretsus through their ability to coordinate informally a certain number of key activities (R&D, export contracts), to transfer expertise through personnel rotation, and to build strong supplier–distributor chains.

The Asian *national holdings* groups have been formed more recently as an expression of industrial independence in order to capitalize on domestic markets and public endowment. Some of these are government-owned like Petronas in Malaysia, Singapore Airlines, Singapore Technology, Gresik in Indonesia, or private like Siam Cement in Thailand or San Miguel in the Philippines. Their business portfolios tend to be less diversified than the ones of the entrepreneurial conglomerates, and their value creation capabilities stem from their "nationality." . . .

GROUP MANAGEMENT: A COMPARISON

In order to proceed to a comparison of the ways groups organize themselves to control and coordinate their activities, one needs to define the key dimensions which capture the most significant differences. In the management literature, various parameters have been proposed to study organizational differences, and the objective of this article is not to review previous research, but to propose what seem to be the most salient measures of differences. Two dimensions are considered as the most important ones:

a. First, the way corporations organize the respective roles of headquarters, the "center," and business units, whether those are divisions or subsidiaries. This dimension is referred to as *Organizational Setting.*

b. Second, the way headquarters ensure that business units' performances and behavior are in line with corporate expectations. This is referred to as *Corporate Control.*

ORGANIZATIONAL SETTING

Corporations around the world appear to cluster themselves around four types of corporate organizational settings.

In the first type of organization, the center plays an important role in managing synergies. Strategic and operational integration and coordination of business units are considered to be the major sources of competitive advantage. Interdependencies are achieved through a variety of mechanisms, including centralized functions, top-down strategic plans, strong corporate identity, and socialization of personnel. Given this high role assigned to the center of this form of organization, it can be qualified as a *federation*. This form prevails in the first type of European groups identified above, that is, the industrial groups, and in certain national holdings in the Asia Pacific region.

In the second type, the center functions as resource allocator, guardian of the corporate identity, and source of strategic renewal. Business units enjoy a large degree of strategic autonomy provided that their strategies are "negotiated" and fit with the overall "corporate strategic framework" inspired by the center. Bottom-up planning, negotiated strategies, operational autonomy, and central mechanisms of financial and human resources allocation are key characteristics of this type of organizational setting. It differs from the federate organization by the more balanced power sharing between the center and the operating units; for that reason it is referred to, here, as a *confederation*. This form is most often characteristic of the European industrial holdings as well as Asian national holdings.

In the third type, one can find groups organized as a multitude of uncoordinated business units, each of them linked directly or indirectly to the center. The role of the center in those groups can be either "hands on," as in the case of Asian entrepreneurial conglomerates, or "hands off," as in the case of European financial conglomerates. What characterizes these groups is the fact that the relationships between business units and corporate headquarters are composed of a series of one-to-one "contractual" agreements. This form resembles a *constellation* and, as said earlier, is predominantly adopted by Asian and European conglomerates.

Finally, in the fourth type of organizational setting, one can find groups in which there is no center or, on the contrary, there are several centers. Some coordination mechanisms are loose, as in the case of informal meetings, while some are more tightly controlled, as in the case of long-term suppliers' contracts. Japanese Keiretsus are representative of this organizational type. Because it is structured as a network, it is called here the *connexion* type of organization.

CORPORATE CONTROL

Corporate control describes how groups ensure that business units' performance and behaviors are in line with corporate expectations. One can distinguish five major methods of exercising control: control by financial performance only, control by systems, control by strategy, direct subjective control of the persons, and control by ideology.

In groups which rely primarily on *financial controls*, headquarters assign financial goals based on financial standards (return on assets, shareholder value). Performances are monitored and evaluated according to achievement of these financial goals. Rewards and punishments of managers are based on those achievements and, for the group, the strategic value of businesses is assessed on their capacities to produce the "figures." This method of control prevails in European financial conglomerates.

The exercise of *control by systems* is based on the implementation of planning and control mechanisms such as interactive strategic planning sessions, investments decisions using capital budgeting techniques, control reviews, etc. Systems use financial as well as non financial information (strategic, marketing). This mode of control predominates in the European industrial holdings and the European industrial groups.

In the *control by strategy* mode, the emphasis is neither on the financial measurement of performance nor on "systems," but on the appreciation of the strategic trajectory of business units and on their degree of fit with the whole corporation. This is done through task forces, corporate conferences, informal meetings, temporary assignments of key executives to business units, etc. European industrial groups and, to some extent, Japanese Keiretsus practice this form of control, whose purpose is not to measure or enforce, but to make sure that there is a coherent corporate strategic fit.

Personalized control is exercised through a direct interface between the group chairman and business units' key managers. Subjective, holistic forms of assessment are in use. Although some form of measurement and use of systems can be found in these groups, the main concern for unit managers is to behave according to the norms and beliefs of the chairman. Asian entrepreneurial conglomerates practice, nearly exclusively, this form of control.

Finally, with *ideological control* the focus is to make sure that managers have internalized the values of the group and are behaving accordingly. Systems, financial measurements, special relationships with the chairman, if used at all, do not play a dominant role here. What does matter is the development of strong beliefs, norms, values across the organization. Recruitments, socialization, training, rotation of staff are all kinds of process which build and maintain an ideology. This type of control prevails in the Asian national holdings in which strong national and corporate identities constitute the essential glue of group performance. Vertical Keiretsus are also well-known to use extensively this form of control.

COMPARING EUROPEAN AND ASIAN GROUPS

Those two dimensions combined give the opportunity to contrast the Asian groups with their European counterparts in the chart represented in Figure 1. As it appears in this figure, Asian and European large corporations live in a different organizational world. While they share some similarities in the way they control their operations, they differ in the way they design their organizational settings, and vice versa. What is interesting to observe in Figure 1 is that Asian corporations introduce, in any case, an interpersonal feature in their management system.

The Keiretsus are built around the ability of group members to connect to each other in one way or another through personal contacts. In the entrepreneurial conglomerate, the entrepreneur is in direct contact with business units and all relationships are personalized. In the case of national holdings, the personification of rapport is established through ideological means, sense of belonging, and nationalistic stand.

The European groups, by contrast, tend to prefer systematic or administrative features in their corporate management. Financial conglomerates are driven by "numbers," industrial holdings favor complex planning and control mechanisms, while industrial groups adopt structural and regulatory means of coordination. When confronted by a problem of change the typical reaction of a Western corporation will be to find a new "structure" or a new "system." . . .

Western corporate designers adopt an "engineering" approach to building and regulating organizational life. Although over the past 50 years behavioral sciences have brought an immense contribution to the art of management, this has been, most of the time, translated into practice

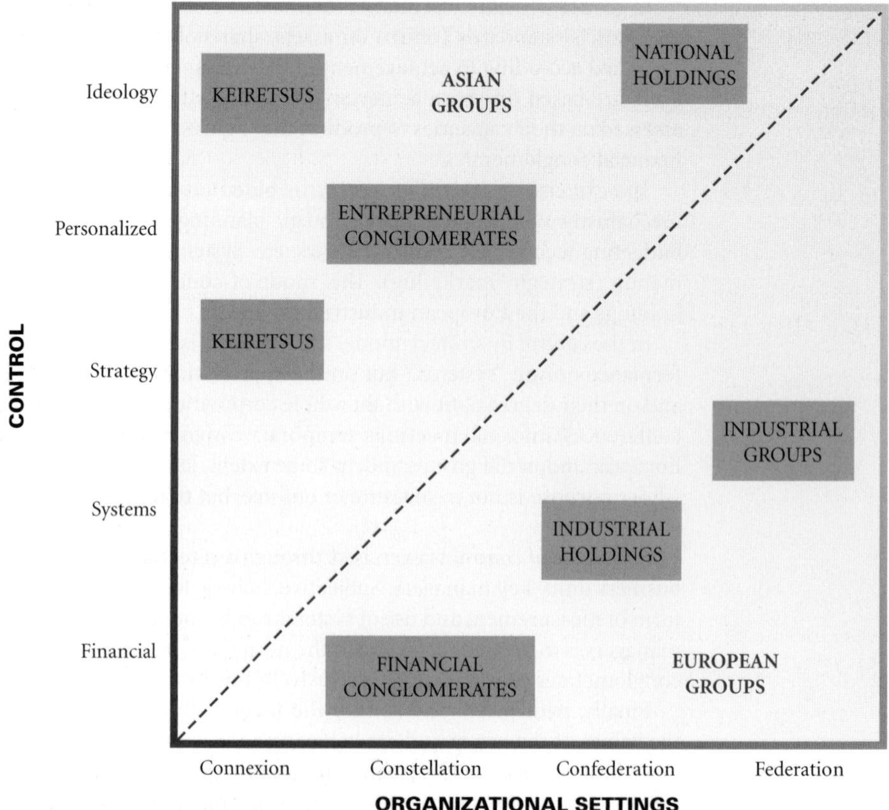

FIGURE 1
ASIAN AND EUROPEAN GROUPS

with an instrumental perspective. Motivation theories have given birth to "management by objectives," experimental psychology using conditioning techniques has been used for the design of rewards and bonus systems, information theory is applied in the setting up of computer systems, etc. The rationale underlying this effort is probably the belief that human behavior can be influenced by the *manipulation* of organizational mechanisms. The main concern of Western managers confronted with a situation of strategic change is to install a new "organization" or a new "management system" which is supposed to align behavior with the new realities.

This instrumental engineering approach is challenged by Asian corporate architects who conceive enterprises as living entities where various individuals and groups obtain mutual benefit through cooperation. Organizations are not seen as independent of the people who compose them and, most of the time, enterprises are compared to "families." In 1984, Chairman Kim Woo Choong, founder of Daewoo, was participating in a session at the Harvard Business School with a group of U.S. senior executives. He was asked by one participant how he could coordinate some 40 subsidiaries without controlling them. Chairman Kim answered that coordination was achieved through "*spiritual linkages*"! (Aguilar, 1967). That does not mean that Asian firms do not use systems for their management, but that personification of interrelationships is given priority over formal systems. One major underlying assumption of Asian managers is that organizational mechanisms are not set up to ""manipulate" people but rather to give a structure to social interactions. In fact, most of the time, people are not rewarded for their performance, as measured in terms of results, but in terms of conformity to behavior. Organizations are not seen as machines (an engineering view) but as a set of "codified" relationships (a biological view).

DECODING ASIAN FIRMS

. . . When the competitive pressure from Asian firms becomes too intense, Western managers try to emulate them. One good example is provided by an article published in 1990 in the *Harvard Business Review* by Charles Ferguson in which the author proposes the creation of Western Keiretsus between U.S. and European countries in the computer industry! This proposition reflects an engineering view of the organizational world: the machine "works" in Japan, why don't we import the machine? It is as if we asked U.S. society to renounce individualism. What an ambition! Instead of trying to "import the machine," Western managers should be inspired to gain an understanding of the way the relationships function or don't function in these groups, what social roles do they play, in other terms to "decode" and not to "imitate" Asian organizations. This decoding ability requires three attitudes: (a) getting rid of *a priori* judgments, (b) making the necessary effort to study the social and cultural background of Asian societies, and (c) resisting the temptation of easy translations.

A. GET RID OF A PRIORI JUDGMENTS

More often than not, when presented with Asian cases, particularly successful ones, Western managers give ready-made explanations: Japan Inc. exploited manpower, "workaholism," nationalism, sacrificed generation, etc. Those views are meaningless because they are based on a simplistic engineering causality leading to defeatism or stubborn protectionism. Understanding the functionality of a social structure is the first necessary step in the analysis of organization, while the deciphering of causal links comes second. A rushed application of ready-made causal schemes based on superficial facts does not help to understand Asian partners and competitors.

B. INVEST IN THE STUDY OF CULTURES AND SOCIETIES

One of the dangers of "instrumental" thinking is that it bypasses what is not considered of immediate relevance. Cultural and social knowledge are all too frequently considered to be a waste of time or, at best, as subjects of "executive summaries." Organization and business behavior are part of a historical and cultural heritage which, in the case of Asian societies, is very rich, complex, and heterogeneous. The manager who does not make the necessary efforts to enlighten himself or herself with such knowledge is condemned to go from surprise to surprise if not from disillusion to disillusion.

C. RESIST THE TEMPTATION OF "EASY TRANSLATIONS"

Some managers fall into the trap of adopting, naively, a so-called "Asian" way of doing things. In the early 1980s, a European bank set up a regional office in Singapore, its first commitment in the region. The newly appointed general manager, a very enthusiastic person, decided that he would work "the Chinese way": handshakes, networking, personal trust, etc. He found himself trapped two years later with a portfolio of bad debts amounting to several million U.S. dollars! Such horror stories can only fuel the resistance of corporate boards to commit resources for developing strategies in the Asia Pacific region. . . .

READING 17.3

From Competitive Advantage to Corporate Strategy* BY MICHAEL E. PORTER

Corporate strategy, the overall plan for a diversified company, is both the darling and the stepchild of contemporary management practice—the darling because CEOs have been obsessed with diversification since the early 1960s, the stepchild because almost no consensus exists about what corporate strategy is, much less about how a company should formulate it.

A diversified company has two levels of strategy: business unit (or competitive) strategy and corporate (or companywide) strategy. Competitive strategy concerns how to create competitive advantage in each of the businesses in which a company competes. Corporate strategy concerns two different questions: what businesses the corporation should be in and how the corporate office should manage the array of business units.

Corporate strategy is what makes the corporate whole add up to more than the sum of its business unit parts.

The track record of corporate strategies has been dismal. I studied the diversification records of 33 large, prestigious U.S. companies over the 1950–1986 period and found that most of them had divested many more acquisitions than they had kept. The corporate strategies of most companies have dissipated instead of created shareholder value.

The need to rethink corporate strategy could hardly be more urgent. By taking over companies and breaking them up, corporate raiders thrive on failed corporate strategy. Fueled by junk bond financing and growing acceptability, raiders can expose any company to takeover, no matter how large or blue chip. . . .

A SOBER PICTURE

. . . My study of 33 companies, many of which have reputations for good management, is a unique look at the track record of major corporations. . . . Each company entered an average of 80 new industries and 27 new fields. Just over 70% of the new entries were acquisitions, 22% were start-ups, and 8% were joint ventures. IBM, Exxon, Du Pont, and 3M, for example, focused on start-ups, while ALCO Standard, Beatrice, and Sara Lee diversified almost solely through acquisitions. . . .

---

*Originally published in the *Harvard Business Review* (May–June 1987) and winner of the McKinsey Prize for the best in the *Review* in 1987.

My data paint a sobering picture of the success ratio of these moves. . . . I found that on average corporations divested more than half their acquisitions in new industries and more than 60% of their acquisitions in entirely new fields. Fourteen companies left more than 70% of all the acquisitions they had made in new fields. The track record in unrelated acquisitions is even worse—the average divestment rate is a startling 74%. Even a highly respected company like General Electric divested a very high percentage of its acquisitions, particularly those in new fields. . . . Some [companies] bear witness to the success of well-thought-out corporate strategies. Others, however, enjoy a lower rate simply because they have not faced up to their problem units and divested them. . . .

I would like to make one comment on the use of shareholder value to judge performance. Linking shareholder value quantitatively to diversification performance only works if you compare the shareholder value that is with the shareholder value that might have been without diversification. Because such a comparison is virtually impossible to make, my own measure of diversification success—the number of units retained by the company—seems to be as good an indicator as any of the contribution of diversification to corporate performance.

My data give a stark indication of the failure of corporate strategies.* Of the 33 companies, 6 had been taken over as my study was being completed. . . . Only the lawyers, investment bankers, and original sellers have prospered in most of these acquisitions, not the shareholders.

PREMISES OF CORPORATE STRATEGY

Any successful corporate strategy builds on a number of premises. These are facts of life about diversification. They cannot be altered, and when ignored, they explain in part why so many corporate strategies fail.

COMPETITION OCCURS AT THE BUSINESS UNIT LEVEL

Diversified companies do not compete; only their business units do. Unless a corporate strategy places primary attention on nurturing the success of each unit, the strategy will fail, no matter how elegantly constructed. Successful corporate strategy must grow out of and reinforce competitive strategy.

DIVERSIFICATION INEVITABLY ADDS COSTS AND CONSTRAINTS TO BUSINESS UNITS

Obvious costs such as the corporate overhead allocated to a unit may not be as important or subtle as the hidden costs and constraints. A business unit must explain its decisions to top management, spend time complying with planning and other corporate systems, live with parent company guidelines and personnel policies, and forgo the opportunity to motivate employees with direct equity ownership. These costs and constraints can be reduced but not entirely eliminated.

SHAREHOLDERS CAN READILY DIVERSIFY THEMSELVES

Shareholders can diversify their own portfolios of stocks by selecting those that best match their preferences and risk profiles (Salter and Weinhold, 1979). Shareholders can often diversify more cheaply than a corporation because they can buy shares at the market price and avoid hefty acquisition premiums.

These premises mean that corporate strategy cannot succeed unless it truly adds value—to business units by providing tangible benefits that offset the inherent costs of lost independence and to shareholders by diversifying in a way they could not replicate.

---

*Some recent evidence also supports the conclusion that acquired companies often suffer eroding performance after acquisition. See Frederick M. Scherer, "Mergers, Sell-Offs and Managerial Behavior," in *The Economics of Strategic Planning*, ed. Lacy Glenn Thomas (Lexington, MA: Lexington Books, 1986), p. 143, and David A. Ravenscraft and Frederick M. Scherer, "Mergers and Managerial Performance," paper presented at the Conference on Takeovers and Contests for Corporate Control, Columbia Law School, 1985.

PASSING THE ESSENTIAL TESTS

To understand how to formulate corporate strategy, it is necessary to specify the conditions under which diversification will truly create shareholder value. These conditions can be summarized in three essential tests:

1. *The attractiveness test.* The industries chosen for diversification must be structurally attractive or capable of being made attractive.
2. *The cost-of-entry test.* The cost of entry must not capitalize all the future profits.
3. *The better-off test.* Either the new unit must gain competitive advantage from its link with the corporation or vice versa.

Of course, most companies will make certain that their proposed strategies pass some of these tests. But my study clearly shows that when companies ignored one or two of them, the strategic results were disastrous.

HOW ATTRACTIVE IS THE INDUSTRY?

In the long run, the rate of return available from competing in an industry is a function of its underlying structure [see Porter reading in Chapter 4]. An attractive industry with a high average return on investment will be difficult to enter because entry barriers are high, suppliers and buyers have only modest bargaining power, substitute products or services are few, and the rivalry among competitors is stable. An unattractive industry like steel will have structural flaws, including a plethora of substitute materials, powerful and price-sensitive buyers, and excessive rivalry caused by high fixed costs and a large group of competitors, many of whom are state supported.

Diversification cannot create shareholder value unless new industries have favorable structures that support returns exceeding the cost of capital. If the industry doesn't have such returns, the company must be able to restructure the industry or gain a sustainable competitive advantage that leads to returns well above the industry average. An industry need not be attractive before diversification. In fact, a company might benefit from entering before the industry shows its full potential. The diversification can then transform the industry's structure.

In my research, I often found companies had suspended the attractiveness test because they had a vague belief that the industry "fit" very closely with their own businesses. In the hope that the corporate "comfort" they felt would lead to a happy outcome, the companies ignored fundamentally poor industry structures. Unless the close fit allows substantial competitive advantage, however, such comfort will turn into pain when diversification results in poor returns. Royal Dutch Shell and other leading oil companies have had this unhappy experience in a number of chemicals businesses, where poor industry structures overcame the benefits of vertical integration and skills in process technology.

Another common reason for ignoring the attractiveness test is a low entry cost. Sometimes the buyer has an inside track or the owner is anxious to sell. Even if the price is actually low, however, a one-shot gain will not offset a perpetually poor business. Almost always, the company finds it must reinvest in the newly acquired unit, if only to replace fixed assets and fund working capital.

Diversifying companies are also prone to use rapid growth or other simple indicators as a proxy for a target industry's attractiveness. Many that rushed into fast-growing industries (personal computers, video games, and robotics, for example) were burned because they mistook early growth for long-term profit potential. Industries are profitable not because they are sexy or high tech; they are profitable only if their structures are attractive.

WHAT IS THE COST OF ENTRY?

Diversification cannot build shareholder value if the cost of entry into a new business eats up its expected returns. Strong market forces, however, are working to do just that. A company can enter new industries by acquisition or start-up. Acquisitions expose it to an increasingly efficient merger market. An acquirer beats the market if it pays a price not fully reflecting the prospects of the new unit. Yet multiple bidders are commonplace, information flows rapidly, and investment bankers and other intermediaries work aggressively to make the market as efficient as possible. In recent years, new financial instruments such as junk bonds have brought new buyers into the market and made even large companies vulnerable to takeover. Acquisition premiums are high and reflect the acquired company's future prospects—sometimes too well. Philip Morris paid more than four times book value for the Seven-Up Company, for example. Simple arithmetic meant that profits had to more than quadruple to sustain the preacquisition ROI. Since there proved to be little Philip Morris could add in marketing prowess to the sophisticated marketing wars in the soft drink industry, the result was the unsatisfactory financial performance of Seven-Up and ultimately the decision to divest.

In a start-up, the company must overcome entry barriers. It's a real catch-22 situation, however, since attractive industries are attractive because their entry barriers are high. Bearing the full cost of the entry barriers might well dissipate any potential profits. Otherwise, other entrants to the industry would have already eroded its profitability.

In the excitement of finding an appealing new business, companies sometimes forget to apply the cost-of-entry test. The more attractive a new industry, the more expensive it is to get into.

WILL THE BUSINESS BE BETTER OFF?

A corporation must bring some significant competitive advantage to the new unit, or the new unit must offer potential for significant advantage to the corporation. Sometimes, the benefits to the new unit accrue only once, near the time of entry, when the parent instigates a major overhaul of its strategy or installs a first-rate management team. Other diversification yields ongoing competitive advantage if the new unit can market its product, through the well-developed distribution system of its sister units, for instance. This is one of the important underpinnings of the merger of Baxter Travenol and American Hospital Supply.

When the benefit to the new unit comes only once, the parent company has no rationale for holding the new unit in its portfolio over the long term. Once the results of the one-time improvement are clear, the diversified company no longer adds value to offset the inevitable costs imposed on the unit. It is best to sell the unit and free up corporate resources.

The better-off test does not imply that diversifying corporate risk creates shareholder value in and of itself. Doing something for shareholders that they can do themselves is not a basis for corporate strategy. (Only in the case of a privately held company, in which the company's and the shareholder's risk are the same, is diversification to reduce risk valuable for its own sake.) Diversification of risk should only be a by-product of corporate strategy, not a prime motivator.

Executives ignore the better-off test most of all or deal with it through arm waving or trumped-up logic rather than hard strategic analysis. One reason is that they confuse company size with shareholder value. In the drive to run a bigger company, they lose sight of their real job. They may justify the suspension of the better-off test by pointing to the way they manage diversity. By cutting corporate staff to the bone and giving business units nearly complete autonomy, they believe they avoid the pitfalls. Such thinking misses the whole point of diversification, which is to create shareholder value rather than to avoid destroying it.

CONCEPTS OF CORPORATE STRATEGY

The three tests for successful diversification set the standards that any corporate strategy must meet; meeting them is so difficult that most diversification fails. Many companies lack a clear concept of corporate strategy to guide their diversification or pursue a concept that does not address the tests. Others fail because they implement a strategy poorly.

My study has helped me identify four concepts of corporate strategy that have been put into practice—portfolio management, restructuring, transferring skills, and sharing activities. While the concepts are not always mutually exclusive, each rests on a different mechanism by which the corporation creates shareholder value and each requires the diversified company to manage and organize itself in a different way. The first two require no connections among business units; the second two depend on them. . . . While all four concepts of strategy have succeeded under the right circumstances, today some make more sense than others. Ignoring any of the concepts is perhaps the quickest road to failure.

PORTFOLIO MANAGEMENT

The concept of corporate strategy most in use is portfolio management, which is based primarily on diversification through acquisition. The corporation acquires sound, attractive companies with competent managers who agree to stay on. While acquired units do not have to be in the same industries as existing units, the best portfolio managers generally limit their range of businesses in some way, in part to limit the specific expertise needed by top management.

The acquired units are autonomous, and the teams that run them are compensated according to unit results. The corporation supplies capital and works with each to infuse it with professional management techniques. At the same time, top management provides an objective and dispassionate review of business unit results. Portfolio managers categorize units by potential and regularly transfer resources from units that generate cash to those with high potential and cash needs. . . .

In most countries, the days when portfolio management was a valid concept of corporate strategy are past. In the face of increasingly well-developed capital markets, attractive companies with good managements show up on everyone's computer screen and attract top dollar in terms of acquisition premium. Simply contributing capital isn't contributing much. A sound strategy can easily be funded; small to medium-size companies don't need a munificent parent.

Other benefits have also eroded. Large companies no longer corner the market for professional management skills; in fact, more and more observers believe managers cannot necessarily run anything in the absence of industry-specific knowledge and experience. . . .

But it is the sheer complexity of the management task that has ultimately defeated even the best portfolio managers. As the size of the company grows, portfolio managers need to find more and more deals just to maintain growth. Supervising dozens or even hundreds of disparate units and under chain-letter pressures to add more, management begins to make mistakes. At the same time, the inevitable costs of being part of a diversified company take their toll and unit performance slides while the whole company's ROI turns downward. Eventually, a new management team is installed that initiates wholesale divestments and pares down the company to its core businesses. . . .

In developing countries, where large companies are few, capital markets are undeveloped, and professional management is scarce, portfolio management still works. But it is no longer a valid model for corporate strategy in advanced economies. . . . Portfolio management is no way to conduct corporate strategy.

RESTRUCTURING

Unlike its passive role as a portfolio manager, when it serves as banker and reviewer, a company that bases its strategy on restructuring becomes an active restructurer of business units. The new businesses are not necessarily related to existing units. All that is necessary is unrealized potential.

The restructuring strategy seeks out undeveloped, sick, or threatened organizations or industries on the threshold of significant change. The parent intervenes, frequently changing the unit management team, shifting strategy, or infusing the company with new technology. Then it may make follow-up acquisitions to build a critical mass and sell off unneeded or unconnected parts and thereby reduce the effective acquisition cost. The result is a strengthened company or a transformed industry. As a coda, the parent sells off the stronger unit once results are clear because the parent is no longer adding value, and top management decides that its attention should be directed elsewhere. . . .

When well implemented, the restructuring concept is sound, for it passes the three tests of successful diversification. The restructurer meets the cost-of-entry test through the types of company it acquires. It limits acquisition premiums by buying companies with problems and lackluster images or by buying into industries with as yet unforeseen potential. Intervention by the corporation clearly meets the better-off test. Provided that the target industries are structurally attractive, the restructuring model can create enormous shareholder value. . . . Ironically, many of today's restructurers are profiting from yesterday's portfolio management strategies.

To work, the restructuring strategy requires a corporate management team with the insight to spot undervalued companies or positions in industries ripe for transformation. The same insight is necessary to actually turn the units around even though they are in new and unfamiliar businesses. . . .

Perhaps the greatest pitfall . . . is that companies find it very hard to dispose of business units once they are restructured and performing well. . . .

TRANSFERRING SKILLS

The purpose of the first two concepts of corporate strategy is to create value through a company's relationship with each autonomous unit. The corporation's role is to be a selector, a banker, and an intervenor.

The last two concepts exploit the interrelationships between businesses. In articulating them, however, one comes face-to-face with the often ill-defined concept of synergy. If you believe the text of the countless corporate annual reports, just about anything is related to just about anything else! But imagined synergy is much more common than real synergy. GM's purchase of Hughes Aircraft simply because cars were going electronic and Hughes was an electronics concern demonstrates the folly of paper synergy. Such corporate relatedness is an ex post facto rationalization of a diversification undertaken for other reasons.

Even synergy that is clearly defined often fails to materialize. Instead of cooperating, business units often compete. A company that can define the synergies it is pursuing still faces significant organizational impediments in achieving them.

But the need to capture the benefits of relationships between businesses has never been more important. Technological and competitive developments already link many businesses and are creating new possibilities for competitive advantage. In such sectors as financial services, computing, office equipment, entertainment, and health care, interrelationships among previously distinct businesses are perhaps the central concern of strategy.

To understand the role of relatedness in corporate strategy, we must give new meaning to this often ill-defined idea. I have identified a good way to start—the value chain. [See Readings 4.1 and 4.2.] Every business unit is a collection of discrete activities ranging from sales to accounting that allow it to compete. I call them value activities. It is at this level, not in the company as a whole, that the unit achieves competitive advantage.

I group these activities in nine categories. *Primary* activities create the product or service, deliver and market it, and provide after-sale support. The categories of primary activities are inbound logistics, operations, outbound logistics, marketing and sales, and service. *Support* activities provide the input and infrastructure that allow the primary activities to take place. The categories are company infrastructure, human resource management, technology development, and procurement.

The value chain defines the two types of interrelationships that may create synergy. The first is a company's ability to transfer skills or expertise among similar value chains. The second is the ability to share activities. Two business units, for example, can share the same sales force or logistics network.

The value chain helps expose the last two (and most important) concepts of corporate strategy. The transfer of skills among business units in the diversified company is the basis for one concept. While each business unit has a separate value chain, knowledge about how to perform activities is transferred among the units. For example, a toiletries business unit, expert in the marketing of convenience products, transmits ideas on new positioning concepts, promotional techniques, and packaging possibilities to a newly acquired unit that sells cough syrup. Newly entered industries can benefit from the expertise of existing units, and vice versa.

These opportunities arise when business units have similar buyers or channels, similar value activities like government relations or procurement, similarities in the broad configuration of the value chain (for example, managing a multisite service organization), or the same strategic concept (for example, low cost). Even though the units operate separately, such similarities allow the sharing of knowledge. . . .

Transferring skills leads to competitive advantage only if the similarities among businesses meet three conditions:

1. The activities involved in the businesses are similar enough that sharing expertise is meaningful. Broad similarities (marketing intensiveness, for example, or a common core process technology such as bending metal) are not a sufficient basis for diversification. The resulting ability to transfer skills is likely to have little impact on competitive advantage.
2. The transfer of skills involves activities important to competitive advantage. Transferring skills in peripheral activities such as government relations or real estate in consumer goods units may be beneficial but is not a basis for diversification.
3. The skills transferred represent a significant source of competitive advantage for the receiving unit. The expertise or skills to be transferred are both advanced and proprietary enough to be beyond the capabilities of competitors. . . .

Transferring skills meets the tests of diversification if the company truly mobilizes proprietary expertise across units. This makes certain the company can offset the acquisition premium or lower the cost of overcoming entry barriers.

The industries the company chooses for diversification must pass the attractiveness test. Even a close fit that reflects opportunities to transfer skills may not overcome poor industry structure. Opportunities to transfer skills, however, may help the company transform the structures of newly entered industries and send them in favorable directions.

The transfer of skills can be one time or ongoing. If the company exhausts opportunities to infuse new expertise into a unit after the initial post-acquisition period, the unit should ultimately be sold. . . .

By using both acquisitions and internal development, companies can build a transfer-of-skills strategy. The presence of a strong base of skills sometimes creates the possibility for internal entry instead of the acquisition of a going concern. Successful diversifiers that employ the concept of skills transfer may, however, often acquire a company in the target industry as a beachhead and then build on it with their internal expertise. By doing so, they can reduce some of the risks of internal entry and speed up the process. Two companies that have diversified using the transfer-of-skills concept are 3M and PepsiCo.

SHARING ACTIVITIES

The fourth concept of corporate strategy is based on sharing activities in the value chains among business units. Procter & Gamble, for example, employs a common physical distribution system and sales force in both paper towels and disposable diapers. McKesson, a leading distribution company, will handle such diverse lines as pharmaceuticals and liquor through superwarehouses.

The ability to share activities is a potent basis for corporate strategy because sharing often enhances competitive advantage by lowering cost or raising differentiation. . . .

Sharing activities inevitably involves costs that the benefits must outweigh. One cost is the greater coordination required to manage a shared activity. More important is the need to compromise the design or performance of an activity so that it can be shared. A salesperson handling the products of two business units, for example, must operate in a way that is usually not what either unit would choose were it independent. And if compromise greatly erodes the unit's effectiveness, then sharing may reduce rather than enhance competitive advantage. . . .

Despite . . . pitfalls, opportunities to gain advantage from sharing activities have proliferated because of momentous developments in technology, deregulation, and competition. The infusion of electronics and information systems into many industries creates new opportunities to link businesses. . . .

Following the shared-activities model requires an organizational context in which business unit collaboration is encouraged and reinforced. Highly autonomous business units are inimical to such collaboration. The company must put into place a variety of what I call horizontal mechanisms—a strong sense of corporate identity, a clear corporate mission statement that emphasizes the importance of integrating business unit strategies, an incentive system that rewards more than just business unit results, cross-business-unit task forces, and other methods of integrating.

A corporate strategy based on shared activities clearly meets the better-off test because business units gain ongoing tangible advantages from others within the corporation. It also meets the cost-of-entry test by reducing the expense of surmounting the barriers to internal entry. Other bids for acquisitions that do not share opportunities will have lower reservation prices. Even widespread opportunities for sharing activities do not allow a company to suspend the attractiveness test, however. Many diversifiers have made the critical mistake of equating the close fit of a target industry with attractive diversification. Target industries must pass the strict requirement test of having an attractive structure as well as a close fit in opportunities if diversification is to ultimately succeed.

CHOOSING A CORPORATE STRATEGY

... Both the strategic logic and the experience of the companies I studied over the last decade suggest that a company will create shareholder value through diversification to a greater and greater extent as its strategy moves from portfolio management toward sharing activities. ...

Each concept of corporate strategy is not mutually exclusive of those that come before, a potent advantage of the third and fourth concepts. A company can employ a restructuring strategy at the same time it transfers skills or shares activities. A strategy based on shared activities becomes more powerful if business units can also exchange skills. ...

My study supports the soundness of basing a corporate strategy on the transfer of skills or shared activities. The data on the sample companies' diversification programs illustrate some important characteristics of successful diversifiers. They have made a disproportionately low percentage of unrelated acquisitions, *unrelated* being defined as having no clear opportunity to transfer skills or share important activities. ... Even successful diversifiers such as 3M, IBM, and TRW have terrible records when they strayed into unrelated acquisitions. Successful acquirers diversify into fields, each of which is related to many others. Procter & Gamble and IBM, for example, operate in 18 and 19 interrelated fields respectively and so enjoy numerous opportunities to transfer skills and share activities.

Companies with the best acquisition records tend to make heavier-than-average use of start-ups and joint ventures. Most companies shy away from modes of entry besides acquisition. My results cast doubt on the conventional wisdom regarding start-ups. . . . successful companies often have very good records with start-up units, as 3M, P&G, Johnson & Johnson, IBM, and United Technologies illustrate. When a company has the internal strength to start up a unit, it can be safer and less costly to launch a company than to rely solely on an acquisition and then have to deal with the problem of integration. Japanese diversification histories support the soundness of start-up as an entry alternative.

My data also illustrate that none of the concepts of corporate strategy works when industry structure is poor or implementation is bad, no matter how related the industries are. Xerox acquired companies in related industries, but the business had poor structures and its skills were insufficient to provide enough competitive advantage to offset implementation problems.

AN ACTION PROGRAM

... A company can choose a corporate strategy by:

1. Identifying the interrelationships among already existing business units. ...
2. Selecting the core businesses that will be the foundation of the corporate strategy. ...
3. Creating horizontal organizational mechanisms to facilitate interrelationships among the core businesses and lay the groundwork for future related diversification. ...

4. Pursuing diversification opportunities that allow shared activities. . . .
5. Pursuing diversification through the transfer of skills if opportunities for sharing activities are limited or exhausted. . . .
6. Pursuing a strategy of restructuring if this fits the skills of management or no good opportunities exist for forging corporate interrelationships. . . .
7. Paying dividends so that the shareholders can be the portfolio managers. . . .

CREATING A CORPORATE THEME

Defining a corporate theme is a good way to ensure that the corporation will create shareholder value. Having the right theme helps unite the efforts of business units and reinforces the ways they interrelate as well as guides the choice of new businesses to enter. NEC Corporation, with its "C&C" theme, provides a good example. NEC integrates its computer, semiconductor, telecommunications, and consumer electronics businesses by merging computers and communication.

It is all too easy to create a shallow corporate theme. CBS wanted to be an "entertainment company," for example, and built a group of businesses related to leisure time. It entered such industries as toys, crafts, musical instruments, sports teams, and hi-fi retailing. While this corporate theme sounded good, close listening revealed its hollow ring. None of these businesses had any significant opportunity to share activities or transfer skills among themselves or with CBS's traditional broadcasting and record businesses. They were all sold, often at significant losses, except for a few of CBS's publishing-related units. Saddled with the worst acquisition record in my study, CBS has eroded the shareholder value created through its strong performance in broadcasting and records.

Moving from competitive strategy to corporate strategy is the business equivalent of passing through the Bermuda Triangle. The failure of corporate strategy reflects the fact that most diversified companies have failed to think in terms of how they really add value. A corporate strategy that truly enhances the competitive advantage of each business unit is the best defense against the corporate raider. With a sharper focus on the tests of diversification and the explicit choice of a clear concept of corporate strategy, companies' diversification track records from now on can look a lot different.

CHAPTER 18

Managing Otherwise

We close the readings of this book in the spirit we have tried to create throughout, only, perhaps, more so: to open up perspectives to new, unconventional ideas. Hence, we call this chapter "Managing Otherwise." It is a context onto itself.

The first reading takes us beyond the five forms of organizing introduced by Mintzberg at the beginning of the last five chapters. That was playing jigsaw puzzle—choosing the right structural form to fit in. But perhaps designing organizations has to be more like playing Lego: using the forms as forces to be combined in all sorts of creative ways. Here Mintzberg brings some closure to our discussion of the different configurations of this section. Called "Beyond Configuration," it is, in a sense, the final chapter of his book on structure, except that it was written more recently and edited for this text. The reading seeks to do just what its title says: make the point that although the different forms (configurations) of the last chapters can help us to make sense of and to manage in a complex world, there is also a need to go beyond configurations, to consider the nuanced linkages among these various forms. Mintzberg proposes that this be done by treating all the forms as a framework of forces that acts on every organization and whose contradictions need to be reconciled. By so doing, we can begin to see the weaknesses in each form as well as the times when an organization is better off to design itself as a combination of two or more forms. This reading also discusses how the forces of ideology (representing cooperation—pulling together) and of politics (representing competition—pulling apart) work both to promote change and to impede it, and how the contradictions among these two must also be reconciled if an organization is to remain effective in the long run.

Next comes a colorful reading by James March of Stanford University about the difference between organizations that *exploit* existing situations and those that *explore* in the hope of creating new ones. March also addresses "the perils and glories of imagination."

Next comes a reading by Gary Hamel, who sets out to upset all that is sacred about strategy, including how it gets created. Indeed, conventional views of how that happens, in Hamel's opinion, get in the way of strategic innovation, which is what he believes really counts: how you break away from the pack rather than analyzing your way into the middle of it. Hamel suggests how this might happen, continuing to upset all the sacred cows of the field.

Ricardo Semler, head of Semco, the Brazilian firm that bears his name, has published a popular book called *Maverick* and a series of startling *Harvard Business Review* articles, the latest of which, "How We Went Digital without a Strategy," is reproduced here. In the first sentence, he writes that he owns a $160,000,000 company "and I have no idea what business it's in." That is just Semler's opening shot! If Hamel seemed provocative, try Semler! This is not every company by a long shot, but it could be a part of every company that wants to move forward.

Mintzberg takes on in a similar vein the nature of managing itself in the next reading. Enough of "loud" managing, he says—enough of the hype of "globalization" and "shareholder value" and "empowerment" and "change." Enough heroic leadership. Time for "managing quietly," by inspiring not empowering, caring not curing, infusing not intruding, initiating not imposing.

The last reading in this chapter, "Managing Effectively", is excerpted from Henry Mintzberg's book "Managing". It looks at the perennial question of effective management. Management is nothing if it is not effective. Clearly, it is central to the strategy process, as it is in every other aspect of the organization. It is also a subject that has generated a vast amount of publications, and arguably is the main justification for MBA programs. Mintzberg argues that much of what has been said about managing effectively is based on misunderstanding, not so much of the nature of managerial work (which he tackles in Chapter 2), but of human beings in general. Because people are always flawed in some way, managerial effectiveness will depend on a match between the person and the context in which they manage. Inevitably, this means that selecting, assessing, and developing managers is the crucial issue facing managerial effectiveness, rather than a list of desirable qualities candidates for managerial positions must possess before they assume their position. It also means that we have to radically rethink the purpose and mission of business schools.

USING THE CASE STUDIES

New ideas in strategy usually come from managers who go against conventional wisdom. Guy LaLiberté takes the conventional concept of the circus and transforms it beyond recognition. Candida Gertler and Yana Peel create a new model of arts philanthropy. Several of the cases deal with managers who have developed new ways of doing strategy. The Natura case describes a Brazilian company where three presidents share equally the decision-making power. In the Haier case, newly appointed CEO Zhang Ruimin puts in place an "80:20" principle under which 20% of employees who are managers are held responsible for 80% of the results, good or bad. Rewards for good performance are quite standard in most companies, but what makes Ruimin's approach unique is holding the top 20% accountable for poor results. In "How We Went Digital without a Strategy," Semler suggests employees, throughout the organization, can hold themselves and each other accountable without complex systems of supervision. In his reading, Hamel argues that innovation in strategy should focus on the "how" of the strategy process rather than the "what" of its content. It is significant in this respect that the Natura and Haier cases deal with industries and products that are not particularly glamorous. None of these companies stake their fortunes on finding lucrative niches or hot products.

The "Disposable Organization" by March explores the obstacles to strategic experimentation. On the other hand, the "Beyond Configuration" reading by Mintzberg suggests that escaping the intrinsic contradictions of organizing is the main impetus to strategic creativity. Semco, Outset, and Pixar cases support Mintzberg's optimism, but Cadbury Schweppes' running up against the limits of creating a globally diversified corporation support March's pessimism.

Strategy innovation, however, can have modest beginnings. The case of "A Restaurant with a Difference" deals with a couple exploring a new business idea: a learning restaurant. What is contemplated is certainly far smaller in scale than the learning organization championed by Ricardo Semler. However, as Mintzberg points out in "Managing Quietly," original thinking in management often takes place away from the limelight. In fact, original thinking in strategy may not be revolutionary at all. It just has to be an idea that makes all the difference. Managing effectively (or ineffectively) can be observed in many of the cases. Sukhinder Singh makes one mistake after another. He often changes his mind. To the casual observer he may appear indecisive. But if we look beyond his reactions to events we see constancy motivated by a passion for his business, and a deep sense of responsibility to the family. When managerial effectiveness is ambiguous, as it is in the case of Novomed's Mathias Jones, asking where it is going wrong can be as instructive as looking at clearly effective managers.

READING 18.1

Beyond Configuration* BY HENRY MINTZBERG

"Lumpers" are people who categorize, who synthesize. "Splitters" are people who analyze, who see all the nuances. From the standpoint of organization, both are right and both are wrong. Without categories, it would be impossible to practice management. With only categories, it could not be practiced effectively.

The author was mostly a lumper until a colleague asked him if he wanted to play "jigsaw puzzle" or "LEGO" with his concepts. In other words, do all these concepts fit together in set ways and known images (puzzle), or were they to be used creatively to create new images? The remainder of this reading is presented in the spirit of playing "organizational LEGO." It tries to show how we can use splitting as well as lumping to understand what makes organizations effective as well as what causes many of their fundamental problems.

FORMS AND FORCES

The configurations described in the chapters of this section of the book are *forms*, and they are laid out at the nodes of a pentagon in Figure 1. Many organizations seem to fit naturally into one of the original five, but some do not fit, to the lumpers' chagrin. To respond to this, five *forces* have been added, each associated with one of the original forms:

- *Direction* for the entrepreneurial form, for some sense of where the organization must go. This is often called "strategic vision." Without direction the various activities of an organization cannot easily work together to achieve common purpose.
- *Efficiency* for the machine form. This ensures a viable ratio of benefits gained to costs incurred. Lack of concern for efficiency would cause all but the most protected organization to fade.
- *Proficiency* for the professional form. Organizations need this to carry out tasks with high levels of knowledge and skill. The difficult work of organizations would otherwise simply not get done.
- *Accountability* for the diversified form. If individual units in an organization are not accountable for their efforts in particular markets, it becomes almost impossible to manage a diversified organization.
- *Learning* for the innovative or adhocracy form. Organizations need to be able to learn, to discover new things for their customers and themselves—to adapt and to innovate.

Two other forces exist that are not necessarily associated with a particular form:

- *Cooperation*, represented by ideology. This is the force for pulling together.
- *Competition*, represented by politics. This is the force for pulling apart.

For the lumpers we now have a *portfolio of forms*, and for the splitters we now have a *system of forces*. Both views are critical for the practice of management. One represents the most fundamental forces that act on organizations. All serious organizations experience all seven of them, at one time or another, if not all the time. The other represents the fundamental forms that organizations can take, which some of them do some of the time. Together, these forces and forms appear to constitute a powerful diagnostic framework by which to understand what goes on in organizations and to prescribe effective change in them.

When one force dominates an organization, it is drawn toward the associated *configuration*, but must deal with *contamination*. When no force dominates, the organization is a balanced

*Adapted from a chapter of this title in *Mintzberg on Management: Inside Our Strange World of Organizations* (Free Press, 1989) by H. Mintzberg; an article similar to this chapter was published in the *Sloan Management Review*.

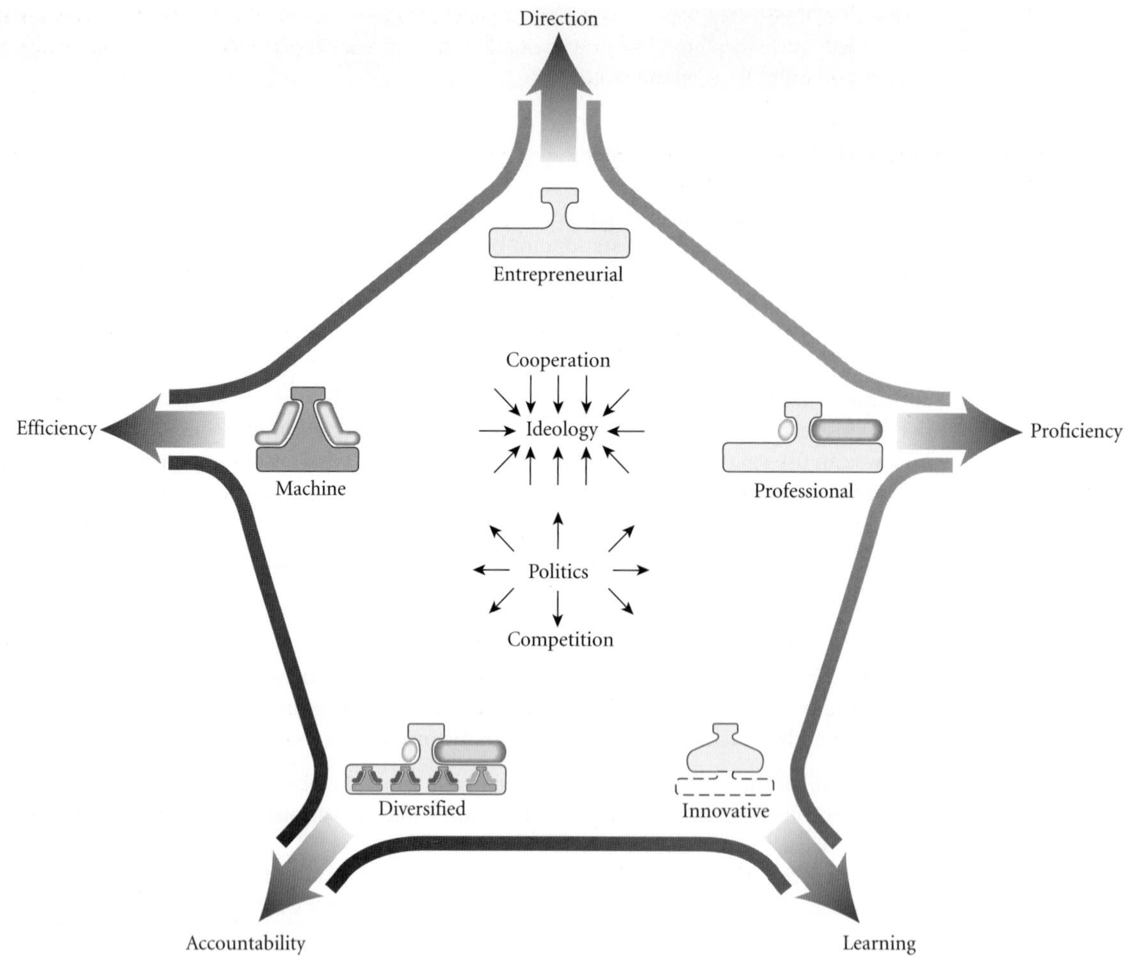

FIGURE 1 AN INTEGRATING PENTAGON OF FORCES AND FORMS

combination of forces, including periods of *conversion* from one form to another. But then there is a problem of *cleavage*. Contamination and cleavage require the management of *contradiction*, which is where ideology and politics come in. We shall discuss each of these notions shortly.

Dominant forces drive an organization to one of the pure forms discussed earlier—entrepreneurial, machine, professional, diversified, innovative. These are not "real," but are abstract models designed to capture some reality. Some organizations *do* match the pure forms closely. If the form fits, the organization should wear it. Configuration has benefits: the organization achieves a sense of order, or integration. Configuration also helps outsiders understand an organization. The consistency of configuration keeps workers from being confused. For classification, for comprehension, for diagnosis, and for design, configuration seems to be effective. But only so long as everything holds still. Introduce the dynamics of evolutionary change and, sooner or later, configuration becomes ineffective.

CONTAMINATION BY CONFIGURATION

The harmony, consistency, and fit that is configuration's greatest strength is also its greatest weakness. The dominant force can become so strong that it drives out everything else. For example, control in machine organizations may contaminate the innovators in research. Machine organizations recognize this when they put their research and development facilities away from the head office, to avoid the contaminating effects of the central efficiency experts. The opposite case is also well known—the "looseness" in adhocracies may contaminate the efforts of the accountants concerned with efficiency. This contamination may be a small price to pay for being coherently organized, until things go out of control.

CONFIGURATION OUT OF CONTROL

When the need arises for change, the dominating forces may act to hold the organization in place. The other forces may have atrophied, and so the organization goes out of control. For instance, the machine organization in need of a new strategy may have no entrepreneurs and no innovators left to give it its new direction. Miller and Kets de Vries (1987) have developed five organizational "neuroses" that correspond roughly to what can happen in extreme cases of contamination in the five forms. Each is an example of a system that may once have been healthy but has run of control.

- *Dramatic:* the entrepreneur, freed from other forces, may take the organization on an ego trip. This can even occur in large diversified organizations that are dominated by strong CEOs.
- *Compulsive:* this happens when there is completeness of control in machine organizations. This is the classic overbearing bureaucracy.
- *Paranoid:* paranoia is often a collective tendency in some professional organizations like universities and hospitals. Professors and doctors are always suspicious that their peers, or worse, "the administration," are planning to undermine their efforts.
- *Depressive:* this can be the result of an obsession with the bottom line in diversified organizations. Being a cash cow that is constantly being "milked" is very bad for morale.
- *Schizoid:* the need to innovate, and to get the commercial benefits from innovation, means that adhocracies can be in constant oscillation between divergent and convergent thinking.

In other words, behaviors that were once functional become dysfunctional when pursued to excess.

CONTAINMENT OF CONFIGURATION

Truly effective organizations thus do not exist in pure form. What keeps a configuration effective is not only the dominance of a single force but also the constraining effects of other forces. This is *containment*. To manage configuration effectively is to exploit one form but also to reconcile the different forces. Machine organizations must exploit their efficiency but must still allow for innovation. Innovative forms must exploit their power to create, but must find a way to remain somewhat efficient.

COMBINATION

Configuration is nice if you can have it. But some organizations all of the time, and all organizations some of the time, are unable to have it. They must instead balance competing forces. Organizations like this can be called *combinations*; instead of being a node in the pentagon, they are somewhere within it.

KINDS OF COMBINATIONS

When only two of the five forces meet in rough balance, that is a *hybrid*. A symphony orchestra is an example, being a rough balance of entrepreneurial and professional forms. Some organizations experience *multiple combinations*. Apple Computer in Canada was once described as a combination of adhocracy (a legacy of its founder, Steve Jobs), machine (for efficiency in production and distribution), entrepreneurial (in the person of a dynamic sales manager), and professional (in marketing and training).

CLEAVAGE IN COMBINATIONS

If configuration encourages contamination, sometimes combination encourages *cleavage*. Instead of one force dominating, two or more confront each other to the point of paralyzing the organization. A common example from business organizations is the innovative drive of R&D against the machine-like drive of production.

Despite the problems created by having to balance forces, combination of one kind or another is probably necessary in most organizations. Effective organizations usually balance many forces. Configuration merely means a tilt toward one force; combination is more balanced.

CONVERSION

The preceding discussions of configuration and combination implied stability. But few organizations stay in one form or combination; they undergo *conversion* from one configuration or combination to another. Often these result from external changes. For example, an innovative organization decides to settle down as a machine to exploit an innovation. Or a suddenly unstable market makes a machine become more innovative. Conversions are often temporary, as in the machine organization that becomes an entrepreneurial organization during a crisis.

CYCLES OF CONVERSION

The forces that may destroy the organization may instead drive it to another, perhaps more viable, configuration. For example, the entrepreneurial form is inherently vulnerable, because of its reliance on a single leader. It may work well for the young organization, but with aging and growth a dominant need for direction may be displaced by that for efficiency. Then conversion to the machine form becomes necessary—the power of one leader must be replaced by that of administrators.

The implication is that organizations go through stages as they develop, sequenced into so-called life cycles. The most common life cycle is the one mentioned above. It begins with the entrepreneurial form and moves down along the left edge of the pentagon. Growth leads to the machine form, and even greater growth leads ultimately to the diversified form. Another life cycle, depicted along the right edge of the pentagon, occurs for firms dependent on expertise. They move from the entrepreneurial form to either the professional form (if they can standardize their services) or the innovative form (if their services are more creative). Another common conversion is when an innovative form decides to exploit and perfect the skills it has developed and settles into a professional form, a common conversion in consulting.

Ideology and politics play a role in conversion. Ideology is a more important form in young organizations. That is because cultures can develop more easily there, especially with charismatic leadership in the entrepreneurial stage. By comparison, it is extremely difficult to build a strong and lasting culture in a mature organization. Politics, by contrast, typically spreads as the energy of the young organization dissipates and its activities become more diffuse. As the organization becomes more formalized, its culture is blunted, and politics becomes a more important force.

CLEAVAGE IN CONVERSION

Some conversions are easy because they are so overdue. But most are more difficult and conflictual, requiring periods of transition, prolonged and agonizing. As the organization in transition sits between its old and new forms, it becomes a kind of combination. The forces that create the conversion also create the possibility of cleavage. How does the organization deal with these contradictions?

CONTRADICTION

Organizations that have to reconcile contradictory forces, especially in dealing with change, often turn to the cooperative force of ideology or the competitive force of politics. Indeed, these two forces themselves represent a contradiction that must be managed if an organization is not to run out of control.

While it is true that each can dominate an organization, and so draw it toward a missionary or political form, more commonly they act differently, as *catalysts*. Ideology tends to draw behavior inwards toward a common core; politics drives behavior away from any central place. One force is centripetal, the other centrifugal. Both can act to promote change or also to prevent it. Either way, they sometimes render an organization more effective, sometimes less.

COOPERATION THROUGH IDEOLOGY

Ideology (or strong culture) represents the force for cooperation in an organization, for collegiality and consensus. It encourages members to look inward, to take their lead from the imperatives of the organization's own vision. One important implication is that infusion of ideology renders any particular configuration more effective. People get fired up to pursue efficiency or proficiency or whatever else drives the organization. When this happens to a machine organization—as in a McDonald's, very responsive to its customers and very sensitive to its employees—we have a "snappy bureaucracy." Bureaucratic machines are not supposed to be snappy, but ideology changes the nature of their quest for efficiency.

Another implication is that ideology helps an organization manage contradiction and so to deal with change. The innovative machine and the tightly controlled innovative organization are inherent contradictions. These organizations handle their contradictions by having strong cultures. Such organizations can more easily reconcile their opposing forces because what matters to their people ultimately is the organization itself, more than any of its particular parts, like efficient manufacturing or innovative R&D. This is how Toyota gets efficiency and high quality at the same time.

LIMITS TO COOPERATION

Ideologies sound wonderful, but they are difficult to build and sustain. And established ideologies can get in the way of organizational effectiveness. They may discourage change by forcing everyone to work within the same set of beliefs. This has implications for strategy. Change *within* strategic perspective, to a new position, is facilitated by a strong ideology. But change *of* perspective—fundamental change—is discouraged by it.

COMPETITION THROUGH POLITICS

Politics represents the force for competition in an organization, for conflict and confrontation. It too can infuse any of the configurations or combinations, in this case aggravating contamination and cleavage. In a configuration, the representatives of the dominant force "lord it" over others. This could lead to contamination. In a combination, representatives of the various forces relish opportunities to do battle with each other, aggravating the cleavage.

One problem facing strategic managers is that politics may be a more "natural" force than ideology. Left to themselves, organizations seem to pull apart rather easily. Keeping them together requires considerable and constant effort.

BENEFITS OF COMPETITION

If the pulling together of culture discourages people from addressing fundamental change, then the pulling apart of politics may become the only way to ensure that happens. Change requires challenging the status quo. Politics may facilitate this; if there are no entrepreneurial or innovative forces stimulating strategic change, it may be the *only* available force for change.

Both politics and ideology can promote organizational effectiveness as well as undermine it. Ideology can be a force for revitalization, energizing the organization and making its people more responsive. But it can also hinder fundamental change. Likewise, politics often impedes necessary change and wastes valuable resources. But it can also promote important change that may be available in no other way. It can enable those who realize the need for change to challenge those who do not.

COMBINING COOPERATION AND COMPETITION

The last remaining contradiction is the one between ideology and politics themselves. Ideology and politics themselves have to be reconciled. Pulling together ideologically infuses life; splitting apart politically challenges the status quo. Only by encouraging both can an organization sustain its viability. Ideology helps secondary forces to contain a dominant one; politics encourages them to challenge it.

The balance between ideology and politics should be a dynamic equilibrium. Most of the time ideology should be pulling things together, contained by healthy internal competition. When fundamental change becomes necessary, however, politics should help pull the organization apart temporarily.

COMPETENCE

What makes an organization effective? The "Peterian" view (named after Tom Peters of *In Search of Excellence* fame) is that organizations should be "hands on, value driven." The "Porterian" view (named after Michael Porter) says that organizations should use competitive analysis. To Porter, effectiveness resides in strategy, while to Peters it is the operations that count. One says do the right things, the other says do things right. But we need to understand what takes an organization to a viable strategy in the first place, what makes it excellent there, and how some organizations are able to sustain viability and excellence in the face of change.

Here are five views to guide us in our search for organizational effectiveness:

CONVERGENCE

First is the *convergence* hypothesis. Its motto is that there is "one best way" to design an organization. This is usually associated with the machine form. A good structure is one with a rigid hierarchy of authority, with spans of control no greater than six, with heavy use of strategic planning, MIS, and whatever else happens to be in the current fashion of the rationalizers. In *In Search of Excellence*, by contrast, Peters and Waterman argued that ideology was the key to an organization's success. We cannot dismiss this hypothesis—sometimes there *are* proper things to do in most, perhaps all, organizations. But we must take issue with its general thrust. Society has paid an enormous price for "one best way" thinking over the course of the last century, on the part of all its organizations that have been drawn into using what is fashionable rather than functional. We need to look beyond the obvious, beyond the convergence hypothesis.

CONGRUENCE

Beyond convergence is the *congruence* or "it all depends" approach. Introduced into organization theory in the 1960s, it suggests that running an organization is like choosing dinner from a buffet table—a little bit of this, a little bit of that, all selected according to specific needs. Organizational effectiveness thus becomes a question of matching a given set of internal attributes, treated as a kind of portfolio, with various situational factors. The congruence hypothesis has certainly been an improvement, but like a dinner plate stacked with an old assortment of foods, it has not been good enough.

CONFIGURATION

The motto of the *configuration* hypothesis is "getting it all together." Design your organization as you would a jigsaw puzzle, fitting the organizational pieces together to create a coherent, harmonious picture. There is reason to believe that organizations succeed in good part because they are consistent in what they do; they are certainly easier to manage that way. But, as we have seen, configuration has its limits, too.

CONTRADICTION

While the lumpers may like the configuration hypothesis, splitters prefer the *contradiction* hypothesis. Their call is to manage the dynamic tension between contradictory forces. They point to the common occurrence of combinations and conversions, where organizations are forced to manage contradictory forces. This is an important hypothesis—together with that of configuration (which are in their own dynamic tension) it is an important clue to organizational effectiveness. But still it is not sufficient.

CREATION

The truly great organization transcends all of the foregoing while building on it to achieve something more. It respects the *creation* hypothesis. Creativity is its forte, "understand your inner nature" is its motto, LEGO its image. The most interesting organizations live at the edges, far from the logic of conventional organizations, where as Raphael (1976: 5–6) has pointed out in biology (for example, between the sea and the land, or at the forest's edge), the richest, most varied, and most interesting forms of life can be found. This might be called the "Prahaladian" view (after C. K. Prahalad, and his ideas of "strategic intent" discussed in Chapter 3). Don't just do the right things right, but keep doing them! Such organizations keep inventing novel approaches that solve festering problems and so provide all of us with new ways to deal with our world of organizations.

READING 18.2

Organizational Adaptation* BY JAMES G. MARCH

. . . Almost every theory of organization presumes a tendency for environmental change to be reflected in organizational change. Environments and history shape organizational forms and practices, although they do so inefficiently . . . and often jerkily. . . . As a result, specific changes in the world are seen as likely to lead to specific changes in organizations as they seek to survive and are selected by their competitive environments. For example, increases in global connectedness and uses of modern information technology are often seen as likely to lead to increased uses of non hierarchical networks in coordinating activities, and increases in the importance of knowledge and in the rate of change in its content are often seen as likely to lead to a decreased emphasis on learning by doing and an increased emphasis on access to external sources of knowledge.

At a more general level, however, stories of rapid environmental change invite a prediction that future environments will favor organizations that are able to be flexible and to adapt quickly to change. Organizations that fail to adapt seem destined to expire as the world around them changes. This has led to considerable enthusiasm for designing organizations that are capable of learning, of adapting to the changes they face. . . .

Adaptiveness involves both the exploitation of what is known and the exploration of what might come to be known (March, 1991, 1994b). *Exploitation* refers to the short-term improvement, refinement, routinization, and elaboration of existing ideas, paradigms, technologies, strategies, and knowledge. It thrives on focused attention, precision, repetition, analysis, sanity, discipline, and control. Exploitation is served by knowledge, forms, and practices that facilitate an organization's well-being in the short run. It emphasizes improving existing capabilities and technologies. It profits from close attention, systematic reason, risk aversion, sharp focus, hard work, training, and refined detail. It includes locating and developing competencies and

---

*Reprinted with deletions from an article originally entitled "The Future Disposable Organizations and the Rigidities of Management," *Organization*, November 1995.

tying those competencies together to produce joint products. It includes managing the capabilities of an organization, facilitating communication and coordination, tightening slack. It includes defining and measuring performance and linking activities powerfully to performance measures.

Exploitation is also served by a pursuit of legitimacy. People in organizations and people with whom they deal are driven by understandings of appropriate behavior. They try to act appropriately and they expect others to do so also. Exhibiting proper organization forms and acting in an appropriate manner generate support and thereby aid survival. . . . As organizations seek technical efficiency and legitimacy, they focus energy on relatively short-run concerns. They refine capabilities, reduce costs, and adopt standard procedures. They mobilize efforts to achieve clearly defined, short-term objectives. Some modern terms are reengineering, downsizing, and total quality management.

Exploration refers to experimentation with new ideas, paradigms, technologies, strategies, and knowledge in hopes of finding alternatives that improve on old ones. It thrives on serendipity, risk taking, novelty, free association, madness, loose discipline, and relaxed control. The characteristic feature of exploration is that it is risky. Success is not assured, indeed is often not achieved. Even when exploration is successful, its rewards are often slow in coming and not necessarily realized by the parts of the organization that have paid the costs. Exploratory risk taking appears to be more likely when an organization is falling somewhat behind its target aspirations than when it is achieving them. It is stimulated by failure. It is sometimes also stimulated, largely unintentionally, by organizational slack and by illusions that organizational actors have about their abilities to overcome risks. . . .

Adaptiveness requires both exploitation and exploration. A system that specializes in exploitation will discover itself becoming better and better at an increasingly obsolescent technology. A system that specializes in exploration will never realize the advantages of its discoveries. . . .

The dynamics of learning tend to destroy the balance. . . . In general, returns to the exploitation of existing knowledge are systematically closer in time and space than are returns to the explorations of possible new knowledge. This produces two well-known "traps" of adaptive systems. The first is the "failure" trap. In the failure trap, an organization fails, tries a new direction, fails again, and tries still another direction, and so on. The process leads to an endless cycle of failure and exploration. The cycle is sustained by the fact that most new directions are bad ideas and that most new ideas that are good ideas usually require practice and time in order to realize their capabilities. In the short run, even good ideas fail and are rejected. The failure trap leads to impatience with a new course of action and an excess of exploration.

The second trap is a "success" trap. When an organization succeeds, it repeats actions that appear to have produced the success. As a result of repeating actions, it becomes more proficient at the technology involved. As a result of the greater proficiency, it is likely to be successful again, and so on. The process leads to an endless cycle of success, increased competence, and local efficiency. New good ideas or technologies are not tried, or if tried do not do as well as the existing technology (because of the disparity in competence with the two). The success trap leads to a failure to experiment adequately. . . .

Within this short story of organizational change can be seen a fundamental dilemma of organizations. Exploitation and exploration are linked in an enduring symbiosis. Each requires the other in order to contribute effectively to an organization's survival and prosperity. At the same time, however, each interferes with the other. Exploitation undermines exploration. It discourages the experimentation and variation that are essential to long-term survival. It results in sticking to one (currently effective) capability to such an extent that there is little exploration of others, or in failing to stick to one (currently ineffective) capability long enough to determine its true value. In a similar fashion, exploration undermines exploitation. Efforts to promote experimentation encourage impatience with new ideas, technologies, and strategies. They are likely to be abandoned before enough time has been devoted to developing the competence that would make them useful. The impatience of exploration results in unrealized dreams and unelaborated discoveries. As a result of the ways in which exploitation and exploration tend to extinguish each other, organizations persistently fail to maintain an effective balance between the two. . . .

THE PERILS AND GLORIES OF IMAGINATION

Enthusiasts for foretelling the future face a grim reality. Predictions about the future of organizations are predictably bad. Well-informed, careful analysts do not have a much better record than do consultants of tea leaves. This is not because tea leaf consultation has a good record but because analysis has a poor one. Even Marx, who was considerably smarter than most of us, didn't get it entirely right. Organizational futurology is a profession in which reputations are crafted from the excitements of novelty, fear, and hope. They are destroyed by the unfolding of experience.

Imaginations of possible organizations are justified not by their potential for predicting the future (which is almost certainly small) but by their potential for nurturing the uncritical commitment and persevering madness required for sustained organizational and individual rigidity in a selective environment. Many observers have noted the role of imagination in stimulating discoveries, but from this point of view its primary role is less in creating new ideas than in protecting them from disconfirmation. Imagination is unlikely to be more correct than convention, but it is more lucid, more autonomous, and more compelling.

Clarity of vision protects deviant imaginations from the disconfirmations of experience and knowledge. Attachment to a fantasy converts the ambiguities of history into confirmations of belief and a willingness to persist in a course of action. This self-sustaining character of imagination protects commitment from the importunities of reality. Soothsayers of the future create sheltered worlds of ignorance, ideology, and faith. Within the shell that they provide, craziness is protected long enough to elaborate its challenge to orthodoxy.

> I began to wonder whether anything truly existed, whether reality wasn't an unformed and gelatinous substance only half-captured by my senses . . . . I was consoled by the idea that I could take the gelatin and mold it to create anything I wanted, . . . a world of my own populated with living people, a world where I imposed the rules and could change them at will. In the motionless sands where my stories germinated, every birth, death, and happening depended on me. I could plant anything I wanted in those sands; I had only to speak the right word to give it life. At times I felt that the universe fabricated from the power of the imagination had stronger and more lasting contours than the blurred realm of the flesh-and-blood creatures around me. (Eva Luna in Allende, 1989, pp. 187–188)

The modern word is "vision," and its overtones of dreams are appropriate. Imaginations of the future are stronger and more lasting than the blurred realm of the flesh-and-blood creatures around us, and that power protects exploration from its enemies . . . .

As Eva Luna reminds us, intellectual passions for reasoned intelligence and constrained imagination have never entirely extinguished a human aesthetic based on fantasy. A commitment to arbitrarily imagined worlds has elements of simple beauty in it. . . . From this perspective, the occasional argument between those who imagine individual organizations as changing and enduring and those who imagine them as rigid and disposable is an argument not only about the truth but also about the beauty and justice of possible fantasies of human existence, thus perhaps worth taking seriously.

READING 18.3

Strategy Innovation and the Quest for Value* BY GARY HAMEL

. . . I believe that only those companies that are capable of reinventing themselves and their industry in a profound way will be around a decade hence. The question today is not whether you can reengineer your processes; the question is whether you can reinvent the entire industry model—as Amazon.com has been attempting to do in book selling. . . .

---

*Reprinted with deletions from "Strategy Innovation and the Quest for Value," G. Hamel, *Sloan Management Review*, Winter 1998, 7–14.

In industry after industry, it is the revolutionaries—usually newcomers—who are creating the new wealth. Of course, there are examples of incumbents like Coca-Cola and Procter & Gamble that are able to continually reinvent themselves and their industry, but all too often, industry incumbents fail to challenge their own orthodoxies and succumb to unconventional rivals.

The point seems incontestable: *in a discontinuous world, strategy innovation is the key to wealth creation*. Strategy innovation is the capacity to reconceive the existing industry model in ways that create new value for customers, wrong-foot competitors, and produce new wealth for all stakeholders. Strategy innovation is the only way for newcomers to succeed in the face of enormous resource disadvantages, and the only way for incumbents to renew their lease on success. And if one redefines the metric of corporate success as *share of new wealth creation* within some broad opportunity domain—e.g., energy, transportation, communication, computing, and so on—the innovation imperative becomes inescapable.

Today, many companies are worrying about EVA (economic value added), but EVA—earning more than your cost of capital—is just the starting point. The goal is not to earn more than your cost of capital; the goal is to capture a disproportionate share of industry wealth creation. There are many semiconductor companies that earn more than their cost of capital, but it is Intel that has created and captured much of the new value in the microprocessor industry during the past decade. Of course Intel earns its cost of capital, but it earns much more than that. . . .

Growth is the scoreboard, but it is definitely not the game. Focusing on growth, rather than on the game of strategy innovation, is likely to destroy wealth rather than create it. The reason is simple. There are as many stupid ways to grow as there are to cut: acquisitions that destroy value (Sony and Matsushita in Hollywood), market share battles that lower industry profitability (the airlines' perennial favorite), and megabucks blue-sky projects (think Apple and the Newton) are just a few examples that should illustrate the danger of go-for-broke growth strategies. Needless to say, companies pursuing value-destroying growth won't make it onto any list of star performers.

When we dig deeper, we find that . . . extraordinarily successful companies . . . grew by radically changing the basis for competition in their industries. They either invented totally new industries or dramatically reinvented existing ones. This is true for Home Depot, Amgen, Nike, Intel, Compaq, the Gap, and most of the other companies on the super-star list. They all developed nonlinear strategies.

IS STRATEGY IRRELEVANT?

So if strategy innovation is key to creating new wealth, why is "strategy" no longer a "big idea" in most companies? Why does it seem to command so little of top management's time and attention? And why are planners an increasingly endangered species?

The competitive environment faced by companies today is far, far different from that which gave birth to the concept of strategy some thirty years ago. But, while the rapidly shifting strategy environment has partially devalued some traditional strategy concepts, such as industry structure analysis, it has also provided the impetus for much new thinking. Indeed, the changing context for strategy has provoked a huge amount of new thinking on the *content* of strategy. The new themes in the strategy world include: foresight, knowledge, competencies, coalitions, networks, extra-market competition, ecosystems, transformation, renewal. All these subjects are intensely contemporary.

So strategists certainly can't be accused of being ignorant of the new competitive realities. But as informed as they may be, impactful they are not. Why? Because managers simply do not know what to do with all the wonderful concepts, frameworks, and buzzwords that tumble from the pages of the *Harvard Business Review*, that jam the business aisles of bookstores, and that glisten in the slickly edited pages of business magazines.

Strategists may have a lot to say about the context and content of strategy, but, in recent years, they have had precious little to say about the *conduct* of strategy—that is, the task of strategy making. No one seems to know much about how to create strategy. Managers today know how to embed quality disciplines, how to reengineer processes, and how to reduce cycle times, but they don't know how to foster the development of innovative wealth-creating strategies.

So, while there has been enormous innovation around the content of strategy—management has an ever-expanding list of "strategic" issues to address—there has been no corresponding innovation around the conduct of strategy. Let's face it, the annual strategic planning process in most companies has changed hardly at all during the past decade or two.

It's ironic; never has a capacity for deep strategic thinking been so necessary as in today's turbulent times, and yet never, in the past two decades, has strategy's "share of voice" been lower in the corridors of corporate power. . . .

WHAT ARE THE SECRETS OF STRATEGY CREATION?

The strategy industry—all those consultants, business school professors, authors, and planners—has a dirty little secret. Everyone knows a strategy when they see one—be it Microsoft's, Nucor's, or Virgin Atlantic's. We all recognize a great strategy after the fact. In the case study method, professors hold strategies up to be admired, or ridiculed, by preternaturally wise MBA students. Their post hoc explanations of the competitive success and failure that ensue are stunningly beautiful. We are great at pinning down butterflies. But our case libraries and business magazines, with their stories of corporate success and failure, are museums filled with dead specimens. Simply put, we all know strategy as a "thing"— once someone else has bagged it and tagged it. We also understand planning as a "process." But the planning process doesn't produce strategy, it produces plans—a point that Henry Mintzberg has made on more than one occasion.

Anyone who claims to be a strategist should be intensely embarrassed by the fact that the strategy industry doesn't have a theory of strategy creation! It doesn't know where bold, new value-creating strategies come from. . . .

The questions we must address are these: How can we create a Cambrian explosion of innovative strategies inside the firm? What does it take to invent new strategy "S curves"? To answer these questions, we must have a theory of strategy innovation. Developing such a theory is a grand project. All I can do here is to offer a few starting propositions.

I agree with Mintzberg that strategy "emerges." But I don't believe the emergent nature of strategy creation prevents us from aiding and abetting the process of strategy innovation. We are not helpless. The reason I don't believe we're helpless is because strategy doesn't simply emerge—rather, it is *emergent*, in the same full-bodied sense that life itself is emergent. One of the things we're learning from complexity theorists is that by creating the right set of preconditions, one can provoke emergence. Stuart Kauffman, a pioneer in complexity theory, has suggested that life began with an "autocatalytic" system—a self-reinforcing set of chemical reactions. Whether you agree or disagree, the analogy may be useful. What, we must ask, would catalyze the emergence of new, viable strategies in a successful, though complacent, organization? My guess is that the answer, while perhaps subtle, will nevertheless be easier to come by than the mystery of life.

Once you start thinking of strategy as an emergent phenomenon, you realize that we have often attacked the wrong end of the problem. Strategists and senior executives have too often worked on "the strategy," rather than on the preconditions that could give rise to strategy innovation. In essence, they've been trying to design complex, multicell organisms, rather than trying to understand and create the conditions from which such organisms will emerge. . . .

Two great forces of nature seem to be counterposed. On the one hand, there is the general trend toward entropy. When we convert fossil fuel into heat, to power our cars or heat our homes, we are turning highly ordered energy—complex carbon molecules—into "disordered" energy—heat, as well as a variety of pollutants. These things can never be "put back together." The second law of thermodynamics suggests that we are sliding inevitably toward chaos. Not only does the law characterize physical systems, it often seems to characterize human systems. Many organizations seem to be affected by a kind of "institutional entropy" in which energy, enthusiasm, and effectiveness slowly dissipate over time.

Yet we see order all around us: the New York Stock Exchange, Toyota's supplier network, a great university, or, most miraculous of all, ourselves. A human being is an almost infinitely more ordered thing, and a much, much more complex system, than a single-celled organism. Order seems to be the second great force in nature. And while entropy may be inevitable in physical systems, there is nothing to suggest that it is inevitable in biological or human systems. . . .

While a complex living system, and the order it possesses, is probably not the product of random variation, neither can it be designed top-down. The New York Stock Exchange couldn't be designed top-down. Neither could life on the Internet, nor a human being, nor a complex but internally consistent strategy. What is going on in all these cases is what Kauffman calls "order without careful crafting." "Order *without* careful crafting"— I'd like to suggest that this is the goal of strategizing.

Order arises from simple, deep rules. Craig Reynolds has shown that with three simple rules, one can richly simulate the behavior of a flock of birds in flight. So it's not that there is *no* crafting, *no* design, only that it works at the level of preconditions and broad parameters—not at the level of a detailed design. So while there was a simple architecture underlying the Internet, no one could have envisioned all the rich permutations of Net-based life that would emerge in the new on-line biosphere. . . .

Like all forms of complexity, strategy is poised on the border between perfect order and total chaos, between absolute efficiency and blind experimentation, between autocracy and complete *adhocracy*. . . .

Let me ask a question of those who've ever sat through a business school case study: Have you ever gotten halfway through a brilliant exposition of a company's strategy and thought to yourself, "Did they really have this thing figured out ahead of time? Isn't this just luck? Isn't this 20/20 hindsight? What about all the failures?" Sure, you have. These impertinent questions lie at the heart of our search for a theory of strategy creation. Is a great strategy luck, or is it foresight? Of course, the answer is that it is both. Circumstance, cognition, data, and desire converge, and a strategy insight is born. The fact that strategy has a significant element of serendipity to it shouldn't cause us to despair. The alternatives are not the "big brain" design school of strategy, nor the "muddle along" process school. The question is, how can we increase the odds that new wealth-creating strategies emerge? How can we make serendipity happen? How can we prompt emergence?

HOW DOES STRATEGY EMERGE?

The most fundamental insight of complexity theory is that "complex behavior need not have complex roots," as Christopher Langton has so succinctly put it. So what are the simple roots of strategy creation? My experience, and that of my colleagues at Strategos, in helping companies improve their capacity for strategizing suggests that there are five preconditions for the emergence of strategy. . . .

1. *New voices*. Bringing new "genetic material" into the strategy process always serves to illuminate unconventional strategies. Top management must give up its monopoly on strategy creation, and previously underrepresented constituencies must be given a larger share of voice in the strategy creation process. Specifically, I believe that young people, newcomers, and those at the geographic periphery of the organization deserve a larger share of voice. It is in these constituencies where diversity lurks. So strategy creation must be a pluralistic process, a deeply participative undertaking.
2. *New conversations.* Creating a dialogue about strategy that cuts across all the usual organizational and industry boundaries substantially increases the odds that new strategy insights will emerge. All too often, in large organizations, conversations become hard-wired over time, with the same people talking to the same people about the same issues year after year. After a while, individuals have little left to learn from each other. Opportunities for new insights are created when one juxtaposes previously isolated knowledge in new ways.
3. *New passions.* Unleashing the deep sense of discovery that resides in almost every human being, and focusing that sense of discovery on the search for new wealth-creating strategies is another prerequisite. I believe the widespread assumption that individuals are against change is flat wrong. People are against change when it doesn't offer the prospect of new opportunity. There is much talk today about return on investment, but I like to think in terms of return on emotional investment. Individuals will not invest emotionally in a firm and its success unless they believe they will get a return on that investment. All my experience suggests that individuals will eagerly embrace change when given the chance to have a share of voice in inventing the future of their company. They will invest when there's a chance to create a unique and exciting future in which they can share.

4. *New perspectives.* New conceptual lenses that allow individuals to reconceive their industry, their company's capabilities, customer needs, and so on substantially aid the process of strategy innovation. To increase the probability of strategy innovation, managers must become the merchants of new perspective. They must search constantly for new lenses that help companies reconceive themselves, their customers, their competitors, and, thereby, their opportunities.
5. *New experiments.* Launching a series of small, risk-avoiding experiments in the market serves to maximize a company's rate of learning about just which new strategies will work and which won't. The insights that come from a broad-based strategy dialogue will never be perfect. While much traditional analysis can be done to refine those insights into viable strategies, there is much that can be learned only in the marketplace.

So where does this leave us? We should spend less time working on strategy as a "thing" and more time working to understand the preconditions that give rise to the "thing." Executives, consultants, and business school professors must rebalance the attention given to context, content, and conduct in favor of conduct.

In focusing on the conduct of strategy, not only are we trying to *discover* something—the hidden properties of strategy emergence—we are also trying to *invent* something. Like those long-ago Neanderthals trying to figure out the principles of cooking . . . we need to invent an oven—a *strategy oven*. . . .

READING 18.4

How We Went Digital without a Strategy* BY RICARDO SEMLER

I own a $160 million South American company named Semco, and I have no idea what business it's in. I know what Semco does—we make things, we provide services, we host Internet communities—but I don't know what Semco is. Nor do I want to know. For the 20 years I've been with the company, I've steadfastly resisted any attempt to define its business. The reason is simple: once you say what business you're in, you put your employees into a mental straitjacket. You place boundaries around their thinking and, worst of all, you hand them a ready-made excuse for ignoring new opportunities: "We're not in that business." So rather than dictate Semco's identity from on high, I've let our employees shape it through their individual efforts, interests, and initiatives.

That rather unusual management philosophy has drawn a good deal of attention over the years. Nearly 2,000 executives from around the world have trekked to São Paulo to study our operations. Few, though, have tried to emulate us. The way we work—letting our employees choose what they do, where and when they do it, and even how they get paid—has seemed a little too radical for mainstream companies.

But recently a funny thing happened: the explosion in computing power and the rise of the Internet reshaped the business landscape, and the mainstream shifted. Today, companies are desperately looking for ways to increase their creativity and flexibility, spur their idea flow, and free their talent—to do, in other words, what Semco has been doing for 20 years.

I don't propose that Semco represents the model for the way businesses will operate in the future. Let's face it: we're a quirky company. But I do suggest that some of the principles that underlie the way we work will become increasingly common and even necessary in the new economy. In particular, I believe we have an organization that is able to transform itself continuously and organically—without formulating complicated mission statements and strategies, announcing a bunch of top-down directives, or bringing in an army of change-management consultants. As other companies seek to build adaptability into their organizations, they may be able to learn a thing or two from Semco's example.

---

*Reprinted with deletions from "How We Went Digital without a Strategy," R. Semler, *Harvard Business Review*, September–October 2000, 51.

TRANSFORMATION WITHOUT END

Over the last ten years, Semco has grown steadily, quadrupling its revenues and expanding from 450 to 1,300 employees. More important, we've extended our range dramatically. At the start of the '90s, Semco was a manufacturer, pure and simple. We made things like pumps, industrial mixers, and dishwashers. But over the course of the decade, we diversified successfully into higher-margin services. Last year, almost 75% of our business was in services. Now we're stretching out again—this time into e-business. We expect that more than a quarter of our revenues next year will come from Internet initiatives, up from nothing just one year ago. We never planned to go digital, but we're going digital nonetheless.

You may wonder how that's possible. How do you get a sizable organization to change without telling it—or even asking it—to change? It's actually easy—but only if you're willing to give up control. People, I've found, will act in their best interests, and by extension in their organizations' best interests, if they're given complete freedom. It's only when you rein them in, when you tell them what to do and how to think, that they become inflexible, bureaucratic, and stagnant. Forcing change is the surest way to frustrate change.

Enough lecturing. Let me give you a concrete example of how our transformation has played out. Ten years ago, one of the things we did was manufacture cooling towers for large commercial buildings. In talking with the property owners who bought these products, some of our salespeople began to hear a common refrain. The customers kept complaining about the high cost of maintaining the towers. So our salespeople came back to Semco and proposed starting a little business in managing cooling-tower maintenance. They said, "We'll charge our customers 20% of whatever savings we generate for them, and we'll give Semco 80% of those revenues and take the remaining 20% as our commission." We said, "Fine, give it a shot."

Well, the little business was successful. We reduced customers' costs and eliminated some of their hassles, and they were happy. In fact, they were so happy that they came back and asked if we'd look after their air-conditioning compressors as well. Even though we didn't manufacture the compressors, our people didn't hesitate. They said yes. And when the customers saw we were pretty good at maintaining compressors, they said, "You know, there are a lot of other annoying functions that we'd just as soon off-load, like cleaning, security, and general maintenance. Can you do any of those?"

At that point, our people saw that their little business might grow into quite a big business. They began looking for a partner who could help bolster and extend our capabilities. They ended up calling the Rockefeller Group's Cushman & Wakefield division, one of the largest real-estate and property-management companies in the United States, and proposing that we launch a 50–50 joint venture in Brazil. Cushman wasn't very keen on the idea at first. People there said, "Property management by itself isn't a very lucrative business. Why don't we talk about doing something that involves real estate? That's where the money is."

We spent some time thinking about going into the real-estate business. We didn't have any particular expertise there, but we were willing to give it a try. When we started asking around, though, we found that no one in the company had much interest in real estate. It just didn't get anyone excited. So we went back to the Cushman folks and said, "Real estate sounds like a great business, but it's not something we care about right now. Why don't we just start with property management and see what happens?" They agreed, though not with a lot of enthusiasm.

We ponied up an initial investment of $2,000 each, just enough to pay the lawyers to set up a charter. Then we set our people loose. In no time, we had our first contract, with a bank, and then more and more business came through the door. Today, about five years later, the joint venture is a $30 million business.

It's also the most profitable property-management business within Cushman & Wakefield. The reason it has been so successful is that our people came into it fresh, with no preconceived strategies, and they were willing to experiment wildly. Instead of charging customers in the traditional way—a flat fee based on a building's square footage—they tried a partnership model. We'd take on all of a property owner's noncore functions, run them like a business, and split the resulting savings. . . .

Most manufacturers would probably consider a shift from making cooling towers to managing buildings pretty radical. Before making such a leap, they'd do a lot of soul-searching about their core businesses and capabilities. They'd run a lot of numbers, hold a lot of meetings, do a lot of planning. We didn't bother with any of that. We just let our people follow their instincts and apply their common sense, and it worked out fine.

GOING TO THE NET

Our recent move into the digital space has proceeded in much the same way, with our people again taking the lead. In fact, some of the eight Internet ventures we've launched grew directly out of our earlier service initiatives. As our facility-management business expanded, for example, we extended it, through a joint venture with Johnson Controls, to managing retail facilities. As our people began to work closely with store managers, they began to notice the huge costs retailers incur from lost inventory. One employee came forward and asked for a paid leave to study opportunities in that area. We gave him a green light, and within a year he had helped us set up a joint venture with RGIS, the largest inventory-tracking company in the world. Less than two years later, the venture had become the biggest inventory-management business in South America. Now it is branching out into Web-enabled inventory control, helping on-line companies coordinate the fulfillment of electronic orders.

Our work in property management also brought us face to face with the disorganization and inefficiency of the construction business. Here, too, our people saw a big business opportunity, one that would build on the unique capabilities of the Internet. A number of the members of our joint ventures with Cushman & Wakefield and Johnson Controls banded together, with Semco's support, to set up an on-line exchange to facilitate the management of commercial construction projects. All the participants in a building project—architects, banks, construction companies, contractors, and project managers—can now use our exchange to send messages, hold real-time chats, issue proposals and send bids, and share documents and drawings. . . .

That business, which we're operating as a 50–50 joint venture with the U.S. Internet software company Bidcom, has itself become a springboard for further new initiatives. One of the most exciting is the creation of a South American Web portal for the entire building industry. . . . We make money by charging transaction fees on all the business that takes place through the portal. . . .

MANAGEMENT WITHOUT CONTROL

Semco's ongoing transformation is a product of a very simple business philosophy: give people the freedom to do what they want, and over the long haul their successes will far outnumber their failures. Operationalizing that philosophy has involved a lot of trial and error, of taking a few steps forward and a couple back. The company remains a work in progress—and I hope it stays that way forever.

As I reflect on our experience, though, I see that we've learned some important lessons about creating an adaptive, creative organization. I'll share six of those lessons with you. I won't be so presumptuous as to say they'll apply to your company, but at least they'll stir up your thinking.

FORGET ABOUT THE TOP LINE

The biggest myth in the corporate world is that every business needs to keep growing to be successful. That's baloney. The ultimate measure of a business's success, I believe, is not how big it gets, but how long it survives. Yes, some businesses are meant to be huge, but others are meant to be medium-sized, and still others are meant to be small. At Semco, we never set revenue targets for our businesses. We let each one find its natural size—the size at which it can maintain profitability and keep customers happy. It's fine if a business's top line stays the same or even shrinks as long as its bottom line stays healthy. Rather than force our people to expand an existing business beyond its natural limits, we encourage them to start new businesses, to branch out instead of building up.

NEVER STOP BEING A START-UP

Every six months, we shut down Semco and start it up all over again. Through a rigorous budgeting and planning process, we force every one of our businesses to justify its continued existence. If this business didn't exist today, we ask, would we launch it? If we closed it down, would we alienate important customers? If the answers are no, then we move our money, resources, and talent elsewhere. We also take a fresh look at our entire organization, requiring that every employee—leaders included—resign (in theory) and ask to be rehired. All managers are evaluated anonymously by all workers who report to them, and the ratings are posted publicly. It has always struck me as odd that companies force new business ideas and new hires to go through rigorous evaluations but never do the same for existing businesses or employees.

DON'T BE A NANNY

Most companies suffer from what I call boarding-school syndrome. They treat their employees like children. They tell them where they have to be at what time, what they need to be doing, how they need to dress, whom they should talk to, and so on. But if you treat people like immature wards of the state, that's exactly how they'll behave. They'll never think for themselves or try new things or take chances. They'll just do what they're told, and they probably won't do it with much spirit.

At Semco, we have no set work hours, no assigned offices or desks, no dress codes. We have no employee manuals, no human resource rules and regulations. We don't even have an HR department. People go to work when they want and go home when they want. They decide when to take holidays and how much vacation they need. They even choose how they'll be compensated . . . . In other words, we treat our employees like adults. And we expect them to behave like adults. If they screw up, they take the blame. And since they have to be rehired every six months, they know their jobs are always at risk. Ultimately, all we care about is performance. An employee who spends two days a week at the beach but still produces real value for customers and coworkers is a better employee than one who works ten-hour days but creates little value.

LET TALENT FIND ITS PLACE

Companies tend to hire people for specific jobs and then keep them stuck in one career track. They also tend to choose which businesses people work in. The most talented people, for instance, may be assigned automatically to the business unit with the biggest growth prospects. The companies don't take into account what the individual really wants. The resulting disconnect between corporate needs and individual desires shows up in the high rates of talent churn that afflict most companies today.

We take a very different approach. We let people choose where they'll work and what they'll do (and even decide, as a team, who their leaders will be). All entry-level new hires participate in a program called Lost in Space. They spend six months to a year floating around the company, checking out businesses, meeting people, and trying out jobs. When a new hire finds a place that fits with his personality and goals, he stays there. Since our turnover rate in the last six years has been less than 1%—even though we've been targeted heavily by headhunters—we must be doing something right.

MAKE DECISIONS QUICKLY AND OPENLY

The best way for an organization to kill individual initiative is to force people to go through a complicated, bureaucratic review and approval process. We strive to make it as easy as possible for Semco employees to propose new business ideas, and we make sure they get fast and clear decisions. All proposals go through an executive board that includes representatives from our major business units. The board meetings are completely open. All employees are welcome to attend—in fact, we always reserve two seats on the board for the first two employees who arrive at a meeting. Proposals have to meet two simple criteria that govern all the businesses we launch. First, the business has to be a premium provider of its product or service. Second, the product or service has to be complex, requiring engineering skills and presenting high entry barriers. Well-considered proposals that meet those standards get launched within Semco. Even if a proposed business fails to meet both criteria, we'll often back it as a minority investor if its prospects look good.

PARTNER PROMISCUOUSLY

To explore and launch new businesses quickly and efficiently, you need help; it's pure arrogance to assume you can do everything on your own. I'm proud to say that we partner promiscuously at Semco. Indeed, I can't think of a single new business we've started without entering into some kind of alliance, whether to gain access to software, draw on a depth of experience, bring in new capabilities, or just share risk. Partnerships have provided the foundation for our experiments and our expansion over the years. Our partners are as much a part of our company as our employees.

STAYING FREE

I travel a lot in my job, and recently I've been spending time in Silicon Valley. I've been visiting Internet companies, talking with technology visionaries, and participating in panel discussions on the future of business. The new companies and their founders excite me. I see in them the same spirit we've nurtured at Semco—a respect for individuals and their ideas, a distrust of bureaucracy and hierarchy, a love for openness and experimentation.

But I'm beginning to see troubling signs that the traditional ways of doing business are reasserting their hegemony. Investors, I fear, are starting to force young start-ups into the molds of the past—molds that some thought had been broken forever. CEOs from old-line companies are being brought in to establish "discipline" and "focus." Entrepreneurs are settling into corner offices with secretaries and receptionists. HR departments are being formed to issue policies and to plot careers. Strategies are being written. The truly creative types are being caged up in service units and kept further and further from the decision makers.

It's sad and, I suppose, predictable. But it isn't necessary. If my 20 years at Semco have taught me anything, it's that successful businesses do not have to fit into one tight little mold. You can build a great company without fixed plans. You can have an efficient organization without rules and controls. You can be unbuttoned and creative without sacrificing profit. You can lead without wielding power. All it takes is faith in people.

READING 18.5

Managing Quietly* BY HENRY MINTZBERG

A prominent business magazine hires a journalist to write about the chief executive of a major corporation. The man has been at the helm for several years and is considered highly effective. The journalist submits an excellent piece, capturing the very spirit of the man's managerial style. The magazine rejects it—not exciting enough, no hype. Yet the company has just broken profit records for its industry.

Not far away, another major corporation is undergoing dramatic transformation. Change is everywhere, the place is teeming with consultants, people are being released in huge numbers.

---

*Reprinted with deletions from "Managing Quietly," H. Mintzberg, *Leader to Leader*, Spring 1999, 24–30.

The chief executive has been all over the business press. Suddenly he is fired: the board considers the turnaround a failure.

Go back five, ten, twenty or more years and read the business press—about John Scully at Apple, James Robinson at American Express, Robert McNamara at the Defense Department. Heroes of American management all . . . for a time. Then consider this proposition: maybe really good management is boring. Maybe the press is the problem, alongside the so-called gurus, since they are the ones who personalize success and deify the leaders (before they defile them). After all, corporations are large and complicated; it takes a lot of effort to find out what has really been going on. It is much easier to assume that the great one did it all. Makes for better stories too.

If you want to test this proposition, try Switzerland. It is a well-run country. No turnarounds. Ask the next Swiss you meet the name of the head of state. Don't be surprised if he or she does not know: the seven people who run the country sit around a table, rotating that position on an annual basis.

MANAGEMENT BY BARKING AROUND

"Forget what you know about how business should work—most of it is wrong!" screams the cover of that book called *Reengineering the Corporation*. Just like that. "Business reengineering means putting aside much of the received wisdom of two hundred years of industrial management," say the authors. Never mind that Henry Ford and Frederick Taylor, to name just two, "reengineered" businesses nearly a century ago. The new brand of reengineering "is to the next revolution of business what the specialization of labor was to the last" (meaning the Industrial Revolution). Are we so numbed by the hype of management that we accept such overstatement as normal?

There is no shortage of noisy words in the field of management. A few favored standbys merit special comment.

- *Globalization:* The Red Cross Federation headquarters in Geneva, Switzerland, has managers from over fifty countries. The Secretary General is Canadian, the three Under Secretary Generals are British, Swedish, and Sudanese. (There used to be a Swiss manager, but he retired recently.) The closest I know to a global company is perhaps Royal Dutch Shell, most of whose senior management comes from two countries—twice as many as almost any other company I can think of. But still a long way from the Red Cross Federation. Global coverage does not mean a global mindset.

  And is "globalization" new? Certainly the word is. They used to call it other things. At the turn of the century, the Singer Sewing Machine Company covered the globe (and that included some of the remotest parts of Africa) as few so-called global companies do today.
- *Shareholder value:* Is "shareholder value" new as well, or just another old way to sell the future cheap? Is this just an easy way for chief executives without ideas to squeeze money out of rich corporations? This mercenary model of management (greed is good, only numbers count, people are human "resources" who must be paid less so that executives can be paid more, and so on and on) is so antisocial that it will doom us if we don't doom it first.
- *Empowerment:* Organizations that have real empowerment don't talk about it. Those that make a lot of noise about it generally lack it: they have been spending too much of their past disempowering everybody. Then, suddenly, empowerment appears as a gift from the gods.

  In actual fact, real empowerment is a most natural state of affairs: people know what they have to do and simply get on with it, like the worker bees in a beehive. Maybe the really healthy organizations empower their leaders, who in turn listen to what is going on and so look good.
- *Change management:* This is the ultimate in managerial noise. Companies are being turned around left and right—all part of today's *managerial correctness*, which, in its mindlessness, puts political correctness to shame.

On March 2, 1998, *Fortune* put on display "America's Most Admired Corporations." But the accompanying article said hardly anything about these corporations. It was all about their leaders. After all, if the corporations succeeded, it must have been the bosses.

Lest that not have been enough, another article touted America's most admired CEOs. One was Merck's Raymond Gilmartin: "When Merck's directors tapped Gilmartin, 56, as CEO four years ago, they gave him a crucial mission: Create a new generation of blockbuster drugs to replace important products whose patents were soon to expire. Gilmartin has delivered."

You would think he had his hands full managing the company. Yet there he apparently was, in the labs, developing those drugs. And in just four years at that. From scratch.

"There is, believe it or not, some academic literature that suggests that leadership doesn't matter," we are told by the astonished *Fortune* writer. Well, this academic is no less astonished: there are, believe it or not, some business magazines so mesmerized with leadership that nothing else matters. "In four years Gerstner has added more than $40 billion to IBM's share value," this magazine proclaimed on April 14, 1997. Every penny of it! Nothing from the hundreds of thousands of other IBM employees. No role for the complex web of skills and relationships these people form. No contribution from luck. No help from a growing economy. Just Gerstner.

Years ago, Peter Drucker wrote that the administrator works within the constraints; the manager removes the constraints. Later, Abraham Zaleznik claimed that managers merely manage; real leaders lead. Now we seem to be moving beyond leaders who merely lead; today heroes save. Soon heroes will only save; then gods will redeem. We keep upping the ante as we drop ever deeper into the morass of our own parochialism.

THE PROBLEM IS THE PRESENT

Let's go back to that book on reengineering, the same page quoted earlier: "What matters in reengineering is how we want to organize work *today*, given the demands of *today's* market and the power of *today's* technologies. How people and companies did things yesterday doesn't matter to the business reengineer" (italics added).

Today, *today*, always *today*. This is the voice of the obsessively analytic mind, shouting into today's wind.

But if you want the imagination to see the future, then you'd better have the wisdom to appreciate the past. An obsession with the present—with what's "hot" and what's "in"— may be dazzling, but all that does is blind everyone to the reality. Show me a chief executive who ignores yesterday, who favors the new outsider over the experienced insider, the quick fix over steady progress, and I'll show you a chief executive who is destroying an organization.

To "turn around" is to end up facing the same way. Maybe that is the problem: all this turning around. Might not the white knight of management be the black hole of organizations? What good is the great leader if everything collapses when he or she leaves? Perhaps good companies don't need to be turned around at all because they are not constantly being thrust into crises by leaders who have to make their marks today. Maybe these companies are simply managed quietly.

MANAGING QUIETLY

What has been the greatest advance ever in health care? Not the dramatic discoveries of penicillin or insulin, it has been argued, but simply cleaning up the water supply. Perhaps, then, it is time to clean up our organizations, as well as our thinking. In this spirit I offer a few thoughts about some of the quiet words of managing.

- *Inspiring:* Quiet managers don't empower their people— "empowerment" is taken for granted. They *inspire* them. They create the conditions that foster openness and release energy. The queen bee, for example, does not make decisions; she just emits a chemical substance that holds the whole social system together. In human hives, that is called *culture*.

  Quiet managers strengthen the cultural bonds between people, not by treating them as detachable "human resources" (probably the most offensive term ever coined in management, at least until "human capital" came along), but as respected members of a cohesive social system. When people are trusted, they do not have to be empowered.

  The queen bee does not take credit for the worker bees' doing their jobs effectively. She just does her job effectively, so that they can do theirs. There are no bonuses for the queen bee beyond what she needs.

Next time you hear a chief executive go on about teamwork, about how "we" did it by all pulling together, ask who among the "we" is getting what kind of bonus. When you hear that chief boasting about taking the long view, ask how those bonuses are calculated. If cooperation and foresight are so important, why have these few been cashing in on generous stock options? Do we take the money back when the price plummets? Isn't it time to recognize this kind of executive compensation for what it is: a form of corruption, not only of our institutions, but of our societies as democratic systems?

- *Caring:* Quiet managers care for their organizations; they do not try to slice away problems as surgeons do. They spend more time preventing problems than fixing them, because they know enough to know when and how to intervene. In a sense, this is more like homeopathic medicine: the prescription of small doses to stimulate the system to fix itself. Better still, it is like the best of nursing: gentle care that, in itself, becomes cure.
- *Infusing:* "If you want to know what problems we have encountered over the years," someone from a major airline once told me, "just look at our headquarters units. Every time we have a problem, we create a new unit to deal with it." That is management by intrusion. Stick in someone or something to fix it. Ignore everyone and everything else: that is the past. What can the newly arrived chief know about the past, anyway? Besides, the stock analysts and magazine reporters don't have the time to allow the new chief to find out.

  Quiet managing is about *infusion*, change that seeps in slowly, steadily, profoundly. Rather than having change thrust upon them in dramatic, superficial episodes, everyone takes responsibility for making sure that serious changes take hold.

  This does not mean changing everything all the time—which is just another way of saying anarchy. It means always changing some things while holding most others steady. Call this *natural* continuous improvement, if you like. The trick, of course, is to know what to change when. And to achieve that there is no substitute for a leadership with an intimate understanding of the organization working with a workforce that is respected and trusted. That way, when people leave, including the leaders, progress continues.
- *Initiating:* Moses supplies our image of the strategy process: walking down the mountain carrying the word from on high to the waiting faithful. Redemption from the heavens. Of course, there are too many people to read the tablets, so the leaders have to shout these "formulations" to all these "implementors." All so very neat.

  Except that life in the valleys below is rich and complicated. And that is what strategy has to be about—not the neat abstractions of the executive suite, but the messy patterns of daily life. So long as loud management stays up there disconnected, it can shout down all the strategies it likes: they will never work.

  Quiet management is . . . about rolling up sleeves and finding out what is going on. And it is not parachuted down on the organization; it rises up from the base. But it never leaves that base. It functions "on the floor," where the knowledge for strategy making lies. Such management blends into the daily life of the corporation, so that all sorts of people with their feet planted firmly on the ground can pursue exciting initiatives. Then managers who are in touch with them can champion these initiatives and so stimulate the process by which strategies evolve.

  Put differently, the manager is not the organization any more than [a painting of a pipe is a pipe] . . . .A healthy organization does not have to leap from one hero to another; it is a collective social system that naturally survives changes in leadership. If you want to judge the leader, look at the organization ten years later.

BEYOND QUIET

Quiet management is about thoughtfulness rooted in experience. Words like wisdom, trust, dedication, and judgment apply. Leadership works because it is legitimate, meaning that it is an integral part of the organization and so has the respect of everyone there. Tomorrow is appreciated because yesterday is honored. That makes today a pleasure.

Indeed, the best managing of all may well be silent. That way people can say, "We did it ourselves." Because we did.

READING 18.6

Managing Effectively BY HENRY MINTZBERG

Now this is not the end.
It is not even the beginning of the end.
But it is, perhaps, the end of the beginning.

Winston Churchill

Welcome to the end of the beginning. This chapter considers the tricky subject of managerial effectiveness. Trying to figure out what makes a manager effective, even just trying to assess whether a manager has been effective, is difficult enough. Believing that the answers are easy only makes the questions that much more difficult. Managers, and those who work with them, in selection, assessment, and development, have to face the complexities. Helping to do so is the purpose of this chapter.

Before I scare you away, let me add that I had a good time writing this chapter. Perhaps the complexity led me into a kind of playfulness— about the inevitably flawed manager, the perils of excellence, what we can learn from happily managed families, and more. So I suspect, or at least hope, that you will have a good time reading this chapter.

THE MANY QUALITIES OF THE SUPPOSEDLY EFFECTIVE MANAGER

Lists of the qualities of effective managers abound. These are usually short—who would take dozens of items seriously? For example, in a brochure to promote its EMBA program entitled "What Makes a Leader?" the University of Toronto business school answers: "The courage to challenge the status quo. To flourish in a demanding environment. To collaborate for the greater good. To set clear direction in a rapidly changing world. To be fearlessly decisive" (Rotman School, n.d., circa 2005).

But this list is clearly incomplete. Where is native intelligence, or being a good listener, or just plain having energy? Surely these are important for managers, too. But fear not—they appear on other lists. So if we are to trust any of these lists, we shall have to combine all of them.

This, for the sake of a better world, I have done in Table 1. It lists the qualities from various lists that I have found, plus a few missing favorites of my own. This composite list contains fifty-two items. Be all fifty-two and you are bound to be an effective manager, if not a human one.

THE INEVITABLY FLAWED MANAGER

All of this is part of our "romance of leadership", that on the one hand puts ordinary mortals on managerial pedestals ("Rudolph is the perfect person for the job—he will save us!"), and on the other hand allows us to vilify them as they come crashing down ("How could Rudolph have failed us so?"). Yet some managers do stay up, if not on that silly pedestal. How so?

The answer is simple: successful managers are flawed—we are all flawed—but their particular flaws are not fatal, at least under the circumstances. (Superman was flawed, too—remember Kryptonite?). Peter Drucker commented at a conference that "the task of leadership is to create an alignment of strengths, so as to make people's weaknesses irrelevant." He might have added "including the leader's own."

If you want to uncover someone's flaws, marry them or else work for them. Their flaws will quickly become apparent. So will something else (at least if you are a mature human being who has made a reasonably good choice): that you can usually live with these flaws. Managers and marriages do succeed. The world, as a consequence, continues to unfold in its inimitably imperfect way.

Fatally flawed are those superman lists of managerial qualities, because they are utopian. Much of the time they are also wrong. For example, managers should be decisive—who can argue with that? For starters, anyone who followed the machinations of George W. Bush, who learned the importance of being decisive by reading case studies in a Harvard classroom. The University of Toronto list calls this quality "fearlessly decisive." Going into Iraq, President Bush certainly was that. As for some of the other items on that list, this president's arch enemy in Afghanistan certainly "had the courage to challenge the status quo," while Ingvar Kamprad, who

TABLE 1 COMPOSITE LIST OF BASIC QUALITIES FOR ASSURED MANAGERIAL SUCCESS

courageous *committed* curious confident *candid*	charismatic passionate *inspiring* visionary
reflective *insightful* open-minded/tolerant (of people, ambiguities, and ideas) innovative communicative (including being a good listener) connected/informed perceptive	energetic/enthusiastic upbeat /optimistic ambitious tenacious/ persistent /zealous
thoughtful/intelligent /*wise* analytic/objective pragmatic decisive (action-oriented) proactive	collaborative/participative/cooperative *engaging* supportive/sympathetic/empathetic stable dependable fair accountable ethical /honest consistent flexible balanced integrative Tall

(*Source:* Compiled from various sources; my own favorites in italics)

built IKEA into one of the most successful retail chains ever, reportedly took fifteen years to "set clear direction in a rapidly changing world." (Actually, he succeeded because the furniture world was not rapidly changing; he changed it.)

So perhaps we need to proceed differently.

SELECTING, ASSESSING, AND DEVELOPING EFFECTIVE MANAGERS

Managers as well as the people who work with them are generally concerned about how to select managers who will be effective, how to access whether they are actually being effective, and how they can be developed for greater effectiveness. The findings of this book are used to consider each of these in turn.

SELECTING EFFECTIVE MANAGERS

This subject has received considerable attention, which does not need to be repeated here. I would just like to add a few thoughts of my own.

Choosing the Devil You Know The perfect manager has yet to be born.

If everyone's flaws come out sooner or later, then sooner is better. So managers should be selected for their flaws as much as for their qualities. The inclination has instead been to focus on people's qualities, sometimes a single one that blinds us to everything else. "Sally's a great networker" or "Joe's a visionary," especially if the failed predecessor was a lousy networker or devoid of strategic vision. No one should ever be selected for a managerial job without making every reasonable and ethical effort to identify his or her flaws—the devil in the candidate.

There is, by the way, one fatal flaw that is wholly common today, yet rather easy to ferret out. Any candidate for a chief executive position who insists on compensation far in excess of others in the company, and, worse, who insists on special protection in the event of failure or firing, should be rejected out of hand. After all, hasn't this candidate already pronounced on how important it will be to "build the team," treat "people as the company's greatest asset," take "the long view"? Imagine how instituting this would change the corporate landscape.

And then these flaws should be carefully judged against the managerial job and situation in question, to avoid surprises, especially from flaws that might later prove fatal. Since flaws are that in context only, performance in a previous managerial job may give no indication of a looming problem in the next one. Of course, figuring this out may be no easy matter: people's qualities are often misjudged, as are the criteria needed for success in a particular job. But there is a surprisingly simple yet rarely used way to mitigate this.

Voice to the Managed Managing happens on the inside, within the unit (through the roles of controlling, leading, doing, and communicating), and on the outside, beyond the unit (through the roles of linking, dealing, and communicating). Yet it is usually people outside the unit who control the selection of its manager, whether that be the board in the choice of chief executive or senior managers in the case of junior ones. What sense does this make, especially when it is so much easier to impress outsiders, who have not had to live with the candidates on a daily basis? Charm may be one criterion for selection, but hardly the main one. As a consequence, too many organizations these days end up with managers who "kiss up and kick down"— overconfident, smooth-talking individuals who have never exhibited the most basic form of leadership.

If one simple prescription could improve the effectiveness of managing monumentally, it is giving voice in the selection processes to those people who know the candidates best—namely, the ones who have been managed by them. Some companies also have outside candidates interviewed by members of the unit, to get their sense of the fit. This could be especially pertinent in the selection of chief executives, where blind optimism seems to be so prevalent.

Can people be trusted to assess candidates for the position of their own manager? There is no doubt about the possibility of bias. But is that worse than trusting inadequately informed outsiders? I am not calling here for the election of managers, only for a balanced assessment by insiders and outsiders together. Indeed, this is common practice in hospitals, universities, and law offices.

There is one famous company, for decades the leader in its field, whose chief executive is elected by a closed vote of its senior managers. I have asked many groups of businesspeople, all of whom know this company, to guess which it is. Rarely does anyone get it. The answer is McKinsey & Company, whose executive director is elected to a three year term by a vote of the senior partners. This seems to have worked well for McKinsey. Has any McKinsey consultant ever proposed it to a client?

Considering an Outside Insider There seems to be some tendency of late, at least for senior positions, to favor outsiders: the new broom that can sweep clean. Unfortunately, the sweeping may be done by the devil the selection committee does not know, while the sweeper may not know enough to distinguish the real dirt. So the danger arises, especially in this age of heroic leadership, that the new broom will sweep out the heart and soul of the enterprise. Perhaps we need a little more attention in selection processes to the devils we do know, because they know the dirt.

In fact, selection committees can get the fresh look of an outsider, unbeholden to the powers within, as well as the knowledge of an insider, by choosing both: someone who quit in disgust—an outside insider. Such a person knows the situation, voted with his or her feet against it, and so may be ideal to drive a turnaround: a new broom that knows the old dirt. Moreover, there will be insiders who can assess this person's qualities and flaws. Steve Jobs of Apple comes to mind here: he didn't quit in disgust—he was fired from the company he built. But he was able to come back and turn it around.

To return to a point near the introduction to this chapter, we make a great fuss about leadership these days. But all too often we attribute leadership qualities to people we hardly know. Consider "young leaders"— to my mind an oxymoron. How can anyone be so designated before he or she has been tested in the crucible of experience? Who can know what flaws lurk below the surface? Indeed, this very designation can encourage hubris and thereby spoil what might have become real leadership. To repeat, leadership is a sacred trust earned from the respect of those people on the receiving end of it.

ASSESSING MANAGERIAL EFFECTIVENESS

You are a manager; you want to know how you are doing. Other people around you are even more intent on finding out how you are doing. There are lots of easy ways to assess this. Beware of all of them. The effectiveness of a manager can only be judged in context. This proposition sounds easy enough, until you take it apart, which I shall do in eight subpropositions.

For starters, (1) managers are not effective; matches are effective. There is no such thing as a good husband or a good wife, only a good couple. And so it is with managers and their units.

There may be people who fail in all managerial jobs, but there are none who can succeed in all of them. That is because a flaw that can be tolerable in one situation—indeed, be a positive quality—can prove fatal in another. It all depends on the match between the person and the context, at the time, for a time, so long as it lasts. The effective manager is the one, not with the good style, but with the necessary style. Thus, (2) there are no effective managers in general, which also means (3) there is no such thing as a professional manager—someone who can manage anything.

Of course, managers and their units succeed and fail together. So (4) to assess managerial effectiveness, you also have to assess the effectiveness of the unit. The purpose of the manager is to ensure that the unit serves its basic purpose. As Andy Grove of Intel put it: "A manager's output = the output of his organization + the output of neighboring organizations under his influence" (1983: 40).

This is a necessary condition for assessing managerial effectiveness, but it is not a sufficient one. (5) A manager can be considered effective only to the extent that he or she has helped to make the unit more effective. Some units function well despite their managers, and others would function a lot worse if not for their managers. Beware of assuming that the manager is responsible for whatever succeeds or fails in the unit. History matters; culture matters; markets matter; weather matters. As for the manager, it is personal impact that matters, not unit or organizational performance per se.

This means that many of the numerical measures of performance (growth in sales, reductions in cost, etc.) tell us nothing directly about the manager's effectiveness. How many managers have succeeded simply by maneuvering themselves into favorable jobs, making sure they did not mess up, and then taking credit for the success?

Even if a manager can be shown to have influenced the unit for better or for worse, (6) managerial effectiveness is always relative, not only to the situation inherited, but also in comparison with other possible people in that job. What if someone turned down for the job would have done a lot better, perhaps because it was an easy job to do? Of course you can drive yourself crazy asking such questions. Who would ever know? But if you want to assess managerial effectiveness—truly do so—then you can't avoid this proposition any more than the others.

To further complete matters, (7) managerial effectiveness also has to be assessed for broader impact, beyond the unit and even the organization. What about the manager who makes the unit more effective at the expense of the broader organization? For example, the sales department sold great quantities of product, but manufacturing couldn't keep up, and so the company went into turmoil. But can you blame the sales manager? After all, he or she was only doing the job. Isn't general management responsible for these broader perspectives?

Viewed conventionally—which means bureaucratically—the answer is yes. In bureaucracies, all responsibilities are neatly apportioned. In the real world of managing, the partial answer is no. Organizations are flawed too; unexpected problems can arise anywhere and often have to be addressed wherever that is. No responsible manager can afford to put on blinders, doing the assigned job without looking left or right . . . A healthy organization is not a collection of detached human resources who simply look after their own turf; it is a community of responsible human beings who care about the entire system and its long-term survival (Watson 1994: 38).

But we cannot stop here. How about what is right for the organization being wrong for the world around it? Albert Speer was a brilliant manager, hugely effective in organizing armament production in Nazi Germany (Singer and Wooton, 1976). After the war, the Allied forces put him in jail anyway. Speer might have been a lot more effective for the world, maybe also for the German people, had he been a lot less effective in organizing his unit—or, better still, if he had chosen to manage something else.

We make a great fuss about holding managers responsible and accountable, but do not give nearly enough attention to asking, responsible for what, accountable to whom? Imploring managers to be "socially responsible" is fine so long as we take it beyond the easy rhetoric into the difficult conflicts that such behavior has to address.

Some economists have an easy reply to this. Let each business look after its own business, and leave the social issues to government (Friedman, 1962). This is a neat distinction that keeps economic theory clean; unfortunately, it has made a mess of society. Is there an economist prepared to argue that social decisions have no economic consequences? Not likely: everything costs something. Well, then, can any economist argue that there are economic decisions that have no social consequences? And what happens when managers ignore them, beyond remaining within the limits of the law?

Put together all these propositions, and you have to ask, How can anyone who needs to assess a manager possibly cope with all this? The answer here, too, is simple, in principle: use judgment. (8) Managerial effectiveness has to be judged and not just measured.

We can certainly get measures of effectiveness for some of these things, notably aspects of unit performance, at least in the short term. But how are we to measure the rest, and, in particular, where is the composite measure that answers the magic question?

If you think that eight propositions to assess managerial effectiveness is a little excessive, not to mention academically detached, then think about the excessiveness and detachedness of the executive bonuses that ignored most of them. They relied on the simplest of measures, such as increases in the stock price in the relative short run. Executive impact has to be assessed in the long run, and we don't know how to measure performance in the long run, at least as attributable to specific managers. So executive bonuses should be eliminated.

Period.

DEVELOPING MANAGERS EFFECTIVELY

So how should managers be developed? In 1996, we set out to rethink the world of management education and development, and as a consequence change how management is practiced—toward what is described in "Managing." We began in our own place, with "management" education in the business school. Some of us at McGill University in Montreal had serious reservations about MBA programs.

The conventional MBA is just that: it is about business administration.

It does a fine job of teaching the business functions, but little to enhance the practice of managing. Indeed, by giving the impression that the students have learned management and are prepared for leadership, it encourages hubris. Moreover, it relies on learning from other people's experience, whether more directly in the discussion of cases, or less directly in the presentation of theory—the distillation of experience through research.

We teamed up with the colleagues from around the world* to create the International Master's in Practicing Management (www.impm.org).

This set the groundwork for a series of initiatives that followed. Four are discussed briefly in the accompanying box, after laying out the premises that lie behind them. All of this can be thought of as natural development.

1. Managers, let alone leaders, cannot be created in a classroom. If management is a practice, then it cannot be taught as a science or a profession. In fact, it cannot be taught at all. MBA and other programs that claim to do so too often promote hubris instead, with destructive consequences. Some of the best managers/leaders have never spent a day in such a classroom, while no shortage of the worst sat there obediently for two years.**

---

*At Lancaster University in England, Insead in France, the Indian Institute of Management at Bangalore, and a group of colleagues in Japan.

**See *Managers Not MBAs* (Mintzberg, 2004: 1–194). Pages 114–119 report a study done by Joseph Lampel and me. We took a list of Harvard Business School superstars published in a book by a long-term insider in 1990, and tracked for over a decade the performance of the nineteen corporate chief executives on that list, many of them quite famous. Ten were outright failures (the company went bankrupt, the CEO was fired, a major merger backfired, etc.); another four had questionable records at best. Just five of the nineteen seemed to do fine.

2. Managing is learned on the job, enhanced by a variety of experiences and challenges. No one gets to practice surgery or accounting without prior training in a classroom. In management, it has to be the opposite. As we have seen, the job is too nuanced, too intricate, too dynamic to be learned prior to practice. So the logical starting point is to ensure that managers get the best experience possible. As Hill (2003: 228) has pointed out, the first managerial assignment can be key, because that is when managers "are perhaps most open to experiences and learning the basics" (Hill, p. 288). Beyond that, the learning can be enhanced by a variety of challenging assignments supported by mentors and peers (Hill, p. 227).
3. Development programs come in to help managers make meaning of their experience, by reflecting on it personally and with their colleagues. The classroom is a wonderful place to enhance the comprehensions and competencies of people who are already practicing management, especially when it draws on their own natural experience.

   It has been said of bacon and eggs that while the chicken is involved, the pig is committed. Management development has to be about commitment: to the job, the people, and the purpose, to be sure, but also to the organization, and beyond that, in a responsible way, to related communities in society.

   As noted earlier, management development is about getting the meaning of experience, and that means busy managers have to slow down, step back, and reflect thoughtfully on their own experience. Accordingly, development should take place as managers go back and forth between the activities of their work and the reflections of a quieter place. This can be away at a formal program, or just getting away at work itself (e.g., an uninterrupted lunchtime). Either way, we have found that the key to this is small groups of managers sitting together at round tables and sharing experiences.
4. Intrinsic to this development should be the carrying of the learning back to the workplace, for impact on the organization. A major problem with management development is that it usually happens in isolation. The manager is developed, perhaps even changed, only to return to an unchanged workplace. Management development should also be about organization development: teams of managers should be expected to drive change in their organization.
5. All of this needs to be organized according to the nature of managing itself—for example, in terms of the managerial mindsets. Most management education and much management development is organized around the business functions. This is fine for learning about business, but marketing + finance + accounting, etc., does not equal management. Moreover, a focus on the business functions amounts to a focus on analysis. This is certainly an important mindset for managers, but only as one among others. Being the easiest one to teach should not make it the main one to learn. We have more than enough calculating managers already. We need ones who can deal with the calculated chaos of managing—its art and craft—which highlights the importance of reflection, worldliness, collaboration, and action.

To repeat, management is not going to be taught to anyone—not by any professor, not by any expert in development, not by any formal coach or even by a manager's own manager. Managers have to learn primarily through their own efforts. We have seen how this can be facilitated in a classroom, but we have also learned how much more powerful this can be when it happens spontaneously at work, as managers reflect on their experience, learn from each other, and together drive improvements in their organizations and societies. The message of our own experience is that nothing is quite so powerful, or so natural, as engaged managers who are committed to developing themselves, their institutions, and their communities.

MANAGING, NATURALLY

If management development can become more natural, then surely there is hope for management itself.

WHICH SPECIES IS OUT OF CONTROL?

As human beings, we presumably began in caves or the like, from which bands of us—communities, if you like—went out to hunt and gather, or else to fight those who were hunting and gathering in our place. We were probably organized much like geese are organized today: the strongest member took the lead and then ceded it as another became stronger. This did not mean that leadership, charisma, empowerment, management, and all the rest did not exist, only that they blended into social processes in a natural way. Luckily for them they lacked the benefit of thousands of books glorifying all this, and so they just got on with it.

Over the years, we became increasingly organized, and perhaps increasingly perverse as well. First, I suppose, came group leaders, who fought the enemies best, some of these leaders eventually turning around to intimidate their followers. Over the millennia, this evolved into chiefs, lords, priests, pharaohs, caesars, emperors, kings, queens, shoguns, czars, maharajahs, sheiks, sultans, viceroys, dictators, führers, prime ministers, and presidents, not to mention managers, directors, executives, bosses, oligarchs, CEOs, COOs, CFOs, and CLOs.

Shouldn't all these labels be telling us something—namely, that we are the species out of control? . . . We have taken something straightforward and made it convoluted, by putting "leaders" on pedestals, in the process undermining plain old management: by turning human beings into human resources; by fooling ourselves into believing that management is a profession and so pretending that we can create managers in a classroom. . . . .

If you really want to understand management, then you would do well to get down on the ground . . . Then maybe you can work "up" from there, to the abstractions of management that so mesmerize us—where people earn larger incomes ostensibly because their work is more important but perhaps really because they have to cope with that much more nonsense, no small measure of it imposed by their own formalized systems.

MANAGING NATURALLY

Isn't it time to wake up to our humanity and get past our childish obsession with leadership? Can't we just be as sensible as bees in a hive? What could be more natural than to see our organizations not as mystical hierarchies of authority so much as communities of engagement, where every member is respected and so returns that respect? (See "Rebuilding Companies as Communities," Mintzberg, 2009). Sure, we need people to coordinate some of our efforts, provide some sense of direction in complex social systems, and support those who just want to get useful work done. But these are managers who work with us, not rule us.

> Management is a very practical, down-to-earth activity. There are no profound truths about it to be discovered and there are no hidden secrets to be uncovered about how to do it. Management is a very simple activity which involves bringing together people and resources to produce goods or services. . . . The message is to lighten up a bit—be playful, agile and alert. (Watson 1994: 215 –216)

Richard Boyatzis of Case Western Reserve University has written, "There appears to be no images, metaphors, or models for management from natural life," and so "management is an unnatural act, or at least there is no guidance for being a manager" (1995: 50). I have agreed from the outset that there is no guidance for being a manager, and certainly managing is an awful lot more complicated—intellectually and socially if not physically—than leading a pack of geese or emitting a chemical substance to hold together a beehive.

But I believe that managing is a perfectly natural act that we make unnatural by disconnecting it from its natural context, and then not seeing it for what it is.

If management and leadership are natural acts, then are we wasting our time trying to find, let alone create, great managers and leaders? Perhaps we should instead be appreciating that reasonably normal people, flawed but not fatally so in their positions, can simply get on with their managing and leading, and so be rather successful. To express this more forcefully, to be a successful manager, let alone—dare I say—a great leader, maybe you don't have to be wonderful so much as more or less emotionally healthy and clearheaded.

Sure, there are some rather different kinds of people—narcissists, for example—who succeed for a time, particularly under difficult circumstances.

But show me one of these and I'll show you many others who failed miserably, while creating those difficult circumstances in the first place.

Imagine if we simply recognized good managers to be ordinary, natural leaders, in the right place, uncontaminated by MBA training and all that "leadership" hype. The man who put management on the map said simply, "No institution can possibly survive if it needs geniuses or supermen to manage it. It must be organized in such a way as to be able to get along under a leadership composed of average human beings" (Drucker 1946: 26).

Consider that little boy in the Hans Christian Andersen story who announced that the emperor wore no clothes. He could have been proclaimed a great leader. Was he? Was he even particularly insightful? Or especially courageous? Maybe he just did the most natural thing of all, unlike all those people around him (including the emperor).

How to get to such natural leadership? As Peter Drucker noted, we can start by stopping to build organizations that are dependent on heroic leadership. No wonder we can't get past them: when one hero fails, we search frantically for another. Meanwhile, the organization—school, hospital, government, business—flounders. By the excessive promotion of leadership, we demote everyone else. We create clusters of followers who have to be driven to perform, instead of leveraging the natural propensity of people to cooperate in communities.

In this light, effective managing can be seen as engaging and engaged, connecting and connected, supporting and supported.

We also make a great fuss about democracy in our societies, yet this also relies obsessively on leadership. In our organizations—where we spend so much of our time, with so much influence on the rest of our lives—we do not even have democracy, these days rarely even community. Mostly we have autocracy—and it is spilling into our governments, too.

So I like to believe that the subject of this book strikes at the heart of our lives today—our increasingly "organized" lives. We need to rethink management and organization, as well as leadership and communityship, by realizing how simple, natural, and healthy they all can be.

BIBLIOGRAPHY FOR READINGS

Abbeglen, J. C., & G. Stalk, Jr., *Kaisha, The Japanese Corporation*. New York: Basic Books, 1985.

Abernathy, W. J., & J. M. Utterback, "Patterns of Industrial Innovation," *Technology Review*, 1978: 40–47.

Abernathy, W. J., & K. Wayne, "Limits on the Learning Curve," *Harvard Business Review*, September–October 1974: 109–119.

Abrahamson, E., "Change without Pain," *Harvard Business Review*, July–August 2000, 78: 75–79.

Ackerman, R. W., *The Social Challenge to Business*. Cambridge, MA: Harvard University Press, 1975.

Aguilar, F. J., *Scanning the Business Environment*. New York: Macmillan, 1967.

Alinsky, S. D., *Rules for Radicals: A Practical Primer for Realistic Radicals*. New York: Vintage Books, 1989.

Allen, S. A., "Organizational Choices and General Management Influence Networks in Divisionalized Companies," *Academy of Management Journal*, 1978: 393–406.

Allende, I., *Eva Luna*. New York: Bantam Books, 1989.

Allison, G. T., *Essence of Decision: Explaining the Cuban Missile Crisis*. Boston, MA: Little Brown, 1971.

Ansberry, C., "Kodak, Sanofi Plan Alliance in Drug Sector," *Wall Street Journal*, January 9, 1991: A3.

Argryis, C., & D. A. Schon, *Organizational Learning: A Theory of Action Perspective*. Reading, MA: Addison-Wesley, 1978.

Ashby, W. R., *Design for a Brain*. New York: Wiley, 1954.

Astley, W. G., "Toward an Appreciation of Collective Strategy," *Academy of Management Review*, 1984, 9(3): 526–533.

Astley, W. G., & C. J. Fombrun, "Collective Strategy: Social Ecology of Organizational Environments," *Academy of Management Review*, 1983, 8(4): 576–587.

Bacon, J., *Corporate Directorship Practices: Membership and Committees of the Board*. Conference Board and American Society of Corporate Secretaries, Inc., 1973.

Baden-Fuller, C., & J. M. Stopford, *Rejuvenating the Mature Business: The Competitive Challenge*. Boston, MA: Harvard Business School Press, 1992.

Baden-Fuller, C., et al., "National or Global? The Study of Company Strategies and the European Market for Major Appliances," London Business School Center for Business Strategy, Working Paper Series No. 28 (June 1987).

Bahrami, H., "The Emerging Flexible Organization: Perspectives from Silicon Valley," *California Management Review*, Summer 1992, 34(4): 33–52.

Barnard, C. I., *The Functions of the Executive*. Cambridge, MA: Harvard University Press, 1938.

Barr, P. S., J. L. Stimpert, & A. S. Huff, "Cognitive Change, Strategic Action and Organizational Renewal," *Strategic Management Journal*, 1992: 15–36.

Barreyre, P-Y. "The Concept of "Impartition" Policy in High Speed Strategic Management", *Papier de recherché*, Grenoble: C.E.R.A.G, 84(7), 1984.

Bartlett, C. A., & S. Ghoshal, "Managing across Borders: New Strategic Requirements," *Sloan Management Review*, Summer 1987: 7–17.

Bartlett, C. A., & S. Ghoshal, "Matrix Management: Not a Structure, a Frame of Mind," *Harvard Business Review*, July/August 1990, 68(4): 138–146.

Beatty, R. W., & D. O. Ulrich, "Re-Energizing the Mature Organization," *Organisational Dynamics*, Summer 1991: 16–30.

Beckhard, R., *Organizational Development: Strategies and Models*. Reading, MA: Addison-Wesley, 1969.

Beer, M., R. A. Eisenstat, & B. Spector, "Why Change Programs Don't Produce Change," *Harvard Business Review*, 1990: 158–166.

Bettis, R. A., "Performances Differences in Related and Unrelated Diversified Firms," *Strategic Management Journal*, 1981: 379–394.

Bhide, A., "Hustle as Strategy," *Harvard Business Review*, September–October 1986.

Blau, P. M., & P. A. Schoenherr, *The Structure of Organizations*. New York: Basic Books, 1971.

Bleeke, J., & D. Ernst, "Is Your Strategic Alliance Really a Sale?" *Harvard Business Review*, 1995: 97–105.

Bolman, L. G., & T. Deal, *Reframing Organizations: Artistry, Choice, and Leadership*, 2nd ed. San Francisco: Jossey-Bass Publishers, 1997.

Boston Consulting Group, *Perspective on Experience*. Boston, 1972.

Boston Consulting Group, *Strategy Alternatives for the British Motorcycle Industry*. London: Her Majesty's Stationery Office, 1975.

Bower, J. L., "Planning within the Firm," *The American Economic Review*, 1970: 186–194.

Bowers, T., & M. Singer, "Who Will Capture Value in On-Line Financial Services," *The McKinsey Quarterly*, 1996: 78–83.

Bowman, E. H., "Epistemology, Corporate Strategy, and Academe," *Sloan Management Review*, Winter 1974, 15(2): 35–50.

Boyatzis, R. E., *The Competent Manager*. New York: Wiley, 1982.

Braybrook, D., & C. E. Lindblom, *A Strategy of Decision: Policy Evaluation as a Social Process*. New York: New York University Press, 1963.

Brook, P., *The Empty Space*. Harmondsworth, Middlesex: Penguin Books, 1968.

Brown, J. S., & P. Duguid, "Organizational Learning and Communities of Practice: Towards a Unified View of Working, Learning, and Organization," *Organization Science*, 1991: 40–57.

Brown, S. L., & K. M. Eisenhardt, *Competing on the Edge: Strategy as Structured Chaos*. Boston: Harvard Business School Press, 1998.

Brunsson, N., "The Irrationality of Action and the Action Rationality: Decision, Ideologies, and Organizational Actions," *Journal of Management Studies*, 1982, 1: 29–44.

Burns, T., "The Directions of Activity and Communication in a Departmental Executive Group," *Human Relations*, 1954: 73–97.

Burns, T., "Micropolitics: Mechanisms of Institutional Change," *Administrative Science Quarterly*, 1961: 257–281.

Burns, T., & G. M. Stalker, *The Management of Innovation*, 2nd ed. London: Tavistock, 1966.

Business Week, February 18, 1967.

Business Week, October 31, 1983.

Buzzell, R. D., B. T. Gale, & R. G. M. Sultan, "Market Share—A Key to Profitability," *Harvard Business Review*, January–February 1975: 97–106.

Campbell, A., & M. Goold, *Strategy and Style: The Role of the Centre in Managing Diversified Corporations*. Oxford: Basil Blackwell, 1987.

Chandler, A. D., *Strategy and Structure: Chapters in the History of the Industrial Enterprise*. Cambridge, MA: M.I.T. Press, 1962.

Chandy, R., & G. Tellis, in J. Useem, "Internet Defense Strategy: Cannibalize Yourself," *Fortune*, September 6, 1999: 121–134.

Channon, D. F., "The Strategy, Structure and Financial Performance of the Service Industries," Working Paper, Manchester Business School, 1975.

Christensen, C. M., & R. S. Rosenbloom, "Explaining the Attacker's Advantage: Technological Paradigms, Organizational Dynamics, and the Value Network," *Research Policy*, 1995: 233–257.

Christenson, C. R., K. R. Andrews, & J. L. Bower, *Business Policy: Text and Cases,* 4th ed. Homewood, IL: Richard D. Irwin, 1978.

Clausewitz, C. von., *On War.* Princeton, NJ: Princeton University Press, 1989.

Clemmer, J., *Pathways to Performance: A Guide to Transforming Yourself, Your Team, and Your Organization.* Toronto: Macmillan Canada, 1995.

Cohen, M. D., J. G. March, & J. P. Olsen, "A Garbage Can Model of Organizational Choice," *Administrative Science Quarterly,* March 1972, 17(1): 1–25.

Cole, A. H., *Business Enterprise in Its Social Setting.* Cambridge, MA: Harvard University Press, 1959.

Coleman, J. S., *The Foundations of Social Theory.* Cambridge, MA: Harvard University Press, 1990.

Copeman, G.H., *The Role of the Managing Director.* London: Business Publications, 1963.

Crozier, M., *The Bureaucratic Phenomenon.* Chicago: University of Chicago Press, 1964.

Cvar, M.R., "Case Studies in Global Competition: Patterns of Success and Failure," in M. E. Porter, ed., *Competition in Global Industries.* Boston, MA: Harvard Business School Press, 1986: 483–516.

Cyert, R. M., & J. G. March, *A Behavioral Theory of the Firm.* Englewood Cliffs, NJ: Prentice Hall, 1963.

Davis, S. M., *Future Perfect,* Reading, MA: Addison-Wesley Publishing Co., 1978.

Day, G. S., & P. Nedungadi, "Managerial Representations of Competitive Advantage," *Journal of Marketing,* 1994: 31–44.

de Gues, A. P., "Planning as Learning," *Harvard Business Review,* March–April 1988: 70–74.

De Pree, M., *Leadership is an Art.* New York: Dell Publishing, 1989.

Delbecq, A., & A. Filley, *Program and Project Management in a Matrix Organization: A Case Study.* Madison, WI: Graduate School of Business, University of Wisconsin, 1974.

Dickhout, R., M. Denham, & N. Blackwell, "Designing Change Programs That Won't Cost You Your Job," *The McKinsey Quarterly,* 1995: 101–116.

Doeringer, P. B., & M. J. Poire, *Internal Labor Markets and Manpower Analysis.* Lexington, MA: D. C. Heath, 1971.

Douglas, S. P., & Y. Wind, "The Myth of Globalization," *Columbia Journal of World Business,* Winter 1987: 19–29.

Doz, Y. L., & H. Thanheiser, "Embedding Transformational Capability," *ICEDR, October 1996 Forum Embedding Transformation Capabilities,* INSEAD, Fontainebleau, France, 1996.

Drucker, P. F., *Concept of the Corporation.* New York: Day, 1946.

Drucker, P., *Management: Tasks, Responsibilities, Practices.* New York: HarperCollins, 1974.

Drucker, P., "The Coming of the New Organization," *Harvard Business Review,* January–February 1988: 1–19.

Drucker, P., "The Network Society," *Wall Street Journal,* March 29, 1995: 12.

Essame, H. P., *A Study in Command.* New York: Charles Scribner's Sons, 1974.

Evered, R., "So What Is Strategy?" Working Paper, Naval Postgraduate School, Monterey, 1983.

Fahey, L., & R. M. Randall, *Learning from the Future: Competitive Foresight Scenarios.* New York: John Wiley & Sons, 1998.

Farago, L. P., *Patton: Ordeal and Triumph.* New York: I. Obolensky, 1964.

Ferguson, C., "Computers and the Coming of US Keiretsus," *Harvard Business Review,* July–August 1990.

Firsirotu, M. Y. S., "Strategic Turnaround as Cultural Revolution: The Case of Canadian National Express," Doctoral Dissertation, Faculty of Management, 1985.

Foch, F., *The Principles of War.* Translated by J. de Morinni. New York: AMS Press, 1970.

Fonfara, K., "Relationships in the Complex Construction Venture Market," *Advances in International Marketing,* 1989: 235–247.

Forrester, J. W., "A New Corporate Design," *Industrial Management Review,* 1965, 7(1): 5–17.

Forrester, J. W., "Counterintuitive Behavior of Social Systems," *Technology Review,* 1971, 73(3): 52–68.

Franklin, B., *Poor Richard's Almanac.* New York: Ballantine Books, 1977.

Friedman, M., *Capitalism and Freedom.* Chicago: University of Chicago Press, 1962.

Fritz, R., *Creating.* New York: Ballantine, 1990.

Fritz, R., *Path of Least Resistance,* Revised and expanded edition. New York: Fawcett, 1989.

Galbraith, J. K., *American Capitalism: The Concept of Countervailing Power.* Boston, MA: Houghton Mifflin, 1952.

Galbraith, J. K., *The New Industrial State.* Boston, MA: Houghton Mifflin, 1967.

Galbraith, J. R., *Designing Complex Organizations.* Reading, MA: Addison-Wesley Publishing Co., 1973.

Galbraith, J. R., *Organization Design.* Reading, MA: Addison-Wesley, 1977.

Galbraith, J. R., & D. Nathanson, *Strategy Implementation.* St. Paul, MN: West Publishing, 1978.

Gerth, H. H., & C. Wright Mills, eds., *From Max Webber: Essays in Sociology.* New York: Oxford University Press, 1958.

Ghemawat, P., *Commitment: The Dynamic of Strategy.* New York: Free Press, 1991.

Gilbert, X., & P. Strebel, "Strategies for Outpacing the Competition," *The Journal of Business Strategy,* June 1987: 28–36.

Glueck, W. F., *Business Policy and Strategic Management,* 3rd ed. New York: McGraw-Hill, 1980.

Goold, M., "Learning, Planning, and Strategy: Extra Time," *California Management Review,* 1996: 100–102.

Gosselin, R., "A Study of the Interdependence of Medical Specialists in Quebec Teaching Hospitals." Ph.D. thesis, McGill University, 1978.

Green, P., *Alexander the Great.* New York: Praeger Publishers, 1970.

Greenleaf, R. K., *Servant Leadership.* Mahwah, NJ: Paulist Press, 1977.

Grove, A., *Only the Paranoid Survive.* New York: Doubleday, 1996.

Grove, A. S., *High Output Management.* New York: Random House, 1983.

Guest, R. H., *Of Time and the Foreman. Personnel,* May 1956: 478.

Hamel, G., & C. K. Prahalad. *Competing for the Future.* Boston, MA: Harvard Business School Press, 1994.

Hannan, M. T., & J. Freeman, "The Population Ecology of Organizations," *American Journal of Sociology,* 1977, 82(5): 929–964.

Hariharan, S., & C. K. Prahalad, "Strategic Windows in the Structuring of Industries: Compatibility Standards and Industry Evolution," in H. Thomas, D. O'Neal, R. White, & D. Hurst, *Building the Strategically Responsive Organization.* New York: John Wiley & Sons, 1994: 289–308.

Harrigan, K., & W. Newman, "Bases of Interorganization Cooperation: Propensity, Power, Persistence," *Journal of Management Studies,* 1990: 417–434.

Haspeslagh, P., "Portfolio Planning: Uses and Limits," *Harvard Business Review,* 1982: 58–73.

Hayes, R. H., & W. J. Abernathy, "Managing Our Way to Economic Decline," *Harvard Business Review,* July–August 1980: 67–77.

Hayes, R. H., & D. A. Garvin, "Managing as If Tomorrow Mattered," *Harvard Business Review,* May–June 1982: 70–79.

Henderson, B., *Henderson on Corporate Strategy.* Cambridge, MA: Harvard University Press, 1980.

Hill, L. A., *Becoming a Manager: How New Managers Master the Challenges of Leadership,* 2nd, expanded edition. Boston: Harvard Business School Press, 2003.

Hofer, C. W., & D. Schendel, *Strategy Formulation: Analytical Concepts.* St. Paul, MN: West Publishing Co., 1978.

Hogarth, R., & H. Kunreuther, "Risk, Ambiguity and Insurance," *Journal of Risk and Uncertainty,* 1989: 5–35.

Hout, T. M., E. Porter, & E. Rudden, "How Global Companies Win Out," *Harvard Business Review,* September–October 1982: 98–108.

Hunt, R. G., "Technology and Organization," *Academy of Management Journal,* 1970: 235–252.

Huy, Q. N., "Time, Temporal Capability and Change," *Academy of Management Review,* October 2001, 26: 601–623.

Huy, Q. N., "Emotional Balancing of Organizational Continuity and Radical Change: The Contribution of Middle Managers," *Administrative Science Quarterly,* March 2002, 47: 31–69.

Iacocca, L., with W. Novack, *Iacocca: An Autobiography.* New York: Bantam Books, 1984.

Irving, D., *The Trail of the Fox.* New York: E.P. Dutton, 1977.

Itami, H., & T. W. Roehl, *Mobilizing Invisible Assets.* Cambridge, MA: Harvard University Press, 1987.

James, D. C., *The Years of MacArthur.* Boston, MA: Houghton Mifflin, 1970.

Jensen, M., "The Eclipse of the Public Corporation," *Harvard Business Review,* September–October 1989.

Johnson, S., & Jones, C., "How to Organize for New Products", *Harvard Business Review,* (May–June) 1957: 49–62.

Jomini, H., *The Art of War.* Translated from the French by G.H. Wendell and W.P. Craighill. The West Point Military Library. Westport, CT: Greenwood Press. 1971.

Kahneman, D., & A. Tversky, "Prospect Theory," *Econometrica,* 1979: 283–291.

Kahneman, D., & D. Lovallo, "Timid Choices and Bold Forecasts: A Cognitive Perspective on Risk Taking," *Management Science,* 1993: 17–31.

Kahneman, D., J. L. Knetsch, & R. Thaler, "Experimental Tests of the Endowment Effect and the Coase Theorem," *Journal of Political Economy,* 1990: 1325–1348.

Kanter, R. M., *The Change Masters.* New York: Simon & Schuster, 1983.

Kauffman, S., *At Home in the Universe.* New York: Oxford University Press, 1995.

Kotter, J. P., "Leading Change: Why Transformation Efforts Fail," *Harvard Business Review,* 1995: 59–67.

Land, E., "People Should Want More from Life . . . ," *Forbes,* June 1, 1975.

Langley, A., H. Mintzberg, P. Pitcher, E. Posada, & J. Saint-Macary, "Opening Up Decision Making: The View from the Black Stool," *Organization Science,* 1995.

Lapierre, R., "Le Changement Stratégique: Un Rêve en Quéte de Rêe." Ph.D. Management Policy course paper, McGill University, 1980.

Learned, E. P., D. N. Ulrich, & D. R. Booz, *Executive Action.* Boston, MA: Harvard Business School, 1951.

Lenin, V. I., *Imperialism. The State and Revolution.* New York: Vanguard Press, 1927.

Levitt, T., "The Globalization of Markets," *Harvard Business Review,* May–June 1983: 92–102.

Lewin, K., *Field Theory in Social Science.* New York: Harper & Row, 1951.

Liddell Hart, B. H., *Strategy, the Indirect Approach.* London: Faber and Faber, 1954.

Lindblom, C. E., *The Policy-Making Process.* Englewood Cliffs, NJ: Prentice Hall, 1968.

Lindblom, C. E., "The Science of 'Muddling Through.'" *Public Administration Review,* Spring 1959: 79–88.

Lodge, G. C., *The New American Ideology.* New York: Knopf, 1st edition 1975.

Machiavelli, M., *The Prince & The Discourses.* Translated by Luigi Ricci, Revised by E.R.P. Vincent, Introduction by Max Lerner. McGraw-Hill, 1950.

Mair, A., "The Honda Motor Company, 1967–1995: Globalization of an Innovative Mass Production Model," in M. Freyssenet, A. Mair, K. Shimizu, & G. Volpato, eds., *One Best Way? Trajectories and Industrial Models of the World's Automobile Producers, 1970–1995.* Oxford: Oxford University Press, 1998a.

Mair, A., "Reconciling Managerial Dichotomies at Honda Motors," in R. de Wit and R. Meyer, eds., *Strategy: Process, Content, Context,* 2nd edition. London: International Thomson Business Press, 1998b.

Majone, G., "The Uses of Policy Analysis," in *The Future and the Past: Essays on Programs,* Russell Sage Foundation Annual Report, 1976–1977: 201–220.

Makridakis, S., *Forecasting, Planning, and Strategy for the 21st Century.* New York: The Free Press, 1990.

Malone, M. S., *Intellectual Capital: Realizing Your Company's True Value by Finding its Hidden Brainpower.* New York: HarperBusiness, 1997.

Mao, Z., *Basic Tactics.* London: Pall Mall Press, 1967.

March, J. G., & H. A. Simon, *Organizations.* New York: John Wiley, 1958.

March, J. G., & J. P. Olsen, *Ambiguity and Choice in Organizations.* Bergen, Norway: Universitetsforlaget, 1976.

March, J. G., "Exploration and Exploitation in Organizational Learning," *Organization Science,* 1991, (2): 71–87.

March, J. G., *Three Lectures on Efficiency and Adaptiveness.* Helsinki: Swedish School of Economics and Business Administration, 1994.

Martin, L. C., "How Beatrice Foods Sneaked Up on $5 Billion," *Fortune,* April 1976: 119–129.

Mason, R., & I. Mitroff, *Challenging Strategic Planning Assumptions.* New York: John Wiley, 1981.

Mathews, J. A., "Holonic Organizational Architectures," *Human Systems Management,* 1996: 1–29.

Matloff, M., & E. M. Snell, *Strategic Planning for Coalition Warfare (1941–42).* Washington, DC: Office of the Chief of Military History, Department of the Army, 1953.

McDonald, J., *Strategy in Poker, Business & War.* New York: W.W. Norton, 1950.

Mezias, S. J., & M. A. Glynn, "The 3 Faces of Corporate Renewal: Institution, Revolution and Evolution," *Strategic Management Journal,* February 1993, 14: 77–101.

Miller, D., "Configurations of Strategy and Structure: Toward a Synthesis," *Strategic Management Journal,* 1986: 233–249.

Miller, D., & M. Kets De Vries, *The Neurotic Organization.* San Francisco: Jossey-Bass, 1984.

Miller, D., & P. H. Friesen, "Archetypes of Strategy Formulation," *Management Science,* May 1978: 921–933.

Miller, D., & P. H. Friesen, *Organizations: A Quantum View.* Englewood Cliffs, NJ: Prentice Hall, 1984.

Mintzberg, H., "Research on Strategy-making," *Proceedings of the 32nd Annual Meeting of the Academy of Management,* 1972.

Mintzberg, H., *The Nature of Managerial Work.* Prentice-Hall, 1973.

Mintzberg, H., & J. A. Waters, "Of Strategies, Deliberate and Emergent," *Strategic Management Journal,* 1985, 6(3): 257–272.

Mintzberg, H., "Crafting Strategy," *Harvard Business Review,* July–August 1987, 65: 66–75.

Mintzberg, H., "Learning 1, Planning 0: Reply to Igor Ansoff," *Strategic Management Journal,* 1991: 464–466.

Mintzberg, H., *The Rise and Fall of Strategic Planning.* New York: Free Press, 1994.

Mintzberg, H., "Introduction: CMR Forum: The 'Honda Effect' Revisited," *California Management Review,* 1996a: 78–79.

Mintzberg, H., "Reply to Michael Goold," *California Management Review,* 1996b: 96–99.

Mintzberg, H., *Managers Not MBAs: A Hard Look at the Soft Practice of Managing and Management Development.* San Francisco: Berrett-Koehler, 2004.

Mintzberg, H., "Rebuilding Companies as Communities," *Harvard Business Review,* July–August 2009.

Mintzberg, H., & J. A. Waters, "Tracking Strategy in an Entrepreneurial Firm," *Academy of Management Journal,* 1982: 465–499.

Mitroff, I., *Break-Away Thinking.* New York: John Wiley & Sons, 1988.

Montgomery, B. L., *The Memoirs of Field-Marshal the Viscount Montgomery of Alamein.* Cleveland: World Publishing Co., 1958.

Moran, P., & S. Ghoshal, "Value Creation by Firms," in J. B. Keys and N. Dosier, eds., *Academy of Management Best Paper Proceedings,* 1996.

Morgan, G., *Images of Organizations.* Beverly Hills, CA: Sage, 1986.

Moyer, R. C., "Berle and Means Revisited: The Conglomerate Merger," *Business and Society,* Spring 1970: 20–29.

Nadler, D., & M. L. Tushman, *Strategic Organization Design.* Homewood, IL: Scott Foresman, 1986.

Nahaplet, J., & S. Ghoshal, "Social Capital, Intellectual Capital, and the Organizational Advantage," *Academy of Management Review,* 1998: 242–266.

Napoleon, I., "Maximes de Guerre," in T. R. Phillips, ed., *Roots of Strategy.* Harrisburg, PA: The Military Service Publishing Company, 1940.

Nathanson, D., & J. Cassano, "Organization Diversity and Performance," *The Wharton Magazine,* Summer 1982: 18–26.

Neustadt, R. E., *Presidential Power: The Politics of Leadership.* New York: Wiley, 1960.

Noël, A., "Strategic Cores and Magnificent Obsessions: Discovering Strategy Formation through Daily Activities of CEOs," *Strategic Management Journal,* 1989, 10(1): 33–49.

Nonaka, I., "The Knowledge Creating Company," *Harvard Business Review,* November-December 1991, 69(6): 96–104.

Nonaka, I., & H. Takeuchi, *The Knowledge-Creating Company: How Japanese Companies Create the Dynamics of Innovation.* New York: Oxford University Press, 1995.

Ohmae, K., *The Mind of the Strategist.* New York: McGraw-Hill, 1982.

O'Neill, H. M., & J. Lenn, "Voices of Survivors: Words that Downsizing CEOs Should Hear," *The Academy of Management Executives,* 1995, 9(4).

Pascale, R., M. Millemann & L. Gioja, "Changing the Way We Change," *Harvard Business Review,* November–December 1997, 75: 126–139.

Pascale, R. T., "Perspectives on Strategy: The Real Story behind Honda's Success," *California Management Review,* 1984: 47–72.

Pascale, R. T., "Reflections on Honda," *California Management Review,* 1996: 112–117.

Perrow, C., *Complex Organizations: A Critical Essay.* New York: Scott Foresman, 1970.

Peters, T. J., "A Style for All Seasons," *Executive,* 1980, 6(3): 12–16.

Peters, T. J., & R. H. Waterman, *In Search of Excellence: Lessons from America's Best Run Companies.* New York: Harper & Row, 1982.

Pfeffer, J., & G. R. Salancik, *The External Control of Organizations: A Resource Dependence Perspective.* New York: Harper & Row, 1978.

Phillips, T. R., ed., *Roots of Strategy.* Harrisburg, PA: The Military Service Publishing Company, 1940.

Piore, M. J., "Dualism as a Response to Flux and Uncertainty," *Dualism and Discontinuity in Industrial Societies,* S. Berger and M. J. Piore, eds., New York: Cambridge University Press, 1980.

Piore, M. J., & C. F. Sabel, *The Second Industrial Divide: Possibilities for Prosperity,* New York: Basic Books, 1984.

Porter, M. E., *Competitive Strategy: Techniques for Analyzing Industries and Competitors.* New York: Free Press, 1980.

Porter, M. E., *Competitive Advantage: Creating and Sustaining Superior Performance.* New York: Free Press, 1985.

Porter, M. E., "Competition in Global Industries: A Conceptual Framework," in M. E. Porter, ed., *Competition in Global Industries.* Boston, MA: Harvard Business School Press, 1986.

Porter, M. E., "What Is Strategy?" *Harvard Business Review,* 1996: 61–78.

Prahalad, C., & G. Hamel, "Strategy as Stretch and Leverage," *Harvard Business Review,* March–April 1993.

Prahalad, C., & G. Hamel, "The Core Competence of the Organization," *Harvard Business Review,* March–April 1990, 68(3): 79–91.

Pugh, D. S., D. J. Hickson, & C. R. Hinings, "An Empirical Taxonomy of Structures of Work Organizations," *Administrative Science Quarterly,* 1969: 115–126.

Pugh, D. S., D. J. Hickson, C. R. Hinings, & C. Turner, "Dimensions of Organizational Structure," *Administrative Science Quarterly,* 1968, 13: 65–105.

Pugh, D. S., D. J. Hickson, C. R. Hinings, K. M. MacDonald, C. Turner, & T. Lupton, "A Conceptual Scheme for Organizational Analysis," *Administrative Science Quarterly,* 1963–1964, 8: 289–315.

Purkayastha, D., "Note on the Motorcycle Industry 1975." Copyrighted Case, Harvard Business School, 1981.

Quinn, J. B., *Strategies for Change: Logical Incrementalism.* Homewood, IL: Irwin, 1980a.

Quinn, J. B., "Managing Strategic Change," *Sloan Management Review,* Summer 1980b: 3–20.

Quinn, J. B., & P. C. Paquette, "Technology in Services: Creating Organizational Revolutions," *Sloan Management Review,* 1990: 67–78.

Quinn, J. B., "Honda Motor Company." In Mintzberg, H., & J.B. Quinn, *The Strategy Process: Concepts, Contexts, Cases.* 2nd ed. Upper Saddle River, NJ: Prentice Hall International, 1991: 284–299.

Quinn, J. B., *The Intelligent Enterprise.* New York: Free Press, 1992.

Quinn, J. B., "Honda Motor Company 1994." In Mintzberg, H., & J. B. Quinn, *The Strategy Process: Concepts, Contexts, Cases.* 3rd ed. Upper Saddle River, NJ: Prentice Hall International, 1996: 849–863.

Raphael, R., *Edges.* New York: Alfred A. Knopf, 1976.

Reeser, C., "Some Potential Human Problems in the Project Form of Organization," *Academy of Management Journal,* 1969: 459–467.

Rhenman, E., *Organization Theory for Long-Range Planning.* London: John Wiley, 1973.

Roach, S. S., "In Search of Productivity," *Harvard Business Review,* 1998: 153–159.

Rotman School of Management. (ca. 2005). *The Origin of Leaders.* Pamphlet, University of Toronto.

Royer, I., "Why Bad Projects Are So Hard to Kill," *Harvard Business Review,* 2003, 81(2): 48–56.

Rumelt, R. P., *Strategy, Structure and Economic Performance.* Boston, MA: Harvard Business School Press, 1974.

Rumelt, R. P., "A Teaching Plan for Strategy Alternatives for the British Motorcycle Industry," in *Japanese Business: Business Policy.* New York: The Japan Society, 1980.

Rumelt, R. P., "Diversification Strategy and Profitability," *Strategic Management Journal,* 1982: 359–370.

Sakiya, T., "The Story of Honda's Founders," *Asahi Evening News,* June–August 1979.

Sakiya, T., *Honda Motor: The Men, the Management, the Machines.* 2nd ed. Tokyo: Kodansha International, 1981.

Sakiya, T., *Honda Motor: The Men, the Management, the Machines.* Tokyo: Kodansha International, 1982.

Salter, M. S., & W. A. Weinhold, *Diversification through Acquisition.* New York: Free Press, 1979.

Sathe, V., "From Surface to Deep Entrepreneurship," *Human Resource Management,* 1988, 27(4): 389–411.

Sayles, L. R., *Managerial Behavior: Administration in Complex Organizations.* New York: McGraw-Hill, 1964.

Sayles, L. R., *The Working Leader: The Triumph of High Performance over Conventional Management Principles.* New York and Toronto: Free Press, 1993.

Schelling, T. C., *The Strategy of Conflict.* New York: Oxford University Press, 1963.

Schelling, T. C., *The Strategy of Conflict,* 2nd ed. Cambridge, MA: Harvard University Press, 1980.

Schoemaker, P. J. H., "Choices Involving Uncertain Probabilities: Test of Generalized Utility Models," *Journal of Economic Behavior and Organization*, 1991a: 295–317.

Schoemaker, P. J. H., "When and How to Use Scenario Planning: A Heuristic Approach with Illustration," *Journal of Forecasting*, 1991b: 549–564.

Schön, D., *The Reflective Practitioner*. New York: Basic Books, 1983.

Selznick, P., *Leadership in Administration: A Sociological Interpretation*, Evanston, IL: Row, Peterson, 1957.

Senge, P. M., *The Fifth Discipline: The Art and Practice of the Learning Organization*. New York: Doubleday, 1990.

Shimizu, R., *The Growth of Firms in Japan*. Tokyo: Keio Tsushin, 1980.

Shubik, M., *Game Theory and Related Approaches to Social Behavior*. Huntington, NY: R.E. Krieger Publishing Co, 1975.

Silbiger, S., *The 10-Day MBA*. London: Piatkus, 1994.

Simon, H. A., *Administrative Behavior*. New York: Macmillan, 1947 and 1957.

Simon, H. A., "The Architecture of Complexity," *Proceedings of the American Philosophical Society*, 1962: 122–137.

Simons, R., "The Role of Management Control Systems in Creating Competitive Advantage: New Perspectives," *Accounting, Organizations and Society*, 1990, 15(112): 127–143.

Simons, R., "Strategic Orientation and Top Management Attention to Control Systems," *Strategic Management Journal*, 1991, 12(1): 49–62.

Singer, E., & L. M. Wooton, "The Triumph and Failure of Albert Speer's Administrative Genius," *Journal of Applied Behavioral Science*, 1976, 12(1): 79–103.

Smircich, L., & C. Stubbart, "Strategic Management in an Enacted World," *Academy of Management Review*, 1985: 724–736.

Smith, C. G., & A. C. Cooper, "Entry into Threatening New Industries: Challenges and Pitfalls," in H. Thomas, D. O'Neal, R. White, & D. Hurst, eds., *Building the Strategically Responsive Organization*. New York: John Wiley & Sons, 1994.

Smith, L., "The Boardroom Is Becoming a Different Scene," *Fortune*, May 8, 1978: 150–188.

Smith, W., "Product Differentiation and Market Segmentation as Alternative Marketing Strategies", *Journal of Marketing*, 21, 1956: 3–8.

Snow, C., R. Miles, & H. Coleman, "Managing the 21st Century Network Organizations," *Organizational Dynamics*, 1992: 5–20.

Spencer, F. C., "Deductive Reasoning in the Lifelong Continuing Education of a Cardiovascular Surgeon," *Archives of Surgery*, 1976: 1177–1183.

Spencer, F. C., "The Significance of Myocardial Preservation and Subclinical Myocardial Infarction Following Coronary Bypass," *Annals of Thoracic Surgery*, September 1978, 26(3): 197–198.

Sperry, R., "Message from the Laboratory," *Engineering and Science*, 1974: 29–32.

Stalk, G., & T. M. Hout, *Competing against Time*. New York: The Free Press, 1990.

Stalk, G., P. Evans, & L. Shulman, "Competing on Capabilities: The New Rules of Corporate Strategy," *Harvard Business Review*, 1992: 57–69.

Stevenson, H. H., "Defining Corporate Strengths and Weaknesses," *Sloan Management Review*, Spring 1976, 17(3): 51–68.

Stewart, R., *Managers and Their Jobs*. London: Macmillan, 1967.

Sun Tzu, *The Art of War*. New York: Oxford University Press, 1963.

Taylor, F. W., *Scientific Management*. New York: Harper, 1911.

Taylor, W. H., "The Nature of Policy Making in Universities," *The Canadian Journal of Higher Education*, 1983: 17–32.

Teece, D. J., "Economies of Scope and Economies of the Enterprise," *Journal of Economic Behavior and Organization*, 1980: 223–247.

Terkel, S., *Working*. New York: Pantheon Books, 1972.

Thompson, J. D., *Organizations in Action*. New York: McGraw-Hill, 1967.

Thompson, V. A., *Modern Organizations*. New York: Alfred A. Knopf, 1961.

Tichy, N. M., & S. Sherman, *Control Your Destiny or Someone Else Will: How Jack Welch Is Making General Electric the World's Most Competitive Corporation*. New York: Doubleday, 1993.

Tilles, S., "How to Evaluate Corporate Strategy," *Harvard Business Review*, July–August 1963: 111–121.

Time, "The Most Basic Form of Creativity," June 26, 1972.

Toffler, A., *Future Shock*. New York: Bantam Books, 1970.

Tregoe, B., & I. Zimmerman, *Top Management Strategy*. New York: Simon & Schuster, 1980.

Tuchman, B., *The Guns and August*. New York: Random House, 1962.

Turner, J. R., & A. Keegan, "The Versatile Project-Based Organization: Governance and Operational Control," *The European Management Journal*, 22(3), 1999: 296–309.

Tushman, M., & C. A. O'Reilly III, *Winning through Innovation: A Practical Guide to Leading Organizational Change and Renewal*. Boston, MA: Harvard Business School Press, 1997.

Urban, G. L., T. Carter, S. Gaskin, & Z. Mucha, "Market Share Rewards to Pioneering Brands: An Empirical Analysis and Strategic Implications," *Management Science*, June 1986, 32(6): 645–659.

Vancil, R. F., "Strategy Formulation in Complex Organizations," *Sloan Management Review*, Winter 1976: 1–18.

Vancil, R. F., & P. Lorange, "Strategic Planning in Diversified Companies," *Harvard Business Review*, January–February, 1975: 81–90.

Varner, V. J., & J. I. Alger, eds., History of the Military Art: Notes for the Course. West Point, NY: U.S. Military Academy, Department of History, 1978.

von Bülow, D. F., *The Spirit of the Modern System of War*. Translated by C.M. deMartemont. London: C. Mercier and Co., 1806.

von Clausewitz, C., *On War*. Translated by M. Howard and R. Raret. Princeton, NJ: Princeton University Press, 1976.

von Neumann, J., & O. Morgenstern, *Theory of Games and Economic Behavior*. Princeton, NJ: Princeton University Press, 1944.

Wack, P., "Scenarios: Uncharted Waters Ahead," *Harvard Business Review*, September–October 1985: 73–89.

Waterman, R. H., T. J. Peters, & J. R. Phillips, "Structure Is Not Organization," *Business Horizons*, June 1980: 14–26.

Watson, T. J., *In Search of Management: Culture, Chaos and Control in Managerial Work*. London: Routledge, 1994.

Weber, M., *The Protestant Ethic and the Spirit of Capitalism*. Upper Saddle River, NJ: Prentice Hall, 1977.

Weick, K. E., "Educational Organizations as Loosely Coupled Systems," *Administrative Science Quarterly*, 1976: 1–19.

Weick, K. E., *The Social Psychology of Organizing*. Reading, MA: Addison-Wesley, 1st edition 1969, 2nd edition 1979.

White, T. H., *In Search of History: A Personal Adventure*. New York: Warner Books, 1978.

Williamson, O. E., *Markets and Hierarchies: Analysis and Antitrust Implications*. New York: Free Press, 1975.

Williamson, O. E., *The Economic Institutions of Capitalism*. New York: Free Press, 1985.

Williamson, O. E., "Comparative Economic Organization: The Analysis of Discrete Structural Alternatives," *Administrative Science Quarterly*, 1991: 269–276.

Wise, D., "Apple's New Crusade," *Business Week*, November 26, 1984.

Womack, J. P., D. T. Jones, & D. Roos, *The Machine that Changed the World*. New York: Rawson Associates, 1990.

Worthy, J. C., *Big Business and Free Men*. New York: Harper & Row, 1959.

Worthy, J. C., "Organizational Structure and Employee Morale," *American Sociological Review*, 1950: 169–179.

Wrigley, L., "Diversification and Divisional Autonomy," DBA dissertation, Graduate School of Business Administration, Harvard University, 1970.

Yoshino, M. Y., "Global Competition in a Salient Industry: The Case of Civil Aircraft," in M. E. Porter, ed., *Competition in Global Industries*. Boston, MA: Harvard Business School Press, 1986.

Young, D., *Rommel: The Desert Fox*. New York: Harper & Row, 1974.

Cases

CASE 1

Robin Hood

It was in the spring of the second year of his insurrection against the High Sheriff of Nottingham that Robin Hood took a walk in Sherwood Forest. As he walked he pondered the progress of the campaign, the disposition of his forces, the Sheriff's recent moves, and the options that confronted him.

The revolt against the Sheriff had begun as a personal crusade; it erupted out of Robin's conflict with the Sheriff and his administration. However, alone Robin Hood could do little. He therefore sought allies, men with grievances and a deep sense of injustice. Later he welcomed all who came, asking few questions and only demanding a willingness to serve. Strength, he believed, lay in numbers.

He spent the first year forging the group into a disciplined band, united in enmity against the Sheriff, and willing to live outside the law. The band's organization was simple. Robin ruled supreme, making all important decisions. He delegated specific tasks to his lieutenants. Will Scarlett was in charge of intelligence and scouting. His main job was to shadow the Sheriff and his men, always alert to their next move. He also collected information on the travel plans of rich merchants and tax collectors. Little John kept discipline among the men and saw to it that their archery was at the high peak that their profession demanded. Scarlock took care of the finances, converting loot to cash, paying shares of the take, and finding suitable hiding places for the surplus. Finally, Much, the Miller's son, had the difficult task of provisioning the ever-increasing band of Merrymen.

The increasing size of the band was a source of satisfaction for Robin, but also a source of concern. The fame of his Merrymen was spreading, and new recruits poured in from every corner of England. As the band grew larger, their small bivouac became a major encampment. Between raids the men milled about, talking and playing games. Vigilance was in decline, and discipline was becoming harder to enforce. "Why?" Robin reflected, "I don't know half the men I run into these days."

The growing band was also beginning to exceed the food capacity of the forest. Game was becoming scarce, and supplies had to be obtained from outlying villages. The cost of buying food was beginning to drain the band's financial reserves at the very moment when revenues were in decline. Travelers, especially those with the most to lose, were now giving the forest a wide berth. This was costly and inconvenient to them, but it was preferable to having all their goods confiscated.

Robin believed that the time had come for the Merrymen to change their policy of outright confiscation of goods to one of a fixed transit tax. His lieutenants strongly resisted this idea. They were proud of the Merrymen's famous motto: "Rob the rich and give to the poor." "The farmers and the townspeople," they argued, "are our most important allies." "How can we tax them, and still hope for their help in our fight against the Sheriff?"

Robin wondered how long the Merrymen could keep to the ways and methods of their early days. The Sheriff was growing stronger and better organized. He now had the money and the men, and was beginning to harass the band, probing for its weaknesses. The tide of events was beginning to turn against the Merrymen. Robin felt that the campaign must be decisively concluded before the Sheriff had a chance to deliver a mortal blow. "But how," he wondered, "could this be done?"

Robin had often entertained the possibility of killing the Sheriff, but the chances for this seemed increasingly remote. Besides, killing the Sheriff might satisfy his personal thirst for revenge, but it would not improve the situation. Robin had hoped that the perpetual state of unrest, and the Sheriff's failure to collect taxes, would lead to his removal from office. Instead, the Sheriff used his political connections to obtain reinforcement. He had powerful friends at court and was well regarded by the regent, Prince John.

Prince John was vicious and volatile. He was consumed by his unpopularity among the people, who wanted the imprisoned King Richard back. He also lived in constant fear of the barons who had first given him the regency, but were now beginning to dispute his claim to the throne. Several of these barons had set out to collect ransom that would release Richard the Lionheart from his

---

Prepared by Joseph Lampel, City University London.

jail in Austria. Robin was invited to join the conspiracy in return for future amnesty. It was a dangerous proposition. Provincial banditry was one thing, court intrigue another. Prince John's spies were everywhere. If the plan failed the pursuit would be relentless, and retribution swift.

The sound of the supper horn startled Robin from his thoughts. There was the smell of roasting venison in the air. Nothing was resolved or settled. Robin headed for camp promising himself that he would give these problems his utmost attention after tomorrow's raid.

CASE 2

Napoleon Bonaparte: Victim of an Inferior Strategy?

ON THE ROAD TO PARIS, JUNE 19, 1815[1]

Incomprehensible coincidence of fatalities! Grouchy, why did he not immediately return to the battlefield when I summoned him? And how can it be that my Chief-of-Staff Soult only sends a single messenger to recall him? Berthier surely would have sent 12! My other marshal, Ney, did not fare better. He did not execute my orders; in fact he failed me twice, in as many days. Just like d'Erlon, who, at Ligny, hesitated between following Ney's orders and mine. It was his wavering which allowed Blücher and his Prussians to escape. And that I had to leave my brave Davout behind to secure Paris in my absence may yet have been my greatest misfortune. Masséna, Murat, Desaix, Berthier, Lannes, Bessiéres, or Duroc: you too were sorrowfully missed! How different the outcome would have been, if only I could have counted on some of you!

Following his disastrous defeat at Waterloo, Napoleon's head must have been filled with such thoughts. ". . . The victory was so close, yet kept escaping me. . ." He had done everything possible to bring France to glory, leading his people through more battles and victories than Alexander the Great, Hannibal, and Julius Caesar combined. Undoubtedly, some of his field marshals and generals grew weary and reluctant to follow his aims of continental annexation, yet they largely stood behind him. Despite his practically infallible personal leadership skills and strategic vision, he had still lost. Questions like "Why did it go so wrong at the end? Why did chance escape me in the end?" are likely to have haunted him on the road back to Paris.

FROM CORSICAN TO EMPEROR OF FRANCE, 1769–1821

Born in Ajaccio, Corsica, on August 15, 1769, Napoleon, who was of Italian descent, received a French education at the Royal Military College in Brienne. On July 14, 1789, the French Revolution broke out when the Bastille was attacked, leading to the downfall of the *Ancien Régime* and King Louis XVI. The Revolution promised *Liberté, Egalité, Fraternité* (Liberty, Equality, Fraternity) for all.

Napoleon first distinguished himself at the Siege of Toulon in 1793, then later in putting down a royalist uprising. This latter success led to his nomination at the head of the "Army of Italy" where his talents as a gifted military commander were fully recognized. Following his invasion of Egypt in 1798, Napoleon successfully led a coup and installed himself as the First Consul of France.

An energetic leader and administrator, he restored civil order, balanced the budget, and established modern-day French administration, overseeing the establishment of the *Code Napoléon*. This code represented a wide-sweeping reform and codification of France's laws in areas such as commerce, civil and legal procedure, and penal and rural law. The country, worn out after 10 years of internal and external strife, was grateful to Bonaparte (as he then was called) for consolidating the rights won by the people during the French Revolution. To permanently mark the transition of France to a new era, Napoleon convinced the Senate to crown him *Empereur des Français* (Emperor of the French) in 1804.

Napoleon fought and won many glorious battles of which Austerlitz was perhaps the most significant. It established his credibility. At the height of his power, Napoleon ruled, directly or indirectly, half of Europe. Though he imposed French practices such as the *Code Napoléon* to integrate countries within the French Empire and sometimes even went so far as to appoint family members as new heirs, he was careful to leave conquered countries otherwise intact. He created the Kingdoms of Bavaria and Württemberg, both of which joined the Confederation of the Rhine in 1806, the precursor of today's Germany.

However, Napoleon's use of military might as the principal instrument of policy proved insufficient. Prompted by military difficulties in Spain, his advisors increasingly supported a more balanced implementation of political, diplomatic, and economic policies, in addition to the military ones, to ensure a more integrated Europe. Napoleon, annoyed by such apparent dissension, began to isolate himself from his advisors. This inherent lack of balance in Napoleon's actions, however, would eventually

---

This case was written by Atul Sinha, INSEAD MBA, July 1999, under the supervision of Professors W. Chan Kim, Renée Mauborgne, and Ludo Van der Heyden of INSEAD. It is intended to be used as a basis for class discussion rather than to illustrate either effective or ineffective handling of an administrative situation.

erode his influence. Power and success had started to corrupt Napoleon.

The fateful invasion and disastrous retreat from Russia in 1812 united all of Europe against him, thereby hastening his downfall. Although he fought a brilliant last campaign in France against a much superior enemy, the odds proved impossible to uphold. In April 1814, his marshals refused to follow his orders, forcing Napoleon to abdicate his throne. He was sent into exile to the Island of Elba in the Mediterranean, not far from his native Corsica.

Napoleon's first exile was short-lived. Strongly encouraged by the ineptitude of the new monarch Louis XVIII, the younger brother of Louis XVI, he escaped from Elba in March 1815. He bravely faced the troops sent to capture him and they soon followed him, all the way to Paris, where he was welcomed as a liberator. Back in power, he advocated a new and more democratic constitution, and veterans of his old campaigns flocked to his support. Once restored to the throne, Napoleon sought peace with his allies. They rejected his offer, so he resorted to war. The result was the *Campagne des Cent Jours* (the Hundred Days Campaign) into Belgium, which ended in his definitive defeat at the Battle of Waterloo on June 18, 1815. He was sent into his second and final exile at Saint Helena, a remote island in the South Atlantic Ocean, where he died on May 5, 1821 (see Appendix 1).

NAPOLEON AS A STRATEGIC INNOVATOR IN MILITARY WARFARE

> The Emperor has discovered a new way of waging war; he makes use of our legs instead of our bayonets.
>
> —*Anonymous soldier*

Napoleon injected a radical new way of thinking into prevailing war strategies of the time. Apart from structural and organizational changes, he conceived the following two fundamentally new tactics.

Corps units

Napoleon formed a *corps d'armée* system, which led to increased mobility and flexible formations. These corps units operated like self-sustained armies and were capable of fighting independently for a limited period of time. The units were assigned different roles and equipped in consequence. Mobility was of the essence. The exception was the Emperor's Personal Guard, composed of elite soldiers who had distinguished themselves in prior battles. The Guard was typically held in reserve, but its presence instilled confidence in the soldiers who knew they could count on these elite troops to change the outcome should the battle take a negative turn.

The corps units were coordinated and controlled via "a communication backbone of marshals," providing the primary and direct link with Napoleon. Each corps had its own general or marshal, acting on a clear mission defined by Napoleon, though this mission could change according to battle conditions. Due to the enormous flexibility of this system, Napoleon was able to implement a more dynamic and evolutionary battle strategy. He had an uncanny ability to determine the enemy's weak spot, probe it, and if confirmed, direct all available forces to that spot. He could mix and match the corps as required by battle conditions. The marshals were critical, as they were the primary link of communication with Napoleon.

Time as a strategic weapon

By considering time—and not simply force—as one of the variables, Napoleon introduced enormous flexibility in his strategic approach to every battle. Dynamic configurations offered multiple possibilities as the battle progressed. Strong communication structures allowed him to modify his orders and battle tactics effectively in nearly an on-line basis.

The timely use of flexible corps afforded Napoleon huge advantages in battle. His devastating "assembly (of troops) and concentration (of force)" approach to battles was a direct result. It was more than a simple matter of collecting a vast number of units at a given point. On the eve of the battle, it was imperative that the troops be "assembled" rather than "concentrated." By "assembly" Napoleon meant placing major units within marching distance of the intended battlefield, though not necessarily in physical contact with the enemy or one another. It was important that the forces were not only placed at marching distance from the possible battle site, but also were sufficiently dispersed on the eve of the battle to permit alternative movements without a major realignment of the formations. The initial dispersion then gave way to a more carefully phased concentration as the battle approached, but also to a larger number of options. After lulling the opponent into a false sense of security (by holding back most of his corps at a two-day march from the planned striking point), the Emperor used to "steal a march" by ordering a rapid movement of his corps under the cover of darkness, thereby gaining a full day of preparations over his enemy. For example, certain of his troops marched an amazing 140 km in 48 hours during the Battle of Austerlitz.

Speed, surprise, flexibility, and continual adjustment were some of the key advantages derived from these two innovations. They transformed his army into a single integrated unit, capable of executing an ever-evolving strategy dictated by battle conditions.

LODI: THE PURSUIT OF HIGH AMBITIONS, MAY 10, 1796

> I will lead you into the most fertile plains on earth. Rich provinces, opulent towns, all shall be at your disposal; there you will find honour, glory and riches.[2]

With such statements Napoleon enticed his soldiers and his officers, with the expectation of rewards in return for bravery and obedience on the battlefield. The promise of victory and the opportunity to fight for "their own country and not for the whims of the King" strongly appealed to the French soldiers, who furthermore were commanded by people who, even of aristocratic descent, had risen through the ranks and proven themselves on the battlefield. Everyone worked tirelessly to prepare this campaign against the Austrians. The objective was to force them to the other side of the Po River and out of Lombardy altogether. Chief-of-Staff Berthier, an engineer/geographer, planned the strategic moves in the Alps, while other brilliant young officers such as Augereau, Masséna, and Murat—all of whom would later be given the rank of marshal—trained the soldiers in the new corps system.

As part of a plan to occupy Milan, Napoleon had accomplished the preliminary task of pushing the Austrians back to the Adda River. This was achieved through repeated concentration of forces at critical places and the brilliant execution of his strategy by the generals and their soldiers. All of his commanders acted in exemplary fashion. As this was Napoleon's first major campaign, he regularly met with his officers to explain his ideas and strategies, as well as to receive and integrate their feedback and their knowledge of the terrain and of enemy formations. Highly confident in his soldiers and in himself, Napoleon resolved to defeat the Austrians quickly. A letter to his superiors in Paris demonstrates this:

> My intention is to catch up with the Austrians and beat them before you have time to reply to this letter.[3]

Napoleon now faced the Austrian Army across the Adda River. Capturing the Lodi Bridge was essential to continue his advance toward Milan. Yet, the Austrians had drawn a dozen guns on each side of the bridge. After a stirring speech to his troops, he ordered a column of grenadiers onto the bridge. The first French charge, under a hail of Austrian fire, reached the center of the bridge before falling back. A second charge was quickly organized. This time many senior officers placed themselves at the column's head. Letting loose a cry of "Vive la République!" they charged into the maelstrom and forced the Austrians to abandon the bridge. This battle earned Napoleon the loyalty of his men, who nicknamed him "Le Petit Caporal" in recognition of his personal courage and determination. Napoleon urged them on:

> In two weeks' time you have won six victories, taken 21 flags . . . several forts, and conquered the richest part of Piedmont . . . but soldiers, do not deceive yourselves. You have achieved nothing, for everything remains to be done. Neither Turin nor Milan is in our hands. . . . There remain battles to fight, cities to take, rivers to cross . . . and friends, I promise, you will achieve all![4]

MARENGO, JUNE 14, 1800: SAVED BY HIS GENERALS

During his early days as First Consul, Napoleon continued to ensure that his generals were involved in the early stages of campaign planning. On one occasion, he had worked out a brilliant plan to move his army into the Rhine. However, one general disagreed with the plan, suggesting another strategy. Though the suggestion directly contradicted his own plans, Napoleon took the general's advice instead of treating it as an act of insubordination. He understood the advantages of engaging his officers and liked to discuss strategic plans with them, seeking their reactions and advice. These exchanges were also an opportunity for Napoleon to train and coach his corps commanders in his strategic way of thinking. The increasing complexity of his strategies reinforced his desire to keep them completely aware of the roles and responsibilities of each of the divisions. Napoleon even believed in making the simplest soldier party to his plan and spelling out what was demanded of him. On the eve of a battle, he would typically sleep on the battleground with the soldiers. He believed that the soldier was not a machine to be put into motion, but a reasonable being that must be directed.

His officers' willingness and ability to carry out battle plans autonomously were never more evident than at the Battle of Marengo. For once, Napoleon was facing a situation that he would typically inflict upon his enemies: the Austrians had concentrated their troops in the fields of Marengo. Since his whole strategy rested on the attack, he was caught totally unprepared by the Austrian attack. He needed reinforcements badly and sent an urgent message for help: "I had thought to attack Melas. He has attacked me first. For God's sake, come up if you still can" read Napoleon's hurried note to Officer Desaix.[5] Fortunately, Desaix upon hearing the cannon fire in the valley, had already decided to return to the battlefield, which he reached by 3 p.m., much to Napoleon's and his soldiers' relief.

Upon Desaix's arrival, Napoleon is reported to have asked his dear Desaix what he thought of it. Desaix responded that this battle was certainly lost, but that it was only two o'clock [in fact, it was three o'clock], and there was still time, therefore, to win yet another battle. And with that reply, Desaix charged upon the unsuspecting Austrians who already imagined the battle won. The Austrians were paralyzed by the ferociousness of the French counterattack. In that brief moment of confusion, another French commander, Kellermann, spontaneously ordered his 400 horsemen to charge, leaving the Austrians even more stunned.

The timing proved to be perfect, and Northern Italy was then recovered for the French Republic.

The victory was acquired without Napoleon ever intervening or giving direct orders. Such was the level of understanding of his strategies and the confidence of his generals. Shortly after 9 p.m., Napoleon had won the Battle of Marengo—at a heavy price. Thousands lay wounded or dead, Desaix among them.

"LE BEAU SOLEIL D'AUSTERLITZ": NAPOLEON'S DOMINATION OF BATTLE AT AUSTERLITZ IN 1805

On the eve of the Battle of Austerlitz, most of the 75,000 French soldiers were in their designated positions for their fight against 90,000 Allied Austrian and Russian forces.

As cited previously, Marshal Davout and his army corps were completing a long march of 140 km in only 48 hours to provide Napoleon with reinforcements.

A few days before the famous battle, Napoleon had issued orders for the French troops to retreat whenever they came in contact with the enemy. He willingly let the Allies occupy the heights of Pratzen and deployed his own troops in front of this plateau, Davout on the right, Soult at the center, and Murat and Lannes on the left. He even negotiated only to further suggest French weakness and fear against a superior enemy.

Napoleon's plan was to present to the enemy an intentionally weakened right wing, hoping that this would induce the Allies to attempt to overtake him on that side. In this maneuver the marching allied forces would expose their own flank to the French center, which could then charge upon them. The allied maneuver would also result in weakening their own center, which Napoleon could then attack by sending the troops under his direct command in a march upon the Pratzen plateau. This movement would cut the enemy army in two and would be continued against its weaker half. Simultaneously, the French cavalry would take on the allied right guard. Heavy fog on the morning of the battle would further help the French by hiding their positions from the enemy and adding greater surprise to their movements.

To keep his men updated and informed, a surprisingly open order of the day was issued:

> The positions we occupy are strong, and as they (the Russians) advance to my right they will expose their flank to me. Soldiers I shall direct your battalions myself. I will hold myself far from the firing line, if with your accustomed bravery, you carry disorder and confusion into the ranks of the enemy. But, if victory should for one moment be uncertain you will see your Emperor exposed to the first blows.[6]

Jomini,[7] the famous Austrian author, later said that never in the history of the world had a leader of an army revealed his plan in this way to the whole of his forces. Wherever Napoleon went for inspection that night, he was greeted with the traditional *Vive l'Empereur!* Taking his men into his confidence he would explain the next day's battle plan. This invariably helped raise the army's morale. Though only a few shared his words, all divisions soon knew that such exchanges were taking place. With his formations in place, with strong morale and a very clear plan, with an unsuspecting enemy who furthermore had been lulled into believing that the French were weak, Napoleon had literally won half the battle before it even began.

The ensuing battle was bloody and brutal. And as expected, the allied army fell into Napoleon's trap, was cut in two, and finally pushed back in three different directions. Nearly 27,000 Russians and Austrians died.

The Battle of Austerlitz demonstrated both the capability of Napoleon's marshals to execute complex tactical maneuvers and the effectiveness of the corps system. Since a corps was divided into smaller units, Napoleon could tailor his attack using combinations of different units to trick the Russians. The Battle of Austerlitz was the clearest demonstration of the effectiveness of his deadly war strategies: massive "assembly-and-concentration" principles were applied during his move through Europe, and attacking the central position was effectively exploited in the battle. Napoleon was well aware of his men's needs and motivation and how critical their commitment was to the victory at Austerlitz. As a reward for victory, gold was distributed among the officers. Provisions were made for generous pensions to the widows of the fallen. Napoleon formally adopted orphaned children, permitting them to add "Napoleon" to their baptismal names. *Solidest, je suis content de vous!* The victory bulletin praised his generals and soldiers.

TORN BETWEEN THE DEMANDS OF A PRIME MINISTER AND THE AMBITIONS OF AN EMPEROR, 1807–1811

> I have done enough soldiering. I must now play Prime Minister for a bit,

Napoleon explained as he convened a cabinet meeting in St. Cloud. He had subdued the young Russian Czar, Alexander I, and forced the signing of the "Treaty of Tilsit"[8] to isolate Britain from the Continent. Poland had been invaded and was now occupied. Napoleon ruled an empire that stretched from the Pyrenees to the Niemen and controlled a multinational army of 800,000—an unprecedented number in Europe. Napoleon was at his pinnacle, but not without some pressing problems, like the resignation of Talleyrand, his invaluable Foreign Minister.

Talleyrand was one of the few critical voices Napoleon would listen to. Following his Foreign Minister's departure, Napoleon underwent a worrying and very visible transformation. He shut down the vociferous and critical Tribunat, the French legislative assembly, in August 1807. Thin-skinned to attacks by the press, he threatened to close the newspapers. He enforced strict court etiquette, keeping everyone physically at arm's length. He could only be approached with the approval of Duroc, Grand Marshal of the Palace. A letter, dated April 4 to his brother Louis in Holland, clearly displayed a changed Napoleon: "You govern your nation like a docile, timorous monk. . . . A king issues orders and does not beg."[9]

Napoleon's self-imposed isolation manifested itself in his distance from the regular guests he used to invite for parties. Public functions were reduced to a minimum. Apart from daily contact with his secretary, Méneval, Napoleon's only close confidant was Duroc. Even some of his closest soldier-friends were no longer permitted to address him with the French familiar form of you, *tu*. Though his official business schedule was as frantic as ever, receiving delegations, etc., his daily chats with his older generals were a thing of the past. Some of his marshals and generals were not on speaking terms with one another.

A few of them were upset at not being named marshal or prince, despite their contributions to Napoleon's victories.[10] Apparently, Napoleon's process for promoting generals or assigning titles left a few of them demanding explanations. And the fact that orders to all senior officers came from the desk of the Chief-of-Staff of the Imperial Army, the increasingly loathed Major General Berthier, did little to help matters.

THE FATEFUL ROAD TO MOSCOW AND TO ABDICATION, 1812

When Russia broke the "Treaty of Tilsit," Napoleon recalled his ambassador and declared war on Russia in 1812. For his second campaign on the Russian front, Napoleon's force was the largest Europe had ever seen.

The multilingual army fell under three levels of command, with a first line of 450,000 soldiers reporting to Napoleon. Apart from the main army, Napoleon also disposed of an enormous reserve army of more than 200,000 soldiers. With such a large mass on the move, marching men in formation became extremely difficult. Consequently, many of the corps and reserves were behind schedule. Three great allies of Russia—time, distance, and weather—started to work against the French. From the moment the French army crossed the French–Russian border, enormous bottlenecks took place. Lack of proper food and fatigue were soon demoralizing the army. Soldiers began throwing away their heavy supplies, even including cartridges.

It seemed that Napoleon had overestimated his soldiers' commitment, their limits, as well as the logistical challenges the armies would face. Almost all the marshals, including his Chief-of-Staff, Berthier, argued vehemently against this campaign, saying that invading Russia was madness. They continued their protest during the campaign. Alone in his single-mindedness and supremely confident in his superior intellect and vision, Napoleon kept overruling them. As Caulaincourt, Ambassador to Russia, recalled:

> Time and again, the Emperor repeated that the Russians, whom everyone had claimed to be so numerous, had in fact no more than 150,000 men. . . . [He] added that he was sure that we [Caulaincourt and the other French generals opposing the campaign] had deceived him personally about everything down to the problems of the Russian climate, insisting that winter here was like in France, except that it just lasted longer. These accusations against us were repeated on many occasions. I reiterated to the Emperor, quite in vain as it turned out, that I had not exaggerated in the least, and that as his most faithful servant, I had revealed the full truth about everything. But I failed to make him change his mind.[11]

Nor was Chief-of-Staff, Berthier, spared from Napoleon's wrath. "Wild abuse was heaped on him for his frank advice, as a reward for his constant work and devotion."[12] Napoleon continually complained that Berthier's staff was incompetent, ". . . no one planned ahead." He refused to trust anyone, even Berthier, to make the smallest decision or give the simplest order, without his stamp of approval.

Even his marshals were becoming uncooperative. Napoleon expressed his distrust of Murat. Murat, who disliked fellow marshal Ney, could not agree on battle plans, and even fought with Davout. Their dislike for Berthier grew stronger.

Despite all this, Napoleon was able to keep his men marching toward Moscow. Finally after chasing the Russians for a long time, Napoleon faced them at Borodino Field, about 70 km from Moscow. It proved a Pyrrhic victory: one in every three soldiers died. The next day the French army invaded Moscow, and Napoleon took the Kremlin. After waiting a month for the Czar of Russia to surrender, Napoleon ordered the retreat of his troops on October 19. With nearly two-thirds of the men dead, the survivors started the long march back home through the harsh and wintry Russian landscape, continuously attacked by Russian cavalry. Ney and his cavalry fought bravely and considerably helped the French retreat.

Napoleon now had most of Europe united against him. He faced the Allies at the Battle of Nations in Leipzig in October 1813, but withdrew on the third day against a much superior enemy. The Allies finally entered France and notwithstanding brilliant military leadership during the Campaign of France, where with 70,000 men Napoleon was able to contain 350,000 Allied troops. The Emperor finally was forced into exile on the Island of Elba. Napoleon bid a dramatic farewell to his troops in the *Cour des Adieux* at the *Château de Fontainbleau*[13] on April 20, 1814. His last words to his loyal Guard were *Bring me my eagle.* He kissed the French flag, while many soldiers wept.

THE LAST CAMPAIGN: 100 DAYS TO WATERLOO

A mere nine months later, Napoleon escaped from Elba with the help of some generals and 1,200 soldiers from his personal guard. His arrival in France took the authorities by surprise. The French people, on the other hand, reacted with surprising calmness. Well aware of inflation, steep prices, and King Louis XVIII's incompetence, Napoleon played to the peasants, who were on the verge of losing all the freedoms that had been won during the Revolution. He assured them that they would not lose their lands to the "émigrés"—the aristocrats who were about to return to reclaim their titles and their lands. He seduced the town's people with promises of fiscal reforms. Everywhere he went, he promised peace and prosperity with popular statements such as the following:

> I am coming back to protect and defend the interests that our Revolution has given us. I want to give an inviolable constitution, one prepared by the people and myself together.[14]

French authorities sought out occasions to challenge him. On one such occasion, the French army was ordered to use all means to stop him. Napoleon stepped forward and faced the muskets, baring his chest. With a remarkable mixture of bravado and charisma, he called on the regiment to join him:

> I heard you calling me in my exile and have overcome every obstacle and peril to be here. . . . Take up those colours that the nation has proscribed, those colours around which we have rallied for 25 years, in fending off enemies of France. Put on the same tricolour cocarde that you wore during your finest days . . . [and] take up the eagles that presided over you at Ulm, Austerlitz, Jena, Eylau, and Friedland. . . .[15] Soldiers, come rally around the banner of your leader![16]

Sending up the cry *Vive l'Empereur,* the Fifth Regiment changed sides. In the meantime, the king had issued a warrant for Napoleon, sending Marshal Ney to arrest him. Once confronted with his former commander, Ney changed his mind, pressured by many of his troops to do so, and defected along with 6,000 men. Napoleon made a grand entrance at the Tuileries Palace in Paris on March 20, 1815, and was restored to the throne.[17]

Britain, Austria, Prussia, and Russia met in Vienna on March 25 to sign the Treaty of Vienna and form the Seventh Coalition. To ensure that Napoleon would "be absolutely beyond the possibility of causing trouble," a massive attack on each of France's borders was planned.

Thus began the Campaign of Belgium. Napoleon's plan was to strike first, targeting the combined forces of Wellington and Blücher in the North. But he found it difficult to select his marshals—many were dead, others were unwilling to join him. In the end, he named Marshal Soult as his Chief-of-Staff and Marshals Ney and Grouchy as commanders of the army's wings.

French preparations for the offensive lasted from June 6 to 14. The Imperial Guard and the reserve cavalry were placed within a 30-km area more than 200 km away from the Franco-Belgian border. Executed in complete secrecy, the speed and surprise of his advance into Belgium gave Napoleon a tremendous advantage even before the first bullet was fired.

On the morning of June 15, Napoleon's army converged on the allied armies of his opponents. Since Wellington and Blücher's armies were dispersed over a large area, the key strategy was to occupy a "central position" between them, dividing them so they could be defeated one at a time. By occupying a vital lateral road, the French army would also be able to break the Anglo-Dutch armies' line of communication. Ney would be responsible for containing the Anglo-Dutch forces, while Napoleon and Grouchy would destroy Blücher and his Prussians. They would then join and take on Wellington. If successful, the strategy would culminate in one of Napoleon's finest military victories.

From the very start, however, imperfections started to show the cracks of the French command structure. General Vandamme's corps received their movement orders after a considerable delay from Soult, which created a subsequent delay in crossing the Sambre River. Uncharacteristic chaos reigned in communication orders on June 16 at Ligny. Ney was to contain the Anglo-Dutch forces at a place called Quatre-Bras, while Napoleon and Grouchy would march against the Prussians in Ligny. Ney waited the whole morning for his orders before acting on his own initiative. This proved to be a decisive mistake. Even when Ney finally received Napoleon's orders to return to Ligny to complete the victory against Blücher, one suspects that he had difficulty in understanding the Emperor's "central position" tactic, which created further confusion. After all, Napoleon had planned everything by himself, neglecting to transmit the information to his marshals, and Berthier was no longer there to carefully translate Napoleon's thoughts into clear orders for the marshals. This was the single biggest factor working against Napoleon. "In three hours' time, the campaign will be decided," remarked a then optimistic Napoleon. "If Ney follows his orders through, not a gun of the Prussian army will get away; they will be taken in the very act."[18] But Ney arrived too late, while d'Erlon and his corps spent the day walking back and forth between the two battles. The Prussians escaped, including Blücher who was left wounded on the battlefield, but finally recovered thanks to French delays in pursuing the retreating Prussians into the night.

More misunderstandings compounded the French army's confusion two days later at Waterloo. On the morning of the battle, Napoleon had rejected most of his fellow commanders' advice. Chief-of-Staff Soult's cautious remark that Grouchy should be recalled was discarded; Prince Jerôme's report that Wellington and Blücher were planning to join forces was dismissed as "trivial." Mistakes were made. During one attack, for example, a strange and outdated formation was used, contrary to Napoleon's instructions, resulting in heavy losses for the French. To recover his position, Ney overreacted in a cavalry attack, angering Napoleon. "This is a premature movement which may lead to fatal results," thundered Napoleon, "he [Ney] is compromising us."[19]

Everything that could possibly go wrong had happened, from the very beginning. Though Napoleon had crafted a brilliant strategy, his marshals were failing him. But there was still a chance to defeat Wellington and win the battle. Napoleon's only worry was that Blücher would reinforce Wellington's forces. Napoleon knew that his army would not be able to sustain the onslaught of their combined forces and hoped that Grouchy's corps would prevent Blücher from reaching Wellington. Then the opportunity vanished: Blücher met up with Wellington late in the evening, as he had promised him, and the Battle of Waterloo was over—exactly 100 days after Napoleon's return to France.

APPENDIX 1 A BRIEF NAPOLEONIC CHRONOLOGY*

Aug. 15, 1769	Birth in Ajaccio (Corsica)
May 15, 1779	Entrance in the Military School of Brienne
Oct. 17, 1784	Admission to the *Ecole Militaire* (Military College) in Paris, which he graduates from a year later 42nd out of 58
June 1788	Joins his regiment in Auxonne
Sept. 1789–Feb. 1791	Third stay in Corsica, participates in the island's political turmoil
May 1792	Arrives in Paris
Aug. 10	Assists at the assault on the *Tuileries* Palace
June 11, 1793	Has to leave Corsica with his family and goes to Toulon
Dec. 18	British withdraw from Toulon and he is appointed *Général de Brigade*
Aug. 9, 1794	Arrested, but soon released
Oct. 5, 1795	Participates in defeating a royalist uprising in Paris
Oct. 26	Appointed General of the Army of the Interior
Mar. 2, 1796	Appointed Commander in Chief of the Army of Italy
May 10	*Victory at the Battle of Lodi*
Oct. 17, 1797	Peace with Austria at Campo-Formio
May 19, 1798	Departs for Egypt
July 21	Victory at the Battle of the Pyramids
Aug. 1	Nelson destroys the French fleet at Aboukir
May 10, 1799	Withdraws from Acco after an 8th unsuccessful assault
July 25	Victory at Aboukir
Aug. 23	Leaves the Army to Kléber and returns to France
Nov. 9	Following a coup, Bonaparte is appointed Consul, with Sieyès and Ducos
Dec. 15	Declaration of a new Constitution
Feb. 17, 1800	Appointment of *Préfets*
May 20	*Crosses the Alps with his Army at the Saint Bernard pass*
June 14	*Victory at the Battle of Marengo*
Nov. 1	Publication of the *Parallèle entre César, Cromwell, Monk et Bonaparte*
Dec. 24	Attempt on his life at Rue Saint-Nicaise
July 15, 1801	Signature of the *Concordat*, which re-establishes the Catholic Church
Mar. 25, 1802	Peace of Amiens with England
May 19, 1802	Introduces the *Légion d'Honneur*
May 6, 1803	Break with England
May 18, 1804	*Napoléon Bonaparte* is appointed *Empereur des Français*
May 19	Eighteen amongst his senior officers are named *Maréchaux d'Empire*
Dec. 2	Crowned Emperor in the presence of Pope Pius VII
Oct. 21, 1805	Franco-Spanish fleet defeated at Trafalgar, where Nelson dies
Dec. 2	*Victory at Austerlitz*
July 12, 1806	Creation of the Confederation of the Rhine
Oct. 14	Victories at Jena (Napoleon) and Auerstadt (Davout) against Prussia
Nov. 21	Decrees the *Blocus Continental* against commerce with England
June 14, 1807	Victory at Friedland against Russia
July 7 and 9	Signature of Peace Treaties at Tilsit with Russia and Prussia
Mar. 1, 1808	Creation of the *Noblesse d'Empire* (Imperial Nobility)
May 2	Uprising in Madrid against the French presence in Spain
April 8, 1809	Austria attacks Bavaria
July 6	Victory against Austria at Wagram, Pius VII is arrested
April 2, 1810	*Napoléon* marries Marie-Louise, daughter of the Austrian Emperor
July 10	Holland is integrated into France
Aug. 21	Bernadotte, a former general, is appointed Hereditary Prince of Sweden
June 24, 1812	*La Grande Armée crosses the river Niemen into Russia*
Sept. 7, 1812	*Victory at the Moskova (Borodino)*
Sept. 14	*French enter Moscow*
Oct. 18	*Decision to leave Moscow and return to France*
Nov. 27	*Disastrous crossing at the Berezina River*

APPENDIX 1 A BRIEF NAPOLEONIC CHRONOLOGY* (*continued*)

Dec. 5	*Leaves his retreating army for Paris*
Mar. 13, 1813	Prussia declares war on France, but is defeated at Lützen and Bautzen
June 21	Victory of Wellington at Vittoria, Spain is lost
Aug. 12	Austria declares war
Oct. 16–19	*Battle of Nations at Leipzig, Napoleon retreats, and Germany is lost*
Nov. 16	So is Holland
Jan. 17, 1814	Murat defects and the French domination of Italy is in jeopardy
Jan. and Feb.	*Campaign of France: victories at Brienne, Champaubert, Montmirail, Montereau, and Reims*
Mar. 31	Marmont capitulates in front of Paris
Apr. 6	*Abdicates without conditions in Fontainebleau*
May 4	*Arrival on the Island of Elba for his first exile*
Mar. 1, 1815	*Return on French soil at Golfe-Juan*
Mar. 7	*First French troops rally to Napoleon*
June 16	*Victory against the Prussians at Ligny*
June 18	*Disaster at Waterloo*
Oct. 16	*Beginning of his second and final exile on the Island of Saint Helena*
May 5, 1821	Death of *Napoléon Bonaparte*

*Events in italics are described in more detail in the case.

APPENDIX 2
LIST OF MARSHALS CREATED BY THE EMPEROR NAPOLEON*

Napoleon, Emperor of the French, by a Decree of May 19, 1804, appointed 18 officers of the French Army to be *Marshals of the Empire* (*Maréchaux d'Empire*). Four of them were honorary marshals from the Senate. The other 14 were on the active list.

The four honorary Marshals were:

KELLERMANN, aged 69, son of a merchant.
LEFEBRE, aged 49, son of a miller.
PERIGNON, aged 50, son of a landowner.
SERURIER, aged 62, son of an officer of the Household Troops.

The 14 Marshals on the active list were:

BERTHIER, aged 51, son of a surveying engineer.
MURAT, aged 37, son of an innkeeper.
MONCEY, aged 50, son of a lawyer.
JOURDAN, aged 42, son of a doctor.
MASSENA, aged 48, son of a tanner and soap-manufacturer.
AUGEREAU, aged 47, son of a working mason.
BERNADOTTE, aged 41, son of a lawyer.
SOULT, aged 35, son of a lawyer.
BRUNE, aged 41, son of a lawyer.
LANNES, aged 35, son of a peasant farmer.
MORTIER, aged 36, son of a farmer.
NEY, aged 35, son of a barrel-cooper.
DAVOUT, aged 34, son of an officer.
BESSIERES, aged 36, son of a surgeon.

Eight were subsequently added:

In 1807 VICTOR, aged 43, son of a soldier.
In 1809 MACDONALD, aged 44, son of a soldier.
MARMONT, aged 35, son of an officer.
OUDINOT, aged 42, son of a brewer.
In 1811 SUCHET, aged 41, son of a silk-manufacturer.
In 1812 SAINT CYR, aged 48, son of a tanner.
In 1813 PONIATOWSKI, aged 50, son of a prince.
In 1815 GROUCHY, aged 49, son of a marquis.

*This Appendix is taken from A. G. MacDonnell's excellent book on Napoleon, entitled: *Napoleon and His Marshals*. It was originally published by Macmillan and Co., 1934, and re-edited in the "Prion Lost Treasures," London, 1996.

CASE 3

Heineken

In January 2011, Dutch brewer Heineken announced the acquisition of five breweries in Nigeria, as part of its plan to expand in one of the world's fastest growing beer markets and Africa's second largest. The purchase will raise the firm's market share to approximately 68%, giving it a substantial lead over other competitors. Nigeria's beer market has grown at an annual rate of about 9% over the past 10 years and growing sales in the country have provided a dominant share of Heineken's profits in Africa.

The move came on the heels of the acquisition of a Mexican brewer FEMSA Cervesa for about \$5.4 billion in 2010. The deal made the firm a stronger, more competitive player in the Latin American beer market, which has also become one of the most profitable and fastest growing markets in the world. It allowed the firm to add FEMSA's beer brands such as *Dos Equis, Sol,* and *Tecate* to its already vast array of offerings. Heineken had already been distributing these beers under license from the Mexican brewery in the US to cater to the growing Hispanic segment of the population.

However, the firm made its most high-profile recent acquisition in 2008 when it bought Scottish-based brewer Scottish & Newcastle, the brewer of well-known brands such as *Newcastle Brown Ale* and *Kronenbourg 1664.* Although the purchase had been made in partnership with Carlsberg, Heineken was able to gain control of Scottish & Newcastle's operations in several crucial European markets such as the UK, Ireland, Portugal, Finland, and Belgium, further solidifying Heineken's position as the leading brewer in Europe. But the Dutch-based firm also took over the Scottish brewer's ventures in far flung places such as the US and India.

These decisions to acquire brewers that operate in different parts of the world have been a part of a series of changes that the Dutch brewer has been making to raise its stature in the various markets and to respond to changes that are occurring in the global market for beer. Beer consumption has been declining in key markets as a result of tougher drunk-driving laws and a growing appreciation for wine. At the same time, the beer industry has become ever more competitive, as the largest brewers have been expanding across the globe through acquisitions of smaller regional and national players.

The need for change was clearly reflected in the appointment in October 2005 of Jean-Francois van Boxmeer as Heineken's first non-Dutch CEO. He was brought in to replace Thorny Ruys, who had decided to resign 18 months ahead of schedule because of his failure to show much improvement in performance. Prior to the appointment of Ruys in 2002, Heineken had been run by three generations of Heineken ancestors, whose portraits still adorn the dark-paneled office of the CEO in its Amsterdam headquarters. Like Ruys, van Boxmeer faces the challenge of preserving the firm's family-driven traditions, while trying to deal with threats that have never been faced before.

CONFRONTING A GLOBALIZING INDUSTRY

Heineken was one of the pioneers of an international strategy, using cross-border deals to expand its distribution of its *Heineken, Amstel,* or 170 other beer brands in more than 150 countries around the globe. For years, it has been picking up small brewers from several countries to add more brands and to get better access to new markets. From its roots on the outskirts of Amsterdam, the firm has evolved into one of the world's largest brewers, operating more than 125 breweries in over 70 countries in the world, claiming a little more than 8% of the worldwide market for beer.

In fact, the firm's flagship *Heineken* brand ranked second only to *Budweiser* in a global brand survey jointly undertaken by BusinessWeek and Interbrand a couple of years ago. The premier brand has achieved worldwide recognition according to Kevin Baker, director of alcoholic beverages at British market researcher Canadean Ltd. A US wholesaler recently asked a group of marketing students to identify an assortment of beer bottles that had been stripped of their labels. The stubby green *Heineken* container was the only one that incited instant recognition among the group.

But the beer industry has been undergoing significant change due to a furious wave of consolidation. Most of the bigger brewers have begun to acquire or merge with their competitors in foreign markets in order to become global players. Over the past decade, South African Breweries Plc acquired US-based Miller Brewing to become a major global brewer. US-based Coors linked with Canadian-based Molson in 2005, with their combined operations

Case developed by Jamal Shamsie, Michigan State University. Material has been drawn from published sources. To be used for purposes of classroom discussion.

allowing it to rise to a leading position among the world's biggest brewers. More recently, Belgium's Interbrew, Brazil's AmBev, and US-based Anheuser-Busch have all merged to become the largest global brewer with operations across most of the continents.

Many brewers have also expanded their operations without the use of such acquisitions. For example, Anheuser-Busch had bought equity stakes and struck partnership deals with Mexico's Grupo Modelo, China's Tsingtao, and Chile's CCU. Such cross-border deals have provided significant benefits to the brewing giants. To begin with, it has given them ownership of local brands that has propelled them into a dominant position in various markets around the world. Beyond this, acquisitions of foreign brewers can provide the firm with the manufacturing and distribution capabilities that they could use to develop a few global brands. "The era of global brands is coming," said Alan Clark, Budapest-based managing director of SABMiller Europe.[1]

Since its acquisition of Anheuser-Busch, InBev is planning to include *Budweiser* in its existing efforts to develop *Stella Artois, Brahma*, and *Becks* as global flagship brands. Each of these brands originated in different locations, with *Budweiser* coming from the US, *Stella Artois* coming from Belgium, *Brahma* from Brazil, and *Becks* from Germany. Similarly, the newly formed SABMiller has been attempting to develop the Czech brand *Pilsner Urquell* into a global brand. Exports of this pilsner have doubled since SAB acquired it in 1999. John Brock, the CEO of InBev, commented: "Global brands sell at significantly higher prices, and the margins are much better than with local beers."[2]

WRESTLING WITH CHANGE

Although the management of Heineken has moved away from the family for the first time, they have been well aware of the long-standing and well-established family traditions that would be difficult to change. Even with the appointment of nonfamily members to manage the firm, a little over half of the shares of Heineken are still owned by a holding company which is controlled by the family. With the death of Freddy Heineken, the last family member to head the Dutch brewer, control has passed to his only child and heir, Charlene de Carvalho, who has insisted on having a say in all of the major decisions.

But the family members were behind some of changes that were announced at the time of van Boxmeer's appointment that would support its next phase of growth as a global organization. As part of the plan, dubbed Fit 2 Fight, the Executive Board was cut down from five members to three, all of whom are relatively young. Along with van Boxmeer, the Board is made up of the firm's Chief Operating Officer and Chief Financial Officer. Later, this Board was further cut down to two members. The change is expected to assist the firm in thinking about the steps that it needs to take to win over younger customers across different markets whose tastes are still developing.

Heineken has also created management positions that would be responsible for five different operating regions and nine different functional areas. These positions were created to more clearly define different spheres of responsibility. Van Boxmeer argues that the new structure also provides incentives for people to be accountable for their performance: "There is more pressure for results, for achievement."[3] He claims the new structure has already encouraged more risk taking and boosted the level of energy within the firm.

The Executive Committee of Heineken was also cut down from 36 to 13 members in order to speed up the decision-making process. Besides the three members of the Executive Board, this management group consists of the managers who are responsible for the five different operating regions and six of the key functional areas. Van Boxmeer hopes that the reduction in the size of this group will allow the firm to combat the cumbersome consensus culture that has made it difficult for Heineken to respond swiftly to various challenges even as its industry has been experiencing considerable change.

Finally, all of the activities of Heineken have been overseen by a Supervisory Board, which currently consists of 10 members. Individuals that make up this board are drawn from different countries and cover a wide range of expertise and experience. They set up policies for the firm to use in making major decisions in its overall operations. Members of the Supervisory Board are rotated on a regular basis.

MAINTAINING A PREMIUM POSITION

For decades, Heineken has been able to rely upon the success of its flagship *Heineken* brand, which has enjoyed a leading position among premium beers in many markets around the world. It had been the best-selling imported beer in the US for several decades, giving it a steady source of revenues and profits from the world's biggest market. But by the late 1990s, *Heineken* had lost its 65-year-old leadership among imported beers in the US to Group Modelo's *Corona*. The Mexican beer has been able to reach out to the growing Hispanic Americans who represent one of the fastest growing segments of beer drinkers.

Furthermore, the firm was also concerned that *Heineken* was being perceived as an obsolete brand by many young drinkers. John A. Quelch, a professor at Harvard Business School who has studied the beer industry, said of Heineken: "It's in danger of becoming a tired, reliable, but unexciting brand."[4] The firm has therefore been working hard to increase awareness of their flagship brand among younger drinkers. It launched a video called *The Entrance* as part of a global campaign for Heineken which premiered on the firm's Facebook fan page at the end of 2010 and then become a major success on YouTube. The average age of the Heineken drinker has been reduced from about 40 in the mid-1990s to about 30 as a result of such efforts.

The firm has recently introduced a light beer, Heineken Premium Light, to target the growing market for such beers in the US. In 2010, Heineken also began to roll out a new design for the Heineken bottle that will be used across all 170 countries where it is sold. The firm has also introduced Heineken in other new forms of packaging. It has achieved some success with a portable draught beer system called DraughtKeg. About 20 glasses of beer can be dispensed from this mini keg. A BeerTender system, which keeps kegs fresh for several weeks once they have been tapped, also continues to grow in sales.

At the same time, Heineken has also been pushing on other brands that would reduce its reliance on its core *Heineken* brand. It has already achieved considerable success with *Amstel Light* which has become the leading imported light beer in the US and has been selling well in many other countries. But many of the other brands that it carries are strong local brands that it has added through its string of acquisitions of smaller breweries around the globe. It has managed to develop a relatively small but loyal base of consumers by promoting some of these as specialty brands, such as *Murphy's Irish Red* and *Moretti*.

Finally, Heineken has been stepping up its marketing to Hispanics, who account for one-quarter of US sales. It obtained a license from FEMSA Cervesa to market and distribute its popular brands which include *Tecate* and *Dos Equis* within the US. Benj Steinman, publisher and editor of the Beer Marketer's Insight newsletter, claims that the deal will give a tremendous boost to Heineken. "This gives Heineken a commanding share of the US import business and . . . gives them a bigger presence in the Southwest . . . and better access to Hispanic consumers," he stated.[5] In 2010, the firm decided to acquire the Mexican firm, allowing Heineken to add its brand to its growing portfolio of beers.

Above all, Heineken wants to maintain its leadership in the premium beer industry, which represents the most profitable segment of the beer business. In this category, the firm's brands face competition in the US from domestic beers such as Anheuser's *Budweiser Select* and imported beers such as InBev's *Stella Artois*. Although premium brews often have slightly higher alcohol content than standard beers, they are developed through a more exclusive positioning of the brand. This allows the firm to charge a higher price for these brands. A six-pack of *Heineken,* for example, costs $10, versus around $7 for a six-pack of *Budweiser*. Furthermore, Just-drinks.com, a London-based online research service, estimates that the market for premium beer will expand considerably to $230 billion by 2012.

BUILDING A GLOBAL PRESENCE

Van Boxmeer is well aware of the need for Heineken to use its brands to build upon its existing stature across global markets. In spite of its formidable presence in markets around the world, Heineken has failed to match the recent moves of formidable competitors such as Belgium's InBev and UK's SABMiller, which have grown significantly through mega acquisitions. In large part, it is assumed that the firm has been reluctant to make such acquisitions because of the dilution of family control.

For many years, Heineken had limited itself to snapping up small national brewers such as Italy's Moretti to Spain's Cruzcampo that have provided it with small, but profitable avenues for growth. In 1996, for example, Heineken had acquired Fischer, a small French brewer, whose *Desperados* brand has been quite successful in niche markets. Similarly, *Paulaner,* a wheat beer that the firm picked up in Germany a few years ago, has been making inroads into the US market.

But as other brewers have been reaching out to make acquisitions from all over the globe, Heineken has been running the risk of falling behind its more aggressive rivals. To deal with this growing challenge, the firm has broken out of its play-it-safe corporate culture to make a few big deals. In 2003, Heineken spent $2.1 billion to acquire BBAG, a family-owned company based in Linz, Austria. Because of BBAG's extensive presence in Central Europe, Heineken has become the biggest beer maker in seven countries across Eastern Europe. The more recent acquisition of Scottish & Newcastle similarly reinforced the firm's dominance in Western Europe.

At the same time, Heineken has done major acquisitions in other parts of the world. Its recent acquisitions in Nigeria and Mexico have allowed it to build its position in these growing markets. The firm has also made an aggressive push into Russia with the acquisition of mid-sized brewing concerns. Through several acquisitions since 2002, Russia has become one of Heineken's largest markets by volume. Heineken now ranks as the third-largest brewer in Russia, behind Sweden's Baltic Beverages Holding and InBev.

Rene Hooft Graafland, the company's Chief Financial Officer, has stated that Heineken will continue to participate in the consolidation of the $460 billion global retail beer industry, by targeting many different markets around the world. During the last decade, the firm has also added several labels to Heineken's shelf, pouncing on brewers in far flung places like Belarus, Panama, Egypt, and Kazakhstan. In Egypt, Ruys bought a majority stake in Al Ahram Beverages Co. and hopes to use the Cairo-based brewer's fruit-flavored, nonalcoholic malts as an avenue into other Muslim countries.

A BREAK FROM THE PAST?

The recent acquisitions in different parts of the world—Africa, Latin America, and Europe—represent an important step in Heineken's quest to build upon its existing global stature. In fact, most analysts had expected that van Boxmeer and his team would make efforts to continue to build Heineken into a powerful global competitor. Without providing any specific details, Graafland, the firm's CFO, did make it clear that the firm's management would take initiatives which would drive long-term growth. In his own words: "We are positive that the momentum in the company and trends will continue."[6]

Upon taking over the helm of Heineken, van Boxmeer had also announced that he would have to work on the company's culture in order to accelerate the speed of decision making. This led many people both inside and outside the firm to expect that the new management would try to break loose from the conservative style that has resulted from the family's tight control. Instead, the affable 46-year-old Belgian has indicated that he is trying to focus on changes to the firm's decision-making process rather to make any drastic shifts in its existing culture.

Van Boxmeer's devotion to the firm is quite evident. Heineken's first non-Dutch CEO spent 20 years working his way up within the firm. Even his cufflinks are silver miniatures of a Heineken bottle top and opener. "We are in the logical flow of history," he recently explained. "Every time you have a new leader you have a new kind of vision. It is not radically different, because you are defined by what your company is and what your brands are."[7]

Furthermore, van Boxmeer seems quite comfortable working with the family-controlled structure. "Since 1952 history has proved it is the right concept," he stated about the current ownership structure. "The whole business about family restraint on us is absolutely untrue. Without its spirit and guidance, the company would not have been able to build a world leader."[8]

TABLE 1 FINANCIAL STATEMENTS (IN MILLIONS OF EUROS)

	2010	2009	2008	2007	2006
Revenue	16,133	14,701	14,319	12,564	11,829
EBIT	2,476	1,757	1,080	1,528	1,832
Net Profit	1,436	1,018	347	807	1,211
	2010	2009	2008	2007	2006
Assets	26,549	20,180	20,563	12,968	12,997
Liabilities	16,321	14,533	15,811	7,022	7,477
Equity	10,228	5,647	4,752	5,946	5,520

Source: Heineken.

TABLE 2 GEOGRAPHICAL BREAKDOWN (IN MILLIONS OF EUROS)

	2009	2008	2007
Western Europe	8,432	7,661	5,450
Central & Eastern Europe	3,200	3,687	3,686
Americas	1,541	1,566	2,043
Africa & Middle East	1,817	1,774	1,416
Asia Pacific	305	279	597

Source: Heineken.

TABLE 3 SIGNIFICANT HEINEKEN BRANDS IN VARIOUS MARKETS

US	Heineken, Amstel Light, Paulaner[1], Moretti
Netherlands	Heineken, Amstel, Lingen's Blond, Murphy's Irish Red
France	Heineken, Amstel, Buckler[2], Desperados[3]
Italy	Heineken, Amstel, Birra Moretti
Spain	Heineken, Amstel, Cruzcampo, Buckler
Poland	Heineken, Krolewskie, Kujawiak, Zywiec
China	Heineken, Tiger, Reeb*
Singapore	Heineken, Tiger, Anchor, Baron's
Kazakhstan	Heineken, Amstel, Tian Shan
Egypt	Heineken, Birell, Meister, Fayrouz[2]
Israel	Heineken, Maccabee, Gold Star*
Nigeria	Heineken, Amstel Malta, Maltina, Gulder
Panama	Heineken, Soberana, Crystal, Panama

*Minority interest
[1]Wheat beer
[2]Nonalcoholic beer
[3]Tequila-flavored beer

TABLE 4 LEADING BREWERS (RANKED BY 2009 ANNUAL SALES, IN MILLIONS OF US DOLLARS)

1. Anheuser-Busch InBev, Leuven, Belgium	$36,758
2. SAB Miller, London, UK	$26,350
3. Heineken, Amsterdam, the Netherlands	$21,061
4. Kirin Holdings*, Tokyo, Japan	$19,695
5. Asahi, Tokyo, Japan	$15,824
6. FEMSA, Monterrey, Mexico	$11,435
7. Carlsberg, Copenhagen, Denmark	$11,400
8. Group Modelo, Mexico City, Mexico	$6,257
9. Molson Coors Brewing, Denver, US	$6,191
10. Foster's Group, Melbourne, Australia	$3,826

Source: Beverage World.
*Includes sales of soft drinks

CASE 4

McDonald's

McDonald's announced in January 2011 that its earnings for the fourth quarter in the previous year rose 2.1% in spite of a slowdown in December due to severe weather in the US and Europe. The fast-food giant's same-store sales rose 5% globally and 4.4% in the US from the same period in the prior year. McDonald's attributed these fourth-quarter gains to its increasingly diverse menu as well as its longer store-operating hours.

Part of McDonald's growth has come from the introduction of specialty beverages that are offered in its McCafes. During 2010, the firm began to offer ice-cold frappes and fruit smoothies, which have been quite successful. Expanding into pricier drinks has helped boost the average spent by each customer and lured them to its outlets for snacks during slower parts of the day. McDonald's President and Chief Operating Officer Don Thompson told analysts that sales of frappes and smoothies have been "blowing away the high-end projections."[1] In addition, the introduction of espresso-based drinks has made coffee 5% of total sales, double of what they were in 2006.

On the whole, however, analysts have attributed the continued success of McDonald's to the "Plan to Win" as first outlined by James R. Cantalupo in 2003 after overexpansion caused the chain to lose focus. The core of the plan was to increase sales at existing locations by improving the menu, refurbishing the outlets, and extending hours. The firm also began to add snacks and drinks, two of the few areas where restaurant sales are still growing. "We do so well because our strategies have been so well planned out," said the firm's CEO Jim Skinner in an interview.[2]

McDonald's is aware that it is facing a rapidly fragmenting market, where consumers are looking for much healthier and even more exotic foods. Many analysts therefore believe that the chain must continue to work on its turnaround strategy in order to meet these challenges. But they acknowledge that the firm has pushed hard to transform itself and they are encouraged by the results that it has achieved over the last eight years. "They have experienced a comeback the likes of which has been pretty unprecedented," said Bob Golden, executive vice-president of Technomic, a food service consultancy. "When restaurants start to slide, it really takes a lot to turn them around."[3]

At the same time, Skinner has been monitoring pricing in order to make sure the menu stays affordable without hurting its profit margins. Even as it continues to wrestle with cost increases, McDonald's has maintained the pricing on its Dollar Menu, which generates almost 15% of total sales. In December 2008, McDonald's did decide to replace its $1 double cheeseburger with the McDouble, a similar burger that is less expensive to make because it has less cheese. Steven Kron, an analyst with Goldman Sachs, emphasized the attractiveness of the firm's affordable Dollar Menu: "When people are seeking value, these guys have a very powerful component."[4]

EXPERIENCING A DOWNWARD SPIRAL

Since it was founded more than 50 years ago, McDonald's has been defining the fast-food business. It provided millions of Americans their first jobs even as it changed their eating habits. It rose from a single outlet in a nondescript Chicago suburb to become one of the largest chain of outlets spread around the globe. But it gradually began to run into various problems which began to slowdown its sales growth.

This decline could be attributed in large part to a drop in McDonald's once-vaunted service and quality since its expansion in the 1990s, when headquarters stopped grading franchises for cleanliness, speed, and service. By the end of the decade, the chain ran into more problems because of the tighter labor market. McDonald's began to cut back on training as it struggled hard to find new recruits, leading to a dramatic falloff in the skills of its employees. According to a 2002 survey by market researcher Global Growth Group, McDonald's came in third in average service time behind Wendy's and sandwich shop Chick-fil-A Inc.

McDonald's also began to fail consistently with its new product introductions, such as the low-fat McLean Deluxe and Arch Deluxe burgers, both of which were meant to appeal to adults. It did no better with its attempts to diversify beyond burgers, often because of problems with the product development process. Consultant Michael Seid, who manages a franchise consulting firm in West Hartford, pointed out that McDonald's offered a pizza that didn't fit through the drive-through window and salad shakers that

Case developed by Jamal Shamsie, Michigan State University. Material has been drawn from published sources. To be used for purposes of class discussion.

were packed so tightly that dressing couldn't flow through them.

In 1998, after McDonald's posted its first-ever decline in annual earnings, CEO Michael R. Quinlan was forced out and replaced by Jack M. Greenberg, a 16-year veteran of the firm. Greenberg did try to cut back on McDonald's expansion as he tried to deal with some of the growing problems. But his efforts to deal with the decline of McDonald's were slowed down by his acquisition of other fast-food chains such as Chipotle Mexican Grill and Boston Market.

On December 5, 2002, after watching McDonald's stock slide 60% in three years, the board ousted Greenberg. He had lasted little more than two years. His short tenure had been marked by the introduction of 40 new menu items, none of which caught on big, and the purchase of a handful of non-burger chains, none of which helped the firm to sell more burgers. Indeed, his critics say that by trying so many different things and executing them poorly Greenberg allowed the burger business to continue with its decline. According to Los Angeles franchisee Reggie Webb: "We would have been better off trying fewer things and making them work."[5]

PINNING HOPES ON A NEW LEADER

By the beginning of 2003, consumer surveys were indicating that McDonald's was headed for serious trouble. Measures for the service and quality of the chain were continuing to fall, dropping far behind those of its rivals. In order to deal with its deteriorating performance, the firm decided to bring back retired Vice-Chairman James R. Cantalupo, 59, who had overseen McDonald's successful international expansion in the 1980s and 1990s. Cantalupo, who had retired only a year earlier, was perceived to be the only candidate with the necessary qualifications, despite shareholder sentiment for an outsider. The board had felt that it needed someone who knew the company well and could move quickly to turn things around.

Cantalupo realized that McDonald's often tended to miss the mark on delivering the critical aspects of consistent, fast, and friendly service, and an all-around enjoyable experience for the whole family. He understood that its franchisees and employees alike needed to be inspired as well as retrained on their role in putting the smile back into McDonald's experience. When Cantalupo and his team laid out their turnaround plan in 2003, they stressed upon getting the basics of service and quality right, in part by reinstituting a tough "up or out" grading system that would kick out underperforming franchisees. "We have to rebuild the foundation. It's fruitless to add growth if the foundation is weak," said Cantalupo.[6]

To begin with, Cantalupo cut back on the opening of new outlets, focusing instead on generating more sales from its existing outlets. In fact, he shifted his emphasis to obtaining most of the growth in revenues to come from an increase in sales in the over 30,000 outlets that are already operating around the world. In part, McDonald's tried to draw more customers through the introduction of new products. The chain has had a positive response to its increased emphasis on healthier foods, led by a revamped line of fancier salads. The revamped menu was promoted through a new worldwide ad slogan "I'm loving it," which was delivered by pop idol Justin Timberlake through a set of MTV style commercials.

But the biggest success for the firm came in the form of McGriddles breakfast sandwich which was launched nationwide in June 2003. The popular new offering consisted of a couple of syrup-drenched pancakes, stamped with the Golden Arches, which acted as the top and bottom of the sandwich to hold eggs, cheese, sausage, and bacon in three different combinations. McDonald's has estimated that the new breakfast addition has been bringing in about one million new customers every day.

With his efforts largely directed at a turnaround strategy for McDonald's, Cantalupo decided to divest the non-burger chains that his predecessor had acquired. Collectively lumped under the Partner Brands, these have consisted of Chipotle Mexican Grill and Boston Market. The purpose of these acquisitions had been to find new growth and to offer the best franchises new expansion opportunities. But these acquired businesses had not fueled much growth and had actually posted considerable losses in recent years.

STRIVING FOR HEALTHIER OFFERINGS

As Skinner took over the reins of McDonald's in late 2004, he expressed his commitment to Cantalupo's plans to pursue various avenues for growth. But Skinner felt that one of his top priorities was to deal with the growing concerns about the unhealthy image of McDonald's, given the rise of obesity in the US. These concerns were highlighted in the popular documentary, *Super Size Me*, made by Morgan Spurlock. Spurlock vividly displayed the health risks that were posed by a steady diet of food from the fast-food chain. With a rise in awareness of the high fat content of most of the products offered by McDonald's, the firm was also beginning to face lawsuits from some of its loyal customers.

In response to the growing health concerns, one of the first steps taken by McDonald's was to phase out supersizing by the end of 2004. The supersizing option allowed customers to get a larger order of French fries and a bigger soft drink by paying a little extra. McDonald's has also announced that it intends to start providing nutrition information on the packaging of its products. The information will be easy to read and will tell customers about the calories, fat, protein, carbohydrates, and sodium that are in each product. Finally, McDonald's has also begun to remove the artery-clogging trans-fatty acids from the oil that it uses to make its french fries.

But Skinner was also trying to push out more offerings that are likely to be perceived by customers to be healthier. McDonald's has continued to build upon its chicken offerings using white meat with products such as Chicken Selects. It has also placed a great deal of emphasis upon its new salad offerings. Although the firm had failed to attract many customers in the past with its salads, McDonald's carried out extensive experiments and tests with its new premium versions. It chose higher quality ingredients, from a variety of lettuces and tasty cherry tomatoes to sharper cheeses and better cuts of meat. It offered a choice of *Newman's Own* dressings, a well-known higher-end brand.

McDonald's has also been trying to include more fruits and vegetables in its well-known and popular Happy Meals. In many locations, the firm is offering apple slices called Apple Dippers in place of French fries in the children's Happy Meal. The addition of fruits and vegetables has raised the firm's operating costs, because these are more expensive to ship and store because of their more perishable nature. But Skinner believes that the firm had to push more heavily on fruits and salads. "Salads have changed the way people think of our brand," said Wade Thoma, vice president for menu development in the US. "It tells people that we are very serious about offering things people feel comfortable eating."[7]

The current rollout of new beverages, highlighted by new coffee-based drinks, represents the chain's biggest menu expansion in almost three decades. Under a plan to add a McCafe section to all of its nearly 14,000 US outlets, McDonald's has been offering lattes, cappuccinos, ice-blended frappes, and fruit-based smoothies to its customers. "In many cases, they're now coming for the beverage, whereas before they were coming for the meal," said Lee Renz, the firm's vice president who is responsible for the rollout.[8]

REVAMPING THE OUTLETS

As part of its turnaround strategy, McDonald's has also been selling off the outlets that it owned. More than 75% of its outlets are now in the hands of franchisees and other affiliates. Skinner is now working with the franchisees to address the look and feel of many of the chain's aging stores. Without any changes to their décor, the firm is likely to be left behind by other more savvy fast-food and drink retailers. The firm is in the midst of pushing harder to refurbish—or reimage—all of its outlets around the world. "People eat with their eyes first," said President and COO Don Thompson. "If you have a restaurant that is appealing, contemporary, and relevant both from the street and interior, the food tastes better."[9]

The reimaging concept was first tried in France in 1996 by Dennis Hennequin, now president of McDonald's Europe, who felt that the effort was essential to revive the firm's sagging sales. "We were hip 15 years ago, but I think we lost that," he said.[10] McDonald's is now applying the reimaging concept to its outlets around the world, with a budget of more than half of its total annual capital expenditures. In the US, the changes cost an average of $150,000 per restaurant, a cost that is shared with the franchisees when the outlet is not company owned.

One of the prototype interiors being tested out by McDonald's has curved counters with surfaces painted in bright colors. In one corner, a touch-activated screen allows customers to punch in orders without queuing. The interiors can feature armchairs and sofas, modern lighting, large television screens, and even wireless internet access. The firm is also trying to develop new features for its drive-through customers, which account for 65% of all transactions in the US. They include music aimed at queuing vehicles and a wall of windows on the drive-through side of the restaurant allowing customers to see meals being prepared from their cars.

The chain has even been developing McCafes inside its outlets next to the usual fast-food counter. The McCafe concept originated in Australia in 1993 and has been rolled out in many restaurants around the world. McDonald's has just begun to introduce the concept to the US as it refurbishes many of its existing outlets. In fact, part of the refurbishment has focused on the installation of a specialty beverage platform across all US outlets. The cost of installing this equipment is running at about $100,000 per outlet, with McDonald's subsidizing part of this expense.

Eventually, all McCafes will offer espresso-based coffee, gourmet coffee blends, fresh baked muffins, and high-end desserts. Customers will be able to consume these while they relax in soft leather chairs listening to jazz, big band, or blues music. Commenting on this significant expansion of offerings, Marty Brochstein, executive editor of *The Licensing Letter* said: "McDonald's wants to be seen as a lifestyle brand, not just a place to go to have a burger."[11]

A NEW AND IMPROVED MCDONALD'S?

Even though Skinner's efforts to transform McDonald's have led to improvements in its sales and profits, there are questions about the future of the fast-food chain. The firm is trying out a variety of strategies in order to increase its appeal to different segments of the market. Through the adoption of a mix of outlet décor and menu items, McDonald's is trying to target young adults, teenagers, children, and families. In so doing, it must ensure that it must not alienate any one of these groups in its efforts to reach out to the other. Its new marketing campaign, anchored around the catchy phrase "I'm loving it," takes on different forms in order to target each of the groups that it is seeking.

Larry Light, the head of global marketing at McDonald's since 2002, insists that the firm has to exploit its brand through pushing it in many different directions. The brand can be positioned differently in different locations, at different times of the day and to target different customer segments. In large urban centers, McDonald's can target young adults for breakfast with its gourmet coffee, egg sandwiches, and fat-free muffins. Light explains the adoption of such as multiformat strategy: "The days of mass-media marketing are over."[12]

Nevertheless, the expansion of the menu beyond the staple of burgers and fries does raise some fundamental questions. Most significantly, it is not clear just how far McDonald's can stretch its brand while keeping all of its outlets under the traditional symbol of its golden arches. Chief financial officer Paull acknowledged that burgers continued to be the main draw for McDonald's. "There is no question that we make more money from selling hamburgers and cheeseburgers," he stated.[13]

Above all, Skinner is convinced that McDonald's must do whatever it can to make sure that it keeps its established customer base from bolting to the growing number of competitors such as the California-based In-N-Out chain. The long-term success of the firm may well depend on its ability to compete with rival burger chains. "The burger category has great strength," added David C. Novak, chairman and CEO of Yum! Brands, parent of KFC and Taco Bell. "That's America's food. People love hamburgers."[14]

TABLE 1
INCOME STATEMENT (IN MILLIONS OF DOLLARS)

	YEAR ENDING		
	Dec 31, 2010	**Dec 31, 2009**	**Dec 31, 2008**
Total Revenue	24,075	22,745	23,522
Gross Profit	9,637	8,792	8,639
Operating Income	7,473	6,841	6,332
EBIT	7,451	6,960	6,681
Net Income	4,946	4,551	4,313

Source: McDonald's.

TABLE 2
BALANCE SHEET (IN MILLIONS OF DOLLARS)

	YEAR ENDING		
	Dec 31, 2010	**Dec 31, 2009**	**Dec 31, 2008**
Current Assets	4,369	3,416	3,518
Total Assets	31,975	30,225	28,462
Current Liabilities	2,925	2,989	2,538
Total Liabilities	17,341	16,191	15,079
Stockholder Equity	14,634	14,034	13,383

Source: McDonald's.

TABLE 3
NUMBER OF OUTLETS (IN MILLIONS OF DOLLARS)

	COMPANY			
	Total	**Owned**	**Franchised**	**Affiliated**
2010	32,737	6,399	26,338	3,574
2009	32,478	6,262	26,216	4,036
2008	31,967	6,502	25,465	4,137
2007	31,377	6,906	20,505	3,966
2006	31,046	8,166	18,685	4,195

Source: McDonald's.

TABLE 4 DISTRIBUTION OF OUTLETS (IN MILLIONS OF DOLLARS)

	2010	2009	2008	2007	2006
US	14,027	13,980	13,918	13,862	13,774
Europe	6,969	6,785	6,628	6,480	6,403
Asia Pacific	8,424	8,488	8,255	7,938	7,822
Americas*	3,317	3,225	3,166	3,097	3,047

*Canada & Latin America
Source: McDonald's.

TABLE 5 BREAKDOWN OF REVENUES (IN MILLIONS OF DOLLARS)

	2010	2009	2008	2007	2006
US	8,116	7,043	8,048	7,906	7,464
Europe	9,569	9,273	9,923	8,926	7,638
Asia Pacific	5,065	4,337	4,231	3,599	3,053
Americas*	1,328	1,190	1,290	2,356	2,740

*Canada & Latin America
Source: McDonald's.

TABLE 6 McDONALD'S MILESTONES

1948	Brothers Richard and Maurice McDonald open the first restaurant in San Bernardino, California, which sells hamburgers, fries, and milk shakes.
1955	Ray A. Kroc, 52, opens his first McDonald's in Des Plaines, Illinois. Kroc, a distributor of milk shake mixers, figures he can sell a bundle of them if he franchises the McDonald's' business and install his mixers in the new stores.
1961	Six years later, Kroc buys out the McDonald brothers for $2.7 million.
1963	Ronald McDonald makes his debut as corporate spokes clown using future NBC-TV weatherman Willard Scott. During the year, the company also sells its 1-billionth burger.
1965	McDonald's stock goes public at $22.50 a share. It will split 12 times in the next 35 years.
1967	The first McDonald's restaurant outside the US opens in Richmond, British Columbia. Today there are 31,108 McDonald's in 118 countries.
1968	The Big Mac, the first extension of McDonald's basic burger, makes its debut and is an immediate hit.
1972	McDonald's switches to the frozen variety for its successful french fries.
1974	Fred L. Turner succeeds Kroc as CEO. In the midst of a recession, the minimum wage rises to $2 per hour, a big cost increase for McDonald's, which is built around a model of young, low-wage workers.
1975	The first drive-through window is opened in Sierra Vista, Arizona.
1979	McDonald's responds to the needs of working women by introducing Happy Meals. A burger, some fries, a soda, and a toy give working moms a break.
1987	Michael R. Quinlan becomes chief executive.
1991	Responding to the public's desire for healthier foods, McDonald's introduces the low-fat McLean Deluxe burger. It flops and is withdrawn from the market. Over the next few years, the chain will stumble several times trying to spruce up its menu.
1992	The company sells its 90-billionth burger, and stops counting.
1996	In order to attract more adult customers, the company launches its Arch Deluxe, a "grownup" burger with an idiosyncratic taste. Like the low-fat burger, it also falls flat.
1997	McDonald's launches Campaign 55, which cuts the cost of a Big Mac to $0.55. It is a response to discounting by Burger King and Taco Bell. The move, which prefigures similar price wars in 2002, is widely considered a failure.
1998	Jack M. Greenberg becomes McDonald's fourth chief executive. A 16-year company veteran, he vows to spruce up the restaurants and their menu.
1999	For the first time, sales from international operations outstrip domestic revenues. In search of other concepts, the company acquires Aroma Cafe, Chipotle, Donatos, and, later, Boston Market.
2000	McDonald's sales in the US peak at an average of $1.6 million annually per restaurant, a figure that has not changed since. It is, however, still more than at any other fast-food chain.
2001	Subway surpasses McDonald's as the fast-food chain with the most US outlets. At the end of the year, it had 13,247 stores, 148 more than McDonald's.
2002	McDonald's posts its first-ever quarterly loss, of $343.8 million. The stock drops to around $13.50, down 40% from five years ago.
2003	James R. Cantalupo returns to McDonald's in January as CEO. He immediately pulls back from the company's 10–15% forecast for per-share earnings growth.
2004	Charles H. Bell takes over the firm after the sudden death of Cantalupo. He states he will continue with the strategies that have been developed by his predecessor.
2005	Jim Skinner takes over as CEO after Bell announces retirement for health reasons.
2006	McDonald's launches specialty beverages, including coffee-based drinks.

Source: McDonald's.

CASE 5

Procter & Gamble

Even though Procter & Gamble has already claimed the status of the world's biggest maker of consumer products, CEO Robert McDonald claimed that there were still plenty of opportunities for the firm to grow its business. "There's plenty of room to keep growing," he told investors at the company's headquarters in Cincinnati.[1] In fact, McDonald expected P&G to achieve a 3%–5% net sales growth in the fiscal year that ended in June 2011. The firm had also just announced that it had increased or maintained its market share in most product categories in all regions of the world for the first time in 11 quarters.

These results are impressive, given that P&G had posted its first annual sales decline since 2001 when McDonald took over the firm in the summer of 2009. In order to achieve these results, the firm has cut prices on many of its products as consumers have cut back on their spending to cope with the economic downturn. At the same time, P&G has also been trying to maintain its profits by promoting the features of their higher priced brands. The firm points to the success of Gillette's *Fusion ProGlide* razors as evidence of the willingness of consumers to continue to buy premium products.

P&G has also decided to pursue growth by embarking on its most ambitious plan to expand into emerging markets such as Brazil and India, which have long been dominated by Unilever and Colgate-Palmolive. "We're late to those markets," said McDonald, who spent much of his career overseas. "As a result, we've got to do things smarter."[2] Although emerging markets have accounted for about 30% of P&G's annual sales, they have delivered more than 50% of its recent growth.

Like his predecessor, A.G. Lafley, McDonald has been working hard to push out new products and build upon on P&G's well-known brands. The firm has managed to increase its number of "superbrands," each of which represents global annual sales of over $1 billion. In part by its acquisitions of firms such as Clairol and Gillette, the firm has increased the number of such brands to 23 over the past decade. P&G continues to carefully build upon each of these brands, relying upon innovation to keep adding new products to expand each of them to reach out to more and more customers.

But McDonald has been developing many more ideas about how to make P&G relevant in the 21st century. He has continued to try to shift the focus of his firm away from its traditional reliance on household care. P&G has been making aggressive inroads into health and beauty products, making these areas account for the majority of the firm's sales and profits. Over the past year, the firm has even branched out into services by using franchises to enter into car wash and dry cleaning businesses. In pushing for these changes, P&G is undertaking the most sweeping transformation of the company since it was founded by William Procter and James Gamble in 1837 as a maker of soap and candles.

AN ATTEMPTED TURNAROUND

For most of its long history, P&G has been one of America's preeminent companies. The firm has developed several well-known brands such as *Tide*, one of the pioneers in laundry detergents, which was launched in 1946 and *Pampers*, the first disposable diaper, which was introduced in 1961. P&G built its brands through its innovative marketing techniques. In the 1880s, it was one of the first companies to advertise nationally. Later on, P&G invented the soap opera by sponsoring *Ma Perkins* when radio caught on and *Guiding Light* when television took hold. In the 1930s, P&G was the first firm to develop the idea of brand management, setting up marketing teams for each brand and urging them to compete against each other.

But by the 1990s, P&G was in danger of becoming another Eastman Kodak or Xerox, a once-great company that might have lost its way. Sales on most of its 18 top brands were slowing as it was being outhustled by more focused rivals such as Kimberly-Clark and Colgate-Palmolive. The only way P&G kept profits growing was by cutting costs, which would hardly work as a strategy for the long term. At the same time, the dynamics of the industry were changing as power shifted from manufacturers to massive retailers. Retailers such as Wal-Mart were starting to use their size to try and get better deals from P&G, further squeezing its profits.

In 1999, P&G decided to bring in Durk I. Jager to try and make the big changes that were obviously needed to

Case developed by Jamal Shamsie, Michigan State University. Material has been drawn from published sources. To be used for purposes of class discussion.

get P&G back on track. But the moves that he made generally misfired, sinking the firm into deeper trouble. He introduced expensive new products that never caught on while letting existing brands drift. He also put in place a company-wide reorganization that left many employees perplexed and preoccupied. During the fiscal year when he was in charge, earnings per share showed an anemic rise of just 3.5%, much lower than in previous years. And during that time, the share price slid 52%, cutting P&G's total market capitalization by $85 billion. The effects were widely felt within the firm, where employees and retirees hold about 20% of the stock.

But Jager's greatest failing was his scorn for the family. Jager, a Dutchman who had joined P&G overseas and worked his way to corporate headquarters, pitted himself against the P&G culture. Susan E. Arnold, president of P&G's previous beauty and feminine care division, said that Jager tried to make the employees turn against the prevailing culture, contending that it was burdensome and insufferable. Some go-ahead employees even wore buttons that read "Old World/New World" to express disdain for P&G's past.

A RENEWED EMPHASIS ON PEOPLE

In 2000, Alan G. Lafley received a call from John Pepper, a former CEO who was a board member. He was asked to take over the reins of P&G from Jager, representing a boardroom coup unprecedented in the firm's history. In a sense, Lafley, who had risen up through the ranks of P&G, had been preparing for this job his entire adult life. By the time he had taken charge, Lafley had developed a reputation as a boss who steps back to give his staff plenty of responsibility and to help shape decisions by asking a series of keen questions. As CEO, Lafley refrained from making any grand pronouncements on the future of P&G. Instead, he spent an inordinate amount of time patiently communicating to his employees about the types of changes that he wanted to see at P&G.

Lafley began his tenure by breaking down the walls between management and the employees. Since the 1950s, all of the senior executives at P&G used to be located on the eleventh floor at the firm's corporate headquarters. Lafley changed this setup, moving all five division presidents to the same floors as their staff. Then he turned some of the emptied space into a leadership training center. On the rest of the floor, he knocked down the walls so that the remaining executives, including himself, would share open offices.

Indeed, Lafley's charm offensive so disarmed most P&Gers that he was able to make drastic changes within the company. He replaced more than half of the company's top 30 managers, more than any P&G boss in memory, and trimmed its work force by as many as 9,600 jobs. And he moved more women into senior positions. In fact, Lafley skipped over 78 general managers with more seniority to name 42-year-old Deborah A. Henretta to head P&G's then-troubled North American baby-care division.

In fact, Lafley was simply recognizing the importance of people, particularly those in managerial roles at P&G. Back in 1947, Richard Dupree, who was CEO at the time, had said: "If you leave us our buildings and our brands, but take away our people, the company will fail."[3] For years, the firm has been known to dispatch line managers rather than human resource staffers to do much of its recruiting. For the few that get hired, their work life becomes a career long development process. At every level, P&G has a different "college" to train individuals and every department has its own "university." The general manager's college holds a week-long school term once a year when there are a handful of newly promoted managers.

P&G also maintains a comprehensive database of all of its more than 130,000 employees, each of which is tracked carefully through monthly and annual talent reviews. All managers are reviewed not only by their bosses but also by lateral managers who have worked with them, as well as on their own direct reports. Every February, one entire board meeting is devoted to reviewing the high-level executives, with the goal of coming up with at least three potential candidates for each of the 35–40 tops at the top of the firm, including that of the CEO. For those who might aspire to rise to the executive ranks, P&G tries to give them as broad an experience as possible. "If you train people to work in different countries and businesses, you develop a deep bench," said Moheet Nagrath, head of human resources.[4]

A NEW STRATEGIC FOCUS

Above all, Lafley had been intent on shifting the focus of P&G back to its consumers. At every opportunity that he got, he tried to drill his managers and employees to not lose sight of the consumer. He felt that P&G has often let technology dictate its new products rather than consumer needs. He wanted to see the firm work more closely with retailers, the place where consumers first see the product on the shelf. And he wanted to see much more concern with the consumer's experience at home.

Under McDonald, P&G has continued to place a tremendous amount of emphasis on the ability of its brands to serve the needs of consumers. Over the previous decade, the firm has updated all of its 200 brands by adding innovative new products. It has begun to offer devices that build on its core brands, such as *Tide StainBrush*, a battery powered brush for removing stains and *Mr. Clean AutoDry*, a water-pressure powered car cleaning system that dries without streaking. P&G has also begun to approach its brands more creatively. *Crest*, for example, which used to be marketed as a toothpaste brand, is now defined an oral care brand. The firm now sells *Crest*-branded toothbrushes and tooth whiteners.

Even in a tough economic climate, McDonald has been pushing even harder for P&G to continue to develop its brands by coming up with new ideas that would appeal to consumers. "There's nothing more important that we can do in these tough times than to keep our brands strong, to continue leading innovation and to win the consumer value equation every day," he told shareholders at the 2010 annual meeting.[5] In fact, McDonald insisted that P&G has introduced more new products over the past year than at any other time in his 30 years at the firm. That includes items like *Gillette* razors with a less irritating shave, *Crest* toothpaste with a sensitive shield, and *Downy* fabric softener that promises to keep smelling fresh for a week.

In order to ensure that P&G continues to come up with innovative ideas, McDonald has also been committed to a practice that was introduced by Lafley. The former CEO had confronted head-on the stubbornly held notion that everything must be invented within P&G, asserting that half of its new products should come from the outside. Under the new "Connect and Develop" model of innovation, the firm has begun to get almost 50% of its new product ideas from outside the firm. This can be compared to the 10% figure that existed at P&G when Lafley had taken charge.

A key element of P&G's strategy, however, has been to move the firm away from basic consumer products such as laundry detergents, which can be knocked off by private labels, to higher-margin products. This has been leading McDonald to focus even more strongly on the firm's beauty and personal care business. Under Lafley, P&G made costly acquisitions of Clairol, Wella, and Gillette to complement its *Cover Girl* and *Oil of Olay* brands. But P&G's most dramatic move has been to move into prestige fragrances through licenses with Hugo Boss, Gucci, and Dolce & Gabbana. Although the beauty products division now accounts for about the third of the firm's total revenues, its sales growth has begun to slowdown.

A REVOLUTION STILL IN THE MAKING

Even as P&G has been trying to build upon its well-known brands by pushing out new products, it is now moving into services through franchising. The idea to diversify beyond products came from FutureWorks, a unit that the firm set up to expand sales of its brands, particularly in saturated markets such as the United States. Four years ago, FutureWorks began considering franchise opportunities, looking for service industries where ownership was fragmented and consumers were not satisfied. It came up with several ideas, staring with car washes and dry cleaning. "I think service is yet an untapped area for us," said McDonald in an interview.[6]

The car washes build on *Mr. Clean*, P&G's popular cleaning product. The *Mr. Clean* line, in fact, now stretches from toilet bowl cleaners to do-it-yourself car-wash kits. In expanding the brand to car washes, the firm has worked hard to distinguish its outlets from others by offering additional services such as *Febreze* odor eliminators, lounges with Wi-Fi and big screen televisions, and spray guns that children can aim at cars passing through the wash. The firm has been expanding slowly, starting with a test market in Cincinnati, where P&G is based.

The firm is even more enthusiastic about its entry into dry-cleaning outlets that are named after *Tide*, its best-selling laundry detergent. P&G believes that consumers will be drawn to its franchise stores by the brand name and by the superior service. The stores will include drive-through services, 24-hour pickup, and environmentally benign cleaning methods. The firm also intends to infuse the stores and its dry-cleaning fluids with the scent of the brand that is cozily familiar to most US households. "It smelled really good in there," said a customer. "When I think of *Tide*, I have so many good feelings. I'm surprised that they didn't think of it sooner."[7]

P&G had tried an at-home dry-cleaning product during the late 1990s, which was eventually withdrawn because of lackluster sales. It had also opened dry-cleaning stores, called Juvian, in Atlanta, which were eventually closed. But the firm believed that it had learnt from these failures in the launch of its new franchise outlets. An early pilot store in Kansas generated more than $1 million in annual sales, four times the industry average.

In order to overcome its lack of franchising experience, P&G broke its decades-old practice of internal promotions to hire William Van Epps, who had managed franchising at Pepsico. "We're not stepping into this for spare change," said Nathan Estruth, vice president of FutureWorks. "We believe we can create a sizeable service business for P&G using the franchise business model as a platform across P&G brands."[8]

DAUNTING CHALLENGES

Since he has taken over from Lafley, McDonald pursued the same type of bold moves that he had initiated in order to remake P&G into a company that is admired, imitated, and uncommonly profitable. This has forced him to pay close attention to every aspect of the firm's strategy and organization. As a result of this, McDonald has introduced the concept of "purpose-inspired growth" which is meant to help P&G employees believe that they are not merely pushers of detergents and deodorants, but that they are helping to improve people's daily existence. "It's more than a noble idea," he proclaimed at the firm's 2010 analyst meeting.[9]

But analysts have pointed to the risk that P&G is taking with some of its recent moves, such as its aggressive push into beauty products, including fragrances. They have questioned the ability of a firm that uses a very methodological approach to make and sell mass market goods to be successful in a business that is known to be quirky and fickle. Unlike the conventional practice of established firms to keep trying to come up with brands, as older ones lose their cachet, P&G hopes to apply its brand development methods to sustain its beauty brands over time. "We need to find ways to do brand building," said Hartwig Langer, the firm's president of global prestige products.[10]

The firm is taking even bigger risks with its use of franchises to move into the service business. P&G has not considered using any partners to enter into a new area, despite the threats that it can pose to its carefully developed image. "It's much easier for a brand experience to happen with a service brand than a product brand," said Julia Beardwood, a partner of a consulting firm that has worked with P&G on many projects. "It's harder to have quality control."[11] But the firm insists that it is minimizing its risks by forcing its franchise owners to undertake five weeks of training and requiring some coaching for all of the employees of these outlets.

Above all, McDonald is aware that P&G must seek out new avenues for expansion. Finding new avenues to grow could be the only way to counter P&G's growing reliance on Wal-Mart. Former and current P&G employees say the discounter already accounts for about one-third of P&G's global sales. Meanwhile, the pressure from consumers and competitors to keep prices low will only increase. In a conference call with reporters, McDonald commented on the moves that P&G has been making to confront these challenges: "This is a period of what we would describe as continuity with change."[12]

TABLE 1
INCOME STATEMENT (IN MILLIONS OF DOLLARS)

	YEAR ENDING		
	June 30, 2010	**June 30, 2009**	**June 30, 2008**
Total revenue	78,938	76,694	83,503
Gross profit	41,019	38,004	42,808
Operating income	16,021	15,374	17,083
EBIT	15,993	15,771	317,545
Net income	12,736	13,436	12,075

Source: P&G.

TABLE 2
BALANCE SHEET (IN MILLIONS OF DOLLARS)

	YEAR ENDING		
	June 30, 2010	**June 30, 2009**	**June 30, 2008**
Current assets	18,782	21,905	24,515
Total assets	128,172	134,833	143,992
Current liabilities	24,282	30,901	30,958
Total liabilities	67,057	71,734	74,498
Stockholder equity	61,439	63,382	69,494

Source: P&G.

TABLE 3
BUSINESS SEGMENTS

	KEY PRODUCTS	**BILLION DOLLAR BRANDS**
Fabric care & home care	Air care, batteries, dish care, fabric care, surface care	Ace, Ariel, Dawn, Downy, Duracell, Gain, Tide
Baby care & family care	Baby wipes, bath tissue, diapers, facial tissue, paper towels	Bounty, Charmin, Pampers
Beauty	Cosmetics, deodorants, hair care, personal cleansing, Fragrances, skin care	Head & Shoulders, Olay, Pantene, Wella
Grooming	Blades and razors, face and shave products, home small appliances	Braun, Fusion, Gillette, Mach 3
Health care	Feminine care, oral care, personal health care	Always, Crest, Oral B
Snacks, coffee & pet care	Pet food, snacks	Iams, Pringles

Source: P&G.

TABLE 4
FINANCIAL BREAKDOWN (IN BILLIONS OF $)

	NET SALES		NET EARNINGS	
	2010	2009	2010	2009
Fabric care & home care	23.8	23.1	3.3	3.0
Baby care & family care	14.7	14.1	2.0	1.8
Beauty	19.5	18.9	2.7	2.6
Grooming	7.6	7.4	1.5	1.4
Health care	11.5	11.3	1.9	1.8
Snacks & pet care	3.1	3.1	0.3	0.2

Source: P&G.

TABLE 5
SIGNIFICANT INNOVATIONS

- Tide was the first heavy-duty laundry detergent
- Crest was the first fluoride toothpaste clinically proven to prevent tooth decay
- Downy was the first ultra-concentrated rinse-add fabric softener
- Pert Plus was the first 2-in-1 shampoo and conditioner
- Head & Shoulders was the first pleasant-to-use shampoo effective against dandruff
- Pampers was the first affordable, mass-marketed disposable diaper
- Bounty was the first three-dimensional paper towel
- Always was the first feminine protection pad with an innovative, dry-weave top sheet
- Febreze was the first fabric and air care product that actually removed odors from fabrics and the air
- Crest White Strips was the first patented in-home teeth whitening technology

Source: P&G.

CASE 6

QVC

On January 12, 2011 QVC announced that it had once again secured a top 10 spot in the annual NRF Foundation/American Express Customers' Choice survey. The survey asked more than 9,000 shoppers to identify the leading retailers who provide the very best customer service. "The QVC team is thrilled to be recognized as one of the 10 best customer service retailers in the country for the third year in a row," said Dan McDermott, QVC's senior vice president of customer services.[1] The NRF ranking represents only one of a number of customer service honors QVC received in recent weeks.

Since it was launched in 1986, QVC has rapidly grown to become the largest television shopping network. Although it entered the market a couple of years after rival Home Shopping Network, the channel has managed to build a leading position. By 2010, its reach had extended to over 98 million households. It regularly ships over 175 million packages annually to customers around the world, resulting in almost $7.4 million in sales. It sells to customers who watch its shows across the US, UK, Germany, Japan, and since 2010, also in Italy.

The success of QVC is largely driven by its popular television home shopping shows that feature a wide variety of eye-catching products, many of which are unique to the channel. It organizes product searches in cities all over the US in order to continuously find new offerings that can be pitched at customers. During these events, the firm has to screen hundreds of products in order to select those that it will offer. In one of its recent searches, QVC had to evaluate the appeal of products such as nail clippers that catch clippings, bicycle seats built for bigger bottoms, and novelty items shaped like coffins.

Thousands of entrepreneurs have used QVC's product searches over the years to try and sell their products on the popular home shopping channel. A chance to display their offerings to QVC's national TV audience can transform a one-person operation into a multibillion-dollar business. "The vendors who are our success stories for this past decade have done over $1 billion in sales on QVC over the past ten years," said Marilyn Montross, the channel's director of vendor relations.[2]

But QVC is also trying to entice new customers by battling a perception that direct-response TV retailers sell just hokey, flimsy, or kitschy goods. Its jewelry selection features prestigious brands such as Tacori, which is worn by TV stars. It offers clothing from couture designers such as Marc Bouwer, who has made clothing for Angelina Jolie and Halle Berry. And it has recently added exclusive products from reality stars such as Kim Kardashian and Rachel Zoe. Such vendors have introduced thousands to QVC, often through social media like Facebook and Twitter. "Rachel Zoe brings so many new customers it's staggering," said CEO Michael George.[3]

PURSUING A LEADING POSITION

QVC was founded by Joseph Segel in June 1986 and began broadcasting by November of the same year. In early 1986, Segel had tuned into the Home Shopping Network, which had been launched just two years earlier. He had not been particularly impressed with the crude programming and the down-market products of the firm. But Segel was convinced that another televised shopping network would have the potential to attract a large enough client base. He also felt that such an enterprise should be able to produce significant profits, because the operating expenses for a shopping network could be kept relatively low.

Over the next few months, Segel raised $30 million in start-up capital, hired several seasoned television executives, and launched his own shopping network. Operating out of headquarters that were located in West Chester, Pennsylvania, QVC offered 24-hour-a-day, seven-day-a-week television home shopping to consumers at home. By the end of its first year of operation, QVC had managed to extend its reach to 13 million homes by satellite and cable systems. About 700,000 viewers had already become customers, resulting in the shipping of 3 million orders. Its sales had already topped $100 million and the firm was actually able to show a small profit.

Segel attributed the instant success of his company to the potential offered by television shopping. "Television's combination of sight, sound and motion is the best way to sell a product. It is more effective than presenting a product in print or just putting the product on a store shelf," he stated. "The cost-efficiency comes from the cable distribution

This case was prepared by Jamal Shamsie, Michigan State University. Material has been drawn from published sources. To be used for purposes of class discussion.

system. It is far more economical than direct mail, print advertising, or traditional retail store distribution."[4]

In the fall of 1988, Segel acquired the manufacturing facilities, proprietary technology, and trademark rights of the Diamonique Corporation, which produced a wide range of simulated gemstones and jewelry that could be sold on the QVC's shows. Over the next couple of years, Segel expanded QVC by acquiring its competitors such as the Cable Value Network Shopping channel.

By 1993, QVC had overtaken Home Shopping Network to become the leading televised shopping channel in terms of sales and profits. Its reach extended to over 80% of all cable homes and to 3 million satellite dishes. Segel retired during the same year, passing control of the company to Barry Diller. Since then, QVC's sales have continued to grow at a substantial rate. As a result, it has consistently widened the gap between its sales and those of Home Shopping Network, which has remained its closest competitor.

STRIVING FOR RETAILING EXCELLENCE

Over the years, QVC had managed to establish itself as the world's preeminent virtual shopping mall that never closes. Its televised shopping channel has become a place where customers around the world can, and do, shop at any hour at the rate of more than five customers per second. It sold a wide variety of products, using a combination of description and demonstration by live program hosts. QVC is extremely selective in choosing its hosts, screening as many as 3,000 applicants annually in order to pick three. New hosts are trained for at least six months before they are allowed to get on a show. In addition, most of the products are offered on regularly scheduled shows, each of which is focused on a particular type of product and a well-defined market. Each of these shows typically lasts for one hour and is based on a theme such as *Now You're Cooking* or *Cleaning Solutions*.

QVC frequently entices celebrities such as clothing designers or book authors to appear live on special program segments in order to sell their own products. In order to prepare them to succeed, celebrities are given training on how to best pitch their offerings. On some occasions, customers are able to call in and have on-air conversations with program hosts and visiting celebrities. Celebrities are therefore often schooled in QVC's "backyard-fence" style, which means conversing with viewers the way they would chat with a friendly neighbor. "They're just so down-home, so it's like they're right in your living room demonstrating," said a long-time QVC customer.[5]

In spite of the folksy presentation, the sales are minutely managed. Behind the scenes, a producer scans nine television and computer screens to track sales of each featured items. "We track new orders per minute in increments of six seconds; we can look backward in time and see what it was that drove that spike," said Doug Rose, who oversees programming and marketing.[6] Hosts and guests are prompted to make adjustments in their pitch that might increase sales. A beauty designer was recently asked to rub an eyeliner on her hand, which immediately led to a surge of new orders.

QVC's themed programs are telecast live 24 hours a day, seven days a week, to millions of households worldwide. The shopping channel transmits its programming live from its central production facilities in Pennsylvania through uplinks to a satellite. The representatives who staff QVC's four call centers, which handled more than 180 million calls last year, are well trained to take orders.

Of all the orders placed with QVC, more than 90% are shipped within 48 hours from one of their distribution centers. The distribution centers have a combined floor space of 4.6 million square feet, which is equivalent to the size of 103 football fields. Finally, everyone at QVC works hard to make sure that every item works as it should before it is shipped and that its packaging will protect it during the shipping process. "Nothing ships unless it is quality-inspected first," said Paul Day, the logistics manager for QVC. "Since our product is going business-to-consumer, there's no way to fix or change a product-related problem."[7]

SEARCHING FOR PROFITABLE PRODUCTS

More than 100 experienced, informed buyers comb the world on a regular basis to search for new products to launch on QVC. The shopping channel concentrates on unique products that can be demonstrated on live television. Furthermore, the price of these products must be high enough for viewers to justify the additional shipping and handling charge. Over the course of a typical year, QVC carries more than 60,000 products. As many as 2,000 items are typically offered in any given week, of which about 15% are new products for the network. QVC's suppliers range from some of the world's biggest companies to small entrepreneurial enterprises.

All new products must, however, pass through stringent tests that are carried out by QVC's in-house Quality Assurance Lab. In many cases, this inspection process is carried out manually by the firm's employees. Only 15% of the products pass the firm's rigorous quality inspection on first try and as many as a third are never offered to the public because they fail altogether. In addition, Jeffrey Rayport, author of a book on customer service, states that "QVC staff look for a product that is complex enough—or interesting enough—that the host can talk about it on air."[8]

About a third of QVC's sales come from broadly available national brands. The firm has been able to build trust among its customers in large part through the offering of these well-known brands. QVC also relies upon promotional campaigns with a variety of existing firms for another third of its sales. It has made deals with firms ranging from Dell, Target, and Bath & Body Works for special limited time promotional offerings. But QVC has been most successful with products that are exclusively sold on QVC or not readily available through other distribution channels. Although such products account for another third of its sales, the firm has been able to earn higher margins with these proprietary products, many of which come from firms that are either start-ups or new entrants into the US market.

Most vendors are attracted to QVC because they reap higher profits selling through their channel than they would make by selling through physical stores. Stores typically require vendors to help to train or pay the sales force and participate in periodic sales where prices are discounted. QVC rarely sells products at discount prices. Maureen Kelly, founder of Tarte Cosmetics, said she typically makes more from an eight-minute segment on QVC than she used to make in a month at a high-end department store.

Apart from searching for exclusive products, QVC has also been trying to move away from some product categories, such as home appliances and electronic gadgets, which offer lower margins. It has been gradually expanding into many new product categories that have higher margins such as cosmetics, apparel, food, and toys. Several of these new categories have also displayed the strongest rates of growth in sales for the shopping channel over the past couple of years.

EXPANDING UPON THE CUSTOMER BASE

Since its start-up, QVC's shopping channel has managed to gradually penetrate almost all of the cable television and broadcast satellite homes in the US. But only about 10% of the households that it reaches have actually bought anything from the network. However, QVC has developed a large customer base, many of whom make as many as 10 purchases in a year. QVC devotees often call the live segments to offer product testimonials, are up on the personal lives of their favorite program hosts, and generally view the channel as entertaining. "As weird as it may sound, for people who love the network, it's good company," said Rayport.[9]

QVC is also hoping to attract new customers on the basis of the reasonably strong reputation that surveys indicate that it has established among a large majority of its current buyers. By its initials alone, QVC had promised that it would deliver Quality, Value, and Convenience to its viewers. More than three-quarters of the shopping channel's customers have given it a score of 7 out of 7 for trustworthiness. This has led most of its customers to recommend it to their friends.

QVC has also benefited from the growing percentage of women entering the workforce, resulting in a significant increase in dual-income families. Although the firm's current customer base does span several socioeconomic groups, it is led by young professional families who have above average disposable income. They also enjoy various forms of "thrill-seeking" activities and rank shopping relatively higher as a leisure activity when compared to the typical consumer.

The firm is also trying to increase sales by making it easier for customers to buy its products by adding features such as an interactive service which would allow them to purchase whatever it is offering on its shopping channel with the single click of a remote. QVC also provides a credit program to allow customers to pay for goods over a period of several months. Everything it sells is also backed by a 30-day unconditional money-back guarantee. Furthermore, QVC does not impose any hidden charges, such as a "restocking fee," for any returned merchandise. These policies help the home shopping channel to attract customers for products that they can view but are not able to either touch or feel.

Regular technological developments may, in fact, allow QVC to continue to offer much higher margin products to both existing and new markets. Rose claims that interactivity in all aspects of the firm's business, including its television shopping channel, will only become more pronounced in the future, making it easier for customers to act on what they see. QVC believes that it still has a lot of room to grow, since almost 90% of its audience has not purchased anything from the network.

POSITIONING FOR FUTURE GROWTH

In 1995, QVC launched its own retail web site to complement its television home shopping channel. The web site has provided the firm access to more than 100 million households in the US that have Internet connections. Initially, the site offered more detailed information about QVC offerings. Since then, it has branched out to develop its own customer base by featuring many products that have not been recently shown on its television channel. Over the last few years, QVC has been fine-tuning its web site by offering mobile phone, interactive television, and iPad apps.

By 2010, QVC.com, a once-negligible part of the QVC empire, accounted for about a third of the firm's domestic revenue. CEO Michael George stated that 60% of QVC's new customers in the United States buy on the Internet or on mobile devices. "The online business is becoming such a crucial part of the business for QVC," remarked Douglas Anmuth, an analyst at Barclay's Capital.[10]

Furthermore, QVC.com is now more profitable than QVC's television operation. It needs fewer call-center workers, and while QVC must share profits with cable companies on TV orders, it does not have to pay them on online orders for products which have not been featured on the air for 24 hours. But online shoppers tend to be more interested in the best price than in staying loyal to brands like QVC.

For many of its loyal consumers, however, nothing will ever replace the shopping on television. The web site does not offer the hybrid of talk show and sales pitch that attracts audiences to the QVC shopping channel. Online shoppers also miss out on the interaction between hosts and shoppers and the continuous feedback about the time that they may have to order before an item is sold out. "You know, on Sundays I might find a program on Lifetime Movie Network, but whatever I'm watching, if it's not QVC, when the commercial comes on I'll flip it back to QVC," said one loyal QVC fan. "I'm just stuck on them."[11]

TABLE 1
ANNUAL SALES

2010	7.8 billion
2009	7.4 billion
2008	7.3 billion
2007	7.4 billion
2006	7.1 billion
2004	5.7 billion
2001	3.8 billion
1998	2.4 billion
1995	1.6 billion
1992	0.9 billion
1989	0.2 billion

Source: QVC, Liberty Media.

TABLE 2
INCOME STATEMENT (YEAR ENDED DECEMBER 31)

	2010	2009	2008	2007
	(AMOUNTS IN MILLIONS)			
Net Revenue	$7,807	$7,352	$7,303	$7,397
Cost of Sales	(5,006)	(4,719)	(4,682)	(4,426)
Gross Profit	2,801	2,604	2,584	2,715
Operating Expenses*	(715)	(684)	(703)	(616)
S, G & A Expenses	(415)	(364)	(379)	(447)
Operating Cash Flow	1,671	1,556	1,502	1,652
Stock Compensation	(18)	(16)	(15)	(22)
Depreciation & Amortization**	(523)	(526)	(531)	(516)
Operating Income	$1,130	$1,014	$956	$1,114

*Operating expenses consist of commissions and license fees, order processing and customer service, credit card processing fees, and provision for doubtful accounts.
**Depreciation & amortization includes amortization of intangible assets recorded in connection with the purchase of QVC by Liberty Media.
Source: Liberty Media, QVC.

TABLE 3
GEOGRAPHICAL BREAKDOWN OF REVENUES (YEAR ENDED DECEMBER 31)

	2010	2009	2008	2007
	(AMOUNTS IN MILLIONS)			
U.S.	$5,235	$4,965	$4,911	$5,208
U.K.	599	578	660	707
Germany	956	942	954	870
Japan	1,015	867	778	612

Source: Liberty Media, QVC.

TABLE 4 SAMPLE OF QVC PROGRAMMING

TIME	MONDAY	TUESDAY	WEDNESDAY	THURSDAY	FRIDAY	SATURDAY	SUNDAY
12:00 AM	Barbara Bixby Jewelry	Company's Coming Reed/Barton	Kathy Van Zeeland Accessories	Victor Costa Occasion Gifts of Style	Gifts of Style	Bose Sound Innovation	Kitchen Aid
2:00 AM	Tignanello Handbags	Dennis Basso Boutique	T3 Hair Care	Tacori for Epiphany Jewelry	Late Night Gifts	Linea by Louis Dell'Olio	Ecclissi Watches
5:00 AM	Savings by Jeanne Bice	Steel by Design Jewelry	Chaz Dean Hair and Body Care	Boyds Bears and Friends	Arte d'Argento Silver	Gold Jewelry Special	Practical Kitchen Aid
9:00 AM	Barbara Bixby Jewelry	Slatkin & Co. Home Accessories	Mary Beth Accessories	Susan Style Graver	Denim & Company	AM Style	Great Gifts by KitchenAid
12:00 noon	Q Check Gifts	Q Check Gifts	Q Check Gifts	Q Check Gifts	Q Check Gifts	Judith Ripka Collection	Gifts from David's Kitchen
3:00 PM	Barbara Bixby Jewelry	Dennis Basso Boutique	Bags and Shoes	Great Gifts	Gifts of Style	QVC Beauty Exclusives	Gifts from David's Kitchen
6:00 PM	NFL Shop	Enjoyable Entertaining Reed/Barton	Kathy Van Zeeland Accessories	Philosophy Beauty	Great Gifts	Gifts for Mom	From Dell
8:00 PM	PM Style	Kitchen Gifts Reed/Barton	NARS Cosmetics	Northern Nights Bedding	What's in My Beauty Bag?	Saturday Night Beauty	From Dell
10:00 PM	Tignanello Handbags	Tuesday Night Gifts Reed/ Barton	Designer Couple Handbags	Tacori for Epiphany Jewelry	Gem Fest Special	Temptation Presentable Ovenware	Nintendo Featuring Wii

Source: QVC.

CASE 7

Barbie vs Bratz

Gloria was busy at work in her office, when her seven-year-old daughter Barbara called up and said that she wanted to get some new dolls. Gloria looked at her watch. It was almost lunch time. She herself wanted to take a break and going to a toy store would be quite refreshing for her as well. She hoped to pick up a collector doll from Barbie herself. Quickly, finishing her work, she left the office.

The three-storied huge store was full with people and buzzing with activity. Barbara and Gloria went to the second storey which was entirely dedicated to toys for girls. Barbara at once rushed to the area which showcased dolls. A strange thing happened, which caught Gloria's attention; Barbara rushed past the section which housed Barbie dolls and stopped in front of the section that showcased dolls called Bratz. After spending about 20 minutes exploring various options, Barbara finalized a total of five Bratz dolls and a Bratz play set.

While on their way back, Gloria asked her daughter why she did not choose a Barbie. (Barbara had been an avid Barbie fan and had more than two dozen of them.) Her daughter replied very casually that they were kiddish and not fashionable and that all her friends were buying Bratz and not Barbie. This answer from her daughter surprised and almost shocked Gloria who had grown up playing with Barbies and had even preserved them.

BARBIE'S BEGINNING

Barbie was made by the world's largest toy making company, Mattel. The company (Exhibit 1) was founded by Harold Matson and Elliot Handler in 1945. In its early days, the company originally produced picture frames and dollhouse accessories from picture frame scraps. With the success of its dollhouse accessories, the company turned its attention to toys. Mattel produced its first big toy called the "Uke-A-Doodle" in January 1947, but the big breakthrough came in 1955 with the release of a new toy called the Burp Gun. The television channel ABC-TV approached Mattel for 52 weeks exclusive sponsorship of their new program for kids, The Mickey Mouse Club. Toy advertising till that time was limited to catalogs and trade advertisements and television was a new and unproven medium. The Handlers after consulting their finance department agreed to sponsor the program and paid ABC-TV $500,000. The sponsorship proved to be highly successful and Mattel sold more than 1 million guns that Christmas.

During the 1950s, toys like Yogi Bear, Howdy Doody, and baby dolls were available for children to play with. Ruth had seen her daughter Barbara and her friends playing with adult paper dolls rather than the three-dimensional baby dolls popular at that time. She recalled, "Through their play Barbara imagined their lives as adults. They used the dolls to reflect the adult world around them. They would sit and carry on conversations, making the dolls real people. I thought if only we could take this play pattern and three dimensionalize it, we would have something very special."[1] In 1955, while the Handlers were vacationing in Switzerland, Ruth came across a German adult doll Lilli which had a shapely figure and sported high heels. The dolls instantly struck Ruth and coincided with her imagination of the three-dimensional adult doll which since long she had wanted and had spent years persuading her company to create. Mattel's engineers and designers had always resisted the idea and had believed that a three-dimensional doll would be too expensive to produce and an adult doll with shapely features might be considered too sexy by critics.

Despite the resistance, Ruth finally managed to convince Mattel's development team to create something similar to Lilli. To reduce the cost, the doll was manufactured in Tokyo, Japan. After three years of design work, the doll debuted at the American International Toy Fair in New York in February 1959 (Exhibit 2). It was named Barbie, after Handler's daughter. Barbie was the first ever three-dimensional teenage doll, targeted at girls in the age group of 6–10 years.

The launch according to the *New York Times* was a "crashing bomb." All the buyers objected to her curvaceous

---

This case was written by Vedpuriswar A. and Mankad R., IBS Research Center. It is intended to be used as the basis for class discussion rather than to illustrate either effective or ineffective handling of a management situation. The case was compiled from published sources.

EXHIBIT 1 MATTEL

Mattel Inc, the world's largest toy company, was founded in California in 1945 by Elliot Handler and Harold Matson. The company originally produced picture frames and dollhouse accessories from picture frame scraps. With the success of their dollhouse accessories, the company turned its attention to toys and became publicly owned in 1960. Currently it designs, manufactures, and markets a broad variety of toy products worldwide through sales to retailers and wholesalers and directly to consumers. Mattel's vision is to provide "the world's premier toy brands—today and tomorrow."

Products

Mattel Brands—Include Barbie fashion dolls and accessories, Polly Pocket, Disney Classics, Hot Wheels, Matchbox and Tyco R/C vehicles and play sets, Harry Potter, Yu-Gi-Oh, Batman, Justice League, Megaman and games and puzzles.

Fisher-Price Brands —Include Fisher-Price, Little People, Rescue Heroes, Baby Gear and View-Master, Sesame Street, Barney, Dora the Explorer, Winnie the Pooh, InteracTV, See 'N Say and Power Wheels.

American Girl Brands—Include American Girl Today, The American Girls Collection and Bitty Baby. American Girl Brands products are sold directly to consumers and its children's publications are also sold to certain retailers.

Business Segments

Mattel's reportable segments are separately managed business units and are divided on a geographic basis between domestic and international. The Domestic segment is further divided into Mattel Brands US, Fisher-Price Brands US and American Girl Brands. Products marketed by the International segment, with the exception of American Girl Brands, are generally the same as those developed and marketed by the Domestic segment, although some are developed or adapted for particular international markets. Mattel's products are sold directly to retailers and wholesalers in Canada and most European, Asian, and Latin American countries, and through agents and distributors in those countries where Mattel has no direct presence. Its products are sold in 150 countries in the world.

Source: Compiled from www.mattel.com.

figure. Sears, the biggest buyer of Mattel, refused to place orders. Soon after the launch, Mattel's market research revealed that while kids loved the dolls, their mothers hated it. Disappointed with the feedback of the launch and results of the market research, Mattel lowered the sales projections and reduced factory orders.

But the forecast proved wrong and 35,100 Barbie dolls were sold at $3 each in 1959, making it a smash hit. Mattel had to add production and warehouse capacity in order to keep up with the demand. This took almost three years. In 1961 Barbie's boyfriend Ken, named after Handler's son, was launched in the market. The revenues shot up from $18.3 million in 1960 to $211 million in 1969. Since then there had been no looking back for Barbie, which reigned supreme for more than four decades (Exhibit 3). The majority of the women in US under the age of 50 years had played with Barbie when they were kids and collected vintage Barbie when they became adults. The global sales of

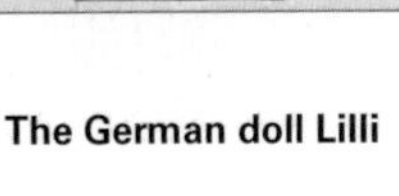

The German doll Lilli

The First Barbie

EXHIBIT 2
THE FIRST BARBIE
Source: www.fiftiesweb.com.

EXHIBIT 3 FOUR DECADES OF BARBIE

As a teenage fashion model, Barbie has worn many fabulous fashions. Beginning with her trademark black and white striped swimsuit and swirled ponytail, over the years as fashion and teenage lifestyle trends have shifted, so has Barbie.

In the early 1960s, she began wearing designer outfits such as Gay Parisienne™, and "Easter Parade," both modeled after Parisian couture fashions. As the 1960s progressed, Barbie took on the style and sophistication of the decade's most famous trendsetter—Jackie Kennedy, wearing stunning fashions. Another popular look for the late 60s was that of the American Girl—a chin-length Dutch-boy hairstyle available in many colors. In addition to the new fashion and hairstyle, American Girl dolls were the first Barbie dolls to have bendable legs. In the late 1960s, Barbie not only got a fashion makeover, but her body style, hair, face sculpting and makeup changed as well. In addition to wearing the popular mod fashions, Barbie doll's body underwent dramatic changes including a new Twist 'N Turn® waist, and a more youthful face with rooted eyelashes.

In the early 1970s, Barbie got bendable wrists, elbows, and ankles. This allowed Barbie to participate in all kinds of new activities, including gymnastics, horseback riding, and ballet. During the 1970s, her fashions included the "prairie" look, the "granny" dress, the "California Girl" suntan, and the zany glitz of the "disco" era. In 1977, Barbie again underwent a major face-sculpting change with the introduction of Superstar Barbie®. This doll featured a wide open-mouthed smile along with bright painted eyes, and looked much friendlier than any of the previous dolls. Barbie wore fashions that mirrored the funky trends found on dance floors across the country, as well as chic designer looks that came in vogue in the late 1970s.

In the 1980s, Barbie collecting became more than a childhood pastime. With Barbie doll's original fans now in their twenties and thirties, Barbie collecting began attracting adult women as well as little girls. For many of these women, Barbie symbolized the innocence of their youth; she was a part of them that was timeless, ageless and they wanted to reconnect with their favorite fashion doll! To meet the needs of these sophisticated adult collectors, Mattel issued Blue Rhapsody® Barbie® in 1986 which marked the beginning of the collector line.

In the 1990s, some of the world's most famous designers began creating fashions for Barbie including Bob Mackie, Nolan Miller, Vera Wang, and Christian Dior just to name a few. In the late 1990s, computer technology boomed, and in 1996, Mattel launched www.barbie.com, the official Barbie website. In 1998, My Design™ was introduced on the site, allowing girls and collectors to decide what their Barbie doll friend would look like by choosing her hair/eye/makeup colors, fashions, accessories, and personality traits.

In 2000, Barbie.com received a brand new look and became a place where girls could play interactive games, make up stories online, and engage in numerous exciting interactive activities!

Now in her fourth decade, the world's ultimate fashion model not only continues to retain her audience from years past, but also ignites the hopes, dreams, and imaginations of a new generation of little girls. Barbie with her humble beginnings as a teenage fashion model has transformed herself into best friend, confidante, and fearless adventurer. With a unique ability to inspire self-esteem, glamour, and a sense of adventure in all who love her, Barbie continues to inspire as she moves into the 21st century.

Source: Compiled from www.barbiecollector.com.

Barbie in 2001 were $1.5 billion and since its launch, more than 1 billion dolls had been sold.

Barbie was the role model for young girls and had become a part and parcel of a girl's fantasy and play world. Barbie was promoted not as a toy alone but as a lifestyle. In addition to the dolls, Barbie was licensed in 30 different product categories ranging from furniture to makeup. There were Barbie conventions, fan clubs, magazines, event for collectors, and its own website. Ruth Handler wrote in her autobiography, "My whole philosophy of Barbie was that through the doll, the little girl could be anything she wanted to be. Barbie always represented the fact that a woman has choices."[2] Each year Mattel created 150 different Barbie dolls and 120 new outfits for them. Since her launch she appeared in various roles: as a teenage fashion model, an astronaut, a surgeon, an athlete, a rock star, a presidential candidate, an engineer, and many others. As one analyst put it,[3] "It is a business-school case study in innovation"[4] (Exhibit 4). A study undertaken concluded that playing with Barbie promoted dramatic play and language development.

Meanwhile, activist groups blamed Barbie time and again, for promoting wrong values. They criticized Barbie for preaching supremacy of good looks and encouraging young girls to be obsessed with dressing and grooming rather than going out and engaging in outdoor activities. In the early 1990s Mattel released a series of talking Barbie, one of which said "*Math class is tough.*" This displeased many women and a New York group called "Barbie Liberation Organization" interchanged the voice boxes inside the dolls with those from the famous male doll G.I. Joe and kept them back on the toy shelves. The altered Barbie now shouted lines like "*Vengeance is mine*" while the boy dolls said things like "*Let's go shopping.*"

Barbie was also held responsible for the new trend among girls and teenagers toward weight control and slim figure. A professor of sociology at the University of West Florida said: "The doll belongs to that chorus of voices extolling not only slimness but also beauty and youthfulness as requisites to feminine success."[5]

KIDS GETTING OLDER YOUNGER (KGOY)

While previously kids till the age of 12 used to play with traditional toys, in the 1990s most of the kids beyond the age of 8 were abandoning them.[6] A new segment "tween" consisting of kids in the age group of 8–12 years had emerged. The traditional toys did not fascinate them. They were interested in products which made them feel more than just a kid. They went shopping with their parents but expected to be treated as adults and influenced the

EXHIBIT 4 BARBIE FACTS

- The full name of Barbie doll is Barbie Millicent Roberts. She hails from Willows, Wisconsin and went to Willows high school
- Barbie has had more than 80 careers and has represented 45 different nationalities
- Barbie is marketed in 150 countries around the world
- If placed head to toe, Barbie dolls and its family members sold since 1959 would encircle the earth more than seven times
- Every second, three Barbie dolls are sold somewhere in the world
- Since 1959, over 1 billion fashions have been produced for Barbie and her friends
- More than 105 million yards of fabric had gone into making Barbie and fashions for her friends, making Mattel one of the largest apparel manufacturers in the world
- Barbie starred in her first movie "Barbie in the Nutcracker" in 2001 and then in "Barbie as Rapunzel" in 2002
- Barbie's website www.barbie.com is the world's number one website for girls with over 8 million users logging every month and spending an average of 42 minutes per visit

Source: Compiled by IBS Ahmedabad, Research Centre.

shopping decision heavily. The time that took for a kid to transit into the tween stage got even shorter. Young boys got more attracted toward technology-enabled games while young girls began to judge their bodies by adult standards at a much earlier age. Very young girls loved Barbie for her fairy-like image and fantastic but unrealistic body proportions, but as they grew older, the allure started fading away. A toy industry analyst said, "Age compression is something we're stuck with. It's the core challenge facing the industry. And it's magnified with Barbie."[7] In 2000, out of the US population a sizable 35 million were tweens. The phenomenon of age compression referred to as KGOY was a significant factor which led to a decline in toy sales.

BRATZ

In June 2001 MGA Entertainment Inc. (MGA) launched "the girls with a passion for fashion,"[8] Bratz dolls with characters named Cloe, Sasha, Jade, and Yasmin. Each of the very fashionable dolls was 10 inches in height, wore flashy outfits, had slightly larger heads, and was priced at $14.99 each. Their first play set was the "Bratz Stylin" Salon "N Spa with Dana." The dolls came with clothing sets for specialized events like a first date, prom, shopping sprees, and beach outings.

The dolls were an instant hit and in the first year itself, $20 million worth of Bratz dolls were sold. According to data provided by NPD Funworld,[9] the Bratz doll set remained the top-selling fashion doll item through the period of January to October 2002 and had pushed the Barbie doll set to number 2. The "People's choice toy of the year"[10] award for 2002 was given to the Bratz doll and the "Bratz Stylin" Salon "N spa with Dana."

An eight-year-old girl who owned three Bratz dolls and wanted a Bratz "Formal Funk Super Stylin" disco play set for her coming birthday, commented: "I used to like Barbie dolls when I was little. But I like Bratz now because they're more fashionable. It makes me feel like a teenager."[11]

MY SCENE BARBIE

In November 2002, Mattel launched a range of dolls named "My Scene" which featured three urban girls, Barbie, Madison, and Chelsea. Priced at $13.99 each, these were extensions of Barbie but more modern than the original one. They wore hipper clothes and offered more accessories to buyers. For the first time, the dolls featured a special sculpted face including extra pouted lips and oversized eyes, which gave them a more stylish look (Exhibit 5). These were targeted at tween girls aged between 8 and 12 years. Mattel's commercial director for Southeast Asia, Geetha Balakrishna, said, "This product is about individual characters, storylines and real city experiences that tweens can identify with as they aspire to be teens."[12] Many other products were also developed under the My Scene brand, which included clothes, accessories, "My Scene Convertible," and three scenes—"My café," "My Boutique," and "My Club."

Isaac Larian, President and Chief Executive Officer of MGA, had publicly referred to "My Scene Barbie" as more of a copy of Bratz and had commented, "I'm flattered and disappointed."[13]

At the 100th Annual American International Toy Fair, among the best-selling toys in 2002, Bratz was the number one doll and the number three best-selling toy. In the top best-selling toys introduced in 2002, Mattel's newly introduced "Rapunzel" Barbie came third and Bratz Funk N Glow Assortment came fifth (Exhibit 6).

In 2002, the US sales of Barbie declined by 2% from the previous year and it further declined by 14% in the first quarter of 2003. The sales of Bratz in 2003 were projected to reach $520 million.

FLAVAS

In July 2003, Mattel made another attempt to woo the tweens with the launch of the highly hip range of dolls called "Flavas." They were a crew of six dolls which were different from each other and reflected the look of real teens. Each of them had a different sculpted face and had different heights which ranged from 10 to 11½ inches (Exhibit 7).

Jerry Bossick, Senior Vice President, Mattel, mentioned, "Younger girls want the fantasy of Barbie. Older girls want a doll that represents realistic aspirations."[14] On competition between Bratz and Flavas, Larian commented, "Bratz are fashionable and trendy. They don't portray the 'bad girl' image that, in my opinion, Flavas does. I don't think

FIRST
CAME BRATZ...
MAKER
DEBUT 2001
NAMES Yasmin, Sasha,
and
MOTTO
a passion for
HER RIDE
...THEN, MY
SCENE BARBIE
MAKER
DEBUT 2002
NAMES Barbie, Madison,
Chelsea, and
Nolee
MOTTO My city.
HER RIDE Vespa
motorscooter

EXHIBIT 5 MY SCENE VS BRATZ

Source: www.businessweek.com.

the majority of kids aged 6–12 aspire to be what Flavas are portraying, nor would this sit well with the majority of parents."[15]

A survey in December 2003[16] revealed that 57% of girls aged 6–8 years and 44% of the girls aged 9–11 years chose Bratz over Barbie. Then they were asked to choose between Bratz, Swan Lake Barbie, My Scene Barbie, and Flavas. Of the girls aged 6–8 years, 33% chose Swan Lake Barbie and another 33% chose Bratz. For 40% of the girls aged 9–11 years, Bratz was their number one doll. Neither of the age group preferred Flavas and rated Swan Lake Barbie as more "cool" than Flavas.[17]

Mattel soon withdrew Flavas from the market.

In December 2003, MGA launched a pair of preadolescent fashion dolls holding hands called "4Ever Best Friends." They were launched with two themes "Beach Party" and "Pajama Party" and each theme contained two dolls with more than 20 accessories such as a hair dryer, a telephone, etc. The dolls were sold in pairs and were priced at $25. Larian commented that Bratz was not competing with Barbie but was meant for girls who did not want to buy Barbie anymore, but "4Ever Best Friends," he said, "It is directly going after Barbie."[18]

In 2004, for the fourth consecutive year, Bratz dolls bagged the "Family Fun Toy of the Year" award. In 2000, Barbie had accounted for more than 90% of the sales of fashion dolls in US. In 2004 Barbie accounted for only 70% of the $1.7 billion worth of sales, the 30% captured by Bratz.[19] Larian commented, "This (Bratz) is the number 1 lifestyle brand for girls age seven to 14. If we keep

EXHIBIT 6 BEST SELLING TOYS IN 2002

TOP 10 BEST SELLING TOYS RANKED ON DOLLARS SOLD ANNUAL 2002

RANK	ITEM DESCRIPTION	MANUFACTURER	INTRO DATE	ARP
1	LeapPad Books Asst.	LeapFrog	July '01	$14.10
2	LeapPad	LeapFrog	Sept '99	$42.31
3	Bratz Asst.	MGA Entertainment	June '01	$13.44
4	Hot Wheels Basic Cars	Mattel	<1986	$0.83
5	Trivial Pursuit 20th Edition	Hasbro Games	June '02	$29.42
6	Spider-Man Dual Web Blaster	Toy Biz	Dec '01	$15.29
7	Star Wars Episode II Asst. 1	Hasbro	March '02	$5.35
8	My 1st LeapPad	LeapFrog	Sept '01	$33.43
9	Rapunzel Barbie	Mattel	June '02	$17.27
10	Yu-Gi-Oh! Collector Tin	Konami	Sept. '02	$19.65

TOP 10 BEST SELLING TOYS RANKED ON DOLLARS SOLD—ITEMS INTRODUCED IN 2002 ANNUAL 2002

RANK	ITEM DESCRIPTION	MANUFACTURER	INTRO DATE	ARP
1	Trivial Pursuit 20th Edition	Hasbro Games	June '02	$29.42
2	Star Wars Episode II Asst. 1	Hasbro	March '02	$5.35
3	Rapunzel Barbie	Mattel	June '02	$17.27
4	Yu-Gi-Oh! Collector Tin	Konami	Sept. '02	$19.65
5	Bratz Funk N Glow Asst.	MGA Entertainment	July '02	$28.03
6	Star Wars II Electric Lightsabers	Hasbro	April '02	$19.66
7	Yu-Gi-Oh! Metal Raider 1st Edition Blister	Konami	July '02	$3.54
8	Yu-Gi-Oh! Magic Ruler Unlimited Blister	Konami	Sept '02	$3.89
9	Bratz Funky Makeover Asst.	MGA Entertainment	July '02	$23.07
10	Bratz Boyz Fall 2002 Asst.	MGA Entertainment	June '02	$12.99

Source: www.npd.com.

Flavas

Bratz

EXHIBIT 7 FLAVAS VS BRATZ

Source: Compiled by IBS Ahmedabad-Research Centre.

innovating, this brand will be around forever. Bratz is the truth, and Barbie isn't anymore."[20]

BARBIE BATTLES

To make Barbie popular across age groups, Timothy Kilpin, Head-Marketing & Design, Girls division, divided the brand into age segments and attached a story line with each line. For instance, a new video "Fairytopia" was released which targeted girls in the age group of 5–7 years. The dresses of dolls and the plastic replica of sets used in the video were offered to them for purchase. Hillary Duff, a celebrity, was signed by Mattel to promote Barbie. Mattel announced on February 12, 2004, two days before Valentine's Day, that after 43 years, the couple of Ken and Barbie were going separate ways and she was now a single Cali (California) girl. Jim Silver, a toy consultant, commented, "The split with Ken was a great publicity gimmick. It brought Barbie lots of attention. The attempt is to reposition Barbie as a single, independent woman and to make her attractive to an older demographic."[21]

Other new products such as the Fashion Fever Barbie line, American Idol[22] Barbie, and the "Jammin' In Jamaica" series for the My Scene line were released which Mattel hoped would attract older girls. Barbie accessories were also updated and had famous labels like Levi's, Aldo, and Sephora. Between 2001 and 2004, Barbie sales had fallen by over 27%[23] (Exhibit 8). The 2004 fourth quarter results of Mattel announced resurgence in sales of the Barbie product line for the first time since 2001.

In April 2005, MGA sued Mattel in federal court, accusing Mattel of unfair competition, intellectual property infringement, and serial copying. MGA charged that Mattel had mimicked the look, themes, and packaging of Bratz in their latest dolls. Mattel considered this as retaliation to its own suit against the creator of Bratz, Carter Bryant in April 2004. Mattel had made out the case with the accusation that Bryant, their former employee, had come up with the idea of Bratz while he was still working with Mattel.

During the first quarter of 2005, Mattel's earnings of Barbie yet again declined by 28%. Barbie sales worldwide fell by 15% and in the US by 25% compared to the previous year. While sales of Fairytopia doll line were strong, sales of My Scene and Fashion Fever dolls remained average and the sales of Cali Girl were disappointing. According to an analyst, "Mattel still feels competition from Bratz. Bratz had some new lines and lower prices. So did Mattel, but not enough to offset that."[24]

In association with the content partner Single Touch Interactive, Mattel offered Nokia mobile phones with a prepaid connection, alongside the My Scene Barbie line in April 2005. These were targeted at the tween girl market. The phone with 30 minutes of airtime featured a full-color screen and voice dialing. After the phone was activated, parents could go to the website, MySceneMobile.com and list small chores they wanted their kid to carry out. Kids completed the chores to note it on the website. Parents could then buy additional minutes for their kids.

On May 5, 2005, Mattel and Benetton Group announced a worldwide exclusive partnership and created a stylish fashion collection for girls called "Barbie loves Benetton." The range consisted of over 50 garments and accessories and featured four contemporary looks from the leading style capitals of the world: London, Paris, New York, and Stockholm. Four special "Barbie loves Benetton" dolls were also created which were dressed similar to the collection and were available at Benetton stores and major toy

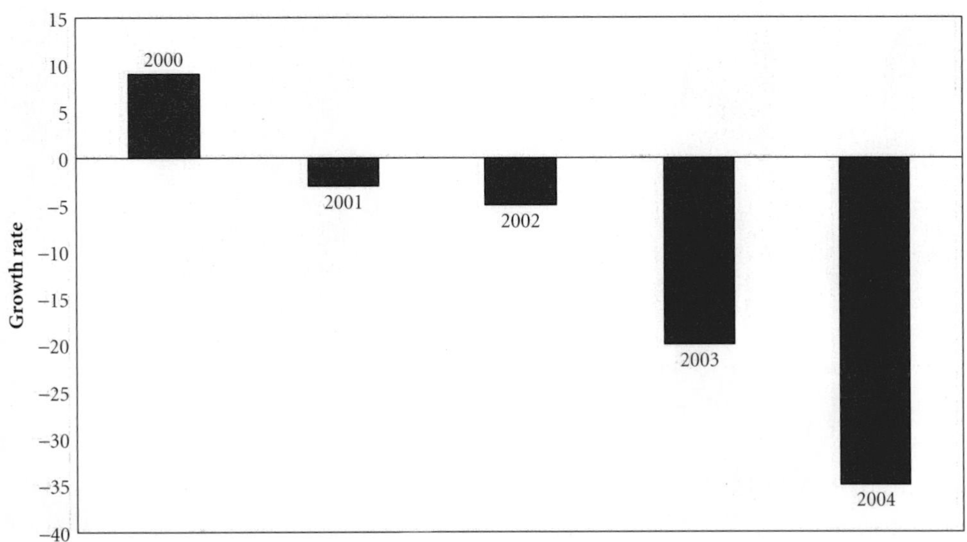

EXHIBIT 8 SALES GROWTH RATE OF BARBIE IN THE US

Source: Compiled by IBS Ahmedabad Research Center based on Annual Reports of Mattel.

retailers (Exhibit 9). Matt Bousquette, President, Mattel Brands, explained, "Both organizations share the same core values as young, fashionable and fun brands that offer the consumer quality products." Mattel believed the partnership would enable the company to reach girls in a unique way.[25] An analyst expressed his doubt on the success of the partnership: "For girls who are older than eight, do they really want to connect with the products and brands that they played with when they were younger?"[26]

CONCLUSION

After dropping Barbara home, Gloria came back to office and tried to focus on her work. But she could not get over what had happened. She really could not understand whether her daughter had outgrown the age of playing with Barbie or, Barbie had outgrown her age and had ceased to fascinate kids like Barbara anymore. She wondered whether the new initiatives taken by Mattel would reinvigorate Barbie and regain customers like Barbara.

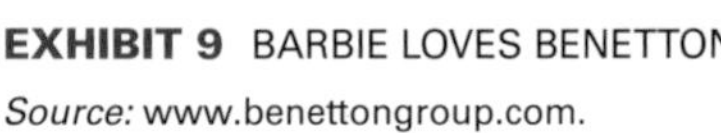

EXHIBIT 9 BARBIE LOVES BENETTON

Source: www.benettongroup.com.

CASE 8

The European Airline Industry: Lufthansa in 2003

In Spring 2003, a management succession was underway at the helm of Lufthansa. At the Annual General Meeting on June 18, Jürgen Weber, the veteran executive who had led the group since 1991, would hand over his responsibilities as CEO and chairman to deputy chairman Wolfgang Mayrhuber, an insider with 30 years' experience at Lufthansa.

Mayrhuber was taking the reins at a crucial point for the company. Investors appeared to have run out of enthusiasm for the business model of the integrated network airline epitomized by Lufthansa. Lufthansa had lost 70% of its stock market value since January 2001. Ryanair, the popular Irish low-cost carrier, had overtaken it as the most valuable airline in Europe, even though its revenues were 20 times smaller than Lufthansa's (Exhibit 1). To make matters worse, several low-cost carriers (LCCs) had entered the German market during 2002, and competition in the segment was intense.

In November 2002, Lufthansa decided to join their ranks. Eurowings Airline, a commuter airline which was 24.9% owned by Lufthansa, had announced the launch of its LCC subsidiary, Germanwings. In preparing for his new role, Mayrhuber had to decide whether Lufthansa's traditional strategy of a global, full-service, vertically integrated network carrier was still appropriate in this deregulated and highly competitive airline industry. How should Lufthansa respond to the emerging threat of the LCCs? What strategic direction should Lufthansa follow to survive and thrive in this new environment?

LUFTHANSA'S EVOLUTION SINCE THE 1990s

Lufthansa had entered the 1990s as a troubled company. Although German reunification provided new business opportunities, the 1991 Gulf War and the ensuing economic recession had a negative impact on the industry. In 1991, the government-owned flag carrier recorded a loss of DM444 million. Despite rising passenger volume, prices fell by 7% and the company was on the verge of bankruptcy. The early 1990s saw major restructuring efforts to boost revenue and cut costs, including a pay freeze and headcount reduction. Lufthansa returned to profitability in 1994. The government reduced its holding to 36% in 1994, and completed the privatization process in 1997. Since then, the company had maintained healthy levels of profitability (posting return on equity in the range of 16–22%), except for losses in 2001 (Exhibit 2).

Source: © Martin Sookias. Pearson Education Ltd.

In its core passenger business, Lufthansa was Europe's largest (and the world's sixth largest) airline in terms of passengers in 2002. With a fleet of 344 aircraft and 34,000 employees, it carried nearly 45 million passengers and generated revenues of about €10 billion. Lufthansa's Frankfurt hub was among the largest in Europe and a second hub in Munich was scaling up. From the mid-1990s Lufthansa had focused on globalization and achieved global scale through alliances and collaboration agreements worldwide. It founded the Star Alliance in May 1997 (together with Air Canada, United Airlines, Thai, and SAS), which soon became the largest airline grouping in the world. In 2003, Star Alliance included 15 members offering more than 10,000 flights per day to 684 airports in 125 countries (Exhibit 3).

This case was written by Javier Gimeno, Associate Professor of Strategy and Management at INSEAD, Karel Cool, BP Professor of European Competitiveness at INSEAD, Herman Fung, INSEAD MBA 2002, and Alessandro Buccella at Roland Berger Strategy Consultants. It is intended to be used as a basis for class discussion rather than to illustrate either effective or ineffective handling of an administrative situation. Please also consult the companion cases, *The European Airline Industry on a Collision Course* (12/2008-5123) and *The European Airline Industry: Ryanair in 2003* (12/2008-5124).

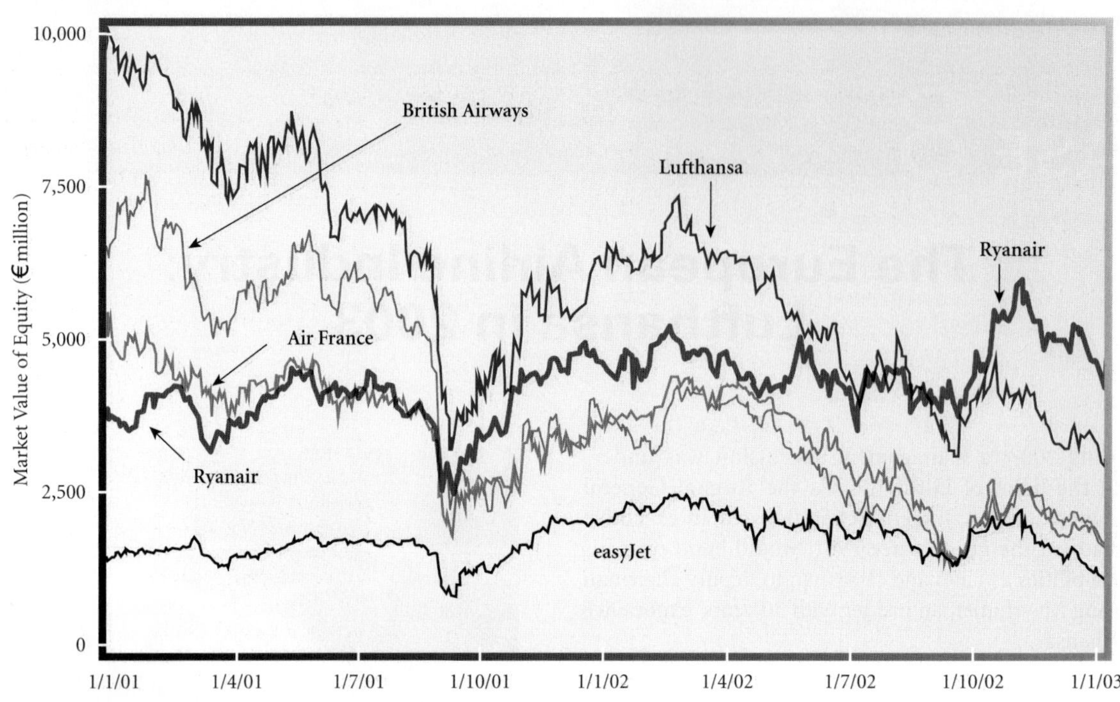

EXHIBIT 1 MARKET VALUE OF EUROPEAN AIRLINES, JANUARY 2001–JANUARY 2003

Source: Datastream.

EXHIBIT 2 CONSOLIDATED CORPORATE FINANCIAL REPORTS, LUFTHANSA GROUP

(DATA IN € MILLION) FINANCIAL YEAR END	2002 31.12.02	2001 31.12.01	2000 31.12.00	1999 31.12.99	1998 31.12.98	1997 31.12.97
Revenues	**16,971.4**	**16,690.0**	**15,200.4**	**12,794.7**	**11,736.6**	**11,048.9**
Profit/Loss from Operating Activities	1,592.1	−315.6	1,482.0	1,012.3	1,454.6	1,089.6
Profit/Loss from Ordinary Activities (inc. Financial Results from Investments and Subsidiaries)	952.4	−744.7	1,215.3	1,002.9	1,269.1	894.1
Net Profit/Loss for the Period	**716.8**	**−633.2**	**689.0**	**630.4**	**731.5**	**550.5**
Current and Other Assets	7,034.1	4,961.9	3,729.4	3,215.5	3,579.0	3,712.0
Non-Current Assets	12,102.8	13,244.0	11,082.0	9,671.6	8,712.6	7,947.7
Total Assets	**19,136.9**	**18,205.9**	**14,810.4**	**12,887.1**	**12,291.6**	**11,659.7**
Current Provisions and Liabilities	6,232.0	6,531.5	4,882.9	3,861.3	3,842.6	3,400.4
Retirement Benefit Obligations	4,019.5	3,700.5	3,354.3	2,993.0	2,760.4	2,577.7
Long-Term Liabilities	4,713.4	4,445.7	2,408.4	2,299.8	2,374.9	2,988.2
Shareholders' Equity	**4,172.0**	**3,528.2**	**4,164.8**	**3,733.0**	**3,313.7**	**2,693.4**
Average Employee Total	94,135	87,975	69,523	66,207	54,867	55,520
Operating Margin (%)	5.6%	−4.5%	8.0%	7.8%	10.8%	8.1%
Return on Net Assets (%)	5.6%	−5.4%	6.9%	7.0%	8.7%	6.7%
Return on Equity (%)	17.2%	−17.9%	16.5%	16.9%	22.1%	20.4%
Net Asset Turnover (Ratio)	1.32	1.43	1.53	1.42	1.39	1.34
Long-Term Debt/Equity (Ratio)	1.13	1.26	0.58	0.62	0.72	1.11

Sources: Lufthansa Annual Report, 2002; company website; Worldscope.

Lufthansa generated revenues of about €5 billion from intra-European destinations, accounting for about 51% of its global airline revenue (compared with 37% for British Airways and 48% for Air France). (Exhibits 4 and 5 provide a geographic breakdown of revenues and traffic for major European carriers.) Analysts estimated that about 33% of intra-European traffic was connecting through one of the hubs, 29% was point-to-point traffic within Germany, and the remaining 38% was point-to-point traffic within Europe.[1]

EXHIBIT 3 STAR ALLIANCE, MARCH 2003

CARRIER	DATE OF ENTRY	AIRCRAFT	EMPLOYEES	HUBS
Air Canada	May 14, 1997 (founder)	328	40,000	Toronto, Montreal, Vancouver (Canada)
Lufthansa	May 14, 1997 (founder)	280	32,000	Frankfurt, Munich (Germany)
SAS Scandinavian Airlines	May 14, 1997 (founder)	199	7,556	Copenhagen, Oslo, Stockholm (Scandinavia)
Thai Airways	May 14, 1997 (founder)	81	26,000	Bangkok, Chiang Mai, Phuket, Had Yai (Thailand)
United Airlines	May 14, 1997 (founder)	559	84,000	Chicago, Denver, San Francisco, Los Angeles, Washington DC (US)
Varig	October 1997	85	16,900	Rio de Janeiro, Sao Paulo (Brazil)
Air New Zealand	March 1999	88	9,500	Auckland, Los Angeles (New Zealand)
All Nippon Airways	October 1999	139	13,000	Tokyo Haneda/Narita, Osaka Itami/Kansai (Japan)
Austrian Airlines	March 2000	94	7,700	Vienna, Innsbruck (Austria)
Singapore Airlines	April 2000	92	14,000	Singapore
Bmi British Midland	July 2000	53	4,800	London Heathrow, Manchester (UK)
Mexicana	July 2000	59	6,500	Mexico City (Mexico)
Asiana Airlines	March 2003	60	6,996	Incheon, Gimpo (South Korea)
Spanair	April 2003 (pending)	54	2,904	Madrid, Barcelona (Spain)
LOT Polish Airlines	October 2003 (pending)	53	4,048	Warsaw (Poland)

Sources: SAS Annual Report, 2002; Star Alliance website.

The passenger airline business, however, only represented about 60% of revenues and 36% of employment at Lufthansa Group in 2002. Following an "Aviation Group" corporate strategy, Lufthansa Group was composed of seven business segments focusing on different aviation-related activities. In addition to the passenger business these included logistics (Lufthansa Cargo), maintenance, repair and overhaul (Lufthansa Technik), catering (LSG Sky Chefs), leisure travel (Thomas Cook AG), IT services (Lufthansa Systems), and service and financial. Many of these units were leaders within their respective industries. Lufthansa Cargo was the second largest cargo company in the world in terms of freight carried, after Federal Express. Lufthansa Technik was the world's largest civilian provider of aeroengineering and maintenance services, serving 370 airlines worldwide. LSG Sky Chefs was the world's largest catering company with a 33% share of the world's catering market and 260 airline customers. Lufthansa had a 50% stake in Thomas Cook AG, the second-largest leisure travel group in Europe, with integrated activities in charter airlines, hotel management, tour operators, and distribution outlets. Lufthansa also had equity stakes in Amadeus, the world's largest global distribution system, and Opodo, a European online travel agency. (Exhibit 6 describes the portfolio of subsidiaries and equity stakes in each segment. Exhibit 7 provides segment financial statistics.)

THE GERMAN SHORT/MEDIUM-HAUL AVIATION MARKET

In the 1980s and early 1990s, like most continental European flag-carriers, Lufthansa had operated with two layers of protection: bilateral agreements and government. Before deregulation, it was estimated that German domestic flights were 20% more expensive than the European average.[2] However, by December 1992 any company with majority European shareholding could run an airline and was free to fly any route between two EU countries. By 1997 EU airlines were allowed to operate domestic flights in any EU country.

Deregulation was received with excitement by both start-up and incumbent airlines. Eurowings was one of the most prominent local challengers. In 1997, the Nuremberg-based airline was charging US$250 for its Nuremberg–Cologne route, versus Lufthansa's US$414.[3] Eurowings grew steadily with annual passenger volume reaching 3.5 million by 2001. In January 2001, Lufthansa acquired 24.9% of Eurowings and turned it into an operating partner with an option to increase its share further to 49%.

In 1992 British Airways (BA) launched its German subsidiary Deutsche BA (DBA), designed to compete head-to-head with Lufthansa on the main domestic routes. DBA unleashed a fierce price war. For example, it offered the Hamburg–Munich service at DM650—more than 30% lower than Lufthansa's price of DM950 (which was later cut to DM840).[4] By 1997 DBA had become Lufthansa's biggest domestic competitor, capturing a market share of 15%, with Lufthansa still holding 80% market share.[5] In response, Lufthansa looked to increase cooperation with its partners and franchisees like Augsburg Airways. It also tried to lower its operating costs which were believed to be 25% higher than British Airways in 1997. Its effort to control staff wages, however, led to a prolonged row with its pilots.

Germany's geography provided it with additional protection. As of 2003, Germany had only 30 civil airports compared with 69 in France and 55 in the UK. Many

EXHIBIT 4 BREAKDOWN OF TRAFFIC VOLUME (MILLION RPKS) BY GEOGRAPHICAL AREA, JANUARY–DECEMBER 2002

	DEUTSCHE LUFTHANSA		BRITISH AIRWAYS		AIR FRANCE		KLM		IBERIA		ALITALIA		SAS		ALL AEA MEMBERS	
Domestic	**5,638**	6.0%	**3,654**	3.7%	**9,656**	9.8%	**0**	0.0%	**8,786**	21.7%	**6,049**	20.4%	**4,283**	17.7%	**51,244**	8.7%
	11.0%		7.1%		18.8%		0.0%		17.1%		11.8%		8.4%		100%	
Intra-European	**18,411**	19.7%	**15,253**	15.4%	**12,056**	12.2%	**10,803**	18.3%	**9,283**	22.9%	**7,503**	25.3%	**9,822**	40.6%	**134,445**	22.8%
	13.7%		11.3%		9.0%		8.0%		6.9%		5.6%		7.3%		100%	
North Africa	**615**	0.7%	**483**	0.5%	**1,734**	1.8%	**426**	0.7%	**163**	0.4%	**868**	2.9%	**0**	0.0%	**5,488**	0.9%
	11.2%		8.8%		31.6%		7.8%		3.0%		15.8%		0.0%		100%	
Middle East	**2,928**	3.1%	**3,905**	3.9%	**1,786**	1.8%	**3,321**	5.6%	**251**	0.6%	**1,282**	4.3%	**0**	0.0%	**17,425**	3.0%
	16.8%		22.4%		10.3%		19.1%		1.4%		7.4%		0.0%		100%	
North Atlantic	**30,131**	32.2%	**38,511**	38.9%	**22,612**	23.0%	**14,771**	25.0%	**5,596**	13.8%	**6,742**	22.8%	**5,958**	24.7%	**163,905**	27.8%
	18.4%		23.5%		13.8%		9.0%		3.4%		4.1%		3.6%		100%	
Mid Atlantic	**3,096**	3.3%	**4,756**	4.8%	**11,933**	12.1%	**8,352**	14.1%	**10,214**	25.2%	**894**	3.0%	**0**	0.0%	**41,666**	7.1%
	7.4%		11.4%		28.6%		20.0%		24.5%		2.1%		0.0%		100%	
South Atlantic	**4,318**	4.6%	**1,775**	1.8%	**7,092**	7.2%	**0**	0.0%	**5,101**	12.6%	**2,366**	8.0%	**0**	0.0%	**25,013**	4.2%
	17.3%		7.1%		28.4%		0.0%		20.4%		9.5%		0.0%		100%	
Sub-Saharan Africa	**3,998**	4.3%	**10,065**	10.2%	**13,701**	13.9%	**7,082**	12.0%	**1,062**	2.6%	**479**	1.6%	**0**	0.0%	**44,030**	7.5%
	9.1%		22.9%		31.1%		16.1%		2.4%		1.1%		0.0%		100%	
Far East Australasia	**24,508**	26.2%	**20,720**	20.9%	**17,611**	17.9%	**14,427**	24.4%	**9**	0.0%	**3,435**	11.6%	**4,107**	17.0%	**106,805**	18.1%
	22.9%		19.4%		16.5%		13.5%		0.0%		3.2%		3.8%		100%	
Short-Medium Haul	**21,954**	23.4%	**19,642**	19.8%	**15,577**	15.8%	**14,550**	24.6%	**9,696**	24.0%	**9,654**	32.6%	**9,822**	40.6%	**157,358**	26.7%
	14.0%		12.5%		9.9%		9.2%		6.2%		6.1%		6.2%		100%	
Long Haul	**66,050**	70.5%	**75,827**	76.5%	**73,275**	74.4%	**44,632**	75.4%	**21,982**	54.3%	**13,915**	47.0%	**10,065**	41.6%	**381,747**	64.7%
	17.3%		19.9%		19.2%		11.7%		5.8%		3.6%		2.6%		100%	
Total Scheduled	**93,643**	100%	**99,123**	100%	**98,508**	100%	**59,181**	100%	**40,464**	100%	**29,618**	100%	**24,170**	100%	**590,348**	100%
	15.9%		16.8%		16.7%		10.0%		6.9%		5.0%		4.1%		100%	

Note: Percentage below RPK number represents firm's traffic as percent of all AEA traffic in the region. Percentage to the right represents region's traffic as percent of total scheduled traffic by airline.
Sources: Association of European Airlines (AEA), Summary of Traffic and Airlines Results 2003.

EXHIBIT 5 GEOGRAPHICAL BREAKDOWN OF AIRLINE REVENUES

Lufthansa Passenger Business

	EXTERNAL REV (€m)		**PASSENGERS ('000)**		**RPK (mil)**		**ASK (mil)**		**LOAD FACTOR (%)**		**NO. OF DESTINATIONS**	
	2002	*2001*	*2002*	*2001*	*2002*	*2001*	*2002*	*2001*	*'02*	*'01*	*'02*	*'01*
Europe	5,022	5,198	34,434	36,292	23,202	24,330	37,146	39,907	62.5	61.0	150	154
N. America	1,965	1,948	4,488	4,499	30,573	31,249	38,310	41,257	79.8	75.7	96	107
S. America	282	371	547	719	4,876	6,201	6,252	7,978	78.0	77.7	10	12
Mid East	202	192	527	523	1,990	1,955	2,782	2,924	71.3	66.9	10	12
Africa	328	306	905	811	4,383	3,956	6,060	5,372	72.3	73.6	18	19
Asia/Pacific	1,918	1,933	2,996	2,810	23,464	22,624	29,199	28,859	80.4	78.4	43	35
Total Scheduled	9,717	9,848	43,897	45,652	88,489	90,316	119,759	126,297	73.9	71.5	327	339
Charters	9	10	52	52	81	73	118	104	68.6	70.5		
Total	9,725	9,858	43,949	45,704	88,570	90,389	118,877	126,400	73.9	71.5		

British Airways

	TURNOVER (£m) BY ORIGINAL SALE		**TURNOVER (£m) BY DESTINATION**		**OPERATING PROFIT (£m) BY DESTINATION**	
	2002/03	*2001/02*	*2002/03*	*2001/02*	*2002/03*	*2001/02*
Europe	4,903	5,402	2,838	3,208	(117)	(244)
United Kingdom	*3,634*	*4,101*	*725*	*863*		
Continental Europe	*1,269*	*1,301*	*2,113*	*2,345*		
The Americas	1,482	1,549	2,763	2,863	223	144
Africa, Middle East & Indian subcontinent	733	789	1,201	1,262	168	91
Far East & Australia	570	600	886	1,007	21	(101)
Total	7,688	8,340	7,688	8,340	295	(110)

Air France

	PASSENGER REVENUE BY AREA OF SALE (€m)		**PASSENGER REVENUE BY DESTINATION (€m)**	
	2002/03	*2001/02*	*2002/03*	*2001/02*
France	4,596	4,524	1,914	2,026
Europe & North Africa	2,093	2,014	2,567	2,558
Caribbean, French Guyana, & Indian Ocean	340	317	994	918
Africa & Middle East	598	539	1,098	975
Americas & Polynesia	1,329	1,336	1,966	1,894
Asia & New Caledonia	757	761	1,174	1,120
Total	9,713	9,491	9,713	9,491

Source: Annual Reports.

German cities had only one airport and it was usually congested. Entrants found it difficult to obtain landing slots, reducing competition on certain routes. For example, in 1997 Lufthansa priced Frankfurt–Berlin, a route with no competition, at about DM900 per round trip, whereas the Cologne–Berlin route, which was a little longer but had competition, was priced at about DM700.[6]

The challenge of LCCs flying into Germany remained insignificant during the 1990s. The first entrant was Debonair in 1996, a short-lived start-up airline based in London–Luton. In 1999, two years after it first flew out of the British Isles, Ryanair entered Germany by flying to Hahn, Frankfurt's second airport, 120 km east of the city. Hahn remained Ryanair's only German destination until 2001. EasyJet did not fly to Germany until it inherited Go's sole German route, Stansted–Munich, in a merger in 2002. Virgin Express, another major player based in Brussels, never opened a route to Germany.

2002: COMPETITION HEATS UP

The situation changed radically during 2002. The year started with the news that Ryanair was to upgrade its operation in Frankfurt Hahn into an operation base in February. Consistent with Ryanair's strategy elsewhere, it

EXHIBIT 6 BUSINESS SEGMENTS OF THE LUFTHANSA GROUP, DECEMBER 2002

SEGMENTS & UNITS	LOCATION	OWNERSHIP STAKE	NOMINAL EQUITY
Passenger Business			
Deutsche Lufthansa AG	Germany	100.0%	€979.9m
Lufthansa CityLine GmbH	Germany	100.0%	€25.6m
Eurowings Lufverkehrs AG	Germany	24.9%	€30.0m
British Midland plc.	UK	30.0%	GB?16.3m
Luxair Societé Luxembourgeoise de Navigation Aérienne S.A.	Luxemburg	13.0%	€13.8m
Air Dolomiti S.p.A. Linee Aeree Regionali Europee	Italy	20.7%	€15m
Logistics			
Lufthansa Cargo AG	Germany	100.0%	€100.0m
Lufthansa Cargo Charter Agency GmbH	Germany	100.0%	€0.1m
time:matters GmbH	Germany	100.0%	€0.1m
Airmail Center Frankfurt GmbH	Germany	40.0%	€0.3m
Maintenance, Repair, and Overhaul			
Lufthansa Technik AG	Germany	100.0%	€220.0m
Aircraft Maintenance and Engineering Corp.	China	40.0%	US$87.5m
Lufthansa Airmotive Ireland Holdings Ltd.	Ireland	100.0%	US$27.1m
Shannon Aerospace Ltd.	Ireland	50.0%	€37.8m
Hawker Pacific Aerospace Inc.	US	100.0%	US$36.0m
AirLiance Materials LLC	US	40.3%	US$15.0m
Lufthansa A.E.R.O. GmbH	Germany	100.0%	€10.2m
HEICO Aerospace Holdings Corp.	US	20.0%	US$36.0m
Lufthansa Technik Shenzhen Comp. Ltd.	China	70.0%	US$5.1m
Lufthansa Technik Budapest Kft.	Hungary	85.0%	HUF1.3bn
Lufthansa Technik Malta Ltd.	Malta	51.0%	€1.2m
Catering			
LSG Lufthansa Service Holding AG	Germany	100.0%	€140.0m
LSG Sky Chefs Deutschland GmbH	Germany	100.0%	€30.7m
LSG Lufthansa Service Europa/Afrika GmbH	Germany	100.0%	DM50,000
LSG Sky Chefs Europe Holding Ltd.	UK	100.0%	GB£42.5m
LSG Sky Chefs US Holding Ltd.	US	100.0%	US$1.0m
LSG Sky Chefs LLC	US	100.0%	US$284.0m
SC International Services Inc.	US	100.0%	US$270.4m
LSG Lufthansa Service Asia Ltd	Hong Kong	100.0%	HK$100.0m
Leisure Travel			
Thomas Cook AG	Germany	50.0%	€303.7m
Condor Flugdienst GmbH	Germany	10.0%	€71.6m
IT Services			
Lufthansa Systems Group GmbH	Germany	100.0%	€20.5m
Lufthansa Systems Infratec GmbH	Germany	100.0%	€10.0m
Lufthansa Systems Airlines Services GmbH	Germany	100.0%	€2.0m
Lufthansa Systems Passenger Services GmbH	Germany	100.0%	€2.0m
Lufthansa Systems Network GmbH	Germany	100.0%	€0.5m
Lido GmbH Lufthansa Aeronautical Services	Germany	100.0%	€4.4m
Lufthansa Systems Berlin GmbH	Germany	100.0%	€1.0m
Lufthansa Process Management GmbH	Germany	100.0%	€0.3m
Service and Financial Companies			
Lufthansa Commercial Holding GmbH	Germany	100.0%	€101.6m
Amadeus Global Travel Distribution S.A.	Spain	18.3%	€33.4m
Lufthansa Flight Training GmbH	Germany	100.0%	€20.5m
START AMADEUS GmbH	Germany	66.0%	€9.3m
Delvag Luftfahrtversicherungs-AG	Germany	100.0%	€4.1m
Lufthansa AirPlus Servicekarten GmbH	Germany	48.8%	€10.0m
Autobahn Tank & Rast Holding GmbH	Germany	31.0%	€10.0m
Opodo Ltd	UK	22.9%	€193.3m

Source: Lufthansa Annual Report, 2002.

EXHIBIT 7 FINANCIAL RESULTS BY BUSINESS SEGMENT OF THE LUFTHANSA GROUP

	PASSENGER BUSINESS		**LOGISTICS/ CARGO**		**MAINTENANCE, REPAIR & OVERHAUL**		**CATERING**		**IT SERVICES**		**LEISURE TRAVEL**		**SERVICE AND FINANCIAL COMPANIES**[b]	
	LUFTHANSA PASSENGER BUSINESS GROUP		LUFTHANSA LOGISTICS GROUP		LUFTHANSA TECHNIK GROUP		LSG SKY CHEFS GROUP		LUFTHANSA SYSTEMS GROUP		THOMAS COOK GROUP[a]			
(Data in € Million)	2002	2001	2002	2001	2002	2001	2002	2001	2002	2001	2002	2001	2002	2001
Revenues	10,461	10,633	2,351	2,438	2,808	2,835	3,076	2,515	557	478	8,063	7,815	156	360
External Revenues	**10,036**	**10,183**	**2,339**	**2,422**	**1,623**	**1,541**	**2,630**	**2,067**	**190**	**126**	**8,063**	**7,815**	**155**	**352**
Segment Result	**516**	**149**	**168**	**66**	**215**	**155**	**8**	**−869**	**54**	**28**	**−120**	**20**	**572**	**148**
Assets	7,265	7,657	1,563	1,694	1,914	1,870	2,614	2,970	146	115	4,743	4,968	794	1,137
Capital Expenditure	632	1,167	9	129	68	65	104	1,380	37	35			234	178
Depreciation	784	795	115	117	82	79	219	652	32	35			43	61
Employees	34,021	33,983	5,207	5,411	16,116	13,194	35,138	28,962	2,916	2,034	27,776	28,388	737	4,391
Return on Sales	4.9%	1.4%	7.1%	2.7%	7.6%	5.5%	0.3%	−34.6%	9.6%	5.8%	−1.5%	0.3%	367.7%	41.0%
Return on Assets	7.1%	1.9%	10.7%	3.9%	11.2%	8.3%	0.3%	−29.3%	36.8%	24.0%	−2.5%	0.4%	72.0%	13.0%

Note: Results include activities of all the units within the group. (a) Results for Thomas Cook reflect the full financial results of the entity. Lufthansa consolidates these results using the equity method, based on its share of 50%. (b) Segment results include operating results of fully owned subsidiaries and financial results of partial equity stakes.
Source: Lufthansa Annual Reports: Worldscope.

undercut competitors' fares by more than 50%. Through the year, Ryanair expanded its routes to/from Frankfurt to 14, claiming to have carried 2 million passengers on those routes in the first year of operations. Ryanair CEO Michael O'Leary declared, "Ryanair's overnight success in the German market has surprised even ourselves. Many German consumers are travelling distances of over 200 kms just to avail themselves of Ryanair's low fares."[7]

On August 29, 2002, TUI, the largest tour operator in Europe, announced its entry into the German LCC arena by launching Hapag-Lloyd Express (HLX) with the slogan "Flying for a price of a taxi." HLX went into operation in December 2002 with eight Boeing 737-700 aircraft chartered from Germania, another TUI subsidiary. HLX's operation was based in Cologne–Bonn and it quickly added a second base in Hanover. By March 2003 it was operating 14 routes connecting to Cologne and 11 to Hanover.

Two weeks after the HLX news, Lufthansa's partner Eurowings announced the launch of Germanwings, which went into operation in November 2002. Germanwings also used Cologne–Bonn as its operation base. Its fleet consisted of five Airbus A319s (140-seater) and one A320 (170-seater). It started with 10 routes and quickly expanded to 19, all connecting to Cologne. These included several routes flying outside the EU, for example, to the Czech Republic and Turkey. HLX and Germanwings were in head-on competition on five routes.

Both airlines offered fares as low as €19.99 on limited seats for all of their flights. Both said that they did not expect to reach break-even before the third year of operations.

The demand for low-fare air travel attracted other existing players. In October 2002, Air Berlin, a large charter operator, launched a new scheduled travel product, the "City Shuttle." It connected 11 major European cities (e.g., Barcelona, Budapest, London–Stansted, Manchester, Warsaw) and seven German airports (including Berlin–Tegel, Düsseldorf, Paderborn, and Hanover) using Boeing 737s. While it did not follow a typical low-cost operation model (it offered in-flight catering, seat reservations, distribution through travel agencies, and a loyalty plan), the ticket price was comparable to its competitors thanks to the lower labor costs of charter airlines.

The sudden increase in competition seemed to deter some intended entrants. Virgin Express was the first casualty. The Brussels-based airline withdrew its plan to start a base in Cologne–Bonn, stating that the group "was not prepared to sustain losses for such a long period."[8] Virgin Express still had no flights into Germany as of March 2003. In May 2002, easyJet had acquired an option to purchase DBA, which was then losing money and was viewed by BA as incompatible with its long-term strategy. The option, which required easyJet to pay €5 million down and €600,000 per month until the exercise date, expired in April 2003. If exercised, easyJet could acquire DBA for an amount between €30 and €39 million on a debt-free basis. In March 2003, easyJet decided to terminate the option, citing two main hurdles: Germany's rigid labor laws, which made it difficult to obtain acceptance of easyJet's employment conditions, and the economic deterioration of the German market due to price competition. However, it was reported that HLX had expressed interest in the acquisition. (Exhibit 8 shows the route structures of Ryanair, HLX, Germanwings, and DBA as of March 2003. A map of Germany is provided in Exhibit 9.)

TRAVEL AND TOURISM IN GERMANY

Germany's travel and tourism market was marked by a significant imbalance between incoming and outbound travelers (Exhibit 10). In 2001, Germany had 18.1 million international arrivals, well behind France's 76.5 million, Spain's 49.5 million, Italy's 39.1 million, Britain's 22.8 million, and even Austria's 18.2 million.[9] However, with 76.8 million departures annually, Germany was the world's second largest tourism spender, 25% above Britain, 160% above France, and 220% above Italy.[10] The industry expected steady growth in both inbound and outbound travel in the next four years at a rate of 2–3% annually.

In Germany, the penetration of air transport was 40.5% of all international arrivals and 60.9% of departures. Land transport represented 34.3% of arrivals and 33.7% of departures. Rail travel accounted for 24.4% of arrivals and 4.9% of departures, with the remainder accounted for by sea travel.[11] The number of domestic travelers, defined as travel involving a stay at a hotel or campsite, was estimated to be 99.3 million in 2001. Of these, only 3.5% used air transport, 76.3% relied on land transport, and 20.2% used rail.

THE LOW-COST CARRIER THREAT TO INCUMBENT AIRLINES

The direct impact of the growth of LCCs on incumbent airlines varied significantly across Europe. In terms of penetration, the UK was most affected (Exhibit 11). Although Ryanair was Irish, London–Stansted was its most important base. EasyJet was established in 1996 out of London–Luton. They became the leaders in the LCC segment with a joint 70–80% market share. In January 2002, the LCC share of international routes involving a British airport was 25%, and only 3% on routes that did not.[12] As a result, BA was the company most immediately affected by the growth of the LCCs. Domestic and European international operations accounted for 10.3% and 28.1% of BA's 2001 turnover, respectively. Damage was most noticeable on the secondary routes (e.g., London–Genoa), where BA permanently lost 12–55% of its passengers.[13]

The LCCs' threat to incumbents came in two areas: loss of market share and yield pressure. One example was the London–Glasgow route. Before easyJet and Ryanair's entry in 1995 and 1997, respectively, BA had enjoyed a duopoly on the route with British Midland, garnering the vast majority of market share. By 2000, BA's market share had fallen to 50%. In May 2001, BA's share dropped to 39%, with Ryanair grabbing 20%, easyJet 15%, and Go 6%.[14] Faced

EXHIBIT 8 LCC ROUTES IN GERMANY AS OF MARCH 2003

ROUTE	SERVED BY	LH	ROUTE	SERVED BY	LH
Frankfurt–London	RY HLX GW DBA	51	Cologne–Munich*	DBA	71
Frankfurt–Bournemouth	RY	0	Cologne–Dresden*	GW	0
Frankfurt–Glasgow	RY	0	Cologne–London	HLX GW	21
Frankfurt–Shannon	RY	0	Cologne–Manchester	HLX	0
Frankfurt–Kerry	RY	0	Cologne–Edinburgh	GW	0
Frankfurt–Milan	RY	56	Cologne–Rome	HLX GW	0
Frankfurt–Rome	RY	41	Cologne–Pisa	HLX	0
Frankfurt–Pisa	RY	0	Cologne–Milan	HLX GW	0
Frankfurt–Prescara	RY	0	Cologne–Venice	HLX GW	0
Frankfurt–Bologna	RY	33	Cologne–Naples	HLX	0
Frankfurt–Barcelona	RY	41	Cologne–Olbia	HLX	0
Frankfurt–Perpignan	RY	0	Cologne–Bologna	GW	0
Frankfurt–Montpellier	RY	0	Cologne–Madrid	GW	0
Frankfurt–Oslo	RY	0	Cologne–Barcelona	GW	0
Frankfurt–Stockholm	RY	7	Cologne–Valencia	HLX	0
Frankfurt–Gothenburg	RY	14	Cologne–Reus	HLX	0
Frankfurt–Malmo	RY	0	Cologne–Lisbon	GW	0
Dusseldorf–Berlin*	DBA	52	Cologne–Marseille	HLX	0
Dusseldorf–Munich*	DBA	93	Cologne–Nice	GW	0
Dusseldorf–London	RY	28	Cologne–Vienna	GW	0
Hamburg–Cologne*	HLX	44	Cologne–Prague	GW	0
Hamburg–Munich*	DBA	91	Cologne–Thessaloniki	GW	0
Hamburg–London	RY	28	Cologne–Istanbul	GW	0
Hamburg–Milan	RY	17	Cologne–Izmir	GW	0
Hamburg–Pisa	RY	0	Hanover–Rome	HLX	0
Hamburg–Stockholm	RY	13	Hanover–Pisa	HLX	0
Hamburg–Nice	DBA	2	Hanover–Milan	HLX	5
Berlin–Cologne*	HLX GW DBA	53	Hanover–Venice	HLX	0
Berlin–Munich*	DBA	91	Hanover–Naples	HLX	0
Berlin–Stuttgart*	DBA	53	Hanover–Olbia	HLX	0
Berlin–London	RY	0	Hanover–Catania	HLX	0
Berlin–Nice	DBA	0	Hanover–Valencia	HLX	0
Friedrichshafen–London	RY	0	Hanover–Bilbao	HLX	0
Stuttgart–Nice	DBA	0	Hanover–Nice	HLX	0
Leipzig–London	RY	0	Munich–London	EJ	42
			Munich–Cardiff	bmi	0
			Munich–East Midlands	bmi	0
			Munich–Malaga	DBA	0

*Denotes domestic routes.
Codes: Ryanair (RY), Hapag–Lloyd Express (HLX), Germanwings (GW), Deutsche BA (DBA), easyJet (EJ), bmibaby (bmi).
Note: LH column stands for number of direct flights served by Lufthansa weekly.
Cities with multiple airports are bundled together in this table.
Sources: Company websites; ATI.

with intense price pressure, in April 2002 it announced a significant price reduction, offering tickets up to 70% cheaper—although Ryanair was still 50% cheaper than that (tax excluded). Seen from a more positive angle, however, the entry of LCCs on a route substantially increased the market size given the lower prices. According to one study in continental Europe,[15] route profitability usually recovered three years after the low-cost entry, although average yield was permanently 20% lower than the original level.

OTHER EUROPEAN CARRIERS' RESPONSES TO THE LCC THREAT

There was an urgent need for Lufthansa to respond to the rising LCC threat. The experiences of other European incumbents provided examples of various defensive strategies, as described in the following. (Exhibits 4, 12, and 13 provide financial and operational information for those European incumbents.)

British Airways, KLM, Alitalia et al: incumbents playing LCC games

Airlines in the US were first to experience competition with LCCs. When Dallas-based Southwest Airlines expanded nationwide during the 1990s, several incumbents responded by creating their own LCC subsidiaries. Continental Lite (by Continental Airlines) was the first such attempt in 1993, but failed painfully amid problems of brand confusion and lack of cost control. The Shuttle by United in 1994, Delta Express in 1996, and MetroJet by US Airways in 1998, also failed due to a combination of union opposition,

EXHIBIT 9 MAP OF GERMANY

creeping costs, brand confusion, and an aggressive reaction by Southwest. Interestingly, American Airlines, the largest airline in the world (also located in Dallas) never tried the concept. Delta announced the launch of Song, a low-cost subsidiary, in January 2003.

In Europe, BA became the first incumbent to adopt the low-fare business model in May 1998. It invested £25 million to set up its own low-fare subsidiary, Go, based at London–Stansted. BA avoided intervening in Go's strategy too heavily, allowing the subsidiary to develop independently. Go sought to differentiate itself from its rivals with better customer services—for example, passengers could buy better food and beverages on board. It was the first LCC to launch full-scale television advertising in the United Kingdom. According to COO Ed Winter, Go intended to achieve "what IKEA had done for furniture, Gap had done for casual clothing, and Swatch had done for watches."[16]

EasyJet reacted aggressively to the news, claiming that the move was anticompetitive and that BA simply intended to eliminate LCCs. It filed a series of court cases against Go, alleging that BA was subsidizing its insurance, advertising, aircraft leasing, and other services. EasyJet advertised strongly against Go, including a promotion campaign that offered free flights to customers who correctly guessed Go's first year losses. Ryanair, on the other hand, welcomed Go's entry but showed a determination to compete vigorously by immediately lowering its fares from London Stansted. Meanwhile, competitors claimed that Go's pricing was unsustainable. Barbara Cassani, Go's CEO, responded that they were simply "promotional prices" for the introductory stage only. In any case, Go's entry heated up the competition among LCCs. As of September 1999, 9 of the 17 (53%) routes operated by Go were in head-on competition with either Ryanair (one route), easyJet (four routes), or Debonair (five routes). In contrast, easyJet had only five of its 23 routes (22%) in head-on competition with other LCCs, and Ryanair only two of its 34 routes (6%).

Go sustained pretax losses of £20 million and £21.8 million in the financial years ending March 31, 1999 and 2000, respectively. But the situation improved rather swiftly and the company recorded its first profitable quarter in September 1999, moving into profit in 2001. However, just as things were showing signs of turnaround, BA decided to sell it off. The new chief executive of BA, Rod Eddington, said: "If you're a full-service network carrier, setting up your own no-frills carrier to compete with your no-frills

EXHIBIT 10 GERMAN TRAVEL MARKET IN 2001

ARRIVALS BY ORIGIN	*'000*
Netherlands	2,642
U.S.	2,117
U.K.	1,697
Italy	1,228
Switzerland	1,086
Austria	887
France	869
Denmark	778
Japan	768
Sweden	758
Total	18,096

DEPARTURES BY DESTINATION	*'000*
Spain	11,883
Italy	10,397
Austria	9,209
France	7,922
Netherlands	2,872
Hungary	2,674
Turkey	2,377
U.K.	2,377
Greece	2,327
U.S.	1,891
Denmark	1,683
Czech Republic	1,683
Switzerland	1,565
Poland	1,069
Total	76,808

Source: World Tourism Organisation, 2002.

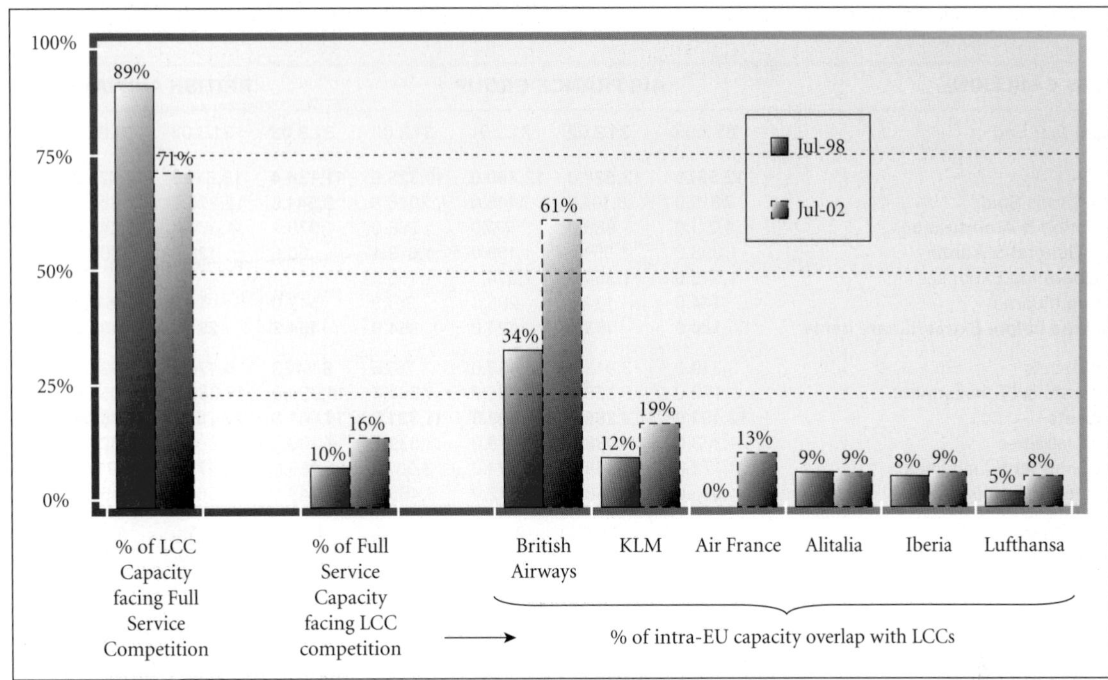

EXHIBIT 11 COMPETITIVE OVERLAP BETWEEN LOW-COST CARRIERS AND FULL-SERVICE CARRIERS, 1998, 2002

Source: EU DGTREN—Analysis of the European Air Transport Industry 2002.

competitors is no solution. What you have to do is fix your own business." In June 2001, a management buyout deal backed by the 3i Group was reached for an estimated £110 million. One year later, easyJet wholly acquired Go for a net price (discounting cash within Go) of £257.6 million.

In January 2000, KLM converted its British regional subsidiary, KLM-UK, into Buzz, a low-cost airline based at London–Stansted. Despite strong growth in traffic, it never turned a profit. Its fleet of BAe 146s put the airline at a cost disadvantage relative to those LCCs operating more efficient jets. In January 2003, Buzz was sold to Ryanair for a mere €5 million net. (A more detailed account is given in the companion case *Ryanair in 2003.*)

Italy's Alitalia planned to get in the game but with a different strategy. Italian cities were always popular destinations for LCCs, and their penetration accelerated from 2002 when Ryanair opened an operating base from Milan–Bergamo. The first local low-cost player emerged when Volare, a regional carrier, announced the start-up of Volareweb.com in 2003. LCCs increased their capacity by 50% in the first 6 months of 2003. Giulio de Metrio, managing director of Alitalia's air transport division, affirmed: "The growth of low-cost carriers to and from Italy has been explosive. This summer it is expected that they will offer almost as many seats between Italy and Western Europe as Alitalia."[17]

Alitalia intended to enter the market but had major difficulty achieving the labor costs needed to start its own low-cost operations. Instead, it sought to join a local partner for an external low-cost project. Volare had once been a likely candidate due to its low-cost model but Alitalia decided against a partnership, reportedly due to pilot union issues within Alitalia. As of April 2003 it began negotiating with Meridiana, a Sardinian-based regional carrier with a more conventional model. However, anticompetitive concerns remained a potential deal-killer as any agreement needed to be approved by the Italian competition authorities. (Exhibit 14 shows the routes operated by major LCCs as of March 2003 in Italy.)

British Airways post-2000: focus on core capabilities

With the increased penetration of LCCs and the economic downturn in 2001, the financial condition of BA declined steeply. Its lowest point was the 2001–02 financial year when it reported pretax losses of £200 million against pretax income of £150 million the previous year. European routes made an operating loss of £244 million, while remaining routes brought an operating profit of £134 million (Exhibit 5). BA blamed its poor performance mainly on the post-September 11 crisis, which hugely affected the turbulent transatlantic aviation market.

BA decided to focus on internal reform and restructuring to achieve better value-for-money for customers and cost reductions of £650 million per year by March 2004.[18] Its intention was to simplify its fleet, fares, and business systems. BA underwent a "Future Size and Shape" program to "strip off unprofitable capacities." In response to the LCCs' challenge, BA would "marry what they do well with what we do best" and revamp its short-haul services

EXHIBIT 12 CONSOLIDATED CORPORATE FINANCIAL REPORTS FOR SELECTED AIRLINE GROUPS

(DATA IN € MILLION)	**AIR FRANCE GROUP**				**BRITISH AIRWAYS**			
Financial Year End	31.3.03	31.3.02	31.3.01	31.3.00	31.3.03	31.3.02	31.3.01	31.3.00
Sales	**12,687.0**	**12,528.0**	**12,280.0**	**10,325.2**	**11,136.4**	**13,611.9**	**14,921.2**	**14,902.5**
Cost of Goods Sold	7,819.0	8,101.0	7,445.0	7,046.8	9,541.5	12,275.2	12,859.4	13,387.2
Depreciation & Amortization	1,211.0	988.0	977.0	788.0	979.2	1,256.7	1,149.9	1,080.2
Selling, General & Admin	1,998.0	1,951.0	1,199.0	1,018.1	66.6	128.9	300.7	295.0
Other Operating Expenses	1,515.0	1,354.0	2,374.0	1,165.0				
Operating Income	144.0	134.0	285.0	307.3	549.0	−49.0	611.1	140.0
Net Income before Extraordinary Items	**120.0**	**153.0**	**421.0**	**354.0**	**104.3**	**−231.8**	**183.3**	**−35.0**
Current Assets	3,319.0	3,913.0	3,433.0	3,767.5	3,947.3	4,176.6	3,933.7	4,320.7
Fixed Assets & LT Investment	9,172.0	9,353.0	8,936.0	7,564.4	14,694.0	18,080.6	18,055.6	18,166.4
Total Assets	**12,491.0**	**13,266.0**	**12,369.0**	**11,331.8**	**18,641.3**	**22,257.2**	**21,989.4**	**22,487.1**
Current Liabilities	4,303.0	4,932.0	4,226.0	3,879.7	4,206.6	5,224.4	5,320.0	5,610.9
Debt & Long Term Liabilities	4,172.0	4,368.0	4,271.0	3,967.0	11,185.6	13,471.5	11,211.0	11,350.2
Shareholders' Equity	4,016.0	3,966.0	3,872.0	3,485.1	3,249.1	3,561.3	5,458.3	5,525.9
Operating Margin (%)	1.14%	1.07%	2.32%	2.98%	4.93%	−0.36%	4.10%	0.94%
Return on Net Assets (%)	1.47%	1.84%	5.17%	4.75%	0.72%	−1.36%	1.10%	−0.21%
Return on Equity (%)	2.99%	3.86%	10.87%	10.16%	3.21%	−6.51%	3.36%	−0.63%
Net Asset Turnover (Ratio)	1.02	0.94	0.99	0.91	0.60	0.61	0.68	0.66
Long Term Debt/Equity	1.04	1.10	1.10	1.14	3.44	3.78	2.05	2.05

(DATA IN € MILLION)	**ALITALIA GROUP**				**SAS GROUP**			
Financial Year End	31.12.02	31.12.01	31.12.00	31.12.99	31.12.02	31.12.01	31.12.00	31.12.99
Sales	**4,736.7**	**5,273.5**	**5,390.9**	**4,806.4**	**7,103.0**	**5,506.6**	**5,366.5**	**4,846.7**
Cost of Goods Sold	1,802.2	2,128.1	2,229.2	1,768.3	6,715.1	5,427.1	4,947.7	4,523.8
Depreciation & Amortization	317.4	301.0	293.1	261.3	323.0	261.6	247.4	226.8
Selling, General & Admin	2,909.3	3,105.0	3,186.3	2,872.2				
Other Operating Expenses	27.0	138.1	116.2	207.5				
Operating Income	−319.2	−398.7	−433.9	−302.9	65.0	−182.0	171.4	96.1
Net Income before Extraordinary Items	**93.1**	**−907.0**	**−256.5**	**7.9**	**−14.4**	**−113.9**	**241.0**	**196.9**
Current Assets	2,054.7	1,388.6	1,715.0	1,412.7	2,183.6	2,179.3	1,806.5	1,738.9
Fixed Assets & LT Investment	3,684.4	3,098.4	2,984.9	2,613.2	4,953.6	4,482.0	3,772.8	3,219.0
Total Assets	**5,739.1**	**4,487.0**	**4,699.9**	**4,025.8**	**7,137.2**	**6,661.3**	**5,579.3**	**4,957.9**
Current Liabilities	1,570.0	1,691.3	1,759.1	1,224.7	2,664.3	2,396.7	1,986.7	1,817.0
Debt & Long Term Liabilities	2,400.3	1,949.6	1,444.4	1,048.6	2,793.7	2,572.2	1,600.1	1,145.8
Shareholders' Equity	1,768.7	846.1	1,496.3	1,752.6	1,679.3	1,692.4	1,992.5	1,995.1
Operating Margin (%)	−6.74%	−7.56%	−8.05%	−6.30%	0.91%	−3.31%	3.19%	1.98%
Return on Net Assets (%)	2.23%	−32.44%	−8.72%	0.28%	−0.32%	−2.67%	6.71%	6.27%
Return on Equity (%)	5.27%	−107.19%	−17.14%	0.45%	−0.86%	−6.73%	12.10%	9.87%
Net Asset Turnover (Ratio)	0.83	1.18	1.15	1.19	1.00	0.83	0.96	0.98
Long Term Debt/Equity	1.36	2.30	0.97	0.60	1.66	1.52	0.80	0.57

Source: Worldscope.

to provide lower prices, better schedules, and greater flexibility. The Q3 2002–03 saw a quick turnaround. Despite a continuous fall in passenger numbers, BA returned to profit, attributing the improvement to its cost reduction initiatives and the "Future Size and Shape" program, which would continue to be its dual focus in future.

Air France: continuous growth and alliance build-up

Things looked quite different across the Channel where Air France, the 54% government-owned flag-carrier, had a much easier time. The LCCs had first arrived in France in 1996 when easyJet and Virgin Express launched new routes to Nice from London–Luton and Brussels, respectively. Ryanair was the first to fly into Paris in 1997 from Dublin using the Beauvais airport located 70 km north of the city center. In subsequent years, new routes to France steadily emerged. As of March 2003, Ryanair operated 10 routes connecting London–Stansted mainly with small towns served by no other airlines, like Pau, Carcassonne, and Perpignan. EasyJet, on the other hand, was more focused on high-density routes, flying five routes into Paris. It repeatedly applied to start a base at Paris-Orly but was regularly turned down by the French government due to lack of slots.

EXHIBIT 13 OPERATING AND FINANCIAL STATISTICS OF SELECTED EUROPEAN AIRLINES

	DEUTSCHE LUFTHANSA AG			BRITISH AIRWAYS PLC			AIR FRANCE			ALITALIA			SAS		
	2000	2001	2002	2000	2001	2002	2000	2001	2002	2000	2001	2002	2000	2001	2002
FINANCIAL YEAR ENDED															
OPERATING STATISTICS	Dec-00	Dec-01	Dec-02	Mar-00	Mar-01	Mar-02	Mar-00	Mar-01	Mar-02	Dec-00	Dec-01	Dec-02	Dec-00	Dec-01	Dec-02
Rev Passengers Carried (000)	44,453	42,655	40,466	35,357	33,088	31,878	39,324	41,845	39,797	25,568	25,147	22,270	23,396	23,242	23,295
Departures	532,851	522,531	500,681	297,825	325,755	311,539	386,978	341,723	368,409	288,265	309,970	268,664	345,388	335,069	297,426
RPK—Revenue Passenger Kms. (million)	92,073	90,316	88,495	116,618	102,237	96,975	93,345	95,161	97,061	40,803	37,350	30,284	22,923	23,295	24,751
ASK—Available Seat Kms. (million)	123,660	126,378	119,746	162,549	144,506	134,028	119,504	123,296	126,422	56,772	51,594	42,167	34,132	35,931	34,626
Average Trip Distance (km)	1,144	1,166	1,173	2,002	1,828	1,866	1,382	1,523	1,445	1,107	1,023	1,014	763	792	785
Average Seats per Aircraft	203	207	204	273	243	231	224	237	238	178	163	155	130	135	148
Financial Statistics ((€ million)															
Passenger Revenues	9,019	8,907	8,569	11,313	10,180	9,156	8,693	8,450	8,424	3,698	3,750	3,193	3,690	3,675	3,597
Freight Revenues	34	40	38	76	66	64	50	35	38	18	15	16	16	15	16
Mail Revenues	0	0	0	0	0	0	53	0	0	10	58	59	32	30	24
Other Revenues	203	137	556	380	418	397	310	801	875	13	122	195	237	212	276
Total Operating Revenues	**9,563**	**9,443**	**9,504**	**12,453**	**11,254**	**10,192**	**9,561**	**9,604**	**9,675**	**3,898**	**4,079**	**3,608**	**4,114**	**4,066**	**4,059**
Total Operating Expenses	**9,128**	**9,615**	**9,082**	**11,718**	**11,279**	**9,594**	**9,046**	**9,193**	**9,430**	**4,143**	**4,335**	**3,729**	**4,004**	**4,203**	**4,072**
Operating Profits	**435**	**−173**	**422**	**735**	**−24**	**598**	**514**	**411**	**244**	**−245**	**−256**	**−121**	**111**	**−137**	**−13**
Operating Margin (%)	4.5%	−1.8%	4.4%	5.9%	−0.2%	5.9%	5.4%	4.3%	2.5%	−6.3%	−6.3%	−3.4%	2.7%	−3.4%	−0.3%
Revenues per Km. (€ cents/km)															
Passenger Revenues per RPK	**9.80**	**9.86**	**9.68**	**9.70**	**9.96**	**9.44**	**9.31**	**8.88**	**8.68**	**9.06**	**10.04**	**10.54**	**16.10**	**15.78**	**14.53**
Other Revenues per RPK	0.26	0.20	0.67	0.39	0.47	0.48	0.44	0.88	0.94	0.10	0.52	0.89	1.24	1.11	1.28
Total Revenues per RPK	**10.39**	**10.46**	**10.74**	**10.68**	**11.01**	**10.51**	**10.24**	**10.09**	**9.97**	**9.55**	**10.92**	**11.91**	**17.95**	**17.46**	**16.40**
Load Factor	74.5%	71.5%	73.9%	71.7%	70.7%	72.4%	78.1%	77.2%	76.8%	71.9%	72.4%	71.8%	67.2%	64.8%	71.5%
Total Revenues per ASK	**7.73**	**7.47**	**7.94**	**7.66**	**7.79**	**7.60**	**8.00**	**7.79**	**7.65**	**6.87**	**7.91**	**8.56**	**12.05**	**11.32**	**11.72**
Operating Profit per ASK	**0.35**	**−0.14**	**0.35**	**0.45**	**−0.02**	**0.45**	**0.43**	**0.33**	**0.19**	**−0.43**	**−0.50**	**−0.29**	**0.32**	**−0.38**	**−0.04**
Expenses per ASK (€ cents/km)															
Fuel & Oil	0.94	1.05	0.89	1.02	1.08	0.92	1.14	0.96	0.90	1.25	1.22	0.99	1.28	1.20	1.00
Flight Deck Crew	0.52	0.52	0.56	0.39	0.45	0.42	0.51	0.62	0.67	0.57	0.69	0.77	1.10	1.15	1.20
Airport Charges	0.28	0.26	0.29	0.30	0.32	0.30	0.24	0.31	0.31	0.18	0.22	0.24	0.64	0.60	0.60
Navigation Charges	0.60	0.44	0.47	0.29	0.33	0.34	0.37	0.31	0.33	0.37	0.40	0.45	0.51	0.53	0.53
Flight Equipment Rentals & Insurance	0.11	0.10	0.14	0.12	0.14	0.10	0.54	0.47	0.29	0.41	0.57	0.27	0.40	0.49	0.65
Depreciation	0.54	0.56	0.57	0.59	0.70	0.68	0.48	0.54	0.59	0.41	0.46	0.56	0.48	0.50	0.48
Maintenance & Overhaul	0.74	0.89	0.90	0.73	0.86	0.86	0.73	0.78	0.83	0.77	0.78	0.91	1.32	1.39	1.51
Station & Ground	1.14	1.07	1.07	0.83	0.94	0.91	0.86	0.85	0.90	0.96	1.09	1.18	1.56	1.56	1.55
Passenger Service	0.45	0.45	0.45	0.51	0.51	0.47	0.44	0.47	0.49	0.39	0.40	0.43	0.94	0.89	0.83
Cabin Attendants	0.54	0.57	0.62	0.58	0.63	0.59	0.46	0.55	0.57	0.52	0.58	0.64	0.86	0.90	0.97
Ticket & Sales & Prom.	0.92	1.38	1.35	1.42	1.32	1.04	1.16	1.05	1.02	1.02	1.41	1.61	2.19	2.13	2.09
General & Administration	0.60	0.31	0.26	0.43	0.53	0.52	0.64	0.55	0.58	0.44	0.60	0.79	0.43	0.37	0.35
Total Operating Expenses	**7.38**	**7.61**	**7.58**	**7.21**	**7.80**	**7.16**	**7.57**	**7.46**	**7.46**	**7.30**	**8.40**	**8.84**	**11.73**	**11.70**	**11.76**

Source: Association of European Airlines, ATI database. Financial statistics for the airline operations of the companies, not for the corporation.

EXHIBIT 14 LCC ROUTES IN ITALY AS OF MARCH 2003

ROUTE	SERVED BY	ROUTE	SERVED BY
Milan–Rome*	VW	Venice–Cologne	HLX 4U
Milan–Cagliari*	VW	Venice–Hanover	HLX
Milan–Catania*	VW	Venice–Madrid	VW
Milan–Brindinsi*	VW	Venice–Paris	VW
Milan–London	RY	Naples–Palermo*	VW
Milan–Cardiff	WW	Naples–London	EJ
Milan–East Midlands	bmi	Naples–Brussels	VW
Milan–Brussels	RY VE	Naples–Cologne	HLX
Milan–Frankfurt	RY	Naples–Hanover	HLX
Milan–Hamburg	RY	Pisa–London	RY
Milan–Cologne	HLX GW	Pisa–East Midlands	bmi
Milan–Hanover	HLX	Pisa–Brussels	RY
Milan–Barcelona	RY	Pisa–Frankfurt	RY
Milan–Bilbao	VW	Pisa–Cologne	HLX
Milan–Valencia	VW	Pisa–Hanover	HLX
Milan–Palma	VW	Pisa–Hamburg	RY
Milan–Copenhagen	ST	Palermo–London	RY
Milan–Stockholm	ST	Palermo–Brussels	VW
Rome–London	RY EJ	Bologna–London	RY
Rome–Brussels	RY VE	Bologna–Frankfurt	RY
Rome–Frankfurt	RY	Bologna–Cologne	VW
Rome–Cologne	HLX GW	Catania–Brussels	VW
Rome–Hanover	HLX	Catania–Cologne	HLX
Rome–Copenhagen	ST	Catania–Hanover	HLX
Rome–Cologne	ST	Genoa–London	RY
Venice–Cagliairi*	VW	Turin–London	RY
Venice–Alghero*	VW	Verona–London	RY
Venice–Oblia*	VW	Trieste–London	RY
Venice–Palermo*	VW	Ancona–London	RY
Venice–Catania*	VW	Pescara–London	RY
Venice–Brindisi	VW	Pescara–Frankfurt	RY
Venice–London	RY EJ VW	Alghero–London	RY
Venice–East Midland	EJ	Olbia–Cologne	HLX
Venice–Bristol	EJ	Olbia–Hanover	HLX
Venice–Brussels	RY VE	Bari–Paris	VW
Venice–Frankfurt	RY VW	Brindisi–Frankfurt	VW

*Denotes domestic routes.

Codes: Ryanair (RY), easyJet (EJ), Virgin Express (VE), Hapag–Lloyd Express (HLX), Germanwings (GW), Volareweb.com (VW), bmibaby (bmi), and Sterling (ST).

Note: Cities with multiple airports are bundled together in this table.

Sources: Company websites; ATI.

LCCs based in France never seemed a major threat. In February 2002, Air Lib, a loss-making French regional airline, established a low-fare subsidiary, AirLib Express. Based at Paris-Orly, the capital's busy second airport, it focused on domestic routes. Despite some promising early results at AirLib Express, Air Lib failed to overcome a financial crisis and filed for bankruptcy in February 2003. In April 2003, the French government allocated the freed slots at Orly among several airlines including Virgin Express and, finally, easyJet.

Air France's reaction to low-cost entry seemed relatively moderate. Aggressive responses and cut-throat price wars were not on its agenda. However, in September 2002 it launched several promotions and rebate programs for frequent travelers on peak-hour flights and one-month advance bookings.

Since 2000 Air France had consistently outperformed its European counterparts financially, particularly in the international arena (Exhibit 12). The Paris Charles de Gaulle airport, with huge infrastructure investment by the government in the 1990s, overtook London Heathrow to become the busiest hub in Europe. Air France attributed its strong performance to a combination of several factors including the superior results and financial strength of Delta Air (its partner in the Skyteam Alliance) over United Airlines and American Airlines (allies of Lufthansa and BA, respectively). Air France now eyed expansion with plans to grow Skyteam by absorbing the KLM/Northwest/Continental group. In February 2002, the French and Italian governments agreed on a 2% equity swap of their flag-carriers prompting rumors that a merger between Air France and Alitalia was being considered.

Scandinavian air system: learning from the LCC experience

Scandinavian air system (SAS), a 50% state-owned (jointly by Sweden, Norway, and Denmark) airline, went through what CEO Jorgen Lindegaard described as a "nightmare period" in 2001 when it posted a record loss of SKr2 billion (US$214 million) for the financial year. The unfolding of the SAS/Maersk scandal surrounding the pricing cartel brought a heavy fine and, more significantly, damaged SAS's reputation. To underline SAS's image as an overpriced airline, Ryanair filed a complaint with the Swedish Competition Authority claiming SAS had been "extorting high fares through its monopoly position." Even Lindegaard admitted, "If you lose that much, you simply lose control of it."[19]

SAS blamed its poor performance on the increasing competition from low-cost airlines. However, there were many ways in which it was vulnerable. It had the most expensive cost structure of all major airlines in the world, mainly due to inferior staff productivity and high labor costs (Exhibit 13). For each 1,000 tonne/km operated, SAS had labor costs of US$370 compared with an average of US$127 for Lufthansa, US$167 for BA, and US$83 for Asian airlines. SAS was also known for its reliance on business-class passengers who traditionally accounted for 30% of its passenger volume and 60% of revenue.[20] When business-class passenger demand shrank in 2001, SAS's financials were severely impacted (Exhibit 12).

The low-cost airlines had launched their Scandinavian challenge in 1996 when Virgin Express opened its Brussels–Copenhagen route. Ryanair entered in 1997, flying from London–Stansted to Oslo and Stockholm Skavsta, the secondary airport 100 km south of city. By the end of 2001, Ryanair was flying 10 routes into Scandinavia, Virgin Express operated two, and easyJet one. Domestically, Copenhagen-based low-fare airline Sterling operated four routes within the region. The share of LCCs in Scandinavia (domestic and international) was 6%, which was low compared to Britain's 30% and Germany's 20%, but was expected to rise.[21]

In 2002, SAS focused its efforts on achieving cost reductions of 25–40%, partly by imitating the tactics of the LCCs. SAS planned to trim up to 3,600 jobs from its workforce of 25,200. Flight hours for cabin crew would be "significantly increased" to improve staff productivity by 20–25%. Seven routes were dropped with another six transferred to regional affiliates. SAS would also dedicate some of its fleet and crew to focus on short-haul point-to-point operations. As a result, it was able to ground 21 aircraft and to improve aircraft utilization by 5%. Probably its most radical move was dropping business class on intra-Scandinavian flights. While still enjoying more flexible terms for ticketing, business travelers got a fare reduction of up to 30% on the less-exclusive services. SAS simplified its pricing structure and introduced one-way prices. To "fit the needs of business travelers," it also introduced a number of promotional fares such as discounted day-return tickets. The company anticipated that these measures would bring it back to profit by 2004.

In December 2002, SAS announced plans for the launch of an LCC unit, Snowflake. SAS would lease four Boeing 737-800s and refit them with the new logo and color schemes. It would initially operate from Copenhagen and Stockholm and fly to tourist spots such as Nice, Alicante, Barcelona, and Malaga. The intention was to leverage SAS's quality brand to attract leisure customers to Snowflake. SAS expressed confidence in avoiding cannibalization, since the routes were those that "SAS normally does not serve, or serves to a small extent." But its competitors remained undeterred. In January 2003, Ryanair announced plans to upgrade Stockholm Skavsta into its fourth operation base in April and start six new routes, including three intra-Scandinavian routes; Ryanair would operate 30 daily flights from Skavsta.

OUTLOOK

The launch of Germanwings did not solve Lufthansa's problem but did at least open up some new options. Now Lufthansa could further invest in the emerging LCC trend by increasing its share of Eurowings, or make its own move to build a new player under its full control. Alternatively, given the dismal record of incumbents entering the LCC segment in the past, Lufthansa could limit its involvement in the segment and refocus on its full-service, vertically integrated business model.

In May 2002, Lufthansa started another experiment by offering six-times-per-week dedicated business flight services between Düsseldorf and Newark. The flight was operated by a charter company, PrivatAir, which used Boeing 737 aircraft with only 48 seats. Lufthansa announced pleasing results and planned to expand similar services to Chicago–Düsseldorf and Newark–Munich routes.

As Wolfgang Mayrhuber prepared to take the helm of Lufthansa, he had various options for responding to the low-cost challenge and enduring the turbulent industry conditions. Whatever his choice, it would be an important step in charting Lufthansa's future strategic direction. One thing was certain: in the changing market environment, Lufthansa could not afford to adopt a wait-and-see stance for too long.

CASE 9

Cadbury Schweppes

It was hardly the Christmas gift that the board of Cadbury Schweppes was expecting as 2007 drew to a close (see Table 1), but there it was nevertheless: a letter from Nelson Peltz, the Chief Executive Officer of Trian Partners, announcing what he intended to do with the 4.5% of the outstanding shares of Cadbury Schweppes he had been accumulating over the past twelve months.

The letter began by reminding the Cadbury Schweppes board of the decline in share price over the past nine months (see Figure 1). The decline, the letter suggested, could be directly attributed to poor margins in the core confectionary business. Notwithstanding the less than stellar share performance, the letter went on to compliment Cadbury Schweppes:

> Trian believes the current management team and Board have made sound strategic judgments in the past, including the acquisition of Adams and the recent decision to separate the beverage and confectionary businesses. And notwithstanding various operational problems that have arisen under the current leadership team, including salmonella issues in the UK, fraud in Nigeria and under-deliverance on past margin targets, Trian continues to believe that the current management team is capable of achieving its plan as well as the actions we are proposing.[1]

Returning to the main theme of under-performance, the letter concluded with a warning:

> However, should Cadbury fail to demonstrate meaningful operational progress in 2008 that translates to the bottom line, Trian will look to become significantly more active in evaluating all of our alternatives as a large shareholder.

CADBURY AND SCHWEPPES: A PREMERGER HISTORY

Cadbury Schweppes is a marriage of two venerable British companies. The Cadbury part of the story goes back to 1824 when a young Quaker, John Cadbury, opened a shop selling tea and coffee, and cocoa and drinking chocolate which Cadbury prepared personally. In 1831 John Cadbury rented a factory, and entered the manufacturing of chocolate. The company expanded rapidly, becoming a market leader and an innovator, bringing to the mass market chocolate-covered nougats, pistache, bonbons delices, pate d'abricot, caramels, avelines, and other delights.

Cadbury became a limited company in 1899. It was the largest confectionary company in Britain, with 2,600 employees in its main Bournville factory. During the first half of the 20th century, the company expanded internationally, starting operations in Ireland, France, Spain, Germany, New Zealand, Canada, Malaysia, and South America.

The Schweppes story begins with Jean Jacob Schweppe, a young Swiss watchmaker and keen amateur scientist, developing the world's first process for manufacturing carbonated mineral water in 1783. Schweppe moved to England at the end of the 18th century where he established a business for producing soda waters and seltzers, which he subsequently expanded to include flavored drinks, and in the 1870s the now famous Schweppes Tonic Water and Ginger Ale. The company expanded operations outside Britain, notably in the US and Australia. In 1897 Schweppes was floated as a public company. As it entered the 20th century, the company continued to expand its product line, as well as modernize its financial and managerial structure.

MERGER AND MOMENTUM

In 1969 Cadbury and Schweppes merged into a single firm. There were obvious synergies to the merger: both companies produced popular food and beverage brands, relying on sophisticated advertising and distribution to expand and increase revenues. Indeed, growth following the merger was rapid. Focusing on core beverage and confectionary businesses, the company expanded rapidly through a string of acquisitions, as well as through organic growth (see Table 2). The acquisitions strategy targeted firms in key markets with the intention of building a global firm that specialized in soft drinks and confectionary products.

In 1993 Dominic Cadbury succeeded Sir Graham Day as chairman of Cadbury Schweppes. The succession marked a return to power of the Cadbury family, and it did not take long for this resurgence to have an impact on the direction of the firm. First came a $232-million investment in Dr Pepper/Seven Up, raising the stake that Cadbury

This case was prepared by Joseph Lampel, City University London.

SHARE PRICE CHART
Price (p)
Grain/Loss (%)
09-Feb-2007 : 8,845,180

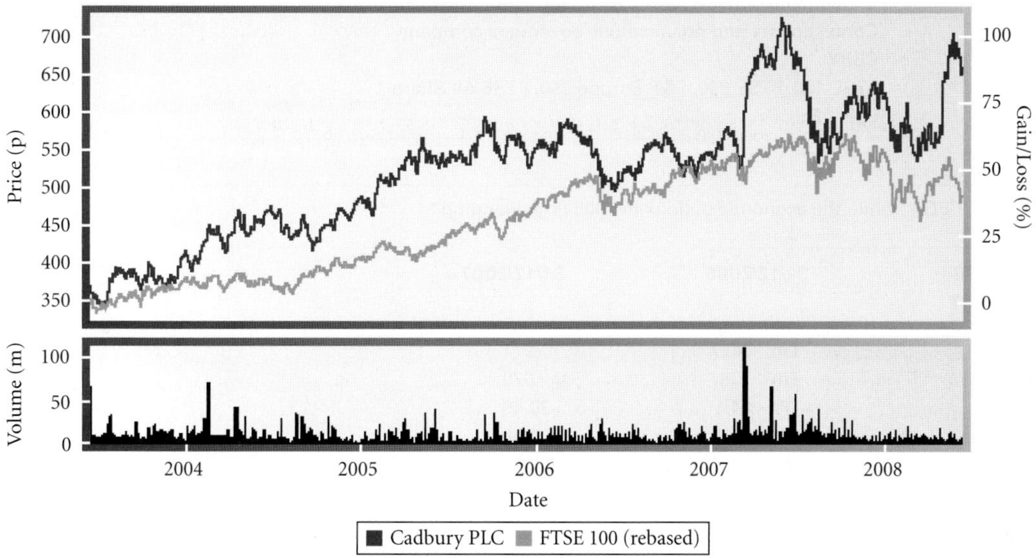

FIGURE 1 CADBURY VERSUS THE FTSE 100

Schweppes already owned to nearly 26%. Then came a surprise $334-million acquisition of the niche soft drink maker A&W. The twin acquisitions were part of a wider strategic push to catapult Cadbury Schweppes to a globally dominant position in the soft drinks industry. But one major obstacle that faced Dominic Cadbury was Cadbury Schweppes' dependence on Coke and Pepsi for about two-thirds of its bottling and distribution in the US and a substantial amount overseas, a dependence that locked the company into a third place globally.

To break this dependence, Cadbury Schweppes signed an agreement with Toronto-based Cott Corp. to produce private label colas and flavored beverages across continental Europe in Cadbury plants. Next came Cadbury Schweppes' boldest move to date, taking control of Dr Pepper/Seven Up. Overcoming resistance from Dr Pepper/Seven Up management, Cadbury Schweppes completed the takeover in 1995, paying £1.1 billion for the acquisition. The acquisition gave the company control of the production and distribution of more than 40% of its beverage volume, allowing for broader distribution of its beverage brands, greater focus on faster growing and more profitable channels, and improvement in cost competitiveness. As a result, Cadbury Schweppes' share of the $49 billion US soft drinks market moved up from 5.6% to 17%.

By the time Dominic Cadbury stepped down as chairman in 2000, the company's growth strategy that he initiated and pursued with persistence and energy seemed to be bearing fruit. Cadbury Schweppes was a truly global company with presence in every major soft drinks and confectionary markets. In his last company annual meeting, Cadbury, who started in the business at 24 as a sales representative, could survey his nine-year tenure as chairman with satisfaction. Cadbury Schweppes share price had risen 50% under his chairmanship, with acquisitions in soft drinks and confectionary, making it number three globally in both sectors.

CADBURY SCHWEPPES ENTERS THE NEW MILLENNIUM

The departure of Dominic Cadbury found the Cadbury Schweppes board without a member of the Cadbury family for the first time in its history. Succession, however, was smooth, with Derek Bonham, the chairman of Imperial Tobacco, becoming chairman. Bonham had cut his teeth as top manager during his tenure as chief executive and deputy chairman of the construction group Hanson. When asked about the contrast between the two firms, he responded: "The images may be different, but running a business comes down to the same things. You still need to know the numbers, assess the economics, watch the productivity measures."[2]

As chairman, Derek Bonham and his chief executive officer, John Sunderland, continued to pursue the strategy developed by Dominic Cadbury. They acquired confectionary and soft drink businesses in France, Spain, China, Argentina, and Australia. They also sought to reinforce Cadbury Schweppes position in the US, the world's biggest soft drinks market, by acquiring Snapple for $1.45 billion dollars. This major acquisition came on the heels of

TABLE 1 COMPANY BACKGROUND AND ANNUAL REPORT

COMPANY BACKGROUND	
Sector	Consumer Goods
Activities	Confectionary and nonalcoholic beverages company
TIDM	CBRY
Index	FTSE 100, FTSE 350, S&P Europe 350, FTSE All Share
Listed	LSE – Full

OUTLOOK

(11/4/2008) RNS: CEO - "while the economic outlook in 2008 is challenging"

LATEST RESULTS - ANNUAL REPORT		31/12/2006	31/12/2007
Turnover	£m	7427	7971
Pre-tax Profit	£m	738	670
EPS (Norm Dil.)	P	34.1	30.49
Dividend	P	13.1	14.9
Notes	Figures from 2004 in accordance with IFRS		

INVESTMENT RATIOS		Co.	FTSE Sector	Market
Price per Earnings Ratio	x	21.21	15.14	11.28
Dividend Yield (pr)	%	2.23	3.56	4.38
Price/Earnings to Growth	f	4.97	3.31	0.32
Return on Capital Employed	%	37.26	42.62	−32.41
Operating Margin	%	13.15	13.13	−1.78
Earning per Share Growth (pr)	%	4.27	5.75	16.39
EV/EBITDA	x	12.64	8.86	10.52
Net Gearing	%	77.39	62.30	91.79
Net Tangible Asset Value PS	p	−102.89	−0.82	1.24
Price to Tangible Book Value (PTBV)	x	−6.34	−4.50	2.22
Price to Cash Flow (PCF)	x	16.59	15.33	11.20
Price to Sales Ratio (PSR)	x	1.71	1.54	2.98

other major acquisitions, notably purchases in France of Orangina the soft drinks producer from Pernod Ricard for £419 million, and the chewing gum and candy unit from Kraft Foods for £200 million.

At the end of 2002, Cadbury Schweppes made its largest acquisition to date, announcing an agreement to purchase the Adams confectionery business from New York City–based pharmaceutical company Pfizer Inc. for $4.2 billion. The acquisition brought into the Cadbury Schweppes fold an organization with 14,300 dependents in 22 countries with 22 factories. It also transformed Cadbury Schweppes in one stroke into the world's leading candy producer and the second-largest chewing-gum maker, behind Chicago-based Wrigley. Some baulked at the price that the company paid: twice Adams' annual sales of £1.25 billion and 18 times operating profits of £148 million. But for Chief Executive John Sunderland, the deal which he had pursued doggedly for some time fulfilled a long-held belief that as an orphan brand in the Pfizer portfolio, Adams represented a not-to-be missed opportunity.

The same year saw the announced departure of Derek Bonham as chairman and the elevation of John Sunderland as his replacement. In turn, chief strategy officer Todd Stitzer, a twenty-year Cadbury Schweppes veteran, became CEO. Stitzer, described by company insiders as the architect of Cadbury's acquisitions strategy, became Cadbury Schweppes' first American CEO. Now that he was in charge, Stitzer turned his attention to reorganizing and consolidating Cadbury Schweppes sprawling multi-continent operations in soft drinks and confectionary. This involved selling noncore operations such as Piasten, Holland House, and Grandam's Molasses. In a surprising move, Cadbury Schweppes also disposed of European Beverages business which makes Orangina and Oasis brands for £1.26 billion. The sale allowed the company to shift resources to the lucrative North American market, in particular, to beef up its distribution system by acquiring the remaining 55% stake in Dr Pepper/Seven Up Bottling Group from its joint-venture partner, the Carlyle group, for £198 million.

TURBULENCE AND UNCERTAINTY

Facing shareholders and analysts in early 2007, Todd Stitzer tried to convey a balanced picture of what had surely been a difficult year. "2006 was a year of contrasts." He told the audience, "We delivered our third year of revenue growth at nearly double our historic growth rate, double-digit emerging market growth, double-digit gum growth, share gains in US CSDs, substantial savings from our Fuel for Growth cost reduction program, and significant operational and strategic progress. Three years in a row."[3]

At the same time, he ruefully admitted, Cadbury Schweppes had experienced a number of highly publicized setbacks that had tarnished the reputation of the firm.

In June 2006 a Health Protection Agency investigation tracked the source of a sudden rash of salmonella poisonings to the Cadbury Schweppes plant at Herefordshire. To make matters worse, the agency accused Cadbury Schweppes management of knowing that contamination had occurred as early as January, but of failing to communicate the relevant facts to regulators. The company insisted that it met all the legal requirements and was under no obligation to inform regulators because in January, at 0.3 cells of salmonella per 100 g of chocolate crumb, the contamination was below the company's own "alert" level of 10 cells per 100 g. Nevertheless, Cadbury Schweppes announced a recall of seven varieties of its Cadbury Dairy Milk chocolate products, and began extensive modifications of manufacturing processes to prevent future contaminations. Later in the year, the company was fined £1 million by a Birmingham court, but the total costs of the incident, according to sources, may have run as high as £30 million in direct costs and another £80 million in lost revenues.

In November 2006, the company's Nigeria-owned operations, Cadbury Nigeria, had deliberately overstated earnings to the tune of N13 and N15 billion. The board of Cadbury Nigeria took immediate action, dismissing its Managing and Finance Directors, and retaining the accountancy firm Price Waterhouse to obtain a complete review of the situation. The company's Public Affairs Manager, Kufre Ekanem, told newsmen that, "Over the number of years, Cadbury Nigeria had assigned itself an ambitious growth target. To achieve these targets, several systems abuses occurred. The overstatements are directly traceable to those systems abuses."

To prove the adage that it never rains but it pours, the salmonella and Nigeria embarrassments were followed by a series of other missteps. In February 2007 Cadbury recalled thousands of Easter eggs which were distributed without nut-allergy warnings, but not before coming under criticism for sending retailers stickers to place on the packaging rather than recalling all the eggs. In the same month, a sales promotion for soft drink Dr Pepper in the US went disastrously wrong. Treasure hunters seeking a $760,000 prize were expected to follow a series of clues to a graveyard in Boston containing the remains of historic American figures such as Samuel Adams. The managers of the graveyard—where Cadbury has buried the winning gold coin—complained and a national outcry ensued. Cadbury admitted to "poor judgment" but maintained that none of the graves was damaged. In March the Advertising Standards Authority banned Cadbury Trebor Bassett's cinema and television commercials for Trident chewing gum, saying they contained offensive racist stereotypes after receiving more than 500 complaints from viewers. The ads were released for broadcasting even though the company's own research showed that one in five black people would find the campaign offensive.

At the same time that Cadbury Schweppes was struggling to contain the fallout from these highly publicized missteps, its stock was fluctuating wildly as it tried to change the strategic direction of the firm. In March 2006 Cadbury Schweppes announced plans to sell off its US drinks business, including big brands such as Dr Pepper, 7Up, Snapple, Mott's, Canada Dry, and Hawaiian Punch. "Separating these two great businesses will enable two outstanding management teams to focus on generating further revenue growth, increasing margin and enhancing returns for their respective shareowners," Todd Stitzer stated in a company statement. But Cadbury was forced to postpone the deal when the credit markets imploded in July. Cadbury's stock had climbed 33% since the start of the year, to a May high of 723.75 pence on the possibility of a $15 billion private equity deal for the drinks unit. Then, when the buyout fell through, shares plunged 30% to a low of 514 pence in August. Finally, in October the company announced that instead of selling its US drinks unit, Cadbury will spin it out to shareholders, creating a new, as-yet-unnamed beverages giant with annual sales of more than $5 billion.

In the meantime, Cadbury had to struggle with increasing commodity prices, higher costs for energy, sweeteners, and other raw materials which lopped off 1.4% from its operating margins. One course of action is for Cadbury to lift margins by seeking a merger with another candy maker. But the list of potential candidates is limited by regulatory concerns. Competition authorities would likely balk at a deal with Mars or Nestle, which compete in many of the same markets as Cadbury. Wrigley and Kraft would similarly shy away from buying the candy maker, as both are currently focused on sorting out their own business problems. Speculating on the choices facing Cadbury Schweppes, Beverage Marketing Corporation chairman and CEO Michael Bellas had this to say:

> There are three scenarios: one is a spin-off, one is a management-led buyout and the third could be a private equity firm taking it over. The other issue that they're going to look at is that some of the brands may make it worth breaking the company apart. There may be some interest in the non-carbs by one group and interests in the carbonated beverages by another. So a lot of different alternatives are in play and the key thing would be to maximize the value to Cadbury.[4]

TABLE 2 CADBURY SCHWEPPES' ACQUISITIONS AND DISPOSALS

YEAR	ACQUISITION AND DISPOSALS	COMMENT
1972	Jeyes group	UK household products firm acquired for £12.4 million
1978	Peter Paul	Purchase of US confectionary firm for $58.2 million propels Cadbury Schweppes to third place in the American market
1982	Duffy-Mott	Acquisition of one of the largest apple juice processors in the world for £41 million
1982	Rioblanco	Acquisition of Spanish soft drink company with 12% market share for £14.2 million
1982	Holland House	Producer of branded nonalcoholic cocktail mixers and specialty products from National Distillers and Chemical Corporation for $8.8 million
1982	Reckitt and Colman Industrial Supply	Floor maintenance equipment with operations in the UK, France, and Ireland for £7.7 million
1984	Cottee's General Foods	Purchase of Australian producer of coffee and fruit juice cordials from General Foods for £16.25 million
1985	Sodastream	Acquisition of the leading producer of in-home soft drinks machines for £ 26.2 million
1986	Typhoo Tea, Kenco Coffee, and Jeyes brands	Sale of units and exit of the general foods and hygiene sector
1986	Canada Dry and Sunkist	Soft drinks units bought from RJR Nabisco for $230 million
1986	Hepburn Spa	Producer of a range of mineral waters and natural lemonade for £1 million
1987	Red Tulip	Australian confectionary brand from Beatrice for $143.5 million
1988	Chocolat Poulain	Acquisition of leading French chocolate bar maker for £94.2 million from Midial, the French food group
1989	Trebor	Largest UK private confectionary firm for £110.3 million
1989	Bassett	UK-based confectionary producer of Liquorice Allsorts, Wine Gums, Jelly Babies, and Dolly Mixtures brands for £91 million
1989	Crush International soft drinks	US producer of carbonated soft drinks from Procter & Gamble for $220 million
1989	E.D. Smith & Sons Ltd.	Canadian producer of Garden Cocktail and Tomato Clam Cocktail juice for $7.6 million
1989	Chocolates Hueso	Spanish confectionary brand
1989	Trinaranjus	Spanish soft drinks producer for £45.25 million
1990	Oasis	French soft drink brand from Source Perrier for £125 million
1992	Aguas Minerales	Acquisition of Mexico's leading mineral producer for £188 million.
1992	Piasten	Purchase of 70% stake in German company making boxed chocolates, liqueurs, and sweets for £43 million
1993	Stani	Argentinean company manufacturing chewing and bubble gums, and other sugar confectionary for $125 million
1994	Industrias Dulciora S.A.	Spanish confectionary company producing gums, jellies, hard candy chews, and panned products for undisclosed sum
1994	Bouquet D'Or	French manufacturer of assorted chocolate assortments and specialist chocolate products for $25.6 million
1995	Dr Pepper/7UP	£1.8 billion pounds for Dr Pepper/Seven Up Allan Candy sugar confectionary in Canada
1996	Neilson Cadbury	Canada's leading chocolate bar manufacturer for $164 million
1997	La Pie Qui Chante	Purchased from Danone for £38 million, making Cadbury Schweppes the number two firm in the French sugar confection market. The company produces boiled sweets, caramels, chews, and jellies
1997	Coca-Cola & Schweppes Beverages	Cadbury Schweppes disposes of its 51% interest in Coca-Cola & Schweppes Beverages for £622.5 million
1997	Jaret	Acquisition of Jaret, a US confectionary distributor
1997	Bim Bim	Acquisition of one of the largest confectionary firms in the Middle East
1998	America Inc.	Joint purchase with Carlyle Group LP of bottling company with US operations. Price $724 million with Cadbury Schweppes holding 40%

1998	Wedel	Acquisition of Poland's leading chocolate company from Pepsico for $76 million
1999	Hawaiian Punch	Purchased from Procter and Gamble for $203 million
2000	Snapple	$1.45 billion acquisition for Snapple, Royal Crown Cola, and Mistic fruit drinks, Diet Rite and Nehi Soda
2000	Hollywood	Acquisition of French producer of chewing gum and candy business from Kraft Foods for £200 million
2000	Mauna La'l	Acquisition of producer of Hawaiian tropical juice producer for undisclosed sum
2000	Wuxi-Lear	Acquisition of Huhtamaki Van Leer's China-based Wuxi-Leaf Confectionery for £1.58 million
2000	Spring Valley	Acquisition of Australian juice and milk-flavored drinks for £11 million
2001	Slush Puppie	Acquisition of Ohio-based Slush Puppie, manufacturer of frozen, noncarbonated beverages, for $16.6 million
2001	Carteret Packaging	US bottling operations for $14.8 million
2001	La Casera	Acquisition of Spanish soft drinks company for £50 million. The acquisition makes Cadbury Schweppes the second largest soft drinks producer in Spain
2001	Orangina	Purchase of Orangina brand and associated assets in Europe, North America, and Australia for £419 million from Pernod Ricard
2001	Mantecol	Acquisition of Argentinian confectionary firm for $23 million
2002	Kent	Purchase of 51% interest in Kent, Turkey's leading sugar confectionary manufacturer, and its distribution arm Birlik, for £67 million
2002	Dandy	The acquisition of Danish chewing gum operations for £201 millions makes Cadbury Schweppes the number two firm in the European chewing gum market.
2002	Nantucket Allserve	Acquisition of American manufacturer of fruit-based beverages from Ocean Spray Cranberries for $100 million
2002	Apollinaris & Schweppes	Cadbury Schweppes buys Brau und Brunnen's 72% interest in the Apollinaris & Schweppes soft drinks joint venture in Germany for around €150 million
2002	Squirt	Acquisition of Mexican soft drinks producer for £35 million gives Cadbury Schweppes the number three position in the Mexican market which is second in size to the US market
2002	Stimorol	Acquisition of Danish chewing gum business for £201 million
2002	Adams	Acquisition of Adams, producer of chocolate bars and chewing gums, from Pfizer for £2.7 billion
2005	Green and Black	Acquisition of UK's leading producer of luxury organic chocolate
2005	Piasten Holland House	Sale of cooking wines company as part of disposal of noncore businesses
2005	Holland House	Sale of cooking wines company as part of disposal of noncore businesses
2005	European Beverages	Cadbury Schweppes sells of European Beverages business which makes Orangina, Oasis, and Schweppes drinks to Blackstone consortium for £1.26 billion
2006	Dr Pepper/Seven Up Bottling (DPSUBG)	Cadbury Schweppes acquires remaining 55% stake in Dr Pepper/Seven Up Bottling Group (BG) from its joint-venture partner the Carlyle group for £198 million
2006	All American Bottling Co.	Acquisition of the third-largest independent bottler in the US, for about $65 million
2006	Cadbury Nigeria	Increased equity holding from 46.4 to 50.02
2006	Grandam's Molasses	Sale of Grandma's Molasses unit to B&G Foods for $30 million
2006	Dan Products	Acquisition of South Africa's leading chewing gum business for £33 million
2006	Bormor	Sale of Cadbury Schweppes South African drinks business for £109
2007	Cottee's Food Allan Candy Cadbury Italia	Sale of three noncore units: Cottee's Food (Australia), Allan Candy (Canada), and Cadbury Italia (Italy) for a total of £250 million
2007	Intergum Sansei South Eastern Beverage	Acquisition of Intergum, the leading chewing gum company, in Turkey, Sansie, Japanese candy maker, and South-Eastern Beverage, a US bottling firm for a total of £300 million
2007	Kandia-Excellent	Romanian confectionary firm for $32 million giving Cadbury Schweppes leading position in the Romanian market

CASE 10

Airbus versus Boeing: Superjumbo and Super risks

It was like a burst of bright sunshine on a cloudy day: On January 25, 2007, Airbus, the premier European aircraft maker, reached a milestone with the 5,000th order for A320 aircraft family, making it the world's most popular passenger aircraft. "The 5,000th order of our A320 aircraft family marks an historic milestone for Airbus and the aviation industry," declared Airbus chief executive officer, Louis Gallois.[1]

Gallois savored the good news, knowing full well that Airbus faced one of the most difficult battles in a history marked by both triumph and tribulation. The past year had seen Airbus beset by heavy turbulence. Its flagship program, the A380 superjumbo, was running more than two years late. The A350, a new mid-size jet designed to take on archrival Boeing, already the subject of several costly redesigns, will require billions of euros in investment before it gets off the ground. And if this was not enough, the continuing weakness of the US dollar—the currency used in sales contract—meant that Airbus had to cut costs just to stand still.

The challenge would have been daunting for the top management of any company, but Airbus was not just any company: It was a multinational European company set up by governments with the specific aim of defying American dominance in commercial aviation. With its various stakeholders and complex ownership structure, it was always a difficult entity to manage. These difficulties were compounded by recent top management shakeup. In June 2006 Noel Forgeard announced his resignation as joint chief executive of EADS and chief executive of Airbus after it emerged that he had made a €2.5 million profit for himself and €400,000 for each of his three children by exercising stock options in March. He was replaced by Christian Streiff. Three months later EADS, the parent company of Airbus, announced delays to A380 delivery, and the resignation of Charles Champion, head of the A380 superjumbo project. Christian Streiff, Airbus's chief executive, in turn tendered his resignation in October of the same year, three months after assuming the job. He was replaced by Louis Gallois, a technocrat and civil servant who won his spurs rescuing the French state-owned rail company SNCF from the edge of insolvency.

THE BIRTH OF THE SUPERJUMBO

The struggle over the world market for large civil aircraft involves billions of dollars and a great deal of national pride. Each aircraft generation takes years to develop, and involves placing enormous bets on market conditions that are almost impossible to predict in advance. Making the wrong bet can severely damage, or even sink, a company. The economic consequences can ripple through the economy of entire regions, and nations, which is the reason why governments provide hundreds of millions of dollars in direct and indirect support of what they consider to be vital national interest.

Boeing is America's biggest exporter, while Airbus is a potent symbol of European industrial prowess. For most of the 1990s the story was that Airbus, the European underdog, was relentlessly pursuing Boeing, the world leader. To many observers nothing symbolized Airbus' challenge to Boeing's decades-old dominance than the decision to launch the A380, the largest commercial aircraft ever produced.

The prospect of building a superjumbo to replace the Boeing 747, the world's largest commercial jet, began to take shape in 1991 when Boeing formed a new unit to study the market for a superjumbo jet that can carry more than 600 passengers. The unit was formed in response to industry demand. United Airlines asked both Boeing and Airbus to consider building a 650-seat superjumbo. Several Asian carriers also expressed interest. At that point, Boeing projected a 5.2% growth in air travel annually to 2005, with much of that growth occurring in the Asian market.

Airbus unveiled its own rough sketches for a superjumbo at the Paris Air Show in June 1991. In late 1991, Boeing countered, offering three options to potential customers for a superjumbo jetliner: a stretched version of the 400-seat 747 jumbo jet, a double-deck 747, and a completely new aircraft that could seat up to 800 passengers. Boeing spokesman Christopher Villiers said no decisions have been made on which planes to build, if any. "We have not ruled out building two jetliners," Villiers said yesterday.[2] His colleague, James Johnson, vice president of Boeing's Everett division, confirmed that the company is considering building two new large jetliners aimed at the growing Pacific Rim market. "We believe a market exists for an airplane larger than the 747-400," said Johnson, "We see significant growth in the traffic forecast on routes between Asia and the U.S."[3]

In private, however, Boeing and Airbus conceded that the market was not large enough to accommodate two superjumbo offerings. The obvious solution was to combine forces, and work together on a single superjumbo jet. In 1993 Boeing and Airbus launched a joint study group to examine the feasibility of the collaboration. Problems arose almost immediately. Boeing was keen to retain a hold on the market for a possible expanded version of its 747 and hence wished any super jumbo to have a minimum capacity of 600, while Airbus partners wanted closer to 500 precisely to stop Boeing monopolizing the 300–500 seat sector. There were also trade and antitrust complications that doomed the potential joint venture.

Boeing and Airbus parted company, but both continued with separate superjumbo projects. For Boeing, however, matters came to a head as the optimism of the early 1990s crumbled under market conditions later in the 1990s. With ailing U.S. airlines yanking orders in record numbers, Boeing underwent the most wrenching downsizing in a decade. More than 28,000 jobs, about 20% of the workforce, were cut—slashing production of commercial jets by 40%. Under these conditions, it was clear to Boeing top management that they could only afford one large aircraft project, and the superjumbo was not the one they decided to pursue. Reflecting on the choice confronting Boeing at this point, Ron Woodward, the president of Boeing Commercial Airplane Group, summed up the company's thinking as follows:

> When we looked at the superjumbo called the Very Large Commercial Transport, we estimated the non-recurring cost to be anywhere from $12 billion to $15 billion. We concluded that there simply wasn't a large enough market to justify that size of investment. Our experience is that the cost to develop derivative airplanes is substantially less than the cost of all-new airplanes. Even so, the non-recurring costs to do major derivatives of our 747—including development expenses and investments in tooling—will be in excess of $5 billion. It's hard to imagine that Airbus can do a totally new airplane for (what they say will be) an $8 billion investment.[4]

Matters came to a head in 1998 during the Farnborough trade show. Boeing claimed that an aircraft of the dimensions being considered by Airbus—able to carry nearly 1,000 all-economy passengers or 620 in three classes—would be economically unviable and potentially unsafe. Ron Woodard, president of Boeing, argued that over the next 20 years there would only be demand for about 470 aircraft with a capacity of 500 seats or more—compared with Airbus' bullish prediction of 1,380. He then went on to suggest that the Airbus forecast was based on the need to justify the huge costs of developing a totally new airliner rather than reality. "Earlier joint studies with Airbus which were terminated only 18 months ago," pointed out Woodward, "had unanimously concluded that to develop a new superjumbo would cost between $12 billion and $15 billion." "We came up with joint numbers and concluded that even half this programme was financial suicide," Woodard told a packed press conference.[5]

"If Boeing truly believes the skies aren't big enough for two super-jumbos," said Airbus' chief operating officer Volker Von Tein, "then I suggest they opt out of the competition."[6] In fact, Boeing had plans of its own to counter Airbus. Boeing's proposed new entry looks like a 747, only more so. The 548-passenger 747-600X would keep the same fuselage width but extend it by 14–85 m, nearly as long as a minimum-size soccer field. Boeing will team it with a longer-range 460-passenger version, the 747-500X, which will have a range of 16,100 km, 2,600 farther than the 747-400. The plane will feature a new, more efficient wing, and engineers will replace the 747's traditional mechanical controls with a computerized fly-by-wire system, pioneered in commercial aircraft by Airbus and used for the first time by Boeing in the hugely popular wide-bodied 777.

For Airbus, strategic logic trumps financial and operating calculations. The company desperately needs a big plane to match the 747, which for 26 years has been a lucrative Boeing monopoly. The 747 not only provides the Seattle plane maker with hefty profits, but because it is included in package deals, it also boosts sales for the rest of Boeing's product line. Says Adam Brown, Airbus' head of strategic planning: "We have no choice. We have to go ahead."[7]

That do-or-die attitude helps explain Airbus' more daring design. The 555-passenger A3XX will be a two-deck, twin-aisle behemoth whose smaller upper section alone will be nearly as big as the entire passenger cabin of the A340, currently the largest plane in the Airbus fleet. A later version could be stretched to hold 650 passengers, and Airbus officials claim the plane will be roomy enough for airlines to add a conference room, a mini-gym, or even a few sleeping compartments on the lower level, if they wish. "We're starting from a clean sheet of paper," says John Leahy, Airbus' senior vice president for sales and marketing. "We're starting from a clean sheet of paper," says John Leahy, Airbus' senior vice president for sales and marketing, adding "They [Boeing] may be in a race, but we're not". "This is a plane that could be around into the middle of the next century."[8]

Airbus faces an organizational challenge: it is not really a company but a loose grouping of France's Aerospatiale, British Aerospace, Spain's CASA, and Germany's Daimler-Benz Aerospace. That structure breeds inefficiencies because work is carried out by national quota rather than by the most efficient constructor. After years of dithering, the four partners in July agreed in principle to convert Airbus into a true corporation by 1999, but ahead lie potentially crippling debates over how to merge and value the different production facilities under one management.

PROSPECTS FOR THE FUTURE

At first sight, one could not find a starker contrast between the position of Boeing and Airbus as they both entered 2007. The first was enjoying strong sales, and was being congratulated for the astute decision to defer entry into the superjumbo market. The second was in turmoil, confronting delays in key projects, and incurring large financial losses. But first impressions can be deceptive. As 2006 drew to a close, Airbus received an unexpected Christmas bonus with a flurry of end-of-year orders, including new A380s. Singapore Airlines increased its order for A380s from 10 to 19 plus six options, while Australian flag-carrier Qantas raised its A380 order from 12 to 20.

The company also announced that the electrical problems on the A380 superjumbo, which have led to major delivery delays, were now fixed. It also said deliveries to Singapore Airlines, its launch customer, were now on track for October.

Boeing, by contrast, began the year with a warning that its program to develop the 787 Dreamliner, its new family of long-range jets, continued to face pressures both from the aircraft being overweight and from key suppliers falling behind schedule. The 787 was well on its way to becoming the company's most successful new aircraft, with 850 orders, worth about $140 billion dollars, in place. But with delivery postponed well into 2009, analysts were asking how profitable the 787 would be if late-delivery penalties are added to other cost concerns.

CASE 11

The Casino Industry

Casinos across the US have suffered as the economic crunch forced people to cut back on their spending. The major casinos in Las Vegas and Atlantic City are therefore working hard to try and recover from their first ever back-to-back losses in 2009 and 2010 (see Table 1). "The picture is not good," said Michael Lawton, senior research analyst for the Nevada Gaming Control Board. "The golden goose is hurting."[1] However, early estimates indicate that casino losses were much smaller during the last year and analysts expect that the industry will return to profitability in 2011. Over the five years to 2016, IBISWorld forecasts that casino revenues and profits will grow at a rate of around 3% each year.

At the same time, there are growing concerns about the growth potential of places such as Las Vegas and Atlantic City over the longer term. The economic slowdown forced potential visitors to put off their travel plans and find some type of casino activity closer to where they live (see Table 2). Even as economic conditions improve, it is not clear how many of these patrons will return to these two major casino destinations. With some form of casinos now allowed in over half of the states, competition is developing all over the country, led by riverboat casinos and Native American casinos. In addition, slot machines are being added at a variety of venues, such as racetracks.

Similar concerns are being raised about the growth of competition in various locations outside the US. Over the years, casinos have been developed in various parts of Europe and Asia, which may compete for the high rollers who have been frequent visitors to Las Vegas and Atlantic City in the past. In 2007, Macau replaced Las Vegas as the leading casino gambling center, after the opening of *Sands Macau*, the first Las Vegas-style casino three years ago. Other Las Vegas-based casinos have also entered this market with lavish properties such as *MGM Grand Macau* and *Wynn Macau*.

In order to deal with this growing competition, casinos in Las Vegas have been developing extravagant new properties. MGM Mirage is just completing work on the *City Center,* which has been at an expense of more than $8 billion. Covering 67 acres, this minicity bordering the Las Vegas Strip includes luxury hotels, condominium units, a convention center, and retail space. Construction is also expected to resume on *Echelon Place* that is being built by Boyd Gaming on the former site of *Stardust*. At $4.4 billion, the 5,000-room *Echelon Place* is eventually expected to be far more expensive than the previous record for a single casino, which was set when Steve Wynn built his $2.7 billion resort.

Casinos in Atlantic City are also vying to retain and grow their business. *Trump Marina* was sold off to Landry's in order to be rebranded as the *Golden Nugget* after a $150 million renovation. Work has also resumed on the $2.8 billion renovation of the *Revel* casino, one of the first to open in Atlantic City after casinos were legalized. New laws have also been passed to allow the development of two smaller boutique casinos.

RIDING THE GROWTH WAVE

Although some form of gambling can been traced back to colonial times, the recent advent of casinos can be traced back to the legalization of gaming in Nevada in 1931. For many years, this was the only state in which casinos were allowed. As a result, Nevada still retains its status as the state with the highest revenues from casinos with annual gambling revenues rising to over $10 billion by 2004. After New Jersey passed laws in 1976 to allow gambling in Atlantic City, this allowed the large population on the east coast easier access to casinos. However, the further growth of casinos has only been possible since 1988, as more and more states have begun to legalize the operation of casinos because of their ability to help generate more commercial activity and create more jobs, in large part through the growth of tourism.

The greatest growth has come in the form of waterborne casinos that have begun to operate in six states that have allowed casinos to develop at waterfronts such as rivers and lakes. By 2010, about 80 such casinos have been generating over $10 billion in annual revenues. Several of the casinos along the Gulf Coast were destroyed or severely damaged by Hurricane Katrina. To encourage casinos to rebuild, Mississippi lawmakers passed a law in 2005 allowing casinos to operate up to 800 feet from the shore,

Case prepared by Jamal Shamsie, Michigan State University. Material has been drawn from published sources. To be used for purposes of class discussion.

TABLE 1 US CASINO INDUSTRY GAMING REVENUES* (IN BILLIONS OF DOLLARS)

2010	30.96
2009	30.74
2008	32.54
2007	34.13
2006	32.42
2005	30.37
2004	28.93
2003	27.02
2002	26.50
2001	25.70
2000	24.50

Source: State Gaming Regulatory Agencies.
*Gaming revenues include the amount of money won by casinos from various gaming activities such as slot machines, table games, and sports betting.

TABLE 2 BREAKDOWN OF GAMING REVENUES BY STATE (IN BILLIONS OF DOLLARS)

2009		
Nevada	10.34[1]	260 Land-Based
New Jersey	3.94[2]	11 Land-Based
Indiana	2.80	1 Land-Based, 10 Riverboats, 2 Racinos
Mississippi	2.47	30 Land-Based Dockside
Louisiana	2.46	1 Land-Based, 13 Riverboats, 4 Racinos
Pennsylvania	1.97	3 Land-Based, 6 Racinos
Missouri	1.73	12 Riverboats
Illinois	1.43	9 Riverboats
Iowa	1.38	7 Land-Based, 7 Riverboats, 3 Racinos
Michigan[3]	1.34	3 Land-Based
New York	1.02	8 Racinos
West Virginia	0.91	4 Racinos
Colorado	0.74	40 Land-Based
Delaware	0.56	3 Racinos
Rhode Island	0.46	2 Racinos
New Mexico	0.24	5 Racinos
Florida	0.22	4 Racinos
South Dakota[4]	0.10	35 Land-Based (Limited Stakes)
Oklahoma	0.09	2 Racinos
Maine	0.06	1 Racino
Kansas	0.02	1 Land-Based

[1]5.50 of this revenue comes from Las Vegas strip.
[2]All of this revenue comes from Atlantic City.
[3]All of this revenue comes from Detroit.
[4]All of this revenue comes from Deadwood.
Source: 2010 AGA Survey of Casino Entertainment.

allowing them to have a stronger foundation to withstand future hurricanes. Most of the damaged casinos in the area had reopened by early 2007.

As casinos have spread to more states, there has also been a growing tendency to regard casino gambling as an acceptable form of entertainment for a night out. Although casinos have tended to draw players from all demographic segments, a recent national survey found that their median age was 47 and their median household income was around $50,000. On the whole, casino gamblers tended to be better educated and more affluent than those who bought lottery tickets. In fact, the bigger casinos attracted a high-roller segment, which could stake millions of dollars and included players from all over the world. Many of the casinos worked hard to obtain the business of this market segment, despite the risk that the sustained winning streak of a single player could significantly weaken the earnings for a particular quarter.

The growth of casino gambling has also been driven by the significantly better payouts that they give players compared with other forms of gambling. Based on industry estimates, casinos typically keep less than $5 of every $100 that is wagered. This compares favorably with racetrack betting which holds back over $20 of every $100 that is wagered and with state-run lotteries that usually keep about $45 of every $100 that is spent on tickets. Such comparisons can be somewhat misleading, however, because winnings are put back into play in casinos much faster than they are in other forms of gaming. This provides a casino with more opportunities to win from a customer, largely offsetting its lower retention rate.

Finally, most of the growth in casino revenues has come from the growing popularity of slot machines. These coin-operated slot machines typically account for almost two-thirds of all casino gaming revenues. A major reason for their popularity is that it is easier for prospective gamblers to feed a slot machine than master the nuances of various table games. Major slot machine manufacturers, such as International Game Technology, have been making the transition to cashless or coin-free gaming by switching to the use of tickets. With the advent of new technology, server-based gaming will allow games on these machines to be changed or updated from a central system.

BETTING ON A FEW LOCATIONS

Although casinos have spread across much of the country, two cities have dominated the casino business. Both Las Vegas and Atlantic City have seen a spectacular growth in casino gaming revenues over the years. Although Las Vegas has far more hotel casinos, each of the dozen casinos in Atlantic City typically generate much higher revenues. Over the last couple of decades, these two locations accounted for almost a third of the total revenues generated by all forms of casinos throughout the US.

Las Vegas clearly acts as a magnet for the overnight casino gamblers, offering several high-end casino hotels with many choices for fine dining, great shopping, and top-notch entertainment. This allows the casinos to generate revenues from offering a wide selection of activities apart from gambling. At MGM Mirage, for example, revenue from nongaming activities has typically accounted for almost 60% of net revenue in recent years. Visitors find it easy to travel to Las Vegas as it is linked by air to many major cities both in the US and around the world.

During the 1990s, Las Vegas had tried to become more receptive to families, with attractions such as circus performances, animal reserves, and pirate battles. But the city has been very successful with its recent return to its sinful roots with a stronger focus on topless shows, hot night clubs, and other adult offerings that have been highlighted by the new advertising slogan, "What happens in Vegas, stays in Vegas." Paul Cappelli, who creates advertising messages, believes that Las Vegas lost its way with the effort to become family friendly. "People don't see Vegas as Jellystone Park. They don't want to go there with a picnic basket," he explained.[2]

For the most part, Las Vegas has continued to show a consistent pattern of growth in visitors. "We still compete with Orlando and New York," said Terry Jicinsky, head of marketing for the Las Vegas Convention and Visitors Authority. "But based on overnight visitors, we're the top destination in North America."[3] In order to accommodate this growth, several of the major resorts such as *Bellagio, Venetian*, and *Mandalay Bay* have added new wings. Even some of the older properties such as *Caesars Palace* have been given an expensive renovation and expanded to include a new Colosseum and a new Roman Plaza.

By comparison, Atlantic City cannot compete with Las Vegas in terms of the broad range of dining, shopping, and entertainment choices. It does, however, offer a beach and a boardwalk along which its dozen large casino hotels are lined. Atlantic City attracts gamblers from various cities in the Northeast, many of whom arrive by charter bus and stay for less than a day. Atlantic City officials point out that one-quarter of the nation's population lives sufficiently close so that they can drive there with just one tank of gas.

The opening of the much-ballyhooed *Borgata Hotel Casino* in 2003 was part of a drive to try and make Atlantic City much more competitive with Las Vegas. "There's no question that this is a Las Vegas-style mega-resort," said Bob Boughner, the CEO of the *Borgata*.[4] After a brief lull, the renovation of the *Revel* casino and the conversion of the *Trump Marina* into the *Golden Nugget* is expected to draw in new visitors.

RAISING THE STAKES

The gradual rise in the number of casinos, including those on riverboats, has led each of them to compete more heavily with each other to entice gamblers. Casinos have had to continuously strive to offer more in order to stand out and gain attention. This is most evident in Las Vegas and Atlantic City, the two destinations where most of the largest casinos are located next to each other. Potential gamblers have more choices when they visit either of these cities than they have anywhere else.

In Las Vegas, each of the casinos has tried to deal with this competition by differentiating itself in several different ways. A large number of them have tried to differentiate on the basis of a special theme that characterizes their casino, such as a medieval castle, a pirate ship, or a movie studio. Others have tried to incorporate into their casinos the look and feel of specific foreign destinations. *Luxor*'s pyramids and columns evoke ancient Egypt, *Mandalay Bay* borrows looks from the Pacific Rim, and the *Venetian*'s plazas and canals recreate the Italian resort.

Aside from ramping up the appeal of their particular properties, most casinos must also offer incentives to keep their customers from moving over to competing casinos. These incentives can be particularly helpful in retaining those high rollers who come often and spend large amounts of money. Casinos try to maintain their business by providing complimentary rooms, food, beverage, shows, and other perks each year that are worth billions of dollars. Gamblers can also earn various types of rewards through the loyalty programs that are offered by the casinos, with the specific rewards being tied to the amount that they bet on the slot machines and at the tables.

Some of the larger casinos in Las Vegas are also trying to fend off competition by growing through mergers and acquisitions. In 2004, Harrah's announced that it was buying casino rival Caesars, allowing it to become the nation's leading operator of casinos, with several properties in both Las Vegas and Atlantic City. This deal came just a month after MGM Mirage had stated that it was buying the Mandalay Resort Group, allowing it to double the number of casinos it held on the Las Vegas Strip. Firms that own several casinos can also pitch each of their properties to a different market and allow all of their customers to earn rewards on the firm's loyalty program by gambling at any of these properties.

Such a trend toward consolidation, however, does not seem to make a serious dent on smaller firms that operate just one or two resorts that appeal to particular types of customers. Steve Wynn's success with *Wynn* has led him to open *Encore*, another glitzy casino resort next to his original property. Similarly, the recently opened 455-room *Palms Hotel Casino* has already become one of the hottest and most profitable properties in Las Vegas. "There will always be a market for a person who doesn't feel comfortable in a big casino setting," said George Maloof, a co-owner of the *Palms Resort*.[5]

RESPONDING TO GROWING THREATS

The growth of Las Vegas and Atlantic City has been matched by the spread of casinos in many other parts of the US. Among these, the largest volume of business is generated by the riverboats that have sprung up in Iowa, Illinois, Mississippi, Louisiana, Missouri, and Indiana. However, the growth of these casinos has not had much effect on the growth of visitors to Las Vegas and Atlantic City. Tom Graves, stock analyst at Standard & Poor's, has expressed his confidence in the attractiveness of Las Vegas: "There's a perception among gamblers that Las Vegas is still the foremost gaming market."[6]

However, all of these casinos are facing growing competition from a variety of sources. Foremost among these is the rise in the number of Native American casinos (see Table 3). The Indian Gaming and Recreation Act of 1988 authorized Native Americans to offer gaming on tribal lands as a way to encourage their self-sufficiency. Of the approximately 550 Native American tribes in the US, more than 200 have negotiated agreements with states to allow gaming on tribal land. Native American casinos are exempt from federal regulations and are not required to pay any taxes on their revenues, but they generally pay a percentage of their winnings to the state in which they are located.

Over the past decade, a large share of the growth in US gaming revenues has come from Native American casinos. The impact of these casinos over the traditional casino industry is likely to increase over the next few years. Several states are reaching agreements to allow the introduction or expansion of Native American casinos because of the additional revenues that they can provide. This has created fears that the growth of these Native American casinos is likely to draw away gamblers from the other types of casinos. In particular, the growth of these casinos in many states such as California and Minnesota may reduce the number of gamblers that make trips to gambling destinations such as Las Vegas and Atlantic City.

The casino industry is also facing growing competition as a result of the move to introduce gaming machines at racetracks (see Table 4). Several states are passing legislation that would allow racetracks to raise their revenues by providing slot machines for their visitors. The introduction of gaming machines at racetracks—sometimes referred to as "racinos"—have been growing in popularity in the six states where they are presently allowed. According to the American Gaming Association, gaming activity at these racetracks has shown considerable growth over the last 5 years.

Finally, all casinos are closely observing the growth of gambling on the Internet. Although Internet gambling is not allowed under legislation in the US, some 2,000 offshore sites generate about $15 billion in revenue. Electronic payment systems have made it possible for gamblers in the US to make bets on these sites without cash, checks, or credit cards. Most casino operators believe that Internet gambling could represent both a threat and an opportunity for them. Placing bets through home computers offers convenience for prospective gamblers and a potentially low-cost business model for firms that already

TABLE 3
STATES WITH NATIVE AMERICAN CASINOS

2009	
Alabama	3
Alaska	3
Arizona	25
California	68
Colorado	2
Connecticut	2
Florida	8
Idaho	7
Iowa	1
Kansas	6
Louisiana	3
Michigan	20
Minnesota	38
Mississippi	2
Missouri	2
Montana	16
Nebraska	6
Nevada	3
New Mexico	22
New York	8
North Carolina	2
North Dakota	12
Oklahoma	106
Oregon	9
South Dakota	11
Texas	1
Washington	33
Wisconsin	33
Wyoming	4

Source: 2010 AGA Survey of Casino Entertainment.

TABLE 4
FAVORITE CASINO GAMES

2009	
Slot machines	59%
Blackjack	18%
Poker	7%
Roulette	6%
Craps	5%

operate casinos. It is widely believed that gambling on the Internet might eventually be legalized, regulated, and taxed. "We frankly find attempts at prohibition to be very shortsighted," said Alan Feldman, senior vice president of MGM Mirage in Las Vegas.[7]

GAMBLING ON THE FUTURE

The competitive pressures that had forced many firms to build new casinos or to renovate existing ones made it difficult for them to deal with the drop in revenues that accompanied the recent economic downturn. In many cases, the heavy spending burdened casino operators with large amounts of debt that became harder to manage when demand for casino gambling began to decline. A few firms around the US, including some in Las Vegas and Atlantic City, ran into financial problems, forcing them to sell off some of their casinos and seek bankruptcy protection. Over the past few years, Trump Entertainment, Tropicana Entertainment, and Station Casinos have all filed for bankruptcy.

So far, such isolated failures have failed to dampen the enthusiasm of most of the firms that are continuing to invest heavily into casinos. Many of these gaming firms view the current economic conditions as a temporary setback that has forced them to place some of the plans for growth on hold. Even as casino revenues have dropped since 2008, 28% of the US adult population still visited a casino, making this form of gaming second in popularity only to lotteries.

If the attraction of gaming continues to show the same level of growth that it has over the past decade, this should allow Las Vegas and Atlantic City to thrive even with the rise of new casinos in other locations. Some observers even believe that the spread of this form of gaming has created a bigger market for the casino resorts in these locations. As more and more people are drawn to casinos, they will be pulled to these centers of gaming. Few places, including Macau, can match Las Vegas or Atlantic City in terms of other forms of entertainment, such as shopping, fine dining, and theater shows.

Nevertheless, there are questions about the possible impact of the proliferation of casinos and the availability of Internet gambling on the revenue growth of gaming centers such as Las Vegas and Atlantic City. But many industry observers believe that these gaming centers will continue to thrive as people who gain a taste for gambling will eventually want to visit Las Vegas or Atlantic City in order to get a feel of the real thing. Jan L. Jones, senior vice president for Harrah's Entertainment, remarked: "Counting Las Vegas down and out, given the entrepreneurial spirit at work here, is just foolish."[8]

EXHIBIT 1 LEADING CASINO OPERATORS

Caesar's Entertainment
2009 Revenue: $8.9 billion
2009 Income: $828 million
Is one of the largest casino operators in the world. Operates casinos across the US, including several that are located in Las Vegas and Atlantic City. Runs several upscale casinos such as *Bellagio, Caesars Palace, Ballys, Paris, Flamingo, Harrahs,* and *Rio* in Las Vegas. Also manages several Native American casinos.

MGM Resorts
2009 Revenue: $5.9 billion
2009 Income: $1.3 billion
Most of its casinos are located in Las Vegas and other parts of Nevada. Runs casinos under the name of *MGM Grand, Bellagio, New York New York, Mirage, Luxor,* and *Monte Carlo,* catering to the high end of the market. Developed the *City Center* project in Las Vegas. Also operates casinos on the Gulf coast and in Illinois and Michigan. Has developed *MGM Grand Macau.*

Las Vegas Sands
2009 Revenues: $4.5 billion
2009 Income: 355 million
Operates the *Venetian* and *Palazzo* in Las Vegas. Has also developed casinos in Macau, spearheaded by the *Sands Macau* and the *Venetian Macao* and a casino in Singapore.

Wynn Resorts
2009 Revenues: $3.0 billion
2009 Income: $21 million
Operates the higher-end *Wynn Resort* and *Encore* casino, both in Las Vegas. Also operates the *Wynn* and *Encore Macau.*

Penn National Gaming
2009 Revenues: $2.37 billion
2009 Income: $265 million
In 2005, merged with Argosy Gaming. Operates mid-priced casinos spread over the US, including riverboats spread over different states. No properties in Las Vegas or Atlantic City. Also operates several racetracks.

Boyd Gaming
2009 Revenues: $1.6 billion
2009 Income: $156 million
Operates casinos in various states around the US. Las Vegas properties that target the middle income segment include *Gold Coast, Orleans,* and *Sam's Town.* Is developing a higher-end casino *Echelon Place* in Las Vegas. Runs the *Borgata* in Atlantic City.

Isle of Capri Casinos
2009 Revenues: $1.1 billion
2009 Income: $43.6 million
Primarily operates riverboat casinos across the US. Also operates casinos in Grand Bahamas and UK.

Station Casinos
2009 Revenues: N/A
2009 Income: N/A
Operates mid-priced casinos in and around Las Vegas. Leading casinos are *Palace Station, Sunset Station,* and *Boulder Station.* Currently reorganizing under bankruptcy protection.

CASE 12

Managing European Wealth

The years 2008 and 2009 were extremely tough years in financial terms, with the global crisis destroying hundreds of billions of dollars of global wealth.

Mainly due to the loss of trust and confidence, more than 25% of HNW clients surveyed withdrew their assets from a wealth management firm or completely switched over to another firm in 2008.

Arvind Sundaresan, CapGemini Consulting.[1]

The "rich" have an increasing appetite for safer, more familiar investments. They are looking to safer investment categories, with cash/deposits and fixed-income securities accounting for up to 50% of the portfolio. During times of heightened economic uncertainty, domestic investments in lower-risk assets are at the forefront of their thinking.

In this environment, restoring trust and confidence in the markets is the priority for industry players. With lower levels of profitability and an increase in low-margin asset allocation, players have to improve client retention and attrition by addressing a heightened demand for transparency and simplicity. Given this context, will the industry consolidate further? And what asset management business models will be profitable in such an environment?

"PERSONAL WEALTH"

Are you still one of the wealthy? Despite the current crisis, there are still many millionaires among us. Count your total personal wealth by starting with the home that you may own, albeit probably jointly with the mortgage lender. Add on the consumer items such as cars, household goods, personal belongings, and even works of art. Deduct any consumer credits that may be outstanding. Include the net worth held in a business or as loaned assets. In the end, you will probably find that most of your wealth is tied up, leaving limited scope for active wealth management.

Add to this initial wealth the remaining value of the future benefits from corporate pension plans and government prescribed or regulated benefit programs and your net worth will likely still increase, unless your entire pension has been depleted in the crisis. Because these claims can only be exercised in the future, they are for the most part beyond the reach of active wealth management.

Counting wealth continues with financial assets that have been acquired, such as voluntary retirement plans or savings programs for children's education. These savings are probably tax-exempt or deferred. Lastly, there is the money invested with banks or insurance intermediaries in other ways, for instance in collective investment schemes such as mutual funds companies and/or in the securities market—either according to your own decisions or with professional advice.

The total sum of the three different categories of net assets represents the individual's or household's economic wealth, although corrections occur as the stock market makes its continuous adjustments. Professional management of wealth is primarily concerned with the third asset category: *voluntary savings available for discretionary placement and investment.*

PROFESSIONAL MANAGEMENT OF WEALTHY INDIVIDUALS

Increasing stratification of the wealth management market is starting to occur as more locally focused retail banks and brokers see the potential of offering high-margin services to a growing base of high net worth clients. While many of these newcomers are aiming investment products at the so-called mass affluent—those with less than US$1 million in investable assets—they offer a credible threat to the traditional service providers to high net worth individuals (HNWIs)—those with more than $1 million in investable assets. Although there is relatively little consensus on the definition of HNWIs, asset managers generally target pooled fund offerings at individuals with investable assets of between $1 million and $5 million (which represents 90% of all HNWIs). And then there is a small elite of asset managers that have chosen to focus on the ultra high net worth market, typically individuals with investable assets in excess of $30 million. Currently, there is a tendency for such individuals to move away from third-party asset managers toward managing their wealth via family offices, employing dedicated professionals to oversee their assets,

Professor Bettina Büchel prepared this note as a basis for class discussion rather than to illustrate either effective or ineffective handling of a business situation.

and sourcing services from a range of providers. The Mid-Tier Millionaires (>$5 million and <$30 million) are caught in the middle with the challenge of having to manage a number of different asset managers as they do not have the resources to manage their assets through family offices.

After a decade of growth

From 2005 to 2007, HNWI grew at an annual rate of 14.9%, expanding from $33.4 trillion to $40.7 trillion. The number of HNWI financial asset wealth individuals worldwide in 2007 reached 10.1 million—an increase of 6% from 2006. The year 2008 showed a completely different picture—the total wealth of HNWI fell by 19.5% to $32.8 trillion (below the 2005 levels) and the number of HNWIs shrank by 14.9% to $8.6 million. In 2008, 2.7 million and 2.6 million HNWIs came from the North American and European markets, respectively (refer to Exhibit 1). The percentages from 2007 to 2008 changed most significantly across three regions: North America (−19%), Europe (−14.4%), and Asia-Pacific (−14.2%). The contraction in the overall HNWI population was exacerbated by the high decline in the ultra-HNWI category (−24.6%) which accounts for 34.7% of global HNWI wealth but only 0.9% of the HNWI population. The industry expects a recovery to an 8% growth rate in the period between 2008 and 2013.

PROFILE OF THE EUROPEAN HNWI

European HNWIs typically have an average age of 59–62 and include a growing number of women. There are large differences within Europe in terms of HNWI population decline in 2008: In the UK, the number shrank by 26.3%, France by 12.6%, and Germany by just 2.7%. In Europe, business ownership and sale of business represents the largest slice of the HNW asset pool (50%), followed by inheritance (19%) and income (13%). These figures differ drastically from the US where the largest source of wealth creation is income (32%), followed by business ownership (26%) and inheritance (16%). In Europe, many of the HNWIs are business owners who hold diversified portfolios.

While European HNWIs have typically sought protection from hyperinflation, high taxation and war, and with needs such as confidentiality, discretion, and stability being of utmost importance (refer to Exhibit 2 for key selection criteria), they are increasingly looking for tailored offerings and trusted advice with the motto "manage with me" rather than "manage for me." Instead of looking for an information provider, HNWIs seek counselor-like advisors similar to institutional investors. They spread their wealth over multiple relationships, entrusting less than 40% to a primary provider. Europeans also take a more medium-term perspective, measuring performance against a range of returns, such as the interest-base rate and local-market indices.

Their portfolios typically consist of more fixed-income and deposit products and fewer equities in comparison with those of North American HNWIs (refer to Exhibit 3 for HNWI assets by investment class). European HNWIs have a legacy of investing assets offshore to maximize tax and estate planning advantages, yet government debt and need for money as well as amnesties on repatriating money have resulted in assets flowing from offshore to onshore. Europeans have also had a tendency to use a number of different specialist advisors (legal, banking, tax, strategic planning, and asset management firms). They are demanding products and reporting to facilitate their imminent wealth transfer.

HOW ASSET MANAGEMENT FIRMS SERVE THEIR CLIENTS

In light of the crisis, dissatisfaction with the current value proposition is leading many HNWIs to seek to retain a greater degree of control over constructing and managing their portfolios or to switch providers. In 2008, many switched their exposure to focus more on cash and deposits, real estate holdings, and safety in home investments. Furthermore, a quarter of HNWIs withdrew assets from their wealth management firms or left the firm altogether, primarily due to a loss of trust and confidence.

Instead of quarterly meetings with investment advisors and printed reports of individual accounts, HNWIs are looking for more frequent reporting, both physical and electronic, reliable on-demand research and analysis, and transparent fee structures. Financial planning firms have three business models: fee-based (56%), fee-only (8%), and commission-based (36%). More financial planners are changing their compensation models from commissions to fees. Advisors benefit from fee-based models as steady revenue is generated even if they are out of the office, and reduces the roller-coaster ride commissions generally create. For a fee, HNWIs demand objective advice, customized solutions, and portfolio risk management services, as well as strategic asset allocation—similar demands to those of institutional investors.

As clients become more interested in gaining greater control over investment decisions by constantly receiving information, asset managers need to develop the array of resources at their disposal to safeguard their existing business. Client relationships are the HNW asset manager's biggest asset. Relationship management is based on the wealth of data embedded in client histories and transaction activity, which can be used to anticipate clients' needs, especially as they are showing increased interest in services such as financial planning for life events and fund management, as well as advice on managing nonliquid financial assets. Financial planners use "values-based planning" to help individuals with complex financial and emotional decisions, such as marriage, loss of parents or spouse, parenting or divorce. Financial planners could leverage groups of specialists to advise clients on wealth transfer, philanthropy and business owner services, and commission attorneys and business analysts to integrate traditional topics of tax and estate planning.

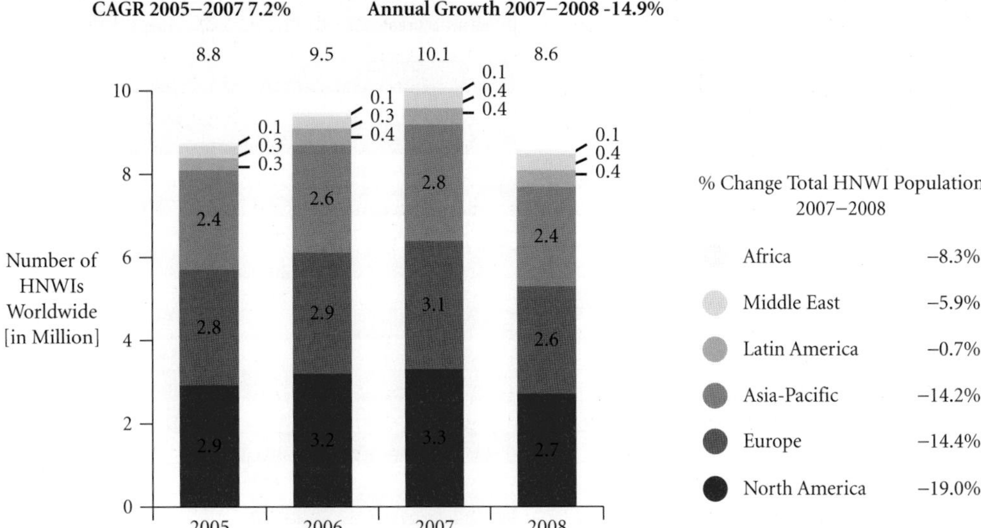

Note: High net worth individuals (HNWIs) have at least US$1 million in investable assets, excluding primary residence, collectibles, consumables, and consumer durables.

Ultra-high net worth individuals (Ultra-HNWIs) hold at least US$30 million in investable assets, excluding primary residence, collectibles, consumables, and consumer durables.

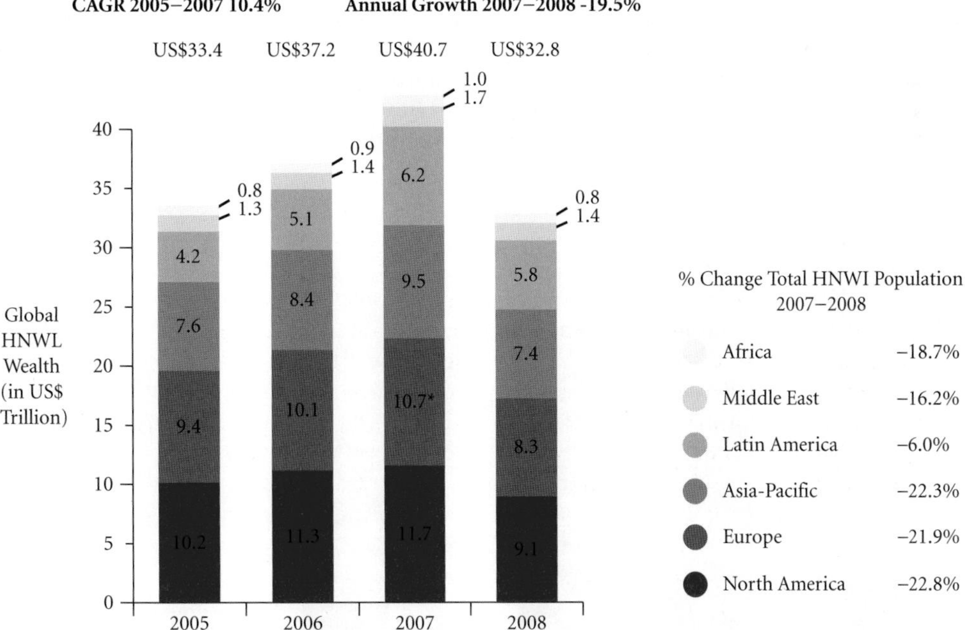

*The 2007 number for Europe was restated from 10.6 to 10.7 as a result of updated data becoming available.

EXHIBIT 1 FINANCIAL ASSET WEALTH OF HNWIS

Source: Capgemini Lorenz curve analysis, 2009.

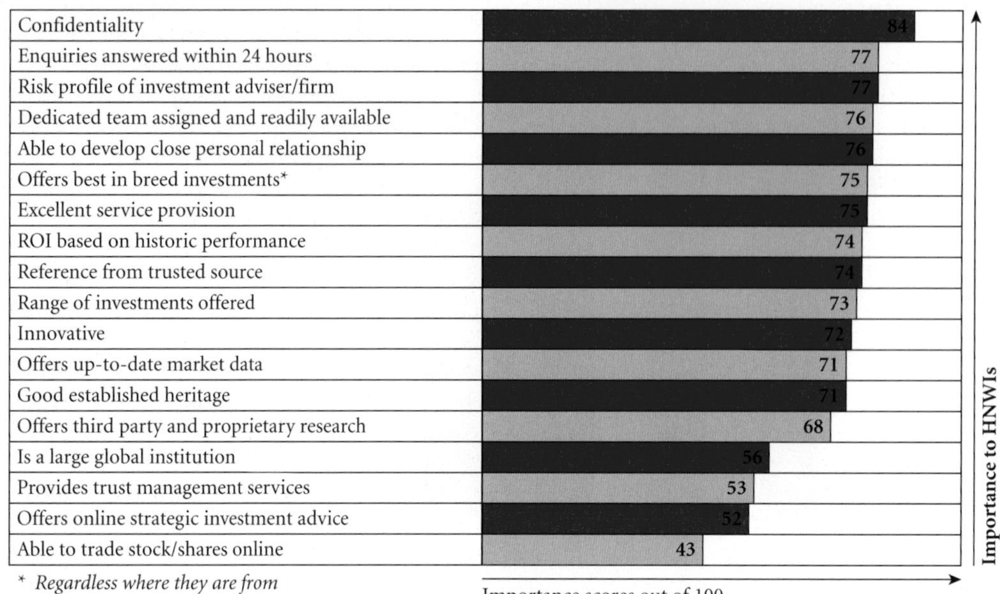

EXHIBIT 2 HNWI'S SELECTION CRITERIA FOR ASSET MANAGERS

Source: World Wealth Report 2002 (Merrill Lynch, Capgemini Ernst & Young).

In a period of loss of trust, advisors have increased communication, offer more simplicity and transparency to help rebuild after the crisis. Given the significant pressure to retain clients and attract new ones, the economics of wealth management business models are being tested. Fifty percent of HNWIs were in the low-margin classes. This, combined with the loss of assets under management, affects the cost base which increased the cost to income ratio in 2008 to 74% from 68% in 2007.

Indeed, the channels available for interaction between HNW asset managers and their clients are continuing to broaden. In Europe, unsurprisingly, all the private banks and the wealth management arms of universal banks have face-to-face services, but almost all have a dedicated website, many have transactional websites, and a quarter of universal bank wealth management companies have a dedicated call center. Investment in websites has been driven primarily to provide another service channel for

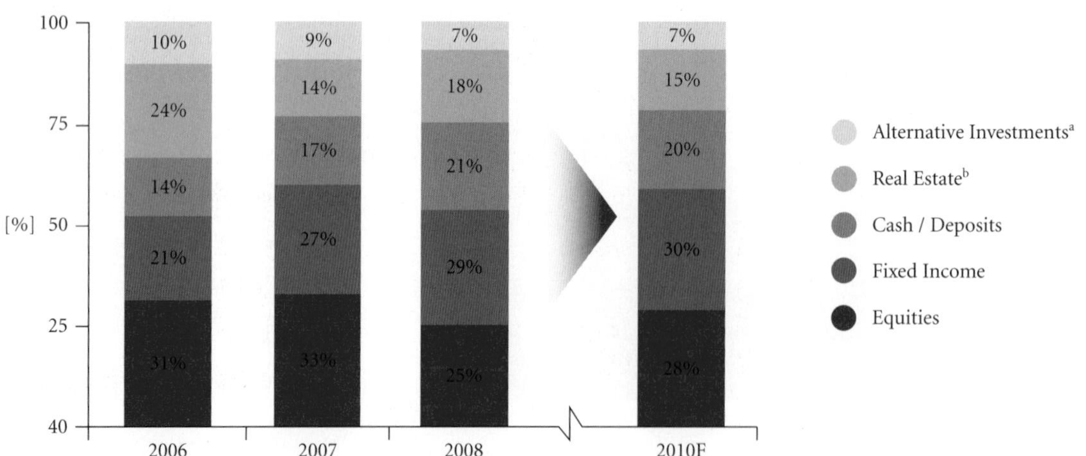

[a]Includes structured products, hedge funds, derivatives, foreign currency, commodities, private equity, venture capital.
[b]Includes commercial real estate, REITs, and other investment properties.

EXHIBIT 3 BREAKDOWN OF HNWI FINANCIAL ASSETS, 2006–2010

Source: Capgemini/Merrill Lynch Financial Advisor Surveys, 2007, 2008, 2009.

existing customers, although it is important to recognize its additional worth as another marketing channel. Wealth managers are expected to maintain the importance of face-to-face contact, especially for new customer acquisition and relationship management, but Internet and call centers are being seen as increasingly helpful means of handling transactions and account maintenance. On average, asset managers invested only 10% of revenues in marketing, with much of the focus of the spend directed at brand building and new product/service launches.

The traditional European distribution channels for investment products—universal banks and insurance companies—still own the majority of the market. Although technology offers the possibility of open-architecture distribution models whereby asset managers can show best-of-breed product and service options from a range of providers, it still has to take hold in the HNWI segment. The platforms essentially help to improve transparency in the client relationship, which the client may want but the provider is often reluctant to give.

Providers need to be aware that to retain clients, there are a number of strategic levers, or drivers, which have significantly different levels of perceived importance for them and for their clients (refer to Exhibit 4). For example, online access and capabilities are deemed important by 66% of clients but only 32% of advisors from within providers; reporting quality by 63% of clients vs. 39% of advisors; due diligence capabilities by 73% vs. 54%; and fee structures by 48% vs. 30%. From a client attrition perspective, the availability of products and investment options is ranked as very important for clients, an area that advisors underestimate.

Investing in technology has never been more important and scale remains the clearest way to lower unit costs. As a result, pure-play administrative specialists have appeared whose quest for greater scale has led them to outsource costly functions such as IT, settlement, and custody. The emergence of third-party back-office players will help the smaller, niche providers survive, as they could not achieve these scale economies on their own. If the back office becomes a level playing field, and any provider can access any product, then producing a superior customer experience will be key.

Although HNWIs rate the ability to choose from a range of cross-border investment products highly, only 70% of asset management firms can provide these products. Only the largest asset managers have the ability to develop tailored, fund-based investment vehicles in-house. It requires having the best portfolio constructors, who need to be retained with competitive remuneration packages. For others, sourcing a broad array of vehicles from third-party providers is the most cost-effective way to match the product capability of the largest asset management houses. The traditional core of mutual funds and bonds is increasingly being squeezed as commodities and innovative products such as hedge funds gain importance (refer to Exhibit 5).

The traditional asset management value proposition bases remuneration on fixed-fee structures—such as a percentage of assets under management—to support a range of value-added services. HNWIs, however, show a decided preference for fee structures that are based wholly or in part on performance-related measures (e.g., minimum-flat fees coupled with result-based incentives or performance-based fees with profit-sharing incorporated). This has to be brought in line with the costs associated with maintaining a $1 million account, which can reach as high as $16,000 per annum for a Swiss private bank. The costs for maintaining a

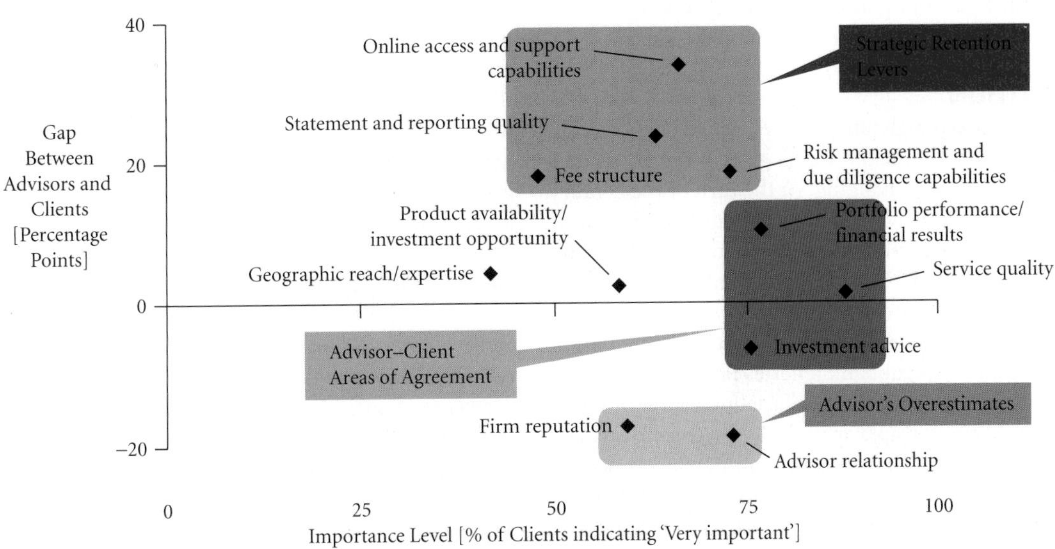

EXHIBIT 4 STRATEGIC LEVERS OF CLIENT RETENTION

Source: Capgemini Analysis, 2009.

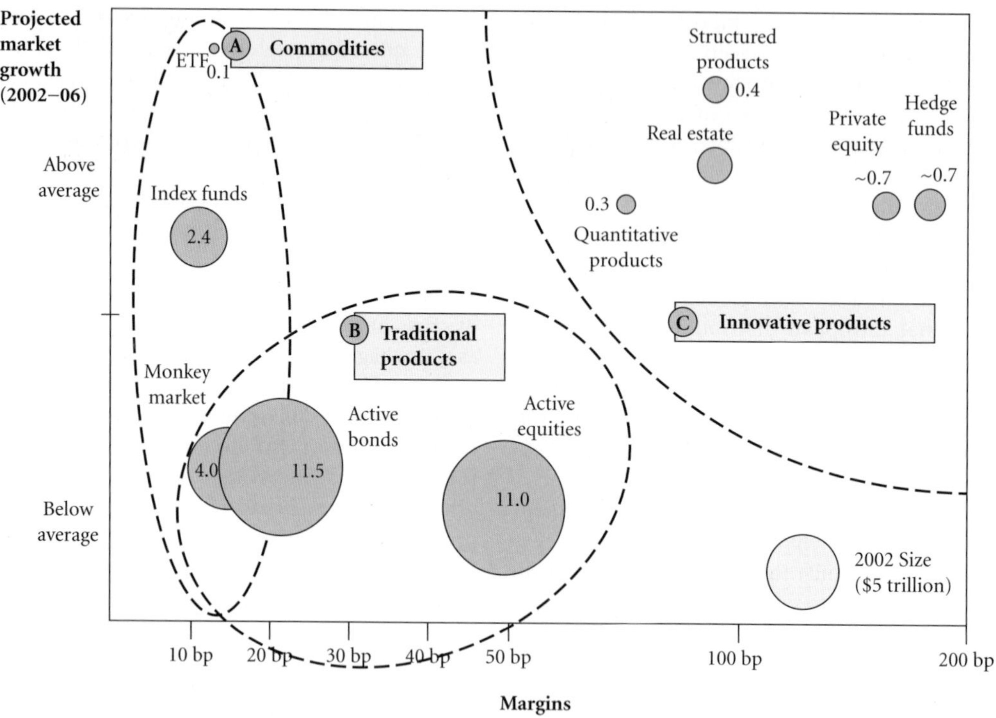

EXHIBIT 5 GROWTH AND RETURN OF INVESTMENT PRODUCTS

Source: Morgan Stanley Industry Report 2004.

HNWI account are split between developing and managing products (45%), administration (35%), and distribution/customer relationship management (20%). Profit margins for asset managers ranged from 10% to 30%.

McKinsey industry benchmarking research reveals three distinctive winning strategies—scale, multi-boutique, and focused-asset players. Firms pursuing one of these strategies generate, on average, pretax profit margins of around 35%—about twice those attained by firms taking a broad approach to any one area (refer to Exhibit 6).

COMPETITION

When viewed from high altitude, the pace of change in the asset management industry seems glacial. But the industry structure is slowly changing. At the turn of the century, an average top-ten player managed about $500 billion in assets; that figure was more than $1 trillion in 2008. While the market for HNWI is still fragmented, with no single wealth management provider having more than a 4% share, predictions of consolidation in the industry are increasing. According to investment bank Jefferies Putnam Lovell:

"Sizable asset management transactions, largely absent in 2008, are likely to reappear in 2009, driven by distressed selling of investment divisions by commercial banks and insurers, consolidation among alternative firms, and opportunistic buying by financial players that are emerging with fewer wounds from a historic and ongoing global credit crisis." The trend toward the separation of banks from their asset management arms will gather momentum in 2009.

"The most active buyers over the past decade, namely commercial and investment banks and insurance companies, are now becoming sellers of, or seeking strategic partnerships for, their asset management businesses. We expect pure-play asset managers and private equity firms to be the biggest beneficiaries of this massive reshaping of the industry," says Aaron Dorr, the firm's New York–based managing director.[2]

With the economy-of-scale advantage offered by global brands, asset management firms started to see the benefits of global presence. From brokers to universal banks, the number of players with a well-established presence in both the US and Europe climbed, with players entering the market through acquisitions, joint ventures, and organic growth. This has led to players establishing themselves across multiple countries in Europe.

SELECTIVE COMPETITOR PROFILES

In 2006 and 2007 Barclays Global Investors (BGI), State Street Global Advisors (SSgA), and Fidelity Investments remained the top three Global Investor Top 100 Asset Managers. Capital Group moved up to fourth place in 2007 (refer to Exhibit 7 for the top 20 asset management firms).

Barclays Global Investors

BGI is one of the world's largest asset managers and a leading global provider of investment management products and services. It transformed the investment industry by creating the first index strategy in 1971 and the first

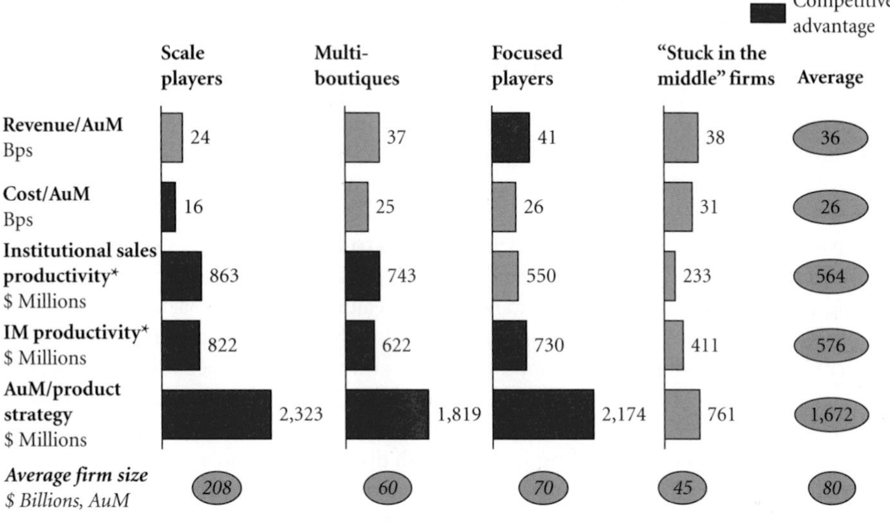

EXHIBIT 6 THREE "WINNING" STRATEGIES OUTPERFORM ON MOST DIMENSIONS

Source: McKinsey/Institutional Investor's US Institute 2004 US Asset Management Benchmarking Survey.

quantitative active strategy in 1978. It is the largest corporate money manager in the world, with over $1.4 trillion under management as of 2009. BGI is headquartered in San Francisco, with research and portfolio management teams in cities including London, Sydney, Tokyo, and Toronto, as well as client service offices in several additional major financial centers in Europe, North America, and Asia.

Fidelity

Fidelity International is a global investment management company with $1.3 trillion in assets under management. Once known primarily as a mutual fund company, Fidelity has adapted and evolved over the years to meet the changing needs of its customers. In addition to more than 300 Fidelity mutual funds, the company offers discount brokerage services, retirement services, estate planning, wealth management, securities execution and clearance, life insurance, and more. It is owned by the Johnson family (49%) and senior executives (51%). As a privately held company, transparency is limited.

Fidelity employs over 30,000 people worldwide and has experienced dramatic organic growth in the last 20 years. With over 450 fund managers and analysts, the company has extensive research resources who carry out in-depth analysis to uncover the best opportunities, following a bottom-up stock picking approach. The company services over 19 million private and institutional investors worldwide, and it has an army of fund managers and support staff to underpin its traditional focus on actively managed funds.

EXHIBIT 7 TOP 15 ASSET MANAGEMENT FIRMS IN 2009

COMPANY AUM ($ trillion)

1. Barclays Global Investors (BARC.L) $1.44
2. State Street Global Advisers SRCKF.PK $1.4
3. Fidelity Investments $1.3
4. Allianz Global Investors (ALVG.DE) $1.3
5. BlackRock (BLK.N) $1.28
6. Axa (AXAF.PA) $1.04
7. Vanguard (excl. sub-advised assets) $0.94
8. BNY Mellon (BK.N) $0.88
9. BNP Paribas/Fortis (BNPP.PA) $0.87
10. Capital Group $0.85
11. Goldman Sachs Asset Management (GS.N) $0.77
12. Legg Mason (LM.N) $0.63
13. Deutsche Asset Management (DBKGn.DE) $0.61
14. Natixis (CNAT.PA) $0.59
15. UBS Global Asset Management (UBSN.VX) $0.51

Source: Reuters, June 2009.

Deutsche Bank

With 77,000 employees, Deutsche Bank serves over 13 million customers in more than 72 countries worldwide. It has three primary divisions: Corporate and Investment Banking (CIB), Private Clients and Asset Management (PCAM), and Group Technology and Operations. One of the largest banks in the world, Deutsche Bank offers retail services primarily in Germany, but operates its investment banking and asset management businesses across the globe—primarily in Europe, but with additional markets in Asia, the Pacific Rim, and the Americas.

The PCAM division comprises Deutsche Bank's investment management business for both private and institutional clients and has $0.61 trillion assets under management. Asset Management provides institutional clients, including pension funds and insurance companies, with a full range of services including traditional asset management, alternative assets, sophisticated absolute return strategies, and real estate asset management. It also provides retail clients across the globe with mutual fund products through the DWS Investments franchises.

Private Wealth Management (PWM) provides HNWIs and families worldwide with a fully integrated wealth management service, encompassing portfolio management, inheritance planning, and philanthropic advisory services. Advisory services are offered in over 85 offices in more than 30 countries.

UBS

UBS is a leading global wealth manager, a leading global investment banking and securities firm, and one of the largest global asset managers. With offices in 50 countries and around 76,000 staff, it is organized in five groups: UBS Investment Banking, UBS Global Asset Management, UBS Wealth Management Americas, Wealth Management and Swiss Bank, and Corporate Center.

In wealth management, UBS's services are designed for high net worth and affluent individuals around the world, whether investing internationally or in their home country. With $0.51 trillion in assets under management, UBS provides tailored, unbiased advice and investment services—ranging from asset management to estate planning and from corporate finance to art banking. As an asset manager, UBS offers innovative investment management solutions in nearly every asset class to private, institutional, and corporate clients, as well as through financial intermediaries. Investment capabilities comprise traditional assets (e.g., equities, fixed income, and asset allocation) and alternative assets (multi-manager funds, funds of hedge funds and hedge funds, real estate, infrastructure, and private equity).

Allianz Global Investors

Allianz Global Investors is part of the Allianz group and is a core business for the group along with insurance and banking. Having grown through numerous acquisitions such as PIMCO, Nicholas-Applegate, and Dresdner, Allianz Global Investors is one of the top five asset management companies worldwide—with access to more than 75 million clients around the globe. With about €1.3 trillion of assets under management, the company employs a staff of almost 5,000, with more than 1,000 investment professionals among them.

Allianz Global Investors offers products covering all major equity and fixed-income investment styles and providing balanced products as well as alternative investment solutions. The company has organized the business into two global lines: Fixed Income and Equities, with PIMCO serving as the global investment platform for Fixed Income and RCM for Equities. Nicholas-Applegate, Oppenheimer Capital, and NFJ Investment Group serve as specialist managers.

Private bankers

Traditionally, private bankers are associated with managing the wealth of the "rich," backed by the personal liability that stands behind the private partnership firm. These providers focus on the special needs that have typically been associated with the HNWI: advice on issues such as succession, international taxation, estate planning, etc. This is combined with discretion and an air of being a confidante in personal and family matters, combined with a touch of exclusivity.

The differentiating characteristics of the private bankers such as Pictet, Lombard Odier, and others are increasingly being challenged by the trend toward onshore private banking, new possibilities offered by information technology, and wealth held by entrepreneurs and younger executives.

STRATEGIC CHOICES

Client needs are the nucleus of any wealth management solution, so firms have to understand and respond to those needs first. To differentiate themselves, firms need to focus on their identity and core competencies, as these need to be in line with what is promised to the customer. As the wealth management market continues to mature and globalize, products and services are becoming more commoditized, making it more difficult to differentiate the product. Having a service delivery model that drives scale can be of significant value. Three types of models are emerging: transactors, investment managers, and wealth planners (refer to Exhibit 8).

While some firms claim to have a single practice orientation, many pursue multiple models in and across regions to capitalize on the strengths of individual advisors. As they expand globally, tension between these different dimensions are likely to occur. The delivery model poses a challenge for operations and IT because of the complexity involved in supporting activities and meeting the demands of managing risk and compliance. In order to deliver global solutions, companies need to combine capabilities including front-, middle-, and back-office services, multicurrency and jurisdiction transactions, accounting and reporting, and full tax optimization and personalized user experiences.

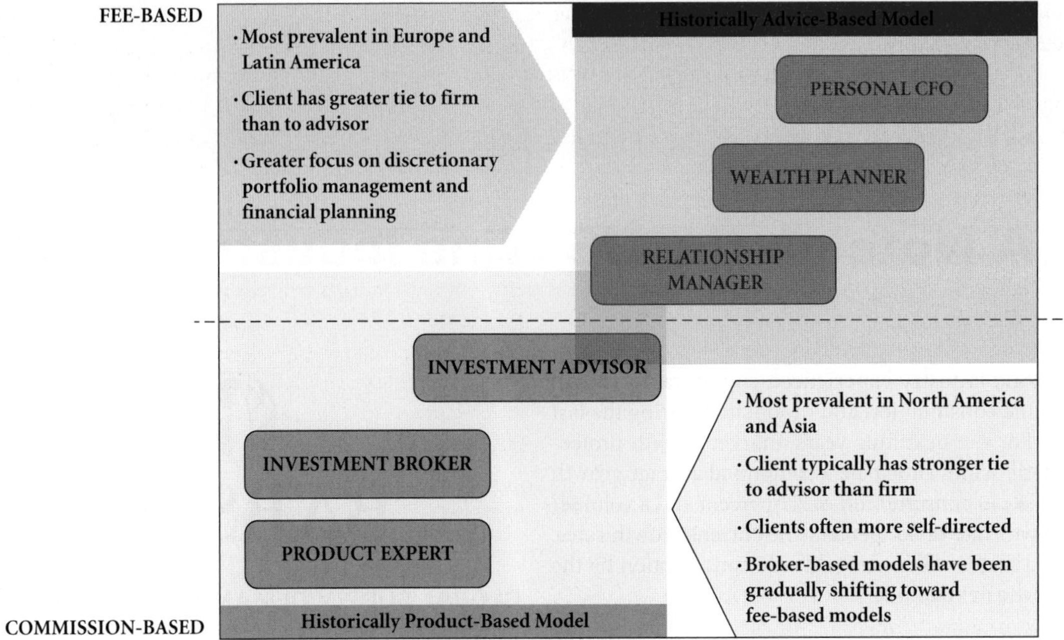

EXHIBIT 8 WEALTH MANAGEMENT PRACTICE ORIENTATION OVERVIEW

Source: World Wealth Report 2008 (Merrill Lynch, Capgemini).

CASE 13

A Note on the US Wine Industry 2007

The US wine industry experienced considerable growth in both wine consumption and production during the last 25 years. For the next four years, market growth projections for still wines anticipate a compound average growth rate (CAGR) in consumption of 7.7 percent and a volume/value growth rate of 4.4 percent. At current growth rates, the United States will lead worldwide consumption by the middle of the next decade.[1]

THE ORIGINS OF WINE

The peoples of the Mediterranean began to emerge from barbarism when they learnt to cultivate the olive and the vine.

—Thucydides, Greek Historian, 5th century BC

As a cultivated product, wine occupies a long and important role in history. The oldest written accounts of winemaking were recorded in the Old Testament, informing us that Noah planted a vineyard, making wine from the fruits of the fields. The Old Testament does not tell us how Noah actually learned to produce wine. Fables provide us with the amusing although likely apocryphal explanation of how wine was discovered.

An ancient Persian fable credits a Princess of the court with the discovery of wine. The Princess, having lost favor with the King, attempted to poison herself by eating spoiled table grapes. She became intoxicated and giddy, falling asleep. Awakening, she found relief from the stresses that had made her life intolerable. The King on discovering the source of her relief, her subsequent conduct changed so remarkably, shared his daughter's discovery with his court and decreed an increase in the production of "spoiled" grapes.[2]

Vineyard cultivation and production of wine spread rapidly from Mesopotamia to Greece. The expansion of Greek civilization followed by the rapid expansion of the Greco Roman civilization throughout Europe led to increasing demand for wine across the Empire. The first known "wine tariffs" were imposed by Roman Emperors seeking to protect the domestic wine industry from imports from France. By the 16th century, explorers were growing grapes in the New World for use in the making of wine. Grape growing and subsequent wine production spread across South America, Australia, and divisions of South Africa. By the late 20th century, the wine industry was global with sales and distribution reaching most alcohol-consuming nations.

GLOBAL SUPPLY/DEMAND

By the early years of the 21st century, global supply was estimated at 300 million hectoliters (mhl) with France, Italy, and Spain being the leading Old World producers and the United States, Australia, and Argentina/Chile the leading New World producers of wine (Metric: 1 Unit = 100 Liters) (see Exhibit 1).

France: In 2007, France remained the largest producer and exporter of wines in the world. By 2004, domestic wine production had reached 57.4 mhl across the six most important wine-growing regions of France: Alsace, Bordeaux, Burgundy, Champagne, Loire, and Rhone. In 2007, domestic production declined to 53.4 mhl. As of 2007, France was the world's largest wine consumer on both an absolute and a per capita basis (see Exhibit 2). However, several factors including health concerns, workplace expectations, and general shifts in consumption patterns had reduced per capita consumption in recent years. Forty percent of wine imports into the United States originated in France.

Italy: As the second largest producer in the world, Italy produced 53 mhl in 2004, with three main wine-growing regions dominating production. However by 2007, domestic production had declined to 46.14 mhl. Both unfavorable weather conditions and a reduction

Source: A Note on the U.S. Wine Industry 2007, Babson College (Cummings, M. & Otley, G. 2010) 660–N10. One time permission to reproduce granted by Babson College on 3rd January 2013. This case was prepared by Professors Michael Cummings and Gary Ottley as a basis for class discussion rather than to illustrate either effective or ineffective handling of an administrative situation. Funding was provided by F. W. Olin Graduate School of Business at Babson College.

EXHIBIT 1 GLOBAL WINE PRODUCTION AND POPULATIONS

WORLD PRODUCTION IN HECTOLITERS (000)

COUNTRY	AVERAGE 2001–03	2004	2005
France	50,034	57,386	52,004
Italy	46,994	53,000	50,556
Spain	35,274	42,988	34,750
United States	24,249	24,947	28,692
Argentina	13,918	15,460	15,222
Australia	10,688	13,810	14,000
China	11,200	11,977	12,366
Germany	8,989	10,047	9,100
South Africa	7,504	9,280	8,410
Chile	5,988	6,300	7,890

POPULATIONS OF MAJOR WINE-PRODUCING COUNTRIES

COUNTRY	2005 POPULATION ESTIMATES (MILLIONS)
China	1,306
United States	295
Germany	82
France	62.9
Italy	58.1
South Africa	47.4
Spain	40
Argentina	39.1
Chile	16
Australia	20.3

in hectares under cultivation contributed to the decline in production. Italy was the world's second largest wine consumer in 2007. Patterns of consumption in Italy mirror the patterns observed in France. Demographic changes including women in the workforce and the move from sit-down meals had contributed to the decline in consumption. Italian wine imports to the United States accounted for 23.7 percent of all wine imports.

Spain: Generally known for bulk wine production, Spain developed domestic capabilities utilizing modern cultivation and production techniques to produce high-quality wines during the later part of the 20th century. As the world's third largest wine producer, Spain's output in 2004 was 43.2 mhl. Due to poor weather and soil erosion, production declined to 39.3 mhl in 2006. Spain was also a large consumer of wine and demographic and lifestyle changes had a particularly pronounced effect there, leading to reduced consumption. The famed Spanish midday dinner had declined as work patterns, including longer commutes and participation of women in the workforce, had shifted demand.

The United States: Domestic production reached 27 mhl in 2004. However by 2008, domestic production had declined to 24.4 mhl. Much of the decline was attributable to adverse weather conditions. Due to the level of domestic production and the quality of the wines, the far West was the preeminent wine-producing region of the United States. Although US domestic production was found in a number of states, the domestic wine industry was concentrated in one state, California. Over 50 percent of domestic wineries reside in California, followed by Washington and Oregon. Indeed, California grows grapes in 46 of its 58 counties with the US government classifying the state into 89 viticulture areas. This large number of classifications was due to the variety of microclimates present in the state. US wine consumption steadily increased over the past 20 years (see Exhibit 3). Industry analysts suggest the increase was linked to increased awareness, growth in disposable income, health perceptions, increased marketing, and availability of affordable wines.

Australia: During the 1990s, Australia emerged as a relative newcomer to the global wine market. Producing 9.5 mhl in 2007, the country was adversely impacted by weather conditions in 2008. Severe drought, high heat, and generally unstable weather patterns had reduced domestic production. Demand was growing at approximately the rate of domestic economic growth.

Argentina/Chile: Both countries had developed robust domestic production capabilities with a combined output of over 25 mhl in 2007 (Argentina produced approximately 15 mhl). Favorable conditions, including the absence of grape vine diseases that affect other wine-producing

EXHIBIT 2 PER CAPITA CONSUMPTION OF "NEW WORLD" AND "OLD WORLD" COUNTRIES, 2005

"OLD WORLD"	LITERS PER PERSON	PERCENTAGE GROWTH RATE	"NEW WORLD"	LITERS PER PERSON	PERCENTAGE GROWTH RATE
France	55.9	0.05	Australia	24.7	4.69
Italy	48.2	−1.47	New Zealand	16.7	2.33
Portugal	46.7	1.06	United States	8.7	1.94
Spain	33.7	0.33	South Africa	8.4	−1.14
Austria	28.8	0.6	Argentina	28.8	−0.19
Germany	24.5	0.16	Chile	15.5	2.13
United Kingdom	19.0	3.26			

Sources: IBIS Reports, www.wineinstitute.org.

EXHIBIT 3 WINE CONSUMPTION IN THE UNITED STATES (1990–2007)

YEAR	TOTAL WINE PER RESIDENT[1] (GALLONS)	TOTAL WINE GALLONS[2] (MILLIONS)	TOTAL TABLE WINE GALLONS[3] (MILLIONS)
2007	2.47	745	650
2006	2.39	717	628
2005	2.33	692	609
2004	2.26	665	589
2003	2.20	639	570
2002	2.14	617	552
2001	2.01	574	512
2000	2.01	568	507
1999	2.02	543	475
1998	1.95	526	466
1997	1.94	519	461
1996	1.89	500	439
1995	1.77	464	404
1994	1.77	459	395
1993	1.74	449	381
1992	1.87	476	405
1991	1.85	466	394
1990	2.05	509	423

[1]All wine types, including sparkling wine, dessert wine, vermouth, other specialty wines, and table wine. Based upon Bureau of the Census estimated resident population data. Per capita consumption will be higher if based on legal drinking age population.
[2]History revised.
[3]Because of changes in reporting, these numbers include all still wines not over 14 percent alcohol. History revised.
Source: The Wine Institute (http://www.wineinstitute.org/resources/statistics/article86).

regions, allowed both countries, Chile in particular, to boost per hectare production. By 2007, both countries had shifted from bulk wine production to higher-quality wines. Demand was static in Argentina and was exhibiting modest growth in Chile.[3]

THE US WINE INDUSTRY

We could in the United States make as great a variety of wines as are made in Europe, not exactly of the same kinds, but doubtless as good.

—Thomas Jefferson

The number of bonded US wineries[4] more than doubled from 1999 to 2007. By 2007, there were 5,958 wineries of various sizes operating. This was a much more rapid increase in wineries when compared to prior decades. By contrast, from 1983 to 1993, winery growth was less than 50 percent. The increase in wineries mirrored the increase in domestic consumption of wines during the last 25 years.

By 2008, US industry concentration was characterized as medium with the top four producers holding approximately 60 percent market share, an industry concentration that was far different from the rest of the world where concentration was low. The market has three distinct product segments, with table wine (still wine) the dominant product offering with an 88 percent market share. Other varieties, such as brandy and sparkling wine, shared the remaining 12 percent of the market.

CALIFORNIA WINE INDUSTRY ORIGINS

California dominated the wine industry because it was the only state that possessed the abundant resources required for scale production of wine. Reliable rainfall, warm climate, excellent soil, available land, and low incidence of frost endowed California with the perfect factors necessary to establish a successful wine industry. While the California wine industry traces its founding to the mid-1800s, wine production was largely confined to smaller operations or large-scale jug wine production throughout the first 50 years of the 20th century. However, in the late 1960s, California vineyards began to produce higher-quality wines. Pioneers such as Robert Mondavi dreamed of producing quality wines to compete with the world's best wines produced in France. Until the 1970s, French wines dominated the quality wine market. California wines had little chance to challenge the long-established cachet associated with French wines.

THE JUDGMENT OF PARIS

A British wine merchant, Steven Spurrier, organized a blind wine-taste testing in Paris in 1976. The event was judged by nine French wine experts, including the country's leading sommelier and the editor of the most influential wine publication in France. The blind-taste test included the finest French wines such as Mouton Rothschild and Haut-Brion. To the horror of the French, when the scores were tallied up, the number one Chardonnay and the number one Cabernet Sauvignon were from Napa. The unthinkable had occurred; the upstart American wineries produced a product judged superior to the iconic French brands. One aggrieved Bordeaux chateau owner later told Spurrier, "You've spat in our soup."[5] Suddenly California wines had established their place in the world of premium wines.

CALIFORNIA WINE INDUSTRY: 32 YEARS LATER

California had 474 bonded wineries operating in 1940 (see Exhibits 4 and 5 for select financial data on the industry). By 1975, the year before the Judgment of Paris consolidation, failure had reduced the number of operating wineries to 330. Following the seminal 1976 Paris event, the number of wineries started to increase each year. Twenty years later the number grew to 877. Beginning in 1998, California experienced an explosion in the number of bonded wineries, growing from 1,185 to 2,687 by 2007.[6] Wine shipments from California wineries had grown as a result (see Table 1).

The growth in wineries was not limited to the well-known regions of Napa and Sonoma, although in these areas growth was in fact considerable. Within these regions, small wineries along the Russian River experienced growth alongside the established name brands of Gallo, Kendall-Jackson, and Robert Mondavi. From the Monterey area

EXHIBIT 4 WINE INDUSTRY FINANCIAL PROFILE—SUB S-CORP FIRMS

(*n* = 1279 SUB S-CORP FIRMS; IN MILLIONS OF DOLLARS)

	2005	2006	2007
Sales	7,621.6	6,521.1	6,458.4
Cost of goods	4,177.1	3,149.7	3,235.0
Gross profit	3,504.5	3,371.4	3,233.4
Officers comp	61.7	54.1	56.8
salaries	477.1	372.4	362.3
Rent	77.7	63.3	65.9
Taxes	457.3	844.5	846.7
Advertising	467.2	402.4	379.5
Benefits	101.4	84.8	76.9
Other SG&A	677.6	571.3	397.2
EBITDA	1,184.4	978.8	1,041.1
Interest paid	393.3	291.4	217.7
Amort/dep	338.4	265.4	255.1
Pre-tax	452.7	421.9	568.4
Cash	265.2	155.4	207.4
A/R	864.0	1,996.0	1,204.3
Inventory	2,767.0	2,223.6	2,206.5
Other CA	945.0	361.5	389.7
Fixed assets	4,133.0	3,581.1	3,647.5
Other assets	5,382.0	1,380.2	1,526.6
Total assets	14,356.2	9,697.8	9,182.0
A/P	901.6	307.4	596.8
Loans/notes	1,052.4	263.8	207.5
Other CL	817.0	1,144.4	1,109.2
Long-term liabilities	3,421.2	3,317.7	4,691.1
Net worth	8,164.0	4,664.5	2,577.4
Total liabilities/ NW	14,356.2	9,697.8	9,182.0

Source: Biz Miner 2007.

EXHIBIT 5 WINE INDUSTRY FINANCIAL PROFILE

(*n* = 9 FIRMS, REVENUES BETWEEN $50 AND $100 MILLION)

	2005	2006	2007
Sales	67,030.0	66,313.6	64,883.3
Cost of goods	36,015.2	37,334.6	38,112.5
Gross profit	31,014.8	28,989.1	26,770.9
Officers comp	898.2	1,061.0	778.6
Salaries	4,028.5	3,912.5	3,133.9
Rent	703.8	769.2	668.3
Taxes	5,523.3	5,610.1	5,430.8
Advertising	1,568.5	1,823.6	1,914.1
Benefits	730.6	742.7	545.0
Other SG&A	3,656.9	4,111.4	4,619.7
EBITDA	13,902.0	10,948.4	9,680.6
Interest paid	1,508.2	1,465.5	837.0
Amort/dep	3,753.7	4,270.6	2,556.4
Pre-tax	8,640.2	5,212.3	6,297.2
Cash	2,215.9	1,922.6	4,441.1
A/R	10,744.6	9,797.3	8,005.1
Inventory	30,843.0	32,090.6	21,796.3
Other CA	2,562.9	2,441.8	1,639.5
Fixed assets	26,995.7	29,626.6	23,661.8
Other assets	11,543.4	10,292.5	11,821.5
Total assets	84,905.5	86,171.4	71,365.3
A/P	7,250.9	7,324.6	5,302.4
Loans/notes	17,566.9	15,683.2	5,880.5
Other CL	7,013.3	5,687.3	5,773.5
Long-term liabilities	13,202.8	14,261.4	16,956.4
Net worth	39,871.6	43,214.9	37,452.5
Total liabilities/NW	84,905.5	86,171.4	71,365.3

Source: Biz Miner 2007.

down to Santa Barbara and San Luis Obispo, numerous wineries were established. The growth was not limited to these nationally and internationally known regions of California, however. Other, less well-known, areas began to establish large numbers of operating wineries. Around Sacramento, Nevada County, El Dorado, Calaveras, and Amador established wineries were producing well-known brands. Central in this area of developing wineries was Lodi.

Lodi

Lodi is located in the San Joaquin Valley 35 miles south of the capital city of Sacramento. Long overshadowed by the more well-known wine-producing regions of Napa, Sonoma, and Santa Barbara, the Lodi area was one of the first in California to cultivate grapes for wine production. Massachusetts native George West established the first commercial winery in Lodi in 1858. Endowed with fertile soil and an excellent microclimate for growing grapes, Lodi produces twice the quantity of grapes of Napa and Sonoma combined.

Despite the Lodi area's prodigious production of grapes, the area was not well-known outside of California. Until

TABLE 1 CALIFORNIA WINERY SHIPMENTS* (MILLIONS OF GALLONS)

YEAR	CALIFORNIA WINERY SHIPMENTS TO ALL MARKETS IN THE UNITED STATES AND ABROAD	CALIFORNIA WINERY SHIPMENTS TO THE US MARKET
2007	554.0	456.5
2006	541.1	449.2
2005	532.8	441.2
2004	521.7	428.2
2003	493.5	417.0
2002	464.3	401.0
2001	449.1	387.0
2000	445.9	392.0
1999	443.1	397.0
1998	432.5	385.0
1997	423.1	384.0

*Includes table, champagne/sparkling, dessert, vermouth, other specialty wines, sake, and others. Includes foreign bulk shipped by California wineries.
Source: The Wine Institute (http://www.wineinstitute.org).

the late 1990s, the region grew large quantities of grapes that were sold to nationally known wine companies such as Gallo. By 2000, local industry experts estimated there were four or five local wineries operating in the area. Farmers were principally price takers, selling their crops annually via contract to large domestic wine producers.

In the late 1990s, farmers began to expand into wine production. By 2008, the area had grown to over 75 operating wineries. These operations ranged from small wineries producing 400 cases a year to large operations producing in excess of 150,000 cases per year. As local wineries sprung up over the last decade, there was variation in the configuration of the wineries. The largest wineries produce much of their own grapes as well as crush, store, bottle, and pack the wines. By 2008, there was considerable variation in the amount of integration among the local competitors. It is not uncommon to find some wineries that contract-purchase grapes, contract-crush grapes, and contract-bottle the wines. Other wineries purchase grapes, using the raw grapes to crush, mix, and bottle their wines. Each winery's configuration varies and is generally a function of time of entry into the business, capital availability, expertise of the founders, and ambitions of the founders. Irrespective of the winery configuration, all winery owners were aware of the inherent risk in the business. Despite the apparent risk, Lodi winery owners were almost uniformly passionate about their product and deeply committed to the success of the venture.

California wine industry challenges

While many of the challenges facing the California wine industry were ubiquitous throughout the US wine industry, no other region produced the quantity of wine produced by California. More than 90 percent of all wines produced in the United States originate in California. In 2008, the industry was estimated to produce upward of $51.8 billion in economic value for the state, employing over 309,000 in wine and wine-related businesses. Industry advocacy was aimed at influencing the legislation that has the potential to negatively impact the industry; the most pressing was "sensible and reasonable immigration reform."[7] Local growers were highly dependent upon migrant labor during the harvesting season, and expressed deep concerns regarding any potential reduction in this important resource.

Fair taxation and science-based regulation were other critical areas of concern. Regulation of wine and spirits was highly problematic for the industry. Industry experts were particularly concerned about increased taxation at the state level. States hungry for increased revenue often view increases in "sin taxes" as a method of raising cash quickly. More importantly, the industry has been vulnerable to wide variation in taxation and regulation at the federal, state, and local levels. State excise taxes vary from as little as $0.20 per gallon in California to $1.80 in Washington. Federal excise taxes increase in relation to the percentage of alcohol contained in the product. Small wine producers may qualify for a tax credit of up to $0.90 per gallon on the first 100,000 gallons if production does not exceed 150,000 gallons. The credit is reduced by 1 percent for every 1,000 gallons produced between 150,000 and 250,000 gallons.[8]

The industry also has to contend with 50 different sets of state regulations, many of which directly impact the wine industry. Seven states prohibit wine-tasting on premises that sell to retail customers. This was a tremendous roadblock for an industry where educating the consumer was critical to the long-term sustainability of the industry.

Finally, liberalization of direct-to-consumer shipping represented one of the thorniest yet most promising avenues for the industry to increase customer acceptance. All 50 states control distribution through complex sets of regulations that vary by state. Some states allowed direct-to-consumer shipping; however, if a specific town does not allow liquor sales, shipments must go to the closest town. Other states allowed direct shipments only to counties that allow liquor sales—meaning that in some states, entire counties were excluded. Finally, some states excluded business-to-consumer (B to C) shipments entirely.

Distribution

Distribution of wine and spirits passes through a well-established three-tier system in most states. Laws governing the three-tier system were enacted at the end of Prohibition to prevent organized crime from controlling the industry. The three-tiers in the system are producers, wholesale distributors, and retailers, and the vast majority of wine made in the United States is distributed via this system. Under the Federal Alcohol Act of 1933, the three tiers must be kept distinct and separate; operators within the system can, in general, only operate in one or two tiers, but not all three. Complete vertical integration covering all three levels was, therefore, prohibited. This generally means that a supplier must appoint a wholesaler in and for each state in which the product is to be sold.[9]

As of 2008, the basic system was still in place, although idiosyncrasies existed in many states. For example, Louisiana allowed permit issuance to any businesses except donut shops while Indiana did not issue licenses to supermarkets or big box retailers unless there was a pharmacy in the store.[10]

The wine and spirits wholesale industry was highly fragmented with the largest firm, Southern Wine and Spirits, controlling an estimated 11.8 percent of the market. The seven largest wholesalers, including Southern Wine and Spirits, held approximately 28 percent market share. The remaining 72 percent was divided among an estimated 1,815 competitors. According to industry experts, the most successful distributors depend upon an anchor company to support their activities. For instance, in Massachusetts, the most successful wholesalers were anchored by a single large relationship with companies such as Gallo, Diageo, or Fosters. Wholesalers then fill in their lines with smaller brands designed to augment their large anchor firm's products. Most distributors were small to medium in size with

TABLE 2 TYPICAL (EXAMPLE) MARKUPS FOR WINE

Retail price	$19.99
Wholesale price	$13.33
Winery price	$9.16

limited sale forces. Of the estimated 1,900 distributors, over 1,000 employ less than 20 staff members.

Table 2 shows an example of typical prices at each level of the three-tier system.

Wholesalers required sample cases for tasting and testing by retail and restaurant prospects. Successful wineries typically provided additional marketing support funds to the wholesalers, often with some level of matching by the wholesaler. Support funds were used for print ads, point-of-sale displays, and wholesaler sales force incentives. Sales force incentives were critical since sales representatives established valuable relationships with retailers, thereby influencing which products were prominently displayed in stores. Support funds ranged from $1.00 to $4.00 per bottle.[11]

In 2005, a US Supreme Court decision opened up an additional channel of distribution. The Granholm decision permitted direct sales via the Internet to wine producers. The Court ruled that laws prohibiting interstate shipping were discriminatory, and that if states allowed *intra*state shipping, then they must allow *inter*state shipping. Several states emerged as strong B to C states: New York, Florida, Virginia, and Ohio exhibit strong B to C sales activity. Direct-to-consumer wine sales increased 7.4 percent in 2007.[12]

While opening up this new distribution path, the Granholm decision has been attributed to leading "a significant shift away from Californian wines that accounted for 54 percent of total wine sales in 2004 to 41 percent in 2007, even though volume increased 5 percent out of this state in 2007."[13]

COMPETITION

There are many wines that taste great, but do not drink well.

—Michael Broadbent

Four major companies dominated the winery industry tier, controlling over 50 percent of the US market. A second-tier group of wineries controlled relatively small market shares under 3 percent each. The balance of the market was highly fragmented among the large number of small wine producers.

GALLO WINERY

Privately held Gallo was the largest US winery by market share (27 percent) with estimated 2006 sales revenue of $2.7 billion.[14] Gallo was unique among competitors, controlling not only large grape-growing capacity and wine production but also producing its own glass bottles, caps, some portions of in-bound logistics, and, in states where it is allowed, the wholesale distribution.

Gallo grew rapidly during the 1940s and 1950s, introducing brands such as Thunderbird, Boone's Farm Apple Wine, and Ripple. Known as a large-scale jug wine manufacturer through the 1970s, Gallo began to move into the production of varietals during the later part of the 1970s. By 2002, Gallo was selling wines ranging from inexpensive table wines to super premium wines retailing for $50 per bottle. Holding prime acreage in Napa and Sonoma, Gallo produces such well-known brands as Turning Leaf and Gossamer Bay.

CONSTELLATION BRANDS

With an estimated market share of 17 percent, Constellation Brands was the second largest US competitor. The company had grown through a series of aggressive acquisitions including Robert Mondavi, Fortune Brands, and Ravenswood Winery. Constellation's brands range from low-priced table wines such as Almaden to premium wines such as Clos du Bois and Ravenswood products. The firm made several smaller acquisitions aimed at filling in gaps in its product lines in the $4.00 to $10.00 per bottle segment. Sales in 2006 were $3.8 billion. The firm recently divested several lower price-point brands. (See Exhibit 6 for select financial data from Constellation.)

FOSTER'S GROUP

The Australian brewing and wine company had an estimated 5.7 percent share of the US wine market by 2007. Foster's leveraged its US distribution to drive sales of imported Australian brands as well as its acquired US brands produced under the Beringer and Stag Leap labels. Estimated sales for 2006 were $1.2 billion.

THE WINE GROUP

The privately held Wine Group had an estimated 3.3 percent share of the US wine market. The firm, once a division of Coca-Cola, competed primarily in the low-end segment of the market, producing such brands as Mogen David, Franzia Brothers, and Tribuno. Estimated 2004 sales were 42 million cases, generating sales revenue of $310 million.

NICHE PLAYERS

During the late 1990s while large players emerged to consolidate the industry, large numbers of niche wines emerged, produced by small wineries with nontraditional configurations. These wineries produce a wide range of brands, from inexpensive table wines to super premium wines. As one distributor noted, "It is a difficult decision to decide which brands to carry. However, there is an incentive for distributors to pay attention to new wines."[15] The distributor went on to point out that the number one selling red zinfandel in the $12 to $20 price range was produced in Lodi by a small independent winery, Michael-David Winery.

WINERY OPERATIONS

Wine is a living liquid containing no preservatives. Its life cycle comprises youth, maturity, old age, and death. When not treated with reasonable respect it will sicken and die.

—Attributed to Julia Child

EXHIBIT 6 CONSTELLATION BRANDS' SELECT FINANCIAL DATA (2004–08)

YEAR	2004	2005	2006	2007	2008
Net sales	3,552.0	4,087.0	4,603.0	5,216.0	3,654.0
Gross profit	992.6	1,140.6	1,368.9	1,564.4	1,357.3
Operating income	535.3	584.9	756.6	811.9	598.0
Net income	220.4	276.5	325.3	−613.3	−301.4
Cash	37.1	17.6	10.9	33.5	20.5
A/R	635.9	849.6	771.9	881.0	731.6
Inventory	1,261.4	1,607.7	1,704.4	1,948.1	2,179.5
Total current assets	2,071.5	2,734.0	2,700.9	3,023.3	3,199.0
Net plant & equipment	1,097.4	1,596.4	1,425.3	1,750.2	2,035.0
Goodwill	1,540.6	2,182.7	2,193.6	3,083.9	3,123.9
Total assets	5,558.7	7,804.2	7,400.6	9,438.2	10,052.8
Current liabilities	1,029.8	1,138.1	1,298.1	1,591.1	1,718.3
Total liabilities	3,181.1	5,024.3	4,425.4	6,020.7	7,786.9
Equity	2,377.6	2,779.9	2,975.2	3,417.5	2,765.9
Total liabilities and net worth	5,558.7	7,804.2	7,400.6	9,438.2	10,052.8

Source: Capital IQ.

The basic process of wine production had changed little over the centuries. However, beginning with the monks during the Middle Ages continuing to the present, continuous process improvements along with improved transport have allowed scale production and distribution. Winery operations vary greatly in both scale and scope in the United States and indeed around the world.

The traditional winery grows and harvests grapes for processing, often supplementing in-house harvest with contract-purchased grapes. The winemaker (or oenologist, the technical term) oversees every stage of the wine production process—from the analysis of the soil used for planting grapes and the selection and planting of the grape varietals, to the selection of the barrels the wine is stored in, and the decision to when (or whether) to blend and/or bottle. Winemaking is a learned skill; it is an exacting, detail-oriented occupation that combines the physical labor of farming with the measured precision of laboratory science. It is the pivotal role in winery operations, and good winemakers earn strong reputations and are sought after by winery owners.

Grapes are picked both manually and mechanically, placed in the crusher-destemmer to remove stems and crush, mixed depending upon the type of wine being produced, pumped through filtration systems, and then stored. Storage for scale production is in large temperature-controlled tanks where the product is aged.[16] Smaller quantity vintage vines are often stored in the more traditional oak casks. Once the product has reached the desired age, the product is bottled, labeled, capped, packed 12 bottles to a case, and stored as the finished product.

Scale production requires both a substantial capital and time commitment. Land acquisition, capital investment in plant and equipment, start-up working capital to fund the two- to three-year cycle from bud-break to final product, and branding require considerable capital investments. While labor is a significant cost at harvest, scale wineries operate with surprisingly few employees. The vineyards are labor intensive while the capital-to-labor ratio in the winery is low.

NONTRADITIONAL WINERY CONFIGURATIONS

Numerous variations on the traditional winery exist. One variation is the contract production of wine by purchasing grapes, contract crush, filtering, and bottling, with the brand owner concentrating solely on the marketing. An even more abbreviated model is the purchase of excess bottled wines from various vineyards, where the brand owner takes possession of the finished product and simply affixes his own label. This configuration has existed for over 100 years in France, where wine merchants contract for finished product under their own labels.

Recently, small wineries that purchased grapes had acquired full in-house production and storage capabilities. Almost all small-scale wineries contract-bottle their product using mobile bottling lines that were driven on the premise only for the time bottling operations was required (owning a bottling line required a capital investment of between $100,000 and $150,000, a substantial investment for the small wine-making operation).

Alternating proprietors

Beginning in the mid-1980s, the Bureau of Alcohol, Tobacco and Fire Arms defined approved alternative methods and procedures to allow two qualified proprietors to alternate the use of a wine facility. Two bonded wineries essentially share the facility where the alternating proprietor when in possession of the facility was fully in charge of overseeing the wine production. In most cases, there was a clean divide between the host proprietor and the tenant proprietor.

When the tenant proprietor was using the facility, he or she was responsible for production, bottling, and storing, as well as for managing the business. Storage within an alternating proprietorship must clearly label each separate proprietor's storage area.[17]

Tenant proprietors exercise full control of the wine production process without the large capital expenditures associated with the more traditional winery. Once the tenant proprietor completes production, the costs associated with operating the winery revert to the host proprietor.

NICHE WINERY SALES AND DISTRIBUTION

Many small wineries were not completely dependent upon the three-tier distribution system. Wineries sold product by operating tasting rooms where tourists, after sampling the vintner's wines, often purchased a quantity directly from the winery. In addition, wineries sold to local grocery stores and restaurants, delivering the product in their own vans or trucks. The discount on these accounts was generally 33 percent versus the 50 percent discount of the three-tier system. Recently, a limited group of wineries were sold through the Internet.

OPPORTUNITIES FOR ENTERING THE CALIFORNIA WINE BUSINESS

There were over 100 wineries for sale on any given day in California. The winery configurations offered for sale vary from brand-only sales to fully integrated wineries. Prices vary widely depending upon the wineries' asset base and owner expectations.

CASE 14

Warner Brothers

On July 16, 1999, the entertainment world awoke to the sudden news of the resignations of Robert A. Daly and Terry Semel, the cochairmen of Warner Brothers (WB). Their resignations represented the end of one of the most stable and successful relationships with a studio in Hollywood history. Under Mr. Daly and Mr. Semel's leadership, Warner had dominated the film industry, seemingly unaffected by the problems besetting its rivals, which tend to careen from surprise blockbuster to major write-off, from old management to new.

Blessed with the longest running management team in the movie business, Warner had consistently outperformed its competitors. Their movies were always equipped with the best crews, effects, and talents that money could buy. For many years, there had been no reason for Mr. Daly or Mr. Semel to move away from this tried and true strategy of reliance on star-driven high-budget event films. For 16 of the 19 years that they reigned, the firm had ranked among the top three studios in terms of US market share. It was placed first eight times and second five times during this period.

But in the last few years, Mr. Daly and Mr. Semel had been subject to increased criticism because of the lackluster performance of their film slate, as reflected by Warner's declining market share. The duo's simple strategy of casting top stars in big event movies did not seem to be working as well. Their most recent expensive flops included big star vehicles as *Father's Day, The Postman,* and *The Avengers*. The studio's deteriorating track record with big-budget star-driven vehicles suggested that the elements that a movie needed to have for success in the market were changing. Even New Line Cinema, a recent acquisition of Time Warner, was scoring bigger and bigger successes with low-to-medium budget movies with relatively fresh, not as yet discovered, stars and directors.

Both Mr. Daly and Mr. Semel denied that their decision had been influenced by Warner's declining performance. They emphasized that they were leaving the studio to pursue other possible opportunities. But industry observers believed that the exit of these two Warner executives was prompted by their concerns about the changes that were confronting the film studios. If these changes continue to take hold, they would raise serious questions about the benefits of Mr. Daly and Mr. Semel's free spending approach to making movies. Recent hits such as *Analyze This* and *The Matrix* were championed not by the top duo, but by the newly recruited production chief, Lorenzo di Bonaventura. Warner's expensive big-event film for the summer *Wild Wild West* opened to a weak box office and dismal reviews, making it unlikely to make much money for the studio.

"They did a great job for the last 19 years," said Gordon Crawford, senior vice-president of Los Angeles–based Capital Research and Management Company, one of Time Warner's large shareholders. "On the other hand, from a Time Warner perspective, they weren't going to take the company forward for the next 20 years, so it was inevitable that the Bob and Terry show would come to an end at some point. The company can discuss restructuring now, because it was never going to happen with Bob and Terry there."

HERITAGE OF THE MOGULS

Both Mr. Daly and Mr. Semel had been trained at the knee of legendary Time Warner Chairman Steven J. Ross, one of the last great movie moguls who died in 1992. Mr. Ross gave his executives independence and a relatively free rein and, perhaps more important, was an extravagant spender whose largess endeared him to stars, directors, and producers. He relished the glitz of Hollywood, cultivating top talent with gifts and perks.

The philosophy was well thought out. Mr. Ross believed that his studio would benefit from ongoing relationships with top stars, directors, and producers because they were essential for the success of movies. Mr. Daly and Mr. Semel learned the formula well. They courted big-name talent and used them to create big movies that they believed the public would flock to see. The lavish gifts and perks were designed to attract and keep such highly regarded talent at the studio as part of its expanded family.

To Mr. Daly and Mr. Semel, the Warner family consisted of a select group of top movie talent with whom they had carefully cultivated a strong relationship. Their films usually resulted from extravagantly high-priced deals that

---

This case was prepared by Jamal Shamsie, UCLA, to be used for class discussion. Material has been drawn from published sources.

they regularly made with the same big-budget and big-star movie producers like Jerry Weintraub, Jon Peters, and Joel Silver. For the most part, these films also tended to draw on the same stars and directors that had created hits in the past. "Bob and Terry are the only two guys in our era who achieved a kind of old-Hollywood continuity with movie stars and world-class filmmakers, whether it was Stanley Kubrick, Clint Eastwood, Mel Gibson, Oliver Stone, Barry Levinson, Kevin Costner, or Dick Donner," said producer Bill Gerber, a former WB copresident of production.

The continuity was based on the loyalty of this top talent, which was amply rewarded by the studio. Even by Hollywood standards, Warner's practices under Mr. Daly and Mr. Semel appeared to have set new standards for excessiveness. However, in the flush times of the mid-1980s to the early 1990s, when the studio produced hits, the extravagances were accepted by the company's hierarchy as the way Hollywood does business. It was Mr. Daly and Mr. Semel, after all, who seemed to possess the magic key that opened doors to success while all around them studio chieftains lost their heads in corporate upheavals.

Their focus on heavy spending in order to be able to make star-studded event films with top directors and producers worked for many years. Warner excelled at making a wide range of such movies. It not only turned out such lucrative movie franchises as *Batman* and *Lethal Weapon,* it created dazzling special-effects films such as *Twister* and *Contact* and mounted thrilling dramas like *The Fugitive*. At the same time, it managed to deliver gritty, thought-provoking films such as Clint Eastwood's Oscar-winning western *Unforgiven* and films with social and political themes such as Spike Lee's *Malcolm X*, Oliver Stone's *JFK*, and Roland Joffe's *The Killing Fields*.

But cracks were beginning to appear in this blockbuster strategy, particularly over the last couple of years. Expensive star-studded flops like *The Postman* with Kevin Costner, *Father's Day* with Robin Williams and Billy Crystal, *Mad City* with Dustin Hoffman and John Travolta, Clint Eastwood's *Midnight in the Garden of Good and Evil, The Avengers* with Uma Thurman and Ralph Fiennes, Barry Levinson's *Sphere,* and the animated *Quest for Camelot* had begun to raise questions about the duo's strategy. It appeared as if Mr. Daly and Mr. Semel were backing films that were no longer able to command the revenues that they might have attracted in the past.

A SEISMIC INDUSTRY SHIFT

Over the last couple of years, movie studios have come under tremendous pressure to cut costs to bolster thin profit margins by making fewer, cheaper, lower-risk films (see Exhibit 1). In particular, studios have begun to cut back on the expensive gambles on star-studded vehicles that Mr. Daly and Mr. Semel were known for. Fewer higher budget films are being grabbed by the studios and these movies are being approved only when a partner has been found to share the financial risk. "Everybody has been forced to see the cold realities of the very narrow profit margins of the movie business," said Brian Glazer, producer of films like *Ransom* and *Apollo* 13.

To some degree, the studios were also beginning to question the necessity of star-driven big-event movies. In recent years, most of the industry profits have come from films like *There's Something About Mary, The Wedding Singer, Rush Hour,* and *Waterboy*. All of these have tended to be more modestly budgeted movies with unknown directors and upcoming stars. The public flocked to see these movies because of their interest in fresh faces that were associated with an easily identifiable concept.

Industry observers claim that the success of these new kinds of films has signaled seismic shifts in the market. Gradually, the studios were trying to figure out newer ways of catering to the younger audiences, particularly males aged 15–25, who are most likely to generate the biggest box office bucks. As other entertainment options have continued to develop, it has become harder to draw this target market to movies (see Exhibit 2). Studios that had some degree of success have attempted to push for fresher approaches that could appeal to this younger audience whose tastes have become harder to define.

Given these changes, Mr. Daly and Mr. Semel were being criticized for their continued reliance on a team of older stars, directors, and producers who churned out weak or formulaic movies. Their emphasis on packaging films around top talent has left them with little experience in finding and nurturing difficult or risky scripts into breakout hits. Both Mr. Daly and Mr. Semel have therefore been reluctant to seek out more adventurous material and take chances with unproven talent. As a result, Warner's films have been weighed down with tired concepts, aging stars, and over-the-hill producers that have had scant appeal for the young audience that other studios were pursuing.

Mr. Daly and Mr. Semel have also faced an uphill task in producing successes from their existing franchises. The last installments of the studio's most successful franchises, *Batman* and *Lethal Weapon,* seem to have played themselves out, leaving it unclear how successfully they can still be reworked. The duo has been unable to develop any new franchises even though they have tried to dust off the scripts of old hit TV shows. Although *Maverick* worked with Mel Gibson and Jodie Foster, *The Avengers* starring Ralph Fiennes and Uma Thurman was a clear flop, and the recent *Wild Wild West,* with the bankable Will Smith and Kevin Kline, does not seem likely to lead to a franchise.

Even as their strategy looked like it was coming apart, Mr. Daly and Mr. Semel seemed unable to make the necessary changes to their filmmaking methods. By sticking with their tried and true methods, the two of them left the cheaper, more adventurous films without stars to other studios like Miramax and New Line Cinema, which is now owned by Time Warner. These firms had mastered a new strategy of creating hits from lower budgeted movies with the likes of Mike Meyers, Adam Sandler, Gwyneth Paltrow,

With the Cost of Films Going Up . . .

Millions of Dollars

80 60 40 20 0

1990 1991 1992 1993 1994 1995 1996 1997 1998

Average marketing and production costs of feature films at major studios.

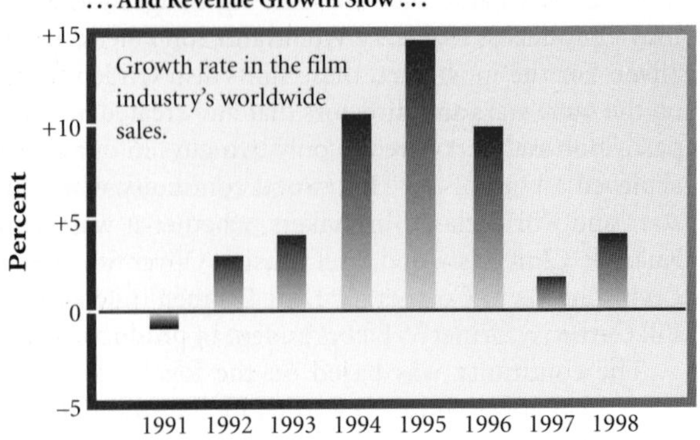

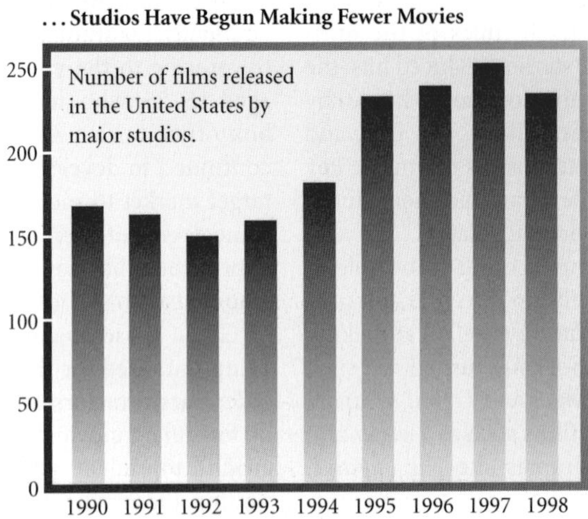

EXHIBIT 1

Sources: Motion Picture Association of America: Paul Kagan Associates.

EXHIBIT 2
FILM MARKET SHARE

YEAR	SHARE (%)	RELATIVE POSITION
1992	19.1	1st
1993	18.9	1st
1994	16.4	2nd
1995	16.5	2nd
1996	15.7	2nd
1997	10.8	4th
1998	11.1	3rd

and Cameron Diaz. New Line was triumphant with youth-oriented fare such as *Austin Powers: The Spy Who Shagged Me* and *Rush Hour*. Miramax, on the other hand, claimed the market for more adult-oriented films with *Shakespeare in Love* and *The English Patient*.

Referring to the strategy that Mr. Daly and Mr. Semel had stuck with over the years, a top producer who spoke on condition of anonymity stated: "They're relying on old horses that haven't been delivering for years. A studio is like a living organism. You have to keep bringing in new talent, new players, reinventing yourself. And this hasn't happened at Warners."

PLOTTING A NEW COURSE

The decision by Mr. Daly and Mr. Semel to leave immediately cast the normally stable WB studios in turmoil. Their departure is expected to represent the end of an era which was characterized by high-octane film franchises, star-producing deals, and legendary perks to top producers and directors. Speaking for Time Warner, chairman Gerald M. Levin said he was saddened by the decision. "There is never a good time to lose this kind of talent," he said, "but our film, TV and music businesses, and our company as a whole, are in excellent shape, and there is tremendous depth of management throughout our organization."

Under Daly and Semel, Warner had already started to cut back costs in many areas. The studio had made news when it recently shelved two big-budget action films: a new version of *Superman,* which was to star Nicholas Cage and Kevin Spacey, and a proposed Arnold Schwarzenegger movie *I Am Legend*. It also terminated expensive production deals with established producers such as Arnon Milchan, Arnold Kopelson, and Mel Gibson. This has allowed the studio, with the help of production chief di Bonaventura, to turn to directors and producers who are outside the tight in-group that have managed to dominate the studio's offerings for years.

In order to reduce its risk exposure, Warner has also increased the number of films that it is cofinancing with other firms. The studio used some form of cofinancing on 12 of the 21 movies that it released in 1999. The most prominent deals were with Village Roadshow Pictures and Bel Air Entertainment. Both of these firms were headed by WB veterans who had already served some years with the studio.

But none of these changes provide any clear signal about the kind of studio that WB is moving toward. "Everything we've had with Bob and Terry dates back so long," said veteran filmmaker Dick Donner. "This place was just home. It's strange to think they would be gone. Sure, I'll miss them in the business world. But it's so much more than that. This is the place you chose to be because of them . . . I would say their legacy is this: They continued the history of the great American studios. They never let that down. Whoever comes in will have to follow that."

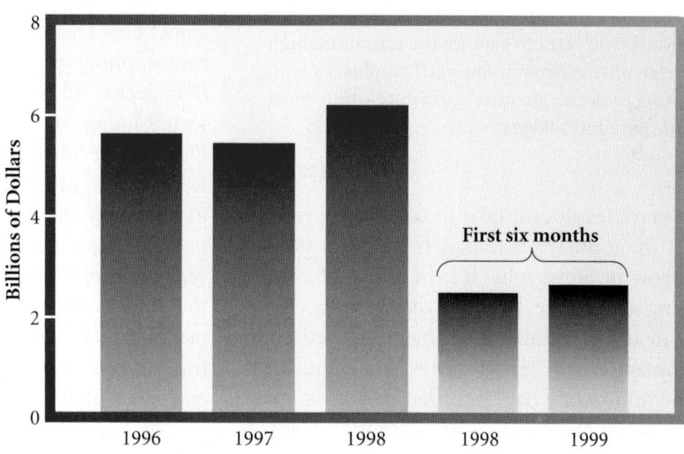

EXHIBIT 3
FILM AND TELEVISION REVENUES

CASE 15

The Making of the iPod

> . . . turn over your iPod, and you'll find six words engraved on the back that foretell the future of competition, "Designed in California. Made in China." Despite the equal billing, the remarkable success of Apple's music business owes relatively little to the company's network of Asian subcontractors. It is a credit instead to the imagination of Apple's designers, marketers and lawyers. . . . The point . . . is this: If you want to capture the economic high ground in the *creative economy,* you need employees who are more than acquiescent, attentive and astute—they must also be zestful, zany and zealous.
>
> —Gary Hamel[1]

How many geniuses does it take to completely rethink an industry? If the industry is music, the answer is four! Five, if you throw in Steve Jobs. It's the iPod, of course, that we're talking about here. In just a very brief period of time, the now nearly ubiquitous iPod has rendered audio CDs virtually obsolete, put "record stores" out of business, reconceived the notion of what "recorded" music is, made the term "disc" jockey meaningless, and essentially blown-up the entire value chain that brought music to the masses. Not bad for four (or five) guys and a few months of effort!

What the iPod also represents is the power of great teams to create big change. This is the story of how that happened.

FROM STATIONARY JUKEBOX TO PERSONAL JUKEBOX TO iPOD

Beginning even before Edison's 1877 invention of the phonograph,* the history of recorded music is a busy one, involving huge shifts in musical tastes, technology, and distribution, all of which have earned it a reputation as a "fast clockspeed"[2] industry. During this relatively short historical period, the primary medium for recording has passed from tin-foil cylinders, to wire, to vinyl discs of various sizes (78 rpm, 33 rpm, and 45 rpm), to tape (again, of various sizes and packaging: reel-to-reel, 8 track, and cassettes), to discs again (CDs and mini-CDs), and eventually, to digitally compressed files, such as MP3. At each stage in this journey, the different technologies in play were matched with different corporate players in a Darwinian struggle to establish standards and win the customers' hearts, minds, and pocketbooks.

The achievement of "portability" in music has also evolved hand-in-hand with the recording technologies. It is hard to believe that as recently as a hundred years ago, the only place that one could hear music was in the company of musicians. That changed with the introduction of gramophones, radios, phonograph players, and then, later, jukeboxes and tape decks. All of these, however, were largely "stationary" technologies, not easily moved out of the home (or car). Despite the introduction of Texas Instrument's inspired Regency TR-1 transistor radio in 1954, the real breakthrough in portability for recorded music started in the 1970s with portable tape players—the notorious "boom boxes"—and really became "personal" in 1979, with the introduction of the Sony Walkman. Throughout this migration to personal portability, the entire value chain connecting the artist to the consumer was in motion with different corporate actors entering and departing from the economic stage.

The advent of electronic digitalization technologies led, inexorably, to the capturing of sound in digital rather than analog fashion and ultimately resulted in the contemporary dominant medium for sound recording, storage, and transfer: MP3, which is a format for compressing music files.[3] Most MP3 files were initially transferred from personal computer to personal computer, over such infamous websites as Napster and Gnutella, but the real possibilities were in the development of compressed musical files that could be stored on miniature, personal jukeboxes, if such devices could be produced. The first mass-market entry of these was the Rio,[4] launched by Diamond Multimedia in 1998. The Rio was "a black, rectangular device resembling a walkie-talkie that had shrunk in the dryer."[5] It held 24 songs, with 12 hours of battery power, and it sold for less than $200.* Hit, immediately, by an intellectual

*A Frenchman, Leon Scott, is generally credited with the first recording of sound, in 1857. See David L. Morton, Jr. *Sound Recording: The Life Story of a Technology,* Baltimore, Johns Hopkins Press, 2004.

Professor William A Fischer prepared this case as a basis for class discussion rather than to illustrate either effective or ineffective handling of a business situation.

*Price estimate from Coleman, Mark. *Playback.* New York: Da Capo Press, 2003, p. 200.

property infringement lawsuit by the Recording Industry Association of America, the Rio failed to deliver on its market promise in either 1998 or 1999, although eventually several hundred thousand units were sold.[6] At around the same time, a "personal jukebox" project team was working at Digital Equipment Corporation (DEC) to take the personal portability concept even further. They were successful in getting to the point where you could hold a couple of hundred tunes in your hand, and they had solved essential problems of "energy management, sound processing, navigation and integration with personal computers."[7] However, the acquisition of DEC by Compaq, followed by the acquisition of Compaq by Hewlett-Packard, placed the entire project in a hopeless situation, leading it to eventually being sold to a Korean company HanGo. The resulting product was ultimately introduced to the market as the PJB-100, in November 1999, but it was slow, had poor user interface, and was expensive: Although *Popular Mechanics* trumpeted it as "the MP3 that changes everything," the reality was that it was fated to fail, leading one observer to lament:

> Like the wizards of Xerox PARC, another Palo Alto research division of a great company whose head was located eastward, the DEC scientists will dwell forever in a destination that they never booked – the limbo populated by creators doomed to see their great ideas realized, and hugely improved upon, by companies with more visionary bosses.[8]

APPLE ENTERS PORTABLE MUSIC

Unlike Diamond Multimedia or DEC, Apple was most decidedly not thinking about portable personal music as the 20th century drew to a close. Instead, Jobs was fascinated by the potential of video transfer, which led, in Apple's case, to the development of FireWire in the early 1990s. FireWire allowed the rapid transfer of massive amounts of digital information from one device to another. Such speed was necessary for video transfer and became an important part of Apple's development of iTV. From this idea, came Apple's Digital Hub strategy, which was announced at Macworld in January 2001:

> The idea was to produce the world's greatest portfolio of consumer software, available only to those smart enough, cool enough, and thinking-different enough to buy an Apple computer.[9]

Digital Hub ushered in iMovie, but while Apple was concentrating on video, the target consumer market was learning how to rip and share music, and the then current version of iMacs, without CD-burners, were fast losing the customers' attention. When Apple realized it had misread the market, it somewhat reluctantly added iTunes to its portfolio, a move occasioned by a $195million quarterly loss announced in January 2001.[10] This was the first quarterly loss incurred by Apple since Jobs had returned to take on the CEO role in July 1997, and it was a real wake-up call.

THE BIRTH OF THE iPOD

Given Apple's widespread reputation for innovation and trendiness, its failure to anticipate the importance of music in the lives of personal computer (PC) users was completely uncharacteristic, but the origins of its mistake might perhaps be traced back to much earlier, controversial personnel decisions at the very top of the organization.

The story begins in 1985, when Steve Jobs, a founder of Apple, had been unceremoniously marginalized by the firm's board for being " . . . unproductive and uncontrollable." After a failed power struggle with the then-CEO (and former PepsiCo boss) John Scully, Jobs quit before he could be fired.[11] In 1996, 11 years later, Apple was in complete disarray, and the company once again turned to Jobs and invited him to return to revolutionize Apple's product line.[*] He began by reducing and simplifying the number of offerings.

Jobs' "master-stroke" following his return was the introduction of the translucently colorful iMacs, which represented a dramatic aesthetic statement about what Apple thought about itself, relative to its drab competitors. One big technical departure from industry norms, besides "color," was the elimination of an integral floppy disc drive. While it had both aesthetic and technical benefits, this choice flew in the face of the wave of CD burning and sharing activities that were sweeping across communities of young people at the time, severely limiting the attractiveness of iMacs to this important customer segment. Once convinced that music acquisition, filing, playing, and sharing was, in fact, an important and durable attribute of PC performance, Jobs began, in his typically full-speed-ahead fashion, to launch an imaginative effort to catch up to the rest of the industry and regain Mac's attractiveness to their customer base. In an unusually candid admission, Jobs told *Fortune* magazine: "I felt like a dope. I thought we had missed it. We had to work hard to catch up."[12]

In this instance, again somewhat uncharacteristically for a company that prided itself in doing everything, Apple went off in search of a ready-made solution. Eventually, it licensed the SoundJam MP music player, which had been written by a trio of programmers including Jeff Robbin, who had previously worked at Apple as a systems software engineer on the much-awaited, but ill-fated, Copland operating system project.[†] Along with the rights to SoundJam, Apple rehired Robbin to turn the software into iTunes.[‡] SoundJam had, in fact, been written in response to a National Public Radio program that had introduced the

[*] In July 1997, Steve Jobs responded to Apple's board's request to serve temporarily as CEO, following the dismissal of Gilbert Amelio. (Kahney, Leander. *Inside Steve's Brain.* New York: Portfolio, 2008, pp. 20–23.)

[†] In development from 1994 to 1996, Copland was slated to be Mac OS 8, but it was eventually abandoned in favor of the exiled Steve Jobs' NeXT operating system.

[‡] See the Wikipedia entry for Jeff Robbin.

Rio MP3 player as an exciting new way to listen to music, and ended with the observation: "Don't get excited Mac users, cause it won't work with Macs."[13] SoundJam was designed to work with the Mac, but it was not a typically elegant Apple program, "Steve Jobs would not tolerate a program that was ugly or acted ugly."[14] Once SoundJam was brought into Apple, this lack of elegance had to change! Despite the misreading of the market and the late response, Robbin captured the intensity of Jobs' commitment to the new vision when he recalled:

> When Apple decides to take something on, you know, we really take it on full throttle. . . . Even in this first version of iTunes, it was about bringing digital audio to the masses. It was about tying it in with the iMac, and CDs, and CD burning, and it was just about digital audio as being a focus for the company.[15]

iTunes was completed in its first commercial version in four months and introduced in January 2001, at the Macworld Conference & Expo. The big loser in the development of iTunes was another spin-off of former Apple employees, Audion, which also had a music filing system of its own. Despite the competitive loss to SoundJam, Cabel Sasser, CEO of Audion, reflected:

> iTunes was of course brilliant. It was a way to take a complicated digital music collection and make it easy. Sure, it was limited, but man, it was easy. . . . iTunes is, you know, actually pretty awesome.[16]

And "awesome" spelled the end of Audion's competitive efforts but not Apple's. After fixing iTunes so that the Mac could work effortlessly with almost any MP3 player, Apple's leadership realized that the rest of the "portable music value chain" was mediocre. While file saving and transfer were now fast and easy, the players themselves were expensive, unattractive, unengaging, and slow, with a short battery life. Greg Joswiak, who went on to become vice president of iPod product marketing, put it this way, "That means no telling your friends how cool it is. Because it isn't cool."[17] "The products stank."[18]

A lot of things had to come together at the same time in order to rectify this value-chain problem, if the iPod was to become as successful as it did in such a short time. An example of how Apple moved quickly along the entire value chain to take command over what Jobs calls "vectors in time"—the ways in which a technology advances over time across a broad set of devices and approaches[19]—can be seen in a visit that Jon Rubenstein made to Toshiba to look at hard drive advances. On that visit, he chanced upon a new 1.8-inch drive that Toshiba had just developed. According to Rubenstein, who was then Apple's senior vice president of hardware, and who had come to Apple from NeXT, where he had also been Job's chief hardware person: "[Toshiba] said that they didn't know what to do with it . . . I went back to Steve and I said, 'I know how to do this (i.e. a small portable music device). I've got all the parts.' So Jobs said, 'Go for it.' "[20] This was the mandate to create the team that would create the iPod.

REDEFINING APPLE'S INNOVATIVE CULTURE

Ask anyone to identify the most "innovative" firms that they can think of, and Apple is sure to be on the list. Today, with the iPod and iPhone, we take this for granted, but even in the 1990s, this was true. After all, Apple had a legitimate claim to have given us the personal computer, and it had, at the very least, created one of the most "beloved" technologies of contemporary times—the Mac. At the heart of that success was an "innovative culture" envied by many. Steve Wozniak, Apple's cofounder, recalled:

> There are occasionally short windows in time when incredibly important things get invented that shape the lives of humans for hundreds of years. The development of the Macintosh computer was one of these events, and it has changed our lives forever. It's chilling to recall how this cast of young and inexperienced people who cared more than anything about doing great things created what is perhaps the key technology of our lives.[21]

A visit to the Apple campus in those days, especially the "Good Earth" building (named after the Good Earth Chinese restaurant next door) where the Mac team was lodged, was a visit to a different corporate planet. Nerf balls and pirate flags were part of the décor, and the overall impression was one of absolute freedom, if not chaos. Don Norman, who was the head of Apple's Advanced Technology Group, remembers it well:

> When I joined Apple in 1993, it was wonderful. You could do creative, innovative things. But it was chaotic. You can't do that in an organization. You need a few creative people, and the rest get the work done.

According to Norman, Apple's engineers were rewarded for being imaginative and inventive, not for the difficult job of knuckling down and making things work. They would invent all day, but rarely did what they were told. Orders would be handed down, but incredibly, six months later nothing had happened. It was ridiculous.[22]

In fact, there was more than a bit of "counter-culture" DNA in Apple's roots. In a 2001 interview with *New York Times* reporter and Silicon Valley historian, John Markoff, Jobs suggested, "that taking LSD was one of the two or three most important things he had done in his life, and that. . . . His countercultural roots often left him feeling like an outsider in the corporate world of which he is now a leader."[23]

Yet, when Jobs returned to Apple in 1997 to take control, some things needed to change, including the chaos, if the company was to remain viable. Jobs ordered the cessation of work on all but the most essential products, reducing the entire product portfolio to just four pieces: two notebooks and two desktops, one of each aimed at the professional and consumer markets.[24] The idea was to never compete in the commodity market where most mainstream PC manufacturers had unwittingly found themselves. As Jobs put it, "The world doesn't need another Dell or Compaq,"[25] Apple would sell premium products for premium margins.

Gone were all the distractions, including some "neat" and beloved products, such as the Newton, Apple's entrant into the fledgling PDA market.

BUILDING THE iPOD TEAM

Killing products, however, did not have to mean losing the talent associated with those product teams, and Jobs was a great believer in building an organization around "A teams [i.e., great teams]." "If we could make four great product platforms [he observed in 1998] that's all we need. We can put our A team on every single one of them instead of having a B or a C team on any."[26]

The iPod team reflected Job's belief in "A teams." Rubenstein was a key member of the team, in charge of hardware. A New Yorker by birth, Rubenstein had worked at Hewlett-Packard and Ardent Computing (a Silicon Valley start-up) and had been recruited by Jobs, personally, to run hardware engineering at NeXT. After selling yet another business to Motorola, Rubenstein was recruited to Apple again by Jobs because in Rubenstein's words, "Apple was the last innovative, high-volume computer maker in the world."[27] It was, in fact, Rubenstein's decision to launch the iMac without a floppy disc,[28] which had contributed to the dilemma that the organization now faced. In later years, Rubenstein was honored by entry into the National Academy of Engineering and by being made a Senior Member of the IEEE (Institute of Electrical and Electronic Engineers).

Design had always held a special place of honor at Apple, and for the iPod A team, Jobs chose Jonathan Ive who was head of Apple's design group. Jobs said of Ive and his team, "I've found . . . the best industrial design team I've ever seen in my life."[29] Ive had already won the London Design Museum's Designer of the Year award twice and worked with what he referred to as "a heavenly design team," where "one of the hallmarks of the team is inquisitiveness [and] being excited about being wrong because that means you've discovered something new."[30]

The third (not counting Jobs) key member of the iPod team came from outside of the organization. Tony Fadell was skiing at Vail when he received a phone call from Rubenstein to come and work at Apple on an unnamed project. It was spring 2001, and Jobs wanted the new portable music device on store shelves in time for Christmas. This meant creating a new team to pull this all together and neither Rubinstein nor Jobs wanted to disrupt any of the other ongoing Mac projects. So they looked outside of Apple and found Fadell who was 32 years old and had developed gadgets for General Magic (where he worked with Mac founders Andy Hertzfeld and Bill Atkinson)[31] and at Philips (where he headed up their handheld PDA work). He was offered an eight-week contract by Rubenstein, after which:

> . . . he was put in charge of a small team of engineers and designers, who put the device together quickly. The team took as many parts as possible off the shelf: the drive from Toshiba, a battery from Sony, some control chips from Texas Instruments. The basic hardware blueprint was bought from Silicon Valley startup PortalPlayer.[32]

It was Fadell who really pulled the whole spectrum of activities, from FireWire to iTunes, together, along with the hardware, to achieve Jobs' ambition. After failing to build what he called "the Dell of consumer electronics," in a start-up named Fuse, Fadell was ready to bring system thinking to the iPod project. In Fadell's opinion:

> I think the definition of product has changed over the decades. The product now is iTunes Music Store and iTunes, and the iPod and the software that goes into the iPod. A lot of companies don't really have control, or they can't really work in a collaborative way to truly make a system. We're really about a system.[33]

Michael Dhuey, the fourth "A team" member, was an Apple III, Lisa, Macintosh, and Mac II veteran hardware engineer, who had the job of designing the electronics hardware for the device in eight months. Although daunting in both physical and schedule challenges, Dhuey was given free rein by Apple to get the job done. "I was told, 'We need this project. It has to be ready by Christmas, so make sure it gets done. And don't screw up.' "[34]

THE WAY THEY WORKED

From the very start, the ambitions for the iPod were extraordinary. For the hardware: *A thousand songs in your pocket*; for the software: *so easy that your Mother could do it*; and for the project: *and on the shelves in eight months!* What is so exquisite about these objectives is that they are simple, clear, understood by everybody, precise, and yet broad enough so that the team could get to work without feeling constrained by the way the vision was presented—they were both totally focused and liberated at the same time!

The space that they worked in was also important. Jonathan Ive's design team had always worked in quarters that were described as having " . . . very little personal space. There are no cubicles or offices. The studio is a large open space with several communal design areas. . . . 'By keeping the core team small and investing significantly in [prototyping] tools and process, we can work with a level of collaboration that seems particularly rare. In fact, the memory of how we work will endure beyond the products of our work.' "[35]

Prototyping was also a continuing theme that ran through the iPod team experience. Early on, when Apple was searching for software "fixes," Pixo, yet another spin-off by ex-Apple employees, pitched their integrated iTunes "experience" by using an existing MP3 player, running Pixo-iTunes software, and actually playing Eric Clapton.[36] iPod team members had prototype devices of their own to take home and test under a variety of "live" situations. One illustration of how important prototyping was to the eventual outcome is the story of how Tony Fadell won Steve Jobs' buy-in on the device:

Working day and night through the course of his [eight-week] contract, Fadell played with cardboard and foam, moving things around in various patterns to show himself what a player might look like. Eventually, he came up with a box the size of a pack of Marlboros with a cell-phone-sized screen at the top and push buttons at the bottom. He weighed down the gadget with fishing weights, to approximate what it might feel like. Then it was time to meet with Jobs. Fadell and Rubenstein knew Jobs liked to get prototypes in groups of three, so they sent up two as "sacrificial lambs" . . . The third one, they hid under a wooden bowl in the conference room . . . It turned out that they knew Jobs pretty well. He quickly dismissed the first two, but the third one left him speechless.[37]

STEVE JOBS AND INNOVATION LEADERSHIP

Leadership is an essential part of every innovation success story, and the iPod is no exception. Yet Steve Jobs was not known for having a "light-touch" when it came to leadership style. In fact, Stanford University professor, Robert I. Sutton, has written:

It sometimes seems as if his full name is "Steve Jobs, that asshole." I put "Steve Jobs" and "asshole" in Google and got 89,400 matches. I asked some insiders to nominate the most (allegedly) demeaning leaders in entertainment and high technology to get some "comparative assholes," because Jobs' companies are in these industries. Michael Eisner, former Disney CEO, was mentioned constantly, yet "Michael Eisner" and "asshole" produced a relatively paltry 11,100 Google hits. And, in high technology, Oracle's infamously difficult "Larry Ellison" and "asshole" generated a mere 750 hits.

The scariest—and most entertaining—stories come directly from people who have worked for Jobs. *Wired* magazine summed up a reunion of 1,300 ex-Apple employees in 2003 by saying that even though Jobs didn't attend, he was the main topic of conversation: "Everyone has their Steve-Jobs-the-asshole story."[38]

To be fair to Jobs, and to Sutton, these quotes come from a chapter entitled "The Virtues of Assholes," which argues that sometimes difficult people can add, rather than subtract value from a talented team.

According to *Time* magazine, Jobs:

. . . needs . . . control because he is fastidious about technology . . . and he recognizes that in an increasingly networked world, in which gadgets can't just do their own thing but have to talk to one another, that conversation will go better if [he] has scripted both sides of it. "One company makes the software. The other makes the hardware . . . It's not working," Jobs says. "The innovation can't happen fast enough. The integration isn't seamless enough. No one takes responsibility for the user interface. It's a mess."[39]

This no-nonsense approach to control was hugely evident on the day before the introduction of the iPod (then called the P68). Having not seen the whole thing together in one piece before this (which, in itself is an interesting insight into someone typically thought of as a "control freak"), Jobs was completely frustrated by the earplugs. "This feels like crap!" Steve growled at the engineer from the industrial design department. He repeatedly plugged and unplugged the headphones from the preproduction iPod and looked as if he might fling it across the room. " . . . these headphone jacks all have to be replaced by tomorrow."[40] "Find a way to fix it."[41]

According to Mike Evangelist, then product manager for iDVD:

The real magic of Apple is that: "Everything had to be just right . . . no not 'just right,' it had to be great."[42]

The magic of Apple is that this stuff is largely invisible. At the unveiling on Tuesday, none of these details had the slightest impact on the response of those in attendance; at least not taken individually. But taken together, along with the countless other little details which had been considered and worked on and improved before the world saw the product, they contributed to the Apple difference.[43]

According to *Time* magazine, there are two lessons to be learned from stories like this:

. . . one about collaboration, one about control. Apple employees talk incessantly about what they call "deep collaboration" or "cross-pollination" or "concurrent engineering." Essentially, it means that products don't pass from team to team. There aren't discrete, sequential development stages. Instead, it's simultaneous and organic. Products get worked on in parallel by all departments at once—design, hardware, software—in endless rounds of interdisciplinary design reviews. Managers elsewhere boast about how little time they waste in meetings; Apple is big on them and proud of it. "The historical way of developing products just doesn't work when you're as ambitious as we are," says Ive. "When the challenges are that complex, you have to develop a product in a more collaborative, integrated way."[44]

The second lesson . . . is about control, and to that extent, it's a lesson about Jobs himself. He is one of the technology world's great innovators but not because he's an engineer or a programmer. He doesn't have an MBA either. He doesn't even have a college degree. [He dropped out of Reed College after one semester.] Jobs has a great native sense of design and a knack for hiring geniuses, but above all, what he has is a willingness to be a pain in the neck about what matters most to him.[45]

As Rubinstein put it, "With Steve pushing me, I [could] achieve things I wouldn't be able to do on my own."[46]

The quest for excellence in all things has marked Steve Jobs and Apple from the start. After all, this is a company that had marketed consumer electronic products using associations with such luminaries as Pablo Picasso, Maria Callas, Albert Einstein, and Mahatma Gandhi. Not many other firms had such high expectations of their customers as Apple did. In Jobs' mind, "Young people like (such associations) because they feel like they're not being talked down to."[47]

CONTENT: THE LAST PIECE OF THE PUZZLE

The Apple iPod was introduced in late 2001. It weighed 6.5 ounces, had a 5-gigabyte hard drive, held 66 hours of music (roughly 1,300 tracks), and cost $399.[48] At the same time, iTunes was available for transferring CD tracks from a Macintosh, but not from a PC, and technically, the legality of the transfers was in question.

One of the biggest impediments to achieving the portability of recorded music has been, for years, the reluctance of the intellectual property holders (record labels and artists) to release their hold over their music far enough so that it could be copied outside of their controlled channels and ported onto personal players. As was the case with David Sarnoff and RCA's radio apparatus, there was little point in having an iPod if there was nothing to listen to, and the lesson from the IP-holders' war against Napster was clear: *They owned the content* beyond legitimate personal listening, and they certainly held rights when "sharing" was involved. Jobs realized that this limited the potential market for iPods, and it had to be changed. The value chain that he had in mind was not to manufacture devices, but to *"rewire" the listening experience*. Although his first inclination was to employ an outer wrapping that said, "Don't steal music!" in multiple languages,[49] it quickly became clear that a much more heroic effort would be needed to win-over the IP holders.

In January 2002, two vice presidents from Warner Music traveled to Cupertino to meet with Jobs. At that meeting, he reportedly castigated them, and their industry, for:

> . . . not getting it . . . for trying to suck out all the money from digital music for themselves . . . *His* customers—*Apple's* customers—deserved better. They needed an easy-to-use music store.[50]

At a subsequent meeting with Roger Ames, then Chairman and CEO of Warner Music, Jobs unveiled the iTunes Store, which met with almost immediate acceptance from Warner and led to a content-licensing agreement. Warner suggested that tracks sell for 99 cents as a "hook" to attract customers, of which Apple would receive 22 cents. Shortly thereafter, the biggest record label, Universal, also bought in, as did Sony eventually.[51]

The iTunes music store opened on April 28, 2003, with a catalog of 200,000 songs all selling at 99 cents each, and in October 2003, became available on PCs as well.[52]

By January 2009, iTunes had grown to become the largest online music seller in the world, having sold more than six billion songs worldwide,* and gaining widespread recognition for being a maker/breaker of popular music, in much the same way that MTV was in the 1990s.[53] Undoubtedly, as a result of the iTunes music store, Apple now occupied one of the most powerful places in the music value chain. Bono, the lead singer of the popular group U2, suggested that working with Apple was like "dealing with the devil":

> The devil here is a bunch of creative minds, more creative than a lot of people in rock bands. The lead singer is Steve Jobs. In the band on lead guitar, [Apple senior vice president] Jonny Ive. A beautiful spirit. A man who has helped design the most beautiful art object in music culture since the electric guitar. That's the iPod. . . .[54]

By 2007, Jobs was calling for the music industry to "drop all anti-piracy software limitations from online music sales," so that any digital player could play music purchased from any store, and any store could sell music that is playable on all players."[55] EMI Music responded positively to this, ending its Digital Rights Management restrictions, and increasing the fidelity of its offered tracks, from 128 to 256 kilobits per second. At the same time, Apple raised the price of such unprotected "premium tracks" from 99 cents to $1.29. The new distribution of revenues from tracks sold became "36% to the [iTunes music store], 30% for the digital distributor, 17% to the label, and 17% to the artist."[56] By 2009, Apple, in a compromise settlement with the music labels, moved to a three-tier pricing arrangement—69 cents, 99 cents, and $1.29—in return for an end to Digital Rights Management restrictions.[57]

---

*Six billion statistics from January 6, 2009, keynote speech by Phil Schiller at Macworld 2009.

CASE 16

Arnold Schwarzenegger (A): Strategy or Sheer Willpower?

On a rainy day in October, 2011, a crowd gathered in Thal, Austria, to watch Arnold Schwarzenegger, world champion bodybuilder, movie star, and former governor of California, unveil a giant, buff bronze statue of himself in front of the house in which he grew up, now a museum dedicated to his humble origins and rise to international fame.

The trip back to his birthplace came three months after Maria Shriver, Schwarzenegger's wife of 25 years, filed for divorce when news that he had fathered a child with a member of the household staff, made headlines around the world. Schwarzenegger had expected to leave the California governor's mansion to pursue a variety of high-profile film and media projects. The scandal put these plans indefinitely on hold. His detractors doubted the chances of a fourth act in Schwarzenegger's extraordinary career. His supporters insisted that he had weathered worse, always coming on top by stamina and an exceptional ability to adapt and learn. Speaking after the unveiling to the crowd and the assembled media, Schwarzenegger was perhaps addressing both sides when he sought to sum up the lessons of his life:

> My personal success has less to do with millions of dollars or with the headlines in the media that are not always positive and also not with being clapped on the shoulder by Barack Obama and other world names. Personal success is the result of determination, hard work and stubbornness. For me, this is not only a museum, it is also a symbol of will. Everyone has a chance.[1]

EARLY DAYS

The man described by the Guinness Book of Records as "The most perfectly developed man in the history of the world" was born on July 30, 1947, in an isolated village in postwar Austria. His childhood is told as a story of tough living conditions with a strict disciplinarian upbringing. The Schwarzenegger home was not equipped with a phone, fridge, or indoor plumbing until the young Arnold Schwarzenegger was 14. Both he and his older brother, Meinhard, were brought up by their mother Aurelia. Their father, Gustav, was the police chief of the town of Graz and a curling champion. He insisted that his children should be raised with strict disciplinarian values, and pushed them both to achieve athletic excellence. Years later, Schwarzenegger had this to say about his father:

> He was so strict. In many ways, too strict. I remember overhearing my father telling my mother that he'd just read a newspaper article that said American fathers want to be friends with their children. He thought that was such nonsense—the idea of a parent and a child being friends. He was police chief for all the villages that surrounded my hometown of Graz in Austria. He wasn't mean, not really, but he was a bit of a police chief at home.[2]

As a boy, Schwarzenegger would rise at 6 AM and do chores, and then sit-ups and squats before breakfast. He was allowed out on Sunday evenings, but legend has it that he had to write a ten-page essay on his activities before going to bed. While training for a local soccer team, Schwarzenegger started to lift weights. Lacking the money to pay for membership in a sports club, he equipped his own exercise room in the basement of his parents' home. The hard training paid off when in 1961 he met Kurt Marnul, the former Mr. Austria. Marnul was impressed with Schwarzenegger's body and asked him to train in the Athletic Union in Graz. Later he was to say that it was at this time that he formed his ambition to become the greatest bodybuilder of all time. He worked toward this with extraordinary drive and dedication, and was even known to break into the gym and train to the point of near collapse from exhaustion.

At age eighteen, Schwarzenegger started his National Service. However, within one month he skipped camp without permission to attend the "Mr. Junior Europe" bodybuilding contest in Stuttgart. He won, with a perfect score, but instead of celebrating he spent seven days in military prison for breaking discipline. In 1966, he left the army to study marketing at the University of Munich, and while there accepted a personal invitation to train at that city's prestigious Putzingger gym. In September he traveled

---

This case was prepared by Joseph Lampel and Daniel Ronen. Cass Business School, City University London.

to London where he worked for £30 per week. While there he entered the amateur "Mr. Universe" contest, coming second overall. Second place, however, was not good enough for Schwarzenegger. With his characteristic dedication, he returned the following year to take first place.

MOVING TO AMERICA

Following his success as an amateur, Schwarzenegger decided to take the next step and become a professional bodybuilder. In 1968, Schwarzenegger won the professional bodybuilding contest "Mr. Universe," becoming the youngest ever to hold the title. This achievement was marred by the deaths of his brother in a car crash, and shortly afterward his father of a fatal stroke. The same year, however, he received an invitation from bodybuilding champion and muscle entrepreneur Joe Weider to come to the United States, officially to study Business and Economics. Weider, the son of a Polish pants presser, started working out as a teenager, to defend himself against bullies in his Montreal neighborhood. Four years later, he won the first of his many weight lifting awards. When other aspiring bodybuilders kept asking him for advice, Weider saw an opportunity and mimeographed 400 copies of a 12-page newsletter which he called "Your Physique."

From this modest start, Weider built his Weider Health & Fitness Corp., a privately held health products and publishing empire. Along with the magazines, Weider Health & Fitness also sells food supplements and a full line of exercise equipment, worldwide. Weider's lasting achievement, however, was gaining public acceptance for bodybuilding as a sport which is distinct from weight lifting. In this he had the help of his brother, Ben Weider, president of the International Federation of Bodybuilders, an organization they cofounded in 1946. The federation has 176 national affiliates, and is recognized by over 90 National Olympic Committees. In 1965, it launched the "Mr. Olympia" contest, followed by "Ms. Olympia" contest in 1980. Both contests are regarded as the pinnacle of professional bodybuilding awards.

Over the years, Weider's competitors have criticized the business relationship between Ben and Joe Weider, suggesting that a mutually beneficial coordination between the bodybuilders promoted in the magazines, and the bodybuilding contests run by International Federation of Bodybuilders, often biases contest judging. No evidence for improper behavior has ever been revealed.

Joe Weider makes no secret of his approach to developing bodybuilding talent. Weider made agreements with promising young bodybuilders in need of income, usually guaranteeing them weekly salaries in return for endorsements. Schwarzenegger was one of these bodybuilders. As Schwarzenegger recalled later, the relationship eased his transition into the United States: "I got money from Weider for writing articles for his muscle magazines. I wrote each month in German how I trained, and gave it to a translator. In return, Weider gave me an apartment for free and a leased Volkswagen and $60 a week spending money. That's what I lived on for the first two years."[3]

Charles Gains, coauthor of *Pumping Iron: The Art and Sport of Bodybuilding*, a book that took bodybuilding into the mainstream, and also brought Schwarzenegger to the attention of the public, puts this arrangement in a wider context: "Joe is a kingmaker. He can make bodybuilders, and he can break them, by leaving them out of his magazine. You can be the new Arnold Schwarzenegger, but if he doesn't give you any press, that's it."[4]

In the United States, with the backing of Weider, Schwarzenegger began his great run of championship success, winning Mr. World, and then ultimately every Mr. Universe title from 1968 until his retirement in 1975. Against all expectations, he emerged from retirement to win the Mr. Universe title in 1980. But it is the 1975 Mr. Olympia contest that is probably best remembered for the cult film *Pumping Iron*. The film showed Schwarzenegger using psychology and humor to unsettle and defeat his rivals, something that was not typical of the sport at that time. He not only dominated the film, as he did the contest, but also showed film presence that foreshadowed his next career move.

BREAKING INTO THE MOVIES

Schwarzenegger had long had his eye on the movie business. At one point he was offered $50,000 a year to manage a gym, a common transition from active bodybuilding to semi-retirement in the industry. He turned the offer down. "I said no," he recalled later, "because managing a gym would not have brought me closer to working in films. And that is what I wanted to do."[5] Schwarzenegger drew inspiration from Reg Park, the legendary English bodybuilder and a personal friend who played Hercules in several movies in the early 1960s. In 1970, he took the plunge and starred in the low budget film *Hercules in New York*. In the film, Schwarzenegger's thick Austrian accent was dubbed over and he used the stage name Arnold Strong. The movie was panned by the critics, and generally ignored by the public.

Disappointed, but undaunted Schwarzenegger fell back on the success of *Pumping Iron*. He began to mix with celebrities, was regularly interviewed on mainstream television programs such NBC's "Today" show, and was featured prominently in publications such as *Sports Illustrated*.

Although Schwarzenegger was best known for his bodybuilding achievements, bodybuilding was not Schwarzenegger's main income. Putting his education to good use, he made his first million from a bricklaying business he established with fellow bodybuilder Franco Columbu. He used these proceeds to finance a series of fitness books and cassettes, whose subsequent success financed the purchase of an apartment block and a series of lucrative real estate deals.

In 1977, Arnold Schwarzenegger met his future wife, Maria Shriver at a Pro-Celebrity tennis tournament. The courtship caught many by surprise. Maria, niece of President

John F. Kennedy, was a politically active TV journalist of the famous Democrat dynasty, whereas Schwarzenegger was a staunch Republican. They married in 1986, and went on to have four children.

It was at this point in his life that he began to pursue his movie career in earnest. He first featured in vaguely comic bit parts, as a thug in *The Long Goodbye* and as a bodybuilder starring alongside Jeff Bridges and Sally Field in *Stay Hungry,* a role for which he won a Golden Globe. He played a bit part in the ensemble comedy *Scavenger Hunt,* showed up as the handsome stranger in *Western Cactus Jack,* and as the muscle-bound Mickey Hargitay in *The Jayne Mansfield Story*. All the while, he was gaining experience of the film industry and building a network of contacts.

In 1982, Schwarzenegger got to play the part that was to make him a star: the lead character in *Conan the Barbarian.* The visual nature of the film and limited dialogue suited him perfectly. As he was to comment later:

> Naturally, when you go into this profession, you use your assets. If your assets are your looks, or your asset is your voice, or if your asset is your body, or the muscularity of the body, or whatever your assets are, you use that first, then you have to follow through with your talents, of course. So in the beginning, I took a lot of acting lessons and studied acting very carefully and sort of worked my way up the same way I did bodybuilding.[6]

The success of *Conan the Barbarian* was followed up by films of the same genre, *Conan the Destroyer* and *Red Sonja.* This led to his breakthrough role as the robot in James Cameron's *The Terminator*. The budget for *The Terminator* was just $6.5 million, but it was to become one of the great films of the 1980s, grossing close to $80 million worldwide. Reminiscing on the making of the film much later, Cameron recalled: "With Arnold, the film took on a larger-than-life sheen. I found myself on the set doing things I didn't think I would do, scenes that were supposed to be purely horrific that just couldn't be, because now they were too flamboyant."[7] While using Schwarzenegger's physical presence to great effect, Cameron was careful not to rely on his more conventional acting skills. Schwarzenegger's longest speech is 18 words, and a large proportion of what he did say could be memorized like an advertising slogan. The one-liners that were to become his trademark began with *The Terminator* "I'll be back" and continued with "I lied" (*Commando*); "Consider that a divorce" (*Total Recall*); and "Hasta la vista, baby" (*Terminator 2*).

With the success of *The Terminator,* Schwarzenegger defined his acting image as an action hero. He therefore continued making action movies including a number of military and sci-fi hits, all with the same format—Arnold Schwarzenegger as the star, lots of big guns, explosions, and sharp witty one-liners. His box office draw was secure. For most actors, let alone a former Austrian bodybuilder with a heavy accent, this would have been sufficient, but Schwarzenegger fully understood the risk that came with his success: Increasingly being forced into playing the same action role in a succession of films that exploited his image. To forestall this threat he sought a parallel career in comedy. As he put it:

> The question is: will I be able to grow as an actor without losing my fans who hold specific expectations of me? You must give your fans what they expect. But then you slowly add on. You give them a little bit of something else, something new. You put a little more clothes on in each movie and show another side of you—more humor, say, or sensitivity. Eventually, I want to do a movie that's entirely comedy.[8]

Schwarzenegger began to seek out movie projects that gave him a chance to expand his image. His new comic persona cleverly winked at all the jokes and Teutonic imitations that now became the staple of television talk and comedy shows. Starting with his role as a bashful intellectual in *Twins,* then in *Kindergarten Cop,* and *Junior,* he has debunked the very image he took so much effort creating (see Exhibit 1).

EXHIBIT 1 ARNOLD SCHWARZENEGGER

	FILMS	
Year	**Genre**	**Film**
1970	Action	*Hercules in New York*
1973	Drama	*Long Goodbye, The*
1976	Drama	*Stay Hungry*
1979	Comedy	*Villain, The*
1979	Comedy	*Scavenger Hunt*
1980	Drama	*Jayne Mansfield Story, The*
1982	Action	*Conan the Barbarian*
1984	Action	*Conan the Destroyer*
1984	Action	*Terminator, The*
1985	Action	*Red Sonja*
1985	Action	*Commando*
1986	Action	*Raw Deal*
1987	Action	*Predator*
1987	Action	*Running Man, The*
1988	Action	*Red Heat*
1988	Family	*Twins*
1990	Action	*Total Recall*
1990	Family	*Kindergarten Cop*
1992	Action	*Terminator 2: Judgment Day*
1992	Family	*Christmas in Connecticut*
1993	Family	*Last Action Hero*
1994	Action	*True Lies*
1994	Family	*Junior*
1996	Action	*Eraser*
1996	Family	*Jingle All the Way*
1996	Action	*T2 3-D: Battle Across Time*
1997	Family	*Batman & Robin*
1999	Action	*End of Days*
2000	Action	*6th Day, The*
2001	Family	*Dr. Doolittle 2*
2002	Action	*Collateral Damage*
2002	Family	*Liberty's Kids*
2003	Action	*Terminator 3: Rise of the Machines*
2003	Action	*Rundown, The*
2004	Family	*Around the World in 80 Days*

Schwarzenegger was now a household name, and an international celebrity. With his image firmly placed in the nice-guy family genre, he made a foray into the world of politics, taking on positions with the American government as Chairman of the President's Council on Physical Fitness and Sports in 1990, and the weight lifting trainer for the Special Olympics weight training team. However, his core acting activity remained and in 1992, he starred in the blockbuster *Terminator 2*.

But then came his first major film debacle, *Last Action Hero*. Despite fitting the family movie formula perfectly, it did badly at the box office, in part because it opened opposite *Jurassic Park*. However, with his reputation still intact, Schwarzenegger quickly made his comeback with a James Bond-like character in *True Lies* and as a US marshal in *Eraser*. On screen, Schwarzenegger was becoming much more relaxed and witty, as he had been all those years before when he was playing himself in *Pumping Iron*. Possibly feeling that his box office draw was strong enough, he started experimenting with different roles, including the villain in *Batman and Robin* and an alcoholic policeman in *End of Days*.

Despite his busy acting schedule, he had continued to develop his business interests including ownership of Oak Productions, Schatzi on Main, World Gym Enterprises, Planet Hollywood Inc. (major co-owner), and All Star Fitness Products. In addition, he had invested his bodybuilding and movie earnings in an array of stocks, bonds, privately controlled companies, and real estate holdings in the United States and worldwide. He has been conservatively estimated to be worth between \$100 and \$200 million, but others believe that his financial worth is anywhere in between US\$800 and \$900 million.

ENTERING CALIFORNIA POLITICS

In 2003 Schwarzenegger's career changed direction once again. California was going into a midterm snap recall election caused by the incumbent governor failing to deliver on key areas of policy. With campaigning limited to only eight weeks, Schwarzenegger sought advice from those he trusted most, including his politically astute wife. He announced his candidacy as a Republican candidate for Governor of California on *The Tonight Show with Jay Leno*. Campaigning energetically, and using his extraordinary name recognition to attract new voters, Schwarzenegger scored a convincing victory.

In the euphoria that followed his improbable ascent to the governorship of the richest and most populous state in America, Schwarzenegger adopted a bold platform that included cuts in the state budget, and restrictions on the power of the public service unions. He also broke with past conventions when taking office, instructing his aids not to prepare a daily schedule, and instead to make himself available to people based on the important issues of the day. Schwarzenegger believed that removing the carefully managed environment in which governors normally operate, would give him a direct feel for the issues that concerned his constituents.

Schwarzenegger started his term in office determined to translate his campaign pledges into action. He energized his staff, and applied his well-known charm and charisma to wooing the Democrats who controlled the state legislature. He also declined the salary of the office, and insisted on using his own private jet for travel. Scrupulously obeying state laws on smoking, he had a tent erected near his office so he could work while indulging his well-known love for cigars.

Politically he took a mixed stance on issues, supporting those which made sense to him and rejecting those policies which did not fit with his view of the world or values. His positions on economic issues were conservative but his social stances were liberal. However, he broke one of his major campaign promises, to reduce the power of special interest groups, when in the first three years of office he accepted over \$90 million in donations, including major contributions from estate developers, financiers, retailers, insurers, and oil and energy giants. He also failed to address other key issues such as environmental problems, escalating health insurance costs, and high gasoline prices. So despite using his profile and charm to woo several high-profile stars from industry and commerce to work with him on state business, Schwarzenegger started to lose public support.

Schwarzenegger became increasingly frustrated with the slow pace of change, and what he regarded as conflicting power centers within the state government and administration. In November 2005, against the advice of his wife, Schwarzenegger called a Special Election, asking voters to back a range of measures on social and economic issues. The proposals reflected Schwarzenegger's "get it done" common sense approach to politics. Up against a coalition funded by more than \$200 million, all eight of his proposals were defeated, severely denting Schwarzenegger's reputation for winning.

Schwarzenegger was humiliated and took personal responsibility for the defeat. He also changed tack, moving toward the political center. Against the advice of fellow Republican strategists he appointed a Democrat, Susan Kennedy, as his chief of staff. He also apologized to the public for driving through the special election in spite of strong opposition, and made conciliatory overtures to Democratic lawmakers, whom he had previously dismissed as "girlie men" and "losers." The result was legislation increasing the minimum wage, something Schwarzenegger had previously opposed, as well as a bipartisan plan for emergency funding on prescription drugs and a landmark law to curb global warming.

REELECTION AND GLOBAL PRESENCE

In November 2006, Arnold Schwarzenegger faced the electorate as the Republican candidate for the Governorship in a predominately Democratic state. But whereas in 2003 he rode a popular revolt against the then governor Gary Davis to the governor's mansion in Sacramento, this time he was campaigning as a full-fledged politician, not as a movie star taking on the political establishment.

As election results came in, supporters at Schwarzenegger's election headquarters in the Beverly Hilton were jubilant. Flanked by First Lady Maria Shriver and their children, Schwarzenegger, who spoke two hours after he was declared the victor, thanked voters and said he would not let them down: "I love doing sequels, but this is my favorite sequel," said Schwarzenegger. "In the next four years, I promise to protect your values and I will protect your dreams."[9]

With California deep in debt these were brave declarations. Schwarzenegger cut billions from state programs in the face of fierce resistance from public sector unions, and raised sales tax by 1% to raise revenues. He also declared two Fridays per month as furlough days for state workers, meaning that they will not come into work and will not be paid. These measures deferred rather than fundamentally addressed California's fiscal crisis. On the other hand, Schwarzenegger had more success with electoral reforms, passing legislations that had previously failed in 2005.

Confronting a difficult economic and political environment at home, Schwarzenegger spent more time abroad. He toured the world promoting trade and investment. He also used his fame and access to world leaders to promote his environmental message, in particular his campaign against global warming, and his belief that a "hydrogen economy" is the only long-term solution that can address the environmental crisis facing the world.

As Schwarzenegger neared the end of his tenure as governor, pundits debated his legacy. The *Los Angeles Times,* a newspaper that traditionally had been critical of Schwarzenegger governorship, reflected the mixed verdict:

> Schwarzenegger mirrored the mindset of early 21st century California: skeptical of partisan politics, unwilling to sever links with our historic commitment to growth and environmental and social responsibility, and sometimes at loose ends when confronting the depth of our budget problems. He leaves office having failed to "blow up the boxes of government," as he vowed to do, and with a budget in desperate shape. But he set a new political course for California. The state, if not better off for the recall, appears no worse for it either—in large part because Schwarzenegger grew beyond the action hero who ran in 2003.[10]

For much of the summer of 2011, Schwarzenegger's official website was reduced to a single page, with an image of him playing chess under the caption "stay tuned for my next move."

CASE 17

Novomed Loses a Client

Losing a client is hard; looking back and asking why is even harder. Mathias Jones looked around the table at his management team and wondered whether it was worthwhile to raise the subject. He had originally called the meeting to discuss Novomed's plans for launching a new product which potentially had far-reaching implication for the firm's strategy, but here he was trying to deal with an unforeseen crisis. The question was where to begin, and the next question was what direction should the discussion take?

Some events are clear-cut. The call from Sarah Hardcastle, the President of Beltronics, and one of Novomed's most important clients, did not come out of the blue. There had been problems of quality, and deliveries were intermittently late, but Jones had been told that these problems were minor, and in each case they were fixed almost immediately.

This did not, however, impress Sarah Hardcastle who lived up to her tough reputation as a demanding customer. "I am sorry Mathias," she said, "We have brought these problems to your attention before." "I know you did your best to fix these problems, but in our business this is not good enough. And I have therefore decided to go with another supplier." "I want to assure you that this is not an easy decision. We have been doing business with you for a long time, and we have a lot of respect for you guys, but respect is not the same as satisfaction."

The loss of Beltronics hit hard. Not only because it was a large client, but also because it was a leading manufacturer. It was a firm that made news, the kind of news that Novomed could do without.

Jones knew that this time he could not let matters rest. Something had to be done, or more precisely somebody had to pay the piper. So although he was busy preparing for the upcoming launch of an exciting new product that could potentially take the industry by storm, he called his secretary and asked her to immediately make an appointment with all his key staff members.

The first to arrive was Vince Montblanc, the head of strategic planning. Vince had been with Novomed for almost 20 years. He knew every nut and bolt of the operation. "As far as I am concerned," said Vince, "this should not have happened." "Our plan for the year set clear goals for quality and delivery improvement." "We have earmarked funds to make these improvements, and I have sent out memos to the people concerned again and again." "Nobody can say that this is a failure on the part of the planning department!"

Later that afternoon Jones saw his operations manager. Tim Collins was a young engineer with impressive operating experience. He had not been long with the company, but he came highly recommended from his last post.

"I'll tell you why this happened," he said to Jones. "We do not have a consistent policy when it comes to finding the right combination of cost and quality." "You call for parts and it takes forever for them to arrive." "You call and ask why the parts are not arriving and you get this harassed person on the other side of the line saying that the parts we order require extra machining." "To rub it in, he tells me that we could have had the parts earlier and cheaper were it not for our unique quality standards." "He says 'unique' with a sarcastic tone—leaving unsaid more explicit comments about our maintenance practices I have heard elsewhere." "I am tempted to tell him to give me what he has in stock, but I am worried about what this will do to my evaluation." "So there you are. Give me clear guidelines, or even better give purchasing clear guidelines."

The first two meetings had been useful, but not conclusive. Jones looked forward to seeing his finance director, May Finley. Finley had been with a company for about four years. She had an MBA from a good business school, and was one of Jones' close confidants. "What I have to say," she told Jones, "will not come as a surprise." "We have a measure for just about everything in this place, but we do not act on these measures." "Sure we review the measures at every meeting. But all we do is go through the motions." "Give me some power and I will make this place really move."

The last person to see Jones was his human resource manager. Tom Mizrachi had spent most of his career at a well-known multinational corporation. He found his new company small by comparison, but he was doing his best to introduce world-class best practices just the same.

"The problem, as I see it," he said after much hesitation, "is that we do not recruit problem solvers." "We recruit people we like, and by extension, people who join us come because they like us. But the people that fit in are not necessarily the people that get things done. You need people who are willing to thump the table a bit more. I have no idea what we can do in the short run, but in the medium and long term my recommendation is that we revamp our interviewing and evaluation process. Get the right people, and then make sure that they are given the right incentives. And when I say incentives, I mean it in the positive as well as the negative. People have to know that if they fail, we pay a price, and when we pay a price they will also pay a price."

As Jones was rushing into the meeting he ran into Greg Allard, his product development manager. "I wanted to talk to you about the Beltronics fiasco," said Jones, "but you were not in your office for the last two days." "Ah, yes, I heard about it," said Greg. "If I were you, I would forget about it." "I foresee plenty of new customers when our new product is launched. I bet that even Beltronics will come crawling back."

Jones thought that Allard had a point, but he was still uneasy about Beltronics. New clients are all well and good, but surely not at the expense of losing the old ones. He wanted answers. Looking back on his conversations with his key managers he could not form clear answers as to why things had gone so badly wrong with Beltronics. He was sure, however, that sooner or later he would have to confront the issue head-on. The only question was when and how.

CASE 18

Whisky Exchange

The *Whisky Exchange* is the world's largest specialist online retailer of Scotch whisky. Formed as an offshoot of a small store, this family-run business is located in London with a worldwide customer base, and a dedicated following among the whisky connoisseur community. In addition to retail, the company bottles whisky under its own brands and supplies other spirits to the UK entertainment and hospitality industries.

Speaking to the case writers in April 2009, Sukhinder Singh, the founder and managing director of the Whisky Exchange, reflected on the competitive position of the company.

> I honestly do not know what my competitors are doing in terms of turnover and traffic. What I do know is that I am the most powerful whisky retailer on the planet. We have a vast product range of approximately two to two-and-half thousand different whiskies. Nobody else can do that. If you go into any other shop you'd be lucky to find 500–600 whiskies.

Whisky Exchange is one part, albeit the most successful part, of the parent company, "Speciality Drinks Limited." In the past several years, Singh has been expanding the company's product line under the umbrella of *Specialty Drinks Limited*. Looking into the future of the company, he is convinced that he can repeat his success with whisky, in the spirits market:

> If I compare The Whisky Exchange with *Specialty*, in other words whisky with spirits, then whisky is the majority—about 2 to 1 at the moment. But other spirits are growing rapidly. So while I know that the whisky side will increase and get better, because we are putting a lot of time and energy into that side of the business, I also know that we are just beginning with other spirits. If you look at the market for mixed spirits compared to whiskies, it is a lot bigger. My feeling is that, in time, the mixed spirits side could be a lot bigger than The Whisky Exchange side. It's another part of the business, but for me it works because it's still alcohol, it's still drinks.

DISCOVERING WHISKY

Looking back, Sukhinder Singh traces his passion for whisky to his early experiences when as a child he spent time in his parents' liquor stores. He grew up looking at the liquor bottles, fascinated by the colored liquids, and this eventually led to him collecting miniature bottles of spirits. Joining a miniature bottle club in his teens, Singh found that most serious collectors focused on whisky. He quickly acquired the collecting "bug," amassing a collection of 400–500 "miniatures." This grew even further when he was offered a large collection of 8,000 miniatures, at what he considered to be a very reasonable price. Splitting the collection, he kept the single malt and blended whisky, and over the next few years, sold the rest. He now had a collection of 2,000–3,000 whisky miniatures. This collection was narrowed further to 400 single malt bottles, which he considered the most collectable, and sold the rest. To acquire more single malt bottles, Singh began to advertise in magazines, looking for miniature collections to buy. As with his first major acquisition, he would drive up and down the country buying collections, keeping the single malts, and then selling the rest to other collectors in the club.

COMBINING A HOBBY WITH BUSINESS

In 1988, Singh went to City University London to study Property Evaluation and Finance. Graduating in 1991, in the middle of the property crash, Singh quickly discovered that there were few prospects for property surveyors. The obvious option was to work in the family business, as he had during his university holidays. Singh's family owned three liquor stores in the greater London area, and had recently expanded the main store in Hanwell by buying the property next door. Singh lobbied and received approval from his father to take over the project of converting the two stores into a single liquor shop. No expense was spared in the conversion, and they were rewarded not only in sales, but in the winning of a prestigious industry award from *Off License News*.

Although Singh was spending more time on retailing wines and spirits, his interest in single-malt miniature whisky collecting endured. At one point, while on a trip to Scotland to buy a miniature collection, he saw an old bottle of whisky from the so-called "lost" Kirkliston distillery that closed in the 1920s–1930s. As he put it later, "I saw this one bottle, and I kept thinking, 'that's beautiful, that's beautiful'. So I bought the collection and eventually persuaded him to sell me the bottle." This bottle was to be a turning point in his collecting habits.

Prepared by Joseph Lampel and Daniel Ronen. Not to be used or reproduced without authors' permission.

After this, Singh became more serious about whisky. He started collecting big bottles of single malt whisky, and began to drink whisky more regularly, gaining a greater appreciation of the nuances of different whiskies in the process. At this point, Singh conceived the idea of aiming to collect one bottle from each Scottish distillery. He would frequent auctions and advertise for individual whisky bottles as well as entire collections. He also parlayed his contacts among miniature bottle collectors who were interested in big whisky bottles into business relations, many of which developed into long-lasting friendships. As his reputation for discovering rare whiskies spread, he would phone or fax information about new whisky discoveries among his network. This especially took off when Singh stumbled on a 2,000-bottle limited edition whisky called "Black Bowmore," so called because not only was it packaged in a black wooden box, but unusually the whisky itself was black. As the word spread about this unusual 1993 bottling, Singh began to receive calls from all over asking where they could find this "Black Bowmore." Recognizing the opportunity, he scoured every whisky retailer in London for available stocks, clearing their shelves in the process. Selling them on, he made a handsome profit from this venture.

Increasingly, Singh began to add retailing to his collecting. He was going to auctions, regularly frequenting a circle of whisky shops, and visiting distillers in Scotland. He looked for single malts for his collection and private deals with collectors, but also for whisky that could be sold at his parents' retail shops, which were facing difficult times.

Higher taxation on alcohol and the entry of supermarkets into the spirits market was putting relentless pressure on their retail shop margins. More and more consumers were traveling to France to take advantage of far lower alcohol taxes across the Channel. At the same time, deregulation was allowing supermarkets to offer spirits alongside other food and beverages. Small retailers, such as the Singh family, could not compete with the bulk buying that allowed supermarkets to drive down prices. When the head of the family fell ill, selling the store became urgent for personal as well as business reasons.

TAKING THE PLUNGE

With their parents' store sold, Sukhinder Singh and his brother Raj, who had just finished university, decided to enter whisky retailing by opening a store in central London. They first explored an opportunity to buy a well-known whisky store in Soho. After carefully examining the accounts they made an offer that included stock, fixtures, and all fittings. The owner initially agreed, but later came back saying he wanted to keep the air-conditioning, coffee machine, tables, and chairs. The Singhs walked away from the deal, and refused to complete even when the owner had a change of heart and agreed to the original terms two weeks later.

The experience made the Singhs look more carefully at the basic economics of whisky retailing. The brothers began to realize why so many specialist spirit stores in central London went bankrupt. Between the high rents and difficult logistics in a highly congested area, stores found it difficult to break even, let alone make a profit. To survive, stores usually added cigars, wine, and spirits to their whisky lines, and even then, often struggled along with some difficulty.

The Singhs looked at other options for retailing whisky that did not involve setting up a costly retail establishment. The Internet, just emerging at the time, caught their attention. They approached one of Raj Singh's friends who was a web designer and asked him to create a website for retailing whisky. But their main emphasis remained direct retailing. With this in mind, they bought a small warehouse around the corner from their old store in Hanwell with money borrowed from their parents.

Within months of launching the website, the Singhs were receiving an increasing volume of online orders, mainly from Japan, but also from countries in Continental Europe, in particular Germany. Reflecting back, Sukhinder Singh comments on the conjunction of technology and markets that laid the foundation for subsequent growth:

> I think at that time we were very fortunate because the phenomenon of limited edition whiskies was very new. Most of this stuff didn't make it overseas, and if it did, it wasn't well distributed. Outside Central London there were no such things as whisky shops. There were just general liquor stores with better whisky selections. But that was it. So at that time whisky was actually very difficult to find. Because we were on the web, everyone was now contacting us. At this point, however, most of our sales were not to customers but to bars. In Japan, for example, they have hundreds of whisky bars that are constantly looking to give their consumers new products. It was easy to find us on the internet, and easy to get in touch with us. Seven to eight months after the website opened we were shipping 12 mixed boxes a week to certain bars, with an average price per bottle of 60–100 pounds. It was fantastic.

Importantly for Singh, operating costs could be kept low. Aside from basic expenses such as electricity, phone, fax, and municipal taxes, there were no other major outlays. Labor costs were also kept to a minimum. Sukhinder and his brother did the processing, packing, and shipping themselves. As business grew, they hired additional help, a friend of Raj who shared their passion for whisky.

The basic business model the brothers developed was based on finding and purchasing whisky they believed will grow in value, purchasing as much of it as they could obtain, and then selling it little by little. Once they were confident that supply of each whisky from other sources was becoming scarce, they increased their prices.

As the business grew, the brothers decided to expand beyond whisky, primarily because Raj Singh had a particular affinity to other spirits. The brothers launched a second website for other spirits, and decided to expand into supplying the on-trade (hotels, bars, and restaurants). As Sukhinder put it later: "We were getting a lot of inquiries from hotels on the whisky side, and felt we could also do the other spirits. There was no one out there with a decent site for other spirits, and we felt that because of the interest we were getting from the on-trade for whisky, why not add other spirits to that?"

What seemed an obvious move at the time, had unanticipated consequences. To meet increasing volume, the brothers decided to move to a facility six times larger than the one they occupied at the time. Scaling up, however, was not as straightforward as they envisaged. As Sukhinder describes it:

> We did not anticipate the impact moving to so much larger premises would have. It was a complete logistical nightmare. Whereas before we had a really nice compact unit with about two-and-half thousand square-feet, we now had six times that, with one and half floors. In the old premises it was very cozy with literally everyone in one room, a showroom upstairs and a warehouse. Everyone knew what was happening, and we all helped each other. In the new premises we were going up and down the floors like a yo-yo. In addition, expenses went through the roof. Our bills were five times bigger. The local tax rates were more expensive. With this being a new building, there were fire alarms, smoke alarms, and annual policies for security. Compliance with Health and Safety rules for the fit-out took six months alone. We also hired more staff. When we were in the other place there were seven of us. After the move to the new premises, there were twenty-five of us. So the first year was really tough. We went from a respectable turnover of six and half million pounds to five or at best five-and-half million pounds.

Surveying the situation after the move to the new facilities, Sukhinder Singh realized that the Internet was the cornerstone of his operations. The system on which they depended currently, however, was an off-the-shelf web-shopping package that was inadequate for their growing needs. The brothers initially contracted with a major web design company, but after investing considerable sums, had to suspend the work with only 50% of the project completed. They found that due to its size, the contractor was just not responsive enough for the constant website updating required by The Whisky Exchange. To finish the job, the brothers hired a full-time website design expert to sort out the problems left by the external contractor, and to maintain the system. The next step was to recruit a full-time editor, to update product information and trade lists for the company's range of 2,000 products, and add the 20 new products added each week.

SOURCING AND BRANDING WHISKY

For Sukhinder Singh, Whisky Exchange occupied a unique position between the distilleries and the final consumers. As a rule, distilleries usually bottled just 5% of their output as single malt whisky, with the rest going into blended whiskies. Some of the distillery's single malt reached the market under the distillery's own brand, and some was sold to independent bottlers. Consumers were familiar with, and generally had confidence in, the distillery labels, but were unfamiliar and more distrustful of the quality of whisky bottled by independent bottlers. Whisky Exchange, or more specifically Sukhinder Singh, started to draw on his knowledge and experience of judging the quality of whisky sold by independent bottlers, to buy the best of these bottlings which by their nature were of limited volume. As he put it:

> When buying, I personally assess and decide how much of a particular whisky we will take, and make an offer. When a rare whisky is good, and at a reasonable price, I have been known to make an offer for the entire stock, asking the company "How much stock do you have?" They say "We have just 1,800/2,000 bottles." I say "I want the lot, any objection?" Sometimes they will say "By all means, take the lot!" A month later they are phoning me back asking if they can buy some of it back because everybody wants it.

Although lucrative, finding sufficient volume of good quality whisky from independent bottlers proved difficult. Sukhinder Singh decided to bypass the independent bottlers and go directly to the distilleries, bottling whisky for private customers often under Whisky Exchange labels. For Sukhinder Singh, this was a logical development. As he put it:

> The name of the distillery on the bottle is not important, you're buying the whisky for the taste. Who cares what the name is on the label? Does it really matter? I don't think so. You drink whisky for pleasure, just like you eat for pleasure. So, with one of our own bottling ranges, I keep the flexibility to declare or not to declare which distillery is behind our brand. For example, I can take different age stocks of Ardbeg whisky, marry them together, and not write the name of the distillery. Sometimes, the distillery may stipulate when selling us product, that they want the product to remain anonymous, so as not to impact on their own distillery bottlings. At other times, we are allowed to name the distillery. Our Single Malts of Scotland labels include details of the distillery, cask number, distillation and bottling dates, number of bottles from the cask, and cask type. When developing these brands I keep in mind the difference between the specialist sector, and the mass market served by very large companies such as Diageo. For example the "Port Askaig" brand we created is definitely more of a commercial brand of the type done by Diageo. On the other hand, our "Single Malts of Scotland" is more for a connoisseurs' market because it's all about the cask selection and being a good example of a whisky from a particular distillery.

LOOKING TO THE FUTURE

By 2010, Whisky Exchange was the largest online single malt retailing operation in the world. Alongside these online operations, they opened a successful whisky retail shop in Vinopolis, a permanent wine and spirits tasting exhibition venue in London's South Bank area near London Bridge. The venue also allows Singh to showcase his own high-end whisky products, with positioning to reflect Singh's views on how premium whisky should be packaged and sold, as well as setting price expectations to encourage the collector market.

At the same time, Singh was expanding his spirits business into gin and rum. The company had recently imported a rum called "Diplomatico" from Venezuela that both the Singh brothers believe had great market potential. To handle more new spirits brands, and to bring their own brands under a single-marketing umbrella, the brothers set up a separate company to take on more agency brands, including tequila, gin, liquors, three different rums, and the company's own whisky brands, Elements, Single Malts of Scotland, and Port Askaig.

AFTERMATH

More than a year after Sukhinder Singh met the case writers, a new whisky price world record was set when he was reported to have paid £100,000 for a single bottle of 64-year-old Dalmore Trinitas single malt. Mahesh Patel, the US property developer who bought the second bottle of the three Dalmore Trinitas was enthusiastic: "Whisky is my passion. I love it. I have over 1,000 bottles in my collection, and the Dalmore Trinitas is now the jewel in the crown."[1] Commenting on the record purchase, John Beard, the CEO of Whyte & Mackay, owners of the distillery that organized the release, had this to say: "There is an emerging whisky investment market for high net worth individuals. This is a huge leap on from our previous record and as we have already sold two, I am wondering if we have priced it high enough."[2]

Sukhinder Singh seemed to concur. In what many regarded as a major coup, he secured rights for the third of the three Trinitas bottles to be sold exclusively through the Whisky Exchange. He had come a long way since he was collecting and selling miniature whiskies, and his latest move suggested that he was once again looking for new horizons.

EXHIBIT 1
THE WHISKY EXCHANGE CASE TIMELINE

1985	Sukhinder Singh joins miniature bottle club and started collecting whisky miniatures.
	Purchased single collection of 8,000 bottles, keeping the single malt whiskies and selling off the rest to other collectors in the club.
1988	Singh Goes to City University London to study Property Evaluation and Finance.
1991	Singh goes to work in the family business liquor store.
	Develops a shop which subsequently wins award from *Off License News*.
	Advertizes in press for whisky collections to buy.
	Starts traveling nationwide buying whisky miniature collections.
	Singh buys full size bottle of "Kirkliston" malt whisky. Starts to collect full-size bottles.
	Through the shop, Singh starts buying limited edition whiskies for sale to club members and small but growing list of private customers, mostly overseas.
1993	Black Bowmore is released. Kick starts whisky "collector" market. Singh buys stock from other retailers, resells with a margin.
	Shop starts to expand its standard whisky range.
	Rise in bootlegging from overseas, and growth of supermarket alcohol retail hits shop profitability.
	Brother Raj finishes university studies and joins the family business.
	Father falls ill. Starts process to sell the business.
	Raj and Sukhinder Singh look at buying whisky shop in central London. Deal falls through.
	Decide to set up an online whisky retailer. Buy small warehouse near family shop.
	Family business is sold.
1999	The Whisky Exchange website goes live.
	Strong sales growth, especially from Japan and Germany.
	Good business profitability with low operating costs.
	Increase range to include non-whisky spirits.
	Move to much larger premises in west London.
	Whisky Exchange experiences difficulty in setting up and managing the larger operation.
	The company suffers fifteen percent drop in turnover.
	Whisky Exchange sees massive increase in operating costs. Profitability collapses.
	Singh starts redevelopment of the website. Failure. Dismisses the web designer.
	Singh invests in website redevelopment with large IT company.
2005	TWE retail store opens at Vinopolis on London's South Bank.
	Whisky Exchange recruits web project manager. Did not resolve the problems.
	Recruit in-house web team.
	Starts taking on new brands as an agent.
2008	Whisky Exchanges launches *Elements of Islay* range of whiskies (TWE own brand).
	Expand *Specialty Spirits,* recruit dedicated team to develop non-whisky sales, and sign UK agency rights for numerous new brands.
2009	Whisky Exchange wins Best Independent Spirits Retailer award.
	The company launches *Port Askaig* range of whiskies (TWE own brand).
2010	Sukhinder Singh acquires £100,000 bottle of 64-year-old Dalmore Trinitas.

CASE 19

Outset Contemporary Art Fund (A)

Candida Gertler, cofounder and director of Outset Contemporary Art Fund, a London-based philanthropic organization for the arts (www.outset.org.uk), was having difficulty believing the e-mail she had just received from Outset's new Turkish affiliate, Saha Outset. For months now, Gertler and her team had been making their expertise and experience freely available to their Turkish colleagues in order to facilitate the September 2011 launch of Saha Outset at the Istanbul Biennial—the most important contemporary art event in the Turkish cultural calendar. As far as she was aware from frequent exchange of emails and personal conversations, the setting up of Saha Outset, the newest Outset affiliate, was proceeding smoothly. Business cards had been designed in London that accommodated the Turkish character of the local chapter; plans for the launch party were being finalized; and a press conference was scheduled.

All the arrangements were in place for Gertler, accompanied by 15 Outset patrons who were committed to support Saha Outset, to attend the formal launch of the alliance. At this point, however, the following email from one of Saha Outset's founders suggested that the plans would have to be revised:

> Mon, 18 Jul 2011
>
> Dear Candida,
>
> I'm glad you are excited and looking forward to the Istanbul trip during the Biennial. We will be more than happy to host you in the best way possible to make it a memorable experience.
>
> We are in the last stages of legalizing Saha's set up and have had our first board meeting this weekend. According to Turkish law there are very clear guidelines in running a fund and it is a very democratic decision making process. As you know, at the beginning of this journey [we] did not maybe fully understand the scope of our initiative, but now as we are a group of nine committed individuals who each in their own right have been involved with art in one way or another, we feel we can make a difference for Turkish art. After lengthy discussions and voting we have decided to launch under the name SAHA Association as it was felt (mainly by the other six founding members) that keeping it rooted to Turkey will make us stronger in the long run. We are grateful to you for always making us feel that we would have been independent in our decisions but the association has taken a life of its own. Having said all this, I would like to emphasize that we would always be ready for collaborations with Outset and during our press launch we would feel confident to announce to press that Saha will be in close collaboration with Outset on some major projects.
>
> I hope that I have made our intentions clear to you and that you will accept Saha, as a friendly counterpart to Outset. At the end of the day we share the same goals and we very much look forward to joining our sources in future projects.
>
> All my best wishes
>
> (Signed)

Candida Gertler was very surprised by this unexpected email. In response, she composed a message addressed to all of Saha's founding members. In her email she reminded members that the initial contact that led to the formation of Saha Outset started when they approached Outset for advice on how to build a philanthropic organization. She also reminded the founders that the pros and cons of publicly linking the Turkish organization to Outset had been extensively discussed during the numerous emails, phone calls, and meetings, that preceded the launch of Saha Outset, with a definite willingness by the founders to take the path of affiliation. The email went on to recount in some detail the subsequent support that Outset provided for the fledgling Turkish affiliate. Most notably, sharing information on how Outset is run, providing advice on how to bring the Outset model to Turkey, and arranging for professional help in designing a logo for Saha Outset. She concluded with the following expression of disappointment at the unexpected U-turn:

> With your recent announcement that you wish to operate as a separate organization, entirely independent of Outset, I feel an even bigger sense of regret. Whilst it is a decision I of course respect, I feel that mine and my team's efforts have been at best wasted, and at worst misused. I am baffled as to why it was left to such a late stage—and with our trip so imminent—for you to come to this conclusion.

Reflecting on her disappointment some time later, Gertler noted that Outset's relationships to its affiliates was always based on trust. Asked by the case writer if she

---

This case was prepared by Joseph Lampel, City University London.

was thinking of changing this policy, she admitted that she was considering asking new applicants to sign contracts that set out the affiliate's relationship to Outset London. In the meantime, she was asking individuals who expressed interest in becoming affiliates to become Outset patrons as a first sign of commitment.

THE ORIGINS OF OUTSET

Looking back at how Outset got started, Candida Gertler singled out her frustration with the limited opportunities of engaging with the art world that were available when she moved to London in the 1990s. There were art courses at Sotheby's and Christie's for learning about art, and museum patron groups that brought people into regular contact with the art world. None, however, were set up for long-term patronage engagement with art and the art world.

A former journalist with Spiegel TV in Germany, Gertler left her profession to raise a family. With little time to spare, she was looking for courses that would deepen her knowledge of contemporary art without having to enroll in a university degree. During this time, Gertler began to notice that a number of the people she encountered during her daily life shared her enthusiasm for contemporary art, but much like her had busy lives that made it difficult to pursue full time regularly scheduled programs.

Gertler reasoned that morning or lunch lectures on contemporary art delivered by carefully selected speakers in the privacy of her living room would be of interest to these individuals. With this in mind, she approached three speakers she met during her Sotheby's and Christies' courses to give private lectures to small groups at a mutually agreed time. The events proved a success. But more importantly, what began as lectures on contemporary art, gradually evolved into funding support for projects in which some of the speakers were involved. Gertler discovered that many of the people who attended these lectures were willing to make donations to art projects that she brought to their attention.

The sums involved were relatively small. Each participant would contribute £35 to £50 toward a project. In total these contributions were modest, but the novelty of Gertler's approach caught the attention of established charities. Gertler was asked by several organizations to use her contacts to put together art events. These events, remarked Gertler much later, made her realize that there were "a lot of people doing things who needed an audience, and people who wanted to be an audience and didn't know where to go." She decided to cater to both sides by packaging the ad hoc events into lecture series, charging each participant £350.

THE FRIEZE–TATE PROJECT

Initially, the lectures were first held in Gertler's living room, but gradually the group began to gather in other venues. Visits to galleries organized by the speakers were a natural first step. Such visits introduced participants to collectors, leading in some instances to collectors organizing viewings for participants. It was during one of these events that Candida Gertler met Yana Peel, the cofounder of Outset. Intrigued by Gertler's approach to arts philanthropy, Peel expressed interest in joining the fund-raising scheme, starting with an event at the recently opened White Cube Gallery in Hoxton Square, and subsequently at the home of Charles Saatchi—one of Britain's preeminent art collectors, and owner of Saatchi Gallery. At the time of the meeting, Peel worked at the London office of Goldman Sachs, but spent much of her spare time in the London arts scene. She felt that Gertler's approach could be substantially expanded by explicitly targeting what were called "resource rich, but time poor" professionals—high net worth individuals that are interested in the arts but lack the time needed to gain access to the rapidly changing contemporary arts scene.

The first event that the two organized was hosted by Norman Foster, one of Britain's best-known architects, and his wife Elena in their private home. Gertler and Peel asked each of the 30 people who came for £5000. The money was to be donated to the Tate Gallery, which in turn would purchase a work of art in the recently launched Frieze arts fair.

The Frieze art fair was the creation of Amanda Sharp and Matthew Slotover, the publishers of *frieze* magazine. They approached Gertler for advice, and expressed a desire to link philanthropic projects to what is essentially a commercial art fair. Peel was then introduced to Sharp and Slotover as they were discussing the final stage of planning for the launch of Frieze. Few people in the art world held out much hope that the new art fair could carve out a viable niche. Not only did Gertler and Peel think otherwise, they were also keen to put the resources of the newly established Outset art fund behind the venture.

Art fairs are often judged by the prestige and price negotiated for the art works that are put up for sale. Established art fairs attract well-known dealers, and feature art works that get noticed and command high prices. This promotes their visibility, which in turn ensures their position as premier art fairs. New art fairs therefore face a hurdle that often seems insurmountable: To create the visibility needed to attract well-known dealers and collectors, they must feature important works by emerging artists. However, to feature important works by emerging artists they must ensure that the prices paid will compare favorably with prices for the same works in established art fairs, or at the very least, that the art works displayed should be acquired by high-profile buyers.

Slotover and Sharp suggested, and Gertler and Peel concurred, that persuading a prestigious museum to purchase important works of art during the first Frieze fair by making a substantial donation would go a long way toward putting Frieze on the map, while at the same time supporting acquisitions of art works by publicly funded institutions. They approached the Tate, Britain's foremost modern art gallery, with this idea. Officially designated by an Act of Parliament to house the UK's national collection of contemporary art, the gallery's stamp of approval carries weight not only in the UK, but in the wider global art world as well.

Tate's response to Gertler and Peel's proposal was at first distinctly cool. Gertler and Peel, however, persevered. Working their way through the Tate's bureaucracy, they were eventually granted a meeting with Sir Nicholas Serota, the head of the Tate. Serota was not only very open to accepting the donation, he was also among the first in the art world to appreciate that Gertler and Peel's offer represented a new idea in arts philanthropy.

Most donations solicited by galleries such as the Tate or the Serpentine are usually made by individual patrons, with the maximum of £1,000 per person. Gertler and Peel proposed a new model based on group donations. The advantage of this model was not only that it multiplies the amounts donated per each event organized, but also that it allowed galleries to create a direct link between new donors and the work of art they sponsored. In other words, whereas traditionally donors had to be content with the knowledge that they benefited the gallery, without necessarily seeing how their funds were specifically used, the collective donation model created a psychological link between the donors and the acquired art works—a link that often led to greater donor engagement, not only in the gallery, but also in the work of the sponsored artists.

The immediate benefit to the Tate was a donation by Outset of £150,000 to be used by the gallery to purchase art works exhibited in the Frieze fair. Beyond stipulating that the donation could only be used to purchase art works at the Frieze, the only other condition that Gertler and Peel attached to the donation was that the Tate team making the selection of the art works will be joined by two external curators. This reflected Gertler and Peel's conviction that Outset should support projects that brought patrons, and local galleries, closer to art in other parts of the world.

The first Frieze art fair in 2003 was a great success for the founders, Amanda Sharp and Matthew Slotover. But it was also a major turning point for Outset. As Gertler put it: "The first Frieze art fair was a real big cornerstone for us. I think that it gave us the credibility on which we then built, engaging with other museums, gaining more support, and attracting new patrons." In the years to come, Outset would work with many other galleries and museums, but arguably the relationship with the Tate remained the organization's most important association. Since 2003 Outset has enabled the Tate to purchase numerous works of art for the collection; of these, 90 works by 60 significant international artists were purchased at the Frieze fair.

THE OUTSET APPROACH TO PROJECTS

Funding the Tate art purchase in the first Frieze fair was a seminal experience for Outset. Whereas previously the organization focused its energies on supporting a variety of projects in the arts, the Tate–Frieze experience showed that Outset could become an important broker as well as fundraiser. Gertler and Peel perceived a new role for Outset: connecting an expanded audience to art institutions such as museums, galleries, and art fairs through projects sponsored by Outset. Each time Outset sponsored a project, new links were forged—between Outset and the gallery, museum, biennale, or the art fair that were involved, and among these institutions as well. But this process did not stop there. Each project also built relationships between Outset's patrons and these institutions, and beyond relationships with institutions they often also built relationships between patrons and artists. In effect, Outset projects built relationships, and relationships led to more projects, which in turn made these relationships even stronger. Using Outset experience with the Whitechapel Gallery, Gertler described the process as follows:

> Once you've supported an exhibition, let's say in the Whitechapel, you start to get to know the director, you get to know the curators, and you get to know the gallery's programs. Later, they come to you and say "the municipality has given us a building. We now need funding for development, for capital campaigns. Would you be able to give us £50,000 for a project gallery?" Now, you have done the exhibition, and you got to know the institution. Of course, you are not going to stop here. You follow up, and you continue to develop your activity. You say "OK, I will sponsor your project gallery." So Outset puts up the first £50,000 towards building the project gallery. But we also think, "why not get our patrons to come and do a hardhat tour? Let them see what other things are still outstanding that can be sponsored. They can put their name on it, or make an anonymous donation." It all works with these relationships. With being recognized; with feeling part of a network of people who are helping develop the arts.

THE OUTSET MODEL AT WORK

Both Gertler and Peel concede readily that they did not foresee the transformation of Outset from a partnership that organized fund-raising events into an important broker in the art world. As Yana Peel puts it: "There was no master plan when we started. It was very much knowing that we were going to be supporting new art. Our mission has always been about bringing private funding to the arts for the benefit of the public. That hasn't changed in nine years. What has changed is the way we've gone about it."

Although Outset does not follow a master plan, it nevertheless follows a set of principles that have emerged from constant experimenting. Gertler describes the basic approach as follows:

> When we look at a project we always start with the quality of the artist who is being presented to us, usually by curators. Once we've identified that a project is desirable from a public institution's point of view, from the curator's point of view, and that the artist is either somebody we have already worked with or somebody emerging who is very much being respected in the artistic community we have another obligation, which is the obligation to our patrons. Because we have to think about how this is going to translate into an experience for the

> patron which will educate, but will also be a unique and special, an experience that will stretch the envelope, stretch one's boundaries. There must be this unique selling point about the project which will make us decide.

For Gertler and Peel, making decisions on which projects Outset should support is a process that moves back and forth between the individuals and institutions that make up the field in which they operate, in what Gertler calls a "magic triangle." As she puts it: "Our approach is very much what I call the magic triangle, moving between the public institution, the collector, the art consumer; or between the patrons, the gallery and the artist." The resulting pattern that has defined Outset since its inception is a complex interplay of following key actors and building blocks.

Donor and funding base

As Outset evolved from an organization supported by individual patrons who pooled together their contributions, into a broker that is engaged in support of multiple projects, both in the UK and internationally, it also diversified its donor and funding base. Currently, Outset's donor and funding base is made up of six distinct categories, as outlined in Exhibit 1. Three of these categories consist of funding directed at specific areas. These include the Outset production fund, Outset family fund, and Outset regional development fund. The other three categories classify Outset's donors. The first category consists of "patrons," a general category of donors who are involved with Outset. The second consists of "associates," young professionals with a strong interest in the arts. The third category is made up of "corporate partners," firms that have lent their support to Outset activities.

During the early days of Outset, Gertler and Peel struggled to overcome the divisions between individuals who were accepted into the tightly knit circles of decision makers in the art world, and others who were invited to participate in gallery openings and fund raising, but rarely came into contact with the artists or the curators. As Gertler recalls: "I was a patron of the Tate, and Yana was a patron at the Serpentine Gallery. It was nice to be invited to openings, but there was no real engagement with the art world per se. It was usually black tie dinners or cocktail parties in the gallery, but you never met the artist, you never got to see the art as it got made."

When Gertler and Peel started Outset, they turned for support to people like themselves who were interested in the arts, had the means to become patrons, but were usually relegated by galleries and museums to the role of passive consumers. Outset offered these individuals the prospect of active engagement with the arts. But to create this active engagement, Gertler and Peel had to tackle the pervasive sense of inexperience that most people feel when they come face-to-face with contemporary art in museum or gallery settings.

For example, some of the patrons that Gertler recruited for her first lecture series were fellow parents at the school gates. Many of these were interested in the arts, but unsure on how to actively pursue this interest. The lecture series, and later Outset's project sponsorship, provided a comfortable social environment in which these people could engage with the arts in London. As they became more familiar with artists and the arts, they also became more active as patrons, which in turn increased the ability of Outset to undertake more projects.

Yana Peel, by contrast, reached out to her professional contacts building an affluent donor base "who wanted the best brought to their doorstep." For these "time poor, cash rich," as Peel described these donors, Outset provided a highly personal way of engaging with the arts that would have been normally difficult to sustain given their busy schedule and wide range of other commitments. Because Gertler and Peel knew their patrons personally, they could match them with projects that would be of particular interest. They also nourished this engagement by keeping them informed on the progress of the projects in a biannual newsletter. But more importantly, by arranging private viewing of exhibitions that were the beneficiaries of Outset funding or by taking donors to meet sponsored artists in their studios, Outset was breaking with the traditional ideas of charitable giving to the arts that treats donors as VIPs, but expects little more from them. As Yana Peel puts it:

> I think what we are really dealing with is a new type of philanthropist, an engaged philanthropist. It is not just giving because your parents used to give to the public art fund, or to the national museum so that a great Poussin would be saved. I think we have a different proposition. What we bring to people is a selection of the best. In this age of increasing information there is so much information all the time that there really is a value to that professional overlay of someone who is a conduit; someone who is a filter, who says you are getting all these invitations—everyone wants you to give, everyone wants you to see everything. These are the twelve things that we think are really meaningful and interesting—trust us we are not going to waste your time because we know it is a very scarce resource.

Gertler and Peel believe that Outset's special contribution to their patrons' engagement with the arts consists in going against their inevitable tendency to fall back on established museums and galleries. "Outset," comments Peel, has always been intent on taking "people outside their comfort zone." This was the inspiration for the name of the venture in the first place. As she puts it: "we call it Outset because it is not about being part of the 'in set.' The 'in set' hangs out in White Cube, the in set hangs out in gala events. We want to go to Hoxton, we want to go to Dino Chapman's studio. But we also wanted to be the 'out set' of a journey. We wanted to be the beginning of their journey in the arts . . . ."

Development officers

The journey that culminated in a successful project often started with Outset lining up willing patrons with galleries and museums that are in need of funds to create new work

EXHIBIT 1* OUTSET DONOR AND FUNDING BASE

Production fund

The Outset Production Fund was launched by a group of Outset supporters seeking deeper engagement with the process of production and institutional collecting. The fund facilitates the creation of new works by emerging and mid-career artists with a view toward institutional donation in the UK and abroad. Projects are selected on an application basis and reviewed in consultation with Outset's broad network of international advisors. To date the Production Fund has helped realize ambitious projects by leading artists including Francis Alys, Yael Bartana, Candice Breitz, and Steve McQueen and donated works to public collections in Europe, Israel, Russia, and the US.

Production Fund Partners attend Outset supporters' program of events, international trips and project review mornings with artists and curators.

Leili Huth is chair of the Production Fund.

Regional development

The aim and ambition of Outset's Regional Development is to encourage and build the institutional frameworks and structures that enable private support to flourish in the regions.

Individual strategies will be developed with institutions outside London to establish and implement active patrons groups. Outset will liaise primarily with the respective Development and Education departments and any support groups they have previously established.

Outset's long-term goal is to align the regional networks with the overall program Outset delivers.

Corporate partners

Since its inception, Outset has worked with a range of corporate partners.

Responding to their desire to have an impact in the arts, while creating meaningful relationships within the artistic community, the partners are deeply committed to Outset's remit of supporting new art.

Outset corporate partners' engagement is directed toward specific areas of the Fund's activities allowing for a focused relationship with the organizations Outset support and the publicities with which it engages. Current corporate partners include Le Méridien, Northern Trust, Leviev and Sotheby's. Previous corporate partners include Tiffany & Co., McLaren, and Laurent Perrier.

Patrons

The commitment of Outset patrons allows the organization to fulfill its remit of supporting new art. Since 2003, the patrons' passion and engagement have allowed significant funds to be directed toward the development of artistic and institutional practices.

Outset patrons have supported a range of organizations and initiatives that includes exhibition and education programs as well as publications, residencies, and symposia. Outset patrons have supported London's leading visual arts organizations as well as a number of institutions throughout the UK and abroad. Projects are selected by Outset directors and their advisors and funded through the donations of patrons and corporate partners.

Outset patrons attend the supporters' program of events, including curator-led tours of museums and galleries, studio visits, research events, and international trips.

Family

Outset Family was founded in 2010 by Outset Production Fund Partner Micaela Boas. It is aimed at families with children between the ages of 2 and 8 and focuses on funding innovative art education programs.

Since its inception, Outset Family has supported the creation of "The Art Room" at the Robert Blair Primary School as well as "Get The Message" at Camden Arts Centre, London.

Outset Family members have the opportunity to introduce their children to London's vibrant visual arts community while supporting art education programs for underprivileged communities. Outset families are offered a range of activities including private tours of exhibitions at London's leading museums and galleries alongside workshops and visits to artists' studios.

Associates

The Outset Associates are comprised of a group of dynamic young professionals with a keen interest in the arts.

Since 2008 Outset Associates have been collaborating with Modern Art Oxford, one of the leading venues for the presentation of international contemporary art in the UK. The initiative brings vital additional funds to the gallery by sponsoring two major annual productions, thus directly supporting the exhibition program.

Outset's involvement with Modern Art Oxford allows Associates to receive all of the gallery's benefits of patronage as well as a special program designed to suit their schedule. Events include private tours of London exhibitions, artist studio visits, and the opportunity to engage with the international art community. Outset Associates has also shaped the idea of the Outset regional development project.

* *Source:* Outset communications (http://www.outset.org.uk/about/outset-uk/).

for an exhibition or acquire new works of arts. Major galleries and museums employ development officers whose job is to solicit individual donations. Gertler and Peel struck a mutually beneficial relationship with development officers. Outset would offer another source of funding, in exchange for the access to the inner workings of the museums and galleries that development officers could provide, and Outset badly needed. As Gertler describes it:

> the development officers and us had the same objectives. They were trying to do the same thing but with less tools. For them it was all about exclusivity, black tie dinners and such. Whereas for us it is all about mingling and mixing up

different groups of people because that is when you get the tension, and the excitement around bringing these people together. At the same time, we were very much in need of the support of development officers because we needed the back office. We needed their knowledge of what was possible and what was not possible within a big ship like Tate for example. We needed to know all the technicalities, the way their institution functions. I now take it for granted that I know how these things work, but when we started we had no idea. So it was a real collaboration. We were offering them what they needed, and didn't have, and they offered us what we didn't know . . .

Curators

From the early days of Outset, Gertler and Peel have courted and closely worked with curators, experts that specialize in organizing and managing exhibitions and art collections. Although curators rarely achieve the public profile of dealers and collectors, they play a key role in selecting and interpreting art works. In contemporary art, curators have acquired a pivotal gate-keeping position, largely because of the influence they derive from identifying and championing new artists and new trends. When curators select certain art works for exhibition in prestige galleries or important art fairs, they often also transform the artists' reputation, and in some instances can even create new trends. Their interpretation of the selected art works, usually in a specially prepared exhibition catalog, amplifies their influence even further. In effect, curators position the art works for viewing by the public, and then create the context that shapes how the art works are interpreted and understood.

Gaining the trust and cooperation of curators has been crucial for Outset's credibility in the art world. Making the first Tate contribution conditional on recruiting two external curators was an important step in this direction. Outset signaled to the curator community that the organization will look to the advice of curators when developing projects. Discussing the close relationship between Outset and curators, both those that are permanently attached to museums and galleries as employees, and "freelancers" who contract their expertise on a case-by-case basis, Gertler remarks:

> Outset is very much curator led. We were always focusing on curators. We invited curators to choose the works; we ask them to come on trips with us; we take their guidance on which projects we support. We hardly ever take the direct approach to the artist. We want to know what the curator thinks, and depending on how he or she develops their vision that's what will guide us as to which projects we support.

Inviting curators on trips at Outset expense has become an important part of building relationships between Gertler, Peel, on the one hand, and curators and other professionals, on the other, but also between curators and Outset patrons. The ensuing interaction between curators and patrons can lead to sponsorship of specific projects, but also to patrons making their expertise and connections available to curators on a more permanent basis.

When Gertler first invited curators to come on trips she encountered skepticism from some curators who questioned Outset's motives. As it became clear that the trips came with no strings attached, this attitude changed. As Gertler puts it:

> we now have the trust of the curators, they are not there for anything else other than their benefit. We are there as part of their entourage. We want to follow them; we want to learn from them; we want to learn what their vision is, and then make our own decision as private individuals.

The artists

Outset consciously avoids artists that are established and commercially successful. These artists can fund their own activities from sale of their works. Instead, Outset prefers to support artists whose work has not crossed over into the commercial art markets. Such artists may be well known in the art world, but their work may be too complex and difficult to set up in private residences of collectors who account for the bulk of the commercial art market.

One would have expected Outset to form close relationships with these artists early on in the life of the organization. In reality, this took time. In the early days of Outset, some artists welcomed patrons to their studios. As Outset gained credibility, there was greater willingness to trust Outset as a creative partner. For Outset this meant greater engagement with the artist—supporting his or her work even before it coalesced into clearly defined work of art. It also played to the strength of Outset as a flexible two-person operation, with the ability to respond quickly to requests by artists. As Gertler puts it:

> I think that what makes Outset rare is the fact that we are very unbureaucratic. If you write an application to the Arts Council, or to other funding bodies such as the Henry Moore Foundation, you are faced with a lot of paperwork, with deadlines, with all sorts of application bureaucracy. With us it is a phone call, an e-mail, a meeting in the café where we see the urgency of a project, and how much of a difference our initial funding could make. We just have huge flexibility in how to say yes.

This flexibility has gone hand-in-hand with building enduring relationships with particular artists across a number of projects. Increasingly, Outset is evaluating support for projects in the context of the artist's career, rather than on a case-by-case basis. As Gertler sees it, an important advantage to becoming part of an artist's career is that it allows Outset to connect with other projects, and by extension form relationships with more institutions, events, and individuals. She gives the example of Yael Bartana, an Israeli artist, to make her point. Outset first supported Bartana at the 2011 Venice Biennale when she presented at the Polish pavilion. Bartana has worked closely with Artur Żmijewski who has been selected to curate the 2012 Berlin Biennale, an event whose catalogue is being supported by Outset. The relationship between Bartana and Żmijewski has led to a panel discussion in London that Outset is now sponsoring regularly.

EXPANDING BEYOND ART

Over the years Outset has brought its model of collective charitable giving to other areas such as education, design, and dance. The first step in this direction took place during the first Tate–Frieze project. When contributions to the first Frieze fund exceeded the set target of £150,000, Gertler and Peel decided to use the surplus to fund an educational art program for children. This was followed by funding for dance and design. Branching from art into these areas was often a natural extension of Outset core activities. The move into dance, for example, came about at the request of an artist who was collaborating with a choreographer at Sadler's Wells, one of Britain's best-known dance venues. Similarly, funding for design came as a result of artists working on set designs for the Royal Opera and the Old Vic. In 2011 Outset launched the "Outset Design Fund." The bulk of support from this fund has gone toward sponsoring projects by the Victoria and Albert Museum in South Kensington, London.

Design has been Yana Peel's special area of interest. Peel sees a common thread running through Outset's support for art and design. As she puts it: "For us it is always important to use art as an anchor. We have moved into art plus dance, or art plus design, as it were. Visual art is very much at our core but around that periphery we realize that there are interesting collaborations that artists very much want to have, and that we are very keen to facilitate."

Notwithstanding her commitment to design, Peel feels that Outset should be mindful of the boundaries that separate the art and design. As she puts it:

> We are not trying to confuse the worlds of art and design. We are not suddenly going to be doing art plus knitting, art plus book reading, art plus this or that. But I think there are really interesting junctions, and that artists don't want to be pigeonholed into just art, art, art. They want to be able to facilitate different sorts of environments.

THE GLOBALIZATION OF THE OUTSET MODEL

Outset currently has affiliates in Germany, Israel, India, and the Netherlands. The affiliates use the Outset name, and maintain a strong relationship with Outset UK, but are independent in other respects. In general, the formation of the Outset affiliates owes more to circumstances than to deliberate planning. The first Outset affiliate was formed in Munich, Germany, in 2006, by Kerstin Traube. Traube was one of Outset patron's in London. When she moved to Germany she decided to found an affiliate modeled on Outset. The next Outset affiliate was formed in Israel in 2008 through a joint effort of Candida Gertler and Vered Gadish. This was followed by the formation of Outset India in 2011 by Feroze Gujral. Outset's next affiliate was formed in 2012 in Amsterdam by Gwen Neumann. Neumann was codirector of Outset Germany from 2009 to 2011, before she founded Outset Netherlands.

When Yana Peel moved to Hong Kong in 2009 it was unclear if she would attempt to set up an Outset affiliate. This proved to be more difficult than she originally envisaged. Although Hong Kong is affluent and cosmopolitan, Peel discovered that the city lacked the history and institutional infrastructure that would support the Outset model. As she put it:

> When I arrived in Hong Kong my immediate assumption was "OK, one could probably do the same thing here." However, Hong Kong has no institutions for displaying or producing or showing contemporary art. There are no museums that would show art that Candida and I, or our patrons would be interested in. There is no one showing Damien Hirst, no one showing Jeff Koons, no one showing Steve McQueen. Hong Kong is not rich in cultural institutions. So you can't have a breakfast at the Tate, and you can't meet the director of the Serpentine, and you can't go to the East End and spend some time with some emerging artist.

Frustrated in her efforts to transplant Outset in Hong Kong, Peel changed tack and joined the board of the government-supported gallery, Para/Site. Her efforts at persuading the board to experiment with the Outset model met with limited success. In 2011, Peel stepped down as Outset UK director and trustee, to assume the directorship of the Victoria and Albert Museum Design Fund, and Intelligence Squared Asia, a forum for political, economic, and cultural debate.

OUTSET MOVES FORWARD

The Saha Outset experience had raised questions about Outset's future policy toward new affiliates that Candida Gertler is still grappling with. Interest in becoming Outset affiliates is still strong (see Exhibit 2). Surprisingly, in light of the economic crisis, a group in Greece approached Gertler with a view toward forming an Outset affiliate. There is also a recently formed Outset affiliate in Scotland—a venture that Gertler was very interested in pursuing as a first step toward expanding Outset's presence in other parts of the UK.

Gertler's ambitions for Outset do not stop there. She has recently written to 25 organizations asking if they would be interested in a loose collaboration under the "International Production Fund." The main purpose of the fund will be to provide biennales with the support that their curators need to realize their vision for the event. This support will extend beyond the biennales to exhibited works that will be donated to museums.

Early in 2012, Outset was commissioned by their Frieze–Tate sponsor, Le Méridien Hotels and Resorts, to hold one of their panel series in Istanbul, in May of that year. Inevitably, in light of her experience with the launch of Saha in 2011, Gertler had to consider whether Outset should take this opportunity to reestablish the relationship with Saha. In March 2012, Nick Aikens, Outset's international projects director, extended the following email invitation to Saha:

> I am writing as Outset will be in Istanbul to host a panel discussion in May as part of the Outset/Le Méridien panel series. All of us at Outset wanted to reach out to Saha in

the context of our activity in Istanbul in May as it seems the perfect opportunity for a dialogue between the two organizations. As we discussed in our last communications we are of course working towards the same goals so it would benefit both organizations to share knowledge and information about relevant projects.

The response from one of Saha's founding members was both positive and friendly:

Dear Nick, It's nice to hear from you. It is exciting that you will be organizing a panel, and a dedicated project in Istanbul. We would love to know more about them. We have always felt that a dialogue between Outset and Saha would be beneficial to both parties.

EXHIBIT 2 OUTSET'S INTERNATIONAL AFFILIATES

Outset Germany

Outset Germany was founded in 2006 by Kerstin Traube and currently has a growing group of patrons consisting of contemporary art enthusiasts eager for a deeper involvement with the arts. Outset enjoys continued support from Le Méridien. From 2006 to 2009 Outset Germany's funding was directed primarily toward education projects at the city's two major contemporary art institutions, Haus der Kunst and the Pinakothek der Moderne. Outset Germany also runs an acquisitions fund for public institutions which has enabled the gifting of works to the Staatliche Graphische Sammlung, the Pinakothek der Moderne and the Neue Nationalgalerie, Berlin. Patrons of Outset Germany are invited to attend a program of events that includes curator-led tours of museum exhibitions, talks and discussions with leading art professionals, as well as national and international trips.

Outset Israel

Outset Israel was founded in September 2008 by Candida Gertler and Vered Gadish. It is a philanthropic platform dedicated to the funding and promotion of Israeli contemporary art projects destined for eventual donation to leading public collections and museums in Israel and beyond. Since its inception at ArtTLV 08, Outset Israel and its patrons have sought to engage international art professionals with the growing talent pool of Israeli artists. The organization conducts research trips to Israel for international curators as well as taking Israeli curators abroad. Outset Israel also holds public lectures and events, bringing leading art figures to Israel.

Outset India

Outset India was founded in 2011 by Feroze Gujral. It is a philanthropic organization dedicated to providing a platform for contemporary art in India, and for Indian artists abroad. The organization aims to offer vital support for artists and art organizations at an exciting time for contemporary art in India. Outset India's activities will include the production of new works, public donations, and publications. It aims to create a group of patrons seeking a deeper engagement with contemporary art. Through a program of tours, trips, and events Outset patrons will forge strong relationships with artists, curators, and art world professionals both in India and internationally.

Outset Netherlands

Outset Netherlands was founded in 2012 by Gwen Neumann. At a crucial moment for arts funding in the country, Outset NL seeks to engage patrons in supporting public museums, galleries, and projects.

The organization will focus on the production of new works of art and their subsequent donation to public collections, institutional acquisitions, exhibition programs, and publications. The organization seeks to engage with artists at a pivotal moment in their career, working with them to realize ambitious projects within the public realm. Patrons of Outset NL seek a deeper understanding of the artists and organizations the Fund works with while playing an active role in strengthening the international landscape of contemporary art. Patrons are invited to attend an extensive program of events that include curator-led tours of exhibitions, studio visits, and international trips with leading art professionals in conjunction with our partners.

Outset Greece

Outset Greece was established in 2012 in collaboration with NEON, founded by contemporary art collector Dimitris Daskalopoulos, at a time when Greece holds a unique position on a global scale. It is a real-life laboratory for studying high intensity political, financial, and social integration issues, covered extensively by the global media. At the same time, there is a restless local artistic community, which responds to the new realities through contemporary art. Outset Greece provides the platform for this constructive dialogue to flourish between artists, society and institutions. Projects supported include exhibitions, talks and debates, collaborative workshops and local community initiatives related to contemporary art. In Greece, Outset's sole patron is NEON.

Outset Scotland

Outset Scotland was founded in October 2012 by Kirstie Skinner, with the aim of bringing private individuals and corporate partners together to fund contemporary art activity in Scotland. It supports selected artists' commissions, exhibitions, and education programmes, and seeks to augment Scotland's public collections of contemporary art with gifted artworks.

Outset Scotland works with beneficiary organisations and public collections to identify projects that are strategically important for them and the artists involved. It selects projects that will prove inspiring for patrons and for wider audiences, and that might offer scope to encourage philanthropy – an area that is currently underdeveloped in Scotland.

In supporting such stimulating projects, and enjoying Outset Scotland's programme of special visits and encounters, patrons acquire a detailed understanding of the contemporary art landscape in Scotland and further afield, and gain unparalleled insight into the motivations and ambitions of its participants.

EXHIBIT 3:
ART WORKS/ART EVENTS THAT OUTSET HAS SUPPORTED OVER THE PAST FEW YEARS

The Big Bamboozle, Camden Arts Centre, 2013
Theatre Royal Haymarket Masterclass Trust, Hospital School, Great Ormond Street Hospital, 2013
'House of Voltaire', Studio Voltaire, 2012
'Seduced by Art: Photography Past & Present', The National Gallery, London, 2012–2013
RCA/Outset Visual Cultures Lecture Series, Royal College of Art, London, 2012–2013
'Adi Nes: The Village', Jewish Museum London, 2012–2013
Outset/Frieze Art Fair Fund To Benefit The Tate Collection
Susan Hiller, documenta (13), Kassel, 2012
Goshka Macuga, documenta (13), Kassel, 2012
The Penzance Convention, The Exchange, Penzance, Cornwall, 2012
Latifah Echakhch, Frieze Projects, New York, 2012
Forget Fear, Reader of the 7th Berlin Biennale, KW Institute, Berlin, 2012
'A Joyful Archipelago', Curated by Olga Grotova, London, 2012
Shezad Dawood (b.1974) 'Piercing Brightness', Modern Art Oxford, 2012
Zarina Bhimji, Whitechapel Gallery, London, 2012
Collaboration between Hofesh Shechter and Antony Gormley: 'Survivor', Barbican, London, 2012
Calvert 22, The Forgetting Of Proper Names, 25 January–18 March 2012
Elmgreen & Dragset, 'Happy Days in the Art World', Performa 11, New York, 2011
Undance, 'Twice through the Heart', Sadler's Wells, London, 2011
Frances Stark, 'My Best Thing', ICA, London, 2011
Nathalie Djurberg with Music by Hans Berg, 'World of Glass', Camden Arts Centre, London, 2011
Haroon Mirza, 'I Saw a Square Triangle Sine', Camden Arts Centre, London, 2011
Emma Hart, 'To Do', Matt's Gallery, London, 2011
'The Peripatetic School: Itinerant Drawing from Latin America', curated by Tanya Barson, Drawing Room, London, 2011
'Infinite Freedom Exercise (near Abadan, Iran)' John Gerrard (b.1974), Manchester International Festival, 2011
Smadar Dreyfus, 'School', Folkestone Triennial, 2011
Picasso Talks, 'Picasso in Palestine', International Art Academy Palestine, 2011
AO& 'Old Acquaintance Should Be Forgot', London Residency, 2011
Karla Black (b.1972) Scottish Pavilion, 54th Venice Biennale, 2011
Yael Bartana: 'Zamach (Assassination)', Polish Pavilion, 54th Venice Biennale, 2011
Roman Ondak – Time Capsule, Modern Art Oxford, March, 2011
V&A Aquisitions, Outset Design Fund, 2011
Exhibition Partner, Chisenhale Gallery, 2011
Curatorial/Knowledge in the Middle East, Goldsmith's College, University of London, 2011–2014
Get the Message – Camden Arts Centre, 2011
The Outset Art Room, Robert Blair Primary School, 2011

CASE 20

Johnson & Johnson

On January 26, 2011, health care conglomerate Johnson & Johnson (J&J) announced that earnings had declined in the fourth quarter of the previous year, and lowered its estimates for its earnings for 2010 (see Table 1). The firm claimed that the weaker results could be attributed to the depressed economy and to a string of product recalls. Sales figures do indicate that Johnson & Johnson has clearly been hurt by 17 recalls since September 2009, covering several over-the-counter medicines, a batch of contact lenses, and some hip replacements (see Table 2).

The most serious problems have surfaced at McNeil Consumer Healthcare, which has had to recall many of its products, including one for an estimated 136 million bottles of children's Tylenol, Motrin, Benadryl, and Zyrtec—the biggest children's drug recall of all time—that were potentially contaminated with dark particles. Johnson & Johnson has been excoriated by the Food and Drug Administration for failing to catch McNeil's quality problems. The agency slapped one of McNeil's plants with a scalding inspection report, causing the company to close down the factory until 2011.

In response to these problems, Johnson & Johnson recently announced that it intended to revamp its quality controls, creating a single framework for its consumer, pharmaceutical, and medical-device divisions. Ajit Shetty, the corporate vice president responsible for supply chain operations, will oversee the new system, reporting directly to William C. Weldon, the firm's chief executive. The company said it also planned to appoint chief quality officers for each of its three major divisions.

The decision to create a more centralized form of quality control was a difficult one for Weldon. The firm has relied heavily on acquisitions to grow over the years, resulting in a collection of as many as 250 different operating companies that are spread over 60 countries. Johnson & Johnson has been committed to providing each of these units as much autonomy as possible in order to preserve an entrepreneurial culture throughout the organization. "The company really operates more like a mutual fund than anything else," commented Pat Dorsey, director of equity research at Morningstar.[1]

In spite of the benefits that Johnson & Johnson may derive from such an arrangement, Weldon had already been thinking about taking steps to be more actively involved with its far-flung business units. He recently told investors that he has been particularly concerned about pushing for more internal growth: "We'll come at it from a variety of different ways, to accelerate top and bottom-line growth."[2] Given the scope of the businesses that J&J manages, he believes that the best opportunities may come from increased collaboration between its different units. But even as he has been pushing for some form of stronger direction for its units, Weldon does not want to threaten the strong entrepreneurial spirit that has been the basis of much of its success. The concerns over quality control have pushed the firm to try to find a more effective method of running its businesses without stripping them of their relative autonomy.

CULTIVATING ENTREPRENEURSHIP

Johnson & Johnson has relied heavily upon acquisitions to enter into and to expand into a wide range of businesses which fall broadly under the category of health care. Over the last decade alone, the firm has spent nearly $50 billion on 70 different purchases. Since 2008, J&J has made eight acquisitions, including a $1.1 billion acquisition of Mentor Corporation, a leading supplier of products for the global aesthetic market. The acquisition allowed the firm to make a substantial move into the growing field of cosmetic drugs and devices. "It's a natural extension of where J&J would want to go," said Michael Weinstein, an analyst who specializes in the medical sector for J.P. Morgan Chase & Company.[3]

As it has grown, Johnson & Johnson has developed into an astonishingly complex enterprise, made up of over 250 different businesses that have been broken down into three different divisions (see Exhibit 1). The most widely known of these is the division that makes consumer products such as *Johnson & Johnson* baby care products, *Band-Aid* adhesive strips, and *Visine* eye drops. The division grew substantially after J&J acquired the consumer health unit of Pfizer in 2006 for $16.6 billion, the biggest in its 120-year-old history. The acquisition

This case was developed by Jamal Shamsie, Michigan State University. Material has been drawn from published sources. To be used for purposes of class discussion.

TABLE 1
INCOME STATEMENT (IN MILLIONS OF DOLLARS)

	YEAR ENDING		
	Jan 2, 2011	Jan 3, 2010	Dec 28, 2009
Total revenue	61,587	61,897	61,897
Gross profit	42,795	43,450	43,450
Operating income	16,527	15,590	15,590
EBIT	17,402	16,206	16,206
Net income	13,334	12,266	12,266

Source: Johnson & Johnson.

TABLE 2
BALANCE SHEET (IN MILLIONS OF DOLLARS)

	YEAR ENDING		
	Jan 2, 2011	Jan 3, 2010	Dec 28, 2009
Current assets	47,307	39,541	39,541
Total assets	102,908	94,682	94,682
Current liabilities	23,072	21,731	21,731
Total liabilities	46,329	44,094	44,094
Stockholder equity	56,579	50,588	50,588

Source: Johnson & Johnson.

EXHIBIT 1
SEGMENT INFORMATION

Johnson & Johnson is made up of over 250 different companies, many of which it has acquired over the years. These individual companies have been assigned to three different divisions:

Pharmaceuticals
Share of firm's 2009 sales: 36%
Share of firm's 2005 sales: 44%
Share of firm's 2001 sales: 46%
Share of firm's 2009 operating profits: 44%
Share of firm's 2005 operating profits: 48%
Share of firm's 2001 operating profits: 63%

Medical devices
Share of firm's 2009 sales: 38%
Share of firm's 2005 sales: 38%
Share of firm's 2001 sales: 35%
Share of firm's 2009 operating profits: 46%
Share of firm's 2005 operating profits: 40%
Share of firm's 2001 operating profits: 25%

Consumer products
Share of firm's 2009 sales: 25%
Share of firm's 2005 sales: 18%
Share of firm's 2001 sales: 20%
Share of firm's 2009 operating profits: 15%
Share of firm's 2005 operating profits: 12%
Share of firm's 2001 operating profits: 12%

Source: J&J.

allowed the firm to add well-known products to its lineup such as *Listerine* mouth wash and *Benadryl* cough syrup (see Exhibit 2).

But Johnson & Johnson has reaped far more sales and profits from its other two divisions. Its pharmaceuticals division sells several blockbuster drugs such as anemia drug *Procit* and schizophrenia drug *Risperdal.* Its medical devices division is responsible for best-selling products such as *Depuy* orthopedic joint replacements and *Cyper* coronary stents. These two divisions tend to generate operating profit margins of around 30%, almost double those generated by the consumer business.

EXHIBIT 2
KEY BRANDS

Pharmaceuticals
RISPERDAL for schizophrenia
PROCRIT for anemia
REMICADE for rheumatoid arthritis
TOPAMIX for epilepsy
DURAGESIC for chronic pain
DOXIL for ovarian cancer
HALDOL for psychosis
NATRECOR for heart failure
ELMIRON for bladder pain

Medical devices
DEPUY orthopedic joint reconstruction products
CORDIS CYPHER stents
ETHICON surgery products
LIFESCAN diabetic testing products
VERIDEX diagnostic devices
ANIMAS insulin pumps
ACUVUE contact lenses

Consumer products
BAND AID bandages
JOHNSON & JOHNSON baby care products
NEUTROGENA skin and hair care products
LISTERINE oral health care
TYLENOL pain killers
ROLAIDS anti-acids
BENADRYL cold and cough syrups
BEN GAY pain relief ointments
TUCK'S hemorrhoidal ointments
VISINE eye drops
ROGAINE hair regrowth treatments
STAY FREE women's health products
SPLENDA sweeteners

Source: J&J.

To a large extent, however, Johnson & Johnson's success across its three divisions and many different businesses has hinged on its unique structure and culture. Most of its far-flung business units were acquired because of the potential demonstrated by some promising new products in its pipeline. Each of these units was therefore granted near-total autonomy to develop and expand upon their best-selling products. That independence has fostered an entrepreneurial attitude that has kept J&J intensely competitive as others around it have faltered. The relative autonomy that is accorded to the business units has also provided the firm with the ability to respond swiftly to emerging opportunities.

Johnson & Johnson has been quite proud of the considerable freedom that it has given to its different business units to develop and execute their own strategies. Besides developing their strategies, these units have also been allowed to work with their own resources. Many of the businesses even have their own finance and human resources departments. While this degree of decentralization makes for relatively high overhead costs, none of the executives that have run J&J, Weldon included, has ever thought that this was too high a price to pay. "J&J is a huge company, but you didn't feel like you were in a big company," recalled a scientist who used to work there.[4]

RESTRUCTURING FOR SYNERGIES

In spite of the benefits that Johnson & Johnson has derived from giving its various enterprises considerable autonomy, there have been growing concerns that they can no longer be allowed to operate in near isolation. Weldon has begun to realize that J&J is in a strong position to exploit new opportunities by drawing on the diverse skills of its various business units across the three divisions. He is well aware that his firm can benefit from the combination of its knowledge in drugs, devices, and diagnostics, since few companies can match its reach and strength in these basic areas.

Indeed, Johnson & Johnson has top-notch products in each of the areas in which it operates. It has been spending heavily on research and development for many years, taking its position among the world's top spenders. It currently spends about 12% of its sales or almost $7 billion on about 9,000 scientists working in research laboratories around the world (see Exhibit 3). This allows each of the three divisions to continually introduce promising new

EXHIBIT 3
RESEARCH EXPENDITURES (IN MILLIONS OF DOLLARS)

2009	6,986
2008	7,577
2007	7,680
2006	7,125
2005	6,462

Source: J&J.

products. Its pharmaceutical division, for example, is currently working on a drug to prevent strokes and one to treat prostate cancer.

Weldon believed, however, that Johnson & Johnson can profit from this convergence by finding ways to make its fiercely independent businesses work together. In his own words: "There is a convergence that will allow us to do things we haven't done before."[5] Through pushing the various far-flung units of the firm to pool their resources, Weldon believes that the firm could become one of the few that may actually be able to attain that often promised, rarely delivered idea of synergy.

Even as Weldon has been supportive of the efforts underway at each of the divisions, he is also pushing for all of its units to work with each other to address different health problems. He has appointed one of its rising stars, Nicholas Valeriani, to head a new Office of Strategy and Growth that would attempt to get business units to work together on promising new opportunities. "It's a recognition that there's a way to treat disease that's not in silos," Weldon stated, referring to J&J's largely independent businesses.[6]

Such a push for communication and coordination would allow Johnson & Johnson to develop the synergy that Weldon was seeking. But any effort to get the different business units to collaborate must not quash the entrepreneurial spirit that has spearheaded most of the growth of the firm to date. Jerry Caccott, managing director of consulting firm Strategic Decisions Group, emphasized that cultivating those alliances "would be challenging in any organization, but particularly in an organization that has been so successful because of its decentralized culture."[7]

BENEFITING FROM COLLABORATION

Weldon, like every other leader in the company's history, has worked his way up through the ranks. His long tenure within the firm has turned him into a true believer in the Johnson & Johnson system. He certainly does not want to undermine the entrepreneurial spirit that has resulted from the autonomy that has been given to each of the businesses. Consequently, even though Weldon may talk incessantly about synergy and convergence, he was cautious in the actual steps he has taken to push J&J's units to collaborate with each other.

For the most part, Weldon has confined himself to taking steps to foster better communication and more frequent collaboration among Johnson &Johnson's disparate operations. "They are the experts who know the marketplace, know the hospitals," he once said of the people who work in the firm's various business units.[8] Besides the appointment of Valeriani, he has worked with James T. Lenehan, vice-chairman and president of J&J, to set up groups that draw people from across the firm to focus their efforts on specific diseases. Each of the groups has been reporting every 6 months on potential strategies and projects.

Perhaps the most promising result of this new collaborative approach has been J&J's drug-coated stent, called *Cypher*. The highly successful new addition to the firm's lineup was a result of the efforts of teams that combined people from the drug business with others from the device business. They collaborated on manufacturing the stent, which props open arteries after angioplasty. Weldon claims that if J&J had not been able to bring together people with different types of expertise, it could not have developed the stent without getting assistance from outside the firm.

Even the company's fabled consumer brands have been starting to show growth as a result of increased collaboration between the consumer products and pharmaceutical divisions. Its new liquid *Band-Aid* is based on a material used in a wound-closing product sold by one of J&J's hospital-supply businesses. And J&J has used its prescription antifungal treatment, *Nizoral,* to develop a dandruff shampoo. In fact, products that have developed in large part out of such a form of cross-fertilization have allowed the firm's consumer business to experience considerable internal growth.

Some of the projects that Johnson & Johnson is currently working on could produce even more significant results. Researchers working on genomic studies in the firm's labs were building a massive database using gene patterns that correlate to a certain disease or to someone's likely response to a particular drug. Weldon encouraged them to share this data with the various business units. As a result, the diagnostics team has been working on a test that the researchers in the pharmaceutical division could use to predict which patients would benefit from an experimental cancer therapy.

DEALING WITH SETBACKS

Even as Johnson & Johnson has been trying to get more involved with the efforts of its business units, it has run into problems with quality control with several over-the-counter drugs that are made by McNeil Consumer Healthcare. Since 2008, FDA inspectors have found significant violations of manufacturing standards at two

McNeil plants, leading to the temporary closure of one of these. These problems have forced the firm to make several recalls of some of its best selling products. Weldon admitted that problems had surfaced, but he insisted that these were confined to McNeil. In a recent interview he stated: "This is one of the most difficult situations I've ever had to personally deal with. It hits at the core of who J&J is. Our first responsibility is to the people who use our products. We've let them down."[9]

Quality problems have arisen before, but they were usually fixed on a regular basis. Analysts suggest that the problems at McNeil may have been exacerbated in 2006 when J&J decided to combine it with the newly acquired consumer health care unit from Pfizer. The firm believed that it could achieve \$500–\$600 million in annual savings by merging the two units together. After the merger, McNeil was also transferred from the heavily regulated pharmaceutical division to the marketing-driven consumer products division, headed by Collen Goggins. Because these consumer executives lacked pharmaceutical experience, they began to demand several changes at McNeil that led to a reduction in emphasis on quality control.

Weldon is well aware of the threat faced by Johnson & Johnson as a result of its problems with quality. He is especially concerned about the allegation by the FDA that the firm initially tried to hide the problems that it found with Motrin in 2009, hiring a contractor to quietly go around from store to store, buying all of the packets off the shelves. McNeil's conduct surrounding the recalls has led to an inquiry by both the House Committee on Oversight and Investigations and by the FDA's office of criminal investigations.

Various changes are underway at McNeil to resolve these quality issues. Goggins was pushed out of her post as senior executive in charge of all consumer businesses. Weldon has allocated more than \$100 million to upgrade McNeil's plants and equipment, appoint new manufacturing executives, and hire a third-party consulting firm to improve procedures and systems. Bonnie Jacobs, a McNeil spokeswoman, wrote in a recent e-mail: "We will invest the necessary resources and make whatever changes are needed to do so, and we will take the time to do it right."[10]

The problems at McNeil, coupled with the recalls of contact lenses and hip replacements, have led Johnson & Johnson to make changes to its corporate oversight of its supply chain and manufacturing. In August 2010, the firm appointed Shetty, a longtime executive, to oversee the new systems of company-wide quality control that involves a single framework for quality across all of the operating units and a new reporting system. The need for these changes was highlighted by Erik Gordon, a professor at the Ross School of Business at the University of Michigan: "Nothing is more valuable to Johnson & Johnson than the brand bond of trust with consumers."[11]

IS THERE A CURE AHEAD?

Weldon realizes that the recalls have presented additional challenges for Johnson & Johnson which is already facing a tougher economic environment. Sales of its various consumer products such as *Tylenol, Benadryl,* and *Rolaids* have shown a substantial decline over the last 6 months of 2010. Weldon has been working hard to reassure analysts, investors, and consumers that it was already dealing with its quality problems. But Les Funtleyder, who invests in health stocks for his investment firm said: "These problems are accumulating. At some point investors are going to start to question J&J's management."[12]

But the firm's diversified portfolios of products that are spread across various areas of heath care have helped it to weather the various problems that it has encountered. In particular, Johnson & Johnson has managed to offset its loss of sales in over-the-counter medications with relatively strong sales from pharmaceuticals and devices. "With interests spread out all over the health-care industry, J&J does not live or die by any one product," remarked Herman Saftlas, a pharmaceutical analyst for Standard & Poor's.[13]

Moving forward, Weldon is hoping to strike a balance between direction and freedom for Johnson & Johnson's business units as he pushes to get the firm to start to grow again. Until the first quarter of 2009, the firm had managed to increase its earnings, adjusted for special items, for 94 consecutive quarters. Weldon believes that he can only resume Johnson & Johnson's record growth by pushing its businesses to work more closely together than they have ever done in the past. The firm can tap into many more opportunities when it tries to bring together the various skills that it has managed to develop across different divisions.

At the same time, Weldon has become acutely aware of the problems that can arise when the corporate managers start to push the business units to become more effective or efficient. To a large extent, the quality problems at McNeil can be attributed to the decision by J&J to merge it with the consumer health care unit that it had acquired from Pfizer. The larger merged unit was then moved away from the pharmaceutical division and subjected to more centralized control within the consumer division. As a result of all of these efforts to wring more profits out of McNeil, the firm had to resort to a string of recalls that have tarnished the image of J&J.

Above all, Weldon is acutely aware that much of Johnson & Johnson's success has resulted from the relative autonomy that it has granted to each of its business units. He knows that even as he strives to push for more control and direction, he does not want to threaten the entrepreneurial spirit that has served his firm so well. But it is clear to Weldon that he has to rethink the process by which his firm manages its diversified portfolio of companies in order to ensure that there are no further threats to its reputation. "This is a company that was purer than Caesar's wife, this was the gold standard, and all of a sudden it just seems like things are breaking down," said William Trombetta, a professor of pharmaceutical marketing at Saint Joseph's University in Philadephia.[14]

CASE 21

Netflix

INTRODUCTION

In late February 2005, Netflix, the pioneer of the video rental business, had to be bothered by the impending threat posed by Wal-Mart, Inc., Blockbuster, and possibly Amazon .com. By the end of February 2005, both Wal-Mart and Blockbuster had taken their DVD rental services online in an attempt to copy the Netflix business model.

The Neflix model was designed to provide an online library of DVD titles that allowed subscribers to "check out" titles as they pleased with neither late fees nor shipping fees. For a flat monthly fee, customers rented a prescribed number of DVDs at a time, exchanging the movies at their leisure. The total number of DVDs rented depended on how quickly the customer returned the titles. After customers finished watching a selection, they mailed the DVD to Netflix via the United States Postal Service in a prepaid envelope. As soon as Netflix received the movie, the company sent the customers the next DVD selection in their "queue" or list of preselected titles.

The online video-retailer model proved valuable to customers and Netflix soon mailed more than one million DVDs a day. When Reed Hastings, chief executive officer (CEO) of Netflix, was asked in 2003 in an interview, "What motivates you these days?" he responded, "The dream 20 years from now [would be] to have a global entertainment distribution company that provided a unique channel for film producers and studios. . . . As Starbucks is for coffee, Netflix is for movies."[1]

However, there were additional questions for Netflix. Its stock had lost 78 per cent of its value in the last year (Exhibit 1). Was it because the market feared that the company would lose its competitive advantage to Wal-Mart and Blockbuster? Was there a strategic plan for Netflix to reverse this decline?

There were still other issues. In 2004, Amazon.com had sales of \$6.9 billion, and Wal-Mart had sales of \$258 billion. Given the price of Netflix stock, what would happen if Amazon.com or Wal-Mart initiated a hostile takeover of Netflix?

Finally, in September 2004, a *Newsweek* article commented on the proposed partnership with TiVo that would enable Netflix to upload movies over the Internet directly to a subscriber's TiVo box instead of sending them by mail. The article said Netflix would then deliver most of its rentals over the Internet. If so, would the company plan to keep its distribution centers? How would it use these channels? Clearly, there were questions about Netflix's strategic direction going forward.

COMPANY OVERVIEW

Based in Los Gatos, California, in the heart of Silicon Valley, Netflix launched subscription services to customers in 1999. Initially, Hastings provided a service similar to traditional DVD rental shops by utilizing rental fees for each DVD checked out as well as charging late fees. However, in late 1999 he switched to a flat-fee model when the previous business model did not catch on with consumers. According to his own admission, Hastings owed a \$40 late fee to Blockbuster for *Apollo 13* and was too embarrassed to tell his wife about it.[2] While driving to a local gym where he was a member and paid a monthly fee, he got the idea of a subscription model for video rental.

Netflix's goal was to provide a premier, filmed-entertainment subscription service to a large and growing subscriber base. The company expected 5 per cent of all US households to become Netflix members by 2006, resulting in five million members (company sources believed six million members were possible) and generating \$1 billion in revenue.[3]

Professor Sayan Chatterjee, Elizabeth Carroll, and David Spencer wrote this case solely to provide material for class discussion. The authors do not intend to illustrate either effective or ineffective handling of a managerial situation. The authors may have disguised certain names and other identifying information to protect confidentiality.

Version: (A) 2010-02-03

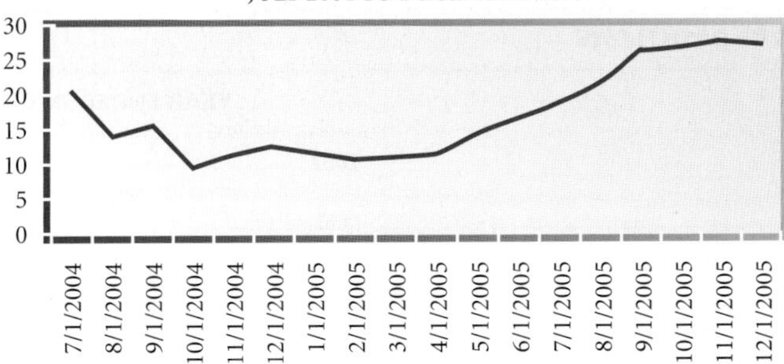

EXHIBIT 1 NETFLIX STOCK PRICE PERFORMANCE, JULY 2004 TO DECEMBER 2005

Source: Chart created by author from data available at S&P Compustat.

Businessweek called Netflix one of the most successful dot-com ventures to date. In its first three years, Netflix acquired 670,000 subscribers.[4] By the end of 2004, Netflix had 2.6 million subscribers—a figure on target with the company's growth projections. For 2005, the company expected to reach or surpass four million subscribers. Despite increased competition, customer defection (or "churn") dropped from 5 per cent to 4.7 per cent between the first and second quarters of 2005. Although Netflix experienced losses in the first few years of operation, it had a 2004 net income of $21 million (see Exhibit 2).

EXHIBIT 2 NETFLIX INCOME STATEMENT (IN THOUSANDS, EXCEPT PER SHARE DATA)

	YEAR ENDED DECEMBER 31					
	1999	**2000**	**2001**	**2002**	**2003**	**2004**
Revenues						
Subscription	$4,854	$35,894	$74,255	$150,818	$270,410	$500,611
Sales	152	—	1,657	1,988	1,833	5,617
Total revenues	5,006	35,894	75,912	152,806	272,243	506,228
Cost of revenues						
Subscription	4,217	24,861	49,088	77,044	147,736	273,401
Sales	156	—	819	1,092	624	3,057
Total cost of revenues	4,373	24,861	49,907	78,136	148,360	276,458
Gross profit	633	11,033	26,005	74,670	123,883	229,770
Operating expenses						
Fulfillment	2,446	10,247	13,452	19,366	31,274	56,609
Technology and development	7,413	16,823	17,734	14,625	17,884	22,906
Marketing	14,070	25,727	21,031	35,783	49,949	98,784
General and administrative	1,993	6,990	4,658	6,737	9,585	16,287
Restructuring charges	—	—	671	—	—	—
Stock-based compensation	4,846	9,714	6,250	8,832	10,719	16,587
Total operating expenses	30,768	69,501	63,796	85,343	119,411	211,173
Operating income (loss)	(30,135)	(58,468)	(37,791)	(10,673)	4,472	18,597
Operating income (expense)						
Interest and other income	924	1,645	461	1,697	2,457	2,592
Interest and other expense	(738)	(1,451)	(1,852)	(11,972)	(417)	(170)
Net income (loss)	$(29,949)	$(58,274)	$(39,182)	$(20,948)	$6,512	$21,019
Net income (loss) per share						
Basic	$(10.74)	$(20.61)	$(10.73)	$(0.74)	$0.14	$0.40
Diluted	$(10.74)	$(20.61)	$(10.73)	$(0.74)	$0.10	$0.32
Weighted-average shares outstanding						
Basic	2,788	2,828	3,652	28,204	47,786	51,988
Diluted	2,788	2,828	3,652	28,204	62,884	64,713

Source: Netflix 2003 Annual Report; Press Release "Netflix announces Q4 result" January 24, 2005.

EXHIBIT 2 NETFLIX INCOME STATEMENT (IN THOUSANDS, EXCEPT PER SHARE DATA) (*continued*)

CONSOLIDATED STATEMENTS OF CASH FLOWS

	YEAR ENDED DECEMBER 31		
	2002	2003 (THOUSANDS)	2004
Cash flows from operating activities			
Net income (loss)	$(20,948)	$6,512	$21,019
Adjustments to reconcile net income (loss) to net cash provided by operating activities			
Depreciation of property and equipment	5,919	4,720	5,871
Amortization of DVD library	17,417	43,125	80,346
Amortization of intangible assets	3,141	3,146	1,987
Noncash charges for equity instruments granted to nonemployees	40	–	–
Stock-based compensation expense	8,832	10,719	16,587
Stock option income tax benefits	–	–	176
Loss on disposal of property and equipment	–	–	135
Loss on disposal of short-term investments	–	–	274
Gain on disposal of DVDs	(1,674)	(1,604)	(2,912)
Noncash interest expense	11,384	103	44
Changes in operating assets and liabilities			
Prepaid expenses and other current assets	(44)	(290)	(9,130)
Accounts payable	6,635	12,304	17,121
Accrued expenses	4,558	2,523	1,506
Deferred revenue	4,806	8,581	13,612
Deferred rent	48	(47)	359
Net cash provided by operating activities	40,114	89,792	146,995
Purchases of short-term investments	(43,022)	(1,679)	(586)
Proceeds from sale of short-term investments	–	–	45,013
Purchases of property and equipment	(2,751)	(8,872)	(14,962)
Acquisitions of DVD library	(24,070)	(55,620)	(102,971)
Proceeds from sale of DVDs	1,988	1,833	5,617
Deposits and other assets	554	(339)	(492)
Net cash used in investing activities	(67,301)	(64,677)	(68,381)
Proceeds from issuance of common stock	88,020	6,299	6,035
Repurchases of common stock	(6)	–	–
Principal payments on notes payable and capital lease obligations	(17,144)	(1,334)	(436)
Net cash provided by financing activities	70,870	4,965	5,599
Effect of exchange rate changes on cash and cash equivalents	–	–	(222)
Net increase in cash and cash equivalents	43,683	30,080	84,567
Cash and cash equivalents, beginning of period	16,131	59,814	89,894
Cash and cash equivalents, end of period	$59,814	$89,894	$174,461

Source: Netflix 2004 Annual Report.

Netflix's strongest growth, as well as keenest competition, was in the San Francisco Bay Area, which was the company's launching point for operations. Household penetration in the Bay Area was 7.2 per cent in March 2004 compared to 4.6 per cent penetration the previous year.[5] This growth occurred despite the existence of a Wal-Mart distribution center (allowing one-day movie deliveries) and a Blockbuster that offered an in-store subscription program.

The fully diluted earnings per share for fiscal year 2004 were 32 cents, up from 10 cents per share for 2003. Netflix's revenue for fiscal year 2004 was $506.2 million.[6]

CHIEF EXECUTIVE OFFICER

At age 44, Hastings had held the position of CEO since September 1998, in addition to serving as the president and chairman of the board since Netflix's founding. Hastings served in the US Peace Corps at a high school in Swaziland and then went on to receive his bachelor's degree at Bowdoin College in 1983. In 1988, he obtained a master's in Computer Science from Stanford University and began working for Pure Atria Software, a maker of software development tools. In October 1991, three years after joining the company, Hastings became the CEO of Pure Atria

Software. From June 1998 through 1999, Hastings created Netflix while serving as the CEO of Technology Network, a political service organization for the technology industry.[7]

THE MOVIE RENTAL INDUSTRY

In 2003, Adams Media Research estimated that the total domestic video industry, including both sales and rentals of DVDs and video cassettes, was $24.4 billion.[8] Using internal research, Netflix estimated that video sales and rental revenues were a record-breaking $11.3 billion in the first half of 2004. However, this number represented $7.2 billion on in-sales (92 per cent of which were DVD sales), compared to $4.2 billion in rental revenue. Overall rental revenues, including both the video and DVD segments, decreased 13 per cent from the same period in 2003. This suggested that the increasing trend of consumers purchasing DVDs based upon price reductions might be affecting the rental market.

Although the overall market for movie rentals declined, the DVD rental portion was still growing, indicating the increasing popularity of DVDs at the expense of videocassettes. However, analysts anticipated that the DVD rental market's growth would begin to decelerate. J.P. Morgan and Associates predicted a 27.2 per cent growth rate in 2004 versus a 51 per cent growth rate in 2003.[9] This was not wholly unexpected as market penetration began to plateau while customers continued purchasing DVDs. The movie rental market share of Internet-based companies such as Netflix increased from 8.3 per cent at the end of 2003 to 13.3 per cent by mid-2004.[10] However, in the online market, Netflix held a commanding share (see Exhibit 3). The growth potential of the market itself was nicely tuned to the common lifestyle at the time. The cost of popcorn in a multiplex cinema was quite high and ticket prices were rising, making a night at the movies a rather expensive outing.

MARKETING AND DISTRIBUTION

Target market

As with any online retailer, Netflix required customers to have access to the Internet and a willingness to make rental purchases online. Target customers also owned or had access to DVD players. By the end of 2003, approximately half of all U.S. households owned at least one DVD player.[11] The typical Netflix customer desired DVD rental convenience through a wide selection of movie titles and fast delivery. In published reports, Hastings segmented customers into three categories: those who sought better value, those who sought better selection, and those who sought convenience.[12] Approximately 27 per cent of Netflix subscribers lived in rural areas, thus falling into the convenience category.[13] These customers generally did not have easy access to satellite or cable TV, or video stores.

Netflix desired customers who were less prone to churn. The longer customers stayed with Netflix, the less likely they would be to discontinue the service. Netflix's internal research identified the number one reason for churn was that customers believed they were not watching enough movies to justify the expense of the service. Consequently, Netflix targeted potentially high movie-watching customers and promoted the benefits of the Netflix business model to induce them to watch more movies. The company also sought customers who wanted to watch not only current blockbuster movies but also older movies from the Netflix catalogs. For this reason, Netflix initially catered to movie aficionados. Over time, however, the target market shifted toward a broader range of movie watchers.

A 2004 survey by Lyra Research indicated that Netflix customers typically rented more movies than the average population. The firm surveyed more than 1,000 active renters; results indicated users of traditional outlets averaged 10 rentals per month while Netflix renters averaged 15 rentals a month.[14] The study also indicated that the more DVDs a person owned, the higher the number of DVDs the person would rent.

By August 2004, Netflix captured 12.5 per cent of the $10 billion movie rental business. Netflix also accounted for 30 per cent of the independent film rental market. Netflix's relationship with independent film distributors was critical to its ability to provide a wide selection of titles in this genre. Customers found titles at Netflix that were not available in traditional outlets, large portions of which were independent films. Based on the list of the top 10 movies rented at the respective venues during 2003, Netflix's subscribers and Blockbuster's storefront customers rented very different titles.[15]

Promotion

Netflix promoted its service through various methods, including Internet and television advertising and promotional inserts with most leading DVD player manufacturers. These efforts encouraged consumers to subscribe to its service and included a 14-day free trial period. At the end of the trial period, subscribers were automatically enrolled as paying subscribers unless they canceled their subscriptions. Approximately 90 per cent of trial subscribers became paying subscribers.[16]

Online advertising via paid search listings, permission-based e-mails, banner ads, and text on popular web portals and other web sites were Netflix's largest source of new subscribers. During 2003, online and word-of-mouth advertising accounted for approximately 85 per cent of all new trial subscriber acquisitions.[17] Despite beating top-line forecasts, in June 2004, Netflix failed to meet earnings estimates due mainly to escalating online advertising rates.

EXHIBIT 3 MARKET SHARE FOR ONLINE RENTALS AT THE END OF 2004

Netflix	78%
Blockbuster	15%
Wal-Mart and others	7%

Source: Verne Kopytoff, "Netflix in for Blockbuster battle," *The San Francisco Chronicle,* January 31, 2005.

Distribution strategy

Netflix aimed to improve accuracy and reduce delivery time for DVDs to reach subscribers, focusing first on the distribution centers. Initially, Netflix's only distribution center was near San Francisco, which meant DVDs spent days in the mail. Hastings commented, "It wasn't a very consumer-satisfying experience."[18] During a time when only one in 10 households owned a DVD player, Netflix struggled to expand nationally and establish more distribution centers. Over time, the company opened distribution centers near major metropolitan areas. According to Netflix's vice president of corporate communications, Ken Ross, by February 2005, Netflix's 35 domestic distribution centers essentially guaranteed one business day delivery within a nearly 100 mile radius from each distribution center. At the distribution centers, workers earned $8.50 to $10.50 an hour by applying mailing labels by hand.[19]

In addition to the distribution centers, Netflix made additional distribution-related improvements as well. The company abandoned an extensive conveyor belt system in favor of using trolleys to move the DVDs, which proved to be more efficient. The company also designed its patented red Netflix envelopes to minimize weight, maximize DVD protection, and increase the speed at which the United States Postal Service processed them.

IT and software

Netflix emphasized technology as a tool for differentiation. For example, Netflix invested in software known as CineMatch—a recommendation engine that was a combination of 29,000 unique lines of code and a database of 315 million film ratings. CineMatch offered personalized film recommendations based on subscribers' previous rental patterns. However, customer feedback was critical for the software to run optimally, as CineMatch was more effective at suggesting movies once it determined subscribers' preferences. The system also enabled easier browsing of the 30,000 titles Netflix offered and allowed customers to share feedback on their selections. Another key feature of the software was its link to the Netflix inventory, thus ensuring CineMatch would not suggest out-of-stock films to customers. As a result of the interactive feedback feature, Netflix customers had the potential to influence the success of films, especially in the independent genre. While popular, newly released movie rentals were much less correlated with the recommendation software, relatively unknown movies benefited greatly. Netflix customers often recommended films that were not supported by large-scale studio advertising. For example, the Spanish-language film *Talk to Her*, a critically acclaimed independent production, received high Netflix ratings; consequently, *Talk to Her* was rented more often in its first six months on Netflix as compared to the latest mainstream blockbuster movies listed on Netflix during the same time period. By recommending independent films such as *Talk to Her*, not only did Netflix give mainstream customers the opportunity to expand their tastes, but it also positioned itself as a potentially unique outlet for independent films of diverse genres (see Exhibit 4).

EXHIBIT 4 NETFLIX'S SELECTION SPANNED 250 GENRES, INCLUDING THESE CATEGORIES

Action and adventure	Horror
Anime	Independent
Children and family	Music and concert
Classics	Romance
Comedy	Sci-Fi and fantasy
Documentary	Special interest
Drama	Sports
Foreign	Television
Gay and lesbian	Thrillers

Source: www.netflix.com, February 2005.

"Netflix [was] without question one of the most efficient and convenient resources for consumers who [wanted] niche and independent films," said Fritz Friedman, a spokesman at Columbia Tri-Star Home Entertainment, the studio that distributed *Talk to Her*.[20]

Netflix also introduced additional services to further enhance subscriber customization opportunities. In January 2005, Netflix launched "Friends," a feature that enabled users to create a network to share what they were watching, as well as invite others to post reviews and film ratings. The average customer rated approximately 150 movies, thus enhancing the service; as such, subscribers were offered custom-tailored recommendations linked not only to past rentals but also to past reviews. The Friends feature, which included more than 10 per cent of the membership base, allowed Netflix to more deeply engage customers in its service while providing a potential means to detect future spikes in demand. In addition to Friends, Netflix also launched Profiles, which was a service that gave different members of a family the ability to create individual movie lists under their own profiles. This service further increased subscriber customization options.

PATENTS

Apart from the patented red envelope, Netflix received approval for a patent from the United States Patent and Trademark Office in June 2003. The patent essentially protected three unique characteristics of the Netflix business model:

1. A computer-implemented approach for renting items to customers in which customers specified what items to rent using item selection criteria involving movie types as well as when the customers wished to receive the specified items.
2. "Max Out" approach to renting, which allowed up to a specified number of items to be rented simultaneously to customers.
3. "Max Turns" approach to renting, which allowed up to a specified number of item exchanges to occur during a

specified time regardless of the number of items rented per turn.[21]

Netflix used Max Out and Max Turns in combination to set its rental policy. Max Out was used to limit the amount of DVDs customers rented at any point in time. Further, the company used Max Turns to restrict the amount of times customers turned over their DVDs per month.

Thoughts about the patent were mixed. Some analysts felt that patent right infringement could not be prosecuted. Moreover, because the patent was public information, competitors would find ways to design their models around the patent. Other analysts were not so sure and felt that if the patent were enforced, Netflix could turn all its competitors—regardless of the rented items—into paying licensees or cause them to cease operations based on the patents.

However, Netflix had no immediate plans to enforce its patent. According to the 2004 10-K filing, Netflix was focused on keeping competitors at bay using its operational excellence.[22] In contrast, Amazon.com developed and patented the "one-click technology," a business method patent. When Barnes & Noble used the patented technology, Amazon.com took Barnes & Noble to court on infringement charges and successfully defended its patent.

ECONOMICS OF THE RENTAL BUSINESS

For most retailers, the primary metric for success was inventory turns. Surprisingly, getting the maximum utility from its movie inventory was by no means the central focus for Netflix—it did not even report inventory figures (see Exhibit 5). Instead, Netflix acquired its DVD titles outright and amortized the expenses. Netflix realized it could make money if it grew its subscriber base and reduced churn.

Accordingly, Netflix worked with more than 50 studios and distributors to amass its large selection of DVDs for consumers. Netflix had a revenue-sharing arrangement for most of its titles. This was similar to the arrangements between movie theaters and film studios whereby the studios received a percentage of the ticket sales. Typically, this percentage was higher for new releases and lower for reruns. Likewise, DVDs were most popular when first released. Netflix did not charge subscribers a rental fee for each DVD rented. Therefore, Netflix created an arrangement with the film studios so that each time a popular title was rented, it cost Netflix $1.25 under the revenue-sharing agreement. Less popular movie titles could cost Netflix $0.50 or less and some movies even had zero revenue-sharing costs. Most of the lower-cost titles were in Netflix's catalogs, some of which it owned (i.e., zero revenue sharing). Consequently, Netflix wanted to introduce new subscribers to its catalog—especially the unique content and the independent studio releases.

Netflix offered its subscription rentals at multiple price points along with a greater range of service options than those provided by Blockbuster or Wal-Mart. For example, a Netflix subscriber would pay $9.99 a month to have one movie at a time. For $17.99 a month, a Netflix subscriber could have three titles out at a time. Netflix changed its pricing in reaction to competitors' pricing moves.

While Netflix was known for its quick turns (sending out a title as soon as it received the previous one), the company sometimes deliberately favored servicing lighter users, who rented three to four movies per month, versus heavier users, who averaged 12 to 15 movies per month. Netflix used this load-balancing process when the following issues were present:

- availability of new titles (not having enough copies to meet demand); or

EXHIBIT 5 NETFLIX BALANCE SHEET

PERIOD ENDING	31-DEC-04	31-DEC-03
Assets		
Current assets		
Cash and cash equivalents	174,461	89,894
Short-term investments	–	45,297
Net receivables	–	–
Inventory	–	–
Other current assets	12,885	3,755
Total current assets	**187,346**	**138,946**
Long-term investments	–	–
Property plant and equipment	18,728	9,772
Goodwill	–	–
Intangible assets	43,119	25,186
Accumulated amortization	–	–
Other assets	2,600	2,108
Deferred long-term asset charges	–	–
Total assets	**251,793**	**176,012**
Liabilities		
Current liabilities		
Accounts payable	62,906	44,279
Short/current long-term debt	68	416
Other current liabilities	31,936	18,324
Total current liabilities	**94,910**	**63,019**
Long-term debt	–	44
Other liabilities	–	–
Deferred long-term liability charges	600	241
Minority interest	–	–
Negative goodwill	–	–
Total liabilities	**95,510**	**63,304**
Stockholders' equity		
Misc. stocks options-warrants	–	–
Redeemable preferred stock	–	–
Preferred stock	–	–
Common stock	53	51
Retained earnings	(131,698)	(153,293)
Treasury stock	–	–
Capital surplus	292,843	270,836
Other stockholder equity	(4,915)	(4,886)
Total stockholder equity	**156,283**	**112,708**
Net tangible assets	**$113,164**	**$87,522**

Source: Netflix 2003 and 2004 Annual Reports.

- when a distribution center was overloaded (too much demand from a particular distribution center leading to capacity constraints for mailing out the DVDs).

This load-balancing practice, labeled by some as "throttling," led to some dissatisfaction as the customer base increased.

The other cost to note is that postage costs were determined by the United States Postal Service.

COMPETITION

The most direct threats to Netflix came from Wal-Mart and Blockbuster (see Exhibits 6–8). Each competitor initiated its own version of a DVD online rental service that operated, in principle, identically to the Netflix business model. As expected, Wal-Mart was the price leader, offering the lowest price for an equal number of DVDs. Blockbuster planned to incorporate its 8,500 company-owned and franchised stores as an option for returning movies. In addition, Blockbuster offered two free in-store rentals per month (see Exhibit 9).

Although the competitors did not publicly state their membership numbers, *Businessweek* estimated that Netflix had at least five times as many DVD-by-mail subscribers as Wal-Mart Stores, Inc., and about three times as many as Blockbuster.[23]

EXHIBIT 7 EXCERPTS FROM COMPETITORS' INCOME STATEMENTS

BLOCKBUSTER		
PERIOD ENDING	**31-Dec-04**	**31-Dec-03**
Total revenue	**6,053,200**	**5,911,700**
Cost of revenue	2,441,400	2,389,800
Gross profit	**3,611,800**	**3,521,900**
WAL-MART		
PERIOD ENDING	**31-Jan-05**	**31-Jan-04**
Total revenue	**287,989,000**	**258,681,000**
Cost of revenue	219,793,000	198,747,000
Gross profit	**68,196,000**	**59,934,000**

Source: Wal-Mart and Blockbuster 2003 and 2004 Annual Reports.

EXHIBIT 6 EXCERPTS FROM COMPETITORS' BALANCE SHEETS

BLOCKBUSTER		
PERIOD ENDING	**31-Dec-04**	**31-Dec-03**
Assets		
Total current assets	1,217,700	960,300
Total assets	3,863,400	4,854,900
Liabilities		
Total current liabilities	1,449,400	1,327,800
Total liabilities	2,800,500	1,605,600
Total stockholder equity	1,062,900	3,249,300
Net tangible assets	($567,700)	$232,800
WAL-MART		
PERIOD ENDING	**31-Jan-05**	**31-Jan-04**
Assets		
Current assets		
Total current assets	**38,491,000**	**34,421,000**
Total assets	**120,223,000**	**104,912,000**
Liabilities		
Current liabilities		
Accounts payable	35,107,000	31,051,000
Short/current long-term debt	7,781,000	6,367,000
Other current liabilities	–	–
Total current liabilities	**42,888,000**	**37,418,000**
Stockholders' equity		
Common stock	423,000	431,000
Retained earnings	43,854,000	40,206,000
Treasury stock	–	–
Capital surplus	2,425,000	2,135,000
Other stockholder equity	2,694,000	851,000
Total stockholder equity	**49,396,000**	**43,623,000**
Net tangible assets	**$38,593,000**	**$33,741,000**

Source: Netflix 2003 and 2004 Annual Reports.

Blockbuster

Blockbuster launched its Blockbuster Online service in August 2004 as a direct result of an attempt to transform itself from a brick-and-mortar movie rental store into an "anywhere-anytime entertainment destination that eventually will enable customers to rent, buy or trade movies and games, new or used, in-store and online."[24]

Blockbuster was a giant in the movie retail industry (both rental and sales of DVDs and video), with 40 per cent market share.[25] With 23 distribution centers, Blockbuster hoped to utilize its extensive store network as distribution sites.[26] Blockbuster also had partnerships with America Online and Microsoft's MSN, which translated into a reach of 75 per cent of the US Internet audience.[27] In terms of rental offerings, Blockbuster offered video game rentals, while Netflix did not. However, although both Netflix and Blockbuster claimed to carry more than 25,000 DVD titles online, the overwhelming response from customers was that beyond recently released, mainstream movies and select classics, Blockbuster was inferior to Netflix in terms of a comprehensive list of DVDs. Analysts estimated Blockbuster lost $120 million entering the online business.

As one critic of Blockbuster stated, "Blockbuster simply [could] not compete with the depth of Netflix's inventory. All Blockbuster [had was] current tripe and crap that [was] up to 10 years old. This [was] from a 10 year member of Blockbuster — I [was] not their enemy."[28] Another

EXHIBIT 8
COMPARISON OF ONLINE DVD RENTAL COMPETITORS

RANK	NETFLIX	WAL-MART	BLOCKBUSTER	
Movie selection	IIII	III	III	IIII = Excellent
Subscription plan selection	III	III	III	III = Above average
Movie search interface	IIII	III	III	II = Average
Movie availability	IIII	III	II	I = Below average
Speed of delivery	IIII	III	II	
Monthly fees				
Subscription plans	4	3	3	
Free trial	14 days	30 days	14 days	
Inventory selection				
Number of movie titles	30,000	17,000	25,000	
Movie searching browsing categories				
By title	Yes	Yes	Yes	
By actor	Yes	Yes	Yes	
By director	Yes	Yes	Yes	
By genre	Yes	Yes	Yes	
By studio	Yes	Yes	No	
By MPAA rating	No	Yes	Yes	
Coming soon	Yes	Yes	Yes	
Recommended	Yes	Yes	Yes	
AFI top 100	Yes	No	No	
Academy awards	Yes	Yes	No	
Additional features				
Preview trailers	Yes	No	No	
Option to buy	No	Yes	Yes	
Movie ratings	Yes	Yes	Yes	
Movie reviews	Yes	Yes	Yes	
Family editing	No	No	No	
Personalized movie recom.	Yes	No	Yes	

Note: MPAA—Motion Picture Association of America; AFI—American Film Institute.
Source: www.online-dvd-rental-reviews.com, accessed July 2004.

EXHIBIT 9
2004 RENTAL FEE COMPARISON FOR WAL-MART, NETFLIX, AND BLOCKBUSTER

NO. OF MOVIES RENTED	WAL-MART (PRICE/MONTH)	NETFLIX (PRICE/MONTH)	BLOCKBUSTER (PRICE/MONTH)
2	$12.97	$11.99	N/A
3	$17.36	$17.99	$14.99
4	$21.94	N/A	N/A
5	N/A	$29.99	$27.49
8	N/A	$47.99	$37.49

Source: I4U News, "Walmart, Netflix or Blockbuster DVD Rental?" posted by Luigi Lugmayr on June 11, 2003, www.i4u.com/article414.html.

critic said, "I [agreed] that the selections offered by Netflix [were] far superior to Blockbuster. I [could] find just about anything on Netflix; from old GI Joe cartoons to the complete seasons of Alias."[29]

Wal-Mart

Wal-Mart offered its online DVD rental service through Walmart.com. Wal-Mart provided a selection of more than 15,000 DVD titles and subscribers could drop off the DVDs at Wal-Mart stores. Wal-Mart attacked Netflix on Yahoo! and other websites, mainly from a price standpoint. The company also expanded its selection of titles and number of distribution centers. The opening of five new distribution centers in June and July 2004 gave Wal-Mart a total of 14 distribution centers. As Wal-Mart had already processed and shipped DVDs from existing facilities, it hoped the addition of the new distribution centers would reduce delivery times, which averaged between two and five days.[30]

Wal-Mart was not as reliant on online advertising as Netflix. Taking advantage of its widespread presence, Wal-Mart advertised its online DVD rental service to its 100 million weekly retail store shoppers. Wal-Mart also advertised the rental service along with complementary products, such as DVD players, that it sold in its stores.

Despite these apparent advantages, a critic of Wal-Mart explained: "I have tried both. I picked a huge list with

Wal-Mart and nearly every DVD was a very long wait. I sent an email asking why that was and got no response back at all. I am now happily using Netflix. . . . One distribution center in Georgia [was] not enough to service an entire country as large as ours. Netflix use[d] several. . . . I am a Wal-Mart employee. It's a shame I have to use the competition."[31]

Amazon

Amazon.com, Inc. presented a new threat by opening an online DVD rental-by-mail service in the United Kingdom.[32] Expansion into the US market would most likely follow. "Amazon customers have been asking for the service, and we believe we're well-positioned to offer a great customer experience," an Amazon spokeswoman said.[33] However, analyst Michael Pachter of Wedbush Morgan Securities Inc. indicated that Amazon faced the challenges of distance, sales tax, and outsourcing. Increasingly, online retailers were under pressure to collect state sales tax on web transactions if the company operated any stores or distribution centers in the states in which customers purchased items. If Amazon established 30 distribution centers to compete with Netflix, its customers could potentially have to pay state sales tax on all Amazon.com purchases. One possible solution to this problem was to outsource distribution.

Video on demand

Videocassette rentals were expected to decrease as customers continued to favor the improved quality and pricing of DVD technologies. Video rental services, both traditional and Internet-based, were facing several challenging developments. Video on demand (VOD) allowed customers to order movies through their cable service. However, the movie studios, which received 51.8 per cent of movie revenue from home videos, still released film to DVD before VOD.[34] It is interesting to note that this percentage was higher than all the other channels combined. Theater was 23.1 per cent, TV and cable was 14 per cent, premium channels was 9.3 per cent, and VOD/PPV was only 1.8 per cent.

Starz Encore Group and RealNetworks offered unlimited movie downloads for $12.95/month subscriptions.[35] Recent technological advances made this offering attractive. The 2004 Consumer Electronics Show highlighted a new product that placed approximately 300 hours of "near DVD quality" video onto its hard drive. This product, the GMINI series, was a small handheld device capable of recording and playing back movies, TV shows, and digital photos on its screen or on a TV.[36] By 2006, Movielink, owned by the studios themselves, offered the broadest selection of movies through digital download. As digital distribution of movies was not "windowed" to all channels (a practice by studios of releasing movies in different formats at different points in time after the initial screening), Movielink had the advantage over its VOD competitors due to its exclusive rights. However, Movielink's 1,500 titles were less than 4 per cent of the DVD titles owned by Netflix.

NETFLIX COMPARED TO ITS COMPETITORS

In an online discussion thread, feedback from customers who had tried both Netflix and Wal-Mart services provided interesting commentary. They often cited Netflix's large selection of movies; a common point was that Netflix not only stocked sufficient levels of new releases, but also carried titles that were not as popular with the masses and were difficult to find through mainstream outlets. On the contrary, the bulk of Wal-Mart's DVD stock was comprised of new releases and mainstream films. Consumers also generally agreed that Netflix provided better services in terms of distribution. Wal-Mart customers complained it sometimes took four to five days to receive a DVD once the company indicated it was shipped.[37] In contrast, Netflix had overnight delivery to nearly 90 per cent of its subscribers. If a movie did not arrive in the mail and a subscriber complained, Netflix shipped another one and simply asked the subscriber to return the first one if it arrived at a later date. Even though Wal-Mart did not have the distribution center infrastructure to match Netflix, Wal-Mart was still a worrisome competitor by virtue of its sheer size.

CONFRONTING THE COMPETITION

In response to the competition, Netflix increased its marketing campaign. This created rising subscriber acquisition costs as the company committed marketing dollars through online advertising and television commercials. The cost per new trial subscriber was projected to grow from $35.12 in the second quarter of 2004 to between $37 and $39 in the third quarter of 2004 (see Exhibit 10). A 24 hour customer service center was available to subscribers who needed to speak with customer service representatives, which further increased costs.

In September 2004, *Newsweek* magazine reported that Netflix and TiVo were planning to unveil a partnership whereby subscribers of both companies would be able to download Netflix movies over the Internet directly into their TiVo boxes instead of receiving Netflix DVDs by mail.[38] Under the plan, subscribers would have access to unlimited downloads and unlimited DVDs with one subscription. Netflix CEO Reed Hastings predicted that by the end of the decade Netflix would deliver most of its rentals over the Internet, supplanting its distribution centers and patented red envelopes (see Exhibit 11).

GOING FORWARD

In summary, would the competitive strategies that Netflix had put into place keep competitors such as Wal-Mart and Blockbuster at bay? Would Netflix's weakened stock price invite a takeover offer? What about the threat from VOD? There were reasons for skepticism about VOD, as only a small number of TVs were connected to the Internet, most of which were through cable companies. That could

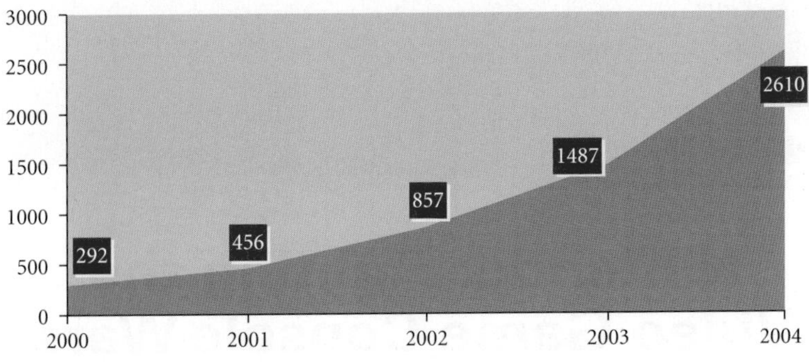

EXHIBIT 10 NETFLIX SUBSCRIBER GROWTH, 2000–2004

Note: Subscribers in thousands.
Source: Netflix 2004 Annual Report.

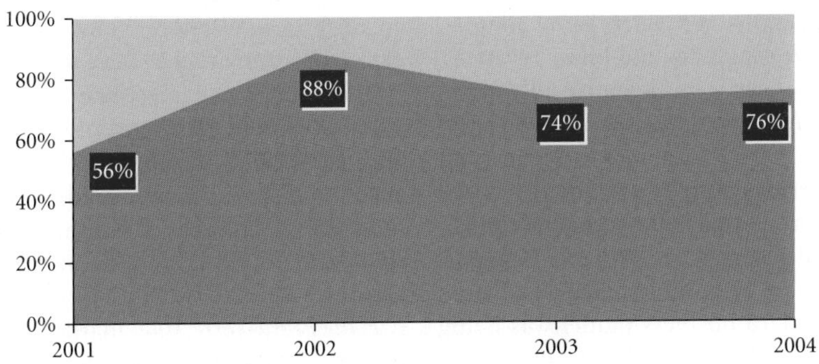

EXHIBIT 11 NETFLIX SUBSCRIBER GROWTH, 2001–2004

Note: Subscriber growth is in percentage increase from previous year.
Source: Netflix 2004 Annual Report.

change with advancements in Wi-Fi-enabled DVD players and future game consoles that would also function as DVD players. However, when DVDs moved to high definition, the download time would increase even with conventional broadband Internet. What would happen if households were equipped with fiber optics? Finally, the movie studios would probably remove digital distribution from the exclusive window and offer it to other vendors by 2010. Were Wal-Mart and Blockbuster really the threat or could Netflix be blindsided by something else?

CASE 22

Nintendo: Fighting the Video Game Console Wars

It was a moment of truth for Nintendo, the video games industry's most iconic company. Despite the recent success of its flagship product, the Wii video game console, Nintendo was facing decreasing sales and lower revenues. The company's hardware sales were down by 10 million units compared to 2009, and software sales were down by 30 million units compared to 2009. Income was in decline, and shares seemed to be in permanent retreat. Nintendo's stock had retreated to levels not seen since the company's mediocre performance before the launch of the Wii (see Figure 1).

Nintendo's problems were taking place at a time when the industry's standard business model was being transformed by online social and mobile gaming—market segments that Nintendo had been slow to enter. For many observers, Nintendo's problems could be traced to Nintendo's conservative management style and incremental innovation policy. Nintendo was still very much a family-owned and managed business. Long time CEO Hiroshi Yamauchi, great-grandson of Nintendo founder Fusajiro Yamauchi, continued the top-down management style that traditionally prevailed in the company. He moved away from day-to-day control of operations when in 2002, Satoru Iwata, until then Head of Corporate Planning, took over as the first ever non-family President in the history of the company.

Iwata went on to successfully turn around Nintendo's fortunes with the Wii console launched in 2006. He was now determined to do it again with the Wii U, Nintendo's next generation video game console. To create maximum buzz, Iwata chose the June 2011 Electronic Entertainment Exposition (E3) in Las Vegas to make the announcement. The game plan was clear: Nintendo was out to remind industry analysts, and through them shareholders, that the Wii U could count on the 87 million owners of Wii consoles to rebuild its market position.

SWIMMING UPRIVER

The company behind some of contemporary entertainment's most famous fictional characters such as *Mario* and *Donkey Kong* began life as a playing cards company in Japan in 1889. When Hiroshi Yamauchi took over presidency from his great-grandfather Fusajiro Yamauchi in 1949, Nintendo moved from playing cards to electronic toys to handheld gaming devices (*Game & Watch*) and arcade games (*Donkey Kong*) before entering the video game console market in the early 1980s.

American companies such as Coleceo and Atari dominated the video game console industry in the late 1970s and early 1980s, producing the first, and then second, generation of video game hardware. By 1983 however, the industry was in crisis. An influx of new video game consoles with poor quality, questionable publishing practices, and the commercial failure of movie tie-in games such as *E.T. the Extra-Terrestrial*, marketed by Atari, led to the loss of consumer trust and consequently the collapse of sales.

It was against this background that Nintendo released its 8-bit cartridge-based Nintendo Entertainment System (NES) video game console in 1983, first in Japan, and two years later in the US. Almost immediately, sales of the NES took off in Japan, but success in the US was much harder to achieve. The 1983 sales crash was still vivid in the memory of distributors, retailers, and most importantly, consumers. As the first company to launch new hardware after the crash, Nintendo faced an uphill struggle. Nintendo had to rebrand the NES twice, sell the console to retailers on a consignment basis, and spend $5 million dollars on marketing during launch in the New York area alone. To reassure retailers that unlike many other console makers that went out of business, Nintendo was here to stay, the company also offered buy-back guarantees for its products. Gradually retailers started stocking and eventually selling the new video game console. The efforts paid off, not only for Nintendo, but also for the infant industry that had been struggling under adverse publicity and consumer skepticism.

Nintendo's NES differentiated itself from the home computer industry by innovative controller design and processing chip utilization that delivered exceptionally sharp graphics. However, these advantages were soon challenged by the 1986 introduction of the Sega Master System

---

This case was prepared by Joost Rietveld, Cass Business School, under the supervision of Professor Joseph Lampel, Cass Business School.

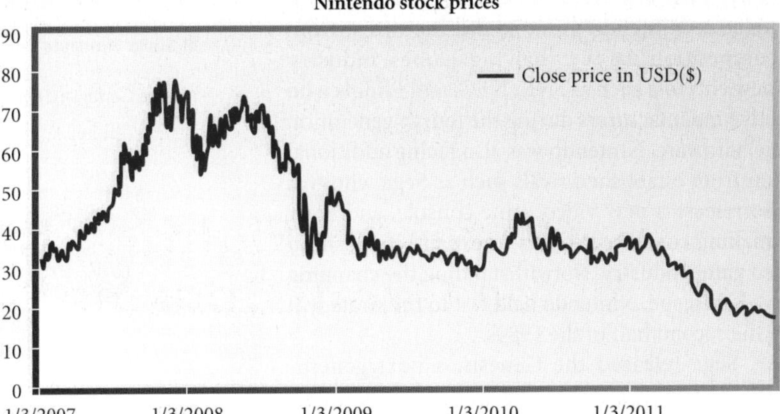

FIGURE 1 NINTENDO'S STOCK PRICE ($) IN THE PERIOD JANUARY 1, 2007–DECEMBER 30, 2011

in the US. Sega's console imitated NES's controller design, but used a processing chip that was twice as powerful. The company was no stranger to the video games industry, having been active both in the Japanese coin-op arcades and the video game console markets.

Sega's Master System challenged Nintendo in the hardware market. However, contrary to other hardware manufacturers, Nintendo considered hardware as less important than software. The company put software development at the top of its agenda, whereas, to quote the company's president Hiroshi Yamauchi, hardware was a "necessary evil"—necessary for delivering superior software performance, but not Nintendo's main business. Putting software first meant drawing on Japan's longstanding tradition in animation to create visually appealing games. Employees with a background in art and animation, rather than engineering, as was common in the US, allowed Nintendo to differentiate itself by focusing on character and plotline development. This led to iconic video game franchises such as "*The Legend of Zelda* (1987)," "*Metroid* (1986)," and "*Mike Tyson's Punch Out* (1987)," games that sold in excess of a million cartridges and with highly profitable sequel spin-offs.

Nintendo further consolidated its strong software library by forging exclusive partnerships with Japanese software developers such as Bandai, Capcom, Hudson, Konami, and Taito. The company set a maximum amount of five games published per year for each publisher, in addition to imposing a two-year exclusivity clause that prevented the release of games on other platforms. Nintendo also set minimum quantity production orders for cartridges. With these restrictions the company was signaling to game publishers that they are expected to meet consumer quality expectations if they wish to do business with Nintendo. However, while the new policies delivered better quality, they also led to discontent among game publishers who chafed under Nintendo's restrictive licensing practices.

The period between 1986 and 1991 marked an era in which Nintendo further refined its business practices. To protect its video game consoles against unlicensed publishing practices, Nintendo prohibited production of cartridges by companies other than itself. Starting in 1991 Nintendo also discontinued working with its distributor, Mattel, deciding instead to bring in-house all marketing and distribution activities. External software development support for Nintendo's system increased as game publishers were attracted to the console's growing customer base. To retain consumer interest, Nintendo launched *Nintendo Power,* a magazine aimed at young consumers, which at its peak had 4 million subscribers. This customer loyalty program paid off handsomely for the company as it used the publication as a vehicle for product announcements and advertisements. Total console sales for the NES reached 61.91 million NES units worldwide. By 1989, Nintendo was generating ¥34,271 million ($446 million) in profits. In the third generation video game consoles, Nintendo attained an 83% worldwide market share, largely due to its exceptional in-house game design capabilities, and strong alliances with external game development companies (see Figure 2).

3rd generation (74,910,000 units)

■ Nintendo Entertainment System (NES) (1985)

■ Sega Master System (SMS) (1986)

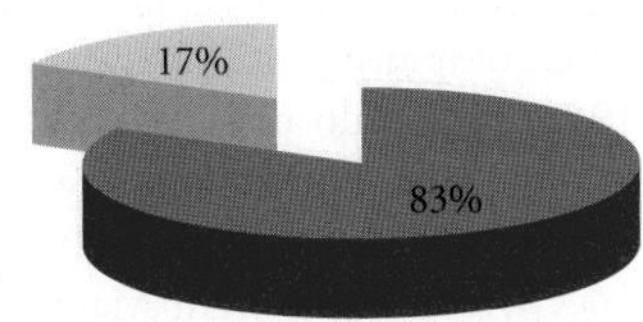

FIGURE 2 MARKET SHARES FOR VIDEO GAME CONSOLES, THIRD GENERATION HARDWARE

JOCKEYING FOR POSITION

As confidence at Nintendo grew, so did the threat from outside competition as the thriving games industry attracted new entrants such as SNK, NEC, and Philips who became active manufacturers during the fourth generation video game hardware. Nintendo was also facing additional competition from established rivals such as Sega who was planning to release a new video game console, and Sony who was making concerted efforts to expand its position in the video game industry. Notwithstanding the changing competitive landscape, Nintendo held fast to the strategy it set during the second half of the 1980s.

In 1989, Sega released the Genesis, a next generation 16-bit video game console that was more than four times as powerful as Nintendo's 8-bit NES console. Sega also made its Genesis console backward compatible, i.e. its users could switch to the new console without making their existing games collection obsolete. Additionally, Sega successfully imitated Nintendo's game development strategy by establishing alliances with external developers, and developing iconic games in-house such as "Sonic The Hedgehog." Sonic The Hedgehog for the Genesis sold over 15 million copies and the franchise still is Sega's best-selling franchise to date.

Nintendo was slow to respond to Sega's challenge. Riding on the success of the NES, Nintendo delayed releasing a successor to the NES until 1991, out of fear of cannibalizing its own market. When Nintendo released the SNES, the new video game console lacked the backward compatibility that made older games playable on the new system. Nintendo watched its market leadership slipping away as Sega's Genesis sales kept rising, fueled by a strong line-up of games.

What turned the tide for the company was the release of the bestseller game *Donkey Kong Country* in 1994. The technically superior game was based on one of Nintendo's iconic franchises from its NES heyday. The release marked a turning point for Nintendo's fortunes. The company recaptured market leadership in the important American and Japanese markets and in most of the European countries. After *Donkey Kong Country*'s release, SNES console sales rose dramatically, accumulating 49 million units worldwide by comparison to Sega's 28.5 million Genesis console units. This reversal of fortunes was especially significant in the US where Sega only managed to obtain a market share of 37%, whereas Nintendo essentially captured the remaining 63% (see Figure 3).

4th generation (77,640,000 units)

■ Super Nintendo Entertainment System (SNES) (1991)

■ Sega Genesis (GEN) [Mega Drive] (1989)

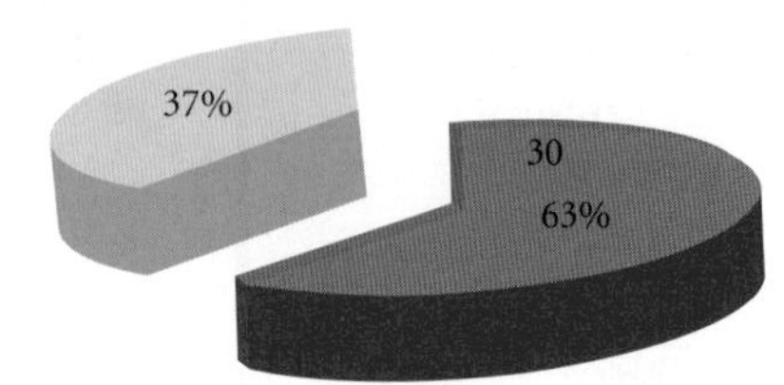

FIGURE 3 MARKET SHARES FOR VIDEO GAME CONSOLES, FOURTH GENERATION HARDWARE

Although Nintendo was rapidly regaining its former strength, the company was not resting on its laurels. In January 1989, Nintendo concluded a strategic partnership with Sony aimed at developing a CD-ROM-based add-on for the SNES. Sony was already a component supplier, or Official Equipment Manufacturer (OEM) to Nintendo, providing the sound chip for the SNES. By 1991 negotiations on a cross-compatible CD-based console project had reached a critical stage. The two sides agreed that Nintendo would secure technical compatibility with a Sony CD-ROM peripheral for its SNES console. For its part Sony would produce its own console, code-named Play Station. The Play Station was expected to play technically and graphically advanced CD-ROM games, on top of SNES cartridge-based games. In a break with past practice, Nintendo allowed Sony to retain licensing rights and publishing profits derived from all CD-ROM games, regardless of platform.

Nintendo's concessions made this agreement irresistibly attractive to Sony. Reflecting back on the deal, Ken Kutaragi, Sony's director responsible for the Play Station project, emphasized the magnitude of the opportunity:

> We could join forces with the best-performing company in the field. We would sell them our technology, establish a track-record, and use that as the springboard to future success[1]

Sony announced the joint venture with Nintendo during the 1991 Consumer Electronics Show in Chicago. The very next day one of Sony's main rivals, Philips, unexpectedly made a similar announcement claiming that it too was developing a CD-ROM peripheral for Nintendo's SNES console. Nintendo would support Philips' CDi system with licensed software from Nintendo's library of successful franchises. The deal with Philips differed from the one that Nintendo had concluded with Sony in that Nintendo would retain licensing rights for the disk-based video games.

By the time the Nintendo–Philips alliance was announced, the Nintendo–Sony relationship was no longer in the cards. Nintendo discontinued negotiation with Sony, much to the dismay of Sony who made every effort to revive the contract. Finally, by 1992, Sony decided to go it alone, using proprietary technology to develop its own video game console. Nintendo's partnership with Philips, on the other hand, was subsequently abandoned. The disk-based peripheral for SNES was never launched, and Philips' CDi system, lacking SNES compatibility altogether, was a commercial failure.

Having called off one alliance, and been disappointed in another, Nintendo decided to go it alone. Discontinuing disk-based hardware development, Nintendo instead released its third cartridge-based video game console, the N64, in 1996. It was not until 2001, more than ten years after the agreements with Sony and Philips, and long after the other competitor, Sega, had released CD add-ons to its consoles, that Nintendo released a disk-based video game console. Consequently, Nintendo was now trailing far behind old rival Sega, and the newly arrived competitor, Sony. Nintendo's technological disadvantage put off consumers who wanted the latest technology in their video game consoles. It also affected relationships with the company's longstanding software suppliers who were increasingly critical of Nintendo's lack of innovation.

While Nintendo focused on incremental innovation, Sony used 3D graphics and disk-based game distribution as a springboard to change the market. Sony managed to convince game publishers to supply Sony with quality content by offering technically superior hardware. Equally important, Sony offered less-restrictive terms, and developed a more mutually beneficial business model for software distribution. No longer did game publishers need to give up exclusivity for their content, and the up-front investment required for producing CDs was much lower than cartridge production. As a result, many long-term Nintendo licensees, among them Namco, Square, Enix, and Konami, moved over to Sony, publishing numerous hit products on the PlayStation platform. In an ironic reversal of fortunes, Sony, who five years earlier was snubbed by Nintendo, had gone from being a Nintendo component supplier to becoming its main rival.

Nintendo had traditionally positioned its consoles as toys, targeting primarily children and adolescents. Sony by contrast saw the PlayStation console as targeting "young adults," between 21 and 29, who spend heavily on entertainment. This paid off for Sony's PlayStation, which became the best-selling video game console with over 102 million units sold. By contrast, despite the growing market for video games, Nintendo lagged far behind. The N64 console sold fewer than 33 million hardware units during its lifetime. Only 225 million games were sold on the N64 platform, less than half of the games sold on the NES console. Sony now had 71% of the market, while Nintendo was far behind with 23% market share in the fifth generation video game consoles (see Figure 4).

Nintendo seemed to be in inexorable decline. By the time the firm released the Nintendo GameCube, its own disk-based video game console in 2001, developers had overwhelmingly switched to Sony, and new entrant Microsoft, who had launched its Xbox console late 2001 in the US. To make matters worse, GameCube lacked technically innovative hardware design, and according to industry experts was confusingly marketed without communicating a clear-value proposition to consumers. GameCube sold just over 21 million units, making it Nintendo's worst-selling consoles. Sony, on the other hand, reinforced its market position with the backward compatible, DVD enabled, PlayStation 2. The console sold 150 million units, by far the best-selling game console in the video games industry to date. This pushed Nintendo's market share in the sixth generation video game consoles to 11%, in marked contrast with Sony's 73% market share (see Figure 5).

While the console market had grown 275% since the NES era, GameCube sales were only a third of Nintendo's first console, and accumulated software sales were less than half compared to NES' game sales. Operating profits had not increased since 1993, and stock growth was sluggish. For Nintendo's top management it became increasingly clear that the company needed to overhaul its strategy if it wished to stay in the home console business.

THE COMEBACK

In May 2002, Satoru Iwata, until then Head of Corporate Planning, took over as the first ever nonfamily President in the history of the company. Iwata was a recent arrival at Nintendo. Originally from Nintendo's long-time software partner HAL Laboratory, Iwata had plenty of opportunities

5th generation (144,230,000 units)

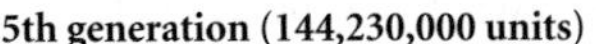

Nintendo 64 (N64) (1996)
Sony PlayStation (PSone) (1995)
Sega Saturn (SAT) (1995)

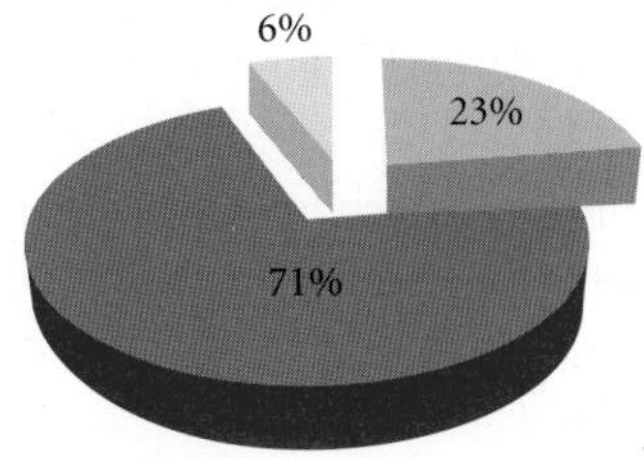

FIGURE 4 MARKET SHARES FOR VIDEO GAME CONSOLES, FIFTH GENERATION HARDWARE

6th generation (204,510,000 units)

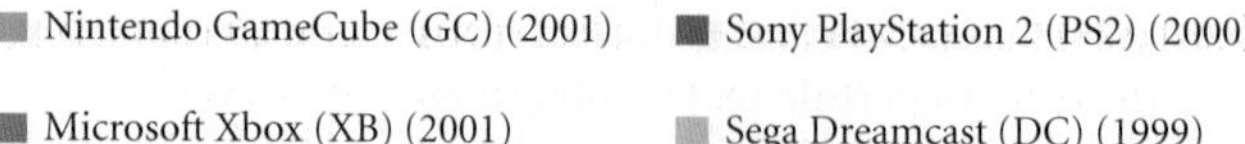

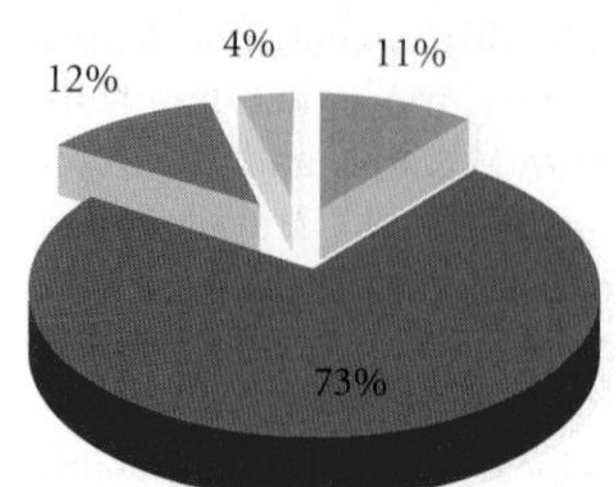

FIGURE 5
MARKET SHARES FOR VIDEO GAME CONSOLES, SIXTH GENERATION HARDWARE

to observe Nintendo's decision making at close quarters. Upon assuming the presidency, he set about changing the traditional top-down management style of the company. Reflecting on the magnitude of the challenge facing Iwata, Nintendo's Creative Director, and creator of game franchises such as *Mario, Zelda,* and *Donkey Kong,* Shigeru Miyamoto had this to say about the changes that the new president was effecting:

> . . . in a sense, Nintendo's history had always been dictated by the single person at the top, and there were aspects of that tendency that were rather stuffy. But Iwata coming in with his outsider's perspective improved the ventilation, so to speak, and I get the feeling that the employees' understanding of management's policies became much deeper thanks to that.[2]

Iwata wanted to extend gaming to a wider population, just as the NES and PlayStation consoles had done before, by adopting what he called "Gaming for Everyone." Achieving this goal required the development of game consoles that were easy to use and offered entertainment value for everyone in the family. Before implementing the new strategy to a video game console, the "Gaming for Everyone" strategy was tested on Nintendo's next generation handheld device, the Nintendo DS, which was released in 2004.

Development of the DS coincided with Iwata's focus on decreasing the boundaries between the hardware design and software design departments. The goal, as creative Director Shigeru Miyamoto put it, was to encourage greater involvement of software development teams in hardware design decisions:

> Collaboration between the hardware teams and software teams became much stronger once we started to do the DS. I'd always thought of that as a strength of ours, but it was really with the DS that the company started to move.[3]

The DS project marked a return to Nintendo's former role as industry leader. The DS quickly became the best-selling handheld gaming device in the history of the video games industry, selling over 147 million units and 851 million games, cumulatively. Nintendo's "Gaming for Everyone" strategy is illustrated by the DS' software line-up. The DS reached out to women and younger kids with accessible titles such as the brain training game, *Brain Age* (18.96 million units sold), and virtual pet, *Nintendogs* (23.64 million units sold).

Whereas innovation in the video game console market traditionally revolved around graphical prowess, for its latest video game console Nintendo concentrated its R&D efforts around off-screen innovation. The resulting console, the Nintendo Wii, was designed around controller-centric innovation using motion sensitive technology to control games rather than player input via buttons. Nintendo set itself apart from main competitors Sony and Microsoft who focused their efforts on on-screen improvements in an arms race for the best graphics. Nintendo's game development divisions were put to work to create a series of games representing real-life pastime activities (including running, bowling, boxing, and golfing), which supported and utilized the console's motion-sensitive remote-like controller.

Despite a year's head start for Microsoft's Xbox 360 console, Nintendo's Wii quickly regained market leadership over Microsoft, selling over 87 million units and 729.53 million games by the end of 2011. Wii's success is underpinned by a strong software line-up of accessible games that mimic pastime activities utilizing the motion-sensitive controller. Nintendo's *Wii Sports* sold 76.76 million copies, *Wii Play* sold 28 million copies, and *Wii Fit* sold 22.67 million copies. All of these games target consumers that were not traditionally considered as part of the gaming market. Nintendo's digital strategy of selling back-log video games from previous generations as paid-for downloads proved successful too. By early 2008, roughly a year after Wii's market introduction, Nintendo had sold over 16 million digital games. The impact on Nintendo's market share and financial performance was dramatic. The company's market share surged to 45% in the seventh-generation video game consoles, while Sony's share fell to 27% (see Figure 6). Likewise, profits rose sharply, reaching ¥279,089 million ($3,645 million) in 2009.

In response to Nintendo's success, Sony and Microsoft gradually followed suit, applying Nintendo's strategies to their own consoles. Microsoft's motion-sensitive Kinect peripheral sold over 10 million units within half a year of its release in 2010. For its part, Sony's rerelease of its PlayStation 2 console with updated graphics, under the *HD collection* label, has been positively received by consumers. This has allowed Sony to reinvigorate sales of its *God of War, Tomb Raider,* and *Metal Gear Solid* franchises in HD on the PlayStation 3. Ironically, however, while Microsoft and Sony were successfully deploying a similar strategy as Nintendo's, i.e. targeting "new" audiences and rereleasing games from their backlog catalogs, Nintendo's biggest threat was coming not from familiar rivals but from new entrants.

LOOKING TO THE FUTURE

The video game console was the foundation of Nintendo's video game strategy. However, as technologically advanced mobile phones and tablet devices were becoming an increasingly effective means for distributing video games, the company faced competition from new entrants such as Apple and Facebook. These companies could use these new distribution channels, and their large customer base, to outflank companies such as Nintendo who relied heavily on consoles to defend their market position. In 2008, Apple created a viable platform for games on its mobile operating system (iOS). Within a year, Apple was selling approximately 5 million games every day on the mobile App store to a customer base of 63 million gamers. The challenge to the video console became even more direct after Apple introduced the iPad. With over 55 million units sold, and 90,000 dedicated applications, the Apple iPad is a threat that Nintendo cannot ignore. At the same time, Facebook's social gaming platform launched in 2007 proved wildly successful with the company's 800 million active customer base. One out of four users visits the social network for gaming purposes.

The popularity of these emerging markets for gaming has come at the expense of growth in the traditional console games market. Nintendo's Wii year-to-date sales figures are down 11% for hardware and 21% for software. For the first time since entering the video game console market, Nintendo is projecting an operating loss for the financial year ending March 31, 2012 (see Figure 7). Nintendo is seeing its customers migrating to the Apple and Facebook platforms. But what is of greater concern in the long run is the trend among game developers and publishers to focus on mobile and social games—a move that threatens to starve Nintendo of the new games it needs to keep customers buying new consoles (see Figure 8).

Plunging sales, and the advent of Facebook's and Apple's gaming platforms, have led to investors rapidly losing trust in Nintendo's ability of replicating its unprecedented performance with its next generation gaming devices. As share prices hit a five-year low, Iwata confronts pressures to move into the rapidly expanding mobile and social gaming markets. But abandoning hardware production for game distribution on third-party platforms goes against Nintendo's long tradition of joint production of gaming devices and software.

It was against this background that Nintendo announced a special investor event shortly after the E3 2011 conference. Nintendo's creative director, Shigeru Miyamoto, took the stage at the event on September 13th in Japan. Miyamoto was intent in dispelling perception that the Wii was losing out to social gaming platforms. Showcasing the console's swansong, "*The Legend of Zelda: Skyward Sword,*" was meant to signal Nintendo's commitment to the Wii. Subsequently, an impressive list of internally developed games based on Nintendo's hit franchises was announced. While the scope of the announcements was "unprecedented," the absence of Nintendo's popular franchises on the Apple and Facebook platforms left industry analysts and shareholders alike unimpressed. In the days that followed, Nintendo's share declined further.

7th generation (195,720,000 units)

■ Nintendo Wii (Wii) (2006) ■ Microsoft Xbox 360 (X360) (2005)

■ Sony PlayStation 3 (PS3) (2007)

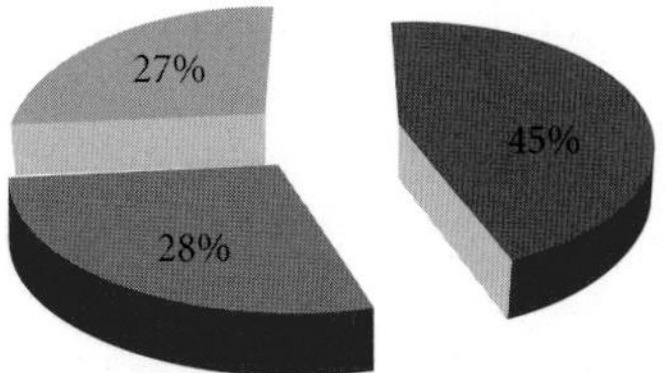

FIGURE 6
MARKET SHARES FOR VIDEO GAME CONSOLES, SEVENTH GENERATION HARDWARE

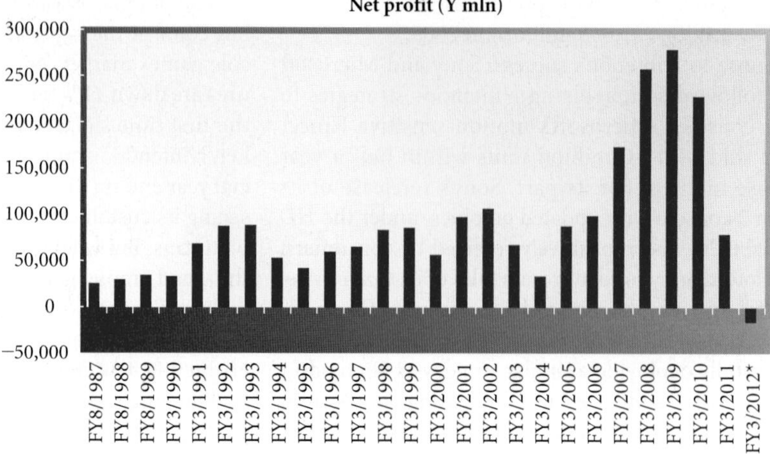

FIGURE 7 NINTENDO'S NET PROFIT (IN MILLION YEN) IN THE PERIOD 1987–2012

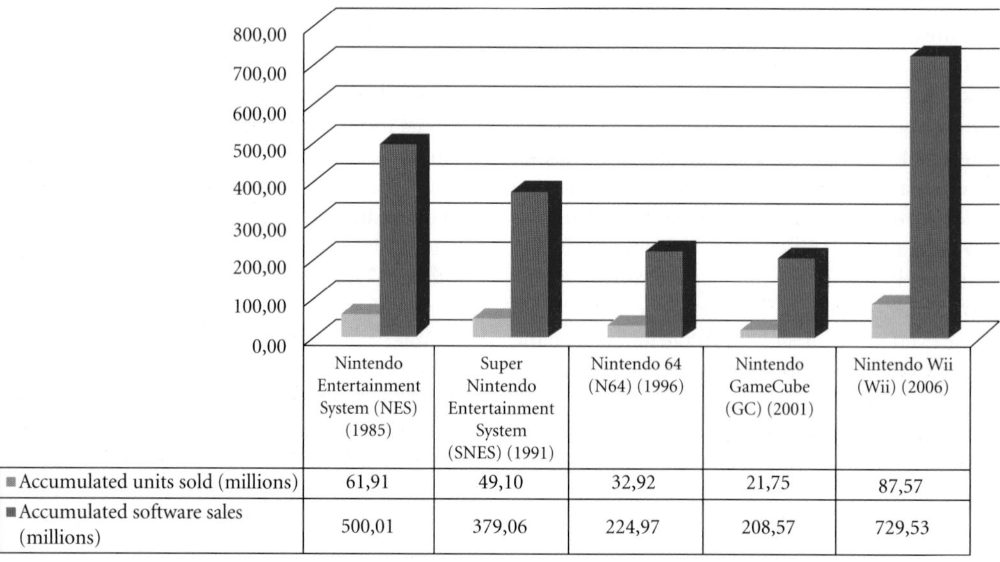

	Nintendo Entertainment System (NES) (1985)	Super Nintendo Entertainment System (SNES) (1991)	Nintendo 64 (N64) (1996)	Nintendo GameCube (GC) (2001)	Nintendo Wii (Wii) (2006)
■ Accumulated units sold (millions)	61,91	49,10	32,92	21,75	87,57
■ Accumulated software sales (millions)	500,01	379,06	224,97	208,57	729,53

FIGURE 8 HARDWARE–SOFTWARE RATIOS FOR NINTENDO VIDEO GAME CONSOLES

REFERENCES

Asakura, R. 2000. *Revolutionaries at Sony: The Making of the Sony PlayStation and the Visionaries Who Conquered the World of Video Games*. McGraw-Hill, New York.

Inoue, O. 2010. *Nintendo Magic: Winning the Videogame Wars*. Vertical, Inc., New York.

Kent, S.L. 2001. *The Ultimate History of Video Games: From Pong to Pokémon and Beyond - The Story Behind the Craze that Touched Our Lives and Changed the World*. Three Rivers Press, New York.

CASE 23

Wipro Consulting Services in 2008: Building an Optimal Global Configuration in Business and IT Consulting Industry

As the Wipro Consulting Services (WCS) board met at Wipro Headquarters in Bangalore, India, in December 2008, to review the progress the consulting division had made since being set up in June 2008, T.K. Kurien, president of WCS, commenced his address by setting out the exciting pathway for WCS:

> Innovation remains a key focus for companies seeking to spur growth, and delivering innovation is our fundamental value proposition. Built on a combination of process excellence, quality frameworks and service delivery innovation, we are seeing exceptional demand for our consulting expertise. Our customers are now asking for higher-level advisory services to complement our world-class IT and BPO services. WCS is thus uniquely positioned to help clients in setting the agenda for strategic cost reduction, capital efficiency, and improve customer experience in transformation-related programs.

Sitting next to Kurien was Kirk Strawser who had joined WCS early during that week as its global head of consulting services from Capgemini consulting. Having listened to Kurien and other speakers, he then spoke out, striking a note of caution:

> Innovation on its own is not sufficient. We need to do a number of things before we get there. First we need to emphasize our cost leadership. Clients want industry specific, integrated solutions (Consulting, IT, Product Engineering, BPO) delivered using innovative, accelerated approaches that drive measurable improvements in critical metrics such as free cash flow and return on equity. Second we need to really work on our global delivery capability. We need to start hiring young bright MBA graduates from top Indian business schools, train them as analysts for a year in India by assigning them to the consulting team and then rotate them globally on live engagements. Third we need to start engaging with potential customers who have no transactional history with the Wipro Technologies.

The technology consulting business which had started as a strategic initiative within Wipro Technologies eight years ago in the backdrop of 2001. IT slowdown had now matured into a thriving business. To fully take advantage of the opportunities this sector had to offer, Wipro had set up WCS as a dedicated organization with its own structure. But to become a business leader in technology consulting, WCS needed to go further. It needed the independence and strategic focus that come from operating as a separate unit within Wipro, while at the same time taking advantage of its parent's prowess in technology and impressive customer base.

How far could the WCS leadership go in developing its own identity, committing resources to scale up, and developing its own model for global delivery? WCS leadership had their plates overflowing in that meeting and everyone knew that the time was running out and they needed to act and act fast!!

ORGANIZATION OVERVIEW

Wipro Technologies Ltd

Wipro Technologies Ltd (parent organization of Wipro Consulting Services), headquartered in Bangalore, India, employed 95,000+ people across 50+ offices spread across the globe. The services offered by Wipro Technologies were aligned to various industry domains such as banking and insurance, embedded systems, enterprise applications, networking, telecom solutions, and web-based applications, and categorized into the following four broad areas:

- *IT Services:* Wipro IT services serve the IT needs of the entire business value chain. It offers services ranging from business intelligence, service-oriented architecture, enterprise applications (CRM, ERP, SCM), and quality consulting to industries ranging from automotive electronics, finance to medical devices.
- *Product Engineering Services (PES):* Wipro is the largest independent provider of R&D services in the world. Using the "Extended Engineering" model for leveraging R&D investment and accessing new knowledge and experience across the globe, people, and technical infrastructure, Wipro helps firms to introduce new

This case was prepared by Joseph Lampel, Ajay Bhalla, and Kaivalya Vishnu © 2011.

products rapidly. Wipro PES business had 14 Centres of Excellence (CoE) in domains such as grid computing, wireless network devices, automotive infotainment, and gaming and animation.

- *Technology Infrastructure Services (TIS):* TIS provides global remote infrastructure services such as infrastructure consulting, system integration, data center management, IT help desk services, IT infrastructure security services, remote management, and telecom infrastructure services for customers spread across the globe. TIS set up the world's first Global Command Centre (GCC) in 2002 to provide remote monitoring and management services based on customer-specific service level agreements (SLAs) to manage customers' IT infrastructure.
- *Business Process Outsourcing (BPO):* Wipro's BPO service offerings include business process re-engineering, integrating technology with BPO, and knowledge services. Wipro emerged as one of the largest BPO providers when it acquired Spectramind in 2002. In 2008, it had over 19,000 people operating out of 9 different locations globally. It delivers process-specific solutions in areas like finance and accounting, HR, loyalty, and knowledge services to customers in various industries including banking, insurance, travel, telecom, and health care.

Wipro Consulting Services

WCS as an independent consulting organization was formally formed in 2007–2008 to provide a range of consulting services including *Business Process Consulting, Technology Consulting,* and *Quality Consulting* across several industry verticals. These services were centered on the theme of providing consulting based on practical business and technology frameworks that helped organizations craft a vision for their business. By the end of 2008, WCS employed approximately 1,200+ people across three geographic areas—EU, North America, and JIMEA (Japan, India, Middle East, and Asia)—and had revenues in excess of $100 million.WCS actively positioned itself as a leading consulting organization in the following key consulting practice areas:

- Strategic business consulting services, which focused on enhancing business performance of its clients by streamlining processes, reducing organizational risk, and leveraging the global sourcing/outsourcing organizational model
- Business process consulting practice, which had a set of targeted offerings that encompassed an entire gamut of operations and technology needs of an enterprise
- Business process improvement, enterprise application package selection, business case for technology investment/outsourcing, and IT strategy
- Quality consulting that endeavored to improve IT value and IT governance for customers, using custom built process solutions, giving customers a 360-degree all round solution to address all their process needs
- The technology management service, which helped clients in improving the alignment of business and technology through efficient business processes, thereby helping them to reduce cost and enhance business value of IT

INDUSTRY LANDSCAPE: AN OVERVIEW

Wipro Technologies competed with technology service providers, which were categorized in the following two broad categories:

- "Global" players that included firms like IBM, Accenture, EDS, HP, and Cap Gemini. These firms occupied more than 90% of the global consulting market. They used the resource and cost advantage of their offshore presence in countries like India, the Philippines, Russia, and Eastern Europe to reinforce their global dominance.
- "Indian" players that included firms like TCS, Infosys, Wipro, HCL, Cognizant, and Satyam. These firms had started their operations as low-cost IT service providers and then branched into consulting to position themselves as end-to-end technology service providers by adopting practices like "global delivery models," "service integration," and "technology rationalization."

Leading "global" players

IBM business consulting service IBM, one of the biggest and most well-established consulting companies, had a large global presence with significant depth and breadth of skills and services. The company's major operations comprised a global services segment (which included business consulting services), a systems and technology group, a personal systems group, a software segment, a global financing segment, and an enterprise investment segment. IBM leveraged global delivery through offshore delivery centers. The firm had three primary offshore hubs located in India, Brazil, and China that offered significant scale in application services. Based on the skills required, these primary delivery centers in-turn channeled offshore work to centers located in secondary locations in Mexico, Belarus, the Philippines, Romania, and Argentina. Given the scale of its global operations, IBM faced challenges in integrating its global delivery approach across all its practices and reducing complexity in using appropriate sales channels to drive work to its global delivery in some markets.

For the fiscal year ended December 31, 2007, IBM's services revenue increased by 12% to $54 billion. IBM's business consulting services had roughly 80,000+ consultants located across the world.

Accenture By the end of 2008, Accenture, a management consulting, technology services, and outsourcing organization with headquarters in New York, had more than 110 offices in 48 countries including service operations in India, the Philippines, Spain, China, the Czech

Republic, Slovakia, Brazil, and Australia. The company's business was structured around five operating groups that comprised 17 industry groups serving clients across the world. The company's offerings included discrete project services and long-term outsourcing contracts for carrying out ongoing maintenance and management for large multinational firms. Accenture's consulting services included strategy and business architecture, customer relationship management, finance and performance management, human performance, learning procurement, and supply chain management.

Accenture claimed it possessed world-class industry and process depth on front-end projects while maintaining low-cost destinations globally, beyond India. The firm had longstanding client relationships, a strong brand, depth and breadth of expertise, and capital resources. For the year ending August 31, 2007, Accenture revenue rose by 13% to approximately $16 billion.

Cap Gemini Cap Gemini was headquartered in Paris, France, and operated in 36 countries with more than 80,000 employees. Its service offerings were divided along the four service lines: consulting services, technology services, outsourcing services, and local professional services. It promoted its key strengths in developing IT strategy and managing technology-related change programs. It had built business consulting practices in the areas of marketing and sales, finance and HR transformation, supply chain management, and IT-enabled transformation consulting.

For the year ending 2007, Cap Gemini's consolidated revenue was €8,703 million out of which 8.7% was from purely business consulting services and 36% came from technology-related consulting services.

Leading "Indian" players

Tata Consultancy Services Tata Consultancy Services (TCS), headquartered in Mumbai, India, and a subsidiary of the Tata group, was the largest offshore IT service provider in India. TCS commenced operations in 1968 and had leveraged the offshore model for more than 30 years. TCS had global service delivery locations in Hungary, Brazil, Uruguay, and China. In addition to consulting, TCS offered IT services, asset-based solutions (e.g., FIG and Quartz software for the banking and financial services industry), IT infrastructure (e.g., complete outsourcing of IT networks), engineering and industrial services, and BPO solutions for large multinational clients. TCS went public in 2004.

TCS derived much of its strength from a partnering relationship it had built with various system integrators and technology product companies. TCS had performed consulting work on an ad hoc opportunistic basis for many years, but only recently established a consulting strategy and created a Global Consulting business unit in 2004. TCS employed about 120,000 employees and had offices in more than 40 countries. TCS's parent firm Tata group was made up of 90 companies and the group accounted for more than 3% of India's GDP.

Infosys Infosys Technologies was started in 1981 and by the end of 2008 was a US$4-billion company. Infosys defined, designed, and delivered a complete range of IT-enabled business solutions to 2,000+ global customers. Infosys' service offerings spanned business and technology consulting, application services, systems integration, product engineering, custom software development, maintenance, reengineering, independent testing and validation services, IT infrastructure services, and BPO solutions. It had over 100,000 employees, and had built a global footprint with over 50 offices and had offshore development centers in locations other than India, such as China, Australia, the Czech Republic, Poland, the UK, Canada, and Japan. Infosys leveraged existing customers and took pride in building strategic long-term client relationships which was demonstrated by the fact that over 97% of its revenues came from existing customers. The firm had pioneered the Global Delivery Model (GDM), which had contributed to the rise of offshore outsourcing. The GDM was based on the principle of taking work to the location where the best talent was available, where it made the best economic sense, with the least amount of acceptable risk.

Infosys launched its consulting division "Infosys Consulting (IC)" as a wholly owned US subsidiary in April 2004 and employed about 1,500+ employees. IC had applied the GDM model to integrate the business consulting and technology implementation lifecycle. Called the 1-1-3 model, it gave the client one IC resource onsite, one Infosys Technologies resource onsite, and three Infosys Technologies resources offshore (in India or other Infosys offshore centers in China, Australia, Mauritius, Czech Republic).

EVOLUTION OF WCS

In the period 2002–2008, Wipro Technologies underwent massive transformation at various levels of the organization. It had grown from a medium-size IT offshore company into an amorphous organization consisting of several business units which provided a range of services spanning from low-end application development to high-end R&D and consulting services.

Two distinct business propositions coexisted, and were embedded within various business units. First, Wipro competed in highly competitive transactional services such as BPO. It had invested heavily to be one of the top three offshore BPO service providers. In parallel, Wipro was pushing forward in positioning the firm as a high value-added independent R&D services provider. The firm had invested in building 55+ "Centers of Excellence" that created solutions around specific needs of industries such as automotive, financial services, telecommunications, and health care.

WCS management had recognized that the prevailing organization structure in 2006 (see Exhibit 3) was highly fragmented and there were cases when various regional practices and business units, instead of complementing each other, appeared to compete against each other. This combined with ad hoc vertical alignment and lack of cohesion with customer accounts was giving rise to internal tension that threatened the organizational alignments. The management believed a new organizational structure, which could consolidate the overlapping capabilities and restore the internal alignments, was very much needed.

The consulting capability had evolved from a small business start-up in 2001, offering services to regional clients, into an organization which by the end of 2008 was aiming to compete head-on with large industry players like IBM and Accenture. The eight years of this sheer hard work and commitment had seen Wipro's consulting business grow from less than 100 consultants to a more than 1,200-strong global organization which in 2008 did business in the region of $100 million. The growth in terms of timeline is illustrated in Figure 1.

The following three phases illustrate the evolution of WCS:

1. The **incubation** phase that began during the slowdown in the IT spending period of 2000/01. This was the first time period when Wipro leadership saw the first signs of consulting competencies emerging out of horizontal business units and it consciously decided to actively nourish and encourage this emergence.
2. The **bubbling** and **collaboration** phase from 2002 to 2006 which saw the emergence of various bubbles of competencies which encouraged Wipro's horizontal business units to collaborate with each other to provide value-added consulting and advisory services to the universe of Wipro customers (Wipro used the term "universe of customers" internally to refer to all its customers spanning across various business units within Wipro Technologies, ranging from BPO to IT Services).
3. **Organizational design** phase, which began in late 2006 and culminated in early 2008 with the formal launch of Wipro Consulting Services (WCS) as a separate organization. In this phase Wipro's leadership embarked on the process of consolidating the emerged consulting bubbles in various business units like Wipro InfoTech, Quality Consulting Group, Wipro Consulting Group, etc. The objective of the eventual separation of the consulting business from IT services business took place.

The incubation phase

Back in 2001–2002 the bursting of the dot-com bubble and the attack on September 11 brought the IT boom to a virtual halt. Clients no longer latched onto new technologies, or welcomed upgrades. Instead, they were more inclined to adopt a wait-and-see attitude, investing only when IT could be shown to have clear benefits for business outcomes.

To counter the resulting downturn, leading IT service providers began to explore a range of strategic options, such as moving up the value chain, and using their expertise into taking up a more strategic role in helping their customers to overcome the difficult business environment. This was the time to "help" businesses through change and not just "*sell*" products and "push off" kind of services.

Besides the slowdown due to external factors, Wipro benefited from a growing disillusionment with consulting and consultants. Many customers increasingly voiced the opinion that consulting was not only failing to add value, but that consultants did their best to avoid taking responsibility for poor results. There was clear and pressing demand for consultants that understood the client's business, took ownership of the technology change program, and demonstrated a clear return on investment by changing the business outcome. Some at Wipro believed that the company should capitalize on the new mood, and move to build on Wipro's expertise in systems developments to create consultancy that not only provided advice, but also offered to implement the advice as well. This new model of client–consultant interaction implied a move from transactional to collaborative relationship, and even beyond, to a partnership where risks would be shared based on the business outcome.

In the third quarter of 2002, Wipro posted a poor 2% profit. To meet shareholders' expectations, Wipro leadership decided to nurture consulting capabilities on the back of their existing IT-based capabilities. The intent was to demonstrate to the customers that Wipro's technology implementation projects were not just limited to routine "going concern" but instead could add real economic

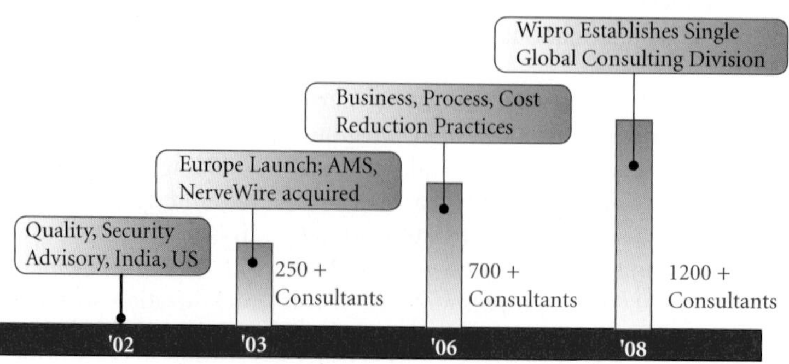

FIGURE 1
WCS EVOLUTION: THE TIMELINE

values to their businesses. As the initiative gained momentum, it also became evident that this will not only improve Wipro's own bottom line but may also open up the doors for many new technology implementation projects for existing services.

Consulting was thus incubated, nurtured, encouraged, and developed in an environment of collaborative relationships among the business unit. On its part, the parent organization provided the infrastructure, the resources, and leadership team to develop and sustain the growth of consulting within various Wipro business units.

The bubbling and collaboration phase

Mark Payne, who headed WCS in Europe, likened the growth of WCS to the emergence of consulting bubbles emerging from the repertoire of knowledge and services that Wipro was good at. Mark Payne pointed out: "Targeting the consulting opportunities in the areas where it is already strong was a strategic masterstroke." This encouraged "bubbles" of consulting competencies to develop in business areas like quality, software process improvements, business transformation, and IT-driven enterprise change. All in all, Wipro's consulting services fell into the following three areas:

1. *Plan and manage:* This entailed identifying the IT infrastructure and application needs and the appropriate governance structure to improve the overall business performance.
2. *Rationalization and streamlining of enterprise IT infrastructure:* This practice focused on consolidation of IT investment to eliminate redundancies and overlap and making the technology framework efficient and seamless for business operation.
3. *Enhanced operational efficiency:* This practice enabled customers to improve the operational efficiency through smart management of people, process, and technology.

Wipro InfoTech in Asia Pacific and the Middle East was already well known and well regarded by Wipro's current customers for IT services. Similarly three other groups—*Quality Consulting group, Wipro Consulting group,* and *Business Process Modeling group*—offered additional services to customers wherever Wipro sensed an opportunity to provide value-added consulting.

For customers, this brought considerable business benefits, since they could now outsource not just the software development but also the entire governance and management of technology to Wipro. Wipro was soon advising customers on technology decisions, which in return further opened up new projects for its IT services. Wipro was climbing the sourcing maturity curve, providing high quality consulting, gaining industry credibility, and the confidence and trust of customers.

Following the early incubation phase, Wipro encouraged all four service units to evolve and develop the consulting capabilities within their areas of core competencies (e.g., quality, process, change management, and CRM) that could be implemented across various industries such as banking, insurance, telecommunications, and oil and gas. This meant hiring senior consultants with significant industry experience (e.g., in UK it hired consultants who had considerable experience in retail banking operations). Furthermore, it also took steps to promote collaboration among all four business units, by forming a joint sales and marketing unit. This helped Wipro Technologies to position itself as an end-to-end technology provider with an inherent capability of providing consulting services.

Revenues from consulting engagements grew rapidly (see Exhibit 1) but by the end of 2006, Wipro's leadership realized that while consulting on its own was a significant business, it was still embedded in Wipro Technologies in a very fragmented manner and lacked focus and cohesion. Such a scenario introduced various overlapping capabilities. For instance, various units within Wipro Technologies (InfoTech, Enterprise Solutions, and Enterprise Application Services) had invested in building competence in offering enterprise architecture consulting. Each unit also had retained its own support activities, such as marketing, HR, and training and development. This introduced internal duplication, and sent conflicting signals to clients as to which unit they should approach to discuss their emerging business requirements.

The organizational design phase: the WCS federation

By late 2006, it was a common viewpoint among its leadership team that consulting needed to create an organization design that matched people, information and technology

Wipro - Revenues from IT services

(USD in Million) except share date

Year ended 31st March					
Particulars	2007	2006	2005	2004	2003
Total IT Revenues	3,127.84	2,185.32	1,699.13	1,218.05	797.51
Growth	43%	29%	39%	53%	

EXHIBIT 1 WIPRO TECHNOLOGIES—IT SERVICES REVENUES

to the purpose, and vision and strategy of the organization. Payne summed up the challenge facing management at point as follows:

> Management had a key dilemma to resolve which resulted from several models or trends that different organizations across the world had followed in trying to extend their businesses across the value chain.

There were two options: First, consulting capability could be developed and then spun off as a completely separated company, which would have no operational connectivity to its parent. Second, consulting could be viewed as a captive unit, an offshoot of an existing business unit that continues to evolve its consulting capabilities and operates under a strong supervision of its parent and borrows the shared operations like marketing and HR from its parent.

After much deliberation, Wipro's leadership decided that it needed to combine the best of the two models and came up with the idea of "The Federated structure" which was to provide the fundamental autonomy to its consulting business but still maintain the loose coupling to its parent—Wipro Technologies. "This was the model that suited WCS the most," recalled Mark Payne. It allowed WCS to be launched as an independent profit and loss-based distinct unit governed through a matrix of geographical segmentation, industry verticals, and consulting practices that will collaborate with each other in a federal structure.

The new structure (see Exhibit 2) in comparison to the old (see Exhibit 3) illustrates the transformation that took place during the formalization of consulting business into WCS. Wipro developed a matrix structure for WCS, which consisted of horizontal services (e.g., functional capabilities such as process engineering, quality, change management, and CRM) aligned with industry verticals (Oil & Gas, Banking, and Telecommunications). It operated under three geographic heads located in London (EU), Texas (North America), and Tokyo (JIMEA).

The consolidation of competencies into a new federated matrix structure was seen as Wipro's unique strength, enabling the firm to add depth, flexibility, and sense of collective purpose. It also encouraged staff to kick-start internal initiatives, such as leveraging existing quality models like Six Sigma pioneered by Wipro Technologies into new business areas.

The new structure also enhanced communication and information flow among the people. Under Dr. Anurag Srivastava's leadership the firm put in place a framework, which it called *"Execution Excellence,"* an amalgam of shared operational services like sales, marketing, and Programme Management Office (PMO), structured to improve communication. The firm also recognized that it needed to continuously focus on building and disseminating new knowledge. By mid-2008, WCS therefore created a unit called "Intellectual Capital Enhancement (ICE)" whose sole purpose was to gather, generate, and disseminate knowledge among its employees.

THE NEXT FRONTIER: IS WCS READY?

In the long term if WCS aimed to become a top global consulting brand, a highly trusted advisory firm for its clients, it needed to reflect the value that a trusted advisor can bring in. For this to happen Wipro's top management believed that the company had to shift from the competency mode to a problem-solver mode. WCS was focusing its strategy on the following three dimensions in order to make this happen (Figure 2):

- *Branding and positioning* to give a sense of purpose and strategic direction.
- *Scaling* to ensure that it can deliver.
- *Differentiation* to distinguish itself from competitors.

Branding and positioning

WCS was consciously trying to avoid positioning itself in the "strategy consulting" space (WCS used the term "strategy consulting space" to refer to management consulting firms such as McKinsey and BCG which helped organizations with specific needs around corporate or business unit strategy). WCS leadership believed that it needed to position the firm as a trusted advisor that enabled clients to improve revenues or overall business performance based on implementing new technology or leading the technology-based change programs.

To enable this positioning, WCS leveraged the parent to get an opening into its existing client and then up-selling its established consulting practices. The firm believed that this was a successful tactic because most of the customers were already familiar with the firm's focus on quality and its core competence in working on projects, which involved integrating client legacy systems and new technologies offering.

It had been able to move quickly from the traditional "transactional" relationship to a "collaborative" or "partnership" based relationship because its consulting capabilities (like process quality, technology change programs, and technology rationalization) were more or less an extension of the services it had been providing to its customers (in the earlier guise of entities like Wipro InfoTech or QCG). Using Wipro's technology expertise WCS was attempting to position itself as a partner who will bring the expertise on how the clients could use technology to transform their businesses. David Taylor, one of WCS's partners, pointed out that using this proposition, it had gained the preferred consulting partner status with one of the largest general insurance providers in the UK where Wipro Technologies had already been acting as a technology partner:

> The market for general insurance in UK is considered fast moving and extremely price sensitive. Firms have to constantly update their products. WCS worked with technology specialists from Wipro Technologies in developing a new internet portal which enabled the insurance provider to monitor competitor prices, product features, adjust its pricing and features, and push this information to both internet and for the telephone channels.

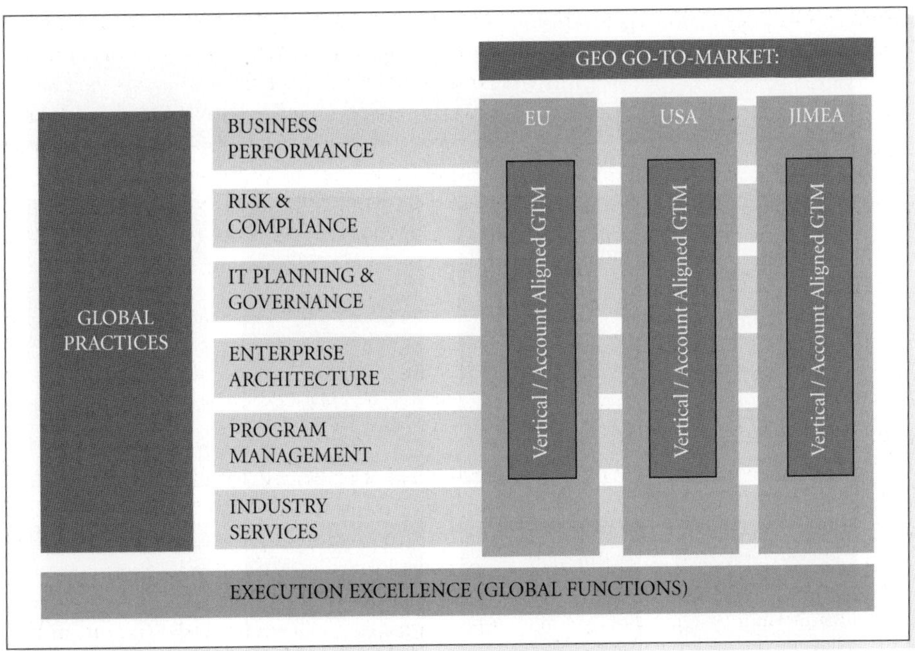

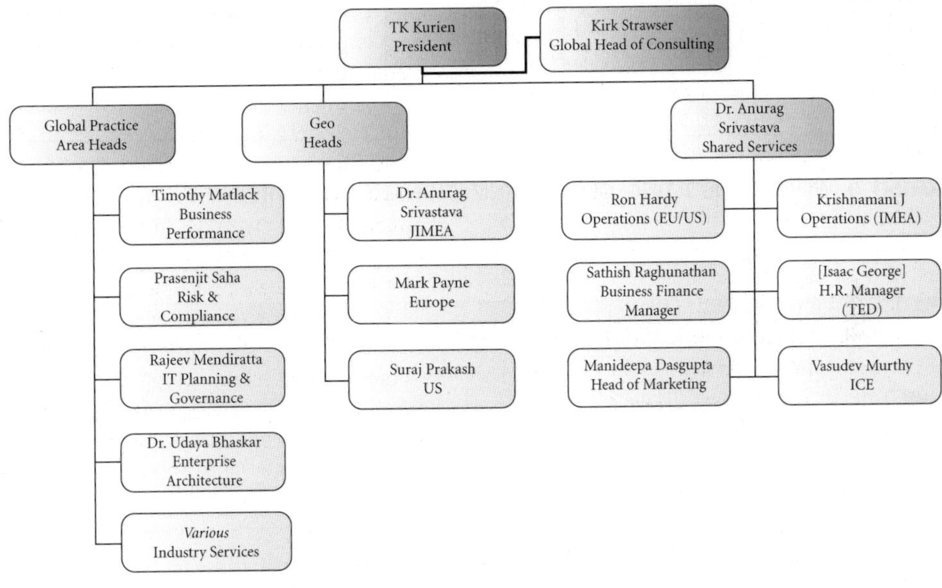

EXHIBIT 2 WIPRO CONSULTING: NEW ORGANIZATIONAL STRUCTURE

Organizational extension and scaling

The WCS leadership regarded the federated organizational model as essential to avoiding the "one size fits all" trap. The federated organizational model provided a fair degree of autonomy to different regional units while remaining global in nature. The evolution of WCS illustrated this key point. On the one hand WCS had expanded globally to attain the economies of scale and consistent global brand, but on the other hand, it needed to embed itself in the local culture, since demonstrating local knowledge in client relationships, which were collaborative, was central to securing trust, and winning repeat engagements.

Tim Matlack (who headed consulting practices in North America) pointed toward Wipro's experience in using this localized strategy to expand Wipro InfoTech's

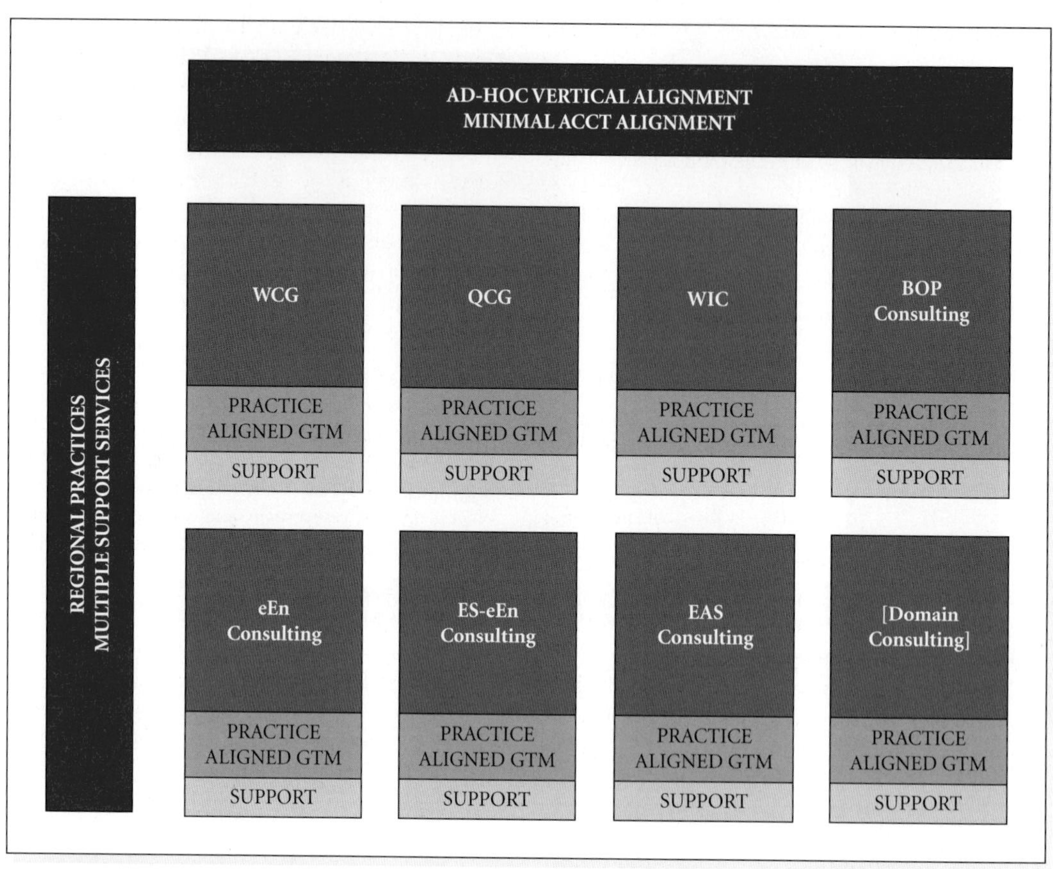

EXHIBIT 3 WIPRO CONSULTING: OLD ORGANIZATIONAL STRUCTURE

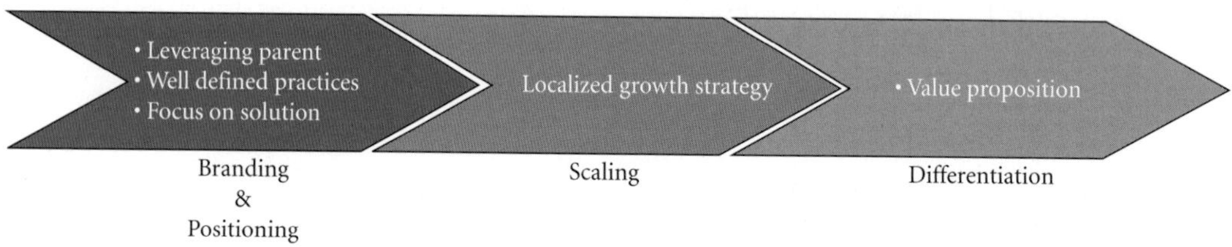

FIGURE 2 WCS: STRATEGIC RESPONSE TO CHALLENGES

market share in the Middle East and elsewhere strongly shaped its current globalization strategy. When operating in different geographies, Matlack believed that WCS recognized the need to invest in building client relationships at local level, and had accordingly customized its business strategy in those regions.

Consulting was considered a mature business in advanced economies such as the US and Europe with strong brands such as IBM, Accenture, and Sapient holding dominant market position. In order to become a global player, WCS needed to follow suit, and strengthen its brand. The $600 million acquisition of Infocross signaled its commitment to becoming a global consulting brand in this region. It also acquired American Management Services (AMS) and Nervewire to expand its consulting capability. Payne and Matlack both were of the opinion that WCS would continue to look for niche acquisitions in these regions in its quest to become a leading technology consulting brand.

However, Wipro management had deliberately opted for organic growth in other geographical regions. In the case of WCS expansion in Japan, India, Middle East, and Asia (JIMEA), the consulting team had grown from 4–5 people in 2001/02 to 500+ now. Srivastava who had headed the JIMEA team from inception pointed that the ability to understand regional cultural differences and adapt accordingly were central to success of WCS in this region. He claimed:

> In this region, clients' emphasis is more on the capabilities and the value system that a consultant can bring in. Also power, proximity and local knowledge are important aspects in this region. Organic growth through the recruitment of local talent works much better than alien acquisitions. Acquisition poses a huge challenge, as the problem of integration is compounded in this region than it would be in other regions.

THE KEY DIFFERENTIATOR: VALUE PROPOSITION OF WCS

> In our way of working, we attach a great deal of importance to humility and honesty. With respect for human values, we promise to serve our customers with integrity . . . .
>
> —Azim Premji

During the evolution of WCS, the firm combined its IT services strengths with strong customer centric approach, modesty when approaching customer needs, and respect toward customers' internal culture. These core values are reinforced by several mechanisms such as monthly governance pack (see Exhibit 4) and client feedback mechanisms (see Exhibit 5).

WCS prided itself on its ability to manage internal change at client organizations. While working with clients, it attempted to align itself with the customer's value system, and aimed to facilitate change from within. It did this by encouraging customers to evolve their best practices, and to rely as much as possible on their own people and culture. Srivastava believed that this approach was a marked departure from the tendency of consultants to emphasize the technical and business aspects at the expense of the cultural issues that inevitably emerge during change. He explained:

> Wipro was quick to realize that tensions emerge in client firm's business value chain if one tries to copy and paste an external culture onto an organization, all in the name of best practices. If the change does not come or appear to come from within, the forces of FUD (Fear, uncertainty and doubt) combine to create staff resentment and stiff resistance, and this has adverse impact on our ability to deliver as a provider.

Srivastava believed that resentment and resistance were less likely to happen if consultants acted more as facilitators who encouraged the client organization to refine and reform its own culture. He promoted the view internally that the true value of consulting consisted of helping a client firm evolve a set of best practices, which the client can

Wipro Monthly TD Governance Meeting

Contents

- Current State of the Relationship:
  - Summary
  - Thought Leadership
  - Commendations Received
  - Relationship Development
  - Quality Update - Plan, Scope & Metrics
  - Transition Status
  - Key Operating Metrics
  - Trends & Predictability
- Operating Plan
  - 30-60-90 day plan
  - Balanced Score card
- Supporting Material
  - Relationship Indicators
  - Release Schedule - Projects in RED and AMBER
  - Platform Monthly Status
  - Contractor Replacement
- Closed Actions

EXHIBIT 4 MONTHLY GOVERNANCE PACK

Customer Feedback Form

1. PROJECT DETAILS				
Project Name	CLIVE – Interim DR Scanning	Capital One	Sponsor	Suzanne Smith
Planned End Date	6th December 2008		Single Point of Contact	Linda McConnachie
Actual End Date	Ongoing			
Planned Effort	N/A	Wipro	Single Point of Contact	Asheesh Malhotra
Planned Budget			Team List	Wipro: Daniel Marshall Parag Acharya
Project Overview				

2. OVERALL CUSTOMER RATING FOR THE ENGAGEMENT (Scale of 0 – 5)	
A simple response of: X 5 - *Extremely satisfied* ☐ 4 - *Satisfied* ☐ 3 - *Neither satisfied nor dissatisfied* ☐ 2 - *Dissatisfied* ☐ 1 - *Extremely dissatisfied* ☐ 0 - *Cannot rate* *(ratings can also be given in decimals e.g.: 4.5)	OVERALL CUSTOMER RATING FOR THE ENGAGEMENT ----4---- COMMENTS (IF ANY) The team was very engaged with the business SMEs and Project Manager. Having been involved in previous inbound correspondence processes resulted in being able to get up to speed with what was required quickly.

EXHIBIT 5
CLIENT FEEDBACK FORM

subsequently own. WCS emphasized in its internal training and meetings that consultants should therefore be working to fill the knowledge gaps in a client's intellectual space and should not attempt to manufacture it from scratch.

To establish itself as a differentiator with unique value proposition, WCS was also working on developing its version of the global delivery model, which Strawser believed would provide the firm with both cost and resource advantage that competitors would find difficult to imitate in the near term. Strawser was working on a plan to implement it in two ways: first, by conducting the back-end industry research in India; and second by recruiting MBA graduates from top Indian business schools, training them for a year as industry and solution specialists (e.g., CRM experts in telecommunications sector), and assigning them to client engagements across various global locations. WCS leadership was in agreement with Strawser that there were potential advantages in terms of extending the knowledge base by sourcing best talent at much lower cost; however, it would require a dramatic shift from both preferred the model of hiring staff from within with longer tenure, and client need to access industry experts with considerable experience.

FUTURE CHALLENGES

As in the past, the 2008 WCS meeting closed with a celebration dinner. Gathering for drinks before dinner, Kurien, Strawser, Payne, Matlack, Srivastava, and other board members discussed the repercussions of the economic crisis roiling the world markets. With deep global recession looming large and corporate budgets under severe pressure, technology firms will be judged by their ability to meet customer expectations more than ever. They agreed that WCS would need to address the following five challenges to increase the chances of its success:

1. First, the firm needs to commit resources to recruiting senior consultants with significant industry experience to augment its knowledge base in high-growth segments such as Oil & Gas, Telecom, and Media. It has to assign these industry specialists with the task of developing generic solution frameworks in areas such as supply chain management, vendor/contract management, dealer network management, and risk management.
2. Second, WCS needs to keep pace with new knowledge, not only at the industry level, but also with new solutions, such as CRM, and new technologies.

3. Third, WCS needs to reexamine the global delivery model as a source of differentiation in the technology consulting industry. The model (which combined on-site presence with global delivery channels located in nearshore and offshore centers) was a de facto standard for Wipro Technologies and its industry peers in the process-driven IT development and support industry; however, it had not been used in the technology consulting industry in the same way WCS was planning to implement.
4. Fourthly, WCS needed to reevaluate its reliance on Wipro Technologies for brand recognition. But developing a separate brand may lead to duplication of competencies and result in tension between WCS and the parent firm.
5. Finally, the high-end consulting market demands a strong relationship at board level and senior management level. WCS and its parent, Wipro Technologies, lacked these relationships. To nurture this competence required patience, a long-term perspective on building relationships.

CASE 24

Tiscali UK: The Rocky Road to Offshoring

Founded in January 1998 in Sardinia, Italy, by Renato Soru, Tiscali began life as a fixed-line telephone operator. Following listing on the Milan stock exchange in October 1999, it embarked on a pan-European expansion plan, acquiring Internet service provider (ISP) firms such as France-based Liberty Surf, UK-based LineOne, Tiny Online and Gateway, Germany-based SurfEU, and the Netherlands-based World Online. With these acquisitions, Tiscali became the second largest service provider in Europe in terms of the active users (4.9 million) with the largest geographical footprint in Europe. The largest of these acquisitions was the LineOne acquisition in the UK in the summer of 2001, which gave Tiscali 1.85 million registered subscribers. Tiscali merged its three UK ISPs to form Tiscali UK as an independent subsidiary operation. With the emergence of broadband in 2002, Tiscali management began to focus on making a transition from dial-up to broadband services. The firm rapidly moved to become the low-cost broadband provider for B2C and B2B markets, pricing its services significantly lower than offered by much bigger competitors such as BT or AOL.

In January 2005, a new government policy allowed operators such as Tiscali to install their own hardware on BT exchanges, thus connecting directly to the consumer's phone line via BT owned local loop—the copper lines running from exchange centers to households and businesses. This directly benefited ISPs such as Tiscali who could bundle broadband and voice products, and enter the new area of "double-play" services, which offered customers the convenience of a single Internet and telephone provider. In August 2006, Tiscali entered the "Triple-Play" market when it acquired HomeChoice, a company that offered a bundled broadband and video-on-demand service to customers. By the end of 2008, Tiscali was the fourth largest ISP in the UK with the customer base of 1.9 million and a market share of 12% after BT, Virgin Media, and The Carphone Warehouse.

EVOLUTION OF OFFSHORING IN TISCALI

The emergence and subsequent growth of offshoring in Tiscali occurred against the background of Tiscali's evolution as an organization. Tiscali first looked to offshoring to reduce costs in support activities such as routine customer queries. Subsequently, Tiscali expanded the use of offshoring to include core operations such as developing software applications, and development of a new billing system for B2B customers. For the most part, offshoring took place in vendor-operated dedicated facilities in India, usually on a fee-for-service basis. In several cases, for instance, during the early development phase of billing platform, offshoring operated in reverse, with vendors sending personnel over to London for project work on the basis of billable hours plus the cost of software.

As a double, and later triple-play services provider, Tiscali operated in a heavily technology-driven business. To meet the demands of this environment Tiscali created a separate technology department (TD). The TD was responsible for a diverse set of activities, such as order management, service assurance, and management reporting activities. In order to carry out these activities, the TD was organized into various small teams, with each team being responsible for a different set of activities. The teams were required to communicate effectively with different Tiscali departments to make sure that they provide and receive necessary inputs quickly and efficiently to carry out various activities (Figure 1). For instance, Customer Operations Support (COPS) was responsible for multiple activities such as providing telephone-based customer support, managing customer orders, customer billing, payment collection, credit control, service upgrade management, and customer technical issues escalation and resolution. It relied on TD for providing tools such as training modules for call center service agents, and diagnostic tools for customer support agents dealing with technical queries.

Any interruption in TD activities affected the performance of the other departments' activities, and likewise problems with other departments had a knock-on effect on TD activities (see Table 1 for description of activities performed by TD and dependence of activities performed by other departments on TD).

As Tiscali moved from being a pure dial-up ISP firm to broadband and later to double- and triple-play provider, it progressively increased its reliance on offshoring. The

This case was prepared by Joseph Lampel and Ajay Bhalla, City University London.

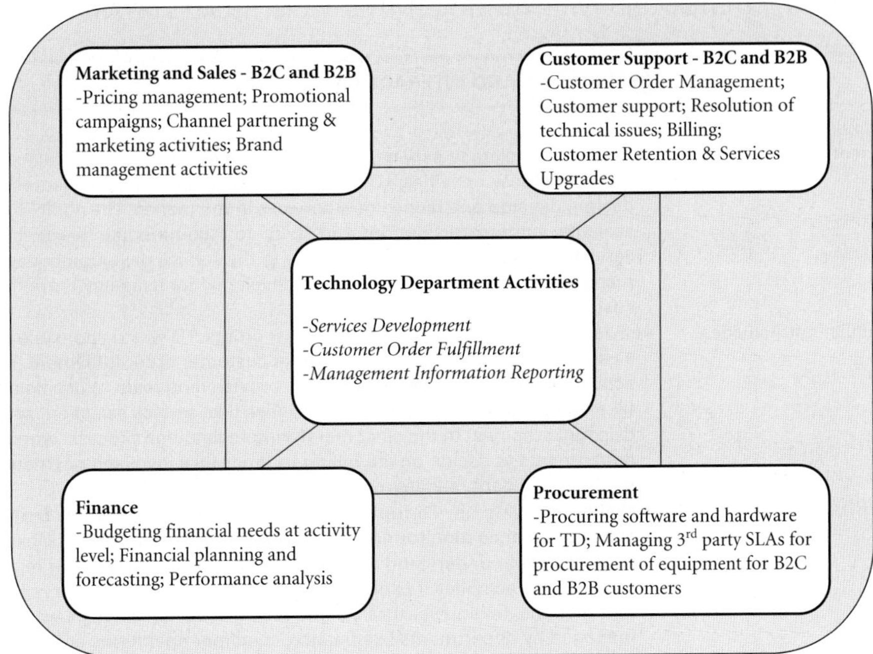

FIGURE 1 TISCALI TD DEPENDENT CONFIGURATION

evolution of offshoring in Tiscali corresponds to a move from low-value to high-value added of this strategy (see Table 2 for a summary of the evolution of offshoring). This evolution falls into the following three distinct time phases:

Phase 1: Business consolidation period, April 2001–October 2002.

Phase 2: Broadband and voice period, November 2002–July 2006.

Phase 3: Voice, video and data "Triple-play" period, August 2006 onward.

PHASE 1: TISCALI EVOLUTION (APRIL 2001–OCTOBER 2002)

For the first two years, following the acquisitions of the three ISPs, Tiscali's UK focus was business consolidation and company reorganization. Cost reduction and rationalization took center stage. Tiscali cut staff and eliminated overlapping of roles and improved on operating cost efficiency. Reorganization also led to the formation of small teams charged respectively with marketing, sales, technology, and customer support responsibilities, allowing Tiscali to keep the interactions between different teams on a relatively informal basis. Thus, whereas other ISPs were preoccupied with creating and managing internal processes, Tiscali could focus management time on achieving business targets.

Key to achieving these targets was consolidation of the systems and platforms inherited from acquisitions into a single integrated infrastructure. The integrated infrastructure produced substantial operating cost reduction, higher network utilization, less network support and service management activities, etc. The new capabilities allowed Tiscali to launch various flavors of narrowband service packages such as their popular unmetered anytime Internet access, and to create various packages suited for different needs of the customers.

But as Tiscali was expanding its offerings and enjoying sales growth, it was also experiencing rapid rise in the costs of providing technical support for new and existing customers. Previously Tiscali expensed this support out of its own resources. But as the customer base increased it began exploring the option of charging customers for technical support with the aim of transforming technical support from a cost center to a fully self-sustaining unit. It was at this juncture that offshoring became an increasingly attractive option.

Offshoring customer services (March 2002–February 2008)

Initially, Tiscali sought a revenue-sharing arrangement with an onshore call service operator that would provide technical support to Tiscali's customers. However, in the UK, none of the call centers were prepared to work on a revenue-sharing basis. This led Tiscali to look to offshore call centers in India. For technical support, Tiscali selected two different offshore vendors–IBM Daksh and Codec in India, based on their capability and pricing. IBM Daksh had considerable capabilities in dealing with routine customer service queries, while Codec in Bangalore had proven expertise in running technical help desk facilities. When it came to selecting which activities should be

TABLE 1 TD ACTIVITIES AND INTERACTION WITH OTHER ACTIVITIES WITHIN TISCALI'S DEPARTMENTS

	DESCRIPTION AND INTERACTION
Technology Department (TD) Activities	
Services Development Activities	Activities that relate to services innovation and diversification of telecom services. As part of these activities. TD interacted with different departments to conceptualize, design, develop and launch new services in the market. The ability to design flexible, scalable, automated solutions and ability to accommodate new technologies and services, backup facilities added value to the service development activities, e.g. it managed a call center portal which it developed for usage by more than 1500 offshore customer service agents.
Customer Order Fulfillment Activities	Activities ensuring fulfillment of customer orders. TD was responsible for activities such as an providing automated platform for customer order fulfillment. The other related activities include working with service provisioning team to decide on the mode (like online portal, telephone) and facilities (like service selection, service pricing, discount schemes) to the customer during registration process: working with billing departments to decide on the billing facilities (like invoicing payment collection method, bad debt management).
Management Information Systems Activities	Activities involving Key Performance Indicator (KPI) reports, which facilitated resourcing, and performance monitoring. These activities included working closely with different departments to understand their daily/weekly/monthly reporting requirements. As part of these activities it captured information on new customer registrations, service terminations, revenue assurance and billing collections, which were fed into activities managed by departments like finance, customer operations and marketing.
Services Management and System Integration Activities	Activities that ensured that all operations are up and running efficiently. These were a critical set of activities needed to meet service level agreements (SLAs),and involved providing tools to customer operations so that they could detect and diagnose any problem in customer service. It also provided a mechanism of escalating the issues to technical team for further technical support.
Other Value Chain Activities	
Finance Department Value Adding Activities	Activities related to arranging, controlling, and budgeting. The finance activities depended on TD to assess the profit margins on different services and to decide on technical activities budget for projects development and operations management. The other activities included getting information from TD like monthly/yearly payment collection, bad debts, billing settlement information, so that finance department could run forecasting models.
Marketing and Sales Value Adding Activities	Activities included brand management, managing advertising campaign, pricing management, and promotions management. The efficiency of marketing and sales activities depended on the efficiency of TD to roll out quality services quickly so that marketing and sales could target new customer segments and run promotions to retain existing customers.
Customer Support Operations Value Adding Activities	Activities involved customer order management, call center support, technical support, customer billing & invoicing issue resolution, payment collection, credit control, customer retention and service upgrade management. There was dependence on TD for many of its ad-hoc requirements like monthly technical issues resolution reports. The COPS needed quick turnaround from TD to resolve high-level technical issues, provide training, and develop user manuals to increase customer satisfaction
Procurement Value Adding Activities	Activities involved cost-effective purchasing of necessary software and hardware for TD. In order to carry out these activities it needed to work closely with TD to understand requirements for the software and hardware, and then negotiate with the 3rd party providers to procure the necessary items at competitive prices.

offshored, Tiscali management decided to focus on routine queries. With this in mind, order taking, status queries, and billing and product upgrade queries were routed to IBM Daksh in Delhi and Pune. Service connection queries and services troubleshooting activities such as running diagnostics test and escalating complaints to the technical team for resolutions were on the other hand routed to the Codec call center in Bangalore.

Tiscali was not involved in recruitment or training of customer service agents, seeing this as the offshore vendor's responsibility. Instead, Tiscali confined its role to providing agents with "scripted flow charts" that used codified responses to a set range of customer queries that in principle should enable agents to carry out troubleshooting in each activity. This solution, however, ran into difficulties when soon after offshoring, Tiscali managers realized that staff at the India-based call centers and customers had difficulties understanding each other, largely because of different accents and intonation. Resolving customer queries led to delays that were costly for customers since they

TABLE 2 EVOLUTION OF OFFSHORING WITHIN TISCALI AND THE IMPACT ON TISCALI CONFIGURATION

PERIOD	OFFSHORED ACTIVITIES	INTERACTIONS WITH OTHER DEPARTMENTAL ACTIVITIES	KEY ISSUES	OFFSHORING IMPACT
PHASE 1 March 2002-Current B2C Call Center (CC) Offshored to IBM Daksh in Delhi, Pune and Codec Bangalore	- Customer service related to ordering/ upgrading/ terminating the services - Manage query handling on billing/ service status/ network speed/ customer complaints/ problem escalations	**COPS – TD linkages** - To gather requirements from COPS for supporting CC operations - To arrange training and user manuals for CC staff - To get KPIs reports regarding new customers joining/ leaving/ upgrades/ complaints, etc. **Marketing and Sales (Pricing) – TD linkages** Configure products and services on the CC portal Configure promotions and discounts on the CC portal	- CCs staff lack knowledge of products offered by Tiscali - Customer complaints lead to drop in Tiscali managements' confidence in quality of service from India based CCs - Tiscali decides not to offshore B2B and B2C retention call center - High focus on supporting and providing training to offshore CC employees	- Enables Tiscali to have a low-cost self-sustaining B2C call center in India - Tiscali was able to extend use of CC for other products like ADSL and residential telephone services
PHASE 2 December 2002 Broadband Applications Development to Wipro	- Application for Broadband Services provisioning on BT network - Development of B2B Broadband Order Management Portal	**Marketing and Sales (Pricing) – Offshore vendor linkages** - Gather information to configure products and services on the CC portal - Configure promotions and discounts on the CC portal **TD - Offshore vendor** - Gather requirements on features and functionality of the broadband services and portal	- Effective setup of team comprising of offshore-onsite resources - Good coordination between Wipro onsite and offshore team - Effective, frequent and informal coordination between the offshore vendor team and in-house TD	- Enabled launch of competitively priced broadband services - Broadband products huge success in the market. Tiscali brand awareness increased manifold
January 2003 B2B Billing System	Integrated Billing System to bill B2B customers	**Marketing and Sales (Pricing) – Offshore Vendor Linkages** - Gather information to configure products and services on the Tiscali B2B order management portal - Gather information to develop features enabling setting pricing through BOSE portal; setting volume discounts, term discounts **Billing – Offshore Vendor linkages** - Understand various types of customer services, pricing and invoicing, processing credits - Understanding recurring billing issues faced by customers **TD - Offshore vendor** Understand call detail record formats and rating logic to break call detail records into billable format	- Severe delay in delivery of the billing system - Constantly changing offshore team members - Lack of full view of the ongoing development - Lack of scoping project requirements effectively often escalated - Ambitious project of having a versatile billing system - Fee for service contract where offshore vendor is paid on time and material basis leads to internal anxiety as project is delayed	- Cost overrun of more than £1.5 million - Sales team not able to launch versatile billing system - Discussion to scrap project - Reorganization of Development team - Replacement of project managers - Sales team hires consultants to deploy alterative billing system - Tiscali looks for alternative partner

TABLE 2 EVOLUTION OF OFFSHORING WITHIN TISCALI AND THE IMPACT ON TISCALI CONFIGURATION (*continued*)

PERIOD	OFFSHORED ACTIVITIES	INTERACTIONS WITH OTHER DEPARTMENTAL ACTIVITIES	KEY ISSUES	OFFSHORING IMPACT
May 2004-Current Technical application support team	Application Support	**COPS – Offshore Vendor team linkages** - Managing high level complaints - Gather requirements for reports - Fixing customer data/information - Configuring products and services on COPS portal **Marketing and Sales – Offshore Vendor team linkages** - Configuring channel partners - Configure products on service systems - Configuring pricing **TD – Offshore Vendor team linkages** - Understanding technical design from tech team - Provide training to offshore team as required	- Lack of process in managing off-shore resources and requirements - In-house team preoccupied with ongoing projects. Often declines to support the App Support Team - Lack of process to manage knowledge transition - Delay in service due to lack of documents and codified knowledge - Transfer of technical issues back and forth - Focus on development of services and training	- Replacement of project manager - Monthly tracking introduced - Manage time difference by enabling offshore team members to support the operation during UK time
PHASE 3 December 2006-January 2008 IPTV Integration	Activities enabling systems to provide triple-play services	**Marketing and Sales Team – Offshore vendor linkages** - To provide information on new products - To provide pricing information to be configured on the system **HomeChoice Tech – Offshore vendor linkages** - To provide interface to enable use of legacy systems - To provide products and services details to enable migration of customers on Tiscali platform **COPS – Offshore vendor linkages** - Enabling IPTV related customer support features on call center portal to have an integrated service	- Delay in delivery of MPF platform - Multiple bureaucratic layers between HomeChoice and Tiscali - Multiple processes followed to integrate systems and develop new services - Focus on implementing full software development cycle methodology leading to increase in the time taken to implement	- Delays in delivery lead- to delay in market entry and loss of market share - Decides to be less process oriented

TD=Technology Department; COPS: Customer Service Operations; CC: Call Center.
IPTV: Internet Protocol Television is a system where using Internet Protocol delivers a digital television service over a network infrastructure.
MPF: Metallic Path Facility gives private service providers exclusive use of residential telephone line.

were charged for the service on the basis of call duration. Inevitably, customer complaints about the quality and cost of Tiscali's support services followed.

The head of customer operations team sought to address this problem by liaising more closely with the technical department. A task force made up of a two-person team from customer operations and two members from the technical department was set up to bridge the gap between the offshoring vendor and Tiscali's operations. But their main effort was confined primarily to preparing training manuals for offshore staff, and developing off-the-shelf packages that target well understood problems where assistance could be easily routinized.

These difficulties called into question Tiscali's approach to offshoring. Of particular concern to Tiscali's top management was the potentially negative impact of offshoring on high revenue-generating B2B customers. During the monthly Tiscali management board meeting in October 2007, executives discussed the operational challenges emerging as a result of growth in B2B and residential customer numbers. There was general consensus that increasing numbers in both customer segments, and the cost of supporting B2B customers from the UK, were putting huge pressure on operating margins. Tiscali managers reviewed offshoring options closer to home market to relieve these pressures. Following this discussion, in January 2008 Tiscali formed a three-year, £66 million pounds agreement with Transcom, a European vendor. Transcom was to provide customer operations activities, such as billing support and collection, aimed at Tiscali's B2B customer base from Lithuania. Tiscali managers were also planning to enhance the call center portal to facilitate offshore retention activities targeted at the residential customer base to an existing facility in India.

PHASE 2: TISCALI EVOLUTION (NOVEMBER 2002–JULY 2006)

Broadband services development (October 2002–March 2003)

In the last quarter of 2002, Tiscali entered the broadband market by launching broadband services based on BT Wholesale ADSL offerings. Managers recognized that as long as BT was the sole network provider, and was offering identical access to all market entrants, competing on service differentiation was not feasible. Thus, competition among broadband providers was increasingly focusing on price, which in turn meant maintaining a low-cost position. To sustain a low-cost positioning, Tiscali needed to lower the cost of developing new application services for broadband users. This led managers to search for offshore providers, primarily in India, that would enable Tiscali to lower the costs of development and speed up the delivery of its services. Ultimately, Tiscali selected Wipro, an India-based provider, because of its experience within the telecommunication sector.

The first project involved Wipro developing the broadband applications tools such as broadband order management and provisioning system that are crucial for enabling upgrade of the narrowband to broadband services for both B2B and B2C customers. Tiscali formed a small team in TD consisting of four people from the core technical team and six people from Wipro. The Wipro team had five members based offshore and one member on-site responsible for coordination with Tiscali in-house team to select application modules to send offshore for development or testing. The team was successful in completing the project within three months. That allowed Tiscali to launch broadband services more quickly than other service providers.

In the first three months after the launch, Tiscali was getting 2000 new broadband orders every day. As a result, Tiscali's brand awareness rose from 4% in 2001 to 80%. But the increasing demand forced Tiscali's finance department to allocate more funds to TD to scale up infrastructure to support high volumes of orders. To accommodate increasing broadband orders, the COPS team ramped up its offshore CC operations. Within Tiscali the successful launch of the project vindicated the use of offshore providers, but other managers cautioned that success was not due simply to offshoring, but also careful requirement specifications and effective coordination between on-site and offshore units.

B2B billing system development (January 2003–December 2004)

Having secured a reliable offshore provider for development of complex applications Tiscali managers began to ramp up its entry into the B2B market. In principle, this market generates higher average revenue per user (ARPU) than residential customers, and significantly, it represents a more stable income stream because as a rule, customers are less willing to suffer the disruption that switching to other providers entails.

The key to this market, however, was superior service. Under the plan put forward, Tiscali would be the first to offer B2B customers the opportunity to bundle together different products and services. To support this offering, TD needed to develop a new billing system labeled in Tiscali as "Billing Operations & Support Environment (BOSE)." The system would enable Tiscali to bill B2B customers for various services such as dial-up, non-geographic numbers, Broadband, Co-Location, and Domain Name Services. The development team also needed to migrate existing customers from the old billing system to the new one, and ensure that management information system worked with the new billing system.

Tiscali turned to Wipro to deliver the project in six months. The Wipro team had been working for Tiscali for just over two months, and had delivered the broadband services project budget, well ahead of schedule. Furthermore, the Wipro account manager had developed a good relationship with the CTO, and gave assurances that Wipro would deliver again. The project kicked off in January 2003 with a budget estimate of £300,000, and expected a delivery period of six months. To carry out the development work Tiscali asked Wipro to form an onshore team including two billing specialists with background in telecommunications that were to work as freelance contractors along with the Wipro team.

The project was central to the success of Tiscali in this crucial market segment, and Tiscali managers decided the Wipro team needed to be based at Tiscali's premises. The decision to base the development team onshore was also driven by the fact that as part of the system development, the Wipro team was required to interact with various departments to collect information to establish requirements and subsequent application design. These departments were marketing and sales (with pricing team to understand pricing and discounting features, promotions, etc.), billing team within COPS (to understand customer, pricing configuration requirement, invoicing, credits, etc.), service provisioning department (to understand services and their features configurations requirement), and TD team (to understand call detail record formats, call mediation and rating logic which breaks call detail records into billable format). The finance team was involved in budget allocation and financial monitoring for the project. In all, the project team size was initially set to nine development members (all on-site) and one project manager to coordinate activities between different departments.

Within a few months of initiation the project ran into serious difficulties. Tiscali's managers concluded that they had placed excessive confidence in Wipro's management skills. Wipro was blamed for constantly rotating the key individuals in the project team from offshore without ensuring the necessary knowledge transfer. In their defense, Wipro's managers responded that Tiscali had signed up Wipro on an agreed rate, and not for overseeing project management. They also pointed out that Tiscali's failure to provide adequate internal project-progress monitoring compounded the problem. More generally, Wipro argued that Tiscali's push to expand its product range led the firm to change project requirements which ultimately had negative consequences for their ability to deliver the project on budget and on time.

It was becoming clear to both Wipro's and Tiscali's managers that expecting the project to deliver billing support for all the services that Tiscali was developing and launching was far too ambitious. Tiscali's managers believed that it was Wipro's responsibility to understand and implement the complex logic of billing various services. Since there was no well-defined project scope, the request for additional new features and services from various departments such as marketing and sales and TD resulted in an ever-increasing feature list. This combined with lack of planned phased deliveries of the software led to an open-ended project. Furthermore, error in the data migration from the legacy system to the new system resulted in wrong bills being generated and sent to customers. Although Wipro was responsible for the problem, customer complaints were directed at the billing support team within the COPS team.

Facing considerable pressure from the board, Tiscali's CTO gave Wipro room to scale up resources needed to deliver the project. As a result, Wipro's on-site team grew to more than 25 members, and project costs ballooned to more than £100,000 per month. Delivery dates, however, were still being postponed. This had a serious knock-on effect on other departments such as Marketing and Sales, which also had to postpone their plans and activities in the B2B customer segment.

At a board meeting in December 2003, the head of finance expressed concern at the mounting costs, pointing out that the total software development costs had crossed £1.3 million, with BOSE project development alone costing in excess of £800,000. The finance department openly questioned the original decision, suggesting that TD could have bought a cheaper "off-the-shelf" billing product from the market. The finance department began to impose more stringent controls on the project, instructing the TD to reduce Wipro project headcount.

The sales department had been waiting for rollout of the billing system so that they could offer customers discounts, promotions, and more attractive service packages. Unfortunately, with the upsurge of B2B broadband orders, they could not wait any longer for development activity on the billing system to finish, and decided instead to hire another team of external consultants to develop a separate ADSL billing system specifically designed to bill the customers for broadband services. Though this alternate system was limited in terms of features compared to what Wipro envisaged, it enabled the sales team to move forward with sales of broadband services to its customers.

The TD was coming under tremendous pressure to put its house in order. Tiscali's CTO moved to dismiss one of the external billing consultants and the Wipro project manager and placed an internal project manager on the project. Tiscali also asked Wipro to shift 80% of the work to its offshore facility to cut on the cost of development. The Wipro on-site team was reduced to 6 members on-site, and 15 members were now working at its Bangalore facility. A weekly teleconference mechanism was set up where teams from sales, billing support team, and development team would sit and discuss weekly progress of the project. With total cost of Wipro resources on this project reaching around £1 million, Tiscali started negotiating fresh billing rates with Wipro. Wipro refused to lower these to the level stipulated by Tiscali managers, resulting in the decline of Wipro on-site resources at Tiscali. Wipro was seen as a liability by Tiscali managers, and in March 2004, Tiscali decided to replace Wipro with Mahindra British Telecommunications (MBT). MBT offered Tiscali billing rates that were 25% lower than Wipro, and was known to have extensive expertise in telecommunications, in part because of its long-standing strategic partnership with BT.

Within six weeks, MBT took over from Wipro and started working on BOSE. MBT also continued with Tiscali's preferred hybrid model of outsourcing, with 80% of resources working offshore and 20% deployed on-site. With MBT assuming total ownership of BOSE, it also started to work with the B2B sales department with a view to delivering further enhancements in the system. By January 2005, with the active participation of the billing team (in highlighting the billing-related issues and giving suggestions to fix them), the sales team (in cutting down complex sets of billing rules), and the finance team (by providing adequate funds), BOSE was finally rolled out successfully.

Application support (May 2004–February 2008)

By mid 2004, with aggressive pricing strategy in place, Tiscali was growing rapidly, signing up 150,000 B2C broadband customers every quarter. Growing customer numbers in turn posed a serious challenge for COPS, which in turn put pressure on the Marketing and Sales departments. The latter departments were especially concerned about damage to the Tiscali brand caused by poor service support. With TD recovering from budget overrun from the BOSE project, and MBT gaining internal reputation for leading the turnaround, Tiscali approached MBT to lower the cost of application support for a variety of activities. The proposal was to offshore activities such as enhancing software applications to reflect promotions and aggressive discount schemes, developing software documentation, and troubleshooting problems reported by B2C customers with use of services such as web mail, website hosting. TD was central to the success of this initiative, as it would provide training to kick-start the project and subsequently feed the technical design of the applications to the offshore team; and document and report any technical bugs on a routine basis. MBT proposed the formation of a separate offshore application support team of 10 people in Bangalore with one project manager based on-site in the London office to coordinate the activities. Tiscali sent four members from its in-house core technology team to Bangalore to lead the training of the offshore team.

The offshore team was expected to interact with COPS, marketing and pricing teams, and internal TD. For instance, COPS managers relied on the offshore team for troubleshooting problems reported by B2C customers. Marketing and Sales functions also relied on the offshore team for activities such as price setting, and support for the automated self-service selling environment for B2C and B2B customers. The latter involved frequently updating the various options that allowed customers to create a bespoke package. Tiscali managers saw the offshore team as an extension of internal TD, and expected quick turnarounds. As the burden on the application support team increased, its ability to meet the requirements of other departments became increasingly constrained. The MBT on-site project manager argued for a larger team as a solution to address the productivity issues, leading Tiscali to increase the offshore team size to 30.

However, performance issues persisted. The dependence of sales, COPS, and TD on the offshore application team was having an adverse affect on Tiscali's operations. For instance, the sales team often found itself waiting for the offshore application team to integrate new service options, or add new promotional offers. Failure to quickly add promotions, or even worse, getting them wrong, led to customer complaints which in turn added to pressure on COPS. The COPS team was also dependent on the offshore team for a range of activities such as upgrading software tools and documentation used by call center staff to resolve customer queries, providing reports on customer orders and complaints. Often these requirements were fed to the MBT on-site project manager, but in many instances individual managers bypassed this manager, placing requests directly with the individual offshore team members in order to speed up delivery. Managers from TD, in turn, complained that the offshore team frequently failed to document the enhancements it made to the applications, or resolve issues according to the priority assigned.

In an industry where customers could opt out of the standard 12-month contract if adequate service level is not maintained, the growing volume of customer complaints was a cause of increasing concern to Tiscali's top management. Accordingly, TD started monitoring the extent of the problem by closely keeping tabs on the monthly figures of problem resolutions carried out by the application support. It also fired the MBT on-site offshore manager and promoted the most energetic member of the offshore team as on-site offshore manager. Tiscali also bought into MBT's recommendation to introduce a parallel application support team on-site with a mandate to respond to urgent requests from sales and COPS team. Reflecting on his experience, the MBT account manager pointed out:

> When Tiscali engaged us, we found there was no overarching structure in place to understand how technology interfaced with their business processes. We had had success with the billing systems development project, and that had given us some confidence that we understood how the company worked. I think, every time complications occurred during the application development, we had to do lot of fire-fighting at our end to understand the source and impact of the problem across the company, from COPS to TD to our development team.

PHASE 3: TISCALI EVOLUTION (AUGUST 2006–FEBRUARY 2008)

In the early part of 2006, the UK market was seeing the emergence of triple-play service providers offering a combination of voice, data, and digital television. Tiscali wanted to deliver triple-play services rapidly to increase average revenue per customer. In August 2006, Tiscali acquired HomeChoice, a video-on-demand services provider. Tiscali managers recognized that the company faced the challenge efficiently integrating the systems, processes, and people of both the organizations. The challenge was particularly acute for TD. As Tiscali's CTO recounted:

> Towards the end of 2006, we endeavored to integrate Tiscali and HomeChoice. The integration process progressed very slowly and took much longer than we expected. It disrupted normal functioning of the TD. We hired 1/3 staff from HomeChoice. Unlike us, TD in HomeChoice was very structured and process oriented which prompted a cultural shift in the TD.

During the same period OFCOM, the regulator for the UK communications industries, pushed deregulation by opening access to BT infrastructure. As part of what came to be known as the Metallic Path Facility policy (MPF), OFCOM required BT to give all voice and data service providers direct access to copper lines from customer premises to the BT exchange. Above all, the MPF platform allowed Tiscali the opportunity to move ahead with triple-play offerings. But doing so required a major revamping of Tiscali's infrastructure and management processes. In the first quarter of 2007, Tiscali hired Logica CMG to conduct a review of TD's performance. The review suggested that TD needed to change the whole service delivery model to a "waterfall" model of software development. This required Tiscali and its offshore partner to follow a sequential software development process from initial requirement specification to design, to implementation, integration, validation, and then installation and subsequent maintenance. While discussing the revamp of TD's operation, the management also reevaluated Tiscali's offshoring strategy. The main question confronting the management was whether to continue with MBT or seek a new offshoring partner. The CTO called a meeting of all department managers to review the matter. There was general consensus that though Tiscali had experienced delays in the application development projects managed by MBT, finding a new partner required a lengthy evaluation exercise that would be best to avoid.

In November 2006, therefore, Tiscali awarded MBT the MPF platform rollout project, which was critical to Tiscali's success in the triple-play market. MBT carried out all key development activities at its offshore facility, but in an attempt to conform to the new process-oriented approach adopted by TD, it expected Tiscali to carry out testing onshore. However, no proper test environment existed onshore, and TD scrambled to conduct testing. The new process orientation, however, greatly hampered these efforts. Under pressure to implement this new orientation, TD found it difficult to contain development costs and meet schedules. The project, which was expected to last no more than three months, took eight months to be completed.

The delay in the project put Tiscali in a difficult strategic position. The company not only had to continue serving existing customers using the higher cost BT platform instead of the much cheaper MPF platform, but it also had to sign new customers at prices that were lower than originally anticipated. The impact on Tiscali's low-cost strategy was significant, and was felt by other areas within the company. The finance department was forced to revise initial returns on investment forecast used for borrowing funds to meet MPF equipment and installation costs. Higher than expected operating costs were also curtailing the revenue forecasts of the sales department. But even more serious was the impact on the ability of the sales department to offer customers the full range of bundled services.

The delay in the MPF project also adversely impacted a related IPTV platform-integration project launched soon after HomeChoice acquisition. The project involved transferring all of HomeChoice's 45,000 customers to Tiscali's MPF platform. In practice, this meant developing an interface between Tiscali and HomeChoice's platform that allowed for delivery of on-demand digital television. The integration was estimated to take six months, and was to be managed onshore with in-house resources. The subsequent yearlong delay was a major strategic setback for Tiscali. It not only meant that Tiscali had forfeited the opportunity to reposition itself early as triple-play provider, but was once again forced to heavily discount its prices in order to retain market share. Unfortunately, as a late mover Tiscali soon discovered the limits of price discounting in a market where bundling triple-play services is competitively crucial. By October 2007, Tiscali had lost 15,000 customers. In retrospect, Tiscali managers placed much of the blame on a combination of decisions-shifting development to a process-oriented approach, while at the same time increasing reliance on offshore vendors to deliver projects on time and on budget.

CASE 25

Pixar

When nominations for the Academy Awards were announced in January 2011, *Toy Story 3* received nominations for best picture and for best animated feature. This represented the second consecutive film from Pixar Animation Studios that was nominated in both categories. The latest offering from the studio had already been heralded by almost all of the critics as soon as it had been released during the prior summer. It had also become the first animated feature to gross more than $1 billion in theaters worldwide, landing it in the top spot among the highest-earning animated films of all time. Although Pixar has not won for the best picture, it has already claimed its four Oscars for best animation, which represents half of the eight trophies that have been handed out since the category was added in 2001.

The recent string of successful releases—*Ratatouille, Wall-E*, and *Up*—suggests that Pixar has continued to flourish despite its 2006 acquisition by the Walt Disney Company for the hefty sum of $7.4 billon. The deal was finalized by Steve Jobs, the Apple Computer chief executive who also heads the computer animation firm. Jobs had developed a production and distribution pact with Disney, under which the two firms split the profits that Pixar films generated from ticket sales, video sales, and merchandising royalties. But the deal was set to expire after the release of *Cars* in the summer of 2006. Disney CEO, Bob Iger, worked hard to clinch the deal to acquire Pixar, whose track record has made it one of the world's most successful animation companies.

Both Jobs and Iger realized, however, that they must try and protect Pixar's creative culture while they also try to carry some of this over to Disney's animation efforts. Even though Pixar has continued to operate independently of Disney's own animation studios, its key talent has overseen the combined activities of both Pixar and Disney. As part of the deal, Jobs gained considerable influence over Disney by assuming the position of a nonindependent director and becoming its largest individual stockholder.

In order to ensure that Pixar manages to preserve its free-wheeling entrepreneurial culture, Jobs sits on a committee that includes other top talent from the animation studio whose key task is to protect its unique approach to making movies. Pixar's lengthy process of crafting a film stands in stark contrast to the production-line approach that has been pursued by Disney. This contrast in culture is best reflected in the Oscars that the employees at Pixar have displayed proudly, but which have been painstakingly dressed in Barbie doll clothing.

Above all, everyone at Pixar remains committed to making films that are original in concept and execution, despite the risks involved. They have begun to make some sequels, but only when they are able to come up with a new and compelling story that can make use of the old characters. However, it is not clear how long Pixar can keep generating hits, given their reliance on a high level of creativity. These concerns have continued to grow since no other studio has managed to generate such an unbroken string of successful films (see Exhibit 1).

PUSHING FOR COMPUTER ANIMATED FILMS

The roots of Pixar stretch back to 1975 with the founding of a vocational school in Old Westbury, New York, called the New York Institute of Technology. It was there that Edwin E. Catmull, a straitlaced Mormon from Salt Lake City who loved animation but couldn't draw, teamed up with the people who would later form the core of Pixar. "It was artists and technologists from the very start," recalled Alvy Ray Smith, who worked with Catmull during those years. "It was like a fairy tale."[1]

By 1979, Catmull and his team decided to join forces with famous Hollywood director, George W. Lucas, Jr. They were hopeful that this would allow them to pursue their dream of making animated films. As part of Lucas's film-making facility in San Rafael, California, Catmull's group of aspiring animators was able to make substantial progress in the art of computer animation. But the unit was not able to generate any profits and Lucas was not willing to let it grow beyond using computer animation for special effects.

Catmull finally turned in 1985 to Jobs, who had just been ousted from Apple. Jobs was reluctant to invest in a firm that wanted to make full length feature films using computer animation. But a year later, Jobs did decide to buy Catmull's unit for just $10 million, which represented

This case was developed by Jamal Shamsie, Michigan State University. Material has been drawn from published sources. To be used for purposes of class discussion.

EXHIBIT 1
PIXAR MILESTONES

1986	Steve Jobs buys Lucas's computer group and christens it Pixar. The firm completes a short film, *Luxo Jr.*, which is nominated for an Oscar.
1988	Pixar adds computer-animated ads to its repertoire, making spots for Listerine, Lifesavers, and Tropicana. Another short one, *Tin Toy*, wins an Oscar.
1991	Pixar signs a production agreement with Disney. Disney is to invest $26 million; Pixar is to deliver at least three full-length, computer-animated feature films.
1995	Pixar releases *Toy Story*, the first fully digital feature film, which becomes the top-grossing movie of the year and wins an Oscar. A week after release, the company goes public.
1997	Pixar and Disney negotiate a new agreement: a 50–50 split of development costs and profits of five feature-length movies. Short *Geri's Game* wins an Oscar.
1998–99	*A Bug's Life* and *Toy Story 2* are released, together pulling in $1.3 billion in box office and video.
2001–04	A string of hits from Pixar: *Monsters Inc., Finding Nemo,* and *The Incredibles.*
2006	Disney acquires Pixar and assigns responsibilities for its own animation unit to Pixar's creative brass. *Cars* is released and becomes another box office hit.
2009	*Wall-E* becomes the fourth film from Pixar to receive the Oscar for a feature-length animated film.

Source: Pixar.

a third of Lucas' asking price. While the newly named Pixar Animation Studios tried to push the boundaries of computer animation over the next five years, Jobs ended up having to invest an additional $50 million—more than 25% of his total wealth at the time. "There were times that we all despaired, but fortunately not all at the same time," said Jobs.[2]

Still, Catmull's team did continue to make substantial breakthroughs in the development of computer-generated full-length feature films. In 1991, Disney ended up giving Pixar a three-film contract that started with *Toy Story*. When the movie was finally released in 1995, its success surprised everyone in the film industry. Rather than the nice little film Disney had expected, *Toy Story* became the sensation of 1995. It rose to the rank of the third highest-grossing animated film of all time, earning $362 million in worldwide box office revenues.

Within days, Jobs had decided to take Pixar public. When the shares, priced at $22, shot past $33, Jobs called his best friend, Oracle CEO Lawrence J. Ellison, to tell him he had company in the billionaire's club. With Pixar's sudden success, Jobs returned to strike a new deal with Disney. Early in 1996, at a lunch with Walt Disney chief Michael D. Eisner, Jobs made his demands: an equal share of the profits, equal billing on merchandise and on-screen credits, and guarantees that Disney would market Pixar films as they did its own.

BOOSTING THE CREATIVE COMPONENT

With the success of *Toy Story*, Jobs realized that he had hit something big. He had obviously tapped into his Silicon Valley roots and turned to computers to forge a unique style of creative moviemaking. In each of their subsequent films, Pixar has continued to develop computer animation that has allowed for more lifelike backgrounds, texture, and movement than ever before. For example, since real leaves are translucent, Pixar's engineers developed special software algorithms that both reflect and absorb light, creating luminous scenes among jungles of clover.

In spite of the significance of these advancements in computer animation, Jobs was well aware that successful feature films would require a strong creative spark. He understood that it would be the marriage of technology with creativity that would allow Pixar to rise above most of its competition. To get that, Jobs fostered a campus-like environment within the newly formed outfit similar to the freewheeling, charged atmosphere in the early days of his beloved Apple, where he also returned as acting CEO. "It's not simply the technology that makes Pixar," said Dick Cook, President of Walt Disney studios.[3]

Even though Jobs has played a crucial supportive role, it is Catmull, now elevated to the position of Pixar's president, that has been mainly responsible for insuring that the firm's technological achievements help to pump up the firm's creative efforts. He has been the keeper of the company's unique innovative culture, which has blended Silicon Valley techies, Hollywood production honchos, and artsy animation experts. In the pursuit of Catmull's vision, this eclectic group has transformed their office cubicles into tiki huts, circus tents, and cardboard castles with bookshelves that are stuffed with toys and desks that are adorned with colorful iMac computers.

Catmull has also been working hard to build upon this pursuit of creative innovation by creating programs to develop the employees. Employees are encouraged to devote up to four hours a week, every week, to further their education at Pixar University. The in-house training program offers 110 different courses that cover subjects such as live improvisation, creative writing, painting, drawing, sculpting, and cinematography. The school's dean is Randall E. Nelson, a former juggler who has been known to perform his act using chainsaws so students in animation classes have something compelling to draw.

It is such an emphasis on the creative use of technology that has kept Pixar on the cutting edge. The firm has turned out ever more lifelike short films, including 1998's Oscar-winning *Geri's Game*, which used a technology called subdivision surfaces. This makes realistic simulation of human skin and clothing possible. "They're absolute geniuses," gushed Jules Roman, cofounder and CEO of rival Tippett Studio. "They're the people who created computer animation really."[4]

BECOMING ACCOMPLISHED STORYTELLERS

A considerable part of the creative energy goes into story development. Jobs understands that a film works only if its story can move the hearts and minds of families round the world. His goal is to develop Pixar into an animated movie studio that becomes known for the quality of its storytelling above everything else. "We want to create some great stories and characters that endure with each generation," Jobs has recently stated.[5]

For story development, Pixar relies heavily on 43-year-old John Lasseter, who goes by the title of vice president of the creative team. Known for his Hawaiian shirts and irrepressible playfulness, Lasseter has been the key to the appeal of all of Pixar's films. Lasseter gets very passionate about developing great stories and then harnessing computers to tell these stories. Most of Pixar's employees believe it is this passion that has allowed the studio to ensure that each of its films has been a commercial hit. In fact, Lasseter is being regarded as the Walt Disney of the 21st century.

When it's time to start a project, Lasseter isolates a group of eight or so writers and directs them to forget about the constraints of technology. The group bounces ideas off each other, taking collective responsibility for developing a story. While many studios try to rush from script to production, Lasseter takes up to two years just to work out all the details. Once the script has been developed, artists create storyboards and copy them onto videotapes called reels. Even computer-animated films must begin with pencil sketches that are viewed on tape. "You can't really shortchange the story development," Lasseter has emphasized.[6]

Only after the basic story has been set does Lasseter begin to think about what he'll need from Pixar's technologists. And it's always more than the computer animators expect. Lasseter, for example, demanded that the crowds of ants in *A Bug's Life* not be a single mass of look-alike faces. To solve the problem, computer expert William T. Reeves developed software that randomly applied physical and emotional characteristics to each ant. In another instance, writers brought a model of a butterfly named Gypsy to researchers, asking them to write code so that when she rubs her antennas, you can see the hairs press down and pop back up.

At any stage during the process, Lasseter may go back to potential problems that he may see with the story. In *A Bug's Life*, for example, the story was totally revamped after more than a year of work had been completed. Originally, it was about a troupe of circus bugs run by P.T. Flea that tries to rescue a colony of ants from marauding grasshoppers. But because of a flaw in the story—why would the circus bugs risk their lives to save stranger ants?—codirector Andrew Stanton recast the story to be about Flik, the heroic ant that recruits Flea's troupe to fight the grasshoppers. "You have to rework and rework it," explained Lasseter. "It is not rare for a scene to be rewritten as much as 30 times."[7]

PUMPING OUT THE HITS

In spite of its formidable string of hits, Pixar has had difficulty in stepping up its pace of production. Although they may cost 30% less, computer-generated animated films do still take considerable time to develop. Furthermore, because of the emphasis on every single detail, Pixar used to complete most of the work on a film before moving on to the next one. Catmull and Lasseter have since decided to work on several projects at the same time, but the firm has not been able to release more than one movie in a year.

In order to push for an increase in production, Pixar has more than doubled its number of employees over the last decade. It is also turning to a stable of directors to oversee its movies. Lasseter, who directed Pixar's first three films, is supervising other directors who are taking helm of various films that the studio chooses to develop. *Monsters Inc.*, *Finding Nemo, The Incredibles*, and *Ratatouille* were directed by some of this new talent. But there are concerns about the number of directors that Pixar can rely upon to turn out high-quality animated films. Michael Savner of Bane of America Securities commented: "You can't simply double production. There is a finite amount of talent."[8]

To meet the faster production pace, Catmull has also added new divisions including one to help with the development of new movies and one to oversee movie development shot by shot. The eight-person development team has helped to generate more ideas for new films. "Once more ideas are percolating, we have more options to choose from so no one artist is feeling the weight of the world on their shoulders," said Sarah McArthur, Pixar's vice president of production.[9]

Finally, Catmull is also turning to new technology in order to help ramp up production (see Exhibit 2). His goal is to reduce the number of animators to no more than 100 per film. Toward this end, Catmull has been overseeing the development of new animation software, called Luxo, which has allowed fewer people to do more work. While the firm's old system did allow animators to easily make a change to a specific character, Luxo adjusts the environment as well. For example, if an animator adds a new head to a monster, the system would automatically cast the proper shadow.

Catmull is well aware of the dangers of growth for a studio whose successes came out of a lean structure that wagered everything on each film. It remains to be seen whether Pixar can keep drawing on its talent to increase

EXHIBIT 2
PROPRIETARY SOFTWARE

Marionette
An animation software system used for modeling, animating, and lighting.

RingMaster
A production management software system for scheduling, coordinating, and tracking a computer animation project.

RenderMan
A rendering software system for high-quality, photo-realistic image synthesis.

Source: Pixar.

production without compromising the high standards that have been set by Catmull and Lasseter. Jobs has been keen to maintain the quality of every one of Pixar's films by ensuring that each one gets the best efforts of the firm's animators, storytellers, and technologists. "Quality is more important than quantity," he recently emphasized. "One home run is better than two doubles."[10]

In order to preserve its high standards, Catmull has been working hard to retain Pixar's commitment to quality even as it grows. He has been using Pixar University to encourage collaboration among all employees so that they can develop and retain the key values that are tied to their success. And he has helped devise ways to avoid collective burnout. A masseuse and a doctor now come by Pixar's campus each week, and animators must get permission from their supervisors if they want to work more than 50 hours a week.

TO INFINITY AND BEYOND?

The continued success of Pixar's films clearly indicates that it has continued to turn out quality films even after it was acquired by Disney in 2006. This has managed to settle some of the concerns that arose at the time of the acquisition about its possible effect on Pixar's rather unique creative culture. David Price, author of a recent book on the animation firm, stated: "Most acquisitions, particularly in media, are value-destroying as opposed to value-creating and that certainly has not turned out to be the case here."[11]

Along the same lines, Jobs recently expressed his satisfaction with the close relationship that the two animation studios have developed with each other: "Disney is the only company with animation in their DNA."[12] In fact, the acquisition of Pixar was viewed as an attempt by Disney to boost its own animation efforts by acquiring a group in which the talent of the individuals and the quality of the finished product are valued above everything else.

In order to ensure this, Ed Catmull and John Lasseter have been given charge of the combined animation business of both Pixar and Disney. In fact, *Tangled* represents the first Disney film that was completed under the supervision of these Pixar heads. For Lasseter, the new responsibilities for Disney have represented a return to his roots. He had been inspired by Disney films as a kid and started his career at Disney before being lured away to Pixar by Catmull. "For many of us at Pixar, it was the magic of Disney that influenced us to pursue our dreams of becoming animators, artists, storytellers and filmmakers," Lasseter recently stated.[13]

But Catmull and Lasseter continue to face a challenging task. They must ensure that they keep developing hits for Pixar even as they try to turn things around at Disney (see Exhibit 3). Both of them, however, are confident of their ability to instill and maintain a strong sense of creativity. Part of their success lies in their faith in the talent that they recruit and train to work together. This leads to a continuous exchange of ideas and fosters a collective sense of responsibility on all their projects. "We created the studio we want to work in," Lasseter had remarked recently. "We have an environment that's wacky. It's a creative brain trust: It's not a place where I make my movies—it's a place where a group of people make movies."[14]

EXHIBIT 3 LEADING ANIMATED FILMS

All eleven of Pixar's films released to date have ended up among the top animated films of all time based on worldwide box office revenues in millions of US dollars.

TITLE	YEAR	STUDIO	REVENUES
1 Toy Story 3	**2010**	**Pixar**	**$1063**
2 Shrek 2	2004	Dreamworks	$920
3 Ice Age: Dawn of the Dinosaurs	2009	Fox	$887
4 Finding Nemo	**2003**	**Pixar**	**$868**
5 Shrek 3	2007	Dreamworks	$799
6 The Lion King	1994	Disney	$784
7 Up	**2009**	**Pixar**	**$731**
8 Shrek Forever After	2010	Dreamworks	$712*
9 Ice Age: Meltdown	2006	Fox	$655
10 Kung Fu Panda	2008	Dreamworks	$632
11 The Incredibles	**2005**	**Pixar**	**$631**
12 Ratatouille	**2007**	**Pixar**	**$624**
13 Madagascar: Escape 2 Africa	2008	Dreamworks	$604
14 Madagascar	2005	Dreamworks	$533
15 The Simpsons Movie	2007	Fox	$527
16 Monsters, Inc	**2002**	**Pixar**	**$525**
17 Wall-E	**2009**	**Pixar**	**$521**
18 Aladdin	1992	Disney	$504
19 Toy Story 2	**1999**	**Pixar**	**$485**
20 How to Train your Dragon	2010	Dreamworks	$484
21 Shrek	2001	Dreamworks	$483
22 Cars	**2006**	**Pixar**	**$462**
23 Tarzan	1999	Disney	$448
24 Happy Feet	2006	Warner Bros	$384
25 Ice Age	2002	Fox	$383
26 Monsters vs Aliens	2009	Dreamworks	$382
27 Beauty and the Beast	1991	Disney	$377
28 A Shark's Tale	2004	Dreamworks	$367
29 A Bug's Life	**1998**	**Pixar**	**$363**
30 Toy Story	**1995**	**Pixar**	**$362**

Source: IMDB, Variety.

CASE 26

Natura: The Magic Behind Brazil's Most Admired Company

Exame magazine, in charge of a yearly company ranking in Brazil, compared the cosmetics company Natura, winner of the Most Admired Company Award in 1998,[1] to the ideal Brazilian business model:

> A school of Samba [Brazilian dance groups who practice all year to perform in Carnival]. Reasons: its capacity to mobilize for each year, in a synchronized movement, spontaneous and informal, a mass of people highly motivated around a common goal.
>
> —*Exame*, July 8, 1998, "Excelência Perfumada"

Luiz Seabra, Guilherme Leal, and Pedro Passos, the three presidents of Natura, got together at their São Paulo headquarters after the recognition ceremony. The publicity had added pressure to come to a decision on Natura's new growth strategy. Natura had perfected its success formula in recent years: a well-trained and motivated door-to-door direct sales force of 220,000, selling premium, high margin cosmetic and personal care products to middle- and upper-class customer segments in Brazil (an unusual customer base in the direct sales industry). Natura had built a strong brand with the highest consumer loyalty in the industry by incorporating honesty and ethics into its marketing approach. The company's turnover had grown at 37% CAGR[2] in the preceding six years and in 1997 return on capital reached 22.3%, significantly higher than the 4.8% median reached by the largest 500 companies in Brazil, and most Fortune 500 companies. The three presidents feared Natura would be tempted to rest comfortably on its laurels with its 9% sales growth in 1998, which although humble compared to its past performance was still way above the industry average of 2%.

The market environment had only become increasingly competitive. Domestic competition had intensified with the opening of the Brazilian market and the stabilization of the economy in 1994, and Natura's second attempt to internationalize had yet to yield gains. The removal of import tariffs and the creation of trading blocks like Mercosur made the region much more attractive for foreign players. Large corporations already established in Brazil like Avon, P&G, and Gessy Lever had begun to wake up from their slumber and new players had begun to pour into the region. Imports in the sector rose to US$250 million in 1997, more than double the US$118 million in 1996. Global consolidation trends put increasing pressure on Natura. With 36 major mergers and acquisitions in the preceding decade, the industry was becoming increasingly concentrated in the hands of a few major global players. For Natura, the implications were that it had to benchmark itself against international standards of quality and innovation, and face competitors with deeper pockets and diversified product portfolios. The Brazilian consumer now had a more stable income, but had also become more demanding. As a result, Natura's impressive growth and margins were both under threat.

The options for growth meant diverging from Natura's traditional success formula to expand Natura's cosmetics and skin care lines with nutritional supplements and healthcare products or to consider channels outside of direct selling such as stores or the Internet. New product segments could leverage Natura's strong brand and sales force, but would demand a new marketing strategy, a new R&D division, and acquiring expertise in a completely different industry. A change in the sales channel would undermine the current sales force, but may be anticipating future market trends.

As was often the case, each of the three presidents looked at the issue from different angles. Seabra, the founder, was worried it would be hard to provide customers with the same quality of innovative concepts as in cosmetics, and thought broadening the sales channel from direct selling would go against the relationship building philosophy they had expounded for the last 30 years. It would be an act of treason toward Natura's faithful Consultants (the name given to direct sellers at Natura). Leal, CEO and President, on the other hand was enthusiastic. Going into Internet sales was a futuristic concept that had not been tried by competitors in Brazil yet, and could represent unlimited growth. Leal thought an expansion into new segments would require Natura to merge or set a joint venture to acquire know-how. Passos, Natura's COO and President,

This case was prepared by Marcela Escobari, visiting researcher at LBS, under the supervision and guidance of Professor Sumantra Ghoshal and Professor Don Sull. This case is intended to serve as a basis for class discussion rather than to illustrate either effective or ineffective handling of an administrative situation. The cooperation of Natura S.A. and Fundação Dom Cabral is gratefully acknowledged.

was concerned about whether Natura had the resources for these initiatives now, and needed a quick resolution to plan how the new factory they were building would incorporate production lines for nutritional products.

As with all major decisions, Natura's growth strategy would have to be negotiated until consensus was reached. But this time they could not afford the luxury of dragging the decision for a year, as had happened the last time that they were not able to reach consensus.

GLOBAL INDUSTRY DYNAMICS

Growth and consolidation in the global cosmetics industry

The cosmetics and personal care industry was dominated by large established players with increasing global operations. The size of the market reached US$168.2 billion in 1998, a 3% dip from 1997 due to the recession in Latin America and Asia. This was an exception to the impressive growth throughout the 1990s as consumers in industrialized countries traded up to premium brands and the industry expanded with the constant introduction of new products. The future looked promising with industry experts pointing to the emergence of a global middle class of 2–2.5 billion in the next 10–15 years, which would move to luxury labels faster than any previous middle class ever did.[3] The power to capture this growth as well as the recuperation of emerging markets resided with the increasingly smaller number of global giants who had come to dominate the industry. The global market share of the top 20 players had grown to 72% in 1998, with the top 10 companies holding 54%.[4] Over the 1990s, there were 36 acquisitions in the industry valued at US$15 billion. Some of the largest included J&J buying Neutrogena in 1994 for US$1 billion, P&G buying Max Factor in 1991 for the same amount, and Estee Lauder buying Aveda in 1998 for US$300 million, to add a "natural" brand.

Blurring boundaries

The cosmetics industry had been traditionally separated into three main categories based on sales channel and price: the expensive prestige brands sold primarily through department stores or specialized stores; the cheaper mass retail market brands sold through drug stores and supermarkets; and the middle-market direct sales brands sold door-to-door. These divisions were becoming blurred as the larger players tried to reach consumers of all income brackets. Some examples of this included L'Oreal's acquisition of Maybelline, a traditionally prestige company buying a mass-market brand, or Avon, the largest direct sales player, starting to sell through stores in malls to capture wealthier customers.

The strategic priority for most of the players in the industry was to develop and promote "megabrands" on a global basis (like P&G's "Oil of Olay" or Beiersdorf's "Nivea"), lead the industry in R&D, and expand market share through acquisitions and joint ventures.

The prestige sector

The prestige sector included companies with expensive brands such as L'Oreal (sales of US$12.4 billion in 1998), the largest player, and other global companies like Estee Lauder, Chanel, Christian Dior, Clarins, Guerlain, and Shiseido. These players focused on selling status and technological innovation. They tended to spend heavily on advertising and to promote separate brands for specific niche populations. For example, Estee Lauder's *Prescriptives* was targeted toward the professional woman; *Origins* had a natural or "green" positioning; and *M·A·C* appealed to the generation X/glamor crowd, while *Aramis* marketed men's items. Building a prestige brand to compete on its own implied huge investments over long periods of time; hence the preference for expansion through acquisition—both for accessing established brands and for obtaining the benefits of synergies in R&D and administrative expenses.

The mass-market sector

The traditional mass-market brands sold through drugstores and supermarkets by companies like P&G (Cover Girl, Oil of Olay), Unilever, Gillette, Colgate-Palmolive, and Revlon represented the largest segment with 63% of total cosmetics sales. The mass market had become more important with globalization since it was the most accessible channel in foreign countries. Competition had become fierce in this sector with prestige players entering the mass market through acquisitions (i.e., L'Oreal/Maybelline), and the emergence of an "upper mass market," offering products with the scientific advances typically available in prestige products, but at lower prices. The pressure had been felt by players like P&G, which was undergoing a major restructuring, and Revlon, which appeared to be in the process of selling one or more of its businesses.

Direct sales

Direct sales organizations (DSOs) could be categorized as a separate business due to their distinctive strategies in marketing, recruiting, and growth. Throughout history, DSOs had been very successful in attracting a population with restricted access to the formal job market by providing a profitable, flexible, and nurturing work environment. In the cosmetics business, the major DSOs included Avon (US$5.2 billion in sales), Mary Kay (approx. US$1.1 billion), and Amway (US$5.7 billion). They targeted their products to the middle/lower class segments, which were usually also the socioeconomic levels from which they built their sales force. Natura was a rare exception using direct sales to sell prestige products in Brazil.

Avon, the largest player with presence in 131 countries, had traditionally targeted the lower-middle class market, but was trying to shed its grandmotherly image and attract wealthier and younger customers. Avon had set up stands in malls around the US, quite a revolutionary departure from its 113 years of direct selling. Although the experiment had attracted first-time users, it was expected to take business away from its direct sales force.

BRAZILIAN COSMETICS INDUSTRY

When Natura was created in 1969, there was a clear division in the Brazilian cosmetics market: on one side were the cheap mass products found in drugstores and supermarkets and on the other a few luxury products sold in specialized stores. Outside of Avon, which entered Brazil in 1959 with local production facilities, there was almost no foreign competition. Import substitution policies implemented in the 1970s, with prohibitively high import tariffs, spurred domestic production for a virtually captive market. These anarchic policies lasted until the early 1980s when almost every American bank cut off its credit lines to Brazil due to political instability in the region, bringing about a long-lasting recession. In the mid-1980s, attracted by high margins in the sector, giants like P&G and Unilever entered Brazil—where Unilever was operating since the 1960s—investing significant amounts and buying brands and companies. By this time, Natura had built a prestige brand and a loyal customer base.

As Brazil opened its market in the 1990s, more foreign competition flooded in, and many of the Brazilian producers either disappeared or were bought out. Most local companies could not keep up with the innovation necessary to compete. For international players, Brazil was a naturally attractive market—the fifth largest market in the world in hygiene and beauty products consumption (measured in dollars), and the sixth largest in cosmetics. It was also 27th in income per capita, which, given its large population base (170 million), implied huge potential for increased consumption. With the inflow of foreign players, the cosmetics sector became even more concentrated than the food sector. Natura turned down repeated acquisition attempts and was able to thrive in the face of strong competitors.

In 1998, sales of cosmetics and toiletries in Latin America amounted to US$18.5 billion, of which Brazil represented almost half. Consumption in this sector more than doubled in Brazil in the three years after 1994 as inflation came under control, and a new middle class began to emerge. In 1998, the largest player in the industry was Avon, with US$840 million in sales, followed by Natura. Other companies with significant presence include Gessy Lever, O'Boticario, and L'Oreal. Among more upscale newcomers were Christian Dior, Shiseido, and Davidoff.

Avon competed with Natura for the same sales force, but its products were targeted to a lower-income client base, with average prices of one-third of Natura's. Avon had over 500,000 resellers in Brazil, with a much lower productivity than that of Natura's Consultants. In 1996, the average sale for an Avon representative was US$2,450 while Natura's was US$3,432. Product-wise, Natura's closest rival was O'Boticario, a Brazilian company with 1,616 stores, and a strong portfolio in perfumes. O'Boticario positioned its products 10–20% cheaper than Natura's.

BACKGROUND OF NATURA

In 1999, Natura marketed and distributed 300 prestige products across seven main categories: perfume, skin care, hair care, color cosmetics, sunscreen, deodorants, and children's products, targeted at the middle- and upper-class segments. Most of Natura's production took place at a factory in Itapecerica, on the outskirts of São Paulo, which produced 300 SKUs (stock keeping units), and operated at 90–95% capacity. A US$110 million project to be completed in 1999 would replace this factory with more modern facilities and fivefold capacity increase. In 1998, Natura had sales[5] of US$692 million and an EBITDA of US$83 million. Only 3% of sales came from international operations, mostly in Argentina, Chile, and Peru.

History

Luiz Seabra, Natura's founder, was first introduced to the cosmetics world when working for a multinational company at the age of 16. One of his most memorable projects was the launch of an electric shaver, quite a pioneering product in Brazil in the early 1960s. While helping with an innovative marketing scheme, Seabra first learned about the skin as a "live organ." He continued taking courses in physiology, biochemistry, and other topics related to therapeutic cosmetics, quite unusual for an economics student. Following his interests in this subject, he joined Bionat in 1966, a small family laboratory that produced cosmetics. After three years, he decided to quit and start Natura with Berjeaut—son of Bionat's owner.

They founded Natura with US$9,000 and with the idea of incorporating principles of therapeutic treatments in the production of cosmetics. They set up their first store in a garage, using the selling points that still characterized Natura: a personalized approach and products customized to Brazil's humid climate and local skin types.

The birth and fall of the five-company structure

The business only took off when the direct sales approach was implemented. After some failed attempts, Seabra partnered with Yara Amaral, an executive with extensive experience in direct sales, and founded **Pró-Estética**—to distribute products in São Paulo and manage the sales force. Other channels like drugstores and franchises were considered, but Seabra thought that it would be difficult to pass on Natura's therapeutic concepts to store attendants or investors. With distributors, Natura would have to provide high margins, and allow them to determine the way to sell, or invest heavily in publicity to help sales. Without the resources to invest in marketing, and wanting to maintain Natura's image, the direct sales method appeared to be the only viable option. They were surprised to find a large pool of capable women eager to embrace the opportunity offered by Natura. The economic recession at the time created pressure for women to find alternative sources of income, and service an existing demand that had not yet been exploited.

In order to have national distribution, Berjeaut brought in Guilherme Leal and created **Meridiana** in 1979, to distribute Natura's products to the whole country except São Paulo (covered by Pró-Estética) and Rio de Janeiro (covered by an independent distributor). Guilherme was trained in business and, following a change of government, had just lost his job at a public railroad company. As Natura continued to grow in the early 1980s, new partners were brought in and additional companies were founded. Yara Amaral, Beal, and a cosmetics producer founded **YGA** to make color cosmetics and perfumes, and **Éternelle** was created to replace the independent distributor in Rio de Janeiro. Pedro Passos was brought in by Leal to head the industrial area at the YGA factory in 1983. They had worked together at the railroad company, and had continued to play soccer on the same team every week. When asked what he saw in Passos, a production engineer from the Polytechnic Institute in São Paulo, Leal answered, "he was a player with character and a powerful inner drive."

This growing corporate structure helped Natura experience explosive sales growth in the 1980s, aided by Brazil's closed economy, high inflation, and unstable currency that made foreign competition unfeasible. The five-company structure was an effective response to the needs for quick growth and new capital infusion. It also provided an internal competitive dynamic that pushed the company forward.

> Meridiana wanted to surpass Pró-Estética in sales, YGA wanted to surpass Natura in sales. There was a fight to see who had a more important participation in the sales channel. During this time when we were relatively alone in the market, that internal competitive energy forced each [company] to make more innovative products and improve quality, trying to win the attention of the consultants. This internal struggle created energy for growth.
>
> —Pedro Passos, COO and President, Natura

Natura's sales jumped from US$5 million in 1979 to US$170 million in 1989 (43% CAGR). The number of consultants grew from 1,000 to 33,000 for the respective years. Natura's growth was quite unusual during what was seen as the "lost decade" for many Brazilian businesses. During this time, 9 zeros were removed from the currency, 10 failed currency plans were attempted, and 11 finance ministers rotated through office.

Finally, at the height of the economic crisis in 1989, Natura's growth came to a screeching halt. Inflation of 89% per month, costly capital, and the opening of the Brazilian economy contributed to Natura's instability. Earnings slumped and Natura was forced to dismiss 15% of its workforce. As new competitors started to pour in, Natura realized it had limited production capacity, an outdated product portfolio, low quality services to its sales force, and a complex decision-taking process due to the five-company structure. Internal conflicts within the company made it difficult to react to the changing environment.

> The energy created by the 5 companies became negative energy. By 1989 we needed a more long-term plan, to invest in a new factory, technology, professionals—but we couldn't agree on a common strategic plan for the different companies. . . . There were four major partners who owned 80% of the companies, but they weren't the same ones in each company. Decisions became slow, we couldn't agree on new products, new price policies . . . the interests [of the major shareholders] were not homogeneous. We had reached an impasse.
>
> —Pedro Passos, COO and President, Natura

The shareholders had polarized their positions: one group led by Seabra and Leal wanted to invest significantly in growing the business while the others were content with Natura's performance and wanted to cash out. Finally, Seabra and Leal bought out the stakes[6] of the other shareholders and, together with Pedro Passos (a minority shareholder at the time), created the existing triumvirate to lead the company toward growth. Decisions would have to be negotiated and discussed but there was an underlying common goal.

Restructuring and professionalization

A three-year period of transformation followed. The two factories and three distribution centers were merged into one company under one brand—Natura. The headquarters moved to a new factory, with 50% increased capacity, and the production and distribution centers were centralized. The new owners reinvested all profits to develop new operational, information and planning systems and revamp the product line with new technology. The original values and vision of the company were reinforced and the company became increasingly aware of its social responsibilities. Realizing that the company was becoming larger than its owners could handle, a new management team was recruited from multinationals. Nine of the 11 directors in 1999 were brought in from the outside. This move created some tensions with the incumbent middle management and fears of disruption in Natura's culture, although they helped benchmark best practices and incorporate international management tools into the company. Natura was ready for the new boom that came in 1994 with the Real Plan[7] and subsequent economic stabilization. In the following four years, the company grew by over 500%.

The attempt to go international

Going international seemed like a natural growth progression for a company growing at the pace of Natura in the 1980s, and a necessary hedge to the sporadic economic crisis faced by Brazil. After three attempts, Natura realized the difficulties with exporting a brand and an image outside of

Brazil. The first attempt to go abroad was not structured: it began through the initiative of a few ex-Natura managers who started distribution in Bolivia and Chile importing the products from Brazil. In a similar manner, distribution was opened in Peru, Paraguay, and Uruguay on a small scale. In 1994, the effort was revisited with added commitment to Argentina. An ex-manager of Avon was hired to head the office in Argentina, but without much guidance from the headquarters and no background on Natura, it ended a complete failure.

> We didn't have the knowledge where we needed it . . . We created an Avon operation down in Argentina with the Natura brand. It is very different, the concept, the value added, the demonstration [of the product] . . . Our prices in Brazil are normally 3 times higher than Avon, because we have a niche market, quality, and a brand image which support this.
>
> —Guilherme Leal, CEO and President, Natura

The growth in Brazil at the time was so high that there were no internal human resources to devote to Argentina.

> Natura was growing at a rate of 100% per year, and between growing 100% in Brazil where we had an important critical mass and growing 300% starting from zero, it was better to grow at the headquarters. It was a matter of resources; we did have financial resources, but we lacked primarily human resources. The Brazilian operation consumed 110% of their time.
>
> —Breno Lucki, Director of International Operations, Natura

The sales structure used in Brazil was not replicated in Argentina. In an effort to grow the sales channel fast, the incorporation of new consultants was not restricted by a minimum ordering amount. More than 50% of the channel was either "ghost" (invented names to earn the incentives offered to consultants who recruit new consultants) or final customers who wanted to benefit from the discounts. The turnover of consultants was high and sales volume was low. The group realized internationalization was much harder than expected.

The strategy was revisited once again in 1998 and efforts were targeted to Argentina. New managers from Brazil were appointed, and all directors at the headquarters were held accountable with 10% of their bonus linked to the performance of the international operations. In 1999, international sales reached US$20 million and profits were still awaited.

THE "MAGIC" BEHIND NATURA

In 1999, Natura was the largest Brazilian-owned cosmetics company, and the most profitable in the sector. It had a very favorable image among Brazilians, recognized and admired for producing quality products and for being a socially conscious company. The combination had earned Natura the title of best company in the hygiene and cosmetic sector in Brazil for three consecutive years, despite not being the largest player in the sector. Many business analysts had sought to pinpoint the formula of Natura's success, and had often resorted to "Natura's magic" in trying to explain its performance and consistent customer loyalty under difficult circumstances.

Truth in cosmetics

Natura's motto, "Truth in Cosmetics," resonated strongly among employees at all levels. According to Seabra, Natura's founder, "in an industry famed for promises and the pursuit of success at any price, Natura prides itself in offering a truthful approach to consumers." This philosophy translated into products that were clearly labeled and a sales force trained to give informed advice regarding the ingredients and appropriateness of each product. Natura's products must somehow contribute to the "well-being" of its customers, both through its choice of technology and the message behind each product. For example, Natura could not produce hair coloring products, because the process inevitably harms the hair. Same with nail polish; Natura did not include it in their cosmetics line until the R&D department found a formula that did not have formaldehyde and toluene, ingredients that tend to debilitate the nail.

New products and lines were usually launched with a message of how they contributed to customers' well-being, which was incorporated into commercials and the training to consultants. The Mother/Baby (Mama/Bebe) creams, for example, were associated with the Shantalla method, encouraging the touch and caressing that created stronger ties between the child and the mother. Chronos, the "anti-signs" cream, was marketed with the message that beauty was not achieved through the pursuit of youth but through the right attitude toward aging. Natura believed this approach had contributed to its loyal customer base, and was a key differentiation factor for its products.

> We believe we can help transform people's lives and the society. We do what we believe and make a profit from it. The functionality of the product is just one aspect of the necessities it provides . . . we deliver in our products much more than functional answers, we deliver emotions, spiritualism, intellectual ideals that can improve people's lives.
>
> —Guilherme Leal, CEO and President, Natura

Advertising

Natura's marketing campaigns highlighted the theme of "Truth in Cosmetics," which sometimes went against the norms of the industry. For example, its commercial for the Chronos line (anti-wrinkle cream) used Natura consumers over 30 years of age instead of young models, with the implicit message according to Leal that "you will not look like Claudia Schiffer with our products, but you're still beautiful." This campaign, called "Real Pretty Women," exalted middle age beauty, "since outside of technology, a woman's beauty depends on her harmonious relationship with time and the different phases of life."

This campaign had made Chronos one of the most profitable lines in Natura even though the product did not seem very different than most anti-wrinkle lines in the industry. Araujo explained how the way Natura launched this line challenged the logic of the industry:

> We had a big discussion about how to label our products for different age groups. All marketing benchmarks advised against putting the ages on the product since women tend to avoid any product that clearly identifies their age. Natura challenged this notion because it went against its concept of truth.
>
> —Marcelo Araujo, Commercial Director, Natura

> The composition of the product is also differentiated. Lancome has three different products for wrinkles, one with vitamin A, another with vitamin C and another with vitamin D, which sell based on brand recognition. Our product incorporates the three vitamins. Why? Because the three vitamins are good for the skin, and how could we answer to a consumer who asked us why we separate the vitamins . . .
>
> —Philippe Pommez, R&D Director, Natura

Direct sales: win through relationships

Luiz Seabra realized early the power of relationships in people's well-being, and decided to make Natura a vehicle for these rewarding relationships. The direct sales method was an integral part of Natura's business identity, and although alternative methods like franchising, or even catalogue sales had been proposed throughout time, they had so far been discarded. Natura believed that it was the only significant company worldwide to successfully use direct sales to access upper and upper-middle demographic segments.

An army of 220,000 consultants, who received continuous training and the highest commissions in the industry, provided Natura with a significant competitive edge and created a strong barrier to entry to other newcomers. Natura's sales managers believed there were an additional 440,000 informal resellers who sold Natura products. They usually "subcontracted" from active Consultants because they did not qualify themselves or because they wanted to help a family member achieve sales targets. Managers perceived this practice as harmless given Natura's established reputation in the market.

R&D: buy instead of produce in-house

In an industry where constant innovation was the key barrier to entry, Natura knew that it could not compete with its global competitors on creating technology from scratch. Instead, it focused on coming up with innovative concepts and marketing schemes and then tracking patents and buying the technology from universities and research centers around the world. According to Philippe Pommez, Natura's R&D director, this efficient patent tracking system was a sustainable R&D policy because the technology already existed,

> The hard part is not finding the new technology, it is deciding what you are looking for. This is where Seabra's conceptualisation of new products and new lines becomes indispensable.
>
> —Philippe Pommez, R&D Director, Natura

The R&D department had close connections with universities in France and the US. This strategy allowed Natura to be competitively innovative, producing a new product every three working days (an output comparable to companies like 3M). Almost 40% of Natura's revenues were derived from products introduced within the last two years. This was achieved with an R&D department of only 150 people and a budget of around 3.0% of net sales. Most of Natura's competitors spent close to 3.5% of *sales* on R&D. L'Oreal, the producers of Lancôme and Maybelline, spent US$370 million, equivalent to 3% of sales and 48% of net income in 1998, and Shiseido alone spent US$200 million on R&D, four times as much as Natura.

Innovation/product development

Natura's innovation process started with a monthly meeting between the three presidents, the Marketing Director and the R&D director, where new ideas and technological advances would be discussed. New product ideas could be quickly tested in the market because consultants could obtain immediate feedback from the customers. Consultants were encouraged to call clients after the sale of a new product simply to gauge their reactions, and maintain a flowing relationship.

> We can be so quick in putting products in the market because we can get immediate feedback, there's no need to create test groups, etc. The close relationships between customers, consultants and promoters can give us a good notion of the product's acceptance within a week. With one of our perfumes, we realized it would be a failure from the consultants' reactions, even before it was put into the market. It was removed from the catalogs within 3 weeks.
>
> —Philippe Pommez, R&D Director, Natura

Natura's faith in the concepts behind its products often challenged industry precedents. One of Natura's daring ideas was the Mother/Baby product line launched in 1993. Although research showed that J&J, with 90% market share, had an unassailable lock in this market, Natura decided to enter anyway and succeeded in capturing a staggering share of the sector. The marketing strategy that associated the product with creating closer ties between the mother and baby, the appealing packaging, and the brand's reputation for high quality helped the line's entry to this market. Similarly, Natura ventured into the luxury perfumes segment, which was dominated by established international brands, and captured an impressive 30% share, with similar conceptual—rather than technological—innovation.

Natura's presidents believed that it was becoming harder to come up with truly innovative concepts, and they were constantly trying to stop the innovation meetings from becoming a routine.

Values

Luiz Seabra wanted to build Natura as a value-based company from its inception, and his commitment to truth and to the value of relationships had impacted every aspect of the company: its products, training programs, relationships among employees, etc. Natura's self-defined purpose was to provide well-being/being well, "to create and market products and services that promote the individual's harmonious, pleasant relationship with himself/herself and his/her own body (well-being), and at the same time with others and the world (being well)." Seabra acknowledged this might seem like "an oxymoron in today's cosmetics industry," but believed that Natura had projected and been consistent with this philosophy in all its dealings with employees and customers.

Seabra was a firm believer in the power of relationships and demonstrated this in the way he treated his employees and the sales force. He personally called every manager and director on their birthdays, he knew the names of the cleaning personnel in his office, and avoided formality in his interactions with people. His personal conduct had become a source of many of the stories and anecdotes that almost defined the soul of the company. Most employees were ready to expound on Natura's values of transparency and respect in its approach toward employees, customers, and the world around it. Manoel Luiz, manager in the IT services division, joined Natura in 1996 after heading the IT department at Einstein Hospital, São Paulo's most prestigious hospital, and explained his reasons,

> Why am I working here!? . . . I have never seen a company like this one, never. The treatment of all the people, the truth with which we work throughout the chain: with our suppliers, our employees and our resellers. It is everything, treatment, truth, payment, benefits, the vision, the mission. . . . To give you one example, this year our founder-president is living in London, and the 6th of March was my birthday. I went away for the weekend, and when I arrived there was a message from him from London: "I am very sorry I haven't met you but I'm calling to say happy birthday, happy new year of life." It is very different—in the hospital I had to call people by, Mr., Dr., to have some respect, this is not the way that I show respect. These are not the relationships I want in my life.
>
> —Manoel Luiz, Manager in IT, Natura

The office layout of Natura's headquarters reflected this sense of openness and camaraderie. Everybody except the three presidents sat in opaque pink cubicles in a large open space, from directors to customer service attendants. Everybody ate at the same cafeteria and there were no parking spaces reserved for management. Leal proudly contrasted Natura's culture to that of a bank he worked for earlier, where elevators were blocked every morning so the President of the company could ride alone while the rest of the employees watched as they waited.

Commitment to society

According to Leal, the value of a firm was proportional to the quality relationships it had with the entire community, promoting material, emotional, and spiritual enrichment. He was the driving force behind Natura's social endeavors, which centered primarily on community-based educational programs. Some programs were run by Natura employees, while others were managed in conjunction with NGOs to aid public schools. In 1997, Natura Consultants raised US$1.5 million selling T-shirts and cards to fund 46 community education projects, and every year 10% of dividends went to a department that promoted social causes. In 1998, Natura donated an additional US$2.5 million from company profits.

Flexibility for middle management

Middle management enjoyed a very high level of flexibility and autonomy in the organization. Of their annual bonus, half depended on the sales target achieved by the company and the other half was based on achieving the targets of their particular division. Managers devised their own yearly targets and then discussed them with their direct bosses. Because of this freedom to set their own targets, people tended to aim very high—much higher than what they would accept if the targets came down from above.

Although managers set their own targets, they needed to be consistent with Natura's overall goals. Every September, all the managers received Natura's yearly strategic plan devised by a council of top management led by Pedro Passos. The plan described the overall goals for the year, including growth targets in the domestic and international area, growth in new businesses, etc. Each manager then prepared the strategic plan of each area (sales, IT, logistics, manufacturing, etc.) that would help Natura achieve these goals.

> I ask myself, what do I have to do to leverage the goals of Natura? I prepare my plan first. For example, I have to have more availability of the system, more facilities for the Consultants, etc. I discuss it with my director who passes it on to Pedro. Pedro tells us it's good here, it's not enough here . . . It is discussed until everyone agrees.
>
> —Manoel Luiz, Manager in IT, Natura

Sales management

Natura's sales organization had three basic levels: sales manager (20), sales promoters (550), and consultants (220,000). Each sales manager was in charge of 20–30 promoters who covered a specified geographical area. Each promoter was responsible for training and supervising a group of consultants in a neighborhood or a whole city in more dispersed areas.

Wooing new consultants into Natura and keeping them was one of the major jobs of the promoters. Natura fiercely competed with the other major international direct sales companies such as Avon, Amway, and Mary Kay for its share of this autonomous and highly mobile workforce. To do this, Natura offered one of the highest average compensation packages in the direct sales industry, a 30%[8] profit on any product sold. Natura also tried to differentiate itself through the constant and personalized contact with the sales promoter, a complete sales support system, and Natura's positive image in the marketplace. Sales promoters organized "Natura Meetings" for their consultants every 21 days (equals one cycle), which provided continual training and reinforcement of Natura's values. These meetings tended to be fun gatherings where promoters would present promotions of new products, and provide a thorough description of the product, its ingredients, attributes, and target customer. For every meeting, the promoter counted on a video and the newsletter "Natura Consulting" put together by the headquarters for every cycle. Consultants received free courses, free support materials, and were part of an elaborate recognition program, which celebrated both performance and seniority. They could order products directly by phone and receive products at home, free of charge, with one of the fastest services in the world. Avon's sales force, in contrast, needed to send the orders through the promoter only during their periodic meetings.

Natura had two service hotlines that supported promoters on the administrative chores. The CAN (Centro de Atendimento Natura) provided pre- and post-sales support for the consultants, 14 hours a day. With 400 operators receiving 420,000 calls per month, it was one of the largest phone-based support centers in Brazil. They received product orders and provided information on delivery times, bills, promotions, and products. They provided any type of information for Natura's 23 lines, and over 300 products. When a consultant called to place an order, the attendant input the request on the computer, which was electronically sent to the warehouse where products were picked automatically and filled in boxes. Natura was able to send a package 24 hours after the request was made.

Natura's customer service hotline (SNAC) played an important role in collecting feedback from customers. The 40 telephone operators received 50,000 calls a month, regarding all types of customer needs, complaints, feedback, questions about products, etc. To encourage feedback from Brazilian customers unused to these services, these attendants enjoyed a high degree of flexibility and authority in solving customer concerns. Attendants could reimburse or replace a product under any circumstance, they could pay doctor's fees in case of adverse reactions to Natura products, reschedule consultants' debts if appropriate, etc.

Building relationships in the sales structure

Natura differentiated its direct sales operations by emphasizing the development of strong relationships between its consultants and the ultimate consumer. Consultants were trained to create trusting relationships with their clients, to provide personalized advice, and to educate their clients on the benefits of Natura's products. Partly due to this personalized treatment, Natura had the highest consumer loyalty within the industry.

Relationship building was encouraged not only toward clients, but also within the organization's structure. Sales promoters, each in charge of 250–300 consultants in a specific region, had more than a sales coordination role, they served as counselors and friends. The promoter met the consultants at their homes on a one-to-one basis through the interview process and was thereafter available to discuss nonwork-related issues. Unlike the competition, most of the promoter's salary was linked to retention of consultants rather than sales.

During "Natura Meetings" every three weeks, promoters introduced new products and promotions, and took the opportunity to socialize and share experiences. They usually invited a fraction of their consultants—50–60 at any given reunion—to maintain a manageable group. The meetings often took place at the promoter's house, where the whole family participated in the cooking and decoration, creating an intimate and personal atmosphere. The meetings were full of cheering and applauding as almost a quarter of the consultants present received a gift of some sort: for high performance in sales, bringing new consultants or random lotteries. Each promoter was free to incorporate other activities during these reunions. For example, at the beginning of the year, a promoter devoted his/her session to explaining the reasons behind the recent currency devaluation and its repercussions, and on another occasion, he/she celebrated Mother's Day reading poems and singing. Natura had the lowest turnover ratio among all direct sales companies.

Training and development of the workforce

Natura provided continual training programs for the sales force on topics ranging from product portfolio to lectures on ethics and citizenship. Managers could choose from a variety of training programs: in 1998 there was a choice of 58 courses in the areas of corporate management, production security, computer programs, operations, and quality. All managers and directors received an average of 180 hours of training in 1998. Outside of these voluntary programs, all managers were fully introduced to the mission and values of the company, its products, and sales structure. Managers also had the option of participating in an executive management program in one of the most prestigious Business Administration colleges in Brazil.

The sales promoters benefited from an extensive and structured training program: after two formal training sessions in the first three to four months of work, promoters were required to return to the headquarters every two years for a weeklong Advanced Formation Program, taught by experienced promoters, sales managers, and outside experts. New promoters were matched with more experienced promoters in the same region, to build mentoring, and support relationships that often lasted throughout his or her career.

RECRUITMENT

The majority of the managers and directors were recruited through word of mouth or personal recommendations. This method had worked best in finding people that fit Natura's culture. There was also an emphasis on hiring from within, so positions were advertised internally first to provide career advancement opportunities to employees.

THE THREE PRESIDENTS

The three-president structure at the top had been a unique feature of the company since 1995. Internally, most employees believed that the three personalities complemented each other, in a wonderful symbiosis. As Seabra explained,

> Our management team would not be as vigorous and efficient if it was based on the personality of one sole leader. The market is so complex now that a leader must dominate different languages: act with sensibility on one side, and American pragmatism on the other.
>
> —Luiz Seabra, Founder and President, Natura

The distribution of roles among the three was a natural process and reflected their different training and personalities. Seabra's intuition to gauge customers' needs and his charismatic and sincere approach toward the employees were key to Natura's culture. He had an important role in the product innovation committee and was in charge of leading important ceremonies for the sales force. Leal was the acting CEO, who concentrated on the strategy and the future direction of the company, while Pedro Passos maintained tight control over operations, making sure that all existing activities were run smoothly and efficiently. The interaction between the three had few formalisms or manuals, and had been perfected over the years. The three were often described as separate parts of a single body.

> If Leal is the head, and Passos is the arms and legs of the company, Seabra would be the soul and memory of the company's vision.
>
> —*Exame,* July 1998

Three personalities

Many of the concepts behind Natura's product lines and the values that underlie the Company's culture came from Seabra's personal beliefs. Influenced by Jungian and Buddhist philosophy, Seabra was a mystical, soft-spoken character. He built two temples (one Buddhist and the other Shintoist) and a Catholic chapel in his backyard. Probably influenced by the Jungian analyst he visited for over a decade, Seabra tried to look at the world through mythology. When talking to the consultants, instead of using complex marketing jargon to explain what moves the market, Seabra preferred to tell a story of Ananque, the goddess of necessity. Seabra was relatively the most removed from the day-to-day running of Natura, but provided the deeper insights on consumer needs and served as an inspiring force during the innovation meetings.

> Luiz [Seabra] is a man with a big passion that is the philosophy behind Natura. He is a very nice person to work with, because he is very calm and his approach is normally conciliatory.
>
> —Pedro Passos, COO and President, Natura

Seabra was also the key figure in periodic award ceremonies for the promoters and consultants. His presence and moving speeches were usually the most-awaited events in these gatherings. His motivating role was not limited to the stage; he personally called each of the 150 directors and managers to compliment them on their birthday.

> I do this as reverence to life. Not everybody values birthdays this much. I use the occasion to show that life should be celebrated. Because life is sacred.
>
> —Luiz Seabra, Founder and President, Natura

Leal was in charge of the strategic issues. He joined the company in 1979 on the distribution side. Leal looked out for Natura's strategies at all levels. He led the internationalization process, and was looking into other growth alternatives like moving into new products, finding potential partners, and modernizing the company. He constantly sought to institutionalize Natura's successful practices, but also looked outside for new ideas.

> Guilherme [Leal] is different [than Seabra]. He is looking at the future and new trends at all times. He is very provocative—to make the company change. He is not nervous, but loves to constantly put new challenges to the company.
>
> —Pedro Passos, COO and President, Natura

Leal was behind Natura's decision to bring in a new management team and devised Natura's variable compensation system. Leal was usually the one bringing new ideas, challenging the group to take risks, and just *do* things. As he said, "the how will be determined on the way." Passos provided an example of Leal's daring ideas,

> Guilherme, 10 years ago proposed we should go sell in Asia. We didn't even know how to sell in Porto Alegre [south of Brazil], but he wanted to sell in Asia. He challenges our routines with new ideas.
>
> —Pedro Passos, COO and President, Natura

Leal believed that creating positive and respectful working relationships within the company and toward the community was essential for sustainable success. He was the driving force behind Natura's praised social endeavors. When asked about the company's purpose, Leal answered,

> When I was asked about the future of this company twenty years ago, I replied our purpose was to create the largest cosmetics company in the world. This is a small purpose. Now our purpose is even greater, to make the world a better place.
>
> —Guilherme Leal, CEO and President, Natura

Aside from the income from sale of T-shirts and cards, Leal set a fixed percentage of the company's dividends toward social programs. Leal's sense of social responsibility extended outside Natura: he had established ETOS, an association to teach corporate ethics to business people, and had decided to donate most of his net worth to a foundation he was expecting to create in the future.

Leal brought Passos into Natura in 1983 to bring technical expertise to one of the factories. Three years later he became a stockholder and in 1995 a co-president at Natura. Passos was described as pragmatic and efficient. He determined the how-tos of achieving the company's goals and ran the company on a day-to-day basis. In charge of operations, he spent half of his time in the factory in Itapecerica. He reported to the board Natura's strategic plan, capital structure, and human resources policies. The 11 directors reported directly to him.

Passos usually had to put the brakes on Seabra and Leal's running imagination, and looked out for the bottom line. He gave the others a sense of what was too expensive or dangerous. Few in Natura knew the exact day-to-day numbers as he did. According to him, most did not need to know. They needed to know if Natura achieved its broad targets—knowing the details of the ups and downs would bring people's motivations down.

Each president approached issues from different perspectives. Both Leal and Seabra often joined the rest of the employees in the cafeteria or the coffee bar in a corner of the floor. Leal used this time to discuss pending issues, gauge concerns, and had once approved a marketing plan in one of those breaks. Seabra on the other hand went to simply enjoy the company of people, and affirmed, "don't dare to think I do that to capture news about the company."

Meetings

The presidents believed in integrating the decision process across business lines. They merged the original five companies so that all decisions would have to be negotiated and discussed among the three. The percentage of stock they owned did not influence the decision power held by each. Most issues were resolved in a series of meetings at different levels of the organization to encourage teamwork and discussions, although most decisions were still reached in an informal manner, "in the corridor" as they put it. In a recent article on Natura, the authors summarized this system:

> Natura's management style can harmonize informality, intuition, cleverness with the necessary accuracy to control and run the company.
>
> —*Exame,* Business Magazine

Openness and inclusiveness were hard-wired in Natura through a proliferation of committees at all levels of decision-making. At the top, the three presidents met periodically to discuss major strategic issues like whether they should continue with direct sales, whether they should expand in Latin America or Eastern Europe, etc. These meetings began with Leal articulating the issue at hand and its repercussions. Seabra tended to examine the issue from unexpected angles, and Passos provided a reality check and brought everybody down to earth. They often disagreed openly, but not on a personal level. These meetings were not scheduled on a regular basis, but happened "spontaneously."

> There is no process, it's informal and just requires "lending an ear." When one feels we need a rule, we try to create one, for example with the issue of setting up a Board. Otherwise, in reality we go to each other when the heart orders, in the corridors, by telephone, in meetings. It's rarely an economic matter; normally it's a question regarding the climate of the company. A rule, "what's above 5 million must be reached by consensus," that's ridiculous. If it's changing the climate of the company then it's required.
>
> —Guilherme Leal, CEO and President, Natura

The Natura Strategy Planning committee brought together the 10 directors from different business areas with Passos twice a month. They discussed results, followed up on strategies, HR policies (salary, bonus, benefits, etc.), and determined the main strategies that needed to be followed on a five-year horizon. The strategies were communicated to all employees. Every three months the presidents held a meeting first with the 96 senior managers and then with a much broader group of supervisors, to answer any concerns and listen to ideas. Seabra believed that such discussions developed interest and creativity among the workforce. Through these meetings and a monthly publication distributed around the company, all the employees had an opportunity to know about and understand the decisions that were taken and how they were consistent with Natura's values.

There were no set rules for decision-making. Certain issues, like those pertaining to the structure of the company, needed consensual agreement. This had sometimes led to impasses. The decision to separate the production and distribution centers dragged for a year, before consensus was reached.

Yet most decisions were made unilaterally. For example, Passos decided to hire services to install SAP, and Leal found out about this decision, which involved millions of dollars, through the newspapers. On a different occasion, Passos decided to call back a product from the market because of quality problems. It was not a problem the consumer could notably feel: the wax in one of their lipstick products was crystallizing, which made it uncomfortable to wear. Passos gave orders to advise all the consultants of the incident so they could pass it on to customers and reimburse them. According to Passos, this decision was in accordance to Natura's values and thus he did not need to discuss it with other presidents.

Natura surviving its owners

Having three presidents meant that the company could continue running if one decided to take a break, which had resulted in the establishment of "Sabbatical years." In 1997,

Leal took off for a year to Boston, to take some business courses at Harvard, examine some alliance possibilities for Natura, and just take a break. Seabra was on Sabbatical in 1999 in London, perfecting his English, and as he put it, "taking some distance from the protected walls of Natura and experience life, with its joys and hardships." Aside from a refreshing break, it provided a healthy separation where they could more objectively perceive the opportunities and threats facing Natura.

> The company needs to have its identity independent from the identity of its leaders. This is our challenge today, transcend Leal, Seabra, and Passos.
>
> —Guilherme Leal, CEO and President, Natura

Slowly, Leal and Seabra were trying to move away from the day-to-day operations of the company, and institutionalize their legacy. This was difficult since many managers continued to rely on Seabra's inspiration and Leal's leadership. Given that they explicitly discouraged family members from working for the company, there were no family heirs to the throne, and there was no set career path to the top for other managers. A big question in everybody's mind was whether this leadership structure could be duplicated when the original leaders left, and whether the lack of institutionalized processes would affect Natura's ability to survive in the future. The presidents were attempting to deal with these issues,

> We are trying to build a process to make the company less dependent in the founders. We have some targets, to build the board of the company, develop people to substitute Guilherme, Luiz and me. We have a remuneration system to make all employees stockholders, we have a very aggressive stock option plan for directors. In the future we plan to make Natura public to make it easier to substitute the people and the founders, and to involve our executives in our credo and our values.
>
> —Pedro Passos, COO and President, Natura

AVOIDING THE FAILURE OF SUCCESS: HOW TO SUSTAIN GROWTH

The three presidents were gathered at the headquarters ... Leal made the situation clear to the other two: on the growth side, the boom years for Natura were gone, competition was increasing, and margins were falling due to the recession. Natura had bet on a new revamped attempt to internationalize, allocating resources to the Argentinean market in an attempt to replicate the Brazilian formula. Results were mixed and the operation was still in the red. One alternative was to venture into new products in Brazil, which fit the brand's "well-being" theme. It would probably be easier and quicker to build on Natura's brand at home than to export a culture to Argentina. If Natura decided to enter this new market, should it consider a joint venture with an experienced player or acquire a smaller company that had the technology? In the merger option, would they risk becoming a mere division of a multinational? Could they do it alone? Another option was to use alternative sales channels like stores or the Internet to grow more rapidly. Would that affect the "Natura's way"? Did they have the resources to implement these strategies? They were considering an IPO in the following year, which might bring the necessary capital for these projects, but, at the same time, might restrict the power of action they had historically enjoyed. Could Natura survive?

This case was prepared by Marcela Escobari, visiting researcher at LBS, under the supervision and guidance of Professor Sumantra Ghoshal and Professor Don Sull. This case is intended to be used as a basis for class discussion rather than to illustrate either effective or ineffective handling of an administrative situation. The cooperation of Natura S.A. and Fundaçao Dom Cabral is gratefully acknowledged.

EXHIBIT 1 NATURA'S FINANCIAL PERFORMANCE SEVEN YEARS

CONSOLIDATED HISTORICAL INCOME STATEMENTS (US$ MILLION)						
Year ending Dec. 31	**1993**	**1994**	**1995**	**1996**	**1997**	**1998**
Gross sales	**145.7**	**236.8**	**462.6**	**583.1**	**634.9**	**691.5**
Taxes on sales	−54.9	−88.3	−128.0	−160.5	−172.3	−183.5
Net sales	**90.8**	**148.5**	**334.7**	**422.6**	**462.6**	**507.9**
Cost of goods sold	−35.3	−44.6	−128.7	−150.3	−169.3	−190.3
Gross profit	**55.5**	**103.9**	**206.0**	**272.2**	**293.3**	**317.6**
Operating expenses	−31.0	−65.4	−133.5	−184.2	−206.7	−235.2
Operating income—Brazil	**24.5**	38.5	72.5	88.0	86.6	82.4
Operating income—International	−0.4	−2.5	−4.4	−5.8	−6.4	−6.6
Operating income—consolidated	24.1	36.0	68.1	82.2	80.2	75.9
Net interest income (expense)	5.0	5.6	3.5	−0.4	−1.1	−1.8
Gain (loss) on conversion to dollars	−9.8	−8.0	−5.7	−2.9	−3.6	−2.6
Others	−3.0	1.6	—	−4.6	−1.4	−4.7
Extraordinary items	−10.8	−33.7	−1.9	−26.8	−25.3	−25.3
Income tax	−3.1	−3.1	−18.4	−15.2	−16.2	−17.4
Net income	**2.4**	**−1.6**	**45.6**	**32.3**	**32.6**	**24.0**
Items	13.2	32.1	47.5	59.1	57.9	49.3
EBIT	24.1	36.0	68.1	82.2	80.2	75.9
Depreciation and amortization	1.5	2.9	2.2	4.4	5.7	6.6
EBITDA	**25.6**	**38.9**	**70.3**	**86.6**	**85.9**	**82.5**

EXHIBIT 1 NATURA'S FINANCIAL PERFORMANCE SEVEN YEARS (*continued*)

CONSOLIDATED HISTORICAL INCOME STATEMENTS (US$ MILLION)					
Year ending Dec. 31	**1992**	**1993**	**1994**	**1995**	**1996**
Assets					
Current assets					
Cash and cash equivalents	10.9	12.7	12.4	32.5	21.1
Accounts receivables	5.8	7.0	32.1	41.9	57.2
Inventories	6.2	7.6	17.0	25.8	32.0
Other current assets	0.2	0.8	2.1	15.5	13.9
Total current assets	23.1	28.1	63.6	115.7	124.2
Net property, plant & equipment	20.1	58.9	26.3	35.3	60.3
Other assets	2.2	0.9	2.7	3.0	4.6
Total assets	**45.4**	**87.9**	**92.6**	**154.0**	**189.1**
Current liabilities of LT debt					
	0.8	2.0	2.1	0.8	16.9
Accounts payable	2.4	3.8	7.9	13.6	13.4
Taxes payable (tributaries)	4.4	3.4	9.2	17.3	14.5
Social contribution tax	0.8	0.4	1.2	8.8	5.7
Social security tax	1.0	2.4	5.4	4.2	9.1
Other current liabilities	2.1	11.0	10.1	11.0	7.5
Total current liabilities	11.5	23.0	35.9	55.7	67.1
Non-current liabilities					
Long-term debt	0.9	0.3	0.2	1.5	1.7
Other noncurrent liabilities	5.5	16.1	11.3	2.0	7.9
Total noncurrent liabilities	6.4	16.4	11.5	3.5	9.6
Total liabilities	**17.9**	**39.4**	**47.4**	**59.2**	**76.7**
Stockholders' equity					
Common stock	27.6	48.6	45.1	83.3	72.6
Minority interest	0.0	0.0	0.0	0.0	0.0
Shareholder debentures	0.0	0.0	0.0	11.6	39.8
Total stockholders' equity	27.6	48.6	45.1	94.9	112.4
Stockholders' equity	**45.5**	**88.0**	**92.5**	**154.1**	**189.1**

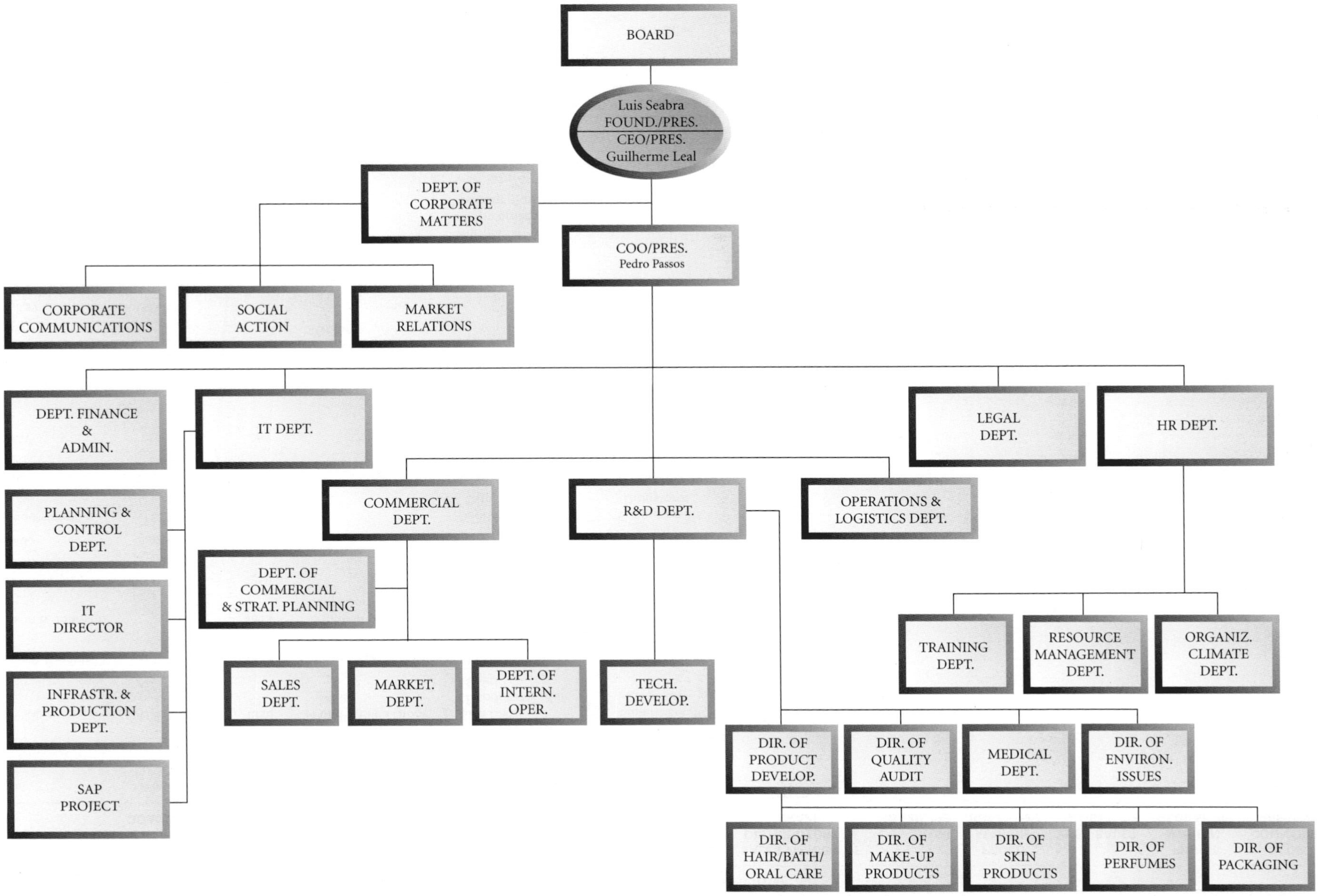

BOARD

Luis Seabra
FOUND./PRES.
CEO/PRES.
Guilherme Leal

DEPT. OF CORPORATE MATTERS

COO/PRES.
Pedro Passos

CORPORATE COMMUNICATIONS

SOCIAL ACTION

MARKET RELATIONS

DEPT. FINANCE & ADMIN.

IT DEPT.

LEGAL DEPT.

HR DEPT.

PLANNING & CONTROL DEPT.

COMMERCIAL DEPT.

R&D DEPT.

OPERATIONS & LOGISTICS DEPT.

DEPT. OF COMMERCIAL & STRAT. PLANNING

IT DIRECTOR

TRAINING DEPT.

RESOURCE MANAGEMENT DEPT.

ORGANIZ. CLIMATE DEPT.

INFRASTR. & PRODUCTION DEPT.

SALES DEPT.

MARKET. DEPT.

DEPT. OF INTERN. OPER.

TECH. DEVELOP.

DIR. OF PRODUCT DEVELOP.

DIR. OF QUALITY AUDIT

MEDICAL DEPT.

DIR. OF ENVIRON. ISSUES

SAP PROJECT

DIR. OF HAIR/BATH/ ORAL CARE

DIR. OF MAKE-UP PRODUCTS

DIR. OF SKIN PRODUCTS

DIR. OF PERFUMES

DIR. OF PACKAGING

EXHIBIT 2 ORGANIZATIONAL CHART—NATURA

EXHIBIT 3 NATURA'S COMPETITORS

MAJOR COMPETITORS (FOREIGN)

	HEAD-QUARTERS	ENTRANCE TO BRAZIL	BRANDS	PRODUCTS	METHOD OF SALES	SALES FORCE/# OF DISTRIBUTORS IN BRAZIL	US$-SALES BRAZIL '98	PROFIT MARGIN-BRAZIL '98	US$-SALES GLOBAL '98	PROFIT MARGIN-GLOBAL '98	# OF COUNTRIES PRESENT
L'Oreal	France	1972	Lancome, Biotherm, Maybelline, Helena Rubinstein	Cosmetics, Personal Care, Skin Care	Department Stores, Specialized Stores				12.4 bn		
Gessy Lever	U.S.A.	1953	Pond's, Elida Gibbs, Lever	Skin Care, Deodorants, Hair, Soap	Supermarkets, Drugstores						
Procter & Gamble	U.S.A.	1988	Oil of Olay, Cover Girl	Make-up, Deodorants, Hair	Supermarkets, Drugstores						
Johnson & Johnson		1953	Johnson & Johnson	Hair, Baby Product Line, Sun Protection	Supermarkets, Drugstores						
Avon	U.S.A.	1959		Cosmetics, Personal Care, Jewellery	Direct Sales	500,000 resellers			5.2bn		131
Shiseido	Japan										
Colgate-Palmolive	U.S.A.			Deodorants, Oral Care	Supermarkets, Drugstores						
Revlon	U.S.A.			Make-up	Supermarkets, Drugstores				(143 mn) loss		
AMWAY		1991		Cosmetics, Personal Care, Nutrition Homecare, Hometech	Direct Sales	70,000 resellers			5.7 bn		49
Estée Lauder	U.S.A.		Clinique, Estée Lauder, Prescriptives, Origins								
Mary Kay Christian Dior Oriflame Davidoff	U.S.A.				Direct Sales						29
Nature's Sunshine		1994		Nutritional Supplements and Natural Cosmetics		150,000 resellers/ 300 distributors					

MAJOR COMPETITORS (LOCAL)

	HEAD-QUARTERS	ENTRANCE TO BRAZIL	BRANDS	PRODUCTS	METHOD OF SALES	SALES FORCE/# OF DISTRIBUTORS IN BRAZIL	US$-SALES BRAZIL '98	PROFIT MARGIN-BRAZIL '98	US$-SALES GLOBAL '98	PROFIT MARGIN-GLOBAL '98	# OF COUNTRIES PRESENT
O'Boticario		1978		Cosmetics, Make-up, Perfumes	Franchise	1,616 stores					
Natura	São Paulo	1969	Chronos, Simbios, Essencial, Mama/Bebe	Cosmetics, Skin Care	Direct Sales	230,000 resellers			69.15	3.5%	

EXHIBIT 4 NATURA'S SHARE IN THE BRAZILIAN COSMETICS MARKET

		BRAZILIAN MARKET		NATURA		
	Year	*Volume (tons)*	*Net income (US$ 000)*	*Volume (tons)*	*Net income (US$ 000)*	*Natura's share of its target market (vol)*
Skin care	1997	21,522	355,016	1,954	64,419	18.2%
	1998	21,561	332,170	1,976	63,304	19.1%
Sun protection	1997	1,589	59,869	130	6,791	10.1%
	1998	1,575	68,190	107	5,329	7.8%
Perfumes	1997	15,823	616,318	1,834	172,090	28.8%
	1998	15,856	598,467	2,028	198,542	33.2%
Deodorants	1997	34,951	400,311	1,297	54,374	13.7%
	1998	28,220	393,262	1,608	64,966	16.5%
Hair	1997	242,752	892,810	3,713	45,916	5.1%
	1998	263,632	882,503	3,716	42,544	4.8%
Soap	1997	210,944	521,100	1,339	33,985	6.5%
	1998	224,275	514,305	1,375	33,204	6.5%
Make-up	1997	513	205,433	42	30,500	14.9%
	1998	580	236,916	44	31,629	13.4%
Total CFT market	1997	636,578	4,245,897			
	1998	669,600	4,256,759			
Total Target market	1997	530,381	3,086,702	10,393	412,019	13.5%
	1998	571,480	3,063,312	10,958	444,417	14.5%

*CFT market refers to Cosmetics, Fragrances, and Toiletries market

PRODUCTIVITY PER RESELLER (BRAZIL)

	DIRECT SALES OF COSMETICS IN BRAZIL (US$ BILLION)	RESELLERS ('000'S)	SALES/RESELLERS (US$)	NATURA RESELLERS ('000'S)	SALES/NATURA RESELLER (US$)
1993	1.2	570	2,105	65	2,241
1994	2.0	708	2,754	70	3,382
1995	3.1	865	3,584	112	4,131
1996	4.0	1,269	3,152	145	3,432
1997	4.0	1,195	3,350	185	3,340
1998	3.8	1,128	3,348	207	4,343

EXHIBIT 5 EMPLOYEE SURVEY ON ORGANIZATIONAL CLIMATE AT NATURA

FACTORS	NATURA 1995	NATURA 1997	NATURA 1999	MARKET	BENCHMARKS
NUMBER OF RESPONSES	*661*	*812*	*990*	*21,079*	*4,895*
Clarity of objectives	46	59	**62**	60	74
Adequacy of structure	42	53	**60**	60	73
Quality of decision process	36	44	**53**	51	65
Integration and communication	41	50	**55**	56	65
Management style	41	49	**55**	54	60
Orientation for personal development	46	54	**65**	51	58
Organizational vitality	64	69	**74**	62	71
Salary	45	54	**56**	50	55
Development of human resources	37	51	**54**	50	62
Image	84	89	**93**	80	85
Quality and productivity	67	74	**80**	75	80
Integration with the community	68	77	**85**	69	80
Partnerships	52	58	**62**	57	65
Average	**51**	**59**	**65**	**59**	**68**

CASE 27

Arista Records

Ending months of tense behind-the-scenes wrangling, Bertelsmann Music Group announced on May 2, 2000, that Antonio "L.A." Reid would take over as president of its Arista Records division from its founder and longtime leader Clive Davis on July 1. Reid's long-rumored ascension had been overshadowed by controversy ever since Davis had stormed out of a meeting in the previous fall at BMG headquarters after being notified about the succession plan by global music chief Strauss Zelnick.

Davis, who has a long-standing reputation for being a notoriously obstinate executive, had perceived the succession plan as a move to push him out of the label he had founded 25 years ago. A Harvard-trained lawyer, Davis had made a long and storied career of nurturing and guiding artists from Janis Joplin and Barry Manilow to Whitney Houston and Carlos Santana. Earlier this year, he won a lifetime Grammy award and was inducted into the Rock and Roll Hall of Fame as its only nonperformer.

At the age of 66, Davis has remained one of the industry's most hands-on label chiefs, often selecting songs for his artists and producing recordings. Six years ago, BMG had rewarded Davis with an unusually rich $50 million contract for transforming his label into a diverse powerhouse that dominated the sales charts with a string of pop, rap, R&B (Rhythm & Blues), light jazz, and country hits. But executives at BMG were becoming increasingly concerned about the future of Arista after Davis left the label. Zelnick explained: "As CEO I have a responsibility to make decisions on what's right for the company, and that includes making sure that we have an appropriate succession plan in place at Arista."

The plan to replace Davis did cause a considerable amount of stir within the music industry. Many artists, among them those who had been groomed by Davis at Arista, expressed their concern about his departure. "It seems that corporations are taking over a lot of the decisions that were once being made by individuals," said Barry Manilow, one of the first artists that had been signed by Davis. "It may make sense to them as a corporation, but when you have talent like Clive Davis, those rules should not apply. When you have someone as brilliant as Clive, you push those corporate rules away and you just let him do his thing."

SUCCESS WITH NEW TALENT

Arista has been remarkable in the growth that it has shown on a consistent basis even during the years in which the recorded music industry had shown lackluster sales. This growth has largely resulted from the appeal of the small and highly selective roster of homegrown talent, which Davis has managed to develop into top acts. At last count, Arista had only about 35 artists on their roster compared to over 200 that can be found at most other major labels. According to Davis: "Our artist roster is a fraction of any competitor that has market share. We pride ourselves in our leanness. We have the highest success ratio."

Indeed, a higher percentage of albums released by Davis's label have turned gold and even platinum than at any other major recording label. Davis feels that a large part of the label's success has been due to its practice of building its acts from the ground up, as opposed to picking them up through acquisitions and mergers. Mr. Davis emphasized: "Historically, we have made every release count. The success ratio of our company has been the highest in history, and we don't do it by buying market share or buying other labels; it's all been homegrown."

The reliance on homegrown talent was made possible due to Arista's remarkable success in breaking new acts. These generally also tend to be more profitable than established stars, who can negotiate bigger advances and more lucrative deals for themselves. In fact, a key aspect of the firm's strategies has been to steadfastly refuse to enter the bidding wars for established talent that have cost other labels millions. Mr. Davis stated: "We're not in the banking business. All of Arista's growth has come from internal development. We have not tried to increase profit by buying labels, and the big artist deals often don't pan out."

But Arista has been relatively successful in grooming new talent because of Davis. He is known as a music man who usually plays it by ear, sensing hits, and nurturing artists, whether it is a Janis Joplin or a Sarah McLachlan. "I can usually tell a hit in 20 seconds," he says of his envied instinct. "I know by then whether the artist has something

---

This case was prepared by Jamal Shamsie, UCLA, to be used for class discussion. Material drawn from published sources.

or whether I should turn off the tape. A song has to evolve through one or two choruses, of course, but you know straightaway. It has to move you. The lyric has to touch the heart."

BMG's Zelnick clearly understood the role that Davis has played in the growth of Arista into a top music label. "The key to Arista's strategy is focusing on a few artists on which Davis and his team really believe, making great records and persevering until they deliver a hit," he stated recently. "We at BMG follow his lead: We believe in a more limited roster than our competitors, more focus and innovative approaches to marketing the records."

Some of these innovative marketing methods were described by Mr. Ari Martin, Arista's senior director of artist development: "When you're launching an album, you have to alert the public, and a lot of analysis goes into finding the most cost-effective ways of getting the word out. We really got to target it." For that, Arista uses an outside market research company to determine the buying habits of music fans, their familiarity with specific artists, and their buying influences. But these data form just one of the inputs into the development of the eventual marketing plan. Adds Mr. Martin: "We realize we're not selling toothpaste. It's not an exact science. So we rely on our instincts more than any numbers we see."

Arista's strategy of building up talent has not gone unnoticed. Mr. Doug Smith, a buyer at Carnegie, Pennsylvania-based National Record Mart, said that Arista has been excellent at setting up albums with singles. "They always have singles on the radio, getting a buzz out there on the street before they release a record," he elaborated. Similarly, Mr. Al Wilson, senior VP of merchandizing at Milford, Massachusetts-based Strawberries, said that when analyzing Arista, "you could take a sarcastic stance and say that they spend enough money to prefab the hits. But how many labels fail at that strategy? The bottom line is that Arista has the ability to spot talent and then do what it takes to roll that talent into hits."

Although most of Arista's success has been in the area of pop music, Mr. Davis claims that he has pursued promising talent in all areas. According to him: "I don't believe in emphasizing areas. When artists excite you, you sign them if you feel that they could be significant." He emphasized that Arista has taken the slow, steady route, not the glitzy route of buying major superstars and creating a staff of hundreds of people. In the words of Davis: "What we stand for is internal growth, all developed from scratch, with a careful, selective approach to signing artists."

SUCCESS THROUGH GREATER DIVERSITY

Davis also asserts that he laid the bedrock for the success of Arista a few years ago when it began to diversify its portfolio in terms of the kinds of music that it offered and the A&R (Artists and Repertoire) sources that generated the music. Much of this diversification was achieved through the establishment of joint ventures with other producers. The firm formed these joint ventures with others who may have the skills to develop talent within a much broader variety of music. In these ventures, Arista has typically relied on their partner to cover A&R, artist development, and artist publicity. For its part, Arista's staff has concentrated mostly on promoting, marketing, and distributing the releases from these joint ventures.

In fact, it was Davis who brought Antonio "L.A." Reid into the Arista fold. He anticipated the changing face of R&B and entered into a joint venture with Reid and Babyface, who formed LaFace. He stated: "They had a vision of starting their own company, and I shared the vision that they could be the Motown of the 90s." The association resulted in the development of successes such as TLC and Toni Braxton. Both of these artists are expected to stay at the top of the box office charts for many years.

Around the same time, the company started Bad Boy Records with Sean "Puffy" Combs. That label has been responsible for the success of many new acts such as Puff Daddy & the Family and the Notorious B.I.G., both of whom released recent best-selling albums. The Notorious B.I.G.'s latest release managed to pass the 1.5 million-unit mark in sales, based on available records.

Arista's next two joint ventures have further expanded its range of acts. Its venture with Dallas Austin resulted in the formation of Rowdy Records. The new label enjoyed considerable success with hot-selling albums from Illegal and Monica. Their partnership with Time Bomb Records has focused on rock music. Under the leadership of Jim Guerinot, this venture has already released albums by new artists such as Elevator Drops and No Knife.

Where it did not seek out strategic ventures, Arista chose to assemble its own repertoire departments from the ground up. For instance, when Arista perceived a need to get into the country music business in the early 1990s, it opened the Arista/Nashville division, headed by Tim DuBois. Since then, Arista/Nashville has become a country powerhouse, boasting a roster that includes Alan Jackson, Brooks & Dunn, Pam Tillis, Diamond Rio, Radney Foster, and BR5-49. Within a few years of its creation, the Nashville division has already grown to account for about 20% of Arista's sales volume.

In general, Mr. Davis attributes much of Arista's success to its adventurous spirit. He claims that other record companies have typically bought other labels in order to increase their market share. In contrast to this approach, Davis states: "We have financed ours from scratch and picked out entrepreneurs, whether they were Puffy Combs with Bad Boy, or Tim DuBois with the Nashville division, or Dallas Austin with Rowdy."

Arista's Vice President and General Manager Roy Lott echoed this sentiment: "I would attribute our success to a decision at the very beginning of the 90s to diversify and expand the repertoire supplying entities that are part of Arista, whether it be our Nashville operation or the current LaFace or Bad Boy ventures, rather than be limited to self-generated A&R, which has continued to grow and be successful."

In order to demonstrate the degree of success that the label has had with its diversification, Mr. Lott referred to Arista's recent hold on the top three spots on the Hot 100 Singles chart. "None of the three records are pop records, and each is from a different product source," he said. "The diversification of A&R and genres of music is contributing to our ability to have success."

SUCCESS AFTER DAVIS?

The appointment of Reid was tied to the decision by Zelnick to buy out the rest of LaFace, bringing it entirely into BMG's Arista division. These moves were regarded as necessary by BMG in order to ensure the survival and growth of Arista beyond Clive Davis. Arista has accounted for about a third of BMG's market share and is considered to be the strongest asset in its US repertoire. "Arista is clearly the jewel in BMG's crown," one industry observer recently remarked.

BMG is clearly confident that Reid has plenty of experience to run Arista. He is also a Grammy-winning producer who started out making hits for such dance acts as Bobby Brown and Paula Abdul. Before being accepted for the position at Arista, Zelnick had Reid complete a 6-week executive course at Harvard Business School. Reid stated that he believes that he can keep Arista on top of the charts by adding to its diversity. "We intend to make Arista the home for many Latin artists, record producers and Latin superstars," he explained.

But the continued success of Arista without Clive Davis will not be an easy task. Industry observers believe Reid will face significant challenges in taking over the reins. The departure of Davis is expected to be followed by an exodus of top executives at the label, including the heads of marketing and promotion as well as its general manager. Some of the artists may also choose to leave for another label, especially if Davis decides to launch his own new label.

Reid did acknowledge that he was stepping into a difficult position. "I'm coming into this job behind one of the most important men ever in the record business—and that's a tall order," he stated. "I think it's fair for people to speculate about it." But he added: "Anybody who knows me knows my passion for music—and hopefully that passion will speak loudly in the success we achieve at Arista in the future."

BMG music chief Zelnick emphasized that he believed Reid would build on the foundations that Davis had laid for Arista. "This was never about an ouster," he stated recently. "I have the greatest respect for Clive Davis. BMG has always said that we have to deal with succession planning and contracts as they come up. Our goal has always been the same: Build upon the company creatively. Build upon Clive's great legacy."

EXHIBIT 1
CLIVE DAVIS: CAREER HIGHLIGHTS

1960	Graduates from Harvard Law School and gets a job at Columbia Records, a division of CBS.
1967	After signing several major artists, like Janis Joplin, Davis becomes president of Columbia Records.
1973	Davis is fired by CBS, allegedly for misuse of funds.
1974	Davis starts Arista Record label with backing from Columbia Pictures, a company unrelated to CBS. Within five years, Davis builds the record label into a major success with artists like Patti Smith and Barry Manilow.
1980	Bertelsmann buys Arista for $50 million.
1990s	Davis has continued to be a trendsetter by reviving the careers of Carlos Santana and Aretha Franklin and cultivating stars like Whitney Houston and Sean "Puffy" Combs.

EXHIBIT 2
ARISTA'S ESTIMATED SALES

FOR YEAR ENDING JUNE	
1996	$325 million
1997	$395 million
1998	$405 million
1999	$425 million
2000	$440 million

EXHIBIT 3
MUSIC INDUSTRY SALES BREAKDOWN

	1999 (%)	**1998 (%)**
Universal	27*	11
BMG	19	12
Sony	16	17
WEA	14	18
EMI	9	13
Polygram		14

*Includes Polygram.

EXHIBIT 4
TOP-SELLING ARISTA ALBUMS

1999		1997	
Santana	Supernatural	Tony Braxton	Secrets
TLC	Fan Mail	Usher	My Way
Sarah McLachlan	Mirrorball	Mace	Harlem World
Puff Daddy	Forever	Soundtrack	Soul Food
1998		**1996**	
Usher	My Way	Puff Daddy	No Way Out
The Notorious B.I.G.	Life After Death	Soundtrack	Waiting to Exhale
Brooks & Dunn	If You See Her	Brooks & Dunn	Borderline
The Lox	Money, Power & Respect	KENNY G	THE MOMENT

CASE 28

HBO

During the winter of 2001, HBO programing Chief Chris Albrecht was trying to figure out how he could continue to build upon the no-strings-attached buzz that his cable channel had begun to generate. The buzz started with *The Larry Sanders Show,* in which Gary Shandling played the fictional host of a late-night talk show. The show's ratings paled in comparison with *Friends,* but it drew the kind of unabashed critical praise that HBO has begun to treasure. It attracted writers to HBO who were willing to trade huge up-front payments and back-end profits for the cachet of appearing alongside a smart, self-referential show. With more recent shows such as *The Sopranos,* a great family drama about crime; *Sex and the City,* a hit comedy of manners with titillating bedroom capers and a fixation on women's shoes; and *Oz,* an innovative, brutal look at prison life HBO has continued to build itself as the literary magazine of series television.

The cable channel had developed a slogan to highlight the distinctiveness of the original programing that it has been putting on the air. The network's ad campaign has been pounding out a clear and consistent message: "It's not TV, it's HBO." In delivering this message, HBO has been trying hard to distinguish itself from the broadcast networks, which could be accused of having sacrificed quality programing for quick-fix schemes that will deliver large enough audiences. Indeed, the growing level of critical acclaim for original HBO shows led to a recent spoof on an episode of *Saturday Night Live,* with a commercial intoning mock blurbs for *The Sopranos*. The message: "If I had a choice between having all the mysteries of the universe revealed to me in a glorious flash of light or watching one episode of *The Sopranos,* I'd hesitate, then I'd watch *The Sopranos*."[1]

Meanwhile, network rivals gnash their teeth when *The Sopranos* or *Sex and the City* claims an Emmy or Golden Globe. HBO may be hitting home runs, the argument goes, but how come nobody points out it's playing with aluminum bats? "If NBC only had to schedule *The West Wing, Law & Order, ER,* and *Friends,* you'd say, 'Wow, they're the boutique network,'" says a veteran TV writer who declined to be named, echoing a commonly held view. Indeed, with uncut movies filling up the lion's share of HBO's broadcast day, the channel is at liberty to be thoughtful and exclusive, ordering 10 or 13 episodes of a series and calling it a season. All the while, its commercial network counterparts scramble each year to fill out schedules, ordering series they only half-believe in and deficit-financing star vehicles that end up being expensive embarrassments.

But executives at HBO also realize that they need to build on their original programing. They believe they are more likely to survive on the basis of shows that people cannot find anywhere else than on the basis of movies that can just as easily be viewed elsewhere. This is not an easy task to accomplish, given that the type of innovative shows that HBO relies upon are hard to come by. Even when Albrecht does come across such shows, it is hard to convince the creators to turn away from the greater revenues that they might be able to get from a more commercial network. But developing the HBO brand has always implied that the channel must struggle to maintain that it is different from ordinary television.

DEVELOPING AN UNCONVENTIONAL SLATE

The typical HBO show comes from a highly respected creative source and deals with a subject that the broadcast networks wouldn't touch. One such show, *Six Feet Under,* which is slated to premiere in June, comes from Alan Ball, the Oscar-winning screenwriter of *American Beauty,* and deals with the business of burying people, seen through a family-run funeral service. The darkly comic pedigree of the series matches Ball's pedigree, which in turn fits the HBO brand: jaded former playwright who grew frustrated with his high-paying, joke-to-joke-to-joke jobs in network TV and wrote what became a mainstream literary hit at the box office.

Six Feet Under is one of two new original shows that HBO intends to roll out in the summer. The other show, *The Mind of the Married Man,* is a half-hour comedy that has been created by stand-up comic-turned-filmmaker Mike Binder. Though it was in development before *Sex and the City* became a hit, the Binder series is bound to be perceived as a male response, given that its three main characters are married men in various stages of thought about love and infidelity. "*Sex and the City* isn't real—it's a fairy-tale release for women," argued Binder. "This show is the naked truth."

This case was prepared by Jamal Shamsie, UCLA, to be used for class discussion. Material drawn from published sources.

Apart from these, HBO claims that it has about 40 scripts in development—everything from a series about hip-hop culture by novelist John Ridley to a comedy about an upscale Los Angeles realtor. Both hip-hop and high-stakes real estate epitomize the HBO milieu. Marry such a subculture and a flawed, dynamic main character and you evidently approximate the HBO brand. One writer who had been working with HBO on the development of a pilot was told to make the main character less likable and not to worry as much about the premise. He recalls that he was told "Just plop us in the world and we'll find our way."

Such notes run decidedly counter to the broadcast networks, where executives usually want likable characters or premises that are apparent early on. They want to ensure that the show will have the elements that are required to make it a commercial hit above everything else. In other words, most of the commercial networks can be accused of slanting their development process to deliver substantial riches down the road. At HBO, the riches can be sacrificed in the interests of getting a show that will receive critical recognition. There is simply the mandate to be "good and different" rather than to do what the other networks do.

As HBO tends to characterize its series development, none of the scripts is more than the gem of an inspiration. Larry David, the writer of *Seinfeld,* was eventually asked to turn his special on HBO into a regular series called *Curb Your Enthusiasm*. Star power is certainly important, but it doesn't carry the day. HBO has passed on a Western miniseries from director Sydney Pollack, for example, and a series about an actor called George Clooney from *Kilroy*. Even Christopher Guest and Eugene Levy, who collaborated on the cult movie comedies *Waiting for Guffman* and *Best in Show,* had their pilot about two B-list theatrical agents turned down.

But that's not to say the HBO development process isn't above the same politics and marketeering that plague broadcast network programing. HBO, for instance, puts its pilots through audience testing, though arguably not as slavishly as the broadcast networks do. And sources say the channel has spent a considerable amount of time and money trying to develop a companion series to *Sex and the City,* an indication that target audiences have crept into HBO's thinking.

"My biggest fear is that they'll develop," says Bob Odenkirk, a writer and performer with a development deal at HBO and the star for four seasons with David Cross of the HBO sketch comedy series *Mr. Show*. To Odenkirk, the channel's growing mainstream popularity is both blessing and curse. "If you attract this whole big crowd of people, you're going to want to keep them. And to keep them you have to give them what brought them there," he explained.

MANAGING BY IMPROVISATION

During the early years of its existence, HBO was largely billed as a movie channel. Its original programing, under Michael Fuchs, was largely confined to one-hour specials with stand-up comedians. The channel was noted for its frugality with spending money on the development of original series. That began to change when Chris Albrecht and Carolyn Strauss took charge of the channel's original programing. Both of them came to HBO after gaining considerable experience scouting talent for comedy clubs. Albrecht even ran the Improv in New York before taking a job at the cable channel. Both of these programing chiefs rose through the ranks, having been at HBO for nearly 15 years.

Albrecht and Strauss together have been making key decisions regarding the original programing that viewers get to see on HBO. These decisions are made on the basis of their years of experience with scouting talent and managing the live entertainment business. The shows have to push the boundaries of what gets defined as conventional entertainment at most of the other television channels. "I say this in a lot of meetings," said Strauss. "The shows have to become a bit bigger than themselves . . . something that resonates in a larger way. I think our best shows do that."

Binder's *The Mind of the Married Man,* for instance, was in and out of development for years. Strauss, for one, was not a supporter, particularly when the project, then called *My Dirty Little Mind,* dwelt on men's sexual fantasies. There were concerns that Binder wasn't the right person to appear in the show and that the material was not likely to grab enough attention. But Albrecht believed in the basic premise of the show and continued to work with Binder to get it into its final form.

Six Feet Under began in-house, with Strauss thinking HBO should explore death in a series. She had been reading Jessica Mitford's *The American Way of Death Revisited,* and she had watched *The Loved One,* the 1965 black comedy based on the novel by Evelyn Waugh. "I started to think, 'Is there a way to do something about death that could be darkly comic?' This is interesting for us, because other places wouldn't do it." Strauss took her idea around town and mentioned it to Ball, who was not only hot off of *American Beauty,* but also coming from a lousy network experience, with his ABC sitcom, *Oh, Grow Up*. Ball wrote a script, gave it to Strauss, and was told to make it darker. "He was still coming out of his ABC experience, so it still had some more conventional sensibilities in there," Strauss explained.

Ball says development at HBO was everything his experience at ABC wasn't. "It seems like there's less levels of bureaucracy to dig through," he stated. "Many times, the lower-level people I would deal with at the networks, I felt like they were second-guessing what their higher-ups would say or think." Writer-producer Thompson added: "To make a good show on HBO is almost easier work. You're living and dying by what you believe in, and you're not being nibbled to death by ducks."[2]

But that doesn't mean that HBO is only likely to stick with those shows that Albrecht or Strauss think highly of. Albrecht described how he had come out of a budget meeting in New York two years ago resolved to cancel *Arli$$,* which premiered in 1996 and stars Wuhl as a sports agent.

The show had failed to deliver strong ratings or deliver the kind of critical accolades that might make ratings a moot issue. In fact, it came as close to a ridiculed show as HBO has ever had.

Asked what prevented him from dropping the show, Albrecht stated that he left the budget meeting and headed to Westchester County to look at a pony for his daughter. On the way, he was on the phone with business affairs, discussing the *Arli$$* cancellation, and when they reached the stables, the driver couldn't help himself. He was begging Albrecht not to cancel the series. "Believe me," Albrecht elaborated, "there are people that are paying for HBO every month that don't watch *The Sopranos* and don't watch *Sex and the City* and don't watch *Curb Your Enthusiasm* that think that *Arli$$* is the best comedy on television."

Everyone agrees that Albrecht thinks differently than most other programing executives. "I look at Tony Soprano, and to me it's Chris Albrecht, in so many ways," said an executive familiar with Albrecht who declined to be named. "His toughness, but also the humanity. He's not your typical network development schmuck. He has a much deeper understanding of the world. . . . He's a textured, somewhat complicated individual. On the other hand, there's a real animal there."

COMPETING FOR IDEAS AND TALENT

Under CEO Jeffrey Bewkes, HBO has raised its budget for original programing to close to $400 million. This 2001 fall, HBO will premiere *Band of Brothers,* a $120 million, 10-part World War II miniseries from Tom Hanks and Steven Spielberg that is based on the book by historian Stephen Ambrose. But while miniseries, original movies, documentaries, and specials fall under the original programing rubric, it is the scripted series that have increasingly come to define the HBO brand. Cable outlets such as Showtime, TNT, and A&E have shown an ability to compete with HBO's original movies and documentaries. But no other channels have been able to match HBO's branded identity in series.

Albrecht and Strauss are trying to develop more series for the HBO channel. Their goal is to schedule original series and miniseries on Sunday nights year-round. They want to be able to segue from a new season of *Oz* to *The Sopranos* to *Sex and the City*. With *Six Feet Under,* Albrecht is also considering building up Wednesdays as an additional night for new series. But shows that HBO wants are hard to come by and harder to grab. Shows that air on HBO do not generate the kind of revenues that other more conventional programing can generate on network television. Often, HBO has to make substantial financial investments into a show in order to obtain it.

In spite of all their efforts, Albrecht and Strauss do still lose some shows to the more commercial networks. Three years ago, HBO appeared to be in business on a comedy pilot called *Action,* about a movie studio chief modeled after hard-driving producer Joel Silver. Albrecht stated that he came up with the germ of the idea and went to Silver, who brought in Chris Thompson, creator of the network sitcom *The Naked Truth* and a writer for *The Larry Sanders Show*. But Thompson and Silver ended up taking the series to Fox, where it died halfway into its first season. Thompson says that the show would have been ideal for HBO, but that there were too many heavy-hitter profit participants in it to make a deal. But it's also true that Silver and Thompson—and by extension, Columbia TriStar, where they were under contract—saw a far bigger pot at the end of the rainbow if *Action* landed at a broadcast network.

Even Brad Grey, who was involved with the development of *The Sopranos,* tried to sell the show to all the major networks before turning to HBO. He had been an executive producer on the highly acclaimed *Larry Sanders Show*. What he wanted, this time, was to develop a critically successful show that would also be a financial hit. "Well, I'll just say it again, that was a mistake, because I shouldn't have taken it to those other companies," Grey said afterward. "I thought at that point, after *Sanders* and after some of the success of HBO, that the networks would embrace a show like *The Sopranos* and give us more leeway creatively."[3]

This leads critics of HBO to charge that it relies heavily on the kind of shows that are not likely to be acceptable on most other networks. They claim that one of the easiest ways to demonstrate that you're "not TV" is to employ nudity, violence, and profanity, something that nearly all HBO original series employ. This is particularly true of reality shows like *G-String Divas,* a behind-the-scenes look at stripper life, and *Real Sex,* a home-movies peek into all manner of sexual appetites. Albrecht definitely agrees that there's violence on *The Sopranos* and *Oz,* and frontal nudity on *Sex and the City,* but he insists that it's only used in the service of the scripts, not for adult males on their couches at night, surfing the cable channels for skin.

"We don't look for things that are taboo," Albrecht adds. "One of the reasons we've held off doing a cop show is I'm not sure that we could do something better than *NYPD Blue* or *Law & Order*. Because there've been so many things done on broadcast networks over the years, it's hard to find subjects."[4] Albrecht claims that *Arli$$* has been a successful show for HBO, because the major networks have been reluctant to do real stories about what happens in sports because of all of their contracts with the major leagues. In referring to a recently canceled ABC show, Albrecht stated: "*Sports Night* had nothing to do with sports."

By picking topics that other networks choose to avoid and giving more creative freedom to proven talent, HBO has been using its original programing to enhance its brand identity. "There's no amount of money spared to do that," said a source familiar with how the network operates. They go to great lengths to unveil new and returning series with proper aplomb. For example, HBO turned the third-season premiere of the Mafia drama *The Sopranos* into a media-hyped event at New York's Radio City Music Hall. But on a more general level, the channel has sold itself to the public not simply as a content provider, but as a lifestyle choice, really, like making time for yoga.

IT'S NOT TV, IT'S HBO

No one denies that HBO's economic model has contributed mightily to its success. Unlike the broadcast networks, HBO derives its revenue from subscribers paying monthly fees of about $12 over their basic cable bills. This means HBO's writer-producers do not have to fear the long arm of standards and practices department. Nor are the network's executives in the "eyeballs business," a term that is used in the industry for trying to attract the most viewers. Instead, HBO continues to search for innovative new shows to keep the percentage of "churn" in the single digits—those viewers who buy the service and then cancel when a particular show that they wanted to view ends its run.

For the final episode of its second season, *The Sopranos* drew an estimated 9 million viewers, unprecedented for an HBO series. Most of its other shows attract around 2 million viewers per airing. This represents a significant achievement, given that HBO is only available in about a quarter of the households. Last year alone, HBO added 1.2 million subscribers, bringing its total base to about 26 million viewers. The increase has helped make HBO a key part of the nearly $7 billion in TV revenue its corporate parent, AOL-Time Warner, reported last year.

But Albrecht and Strauss must find more money to fund the development of more original programing. They are wrestling with raising more revenues by offering some of their original shows for syndication. To begin with, they are not sure what they will be able to get for their programs on the syndication market. Recently, HBO Enterprises, HBO's syndication arm, began offering an edited version of *Sex and the City* to basic cable stations, reportedly at $750,000 an episode, which approaches the astronomical fees garnered in syndication by *Seinfeld*. But the offer was taken off the table amid sentiment that the asking price was exorbitant.

With the huge success of *The Sopranos*, HBO is looking again at the revenues that might be obtained from syndication. The show is the most expensive that the channel has ever put on the air. But this is not an easy issue to address. Beyond the task of making the series palatable to a wider audience, there is another question: Wouldn't letting *The Sopranos* go to a basic cable outlet like TBS diminish the distinction of the HBO brand? Keeping it in the family can only become more crucial for a network having to live up to its boutique image with each new series. In the words of Albrecht: "As the world gets more competitive, and as these series are the things that define us, why would we give them to someone else unless we really needed the money?"

CASE 29

Building Emotional Energy for Renewal: Nissan

TAKING ON THE CHALLENGE

In March 1999, when Renault and Nissan announced their alliance, the press releases from both sides stressed how well the companies complemented each other. Renault's cash injection of $5.4 billion for an equity stake of over 36% in Nissan would reduce the Japanese automaker's crushing debt. It would also provide Renault with access to two huge markets—North America and Asia—where it was virtually absent. Conversely, Renault's market strengths were in Europe and Latin America where Nissan was weak. Likewise in terms of capabilities, Renault would gain access to Nissan's engineering and manufacturing expertise while Nissan would benefit from Renault's marketing and design flair. In theory it looked like a perfect match, but industry analysts had serious reservations about the deal.

The first hitch was Nissan's desperate financial situation: It had posted global losses in six of the previous seven years. In its home market, only 4 out of 43 models were profitable. And its debts were such that in 1998 it had spent $1 billion on interest payments alone, money that should have been reinvested in its aging and rather bland product line. For months, Nissan's chairman, Yoshikazu Hanawa, had tried to secure a relationship with a foreign investor; yet, other carmakers were afraid to touch it. DaimlerChrysler, for one, was put off by the figures and anticipation of Japanese resistance to change.[1] Indeed, one Chrysler insider compared bailing out Nissan to "putting $5 billion into a steel container and throwing it into the ocean."[2]

Then there was Renault's credibility as a rescuer. Its botched merger with Volvo in the early 1990s—fueled by cultural problems—was still fresh in many minds. Renault had been a French government-controlled enterprise until only five years before, and remained 44% state owned. Cultural incompatibility seemed likely, leading one industry analyst to comment, "Much has been made of the culture clash between Daimler and Chrysler, [but] it will be nothing compared to Nissan and Renault. . . . At their core, they are both nationalistic and patriotic, and each believes its way is the right way to do things. We will have quite a teething period for the first year or two as they feel each other out. It's a complex thing to work through."[3] Another observer commented that it was "like relying on the French civil service to revive the Japanese economy."

News of the negotiations provoked a fall in Renault's share price. Many of Nissan's problems were evident. It had too many plants (some running at 50% of their nominal capacity), too many car platforms (25 expensive chassis, compared with Volkswagen's four), too many suppliers (at 3,000, nearly 10 times more than Ford), and too many dealers in Japan.[4] Radical surgery seemed the obvious solution. Yet this ran counter to deeply anchored Japanese business practices such as lifetime employment and close ties with suppliers. Moreover, Renault's stake in Nissan only gave it power of veto, raising the difficulty of pushing through fundamental changes.

The unenviable challenge of trying to make the alliance work fell to Carlos Ghosn, already seen as Louis Schweitzer's number two at Renault, and the main driving force behind Renault's ongoing cost-cutting program.

BUILDING UP THE EXPEDITIONARY TEAM

Born in Brazil of French and Lebanese parents, and trained as an engineer in France, Ghosn was no stranger to cross-cultural challenges. He had held major jobs on four continents and had made his reputation overseeing the restructuring of Michelin's North American operations. Ghosn was then recruited by Louis Schweitzer to restructure Renault and quickly turned the carmaker's fortunes around by implementing an aggressive cost-cutting plan.

Ghosn agreed to work on the Nissan alliance on the condition that he would have full control, and that he would not constantly have to seek approval from France. He also insisted on handpicking the 20 or so executives who would accompany him on this mission. Commenting on the modest size of the team he proposed to take to

---

This case was written by Quy Nguyen Huy, Associate Professor of Strategy at INSEAD. It is intended to be used as a basis for class discussion rather than to illustrate either effective or ineffective handling of an administrative situation. It draws extensively on INSEAD case 02/2003-5095 written by Kathryn Hughes, Jean-Louis Barsoux, and Jean-François Manzoni, as well as other publicly available information.

Nissan, Ghosn said: "To make deep changes inside a company you don't need loads of people, but rather the right catalysts in the right places."[5] His approach to the alliance was for the two companies to work together as distinct partners without having to worry about creating a common culture and combining their businesses.

In the two months preceding his formal appointment, Ghosn went to places where the actual work was done and talked to people who dealt with customers every day such as sales people and service technicians. He also visited research facilities and production plants, gathering input from division managers, engineers, and dealers. He solicited their views earnestly and got candid feedback.[6] He was astonished to find that Nissan factory managers could tell him how many minutes it took to build a car but not how much it cost.

Another troubling sign, Ghosn commented, was that: "Everybody tells you he is achieving his objective, yet the company is in bad shape . . . nobody feels really responsible for the situation of the company, and that's why there [is] no sense of urgency."[7]

Ghosn understood that the success of corporate turnarounds was not simply about making radical changes to the company's operations. He also had to preserve the company's identity and the self-esteem of people affected by the change. Ghosn assured the Nissan workers that the company would remain Japanese. He wanted to show them respect by keeping the strengths of the Japanese culture but to modify elements that offered an opportunity for progress by adopting worldwide best practices.

Ghosn was named Chief Operating Officer on June 25, 1999.[8] Yoshikazu Hanawa was appointed President, and assumed a more ambassadorial role. For the first time, the board meeting was held in English. Ghosn's message was simple but blunt: "Gentleman, we've had 10 years of decline. That's enough," he said. "There is a place for every single person in this company who wants to give the company a chance for recovery, no matter what age, what gender, what citizenship."[9]

In the annual shareholder meeting that immediately followed the board meeting, Ghosn told the audience: "I have not come to Japan for Renault, but for Nissan. I will do everything in my power to bring Nissan back to profitability at the earliest date possible and revive it as a highly attractive company."[10]

During his first week in charge, Ghosn introduced a number of changes. He announced a quasi-stock option incentive plan for its 30 executive officers, including the three new board members from Renault. He also immediately introduced new language policy—decreeing that all top-level meetings be conducted in English and that reports be produced in English. Ghosn backed up the decision with intensive language courses for all Nissan employees. But beyond those efforts he realized that "some key words were not understood in the same way by different Japanese people or even different French people,"[11] so he asked a mixed Renault–Nissan team to establish a dictionary of essential terms. The 100 or so entries included clear definitions of terms such as "commitment," "authority," "objectives," "transparency," and "targets." An open discussion of these notions would help to avoid mixed messages. Ghosn told his top management team: "What we think, what we say, and what we do must be the same. We have to be impeccable in ensuring that our words correspond to our actions. If there are discrepancies between what we profess and how we behave, that will spell disaster."[12]

MOBILIZING MIDDLE MANAGERS

Ghosn quickly set up nine cross-functional teams (CFTs) to generate ideas and recommendations for change. Contrary to convention, these would not be made up exclusively of senior managers, but rather would draw on line middle managers in their 30s and 40s from different departments and divisions.

CFTs of middle managers ensured that the revival plan was the work of the whole company, not only of top management. From his preliminary contacts with Nissan employees, Ghosn had been amazed at the lack of communication across functions, borders, and hierarchical lines.

The CFTs focused on different critical areas such as purchasing, engineering, and R&D. Ghosn wanted selection of CFT members to be based upon talent and demonstrated commitment to Nissan. He took a close personal interest in the selection of the pilots, those who would drive each team's agenda and discussions—since the reforms proposed by the CFTs would form the backbone of Nissan's recovery plan.

Each CFT was piloted by a middle or upper-middle manager chosen for his extensive frontline experience and strong personal credibility. Two senior executives representing different functional areas, whose roles were to remove organizational barriers and facilitate the team's work, sponsored each CFT. Having two senior voices ensured that no single perspective function could dominate and the team would not focus its efforts too narrowly.

The CFTs were peppered with former Renault managers familiar with the process, and team size was limited to 10 members to avoid endless debating. It was clear, however, that 10 people would not be able to review all the operations in their domain, so subteams of 10 people were created to investigate particular issues. Through this cascading effect, the total exercise drew on the efforts of 500 or so people. The teams received three simple guidelines: "One goal: to make proposals in order to develop the business and reduce costs. One deadline: three months for final official decision-making. One rule: no sacred cows, no taboos, no constraints."[13] Ghosn kept repeating, "Only one issue is non-negotiable: the return to profit."[14]

As the CFTs started working, the team members generated a lot of ideas, many of which had never been implemented due to lack of resources. They felt energized as they realized it was up to them to revive Nissan and this might very well be their last chance. Never before in Nissan's history had a small group of middle managers been engaged to perform a drastic reexamination of company practices without spending a lot of time building consensus. As a result, past proposals had tended to be conservative when they finally reached top management. As the teams made their initial recommendations to the executive committee, Ghosn rejected many of them outright and sent them back for more work, telling them that their recommendations were not aggressive enough.

The second time around, members of the CFTs were bolder as they concluded that there would be no place to return to anyway if they failed. They solicited the help of the two executive sponsors to negotiate with the recalcitrant departments. After much tough negotiations, they finally came up with recommendations that met Ghosn's expectations.

Ghosn toured the company telling employees that Nissan had just lost its position as the country's second largest carmaker to Honda, stressing that world sales of the brand in the last seven years had fallen by 800,000 units amounting to "nearly the equivalent of Mercedes' or Mazda's worldwide sales, and more than BMW."

He also said: "If the Nissan Revival Plan succeeds, it will have many fathers. If it fails, it will have only one."[15] He surprised workers by strolling up and down the assembly lines and asking questions, not just of senior engineers and managers but also of workers themselves. And he encouraged the use of email, previously little used at Nissan. Ghosn became aware of the psychological damage wrought by so many years of underperformance: "The biggest challenge when the company has been depressed for a long time is self-confidence. [I had] to help Nissan people believe that they are capable of doing a great job in this industry, that they are capable of rivaling Honda and Toyota in terms of profitability and in terms of growth."[16]

A week before the announcement of the revival plan, Ghosn met with and solicited support from the union leaders. He assured them that employees who were willing to relocate would be guaranteed a job. Those who were unable or unwilling to move would be offered a compensation package by the company.

ANNOUNCING THE PLAN

The CFTs made more than 400 recommendations that were aggregated into a comprehensive plan by the executive committee and its staff. On October 18, 1999, Ghosn unveiled Nissan's restructuring plan to a packed audience of journalists and analysts—the speech was to be simultaneously broadcast to company employees worldwide. The extended quotes that follow are excerpts from a transcript of the speech.[17]

Ghosn got straight to the point. "Nissan is in bad shape . . . losing global market share continuously since 1991." Ghosn outlined his diagnosis of the company's performance problems: (1) Lack of clear profit orientation, (2) insufficient focus on customers and too much focus on chasing competitors, (3) lack of cross-functional, cross-border, intra-hierarchical lines, work in the company, (4) lack of a sense of urgency, and (5) no shared vision or common long-term plan.

Ghosn noted that the Nissan Revival Plan had been elaborated through broad-based debate in CFTs and outlined the key contents of the plan. "There is no problem at a car company that good products can't solve." He went on to describe some of the new product opportunities they had identified which would give rise to several revamps and four new models, including the reincarnation of the celebrated "Z". "Product development," he asserted, "will be at the heart of Nissan's revival."

Ghosn continued: "Our styling has not always been an asset. It has to be more attractive and consistent." He then caused quite a stir in the audience by revealing that he had lured from rival automaker, Isuzu Motors, its 25-year veteran design chief, Shiro Nakamura. Starting today as Nissan's head of design, Ghosn explained, "He will be fully empowered, along with a re-enhanced styling team, with the mission to bring back to Nissan's car design the attractiveness and consistency it urgently needs."

Now came the moment to deliver the proposed treatment. First, there would be a two-pronged attack to cut purchasing costs by 20% over three years. Ghosn explained: "Today, . . . purchasing will be centralized and globalized." The other, more controversial measure, involved Nissan halving the number of its suppliers "which means that our chosen suppliers, existing or new ones, will significantly increase their business with us."

The second target had to do with Nissan's excess capacity. "Taking into account our long-term forecasts, we have decided to reduce by 30% the current capacity." A gasp went through the audience as the corresponding plant closures were announced: three of the company's seven auto assembly plants in Japan plus two engine-transmission factories in Japan. "The plant closures, however painful they are—and they really are—will guarantee the future [of the remaining plants] by allowing them to be industry leaders." Ghosn continued: "We will . . . rationalize . . . the number of Nissan platforms"—going from 24 platforms spread between seven plants to 15 platforms divided by four plants in 2002, and down to 12 by 2004.

"Our target is to develop and optimize our R&D capability and capacity," asserted Ghosn. "We will move to a globally integrated organization . . . in terms of [R&D] strategy, processes, standards and benchmarks. . . . We will empower [the regional R&D centers] to take more responsibility for the entire product line offered in their region, whether they developed it or not." Investment in R&D would be increased from 3.7% of sales in 1998 to 5%.

Ghosn then revealed extensive changes to Nissan's traditional HR practices: "A performance-oriented compensation will be established for management starting in 2000. Bonuses and stock options will be part of the incentives offered to boost Nissan profitability and growth. Performance-based career advancement will be established at the latest by the end of [April] 2000 to make sure we act in a coherent manner across the company."

Of the 148,000 employees, 21,000 people (14%) would be cut from Nissan's consolidated workforce—with domestic employment bearing more than three-quarters of the cut—through attrition, the increased use of part-time employees, spin-offs, and early retirement programs. Ghosn reassured employees that there would be no outright layoffs: "Transfers will be offered to all direct and semi-direct employees. In order to facilitate the transfers, hiring will be strictly limited and monitored by HR." R&D, however, would increase its headcount by 500.

Ghosn admitted: "Establishing the plan represents at most 5% of the challenge; 95% of the challenge now lies in its execution." He rounded off his speech by specifying the commitments of the top management team. First, a return to profit by FY 2000; second, an operating profit of at least 4.5% of sales for FY 2002; and third, to cut the debt in half to $6.3 billion by FY 2002. He declared, "The top management will be accountable for delivering the committed performance—all of it."[18–21]

Immediate reactions to the radical renewal plan were mixed. Predictably, suppliers and dealers denounced Nissan's demands as extreme. The employer's federation condemned the large-scale layoffs. The powerful labor unions, frequently vocal in their response to organizational change proposed by foreigners, requested only that no employees be laid off. According to one insider: "He painted a picture so bleak that suppliers and unions felt compelled to accept change."[22] Some investment analysts doubted Ghosn's ability to deliver on intangibles, such as designing products that people wanted to buy and creating a powerful and consistent brand image. Nissan had tried many restructurings before but had never followed through.[23, 24]

Ghosn was aware that until he had some results to show, his credibility was in straight talk. As he observed: "Credibility has two legs: the first leg of credibility is performance, but [we have nothing to show at the start]; the second leg of credibility is transparency—what I think, what I say, what I do is the same thing. So we have to be extremely transparent."[25]

FOCUSING ON ACTION

Less than two weeks after the NRP announcement, Nissan's stock had fallen 5%.[26] Within days, Ghosn promised to quit along with the executive committee if Nissan failed to post a profit for the year ending March 2001.[27] As Ghosn explained: "It was very important for the credibility of the plan, both internally and externally. The ultimate sacrifice for the top manager is to say 'I'm putting my job on the line if I don't achieve these targets'."[28]

Ghosn also approved the project to build a new $930-million assembly plant in Mississippi intended to supply the US market which accounted for over a third of Nissan's sales. The plant was scheduled to start production in mid-2003 with new models targeted at the American market.[29] Though this investment decision was regarded by some executives as premature, Ghosn told them: "People need to know what the prize is, what are they aiming for, what are the benefits or the advantage to them of changing some established tradition."[30]

While Ghosn praised the loyalty and enthusiasm inside Nissan, he simultaneously pressed employees for top results. When two managers presented their ideas for a new information system at Nissan, Ghosn challenged them to prove that their solution could not be bettered by outside consultants. He sent them away, demanding a response to his queries within three weeks.[31] Ghosn also required that every number had to be checked and reports should be totally clear and verifiable.

He encouraged open debate of major issues and expression of open disagreement, in contrast to the old Nissan way in which proposals were worked out prior to the meetings and no one was supposed to raise questions or objections in the formal meetings. Japanese managers were initially not used to it, but eventually found the new approach more productive.

Ghosn also told Nissan managers to use 5% of their time planning and 95% on implementation, contrary to their habit of planning much of the time. The CEO saw continuous insistence on implementation as the key difference between turnaround success and failure. He stressed action, speed, results, and close follow-up.

Though expected to disband after building the NRP, Ghosn kept the CFTs as part of the management structure to serve as watchdogs for the implementation of the plan and to look for new ways to improve performance—indeed, a tenth team was added to cover investment costs and efficiency.[32] The CFT pilots continued to meet with Ghosn at least once a month, serving as relays to the rest of the workforce but also keeping him informed of progress.

Plant closures took place as planned and in close cooperation with the union leaders. Japanese middle managers and first line supervisors, many of them 30-year veterans, spent a lot of their time meeting with the workers, often in small groups, as they devoted their attention to a massive amount of detail since each person's situation was different and required customized solutions. As they had to relocate most of the workers along with the production lines, plant managers had to coordinate closely with the engineering and manufacturing groups who underwent a lot of changes themselves. Managers ensured that workers who agreed to move would be integrated into the work groups at the new locations.[33, 34]

2000: MAKING HEADWAY

During the 1990s, Nissan managers received bonuses based on production levels rather than profits—which meant there was little incentive to minimize overproduction.

Ghosn insisted that bonus structures be explicitly linked to the operating profit of the company or the subsidiary, with up to 35% of salary to be performance related. At internal meetings with managers, he emphasized that without a demonstrated contribution to cost cuts, no one in purchasing, administration, or engineering would receive a pay increase.[35] Ghosn mandated that within one year of his arrival all promotions were to be based upon performance rather than seniority—and the power and prestige of many senior managers began to evaporate as longstanding supplier relationships were severed. These HR changes were crowned in March 2000 by the extension of the stock option plan to managers worldwide, benefiting about 500 employees.

Ghosn introduced the notions of target (i.e., stretched goals) and commitment that were new to most Nissan managers. Commitment referred to an annual set of objectives to which compensation and promotion were tied. Actual performance was monitored monthly to ensure immediate response to shortfalls from budget. Managers who met their targets could receive cash incentives equal to about a third of their total compensation. Typically, commitment and target comprised two or three specific, and mostly quantitative, goals.

On whistle-stop tours of factories, he probed managers for explanations of sluggish performance improvements or limited cost cuts. He reprimanded one tongue-tied manager whose results were insufficiently promising, with, "This is your responsibility. Brainstorm. Discuss. You will be held accountable for this."[36] He was direct in his dealings with employees, enthusiastically shaking hands with all those who came to his office, regardless of rank.[37]

Contrasting with the complaints and confusion of some of the more established executives, many of the younger executives, especially those who spoke English, saw unexpected new responsibilities and career opportunities coming their way. According to Thierry Moulonguet, VP Finance: "With Carlos Ghosn the rules of the game are simple and clear. That was perfectly understood by the young generation of Japanese managers. He is very approachable. Anyone can send him an email; he looks at all of them. He reacts in an open and straightforward way."[38]

In late March 2000, Ghosn and Moulonguet were designated president and chief financial officer, respectively. The incumbent president, Yoshikazu Hanawa, would assume the largely symbolic role of chairman, serving as a liaison with the Japanese business community. More significant was the decision to eliminate the divisional presidencies in Europe and North America—putting in place instead four management teams including representatives from the major functions who would meet once a month. Ghosn asserted that regional presidencies were conducive to crossed communication and unclear leadership. According to Ghosn, "This reorganization was one of the few changes I made unilaterally."[39]

Ghosn also announced the high profile promotion of two senior VPs, Toshiyuki Shiga and Shiro Tomii, both still in their 40s. With purchasing finance, manufacturing, and R&D already under global management, Ghosn named Shozo Kurihara as chief information officer with global responsibility; likewise, the CEO established a global marketing team to provide him with better marketing intelligence as he lacked a clear picture of how Nissan's models were faring against the competition.

In mid-May 2000, Nissan announced plans to revamp its product line with 22 new models over the next three years. Ghosn insisted that these would be "all-new products, not derivatives," 10 of them destined for the North American market.[40, 41] Ghosn told journalists: "The NRP is on track and it is now time to grow."[42]

At the end of the following October, Ghosn announced Nissan's best half-year results in a decade with a consolidated net profit of over $1.5 billion contrasting with a $3 billion loss for the corresponding period the previous year. The workforce had been cut by 9,000 by September 2000 and purchasing costs had been cut by 10%—with suppliers noting that formerly risk-averse Nissan managers were suddenly more willing to consider suppliers' ideas for cost-cutting design changes.[43] "The revival plan is going further, moving faster and reaching deeper than we previously forecast,"[44] said Ghosn, as the company quadrupled its earlier projections for full-year profits.[45]

Though clearly delighted with the speed of improvement, Ghosn was careful to protect the reputation of his predecessors, telling journalists: "The previous management [was] struggling with survival problems, and therefore it did not have enough time to think about long-term vision."[46] As an outsider, he explained, he was much freer to make drastic reforms.[47]

CREATIVITY AND INNOVATION

Ghosn believed that new, exciting models delivered rapidly would save Nissan. Despite the company's low cash and cost-cutting situation, he approved the upscale remodeling of Nissan's technical center in Tokyo where chief designer Nakamura and his team worked. Nakamura, a graduate of the Art Center College of Design in Pasadena, California, felt that Japanese designers were more concerned with group consensus than individuality, and was determined to include more foreigners in the Japanese design teams.

Nakamura challenged his team create innovative styling and led two-and-a-half years of creativity at levels he had never seen before. Japanese designers worked closely with their US counterparts at Nissan Design America (NDA) based in San Diego. As part of the global teamwork instituted under Ghosn, designers started to be involved in models throughout the life of the car, since engineering changes and marketing demands directly affect design. Designers communicate daily with other team members in Japan, Europe, and North America and frequently met with people from engineering and sales and marketing.

The increased involvement and cross-team coordination meant more work, but most designers, who were strongly stimulated by Ghosn's stretched goals, welcomed the additional work in exchange for the freedom to create all-new vehicles that displayed original styling. The results: new Z-car, the full-size truck, a new sports utility, the new Altima, a new minivan, the Murano cross-over vehicle—more than two dozen new or radically changed models.[48]

On the back of the company's encouraging first half-year profits, Ghosn also announced that Nissan would spend $790 million in conjunction with Renault to develop a viable fuel-cell car. The partnership made a lot of sense given the risks involved and the lack of consensus over what type of fuel cell was most promising. A large number of the 1,000 new engineers that Nissan was set to hire would be channeled toward the five-year fuel-cell program.

2001: NISSAN IS BACK!

When Ghosn first came in, he had kept the existing executives in place, yet made them "very aware" that there would be consequences if they did not meet their targets. In March 2001, there were several senior casualties including one member of the executive committee. Twenty subsidiary presidents were also axed from the domestic dealership network.[49]

On the other hand, there were also many promotions. Among the most notable was the promotion of Shiro Nakamura, now fronting TV ads for the newly redesigned Skyline sedan, from VP of design to SVP. There was also the rapid promotion of Mamoru Yoshida, who had piloted one of the CFTs, to head the group's Canadian operations. One of the recently promoted Japanese managers commented: "In the old system everyone could be promoted, so there was no pressure. . . . For many employees it was a good system but for those with good skills it was no good. If I [had] been replaced by a younger man in the past I would have been shocked. But now I don't think I would care because clearly the person has better skills than mine."[50]

In the same week, Ghosn announced plans to resume dividend payments for the first time since 1998. He also granted a generous 6% salary increase for all employees in recognition that the change in Nissan's fortunes had been the result of a collective effort. After a two-year freeze, the unions had put their demands to Ghosn expecting some negotiation but instead received immediate approval. The decision was so fast and unexpected that it drew widespread attention from the national press.[51]

In May 2001, when announcing Nissan's full-year results at a news conference in Tokyo, Ghosn declared, "Nissan is back!"[52] Sales were up 1.9% to nearly $50 billion; cash generated by the disposal of noncore assets and the sale of securities and real estate had shrunk debt by nearly half (to $7.7 billion), contributing to profit by reducing interest repayments; purchasing costs had been cut by 11%; and the closure of three assembly plants had pushed up domestic capacity utilization rate to 74%. As a result, operating margins had more than tripled from 1.4% to 4.75%, exceeding the NRP goal a year ahead of schedule.[53] Building on this financial recovery Ghosn discussed plans to introduce 22 new models in the following three years while boosting global sales by one million units.

Just past the mid-point of the three-year NRP, Nissan had met or exceeded its self-imposed targets. For example, as of September 2001, procurement costs were down by 18%. The global headcount had been reduced from 148,000 to 128,100 employees.

At the start of February 2002, Nissan confirmed that it would meet all of NRP targets one year ahead of schedule.[54] Jed Connelly, Nissan North America's senior VP of sales and marketing, commented: "One thing that Ghosn brought to the party was a clear focus on our priorities and a clear plan by which to execute those priorities. He has not wavered from day one."[55–57] A French manager commented: "Ghosn knew how to make people feel what they faced was not insurmountable. He got people involved by convincing them that facing challenge would develop them personally, even if they didn't agree initially with him. In the end, the objective appeared so clear and transparent it was difficult to argue against."[58, 59]

Ghosn sought to push the change deeper within Nissan by empowering lower levels of middle management than those involved in the CFTs, believing answers could be found within the organization if people were given freedom to actively find problems and recommend solutions. Known within the company as V-up, the program utilized more than 400 "V-pilots." Similar to CFT pilots, V-pilots were smaller teams with more specific areas of focus. Their challenge was to offer continuous process improvement and field-level problem solutions. By doing so, Ghosn sought to relieve the boredom and frustrations that typically strike middle managers in Japan and encouraged them to lead the changes and fix the company by providing solutions to everyday problems.[60]

Reflecting on the reasons for the success achieved thus far, Ghosn said:

> No matter how promising your resources, you will never be able to turn them into gold unless you get the corporate culture right. A good corporate culture taps into the productive aspects of a country's culture, and in Nissan's case we have been able to exploit the uniquely Japanese combination of keen competitiveness and sense of community. . . . For a turnaround process of this kind to work, people have to believe both that they can speak the truth and that they can trust what they hear from others. Building trust, however, is a long-term project; those in charge have to demonstrate that they do what they say they'll do, and that takes time. But you have to start somewhere. Right from the beginning, I made it clear that every number had to be thoroughly checked. I did not accept any report that was less than totally clear and verifiable, and I expected people to personally commit to every observation or claim they made. I set the example myself: when I announced the revival plan, I also declared that I would resign if we failed to accomplish any of the commitments we set for ourselves.[61]

CASE 30

Even a Clown Can Do It: Cirque du Soleil Recreates Live Entertainment

LE CIRQUE RÉINVENTÉ: CIRQUE DU SOLEIL REINTERPRETS THE PERFORMING ARTS

> Cirque du Soleil began with a very simple dream. A group of young entertainers got together to amuse audiences, see the world, and have fun doing it. Every year, the audience becomes bigger, we continue to discover new places and ideas, and we're still having fun. We also dream of suffusing our new projects with the energy and inspiration that are the essence of our shows. And we want to help young people express their dreams . . . and make them come true.
>
> Guy Laliberté, President and Chief Executive Officer, Cirque du Soleil.

In 1984, a determined Guy Laliberté set out to reinvent the circus industry. This was no small challenge given that the very core of the product was delivering spectacles and surprise on a daily basis. As with many other industries, this one had its share of white elephants and dogs. It was rife with promoters, hustlers, and fire-breathers of all sorts, but had its impassive iron-men as well. An amalgam of strong traditions and a quest for novelty, it was a circus.

From its original incarnation as a troupe called "Le Club des Hauts Talons," so named because of its host of stilt-walkers, Laliberté's Cirque du Soleil rapidly evolved from a pack of underemployed kids into one of Canada's largest cultural exports. Almost 30 million people saw one of the troupe's productions between 1984 and 2000. In that last year alone, approximately 50,000 people took in the Soleil experience, as productions appeared in 120 cities around the world.

From a production which put on its first show in an 800-seater tent purchased with an Arts grant from the Quebec government, it now boasts three separate traveling productions housed in 2,500-seater tents, and four permanent shows in purpose-built theaters in Orlando, Biloxi (Mississippi), and Las Vegas.[1]

THE ORIGINS OF CIRQUE DU SOLEIL

Cirque du Soleil was created in 1984 by a group of young street performers who had pooled their talents to form the "Club des Talons Hauts" two years earlier. Initially part of the celebrations of the 450th anniversary of Jacques Cartier's arrival in Quebec, the brainchild of Guy Laliberté was based on a totally new concept: a mix of the circus arts

FIGURE 1 THE CHARACTER 'TARGET' AT CIRQUE DU SOLEIL'S SHOW 'QUIDAM', 2011, SACRAMENTO, CALIFORNIA

Source: Randy Miramontez/Shutterstock.com.

This case was prepared by Matt Williamson, INSEAD MBA 2000, under the supervision of Professors W. Chan Kim, Renée Mauborgne, and Ben M. Bensaou, all at INSEAD. It is intended to be used as a basis for class discussion rather than to illustrate either effective or ineffective handling of an administrative situation.

and street entertainment featuring wild costumes, staged under "magical" lighting and set to original music. As such, Cirque du Soleil was part of a movement that many call the New American Circus.

Cirque du Soleil scrambled the existing traditions of the circus and the performing arts, and reinvented the wheel. The resulting dream world, populated by operatic, choreographed, and acrobatic sprites was like no other place on earth; a reflection of the arts which inspired it. Sharing elements of dance, circus, and opera, Soleil competes with them all but remains utterly unique. Nor has Soleil failed to draw attention to its novel position as a non-circus; early productions such as *We Reinvent the Circus* and *Nouvelle Expérience* gave warning that the show would be unlike anything ever seen before, under the Big Top or anywhere else.

Cirque du Soleil was not, however, the first to take this new route. Paul Binder and Michael Christiansen, founders of the Big Apple Circus in 1979, and Larry Pisoni, founder of the Pickle Family Circus, brought the more classical one-ring circus back to America after over 100 years, when even the smallest circuses spread their shows over three rings.[2] Also in 1979, Guy Caron established the circus school that would eventually become the Ecole Nationale du Cirque and train a significant number of the original performers in Cirque du Soleil's initial 13-week tour. Each of these key players were outsiders in the tradition-bound world of circus, with roots more akin to the hippie counterculture than anything else. In contrast to the consciously intimate scale and deference to skill and artistry above commercialism of the Pickle Family and Big Apple Circuses, they never hesitated to make theirs a commercial enterprise.

With a US$1.7 million contract from the provincial government of Quebec, the show traveled the province, attracting some powerful fans that it would later need. Closing the first season with a surplus of US$50,000, Laliberté decided to promote his new show and invested heavily in a new tent and other equipment. Although it finished the 1985 season to critical acclaim, Cirque du Soleil was nevertheless US$750,000 in debt from its investments in equipment, despite extending the run several cities beyond the initial route. Rene Levesque, then the Prime Minister of Quebec and an avid fan from the 1984 opening show, saw the cultural value in supporting the enterprise and refinanced the debt.[3]

FIGURE 2 EXTERIOR OF CIRQUE DU SOLEIL, FLORIDA

Source: Steven Greaves, © Dorling Kindersley.

The troupe took another huge gamble, spending all its remaining funds after the 1986 season to join the Los Angeles Arts Festival in 1987, its first serious foray outside of the Quebec region. This time the gamble paid off: Cirque du Soleil was a huge success and almost immediately sold out its later shows. Patronage of celebrities like Steve Martin, David Bowie, Madonna, Elton John, and Francis Ford Coppola helped seal its identity as a sophisticated new form of entertainment.

THE CONTENT AND STYLE OF CIRQUE DU SOLEIL

Cirque du Soleil has a unique approach to developing its shows, setting it apart from most other circuses. "A Cirque du Soleil performance is like no other circus ever seen in the United States or anywhere else. It is relentless in its drive to be nothing short of spellbinding." A thematic line, though frequently rather vague (and intentionally so), is manifested throughout the show in costumes, music, and the types of acts performed. While not rising to the level of a storyline, the theme brings harmony and an intellectual component to the show, without imposing limits on its potential for acts. Rather than taking existing acts and compiling them into a show, Guy Caron, Franco Dragone, and the creative teams at Cirque du Soleil who have followed them, begin with a theme, such as *Saltimbanco* or *Quidam,* and build a show to suit. The result is a seamless entertainment experience for the audience rather than a punctuated series of acts. Moreover, unlike traditional circus, the company has multiple productions; shows have distinctive themes allowing the spectator to see Le Cirque several times.

In creating the performance that rocked the Los Angeles Arts Festival, Caron took his team on a weeklong retreat to focus simply on developing the theme and how it would be conveyed through each component of the show. The theme, rather than simply being a new edition of the circus, is a performance in itself. It serves as the audience's guarantee of a high quality, exotic experience.

The most important element of this thematic drive, and the starting point from which the creative team begins, is an original score. Since the inception of Cirque du Soleil, Rene Dupere has taken the creative director's expression of the theme and transformed it into a full-length original score. The music for a Soleil show drives the selection of the visual performance, lighting, and timing of the acts, rather than the reverse.[4] "In the movement you see the music and in the music you hear the movement," says Caron.[5]

More than just the theme sequencing of a production, Cirque du Soleil represents a true mixture of the performing arts. It is not quite a circus, nor is it quite opera or theater, but it combines elements from them all. While the signature blue and yellow tent and the circus acrobatics and clowns that form much of the show's content are clearly circus, the show takes place on a stage without a ring and seating on three sides.

In constructing the physical dimensions of the show, the creative team draws heavily upon circus arts, featuring jugglers, trampolinists, trapeze artists, teeterboard virtuosos and, of course, clowns. Nevertheless, each act, even each movement, has a purpose within the show and contributes to the development of the overall thematic element. Owing to this singularity of purpose, big name acts have no place in Cirque du Soleil. The presence of a Gunther Gebel-Williams and 40 wild cats or a drum roll leading into a Gaona quadruple somersault would undercut the dreamlike development of the theme.

Performers in Cirque du Soleil, while highly accomplished in their own right, play roles within the larger show. In part because of the outlandish costumes, but also because of the lack of a ringmaster announcing the acts, and a printed program which buries the names of the individual artists in a cast list at the back, individual performers are essentially anonymous to the audience. This was not lost on the initial cast of Cirque du Soleil and many were dismayed to learn that Laliberté might not always include them in future productions.

A final striking detail of the Cirque du Soleil experience, which sets it apart from most traditional circuses, is the complete absence of performing animals. This is a dramatic departure for a medium that originated in a horse ring and has been synonymous with elephants and other wild animal trainers. Leaving animal acts behind, Laliberté has created something new and different, not quite circus but not quite anything else. Circus historian Fred Pfening notes, "There's one question that always annoys me: 'But is it circus?' That's utterly irrelevant. It is what the audience thinks it is. It is Soleil."[6]

THE BUSINESS OF CIRQUE DU SOLEIL

Clearly, the initial vision that drove the founders of the various New American circuses was more artistic than commercial. The family nature of both the Pickle Family Circus and the Big Apple Circus was more reminiscent of a hippie commune than a typical start-up. Somewhat in contrast, Cirque du Soleil took little time to become immensely profitable after its success at the Los Angeles Arts Festival. Unlike the others, Soleil pursued the dual goals of artistry and profit, exemplified in the initial agreement between Caron and Laliberté to lead these two components separately.

Over time, Soleil has come up with a lifecycle strategy that features an opening in Montreal followed by a North American tour, stretching over several years. The show then remains on tour for up to four more years, traveling first through Europe, usually followed by a jaunt through Asia. Instead of traveling to audiences, three permanent shows tap into the continuous flow of potential viewers through such places as Las Vegas and Disney World. *Mystere, La Nouba,* and "*O*" have run in such permanent installations from the beginning, while *Alegria,* one of Soleil's older touring shows, has performed in the riverboat gambling casinos of Biloxi, Mississippi, on what was to be a permanent engagement, only to begin touring anew two years later in the spring of 2001. Surprisingly, not since *Nouvelle Experience* has a Soleil show stopped touring.

Quidam is exemplary of the typical touring Cirque du Soleil show. It was produced for approximately US$5.9 million and first staged in Montreal in April 1996. Following a three-year tour of North America, the show traveled throughout Europe. Expected annual gross revenues at the start of the tour were US$14.6 million, a figure that has been exceeded year after year by a significant amount, according to Soleil staff.

Cirque du Soleil draws its revenue in significantly different fashion from the traditional circus and other shows that take place in civic arenas and sports stadiums. The show derives the great majority of revenues from ticket sales, though sponsor partners and concession sales also contribute to profit margins.

Soleil's focus on providing sophisticated entertainment enables a different approach to ticket pricing. Rather than a family event with free or discounted tickets for children or other age groups, seats are generally sold at full face value. "Sure there are a couple of kids at a Soleil performance, but children make up a much smaller share of the audience. With the Ringling Brothers and Barnum & Bailey's Circus (hereafter referred to as the Ringling Brothers & Co.) the audience is almost all families or kids."[7] Reflecting the adult market for live entertainment, Soleil tickets are available at a substantially higher price, in line with major theater or opera tickets. Tickets for *Dralion*'s 2001 New York engagement sold at US$65–85. VIP packages including food offered in a separate preshow gathering tent sell at up to US$230 per seat. Meanwhile, "*O*" sported the most expensive seat for Vegas-based productions after boosting the price to US$110 per seat in November 2000. It remains one of the hardest tickets to find. Shows are regularly sold out and boast the highest seat occupancy in the industry, consistently approaching 85–95%.

Soleil keeps a traditionally large source of circus revenues—concessions—at arm's length. Not surprisingly, less than 10% of revenues come from concessions at a Soleil show. In keeping with the performance-centered ethic of the troupe, nothing is sold during the performance or inside the tent. For the Ringling Brothers & Co. shows, this figure may be dramatically higher—closer to 20%—as the sales effort is substantially stronger. At the Ringling Brothers & Co. circus, hawkers pass among the seated audience selling food and toys; concession stands are also packed tightly outside the performance space.

Sponsorships are a low-key but significant source of revenue for Soleil. Originally a key revenue earner from the days when the show operated as nonprofit, many of the traveling shows have a primary sponsor, usually associated with the VIP tent. Lincoln Automobiles is the primary sponsor of *Dralion,* with five other corporations taking minor sponsorship roles entitling them to discreet mention in the playbill, advertising, and banners around the tent.[8] For a typical "shrine" circus, or even a larger show such as the Big Apple Circus, a main sponsor guarantees a gate to the circus and sells the tickets independently. Sponsors in this vein are normally powerful local nonprofit organizations who use the event as a major fund-raising opportunity. They view it as a chance to associate themselves with the panache of Soleil and the upscale consumers attending the show. The arrangement is much more like a sponsor at a sporting event such as the Masters or the US Open.

Using its fantastic creative team and seeking to build on the brand the live shows have created, in recent years Soleil has somersaulted into film and other ventures. Beginning with videos of live performances and behind-the-scenes documentaries, the troupe has graduated to film, creating *Journey of Man* in the IMAX format. Pieced together using performers from several of the different productions, the film creates a dreamlike vision of the trajectory of one man's life using the brushstrokes of Soleil's signature costuming and circus arts. Though the IMAX format limits the potential box office take—both the projection equipment and special dimension screens are extremely expensive and limited in numbers—longer-term engagements at the science museums that often host these films enable Soleil to bridge the film barrier by adding a physical dimension through rides and interactive displays that would not be available at a normal cinema. At the Franklin Institute in Philadelphia, for instance, moviegoers willing to pay an additional US$2 can bicycle on a high-wire 10 meters above the heads of other patrons standing in the ticket line.[9]

FINALE

One might think that in the performing arts and the circus the need for innovation is obvious. Yet even in such an innovation-friendly environment, the circus industry had become stagnant, generating "new" acts by dressing up what already existed. Circus families and individual artists created highly developed and ever more challenging variations on the same formula of trained animals and "death-defying" stunts that had been popular in the past century. Irving Feld was well known for pressing performers to add yet another somersault off the flying trapeze or one more tiger to a simultaneous rollover act. Yet the added difficulty and danger faced by the performers were all but lost on the vast majority of the audience. This was novelty but not innovation, adding little of value to the audience's experience yet requiring significant expenditure by the circus company. By reinventing the circus industry, Cirque du Soleil created a phenomenon that has inspired and amazed millions of fans. In the process, it has produced an exciting line of shows that have attracted millions of people, and generated revenues that would have made P.T. Barnum blush (see Exhibits 1 and 2).

EXHIBIT 1
CIRCUS REVENUES

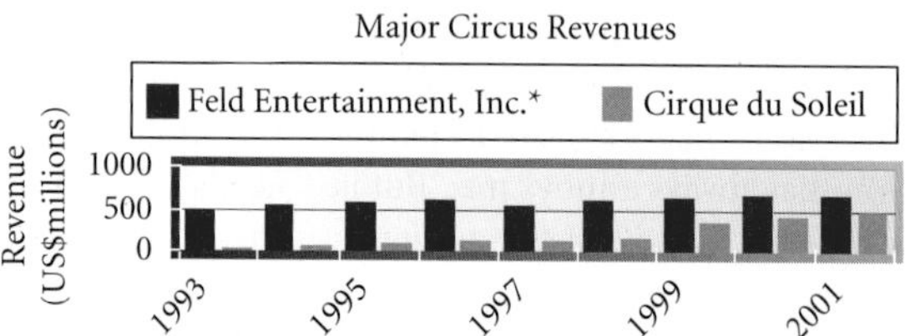

Estimates based on the data of Hoovers Online. Note: RBB&B is a major division of Feld

EXHIBIT 2
CIRQUE DU SOLEIL ATTENDANCE FIGURES

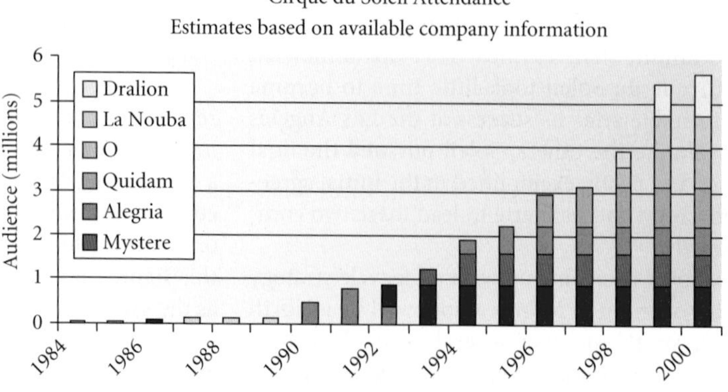

Estimates based on available company information

CASE 31

A Restaurant with a Difference

Since they first met, Mark Rapport and Jenny Lindstrom had often toyed with the idea of leaving their current jobs and venturing out on their own. Given their temperament, their experience, and their current situation, this made a lot of sense. Mark was an award-winning journalist for the Boston Globe who had once roamed the world's trouble spots in search of stories, but now was confined to the newspaper's main office on Morrissey Boulevard, where he read other people's copies and wished he had never been promoted to Senior Foreign Editor. Jenny began her professional life as a mathematician, moved to voice recognition during the 1990s, and eventually became one of the team at Vox Tech which pioneered the first commercial voice recognition programs. The excitement of research and development however came to an end when Vox Tech was acquired some years later by TransCom Solutions, an information technology company whose one-stop approach to computer procurement ("You come to us, we shop for you") made it one of largest IT suppliers of computer software and equipment. However, research and development hardly fitted this strategy, so the voice recognition team was disbanded and Jenny was reassigned to customer support—a job she detested but performed with her usual professionalism.

When they discussed their future business they agreed that there was no point in just starting another business. What they wanted was a business that made going to work each morning an adventure. So many evenings after work they would bounce ideas around. Usually, one put forth an idea they had been mulling over, and the other would raise questions and suggest alternatives. The process was taxing—they often had protracted arguments—but they enjoyed the exploration. For a while they were different, they also complemented each other well. Mark was an intuitive thinker who relentlessly followed his flashes of insight. By contrast, Jenny was an acute observer who systematically developed ideas she usually got from something she heard or saw.

On this particular evening, it was Mark who came home with an idea that had been buzzing in his head all day. Jenny could sense Mark's excitement. Nevertheless, as was their custom they did not discuss business during supper. As soon as the dishes were cleared, Mark leaned forward and began to explain his idea.

"You remember Sam's, the diner across from my office building? You know the one with the neon sign that flashes a soup bowl and a sandwich."

"Yes", said Jenny, "I seem to remember it." "It makes a decent chicken sandwich but the coffee is abysmal."

"Well," said Mark, "I took our Middle East correspondent for lunch today, and I have to tell you it was an unmitigated disaster. He looked at the menu and after some thinking ordered a lamb pastrami sandwich. We waited for almost half an hour and still no sandwich. Forty minutes later with some prodding on my part the sandwich arrives. He bites into the sandwich and the expression on his face says it all. I call the waitress over and tell her: 'You call this a sandwich? How long has this meat been in the freezer?' "

"She apologizes and whisks away the sandwich. However, I am not satisfied. I ask for the manager. He comes over and apologizes again, and tells us that the lunch is on the house. Now I am satisfied, but I am also curious. 'You know', I tell the manager, 'I have been coming here for years, but I have never had this problem before'. The manager nods his head, and says: 'Well, we often have this problem with dishes that are on the menu but that are rarely ordered. At the end of each day the cook checks to make sure that we have enough of everything for the next day, but he does not check to make sure that too much has been left from the previous day. Usually things move fast enough so this is not a problem, but once in a while the food stays in the fridge too long and then I have to eat humble pie. If cooks were not so hard to find I would give this one a piece of my mind, but since he is as temperamental as they come, all I can do is simply remind him to check more carefully and hope for the best'."

"This got me thinking. Why are restaurants so static? Why do places like Sam's have the same menu for years? Clearly, the manager should have dropped this sandwich from the menu long ago, but the menu stays the same and customers that are unhappy or want something different simply go elsewhere."

"What if we were to start a restaurant that was different. A restaurant where the menu changed as demand changed. Think about this Jenny. With today's technology it would

This case was prepared by Joseph Lampel, City University London.

not be so difficult. Each waitress would have an iPad with a dedicated App instead of a paper pad. She would write the order on the iPad and then transmit the order directly to the kitchen. At the end of each week the orders would be totaled and the demand analyzed. Dishes that fell below a certain volume would be deleted from the menu. And using a laser printer we could print a new menu each week at fairly low cost."

As he spoke Mark could see the doubts on Jenny's face. So before she had a chance to speak he decided to bring out his trump card. "You know how much we both love food. Not just finding new dishes in interesting restaurants, but trying out new recipes in our own kitchen. Well, this restaurant will allow us to combine our passion for food with our wish to build a business where we are constantly experimenting and exploring. Each week we will introduce new dishes. If they work out, fine, if not, we will drop them. Think of all the fun we will have, searching for new recipes, trying them out in the kitchen, and then waiting to see how well they are received."

Jenny could contain herself no longer. "It does not sound like fun to me!" she said with some exasperation. "Have you thought of all the problems? A restaurant where the menu changes all the time! Have you given thought to the kitchen operations? Where will we find a cook that will tolerate a constantly changing menu? What about shopping for provisions and ingredients? It is difficult enough to do this at the lowest cost possible when the menu stays the same, how are you going to do this when it changes all the time?"

Mark was on the defensive, but he was not going to give up that easily. "You must know," he said, "that one of the oldest principles of business is that 20 percent of all products account for 80 percent of all the sales. I am sure that restaurants are no exception. It may well be true that kitchen operations will be more expensive, but we will save much more by removing from the menu dishes that add to our inventory and overhead costs."

"This may well be the case," responded Jenny, "but then people rarely eat alone. They often come with partners or friends who may actually want a dish that is not popular. What are you going to do about them? What if they prefer to go elsewhere, and by default take their partners or friends with them?"

"Of course, there are things that still need to be worked out," retorted Mark, "this is the nature of good strategy. You cannot work everything out in advance. It would be foolish to try, and even more foolish to do it and believe that you have succeeded. It is certain that we will have to explore and solve many problems, but in the meantime think about this from a wider perspective: This will be the first restaurant that learns from its customers in this city, perhaps the first in the entire country. Think of the publicity this will generate. This alone will attract tremendous attention. People will come from everywhere to try out our concept. Our initial business is guaranteed, and with it the initial period of time we need to iron out our problems. By the time that buzz begins to fade we will have a working restaurant based on a concept that is truly novel, and furthermore, a restaurant with a difference, a place of work that satisfies our craving for exploration and novelty. Come on, Jenny, where is your spirit of adventure?"

"My spirit of adventure is intact," responded Jenny. "I am simply not persuaded that what you propose is either practical or for that matter truly innovative."

CASE 32

Managing Performance at Haier (A)

FROM BANKRUPT COLLECTIVE ENTERPRISE TO THE COVER OF *FORBES*

One spring day in early 1985, anyone visiting the production facilities of Qingdao Refrigerator General Factory, a home appliance manufacturer in the northeastern Chinese city of Qingdao, would have been forgiven for thinking that company CEO Zhang Ruimin had taken leave of his senses. Just a few months after taking the helm of the company, at the age of 35, this former Qingdao city official in charge of the home appliance sector gathered all factory personnel outside the factory. There, they watched a group of coworkers implement an order from their young CEO: Destroy 76 refrigerators just off the production line.

The refrigerators being pounded to bits had been found to be defective in some way, even though some defects, such as chips in the paintwork, may have seemed minor. The workers who had assembled them were now handed the tools to destroy them. Wielding sledgehammers, the workers, plus Zhang himself, began the noisy demolition of the glistening new refrigerators—products that would have retailed for RMB 1,560[1] each, or four times their annual salary. Some swung their hammers with tears in their eyes. Though his employees may have doubted it that day, Zhang had a very clear message: The company would no longer produce substandard products.

Since that day in 1985, Haier, with its unique performance management system, has often been heralded as a model for the transformation of an ailing socialist enterprise to a thriving multinational. The company was seen as capable not only of succeeding in China but also of competing on the world stage.

QINGDAO HAIER REFRIGERATOR

In 2002, Qingdao Haier refrigerator produced a wide range of household electrical appliances and ranked fifth worldwide in the white goods industry, with a 3.7% global share.[2] Starting from a bleak position, in just under two decades Haier had managed to achieve what its peers had taken on average 95 years to accomplish.[3] Haier's story was one of a remarkable turnaround.

In 1985, what was then the Qingdao Refrigerator General Factory had run up a debt of RMB 1.47 million—equivalent to the combined annual salaries of its nearly 3,000 employees—and was virtually bankrupt. At that time, Haier's performance was similar to that of many other local Chinese enterprises, characterized by bureaucracy and inefficiency, with little regard for cost or quality control or for customer needs.[4]

A shift in the company's fortunes came when Zhang was appointed CEO in 1985. He turned the small loss-making refrigerator factory into a group of more than 100 plants and companies, employing over 20,000 workers. Between 1984 and 2002 Haier's revenues jumped from RMB 3.48 million to RMB 71.1 billion, while profits before tax soared from RMB 2.98 million in 1985 to RMB 240 million in 1995 and RMB 4.47 billion in 2002 (refer to Exhibit 1 *for selected financials for its main business—refrigerators*).

By 2002, Haier was recognized as China's most valuable brand, based on its success in "introducing market competition in the whole electric home appliance industry."[5] The company was a source of national pride, both for its performance in the domestic markets and its increasing successes internationally; in 2001, Haier was ranked as the world's fifth largest maker of white goods—refrigerators, freezers, and washing machines, for example (refer to Exhibit 2). According to the company, this position was held in 2002.

Since it began exporting to the US in the early 1990s, Haier had pursued a strategy of creating, then dominating, market niches. For example, it manufactured compact refrigerators of the kind typically found in college dorms or hotel rooms—and for which it had captured almost half that market in the US. Another niche in the US for Haier was electric wine cellars (refrigerators specially designed to store wine). With this niche marketing strategy, in 2002 Haier achieved US sales of approximately $150 million.

In 2002, Haier exported $445 million worth of goods—over 5% more than the previous year—earning the company the distinction of China's fifth largest exporter overall. Its products were sold in 160 countries, in 12 of the 15 top European retailers, and 8 of the 10 top American ones.

Research Associate Donna Everatt prepared this case under the supervision of Professors Vladimir Pucik and Katherine Xin as a basis for class discussion rather than to illustrate either effective or ineffective handling of a business situation.

EXHIBIT 1 SELECTED FINANCIALS QINGDAO HAIER: REFRIGERATORS (RMB MILLION)

	1999	2000	2001
Turnover	3,974	4,828	11,442
Gross profit	819	870	1,903
Operating profit	346	358	955
Net profit	311	424	618
Net profit growth	70%	37%	46%
Gross margin	21%	18%	17%
Net margin	8%	9%	5%
Dividend yield	1.2%	1.8%	2.6%

Source: Company information.

EXHIBIT 2 GLOBAL BANKING: WHITE GOODS (% VOLUME)

	2000	2001
Whirlpool Corp	8.74	8.09
Electrolux AB	7.69	7.73
Bosch-Siemens Hausgeräte GmbH	5.36	5.60
General Electric Co (GE)	5.07	5.07
Haier Group	2.90	3.72
Sears, Roebuck & Co	3.73	3.71
Maytag Corp	2.83	2.79
Sharp Electronics Corp	2.79	2.77
Merloni Elettrodomestici SpA	2.33	2.46
Matsushita Electric Industrial Co Ltd	2.19	2.19

Source: Euromonitor, 2002.

KEY SUCCESS FACTORS

A summary of Haier's key success factors included:

- *Product diversification:* Haier evolved from one refrigerator model in 1984 to 86 different product categories with over 13,000 specifications, including microwave ovens, air conditioners, small home appliances, TVs, washing machines, and MP3 players.
- *Product innovation to create niche markets:* For example, in China's major cities, living space was limited, families were small,[6] and energy was relatively more expensive. Haier invented a miniature washing machine as a secondary household machine to wash small loads of laundry daily in summer.
- *Marketing initiatives that emphasized product quality and market research:* In contrast to many Chinese manufacturers that competed on price, Haier sought to differentiate its products. In a recent price war in both the domestic and international appliance market, Haier actually increased its price to send a message to the market of Haier's quality and service.
- *Globalization:* By 2002, Haier had set up many overseas production bases, service and sales facilities, procurement networks, and international technology alliances and joint ventures with foreign players to better penetrate international markets.
- *Innovative human resource management practices:* Haier was one of the first Chinese companies to tie salaries, and even job security, to performance. Its organizational strategies included transparency, fairness, and justice.

HAIER GROUP'S MANAGEMENT PHILOSOPHIES

Zhang's management principles integrated Japanese management philosophy, American innovation, and aspects of traditional Chinese culture, as well as Haier's own learning. These policies were introduced into an environment framed at the beginning by the Chinese cultural values of harmony, face, relationships, and hierarchy, as well as by the management practices inherited from state-owned enterprises (SOEs). (Refer to Exhibit 3 for a summary of characteristics of SOE managers.)

Zhang remarked on the importance of effective human resource management policies:

> An enterprise is like a ball being pushed up a hill (F1). Under pressure of market competition and internal stress (F2), the ball needs a strong braking force (F) to prevent it from rolling back down. This braking force is the internal management infrastructure.

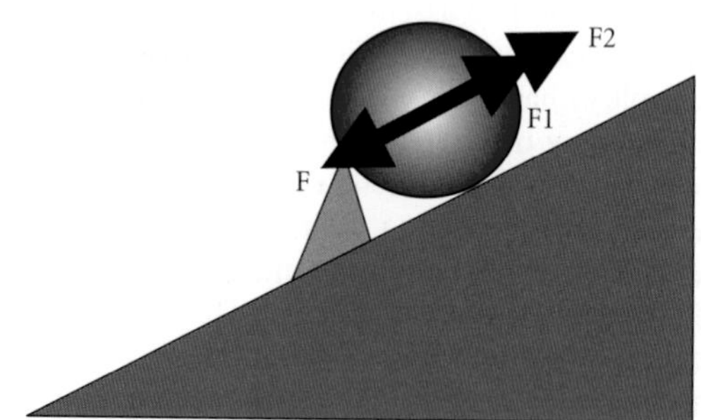

EXHIBIT 3 CHARACTERISTICS OF SOE MANAGERS

Characteristics of managers in Chinese SOEs frequently mentioned in current books and articles on the Chinese economy:

- Information conduits, not decision makers
- Comfortable working only in functional silos
- Risk averse/compliant
- Preference for ambiguity in oversight roles
- Averse to transparency
- Paternalistic[9] and coalitional (*guanxi* networks)
- Reliance on informal contacts
- Not fully appreciative of the market (incomplete buy-in)
- Professionally undereducated
- Inflexible (or constrained by unwieldy economic system)

A sense of urgency

Zhang explained that Haier was prepared for "moving forward in times of danger." He continued:

> We are not safe in that Haier has not achieved its goal so far—a goal that is limitless. Haier has been developing for 18 years, but so far we haven't seen a day of peace and safety. The outside world is always forcing or pushing us to move forward without stopping.

This sense of urgency was heightened by internal competition as well as external. Xiwen Zhou, president of Haier University, explained:

> Each Haier employee is a customer of his fellow workers. For example, Haier's Environmental Testing Laboratory must satisfy the needs of its "customers" in the Design Department by meeting deadlines and producing excellent data and useful test results. The Design Department, in turn, serves customers in the Production Department by innovative and successful designs for the manufacture of goods.

Zhou used another example from a particular division:

> For example, we have 22 vacuuming technicians engaged in different divisions. They used to care only about their own job and their division. There was no communication among business divisions, and creative ideas were not shared. Now we rank them across the Group according to several indexes such as quality, cost and output. Thus everybody knows he is No. 1, No. 2 or No. 3 among the vacuuming technicians, etc., and the sense of competition instantly increases. All the workers are motivated to do better and better.

In this way, Zhang noted that "employees can begin to feel market pressures even though they are inside the organization." Further, he felt that this philosophy had helped Haier avoid two problems that had traditionally characterized Chinese organizations: hierarchy and interpersonal networks (referred to as *guanxi*),[7] or what Zhang called "speed-absorbers."

Another fundamental element of Zhang's performance management system was accountability, at all levels, at all times.

OEC: Overall, every, and control and clearance A guiding principle of Haier's management system was OEC: Overall, Every, and Control and Clearance. The term "overall" meant that all performance dimensions had to be considered. "Every" referred to everyone, every day, and everything. "Control and clearance" referred to Haier's end-of-work procedure each day, which stated that each employee must finish all tasks planned for that day before leaving work. Clearance was conducted through self-assessment and meeting with one's supervisors. The concept of OEC laid the groundwork for a management system that had both breadth and depth: It applied to every aspect of work, every employee, every day.

According to Mianmian Yang, the president of Haier Group:

> It is really hard to keep track of all employees every day. Since Haier started the OEC practice (i.e., a self-management system) in 1989, we have been training our employees and managers to learn how to set up, achieve, and be accountable for the targets that they set for themselves every day. The targets set have to be continuously improved and stretched. We raise the bar all the time. Human beings tend to get used to the status quo. A worker must finish the task he and his supervisors set to be accomplished every day. As a manager, if you can tell the employee—with his agreement and participation—his targets, then he knows what is expected of him. Each employee should set his own challenging targets.

Once the worker knew what was expected of him, his performance was closely monitored, evaluated, and rewarded.

80:20 Principle

Under Haier's "80:20 Principle," the 20% of employees who were managers were held responsible for 80% of company results (good or bad). For example, if a worker was fined for equipment damage, he would be held responsible for 20% of the problem and his supervisor would be held responsible for 80%. This did not directly translate to a 20:80 ratio of fines, bonuses, etc. It was a slogan in Haier that communicated a clear and loud message: Managers have to have the courage and conscientiousness to assume responsibility at Haier.

Racetrack model

A key aspect of Haier's management principles was the system used for performance evaluations and promotions—and demotions—based on the concept of a racetrack. All employees were welcome to compete in work-related "races" such as job openings and promotions. But winners had to keep racing—and keep winning—to defend a title. There was no such thing as a permanent promotion. In keeping with this philosophy, every employee in the Haier Group (except the top eight senior executives) underwent frequent and transparent performance appraisals—going against the traditional Chinese culture in which "face" was extremely important.

TRYING INDIVIDUAL PROFIT AND LOSS

Monthly measures were used to track performance, according to the revenue and profit the managers had earned for the company. A senior manager gave an example:

> Let's take the relationship between a refrigerator division director and a refrigerator production unit manager for example. If the production unit has the capacity to produce 50,000 refrigerators, the division director must provide orders for 50,000 refrigerators to the production unit, enough orders to meet its entire capacity. If you only provide orders for 45,000 refrigerators, then you, the division director, rather than the production unit manager, must be responsible for the lack of orders for 5,000 refrigerators. That is your expense. Similarly,

the division director can earn his income by achieving his target (of 50,000 refrigerators) [and if] the production unit does not meet the quality standards, or delays delivery, the division director can claim for compensation. This would be extra income for his account, as one of his normal income items would be. The claim is a cost to the production unit, but an income to the division director.

Another example was provided:

We have seven refrigerator production units altogether in our refrigerator division. They must share their best experiences to improve the lowest performer. When the average performance level is raised, the unit managers can achieve their incomes.

However, although the unit's income was attributed to the unit manager, that manager also had his own income and expenditure, accounted for in a "bankbook."

Deposit book[8]

Although each manager was accountable for only a small portion of the overall profits, Zhang believed each one could function as a miniature company (MMC), each with his own profit and loss statement, mimicking a company's accounting records. As each MMC profited, so did the Group. Increasing revenues was similar to depositing money in a bank—the more a division profited, the more the manager accumulated in his resource bankbook. As long as a manager stayed with the company, his account existed, regardless of department or division.

Zhou explained the system:

We set basic goals for managers. Only when they meet or exceed those goals will they have money (i.e., savings) in their account, otherwise they have to pay. This is an incentive to do a better job. But this is effective for those who reach their goals first, for the goals we have set for them are merely basic ones. We give them three or five more months, and whoever reaches his goal earlier will receive more income, and the later ones do not receive any income and have to pay.

Let me give you an example. Yongshao Zhang used to be one of our purchasing agents for the logistics department. All he needed to do was buy what you wanted according to your requirements, without taking any responsibility for when these materials were used. Now we have changed the practice, and Zhang has become a purchasing manager. As a manager, he has to ensure that the steel plates he buys are the least expensive in the world and are of the best quality. Moreover, he has to provide the steel plates in time according to the demands of the business divisions, while trying not to store them in the warehouse for long, because he is charged for warehouse space. Zhang's office expenses—including water and electricity, machines, customs declarations, employees' salaries—are all "paid" by him. If the steel plates have quality problems according to the feedback from the market, Zhang Yongshao is entirely responsible. Passive job performance has turned into a practice that actively drives all the units. Passive management has turned into active procedures.

MANAGING PERFORMANCE

Haier used several performance management and motivational tools. One involved a set of colored footprints on the factory floor. Before 1998, a pair of yellow footprints was used as a kind of warning. Every day, a poor performer would stand on the yellow footprints to "reflect." The worker was expected to share how he could improve performance the next day.

Subsequently, the color was changed to green to represent encouragement. Now, a top performer—either worker or manager—would stand on the footprints and explain why he had done a good job or how he accomplished his job by being innovative and what others might learn from this. According to Zida Yu, vice president in charge of research and development promotion, "Our main purpose is to motivate our people effectively."

Another tool used to motivate workers was a board placed in the factory workshop that recorded workers' performance on a daily basis. Under a system of self-management, employees set clear goals for themselves in a brief meeting with their supervisor at the beginning of their shift. At the end of the day, the employee and supervisor met again to assess how well these goals had been fulfilled. Each employee received a colored face, representing an informal grade for the day: red meant "excellent," green denoted "average," and yellow was "below average or below expectations."

Haier had a formal policy for managing those employees who did not meet set expectations. The lowest-performing 10% of employees were dismissed, based on a three-phase system. In the first review (either annual or quarterly), an employee who ranked in the bottom 10% was "asked to be on leave" and sent for job training at Haier's expense. If he remained in the bottom 10% during the second review, he was sent for more training—again on leave, but at his own expense. Continued performance in the bottom 10% in the third review resulted in the employee's dismissal.

The flip side of this approach was the emphasis on recognizing and rewarding successes and creativity. If an employee developed or improved a product, or suggested an efficient new procedure, the innovation carried the employee's name, and notice of it was prominently displayed.

APPRAISING MANAGERS

Although it was more challenging to evaluate the performance of managers than of workers, Haier had developed a system of review based partly on quantifiable results. For a manager responsible for domestic or overseas business development, indicators such as volume of sales and selling speed, share of local market, and share of global market were used. For a division head, the number of product orders, quality, cost, time for delivery, etc., were used. And for a senior manager, strategic business unit results and profit and loss were used.

Each manager's performance was reviewed weekly. The criteria for weekly evaluation involved both achieving quantifiable goals and the degree of innovation and process improvement, for example. At the end of the month, managers received a performance grade of A, B, or C. The results of this evaluation were announced at a monthly meeting for middle- and upper-level managers on the eighth day of the month.

The results of managers' performance ranking were openly displayed at the entrance to the company cafeteria, with a green or red arrow indicating whether their score had gone up or down that month. Haier had been doing this for over 15 years. Promotions or demotions were also published in the *Haier Ren Bao*.

Haier devoted significant resources to training and development. An important part of the appraisal process also included identifying more than 80 of the mid- to upper-level managers in the Group. They were sent on courses at "Haier University" every Saturday morning. The classes, called Interactive Learning sessions, focused on developing an action plan and implementing improvements in operations. The grades received in these courses accounted for about 40% of each manager's performance evaluation.

Developing talent

When new positions opened up, Haier ensured that a wide pool of candidates competed for the position rather than promoting only from among employees of a certain position or tenure. Job rotation was critical to promote employee development and to avoid territorialism. New recruits tried out two or three different jobs before being finally assigned to a position. Later on, even when an employee performed well in a particular post, he was rotated into a new job. The average length of stay in a management position was three years (the maximum term was six years), ensuring that managers understood many different areas of the company.

At the monthly management evaluation meetings, top performers were identified, and those with the most potential were transferred into the Haier talent pool. The competitive threshold was high and selections for the talent pool were drawn from scratch every quarter, and then evaluated separately for every new position. There was no philosophy of "once you're in, you're in" at Haier. However, unlike the general employee pool, the company did not have a fixed percentage of people in the talent pool that had to be eliminated.

A points system was used to assess whether a manager was achieving the performance standards to remain in the talent pool. Five points were allocated for monthly performance, five for accumulative performance, and five for current project reviews. A score of less than 10 for several months in a row would result in a transfer out of the talent pool.

Dealing with low performance of managers

The pressure to perform and improve was relentless. In 2000, 13 of 58 senior managers in the headquarters in Qingdao were identified and penalized at different levels because they were not performing to ever-increasing Haier standards.

The low-performing managers were classified into three categories. If minor improvements in management performance were necessary, managers were "put on medication," which indicated that they needed to change and received training on those specific issues. More serious underperformers were referred to as "IV users" and demoted. Managers with serious performance issues were "hospitalized," and would be removed from their position.

GOING GLOBAL

By 2002, Haier was the only major Chinese manufacturer to have established manufacturing bases internationally. An interesting question was whether the performance management practices that had earned Haier such success in China were transferable to other cultures as it continued with its aggressive pushes toward international expansion.

Many of Haier's performance management philosophies were considered groundbreaking not only for a Chinese company but also for any firm anywhere. How, then, could Haier's performance management systems be applied in other regions of the world?

CASE 33

Sportsmake: A Crisis of Succession

For almost a year following Jim Claymore's death in the crash of his private plane outside Las Vegas, Sportsmake, the sport equipment company he founded and ran, remained rudderless. Claymore was a legend in the industry. A champion pentathlon athlete, he believed that high quality sports equipment at affordable prices should be made available to what he called the "serious non-athlete": the person who pursued athletic activities intensively but noncompetitively.

Out of this vision emerged a range of products, some proprietary and others licensed, which gained a reputation for performance and durability. The company outsourced all its manufacturing, but kept rigorous controls over its designs and quality. As Claymore was fond of telling his staff: "I am comfortable with letting others take the manufacturing margins. Our advantage is in the loop we create between the serious non-athlete and the retailer. So keep your eye on potential equipment for the serious non-athlete and spend your energies convincing the retailer that the equipment we are developing will be a best seller."

The company grew rapidly from sales of $200,000 in 1974, to $20 million in 1984, to current sales of $120 million. In 1996, the company went public. Claymore used the injection of capital to acquire Sportsmake's first retail operation: Hike and Bike—a chain of stores specializing in the newly emerging area of leisure camping and biking. The success of this acquisition led to other acquisitions, not all of them successful. Perhaps the biggest gamble was the acquisition in 1997 of the giant Winter Sportsworld for $400 million. The acquisition put considerable strain on Sportsmake's resources, and proved to be a harder operation to integrate into Sportsmake's ethos and methods of doing business than originally anticipated.

Claymore was known to be a demanding but generous boss. Alternately tyrannical and charming, he frequently popped into people's offices for an informal chat. His subordinates dreaded these chats, but also admitted that they felt strangely elated and energized by the visits. Joe Murphy, a Marketing Manager in the outdoor sports division, described these chats as ". . . a mixture of third-degree questioning by the police and an encounter with a bible thumping evangelist." "You feared what he will find out, but you also felt enthused by his approval. It was quite an experience . . . ."

Immediately after the funeral, the board turned to Roy Claymore, the founder's son, as a possible successor. He took over as interim CEO and did his best to ensure continuity. However, it quickly became clear that his heart was not in it. He notified the board that he intended to step down by the end of the year to resume his former career as medical researcher at the University of South Carolina. With Roy out of the picture, the board began to consider other candidates to head the company. A number of names were brought forward, but after a brief discussion only two remained: Tony Petroski, Vice President in charge of marketing, and Marcia Davenport, Vice President in charge of finance.

The contrast between the two candidates could hardly be greater. Petroski had spent all his career in Sportsmake; starting as Sales Clerk at the age of 17, and ending as Vice President of corporate marketing 32 years later at the age of 49. Davenport, on the other hand, had only recently arrived at Sportsmake. She began as assistant to Stanley Cramer, Sportsmake's Vice President of finance in 1993, and had upon his retirement four years later been given the top finance job in the company.

Petroski's ethos if not his entire personality had been shaped by his years in the company. He first came to the notice of Jim Claymore when, while taking his annual holidays in the Swiss Alps, he managed to obtain a contract for Sportsmake's new high performance skis from one of Switzerland's most exclusive ski resorts. He was subsequently promoted to head the winter sports division, and within five years of his appointment he doubled the sales of the division from 20 million to 40 million.

Petroski's greatest coup as head of winter sports was masterminding the company's entry into the snowboarding market. Petroski was among the first in the United States to detect the potential of snowboarding as a mass sport. After a trip to a ski resort in Vermont he came back to Denver full of enthusiasm for the new sport. He instructed his development team to drop their work on special composite skis and instead concentrate their efforts on designing a snowboard. His staff was accustomed to Toni's "wild ideas," but this time they thought he had truly gone over the edge. As Jack

---

This case was written by Joseph Lampel, City University Business School, London.

Rorty, Chief Equipment Designer, recollected many years later: "some of us were willing to concede that it was possible to downhill on one ski without breaking your neck, but even these people felt that the demand for such equipment was limited. We were dealing with a fad—a winter sport version of the hula hoop. Making high performance skis was our real business, and any distraction was going to cost us dearly."

Petroski had the last laugh on the skeptics. Sportsmake's "Quickboard" became one of the division's most profitable products. It set new industry standards, and was the preferred equipment in many snowboarding competitions.

The episode cemented Petroski's reputation as a man with an uncanny talent for spotting new products. When Jack Lindsay, who had run corporate marketing since 1967, died suddenly in 1987, he was the natural choice for the job. Jim Claymore delivered the news in person. Shaking Petroski's hand he remarked: "Well Toni, the fun is over. Now all you have to do is learn to stomach the bad coffee at head office with the rest of us."

If Petroski was the quintessential company man, Davenport embodied the spirit of the professional manager. Born in California to an affluent real estate developer father and a pediatrician mother, Davenport earned an undergraduate degree in Economics in Berkeley before joining one of the leading retail banks in the San Francisco area. After five years during which she rose to the position of manager of small business loans, she headed east to pursue MBA studies at the Wharton Business School.

Later she often reflected with some nostalgia on her time at the Wharton school. She stood out as one of the brightest and most energetic students, and in spite of the heavy load, she found time for extracurricular activities. Every afternoon she took two hours off to jog and swim, and on weekends she often went on long hikes with her boyfriend (later her husband), John Mercner.

Mercner was in the midst of his law studies at the University of Pennsylvania Law School when the couple met. They decided to look for a job in the New York area. He accepted a position in one of New York's most prestigious law firms, and she accepted a position in the finance department of one of the largest department stores in the city. Their careers, however, did not prosper equally. He found the pressure stifling, and it was increasingly clear that he was not going to make partner. She, on the other hand, rose rapidly to become an assistant to the Vice President in charge of finance. After five years of enjoying life in New York, they both accepted that the time had come to move on. Although Mercner had a number of offers, the best one came from Smith, Prizker, and Cohen, a Denver law firm specializing in energy and transportation. Davenport had a number of offers—none compared with her New York position. After considering the offers, she settled for a position as assistant to the Vice President in charge of finance in Sportsmake.

Davenport knew that accepting Sportsmake's offer was a gamble. Traditionally, Sportsmake promoted from within. It was well-known that Claymore scrutinized each candidate personally, and that he gave disproportionate weight to such things as a person's competitive spirit and commitment to sports. Rumor even had it that managers had been denied promotion because Claymore thought they were mediocre skiers or handled their tennis racket poorly. In her interview with Claymore, Davenport noticed little emphasis on her athletic activities. They chatted briefly in passing about Davenport's addiction to jogging, but in general the conversation revolved around Davenport's New York experience. Like many people before her, Davenport found the interview exhausting yet exhilarating. Ultimately, Claymore's persuasive powers overcame her hesitations and she accepted the offer.

Davenport did not regret her decision. Almost immediately after being hired she was put in charge of what is arguably the most important financial decision in the history of Sportsmake: the decision to go public. Working closely with Claymore, she planned and executed the public offering of Sportsmake's shares. The share began trading at 7 1/4 and within 7 months it had moved up to 9 1/2. Following this success, Davenport became deeply involved in the company's acquisition strategy. She spent much time investigating acquisition targets. Her reports and presentations were highly praised by Claymore who came to rely on her observations and advice. When Stanley Cramer retired in 1997, no one was surprised when she was promoted as his successor. From her new position, she not only supervised routine financial matters, but also became deeply involved in corporate strategy, in particular the integration of Winter Sportsworld, and much discussed and considerably delayed reorganization of Sportsmake.

If a company can be said to hold its collective breath, then Sportsmake was certainly doing just that on the morning of Friday the 26th of November when the board of directors met to discuss and render their decision. For some the choice was clear. Petroski was the embodiment of Sportsmake, and the natural successor in both spirit and talents to the legendary Claymore. For others, however, Petroski was an embodiment of what Sportsmake was rather than what it should become. The future, these people felt, lay with Sportsmake under Davenport—a diversified sports equipment firm which is in the process of transforming itself into a modern and professionally managed corporation.

CASE 34

Reorganization at Axion Consulting (A)

Matt Walsh turned off his computer and was getting ready to leave for home when Marvin Curtis stuck his head into the office and said, "Say Matt, can I see you for a couple of minutes? It is about next week's board meeting."

Despite being in a hurry to catch the late-evening train, Walsh was loath to refuse Curtis's request. They had recently clashed over a decision to hire additional staff and putting him off, regardless of the excuse, could aggravate an already uneasy relationship.

Walsh therefore put down his briefcase, sat back in his chair, and motioned Curtis to sit in the chair opposite him.

"Sorry to barge in so late in the day," said Curtis, "but I thought it important to find out what you think about Howard Fisk's plans for reorganizing Axion."

Walsh was entirely surprised by Curtis's question. He also had his doubts about the planned reorganization, but he was uncertain whether he could honestly share them with Curtis. "What is the problem?" he asked cautiously, thinking it best to find out where Curtis stood before he revealed his own thoughts on the matter.

Curtis needed no encouragement. He had clearly been mulling over the issues for quite a while, and now it all came tumbling out. "I do not wish to be patronizing," he said,

> but as a newcomer, you may not be entirely familiar with the history of Axion. I am sure you know that we began our existence as a small group of economists specializing in policy analysis for the public sector. This was back at the end of the 1980s when the privatization of public services was the rage. Subcontractors were cheaper, but often they did not deliver quality. What governments wanted, and what we delivered, was an evaluation of these services. We were in an excellent position to advise as to which company should get the bid, which bid should be renewed, and which should be refused.
>
> Eventually, however, governments began to do this for themselves, and do it quite effectively. As the market for our basic products matured, we diversified into the more lucrative but also much more competitive area of management consulting. We started hiring MBAs, many with previous consulting experience: a marked departure from our traditional recruitment in departments of economics. The influx of people with different backgrounds was bound to change things. We always had our disagreements—which group of people does not? But we also had enough in common to resolve these differences and get on with the job. But over time, we found that our disagreements were escalating out of hand. Our arguments were not only about issues, they were about values, and identity as well. The economists dismissed the consultants as snake oil salesmen, and the consultants dismissed the economists as woolly brained ivory tower dwellers. We kept trying to patch things up by setting up a balanced executive committee and rotating the presidency, but nothing worked. In the end, we turned to an outsider for salvation, and to transcend the divisions we chose Howard Fisk, a scientist who had spent much of his career in industry. I have to confess that I was not in favor of this appointment, but my voice did not carry the day.

Matt Walsh knew that Curtis was not entirely candid on this point. His opposition was not based on principle alone; it was driven as much, if not more, by personal ambition. Marvin Curtis had wanted the job of president for himself. He was one of Axion's founding partners and an influential member of the executive board. But he also had the sort of acerbic personality that made enemies. It was no secret that he believed a behind-the-scenes deal to look for an outside candidate had denied him his turn at the presidency.

"I may not have been enthusiastic about Howard," continued Curtis,

> but I agree with his central contention: We have to change if we are to survive. My main concern is with the changes he is proposing. I believe that his idea of splitting Axion into business units, each specializing in different areas, will increase our differences, aggravate competition for resources, and reduce our incentives for cross unit cooperation. Why should the Quality Evaluation business unit help E-Commerce if they know that when all is said and done, resources are divided according to how many clients you bring in? And if there is no cooperation between the different units, where is our innovation going to come from? Specializing is good for focus and this produces quick results in the marketplace, but in the long run we will be suppressing the creative flows which made us so successful in the first place.

This case was prepared by Joseph Lampel, City University Business School, London, with the assistance of Daniel Ronen. Not to be used or reproduced without author's permission.

Walsh had been listening intently, but said little. He shared Curtis's concerns, but his views were tempered by the knowledge that he stood to gain from the reorganization. Matt expected to head one of the business units that Howard Fisk proposed to set up. Or at least, that was what he had thought until recently.

For years, Matt Walsh had been trying to set up a group that specializes in R&D management consulting, but he was frustrated by the lack of support. He believed that Axion was ignoring an important area in the emerging knowledge economy. The plan that Fisk unveiled during the last general meeting proposed the setting up of such a group, and Matt Walsh was of course delighted and grateful that Fisk had endorsed his idea. It was also inevitable that he, in turn, reciprocated by giving Fisk his support and endorsement.

However, in the weeks that followed, things began to change. Fisk indicated that perhaps it was not the right time to create an R&D Management consulting unit. Setting up the other business units was consuming more resources than initially anticipated. Fisk had, however, reiterated his commitment to Walsh's proposed unit, and had suggested that Walsh needed to prepare the grounds for it more carefully, by enlisting the support of others in the organization. Walsh followed his advice faithfully by discreetly lobbying for his project whenever possible. He encountered little overt opposition, but he also formed the impression that without a strong ally on the board, his project would remain in limbo. Now that Marvin Curtis was making a clear pitch for his support, he was beginning to wonder if Curtis was that person.

CASE 35

Reorganization at Axion Consulting (B)

Howard Fisk pushed aside the papers in front of him, and looked around the table. "There is one other item of business I would like to raise before you dig into the delicious sandwiches, Jenny so kindly ordered from the deli across the street. As some of you may know, Robert Leonardi, the Managing Director of Perkins & Evans, has announced his intention to step down at the end of the year. What you probably do not know is that key members of the executive committee of Perkins & Evans have recently approached me with the view towards exploring the possibility of a merger between Axion and Perkins & Evans." He paused for a moment, letting the news sink in, and then continued:

> Of course, this is strictly informal at this point, and will go no further if I do not have your support. However, I do not mind telling you that I am excited by the prospects. I think you would all agree that Perkins & Evans is a young and dynamic management consulting company. Their expertise in turning around financially troubled high-technology firms has attracted much press attention. They are slightly smaller than we are, and their client base is more diverse, but to my mind the potential synergy is there, if we are willing to work towards it.

There was nervous murmur around the table. Most of the committee had been caught off guard, and they were venting their surprise in no uncertain terms. Howard Fisk held up his hand, "I know, I know," he said, "more information is clearly in order. I have prepared a dossier with a complete analysis which you can pick up on the way out. Time, however, is of the essence. I must let Perkins & Evans know if we intend to explore the idea further, or whether it is a non-starter. So let me have your views, and do not be afraid to be honest with me. I can certainly take it."

Matt Walsh looked around the table. The executive committee was made up of six people, excluding Howard Fisk. Of the six, two would almost certainly be against any such move, and two would strongly support it. Marvin Curtis had made no secret of his unhappiness about where Axion was going under Fisk, and would therefore oppose the initiative. Bruno Neri, who Curtis had recruited and trained, was likely to echo his mentor's opinion. On the other side, Salma Porter was likely to support the initiative. She was open in her admiration for Fisk's leadership qualities. Joe Wolberg owed his position on the committee to Howard Fisk. In principle, one would expect him to give Fisk his support, but lately he had showed an independent streak, clashing with Fisk over the new knowledge management initiative.

That left Jeremy Gold and Matt Walsh. As far as Walsh was concerned, Gold was an enigma, a highly respected economist, he had left academia to join the fledgling Axion for reasons that were not entirely clear. He had supported Fisk's appointment, but had not prospered under the new regime. His vote could go either way. The same could be said of Matt Walsh himself. He was torn between supporting and opposing Howard Fisk. He appreciated Fisk's dynamism and talent for spotting opportunities, but at the same time he was becoming increasingly alarmed at Fisk's unpredictability and his tendency to embrace initiatives before they were fully explored. He leaned back in his chair and tried to concentrate. Even if his vote did not carry the day, his decision could affect his position and future prospects at Axion.

This case was prepared by Joseph Lampel, City University Business School, London, with the assistance of Daniel Ronen. Not to be used or reproduced without author's permission.

CASE 36

Yahoo!

More than two years after the board of Yahoo hired Carol A. Bartz as chief executive to apply a little shock therapy to the ailing Web portal, the firm appears to be still suffering from many of the same symptoms. Its revenues and profits remain relatively stagnant, its market share has remained low, and there still continues to be a shortage of innovation. Most analysts feel that her turnaround plan has failed to generate any significant results so far, prompting skepticism that she may not have been well suited for the job. "She's been there long enough that you have to question her ability to have the impact that's needed," said Lou A. Kerner, an analyst with Wedbush Securities.[1]

Bartz has long warned that reviving Yahoo would take some time. Shortly after she took charge in January 2009, Bartz had warned that she would be trying to reverse a slide that has been years in the making, one that analysts say was caused by a slow decision-making process that allowed new competitors to capitalize on the various emerging trends among Internet users. During her two years as the head of Yahoo, Bartz has made substantial changes to the organization, including a shuffling of top executives. She has also tried to refocus the firm on its strengths in content areas such as news, sports, and finance and on other popular services such as e-mail and instant messaging.

Many other forms of services which were no longer considered to be central to the firm's strategy, such as personals, job listings, and real estate, have been outsourced and are now largely handled by third parties. By far, Bartz's biggest move has been handing over its search engine and related advertising to Microsoft, its one-time search nemesis. The agreement allows Yahoo to forgo the cost of maintaining search infrastructure while still collecting most of the revenue from the partnership. The firm can now focus on display advertising—banners and other graphical ads—where it remains the industry leader.

In spite of all of these moves, Yahoo's financial results for the third quarter of 2010 showed only slight gains. Despite having an enormous audience of 630 million unique monthly visitors, and consequently making it the most visited website in the world, users are spending less time on the site. This stands in stark contrast to the traffic that is being generated by Google and Facebook, both of which continue to make big gains. "They're treading water right now," said Jordan Rohan, an analyst with Stifel, Nocolaus & Company.[2]

Bartz has acknowledged that much work needs to be done to restore Yahoo to its former glory, but she maintained that the firm was showing several signs of improvement or at least stability. "First you walk, then you run, then you fly," she said in a conference call with securities analysts.[3] Larry L. Cornett, a former Yahoo search executive, said that he was encouraged by the early stages of Yahoo's turnaround, but that Bartz needed to clearly lay out what the company stands for. "Maybe there's some conversations internally, but from the outside, there isn't a crystal-clear definition of what Yahoo means," he explained.[4]

DEALING WITH A SLUMP

After a period of strong growth in the late 1990s, Yahoo saw a steep fall in revenues and profits as advertisers cut back on their spending after the dot-com bust. Under Tim Koogle, Yahoo had developed as a Web portal that relied heavily on advertising revenues for profits. He had been confident that advertisers would continue to pay in order to reach the younger learning and technologically savvy surfers that would use his portal. As advertising revenues dropped off sharply, leading to a steep decline in the firm's stock price, Koogle was replaced in April 2001 by Terry Semel, an experienced Hollywood media executive who had once controlled Warner Brothers.

Semel realized that he had to entice traditional advertisers back to his site. He made an all-out push to court advertising agencies that Yahoo had pushed away with its arrogance during the years before the bust. He also tried to attract back the business of big advertisers such as General Motors, Procter & Gamble, and Coca-Cola by using technology that allowed the website to move beyond static banner advertising, offering eye-catching animation, videos, and other rich-media formats. As advertisers gradually decided to spend again on online advertising after the slump, Yahoo managed to draw many of them back to its site, leading to a dramatic increase in its advertising revenues.

But Semel did not want Yahoo to rely primarily on advertising for its revenues. He began to push for other

This case was developed by Jamal Shamsie, Michigan State University. The material has been drawn from published sources, to be used for purposes of class discussion.

sources of revenue by making acquisitions that would allow his site to offer more premium services that consumers would be willing to pay for. One of the first of these was the buyout of HotJobs.com in 2002, which moved the firm into the online job-hunting business. Semel followed up with the acquisition of online music service Musicmatch Inc., hoping to bring more subscribers into the Yahoo fold. Over the next few years, the firm continued to add to its growing range of services by acquiring firms such as Flickr, a photo-sharing site, and Del.icio.us, a bookmark-sharing site.

By making such smart deals, Semel was able to build Yahoo into a site that could offer surfers many different services, with several of them requiring the customer to pay a small fee. The idea has been to coax Web surfers to spend hard cash on everything from digital music and online games to job listings and premium e-mail accounts with loads of extra storage. Semel hoped that the contribution from such paid services will continue to rise over the next few years, allowing the firm to rely less heavily on advertising. In his own words: "We planted a lot of seeds . . . and some are beginning to grow."[5]

Semel's biggest moves, however, were tied to his efforts to strengthen Yahoo's position in the search area. Yahoo had been using Google to provide these services, but with Google's growing strengths in this area, Semel decided to work upon further developing its own search engine. In 2002, he purchased Inktomi, a strong contender in search engines with whom Yahoo had also worked in the past. A year later, Yahoo also bought Overture Services, a company that specialized in identifying and ranking the popularity of websites and in helping advertisers find the best sites to advertise on. Finally, Semel spent millions of dollars on further improving upon its search advertising system in order to stem the continual loss of search-related advertising revenues to Google.

CREATING A THEME PARK

With the expansion of services, Semel envisioned building Yahoo into a digital Disneyland, a souped-up theme park for the Internet Age. The idea was that Web surfers logging on to Yahoo's site, like customers squeezing through the turnstiles in Anaheim, should find themselves in a self-contained world full of irresistible offerings. Instead of Yahoo being an impartial tour guide to the Web, it should be able to entice surfers to stay inside its walls as long as possible. In order to make such a concept work, Semel believed that the firm should establish strong links between its various sites that would allow its consumers to move effortlessly from one of them to another.

This vision for Yahoo represented a drastic change from the model that had been developed by its original founders. The firm had let managers push for their own pet projects, resulting in an assortment of offerings that operated relatively independently. No one had thought about developing the portal as a whole, much less how the various bits and pieces could work together. Under these conditions, executives fought hard in order to obtain sufficient support for the particular services that each of them had developed. "Managers would beg, borrow, and steal from the network to help their own properties," said Greg Coleman, Yahoo's executive vice president for media and sales.[6]

Semel had been pushing to stitch it all together. He demanded that Yahoo's myriad of offerings from e-mail accounts to stock quotes to job listings interact with each other. Semel called this concept "network optimization" and regarded this as a key goal for his firm. In order to ensure that the various efforts that were being made by managers were tied to each other more closely, he moved swiftly to replace its freewheeling culture with a more deliberate sense of order.

Semel began to pursue this stronger integration by chopping the 44 business units that he had inherited down to only 5. He also made it clear that every initiative proposed by any of the units was expected not only to make money but to also feed Yahoo's other businesses. Consequently, Semel pushed Yahoo away from its earlier emphasis on long brainstorming sessions and initiatives driven by hunches. Instead, he demanded that managers make formal presentations of their new ideas in weekly meetings of a group called the Product Council, with nine managers from all corners of the company. The responsibility of the group was to make sure all new projects bring benefits to Yahoo's existing businesses.

In spite of Semel's efforts to tightly control the growth of Yahoo into new areas, the push to develop a digital theme park has led some of the analysts to question whether the firm has spread itself too thin. Even some people inside Yahoo began to question its goal of providing a broad range of services that can attract an audience that can be sold to advertisers. In a scathing internal memo written in the fall of 2006, Brad Garlinghouse, a senior Yahoo vice president, compared Yahoo's strategy to indiscriminately spreading peanut butter across the Internet. "We lack a focused, cohesive vision for our company," he stated in the memo. "We want to do everything and be everything—to everyone. We've known this for years, talked about it incessantly, but done nothing to fundamentally address it."[7]

SEARCHING FOR A DIRECTION

Garlinghouse's memo was intended to push Yahoo into establishing a clearer vision for the firm to pursue. He had believed that a stronger focus on specific goals would result in more specific responsibilities for individuals and units and speedier decision making for the firm. He had realized that Yahoo's attempts to offer a wide variety of services had led to a proliferation of new executive hires, which eventually contributed to a growth of conflict between various business units. This had made it difficult to move swiftly to make critical decisions, such as making key partnerships and acquisitions to keep up with the changing competitive landscape. The once high-flying Internet pioneer was losing online advertising revenues to search engines such as Google and social networking sites such as Facebook.

Shareholder dissatisfaction with Yahoo's financial performance finally led to the resignation of Semel in July 2007. The firm turned to Jerry Yang, one of its cofounders who had been serving as Chief Yahoo! to improve earnings and profits. When he took over, Yang promised that he would move quickly to come up with a new sweeping plan for Yahoo after a 100-day review of every aspect of its operations. As part of this plan, Yang announced a three-pronged new direction for Yahoo. He wanted his site to be the premier starting point for consumers on the Web, to be a top choice for marketers seeking to place ads on sites across the Web, and to open its technology infrastructure to third-party programmers and publishers. Yang was clearly aware that these goals will require time and investments, but he was upbeat about his firm's progress. "We are seeing early signs of success as a result of this clear new focus," he announced soon after he took charge.[8]

Although these changes were welcomed, analysts were not sure that Yang could move quickly enough before competitors gained more ground and before investors lost patience. "They have six to nine months to prove their initiatives are working," said Mark Mahaney of Citigroup Smith Barney.[9] These concerns were echoed by Jeffrey Lindsay, an analyst with Sanford C. Bernstein. "I have a lot of respect for Jerry Yang," he commented six months after Yang had taken charge. "But so far his changes have been slow and incremental instead of quick and bold. To move at such a slow pace in the Internet market is risky."[10]

It was clear that the many problems that Yahoo was facing would pose a considerable challenge for Yang. In particular, there have been questions about the firm's decision to invest in its own search engine rather than forging a partnership with Google. Similarly, the firm failed to clinch some crucial deals, including one with Facebook, one of the hottest social-networking websites. Rob Sanderson, an analyst at American Technology Research, warns that the firm is at a critical juncture. "They're relevant, and hold their audience pretty well, but the investor and media perception is that Yahoo is another AOL—a once-great company in decline," he explained.[11]

One of the biggest challenges faced by Yang was the offer made by Microsoft in early 2008 to buy Yahoo for $33 a share or approximately $47.5 billion. Yang refused to sell his company for less than $37 a share although these shares had been trading for around $20. Shareholders were upset because they stood to lose about $20 billion by the rejection of Microsoft's offer. "I don't think anything Yahoo puts out there is going to be comparable with what Microsoft was offering," said Darren Chervitz, comanager of the Jacob Internet Fund, which owns about 150,000 shares of Yahoo.[12]

SCRAMBLING FOR A FOCUS

Less than a year and a half after he had assumed control, Yang decided to give up his role as CEO and revert to being the "chief Yahoo," the strategy position that he had held before. After an extensive search, the board appointed Carol Bartz as the new head of the firm. Bartz had been in charge of Autodesk, a computer-aided software design firm, for 14 years before stepping down recently. She was expected to develop a stronger focus for a firm that was perceived to have been drifting, especially during Yang's turbulent leadership. Analysts were generally positive about her appointment, although many suggested that she lacked online media experience.

Bartz was expected to move quickly to reassure investors who were angry with Yahoo's board for refusing to accept Microsoft's bid for the firm. Shortly after she took over, Bartz moved to overhaul the company's top executive ranks, consolidating several positions and creating others in an attempt to make the Web company more efficient. She combined the firm's technology and product groups into one unit and created a customer advocacy group to better incorporate customer feedback. The changes were intended to speed up decision making within the company by making it "a lot faster on its feet," as Bartz wrote in a Yahoo public blog. But Ross Sandler, an analyst with RBC Capital Markets, said the restructuring was more promising because it clarified responsibilities. "There has been confusion at the top for so long," he said. "This should solve that problem."[13]

By July, Bartz had reached an agreement to hand over its search operations to Microsoft, which had invested heavily in relaunching its search engine and renamed it Bing. The terms of the 10-year agreement gave Microsoft access to search technologies that Yahoo had helped to pioneer and develop. Yahoo will transfer many of its talented engineers to Microsoft and lay off 400 employees that ran the search operations. In return, Yahoo will receive 88 percent of the search-related ad revenue for the first five years of the deal, much higher than is standard in the industry.

Reactions to the deal have been mixed. Some Yahoo shareholders have expressed concerns that the company will lose its valuable search experience, which would be difficult to recover from. "It feels kind of like a stab in the chest," said Darren Chervitz, the comanager of the Jacob Internet Fund, which owns about 100,000 shares of Yahoo. "It certainly feels like Yahoo is giving away their strong and hard fought share of the search market for really a modest price. My sense is that Yahoo will regret making this move."[14]

But Bartz insists that the firm could no longer continue to match the level of investment Google and Microsoft have been making in searching, one of the Web's most lucrative and technically complex businesses. "This deal allows Yahoo to invest in what we should be investing in for the future—audience properties, display advertising and the mobile Internet experience," Bartz said in an interview soon after the deal had been finalized. "Our vision is to be at the center of people's lives online."[15]

WAITING FOR A TURNAROUND?

Even though progress has been slow, Bartz has managed to refocus Yahoo on areas such as news, sports, and finance where it has considerable strengths. While she has moved the firm away from other activities she considered to be peripheral, Bartz has invested heavily in content over the last year, hiring dozens of editorial employees and buying Associated Content, a freelance news site, to enhance local news coverage. She also claims to have made progress with revamping the technology behind the Web portal that should make it possible to introduce new services much more quickly in the future. At the same time, Bartz has managed to achieve an improvement in Yahoo's profit margins due to her aggressive moves to cut costs wherever possible.

In spite of these achievements, some investors are losing patience and have begun to demand that Yahoo's board replace Bartz although her contract does not run out until 2012. Besides the slow growth in revenues and profits, they point to the continual turnover among executives at the firm. Three top managers have stepped down over the past couple of months, creating a perception of continuing turmoil and uncertainty. Even with this turnover, Blake Irving, recently hired as the firm's product chief, claimed that employees are not feeling demoralized or rudderless. "What ends up getting picked up on more are the departures than the new people coming in," he said.[16]

The news that some private equity firms are considering a bid to buy Yahoo has created more pressures for Bartz. These efforts are very preliminary, however, as the equity firms are speaking with AOL and the News Corporation about teaming up on a deal. Salim Ismail, a former Yahoo executive who is now executive director of Singularity University, said that Yahoo should convert from a publicly traded company to a private one to escape the pressure of quarterly earnings reports. According to Ismail, this will free up the firm to take the steps needed to abolish the complex organizational structure which is slowing decision making and reducing innovation. "They're putting on a Band-Aid when what they really need is major surgery."[17]

Though concerns continue to surface about the future of Yahoo, many people still think that the firm just needs some time to find a new direction. Peter Thiel, a prominent Silicon Valley investor, maintains that Yahoo should not make any drastic moves. In particular, he believes that more big acquisitions would be misguided especially if they prevent the firm from gradually focusing upon what it does best. Paul Gunning, chief of a digital advertising agency, also claimed that despite some problems that needed to be resolved, Yahoo has remained a great place for marketers to reach consumers. "We're bullish on them," he said.[18]

EXHIBIT 1
INCOME STATEMENT (IN MILLIONS OF DOLLARS)

	YEAR ENDING		
	Dec. 31, 2010	Dec. 31, 2009	Dec. 31, 2008
Total revenue	6,325	6,460	7,209
Gross profit	3,697	3,589	4,185
Operating income	773	387	13
EBIT	1,070	574	96
Net income	1,232	598	424

Source: Yahoo!

EXHIBIT 2
BALANCE SHEET (IN MILLIONS OF DOLLARS)

	YEAR ENDING		
	Dec. 31, 2010	Dec. 31, 2009	Dec. 31, 2008
Current assets	4,346	4,595	4,745
Total assets	14,928	14,936	13,690
Current liabilities	1,626	1,718	1,705
Total liabilities	2,370	2,443	2,439
Stockholder equity	12,558	12,493	11,251

Source: Yahoo!

EXHIBIT 3 SIGNIFICANT MILESTONES

1994	David Filo and Jerry Yang start the company as "Jerry's guide to the World Wide Web," later renaming it Yahoo!
1996	Yahoo goes public, raising $338 million. Filo and Yang ask Tim Koogle, an experienced ex-Motorola executive with an engineering background, to be the new CEO.
1999	Yahoo begins to make major acquisitions, including GeoCities, the third most visited website at the time.
2001	Koogle departs because of sharp drop in firm's stock price as a result of declining advertising revenue. Yang asks Terry Semel to take over the firm.
2001	Yahoo acquires more firms such as HotJobs, a leading Internet job-hunting and placement company.
2002	Yahoo buys Inktomi, a search engine leader.
2003	Yahoo buys Overture Services, a company that specializes in Web search advertising.
2005	Yahoo acquires Flickr, a photo-sharing site and announces that it will link several sites together to create a social-networking group.
2007	Semel is pushed out because of decline in performance. Yang takes over as CEO of the firm.
2009	Yang steps down and Carol Bartz is appointed as the new CEO. Bartz concludes a major deal with Microsoft to cede control of its search business.

Source: Yahoo!

EXHIBIT 4
US VISITORS

Monthly estimates, January–July 2010

Google: 149 million
Yahoo: 136 million
Facebook: 126 million
Microsoft: 58 million

Share of US searches

Monthly estimates, January–July 2010

Google: 64%
Yahoo: 19%
Microsoft: 12%

CASE NOTES

CASE 2
Napoleon Bonaparte: Victim of an Interior Strategy?

1. Marshals Grouchy and Ney commanded, respectively, the right and left wings of the French Army in the battle of Waterloo, which also saw Marshal Soult act for the first time as the Emperor's Chief-of-Staff. Soult had succeeded Berthier, who had been his longtime and favorite chief-of-staff, ever since the first campaign in Italy. He died in 1815, upon hearing of his Emperor's return from exile on the Island of Elba. Masséna, Murat, Desaix, Berthier, Lannes, Bessières, and Duroc were some among Napoleon's superb field marshals and generals who either had died earlier or did not take part in the events at Waterloo.
   Correspondence, Vol. 1, No.91, p. 107. David G. Chandler. *The Campaigns of Napoleon: The Mind and Method of History's Greatest Soldier.* Macmillan, 1973.
2. *Correspondence*, Vol. 1, No. 91, p. 107. David G. Chandler. *The Campaigns of Napoleon: The Mind and Method of History's Greatest Soldier.*
3. David G. Chandler. *The Campaigns of Napoleon: The Mind and Method of History's Greatest Soldier*. Macmillan, 1973, p. 53.
4. Alan Schom. *Napoleon Bonaparte.* Harperperennial Press, 1998, p. 47.
5. Melas was the Austrian commander. Desaix was possibly Napoleon's finest commander.
6. Alistair Horne. *How Far from Austerlitz–Napoleon 1805–1815.* St. Martin's Press, 1997, p. 146.
7. Jomini was a famous Austrian war historian who also fought against Napoleon.
8. The "Treaty of Tilsit" was signed twice, once with the Russians to maintain an alliance between France and Russia, and the second treaty two days later with Prussia, which lost a substantial part of land. A large portion of Germany thus came under French control.
9. Alistair Horne. *How Far from Austerlitz–Napoleon 1805–1815.* St. Martin's Press, 1997, p. 233.
10. Eighteen Marshals of the Empire (*Maréchal d'Empire*) were named by Napoleon in 1804, the day following his nomination as Emperor of the French (*Empereur des Français*). He later introduced other imperial titles, such as Duke and Prince, to further recognize exceptional service in battle.
11. Alan Schom. *Napoleon Bonaparte.* Harperperennial Press, 1998, p. 602.
12. Ibid, p. 603.
13. Fontainebleau became the Imperial Court and an important center for Napoleon.
14. Alan Schom. *Napoleon Bonaparte.* Harperperennial Press, 1998, p. 713.
15. Ulm, Austerlitz, Jena, Eylau, and Friedland were famous victories of Napoleon.
16. Alan Schom. *Napoleon Bonaparte.* Harperperennial Press, 1998, p. 710.
17. Louis XVIII escaped France and sought exile in Belgium.
18. David G. Chandler. *The Campaigns of Napoleon: The Mind and Method of History's Greatest Soldier*. Macmillan, 1973, p. 1041.
19. Ibid, p. 1084.

CASE 3
Heineken

1. Jack Ewing & Gerry Khermouch. Waking Up Heineken. *Business Week*, September 8, 2003, p. 68.
2. Richard Tomlinson. The New King of Beers. *Fortune*, October 18, 2004, p. 238.
3. Ian Bickerton & Jenny Wiggins. Change is Brewing at Heineken. *Financial Times*, May 9, 2006, p. 12.
4. *Business Week*, September 8, 2003, p. 69.
5. Andrew Kaplan. Border Crossings. *Beverage World*, July 15, 2004, p. 6.
6. Christopher C. Williams. Heineken Seeing Green. *Barron's*, September 18, 2006, p. 19.
7. *Financial Times*, May 9, 2006, p. 12.
8. *Financial Times*, May 9, 2006, p. 12.

CASE 4
McDonald's

1. Julie Jargon & Paul Ziobro. McDonald's Cup Runs Over. *Wall Street Journal*, August 10, 2010, p. B8.
2. Janet Adamy. McDonald's to Expand, Posting Strong Results. *Wall Street Journal*, January 27, 2009, p. B1.
3. Neil Buckley. McDonald's Shares Survive Resignation. November 24, 2004, p. 18.
4. *Wall Street Journal*, January 27, 2009, p. B1.
5. Pallavi Gogoi & Michael Arndt. Hamburger Hell. *Business Week*, March 3, 2003, p. 106.
6. *Business Week*, March 3, 2003, p. 105.
7. Melanie Warner. You Want any Fruit with that Big Mac? *New York Times*, February 20, 2005, p. 8.
8. Janet Adamy. McDonald's Coffee Strategy is Tough Sell. *Wall Street Journal*, October 27, 2008, p. B3.
9. Ben Paynter. Super Style Me. *Fast Company*, October 2010, p. 107.
10. Jeremy Grant. McDonald's to Revamp UK Outlets. *Financial Times*, February 2, 2006, p. 14.
11. Bruce Horovitz. McDonald's Ventures Beyond Burgers to Duds, Toys. *USA Today*, November 14, 2003, p. 6B.
12. Big Mac's Makeover. *Economist*, October 16, 2004, p. 65.
13. *Economist*, October 16, 2004, p. 64.
14. *Business Week*, March 3, 2003, p. 108.

CASE 5
Procter & Gamble

1. Ellen Byron. P&G Stays Firm on Sales Outlook. *Wall Street Journal*, December 17, 2010, p. B4.
2. Jennifer Reingold. Can P&G Make Money in Places Where People Earn $2 a Day? *Fortune*, January 27, 2011, p. 89.
3. Mina Kimes. A Tough Job For P&G's New CEO. CNNMoney.com, June 10, 2009.
4. Mina Kimes. P&G's Leadership Machine. *Fortune*, April 13, 2009, p. 22.
5. Anonymous. Purpose-Inspired Growth Strategy is Working, P&G CEO Tells Shareholders. *PR Newswire*, October 12, 2010.
6. Jack Neff. P&G Plots Growth Path Through Services. *Advertising Age*, March 22, 2010, p. 2.

7. Andrew Martin. Smelling an Opportunity. *New York Times*, December 9, 2010, p. B1.
8. Kevin McKeough. Procter's Gamble. *Crain's Chicago Business*, November 8, 2010, p.2.
9. *Fortune*, January 17, 2011, p. 89.
10. Ellen Byron. P&G's Push into Perfume Tests a Stodgy Marketer. *Wall Street Journal*, November 12, 2007, p. A15.
11. *Crain's Chicago Business*, November 8, 2010, p. 2.
12. CNNMoney.com, June 10, 2009.

CASE 6
QVC

1. Anonymous. QVC Continues to be Recognized for Exceptional Customer Service. *PR Newswire*, January 12, 2011.
2. Mary Jo Feldstein. Investors, Entrepreneurs Vie for QVC Appearance. *Knight Ridder Tribune Business News*, February 11, 2005, p. 1.
3. Stephanie Clifford. Can QVC Translate its Pitch Online? *New York Times*, November 21, 2010, p. B7.
4. *QVC Annual Report*, 1987–1988.
5. *New York Times*, November 21, 2010, p. B7.
6. *New York Times*, November 21, 2010, p. B7.
7. Eugene Gilligan. The Show Must Go On. *Journal of Commerce*, April 12, 2004, p. 1.
8. *USA Today*, May 5, 2008, p. 2B.
9. *USA Today*, May 5, 2008, p. 2B.
10. *New York Times*, November 21, 2010, p. B7.
11. *New York Times*, November 21, 2010, p. B7.

CASE 7
Barbie vs. Bratz

1. Belem Ramos. Barbie Doll Revolutionized Toy Industry. www.epcc.edu.
2. Patricia O'Connell. To Ruth Handler, a 21-Barbie Salute. www.businessweek.com, April 30, 2002.
3. Dan Jansen. www.economist.com, December 19, 2002.
4. Life in Plastic. www.economist.com, December 19, 2002.
5. Ibid.
6. New Toys on the Block. www.smh.com, April 12, 2002.
7. Fern Shen. Barbie, Bratz and Age Compression. *Washington Post*, February 17, 2002.
8. The slogan of the Bratz girls.
9. NPD Funworld is the premier source of market information for the toys, PC games, and video games industry.
10. The Toy Industry Association introduced the annual toy of the year awards in 2000, to honor the best toys developed by the international toy industry for consumers in the United States.
11. Bratz or Barbie? *New Straits Times*, February 3, 2004.
12. Hip, Urban 'My Scene Dolls for Tweens. *New Straits Times* (Malaysia), June 21, 2003.
13. Lisa Bannon. Those Troblin' Tweens. *The Wall Street Journal*, November 29, 2002.
14. Elsie Christenson. Flavas of the Week. www.newsweek.com, August 4, 2003.
15. Tim Conolly. Doll Wars: Mattel's Flavas Take on Bratz in a Battle for Tween Girl's Dollars. www.toydirectory.com August 2003.
16. A US based consulting firm for toys and entertainment products sampled over 500 girls in the age group of 6–14 years and asked them about the preference between Barbie and Bratz.
17. Rosette Gonzales. Fashion Dolls Compete in Popularity Contest. February 2004.
18. Abigail Goldman. Maker of Bratz Plans New Dolls to Challenge Barbie. http://biz.thestar.com, December 7, 2003.
19. Andria Cheng. World Barbie Means Business. www.theage.com, April 21, 2004.
20. Is Barbie Past Her Shelflife?, www.news.bbc.co.uk, April 21, 2004.
21. Parija Bhatnagar. Can Mattel Save Barbie?, www.cnn.com, October 18, 2004.
22. American Idol is a famous television reality show.
23. Dorothy Pomerantz. The Barbie Bust. *Forbes*, March 28, 2005.
24. Barbie Breaks Mattel's Heart; Toymaker Profit Falls 28%. www.usatoday.com, April 15, 2005.
25. www.benettongroup.com.
26. op.cit. Can Mattel Save Barbie?.

CASE 8
The European Airline Industry: Lufthansa in 2003

1. *UBS Warburg Report*. Lufthansa. January 23, 2003.
2. Rivals Are Buzzing All Around Lufthansa. *Business Week*, March 3, 1997.
3. Rivals Are Buzzing All Around Lufthansa. *Business Week*, March 3, 1997.
4. Airline Competition in Germany. *The Economist*, February 15, 1997.
5. Ibid.
6. Rivals Are Buzzing All Around Lufthansa. *Business Week*, March 3, 1997.
7. German Success Better than Anticipated: Ryanair. *Air Transport Intelligence News*, June 10, 2002.
8. Virgin Abandons German Plans. *Financial Times (London)*, September 19, 2002.
9. World Tourism Organisation, *Tourism Highlights*, 2002.
10. Ibid.
11. Euromonitor GMI Database, German Market for Travel and Tourism, November 2002.
12. Urs Bingelli et al. Hyped Hopes for Europe's Low-Cost Airlines. *McKinsey Quarterly*, Vol. 4, 2002.
13. Ibid.
14. Scots Drop Sky-High BA for Budget Flights. *Scottish Daily Record*, May 24, 2001.
15. Urs Bingelli et al. Hyped Hopes for Europe's Low-Cost Airlines. *McKinsey Quarterly*, vol. 4, 2002.
16. Dogfight over Europe: Ryanair (C). HBS Case, 2000.
17. Alitalia Mulls Low-Cost Options with Volare Tie-Up. *Airline Business*, March 1, 2003.
18. *British Airways Annual Report*, 2001–02.
19. Interview: Jorgen Lindegaard. *Airline Business*, October 1, 2002.
20. Exit Curtain, Brandy And Papers. *Financial Times (London)*, March 26, 2002.
21. Budget Options: the Entry of SAS into the Low-Cost Sector. *Airline Business*, February 1, 2003.

CASE 9
Cadbury Schweppes

1. Letter to Cadbury Board, Trian Corporation, December 18, 2007.
2. Bonham to take Cadbury chair, Alison Smith, *Financial Times*, March 14, 2000, Tuesday London Edition 2, p. 26.
3. Preliminary 2006 Cadbury Schweppes Earnings Presentation, FD (Fair Disclosure) Wire, February 20, 2007 Tuesday.
4. Jeff Cioletti. The Big Break Up. *Beverage World*, Vol. 126, Issue 4, April 15, 2007.

CASE 10
Airbus vs. Boeing

1. Airbus A320 Family Passes the 5,000th Order Mark, Airbus press release, January 25, 2007.
2. Karen West, Boeing Pares 747 Options down to Three, *Seattle Post-Intelligencer*, November 27, 1991, p. B5.

3. Ibid.
4. Boeing Outlines the "Value" of its 747 Plans, M2 Presswire, September 3, 1996.
5. Boeing Lambasts Airbus Project for Superjumbo, *The Guardian*, September 3, 1996.
6. Jay Branegan, Here Come the Sky Giants Airbus, Boeing and the Looming Battle to Build the Next Flying Behemoth, *Time International*, September 16, 1996, Vol. 148, Issue 12.
7. Ibid.
8. Ibid.

CASE 11
The Casino Industry

1. Cy Ryan. Las Vegas Strip Casinos Post $2.5 Billion Loss Last Fiscal Year. *Tribune Business News*, January 31, 2011.
2. Michael McCarthy. Vegas Goes Back to Naughty Roots; Ads Trumpet Return to Adult Playground. *USA Today*, April 11, 2005, p. B6.
3. *USA Today*, April 11, 2005, p. B6.
4. Gene Sloan. Atlantic City Bets on Glitz: Down-at-the-Heels Resort Rolls the Dice, Wagering a Cool $2 Billion That it Will One Day Rival Las Vegas. *USA Today*, August 29, 2003, p. D1.
5. Christopher Palmeri. Little Guys with Big Plans for Vegas. *Business Week*, August 2, 2004, p. 49.
6. Chris Woodyard & Matt Krantz. Latest Vegas Marriage: Harrah's, Caesars Tie Knot; $5 Billion Deal Marks Strategy to Reach More Gamblers. *USA Today*, July 16, 2004, p. B1.
7. Lorraine Woellert. Can Online Betting Change its Luck? *Business Week*, December 20, 2004, p. 67.
8. Steve Friess. Las Vegas Sags as Conventions Cancel. *New York Times*, February 15, 2009, p. 20.

CASE 12
Managing European Wealth

1. Philip Haddon. Wave of M&A to Reshape Asset Management Industry in 2009. www.citywire.co.uk, January 13, 2009.

CASE 13
A Note on the US Wine Industry 2007

1. US Wine Market Forecast to 2012. marketresearch.com
2. winpros.org.
3. IBIS Report.
4. Bonded wineries are licensed by the US Tax and Trade Bureau for the purpose of collecting taxes on all wine produced and sold in the United States.
5. The Judgment of Paris: Why the French didn't Learn from the Legendary Wine-tasting, Mike Steinberger. www.slate.com, Wednesday, May 24, 2006 (http://www.slate.com/id/2142365/)
6. www.wineinstitute.org. Data based upon bonded winerie. The number includes contract wineries, alternating proprietors and other bonded facilities designed for the collection of taxes.
7. www.wineinstitute.org.
8. IBIS Report.
9. Ibid.
10. Distilled Liquor Council.
11. John Sullivan, industry executive.
12. IBIS Report: Wine & Spirits Wholesaling in the US.
13. Ibid, p. 8.
14. Since Gallo is a privately held company, this is an estimate.
15. John Sullivan, industry executive.
16. To get a more "oaky" taste, oak chips or oak wood dust is often added to wine stored in stainless steel tanks.
17. ttb.gov

CASE 15
The Making of the iPod

1. Gary Hamel & Bill Breen. *The Future of Management*. Harvard Business School Press, Cambridge, MA, 2007, pp. 59–60.
2. Charles Fine. *Clockspeed*. Perseus, New York, 1999.
3. John Alderman. *Sonic Boom*. Perseus, Cambridge, MA, 2001.
4. Ibid, p. 57.
5. Steve Knopper. *Appetite for Self-Destruction*. Free Press, New York, 2009, p. 166.
6. Ibid.
7. Steven Levy. *The Perfect Thing*. Simon & Schuster, New York, 2006, pp. 45–46.
8. Levy. *The Perfect Thing*.
9. Ibid, p. 47.
10. Leander Kahney. *Inside Steve's Brain*. Portfolio, New York, 2008. pp. 225–226.
11. Kahney. *Inside Steve's Brain*.
12. Levy. *The Perfect Thing*. p. 51.
13. www.panic.com/extras/audionstory/popup-sjstory.html.
14. Levy. *The Perfect Thing*, p. 51.
15. Ibid.
16. Ibid, p. 52.
17. Ibid, p. 53.
18. Kahney. *Inside Steve's Brain*. p. 226.
19. Ibid, p. 228.
20. Ibid, p. 229.
21. Steve Wozniak. Foreword. In Andy Hertzfeld, *Revolution in the Valley*. O'Reilly, Sebastopol, CA, 2004.
22. Kahney. *Inside Steve's Brain*. p. 23.
23. John Markoff. *What the Doormouse Said*. Viking, New York, 2005, p. xix.
24. Kahney. *Inside Steve's Brain*. p. 29.
25. Ibid, p. 42.
26. Ibid, p. 35.
27. John Marhoff. Apple and PCs, Both Given Up for Dead, Are Rising Anew. *The New York Times*, April 26, 1999.
28. http://en.wikipedia.org/wiki/Jon_Rubinstein#cite_note-4.
29. Kahney. *Inside Steve's Brain*, p. 34.
30. Ibid, p. 96.
31. Levy. *The Perfect Thing*, p. 54.
32. Leander Kahney. *Straight Dope on the iPod's Birth*. Wired.com, October 17, 2006.
33. Kahney. *Inside Steve's Brain*. p. 258.
34. http://www.designnews.com/article/1720 2007_Engineer_of_the_Year_Finalist_Michael_Dhuey_s_Hardware_Knowledge_Helps_Breathe_Life_Into_iPod_TelePresence.php.
35. Kahney. *Inside Steve's Brain*. pp. 94–95.
36. Levy. *The Perfect Thing*, p. 45.
37. Knopper. *Appetite for Self-Destruction*. p. 168.
38. Robert I Sutton. *The No Asshole Rule*. Warner Business Books, New York, pp. 155–156.
39. Lev Grossman. How Apple Does It. *Time*, Oct. 16, 2005.
40. Making It Look Easy – The Birth of the iPod. Posted on Oct 27, 2005 at 11:36 am in The Book– Jobs Ive Known. Source: http:// writers blocklive.com/making-it-looks-easy-the-original-ipod-2005-10.
41. Making It Look Easy.
42. Ibid.
43. Ibid.
44. Grossman. *How Apple Does It*.
45. Ibid.
46. Levy. *The Perfect Thing*, p. 53.
47. Ibid, p. 52.
48. Mark Coleman. *Playback*. Da Capo Press, New York, 2003, p. 200.
49. Levy. The Perfect Thing, p. 49.

50. Steve Knopper. *Appetite for Self-Destruction*, p. 170.
51. Ibid, pp. 170–175.
52. Ibid, pp. 177–178.
53. Ibid, p. 179.
54. Greg Kot. *Ripped*. Scribner, New York, 2009, pp. 201–202.
55. Ibid, p. 204.
56. Ibid, p. 205.
57. Ibid, p. 207.

CASE 16
Arnold Schwarzenegger

1. Arnold Schwarzenegger Attends Home Museum Inauguration. BBC News Website, October 7, 2011.
2. Advice from Mr Schwarzenegger. Destroy Your Enemy, and Move on Without Any Kind of Hesitation at All. *The Guardian*, July 25, 1997.
3. Arnold does the laughing "If I wasn't happy I'd be an idiot" says Mr. Muscle, Jack Mathews Special to *The Toronto Star*, September 1989, SU2, D5.
4. (Body) Building an Empire. *New York Times*, November 28, 1981.
5. Arnie's Famed Torso Getting the Heave-Ho, John Elder. *Sun Herald*, September 13, 1987.
6. Peter McGough. Anatomy of an American Icon. *Muscle & Fitness*, July 1, 1997, Vol. 58, No. 7.
7. Advice from Mr Schwarzenegger. Destroy your Enemy, and Move on Without Any Kind of Hesitation at All. July 25, 1997 *The Guardian* 6.
8. John Elder. Arnie's Famed Torso Getting the Heave-Ho. *Sun Herald*, September 13, 1987.
9. Gillian Flaccus. Schwarzenegger Coasts to Second Term on Promise to Rebuild California: "I Love doing Sequels". Associated Press, November 7, 2006.
10. The Governor Leaves Office with a Budget in Desperate Shape, but He Set a New Political Course for California, *Los Angeles Times*, December 27, 2010.

CASE 18
Whisky Exchange

1. Dalmore 64 Trinitas Sells for £100,000. *Scotch Malt Whisky*, October 14, 2010.
2. Rare Whisky Fetches £100,000: New Record for Industry set by Sale of Two Bottles of 64-year-old Whyte & Mackay Single Malt for £100,000 each, Zoe Wood. *The Guardian*, Thursday October 14, 2010.

CASE 20
Johnson & Johnson

1. Shirley S. Wang & Rhonda L. Rundle. J&J to Acquire Breast-Implant Maker. *Wall Street Journal*, December 2, 2008, p. B1.
2. Amy Barrett. Staying on top. *Business Week*, May 5, 2003, p. 61.
3. Christopher Bowe. J&J Reveals its Guidant Motive. *Financial Times*, January 25, 2006, p. 17.
4. Peter Loftus & Shirley S. Wang. J&J Sales Show Health Care Feels the Pinch. *Wall Street Journal*, January 21, 2009, p. B1.
5. Avery Johnson. J&J's Consumer Play Paces Growth. *Wall Street Journal*, January 24, 2007, p. A3.
6. Holly Hubbard Preston. Drug Giant Provides a Model of Consistency. *Herald Tribune*, March 12–13, 2005, p. 12.
7. *Business Week*, May 5, 2003, p. 62.
8. Avery Johnson. J&J Realigns Managers, Revamps Units. *Wall Street Journal*, November 16, 2007, p. A10.
9. *Business Week*, May 5, 2003, p. 62.
10. Natasha Singer & Reed Abelson. Can Johnson & Johnson Get its Act Together? *New York Times*, January 16, 2011, p. B4.
11. *New York Times*, January 16, 2011, p. B4.
12. Natasha Singer & Reed Abelson. After Recall of Drugs, a Congressional Spotlight on J.&J.'s Chief. *New York Times*, September 29, 2010, p. B4.
13. Johanna Bennett. J&J: A Balm for Your Portfolio. *Barron's*, October 27, 2008, p. 39.
14. Natasha Singer. Hip Implants are Recalled by J&J Unit. *New York Times*, August 27, 2010, p. B1.

CASE 21
Netflix

1. Jeffrey O' Brien. The Netflix Effect. *Wired News*, December 2002.
2. Alyssa Abkowitz. How Netflix got Started. *Fortune*, January 28, 2009.
3. Press Release, The Netflix Opens New Shipping Centre, Louisville Facility Brings Faster Delivery to Three States. www.netflix.com, May 11, 2004.
4. Jane Black. Reed Hastings, Movies by Mail. *Business Week*, October 1, 2002.
5. Competition Mounts Online: Netflix Welcomes Cyber-rivals. *Video Business*, June 21, 2004.
6. Press Release, Netflix Announced Q4 Results. January 24, 2005.
7. Reed Hastings. www.forbes.com, September 20, 2004.
8. Hollywood Video: 10-K Annual Filing. March 15, 2004.
9. Imran Khan. Netflix Inc- To Rent or Buy that is the Question. *North America Equity Research*, August 13, 2004.
10. David Ranii. Video Stores Look to Reinvent Themselves as Online Rentals, Cable TV Rise. *Knight Ridder Tribune Business News*, September 15, 2004.
11. Freedonia Focus on Household Audio and Video Equipment, May 2004.
12. Tim Mullaney. Reed Hastings' Script for Netflix. *Business Week*, August 2, 2004.
13. Imran Khan. Netflix Inc- To Rent or Buy that is the Question. *North America Equity Research*, August 13, 2004.
14. Holly Wagner. Study: Buyers Big Renters, Too. *Video Store Magazine*, August 29–September 4, 2004.
15. Showdown Begins in Movie-Rental Business; Blockbuster Tries a Remake. *New York Times*, July 26, 2004.
16. Netflix 2003 Annual Report.
17. Ibid.
18. Gary Rivlin. How Long will Netflix Stay in the Picture? *International Herald Tribune*, February 23, 2005.
19. Nicholas Thompson. Netflix Uses Speed to Fend Off Wal-Mart Challenge. *New York Times*, September 29, 2003.
20. Ibid.
21. Reed Hastings et al. United States Patent, June 24, 2003.
22. FORM 10-K for the fiscal year ended December 21, 2004, p. 7. However in 2006 Netflix changed its mind and did file a patent violation lawsuit against Blockbuster.
23. Tim Mullaney and Tom Lowry. Netflix: Moving into Slo-Mo? *Business Week*, August 2, 2004.
24. Press Release, Blockbuster Launches New Online DVD Rental Service. www.blockbuster.com, August 11, 2003.
25. Melinda Saccone. Big Retailers Gobbling up More of the Market. *Video Store Magazine*, October 5–11, 2003.
26. Gary Rivlin. How Long will Netflix Stay in the Picture? *International Herald Tribune*, February 23, 2005.
27. Blockbuster Gets Promo Partners: AOL, MSN Join Online Launch. *Video Business*, August 16, 2004.
28. Discussion thread, Online DVD Rental Service from Blockbuster. www.afterdawn.com, August 2004.
29. Ibid.
30. Competition Mounts Online: Netflix Welcomes Cyber-rivals. Video Business, June 21, 2004.

31. Discussion thread, Walmart, Netflix, or Blockbuster DVD Rental? www.i4u.com, June 11, 2003.
32. Paula L. Stepankowsky. Netflix Executives Pledge to Retain Market Leadership. *Dow Jones Newswires*, January 2005.
33. Who Wins if Amazon Offers Online DVD Rentals? *Internet Retailer*, January 2005.
34. Slowdown Begins in Movie-Rental Business; Blockbuster Tries a Remake. *New York Times*, July 26, 2004.
35. Competition Mounts Online: Netflix Welcomes Cyber-rivals. *Video Business*, June 21, 2004.
36. Freedonia Focus on Household Audio and Video Equipment. May 2004.
37. Discussion thread, Walmart, Netflix, or Blockbuster DVD Rental? www.i4u.com, June 11, 2003.
38. Brad Stone. I Want a Mobile! Now! *Newsweek*, September 13, 2004.

CASE 22
Nintendo

1. R. Asakura. *Revolutionaries at Sony: The Making of the Sony PlayStation and the Visionaries Who Conquered the World of Video Games*. McGraw-Hill, New York, 2000, p. 29.
2. O. Inoue. *Nintendo Magic: Winning the Videogame Wars*. Vertical, Inc., New York, 2010, p. 84.
3. Ibid., p. 82.

CASE 25
Pixar

1. Peter Burrows & Ronald Grover. Steve Jobs: Movie Mogul. *Business Week*, November 23, 1998, p. 150.
2. *Business Week*, November 23, 1998, p. 150.
3. *Business Week*, November 23, 1998, p. 146.
4. *Business Week*, November 23, 1998, p. 146.
5. Marc Graser. Pixar Run by Focused Group. *Variety*, December 20, 1999, p. 74.
6. *Variety*, December 20, 1999, p. 74.
7. *Business Week*, November 23, 1998, p. 146.
8. Andrew Bary. Coy Story. *Barron's*, October 13, 2003, p. 21.
9. Pui-Wing Tam. Will Quantity Hurt Pixar's Quality? *Wall Street Journal*, February 15, 2001, p. B4.
10. Peter Burrows & Ronald Grover. Steve Jobs' Magic Kingdom. *Business Week*, February 6, 2006, p. 66.
11. Brooks Barnes. For Disney and Pixar, a Smooth (so far) Ride. *International Herald Tribune*, June 2, 2008, p. 9.
12. *New York Times*, January 25, 2006, p. C6.
13. Charles Solomon. Pixar Creative Chief to Seek to Restore the Disney Magic. *New York Times*, January 25, 2006.
14. Andrew Bary. Coy Story. *Barron's*, October 13, 2003, p. 21.

CASE 26
Natura

1. Natura was chosen best company of the year by *Exame*, Brazil's major business magazine. It has also been the number one company in the hygiene and cosmetics sector for the last three years, 1997, 1998, and 1999. Exame Maiores e Melhores 98 (Exame Largest and Best 98).
2. Growth rate determined based on US$ figures, which account for devaluation (equivalent to inflation during the period). Inflation and devaluation go relatively hand in hand for the period of 1980–1998.
3. Arnold Browth, chairman of Weiner, Edrich, Brown Inc., discussed major industry trends in the Fragrance Foundation's "View from the Top" ceremony on January 26, 1999.
4. *Euromonitor*, 1998.
5. Sales does not include the 30% mark-up which is the margin received by the Consultants.
6. Seabra and Leal bought 26% stake in Natura for US$25 million from the other important shareholder. The resulting ownership left Seabra with 37.9%, Leal with 36%, Passos with 9%, and the remaining in the hands of minority shareholders.
7. The Real Plan was a currency stabilization program implemented in 1994 by Fernando Henrique Cardoso, the finance minister at the time. The new program of macroeconomic policies was based on a reduction in public expense, increased federal taxes, tighter controls over state-owned banks, and an acceleration of the privatization program. When Cardoso became the president in 1995, his administration took further steps in Brazil's economic liberalization process.
8. Of a product's suggested retail price of R$100, Consultants need to pay R$70 to Natura.

CASE 28
HBO

1. Brownfield, P. (2001). *Call it-Must Buy TV.* February 25, 2001. http://articles.latimes.com/2001/feb/25/entertainment/ca-29862
2. Ibid.
3. Ibid.
4. Ibid.

CASE 29
Building Emotional Energy for Renewal: Nissan

1. Anon. Renissant? *Economist*, March 20, 1999, pp. 65–66.
2. C. Ghosn. Saving the Business Without Losing the Company. *Harvard Business Review*, January, 2002, pp. 3–11.
3. J. B. Treece and S. Farhi. Renault Goes for Broke with Nissan Bid. *Automotive News*, March 22, 1999, p. 43.
4. Anon. "Renissant?" *Economist*, March 20, 1999, pp. 65–66.
5. S. Farhi. Ghosn Sees Fast Start at Nissan. *Automotive News*, April 5, 1999, pp. 1–2.
6. A. Harney. Nissan Prepares for "le cost-killer." *Financial Times*, June 28, 1999, p. 29.
7. A. R. Gold, M. Hirano, and Y. Yokoyama. An Outsider Takes Japan. *The McKinsey Quarterly*, 1, 2001, pp. 94–105.
8. X. Debontride. Carlos Ghosn met en oeuvre a Tokyo une equipe de choc. *Les Echos*, March 29, 1999, p. 12.
9. S. Dabkowski. The Father of Nissan's Revival. *The Agre*, July 12, 2001, p. 3.
10. S. Strom. In a Change, Nissan Opens Annual Meeting to Press. *New York Times*, June 26, 1999, p. C2.
11. N. Mayershohn. Nissan's U-turn to Profits. *Chief Executive*, January, 2002, pp. 12–16.
12. V. Emerson. An Interview with Carlos Ghosn. *Journal of World Business*, Spring 2001, pp. 3–11.
13. C. Ghosn. We don't Have a Choice. (speech transcript). *Automotive News*, November 8, 1999, pp. 36–44.
14. S. Lauer. Carlos Ghosn a l'epreuve de Nissan. *Le Monde*, October 19, 1999, p. 5.
15. M. Naumann. Nissan's Woes Seen as Opportunity for New Operations Chief. *San Jose Mercury News*, July 23, 1999.
16. Carlos Ghosn. Global Leader Series, Speech at INSEAD, Fontainebleau, France, September 24, 2002.
17. C. Ghosn. We don't Have a Choice. (speech transcript). *Automotive News*, November 8, 1999, pp. 36–44.
18. Ibid.
19. S. Strom. Cuts by Nissan are Deeper than Foreseen. *New York Times*, October 19, 1999, p. 1.

20. P. Eisenstein. A Remarkably Un-Japanese way to Reorganize. *Professional Engineering*, November 3, 1999.
21. Nissan Press Release, October 18, 1999.
22. T. Burt. The Ice-breaker Sees Open Waters. *Financial Times*, March 21, 2001, p. 16.
23. A. Harney. Restructuring gives Japan's Workers Culture Shock. *Financial Times*, November 2, 1999, p. 14.
24. G. Wehrfrtiz. Can this Company be Saved? *Newsweek*, November 1, 1999, p. 60.
25. Carlos Ghosn. *Global Leader Series, Speech at INSEAD*. Fontainebleau, France, September 24, 2002.
26. G. Wehrfrtiz. Can this Company be Saved? *Newsweek*, November 1, 1999, p. 60.
27. S. Storm. Betting on a Turnaround. *New York Times*, November 9, 1999, p. 4.
28. A. R., Gold, M. Hirano, and Y. Yokoyama. An Outsider Takes Japan. *The McKinsey Quarterly*, 1, 2001, pp. 94–105.
29. A. Taylor. Nissan's Turnaround Artist. *Fortune*, February 18, 2002, pp. 47–51.
30. V. Emerson. An Interview with Carlos Ghosn. *Journal of World Business*, Spring 2001, pp. 3–11.
31. E. Thornton. Remaking Nissan. *Business Week*, November 15, 1999, pp. 70–74.
32. C. Ghosn. Saving the Business without Losing the Company. *Harvard Business Review*, January, 2002, pp. 3–11.
33. M. Yoshino & M. Egawa. HBS Case 9-303-111: Implementing the Nissan Renewal Plan (paraphrasing Takahashi's statement).
34. N. Kawato and H. Ikematsu. Feelings Mixed on Ghosn Reform. *The Daily Yomiuri*, January 27, 2000, p. 18.
35. E. Thornton. Remaking Nissan. *Business Week*, November 15, 1999, pp. 70–74.
36. T. Larimer. Rebirth of the Z. *Time*, January 15, 2001, pp. 18–20.
37. B. Fulford. Renaissance at Nissan. *Forbes*, October 2, 2001, pp. 80–81.
38. F. Hauter. Carlos Ghosn: "En situation de crise, la tranparence s'impose." *Le Figaro Enterprises*, July 2, 2001, pp. 28–29,
39. C. Ghosn. Saving the Business without Losing the Company. *Harvard Business Review*, January, 2002, pp. 3–11.
40. B. Fulford. Renaissance at Nissan. *Forbes*, October 2, 2000, pp. 80–81.
41. R. Colitt. Nissan to Put $300m into Brazil Deal with Renault. *Financial Times*, May 30, 2000, p. 29.
43. N., Shirouzu, J. B., White, and T. Zaun. A revival at Nissan Shows there's Hope for Japan Inc. *Asian Wall Street Journal*, November 17, 2000, p. 1.
44. S. Strom. Nissan Reports Solid Profit for Half-Year. *New York Times*, October 31, 2000, p. 1.
45. K. Purba. Frenchman Helps Nissan to Surviva. *Jakarta Post*, November 20, 2000, p. 11.
46. Ibid.
47. Ibid.
48. D. Magee. *Turnaround: How Carlos Ghosn Rescued Nissan*. HarperCollins Publishers, 2003, pp. 118–120.
49. E. Nuss. Why Should We Change? The Nissan Revival Plan. INSEAD-The Business Link, 3, 2001, pp. 18–22.
50. D. Ibison. Nissan Puts Merit before Service. *Irish Times*, July 27, 2001, p. 63.
51. F. Hauter. Carlos Ghosn: "En situation de crise, la tranparence s'impose." *Le Figaro Enterprises*, July 2, 2001, pp. 28–29.
52. J. O'Dell. Nissan Proves Comeback with Soaring Earnings. *Los Angeles Times*, May 18, 2001, p. 1.
53. Nissan Annual Report, 2000.
54. T. Zaun. Nissan Nears its Restructuring Targets. *Asian Wall Street Journal*, February 11, 2002, p. 3.
55. N. Mayershohn. Nissan's U-turn to Profits. *Chief Executive*, January, 2002, pp. 12–16.
56. A. Taylor. Nissan's Turnaround Artist. *Fortune*, February 18, 2002, pp. 47–51.
57. I. Williams. Japan's New Superstar. *Sunday Telegraph*, July 1, 2001, p. 29.
58. S. Lauer. Carlos Ghosn a l'epreuve de Nissan. *Le Monde*, October 19, 1999, p. 5.
59. T. Burt and D. Ibison. Interview: Carlos Ghosn, *Financial Times* (ft. com), October 25, 2001.
60. D. Magee. *Turnaround: How Carlos Ghosn Rescued Nissan*. HarperCollins Publishers, 2003, p. 106.
61. Reprinted by permission of *Harvard Business Review*. From Saving the Business without Losing the Company, Carlos Ghosn, Vol. 80, Issue 1, January 2002.

CASE 30
Even a Clown Can Do It: Cirque du Soleil Recreates Live Entertainment

1. Cirque du Soleil is based in Montreal, Quebec, and runs shows around the world. Nevertheless, the majority of its performances take place in the United States.
2. Ernest Albrecht. *The New American Circus*. University Press of Florida, Gainesvilla, FL, p. 2.
3. Ibid, p. 75.
4. Ibid, p. 77.
5. Guy Caron in Ibid, p. 77.
6. Author's interview with circus historian Fred Pfening, May 15, 2001.
7. Author's interview with circus historian Fred Pfening, May 15, 2001.
8. Author's personal observation, May 30, 2001.
9. Author's personal observation, May 5, 2001.

CASE 32
Managing Performance at Haier (A)

1. Chinese Yuan Renminibi (RMB)= US$0.12
2. *Euromonitor*, February 2008.
3. The average age of the world's top five global players in the household electrical market was 95 years (*Euromonitor*, 2001).
4. One of the first rules Zhang set was, "Do no urinate on the factory floor."
5. Annual report of the Beijing Famous-Brand Evaluation Co. Ltd., 2002.
6. Due to China's one-child policy.
7. *Guanxi* refers to the Chinese cultural system of forming social-and business-relationships based on mutual obligation. In other words, "I'll help you now: you help me later."
8. Haier referred to the credits employees earned with their contribution to productivity and/or innovation as income (points), recorded in a book that functioned like a bankbook, which accompanied the employee until the end of his/her career with Haier. At the same time, the employee would pay for resources used. When income was greater than expenses, it was recorded as profit (or value added). When expenses were greater than income, the employee was in debt. Thus, every employee functioned with profit/loss, as a strategic business unit. Each employee earned a salary if he/she made a "profit" (a positive contribution to the company and the unit). An employee's salary was determined by his/her bankbook.
9. Chinese society was hierarchically structured based on Confucian principles of emperor over general, father over son (highly paternalistic), husband over wife, older brothers over younger brothers, for example.

CASE 36
Yahoo!

1. Verne G. Kopytoff. Even under New Captain, Yahoo Seems Adrift. *New York Times*, October 18, 2010, p. B4.
2. Verne G. Kopytoff. Yahoo Profit Rises, but Revenue is Flat. *New York Times*, October 20, 2010, p. B2.
3. *New York Times*, October 20, 2010, p. B2.
4. *New York Times*, October 18, 2010, p. B4.
5. Ben Elgin & Ronald Grover. Yahoo!: Act Two. *Business Week*, June 2, 2003, p. 72.
6. *Business Week*, June 2, 2003, p. 74.
7. Elise Ackerman. Can 'Chief Yahoo' Yang Make it Work This Time as CEO? *Knight Ridder Tribune Business News*. June 24, 2007, p. 1.
8. Miguel Helft. Yahoo to Cut 1,000 Jobs, and Warns on Growth. *New York Times*, January 30, 2008, p. C3.
9. John Swartz. Yahoo Encounters a Fork in Road Toward its Future. *USA Today*, January 28, 2008, p. 2B.
10. *USA Today*, January 28, 2008, p. 2B.
11. Ibid.
12. Miguel Helft. Yahoo Celebrates (for Now). *New York Times*, May 5, 2008, p. C1.
13. Jessica E. Vascellaro. Bartz Remakes Yahoo's Top Ranks. *Wall Street Journal*, February 27, 2009, p. B3.
14. Steve Lohr. Linked Up. Now What? *New York Times*, July 30, 2009, p. B7.
15. *New York Times*, July 30, 2009, p. B7.
16. *New York Times*, October 18, 2010, p. B4.
17. Ibid.
18. Ibid.

NAME INDEX

SUBJECT INDEX